Crossing the Thames Estuary

63 routes with full passage planning tables

Roger Gaspar

Imray Laurie Norie & Wilson

Published by
Imray, Laurie, Norie & Wilson Ltd
Wych House St Ives Cambridgeshire PE27 5BT England
✆ +44(0)1480 462114
Fax +44(0)1480 496109
Email ilnw@imray.com
www.imray.com
2014

All rights reserved. No part of this publication may be reproduced, transmitted or used in any form by any means graphic, electronic or mechanical, including photocopying, recording, taping or information storage and retrieval systems or otherwise without the prior permission of the publisher.
© Roger Gaspar 2014

Roger Gaspar has asserted his right under the Copyright, Designs and Patents Act 1988 to be identified as the author of this work. A catalogue record for this book is available from the British Library.

First edition 2008
Second edition 2014

ISBN 978 184623 628 0

CAUTION
Every effort has been made to ensure the accuracy of this book. It contains selected information and thus is not definitive and does not include all known information on the subject in hand; this is particularly relevant to the plans, which should not be used for navigation. The author believes that his selection is a useful aid to prudent navigation, but the safety of a vessel depends ultimately on the judgement of the navigator, who should assess all information, published or unpublished.

PLANS
The plans in this guide are not to be used for navigation. They are designed to support the text and should at all times be used with navigational charts.

CORRECTIONAL SUPPLEMENTS
This pilot book will be amended at intervals by the issue of correctional supplements. These are published on the internet at our web site www.imray.com and may be downloaded free of charge. Printed copies are also available on request from the publishers at the above address. This work has been corrected to October 2014

Printed in Croatia by Zrinski

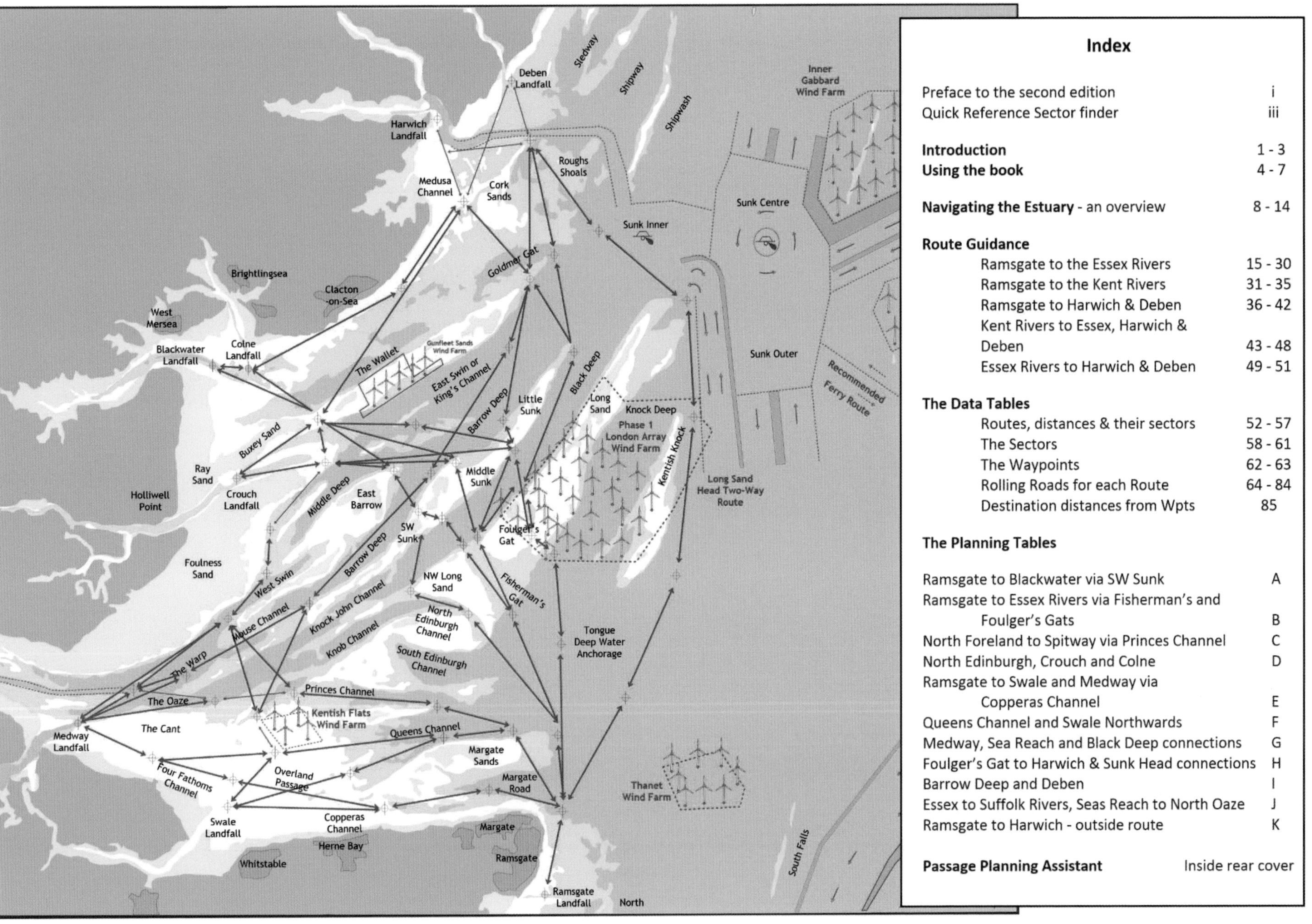
Deben Landfall
Sledway
Shipway
Shipwash
Inner Gabbard Wind Farm
Harwich Landfall
Roughs Shoals
Medusa Channel
Cork Sands
Sunk Inner
Sunk Centre
Goldmer Gat
Brightlingsea
Clacton -on-Sea
West Mersea
Blackwater Landfall
Colne Landfall
The Wallet
Gunfleet Sands Wind Farm
East Swin or King's Channel
Sunk Outer
Recommended Ferry Route
Barrow Deep
Little Sunk
Black Deep
Long Sand
Knock Deep
Phase 1 London Array Wind Farm
Kentish Knock
Buxey Sand
Ray Sand
Middle Sunk
Long Sand Head Two-Way Route
Holliwell Point
Crouch Landfall
Middle Deep
East Barrow
SW Sunk
Foulger's Gat
Foulness Sand
West Swin
Barrow Deep
NW Long Sand
Fisherman's Gat
Mouse Channel
Knock John Channel
North Edinburgh Channel
Tongue Deep Water Anchorage
The Warp
Knob Channel
South Edinburgh Channel
The Oaze
Princes Channel
Kentish Flats Wind Farm
Medway Landfall
The Cant
Queens Channel
Margate Sands
Four Fathoms Channel
Overland Passage
Margate Road
Thanet Wind Farm
Swale Landfall
Copperas Channel
Herne Bay
Margate
Whitstable
Ramsgate
South Falls
Ramsgate Landfall
North

Index

Preface

How to use this Book

1. Read the *Route Guidance* and chose your route of preference;
2. Identify the sectors for your chosen route from the *Data Tables*. Note these on the fold-out *Passage Planning Assistant* inside the rear cover;
3. Go to the *Planning Tables* and chose the right table for your passage;
    - Yellow edged tables for north or westbound
    - Green edged tables for south or eastbound
    - Select the page for your intended average boat speed
    - Select the page for Springs or Neaps
4. Follow the detailed guidance on pages 4 to 7 to use the *Planning Tables* and identify the best start time related to the time of HW Sheerness;
5. Use the further data in the *Data Tables* to note waypoints, distances and navigational marks;
6. When on passage, use the Rolling Route Diagrams as a quick reference.

SOLAS V for pleasure craft - Voyage Planning requirements

"Regulation V/34 - *Safe Navigation and avoidance of dangerous situations* concerns prior planning for your boating trip, more commonly known as voyage or passage planning. Voyage planning is basically common sense. As a pleasure boat user, you should particularly take into account the following points when planning a boating trip.

- ***Weather***: before you go boating, check the weather forecast and get regular updates if you are planning to be out for any length of time.
- ***Tides***: check the tidal predictions for your trip and ensure that they fit with what you are planning to do.
- ***Limitations of the vessel***: consider whether your boat is up to the proposed trip and that you have sufficient safety equipment and stores with you.
- ***Crew***: take into account the experience and physical ability of your crew. Crews suffering from cold, tiredness and seasickness won't be able to do their job properly and could even result in an overburdened skipper.
- ***Navigational dangers***: make sure you are familiar with any navigational dangers you may encounter during your boating trip. This generally means checking an up to date chart and a current pilot book or almanac.
- ***Contingency plan***: always have a contingency plan should anything go wrong. Before you go, consider bolt holes and places where you can take refuge should conditions deteriorate or if you suffer an incident or injury. Bear in mind that your GPS set is vulnerable and could fail at the most inconvenient time. It is sensible and good practice to make sure you are not over-reliant on your GPS set and that you can navigate yourself to safety without it should it fail you."

Preface to the second edition

The inspiration for this book was time spent at the chart table either at anchor in the Blackwater or in Ramsgate planning the best departure time to cross the Estuary. The concept was planned on a wet Wednesday in late November in that post-layup depression that precedes the London International Boat Show. The encouragement came from Colin Jarman whose assistance was second only to the patience of my wife, Judy. To both, continued thanks are due, as indeed, they are to those kind people at Imray.

This book is not intended to rival that excellent Imray publication *East Coast Pilot* by Colin Jarman, Garth Cooper and Dick Holness which I highly recommend: rather to sit and work alongside it providing detailed descriptions and notes on the routes across the estuary and tables that will considerably reduce the time spent planning. Unfortunately for a variety of reasons, the 'Landfall' waypoints used differ from those in *East Coast Pilot* although in some places there are very close.

The object is help you plan your journey across the complex waters of the Thames Estuary quickly, safely, easily and accurately. To do this a series of tables is provided based upon a variety of routes with alternative tables for Springs and Neaps and for a choice of average boat speeds of 4, 5, 6 and 7 knots.

It is thanks to the readership that there is a call for a second edition. That has enabled me to make a number of changes that I hope will be regarded as improvements. First, the number of routes covered is increased from 32 to 63. The main additions are extra choices from Ramsgate to the Kent Rivers via the Queen and Princes Channels, the use of Princes Channel for the Essex Rivers and sectors linking the Essex and Suffolk Rivers. Unfortunately to keep the size of the book to affordable dimensions that has meant the loss of the boat speed table for 3 knots. I hope that is an acceptable compromise.

Secondly, the layout of the book is changed to four sections:

- an explanation of how to use the book and tables;
- a description of the routes and navigational issues likely to be encountered;
- an entirely new section on route data. This puts all the route, sector detail and waypoint information in one place and includes a *rolling road* diagram for each route. The Rolling Road is designed to be open on the chart table or in the cockpit during your passage;
- the planning tables.

Thirdly, I hope that you find the illustrations much improved.

As with the first edition, the concentration is on the 'inside' routes that weave through or across various sands and swatchways. However, this edition now includes the 'outside' route between the Suffolk Rivers and Ramsgate.

Once you have chosen your route from the guidance in the route descriptions, the time planning tables will enable you to plan departure times for the speediest passage, to arrive at key crossing points at your chosen time, or to plan arrival at Landfall waypoints with sufficient time to carry the tide up river to your final destination. The planning tables will provide you with a simple and accurate way to determine the best choices when making the crossing. What is the preferred route? What time do I start to ensure sufficient water through the swatchways or over banks? What is the best compromise to get the most help from the tide and still have sufficient water over the banks?

Please note that this book uses **HW Sheerness** as the datum for tide references for all routes. This is because the majority of tidal data in the Estuary area is so based.

Please visit www.crossingthethamesestuary.com. Not only will necessary corrections and changes be notified there but you will also find an illustrated Notices to Mariners service for the area covered by this book and a range of chartlets based upon surveys which I have carried out. Feedback through the web site is always welcomed.

Thanks are due to many readers for information and feedback but particularly to Bob Darby and Peter Broadley.

Roger Gaspar
West Mersea
August, 2014

Sectors – Quick Reference Page Finder

Introduction

63 Routes and Passage Planning Tables

The crossing of the Thames Estuary provides one of the more complicated navigational problems confronting the UK yachtsman or woman. The numerous banks and shoals, changing marks together with strong currents require a good understanding of the route and the effect of tides.

The usual analogy of the Thames Estuary is to place your left hand on the image of the Estuary on the index page of this book and with your thumb representing the Kent coast and its tip, the North Foreland. You will have an immediate grasp of the shoals confronting you between Essex and Kent.

The Long and Sunk Sands, represented by your first and second fingers, must be crossed or circumvented; the Barrow Sand, represented by your third finger, must be skirted on any passage to the Essex Rivers and, if continuing to the Wallet or the Rivers Colne and Blackwater, the Buxey/Gunfleet Sands, represented by the little finger, must also be crossed. Whether traveling between the Essex, Suffolk or Kent rivers, you have the choice of several routes between the sands.

Any passage plan needs to consider:

- The weather;
- The tides;
- The choice of route, and
- The choice of timing.

The weather is left to you. However, the book provides information on sectors, waypoints, navigational issues, tides and timing for the chosen 63 routes across the Estuary variously between Ramsgate and the Kent, Essex and Suffolk Rivers.

What does this book contain?

This book covers all usual routes between Ramsgate and the Kent, Essex and Suffolk Rivers including, in this edition, the 'outside' route from the Deben and Harwich to Ramsgate.

The aim is to help you make the choice of route and quick, simple and accurate time planning of your chosen passage across the Thames Estuary. At the heart of this book are comprehensive Time Planning charts but to make this all work, the contents include:

- *How to use this book* - guidance on using the book, the data and the planning tables;
- *Route Guidance* – a description of each route, including illustrations of the routes and details of hazards;
- *Data Section* - A section providing quick reference to detail of routes, their sectors, waypoints, distances and a rolling road for each route, and
- *Time Planning Tables* – to calculate passage time and timing for average boat speeds (speed through the water) of 4, 5, 6 and 7 knots.

Using this book – the explanation shows how to use the planning tables to select your best start time, whether it be for a speedy passage, arrival at tidal gates at suitable times or a suitable arrival time.

The **Route Guidance** provides advice on the navigational issues which arise. The routes are chosen firstly to provide a basis for the passage planning tables and are therefore conservative in nature. They are intended to survive minor changes in buoyage and the shape of the shoals.

You should, however, always consider how suitable the exact detail of each route is for you; whether it takes you too close to charted hazards, or, indeed, whether by altering the track by a few degrees, you can reduce the distance to be sailed. As with all advice on route planning, you should compare the suggestions here with an up to date chart and ensure that you have identified and considered all potential hazards. In certain places you will invited to check the companion web site www.crossingthethamesestuary.com for the very latest information.

Each route comprises a number of sectors chosen as the best compromise between hazards. Each sector has a start and end waypoint which may or may not be close to a navigation mark (ATON). The 'Rolling Roads' illustrate the ATONs likely to be seen, **either distant or close-to** while on track between waypoints; inclusion of an ATON in a Rolling Road diagram does not necessarily mean that the track passes close-by.

Introduction

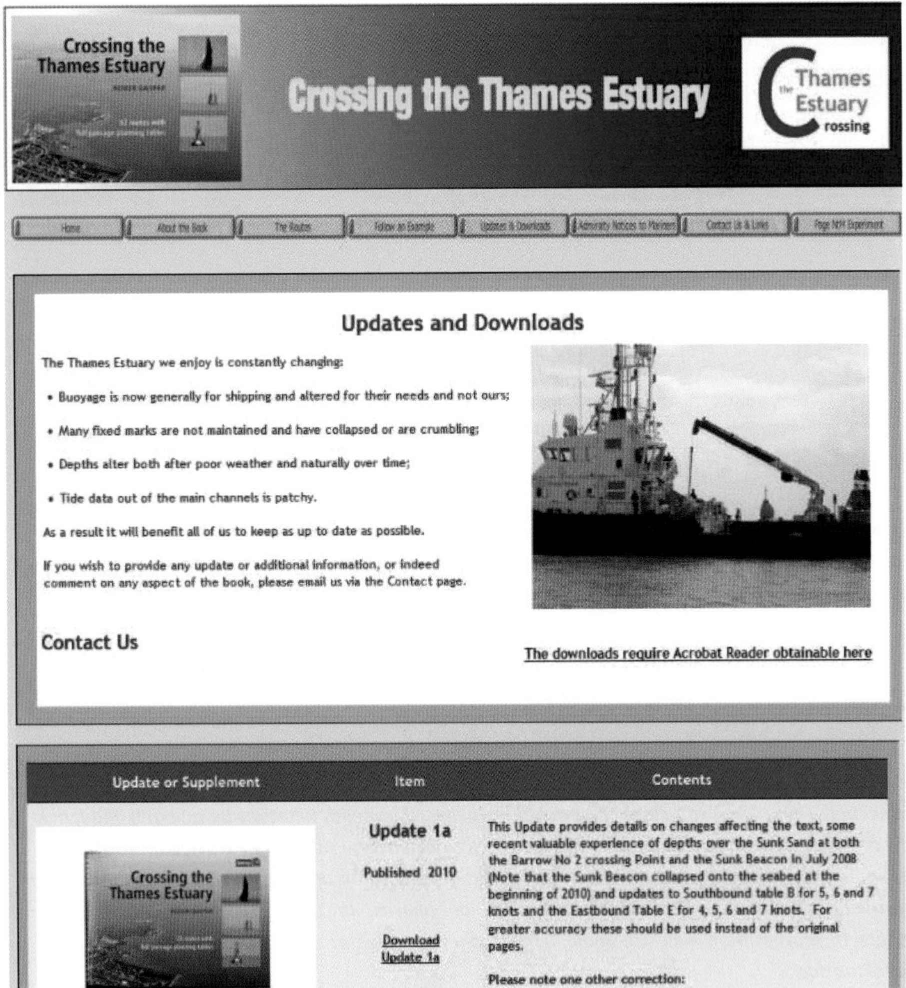

The updates page on www.crossingthethamesestuary.com

Note it is the convention in the Route Guidance to describe the route from the south to north.

The **Route Guidance** breaks down each of the routes into Sectors corresponding to a required change of course or where a different tidal diamond has been used to calculate the effect of the tide.

The **Data Section** provides a quick reference to all relevant data including the sectors comprising each route, track direction and distance for each sector, relevant waypoints and rolling roads. This is in one convenient place for reference.

The **Time Planning** tables are provided in one knot average speeds between 4 and 7 knots. These show, at 15 minute intervals, the duration it will take to sail (or motor) that sector at the chosen average speed allowing for the tide effect. *These are to enable you to plan your start times or arrival times at tidal gates accurately and speedily.* A separate set of tables is provided for North and South Bound (or East/West) journeys and for Springs and Neaps.

How do the tables help your passage planning?

The 63 routes have been selected to serve the most common passages across the Estuary. Each is broken down into a number of sectors reflecting the length of the passage and principal track changes required. For each sector, the planning tables provide, for a start time every fifteen minutes of the day, the time it will take to complete the sector at the given boat speed at that start time. This 'duration' time takes into account the tide effect for that start time. Thus, if you know the time you will start the first sector you will instantly know the time you will arrive at the start of the second sector. By moving from sector to sector for the whole route, you can identify the estimated arrival time in a matter of a minute without recourse to tidal charts. The layout of the tables then allows you to refine your initial plan to calculate the speediest passage or arrival at tidal gates at the right time.

Note that all times relate to HW Sheerness. This enables the reader to use the tables in perpetuity providing the time of high water at Sheerness is known.

Material used in the construction of these tables

All chart work was completed on Admiralty Charts and using Imray's charts in the Meridian chartware package, ID10 North Sea – South and East. The tide data underpinning the Tables is from the following Admiralty Charts:

1975 – Thames Estuary – Northern Part;
1607 – Thames Estuary – Southern Part;
1828 – Dover to North Foreland;
2693 – Approaches to Felixstowe, Harwich and Ipswich;
2052 – Orford Ness to the Naze;
5607-1 and 2 – UKHO Leisure Folio of Thames Estuary, Essex and Suffolk coast.

Tidal data was taken from appropriate tidal diamonds on those charts and NP249, the UK Hydrographic Office's Tidal Stream Atlas and Co-Tidal charts for the Thames Estuary. All chartlets and photographs in this publication are by the author except where otherwise acknowledged. Note that all chartlets in this publication are here to aid understanding of the routes and should **not** be used for navigation.

Interpolations

Source data from Admiralty Charts uses hourly data from -6 hours to +6 hours after HW. Since tidal diamond data for the hour represents the half hour before to the half hour after the quoted time, this suggests that -6:30hrs is the same as +6:30.

However, the tidal cycle is not perfectly symmetrical, successive high waters falling anywhere between 12 hours 5 minutes to 12 hours 45 minutes later. In order that the Planning Tables can be applied regardless of the date, the tables assume that +6 and -6 are the same time. This induces only minimal error. However, this error can be completely removed by finding the difference between the two High Waters on the day in question and factoring in the difference in minutes either as you move from + to – values or dividing the difference by the number of sectors and adding in the result (in minutes) in each sector as you move through the tables.

Compromises

The routes have been selected to be as short as possible whilst avoiding points where depth might become critical for most of us. Each route is broken down into a number of sectors for which distance and duration times are provided. To enable the tables to be as flexible as possible, the beginning and end of sectors are formed of waypoints that may cover more than one route. For example, overall the tables use 57 Waypoints which provide 87 sectors. Note that like waypoints, some sectors are common to more than route. Rather than repeat the sector guidance when it is used in a subsequent route, reference is made back to the page number where the original guidance is give.

No route uses more than 10 sectors, many less and broadly (but not exactly) these correspond with the number of track changes to be expected during each passage. Where there is no track change, a new sector will only have been added in a long track where the use of two different tidal diamonds is required for accurate passage planning calculations.

In order to provide the greatest flexibility with a sensible number of waypoints, they are chosen at key points in safe water. They therefore err on the side of caution. Users, aware of the draught of their vessel and its capabilities, may therefore be able to make some changes which will shorten the passage a little.

It will thus be possible to save a little distance on some passages by amending waypoints for your own personal use. If you do this, it is likely to have little impact on the timing data and frequently in the text it is suggested where this may be done. Equally in places (such as when crossing the Sunk Sand), the text states when a waypoint should be strictly maintained.

Note that whilst every care has been taken in the selection of the waypoints, the Thames Estuary and its shoals and swatchways are in a constant state of change. ***The reader should plot any waypoints used and satisfy themselves that they are safe and satisfactory for their purposes. Any updates required will be notified on the web site at www.crossingthethamesestuary.com.***

Passage Planning using this book

Passage Planning

This section is not intended to replace a training manual on passage planning but ignoring the issue of the weather which must be attended to by the reader, you will want to understand the route you intend to take and the impact of the tides. The Route Guidance part of this book (coming next) will help you decide on your route; this part of the book will help you use the Planning Tables to determine the best start time for your passage bearing in mind tidal gates, best advantage from the tides and arrival estimates to allow you to complete your journey to the ultimate destination beyond the Landfall waypoints.

Remember that passage planning is not an exact science. Tidal rates are averages of rates and headings over an hour at one position and thus constantly alter and never stay precise, either for a whole hour or for the whole of a particular sector. This book will provide you with the rhumb line direction and distance for each sector of your passage which is used for planning purposes. You should always consider the effect of your planned course to steer against charted hazards. Where this is critical advice is given in the Route Guidance.

The tables follow the passage planning convention of assuming a constant average boat speed and the ability to pass through each sector directly on the quoted track. The sector duration time is calculated for every fifteen minutes

Using the Time Planning Tables

The time planning charts pre-calculate the time required to complete each sector taking the tide into account. By linking through the right table for your expected average speed, you can find the best time to start the passage – **in less time than it would take you to draw a tidal vector!**

1. ***Get the right Table***

    a. Select your Route and using the Route tables in the Data section, note the sectors in the Planning Assistant (inside the rear cover – the format is downloadable from the web site);
    b. Chose the set of tables for the direction you are intending to travel (yellow edged tables for North or West Bound; Green edged tables for South or East);
    c. Chose the average speed through the water you are likely to achieve; chose the Spring or Neap table;

2. ***Determine if any High Water time correction for the day is required (number of minutes by which the second High Water is later than 12 hours)***

    There is a choice on how you deal with this: if the difference is not very great, for example 10 minutes, then you can ignore it. This is, after all passage planning! If you prefer you can either add in the difference in time to your duration as you pass from '+' to '-' values in the tables or you can divide the difference by the number of sectors and add in the resulting time difference to the duration time of each sector.

3. ***Using the Table*** *(see illustration opposite)*

    a. Go to your first Sector: select your preferred start *'Time'* in the first left hand column - this is the time you start the sector. If you have no preference, look down the duration column and pick the Start Time with the least duration;
    b. Note the *'Time at end of Sector'* in the third column for that start time;
    c. Move right to the column for your next Sector (in some cases you may need to move to a different table). Find the nearest *'Time'* to match the previous *'Time at end of Sector'*.
    d. Where the *'Time at end of Sector'* is midway between two *'Time'* values, you should choose the earlier time if optimistic about keeping to or exceeding your chosen average speed, or the later *'Time'* if a little pessimistic. Indeed it is perfectly acceptable to add on the difference to the *'Time at end of Sector'*. This will give you even great accuracy.
    e. Repeat the process until you reach the final Sector. The *'Time at end of Sector'* will be your estimated time of arrival. Timing at critical points can be noted as you move through the Table.

Time to cover Sectors (in minutes) at 4.0 kts — All times relate to HW Sheerness

	A1 Ramsgate to North Foreland			A2 North Foreland to East Margate			A3 East Margate to Outer Fisherman			A4 Outer to Inner Fisherman			A5 Inner Fisherman to SW Sunk	
Time	*Duration*	*Time at End of Sector*	*Time*	*Duration*	*Time at End of Sector*	*Time*	*Duration*	*Time at End of Sector*	*Time*	*Duration*	*Time at End of Sector*	*Time*	*Duration*	*Time at End of Sector*
- 3.15	66	- 2:09	- 3.15	45	- 2:30	- 3.15	87	- 1:48	- 3.15	42	- 2:33	- 3.15	59	- 2:16
- 3.00	60	- 2:00	- 3.00	42	- 2:18	- 3.00	86	- 1:34	- 3.00	40	- 2:20	- 3.00	58	- 2:02
- 2.45	53	- 1:52	- 2.45	40	- 2:05	- 2.45	85	- 1:20	- 2.45	40	- 2:05	- 2.45	56	- 1:49
- 2.30	47	- 1:43	- 2.30	38	- 1:52	- 2.30	85	- 1:05	- 2.30	39	- 1:51	- 2.30	54	- 1:36
- 2.15	45	- 1:30	- 2.15	36	- 1:39	- 2.15	84	- 0:51	- 2.15	39	- 1:36	- 2.15	53	- 1:22
- 2.00	44	- 1:16	- 2.00	34	- 1:26	- 2.00	84	- 0:36	- 2.00	38	- 1:22	- 2.00	51	- 1:09
- 1.45	43	- 1:02	- 1.45	33	- 1:12	- 1.45	85	- 0:20	- 1.45	40	- 1:05	- 1.45	51	- 0:54
- 1.30	42	- 0:48	- 1.30	33	- 0:57	- 1.30	86	- 0:04	- 1.30	42	- 0:48	- 1.30	50	- 0:40
- 1.15	42	- 0:33	- 1.15	32	- 0:43	- 1.15	87	+ 0:12	- 1.15	43	- 0:32	- 1.15	50	- 0:25
- 1.00	43	- 0:17	- 1.00	31	- 0:29	- 1.00	88	+ 0:28	- 1.00	45	- 0:15	- 1.00	49	- 0:11
- 0.45	44	- 0:01	- 0.45	32	- 0:13	- 0.45	90	+ 0:45	- 0.45	48	+ 0:03	- 0.45	50	+ 0:05
- 0.30	44	+ 0:14	- 0.30	32	+ 0:02	- 0.30	93	+ 1:03	- 0.30	52	+ 0:22	- 0.30	51	+ 0:21
- 0.15	46	+ 0:31	- 0.15	32	+ 0:17	- 0.15	96	+ 1:21	- 0.15	56	+ 0:41	- 0.15	51	+ 0:36
HW	48	+ 0:48	HW	33	+ 0:33	HW	99	+ 1:39	HW	59	+ 0:59	HW	52	+ 0:52
+ 0.15	49	+ 1:04	+ 0.15	34	+ 0:49	+ 0.15	102	+ 1:57	+ 0.15	63	+ 1:18	+ 0.15	53	+ 1:08
+ 0.30	51	+ 1:21	+ 0.30	36	+ 1:06	+ 0.30	105	+ 2:15	+ 0.30	66	+ 1:36	+ 0.30	54	+ 1:24
+ 0.45	54	+ 1:39	+ 0.45	38	+ 1:23	+ 0.45	109	+ 2:34	+ 0.45	69	+ 1:54	+ 0.45	55	+ 1:40
+ 1.00	56	+ 1:56	+ 1.00	39	+ 1:39	+ 1.00	112	+ 2:52	+ 1.00	73	+ 2:13	+ 1.00	56	+ 1:56
+ 1.15	59	+ 2:14	+ 1.15	42	+ 1:57	+ 1.15	114	+ 3:09	+ 1.15	74	+ 2:29	+ 1.15	56	+ 2:11
+ 1.30	62	+ 2:32	+ 1.30	45	+ 2:15	+ 1.30	116	+ 3:26	+ 1.30	76	+ 2:46	+ 1.30	56	+ 2:26
+ 1.45	65	+ 2:50	+ 1.45	47	+ 2:32	+ 1.45	117	+ 3:42	+ 1.45	77	+ 3:02	+ 1.45	56	+ 2:41
+ 2.00	69	+ 3:09	+ 2.00	50	+ 2:50	+ 2.00	119	+ 3:59	+ 2.00	78	+ 3:18	+ 2.00	56	+ 2:56

Interpolating a mid-value = +2.50

Using the tables - This example in the illustration uses Table A, the Ramsgate to River Blackwater (via Fisherman's Gat and SW Sunk) route, Northbound, Springs, 4kts average boat speed.

An example of using the Planning Assistant from inside the back cover is overleaf.

The table in the example pre-calculates the time it will take to cross each sector at 4 knots, taking into account the rate and direction of the tide. This is done for every 15 minutes of the day for each sector relating the tide to HW Sheerness.

So in the example, leaving the waypoint at Ramsgate at HW Sheerness – 2 hours will take us 44 minutes, arriving at the North Foreland waypoint at 1 hours 16 minutes (-1:16) before HW Sheerness. It is easy to transfer this value to the nearest value as the start time for the next sector – in this case from the North Foreland waypoint to the East Margate waypoint where after 32 minutes, if we maintain our 4 knot boat speed average, we will arrive 43 minutes before HW Sheerness.

So the passage calculation can continue from sector to sector.

It is possible to be precise; for example in sector A5 we are looking for a start time of +1:54 which falls midway between the available values. You can have the choice of working on an optimistic value of the first time of +1:45 or the pessimistic choice of +2:00. Alternative use mental arithmetic to interpolate for the more accurate result of +2:50.

It is perhaps useful to use the tables first on the basis of the 'nearest' values; find the passage start time that provides the best option for you taking into account matters including tidal gates (e.g. avoiding low water over sand banks) or arriving at the destination in daylight. With this done a more precise use of the tables can work out a precise timing. But bear in mind, this is passage planning. It can never be an exact calculation. Tidal rates and direction for an hour are mean values and maintaining an exact boat speed or indeed, steering an exactly straight course is impossible meaning that the result is a sound approximation rather than a timetable. Please not that 'boat speed' means just that; speed through the water, not speed over the ground.

Improving the Passage Plan

This example also uses the Ramsgate to River Blackwater route via Fisherman's Gat and SW Sunk.

The perfect passage on this route would:

a. avoid adverse tide up or down the North Foreland; avoid adverse tide through Fisherman's Gat;

Using the book

Example	Passage Plan 'Quick Reckoner' Table			*All times relate to HW Sheerness*
Route?	**Average Boat Speed?**	**Springs or Neaps?**	**Any time adjustment between successive HWs?**	**Core Route Table?**
Ramsgate to Blackwater via SW Sunk	*4 Knots*	*Springs*	*Not used in this example*	*A*

	Sectors Numbers for this chosen route									
Sectors from Table	*A1*	*A2*	*A3*	*A4*	*A5*	*A6*	*A7*	*A8*		
Insert times from Table - these are the times of starting each sector *Start at any tidal gate and work forwards or backwards, or* *Chose a preferred start or finish time*	*-2:00*	*-1:16* *(Using -1:15)*	*-0:43* *(Using -0:45)*	*+0:45* *(Exact)*	*+1:54* *(Bet +1:45 & +2:00)*	*+2:50* *(Using +2:45)*	*+3:17* *(Using +3:15)*	*+4:39* *(+4:30/ +4:45 ETA -5:11)*		

Using the Planning Assistant (from inside the rear cover)

b. avoid strong or adverse tide across the Black Deep;
c. ensure sufficient height of tide crossing the Sunk Sand;
d. avoid adverse tide from the Sunk Sand to the Spitway;
e. ensure sufficient water in the Spitway; and,
f. leave sufficient flood to carry us to our final destination within the Blackwater.

As you use the Time Planning tables, you will see that achieving all of these is practically impossible at some average speeds due to the nature of the Estuary. Hence a compromise is necessary and you will have to make some choices. Of (a) to (f) in the example, sufficient water at the Sunk Sand and/or Spitway are probably the most crucial and those with shoal draft will, of course, enjoy the greatest flexibility. All the other factors are more to do with speed of passage rather than anything more dramatic such as a grounding but an adverse tide up or down the North Foreland or to or from the Essex Rivers can significantly add to the time of the passage. Hence the need to look for the best timing possible.

Follow an example using the Planning Assistant above

The example above uses -2:00 Sheerness as a start time as it provides for good tidal assistance in the first sector. This gives a reasonably fast passage with the most favourable tide from Ramsgate to the North Foreland and on from there to Fisherman's Gat. The yacht will be at the Sunk Sand close to 3 hours after HW Sheerness by which time the ebb will have been running at the SW Sunk for 3 hours 40 minutes. With a run to the corner of the East Barrow Sands (Sector A6) of about 30 minutes, this plan leaves us facing the remains of the ebb (Sector A7) while we cross the Swin to the Spitway. The plan suggests we will arrive at the Spitway +4:39 after HW Sheerness. Since LW Springs is approximately 42 minutes earlier at the Spitway than at Sheerness we are facing this crossing shortly before low water (+5:20 Spitway) with the remains of the tide still falling. Provided there is sufficient depth for us to cross the Spitway, this timing does leave us in very good shape to carry the new flood into the Blackwater with plenty of time to make destinations at the top of the river such as Heybridge Basin or Maldon.

However, should this leave us too short of water over the Spitway or unhappy with crossing the SW Sunk on a falling tide, an alternative plan is necessary.

There are a number of ways to use the tables to improve the passage plan. Firstly, a scan of the time Planning Table for the intended journey will easily show the impact of a favourable or adverse tide in each sector. The duration column makes this easy.

Because the process of planning is speeded by these tables, it is possible using the 'planning assistant' inside the back cover of this book to select alternative plans for consideration. For example, if height of the water over the Sunk Sand or the Spitway is crucial for you, the passage plan can be worked backed from a suitable time at that point (the *Time at the end of the Sector*) to determine a start time and then forward to judge the estimated time of arrival. Alternative choices that are important to you might be to judge the quickest passage, to ensure you start or finish in daylight or to ensure you arrive at a critical point on a rising tide. The Tables will also make it clear when it is worthwhile to press for a higher average speed during any particular sector, for example, by motor sailing. Here are some examples.

To ensure adequate water at the Sunk Sand:

1. If crossing the Sunk Sand at the SW Sunk swatchway either on a rising tide or close to High Water is the most important factor to you, look at the columns for the Sector covering the start of the SW Sunk Swatchway (A5) and run down the '*Time at end of Sector*' in the previous column until you find the value closest to the time you want to start the sector (i.e. crossing the sand). Let us assume that you want to start crossing the Sunk Sand at half-tide on the flood. LW springs at the SW Sunk is 47 minutes earlier than LW Sheerness so we want to arrive at the SW Sunk at -3:47 Sheerness approximately.

   Find this value in the '*Time at end of Sector*' for sector A5 (here we are using -3:42). Now work backwards, using that '*Time*' to match the '*Time at end of Sector*' in the previous column. Repeat this as shown in the image below until you are in the left hand column and you have found your start time which in this example is +2:15 Sheerness.

Impact of adverse tide:

2. Scanning the tables will illustrate the impact of an adverse tide in each of the sectors. In some cases, an adverse tide can double the time taken to cross a sector. So we might, when going Northbound, seek to carry the favourable tide up the North Foreland and decide to leave Ramsgate at -1:30 Sheerness. At 4 knots average (Springs), we will arrive at the North Foreland waypoint after 42 minutes instead of 118 minutes if we had left at -5:30 Sheerness. The down side of this choice is this will get you to Sector A5 for the SW Sunk Sand on a falling tide with over 4 hours of ebb tide gone.

Other Tidal Gates:

3. Similarly, if your destination is right up the Blackwater and it is important to you to carry the flood all the way from the Spitway, working back from a +5:20 'start of sector time' at the Spitway will give you a start time off Ramsgate of –1:30 Sheerness at 4 knots average, the same as in the example above. So starting at the optimum time at 4 knots on Springs from Ramsgate will also give you the best tide towards the Colne and Blackwater. The issue will be whether that will provide sufficient water for you at the SW Sunk and Spitway. Such is the challenge of the Estuary!

Time to cover Sectors (in minutes) at 4.0 kts — All times relate to HW Sheerness

	A1			A2			A3			A4			A5	
	Ramsgate to North Foreland			North Foreland to East Margate			East Margate to Outer Fisherman			Outer to Inner Fisherman			Inner Fisherman to SW Sunk	
Time	*Duration*	*Time at End of Sector*	*Time*	*Duration*	*Time at End of Sector*	*Time*	*Duration*	*Time at End of Sector*	*Time*	*Duration*	*Time at End of Sector*	*Time*	*Duration*	*Time at End of Sector*
- 6.00	115	- 4:05	- 6.00	62	- 4:58	- 6.00	103	- 4:17	- 6.00	61	- 4:59	- 6.00	58	- 5:02
- 5.45	117	- 3:48	- 5.45	62	- 4:43	- 5.45	102	- 4:03	- 5.45	59	- 4:46	- 5.45	59	- 4:46
- 5.30	118	- 3:32	- 5.30	61	- 4:29	- 5.30	102	- 3:48	- 5.30	57	- 4:33	- 5.30	60	- 4:30
- 5.15	114	- 3:21	- 5.15	61	- 4:14	- 5.15	101	- 3:34	- 5.15	55	- 4:20	- 5.15	62	- 4:13
- 5.00	110	- 3:10	- 5.00	61	- 3:59	- 5.00	100	- 3:20	- 5.00	53	- 4:07	- 5.00	63	- 3:57
- 4.45	106	- 2:59	- 4.45	59	- 3:46	- 4.45	98	- 3:07	- 4.45	51	- 3:54	- 4.45	63	- 3:42
- 4.30	102	- 2:48	- 4.30	57	- 3:33	- 4.30	97	- 2:53	- 4.30	50	- 3:40	- 4.30	63	- 3:27
+ 2.15	72	+ 3:27	+ 2.15	52	+ 3:07	+ 2.15	118	+ 4:13	+ 2.15	79	+ 3:34	+ 2.15	56	+ 3:11
+ 2.30	75	+ 3:45	+ 2.30	54	+ 3:24	+ 2.30	117	+ 4:27	+ 2.30	80	+ 3:50	+ 2.30	56	+ 3:26
+ 2.45	77	+ 4:02	+ 2.45	56	+ 3:41	+ 2.45	117	+ 4:42	+ 2.45	81	+ 4:06	+ 2.45	55	+ 3:40
+ 3.00	79	+ 4:19	+ 3.00	57	+ 3:57	+ 3.00	116	+ 4:56	+ 3.00	82	+ 4:22	+ 3.00	55	+ 3:55
+ 3.15	80	+ 4:35	+ 3.15	58	+ 4:13	+ 3.15	114	+ 5:09	+ 3.15	84	+ 4:39	+ 3.15	55	+ 4:10
+ 3.30	82	+ 4:52	+ 3.30	58	+ 4:28	+ 3.30	113	+ 5:23	+ 3.30	86	+ 4:56	+ 3.30	55	+ 4:25
+ 3.45	85	+ 5:10	+ 3.45	59	+ 4:44	+ 3.45	111	+ 5:36	+ 3.45	89	+ 5:14	+ 3.45	55	+ 4:40
+ 4.00	88	+ 5:28	+ 4.00	59	+ 4:59	+ 4.00	109	+ 5:49	+ 4.00	91	+ 5:31	+ 4.00	54	+ 4:54
+ 4.15	91	+ 5:46	+ 4.15	60	+ 5:15	+ 4.15	108	- 5:57	+ 4.15	87	+ 5:42	+ 4.15	54	+ 5:09
+ 4.30	94	- 5:56	+ 4.30	60	+ 5:30	+ 4.30	106	- 5:44	+ 4.30	84	+ 5:54	+ 4.30	54	+ 5:24
+ 4.45	96	- 5:39	+ 4.45	60	+ 5:45	+ 4.45	104	- 5:31	+ 4.45	81	- 5:54	+ 4.45	54	+ 5:39
+ 5.00	98	- 5:22	+ 5.00	61	- 5:59	+ 5.00	103	- 5:17	+ 5.00	77	- 5:43	+ 5.00	54	+ 5:54
+ 5.15	101	- 5:04	+ 5.15	61	- 5:44	+ 5.15	102	- 5:03	+ 5.15	75	- 5:30	+ 5.15	54	- 5:51
+ 5.30	103	- 4:47	+ 5.30	61	- 5:29	+ 5.30	102	- 4:48	+ 5.30	73	- 5:17	+ 5.30	54	- 5:36
+ 5.45	112	- 4:23	+ 5.45	62	- 5:13	+ 5.45	101	- 4:34	+ 5.45	71	- 5:04	+ 5.45	54	- 5:21
+ 6.00	114	- 4:06	+ 6.00	62	- 4:58	+ 6.00	101	- 4:19	+ 6.00	69	- 4:51	+ 6.00	54	- 5:06

Working the tables in reverse to find a start time

These are just some of the ways in which the tables may be used in relation to one route. Each route will have its own issues and these are covered in the Route Guidance section next.

Remember - all times are based upon HW Sheerness

Note also *that all tidal predictions are just that – predictions. It is not a timetable. These tables complete the calculations for you but normal navigational prudence must remain your responsibility.*

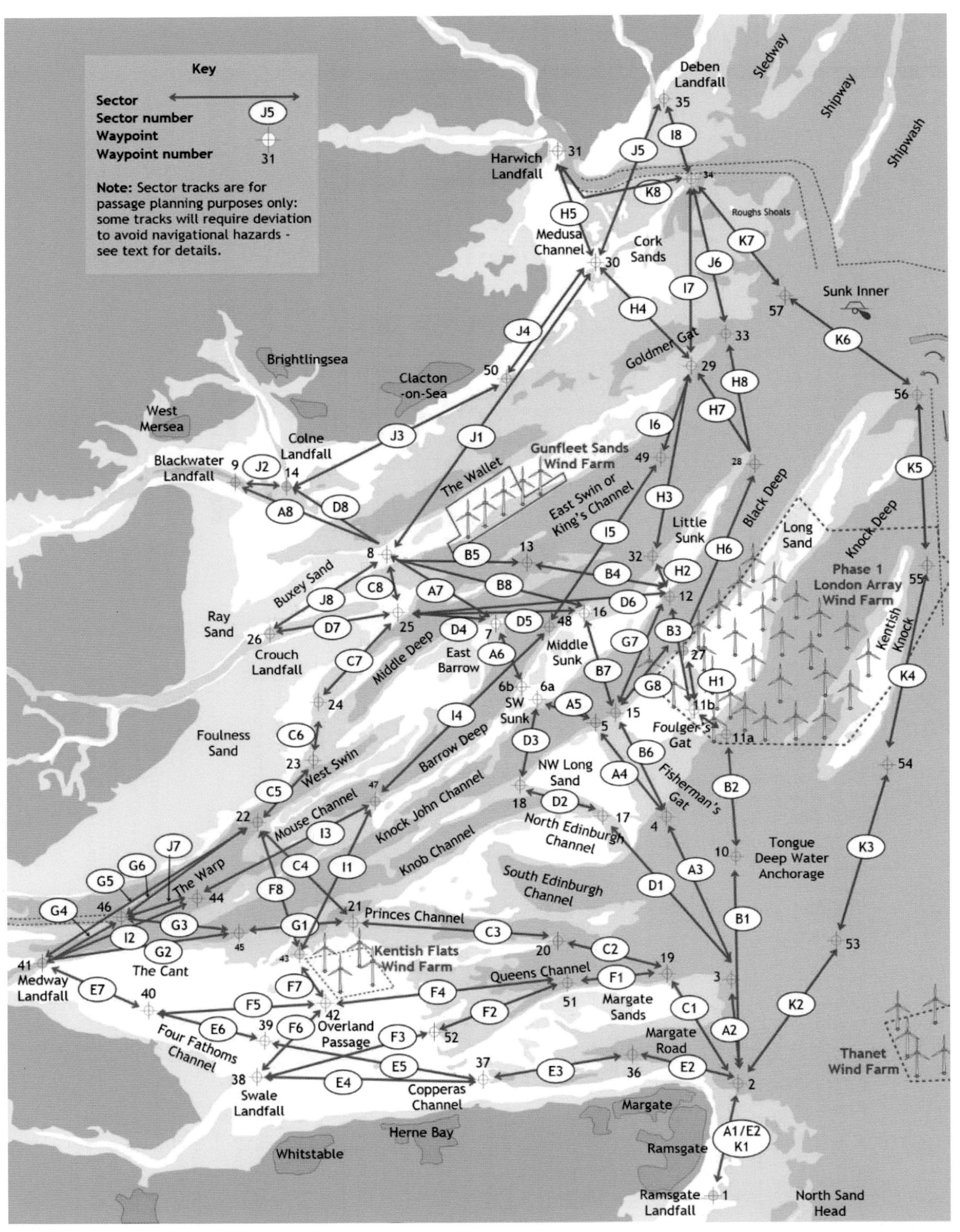
Key
Sector
Sector number
J5
Waypoint
Waypoint number
31
Note: Sector tracks are for passage planning purposes only: some tracks will require deviation to avoid navigational hazards - see text for details.
Deben Landfall
Sledway
Shipway
Shipwash
Harwich Landfall
Roughs Shoals
Medusa Channel
Cork Sands
Sunk Inner
Goldmer Gat
Brightlingsea
Clacton -on-Sea
West Mersea
Colne Landfall
Blackwater Landfall
Gunfleet Sands Wind Farm
The Wallet
East Swin or King's Channel
Little Sunk
Black Deep
Long Sand
Knock Deep
Phase 1 London Array Wind Farm
Kentish Knock
Buxey Sand
Ray Sand
Crouch Landfall
Middle Deep
East Barrow
Middle Sunk
SW Sunk
Foulger's Gat
Foulness Sand
West Swin
Barrow Deep
NW Long Sand
Fisherman's Gat
Mouse Channel
Knock John Channel
North Edinburgh Channel
Tongue Deep Water Anchorage
The Warp
Knob Channel
South Edinburgh Channel
Princes Channel
Kentish Flats Wind Farm
The Cant
Medway Landfall
Queens Channel
Margate Sands
Overland Passage
Four Fathoms Channel
Margate Road
Thanet Wind Farm
Swale Landfall
Copperas Channel
Margate
Herne Bay
Whitstable
Ramsgate
Ramsgate Landfall
North Sand Head

Navigating the Estuary

The complexity of navigating the Thames Estuary lies in the many issues to be considered. There is nothing unusual in these issues – tides, sandbanks, channels, shipping, wind farms and unmarked hazards. These will be encountered anywhere but the Thames Estuary has more than its share. But careful planning can deal with all of these issues, indeed take advantage of some of them and thus provide a much more interesting passage than a featureless cross channel trip from the south coast.

This part of the book provides an overview of the principal navigation issues to be considered. More detailed advice, applicable to particular routes, will be found in the route guidance section which follows.

The Sands and Shoal Waters

The estuary tidal patterns have their unusual side so whether to start talking about the sands or the tides is a moot point. But if the sands were not there, then the passage across the estuary would be simple so let us start with them.

Travelling north from North Foreland, the yachtsman or woman will come in turn to the Margate Sand, then the Long Sand, Sunk Sand, Barrow Sand and the Buxey/Gunfleet Sands.

The Margate Sand

Those bound between Ramsgate and the Essex Rivers will skirt the eastern side of the Margate Sands which is well marked by the East Margate port hand buoy. Those heading from or to the Kent Rivers will either go round the top of the sand by the east and north side and use the Queens or Princes Channel or use the south side via Margate Road, and the Gore and Copperas Channels. The East Margate buoy has not needed moving in recent years but the western side of the sands altered in 2012 with the closure of the East Last swatchway and in consequence, Trinity House moved the buoyage to mark the Copperas Channel. Once through the Copperas Channel to either the Swale or Medway, yachts will encounter the shoal but passable waters off the North Kent coast.

The Long Sand

The Long Sand runs for approximately 25 nm north-east to south-west across the middle of the Estuary from the dangerous Long Sand Head to the Princes Channel. Phase one of the London Array Wind Farm has been built on the Long Sand to the north-east of Fisherman's Gat and across the Knock Deep. Whether phase two as a north-eastern extension will be built remains to be seen. Recent moves of the sand have been a gradual migration and shallowing of the Long Sand Head north-east giving the Black Deep *QR* port hand buoy the dubious honour of being the most moved buoy in the Estuary.

Moving south-west down the sand, the impact of the wind farm on the Sand remains to be seen. Scouring is observed around turbine bases and it has been surmised that the scoured sand will be deposited between the turbines. Foulger's Gat has seen some natural movement towards the north-east and since there is an immovable 'avenue' for yachts through the turbines to use the Gat, it is to be hoped that such movement will be minimal. But since there has been immense seabed activity with the placing of turbine bases and the burying of innumerable power cables it may take a few years for nature to settle down again.

To cross the Long Sand, there are three practical channels: Fisherman's Gat, Foulger's Gat or the North Edinburgh. In theory there is a fourth option of the South Edinburgh but that is un-buoyed and has little advantage over the Princes Channel route which goes round the Long Sand to the west as so is ignored in this guidance. Indeed the North Edinburgh Channel is also now un-marked and whilst once 20 years ago was the principle route for yachts, it is a now a GPS only option and has suffered from the absence of a recent survey. However, in 2014, the Port of London Authority, having finished over two year's extensive work preparing the Sea Reach and Black Deep for the larger London Gateway traffic, is returning to more normal survey programmes which include a current revision of depths at the North Edinburgh. As a consequence, the North Edinburgh remains in the planning tables and advice as an option.

Fisherman's Gat is the most popular route across the Long Sand. It is a stable way across the Sand being extremely well marked, flat with a controlling depth of over 8m at Chart Datum (CD) and now with reduced commercial traffic as a result of the dredging of the Princes Channel several ago. A Precautionary Area remains where Fisherman's Gat joins the Black Deep. Whilst commercial traffic using the Gat appears much reduced, this remains a significant junction for commercial shipping where a ship may need to turn sharply in or out of the Gat to join or leave the main Black Deep route.

Navigating the Estuary

Foulger's Gat is also popular but as a route suffered in 2011 and 2012 from interruptions from the construction of the first phase of the London Array Wind Farm. The Wind Farm is now constructed and commissioned and only unusual maintenance could close down that route – and then only temporarily. Using Foulger's Gat will, however, be more unusual than most swatchways as the Wind Farm developers have left us a dog-legged avenue through the turbines. The avenue is of sufficient width and the turbines are numbered but as you will not be wishing to get that close to the turbines, Trinity House have reinstated the buoyage in the Gat, including the provision of a 'middle' safe water buoy where the pivot of the dog-leg is encountered. It has been reported that identifying the safe water buoys at night against the background of the lights on each turbine is very difficult and that as the safe water buoys are not within sight of each other from the cockpit of a yacht, the turbines can become disorientating at times.

The Sunk Sand

The Sunk Sand is a similar north-east to south-west lying sand running for some 18nm to the north of the Long Sand separated by the Black Deep and Knock John channels. It is unfortunately more troublesome than the Long Sand as in contrast to the buoyage of Fisherman's and Foulger's Gats, it is completely devoid of marks to aid leisure craft.

The choice facing us is crossing at the South-West, Middle or Little Sunk. Of the three, the crossing point at the Little Sunk suffers the least change, is a relatively wide and flat expanse with a controlling depth of 3m. Inevitably, for the Essex Rivers, the Little Sunk adds the most distance – over 4 nm to the overall passage.

The South-West Sunk swatchway is the shortest route to any of the Essex Rivers but this is an area of sand that moves. It is though, generally stable for the season and readers are referred to: www.crossingthethamesestuary.com where the very latest information is maintained including the provision of a chartlet showing depths and recommended waypoints over this part of the sands.

The Middle Sunk area is less volatile than the South-West Sunk but over recent years a shoal 'finger' of sand has built north-east over the top of this route which is best avoided before a course can be struck for the Whitaker or Spitway. The latest position on this route will also be posted on the web site.

Courtesy of Bob Darby

The Foulger's Gat 'avenue' between rows 'A' and 'B' heading for the Long Sand Middle safe water buoy

Barrow Sands

Back in the thirties, the pilot books recommended a half-tide route from the Crouch across the Whitaker Sand to the Swin Middle Light Float which was the ideal starting point to cross the Barrow Sands via the Barrow Beacon and save miles down to the SW Sunk. Such a route has fallen from popularity and whilst the Barrow Beacon still stands, most pass round the east and north side of the Barrow when crossing the middle of the Estuary.

The edges of the sand are not well marked for us with the exception of the West Swin and the southern eastern edge which is marked by the Barrow No 7 *(Fl.G.2.5s)* starboard hand buoy. But the eastern side shallows gently and it is easy to run approximately north or south along the edge watching the echo sounder. With the sands to windward in a south-westerly, there is frequently flat water and an enjoyable sail here.

At the north east corner, it is necessary to beware a shallow 'finger' that has extended north-east. A *Wk awash* (but I have never seen it) has to be left to the west and whilst there is a sort of swatchway to the east of the marked position of the wreck, going too much to the east can take you over the shallowest part of this finger and make the readings on your echo sounder plummet. Simply going further east brings deeper water.

The Buxey/Gunfleet Sands

The Buxey and Gunfleet Sands extend for 20nm, north-east from Holliwell Point on the Burnham/Bradwell peninsula to off the Naze. Moving north-east from Holliwell Point there is a half-tide route across the Ray Sand (the Rays'nd) between the Crouch and Blackwater and further east, the Spitway which separates the Buxey from the Gunfleet. Both these passages are well marked.

The Gunfleet is dominated by the Gunfleet Wind Farm which faces Clacton. This wind farm sits astride the old 1930's position of the Spitway which was once almost due south of Clacton Pier. The current position of the Spitway which is more convenient for the Blackwater and Colne than then, has a controlling depth of about 1.5m. It is to be hoped that it remains or we may be faced with a choice of finding the old swatchway in the middle of the wind farm or a long detour round the head of the Gunfleet.

The East Barrow Beacon

The Tides

In the northern part of the Estuary, the tidal flows are linear and follow the broad shape of the coastline; therefore simply flowing round East Anglia and into the Estuary and our Rivers on the flood and back again on the ebb. In the southern part, the tide floods north up past Ramsgate and for a couple of hours curls round North Foreland to head west to join the last of the south bound flood. Then, at high water up at Sheerness and the mouth of the Thames, this north going tide at the North Foreland stops its westerly curl and heads north. For three hours it joins the main north going ebb from the Estuary. Only +3:30 HW Sheerness, does the tide start to curl back south round the North Foreland.

Coupled with 7 hours flood and 5 hours ebb, this tidal pattern gives us some opportunities. Equally it can provide some adverse tide if planning is neglected. The 5 hour ebb does mean that the tidal rate can be high when the ebb gets into full flow. The highest rates in the estuary can be found in the West Swin and Black Deep where 2.8kts may be encountered on the ebb. Great if you are going the right way although I admit to running down the Black Deep with the wind behind us and over 2.5 knots of tide revelling in a SOG of 10 knots, only to miss the crossing point over the Little Sunk! Whilst it was simple to carry on down the Black Deep to the Sunk Head, the resulting beat into the Naze trying to stay up-wind and up-tide of the South Cork north cardinal buoy on a very wet day was not quite so much fun.

Useful tidal times related to HW Sheerness

-6:30	West going tide starts along the North Kent Coast;
-2:30	North going tide starts at Ramsgate, joins west going tide round the North Foreland;
-1:30	North going ebb starts north-east of a line from Walton-on-the-Naze to Foulger's Gat;
	Some light north-west component in tide at the Sunk Gyratory and the top of the major channels (Black Deep, Barrow Deep, East Swin);
-0:30	West going tide round North Foreland and along North Kent coast stops;
	North going tide from Ramsgate, past North Foreland continues north towards the Long Sand;
	Ebb flowing fully parallel north-east of a line from Walton to Foulger's Gat;
+0:30	East going tide along North Kent coast starts, heads north off North Foreland
	Ebb starts in the Outer Crouch, Blackwater and Colne;

Navigating the Estuary

+1:30 North going tide Ramsgate and North Foreland now heading more north-Easterly;
+3:30 North going tide off Ramsgate stops;
+6:00 LW slack west of a line from Walton to Herne Bay;
+6:30 East going tide along North Kent coast stops;

The Major Channels

Moving north from North Foreland, the major channels into the London River are the Queens and Princes Channels, the Black and Barrow Deeps, the Kings Channel or East Swin (leading to the West Swin) and the Wallet.

Shipping makes use principally of the Princes and Black Deep channels although smaller vessels will be encountered in the Barrow Deep, Fisherman's Gat and the West Swin. The JJ Prior fleet of aggregate carriers will be often found plying their trade to London from Fingringhoe via the Spitway and West Swin while spoil from the London Crossrail project will be brought up the Barrow Deep, round the East Barrow sands and into the newly fully buoyed Crouch for placement on the Wallesea Wetlands (opposite Burnham).

The Princes Channel traffic will be encountered by north-south leisure craft shortly after leaving the East Margate. Generally this is not as busy as the cross-channel TSS routes but it may be worth listening to London VTS on channel 69 while you are between North Foreland and the Barrow Sands.

We can expect the large traffic in the Black Deep to increase – both in size and frequency with the opening of the London Gateway. The London Gateway has been a major development of the old Shell terminals at Hole Haven into 6 deep water berths with 17m of water and 2700 metres of quay. 2012 and 2013 saw major dredging of the Sea Reach, Oaze, Knock John and Black Deep channels to provide a deep water route from the Sunk Gyratory to the Gateway quays. This deep water route is marked with special buoys and will be used by vessel constrained by their draught. We should keep clear! We should be especially careful if our route takes us across the Thames end of the Princes Channel across the Oaze Deep for example when heading for the West Swin. This area is subject to special rules under PLA Bye-Laws to control the safe passing of in-bound and out-bound traffic and is rigorously controlled by London VTS. Leisure craft will not be a priority and should keep a good and early lookout to understand what traffic is moving. Monitoring of London VHS on VHF channel 69 seems essential.

Ships in-bound are required to report their movements at the Sunk Head Tower if using the Black Deep or before entrance to the Princes Channel. Note that special buoys in the centre of these channels mark the deep water. The Port of London Authority provides advice that recreational vessels should avoid using the Black Deep, Fisherman's Gat and Princes Channel. Routes in this book avoid the Knock John and the lower part of the Black Deep. However, crossing it has to happen somewhere and if using their recommended route of Foulger's Gat, the leisure craft has to go somewhere once they arrive at the edge of the Black Deep! Comment on using Princes Channel and the Black Deep channel and the precautions to take is made at the relevant point of in the detailed route guidance.

Note that Fisherman's Gat and Princes Channel have sufficient depth for yachts outside the buoyed channel which we should use.

Finally, mention should be made of the Sunk Gyratory. All of the 'inside' routes in this book avoid the Gyratory but nonetheless as a major maritime 'roundabout' we should be aware of it.

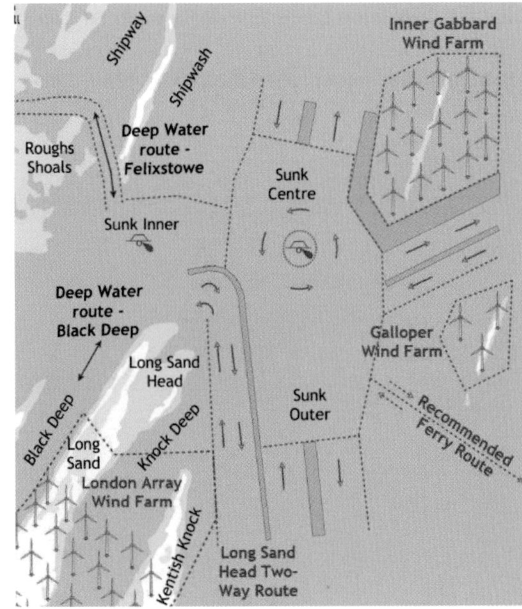

The Sunk Gyratory

The Gyratory comprises two 'roundabouts' and six 'roads' in. Its purpose is to separate major shipping arriving or leaving from Harwich harbour or the London River whether from or to the north, east or south. The main gyratory movement is anti-clockwise round the Sunk centre but the Long Sand Head two-way route provides a route direct into the Black Deep rather like those protected left hand turn lanes at some road roundabouts. The result is that traffic to and from the Black Deep can simply come up the side of the Kentish Knock and turn down the Black Deep without going round either the Sunk Centre or Inner Sunk light floats.

The Sunk Gyratory is really outside the geographical limits of this book as it marks the end of the crossing of the estuary but it will be relevant to people choosing the outside route from the Deben or Harwich Harbour. If trying to stay to the west of the two-way route when using a route outside of the estuary, do give Long Sand Head sufficient sea-room. It has been extending north-east in recent years and a yacht grounding here is always seen as a serious issue.

Wind Farms

The Thames Estuary has four established Wind Farms within it and two additional Wind Farms adjacent to the Sunk Gyratory. A further, huge, Wind Farm is authorised from Suffolk to Norfolk but at the time of publication has yet to commence the construction phase. Notification will be made on the web site as and when this occurs.

The four established Wind Farms within the estuary will be visible on many passages but only two of them are likely to be approached closely; these are the London Array and the Kentish Flats. Thanet will be visible to the east approaching the North Foreland and the Gunfleet will be ever present while crossing the East Swin or Spitway. However, neither will be approached sufficiently closely to hinder passage.

The London Array, however, is different. It sits astride Foulger's Gat with an avenue left for us for transit through the Gat. Being used for the first time in 2014 clear of construction traffic, there are currently some initial concerns about the visibility of navigation marks within the 'avenue' against quite significant light pollution from lights on individual turbines. This has been raised with Trinity House and it remains to be seen how it will be handled. Detailed information on passage using this 'avenue' is included in the relevant route guidance. Planning permission has been given for a Phase Two build on this Wind Farm but immediate plans for development of this extension have been dropped by the owners. Should Phase Two occur, it will expand the Wind Farm along the Long Sand and Knock Deep to the North East but this is unlikely, construction traffic apart, to cause recreational craft any problem.

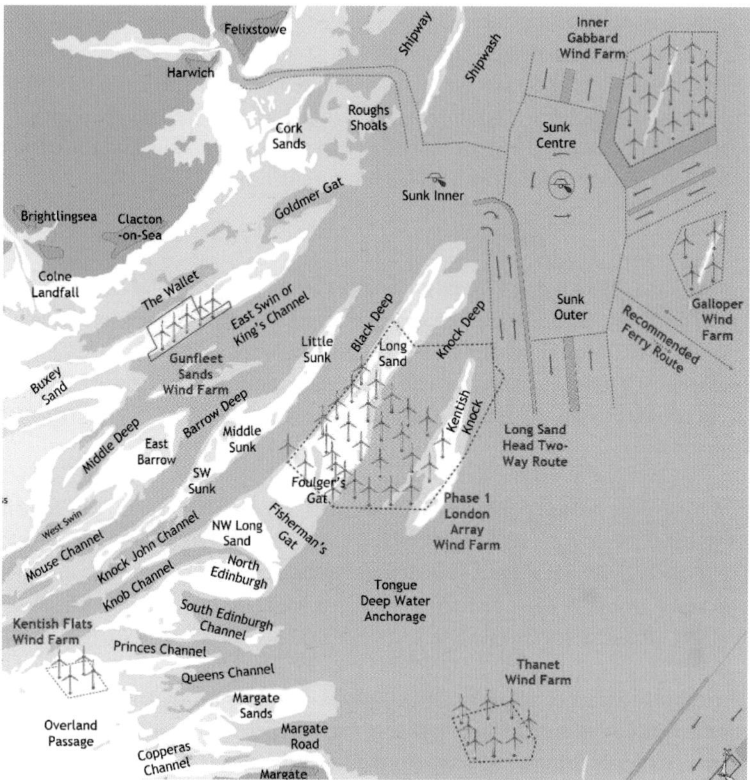

Wind Farms in the Thames Estuary

The main cabling from Wind Farm to shore from the London Array to Kent has required some specific underwater work where it crosses existing power cables. This consists of a rock berm in each of two locations to retain and protect the cables. The locations are on the edge of the Princes Channel where the London Array cable passes over the BritNed power cable (British-Netherlands) and on the Kentish Flats where it crosses the Kentish Flats cables. Both are marked but the latter is of the greatest concern to recreational craft as it reduces depths to less than a metre at chart datum.

Navigating the Estuary

The significance of the risk is illustrated by the provision of three yellow Special Marks and a South Cardinal Buoy at this point. The Kentish Flats Wind Farm sits astride the direct route from the Swale out into the Knob and Knock John Channels and so currently must be left to the east and passage taken up the west side of the Wind Farm between the Wind Farm and the East Spaniard and East Middle Sands. Work is planned to commence on an extension to this Wind Farm to the south and west sides in 2015 and this will make a west side passage doubtful. Certainly we can expect this to be prohibited during construction. Up to date information will be provided on the web site and the current best information is described in the detailed route guidance.

Wind Farm Rules

Once constructed, there is a 50m radius 'advisory caution' zone around each turbine or sub-station platform. Blade clearance is more than sufficient to clear the masts of recreational craft but you should be aware that the cable connection may extend underwater for several metres on one side of the monopole. The cable rises from the seabed into what is called a 'J' tube – so named because of its shape and then up the side of the monopole.

Exclusion zones may be put in place during construction or maintenance. This can either be a 200m or 500m zone depending on the work involved. Since such maintenance or construction may involve divers and underwater cabling, common sense dictates that any work should be given the widest berth. Maintenance warnings can be heard from time-to-time being broadcast on channel 16.

Note also that the effect of all the construction work on the surrounding seabed has yet to be quantified. Scouring around the monopoles has been experienced and the material so scoured may well be deposited between turbines causing uneven depths. Wind Farms are probably best avoided apart from the designated route that is Foulger's Gat through the London Array.

Unmarked Hazards

With the exception of the Copperas Channel and Foulger's Gat buoyed by Trinity House, there is no buoyage in the main estuary just for recreational craft. There is, of course, helpful local buoyage such as the Ray Sand provided by the Crouch Harbour Master and the Walton Backwaters provided by the Walton and Frinton Yacht club but otherwise we use main shipping buoyage. Which is fine except that only the Long Sand cross sand routes are marked for us. Hoped-for transits using distant wind farms do not seem possible.

Back in the 1950's, the Admiralty erected a series of beacons – it seems for surveying training purposes - on the Sunk and Long Sands and whilst these were not placed specifically to mark swatchways, some did help. Unfortunately most of these did not survive far past the Millennium. Beacons at the South-West, Middle and Little Sunk and the NW Long Sand have collapsed and form dangerous wreckage on the sands. Each of those beacons is now an unmarked hazard. The NW Long Sand is unlikely to trouble any recreational craft on a sensible course but the three collapsed Sunk beacons are sufficiently close to current crossing places as to need care. But their position is known and with normal prudence they need not hinder leisure craft. Specific guidance is given in the detailed route guidance.

The estuary sands are the resting place for many ships from the World Wars and aircraft from World War II. Many are known and marked but the sands do change constantly, exposing and covering wreckage from time to time. These changes make it sensible to be prudent when considering a short cut; for example the image below shows a German V12 aircraft engine, probably from a JU88 bomber, at extra low water springs. Charted as a *FOUL*, movement of the sands has exposed it leaving it as a dangerous piece of wreckage until time reverses the process and once more hides it until it is wreckage just below the surface again.

The routes recommended in this book are selected to avoid such hazards.

The Routes

Ramsgate to the Essex Rivers

This section contains detailed guidance on 6 routes between the three Essex Rivers of the Crouch, Blackwater and Colne which between them comprise Routes 1 to 18. Effectively there are six options for crossing the Estuary with variations at the end of the passage depending upon the River of your destination.

All routes start with the *Ramsgate Landfall,* Waypoint No 1 which is adjacent to the Ramsgate No 3 Starboard Hand Buoy *(Fl.G.2.5s)*. Remember to leave yourself time to leave harbour to reach the vicinity of this waypoint as it is easy to take up to an hour easing yourself out of Ramsgate Marina, waiting for permission to leave, hoisting sails or whatever.

The destination landfalls are each deliberately chosen at the entrance or early part of the three Essex Rivers as your ultimate destination up river will vary. Part of your planning criteria will be the extra time needed to reach your berth from the Landfall waypoint. To assist, at the end of this section, approximate distances between the Landfall waypoint and common destinations are provided.

The choices of route

The overall passage distance can vary by up to 10nm depending upon the route chosen so the choice is worth a bit of forethought and really it will be governed by whether you want to cross the Sunk Sand or go round it. Comparable distances are shown on pages 52 and 53 but as a quick reference via Fisherman's Gat and the South-West Sunk is the shortest and the Princes Channel the longest. To avoid crossing the Sunk Sand, the only practical choice is to use the Princes Channel and West Swin which takes you round the western end of the Long and Sunk Sands. It is also not unknown for leisure craft to travel the length of the Wallet or East Swin and go round the eastern end of the Sands but that is so unusual and adds so much distance that this book does not cover that route.

The Princes Channel and West Swin route is by far the longest passage between Ramsgate and the Essex Rivers. It suffers the complication that it is impossible to carry a favourable tide for the whole passage being *Z* in shape. Depths, however, will not be an issue apart from the Spitway for those bound for the Blackwater or Colne (but then this affects all routes to those two rivers) but care will need to be taken to keep out of the way of shipping especially in the

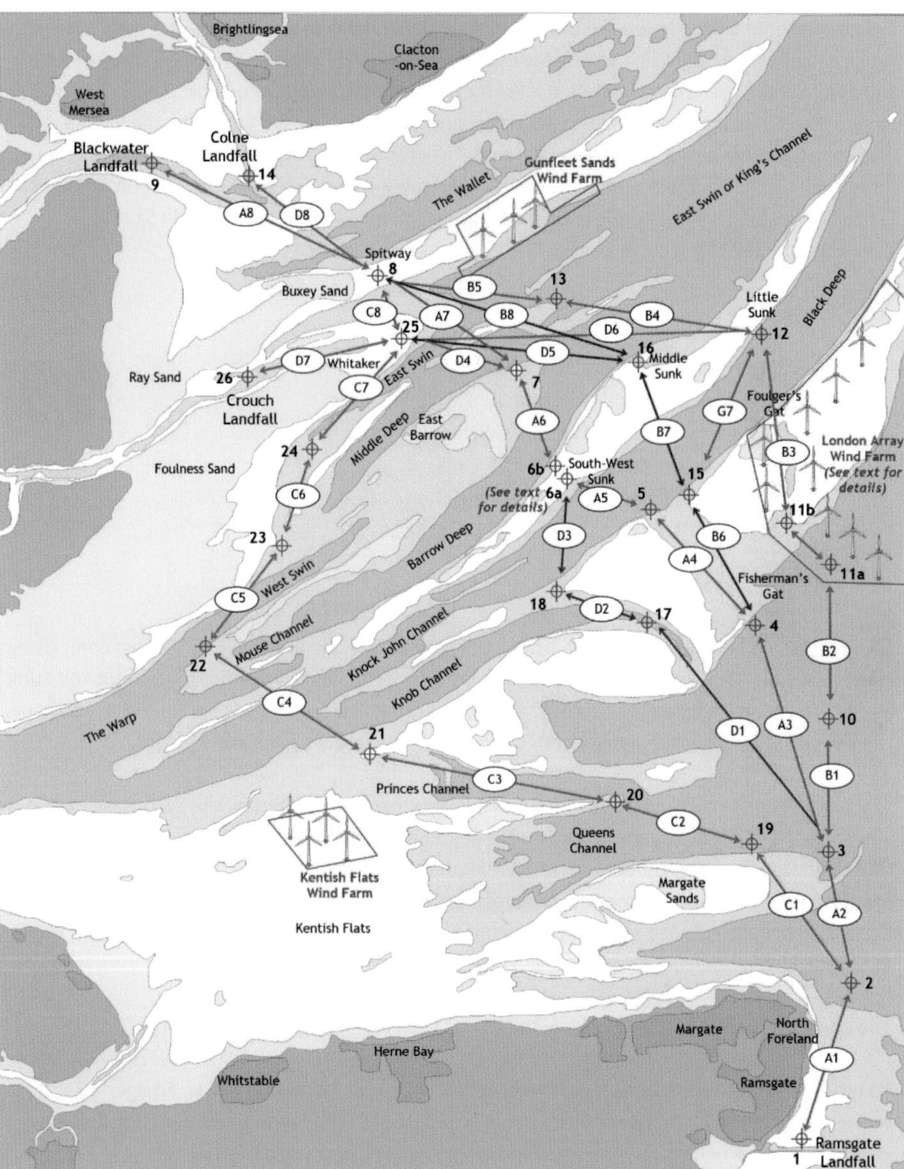

Princes Channel and crossing the Oaze. The five alternatives to the Princes Channel route are much closer to a straight line across the Estuary and thereby shorter. However, they require the Sunk Sand to be crossed either at the South-West, Middle or Little Sunk. This is the critical choice as your option of route over the Long Sand will match where you cross the Sunk Sand. The Long Sand has three options for crossing; Fisherman's Gat, Foulger's Gat or the North Edinburgh Channel. The South Edinburgh is also viable for leisure craft but it is unmarked and is too far west to match any commonly frequented crossing point for the Sunk Sand. Consequently it is not a route covered by this book.

So the choices are:

- Via Fisherman's Gat and the South-West Sunk;
- Via Foulger's Gat and the Little Sunk;
- Via Fisherman's Gat and the Middle Sunk;
- Via Fisherman's Gat and the Little Sunk;
- Via the North Edinburgh channel and the South-West Sunk;
- Via Princes Channel and the West Swin.

Overview

So there are six choices for passage from Ramsgate to any of the three Essex Rivers comprising routes 1 to 18. Those choices are determined by how you wish to deal with the Long and Sunk Sands. There are five choices passing through the Long and Sunk Sands and one alternative via the Princes Channel which avoids both Sands but is inevitably significantly longer.

The main issue for consideration when selecting your route is posed by the Sunk Sand. Once you cross this Sand at any of the three crossing points you will really want to carry the flood tide to your destination on the Crouch, Colne or Blackwater. Given the distance to be travelled up those rivers to your destination, ordinarily you would seek to have crossed the Sunk Sand close to low water. Those readers with deeper draught yachts will thus regard the Sunk Sand as a tidal gate when using the planning tables.

The Long Sand

To cross the Long Sand, there are three practical channels: Fisherman's Gat, Foulger's Gat or the North Edinburgh. In theory there is a fourth option of the South Edinburgh but that is un-buoyed and has little advantage over the Princes Channel route as so is ignored in this guidance. Indeed the North Edinburgh Channel is also now un-marked and whilst once 20 years ago was the principle route for yachts, it is now a GPS only option suffering from the absence of a recent survey. It remains discussed as an option as the Estuary changes and thus in the future such guidance might be useful.

Fisherman's Gat is the most popular route across the Long Sand. It is a stable way across the Sand being extremely well marked, flat with a controlling depth of over 8m LAT now benefitting from slightly reduced commercial traffic as a result of the dredging of the Princes Channel several years ago. Foulger's Gat is also popular but as a route, suffered between 2011 and 2013 from interruptions from the construction of the first phase of the London Array Wind Farm.

The Wind Farm is now constructed and commissioned and only unusual maintenance could close down that route – and then only temporarily. Using Foulger's Gat will, however, be more unusual than most swatchways as the Wind Farm developers have left us a dog-legged avenue through the turbines. The avenue is of sufficient width and the turbines are numbered but as you will not be wishing to get that close, Trinity House have reinstated the buoyage in the Gat, including the provision of a middle safe water buoy where the pivot of dog-leg is encountered.

The Sunk Sand

The Sunk Sand is unfortunately more troublesome than the Long Sand and in contrast completely devoid of marks to aid leisure craft now that the 1950's Beacons at the South-West, Middle and Little Sunk have collapsed. Each of those three beacons is now an unmarked hazard but their position is known and with normal prudence need not hinder leisure craft. The choice facing us is crossing at the South-West, Middle or Little Sunk. Of the three, the crossing point at the Little Sunk suffers the least change, is a relatively wide and flat expanse with a controlling depth of 3m. Inevitably, for the Essex Rivers, the Little Sunk adds the most distance – over 4 nm.

The South-West Sunk swatchway is the shortest route to any of the Essex Rivers but is an area of sand that moves. It is though generally stable for the season and readers are referred to the web site: www.crossingthethamesestuary.com where the very latest information is maintained including the provision of a chartlet showing depths and recommended waypoints.

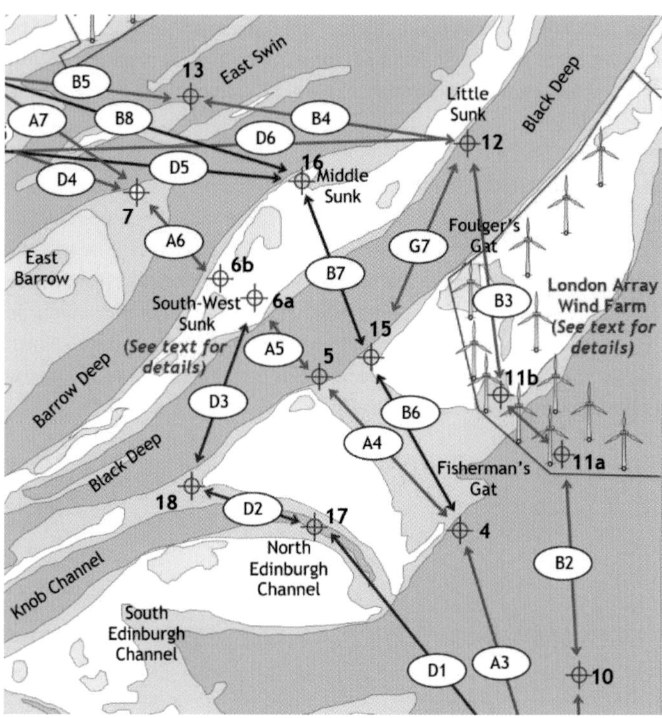

Crossing the Long and Sunk Sands

The Middle Sunk area is less volatile than the South-West Sunk but over recent years a shoal 'finger' of sand has built north-east over the top of this route which needs to be avoided before a course can be struck for the Whitaker or Spitway. The latest position on this route will also be posted on the web site but currently it provides no real advantage over the SW Sunk route.

Linking the choice of crossing point – Long and Sunk Sands

It is quite possible to choose any of the three crossing points of the Long Sand and any of the three across the Sunk Sand. But logic suggests that if you choose the North Edinburgh Channel you will cross the Sunk Sand via the SW Sunk Swatchway. Equally, if you use Foulger's Gat, it only makes sense to cross the Sunk Sand at the Little Sunk. Select Fisherman's Gat however, and you can opt for any of the three Sunk Sand crossings.

The Princes Channel

This route avoids crossing either the Long or Sunk Sand but suffers from the additional distance necessary to 'go round' those Sands. That can add 10 nm to the overall passage and provide a challenge to get the best from the tide as it needs the flood from North Foreland to the SW Barrow, the ebb through the West Swin and then slow progress against the remaining ebb up the Essex Rivers. Coming south has similar issues. Nevertheless, it does remove concerns over crossing the Sands. Commercial shipping will be encountered in the Princes Channel but there is sufficient room at the edges of the Channel to keep clear. Crossing the Knock John Channel on way to the SW Barrow will require a careful lookout for the largest commercial shipping that uses the Thames via the Black Deep and Knock John Channels. The deep water channel is not excessively wide and the crossing of inbound and outbound shipping is carefully controlled by London VTS and so should be accorded priority.

The Routes in detail

Routes 1, 7 & 13 – Ramsgate to the Essex Rivers via Fisherman's Gat and the SW Sunk

Sector A1 – Ramsgate to North Foreland

This 4.75nm sector is common to all routes to and from Ramsgate.

The southerly waypoint is adjacent to the No 3 Starboard Hand Mark (Fl G 2.5s) of the dredged approach channel to Ramsgate. This is chosen because it is convenient to those starting from Ramsgate and sufficiently close for those arriving via the Gull Stream from the Channel. Those coming north outside the Goodwin Sands via the North East Goodwin Buoy can also use the data for this sector without alteration. It should be noted that this waypoint is also adjacent to the recommended point at which yachts should cross the Ramsgate Channel. The northerly waypoint of the sector is an arbitrary position just north of the North Foreland. North Foreland light (*Fl(5)WR.20s57m 19-15M)* bears 209°(T) 1.93nm. This northerly waypoint is used for the routes to and from the Kent Rivers and all of the three routes across to the Long Sand.

The coastline on this sector is slightly elliptical and therefore the track between these waypoints passes close to the beach at Broadstairs. Although, the tides run largely north-south here, there are some inshore components at certain times and this may have effect of taking you to west of the uncorrected track. In practice you are more likely to steer a course parallel to the coast to keep a uniform distance off the shore. Apart from the coastline and associated shallows off the beaches, there are no particular hazards in this Sector but obviously the cliffs provide a significant lee from westerly's and is a lee shore for any wind with east in it.

Note that if coming southwards you intend to pass Ramsgate to continue south, for example for Dover, the south going tide from Ramsgate runs from +4:30 Dover to -1:30 Dover. Converting that to HW Sheerness to link in with the Planning Tables gives +3:30 Sheerness to -3:30 Sheerness, obviously with the best rates in the middle of this period. On the basis that the passage from Ramsgate to Dover is approximately 15nm, a yacht averaging 4 knots through the water would benefit from being off Ramsgate at least by +5:00 Sheerness. At 7 knots up to -5:30 Sheerness should still allow a favourable tide to be carried to Dover.

Sector A2 – North Foreland to East Margate

From this point heading north you will need to have decided which of the three crossing points of the Long Sand you are going to use. This decision in turn will depend upon which crossing point of the Sunk Sand you chose. The routes to the Essex Rivers start to diverge at the North Foreland waypoint depending upon your choice of crossing the Long Sand. For tidal calculation purposes, each of the three routes has two sectors between the North Foreland and the Long Sand as there may be either a strong West or North-East component in the tide.

From the North Foreland waypoint, the first of the two sectors to Fisherman's Gat (and also to the North Edinburgh Channel) use Sector A2 heading from the North Foreland waypoint to a waypoint close to the East Margate port hand buoy *(Fl.R.2.5s)* which bears 252˚(T), 0.45nm. The waypoint is east of the buoy but you should find ample water between the buoy and the sands it marks if necessary; provided, of course, you are not set down too far to the west of the buoy and therefore too close to the Margate Sand.

Sector A3 – East Margate to the Outer Fisherman

Thereafter the Fisherman's Gat route follows Sector A3 to a waypoint about half a mile from the Outer Fisherman east cardinal buoy *(Q(3) 10s)* bearing 025˚(T) 0.66nm. This is an unremarkable sector except that it crosses the track of shipping heading to or from the Queens and Princes Channels.

This course errs on the side of caution (towards the east) to avoid the finger of the Long Sand that extends north-east athwart our course at the bottom of Fisherman's Gat. For those who are not concerned about this finger (least charted depth 2_4), a few degrees to port when heading northbound will shape more directly for the Fisherman No 2 port hand buoy *(Fl R 2.5s).* This continuation of the course from Sector A2 is treated as separate in order to take advantage of a closer and therefore more accurate tidal diamond for the second part of the crossing to the Long Sand.

The tide can be particularly helpful at this point of the passage. The basic ebb in this Sector is North East into the North Sea. The ebb starts off Ramsgate -2:30 Sheerness but is not joined by the waters off the North Kent coast until an hour after HW Sheerness. The effect of this is that any northward journey from Ramsgate has two potential benefits; first from the favourable tide up past the North Foreland and secondly from a continuation of this favourable tide as it remains mainly northward towards the Outer Tongue until the ebb from the North Kent coast starts to push eastwards later. The downside of this is that inevitably you will arrive at both the Long Sand and Sunk Sand on a falling tide!

HMS Bulwark, the Royal Navy's 18,500 tonne Fleet Flagship, an assault command and control warship starts the sharp turn into Fisherman's Gat in May, 2014

Sector A4 – Outer Fisherman to Inner Fisherman

Note that it is not necessary to actually close to the Outer Fisherman east cardinal buoy. This is one part of the passage where Sector A3 can be 'merged' into Sector A4 as you near the Gat in order to save distance. The buoyage in Fisherman's Gat is intended for shipping and marks the controlling depth of 8_2 metres. The reader may be aware of suggestions that leisure craft should not use Fisherman's Gat and it is true that the Port of London Authority have issued a general discouragement to leisure craft saying that the Princes Channel, Black Deep and Fisherman's Gat should be avoided. The inclusion of Fisherman's Gat in that discouragement came before Princes Channel was dredged and now commercial traffic in the Gat is reduced. 'Reduced' note but not eliminated.

Large ships are still using the Gat. The confluence between the Black Deep and Fisherman's Gat is marked as a Precautionary Area to allow for ships turning in and out of this channel and certainly yachts must respect this. Container ships are unlikely to use the Gat because of their draught but even for 'smaller' ships this is a tight 'corner' and they will take up the whole channel. This is not the time for a small yacht to be present in the channel. However, plenty of water exists for yachts outside the buoyed channel and the authorities were content to allow the Gat to be used while Foulger's Gat was closed due to the construction of the London Array Wind Farm. Consequently prudent use leaving the marked channel clear and good observation should prevent any problem arising.

The tidal diamond for Fisherman's Gat is towards the southern part of the swatchway and generally shows a south-east ebb and north-west flood. My experience has been that the ebb can flow strongly southerly from the Black Deep into the Gat particularly when close to the Inner Fisherman for at least for some of the ebb. On several occasions I have experienced the tide running quite hard round this particular corner on the ebb into Fisherman's Gat but the current appeared to reduce quite quickly as we moved into the Black Deep. Such an effect is probably very local and caused by the shape of the Long Sand at this point.

The northerly waypoint of this sector is adjacent to the Inner Fisherman Port Hand Buoy [QR] which guards the shallow part of the north-east corner of the Long Sand.

Sector A5 – Inner Fisherman to the SW Sunk

This short sector of less than 2nm takes you across the Black Deep to the south waypoint for the SW Swatchway. Currently in 2014 this is at 51° 37'70N, 001° 18'80E with a corresponding north side waypoint of 51°38'025N, 001°16'200E giving a rhumb line across the Sunk Sand of 1.65nm at 101°(T)/281°(T) in least depth of 3_9 metres LAT. The Planning Tables make allowance for the distance across the sands.

There are a number of issues to consider in this Sector:

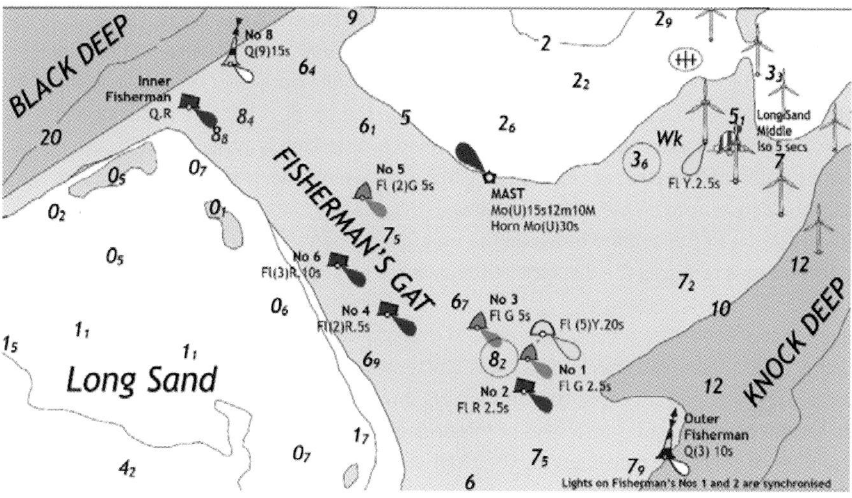

Fisherman's Gat (buoyage as at August 2014)

1. You are crossing a Precautionary Area with shipping using both the Black Deep and Fisherman's Gat. All will be constrained by their draught, particularly large container ships using the Black Deep to and from the new Container Port in the Thames at the London Gateway. Such ships may move quite rapidly in the Black Deep and may have very little under-keel clearance. A good look out is essential and it is worth listening in the London VTS transmissions on Channel 69. Inbound ships must report themselves at Long Sand Head and the approach to Fisherman's Gat. Outbound ships similarly report themselves on leaving Sea Reach;
2. As you cross the Black Deep you will be going athwart the tide which can run strongly through the Precautionary Area. Be prepared to counter cross track error especially in the light of item 3 next;
3. Both waypoints marking the SW Sunk should be strictly adhered to. They will take you across the Sunk Sand between a drying knoll to the south-west and a shallowing area to the north-east. Watching for any cross track error is again worthwhile although the effect of the tide is considerably reduced as you go over the sand.

The Routes – Ramsgate to the Essex Rivers

The SW Sunk is the most volatile part of the Sunk Sand and the swatchway does move. Perhaps more accurately as one swatchway closes, another becomes available. Indeed, the swatchway used from 2009 to 2013 could be seen to gradually close over the four years and in the winter of 2013 with a number of strong winds from the south, it became impassable. However, within a mile the current alternative previous described is available. With a controlling depth of 3_9 metres at chart datum, this is sufficiently deep for most leisure craft reducing the concerns of crossing the swatchway towards low water. An additional benefit is that its position is better aligned between the Inner Fisherman and the corner of the North-East Barrow sands reducing the distance of the passage by over a mile against the 2013 route.

However, readers comparing the coordinates of this swatchway against the 2014 edition of the UKHO chart or data derived from it on a chart plotter will see first, that this swatchway is not shown on the chart, and secondly, that this area is shown as a significant drying patch. The reason for this is that no official surveys of this area of the Sunk Sands have been completed for a number of years and consequently the chart cannot be updated. Nevertheless, CTTE found this swatchway in 2014 and it has been used successfully thoroughly the season. A download of a CTTE chartlet is available at www.crossingthethamesestuary.com where the reader is able to check on the current position with regard to this swatchway.

Attempts are made annually to check on the position of the swatchway and any changes necessary in the quoted waypoints will be notified on the web site at the earliest moment. The final issue for this sector is that tides turn earlier out in the middle of the estuary than they do at Sheerness. As a result note should be taken of the tidal differences table when calculating when the flood will start to flow at the SW Sunk. A useful way of instantly assessing the height of tide is to listen in the London VTS on channel 69. At 15 minutes to and after the hour, they broadcast the height of tide to one decimal point at four gauges in the Estuary: Walton, Margate, Shivering Sands and Southend. Height of water at the SW Sunk will generally be within 0.1 metre of the height of tide at Margate.

Tide at SW Sunk	Relationship to Sheerness times
Mean HW Springs	Approx. - 47 minutes
Mean HW Neaps	Approx. – 37 minutes
Mean LW Springs	Approx. – 47 minutes
Mean LW Neaps	Approx. – 18 minutes

Sector A6 – SW Sunk Swatchway to East Barrow Sands

This is a relative short and simple sector across the Barrow Deep and skirting the east side of the East Barrow Sand. In a strong blow from the south-west, the journey northwards will benefit from calmer waters in the lee of the sands. The sand shallows gently to the west and in clear weather, the route can be quite close to the sand. However, there is an unmarked wreck (*Wk awash)* at 51° 39'.45N, 001° 12'80E (approximately) to avoid and a shallow 'finger' of sand extending north-east from the Sands. The waypoint at the East Barrow Sands is conservative to avoid these two dangers but at the right state of tide, a shoal draft craft can cut inside of this waypoint providing care is taken to stay well clear of the unmarked wreck.

Sector A7 – East Barrow Sands to the Mid-point Spitway

This sector will only apply for craft bound for the Blackwater and Colne – on going sectors for those bound for the River Crouch are dealt with in the River Crouch section later.

The northerly waypoint is set mid-way between the two safe water marks of the Spitway. The track between there and the East Barrow Sands waypoint crosses the Middle Deep and East Swin which is separated by the NE Middle shoal with a least charted depth of 1_2 metres LAT. Those using this track near low water will therefore want to watch their track and may need to shape a small dogleg around the bank. Cutting inside the East Barrow waypoint if the tide and draught permits increases the possibility of a direct track between the waypoints without such a dogleg.

The first mark visible on this track will be the Whitaker east cardinal buoy *(Q(3)10s Bell)* which is a useful visual guide to eliminating cross track error as it is very close to a direct rhumb line between the two sector waypoints. There is ample water to allow yachts to pass the west of the buoy. To the north and well clear of the track will be the Gunfleet Wind Farm.

The Spitway is fully marked by Trinity House with two distinctly different safe water buoys: the Wallet Spitway buoy at the northern end, the Swin Spitway at the southern end. Many leisure craft adhere to the line between the two safe water marks – and indeed if you are transiting the Spitway between the Blackwater and Crouch, this is sensible. However, if bound to or from one of the crossing points over the Sunk Sand, a diagonal passage across the Spitway to the east of the two safe water marks is feasible. CTTE has conducted surveys of the Spitway and a downloadable chartlet is available from the web site.

The Whitaker East Cardinal with the Gunfleet Sands Wind Farm dominating the backdrop

The Spitway itself is shown on UKHO charts as having a least charted depth of 1_5 metres but CTTE has found slightly less depths of 1_3 metres just to the west of the south end of a direct line between the two safe water marks. Curiously there seems to be more concern about depths at the SW Sunk than the Spitway. The SW Sunk is, of course, notorious for changing depths but perhaps the Spitway is considered less of a hazard because it is conveniently marked with Safe Water Marks at either end or because of its great familiarity for those from the Essex Rivers. The point is, though, that depth of water may well be an issue for some here and therefore it is an important tidal gate.

Times of high and low water at the Spitway will also be earlier than the times of high and low water at Sheerness. The relative mean values on Sheerness times are in the column opposite.

Section A8 – Mid-point Spitway to River Blackwater Landfall

This sector only applies for those bound for the River Blackwater. Please see the section on the River Colne for connection from the Spitway to the River Colne Landfall.

Tide at Spitway	Relationship to Sheerness times
Mean HW Springs	Approx. - 42 minutes
Mean HW Neaps	Approx. – 32 minutes
Mean LW Springs	Approx. – 42 minutes
Mean LW Neaps	Approx. – 22 minutes

Once clear of the Spitway, the passage enters its final sector bringing you past the Bench Head starboard hand buoy *(Fl(3)G.10s)* (acknowledged as the entrance to the Blackwater) to the Landfall waypoint.

The Wallet and Swin Spitway safe water buoys

For passage planning purposes this is treated as a single rhumb line of over 8nm but intruding shoals require a little more consideration particularly if you are taking the first of the flood from the Spitway. A direct rhumb line between the mid-point Spitway waypoint and the Blackwater Landfall off Sales Point would take us over the Knoll and later on the passage close to St Peters Flats. To avoid the worst of the Knoll, leave the Knoll north cardinal buoy *(Q)* and Eagle starboard hand buoy (QG) reasonably close to the east. This will take you to the east of the worst shallows of the Knoll. From the Eagle, leave the Colne Bar starboard hand buoy *(FL(2) G.5s)* to the north, the NW Knoll port hand buoy *(Fl (2) R.5 s)* to the south and finally the Bench Head starboard hand buoy *(Fl(3) G.10s)* to the north.

The Blackwater Landfall has Mersea Island to starboard of the track and the Bradwell peninsula to port. The decommissioned Nuclear Power Station at Bradwell will have been a constant visual cue from the Spitway in all but the worst visibility or fog and as you near the waypoint, the stub of the power station baffle wall set out in the River will become visible as a useful aim point.

Over on the Bradwell shore the passage of a different sort – time – is marked with a small stone building with red tiled roof. This is St Peters-on-the Wall, St Cedd's church of the 7th century, itself built on the former back wall of Othona, a Roman fort, part of the half ring of 3rd century defences from the Wash to the Isle of Wight. All of which is now dominated by 21st century technology of a land based wind farm.

St Cedd's 7th church now overshadowed by 21st century technology

From Blackwater Landfall to:	Approximate distance	From Blackwater Landfall to:	Approximate distance
West Mersea	1.23nm	Bradwell Marina	1.63nm
Tollesbury Marina	3.44nm	Marconi	5.48nm
Osea Island	6.10nm	Maylandsea	8.10nm
Heybridge Basin	9.21nm	Maldon	10.53nm

Routes 2, 8 & 14 – Ramsgate to the Essex Rivers via Foulger's Gat and the Little Sunk

Sector A1 – Ramsgate to North Foreland – Page 17

These routes all start with the first sector from Ramsgate to North Foreland previously described and there is nothing to add.

Sectors B1 and B2 – North Foreland to Long Sand Outer

For passage planning purposes, the track, close to 12nm, from the North Foreland waypoint to the Long Sand Outer waypoint at the entrance to the London Array Wind Farm is treated as two sectors in order to apply the tidal affect using two different tidal diamonds. In consequence there is a mid-point waypoint near the edge of the Tongue deep-water anchorage. The track should carry you to the west of any anchored ships waiting pilotage up to the London River.

There are no navigation hazards in these two sectors but shipping passing to and from Princes Channel and Fisherman's Gat may be encountered.

Unfortunately, it is no longer recommended to head directly for the southern end of Foulger's Gat because of the Wind Farm which sits over the whole area. As a result of representation during the planning stage for the Wind Farm, an avenue has been left through the turbines to allow us to use Foulger's Gat but this means entering the wind farm at its south-western corner and first passing north-west between lines A and B of the turbines until Foulger's Gat is reached. Following completion of construction, Trinity House has reinstated the Safe Water buoys marking Foulger's Gat and the end of this sector is the Long Sand Outer safe water buoy *(LFl.10s)* at the entrance to the avenue. Unfortunately first reports suggest that this buoy is very difficult to pick out against the significant light pollution from non-navigation lights on the turbines. Representation has been made to Trinity House and at the time of publication we await a response.

North Side (at southern edge of the Sunk Sand)				
		'Black Deep' CTTE Waypoint 12	51°41'22N, 001°24'97E	Track: 5.73nm Northwards 351°(T) Southwards 171°(T)
	Mo(A)15s	Long Sand Inner	51°38′78N, 001°25′44E	
	Iso.5s	Long Sand Middle	51°35′60N, 001°26′45E	
		'Long Sand Middle' CTTE Waypoint 11b	51°35'56N, 001°26'38E	Turning point
	LFl.10s	Long Sand Outer	51°34′61N, 001°28′34E	Track: 1.36nm Northwards 308°(T) Southwards 128°(T)
		'Long Sand Outer' CTTE Waypoint 11a	51°34'73N, 001°28'10E	
South Side in Knock Deep (between Turbines A10 and B10)				

Coordinates for passage using Sector B3 through the London Array Wind Farm

Sector B3 – Long Sand Outer to Black Deep

This sector is no longer as straight forward as it was when we could transit straight through Foulger's Gat on one track. However, it is still not difficult although in complete contrast to the featureless area we used to sail over. All the coordinates you will require are shown in the table above and the illustration overleaf.

Entering the avenue between turbines A10 and its partner B10 you will now pass the Long Sand Outer safe water buoy *(LFl.10s)* and aim for the new Long Sand Middle safe water buoy *(Iso. 5s)* which is the point where you turn into Foulger's Gat. Depths have shallowed slightly here and are now between 3.8m and 4.5m LAT. Be careful of cutting the corner here. The trend in the past ten years has been for the Long Sand to migrate westwards at this point and we may, in the future, come to regret the London Array's decision to omit Turbine B14 for us rather than B15. It may be ultra-cautious for shallow draft craft but deeper yachts may benefit from treating the Long Sand Middle as a west cardinal mark and leave the buoy to the north and east as you turn.

Heading more northerly you pass up the avenue of 700m-800m width specifically left for us leaving the Sub-Station (SS1) well to the East until Long Sand Inner *(Mo(A)15s)* is past. You are now in the Black Deep and regard should be taken to note any shipping passing up or down this main shipping channel which is less than 2nm wide at this point. The Yellow special marks in the Black Deep mark the Deep Water channel which the larger container ships bound for the London Gateway will require. Listening into London VTS on channel 69 is prudent to get an idea of shipping movements, particularly in poor visibility.

The planning tables accommodate three different sets of tidal information for this section. The first part of the sector from the Long Sand Outer to Long Sand Middle uses the Knock Deep data which will be the primary influence. There is, however, no tidal data available for Foulger's Gat and consequently Fisherman's Gat data is used for the section between Long Sand Middle and Long Sand Inner. The final section of this Sector uses Black Deep tidal information and in this part of the Sector, monitoring of cross track error would be prudent. Depending on your timing, the tide across your track could be significant. However, in terms of passage planning, all these influences are taken into consideration in the Planning Table data.

The northern waypoint of this Sector is on the edge of the Sunk Sand at the Little Sunk positioned midway between the two hazards situated to the north-east and south-west of this crossing point. The two hazards, both unmarked, are the remains of the 1950's Little Sunk beacon to the north-east and two wrecks to the south-west. There is over 1.2nm between these two hazards and better than 3 metres LAT so ample room and depth to cross the Sand which has been relatively flat and stable at this point. This crossing point was used extensively by crew vessels from Brightlingsea for the construction of the Wind Farm and is simple to find with a GPS fix. Unfortunately the Wind Farm turbines do not line up as any useful visual cue.

Downloads of the London Array Wind Farm and Little Sunk illustrations overleaf are available on www.crossingthethamesestuary.com.

The Routes – Ramsgate to the Essex Rivers

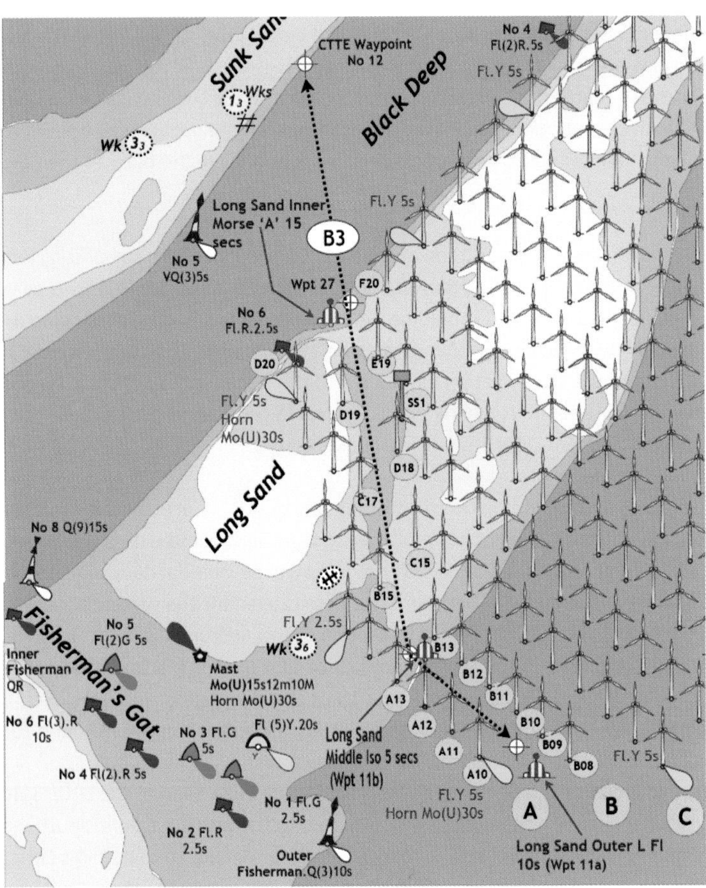

The route through Foulger's Gat

Tide at Little Sunk	Relationship to Sheerness times
Mean HW Springs	Approx. - 50 minutes
Mean HW Neaps	Approx. – 45 minutes
Mean LW Springs	Approx. – 55 minutes
Mean LW Neaps	Approx. – 30 minutes

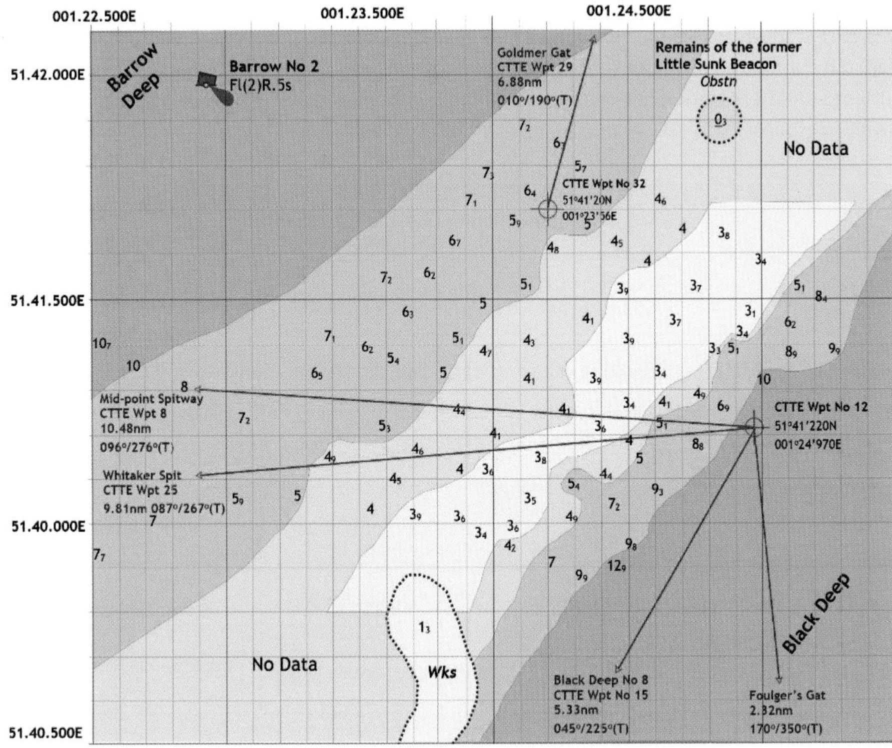

The Little Sunk crossing point (downloadable from web site)

Sectors B4 & B5 – Black Deep to NE Middle: NE Middle to Mid-point Spitway

Note that the tide is earlier here at the Little Sunk than Sheerness and in estimating the turn of the tide, the table overleaf should be applied. The width of the crossing point does mean that from the Black Deep waypoint (CTTE No 12) a course direct to the next waypoint at the NE Middle is feasible. The Barrow No 2 port hand buoy *(Fl(2) R.5s)* and No 3 east cardinal buoy *(Q(3) 10s)* are left well clear to the north-east of the track (note that Waypoint 32 illustrated above is used in routes for the Suffolk Rivers).

This section between the Sunk Sand and the Spitway is treated for planning purposes as separate Sectors for tidal calculation but for practical passage purposes is one track of

10.48nm. Just before the mid-point waypoint, the NE Middle shoal is crossed in not less than 4_1 metres LAT. On this track, the N. Middle north cardinal buoy *(Q)* is distant to the south but towards the end of the second sector, you pass close to the starboard hand buoy 'GFS-WF 5' *(Fl G.5s)* (probably best remembered as the Gunfleet Sands Wind Farm No 5!) which marks the south-west corner of the wind farm from where the two 'extra-large' turbines of the Gunfleet Sands Demo site are situated. This is not a limit mark for the wind farm and craft may pass between it and the turbines subject to the usual wind farm rules if that suits their purpose.

See pages 21 and 22 for further details about crossing the Spitway including times of tide in relation to Sheerness.

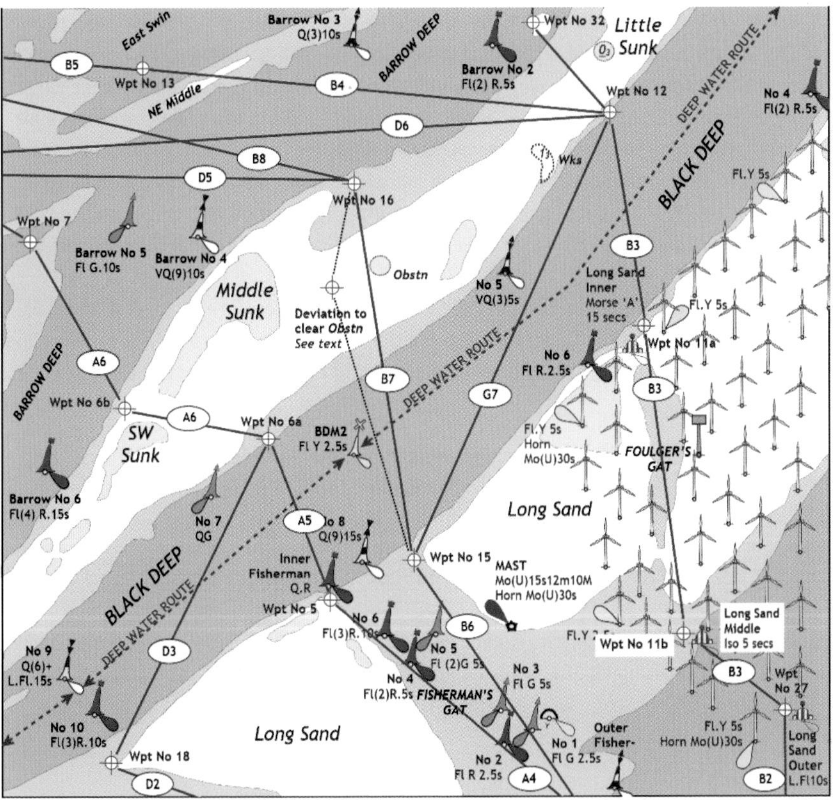

The three Sunk Sand crossing points

Sector A8 – Mid-point Spitway to River Blackwater Landfall

This Sector (as described on page 21) completes the passage.

Routes 3, 9 & 15 – Ramsgate to the Essex Rivers via Fisherman's Gat and the Middle Sunk

This route is included as an alternative should the SW Sunk swatchway disappear in the future. It is identified in the route diagram on page 15 as the middle route across the Sunk Sand but at present it provides no additional benefit over the SW Sunk route. The route uses the first three Sectors of Routes 1, 7 and 13 and then at the Outer Fisherman waypoint, the route uses new sectors between there and the Spitway (or Whitaker Spit for the Crouch).

Sector A1 – Ramsgate to North Foreland – Page 17
Sector A2 – North Foreland to East Margate – Page 18
Sector A3 – East Margate to Outer Fisherman – Page 18

Sector B6 – Outer Fisherman to Black Deep No 8.

In terms of advice there is no difference to that already provided for transiting the Gat. Leisure craft will, however, in avoiding the central buoyed channel in the presence of shipping pass up the north-east side of the Gat with the backdrop of the London Array Wind Farm close, but out of the way to the north-east. The tall control mast *(Mo(U)15s12m10M Horn Mo(U)30s)* also lies to the north-east.

Sector B7 – Black Deep No 8 to Barrow Deep

This sector takes you across the Black Deep and then across the Sunk Sand. You must note that this area of the Black Deep is the Precautionary Area previously described and you must watch for ships transiting the Black Deep and turning in and out of the Gat. Monitor London VTS on channel 69.

Keeping an eye on cross track error across the Black Deep is sensible as tides can run strongly up and down the Black Deep but once over the Sunk Sand the impact is greatly reduced. **Note** that the track used for passage planning purposes is a single track and **MUST** be modified to keep clear of the collapsed Middle Sunk beacon (at 51°39'385N, 001°20'682E). From the Black Deep Waypoint maintaining a track of 343°(T)/163°(T) for 3.08nm to 51°39'320N, 001°19'930E will leave this wreckage about half a nautical mile away to the east. Turning then to 012°(T)/192°(T) for a further 1.18nm will bring you to the Barrow Deep waypoint. The reason for this dogleg is that a shallow finger of the Middle Sunk sand has extended north-eastwards which is best avoided.

Tide at Middle Sunk	Relationship to Sheerness times
Mean HW Springs	Approx. - 48 minutes
Mean HW Neaps	Approx. – 40 minutes
Mean LW Springs	Approx. – 52 minutes
Mean LW Neaps	Approx. – 23 minutes

Sector B8 – Barrow Deep to Mid-point Spitway

This track across the Barrow Deep, Middle Deep and East Swin is close to 8nm. Where the rhumb line crosses the NE Middle shoal there is more than 5m LAT provided the North Middle north cardinal buoy *(Q)* is left to the south-west (port northbound – starboard southbound).

Sector A8 – Mid-point Spitway to Blackwater Landfall – Pages 20 to 22

Guidance for the Spitway and the use of Sector A8 as the final sector to the Blackwater Landfall are as before. See later for connections to the Rivers Colne and Crouch.

Routes 4, 10 & 16 – Ramsgate to the Essex Rivers via Fisherman's Gat and the Little Sunk

This alternative is for those who want to use the Little Sunk crossing point adjacent to the Barrow No 2 but who do not want to pass through the London Array wind farm.

The first four sectors are identical to the previous route: that is Sectors A1, A2, A3 and B6, and the route after waypoint No 12 at the Black Deep is identical to Routes 2, 8 and 14 using Sectors B4, B5 and then A8 for the final sector to the Blackwater. In between Sector G7 provides the link between the waypoints at Black Deep No 8 (CTTE No 15) and the Black Deep (CTTE No 12).

Sector A1 – Ramsgate to North Foreland – Page 17
Sector A2 – North Foreland to East Margate – Page 18
Sector A3 – East Margate to Outer Fisherman – Page 18
Sector B6 – Outer Fisherman to Black Deep No 8 – Page 25

Sector G7 - Black Deep No 8 to Black Deep

Depth is no issue at all in this sector as you are crossing the Black Deep main deep water channel. The two critical issues are staying out of the way of shipping and getting the tide right. Following dredging in preparation for the opening of the London Gateway, the Black Deep now has a central deep water channel marked by yellow special mark buoys one of which, BDM2 *(Fl.Y.2.5s),* will be seen in the middle of the channel off the Black Deep No 8. The Port of London Authority would prefer that we did not use the Black Deep whilst obviously accepting that Foulger's Gat is buoyed principally for leisure craft (which means that we will inevitably begin or end up in the Black Deep). But the Black Deep is a main commercial artery for the country with quite significant 'narrow' channel issues for the larger ships and consequently it is beholden on us to keep well out of the way. This is easily possible by choosing one side of the channel or other as wind or preference serves. Between the two waypoints you will pass Black Deep No 6 *(Fl.R.2.5s)* and No 5 east cardinal buoy *(VQ(3) 5s).*

As to tide, note that the tide can run strongly; over 2kts and therefore, if adverse can significantly increase the time taken to complete this sector at 4 or 5kts. Always review the duration time in the Planning Tables to ensure you avoid the worst impact of the tide on your plan.

Sectors B4/B5 – Black Deep to NE Middle: NE Middle to Mid-point Spitway – Page 23
Sector A8 – Mid-point Spitway to Blackwater Landfall – Pages 20 to 22

Routes 5, 11 & 17 – Ramsgate to the Essex Rivers via Princes Channel and West Swin

The route is provided for those who do not wish to cross the Sunk Sand. It is, however, about 10nm longer than crossing via the SW Sunk and 5nm longer than using the Foulger's Gat and Little Sunk route. The passage will also suffer from more adverse tide than either of the 'crossing' routes.

The route uses the usual start Sector A1 from Ramsgate to North Foreland but thereafter deviates closer to the Margate Sands on route to crossing the Queens Channel to the entrance to Princes Channel. Following Princes Channel until it meets the main north-east/south-west channels, the route crosses the Knob, Knock John and Mouse Channels to the SW Barrow. Travelling north, this part of the route would benefit from the flood tide but unfortunately since it is about 21nm from the North Foreland waypoint to the SW Barrow, getting the best help for those averaging 4 or 5kts boat speed will require Ramsgate to be left before the north going tide is available.

Assuming arrival at the SW Barrow close to HW Sheerness, we will get the ebb to help us up the twelve and a half nautical miles of the West Swin to the Spitway. Here are some of the highest tidal rates in the estuary on the ebb so progress particularly on Springs will be excellent (especially with a prevailing south-westerly). The down side is that you may be reaching the Spitway (or Whitaker Spit for the Crouch) after more than three hours of ebb. If this is an issue, the answer is to construct more alternatives using the Planning Tables to find the best compromise for your average boat speed.

Sector A1 – Ramsgate to North Foreland – Page 17

Sector C1 – North Foreland to Margate Sand

This sector is shaped inside the East Margate port hand buoy *(Fl R.2.5s)* to a waypoint parallel with the northern edge of the Sands. This does pass closer to the Margate Sands but the track is always in at least 6_8 metres LAT.

Sector C2 – Margate Sand to Princes South

This sector crosses the deep water of the Queens Channel. Most shipping seen to close on you will be aiming for the Princes Channel (monitor London VTS on channel 69) but beware that there is a Bunkering Anchorage in the Queens Channel to the south-west of the track and it is possible that some may be heading there.

The Rhumb line between these waypoints is chosen to keep us outside of the designated entrance to Princes Channel. This is marked on charts but not by buoyage.

Sector C3 – Princes South to Princes No 6

This is a track of just short of 7nm along the line of port hand buoys marking the south side of the Princes Channel. There is sufficient water outside of this line of buoys so we may comply with the PLA wish for us to avoid the actual channel.

The Sector starts by leaving the Princes South *(QR sync)* to the north. Note you will quickly come to the north cardinal buoy Brit N *(Q)* at 51° 28′·72N., 1° 17′·50E which marks the rock berm protecting where the power cables for the London Array cross the BritNed (British /Netherlands) power cable. Depth over this berm is 4m at LAT.

Continuing on this sector, Princes No 2 *(Fl(2).R.5s sync)* and Princes No 4 *(Fl(3).R 10s sync)* are left to the north and the drying sands of Ridge and Pan Sand to the south. The end of sector waypoint is just before the Princes No 6 port hand buoy *(Fl(4).R.15s).*

Sector C4 – Princes No 6 to SW Barrow

This track requires care to be taken to avoid shipping. It first crosses the Princes Channel to close on the Shivering Sands Forts. Leaving the Forts, the track crosses first the unmarked Knob Channel and then the Knock John Channel which is the continuation of the Black Deep. The Mouse Channel which is the continuation of the Barrow Deep is next. Consequently there are three channels that you will cross that will contain shipping of varying frequency. There is a lot of sense in crossing the Princes Channel earlier – for example in the previous sector – when there is no traffic and then completing Sector C3 by aiming outside of the starboard hand buoys of Princes Channel for the Shivering Sands.

The track leaves the Oaze Precautionary Area to the south-west which is an area strictly controlled by London VTS to avoid problems with in-bound and out-bound shipping meeting in the narrowest part near the Oaze Yellow Special mark. Whilst this is over 4nm to the south-west of the track, monitor London VTS on channel 69 to understand shipping movements. Ships using the Knock John are required to report their intentions to London VTS, in-bound on passing Sunk Head Tower or Fisherman Outer giving their ETA at Knock John No 1. Out-bound ships report when passing Sea Reach No 1 or the Medway Safe Water buoy giving their ETA at the Knock John No 4.

Sector C5 – SW Barrow to Maplin Edge

Our passage turns here from west to north as we enter the West Swin at the SW Barrow south cardinal buoy *(Q(9).15s)*. The channel is well marked with the West Swin port hand buoy *(QR sync)* and Maplin starboard hand buoy (*QG sync)* and the only real issue is the tide which flows hard – up to 2.7 knots on the ebb on Springs – which can give a very speedy passage.

Sector C6 – Maplin Edge to NE Maplin

The start waypoint for this sector is before the Maplin Edge starboard hand buoy *(Fl.G.2.5s)*. Thereafter the Maplin Bank port hand buoy *(Fl(3)R.10s)* is left to the east with the NE Maplin starboard hand buoy *(Fl.G.5s)* adjacent to the end waypoint. Depths will not be startling as most of this track is shy of the 10m contour line but will be sufficient. You are close to the Shoeburyness Firing range to the west and so may have a lively accompaniment to your passage. Frequent users of the West Swin are the Prior Barges who trade between their base at Fingringhoe on the River Colne and London.

The Bert Prior returning empty to Fingringhoe after passage up the West Swin and Spitway

Sector C7 – NE Maplin to Whitaker Spit

A direct track between waypoints will take you just over the edge of the Whitaker Spit. If the height of tide and your draught does not suit, pilotage via the West Hook Middle port hand buoy *(Fl.R.5s)* and the South Whitaker starboard hand buoy *(Fl(2).G.10s)* should be used. The northerly waypoint of this sector is adjacent to the Inner Whitaker *(VQ(6)+LFl.10s)* north cardinal buoy which marks the entrance to the Whitaker Channel for those bound for the Crouch (see later). Those heading for the Blackwater or Colne have a short sector to the Mid-point Spitway.

Sector C8 – Whitaker Spit to Mid-point Spitway

This short sector of less than two miles is principally cross tide. The track passes close to the Swin Spitway safe water buoy *(Iso.10s Bell)* to meet up with the final sector, A8 (described earlier) to complete the passage to the Blackwater Landfall.

Sector A8 – Mid-point Spitway to Blackwater Landfall – Pages 20 to 22

Routes 6, 12 & 18 – Ramsgate to the Essex Rivers via the North Edinburgh Channel and SW Sunk

Twenty-five years ago this route used to be one of the principal routes of crossing the Long Sand before Fisherman's Gat was buoyed. It fell into commercial disuse because of silting at the southern end and was replaced by Fisherman's Gat. The buoyage within the channel was removed as was that later from the Knob Channel which had provided the channel for shipping to pass into the mouth of the Thames. The Port of London Authority plan to re-survey the area and consequently this route remains described for future eventualities.

The route uses Sectors A1 and A2 from Ramsgate to the East Margate and Sectors A6, A7 and A8 to complete the passage from the southern end of the SW Sunk. In between, Sectors D1, D2 and D3 provide the alternative route across the Long Sand.

Sector A1 – Ramsgate to North Foreland – Page 17
Sector A2 – North Foreland to East Margate – Page 18

Sector D1 – East Margate to North Edinburgh

This sector runs from the East Margate waypoint at the southern end to a waypoint mid-point in the North Edinburgh Channel. The track is in deep water until the edge of the Long Sand is reached. To the west will be seen the remains of the wartime fort, Tongue Sand Tower. In the early part of this track expect to cross the track of shipping bound to and from the Princes Channel. On entering the North Edinburgh maintain a watch on cross track error to remain within the channel.

Sector D2 – North Edinburgh to NW Long Sand

From the waypoint in the mid-point of the North Edinburgh Channel head for the waypoint on the north-west corner of the Long Sand. Some 'trimming' of the corner inside the waypoint is permissible with the right draught and height of tide but resist the temptation at high water to cut right over the sand as the former NW Long Sand beacon has now collapsed and remains as unmarked wreckage at 51°34'724N, 001°18'040E. Note that the tide tends to follow the channel.

Sector D3 – NW Long Sand to SW Sunk (South Side)

This sector leads you diagonally across the Black Deep with the former cautions about shipping still applicable. Indeed shipping heading for the Thames will be concentrating on passing through the quite narrow channel between Black Deep No's 9 & 10 and 11 & 12 and the subsequent even narrower Knock John channel. Black Deep No 10 port hand buoy *(Fl(3).R.10s)* will be left to west and having crossed the Black Deep, the No 7 starboard hand buoy *(QG)* will be left to the north/north-west. To avoid any problems ensure that you go to the SW Sunk waypoint No 6a at 51°37'70N, 001°18'80E before crossing the Sand.

Sector A6 – SW Sunk (north side) to East Barrow Sands – Page 20
Sector A7 – East Barrow Sand to Mid-point Spitway – Page 20
Sector A8 – Mid-point Spitway to Blackwater Landfall – Pages 20 to 22

Connections to the River Colne

All the above routes are identical for the River Colne with the exception of the final Sector. So, if bound for the Colne, replace Sector A8 with Sector D8.

Sector D8 – Mid-point Spitway to Colne Landfall

This sector is 4.29nm in length and a single track from the Mid-point Spitway waypoint will take you to the Colne Bar. Like the pilotage guidance given for Sector A8, this track will take you over the Knoll at a point where there is 2_5 metres LAT leaving the Knoll north cardinal buoy *(Q)* and Eagle starboard hand buoy *(QG)* to the east. The surface can be mildly choppy in this area at some states of the tide but should not prove too troublesome. The Colne Landfall waypoint is adjacent to the Colne Bar starboard hand buoy *(Fl(2).G.5s)*. Distances from the Landfall waypoint to destinations in the Colne are provided in the following table.

From Colne Landfall to:	Approximate distance	From Colne Landfall to:	Approximate distance
Mersea Stone	3.60nm	Brightlingsea	4.16nm
Wivenhoe	7.66nm	Rowhedge	8.05nm
Colchester Hythe	9.87nm		

Connections to the River Crouch

Obviously craft bound for the Crouch will not use the Spitway but rather lead into the Whitaker Channel from the Whitaker Spit waypoint. Different sectors are therefore necessary to link the various Sunk Sand crossing points to the Whitaker Spit waypoint (the Prince Channel route already links to the Whitaker Spit waypoint). These are:

Sector D4 – East Barrow Sands to Whitaker Spit – the SW Sunk route
Sector D5 – Barrow Deep to Whitaker Spit – the Middle Sunk route
Sector D6 – Black Deep to Whitaker Spit – the Little Sunk route

29

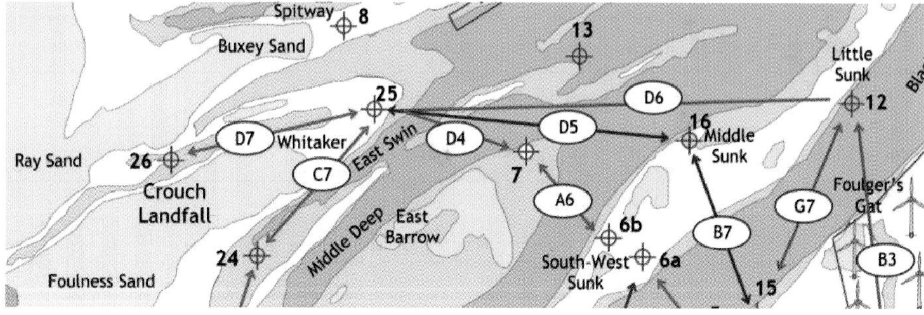

Sectors linking the Sunk Sand crossing points to the Crouch

All sectors obviously vary in length and track but all first cross the Barrow Deep and then the Middle Deep. Sector D6 from the Little Sunk runs close to the North Middle shoal where depths of 1_3 metres at LAT may be encountered. If necessary because of the height of tide the track should be deviated southerly to avoid the worst of this shoal.

The Routes – Ramsgate to the Essex Rivers

Buoyage for the most part will be distant until the end waypoint at the Whitaker Spit is closed when the Inner Whitaker *(VQ(6)+LFl.10s)* north cardinal buoy will be ahead and the S Whitaker starboard hand buoy *(Fl(2).G.10s)* off to the south.

Sector D7 – Whitaker Spit to Crouch Landfall

This final sector for those bound for the Crouch links the Whitaker Spit waypoint to the Crouch Landfall waypoint. The Crouch Landfall waypoint is mid-way between the paired Whitaker channel buoys no's 5 & 6 and no's 7 & 8.The sector is now well marked to save pilotage charges for those ships bringing the spoil from the Thames Crossrail project to the Wallesea project opposite Burnham. The Whitaker Channel is marked with 4 pairs of lateral buoys with synchronised lights and no depth issues will arise provided position within the channel is maintained. Obviously a good look-out is prudent for the Wallesea ship traffic which tends to enter the Whitaker Channel on a rising tide.

From Crouch Landfall to:	Approximate distance	From Crouch Landfall to:	Approximate distance
River Roach entrance	7.13nm	Burnham	9.23nm
Burnham Yacht Harbour	9.80nm	Essex Marina	9.80nm
North Fambridge YS	14.90nm	Fambridge Yacht Haven	16.01nm
Brandy Hole YS	16.62nm	Battlesbridge	19.57nm
Yokesfleet Anchorage	9.76nm	Paglesham	10.59nm

Ramsgate to the Kent Rivers and Thames

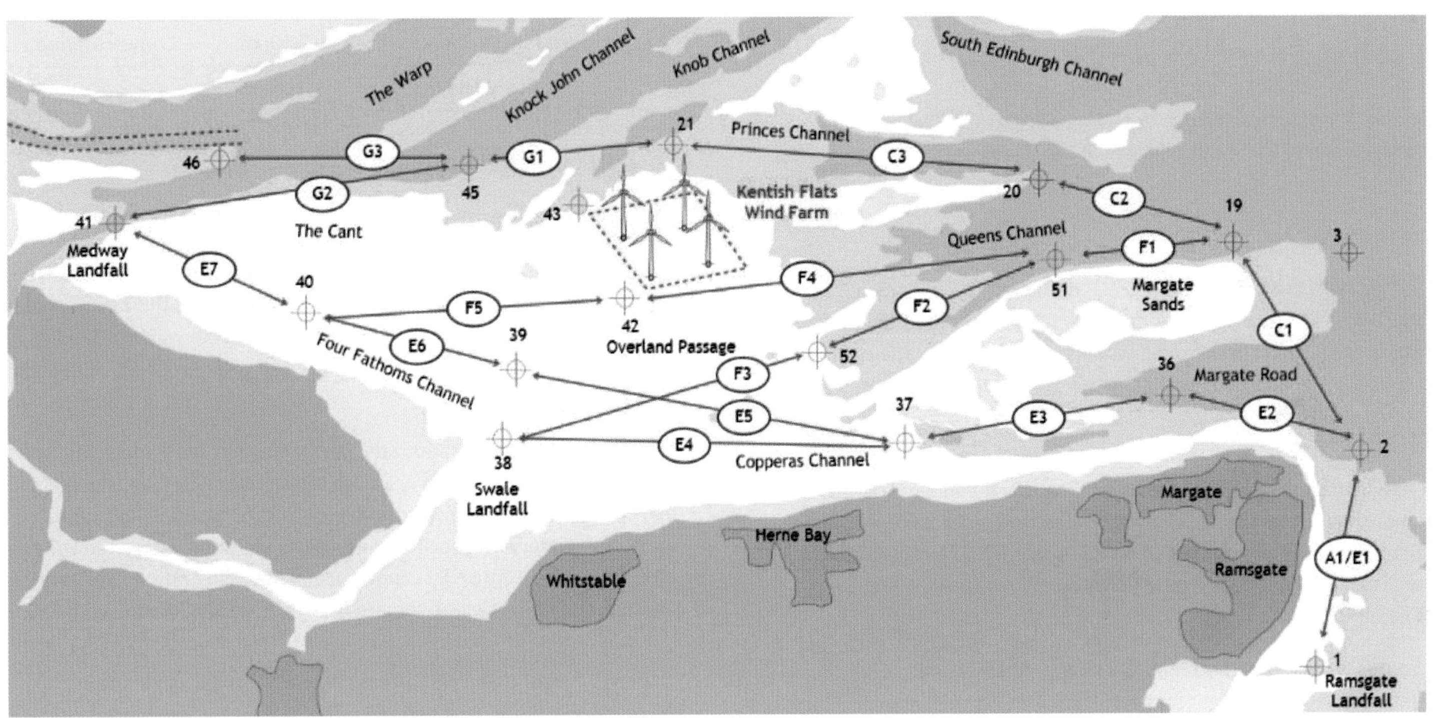

This section contains guidance on 6 routes between Ramsgate and the Swale, Medway and Thames. These comprise Routes 19 to 24 and use a choice of three options: the Copperas Channel, Queens Channel or Princes Channel.

The Copperas Channel is the shortest route to any of the three destinations but only by less than 2nm. It will also be the shallowest route but if seeking to benefit from the lee of the North Kent coast, will provide the most shelter. There is almost no difference in the distance to the Medway and London River between using the Queens or Princes Channel. The latter provides deeper water but will be on the edge of a main shipping channel for most of the passage. There is no particular tidal advantage over the choices; all three routes benefit (or suffer) to a similar extent from the same tidal issues.

The primary issue with the tide affects west-bound passages from Ramsgate. The ideal tidal plan would be to carry the first of the north-going tide from Ramsgate up to the North Foreland (starting at -2:30 before HW Sheerness). However, the west going tide curling round the North Foreland and along the North Kent coast turns foul three hours later at +0:30 Sheerness. With distances between 20 and 30nm depending on the passage, some negative tide is therefore inevitable except for the fastest yachts heading for the Swale.

East-bound passages are not troubled with the same issue. Slack water off the Medway and Swale is HW Sheerness (inevitably) and the south-going tide down past the North Foreland starts +3:30 Sheerness. Indeed it continues to flow south until -2:30 Sheerness.

The Routes in detail

Routes 19 & 21 – Ramsgate to the Kent Rivers via the Copperas Channel

Sector E1 – Ramsgate to North Foreland

This is Sector A1, the common 4.75nm sector starting or ending all routes to and from Ramsgate. However, for convenience of use it is duplicated in the 'E' Table. Please see page 17 for details.

Sector E2 – North Foreland to SE Margate

This is pretty much an East-West track from the North Foreland waypoint to a waypoint 0.13nm due south of the South-East Margate east cardinal buoy *(Q(3).10s)*. The direct planning track passes quite close inshore of Foreness Point and it would be prudent to shape a course at least between the unlit Longnose port hand buoy and diffuser port hand buoy *(Fl R.5s)*.

Sector E3 – SE Margate to Copperas

This track takes the Gore Channel past the South Margate starboard hand buoy *(Fl G.2.5s)* to the north and the Reculver port hand mark *(QR)* to the south. The track goes through the Copperas Channel to the westerly waypoint adjacent to the Copperas *(QG)* starboard hand buoy. Note that the former 'East Last' route has closed up with Trinity House moving the buoyage to the Copperas Channel.

At the westerly waypoint, routes to the Swale and Medway part company.

Connections to the Swale

Sector E4 – Copperas to Swale Landfall (for the Swale)

From Copperas to the Swale Landfall adjacent to the Columbine starboard hand buoy *(Fl.G.2s)* and Whitstable Street port hand buoy *(Fl.R.2s)* depths will not be great with little above 2 metres charted at LAT once the Copperas Channel is left. Perusal of the relevant chart would be prudent.

From Swale Landfall to:	Approximate distance	From Swale Landfall to:	Approximate distance
Faversham Creek	7.50nm	Conyer Marina	10.46nm
Kingsferry Bridge	13.28nm		

Connections to the Medway

Sector E5 – Copperas Channel to the Kentish Flats (for the Medway)

Sectors E5 and 6 are one track split into two Sectors for tidal calculations purposes by an arbitrary waypoint (called *Kentish Flats)*. The track in this Sector threads over the best water from the Copperas Channel waypoint. To the north will be a view of the Kentish Flats Wind Farm to which an extension on the west and southern sides is planned for commencement late in 2014.

There is nothing special about the depth of water here and some isolated spots of under 2 metres least charted depth are close to the track. Clear and to the north of the track, four buoys (3 yellow special marks and a south cardinal buoy) can be seen marking the shoal area where the underwater rock berm protects the point where the London Array power cable passes over the Kentish Flats power cable (see illustration overleaf). As you approach the western end of the Sector you are transiting what is known as the 'Overland Passage'.

Sector E6 – Kentish Flats to Spile

Sector E6 is a continuation of the same track as E5, moving from the Overland Passage to the Four Fathom Channel – 'at High Water Springs' as is noted on Admiralty Charts!

Generally speaking the charted depths are 2+ metres but there are one or two 'fingers' of less than a metre LAT and an isolated *Obstn* at 51˚25'96N, 000˚56'56E has a charted depth of 1_1 metres LAT. This is about half a mile from the westerly waypoint of this sector adjacent to the Spile Starboard hand buoy. You should also note that the Spile starboard hand buoy *(Fl.G.2.5s)* guards a wreck with 1_8 metres over it just to the north of the buoy.

Sector E7 – Spile to Medway Landfall

The track passes over The Cant, a continuation of the shallow plateau that runs for most of the North Kent Coast with charted depth of 2 to 3 metres.

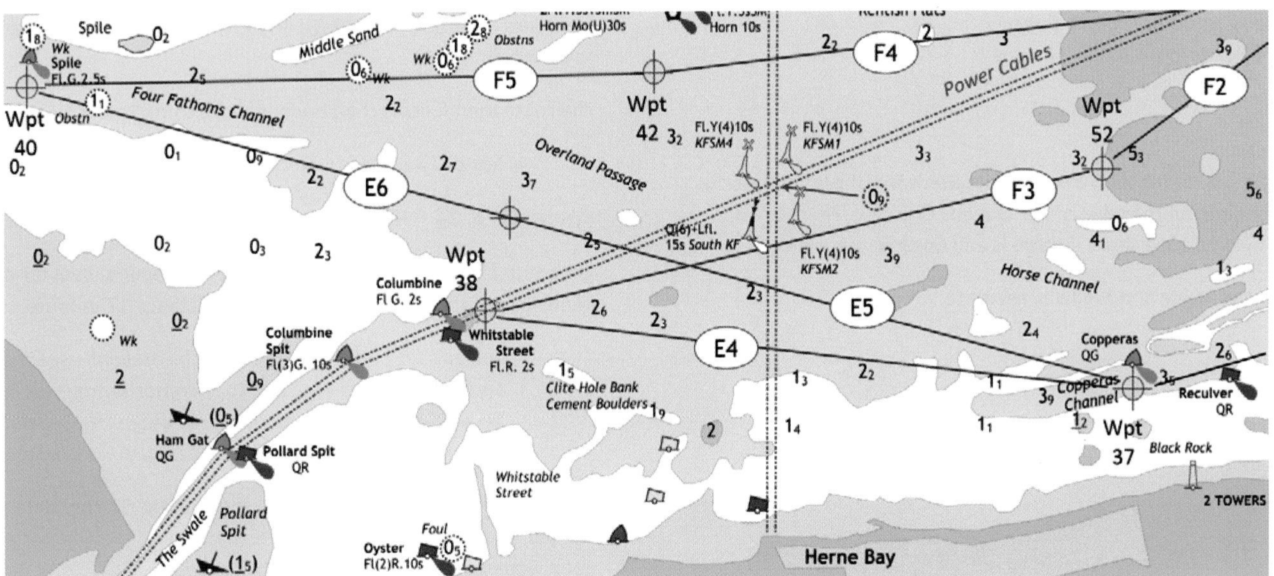

Avoiding the Rock Berms - The four buoys marking the underwater rock berm at the point where the power cables from the London Array (passing diagonally) and the Kentish Flats Wind Farm (passing north-south) cross. Depth at the shallowest part is 0.9 metres LAT. Passing between the buoys is strictly to be avoided.

The easterly waypoint of this Sector is the River Medway Landfall in the buoyed channel, approximately two and a half miles from Garrison Point, between the paired channel buoys no's 5 & 6 and 7 & 8. Note that this waypoint is chosen for passage planning purposes and you should avoid both the marked deep water and secondary route into the Medway. For passage into the Medway beyond this Landfall waypoint, it is suggested you read the advice in the current East Coast Pilot on entering the Medway. This describes the various hazards on east and west side of the channel including the wreck of the wartime ammunition ship the *SS Richard Montgomery*.

The Recommended Yacht Track into the Medway starts south of the marked wreck of the *Richard Montgomery* and runs down the 'London' side of the approach channel between the No 11 starboard hand buoy *(Fl(3).G.10s)* and the Grain Hard starboard hand buoy *(Fl.G.5s)*. This recommended route is intended to keep small craft clear of Garrison Point. To make this route and keep clear of Garrison Point, it would be prudent to run down the east of the Approach Channel until south of the *Richard Montgomery* and then cross when the Channel is clear. It would be useful to monitor Medway VTS on Channel 74 while in this sector.

Note that if bound for the Thames, it is feasible to cross the Medway Channel at the Landfall waypoint, north of the wreck of the *SS Richard Montgomery* and use the Great Nore and Nore Swatchway to enter the Thames. This has the advantage of putting you on the south side of the Yantlet Deep Water route into the Thames where you can meet up with the recommended small craft route on leaving the Nore Swatch.

Routes 20 & 22 – Ramsgate to the Kent Rivers via Queens Channel

This route runs from the North Foreland waypoint round the north of the Margate Sands, skirting the northern edge of the Sands and then either heading in to the Swale Landfall waypoint or taking a more easterly course along the southern side of the Kentish Flats Wind Farm to join up with the previous route to the Medway at the Spile waypoint. It benefits from better water, at least until the Kentish Flats are reached but there is less of a lee in strong south-westerly winds.

The routes starts with the common Sectors E1 *Ramsgate to North Foreland* and C1, *North Foreland to Margate Sands* previously described.

The Routes – Ramsgate to the Kent Rivers and Thames

Sector A1/E1 – Ramsgate to North Foreland – Page 17
Sector C1, North Foreland to Margate Sands – Page 27

Sector F1 – Margate Sands to Wedge

This Sector is common to both those bound for the Swale and the Medway. It runs almost due east-west just north of the Margate Sand on the edge of the Queens Channel. There are no particular issues other than this would be a lee shore if there is any north in the wind.

At the Wedge waypoint, routes for the Swale and Medway separate.

Connections to the Swale

Sector F2 – Wedge to Woolpack

This is a simple sector with nothing particular to characterise it, with at least 5 metres LAT throughout.

Sector F3 – Woolpack to Swale Landfall

This sector brings the passage onto the Kentish Flats where depths will fall to a least charted depth of 2_5 metres LAT. The Woolpack waypoint has deliberately been set a little south so that this track runs south of the buoys marking the rock berm over the power cable crossing point (see illustration on the previous page).

Connections to the Medway

Sector F4 – Wedge to Spaniard

The westerly waypoint retains the name of the Spaniard, taken from the adjacent sand, despite the removal of this buoy by Trinity House. The track runs south past the Wind Farm and well clear north of the four buoys marking the rock berm. Construction work may intrude on this track if the extension of the Wind Farm goes ahead but there is ample room to deviate the track a little south and this will not harm the planning estimate significantly.

Sector F5 – Spaniard to Spile

This track is generally short of 3 metres depth LAT and just south of the Middle Sand there are some shallow wrecks to leave north of the track. There will be little to see except the Spile starboard hand buoy *(Fl.G.2.5s)* ahead and the unlit red and white Middle Sand beacon distant to the north.

The route then follows the previous route using Sector E7 to conclude the passage.

Sector E7 – Spile to Medway Landfall – Page 32

Routes 23 & 24 – Ramsgate to the Medway and Thames via Princes Channel

The route from Ramsgate to the Medway Landfall is ideal for those with concerns over the Kentish Flats and is effectively the same distance. The route uses Sectors previously described:

Sector A1/E1 – Ramsgate to North Foreland – see page 17
Sector C1 – North Foreland to Margate Sands – see page 27
Sector C2 – Margate Sands to Princes South – see page 27
Sector C3 – Princes South to Princes No 6 – see page 27

From the Princes No 6 waypoint, Sectors G1 and G2 complete the passage to the Medway Landfall and Sector G3 completes the passage to the Thames and its waypoint north of the deep water route adjacent to Sea Reach No 1.

Connections to the Medway

Sector G1 – Princes No 6 to Red Sand Towers

This sector tracks through the deeper water between the Kentish Flats and the Princes Channel leaving the Princes No 6 *(Fl(4)R.15s)* and Princes No 8 port hand buoys *(Fl(2)R.5s)* to the north. A finger of the Red Sand intrudes slight near the Princes No 8 but is charted at 4_9 metres LAT. The westerly waypoint is adjacent to the Red Sand Towers marked (although it is sufficiently large at 17m to be noticeable!) by a port hand buoy *(Fl(3) R.10s Bell)*.

Sector G2 – Red Sand Towers to Medway Landfall

Obviously for passage planning purposes, this is a straight track from the Red Sand Towers to the Medway Landfall waypoint between the paired channel buoys no's 5 & 6 and 7 & 8.

However, on passage you will want to shape a course to the outside of the East Cant port hand buoy *(QR)* and then skirt the edge of the Cant, keeping outside of the Yellow buoys marking the Medway Secondary Channel. Again, it is feasible to cross the Medway Channel and make for the Great Nore if proceeding up the Thames.

Red Sand Towers

From Medway Landfall to:	Approximate distance	From Medway Landfall to:	Approximate distance
Queenborough ATL	4.88nm	Whitton Marina	7.84nm
Gillingham Marina	8.13nm	Hoo Marina	8.82nm
Victoria Marina	10.52nm	Rochester Bridge	12.04nm

Connections to the Thames

Sector G3 – Red Sand Towers to Sea Reach No 1

The 'Landfall' waypoint for the Thames is situated to the north of Sea Reach No 1 yellow special buoy *(Fl .Y.2.5s)* so as to be well clear of the Yantlet deep water route into the Thames.

The Routes – Ramsgate to the Kent Rivers and Thames

This sector is recommended if the destination is Leigh-on-Sea or elsewhere on the nearby north Thames.

The track from the Red Sand Towers waypoint needs care. Initially the track crosses the Oaze Deep which is a critical area for shipping using the Black Deep and Princes Channel. If busy, time can be bought by shaping a course via the East Cant port hand buoy *(QR)* (as in Sector G2 above) until the channels are clear. Monitor channel 69 for London VTS or 74 for Medway VTS.

Approximate distances from the Sea Reach No 1 waypoint are:

From Thames Landfall to:	Approximate distance	From Thames Landfall to:	Approximate distance
Ray Gut	6.80nm	Holehaven Creek	12.13nm
Embankment Marina	19.94nm	Thurrock YC	23.71nm
QE II Bridge	27.07nm	Erith YC	29.02nm
Gallions Point Marina	34.69nm	Thames Barrier	36.45nm
Greenwich YC	37.12nm	Poplar Dock Marina	38.33nm
West India Moorings	38.49nm	South Dock Marina	40.69nm
Limehouse Marina	41.74nm	St Katharine Docks	43.22nm

Ramsgate to Harwich Harbour and the Deben

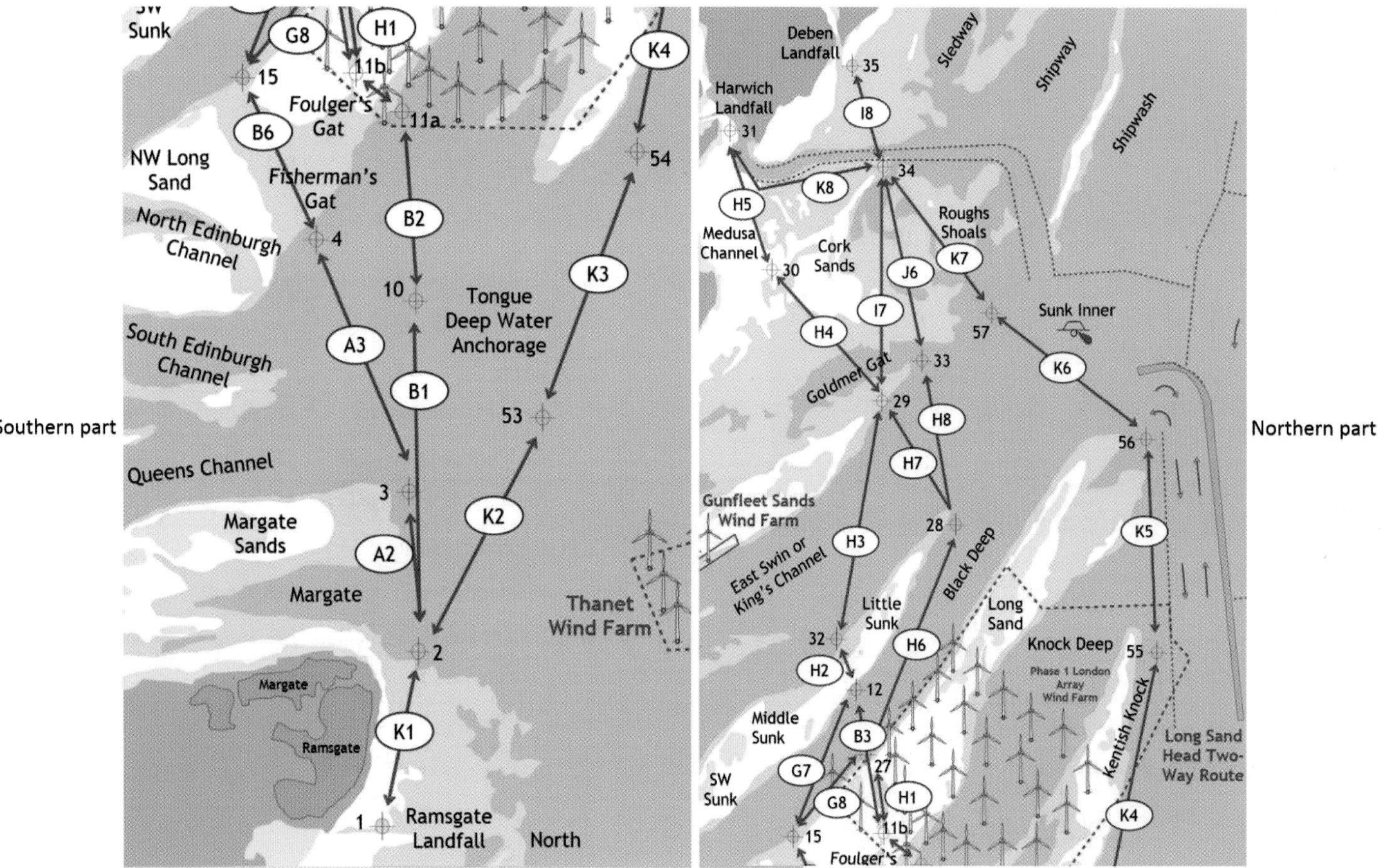

This section contains guidance on 10 routes each between the Ramsgate and Harwich Harbour and the Deben. These comprise Routes 25 to 32 (the 'inside' routes) and 62 and 63 (the 'outside' routes). The inside routes use a choice of Fisherman's or Foulger's Gat to cross the Long Sand and then the Little Sunk or Black Deep to negotiate the Sunk Sand. The outside route does what it says; passes up from Ramsgate to the west of the Thanet wind farm and the east of the Kentish Knock going round the eastern side of the Long Sand Head before shaping a track across the Sunk Inner Precautionary Area and Rough Shoals where the routes to Harwich and the Deben part company. Those for Harwich follow the outside of the Harwich Deep Water Channel and those for the Deben head directly from the Cork Sand Beacon to the Deben Landfall adjacent to the Woodbridge Haven safe water buoy.

There is little tidal advantage between any of the inside or the outside route. Of the inside routes, there is barely two miles difference whether one choses the shortest via Foulger's Gat and the Little Sunk or the longest via Fisherman's Gat and the Black Deep. However, the shortest inside route to Harwich is just over 7nm less than the outside route with the best inside route to the Deben being 5.7nm shorter. Generally the effect of the tide is so similar between the routes that the difference in estimated duration generally just reflects the length of the passage.

The choice will therefore be a preference over the basic nature of the routes. There are two elements to choose. First, the choice between Fisherman's and Foulger's Gat is really whether you would wish to avoid the wind farm. Some have found difficulty at night picking out the light of Long Sand Inner safe water mark *(LFl.10s)* against the general light pollution of the wind farm and have diverted safely and easily to Fisherman's Gat. Fisherman's Gat is buoyed for shipping and the PLA would like us to keep clear of the marked channel which delineates a controlling depth of 8_2 metres LAT. However, there is ample room for yachts to the east of the marked channel and thus this ought not to deter you.

Secondly, after the decision over crossing the Long Sand is the choice of whether to cross the Sunk Sand at the Little Sunk (see page 24 for detail) or transit the Black Deep. Crossing the Little Sunk midway between the hazards which are 1.2nm apart provides a controlling depth of 3_4 metres LAT and is a relatively flat and stable crossing point. Passage up the Black Deep requires us to keep clear of shipping which is set to increase with the opening of the London Gateway container terminal, especially the deep water channel.

The choice for the second element of the passage may be influenced by wind direction. With a wind north of West, passage diagonally across the East Swin will be considerably freer than clearing the Sunk Head and then heading in for Goldmer Gat. One of my more unpleasant memories is beating in from the Sunk Head fighting a losing battle against leeway and the strong spring ebb on a day where the separation from grey sea and grey sky took some concentration. The end result was to end up too close to the South Cork south cardinal buoy *(Q(6)+L Fl. 15s)* and its inevitable infestation of lobster pots. Such an issue is, of course, not so relevant to those bound for the Deben although it still applies to some extent.

Weighing the inside routes against the outside route is principally an issue of the extra distance which will mean more time for the passage. Note also that it involves crossing the Inner Sunk precautionary area with consequential attention necessary to shipping.

The timing of any of these routes can be interesting. Going north, the tide can be worked easily. Take the start of the north going tide off Ramsgate at -2:30 Sheerness; because at this time it is still flooding in the north part of the Estuary, effectively 8 hours of favourable tide is available; albeit that the last hour is moving swiftly towards slack water off the Deben.

Coming south is not so helpful. The first of the flood south down into the Estuary off the Deben and Harwich starts at +5:30 Sheerness but 5 hours later at -2:30 Sheerness, the tide from Ramsgate to the North Foreland has turned to the north. Also the tide south of the Long Sand and Kentish Knock has lost its south-going trend and turned westerly. This will not be too much of a problem at higher average speeds through the water when the destination is Ramsgate but at slower average speeds and for those hoping to make Dover or further into the Channel, a lot of adverse tide will be faced.

The planning tables help in this respect as it is simple to calculate the effect of different start times relative to HW Sheerness. Many bound for Dover in fact start from the Landfall waypoints close to local HW (around -1:00 Sheerness). Because the early part of the route has a significant cross tide component, the adverse effect of the tide can be mitigated and a timing achieved that gets the craft near to the Tongue deep water anchorage as the south-going tide starts to build (around +4:30 Sheerness). An earlier start to the passage (which in consequence will be slightly slower) can provide a later benefit if the destination is south of Ramsgate.

The Routes in detail

Routes 25, 27, 29 & 31 – Ramsgate to the Harwich Harbour and the Deben via either Gat and the Black Deep

The Black Deep route can either be used via Foulger's Gat or Fisherman's Gat whether for Harwich (for the Stour or Orwell) or the Deben.

Via Foulger's Gat

If using Foulger's Gat (route 25 and 29), the passage to either destination starts with the following previously described sectors:

Sector A1 – Ramsgate to North Foreland – Page 17
Sector B1 – East Margate to Tongue DW Anchorage – Page 22
Sector B2 – Tongue Deep Water Anchorage to Long Sand Outer – Page 22

Sector H1 – Long Sand Outer to Long Sand Inner

This sector is identical to Sector B3 described on page 23 except that it terminates adjacent to the Long Sand Inner safe water buoy *(Mo(A)15s)* as soon as the Black Deep is reached. It is

The Routes – Ramsgate to Harwich Harbour and the Deben

therefore shorter in length and uses two (instead of three) tidal diamonds for the purposes of the Planning Tables. This need not concern the reader as the calculations are already completed in the tables but for the purist, there is no tidal data publicly available for Foulger's Gat and therefore data for Fisherman's Gat is used as the nearest relevant diamond. Some variations cannot therefore be excluded. The table below provides the coordinates for transiting the wind farm.

North Side (at southern edge of the Black Deep)				
		'Long Sand Inner' CTTE Waypoint 27	51°38'91N, 001°25'56E	Track: 3.39nm
	Mo(A)15s	Long Sand Inner	51°38′77N, 001°25′43E	Northwards 351°(T) Southwards 171°(T)
	Iso.5s	Long Sand Middle	51°35′60N, 001°26′45E	
		'Long Sand Middle' CTTE Waypoint 11b	51°35'56N, 001°26'38E	Turning point
	LFl.10s	Long Sand Outer	51°34′61N, 001°28′34E	Track: 1.36nm
		'Long Sand Outer' CTTE Waypoint 11a	51°34'73N, 001°28'10E	Northwards 308°(T) Southwards 128°(T)
South Side in Knock Deep (between Turbines A10 and B10)				

Coordinates for passage using Sector H1 through the London Array Wind Farm

Sector H6 – Long Sand Inner to Sunk Head

This sector continues down the Black Deep to the end of the channel at the Sunk Head. At some stage it will be necessary to cross to the northern side of the Black Deep taking care to avoid any traffic which might be using the channel.

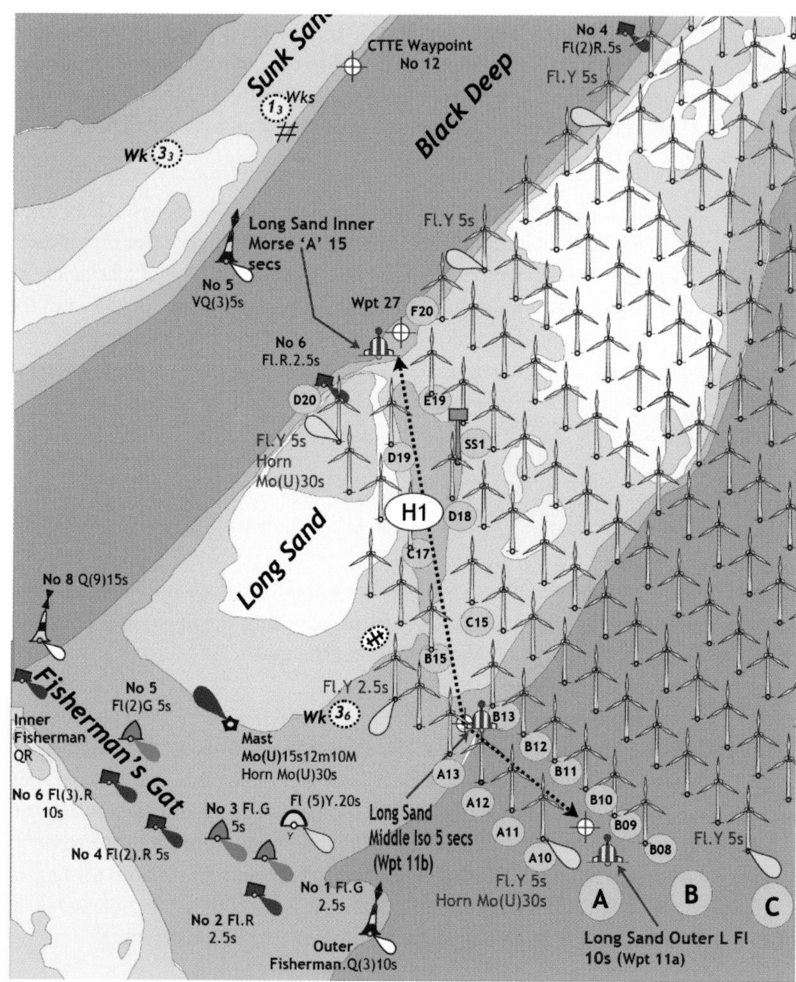

Transiting Foulger's Gat using Sector H1

Tides can run fast here, over 2 knots on springs so progress with the tide can be quite spectacular and progress against the strongest of it to be avoided. The Back Deep No 1 *(Fl.G.5s)* will give advance notice of the approach to the end waypoint. It is not necessary to go to the Sunk Head Tower north cardinal buoy hence the positioning of the end of Sector waypoint where there is sufficient water to cross over the end of the Sunk Head.

However, there has been a report of less water on the Great Sunk and so it would be prudent to make the turn at the waypoint and not before.

At this point routes for Harwich Harbour and the Deben part company.

Connections to Harwich Harbour

The route to Harwich turns north-west and crosses the end of the East Swin and Goldmer Gat before using the Medusa Channel to close on Harwich Harbour entrance.

Sector H7 – Sunk Head to Goldmer Gat

This sector is quite straight forward with no navigational hazards except to beware of cross-track error. Travelling either way, it is not particularly helpful to be set off track; for example travelling north on the ebb, being set down tide of the end waypoint on the ebb merely adds to the tightness of the next sector in keeping well away from the West Rocks and Cork Sand. Coming south with the flood, making the Sunk Head waypoint is necessary to avoid the shallow sand of the Great Sunk.

The end waypoint is an arbitrary location clear of the end of the Gunfleet Sands. This means that there is no natural transit to help check on cross track error and the best visual help will be the North-East Gunfleet east cardinal buoy *(Q(3) 10s)* which will be distant, over 1.5nm to the east.

Sector H4 – Goldmer Gat to the Naze

The Naze waypoint is just under a mile south of the Stone Banks port hand buoy *(Fl.R.5s)* in the Medusa Channel. Leaving the Goldmer Gat waypoint, the Wallet No 2 port hand buoy *(Fl.R.5s)* will be seen distant to port and the South Cork south cardinal buoy *(Q(6)+LFl.15s)* distant to starboard. It is prudent to keep away from the South Cork for two reasons; first it marks the shallow West Rocks and secondly it appears to be very popular with fishermen set on laying lobster pots.

Over two thirds along the track, the Medusa starboard hand buoy *(Fl.G.5s)* will be left to port and you enter the shallow channel with little over 2 metres LAT. If this seems insufficient, bear in mind the exploits of Graeme Spense. He, faced with an impatient Vice-Admiral Nelson on 10th August 1801 who had been refused pilotage assistance from the Harwich Pilots, took the 44m HMS Medusa drawing 16ft out through this channel at high water and down the Wallet bound for the Nore via the Spitway and West Swin.

Sector H5 – the Naze to Harwich Landfall

The positioning of the Naze waypoint is deliberately at the entrance to the Medusa Channel to provide a track into the Harwich Landfall leaving the Stone Banks port hand buoy *(Fl.R.5s)* to starboard.

Beware of poorly marked lobster pots in this area, particularly around the Naze!

From Harwich Landfall to:	Approximate distance	From Harwich Landfall to:	Approximate distance
Halfpenny Pier	1.85nm	Shotley	2.53nm
Wrabness	6.86nm	Mistley	9.53nm
Suffolk Yacht Harbour	4.46nm	Pin Mill	6.29nm
Woolverstone Marina	7.22nm	Fox's Marina	9.41nm
Ipswich Docks	10.40nm		

Connections to the Deben

From the Sunk Head waypoint at the end of Sector H6, three sectors complete the passage to the Deben crossing the East Swin, the Rough Shoals, the Harwich Deep Water route and finally the Cork anchorage to the Deben Landfall at Woodbridge Haven safe water mark.

Sector H8 – Sunk Head to North-East Gunfleet

There is little of concern in this sector. The track crosses the East Swin and like Sector H7, some shipping might be encountered heading into the Sunk Inner precautionary area. The end of sector waypoint to the north is adjacent to the North-East Gunfleet east cardinal buoy *(Q(3)10s)*.

Sector J6 – North-East Gunfleet to Cork Sand Beacon

From the North-East Gunfleet, the track crosses Goldmer Gat (back in the 18th century the principal route south for ships bound for London), the South East Spit (ample water at nearly 7 metres LAT) and the edge of the Roughs Shoals (again ample water).

The Routes – Ramsgate to Harwich Harbour and the Deben

There are no close marks on this track but the towers of Roughs Tower, one of Maunsell's wartime forts and latterly Sealand, will be visible to the east.

Sector I8 – Cork Sand Beacon to Deben Landfall

This Sector starts immediately with an encounter with the Harwich Deep Water Channel. At this point, you should be monitoring Harwich VTS on Channel 71 to gain an understanding of shipping movements that will cross athwart your course. Be aware that shipping in this channel is permitted a maximum speed of 17 knots and that you have just over a nautical mile of traffic separation lanes to cross: at five knots you will be crossing for about 15 minutes. The rules are explicit: *'you shall cross as nearly as practicable at right angles to the Separation Lanes, you shall not impede the passage of a vessel which can safely navigate only within the narrow channel or fairway and you shall not cross if such crossing impedes such a vessel'*.

Harwich Harbour Authority adds that it does not recommend crossing the bows of an oncoming ship and to be aware of the restricted visibility for the master of a large ship as it closes upon a yacht. In poor visibility monitoring Channel 71 is an essential requirement and if you do not have radar and you are in serious doubts as to the commercial movements, Harwich VTS invite you to call them on Channel 71. Whilst Harwich VTS cannot undertake control of small craft in reduced visibility and may move you to a working channel, the operators will give whatever assistance is possible at the time. Bear in mind that the largest container ships in the world uses this port!

The track used on this sector is 340˚/160˚. The Separation Lanes are not exactly parallel but average 265˚/085˚ so the precise 'right angles' to the lanes is 355˚/175˚.

Once clear of the Separation Zone, there are no navigation problems confronting you on the rest of this sector. You may however encounter anchored ships in the Cork Anchorage which lies to the north of the Separation Zone at this point. Remember to check for the latest position of the Woodbridge Haven Buoy at: www.eastcoastpilot.com.

From Deben Landfall to:	Approximate distance	From Deben Landfall to:	Approximate distance
Ramsholt	3.92nm	Waldringfield	6.57nm
Woodbridge	8.98nm		

Via Fisherman's Gat

If using Fisherman's Gat (route 27 or 31), the routes use the previous described Sectors:

Sector A1 – Ramsgate to North Foreland – Page 17
Sector A2 – North Foreland to East Margate – Page 18
Sector A3 – East Margate to Outer Fisherman – Page 18
Sector B6 – Outer Fisherman to Black Deep No 8 – Page 25

Sector G8 – Black Deep No 8 to Long Sand Inner

From the waypoint at the Black Deep No 8, the route turns north-east along the Black Deep and a track should be taken down the side of the channel to the Long Sand Inner safe water buoy *(Mo(A).15s)* passing the Black Deep No 6 port hand buoy *(Fl.R.2.5s)* on the way and with the London Array Wind Farm to the south-east.

Maintaining the side of the channel will keep you clear of any shipping and the central Deep Water route. Monitoring London VTS on VHF channel 69 is advised.

From the Long Sand Inner safe water mark for passage to **Harwich** you will use:

Sector H6 – Long Sand Inner to Sunk Head – see page 38
Sector H7 – Sunk Head to Goldmer Gat – see previous page
Sector H4 – Goldmer Gat to the Naze – see previous page
Sector H5 – The Naze to Harwich Landfall – see previous page

From the Long Sand Inner safe water mark for passage to the **Deben** you will use:

Sector H6 – Long Sand Inner to Sunk Head – see page 38
Sector H8 – Sunk Head to North-East Gunfleet – see previous page
Sector J6 – North-East Gunfleet to Cork Sand Beacon – see previous page
Sector I8 – Cork Sand Beacon to Deben Landfall – see previous page

Routes 26, 28, 30 & 32 – *Ramsgate to the Harwich Harbour and the Deben via either Gat and Little Sunk*

These four routes following the same early passage as the previous section. That is to say that those using **Fisherman's Gat** will follow:

Sector A1 – Ramsgate to North Foreland – Page 17
Sector A2 – North Foreland to East Margate – Page 18
Sector A3 – East Margate to Outer Fisherman – Page 18
Sector B6 – Outer Fisherman to Black Deep No 8 – Page 25
Sector G7 – Black Deep No 8 to Black Deep – Page 26

At the Black Deep waypoint no 12 the route via Foulger's Gat will converge.

Those using **Foulger's Gat** will follow:

Sector A1 – Ramsgate to North Foreland – Page 17
Sector B1 – East Margate to Tongue DW Anchorage – Page 22
Sector B2 – Tongue Deep Water Anchorage to Long Sand Outer – Page 22
Sector B3 – Long Sand Outer to Black Deep – Page 23

All of these four routes then use Sector H2 to cross the Sunk Sand at the Little Sunk and Sector H3 to cross the East Swin to the Goldmer Gat waypoint.

Sector H2 – Black Deep to Barrow No 2

This short sector crosses the Sunk Sand at the Little Sunk. The Black Deep waypoint is on the edge of the sand just in the Black Deep. Note that the sand is steep to on the edge of the Black Deep shelving from 15 metres LAT to a little over 3 metres in less than a third of a mile. This can cause an interesting popple at the edge of the sand in south or south-easterly winds but is soon passed as the sand levels out. It is relatively stable and flat at this point and with 1.2nm between the unmarked hazards either side of this crossing point (see the downloadable illustration on Page 24), it is not unknown for those familiar with the crossing point and aware of their position to sail diagonally across the sand.

The Barrow No 2 waypoint is on the other side of the Sunk Sand about half a mile from the Barrow No 2 port hand buoy *(Fl(2) R.5s)*. It is not necessary to go to the Barrow No 2 buoy. Arrival at the CTTE waypoint will have cleared the Sunk Sand and the next Sector, common to all four routes, can begin immediately.

Sector H3 – Barrow No 2 to Goldmer Gat

This is a straight forward Sector, diagonally crossing the end of the Barrow Deep and East Swin. There will be no close marks but the West Sunk west cardinal buoy *(Q(9)15s)* and Gunfleet Spit south cardinal buoys *(Q(6)+LFl15s Bell)* will be distant to the east and west of the track respectively. Some smaller shipping may be encountered using the Barrow Deep or East Swin.

At the Goldmer Gat waypoint, the routes for Harwich Harbour and the Deben part company.

Connections to Harwich Harbour

Those for Harwich Harbour will use the following previous described Sectors:

Sector H4 – Goldmer Gat to the Naze – Page 39
Sector H5 – the Naze to Harwich Landfall – Page 39

The Belgium Yacht Yxilium over the Little Sunk sailing diagonally for the Black Deep (note the London Array wind farm on the other side of the Black Deep)

Connections to the Deben

Sector I7 – Goldmer Gat to Cork Sand Beacon

The track for this sector passes close to the West Rocks which is marked by the distant South Cork south cardinal buoy *((Q(6)+LFl15s)*. It will prudent to keep an eye on your track and if necessary deviate slightly towards the east. Also keep a careful watch for poorly marked lobster pots which can be frequently encountered over the West Rocks.

In the northerly part of this sector, you will pass over the Cork Hole which is used to test experimental buoys. These will have no relevance to your passage, your goal being a waypoint adjacent to the Cork Sand beacon. Passage to the Deben Landfall waypoint adjacent to the Woodbridge Haven safe water buoy is completed using:

Sector I8 – Cork Sand Beacon to Deben Landfall – Page 40.

Routes 62 and 63 – *Ramsgate to the Harwich Harbour and the Deben via the 'outside' route*

The outside route has no issues with tidal gates or insufficient water. Its disadvantage is principally the extra length which will be a matter of personal choice. There are some issues of note however.

Sector K1 – Ramsgate to North Foreland

This is Sector A1 repeated in table K for convenience of use. See page 17 for details.

Sectors K2 – North Foreland to Thanet and K3 - Thanet to South Knock

These two sectors will cause little problem. The first bisects the gap between the NE Spit east cardinal buoy *(VQ(3).5s)* to the west and the Thanet wind farm to the east marked by the North Thanet north cardinal buoy *(VQ).* Sector K3 continues the northwards passage past the South Knock in deep water to the outside of the Kentish Knock. This sand, like the London Array Wind Farm, lies to the west of the track.

Sectors K4 – South Knock to Kentish Knock and K5 – Kentish Knock to Long Sand Head

Approximately half way along this track, the Kentish Knock east cardinal buoy *(Q(3).10s)* to the east marks the western side and beginning of the Long Sand Head two-way route for shipping. Leaving this route clear to the east and the sands of the Kentish Knock to the west, Sector K4 continues with Sector K5 on the same track aiming for the Long Sand Head north cardinal buoy *(VQ Whis).*

This buoy is the 'inside marker' for shipping using the two-way route and shipping London bound will come up the two-way route and turn 150° to enter the Black Deep (or vice versa). As a traffic zone, we will keep clear of such traffic but note the location of the Long Sand Head to the west.

This is a nasty area of water in a blow and the Long Sand Head has been slowly and steadily extending north-east to give the Black Deep port hand buoy *(QR)* the dubious distinction of being the most moved ATON in the area. Do not get close due south of the Black Deep buoy! A yacht grounding on the Long Sand Head is generally regarded by the Cox'n of the Walton Lifeboat as an inevitable call-out.

Sector K6 – Long Sand Head to South Threshold

This Sector passes north-west/south-east through the Sunk Precautionary Area past the Trinity south cardinal buoy *(Q(6)+LFl.15s)*, the Sunk Inner light float *(Iso.3s11m12M Horn 1(30s) Racon AIS)* to the end waypoint near the South Threshold yellow special mark *(Fl(4).Y.10s).* As a Precautionary Area, expect shipping heading to or from the Black Deep and East Swin into the Sunk Gyratory (see illustration on page 12) and keep clear.

Sector K7 – South Threshold to Cork Sand Beacon

The same north-west/south-east track continues straight to the waypoint at the Cork Sand beacon. The track will cross the Rough Shoals but in good water (better than 5 metres LAT) and leave the Roughs Tower marked by twin west *(VQ(9).10s)* and east *(Q(3).10s)* cardinal buoys to the north-west.

At the Cork sand beacon, the routes for Harwich and the Deben part company; those for Harwich using the recommended Yacht track south of the Harwich Deep water route and those for the Deben using Sector I8 as described at Page 39.

Connections to Harwich Harbour

Sector K8 – Cork Sand Beacon to Harwich Landfall

From the Cork Sand Beacon follow the south side of the Harwich Deep Water route marked by yellow and red port hand buoys. In fact it is possible to turn before reaching the start waypoint and pass mid-way between the Cork Sand Yacht Beacon *(VQ. 2M)* and the Cork Sand Beacon *(Fl(3).R.10s).* As the track reaches Ridge south of the Inner Ridge port hand buoy *(QR)* depths may fall. It has, in the past, become quite shallow at this point but Harwich Harbour Authority responded promptly to dredge the track and reinstate reasonable depths. There is no reason to think that the HHA will not do the same should Ridge build up again.

South of the Deane port hand buoy *(LFl.R.6s)* you can follow the Deep Water route channel markers round to the Harwich Landfall to the west of the Cliff Foot port hand buoy *(Fl.R.5s).* The Planning Tables for this sector accommodates this turn in their calculations.

The Kent Rivers and the Thames to the Essex and Suffolk Rivers

This section contains guidance on a total of 21 routes each from the Kent Rivers (Swale and Medway) and the Thames to the Essex Rivers, Harwich Harbour and the Deben. These comprise Routes 33 to 53. Although this is a significant number of routes with different start and finish points, there are essentially only two choices; using the West Swin, Spitway and Wallet or the Barrow Deep and East Swin. The West Swin route is used for passage to the Essex Rivers.

The principal tidal issue is the 7 hour flood and 5 hour ebb experienced in the lower part of the Estuary. This generally means higher rates of tide on the ebb but also means when heading for the Suffolk Rivers that the flood is encountered in the northern part of the estuary while it is still slack in the lower part. A compromise is therefore inevitable for the longer passages to the Suffolk Rivers.

The Barrow Deep route has no depth issues but the West Swin route has the tidal gate of the Spitway where LW springs can have less than half a metre height of tide and a controlling depth at LAT of 1_5 metres. This will mean careful planning if heading northwards on a falling tide or southwards early on the flood.

For Harwich Harbour and the Deben, the route via the Barrow Deep and East Swin is marginally shorter from the Swale but longer from the Thames or Medway by 4 or 5nm depending on the exact route being used. Compare all the different distances using the Route tables at pages 56 and 57.

The Tides

There are no cross tide components for the Medway routes except for the first Sector (F1) to the SW Barrow. The tide ebbs north-easterly and floods south-westerly so it is either behind you or on the nose in all other sectors. The obvious plan is to take the start of the ebb from the Medway but as you travel northwards so the tide is lost after about five hours. This is not a problem if your destination is one of the Essex Rivers. However, if bound for Harwich or the Deben such a start time will bring you some adverse tide. The planning tables will assist in whether it is better to leave the Medway Landfall waypoint shortly before HW Sheerness or take the adverse tide at the other end of the journey. Of course, leaving the Medway Landfall

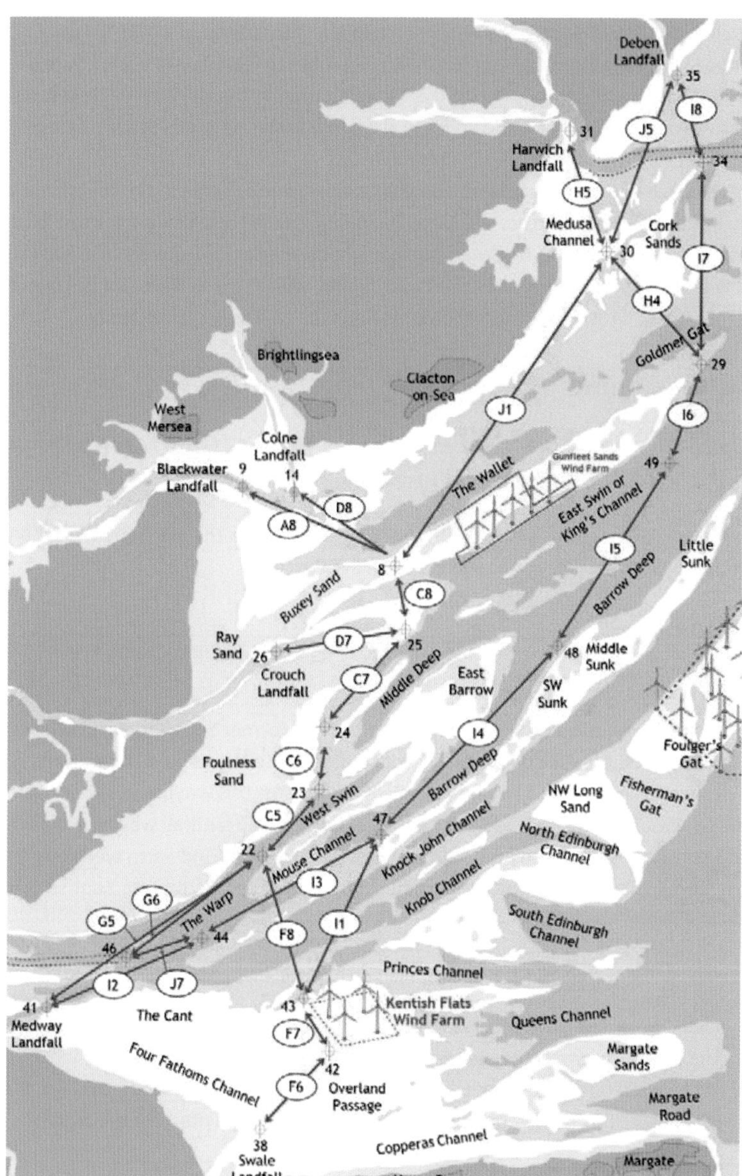

waypoint either at HW Sheerness or before carries the implication of taking on the flood as you make for the start waypoint. Coming south, it is possible to carry some eight hours of favourable tide as the tide turns later at the Medway than at the Harwich or Deben Havens. Depths at the Spitway should not be an issue since low water here will usually be avoided.

The Swale routes have to contend with some cross-tide components in the first three sectors across the Kentish Flats and across the Oaze Deep and The Warp if using the West Swin and Wallet route. This will need to be noted particularly on the sector between the Spaniard and Red Sand waypoints when the Kentish Flats wind farm will lie to the East and the Spaniard shoals to the West. Otherwise the comments about the Medway routes apply.

The Routes in detail

Routes 33 to 35 – The Swale to the Essex Rivers, 40 to 42 – the Medway to the Essex Rivers and 47 to 49 – the Thames to Essex Rivers

All these routes share a common three sector central part from the SW Barrow to the Whitaker Spit. Each River has different connections to the SW Barrow.

From the Swale

Sector F6 – Swale Landfall to Spaniard

Although Trinity House have now permanently lifted the former Spaniard east cardinal buoy, the northerly waypoint is still so named in recognition of the like named shoal to the north-west. The presence of this shoal mandates the necessity for this waypoint rather than a direct rhumb line to the next waypoint to the north. From the Swale landfall waypoint this track crosses the Kentish Flats towards the south-west corner of the Wind Farm well clear to the west of the buoys marking the Rock Berm where the power cable from the Kentish Flats is crossed by that from the London Array.

Sector F7 – Spaniard to Red Sand

Sector F7 passes between the Kentish Flats wind farm to the east and the East Middle Sand to the west. The northerly waypoint (Red Sand) is about a third of a nautical mile west of the boundary of the wind farm and its north-west corner turbine *(Fl.Y.5s 5M Horn)*. An unmarked wreck with 1_8 metres LAT lies to the west of this waypoint so maintaining the track is important.

There are plans to extend the Kentish Flats wind farm on its southern and west sides. This will call this sector into question as the construction work will inevitably make this a restricted area and once completed, there may be insufficient room between the wind farm and the East Middle Sand.

The alternative would appear to be to head north-west from the Swale Landfall waypoint and skirt the western edge of the Middle Sand and cross the Red Sand midway between the Middle Sand beacon and the Spile shoal. However, this is not a route that has yet been tested by CTTE and the construction work has yet to start. Although scheduled to commence in the latter part of 2014, most wind farm companies are reviewing their plans to take up the extension options. The position will be monitored and an update provided on the web site.

Sector F8 – Red Sand to the SW Barrow

This sector crosses the Oaze Deep which is the London end of the Knock John and Black Deep channels and consequently a look-out is essential for shipping and the monitoring of London VTS on Channel 69 prudent. There is no difficulty with depth on this track although it does cross the tail of the Red Sand in about 4 metres LAT and the Oaze Bank in about 3_6 metres LAT. After the Oaze Bank, watch for shipping entering or leaving the Barrow Deep. Tides will generally run across the track.

From the Medway

Sector G5 – Medway Landfall to SW Barrow

This single 8.2nm sector connects the Medway Landfall to the common central section of these routes which starts at the SW Barrow. This sector crosses the Yantlet deep water channel of the Thames close to the Sea Reach No 1 yellow special mark *(Fl.Y.2.5s)*. Care should be taken to avoid shipping, being aware that some may be constrained by their draught. The advice to monitor London VTS on channel 69 is repeated.

From the Thames

Sector G6 – Sea Reach No 1 to SW Barrow

The Sea Reach No 1 waypoint is situated to the north of the Yantlet deep water route so that the routes westward do not take leisure craft into the Deep Water Channel. If coming out of the Thames, the advice is to use the recommended yacht track. This runs south of the Yantlet channel until a crossing point between the paired Sea Reach No 5 and No 4 buoys. This recommended track should be followed and passage along the north side of the deep water route maintained. If heading for the SW Barrow, it is not necessary to go exactly to the CTTE waypoint but in preference to follow the curve of the channel into the West Swin.

The southern edge of the Maplin sands is well marked by the South Shoebury *(Fl.G.5s)* and Blacktail Spit *(Fl(3) G.10s)* starboard hand buoys. For time planning purposes, this sector can be considered to commence due south of the South Shoebury starboard hand buoy.

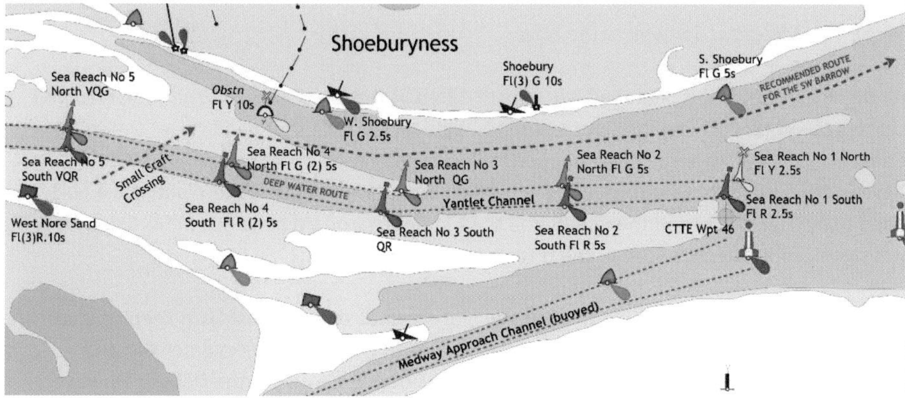

Sea Reach, River Thames

The sectors common to all routes (see also pages 27 & 28)

Sector C5 – SW Barrow to Maplin Edge

From the SW Barrow, the route passes up the West Swin between the Maplin starboard hand buoy *(QG sync Bell)* and West Swin port hand buoy *(QR sync)*. The northerly waypoint of this sector is just before the Maplin Edge starboard hand buoy *(Fl.G.2.5s)*. There are no specific navigational hazards but depending upon your timing some of the highest tidal rates in the estuary can be experienced here.

Sector C6 – Maplin Edge to NE Maplin

This short sector continues up the West Swin. Immediate after starting the sector, the Maplin Edge starboard hand buoy *(Fl.G.2.5s)* is left to the west and the Maplin Bank port hand buoy *(Fl(3) R.10s)* to the east. The bottom is strewn with wrecks and debris in this area but the least depth is over a wreck a little way north with 2_9 metres LAT. The end waypoint is adjacent to the NE Maplin starboard hand buoy *(Fl.G.5s Bell)* taking you to the west of a shoal area separating the West Swin from the Middle Deep.

Sector C7 – NE Maplin to Whitaker Spit

The final of these three sectors common to all routes is a simple track to the Whitaker Spit waypoint. This track does, however, pass over the edge of the Whitaker Spit and pilotage to the West Hook Middle port hand buoy *(Fl.R.5s)* may be necessary as your draught and the height of tide dictates.

The northerly waypoint is past the South Whitaker starboard hand buoy *(Fl(2)G.10s)* adjacent to the Inner Whitaker north cardinal buoy *(VQ(6)+LFl.10s)*. Here the routes part company according to the Essex River of destination.

Connection to the Crouch

Sector D7 – Whitaker Spit to Crouch Landfall – Page 29

Connections to the Blackwater

Sector C8 – Whitaker Spit to Mid-point Spitway

This short unremarkable cross-tide sector connects the West Swin route to the waypoint at the mid-point at the Spitway for those bound for either the Blackwater or Colne. The Spitway depths are discussed on pages 21 and 22. Note the least water found at the Spitway is 1_5 metres LAT although slightly better depths appear to be available to the east of the line between the two buoys. Note also the times of the tide at the Spitway in relation to Sheerness set out overleaf and that a chartlet is available for download from the web site.

The Swin Spitway buoy (Iso.10s Bell)

The Routes – The Kent Rivers and the Thames to the Essex and Suffolk Rivers

Tide at Spitway	Relationship to Sheerness times
Mean HW Springs	Approx. - 42 minutes
Mean HW Neaps	Approx. – 32 minutes
Mean LW Springs	Approx. – 42 minutes
Mean LW Neaps	Approx. – 22 minutes

Sector A8 – Mid-point Spitway to Blackwater Landfall – Page 21

Connections to the Colne

Sector C8 – Whitaker Spit to Mid-point Spitway - above
Sector D8 – Mid-point Spitway to Colne Landfall – Page 29

Routes 36 & 38, 43 & 45, 50 & 52 – The Swale, Medway and Thames to Harwich Harbour and the Deben via the West Swin, Spitway and Wallet

These routes re-use the sectors described above from their starting waypoints to the Spitway. Thereafter there is one common sector through the Wallet to the Naze where the routes to Harwich and the Deben part company.

From the Swale

Sector F6 – Swale Landfall to Spaniard – Page 44
Sector F7 – Spaniard to Red Sand – Page 44
Sector F8 – Red Sand to the SW Barrow – Page 44

From the Medway

Sector G5 – Medway Landfall to SW Barrow – Page 44

From the Thames

Sector G6 – Sea Reach No 1 to SW Barrow – Page 44

Common Sectors

Sector C5 – SW Barrow to Maplin Edge – Page 45 (also Page 27)
Sector C6 – Maplin Edge to NE Maplin – Page 45 (also Page 27)
Sector C7 – NE Maplin to Whitaker Spit – Page 45 (also Page 28)
Sector C8 – Whitaker Spit to Mid-point Spitway – Page 45 (also Page 28)

Sector J1 – Mid-point Spitway to the Naze

All these routes use this Sector which, at over 12nm, is the longest sector used by CTTE. This crosses the Wallet leaving the Gunfleet Sands wind farm to the south and closes the shore off Frinton and Walton where poorly marked lobster pots may be encountered. At night, a tactic I have used to avoid these is to stay in the marked Wallet channel until the Wallet No 4 port hand buoy *(Fl(4)R.10s)* and then head into the Medusa starboard hand buoy *(FIG.5s)*. This will not significantly affect the use of the planning table.

Note, it is quite feasible to avoid the Spitway and continue into the East Swin keeping south of the Gunfleet Sands and its wind farm before heading in either, across Goldmer Gat and through the Medusa Channel for Harwich, or across the Cork Hole for the Deben. However, there is no significant reduction in distance.

Connection to Harwich Harbour

Sector H5 – the Naze to Harwich Landfall – Page 39

Connection to the Deben

Sector J5 – The Naze to Deben Landfall

For the purposes of planning the impact of the tide, this sector uses a track of 027˚(T)/207˚(T) from the Naze to the waypoint adjacent to the Woodbridge Haven Safe Water Mark *(MO(A) 15s)*. However, the sector crosses the Harwich Deep Water Channel to the east of the Pitching Ground and Platters Buoys. This channel is under the authority of the Harwich Haven Authority who recommend crossing to the west of these buoys. Their recommendation is to cross between 51˚55'83N, 001˚20'29E and 51˚55'23N, 001˚20'39E. This complies with the requirement to cross with a heading as near as practical at right angles to the Separation Lane and also at the narrowest part of the Lane.

To achieve this crossing point it will be necessary having left Stone Banks port hand buoy to port to dogleg off the sector track for the Outer Ridge port hand buoy *(R)* on a 3nm track of 013°(T)/193°(T). It will be shallow around the Stone Banks buoy with little over 2 metres LAT but the depth improves in the second part of the track. Having crossed between the recommended waypoints you will be over the Wadgate Ledge which has limited water in places. If this is an issue for you because of your draught and the height of tide, it would be prudent to head for the Wadgate Ledge Beacon *(Fl.(4)G.15s)* and pass it to the south.

Finally be aware that the Woodbridge Haven safe water buoy *(Mo(A)15s)* safe water buoy can be subject to frequent moves and its latest position should be checked on www.eastcostpilot.com

Routes 37 & 39, 44 & 46, 51 & 53 – The Swale, Medway and Thames to Harwich Harbour and the Deben via the Barrow Deep and East Swin

These are alternative routes to the West Swin, Spitway and Wallet previously described. The common sectors are from the Barrow No 10 PHM, along the Barrow Deep, past the Barrow No 4, west cardinal buoy and the Gunfleet Spit south cardinal buoy to the Goldmer Gat waypoint clear of the head of the Gunfleet Sands. At this point, the Harwich Harbour route uses two previously described sectors across Goldmer Gat to the Naze waypoint and from there to a waypoint adjacent to the Cliff Foot PHM outside main Harwich Channel.

Those bound to or from the Deben will use two sectors, also previously described to cross Goldmer Gat and the Cork Hole to the Cork Sand Beacon and from there across the main Harwich Shipping Channel to the waypoint adjacent to the Woodbridge Haven Safe Water Mark.

For those connecting to or from the Medway, the Barrow Deep and East Swin route is longer for both Harwich Harbour and the Deben but has no issues about depth. The West Swin and Wallet route does have the reduced depth of the Spitway but this is unlikely to be a problem unless unusual timing has forced you to be there at low water. Since this would then have the prospect of a foul tide whichever direction you are traveling for half of the passage, your planning will probably have avoided this.

The Swale sailor has little difference in distance between the two core routes. The West Swin and Wallet route is a mile longer for Harwich but nearly a mile shorter for the Deben.

From the Swale

Sector F6 – Swale Landfall to Spaniard – Page 44
Sector F7 – Spaniard to Red Sand – Page 44

Sector I1 – Red Sand to Barrow No 10

From the Red Sand waypoint, Sector I1 runs for nearly 6.5nm to the northerly waypoint adjacent to Barrow No 10 port hand buoy *(Fl(3)R.10s).* This track crosses the Princes Channel Deep Water channel leaving the Princes No 8 port hand buoy *(Fl(2) R.5s)* and the Princes Inner yellow special mark *(Fl.Y.2.5s)* to the west. Beware of shipping using this channel. You are clear of the Princes Channel when you have reached the Shivering Sand Towers which are left to the east.

After the Towers, the Knob and Knock John Channels are crossed with care taken to avoid shipping in the Knock John. The Knob safe water buoy *(ISO 5s Bell)* and the more distant SE Mouse starboard hand buoy *(QG)* are left to the west. Across the Knock John Channel, the No 7 starboard hand buoy *(Fl(4)G.15s),* left to the east, indicates you are approaching Knob Gat passing between the Mouse and Knock John banks. The shallowest water is to the east side of the track which should be avoided particularly as there will be some tidal component setting you towards this bank on the ebb where there is a wreck charted as 0_9 metres LAT.

From the Medway

Sector I2 – Medway Landfall to North Oaze

This Sector leaves the Medway channel and passes north of the Oaze Bank thus crossing the entrance to the Oaze Deep. This is the principle shipping route for vessels bound between the Thames and either the Black Deep or Princes Channel. Care should therefore be taken of such movements and London VTS should be monitored on channel 69. There are no depth issues for yachts in this sector.

Sector I3 – North Oaze to Barrow No 10

From the North Oaze port hand buoy *(QR),* this sector runs for just over 7nm to a waypoint adjacent to the Barrow No 10 port hand buoy *(Fl(3)R.10s).* This passes clear (south) of the Mouse Channel, close to two yellow special buoys *(Fl(5)Y.20s)* and the Barrow No 12 port hand buoy *(Fl2) R.5s)* just to the north.

The Routes – The Kent Rivers and the Thames to the Essex and Suffolk Rivers

From the Thames

Sector J7 – Sea Reach No 1 to North Oaze

Those coming down the Thames should note the comments and illustration on Page 44. From the waypoint north of the Sea Reach No 1, the track is through the Warp and the marked Mouse Channel (which uses Barrow Deep buoy numbering), heading direct for the Barrow No 10 port hand buoy. This will be clear of any Princes or Knock John channel shipping but some may be encountered to or from the Barrow Deep.

Sector I3 – North Oaze to Barrow No 10 – Page 47

Common Sectors

Sector I4 – Barrow No 10 to Barrow No 4

This is a long sector of nearly 8.5nm along the Barrow Deep. Depth will be ample and you will pass the paired channel buoys no's 8 & 9 and 6 & 7 on route to the northerly waypoint adjacent to the Barrow No 4 west cardinal buoy *(VQ(9)10s)*. Precise adherence to this waypoint is not necessary but while the Barrow Deep has nothing like the larger shipping of the Black Deep and Princes Channel, it is used by smaller shipping especially the current regular small bulk carriers servicing the Crossrail to Wallesea (on the River Crouch) contract. These small bulk carriers are taking spoil from the Crossrail project to form the Wallesea Wetlands opposite Burnham. Their normal route from London laden to just over 4 metres is via the Barrow Deep, turning once clear of the East Barrow Sands, back down the Swin to the Whitaker Channel. These craft frequently anchor in the Barrow Deep Anchorage waiting for the tide.

Sector I5 – Barrow No 4 to Gunfleet Spit

This is a similarly uneventful sector between the Barrow No 4 west cardinal buoy *(VQ(9)10s)* and a waypoint off the Gunfleet Spit south cardinal buoy *(Q(6)+LF.15s Bell).* The track crosses the tail of the NE Middle bank but with over 5 metres of water LAT. The Barrow No 3 south cardinal buoy *(Q(3)10s)* marks the NE Middle bank for shipping.

Sector I6 – Gunfleet Spit to Goldmer Gat

From the Gunfleet Spit waypoint, the remains of the Old Gunfleet Lighthouse will be visible nearly a mile away to the north-west. The end waypoint at Goldmer Gat is at the head of the Gunfleet Sand. There are no issues about depth although the track will see reducing depths as it approaches the waypoint over the tail end of the sands. However, this will not entail depths less than 5 metres.

At the Goldmer Gat waypoint, the routes for Harwich Harbour and the Deben will diverge.

The Arctica Hav, one of the Crossrail - Wallesea bulk carriers in the Barrow Deep

Connection to Harwich Harbour

Sector H4 – Goldmer Gat to the Naze – Page 39
Sector H5 – the Naze to Harwich Landfall – Page 39

Connection to the Deben

Sector I7 – Goldmer Gat to Cork Sand Beacon – Page 42
Sector I8 – Cork Sand Beacon to Deben Landfall – Page 40

The Essex Rivers to Harwich Harbour and the Deben

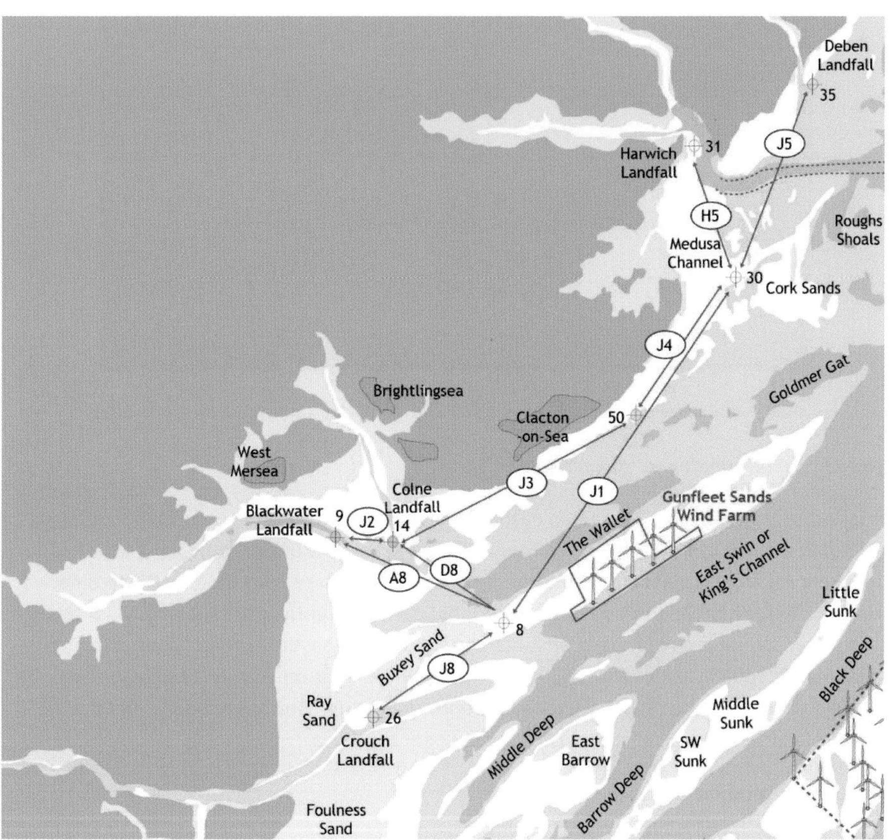

This section contains guidance on routes from each of the Essex Rivers (Crouch, Blackwater and Colne) to Harwich Harbour and the Deben. Guidance is also included here to accompany the Sectors that enable time planning between the Crouch (via the Spitway) and either the Blackwater or Colne. These are routes 54 to 61.

There are no particular mysteries about the tide affecting these routes. The flood and ebb flows south and north past the coast, mean HW at Walton being approximately 23 minutes before HW West Mersea and 43 minutes before HW Burnham.

The Routes in detail

Routes 54 and 57 – The Crouch to Harwich Harbour and the Deben

Sector J8 – Crouch Landfall to Mid-point Spitway

For time planning purposes, this sector is treated as a single rhumb line between the two waypoints. However, this sector uses the Swallowtail channel and this requires a small 'dogleg' to enter the channel. If approaching the Spitway at low water, it may be prudent to aim for the Swin Spitway buoy *(Iso.10s Bell)* rather than directly for the central waypoint.

The Crouch landfall waypoint is between the Whitaker No 7 *(Fl(4) G.10s)* and No 5 *(Fl(3) G.10s)* starboard hand buoys. To enter the Swallowtail aim for the Swallowtail West, west cardinal buoy *(VQ(9)10s)* and then midway between the Swallowtail No 4 yellow can *(Fl(2) Y.10s)* to the south and the Buxey Edge starboard hand buoy *(FlG.10s)* to the north. The sector continues north above the Swallowtail shoal passing the Swallowtail No 3 *(Fl.Y.15s)* and No 2 *(Fl.Y.10s)* yellow can buoys. Once past the Swallowtail No 2, the Swin Spitway buoy will be ahead.

Note the guidance on pages 21 and 22 regarding depths and tides at the Spitway.

Sector J1 – Mid-point Spitway to the Naze – Page 46

At the Naze, the routes for Harwich and the Deben part company.

Connection to Harwich

Sector H5 – The Naze to Harwich Landfall – Page 39

Connection to the Deben

Sector J5 – The Naze to Deben Landfall – Page 46

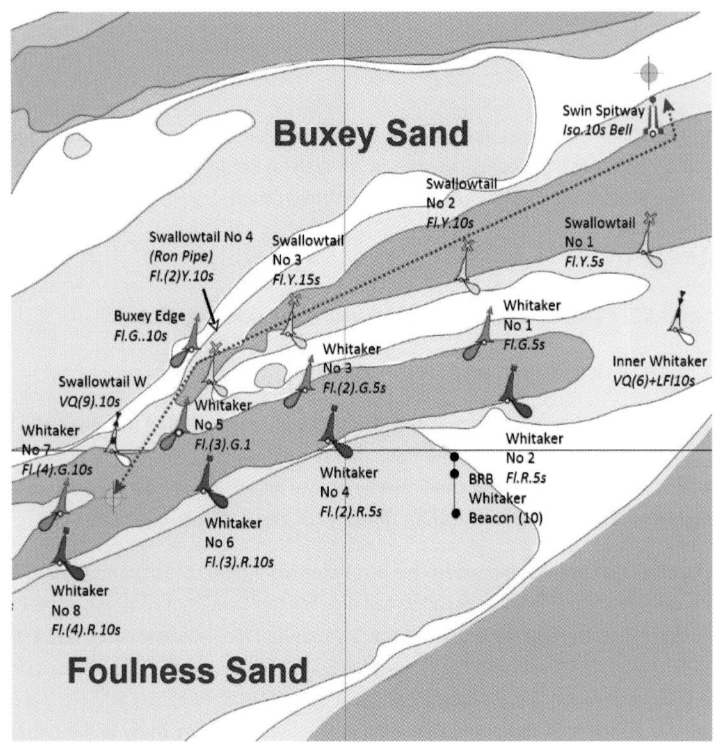

Sector J8 Crouch Landfall to Mid-point Spitway via Swallowtail

Routes 55 & 56 - Blackwater and Colne to Harwich Harbour – routes 58 & 59 - Blackwater and Colne to the Deben

Sector J2 – Blackwater Landfall to Colne Landfall

This is a simple sector of about 4.3nm from the Blackwater Landfall past the Bench Head starboard hand buoy *(Fl(3)G.10s)* to the Colne Bar starboard hand buoy *(Fl(2) G.5s)*. The NW Knoll port hand buoy *(Fl(2)R.2.5s)* will be seen to the south.

Trinity House Vessel Alert servicing the NW Knoll on a perfect summer's day

Sector J3 – Colne Landfall to Holland-on-Sea

This is a long sector of over 8nm to an easterly waypoint off Holland-on-Sea. Pass the Colne Bar starboard hand buoy *(Fl(2)G.5s)* to the south giving the end of the Colne Bar a little room before shaping a course north of the Eagle shoal marked by the eponymous north cardinal buoy *(Q)*. Thereafter the track passes over Priory Spit with slightly less than 3m LAT. If this is a little shallow for you, move further offshore and follow the coastline round. The waypoint is approximately south-west of the Radar Mast between Holland-on-Sea and Frinton-on-Sea. There is no need to close on this waypoint if depth is an issue. Beware of poorly marked lobster pots all along this coast especially as you near the Naze.

Sector J4 – Holland-on-Sea to the Naze

Ahead, a little more than half way along this sector, Walton Pier is visible and beyond it the Naze. There is little more than 2m LAT close inshore but the bottom is relatively consistent and it is easy to move further out to gain extra depth if necessary. At night to avoid lobster pots, I prefer to be much further out aiming for the Medusa buoy before heading for Harwich.

Connection to Harwich

Sector H5 – The Naze to Harwich Landfall – Page 39

Connection to the Deben

Sector J5 – The Naze to Deben Landfall – Page 46

Routes 60 & 61 - The Crouch to the Blackwater and Colne via the Spitway

These sectors are all previously described:

Sector J8 – Crouch Landfall to Mid-point Spitway – Page 49

For the Blackwater

Sector A8 – Mid-point Spitway to Blackwater Landfall – Pages 21 & 22

For the Colne

Sector D8 – Mid-point Spitway to Colne Landfall – Page 29

The Crouch to the Blackwater and Colne via the Ray Sand (Rays'nd)

This is not a route for which any time planning sectors exist but it is an acknowledged short-cut between the Crouch and the other two Essex rivers. Several centuries ago the Ray Sand Channel was probably the main exit from the Crouch. In 1900, 12 foot of water was reported. In 1920, charts showed a fathom and a half and in 1956 in his first edition of East Coast Rivers, Jack Coote reported "a minimum depth of only two or three feet in the southern entrance". By 1988 it was "little or no water"! The sand now dries more than a metre at low water springs. In consequence passage using this route is only possible when there is sufficient height of tide but many yachts and motor yachts continue to use the route when the tide serves.

The Crouch Harbour Master buoys the crossing point with the old circular yellow 'Ray Sand' buoy at 51°39'030N, 000°59'300E and two more recent safe water marks: the Ray Sand Middle at 51°40'000N, 000°59'500E and the Ray Sand North at 51°40'700N, 000°59'500E. All three are unlit and not particularly large. The yellow Ray Sand buoy in particular can be difficult to see.

The worst drying height on the 000°59'500E meridian is drying 1_3 metres LAT. When there is sufficient height of tide, follow this meridian until the Ray Sand North is passed where the water will deepen slightly. The Buxey Beacon will be distant to the East. If bound for the Blackwater now deviate slightly to the east and follow the 001° meridian until the Blackwater is reached. Having had sufficient water to pass over the Rays'nd, craft bound for the Colne should be able to shape a course directly for Brightlingsea from the Ray Sand North Buoy.

A CTTE chartlet of the Ray Sand is available for download from the web site.

The Ray Sand and its buoyage

Routes, distances and their sectors

Ramsgate to the Essex Rivers - Routes 1 to 18

		Via	Distance	Direction	Sectors									
1	**Ramsgate to Blackwater**	Fisherman's Gat and SW Sunk	36.79nm	Northbound	A1	A2	A3	A4	A5	A6	A7	A8		
				Southbound	A8	A7	A6	A5	A4	A3	A2	A1		
				Waypoints	Ramsgate → 1 – 2 – 3 – 4 – 5 – 6a – 6b – 7 - 8 – 9 ← Blackwater									
2		Foulger's Gat and Little Sunk	41.28nm	Northbound	A1	B1	B2	B3	B4	B5	A8			
				Southbound	A8	B5	B4	B3	B2	B1	A1			
				Waypoints	Ramsgate → 1 – 2 – 10 – 11a – 11b – 12 – 13 – 8 – 9 ← Blackwater									
3		Fisherman's Gat and Middle Sunk	38.19nm	Northbound	A1	A2	A3	B6	B7	B8	A8			
				Southbound	A8	B8	B7	B6	A3	A2	A1			
				Waypoints	Ramsgate → 1 – 2 – 3 – 4 – 15 - 16 – 8 – 9 ← Blackwater									
4		Fisherman's Gat and Little Sunk	42.10nm	Northbound	A1	A2	A3	B6	G7	B4	B5	A8		
				Southbound	A8	B5	B4	G7	B6	A3	A2	A1		
				Waypoints	Ramsgate → 1 – 2 – 3 – 4 – 15 – 12 – 13 – 8 – 9 ← Blackwater									
5		Princes Channel and West Swin	46.32nm	Northbound	A1	C1	C2	C3	C4	C5	C6	C7	C8	A8
				Southbound	A8	C8	C7	C6	C5	C4	C3	C2	C1	A1
				Waypoints	Ramsgate → 1 – 2 – 19 – 20 – 21 – 22 – 23 – 24 – 25 – 8 – 9 ← Blackwater									
6		North Edinburgh and SW Sunk	38.91nm	Northbound	A1	A2	D1	D2	D3	A6	A7	A8		
				Southbound	A8	A7	A6	D3	D2	D1	A2	A1		
				Waypoints	Ramsgate → 1 – 2 – 3 – 17 – 18 – 6a – 6b - 7 – 8 – 9 ← Blackwater									
7	**Ramsgate to Colne**	Fisherman's Gat and SW Sunk	32.66nm	Northbound	A1	A2	A3	A4	A5	A6	A7	D8		
				Southbound	D8	A7	A6	A5	A4	A3	A2	A1		
				Waypoints	Ramsgate → 1 – 2 – 3 – 4 – 5 – 6a – 6b – 7 - 8 – 14 ← Colne									
8		Foulger's Gat and Little Sunk	37.15nm	Northbound	A1	B1	B2	B3	B4	B5	D8			
				Southbound	D8	B5	B4	B3	B2	B1	A1			
				Waypoints	Ramsgate → 1 – 2 – 10 – 11a – 11b – 12 – 13 – 8 – 14 ← Colne									
9		Fisherman's Gat and Middle Sunk	34.06nm	Northbound	A1	A2	A3	B6	B7	B8	D8			
				Southbound	D8	B8	B7	B6	A3	A2	A1			
				Waypoints	Ramsgate → 1 – 2 – 3 – 4 – 15 - 16 – 8 – 14 ← Colne									
10		Fisherman's Gat and Little Sunk	37.97nm	Northbound	A1	A2	A3	B6	G7	B4	B5	D8		
				Southbound	D8	B5	B4	G7	B6	A3	A2	A1		
				Waypoints	Ramsgate → 1 – 2 – 3 – 4 – 15 – 12 – 13 – 8 – 14 ← Colne									
11		Princes Channel and West Swin	42.19nm	Northbound	A1	C1	C2	C3	C4	C5	C6	C7	C8	D8
				Southbound	D8	C8	C7	C6	C5	C4	C3	C2	C1	A1
				Waypoints	Ramsgate → 1 – 2 – 19 – 20 – 21 – 22 – 23 – 24 – 25 – 8 – 14 ← Colne									
12		North Edinburgh and SW Sunk	34.78nm	Northbound	A1	A2	D1	D2	D3	A6	A7	D8		
				Southbound	D8	A7	A6	D3	D2	D1	A2	A1		
				Waypoints	Ramsgate→ 1 – 2 – 3 – 17 – 18 – 6a – 6b - 7 – 8 – 14 ← Colne									

		Via	Distance	Direction	Sectors								
13	Ramsgate to Crouch	Fisherman's Gat and SW Sunk	31.42nm	Northbound	A1	A2	A3	A4	A5	A6	D4	D7	
				Southbound	D7	D4	A6	A5	A4	A3	A2	A1	
				Waypoints	Ramsgate → 1 – 2 – 3 – 4 – 5 – 6a – 6b – 7 - 25 – 26 ← Crouch								
14		Foulger's Gat and Little Sunk	36.44nm	Northbound	A1	B1	B2	B3	D6	D7			
				Southbound	D7	D6	B3	B2	B1	A1			
				Waypoints	Ramsgate → 1 – 2 – 10 – 11a – 11b – 12 – 25 – 26 ← Crouch								
15		Fisherman's Gat and Middle Sunk	33.19nm	Northbound	A1	A2	A3	B6	B7	D5	D7		
				Southbound	D7	D5	B7	B6	A3	A2	A1		
				Waypoints	Ramsgate → 1 – 2 – 3 – 4 – 15 - 16 – 25 – 26 ← Crouch								
16		Fisherman's Gat and Little Sunk	37.27nm	Northbound	A1	A2	A3	B6	G7	D6	D7		
				Southbound	D7	D6	G7	B6	A3	A2	A1		
				Waypoints	Ramsgate → 1 – 2 – 3 – 4 – 15 – 12 – 25 – 26 ← Crouch								
17		Princes Channel and West Swin	40.46nm	Northbound	A1	C1	C2	C3	C4	C5	C6	C7	D7
				Southbound	D7	C7	C6	C5	C4	C3	C2	C1	A1
				Waypoints	Ramsgate → 1 – 2 – 19 – 20 – 21 – 22 – 23 – 24 – 25 – 26 ← Crouch								
18		North Edinburgh and SW Sunk	33.53nm	Northbound	A1	A2	D1	D2	D3	A6	D4	D7	
				Southbound	D7	D4	A6	D3	D2	D1	A2	A1	
				Waypoints	Ramsgate → 1 – 2 – 3 – 17 – 18 – 6a – 6b - 7 – 25 – 26 ← Crouch								

Ramsgate to the Kent Rivers – Routes 19 to 23

		Via	Distance	Direction	Sectors					
19	Ramsgate to the Swale	Copperas Channel	21.09nm	Westbound	E1	E2	E3	E4		
				Eastbound	E4	E3	E2	E1		
				Waypoints	Ramsgate → 1 – 2 – 36 – 37 – 38 ← Swale					
20		Queens Channel	22.94nm	Westbound	E1	C1	F1	F2	F3	
				Eastbound	F3	F2	F1	C1	E1	
				Waypoints	Ramsgate → 1 – 2 – 19 – 51 – 52 – 38 ← Swale					
21	Ramsgate to Medway	Copperas Channel	30.47nm	Westbound	E1	E2	E3	E5	E6	E7
				Eastbound	E7	E6	E5	E3	E2	E1
				Waypoints	Ramsgate → 1 – 2 – 36 – 37 – 39 – 40 – 41 ← Medway					
22		Queens Channel & Kentish Flats	31.70nm	Westbound	E1	C1	F1	F4	F5	E7
				Eastbound	E7	F5	F4	F1	C1	E1
				Waypoints	Ramsgate → 1 – 2 – 19 – 51 – 42 – 40 – 41 ← Medway					
23		Princes Channel	31.67nm	Westbound	E1	C1	C2	C3	G1	G2
				Eastbound	G2	G1	C3	C2	C1	E1
				Waypoints	Ramsgate → 1 – 2 – 19 – 20 – 21 – 45 – 41 ← Medway					

Routes, distances and their sectors

Ramsgate to the London River – Route 24

		Via	Distance	Direction	Sectors					
24	Ramsgate to Sea Reach No 1	Princes Channel	29.04nm	Westbound	E1	C1	C2	C3	G1	G3
				Eastbound	G3	G1	C3	C2	C1	E1
				Waypoints	Ramsgate → 1 – 2 – 19 – 20 – 21 – 45 – 46 ← Sea Reach					

Ramsgate to Harwich Harbour (for Stour and Orwell) and the Deben – Routes 25 to 32

		Via	Distance	Direction	Sectors								
25	Ramsgate to Harwich Harbour	Foulger's Gat and Black Deep	39.73nm	Northbound	A1	B1	B2	H1	H6	H7	H4	H5	
				Southbound	H5	H4	H7	H6	H1	B2	B1	A1	
				Waypoints	Ramsgate → 1 – 2 – 10 – 11a – 11b – 27 – 28 – 29 – 30 - 31 ← Harwich								
26		Foulger's Gat and Little Sunk	39.07nm	Northbound	A1	B1	B2	B3	H2	H3	H4	H5	
				Southbound	H5	H4	H3	H2	B3	B2	B1	A1	
				Waypoints	Ramsgate → 1 – 2 – 10 – 11a – 11b – 12 – 32 – 29 – 30 - 31 ← Harwich								
27		Fisherman's Gat and Black Deep	41.19nm	Northbound	A1	A2	A3	B6	G8	H6	H7	H4	H5
				Southbound	H5	H4	H7	H6	G8	B6	A3	A2	A1
				Waypoints	Ramsgate → 1 – 2 – 3 - 4 – 15 – 27 – 28 – 29 – 30 - 31 ← Harwich								
28		Fisherman's Gat and Little Sunk	39.90nm	Northbound	A1	A2	A3	B6	G7	H2	H3	H4	H5
				Southbound	H5	H4	H3	H2	G7	B6	A3	A2	A1
				Waypoints	Ramsgate → 1 – 2 – 3 – 4 – 15 – 12 – 32 – 29 - 30 - 31 ← Harwich								
29	Ramsgate to Deben	Foulger's Gat and Black Deep	40.10nm	Northbound	A1	B1	B2	H1	H6	H8	J6	I8	
				Southbound	I8	J6	H8	H6	H1	B2	B1	A1	
				Waypoints	Ramsgate → 1 – 2 – 10 – 11a – 11b – 27 – 28 – 33 – 34 - 35 ← Deben								
30		Foulger's Gat and Little Sunk	39.89nm	Northbound	A1	B1	B2	B3	H2	H3	I7	I8	
				Southbound	I8	I7	H3	H2	B3	B2	B1	A1	
				Waypoints	Ramsgate → 1 – 2 – 10 – 11a – 11b – 12 – 32 – 29 – 34 - 35 ← Deben								
31		Fisherman's Gat and Black Deep	41.56nm	Northbound	A1	A2	A3	B6	G8	H6	H8	J6	I8
				Southbound	I8	J6	H8	H6	G8	B6	A3	A2	A1
				Waypoints	Ramsgate → 1 – 2 – 3 – 4 - 15 – 27 – 28 – 33 – 34 - 35 ← Deben								
32		Fisherman's Gat and Little Sunk	40.72nm	Northbound	A1	A2	A3	B6	G7	H2	H3	I7	I8
				Southbound	I8	I7	H3	H2	G7	B6	A3	A2	A1
				Waypoints	Ramsgate → 1 – 2 – 3 – 4 - 15 – 12 – 32 – 29 – 34 - 35 ← Deben								

Swale to the Essex and Suffolk Rivers – Routes 33 to 39

		Via	Distance	Direction	Sectors								
33		To the River Crouch	24.07nm	Northbound	F6	F7	F8	C5	C6	C7	D7		
				Southbound	D7	C7	C6	C5	F8	F7	F6		
				Waypoints	Swale → 38 - 42 - 43 - 22 – 23 - 24 - 25 - 26 ← Crouch								
34	Swale to the Essex Rivers	To the River Blackwater	29.93nm	Northbound	F6	F7	F8	C5	C6	C7	C8	A8	
				Southbound	A8	C8	C7	C6	C5	F8	F7	F6	
				Waypoints	Swale → 38 – 42 – 43 – 22 - 23 – 24 – 25 – 8 - 9 ← Blackwater								
35		To the River Colne	25.80nm	Northbound	F6	F7	F8	C5	C6	C7	C8	D8	
				Southbound	D8	C8	C7	C6	C5	F8	F7	F6	
				Waypoints	Swale → 38 – 42 – 43 – 22 - 23 – 24 – 25 – 8 - 14 ← Colne								
36	Swale to Harwich Harbour	West Swin, Spitway & Wallet	37.13nm	Northbound	F6	F7	F8	C5	C6	C7	C8	J1	H5
				Southbound	H5	J1	C8	C7	C6	C5	F8	F7	F6
				Waypoints	Swale → 38 – 42 – 43 – 22 - 23 – 24 – 25 – 8 – 30 - 31 ← Harwich								
37		Barrow Deep & East Swin	38.47nm	Northbound	F6	F7	I1	I4	I5	I6	H4	H5	
				Southbound	H5	H4	I6	I5	I4	I1	F7	F6	
				Waypoints	Swale → 38 – 42 – 43 – 47 - 48 – 49 – 29 – 30 - 31 ← Harwich								
38	Swale to Deben	West Swin, Spitway & Wallet	40.22nm	Northbound	F6	F7	F8	C5	C6	C7	C8	J1	J5
				Southbound	J5	J1	C8	C7	C6	C5	F8	F7	F6
				Waypoints	Swale → 38 – 42 – 43 – 22 - 23 – 24 – 25 – 8 – 30 - 35 ← Deben								
39		Barrow Deep & East Swin	39.30nm	Northbound	F6	F7	I1	I4	I5	I6	I7	I8	
				Southbound	I8	I7	I6	I5	I4	I1	F7	F6	
				Waypoints	Swale → 38 – 42 – 43 – 47 - 48 – 49 – 29 – 34 - 35 ← Deben								

Medway to the Essex and Suffolk Rivers – Routes 40 to 47

		Via	Distance	Direction	Sectors					
40		To the River Crouch	23.16nm	Northbound	G5	C5	C6	C7	D7	
				Southbound	D7	C7	C6	C5	G5	
				Waypoints	Medway → 41 – 22 - 23 – 24 – 25 – 26 ← Crouch					
41	Medway to the Essex Rivers	To the River Blackwater	29.02nm	Northbound	G5	C5	C6	C7	C8	A8
				Southbound	A8	C8	C7	C6	C5	G5
				Waypoints	Medway → 41 – 22 - 23 – 24 – 25 – 8 - 9 ← Blackwater					
42		To the River Colne	24.89nm	Northbound	G5	C5	C6	C7	C8	D8
				Southbound	D8	C8	C7	C6	C5	G5
				Waypoints	Medway → 41 – 22 - 23 – 24 – 25 – 8 - 14 ← Colne					

Routes, distances and their sectors

		Via	Distance	Direction	Sectors						
43	Medway to Harwich Harbour	West Swin, Spitway & Wallet	36.22nm	Northbound	G5	C5	C6	C7	C8	J1	H5
				Southbound	H5	J1	C8	C7	C6	C5	G5
				Waypoints	Medway → 41 – 22 - 23 – 24 – 25 – 8 – 30 - 31 ← Harwich						
44		Barrow Deep & East Swin	41.08nm	Northbound	I2	I3	I4	I5	I6	H4	H5
				Southbound	H5	H4	I6	I5	I4	I3	I2
				Waypoints	Medway → 41 – 44 – 47 - 48 – 49 – 29 – 30 - 31 ← Harwich						
45	Medway to Deben	West Swin, Spitway & Wallet	39.31 nm	Northbound	G5	C5	C6	C7	C8	J1	J5
				Southbound	J5	J1	C8	C7	C6	C5	G5
				Waypoints	Medway → 41 – 22 - 23 – 24 – 25 – 8 – 30 - 35 ← Deben						
46		Barrow Deep & East Swin	41.90 nm	Northbound	I2	I3	I4	I5	I6	I7	I8
				Southbound	I8	I7	I6	I5	I4	I3	I2
				Waypoints	Medway → 41 – 44 – 47 - 48 – 49 – 29 – 34 - 35 ← Deben						

Thames to the Essex and Suffolk Rivers – Routes 47 to 53

		Via	Distance	Direction	Sectors						
47	Sea Reach No 1 to the Essex Rivers	To the River Crouch	19.93 nm	Northbound	G6	C5	C6	C7	D7		
				Southbound	D7	C7	C6	C5	G6		
				Waypoints	Sea Reach → 46 – 22 - 23 – 24 – 25 – 26 ← Crouch						
48		To the River Blackwater	25.78 nm	Northbound	G6	C5	C6	C7	C8	A8	
				Southbound	A8	C8	C7	C6	C5	G6	
				Waypoints	Sea Reach → 46 – 22 - 23 – 24 – 25 – 8 - 9 ← Blackwater						
49		To the River Colne	21.65 nm	Northbound	G6	C5	C6	C7	C8	D8	
				Southbound	D8	C8	C7	C6	C5	G6	
				Waypoints	Sea Reach → 46 – 22 - 23 – 24 – 25 – 8 - 14 ← Colne						
50	Sea Reach No 1 to Harwich Harbour	West Swin, Spitway & Wallet	32.99 nm	Northbound	G6	C5	C6	C7	C8	J1	H5
				Southbound	H5	J1	C8	C7	C6	C5	G6
				Waypoints	Sea Reach → 46 – 22 - 23 – 24 – 25 – 8 – 30 - 31 ← Harwich						
51		Barrow Deep & East Swin	38.04 nm	Northbound	J7	I3	I4	I5	I6	H4	H5
				Southbound	H5	H4	I6	I5	I4	I3	J7
				Waypoints	Sea Reach → 46 – 44 – 47 - 48 – 49 – 29 – 30 - 31 ← Harwich						
52	Sea Reach No 1 to Deben	West Swin, Spitway & Wallet	36.08 nm	Northbound	G6	C5	C6	C7	C8	J1	J5
				Southbound	J5	J1	C8	C7	C6	C5	G6
				Waypoints	Sea Reach → 46 – 22 - 23 – 24 – 25 – 8 – 30 - 35 ← Deben						
53		Barrow Deep & East Swin	38.86 nm	Northbound	J7	I3	I4	I5	I6	I7	I8
				Southbound	I8	I7	I6	I5	I4	I3	J7
				Waypoints	Sea Reach → 46 – 44 – 47 - 48 – 49 – 29 – 34 - 35 ← Deben						

Essex Rivers to Harwich Harbour and Deben – Routes 54 to 59

		Via	Distance	Direction	Sectors			
54	Essex Rivers to Harwich Harbour	River Crouch to Harwich	19.92 nm	Northbound	J8	J1	H5	
				Southbound	H5	J1	J8	
				Waypoints	Crouch → 26 – 8 - 30 - 31 ← Harwich			
55		River Blackwater to Harwich	21.22 nm	Northbound	J2	J3	J4	H5
				Southbound	H5	J4	J3	J2
				Waypoints	Blackwater → 9 – 14 - 50 – 30 - 31 ← Harwich			
56		River Colne to Harwich	16.93 nm	Northbound	J3	J4	H5	
				Southbound	H5	J4	J3	
				Waypoints	Colne → 14 – 50 - 30 - 31 ← Harwich			
57	Essex Rivers to Deben	River Crouch to Deben	23.01 nm	Northbound	J8	J1	J5	
				Southbound	J5	J1	J8	
				Waypoints	Crouch → 26 – 8 - 30 - 35 ← Deben			
58		River Blackwater to Deben	24.31 nm	Northbound	J2	J3	J4	J5
				Southbound	J5	J4	J3	J2
				Waypoints	Blackwater → 9 – 14 - 50 – 30 - 35 ← Deben			
59		River Colne to Deben	20.02 nm	Northbound	J3	J4	J5	
				Southbound	J5	J4	J3	
				Waypoints	Colne → 14 – 50 - 30 - 35 ← Deben			

Between the Essex Rivers – Routes 60 to 61

		Via	Distance	Direction	Sectors	
60	Between the Essex Rivers	River Crouch to Blackwater via Spitway	12.71 nm	Northbound	J8	A8
				Southbound	A8	J8
				Waypoints	Crouch → 26 – 8 - 9 ← Blackwater	
61		River Crouch to Colne via Spitway	8.58 nm	Northbound	J8	D8
				Southbound	D8	J8
				Waypoints	Crouch → 26 – 8 - 14 ← Colne	

Ramsgate to Harwich Harbour and Deben via the Outside Route – Routes 62 to 63

		Via	Distance	Direction	Sectors							
62	The Outside Route	Ramsgate to Harwich	46.16 nm	Northbound	K1	K2	K3	K4	K5	K6	K7	K8
				Southbound	K8	K7	K6	K5	K4	K3	K2	K1
				Waypoints	Ramsgate → 1 – 2 - 53 – 54 – 55 – 56 – 57 – 34 - 31 ← Harwich							
63		Ramsgate to Deben	44.54 nm	Northbound	K1	K2	K3	K4	K5	K6	K7	I8
				Southbound	I8	K7	K6	K5	K4	K3	K2	K1
				Waypoints	Ramsgate → 1 - 2 – 53 – 54 – 55 – 56 – 57 – 34 – 35 ← Deben							

Sector Tables

Showing Sector number and name, coordinates of waypoints, distance and rhumb line course in °true

A1	Ramsgate - North Foreland			
1	Ramsgate Landfall	51°19’50N 001°26’67E	4.75nm	012°(T) Northbound
2	North Foreland	51°24’15N 001°28’19E		192°(T) Southbound
A2	**North Foreland - East Margate**			
2	North Foreland	51°24’15N 001°28’19E	3.08nm	347°(T) Northbound
3	East Margate	51°27’15N 001°27’10E		167°(T) Southbound
A3	**East Margate - Outer Fisherman**			
3	East Margate	51°27’15N 001°27’10E	6.45nm	346°(T) Northbound
4	Outer Fisherman	51°33’42N 001°24’66E		166°(T) Southbound
A4	**Outer Fisherman - Inner Fisherman**			
4	Outer Fisherman	51°33’42N 001°24’66E	3.93nm	311°(T) Northbound
5	Inner Fisherman	51°36’00N 001°19’90E		131°(T) Southbound
A5	**Inner Fisherman - SW Sunk (North Side) ***			
5	Inner Fisherman	51°36’00N 001°19’90E	3.48nm	338°(T) Northbound
6a	SW Sunk (North Side)	51°38’03N 001°16’20E		158°(T) Southbound
A6	**SW Sunk (North Side) - East Barrow Sands ***			
6b	SW Sunk (North Side)	51°38’03N 001°16’20E	2.10nm	329°(T) Northbound
7	East Barrow Sands	51°39’83N 001°14’49E		149°(T) Southbound
A7	**East Barrow Sands - Mid-Point Spitway**			
7	East Barrow Sands	51°39’83N 001°14’49E	4.59nm	302°(T) Northbound
8	Mid-Point Spitway	51°42’23N 001°08’20E		122°(T) Southbound
A8	**Mid-Point Spitway - Blackwater Landfall**			
8	Mid-Point Spitway	51°42’23N 001°08’20E	8.42nm	292°(T) Northbound
9	Blackwater Landfall	51°45’39N 000°55’63E		112°(T) Southbound

* Note: refer to text on Page 21 for pilotage across the SW Sunk swatchway. The time planning tables allow for the distance of the swatchway (1.65nm in 2014).

B1	North Foreland - Tongue DW Anchorage			
2	North Foreland	51°24’15N 001°28’19E	6.56nm	000°(T) Northbound
10	Tongue DW Anchorage	51°30’71N 001°28’10E		180°(T) Southbound
B2	**Tongue DW Anchorage - Long Sand Outer ***			
10	Tongue DW Anchorage	51°30’71N 001°28’10E	4.02nm	000°(T) Northbound
11a	Long Sand Outer	51°34’73N 001°28’10E		180°(T) Southbound
B3	**Long Sand Outer - Black Deep ***			
11a	Long Sand Outer*	51°34’73N 001°28’10E	7.06nm	350°(T) Northbound
12	Black Deep	51°41’22N 001°24’97E		170°(T) Southbound
B4	**Black Deep - NE Middle**			
12	Black Deep	51°41’22N 001°24’97E	5.28nm	276°(T) Northbound
13	NE Middle	51°41’73N 001°16’52E		096°(T) Southbound
B5	**NE Middle - Mid-Point Spitway**			
13	NE Middle	51°41’73N 001°16’52E	5.20nm	276°(T) Northbound
8	Mid-Point Spitway	51°42’23N 001°08’20E		096°(T) Southbound
B6	**Outer Fisherman - Black Deep No 8**			
4	Outer Fisherman	51°33’42N 001°24’66E	3.58nm	325°(T) Northbound
15	Black Deep No 8	51°36’36N 001°21’37E		145°(T) Southbound
B7	**Black Deep No 8 to Barrow Deep**			
15	Black Deep No 8	51°36’36N 001°21’37E	4.17nm	351°(T) Northbound
16	Barrow Deep	51°40’48N 001°20’33E		171°(T) Southbound
B8	**Barrow Deep to Mid-Point Spitway**			
16	Barrow Deep	51°40’48N 001°20’33E	7.74nm	283°(T) Northbound
8	Mid-Point Spitway	51°42’23N 001°08’20E		103°(T) Southbound

* Note: Refer to text on Page 24 for pilotage between the London Array South and Foulger’s Gat Waypoints.

C1	North Foreland - Margate Sand			
2	North Foreland	51°24’15N 001°28’19E	3.68nm	325°(T) Northbound
19	Margate Sand	51°27’14N 001°24’77E		145°(T) Southbound
C2	**Margate Sand - Princes South**			
19	Margate Sand	51°27’14N 001°24’77E	4.31nm	290°(T) Northbound
20	Princes South	51°28’65N 001°18’30E		110°(T) Southbound
C3	**Princes South - Princes No 6**			
20	Princes South	51°28’65N 001°18’30E	6.99nm	273°(T) Northbound
21	Princes No 6	51°29’00N 001°07’12E		093°(T) Southbound
C4	**Princes No 6 - SW Barrow**			
21	Princes No 6	51°29’00N 001°07’12E	5.77nm	303(T) Northbound
22	SW Barrow	51°32’11N 000°59’36E		123°(T) Southbound
C5	**SW Barrow - Maplin Edge**			
22	SW Barrow	51°32’11N 000°59’36E	3.91nm	045°(T) Northbound
23	Maplin Edge	51°34’89N 001°03’77E		225°(T) Southbound
C6	**Maplin Edge - NE Maplin**			
23	Maplin Edge	51°34’89N 001°03’77E	2.62nm	017°(T) Northbound
24	NE Maplin	51°37’39N 001°05’01E		197°(T) Southbound
C7	**NE Maplin - Whitaker Spit**			
24	NE Maplin	51°37’39N 001°05’01E	4.20nm	039°(T) Northbound
25	Whitaker Spit	51°40’66N 001°09’23E		219°(T) Southbound
C8	**Whitaker Spit - Mid-Point Spitway**			
25	Whitaker Spit	51°40’66N 001°09’23E	1.70nm	338°(T) Northbound
8	Mid-Point Spitway	51°42’23N 001°08’20E		158°(T) Southbound

Sector Tables

Showing Sector number and name, coordinates of waypoints, distance and rhumb line course in °true

D1	East Margate - Mid-Point North Edinburgh			
3	East Margate	51°27'15N 001°27'10E	7.14nm	326°(T) Northbound
17	North Edinburgh	51°33'08N 001°20'77E		146°(T) Southbound
D2	**Mid-Point North Edinburgh - NW Long Sand**			
17	North Edinburgh	51°33'08N 001°20'77E	3.21nm	289°(T) Northbound
18	NW Long Sand	51°34'13N 001°15'91E		109°(T) Southbound
D3	**NW Long Sand - SW Sunk (South Side) ***			
18	NW Long Sand	51°34'13N 001°15'91E	4.00nm	027°(T) Northbound
6a	SW Sunk (South Side)*	51°37'70N 001°18'80E		207°(T) Southbound
D4	**East Barrow Sands - Whitaker Spit**			
7	East Barrow Sands	51°39'83N 001°14'49E	3.38nm	284°(T) Northbound
25	Whitaker Spit	51°40'66N 001°09'23E		104°(T) Southbound
D5	**Barrow Deep - Whitaker Spit**			
16	Barrow Deep	51°40'48N 001°20'33E	6.91nm	272°(T) Northbound
25	Whitaker Spit	51°40'66N 001°09'23E		092°(T) Southbound
D6	**Black Deep - Whitaker Spit**			
12	Black Deep	51°41'22N 001°24'97E	9.81nm	267°(T) Northbound
25	Whitaker Spit	51°40'66N 001°09'23E		087°(T) Southbound
D7	**Whitaker Spit - Crouch Landfall**			
25	Whitaker Spit	51°40'66N 001°09'23E	4.26nm	258°(T) Northbound
26	Crouch Landfall	51°39'78N 001°02'53E		078°(T) Southbound
D8	**Mid-Point Spitway - Colne Landfall**			
8	Mid-Point Spitway	51°42'23N 001°08'20E	4.29nm	302°(T) Northbound
14	Colne Landfall	51°44'58N 001°02'42E		122°(T) Southbound

* Note: refer to text on Page 21 for pilotage across the SW Sunk swatchway.

E1	Ramsgate Landfall - North Foreland *			
1	Ramsgate	51°19'50N 001°26'67E	4.75nm	012°(T) Westbound
2	North Foreland	51°24'15N 001°28'19E		192°(T) Eastbound
E2	**North Foreland - SE Margate**			
2	North Foreland	51°24'15N 001°28'19E	4.86nm	268°(T) Westbound
36	SE Margate	51°23'96N 001°20'42E		088°(T) Eastbound
E3	**SE Margate - Copperas**			
36	SE Margate	51°23'96N 001°20'42E	5.85nm	267°(T) Westbound
37	Copperas	51°23'64N 001°11'08E		087°(T) Eastbound
E4	**Copperas - Swale Landfall**			
37	Copperas	51°23'64N 001°11'08E	5.63nm	278°(T) Westbound
38	Swale Landfall	51°24'45N 001°02'17E		098°(T) Eastbound
E5	**Copperas - Kentish Flats**			
37	Copperas	51°23'64N 001°11'08E	5.37nm	285°(T) Westbound
39	Kentish Flats	51°25'05N 001°02'80E		105°(T) Eastbound
E6	**Kentish Flats - Spile**			
39	Kentish Flats	51°25'05N 001°02'80E	4.60nm	285°(T) Westbound
40	Spile	51°26'22N 000°55'68E		105°(T) Eastbound
E7	**Spile - Medway Landfall**			
40	Spile	51°26'22N 000°55'68E	5.05nm	290°(T) Westbound
41	Medway Landfall	51°27'93N 000°48'09E		110°(T) Eastbound

* Note: Sector E1 is identical to Sector A1 but is repeated in Table E for convenience.

F1	Margate Sands - Wedge			
19	Margate Sand	51°27'14N 001°24'77E	4.03nm	270°(T) Northbound
51	Wedge	51°27'14N 001°18'33E		090°(T) Southbound
F2	**Wedge - Woolpack**			
51	Wedge	51°27'14N 001°18'33E	4.94nm	250°(T) Westbound
52	Woolpack	51°25'45N 001°10'89E		070°(T) Eastbound
F3	**Woolpack - Swale Landfall**			
52	Woolpack	51°25'45N 001°10'89E	5.55nm	260°(T) Westbound
38	Swale Landfall	51°24'45N 001°02'17E		080°(T) Eastbound
F4	**Wedge - Spaniard**			
51	Wedge	51°27'14N 001°18'33E	8.63nm	263°(T) Westbound
42	Spaniard	51°26'14N 001°04'62E		083°(T) Eastbound
F5	**Spaniard - Spile**			
42	Spaniard	51°26'14N 001°04'62E	5.59nm	271°(T) Westbound
40	Spile	51°26'22N 000°55'68E		091°(T) Eastbound
F6	**Swale Landfall - Spaniard**			
38	Swale Landfall	51°24'45N 001°02'17E	2.28nm	042°(T) Northbound
42	Spaniard	51°26'14N 001°04'62E		222°(T) Southbound
F7	**Spaniard - Red Sand**			
42	Spaniard	51°26'14N 001°04'62E	2.26nm	330°(T) Northbound
43	Red Sand	51°28'10N 001°02'83E		150°(T) Southbound
F8	**Red Sand - SW Barrow**			
43	Red Sand	51°28'10N 001°02'83E	4.56nm	322°(T) Northbound
22	SW Barrow	51°32'11N 000°59'36E		142°(T) Southbound

Sector Tables

Showing Sector number and name, coordinates of waypoints, distance and rhumb line course in °true

G1	Princes No 6 - Red Sand Towers			
21	Prince No 6	51°29’00N 001°07’12E	4.85nm	268°(T) Westbound
45	Red Sand Towers	51°28’84N 000°59’35E		088°(T) Eastbound
G2	**Red Sand Towers - Medway Landfall**			
45	Red Sand Towers	51°28’84N 000°59’35E	7.09nm	263°(T) Westbound
41	Medway Landfall	51°27’93N 000°48’09E		083°(T) Eastbound
G3	**Red Sand Towers - Sea Reach No 1**			
45	Red Sand Towers	51°28’84N 000°59’35E	4.40nm	282°(T) Westbound
46	Sea Reach No 1	51°29’77N 000°52’37E		102°(T) Eastbound
G4	**Medway Landfall - Sea Reach No 1**			
41	Medway Landfall	51°27’93N 000°48’09E	3.24nm	056°(T) Northbound
46	Sea Reach No 1	51°29’77N 000°52’37E		236°(T) Southbound
G5	**Medway Landfall - SW Barrow**			
41	Medway Landfall	51°27’93N 000°48’09E	8.18nm	059°(T) Northbound
22	SW Barrow	51°32’11N 000°59’36E		239°(T) Southbound
G6	**SW Barrow - Sea Reach No 1**			
22	SW Barrow	51°32’11N 000°59’36E	4.95nm	062°(T) Northbound
46	Sea Reach No 1	51°29’77N 000°52’37E		242°(T) Southbound
G7	**Black Deep No 8 - Black Deep**			
15	Black Deep No 8	51°36’36N 001°21’37E	5.33nm	025°(T) Northbound
12	Black Deep	51°41’22N 001°24’97E		205°(T) Southbound
G8	**Black Deep No 8 - Long Sand Inner**			
15	Black Deep No 8	51°36’36N 001°21’37E	3.66nm	045°(T) Northbound
27	Long Sand Inner	51°38’91N 001°25’56E		225°(T) Southbound

H1	Long Sand Outer - Long Sand Inner			
11a	Long Sand Outer	51°34’73N 001°28’10E	4.75nm	308/351°(T) Northbound
27	Long Sand Inner	51°38’91N 001°25’56E		171/128°(T) Southbound
H2	**Black Deep - Barrow No 2**			
12	Black Deep	51°41’22N 001°24’97E	1.32nm	318°(T) Northbound
32	Barrow No 2	51°42’20N 001°23’56E		138°(T) Southbound
H3	**Barrow No 2 - Goldmer Gat**			
32	Barrow No 2	51°42’20N 001°23’56E	6.88nm	010°(T) Northbound
29	Goldmer Gat	51°48’97N 001°25’49E		190°(T) Southbound
H4	**Goldmer Gat - The Naze**			
29	Goldmer Gat	51°48’97N 001°25’49E	5.07nm	311°(T) Northbound
30	The Naze	51°52’30N 001°19’31E		131°(T) Southbound
H5	**The Naze - Harwich Landfall**			
30	The Naze	51°52’30N 001°19’31E	3.41nm	350°(T) Northbound
31	Harwich Landfall	51°55’67N 001°18’34E		170°(T) Southbound
H6	**Long Sand Inner - Sunk Head**			
27	Long Sand Inner	51°38’91N 001°25’56E	6.85nm	020°(T) Northbound
28	Sunk Head	51°45’35N 001°29’33E		200°(T) Southbound
H7	**Sunk Head - Goldmer Gat**			
28	Sunk Head	51°45’35N 001°29’33E	4.34nm	327°(T) Northbound
29	Goldmer Gat	51°48’97N 001°25’49E		147°(T) Southbound
H8	**Sunk Head - NE Gunfleet**			
28	Sunk Head	51°45’35N 001°29’33E	4.65nm	348°(T) Northbound
33	NE Gunfleet	51°49’88N 001°27’72E		168°(T) Southbound

I1	Red Sand - Barrow No 10			
43	Red Sand	51°28’10N 001°02’83E	6.44nm	027°(T) Northbound
47	Barrow No 10	51°33’80N 001°07’64E		207°(T) Southbound
I2	**Medway Landfall - North Oaze PHM**			
41	Medway Landfall	51°27’93N 000°48’09E	6.30nm	070°(T) Northbound
44	North Oaze PHM	51°30’11N 000°57’56E		250°(T) Southbound
I3	**North Oaze PHM - Barrow No 10**			
44	North Oaze PHM	51°30’11N 000°57’56E	7.29nm	060°(T) Northbound
47	Barrow No 10	51°33’80N 001°07’64E		240°(T) Southbound
I4	**Barrow No 10 - Barrow No 4**			
47	Barrow No 10	51°33’80N 001°07’64E	8.47nm	046°(T) Northbound
48	Barrow No 4	51°39’77N 001°17’28E		226°(T) Southbound
I5	**Barrow No 4 - Gunfleet Spit**			
48	Barrow No 4	51°39’77N 001°17’28E	6.31nm	031°(T) Northbound
49	Gunfleet Spit	51°45’16N 001°22’57E		211°(T) Southbound
I6	**Gunfleet Spit - Goldmer Gat**			
49	Gunfleet Spit	51°45’16N 001°22’57E	4.22nm	025°(T) Northbound
29	Goldmer Gat	51°48’97N 001°25’49E		205°(T) Southbound
I7	**Goldmer Gat - Cork Sand Beacon**			
29	Goldmer Gat	51°48’97N 001°25’49E	6.43nm	001°(T) Northbound
34	Cork Sand Beacon	51°55’40N 001°25’62E		181°(T) Southbound
I8	**Cork Sand Beacon - Deben Landfall**			
34	Cork Sand Beacon	51°55’40N 001°25’62E	2.89nm	340°(T) Northbound
35	Deben Landfall	51°58’12N 001°24’04E		160°(T) Southbound

Showing Sector number and name, coordinates of waypoints, distance and rhumb line course in °true

J1	Mid-Point Spitway - The Naze			
8	Mid-Point Spitway	51°42’23N 001°08’20E	12.20nm	034°(T) Westbound
30	The Naze	51°52’30N 001°19’31E		214°(T) Eastbound
J2	**Blackwater Landfall - Colne Landfall**			
9	Blackwater Landfall	51°45’39N 000°55’63E	4.29nm	101°(T) Eastbound
14	Colne Landfall	51°44’58N 001°02’42E		281°(T) Westbound
J3	**Colne Landfall - Holland-on-Sea**			
14	Colne Landfall	51°44’58N 001°02’42E	8.24nm	066°(T) Eastbound
50	Holland-on-Sea	51°47’93N 001°14’54E		246°(T) Westbound
J4	**Holland-on-Sea - The Naze**			
50	Holland-on-Sea	51°47’93N 001°14’54E	5.28nm	034°(T) Eastbound
30	The Naze	51°52’30N 001°19’31E		214°(T) Westbound
J5	**The Naze - Deben Landfall**			
30	The Naze	51°52’30N 001°19’31E	6.51nm	027°(T) Northbound
35	Deben Landfall	51°58’12N 001°24’04E		207°(T) Southbound
J6	**NE Gunfleet - Cork Sand Beacon**			
33	NE Gunfleet	51°49’88N 001°27’72E	5.67nm	347°(T) Northbound
34	Cork Sand Beacon	51°55’40N 001°25’62E		167°(T) Southbound
J7	**Sea Reach No 1 - North Oaze PHB**			
46	Sea Reach No 1	51°29’77N 000°52’37E	3.26nm	084°(T) Eastbound
44	North Oaze PHB	51°30’11N 000°57’56E		264°(T) Westbound
J8	**Crouch Landfall - Mid-Point Spitway (via Swallowtail)**			
26	Crouch Landfall	51°39’786N 001°02’53E	4.37nm	041/062°(T) Eastbound
8	Mid-Point Spitway	51°42’23N 001°08’20E		242/221°(T) Westbound

K1	Ramsgate - North Foreland			
1	Ramsgate Landfall	51°19’50N 001°26’67E	4.75nm	012°(T) Northbound
2	North Foreland	51°24’15N 001°28’19E		192°(T) Southbound
K2	**North Foreland - Thanet**			
2	North Foreland	51°24’15N 001°28’19E	6.75nm	030°(T) Northbound
53	Thanet	51°30’00N 001°33’59E		210°(T) Southbound
K3	**Thanet - South Knock**			
53	Thanet	51°30’00N 001°33’59E	6.63nm	030°(T) Northbound
54	South Knock	51°35’71N 001°38’98E		Southbound 210°(T)
K4	**South Knock - Kentish Knock**			
54	South Knock	51°35’71N 001°38’98E	5.63nm	001°(T) Northbound
55	Kentish Knock	51°41’34N 001°39’14E		181°(T) Southbound
K5	**Kentish Knock - Long Sand Head**			
55	Kentish Knock	51°41’34N 001°39’14E	6.58nm	001°(T) Northbound
56	Long Sand Head	51°47’92N 001°39’33E		181°(T) Southbound
K6	**Long Sand Head - South Threshold**			
56	Long Sand Head	51°47’92N 001°39’33E	5.91nm	311°(T) Northbound
37	South Threshold	51°51’82N 001°32’17E		131°(T) Southbound
K7	**South Threshold - Cork Sand Beacon**			
37	South Threshold	51°51’82N 001°32’17E	5.41nm	311°(T) Northbound
34	Cork Sand Beacon	51°55’40N 001°25’62E		131°(T) Southbound
K8	**Cork Sand Beacon - Harwich Landfall**			
34	Cork Sand Beacon	51°55’40N 001°25’62E	4.87nm	268/353°(T) Northbound
31	Harwich Landfall	51°55’67N 001°18’34E		172/098°(T) Southbound

* Note: Sector K1 is identical to Sector A1 but is repeated in Table K for convenience.

The Waypoints

WPT No	Latitude	Longitude	Named Used	Description of Location
1	51°19'.50N	001°26'.67E	Ramsgate Approach Channel	**Ramsgate Landfall** - Ramsgate approach channel, adjacent to No 3 SHM
2	51°24'.15N	001°28'.19E	North Foreland	North Foreland Light bears 209°(T), 1.93nm
3	51°27'.15N	001°27'.10E	East Margate	East Margate PHM bears 252°(T), 0.45nm
4	51°33'.42N	001°24'.66E	Outer Fisherman	Outer Fisherman ECB bears 027°(T), 0.53nm
5	51°36'.00N	001°19'.90E	Inner Fisherman	Leaving Fisherman's Gat: Inner Fisherman PHM adjacent
6a	51°37'.70N	001°18'.80E	SW Sunk (South Side)	South side of South West Sunk swatchway – Beware: SW Sunk Beacon destroyed
6b	51°38'.03N	001°16'.20E	SW Sunk (North Side)	North side of South West Sunk swatchway – Beware: SW Sunk Beacon destroyed
7	51°39'.83N	001°14'.49E	East Barrow Sands	Waypoint to clear NE point of East Barrow sands
8	51°42'.23N	001°08'.20E	Mid-point Spitway	Waypoint in the approximate mid-point in the Spitway
9	51°45'.39N	000°55'.63E	River Blackwater, off Sales Point	**River Blackwater Landfall** – Waypoint in River Blackwater, north of Sales Point
10	51°30'.71N	001°28'.10E	Tongue DW Anchorage	Western edge of Tongue DW Anchorage
11a	51°34'.73N	001°28'.10'E	Long Sand Outer	Entrance to London Array 'avenue'
11b	51°35'.56N	001°26'.38E	Long Sand Middle	Turning point within the London Array 'avenue'
12	51°41'.22N	001°24'.97E	Black Deep	In Black Deep, Barrow No 2 PHM bears 299°(T), 1.44nm
13	51°41'.73N	001°16'.52E	NE Middle	Approximate mid-point across the East Swin towards the Spitway
14	51°44'.58'N	001°02'.42E	Colne Bar	**River Colne Landfall** - Adjacent to the Colne Bar Starboard Hand Mark
15	51°36'.36N	001°21'.37E	Black Deep No 8	Adjacent to Black Deep No 8 WCB
16	51°40'.48N	001°20'.33E	Barrow Deep	Barrow No 4 WCB bears 250°(T) 1.87nm (Beware – Sunk Beacon destroyed)
17	51°33'.08N	001°20'.77E	North Edinburgh	Midpoint North Edinburgh Channel
18	51°34'.13N	001°15'.91E	NW Long Sand	Waypoint to clear WNW corner of Long Sand
19	51°27'.14N	001°24'.77E	Margate Sand	Close north-east of the Margate Sand
20	51°28'.65N	001°18'.30E	Princes South	Adjacent to Princes South PHB
21	51°29'.00N	001°07'.12E	Princes No 6	Adjacent to the Princes No 6 PHB
22	51°32'.11N	000°59'.36E	SW Barrow	SW Barrow WCB bears 073° (T), 0.62nm
23	51°34'.89N	001°03'.77E	Maplin Edge	Maplin Edge SHM bears 340°(T), 0.39nm
24	51°37'.39'N	001°05'.01E	NE Maplin	Adjacent to the NE Maplin SHM
25	51°40'.66N	001°09'.23E	Whitaker Spit	South Whitaker SHM bears 191°(T), 0.48nm
26	51°39'.78N	001°02'.53E	Sunken Buxey	**River Crouch Landfall** – Mid-way between Whitaker 5 & 6 and 7 & 8 paired buoys
27	51°38'.91N	001°25'.56E	Long Sand Inner	Adjacent to Long Sand Inner SWM
28	51°45'.35N	001°29'.33E	Sunk Head	Sunk Head NCB bears 030°(T), 1.51nm
29	51°48'.97N	001°25'.49E	Goldmer Gat	NE Gunfleet ECB bears 058°(T), 1.74nm
30	51°52'.30N	001°19'.31E	The Naze	Stone Banks PHM bears 357°(T) 0.90nm
31	51°55'.67N	001°18'.34E	Harwich	**Harwich Harbour Landfall** - Adjacent to Cliff Foot SHM (outside buoyed channel)
32	51°42'.20N	001°23'.56E	Barrow No 2	Barrow No 2 PHM bears 235°(T) 0.49nm
33	51°49'.88N	001°27'.72E	NE Gunfleet	Adjacent to the NE Gunfleet ECB
34	51°55'.40N	001°25'.62E	Cork Sand Beacon	Adjacent to the Cork Sand Beacon
35	51°58'.12N	001°24'.04E	Woodbridge Haven	**River Deben Landfall** – Adjacent to Woodbridge Haven SWB (frequently moved)
36	51°23'.96N	001°20'.42E	SE Margate	SE Margate ECB bears 359°(T), 0.31nm
37	51°23'.64N	001°11'.08E	Copperas	Adjacent to the Copperas SHM

Waypoints and relative times of HW

WPT No	Latitude	Longitude	Named Used	Description of Location
38	51°24'.45N	001°02'.17E	Columbine	**River Swale Landfall** - Columbine SHM bears 246°(T), 0.55nm
39	51°25'.05N	001°02'.80E	Kentish Flats	Spaniard ECB bears 034°(T), 1.16nm
40	51°26'.22N	000°55'.68E	Spile	Adjacent to the Spile Starboard HM
41	51°27'.93N	000°48'.09E	Medway Channel	**River Medway Landfall** - Medway buoyed channel, approx. 2.5nm Garrison Point
42	51°26'.14N	001°04'.62E	Spaniard	South-west of the Kentish Flats Wind Farm
43	51°28'.10N	001°02'.83E	Red Sand	Adjacent to the NW corner of Kentish Flats Wind Farm
44	51°30'.11N	000°57'.56E	North Oaze PHM	Adjacent to the North Oaze PHM
45	51°28'.84N	000°59'.35E	Red Sand Towers	Adjacent to the Red Sand Towers PHB
46	51°29'.77N	000°52'.37E	Sea Reach No 1	Adjacent to the Sea Reach No 1 safe water buoy at the entrance to the Thames
47	51°33'.80N	001°07'.64E	Barrow No 10 PHM	Barrow No 10 PHM bears 068°(T), 0.34nm
48	51°39'.77N	001°17'.28E	Barrow No 4 PHM	Adjacent to the Barrow No 4 WCM
49	51°45'.16N	001°22'.57E	Gunfleet Spit	Gunfleet Spit SCM bears 292°(T), 0.52nm
50	51°47'.93N	001°14'.54E	Holland-on-Sea	Off Holland-on-Sea
51	51°27'.14N	001°18'.33E	Wedge	South side of the Queens Channel with the Margate Sand to the south
52	51°25'.45N	001°10'.89E	Woolpack	At the edge of the Kentish Flats
53	51°30'.00N	001°33'.59E	Thanet	North of the Thanet Wind Farm
54	51°35'.71N	001°38'.98E	South Knock	To the east of the South Knock
55	51°41'.34N	001°39'.14E	Kentish Knock	To the north-east of the Kentish Knock
56	51°47'.92N	001°39'.33E	Long Sand Head	Adjacent to the Long Sand Head North Cardinal Buoy
57	51°51'.82N	001°32'.17E	South Threshold	Within the Sunk Inner area adjacent to the South Threshold Special Mark

Approximate mean times of HW relative to HW Sheerness	
Ramsgate	-1.10
Margate	-0.45
Burnham on Crouch	-0.15
West Mersea	-0.20
Bradwell on Sea	-0.25
Maldon	-0.25
Brightlingsea	-0.40
Walton on Naze	-1.00
Harwich	-0.50
Woodbridge Haven	-1.05

Approximate times of HW and LW mid-estuary relative to HW & LW Sheerness		
Little Sunk	Mean HW Springs	approx. -50 minutes
	Mean HW Neaps	approx. -45 minutes
	Mean LW Springs	approx. -55 minutes
	Mean LW Neaps	approx. -30 minutes
Middle Sunk	Mean HW Springs	approx. -48 minutes
	Mean HW Neaps	approx. -40 minutes
	Mean LW Springs	approx. -52 minutes
	Mean LW Neaps	approx. -23 minutes
SW Sunk	Mean HW Springs	approx. -47 minutes
	Mean HW Neaps	approx. -37 minutes
	Mean LW Springs	approx. -47 minutes
	Mean LW Neaps	approx. -18 minutes
Spitway	Mean HW Springs	approx. -42 minutes
	Mean HW Neaps	approx. -32 minutes
	Mean LW Springs	approx. -42 minutes
	Mean LW Neaps	approx. -22 minutes

Routes 1 to 3 - Rolling Route Diagrams

64

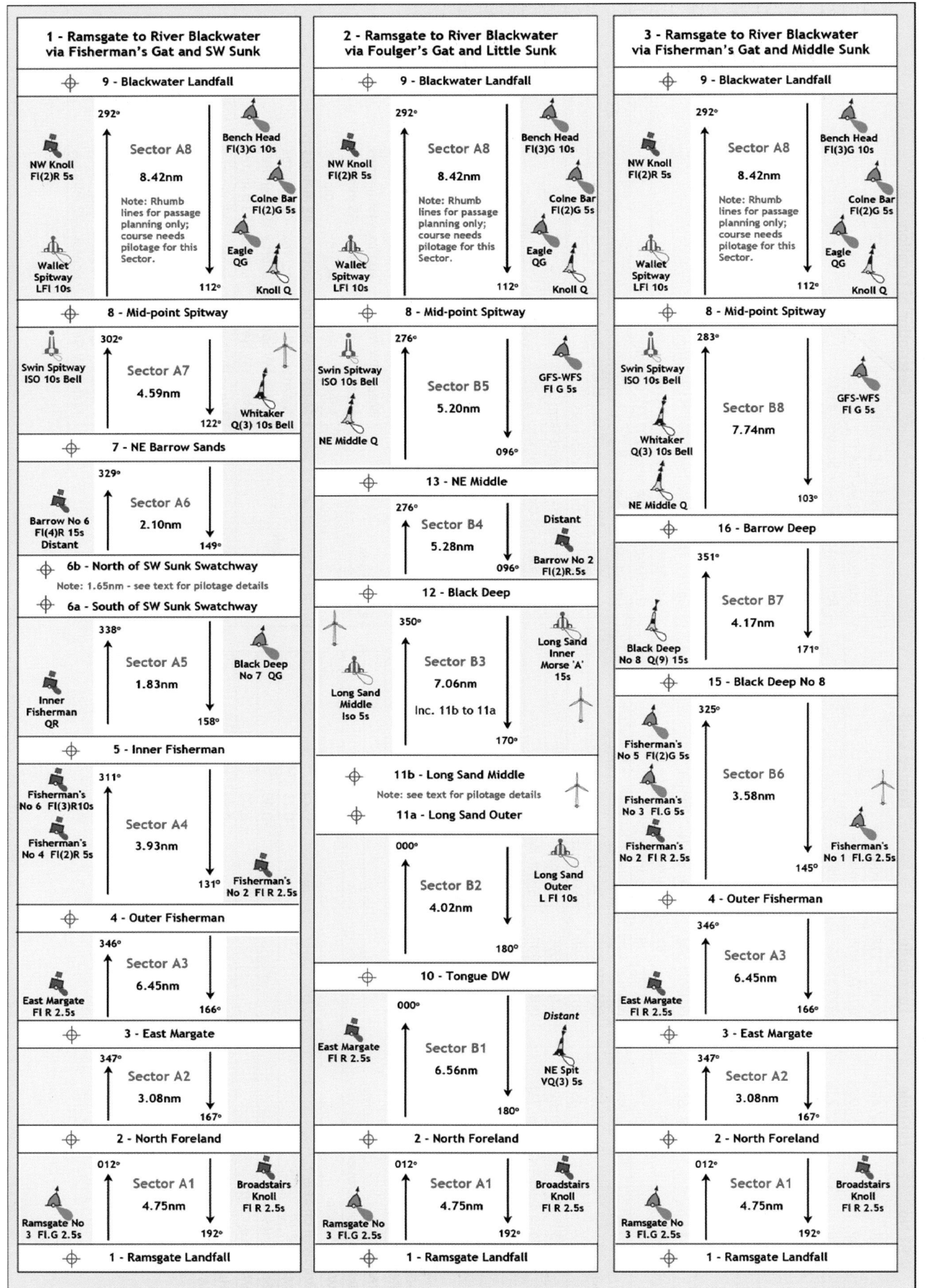

Rolling Route Diagrams - Routes 4 to 6

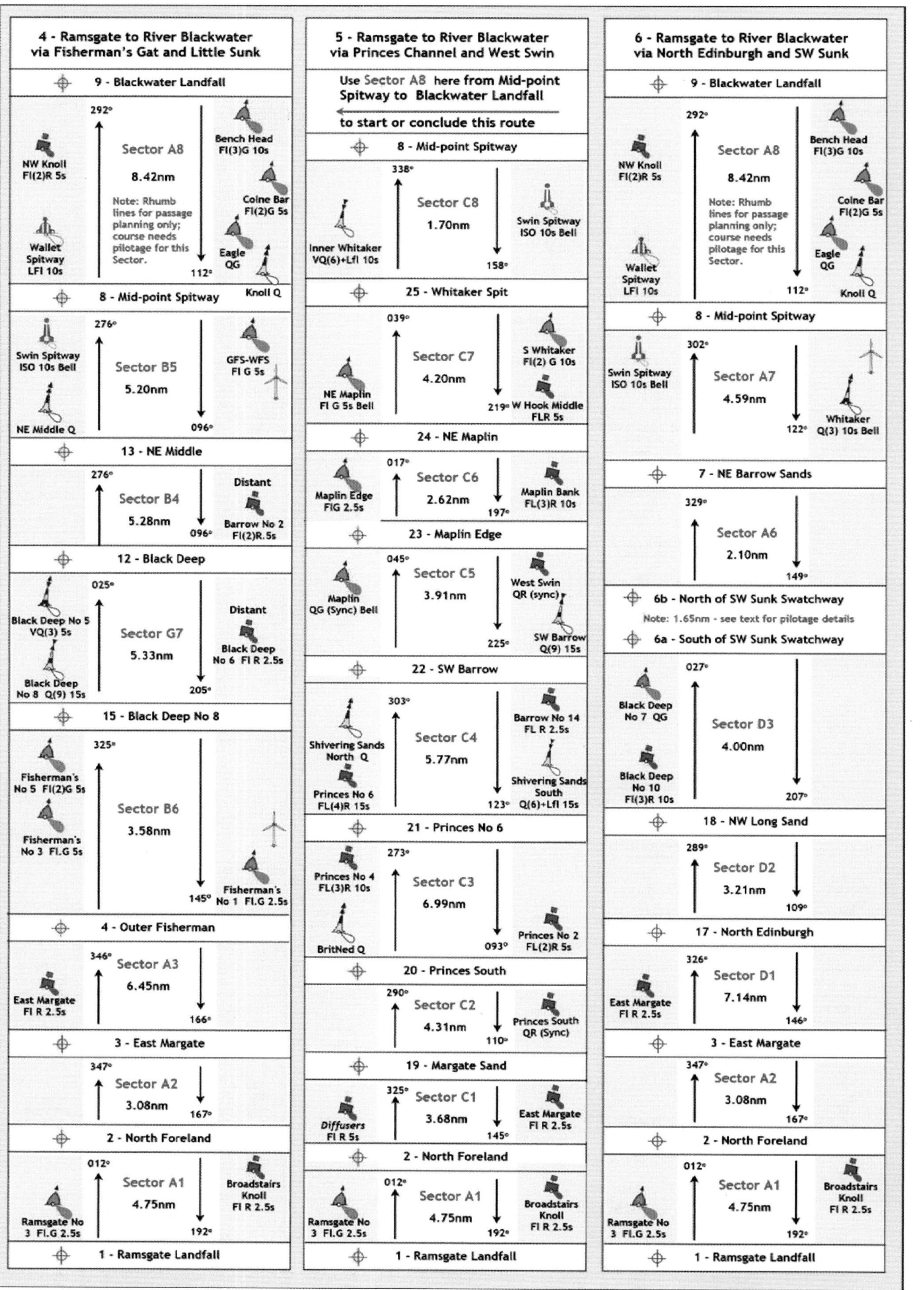

Routes 7 to 9 - Rolling Route Diagrams

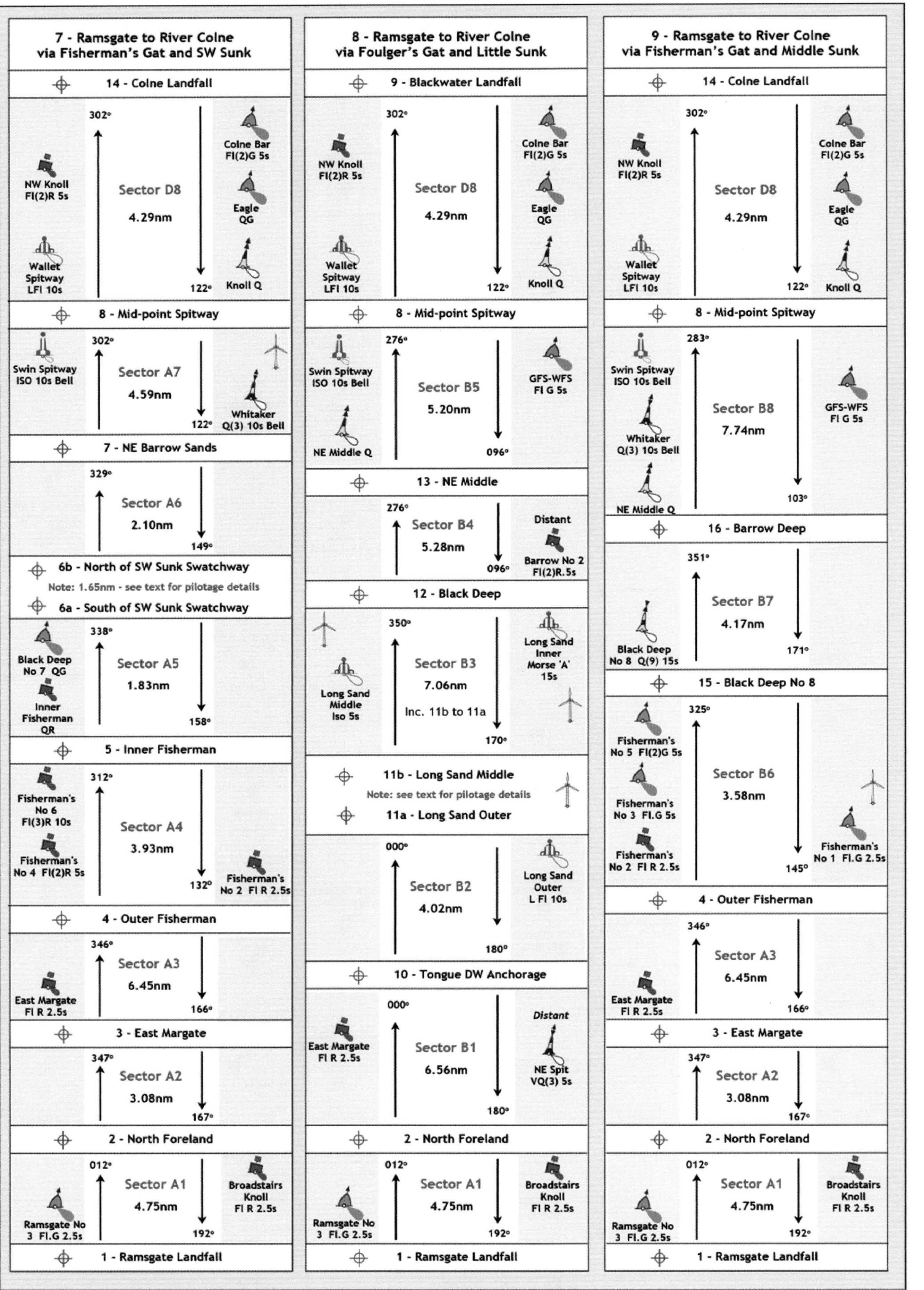

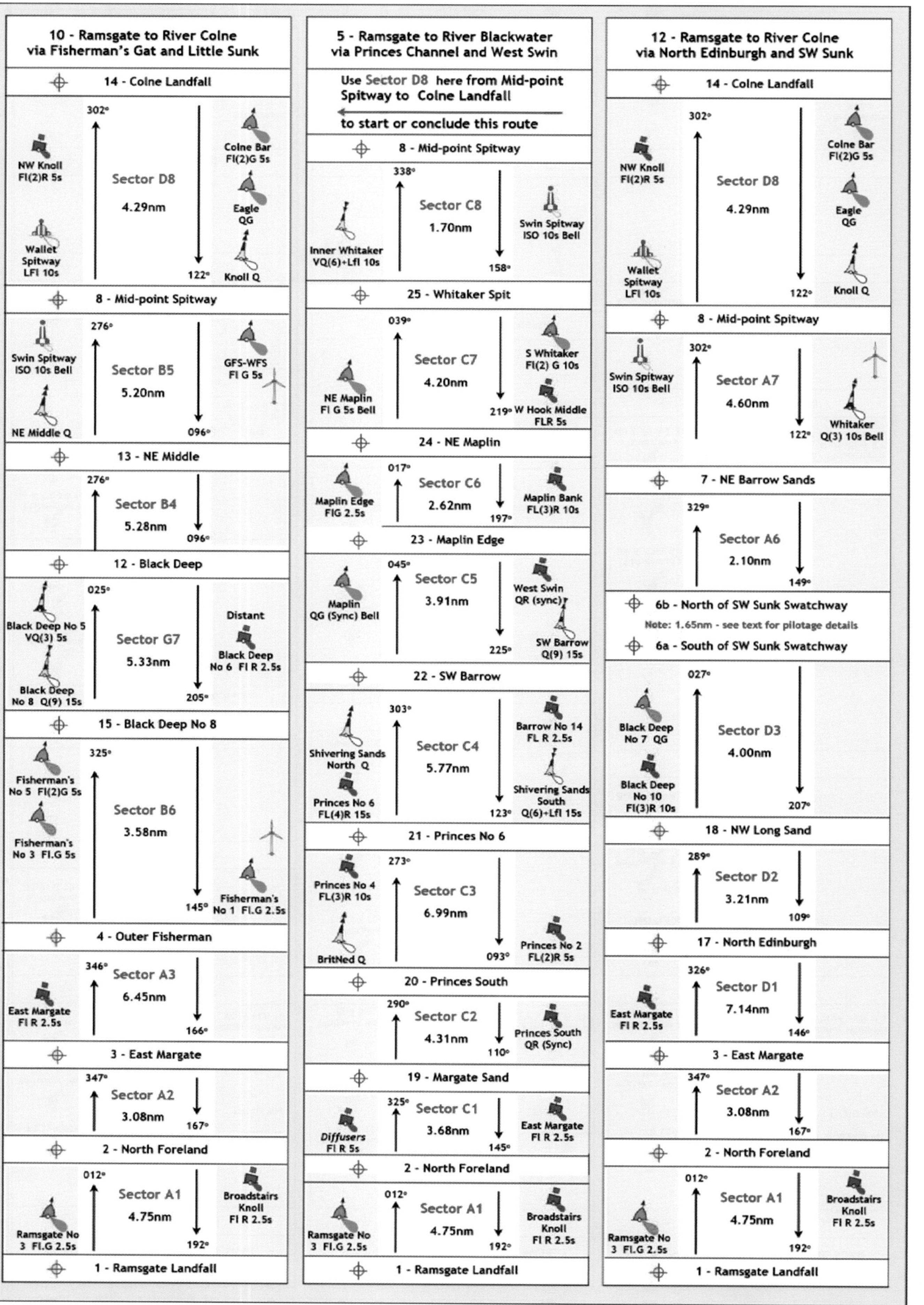
10 - Ramsgate to River Colne via Fisherman's Gat and Little Sunk
14 - Colne Landfall
302°
NW Knoll Fl(2)R 5s
Sector D8
4.29nm
Colne Bar Fl(2)G 5s
Eagle QG
Wallet Spitway LFl 10s
122°
Knoll Q
8 - Mid-point Spitway
276°
Swin Spitway ISO 10s Bell
Sector B5
5.20nm
GFS-WFS Fl G 5s
NE Middle Q
096°
13 - NE Middle
276°
Sector B4
5.28nm
096°
12 - Black Deep
025°
Black Deep No 5 VQ(3) 5s
Sector G7
5.33nm
Distant
Black Deep No 6 Fl R 2.5s
Black Deep No 8 Q(9) 15s
205°
15 - Black Deep No 8
325°
Fisherman's No 5 Fl(2)G 5s
Sector B6
3.58nm
Fisherman's No 3 Fl.G 5s
145°
Fisherman's No 1 FL.G 2.5s
4 - Outer Fisherman
346°
Sector A3
6.45nm
East Margate Fl R 2.5s
166°
3 - East Margate
347°
Sector A2
3.08nm
167°
2 - North Foreland
012°
Sector A1
4.75nm
Broadstairs Knoll Fl R 2.5s
Ramsgate No 3 Fl.G 2.5s
192°
1 - Ramsgate Landfall
5 - Ramsgate to River Blackwater via Princes Channel and West Swin
Use Sector D8 here from Mid-point Spitway to Colne Landfall
to start or conclude this route
8 - Mid-point Spitway
338°
Sector C8
1.70nm
Swin Spitway ISO 10s Bell
Inner Whitaker VQ(6)+LFl 10s
158°
25 - Whitaker Spit
039°
Sector C7
4.20nm
S Whitaker Fl(2) G 10s
NE Maplin Fl G 5s Bell
219°
W Hook Middle FLR 5s
24 - NE Maplin
017°
Sector C6
2.62nm
Maplin Edge FlG 2.5s
Maplin Bank FL(3)R 10s
197°
23 - Maplin Edge
045°
Sector C5
3.91nm
West Swin QR (sync)
Maplin QG (Sync) Bell
225°
SW Barrow Q(9) 15s
22 - SW Barrow
303°
Sector C4
5.77nm
Barrow No 14 FL R 2.5s
Shivering Sands North Q
Princes No 6 FL(4)R 15s
123°
Shivering Sands South Q(6)+LFl 15s
21 - Princes No 6
273°
Sector C3
6.99nm
Princes No 4 FL(3)R 10s
BritNed Q
093°
Princes No 2 FL(2)R 5s
20 - Princes South
290°
Sector C2
4.31nm
Princes South QR (Sync)
110°
19 - Margate Sand
325°
Sector C1
3.68nm
Diffusers Fl R 5s
East Margate Fl R 2.5s
145°
2 - North Foreland
012°
Sector A1
4.75nm
Broadstairs Knoll Fl R 2.5s
Ramsgate No 3 Fl.G 2.5s
192°
1 - Ramsgate Landfall
12 - Ramsgate to River Colne via North Edinburgh and SW Sunk
14 - Colne Landfall
302°
NW Knoll Fl(2)R 5s
Sector D8
4.29nm
Colne Bar Fl(2)G 5s
Eagle QG
Wallet Spitway LFl 10s
122°
Knoll Q
8 - Mid-point Spitway
302°
Swin Spitway ISO 10s Bell
Sector A7
4.60nm
Whitaker Q(3) 10s Bell
122°
7 - NE Barrow Sands
329°
Sector A6
2.10nm
149°
6b - North of SW Sunk Swatchway
Note: 1.65nm - see text for pilotage details
6a - South of SW Sunk Swatchway
027°
Sector D3
4.00nm
Black Deep No 7 QG
Black Deep No 10 Fl(3)R 10s
207°
18 - NW Long Sand
289°
Sector D2
3.21nm
109°
17 - North Edinburgh
326°
Sector D1
7.14nm
East Margate Fl R 2.5s
146°
3 - East Margate
347°
Sector A2
3.08nm
167°
2 - North Foreland
012°
Sector A1
4.75nm
Broadstairs Knoll Fl R 2.5s
Ramsgate No 3 Fl.G 2.5s
192°
1 - Ramsgate Landfall

Routes 13 to 15 - Rolling Route Diagrams

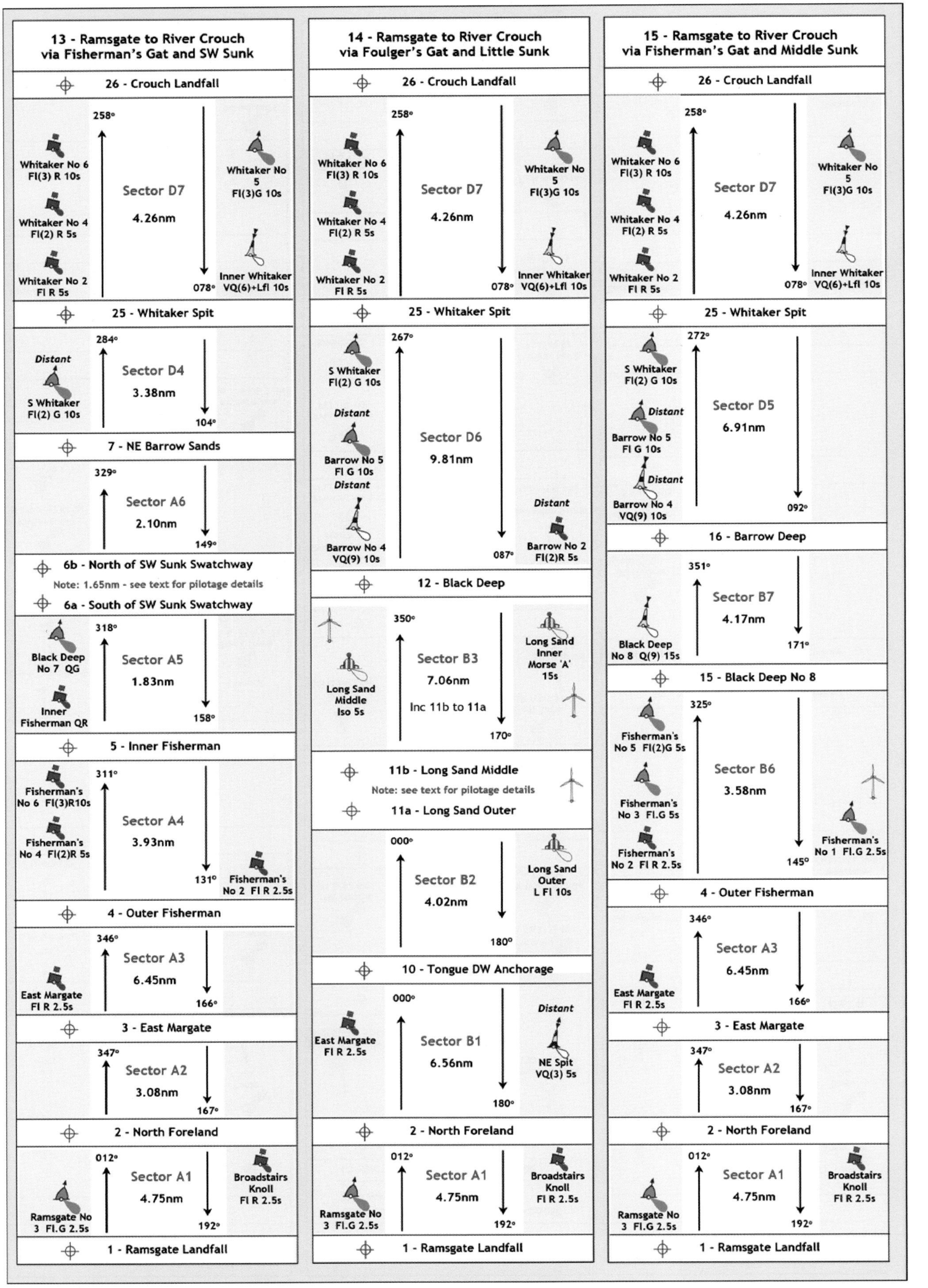

Rolling Route Diagrams - Routes 16 to 18

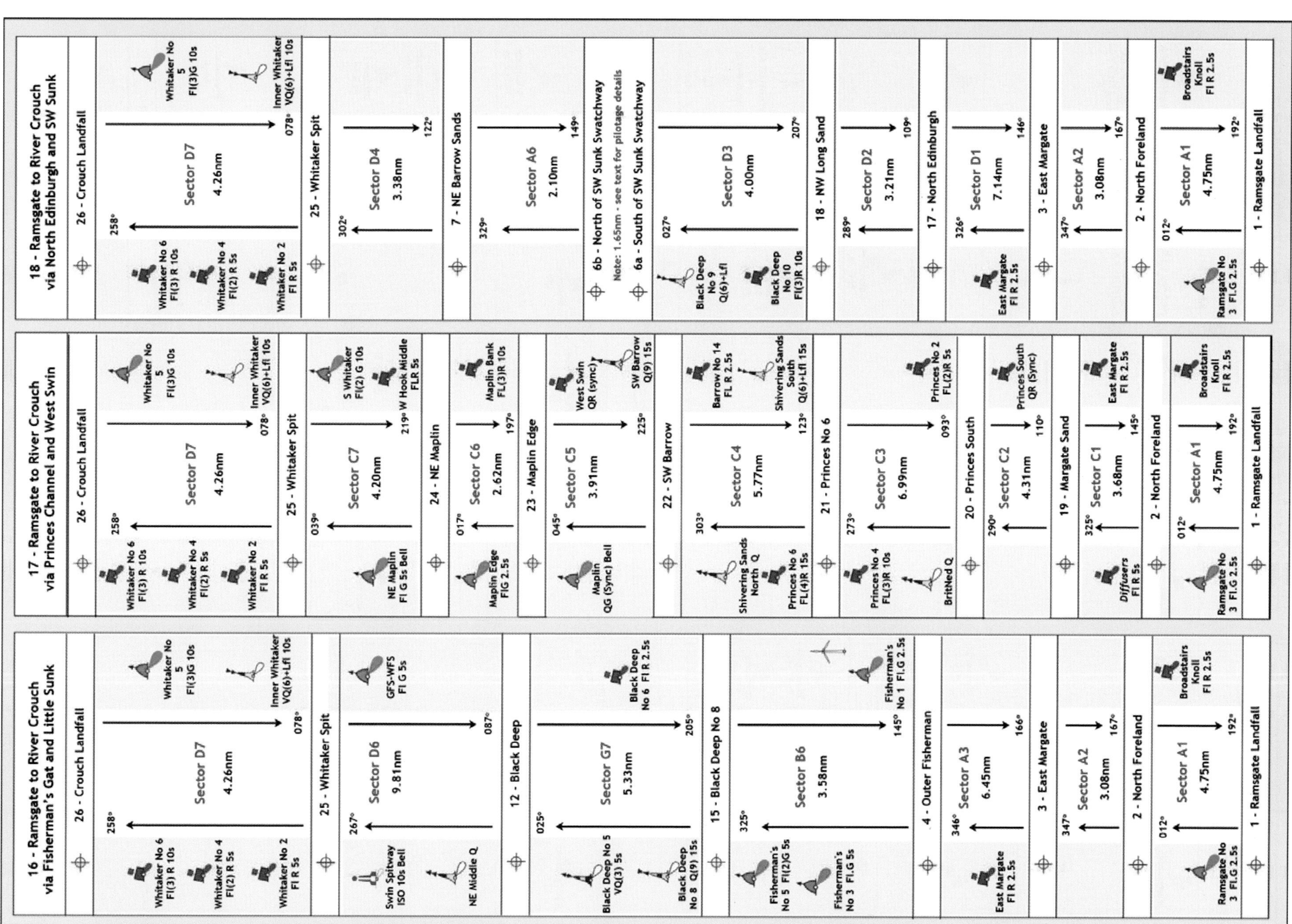

Routes 19 to 21 - Rolling Route Diagrams

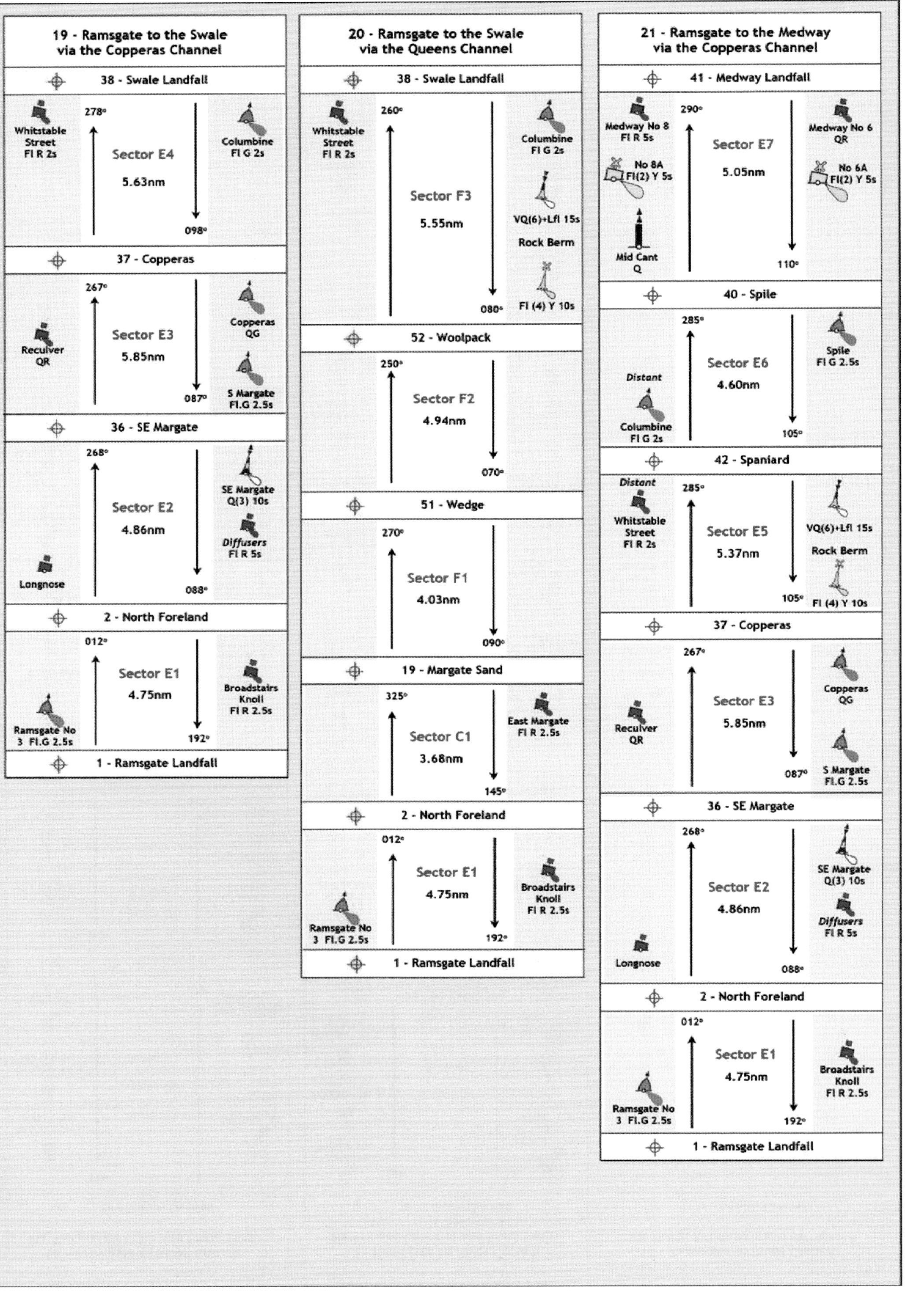

Rolling Route Diagrams - Routes 22 to 24

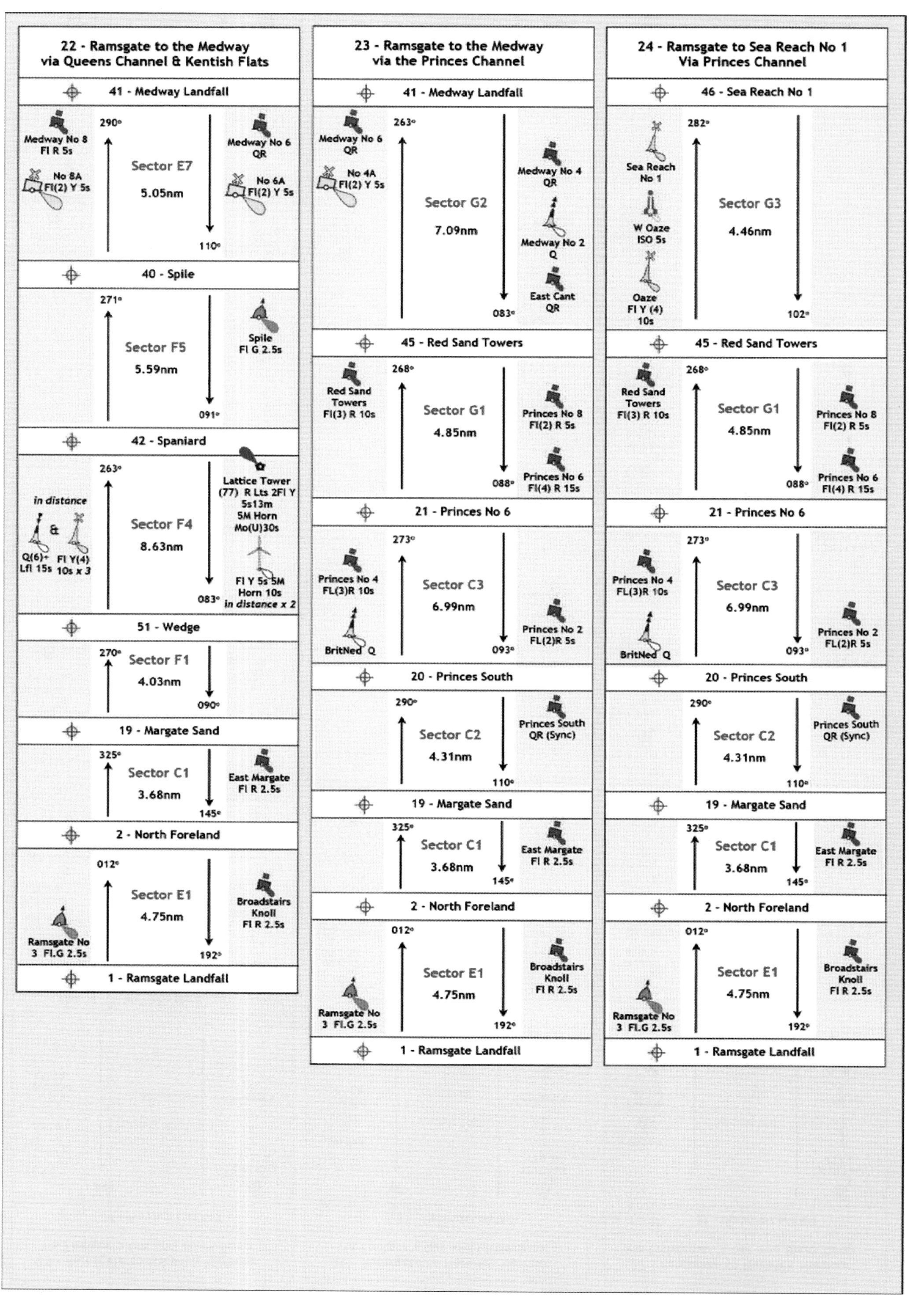

Routes 25 to 27 - Rolling Route Diagrams

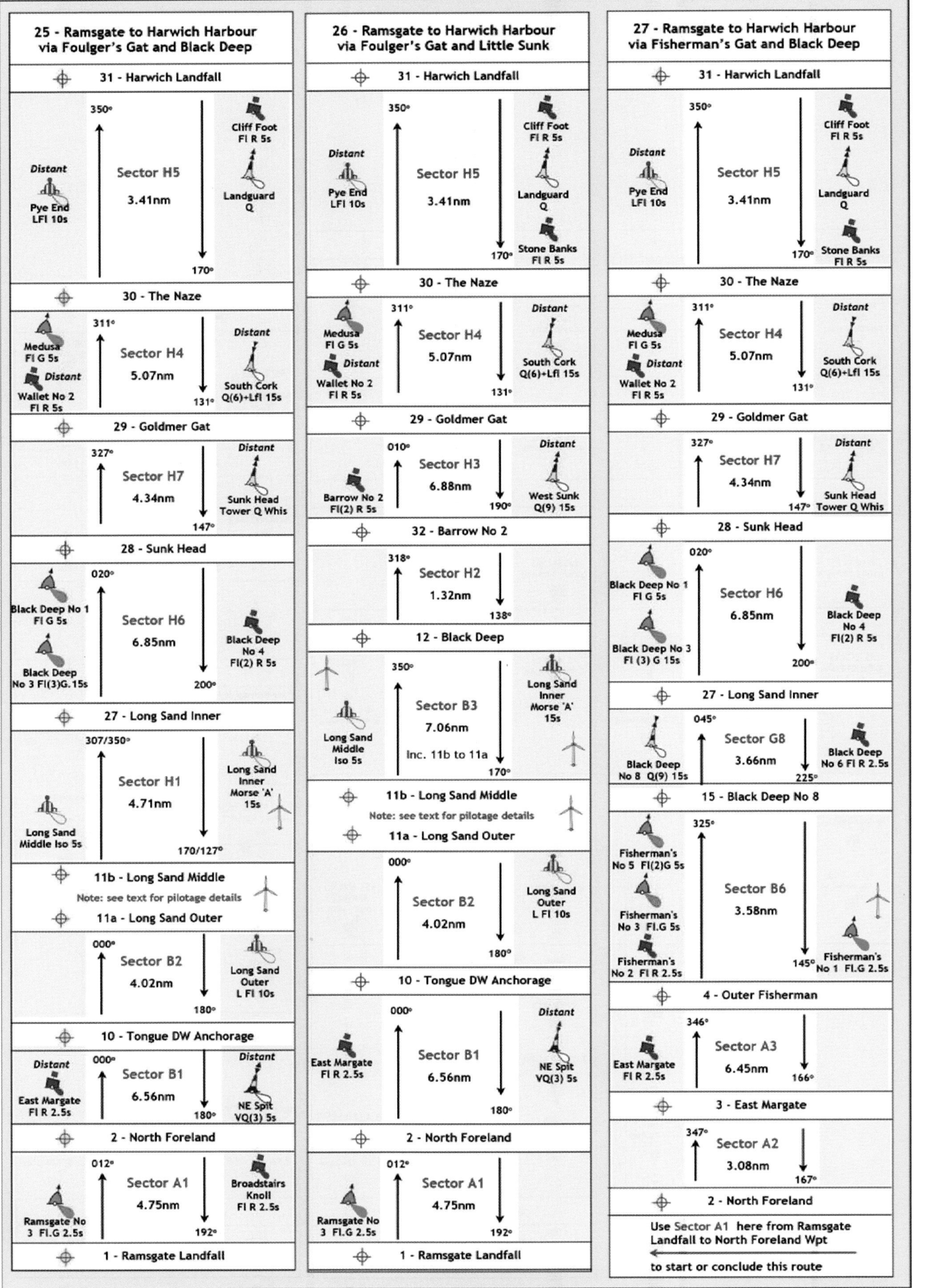

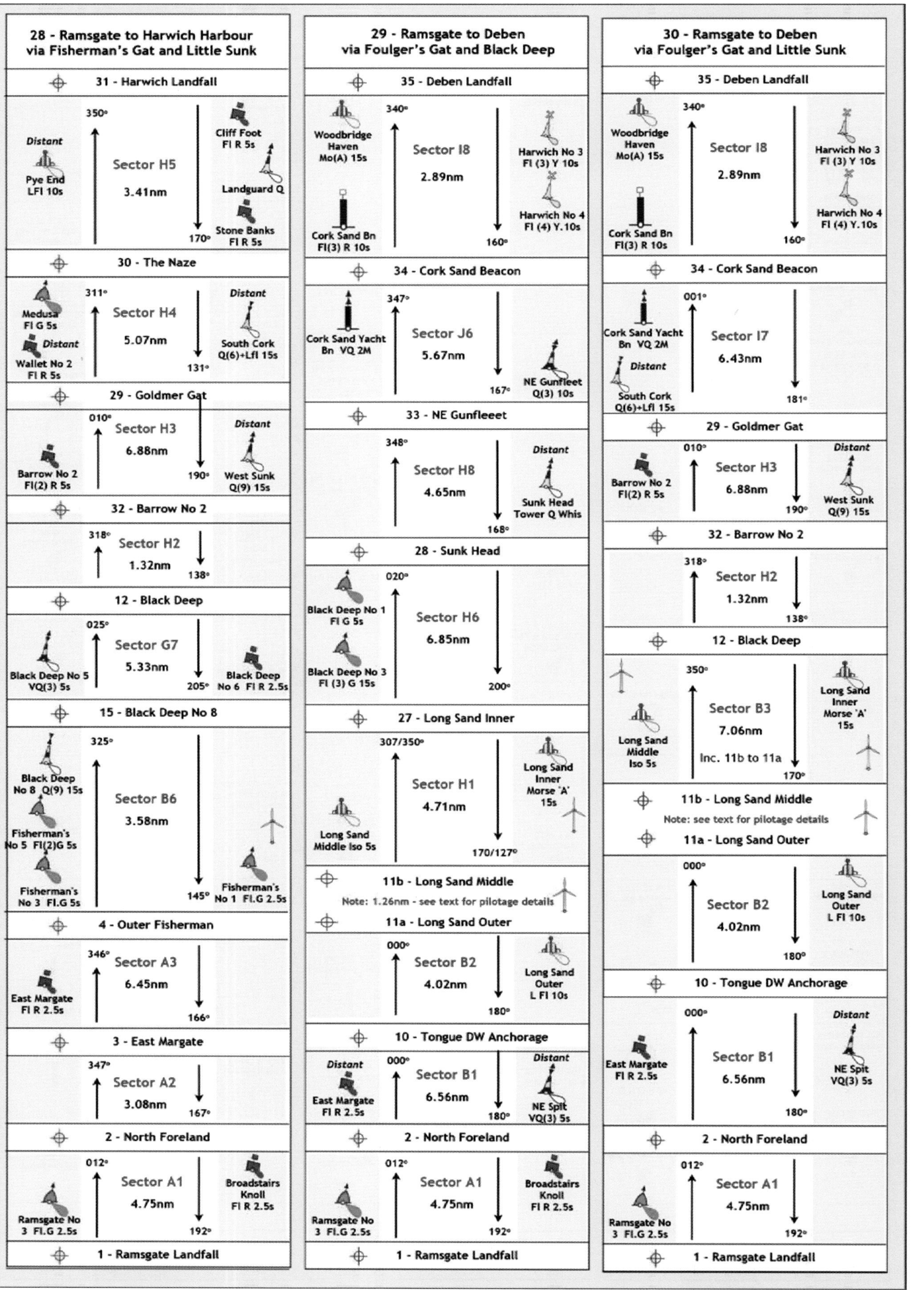

28 - Ramsgate to Harwich Harbour
via Fisherman's Gat and Little Sunk
31 - Harwich Landfall
350°
Distant
Pye End
LFl 10s
Sector H5
3.41nm
Cliff Foot
Fl R 5s
Landguard Q
170°
Stone Banks
Fl R 5s
30 - The Naze
311°
Medusa
Fl G 5s
Distant
Wallet No 2
Fl R 5s
Sector H4
5.07nm
131°
Distant
South Cork
Q(6)+Lfl 15s
29 - Goldmer Gat
010°
Barrow No 2
Fl(2) R 5s
Sector H3
6.88nm
190°
Distant
West Sunk
Q(9) 15s
32 - Barrow No 2
318°
Sector H2
1.32nm
138°
12 - Black Deep
025°
Black Deep No 5
VQ(3) 5s
Sector G7
5.33nm
205°
Black Deep
No 6 Fl R 2.5s
15 - Black Deep No 8
325°
Black Deep
No 8 Q(9) 15s
Fisherman's
No 5 Fl(2)G 5s
Fisherman's
No 3 Fl.G 5s
Sector B6
3.58nm
145°
Fisherman's
No 1 Fl.G 2.5s
4 - Outer Fisherman
346°
East Margate
Fl R 2.5s
Sector A3
6.45nm
166°
3 - East Margate
347°
Sector A2
3.08nm
167°
2 - North Foreland
012°
Ramsgate No
3 Fl.G 2.5s
Sector A1
4.75nm
192°
Broadstairs
Knoll
Fl R 2.5s
1 - Ramsgate Landfall
29 - Ramsgate to Deben
via Foulger's Gat and Black Deep
35 - Deben Landfall
340°
Woodbridge
Haven
Mo(A) 15s
Cork Sand Bn
Fl(3) R 10s
Sector I8
2.89nm
160°
Harwich No 3
Fl (3) Y 10s
Harwich No 4
Fl (4) Y.10s
34 - Cork Sand Beacon
347°
Cork Sand Yacht
Bn VQ 2M
Sector J6
5.67nm
167°
NE Gunfleet
Q(3) 10s
33 - NE Gunfleeet
348°
Sector H8
4.65nm
168°
Distant
Sunk Head
Tower Q Whis
28 - Sunk Head
020°
Black Deep No 1
Fl G 5s
Black Deep No 3
Fl (3) G 15s
Sector H6
6.85nm
200°
27 - Long Sand Inner
307/350°
Long Sand
Middle Iso 5s
Sector H1
4.71nm
170/127°
Long Sand
Inner
Morse 'A'
15s
11b - Long Sand Middle
Note: 1.26nm - see text for pilotage details
11a - Long Sand Outer
000°
Sector B2
4.02nm
180°
Long Sand
Outer
L Fl 10s
10 - Tongue DW Anchorage
000°
Distant
East Margate
Fl R 2.5s
Sector B1
6.56nm
180°
Distant
NE Spit
VQ(3) 5s
2 - North Foreland
012°
Ramsgate No
3 Fl.G 2.5s
Sector A1
4.75nm
192°
Broadstairs
Knoll
Fl R 2.5s
1 - Ramsgate Landfall
30 - Ramsgate to Deben
via Foulger's Gat and Little Sunk
35 - Deben Landfall
340°
Woodbridge
Haven
Mo(A) 15s
Cork Sand Bn
Fl(3) R 10s
Sector I8
2.89nm
160°
Harwich No 3
Fl (3) Y 10s
Harwich No 4
Fl (4) Y.10s
34 - Cork Sand Beacon
001°
Cork Sand Yacht
Bn VQ 2M
Distant
South Cork
Q(6)+Lfl 15s
Sector I7
6.43nm
181°
29 - Goldmer Gat
010°
Barrow No 2
Fl(2) R 5s
Sector H3
6.88nm
190°
Distant
West Sunk
Q(9) 15s
32 - Barrow No 2
318°
Sector H2
1.32nm
138°
12 - Black Deep
350°
Long Sand
Middle
Iso 5s
Sector B3
7.06nm
Inc. 11b to 11a
170°
Long Sand
Inner
Morse 'A'
15s
11b - Long Sand Middle
Note: see text for pilotage details
11a - Long Sand Outer
000°
Sector B2
4.02nm
180°
Long Sand
Outer
L Fl 10s
10 - Tongue DW Anchorage
000°
East Margate
Fl R 2.5s
Sector B1
6.56nm
180°
Distant
NE Spit
VQ(3) 5s
2 - North Foreland
012°
Ramsgate No
3 Fl.G 2.5s
Sector A1
4.75nm
192°
1 - Ramsgate Landfall

Routes 31 to 33 - Rolling Route Diagrams

74

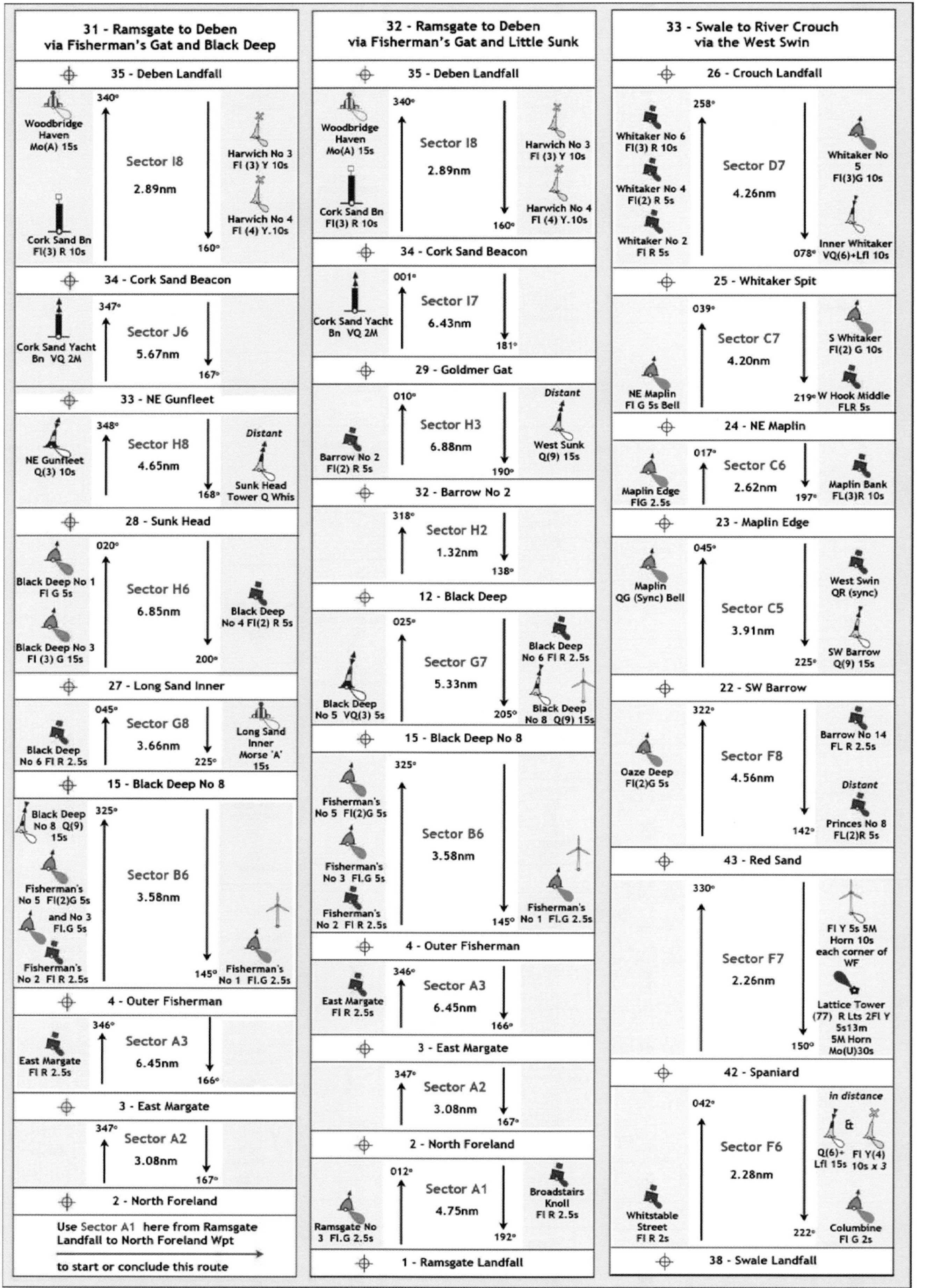

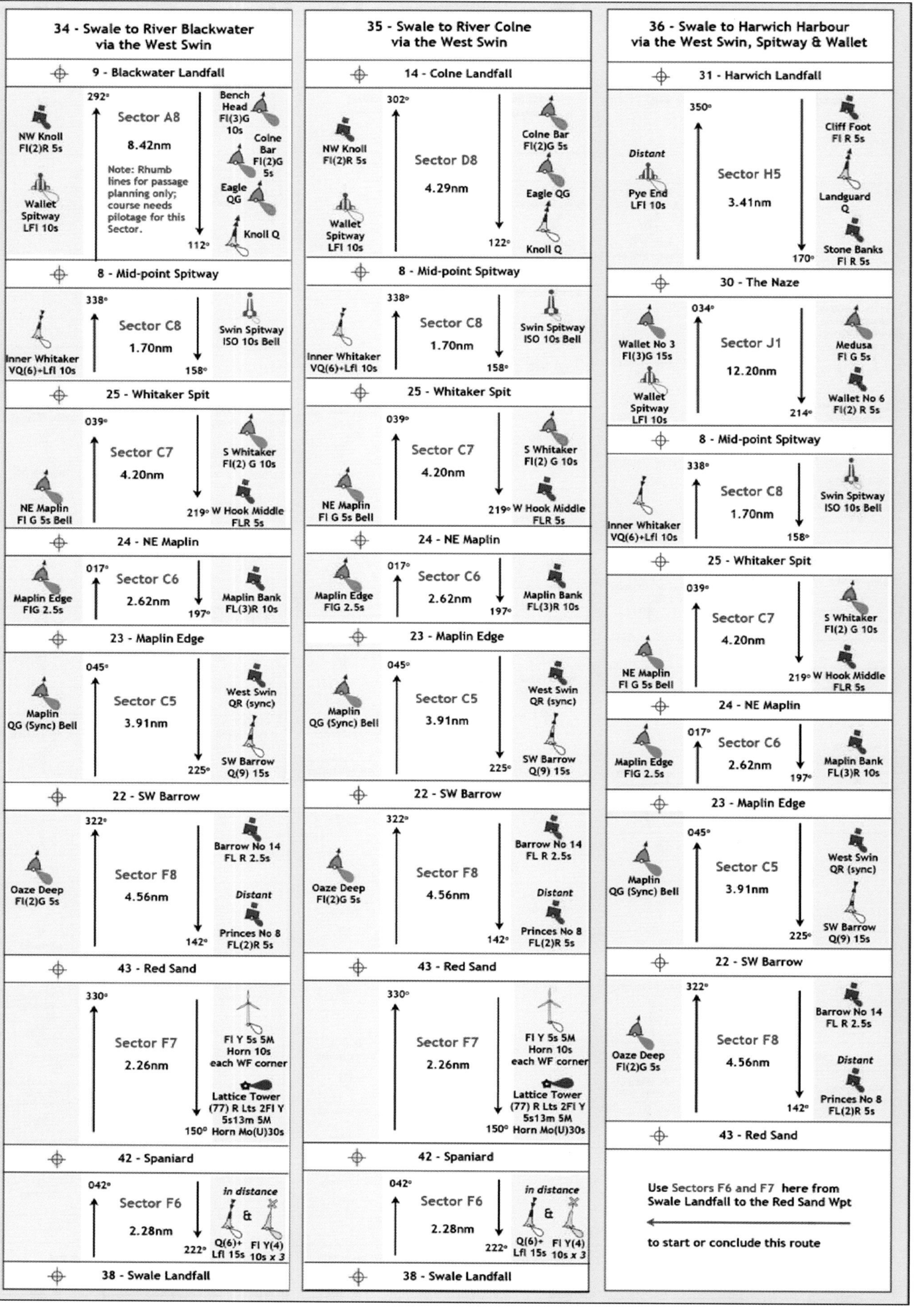

34 - Swale to River Blackwater via the West Swin
9 - Blackwater Landfall
NW Knoll Fl(2)R 5s
Wallet Spitway LFl 10s
292°
Sector A8
8.42nm
Note: Rhumb lines for passage planning only; course needs pilotage for this Sector.
112°
Bench Head Fl(3)G 10s
Colne Bar Fl(2)G 5s
Eagle QG
Knoll Q
8 - Mid-point Spitway
Inner Whitaker VQ(6)+LFl 10s
338°
Sector C8
1.70nm
158°
Swin Spitway ISO 10s Bell
25 - Whitaker Spit
NE Maplin Fl G 5s Bell
039°
Sector C7
4.20nm
219°
S Whitaker Fl(2) G 10s
W Hook Middle FLR 5s
24 - NE Maplin
Maplin Edge FlG 2.5s
017°
Sector C6
2.62nm
197°
Maplin Bank FL(3)R 10s
23 - Maplin Edge
Maplin QG (Sync) Bell
045°
Sector C5
3.91nm
225°
West Swin QR (sync)
SW Barrow Q(9) 15s
22 - SW Barrow
Oaze Deep Fl(2)G 5s
322°
Sector F8
4.56nm
142°
Barrow No 14 FL R 2.5s
Distant
Princes No 8 FL(2)R 5s
43 - Red Sand
330°
Sector F7
2.26nm
150°
Fl Y 5s 5M Horn 10s each WF corner
Lattice Tower (77) R Lts 2Fl Y 5s13m 5M Horn Mo(U)30s
42 - Spaniard
042°
Sector F6
2.28nm
222°
in distance
&
Q(6)+ LFl 15s
Fl Y(4) 10s x 3
38 - Swale Landfall
35 - Swale to River Colne via the West Swin
14 - Colne Landfall
NW Knoll Fl(2)R 5s
Wallet Spitway LFl 10s
302°
Sector D8
4.29nm
122°
Colne Bar Fl(2)G 5s
Eagle QG
Knoll Q
8 - Mid-point Spitway
Inner Whitaker VQ(6)+LFl 10s
338°
Sector C8
1.70nm
158°
Swin Spitway ISO 10s Bell
25 - Whitaker Spit
NE Maplin Fl G 5s Bell
039°
Sector C7
4.20nm
219°
S Whitaker Fl(2) G 10s
W Hook Middle FLR 5s
24 - NE Maplin
Maplin Edge FlG 2.5s
017°
Sector C6
2.62nm
197°
Maplin Bank FL(3)R 10s
23 - Maplin Edge
Maplin QG (Sync) Bell
045°
Sector C5
3.91nm
225°
West Swin QR (sync)
SW Barrow Q(9) 15s
22 - SW Barrow
Oaze Deep Fl(2)G 5s
322°
Sector F8
4.56nm
142°
Barrow No 14 FL R 2.5s
Distant
Princes No 8 FL(2)R 5s
43 - Red Sand
330°
Sector F7
2.26nm
150°
Fl Y 5s 5M Horn 10s each WF corner
Lattice Tower (77) R Lts 2Fl Y 5s13m 5M Horn Mo(U)30s
42 - Spaniard
042°
Sector F6
2.28nm
222°
in distance
&
Q(6)+ LFl 15s
Fl Y(4) 10s x 3
38 - Swale Landfall
36 - Swale to Harwich Harbour via the West Swin, Spitway & Wallet
31 - Harwich Landfall
Distant
Pye End LFl 10s
350°
Sector H5
3.41nm
170°
Cliff Foot Fl R 5s
Landguard Q
Stone Banks Fl R 5s
30 - The Naze
Wallet No 3 Fl(3)G 15s
Wallet Spitway LFl 10s
034°
Sector J1
12.20nm
214°
Medusa Fl G 5s
Wallet No 6 Fl(2) R 5s
8 - Mid-point Spitway
Inner Whitaker VQ(6)+LFl 10s
338°
Sector C8
1.70nm
158°
Swin Spitway ISO 10s Bell
25 - Whitaker Spit
NE Maplin Fl G 5s Bell
039°
Sector C7
4.20nm
219°
S Whitaker Fl(2) G 10s
W Hook Middle FLR 5s
24 - NE Maplin
Maplin Edge FlG 2.5s
017°
Sector C6
2.62nm
197°
Maplin Bank FL(3)R 10s
23 - Maplin Edge
Maplin QG (Sync) Bell
045°
Sector C5
3.91nm
225°
West Swin QR (sync)
SW Barrow Q(9) 15s
22 - SW Barrow
Oaze Deep Fl(2)G 5s
322°
Sector F8
4.56nm
142°
Barrow No 14 FL R 2.5s
Distant
Princes No 8 FL(2)R 5s
43 - Red Sand
Use Sectors F6 and F7 here from Swale Landfall to the Red Sand Wpt
to start or conclude this route

Routes 37 to 39 - Rolling Route Diagrams

76

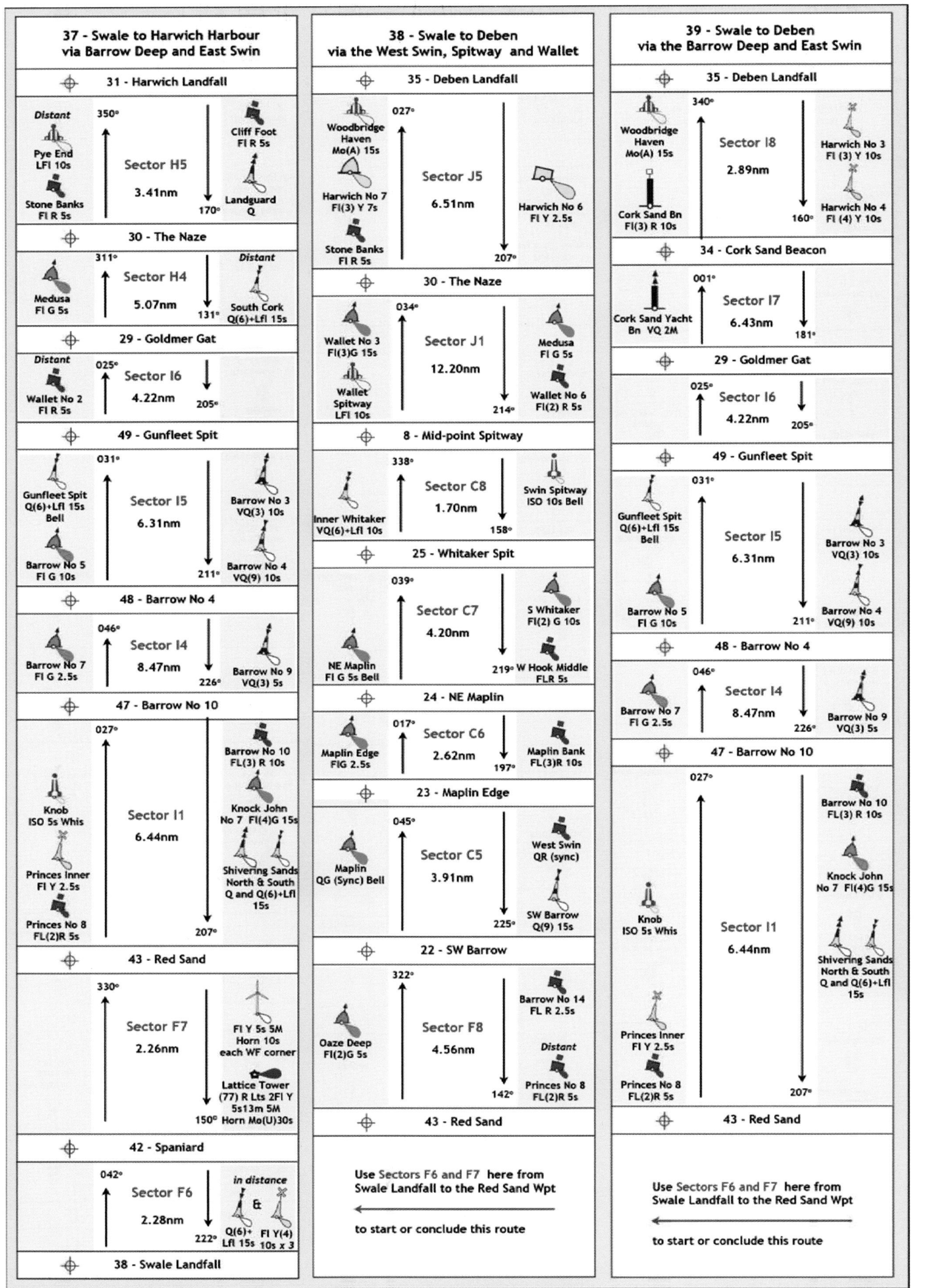

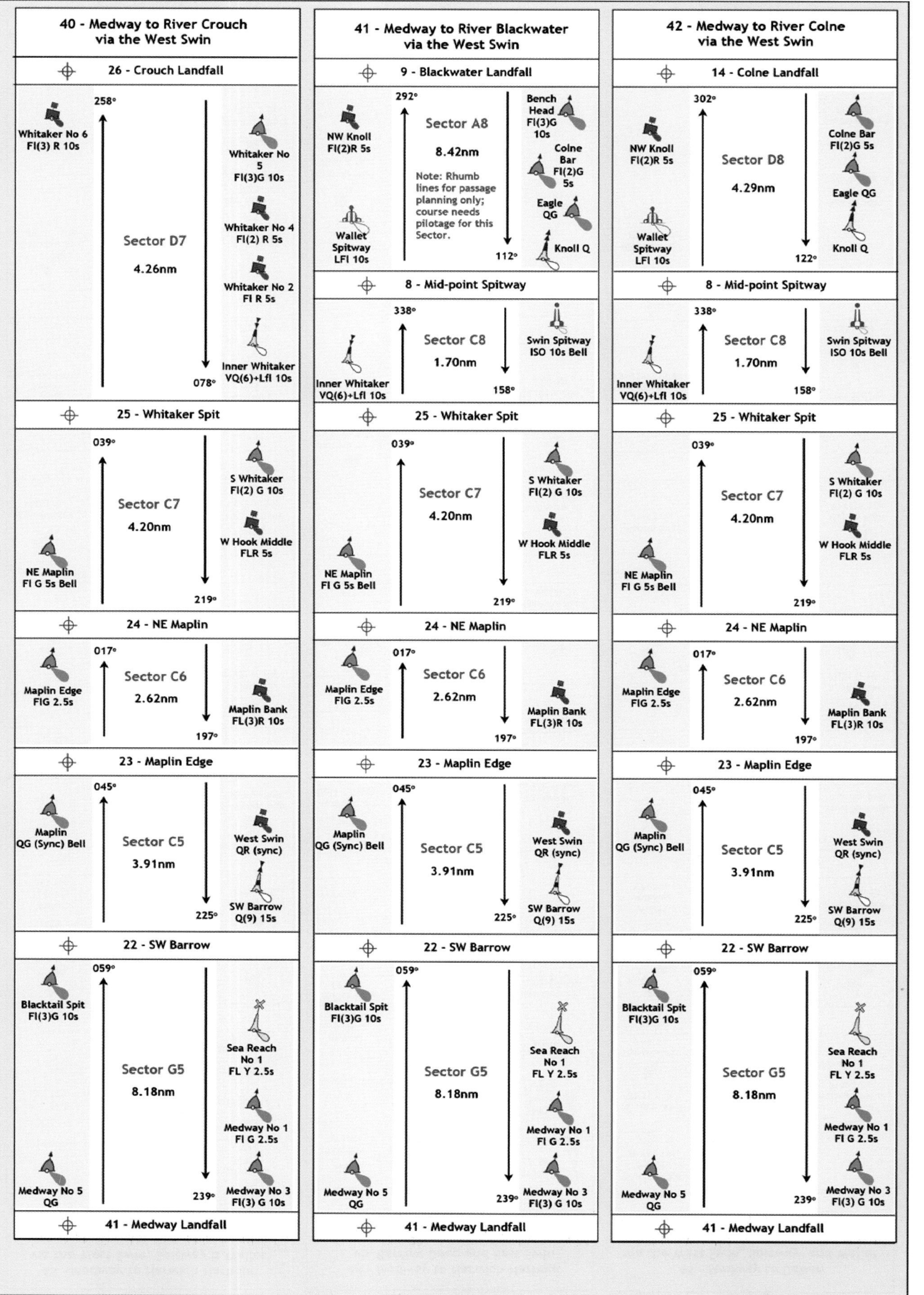
40 - Medway to River Crouch via the West Swin
26 - Crouch Landfall
Whitaker No 6 Fl(3) R 10s
258°
Sector D7
4.26nm
078°
Whitaker No 5 Fl(3)G 10s
Whitaker No 4 Fl(2) R 5s
Whitaker No 2 Fl R 5s
Inner Whitaker VQ(6)+Lfl 10s
25 - Whitaker Spit
NE Maplin Fl G 5s Bell
039°
Sector C7
4.20nm
219°
S Whitaker Fl(2) G 10s
W Hook Middle FLR 5s
24 - NE Maplin
Maplin Edge FlG 2.5s
017°
Sector C6
2.62nm
197°
Maplin Bank FL(3)R 10s
23 - Maplin Edge
Maplin QG (Sync) Bell
045°
Sector C5
3.91nm
225°
West Swin QR (sync)
SW Barrow Q(9) 15s
22 - SW Barrow
Blacktail Spit Fl(3)G 10s
Medway No 5 QG
059°
Sector G5
8.18nm
239°
Sea Reach No 1 FL Y 2.5s
Medway No 1 Fl G 2.5s
Medway No 3 Fl(3) G 10s
41 - Medway Landfall
41 - Medway to River Blackwater via the West Swin
9 - Blackwater Landfall
NW Knoll Fl(2)R 5s
Wallet Spitway LFl 10s
292°
Sector A8
8.42nm
Note: Rhumb lines for passage planning only; course needs pilotage for this Sector.
112°
Bench Head Fl(3)G 10s
Colne Bar Fl(2)G 5s
Eagle QG
Knoll Q
8 - Mid-point Spitway
Inner Whitaker VQ(6)+Lfl 10s
338°
Sector C8
1.70nm
158°
Swin Spitway ISO 10s Bell
25 - Whitaker Spit
NE Maplin Fl G 5s Bell
039°
Sector C7
4.20nm
219°
S Whitaker Fl(2) G 10s
W Hook Middle FLR 5s
24 - NE Maplin
Maplin Edge FlG 2.5s
017°
Sector C6
2.62nm
197°
Maplin Bank FL(3)R 10s
23 - Maplin Edge
Maplin QG (Sync) Bell
045°
Sector C5
3.91nm
225°
West Swin QR (sync)
SW Barrow Q(9) 15s
22 - SW Barrow
Blacktail Spit Fl(3)G 10s
Medway No 5 QG
059°
Sector G5
8.18nm
239°
Sea Reach No 1 FL Y 2.5s
Medway No 1 Fl G 2.5s
Medway No 3 Fl(3) G 10s
41 - Medway Landfall
42 - Medway to River Colne via the West Swin
14 - Colne Landfall
NW Knoll Fl(2)R 5s
Wallet Spitway LFl 10s
302°
Sector D8
4.29nm
122°
Colne Bar Fl(2)G 5s
Eagle QG
Knoll Q
8 - Mid-point Spitway
Inner Whitaker VQ(6)+Lfl 10s
338°
Sector C8
1.70nm
158°
Swin Spitway ISO 10s Bell
25 - Whitaker Spit
NE Maplin Fl G 5s Bell
039°
Sector C7
4.20nm
219°
S Whitaker Fl(2) G 10s
W Hook Middle FLR 5s
24 - NE Maplin
Maplin Edge FlG 2.5s
017°
Sector C6
2.62nm
197°
Maplin Bank FL(3)R 10s
23 - Maplin Edge
Maplin QG (Sync) Bell
045°
Sector C5
3.91nm
225°
West Swin QR (sync)
SW Barrow Q(9) 15s
22 - SW Barrow
Blacktail Spit Fl(3)G 10s
Medway No 5 QG
059°
Sector G5
8.18nm
239°
Sea Reach No 1 FL Y 2.5s
Medway No 1 Fl G 2.5s
Medway No 3 Fl(3) G 10s
41 - Medway Landfall

Routes 43 to 45 - Rolling Route Diagrams

78

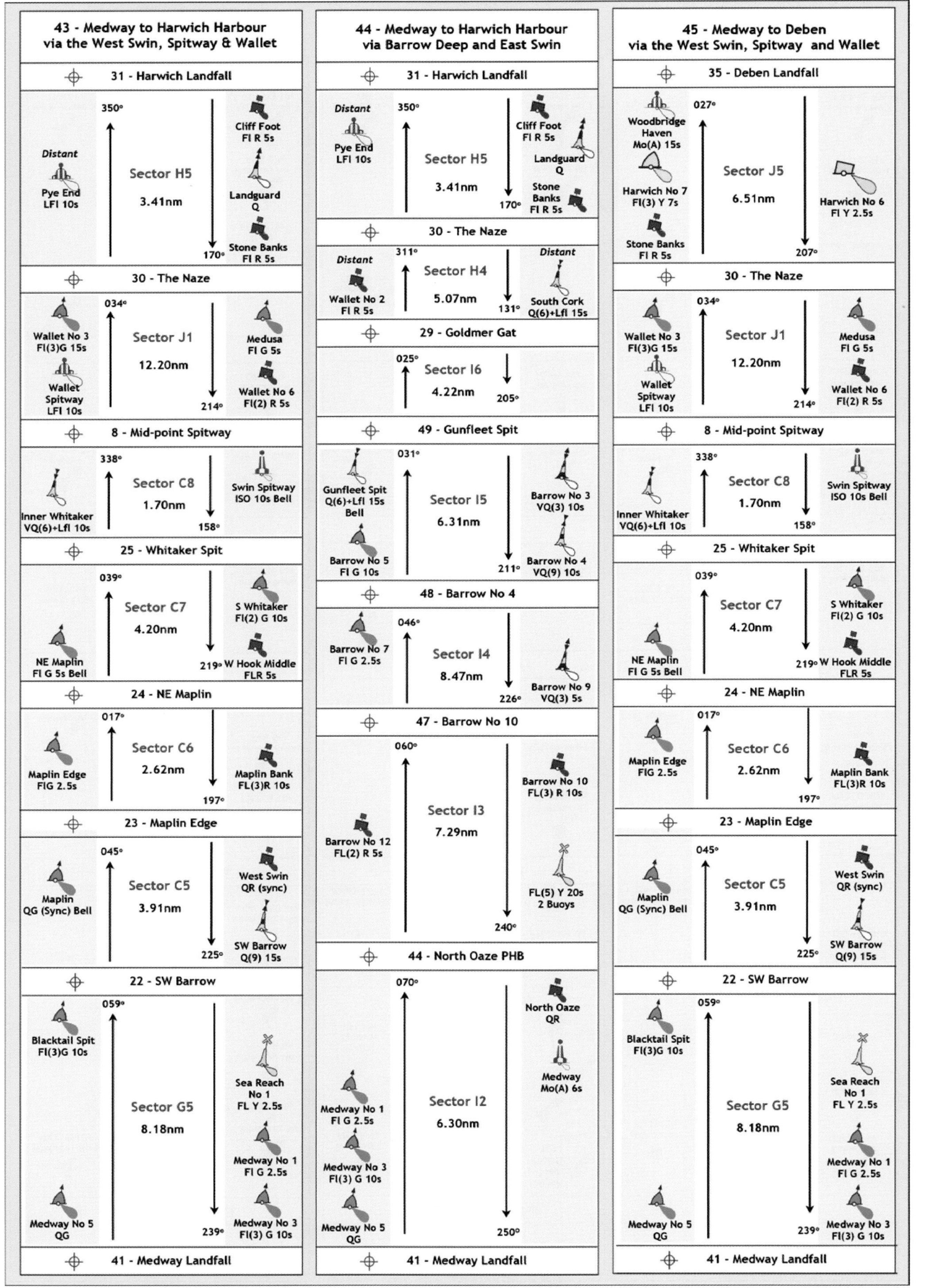

Rolling Route Diagrams - Routes 46 to 48

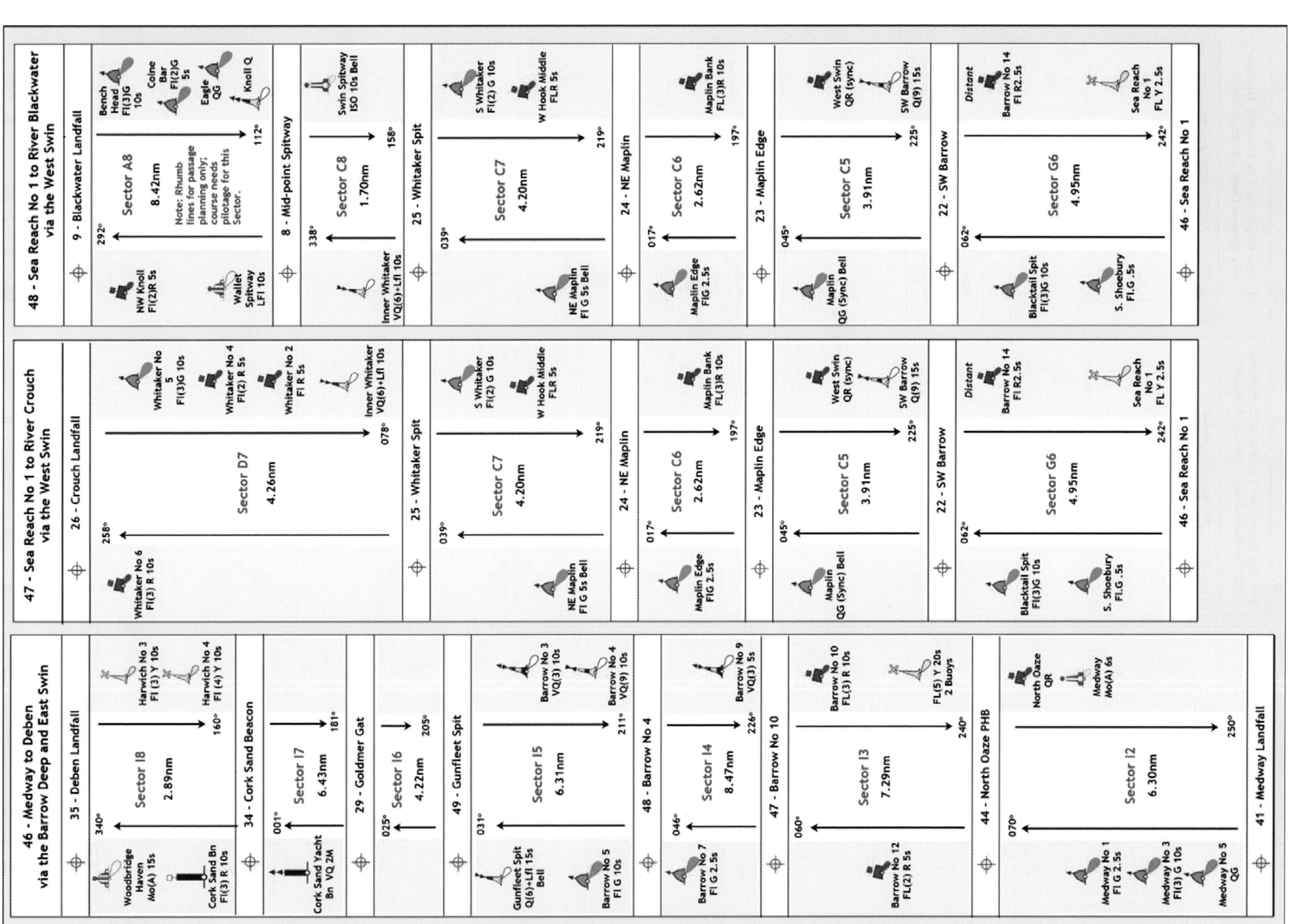

Routes 48 to 51 - Rolling Route Diagrams

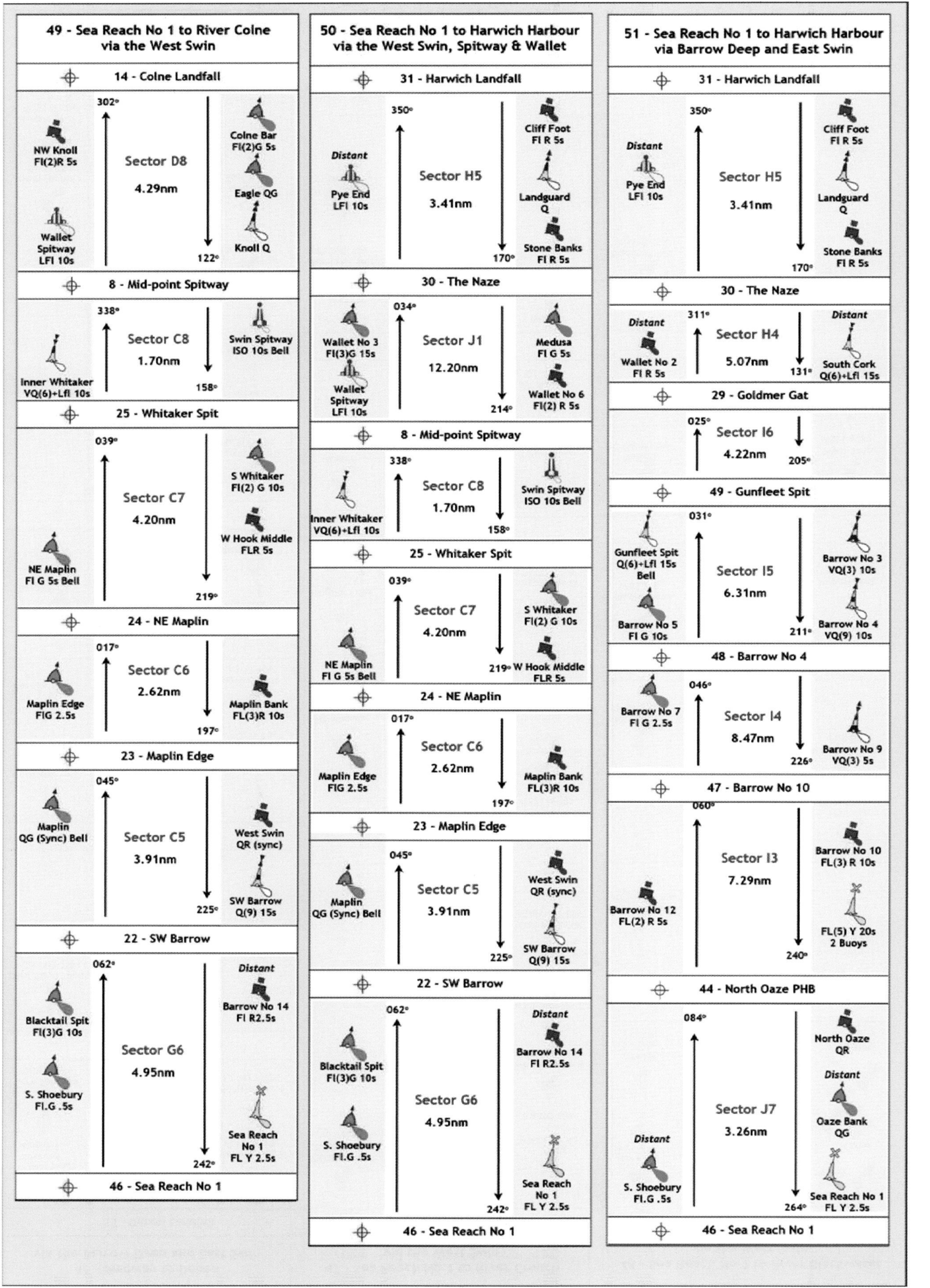

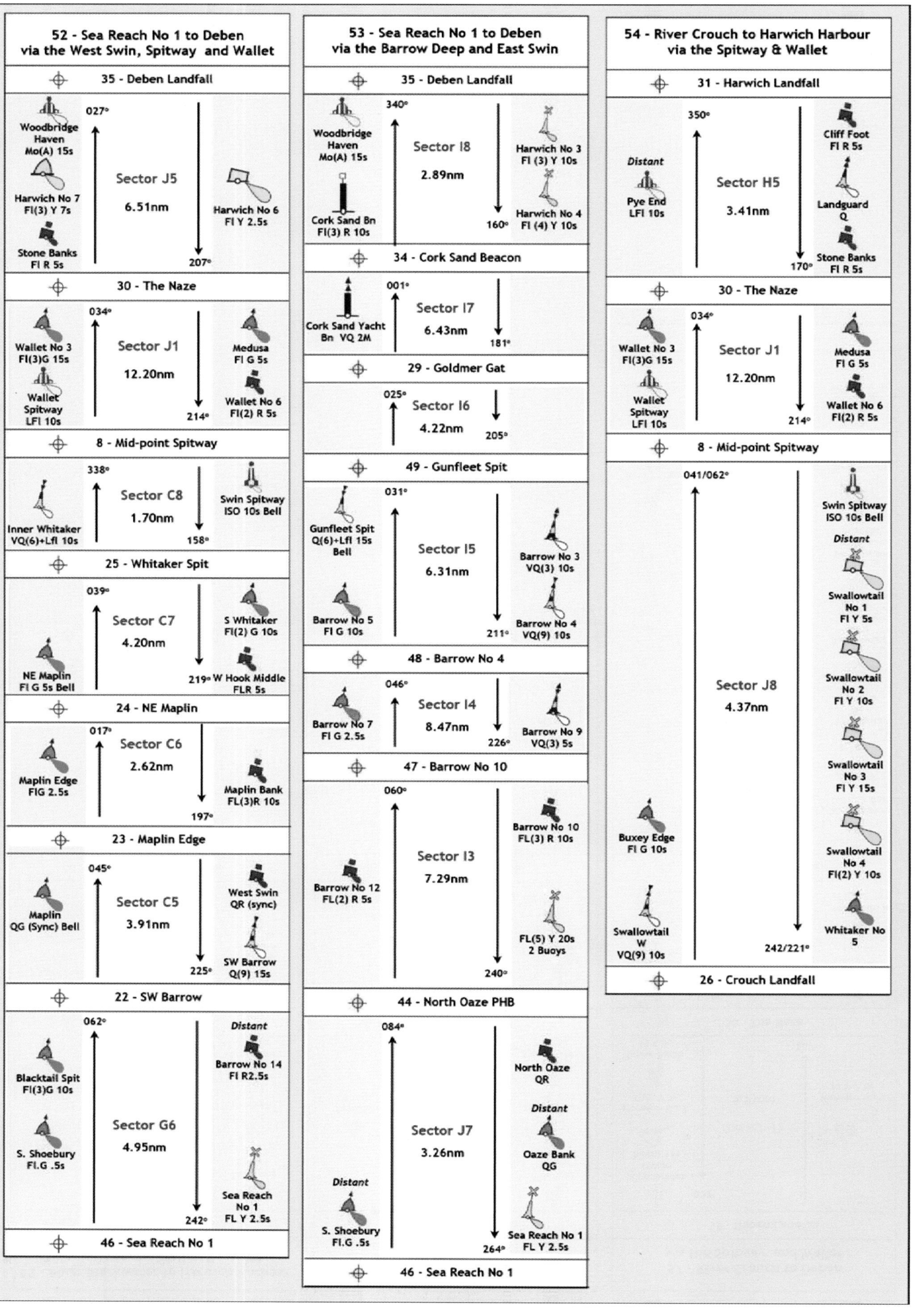

52 - Sea Reach No 1 to Deben via the West Swin, Spitway and Wallet
35 - Deben Landfall
Woodbridge Haven Mo(A) 15s
Harwich No 7 Fl(3) Y 7s
Stone Banks Fl R 5s
027°
Sector J5
6.51nm
207°
Harwich No 6 Fl Y 2.5s
30 - The Naze
Wallet No 3 Fl(3)G 15s
Wallet Spitway LFl 10s
034°
Sector J1
12.20nm
214°
Medusa Fl G 5s
Wallet No 6 Fl(2) R 5s
8 - Mid-point Spitway
Inner Whitaker VQ(6)+LFl 10s
338°
Sector C8
1.70nm
158°
Swin Spitway ISO 10s Bell
25 - Whitaker Spit
NE Maplin Fl G 5s Bell
039°
Sector C7
4.20nm
219°
S Whitaker Fl(2) G 10s
W Hook Middle FLR 5s
24 - NE Maplin
Maplin Edge FlG 2.5s
017°
Sector C6
2.62nm
197°
Maplin Bank FL(3)R 10s
23 - Maplin Edge
Maplin QG (Sync) Bell
045°
Sector C5
3.91nm
225°
West Swin QR (sync)
SW Barrow Q(9) 15s
22 - SW Barrow
Blacktail Spit Fl(3)G 10s
S. Shoebury Fl.G .5s
062°
Sector G6
4.95nm
242°
Distant
Barrow No 14 Fl R2.5s
Sea Reach No 1 FL Y 2.5s
46 - Sea Reach No 1
53 - Sea Reach No 1 to Deben via the Barrow Deep and East Swin
35 - Deben Landfall
Woodbridge Haven Mo(A) 15s
Cork Sand Bn Fl(3) R 10s
340°
Sector I8
2.89nm
160°
Harwich No 3 Fl (3) Y 10s
Harwich No 4 Fl (4) Y 10s
34 - Cork Sand Beacon
Cork Sand Yacht Bn VQ 2M
001°
Sector I7
6.43nm
181°
29 - Goldmer Gat
025°
Sector I6
4.22nm
205°
49 - Gunfleet Spit
Gunfleet Spit Q(6)+LFl 15s Bell
Barrow No 5 Fl G 10s
031°
Sector I5
6.31nm
211°
Barrow No 3 VQ(3) 10s
Barrow No 4 VQ(9) 10s
48 - Barrow No 4
Barrow No 7 Fl G 2.5s
046°
Sector I4
8.47nm
226°
Barrow No 9 VQ(3) 5s
47 - Barrow No 10
Barrow No 12 FL(2) R 5s
060°
Sector I3
7.29nm
240°
Barrow No 10 FL(3) R 10s
FL(5) Y 20s 2 Buoys
44 - North Oaze PHB
Distant
S. Shoebury Fl.G .5s
084°
Sector J7
3.26nm
264°
North Oaze QR
Distant
Oaze Bank QG
Sea Reach No 1 FL Y 2.5s
46 - Sea Reach No 1
54 - River Crouch to Harwich Harbour via the Spitway & Wallet
31 - Harwich Landfall
Distant
Pye End LFl 10s
350°
Sector H5
3.41nm
170°
Cliff Foot Fl R 5s
Landguard Q
Stone Banks Fl R 5s
30 - The Naze
Wallet No 3 Fl(3)G 15s
Wallet Spitway LFl 10s
034°
Sector J1
12.20nm
214°
Medusa Fl G 5s
Wallet No 6 Fl(2) R 5s
8 - Mid-point Spitway
Buxey Edge Fl G 10s
Swallowtail W VQ(9) 10s
041/062°
Sector J8
4.37nm
242/221°
Swin Spitway ISO 10s Bell
Distant
Swallowtail No 1 Fl Y 5s
Swallowtail No 2 Fl Y 10s
Swallowtail No 3 Fl Y 15s
Swallowtail No 4 Fl(2) Y 10s
Whitaker No 5
26 - Crouch Landfall

Routes 55 to 57 - Rolling Route Diagrams

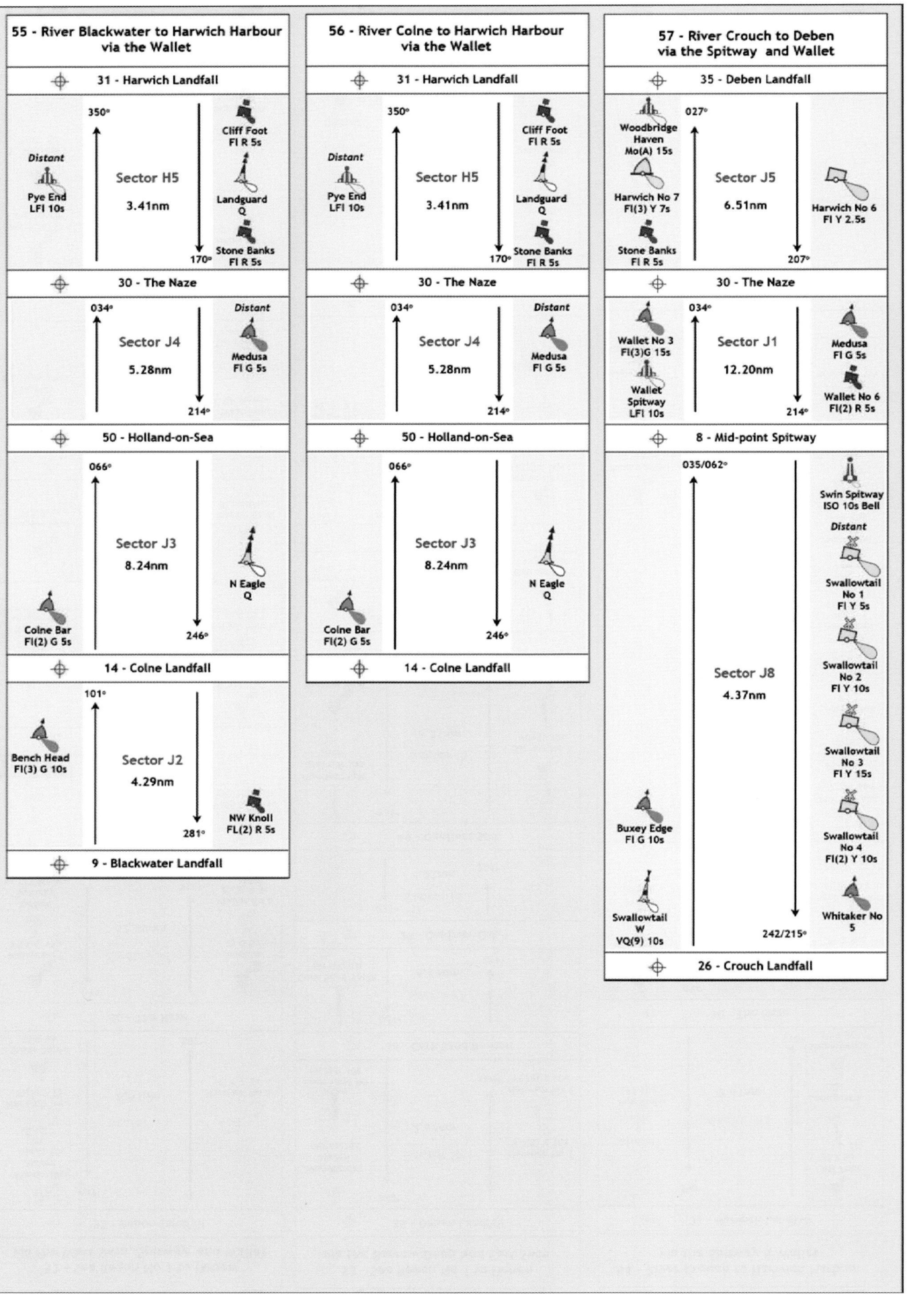

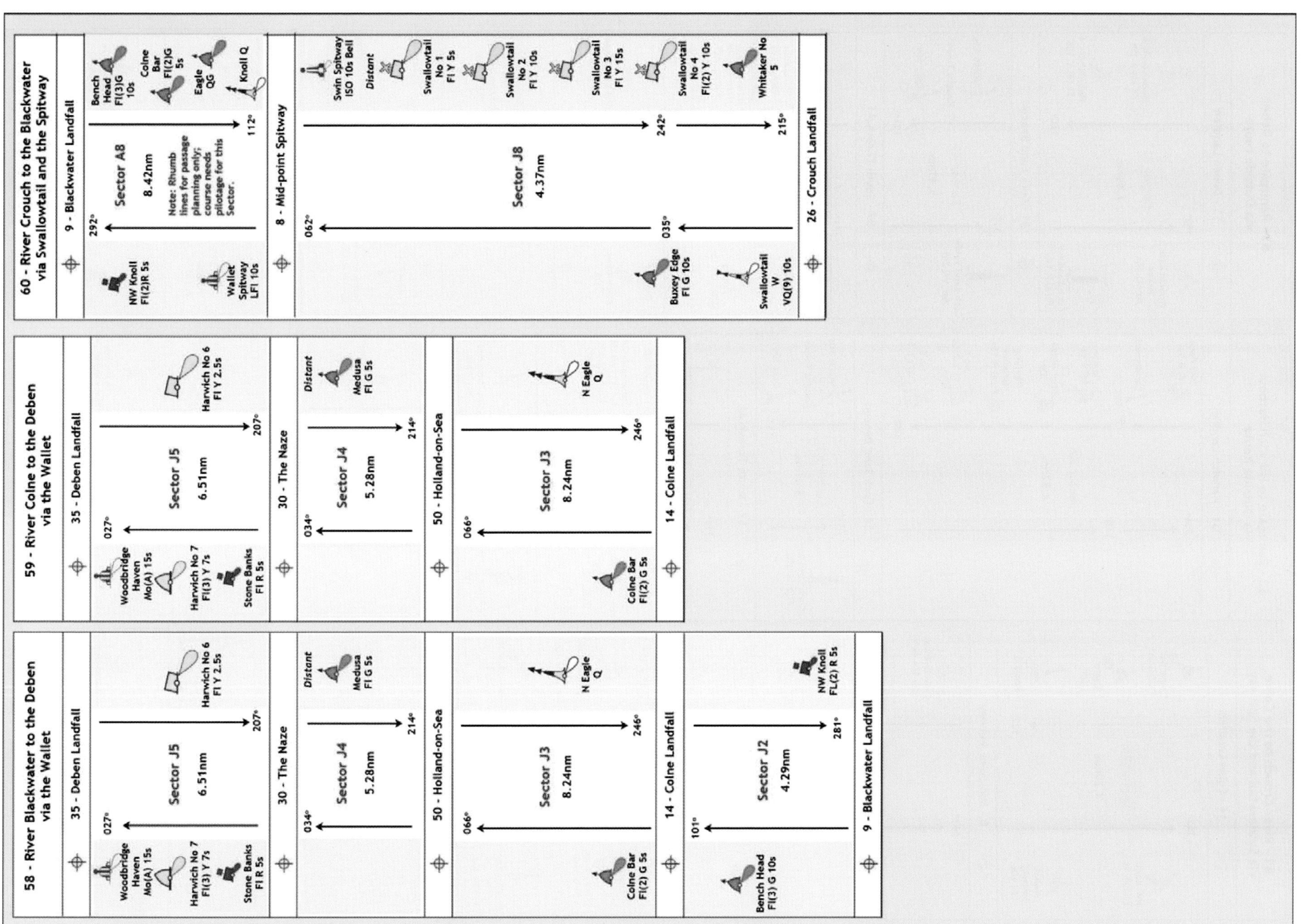

58 - River Blackwater to the Deben via the Wallet
35 - Deben Landfall
Woodbridge Haven Mo(A) 15s
Harwich No 7 Fl(3) Y 7s
Stone Banks Fl R 5s
027°
Sector J5
6.51nm
207°
Harwich No 6 Fl Y 2.5s
30 - The Naze
034°
Sector J4
5.28nm
214°
Distant
Medusa Fl G 5s
50 - Holland-on-Sea
066°
Sector J3
8.24nm
246°
Colne Bar Fl(2) G 5s
N Eagle Q
14 - Colne Landfall
101°
Sector J2
4.29nm
281°
Bench Head Fl(3) G 10s
NW Knoll FL(2) R 5s
9 - Blackwater Landfall
59 - River Colne to the Deben via the Wallet
35 - Deben Landfall
Woodbridge Haven Mo(A) 15s
Harwich No 7 Fl(3) Y 7s
Stone Banks Fl R 5s
027°
Sector J5
6.51nm
207°
Harwich No 6 Fl Y 2.5s
30 - The Naze
034°
Sector J4
5.28nm
214°
Distant
Medusa Fl G 5s
50 - Holland-on-Sea
066°
Sector J3
8.24nm
246°
Colne Bar Fl(2) G 5s
N Eagle Q
14 - Colne Landfall
60 - River Crouch to the Blackwater via Swallowtail and the Spitway
9 - Blackwater Landfall
NW Knoll Fl(2)R 5s
Wallet Spitway LFl 10s
292°
Sector A8
8.42nm
Note: Rhumb lines for passage planning only; course needs pilotage for this Sector.
112°
Bench Head Fl(3)G 10s
Colne Bar Fl(2)G 5s
Eagle QG
Knoll Q
8 - Mid-point Spitway
062°
Sector J8
4.37nm
242°
035°
215°
Swin Spitway ISO 10s Bell
Distant
Swallowtail No 1 Fl Y 5s
Swallowtail No 2 Fl Y 10s
Swallowtail No 3 Fl Y 15s
Swallowtail No 4 Fl(2) Y 10s
Whitaker No 5
Buxey Edge Fl G 10s
Swallowtail W VQ(9) 10s
26 - Crouch Landfall

Routes 61 to 63 - Rolling Route Diagrams

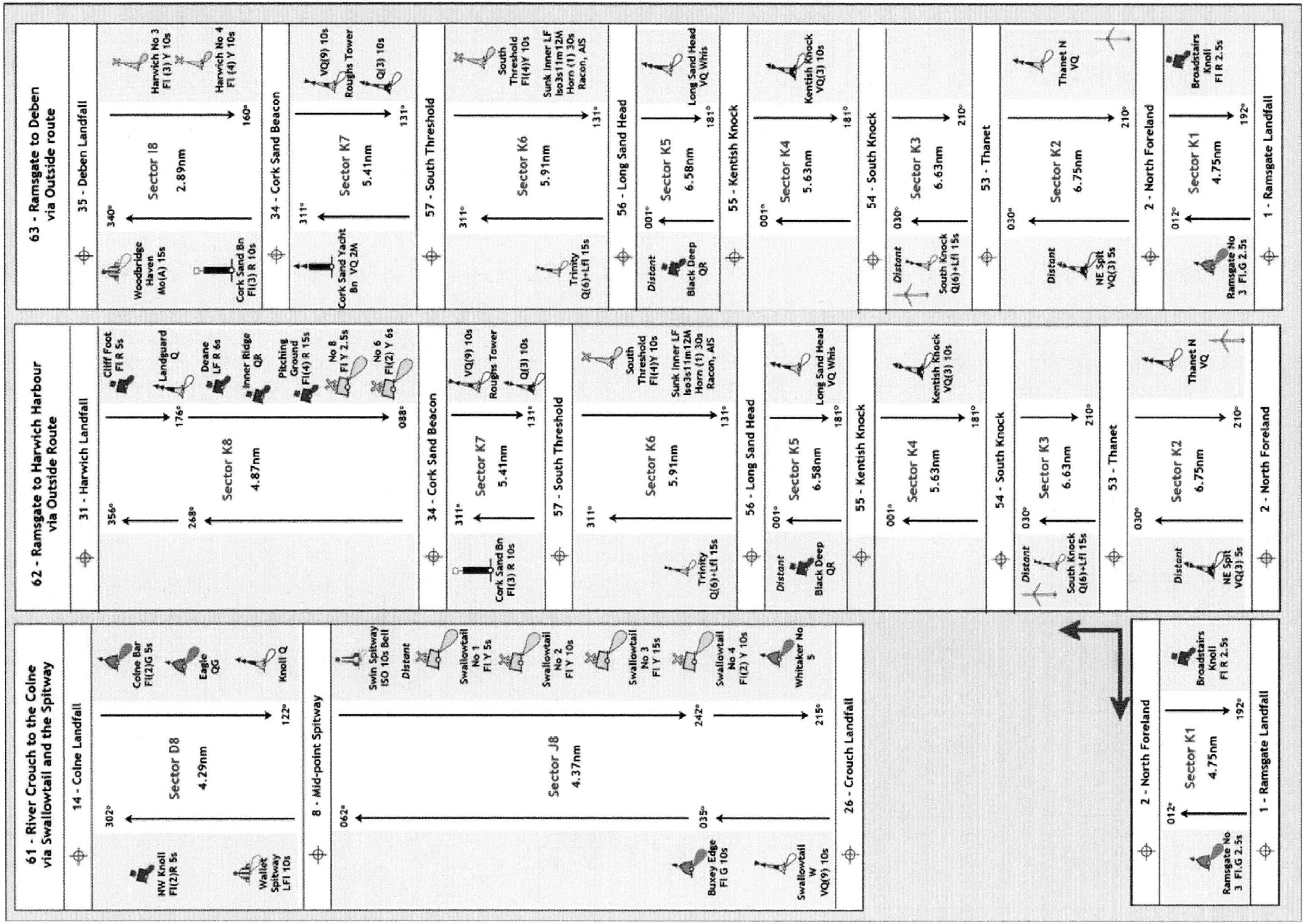

61 - River Crouch to the Colne via Swallowtail and the Spitway

14 - Colne Landfall

Sector D8 — 4.29nm — 302° / 122°

NW Knoll Fl(2)R 5s; Wallet Spitway LFl 10s; Colne Bar Fl(2)G 5s; Eagle QG; Knoll Q

8 - Mid-point Spitway

Sector J8 — 4.37nm — 062° / 035° — 242° / 215°

Buxey Edge Fl G 10s; Swallowtail W VQ(9) 10s; Swin Spitway ISO 10s Bell; *Distant*; Swallowtail No 1 Fl Y 5s; Swallowtail No 2 Fl Y 10s; Swallowtail No 3 Fl Y 15s; Swallowtail No 4 Fl(2) Y 10s; Whitaker No 5

26 - Crouch Landfall

2 - North Foreland

Sector K1 — 4.75nm — 012° / 192°

Ramsgate No 3 Fl.G 2.5s; Broadstairs Knoll Fl R 2.5s

1 - Ramsgate Landfall

62 - Ramsgate to Harwich Harbour via Outside Route

31 - Harwich Landfall

Sector K8 — 4.87nm — 356° / 268° — 176° / 088°

Cliff Foot Fl R 5s; Landguard Q; Deane LF R 6s; Inner Ridge QR; Pitching Ground Fl(4) R 15s; No 8 Fl Y 2.5s; No 6 Fl(2) Y 6s

34 - Cork Sand Beacon

Sector K7 — 5.41nm — 311° / 131°

Cork Sand Bn Fl(3) R 10s; VQ(9) 10s; Roughs Tower; Q(3) 10s

57 - South Threshold

Sector K6 — 5.91nm — 311° / 131°

Trinity Q(6)+Lfl 15s; South Threshold Fl(4)Y 10s; Sunk Inner LF Iso3s11m12M Horn (1) 30s Racon, AIS

56 - Long Sand Head

Sector K5 — 6.58nm — 001° / 181°

Distant; Black Deep QR; Long Sand Head VQ Whis

55 - Kentish Knock

Sector K4 — 5.63nm — 001° / 181°

Kentish Knock VQ(3) 10s

54 - South Knock

Sector K3 — 6.63nm — 030° / 210°

Distant; South Knock Q(6)+Lfl 15s

53 - Thanet

Sector K2 — 6.75nm — 030° / 210°

Distant; NE Spit VQ(3) 5s; Thanet N VQ

2 - North Foreland

63 - Ramsgate to Deben via Outside route

35 - Deben Landfall

Sector I8 — 2.89nm — 340° / 160°

Woodbridge Haven Mo(A) 15s; Cork Sand Bn Fl(3) R 10s; Harwich No 3 Fl (3) Y 10s; Harwich No 4 Fl (4) Y 10s

34 - Cork Sand Beacon

Sector K7 — 5.41nm — 311° / 131°

Cork Sand Yacht Bn VQ 2M; VQ(9) 10s; Roughs Tower; Q(3) 10s

57 - South Threshold

Sector K6 — 5.91nm — 311° / 131°

Trinity Q(6)+Lfl 15s; South Threshold Fl(4)Y 10s; Sunk Inner LF Iso3s11m12M Horn (1) 30s Racon, AIS

56 - Long Sand Head

Sector K5 — 6.58nm — 001° / 181°

Distant; Black Deep QR; Long Sand Head VQ Whis

55 - Kentish Knock

Sector K4 — 5.63nm — 001° / 181°

Kentish Knock VQ(3) 10s

54 - South Knock

Sector K3 — 6.63nm — 030° / 210°

Distant; South Knock Q(6)+Lfl 15s

53 - Thanet

Sector K2 — 6.75nm — 030° / 210°

Distant; NE Spit VQ(3) 5s; Thanet N VQ

2 - North Foreland

Sector K1 — 4.75nm — 012° / 192°

Ramsgate No 3 Fl.G 2.5s; Broadstairs Knoll Fl R 2.5s

1 - Ramsgate Landfall

Approximate distances to destinations up-river from the Landfall Waypoints			
From the Blackwater Landfall		**From the Colne Landfall**	
West Mersea	1.23nm	Mersea Stone	3.60nm
Bradwell	1.63nm	Brightlingsea	4.16nm
Tollesbury Marina	3.44nm	Wivenhoe	7.66nm
Marconi	5.48nm	Rowhedge	8.05nm
Osea Island	6.10nm	Colchester Hythe	9.87nm
Maylandsea	8.10nm		
Heybridge Basin	9.21nm		
Maldon	10.53nm		
From the Swale Landfall		**From the Crouch Landfall**	
Faversham Creek	7.50nm	River Roach entrance	7.13nm
Conyer Marina	10.46nm	Burnham	9.23nm
Kingsferry Bridge	13.28nm	Burnham Yacht Hbr	9.0nm
		Essex Marina	9.80nm
From the Medway Landfall		North Fambridge YS	14.90nm
Queenborough ATL	4.88nm	Fambridge Yacht H'vn	16.01nm
Whitton Marina	7.84nm	Brandy Hole YS	16.62nm
Gillingham Marina	8.13nm	Battlesbridge	19.57nm
Hoo Marina	8.82nm	Yokesfleet Anchorage	9.76nm
Victoria Marina	10.52nm	Paglesham	10.59nm
Rochester Bridge	12.04nm		
From the Harwich Landfall		**From the Thames Landfall**	
Halfpenny Pier	1.85nm	Ray Gut	6.80nm
Shotley Marina	2.53nm	Holehaven Creek	12.13nm
Wrabness	6.86nm	Embankment Marina	19.94nm
Mistley	9.53nm	Thurrock YC	23.71nm
Suffolk Yacht Harbour	4.46nm	QE II Bridge	27.07nm
Pin Mill	6.29nm	Erith YC	29.02nm
Woolverstone Marina	7.22nm	Gallions Point Marina	34.69nm
Fox's Marina	9.41nm	Thames Barrier	36.45nm
Ipswich Docks	10.40nm	Greenwich YC	37.12nm
		Poplar Dock Marina	38.33nm
From the Deben Landfall		West India Moorings	38.49nm
Ramsholt	3.92nm	South Dock Marina	40.69nm
Waldringfield	6.57nm	Limehouse Marina	41.74nm
Woodbridge	8.98nm	St Katherine Docks	43.22nm

The Passage Planning Tables

- Select your route using the guidance in the book and the data tables immediately preceding this page;
- Open pull-out planning guide from rear cover;
- Identify the sectors in your chosen route from the Route lists (pages 52 to 57: enter each Sector number in the planning guide;
- Select average boat speed and Springs or Neaps: yellow edged tables are Northbound or Westbound, green edged tables are Southbound or Eastbound;
- Note any required time adjustment (difference between successive HW times);
- Select start time – if you have no particular requirements, CTTE suggests you start by looking at the first sector duration times and select a time around the shortest duration;
- Note 'End of Sector' times in sequence on the planning guide: each 'End of sector' time = your start time for the next Sector: work through to destination;
- Try to improve this first plan, for example repeat by trying one hour before and one hour later or examine where you are getting a long mid-sector time. Check tidal gates such as low water over the sands.

A - 4 Kts　　Table A - Ramsgate to Blackwater via SW Sunk　　4 Kts - A

Neaps　　All times relate to HW Sheerness　　**Time to cover Sectors (in minutes) at 4.0 Kts**

NORTH BOUND

A1 — Ramsgate to North Foreland

Time	Duration	Time at End of Sector
- 6.00	99	- 4:21
- 5.45	100	- 4:05
- 5.30	101	- 3:49
- 5.15	100	- 3:35
- 5.00	98	- 3:22
- 4.45	97	- 3:08
- 4.30	95	- 2:55
- 4.15	89	- 2:46
- 4.00	84	- 2:36
- 3.45	78	- 2:27
- 3.30	72	- 2:18
- 3.15	68	- 2:07
- 3.00	64	- 1:56
- 2.45	60	- 1:45
- 2.30	56	- 1:34
- 2.15	55	- 1:20
- 2.00	54	- 1:06
- 1.45	53	- 0:52
- 1.30	52	- 0:38
- 1.15	52	- 0:23
- 1.00	53	- 0:07
- 0.45	53	+ 0:08
- 0.30	54	+ 0:24
- 0.15	55	+ 0:40
HW	56	+ 0:56
+ 0.15	57	+ 1:12
+ 0.30	58	+ 1:28
+ 0.45	60	+ 1:45
+ 1.00	62	+ 2:02
+ 1.15	64	+ 2:19
+ 1.30	66	+ 2:36
+ 1.45	67	+ 2:52
+ 2.00	69	+ 3:09
+ 2.15	71	+ 3:26
+ 2.30	73	+ 3:43
+ 2.45	75	+ 4:00
+ 3.00	76	+ 4:16
+ 3.15	78	+ 4:33
+ 3.30	79	+ 4:49
+ 3.45	80	+ 5:05
+ 4.00	81	+ 5:21
+ 4.15	82	+ 5:37
+ 4.30	83	+ 5:53
+ 4.45	85	- 5:50
+ 5.00	87	- 5:33
+ 5.15	88	- 5:17
+ 5.30	90	- 5:00
+ 5.45	96	- 4:39
+ 6.00	97	- 4:23

A2 — North Foreland to East Margate

Time	Duration	Time at End of Sector
- 6.00	55	- 5:05
- 5.45	54	- 4:51
- 5.30	54	- 4:36
- 5.15	54	- 4:21
- 5.00	54	- 4:06
- 4.45	53	- 3:52
- 4.30	52	- 3:38
- 4.15	51	- 3:24
- 4.00	50	- 3:10
- 3.45	48	- 2:57
- 3.30	46	- 2:44
- 3.15	45	- 2:30
- 3.00	43	- 2:17
- 2.45	42	- 2:03
- 2.30	40	- 1:50
- 2.15	39	- 1:36
- 2.00	38	- 1:22
- 1.45	37	- 1:08
- 1.30	37	- 0:53
- 1.15	37	- 0:38
- 1.00	36	- 0:24
- 0.45	37	- 0:08
- 0.30	37	+ 0:07
- 0.15	37	+ 0:22
HW	38	+ 0:38
+ 0.15	39	+ 0:54
+ 0.30	40	+ 1:10
+ 0.45	41	+ 1:26
+ 1.00	42	+ 1:42
+ 1.15	43	+ 1:58
+ 1.30	44	+ 2:14
+ 1.45	46	+ 2:31
+ 2.00	47	+ 2:47
+ 2.15	48	+ 3:03
+ 2.30	49	+ 3:19
+ 2.45	50	+ 3:35
+ 3.00	51	+ 3:51
+ 3.15	51	+ 4:06
+ 3.30	52	+ 4:22
+ 3.45	52	+ 4:37
+ 4.00	52	+ 4:52
+ 4.15	53	+ 5:08
+ 4.30	53	+ 5:23
+ 4.45	53	+ 5:38
+ 5.00	53	+ 5:53
+ 5.15	54	- 5:51
+ 5.30	54	- 5:36
+ 5.45	54	- 5:21
+ 6.00	55	- 5:05

A3 — East Margate to Outer Fisherman

Time	Duration	Time at End of Sector
- 6.00	101	- 4:19
- 5.45	101	- 4:04
- 5.30	100	- 3:50
- 5.15	100	- 3:35
- 5.00	99	- 3:21
- 4.45	98	- 3:07
- 4.30	96	- 2:54
- 4.15	95	- 2:40
- 4.00	93	- 2:27
- 3.45	92	- 2:13
- 3.30	91	- 1:59
- 3.15	89	- 1:46
- 3.00	88	- 1:32
- 2.45	88	- 1:17
- 2.30	87	- 1:03
- 2.15	87	- 0:48
- 2.00	87	- 0:33
- 1.45	88	- 0:17
- 1.30	89	- 0:01
- 1.15	89	+ 0:14
- 1.00	90	+ 0:30
- 0.45	92	+ 0:47
- 0.30	93	+ 1:03
- 0.15	95	+ 1:20
HW	96	+ 1:36
+ 0.15	99	+ 1:54
+ 0.30	101	+ 2:11
+ 0.45	103	+ 2:28
+ 1.00	105	+ 2:45
+ 1.15	106	+ 3:01
+ 1.30	108	+ 3:18
+ 1.45	109	+ 3:34
+ 2.00	111	+ 3:51
+ 2.15	111	+ 4:06
+ 2.30	111	+ 4:21
+ 2.45	110	+ 4:35
+ 3.00	110	+ 4:50
+ 3.15	109	+ 5:04
+ 3.30	109	+ 5:19
+ 3.45	108	+ 5:33
+ 4.00	107	+ 5:47
+ 4.15	105	- 6:00
+ 4.30	104	- 5:46
+ 4.45	103	- 5:32
+ 5.00	101	- 5:19
+ 5.15	101	- 5:04
+ 5.30	100	- 4:50
+ 5.45	100	- 4:35
+ 6.00	100	- 4:20

A4 — Outer to Inner Fisherman

Time	Duration	Time at End of Sector
- 6.00	60	- 5:00
- 5.45	59	- 4:46
- 5.30	57	- 4:33
- 5.15	56	- 4:19
- 5.00	55	- 4:05
- 4.45	54	- 3:51
- 4.30	53	- 3:37
- 4.15	52	- 3:23
- 4.00	51	- 3:09
- 3.45	50	- 2:55
- 3.30	49	- 2:41
- 3.15	47	- 2:28
- 3.00	46	- 2:14
- 2.45	46	- 1:59
- 2.30	45	- 1:45
- 2.15	45	- 1:30
- 2.00	45	- 1:15
- 1.45	46	- 0:59
- 1.30	47	- 0:43
- 1.15	48	- 0:27
- 1.00	49	- 0:11
- 0.45	52	+ 0:07
- 0.30	54	+ 0:24
- 0.15	56	+ 0:41
HW	59	+ 0:59
+ 0.15	61	+ 1:16
+ 0.30	63	+ 1:33
+ 0.45	65	+ 1:50
+ 1.00	67	+ 2:07
+ 1.15	68	+ 2:23
+ 1.30	69	+ 2:39
+ 1.45	69	+ 2:54
+ 2.00	70	+ 3:10
+ 2.15	71	+ 3:26
+ 2.30	71	+ 3:41
+ 2.45	72	+ 3:57
+ 3.00	72	+ 4:12
+ 3.15	72	+ 4:27
+ 3.30	73	+ 4:43
+ 3.45	73	+ 4:58
+ 4.00	73	+ 5:13
+ 4.15	72	+ 5:27
+ 4.30	71	+ 5:41
+ 4.45	71	+ 5:56
+ 5.00	70	- 5:50
+ 5.15	69	- 5:36
+ 5.30	67	- 5:23
+ 5.45	66	- 5:09
+ 6.00	65	- 4:55

A5 — Inner Fisherman to SW Sunk

Time	Duration	Time at End of Sector
- 6.00	55	- 5:05
- 5.45	56	- 4:49
- 5.30	57	- 4:33
- 5.15	57	- 4:18
- 5.00	58	- 4:02
- 4.45	58	- 3:47
- 4.30	57	- 3:33
- 4.15	57	- 3:18
- 4.00	57	- 3:03
- 3.45	56	- 2:49
- 3.30	55	- 2:35
- 3.15	55	- 2:20
- 3.00	54	- 2:06
- 2.45	53	- 1:52
- 2.30	52	- 1:38
- 2.15	52	- 1:23
- 2.00	51	- 1:09
- 1.45	51	- 0:54
- 1.30	50	- 0:40
- 1.15	50	- 0:25
- 1.00	50	- 0:10
- 0.45	50	+ 0:05
- 0.30	51	+ 0:21
- 0.15	51	+ 0:36
HW	51	+ 0:51
+ 0.15	52	+ 1:07
+ 0.30	52	+ 1:22
+ 0.45	53	+ 1:38
+ 1.00	53	+ 1:53
+ 1.15	53	+ 2:08
+ 1.30	53	+ 2:23
+ 1.45	53	+ 2:38
+ 2.00	53	+ 2:53
+ 2.15	53	+ 3:08
+ 2.30	53	+ 3:23
+ 2.45	53	+ 3:38
+ 3.00	53	+ 3:53
+ 3.15	53	+ 4:08
+ 3.30	53	+ 4:23
+ 3.45	53	+ 4:38
+ 4.00	53	+ 4:53
+ 4.15	53	+ 5:08
+ 4.30	53	+ 5:23
+ 4.45	53	+ 5:38
+ 5.00	53	+ 5:53
+ 5.15	53	- 5:52
+ 5.30	53	- 5:37
+ 5.45	53	- 5:22
+ 6.00	53	- 5:07

A6 — SW Sunk to East Barrow Sands

Time	Duration	Time at End of Sector
- 6.00	32	- 5:28
- 5.45	33	- 5:12
- 5.30	33	- 4:57
- 5.15	34	- 4:41
- 5.00	34	- 4:26
- 4.45	35	- 4:10
- 4.30	35	- 3:55
- 4.15	35	- 3:40
- 4.00	35	- 3:25
- 3.45	34	- 3:11
- 3.30	34	- 2:56
- 3.15	33	- 2:42
- 3.00	33	- 2:27
- 2.45	33	- 2:12
- 2.30	32	- 1:58
- 2.15	32	- 1:43
- 2.00	31	- 1:29
- 1.45	31	- 1:14
- 1.30	31	- 0:59
- 1.15	31	- 0:44
- 1.00	31	- 0:29
- 0.45	30	- 0:15
- 0.30	30	HW
- 0.15	30	+ 0:15
HW	30	+ 0:30
+ 0.15	30	+ 0:45
+ 0.30	31	+ 1:01
+ 0.45	31	+ 1:16
+ 1.00	31	+ 1:31
+ 1.15	31	+ 1:46
+ 1.30	31	+ 2:01
+ 1.45	31	+ 2:16
+ 2.00	31	+ 2:31
+ 2.15	31	+ 2:46
+ 2.30	31	+ 3:01
+ 2.45	31	+ 3:16
+ 3.00	31	+ 3:31
+ 3.15	31	+ 3:46
+ 3.30	31	+ 4:01
+ 3.45	31	+ 4:16
+ 4.00	31	+ 4:31
+ 4.15	31	+ 4:46
+ 4.30	31	+ 5:01
+ 4.45	31	+ 5:16
+ 5.00	31	+ 5:31
+ 5.15	31	+ 5:46
+ 5.30	31	- 5:59
+ 5.45	32	- 5:43
+ 6.00	32	- 5:28

A7 — East Barrow to Swin Spitway

Time	Duration	Time at End of Sector
- 6.00	63	- 4:57
- 5.45	63	- 4:42
- 5.30	62	- 4:28
- 5.15	62	- 4:13
- 5.00	61	- 3:59
- 4.45	61	- 3:44
- 4.30	61	- 3:29
- 4.15	61	- 3:14
- 4.00	61	- 2:59
- 3.45	61	- 2:44
- 3.30	60	- 2:30
- 3.15	60	- 2:15
- 3.00	60	- 2:00
- 2.45	61	- 1:44
- 2.30	61	- 1:29
- 2.15	62	- 1:13
- 2.00	62	- 0:58
- 1.45	64	- 0:41
- 1.30	65	- 0:25
- 1.15	66	- 0:09
- 1.00	68	+ 0:08
- 0.45	70	+ 0:25
- 0.30	72	+ 0:42
- 0.15	74	+ 0:59
HW	76	+ 1:16
+ 0.15	77	+ 1:32
+ 0.30	79	+ 1:49
+ 0.45	81	+ 2:06
+ 1.00	82	+ 2:22
+ 1.15	84	+ 2:39
+ 1.30	86	+ 2:56
+ 1.45	88	+ 3:13
+ 2.00	90	+ 3:30
+ 2.15	87	+ 3:42
+ 2.30	84	+ 3:54
+ 2.45	81	+ 4:06
+ 3.00	79	+ 4:19
+ 3.15	77	+ 4:32
+ 3.30	76	+ 4:46
+ 3.45	75	+ 5:00
+ 4.00	74	+ 5:14
+ 4.15	72	+ 5:27
+ 4.30	71	+ 5:41
+ 4.45	70	+ 5:55
+ 5.00	69	- 5:51
+ 5.15	68	- 5:37
+ 5.30	67	- 5:23
+ 5.45	67	- 5:08
+ 6.00	66	- 4:54

A8 — Swin Spitway to Blackwater

Time	Duration	Time at End of Sector
- 6.00	109	- 4:11
- 5.45	107	- 3:58
- 5.30	106	- 3:44
- 5.15	104	- 3:31
- 5.00	103	- 3:17
- 4.45	102	- 3:03
- 4.30	102	- 2:48
- 4.15	101	- 2:34
- 4.00	101	- 2:19
- 3.45	101	- 2:04
- 3.30	101	- 1:49
- 3.15	101	- 1:34
- 3.00	101	- 1:19
- 2.45	103	- 1:02
- 2.30	105	- 0:45
- 2.15	108	- 0:27
- 2.00	110	- 0:10
- 1.45	116	+ 0:11
- 1.30	123	+ 0:33
- 1.15	130	+ 0:55
- 1.00	136	+ 1:16
- 0.45	143	+ 1:38
- 0.30	151	+ 2:01
- 0.15	158	+ 2:23
HW	165	+ 2:45
+ 0.15	166	+ 3:01
+ 0.30	167	+ 3:17
+ 0.45	167	+ 3:32
+ 1.00	168	+ 3:48
+ 1.15	166	+ 4:01
+ 1.30	164	+ 4:14
+ 1.45	162	+ 4:27
+ 2.00	160	+ 4:40
+ 2.15	156	+ 4:51
+ 2.30	153	+ 5:03
+ 2.45	150	+ 5:15
+ 3.00	147	+ 5:27
+ 3.15	144	+ 5:39
+ 3.30	141	+ 5:51
+ 3.45	138	- 5:57
+ 4.00	135	- 5:45
+ 4.15	133	- 5:32
+ 4.30	130	- 5:20
+ 4.45	128	- 5:07
+ 5.00	125	- 4:55
+ 5.15	123	- 4:42
+ 5.30	120	- 4:30
+ 5.45	118	- 4:17
+ 6.00	116	- 4:04

A - 4 Kts

Table A - Ramsgate to Blackwater via SW Sunk

4 Kts - A

Time to cover Sectors (in minutes) at 4.0 kts — All times relate to HW Sheerness — **Springs**

NORTH BOUND

A1 — Ramsgate to North Foreland

Time	Duration	Time at End of Sector
- 6.00	115	- 4:05
- 5.45	117	- 3:48
- 5.30	118	- 3:32
- 5.15	114	- 3:21
- 5.00	110	- 3:10
- 4.45	106	- 2:59
- 4.30	102	- 2:48
- 4.15	95	- 2:40
- 4.00	88	- 2:32
- 3.45	80	- 2:25
- 3.30	73	- 2:17
- 3.15	66	- 2:09
- 3.00	60	- 2:00
- 2.45	53	- 1:52
- 2.30	47	- 1:43
- 2.15	45	- 1:30
- 2.00	44	- 1:16
- 1.45	43	- 1:02
- 1.30	42	- 0:48
- 1.15	42	- 0:33
- 1.00	43	- 0:17
- 0.45	44	- 0:01
- 0.30	44	+ 0:14
- 0.15	46	+ 0:31
HW	48	+ 0:48
+ 0.15	49	+ 1:04
+ 0.30	51	+ 1:21
+ 0.45	54	+ 1:39
+ 1.00	56	+ 1:56
+ 1.15	59	+ 2:14
+ 1.30	62	+ 2:32
+ 1.45	65	+ 2:50
+ 2.00	69	+ 3:09
+ 2.15	72	+ 3:27
+ 2.30	75	+ 3:45
+ 2.45	77	+ 4:02
+ 3.00	79	+ 4:19
+ 3.15	80	+ 4:35
+ 3.30	82	+ 4:52
+ 3.45	85	+ 5:10
+ 4.00	88	+ 5:28
+ 4.15	91	+ 5:46
+ 4.30	94	- 5:56
+ 4.45	96	- 5:39
+ 5.00	98	- 5:22
+ 5.15	101	- 5:04
+ 5.30	103	- 4:47
+ 5.45	112	- 4:23
+ 6.00	114	- 4:06

A2 — North Foreland to East Margate

Time	Duration	Time at End of Sector
- 6.00	62	- 4:58
- 5.45	62	- 4:43
- 5.30	61	- 4:29
- 5.15	61	- 4:14
- 5.00	61	- 3:59
- 4.45	59	- 3:46
- 4.30	57	- 3:33
- 4.15	56	- 3:19
- 4.00	54	- 3:06
- 3.45	51	- 2:54
- 3.30	48	- 2:42
- 3.15	45	- 2:30
- 3.00	42	- 2:18
- 2.45	40	- 2:05
- 2.30	38	- 1:52
- 2.15	36	- 1:39
- 2.00	34	- 1:26
- 1.45	33	- 1:12
- 1.30	33	- 0:57
- 1.15	32	- 0:43
- 1.00	31	- 0:29
- 0.45	32	- 0:13
- 0.30	32	+ 0:02
- 0.15	32	+ 0:17
HW	33	+ 0:33
+ 0.15	34	+ 0:49
+ 0.30	36	+ 1:06
+ 0.45	38	+ 1:23
+ 1.00	39	+ 1:39
+ 1.15	42	+ 1:57
+ 1.30	45	+ 2:15
+ 1.45	47	+ 2:32
+ 2.00	50	+ 2:50
+ 2.15	52	+ 3:07
+ 2.30	54	+ 3:24
+ 2.45	56	+ 3:41
+ 3.00	57	+ 3:57
+ 3.15	58	+ 4:13
+ 3.30	58	+ 4:28
+ 3.45	59	+ 4:44
+ 4.00	59	+ 4:59
+ 4.15	60	+ 5:15
+ 4.30	60	+ 5:30
+ 4.45	60	+ 5:45
+ 5.00	61	- 5:59
+ 5.15	61	- 5:44
+ 5.30	61	- 5:29
+ 5.45	62	- 5:13
+ 6.00	62	- 4:58

A3 — East Margate to Outer Fisherman

Time	Duration	Time at End of Sector
- 6.00	103	- 4:17
- 5.45	102	- 4:03
- 5.30	102	- 3:48
- 5.15	101	- 3:34
- 5.00	100	- 3:20
- 4.45	98	- 3:07
- 4.30	97	- 2:53
- 4.15	95	- 2:40
- 4.00	93	- 2:27
- 3.45	91	- 2:14
- 3.30	89	- 2:01
- 3.15	87	- 1:48
- 3.00	86	- 1:34
- 2.45	85	- 1:20
- 2.30	85	- 1:05
- 2.15	84	- 0:51
- 2.00	84	- 0:36
- 1.45	85	- 0:20
- 1.30	86	- 0:04
- 1.15	87	+ 0:12
- 1.00	88	+ 0:28
- 0.45	90	+ 0:45
- 0.30	93	+ 1:03
- 0.15	96	+ 1:21
HW	99	+ 1:39
+ 0.15	102	+ 1:57
+ 0.30	105	+ 2:15
+ 0.45	109	+ 2:34
+ 1.00	112	+ 2:52
+ 1.15	114	+ 3:09
+ 1.30	116	+ 3:26
+ 1.45	117	+ 3:42
+ 2.00	119	+ 3:59
+ 2.15	118	+ 4:13
+ 2.30	117	+ 4:27
+ 2.45	117	+ 4:42
+ 3.00	116	+ 4:56
+ 3.15	114	+ 5:09
+ 3.30	113	+ 5:23
+ 3.45	111	+ 5:36
+ 4.00	109	+ 5:49
+ 4.15	108	- 5:57
+ 4.30	106	- 5:44
+ 4.45	104	- 5:31
+ 5.00	103	- 5:17
+ 5.15	102	- 5:03
+ 5.30	102	- 4:48
+ 5.45	101	- 4:34
+ 6.00	101	- 4:19

A4 — Outer to Inner Fisherman

Time	Duration	Time at End of Sector
- 6.00	61	- 4:59
- 5.45	59	- 4:46
- 5.30	57	- 4:33
- 5.15	55	- 4:20
- 5.00	53	- 4:07
- 4.45	51	- 3:54
- 4.30	50	- 3:40
- 4.15	48	- 3:27
- 4.00	47	- 3:13
- 3.45	45	- 3:00
- 3.30	43	- 2:47
- 3.15	42	- 2:33
- 3.00	40	- 2:20
- 2.45	40	- 2:05
- 2.30	39	- 1:51
- 2.15	39	- 1:36
- 2.00	38	- 1:22
- 1.45	40	- 1:05
- 1.30	42	- 0:48
- 1.15	43	- 0:32
- 1.00	45	- 0:15
- 0.45	48	+ 0:03
- 0.30	52	+ 0:22
- 0.15	56	+ 0:41
HW	59	+ 0:59
+ 0.15	63	+ 1:18
+ 0.30	66	+ 1:36
+ 0.45	69	+ 1:54
+ 1.00	73	+ 2:13
+ 1.15	74	+ 2:29
+ 1.30	76	+ 2:46
+ 1.45	77	+ 3:02
+ 2.00	78	+ 3:18
+ 2.15	79	+ 3:34
+ 2.30	80	+ 3:50
+ 2.45	81	+ 4:06
+ 3.00	82	+ 4:22
+ 3.15	84	+ 4:39
+ 3.30	86	+ 4:56
+ 3.45	89	+ 5:14
+ 4.00	91	+ 5:31
+ 4.15	87	+ 5:42
+ 4.30	84	+ 5:54
+ 4.45	81	- 5:54
+ 5.00	77	- 5:43
+ 5.15	75	- 5:30
+ 5.30	73	- 5:17
+ 5.45	71	- 5:04
+ 6.00	69	- 4:51

A5 — Inner Fisherman to SW Sunk

Time	Duration	Time at End of Sector
- 6.00	58	- 5:02
- 5.45	59	- 4:46
- 5.30	60	- 4:30
- 5.15	62	- 4:13
- 5.00	63	- 3:57
- 4.45	63	- 3:42
- 4.30	63	- 3:27
- 4.15	63	- 3:12
- 4.00	63	- 2:57
- 3.45	62	- 2:43
- 3.30	60	- 2:30
- 3.15	59	- 2:16
- 3.00	58	- 2:02
- 2.45	56	- 1:49
- 2.30	54	- 1:36
- 2.15	53	- 1:22
- 2.00	51	- 1:09
- 1.45	51	- 0:54
- 1.30	50	- 0:40
- 1.15	50	- 0:25
- 1.00	49	- 0:11
- 0.45	50	+ 0:05
- 0.30	51	+ 0:21
- 0.15	51	+ 0:36
HW	52	+ 0:52
+ 0.15	53	+ 1:08
+ 0.30	54	+ 1:24
+ 0.45	55	+ 1:40
+ 1.00	56	+ 1:56
+ 1.15	56	+ 2:11
+ 1.30	56	+ 2:26
+ 1.45	56	+ 2:41
+ 2.00	56	+ 2:56
+ 2.15	56	+ 3:11
+ 2.30	56	+ 3:26
+ 2.45	55	+ 3:40
+ 3.00	55	+ 3:55
+ 3.15	55	+ 4:10
+ 3.30	55	+ 4:25
+ 3.45	55	+ 4:40
+ 4.00	54	+ 4:54
+ 4.15	54	+ 5:09
+ 4.30	54	+ 5:24
+ 4.45	54	+ 5:39
+ 5.00	54	+ 5:54
+ 5.15	54	- 5:51
+ 5.30	54	- 5:36
+ 5.45	54	- 5:21
+ 6.00	54	- 5:06

A6 — SW Sunk to East Barrow Sands

Time	Duration	Time at End of Sector
- 6.00	34	- 5:26
- 5.45	35	- 5:10
- 5.30	35	- 4:55
- 5.15	36	- 4:39
- 5.00	37	- 4:23
- 4.45	37	- 4:08
- 4.30	38	- 3:52
- 4.15	38	- 3:37
- 4.00	38	- 3:22
- 3.45	37	- 3:08
- 3.30	36	- 2:54
- 3.15	36	- 2:39
- 3.00	35	- 2:25
- 2.45	34	- 2:11
- 2.30	33	- 1:57
- 2.15	33	- 1:42
- 2.00	32	- 1:28
- 1.45	31	- 1:14
- 1.30	31	- 0:59
- 1.15	31	- 0:44
- 1.00	30	- 0:30
- 0.45	30	- 0:15
- 0.30	30	HW
- 0.15	30	+ 0:15
HW	30	+ 0:30
+ 0.15	31	+ 0:46
+ 0.30	31	+ 1:01
+ 0.45	31	+ 1:16
+ 1.00	31	+ 1:31
+ 1.15	31	+ 1:46
+ 1.30	32	+ 2:02
+ 1.45	32	+ 2:17
+ 2.00	32	+ 2:32
+ 2.15	32	+ 2:47
+ 2.30	32	+ 3:02
+ 2.45	32	+ 3:17
+ 3.00	32	+ 3:32
+ 3.15	32	+ 3:47
+ 3.30	32	+ 4:02
+ 3.45	32	+ 4:17
+ 4.00	32	+ 4:32
+ 4.15	32	+ 4:47
+ 4.30	32	+ 5:02
+ 4.45	32	+ 5:17
+ 5.00	31	+ 5:31
+ 5.15	32	+ 5:47
+ 5.30	32	- 5:58
+ 5.45	32	- 5:43
+ 6.00	32	- 5:28

A7 — East Barrow to Swin Spitway

Time	Duration	Time at End of Sector
- 6.00	62	- 4:58
- 5.45	61	- 4:44
- 5.30	61	- 4:29
- 5.15	60	- 4:15
- 5.00	60	- 4:00
- 4.45	60	- 3:45
- 4.30	59	- 3:31
- 4.15	59	- 3:16
- 4.00	59	- 3:01
- 3.45	59	- 2:46
- 3.30	58	- 2:32
- 3.15	58	- 2:17
- 3.00	58	- 2:02
- 2.45	58	- 1:47
- 2.30	59	- 1:31
- 2.15	59	- 1:16
- 2.00	60	- 1:00
- 1.45	61	- 0:44
- 1.30	63	- 0:27
- 1.15	65	- 0:10
- 1.00	67	+ 0:07
- 0.45	70	+ 0:25
- 0.30	74	+ 0:44
- 0.15	77	+ 1:02
HW	81	+ 1:21
+ 0.15	85	+ 1:40
+ 0.30	90	+ 2:00
+ 0.45	95	+ 2:20
+ 1.00	100	+ 2:40
+ 1.15	100	+ 2:55
+ 1.30	99	+ 3:09
+ 1.45	99	+ 3:24
+ 2.00	99	+ 3:39
+ 2.15	95	+ 3:50
+ 2.30	92	+ 4:02
+ 2.45	89	+ 4:14
+ 3.00	86	+ 4:26
+ 3.15	84	+ 4:39
+ 3.30	82	+ 4:52
+ 3.45	79	+ 5:04
+ 4.00	77	+ 5:17
+ 4.15	75	+ 5:30
+ 4.30	73	+ 5:43
+ 4.45	71	+ 5:56
+ 5.00	70	- 5:50
+ 5.15	68	- 5:37
+ 5.30	67	- 5:23
+ 5.45	66	- 5:09
+ 6.00	65	- 4:55

A8 — Swin Spitway to Blackwater

Time	Duration	Time at End of Sector
- 6.00	103	- 4:17
- 5.45	102	- 4:03
- 5.30	100	- 3:50
- 5.15	99	- 3:36
- 5.00	97	- 3:23
- 4.45	96	- 3:09
- 4.30	96	- 2:54
- 4.15	95	- 2:40
- 4.00	94	- 2:26
- 3.45	94	- 2:11
- 3.30	94	- 1:56
- 3.15	94	- 1:41
- 3.00	94	- 1:26
- 2.45	97	- 1:08
- 2.30	101	- 0:49
- 2.15	104	- 0:31
- 2.00	108	- 0:12
- 1.45	119	+ 0:14
- 1.30	131	+ 0:41
- 1.15	143	+ 1:08
- 1.00	155	+ 1:35
- 0.45	163	+ 1:58
- 0.30	171	+ 2:21
- 0.15	179	+ 2:44
HW	188	+ 3:08
+ 0.15	188	+ 3:23
+ 0.30	187	+ 3:37
+ 0.45	187	+ 3:52
+ 1.00	187	+ 4:07
+ 1.15	183	+ 4:18
+ 1.30	180	+ 4:30
+ 1.45	176	+ 4:41
+ 2.00	172	+ 4:52
+ 2.15	167	+ 5:02
+ 2.30	163	+ 5:13
+ 2.45	159	+ 5:24
+ 3.00	154	+ 5:34
+ 3.15	150	+ 5:45
+ 3.30	146	+ 5:56
+ 3.45	141	- 5:54
+ 4.00	137	- 5:43
+ 4.15	134	- 5:31
+ 4.30	130	- 5:20
+ 4.45	127	- 5:08
+ 5.00	123	- 4:57
+ 5.15	121	- 4:44
+ 5.30	118	- 4:32
+ 5.45	115	- 4:20
+ 6.00	112	- 4:08

Table A - Ramsgate to Blackwater via SW Sunk

Neaps — All times relate to HW Sheerness — **Time to cover Sectors (in minutes) at 5.0 Kts**

NORTHBOUND

	A1 Ramsgate to North Foreland		A2 North Foreland to East Margate		A3 East Margate to Outer Fisherman		A4 Outer to Inner Fisherman	
Time	Duration	Time at End of Sector	Duration	Time at End of Sector	Duration	Time at End of Sector	Duration	Time at End of Sector
- 6.00	68	- 4:52	42	- 5:18	79	- 4:41	48	- 5:12
- 5.45	69	- 4:36	42	- 5:03	79	- 4:26	47	- 4:58
- 5.30	69	- 4:21	42	- 4:48	79	- 4:11	46	- 4:44
- 5.15	69	- 4:06	42	- 4:33	78	- 3:57	45	- 4:30
- 5.00	69	- 3:51	42	- 4:18	78	- 3:42	45	- 4:15
- 4.45	68	- 3:37	41	- 4:04	77	- 3:28	44	- 4:01
- 4.30	68	- 3:22	41	- 3:49	76	- 3:14	43	- 3:47
- 4.15	66	- 3:09	40	- 3:35	75	- 3:00	43	- 3:32
- 4.00	63	- 2:57	39	- 3:21	74	- 2:46	42	- 3:18
- 3.45	61	- 2:44	39	- 3:06	74	- 2:31	42	- 3:03
- 3.30	58	- 2:32	38	- 2:52	73	- 2:17	41	- 2:49
- 3.15	56	- 2:19	37	- 2:38	72	- 2:03	40	- 2:35
- 3.00	53	- 2:07	36	- 2:24	71	- 1:49	39	- 2:21
- 2.45	51	- 1:54	35	- 2:10	71	- 1:34	39	- 2:06
- 2.30	48	- 1:42	34	- 1:56	71	- 1:19	38	- 1:52
- 2.15	47	- 1:28	33	- 1:42	71	- 1:04	38	- 1:37
- 2.00	46	- 1:14	32	- 1:28	71	- 0:49	38	- 1:22
- 1.45	46	- 0:59	31	- 1:14	71	- 0:34	38	- 1:07
- 1.30	45	- 0:45	31	- 0:59	72	- 0:18	39	- 0:51
- 1.15	45	- 0:30	31	- 0:44	72	- 0:03	39	- 0:36
- 1.00	45	- 0:15	30	- 0:30	73	+ 0:13	40	- 0:20
- 0.45	45	HW	30	- 0:15	74	+ 0:29	41	- 0:04
- 0.30	45	+ 0:15	31	+ 0:01	75	+ 0:45	43	+ 0:13
- 0.15	46	+ 0:31	31	+ 0:16	76	+ 1:01	44	+ 0:29
HW	47	+ 0:47	31	+ 0:31	77	+ 1:17	46	+ 0:46
+ 0.15	47	+ 1:02	31	+ 0:46	78	+ 1:33	47	+ 1:02
+ 0.30	48	+ 1:18	32	+ 1:02	79	+ 1:49	49	+ 1:19
+ 0.45	49	+ 1:34	33	+ 1:18	80	+ 2:05	50	+ 1:35
+ 1.00	50	+ 1:50	33	+ 1:33	81	+ 2:21	52	+ 1:52
+ 1.15	51	+ 2:06	34	+ 1:49	81	+ 2:36	52	+ 2:07
+ 1.30	53	+ 2:23	35	+ 2:05	82	+ 2:52	53	+ 2:23
+ 1.45	54	+ 2:39	36	+ 2:21	83	+ 3:08	53	+ 2:38
+ 2.00	55	+ 2:55	37	+ 2:37	83	+ 3:23	54	+ 2:54
+ 2.15	56	+ 3:11	38	+ 2:53	83	+ 3:38	54	+ 3:09
+ 2.30	58	+ 3:28	38	+ 3:08	83	+ 3:53	55	+ 3:25
+ 2.45	59	+ 3:44	39	+ 3:24	83	+ 4:08	55	+ 3:40
+ 3.00	60	+ 4:00	40	+ 3:40	83	+ 4:23	55	+ 3:55
+ 3.15	61	+ 4:16	40	+ 3:55	83	+ 4:38	56	+ 4:11
+ 3.30	62	+ 4:32	40	+ 4:10	83	+ 4:53	56	+ 4:26
+ 3.45	62	+ 4:47	40	+ 4:25	83	+ 5:08	56	+ 4:41
+ 4.00	63	+ 5:03	41	+ 4:41	82	+ 5:22	56	+ 4:56
+ 4.15	64	+ 5:19	41	+ 4:56	82	+ 5:37	56	+ 5:11
+ 4.30	64	+ 5:34	41	+ 5:11	81	+ 5:51	55	+ 5:25
+ 4.45	64	+ 5:49	41	+ 5:26	80	- 5:55	55	+ 5:40
+ 5.00	65	- 5:55	41	+ 5:41	80	- 5:40	54	+ 5:54
+ 5.15	65	- 5:40	42	+ 5:57	79	- 5:26	54	- 5:51
+ 5.30	65	- 5:25	42	- 5:48	79	- 5:11	53	- 5:37
+ 5.45	67	- 5:08	42	- 5:33	79	- 4:56	52	- 5:23
+ 6.00	67	- 4:53	42	- 5:18	78	- 4:42	51	- 5:09

	A5 Inner Fisherman to SW Sunk		A6 SW Sunk to East Barrow Sands		A7 East Barrow to Swin Spitway		A8 Swin Spitway to Blackwater	
Time	Duration	Time at End of Sector	Duration	Time at End of Sector	Duration	Time at End of Sector	Duration	Time at End of Sector
- 6.00	43	- 5:17	26	- 5:34	51	- 5:09	91	- 4:29
- 5.45	44	- 5:01	26	- 5:19	51	- 4:54	89	- 4:16
- 5.30	44	- 4:46	26	- 5:04	51	- 4:39	88	- 4:02
- 5.15	44	- 4:31	27	- 4:48	50	- 4:25	87	- 3:48
- 5.00	45	- 4:15	27	- 4:33	50	- 4:10	85	- 3:35
- 4.45	45	- 4:00	27	- 4:18	50	- 3:55	85	- 3:20
- 4.30	45	- 3:45	27	- 4:03	49	- 3:41	85	- 3:05
- 4.15	45	- 3:30	27	- 3:48	49	- 3:26	85	- 2:50
- 4.00	45	- 3:15	27	- 3:33	49	- 3:11	84	- 2:36
- 3.45	44	- 3:01	27	- 3:18	49	- 2:56	84	- 2:21
- 3.30	44	- 2:46	27	- 3:03	49	- 2:41	84	- 2:06
- 3.15	43	- 2:32	26	- 2:49	49	- 2:26	84	- 1:51
- 3.00	43	- 2:17	26	- 2:34	49	- 2:11	84	- 1:36
- 2.45	42	- 2:03	26	- 2:19	50	- 1:55	85	- 1:20
- 2.30	42	- 1:48	26	- 2:04	50	- 1:40	86	- 1:04
- 2.15	41	- 1:34	25	- 1:50	50	- 1:25	87	- 0:48
- 2.00	41	- 1:19	25	- 1:35	50	- 1:10	89	- 0:31
- 1.45	41	- 1:04	25	- 1:20	51	- 0:54	92	- 0:13
- 1.30	40	- 0:50	25	- 1:05	52	- 0:38	96	+ 0:06
- 1.15	40	- 0:35	24	- 0:51	53	- 0:22	100	+ 0:25
- 1.00	40	- 0:20	24	- 0:36	54	- 0:06	104	+ 0:44
- 0.45	40	- 0:05	24	- 0:21	55	+ 0:10	109	+ 1:04
- 0.30	40	+ 0:10	24	- 0:06	56	+ 0:26	113	+ 1:23
- 0.15	41	+ 0:26	24	+ 0:09	57	+ 0:42	118	+ 1:43
HW	41	+ 0:41	24	+ 0:24	59	+ 0:59	122	+ 2:02
+ 0.15	41	+ 0:56	24	+ 0:39	60	+ 1:15	124	+ 2:19
+ 0.30	41	+ 1:11	24	+ 0:54	61	+ 1:31	125	+ 2:35
+ 0.45	41	+ 1:26	24	+ 1:09	62	+ 1:47	127	+ 2:52
+ 1.00	42	+ 1:42	24	+ 1:24	63	+ 2:03	128	+ 3:08
+ 1.15	42	+ 1:57	24	+ 1:39	63	+ 2:18	127	+ 3:22
+ 1.30	42	+ 2:12	24	+ 1:54	63	+ 2:33	126	+ 3:36
+ 1.45	42	+ 2:27	25	+ 2:10	63	+ 2:48	125	+ 3:50
+ 2.00	42	+ 2:42	25	+ 2:25	63	+ 3:03	124	+ 4:04
+ 2.15	42	+ 2:57	25	+ 2:40	63	+ 3:18	122	+ 4:17
+ 2.30	42	+ 3:12	25	+ 2:55	62	+ 3:32	120	+ 4:30
+ 2.45	42	+ 3:27	25	+ 3:10	62	+ 3:47	118	+ 4:43
+ 3.00	42	+ 3:42	25	+ 3:25	61	+ 4:01	116	+ 4:56
+ 3.15	42	+ 3:57	25	+ 3:40	61	+ 4:16	114	+ 5:09
+ 3.30	42	+ 4:12	25	+ 3:55	60	+ 4:30	112	+ 5:22
+ 3.45	42	+ 4:27	25	+ 4:10	59	+ 4:44	110	+ 5:35
+ 4.00	42	+ 4:42	25	+ 4:25	58	+ 4:58	108	+ 5:48
+ 4.15	42	+ 4:57	25	+ 4:40	57	+ 5:12	107	- 5:58
+ 4.30	42	+ 5:12	25	+ 4:55	57	+ 5:27	105	- 5:45
+ 4.45	42	+ 5:27	25	+ 5:10	56	+ 5:41	103	- 5:32
+ 5.00	42	+ 5:42	25	+ 5:25	55	+ 5:55	102	- 5:18
+ 5.15	42	+ 5:57	25	+ 5:40	55	- 5:50	100	- 5:05
+ 5.30	42	- 5:48	25	+ 5:55	54	- 5:36	98	- 4:52
+ 5.45	42	- 5:33	25	- 5:50	54	- 5:21	97	- 4:38
+ 6.00	42	- 5:18	25	- 5:35	53	- 5:07	95	- 4:25

Table A - Ramsgate to Blackwater via SW Sunk

Time to cover Sectors (in minutes) at 5.0 kts — All times relate to HW Sheerness — **Springs**

Time	A1 Ramsgate to North Foreland Duration	A1 Time at End of Sector	Time	A2 North Foreland to East Margate Duration	A2 Time at End of Sector	Time	A3 East Margate to Outer Fisherman Duration	A3 Time at End of Sector	Time	A4 Outer to Inner Fisherman Duration	A4 Time at End of Sector
- 6.00	78	- 4:42	- 6.00	47	- 5:13	- 6.00	81	- 4:39	- 6.00	49	- 5:11
- 5.45	79	- 4:26	- 5.45	47	- 4:58	- 5.45	81	- 4:24	- 5.45	48	- 4:57
- 5.30	80	- 4:10	- 5.30	46	- 4:44	- 5.30	80	- 4:10	- 5.30	46	- 4:44
- 5.15	79	- 3:56	- 5.15	46	- 4:29	- 5.15	80	- 3:55	- 5.15	45	- 4:30
- 5.00	79	- 3:41	- 5.00	46	- 4:14	- 5.00	80	- 3:40	- 5.00	43	- 4:17
- 4.45	78	- 3:27	- 4.45	45	- 4:00	- 4.45	78	- 3:27	- 4.45	43	- 4:02
- 4.30	78	- 3:12	- 4.30	44	- 3:46	- 4.30	77	- 3:13	- 4.30	42	- 3:48
- 4.15	73	- 3:02	- 4.15	43	- 3:32	- 4.15	76	- 2:59	- 4.15	41	- 3:34
- 4.00	69	- 2:51	- 4.00	43	- 3:17	- 4.00	74	- 2:46	- 4.00	40	- 3:20
- 3.45	65	- 2:40	- 3.45	41	- 3:04	- 3.45	73	- 2:32	- 3.45	39	- 3:06
- 3.30	60	- 2:30	- 3.30	39	- 2:51	- 3.30	72	- 2:18	- 3.30	38	- 2:52
- 3.15	56	- 2:19	- 3.15	37	- 2:38	- 3.15	71	- 2:04	- 3.15	37	- 2:38
- 3.00	52	- 2:08	- 3.00	35	- 2:25	- 3.00	70	- 1:50	- 3.00	36	- 2:24
- 2.45	47	- 1:58	- 2.45	34	- 2:11	- 2.45	69	- 1:36	- 2.45	35	- 2:10
- 2.30	43	- 1:47	- 2.30	32	- 1:58	- 2.30	69	- 1:21	- 2.30	35	- 1:55
- 2.15	42	- 1:33	- 2.15	31	- 1:44	- 2.15	69	- 1:06	- 2.15	34	- 1:41
- 2.00	40	- 1:20	- 2.00	30	- 1:30	- 2.00	68	- 0:52	- 2.00	33	- 1:27
- 1.45	39	- 1:06	- 1.45	29	- 1:16	- 1.45	69	- 0:36	- 1.45	34	- 1:11
- 1.30	38	- 0:52	- 1.30	28	- 1:02	- 1.30	70	- 0:20	- 1.30	35	- 0:55
- 1.15	38	- 0:37	- 1.15	27	- 0:48	- 1.15	70	- 0:05	- 1.15	36	- 0:39
- 1.00	38	- 0:22	- 1.00	26	- 0:34	- 1.00	71	+ 0:11	- 1.00	36	- 0:24
- 0.45	39	- 0:06	- 0.45	26	- 0:19	- 0.45	72	+ 0:27	- 0.45	39	- 0:06
- 0.30	39	+ 0:09	- 0.30	26	- 0:04	- 0.30	74	+ 0:44	- 0.30	41	+ 0:11
- 0.15	39	+ 0:24	- 0.15	27	+ 0:12	- 0.15	75	+ 1:00	- 0.15	43	+ 0:28
HW	41	+ 0:41	HW	27	+ 0:27	HW	77	+ 1:17	HW	46	+ 0:46
+ 0.15	42	+ 0:57	+ 0.15	28	+ 0:43	+ 0.15	79	+ 1:34	+ 0.15	48	+ 1:03
+ 0.30	43	+ 1:13	+ 0.30	29	+ 0:59	+ 0.30	80	+ 1:50	+ 0.30	50	+ 1:20
+ 0.45	45	+ 1:30	+ 0.45	30	+ 1:15	+ 0.45	82	+ 2:07	+ 0.45	53	+ 1:38
+ 1.00	46	+ 1:46	+ 1.00	31	+ 1:31	+ 1.00	84	+ 2:24	+ 1.00	55	+ 1:55
+ 1.15	48	+ 2:03	+ 1.15	33	+ 1:48	+ 1.15	86	+ 2:41	+ 1.15	56	+ 2:11
+ 1.30	50	+ 2:20	+ 1.30	35	+ 2:05	+ 1.30	87	+ 2:57	+ 1.30	57	+ 2:27
+ 1.45	52	+ 2:37	+ 1.45	36	+ 2:21	+ 1.45	89	+ 3:14	+ 1.45	58	+ 2:43
+ 2.00	54	+ 2:54	+ 2.00	38	+ 2:38	+ 2.00	91	+ 3:31	+ 2.00	59	+ 2:59
+ 2.15	56	+ 3:11	+ 2.15	39	+ 2:54	+ 2.15	90	+ 3:45	+ 2.15	60	+ 3:15
+ 2.30	59	+ 3:29	+ 2.30	41	+ 3:11	+ 2.30	89	+ 3:59	+ 2.30	60	+ 3:30
+ 2.45	60	+ 3:45	+ 2.45	42	+ 3:27	+ 2.45	89	+ 4:14	+ 2.45	61	+ 3:46
+ 3.00	61	+ 4:01	+ 3.00	43	+ 3:43	+ 3.00	88	+ 4:28	+ 3.00	61	+ 4:01
+ 3.15	62	+ 4:17	+ 3.15	44	+ 3:59	+ 3.15	88	+ 4:43	+ 3.15	62	+ 4:17
+ 3.30	64	+ 4:34	+ 3.30	44	+ 4:14	+ 3.30	87	+ 4:57	+ 3.30	62	+ 4:32
+ 3.45	65	+ 4:50	+ 3.45	45	+ 4:30	+ 3.45	86	+ 5:11	+ 3.45	62	+ 4:47
+ 4.00	65	+ 5:05	+ 4.00	45	+ 4:45	+ 4.00	85	+ 5:25	+ 4.00	63	+ 5:03
+ 4.15	66	+ 5:21	+ 4.15	45	+ 5:00	+ 4.15	84	+ 5:39	+ 4.15	62	+ 5:17
+ 4.30	67	+ 5:37	+ 4.30	45	+ 5:15	+ 4.30	83	+ 5:53	+ 4.30	61	+ 5:31
+ 4.45	69	+ 5:54	+ 4.45	46	+ 5:31	+ 4.45	82	- 5:53	+ 4.45	60	+ 5:45
+ 5.00	70	- 5:50	+ 5.00	46	+ 5:46	+ 5.00	81	- 5:39	+ 5.00	60	- 6:00
+ 5.15	71	- 5:34	+ 5.15	46	- 5:59	+ 5.15	81	- 5:24	+ 5.15	58	- 5:47
+ 5.30	72	- 5:18	+ 5.30	46	- 5:44	+ 5.30	80	- 5:10	+ 5.30	57	- 5:33
+ 5.45	76	- 4:59	+ 5.45	47	- 5:28	+ 5.45	80	- 4:55	+ 5.45	55	- 5:20
+ 6.00	77	- 4:43	+ 6.00	47	- 5:13	+ 6.00	79	- 4:41	+ 6.00	54	- 5:06

Time	A5 Inner Fisherman to SW Sunk Duration	A5 Time at End of Sector	Time	A6 SW Sunk to East Barrow Sands Duration	A6 Time at End of Sector	Time	A7 East Barrow to Swin Spitway Duration	A7 Time at End of Sector	Time	A8 Swin Spitway to Blackwater Duration	A8 Time at End of Sector
- 6.00	45	- 5:15	- 6.00	26	- 5:34	- 6.00	50	- 5:10	- 6.00	86	- 4:34
- 5.45	45	- 5:00	- 5.45	27	- 5:18	- 5.45	50	- 4:55	- 5.45	84	- 4:21
- 5.30	46	- 4:44	- 5.30	27	- 5:03	- 5.30	49	- 4:41	- 5.30	83	- 4:07
- 5.15	47	- 4:28	- 5.15	28	- 4:47	- 5.15	49	- 4:26	- 5.15	81	- 3:54
- 5.00	48	- 4:12	- 5.00	28	- 4:32	- 5.00	48	- 4:12	- 5.00	79	- 3:41
- 4.45	48	- 3:57	- 4.45	29	- 4:16	- 4.45	48	- 3:57	- 4.45	78	- 3:27
- 4.30	48	- 3:42	- 4.30	29	- 4:01	- 4.30	48	- 3:42	- 4.30	78	- 3:12
- 4.15	48	- 3:27	- 4.15	29	- 3:46	- 4.15	48	- 3:27	- 4.15	77	- 2:58
- 4.00	48	- 3:12	- 4.00	29	- 3:31	- 4.00	48	- 3:12	- 4.00	76	- 2:44
- 3.45	47	- 2:58	- 3.45	29	- 3:16	- 3.45	48	- 2:57	- 3.45	76	- 2:29
- 3.30	46	- 2:44	- 3.30	28	- 3:02	- 3.30	48	- 2:42	- 3.30	76	- 2:14
- 3.15	46	- 2:29	- 3.15	28	- 2:47	- 3.15	47	- 2:28	- 3.15	75	- 2:00
- 3.00	45	- 2:15	- 3.00	27	- 2:33	- 3.00	47	- 2:13	- 3.00	75	- 1:45
- 2.45	44	- 2:01	- 2.45	27	- 2:18	- 2.45	48	- 1:57	- 2.45	77	- 1:28
- 2.30	43	- 1:47	- 2.30	26	- 2:04	- 2.30	48	- 1:42	- 2.30	79	- 1:11
- 2.15	42	- 1:33	- 2.15	26	- 1:49	- 2.15	48	- 1:27	- 2.15	81	- 0:54
- 2.00	41	- 1:19	- 2.00	25	- 1:35	- 2.00	48	- 1:12	- 2.00	83	- 0:37
- 1.45	40	- 1:05	- 1.45	25	- 1:20	- 1.45	50	- 0:55	- 1.45	90	- 0:15
- 1.30	40	- 0:50	- 1.30	25	- 1:05	- 1.30	51	- 0:39	- 1.30	96	+ 0:06
- 1.15	40	- 0:35	- 1.15	25	- 0:50	- 1.15	52	- 0:23	- 1.15	103	+ 0:28
- 1.00	40	- 0:20	- 1.00	24	- 0:36	- 1.00	53	- 0:07	- 1.00	109	+ 0:49
- 0.45	40	- 0:05	- 0.45	24	- 0:21	- 0.45	55	+ 0:10	- 0.45	115	+ 1:10
- 0.30	40	+ 0:10	- 0.30	24	- 0:06	- 0.30	57	+ 0:27	- 0.30	121	+ 1:31
- 0.15	40	+ 0:25	- 0.15	24	+ 0:09	- 0.15	59	+ 0:44	- 0.15	127	+ 1:52
HW	41	+ 0:41	HW	24	+ 0:24	HW	61	+ 1:01	HW	133	+ 2:13
+ 0.15	41	+ 0:56	+ 0.15	24	+ 0:39	+ 0.15	63	+ 1:18	+ 0.15	135	+ 2:30
+ 0.30	42	+ 1:12	+ 0.30	24	+ 0:54	+ 0.30	65	+ 1:35	+ 0.30	137	+ 2:47
+ 0.45	43	+ 1:28	+ 0.45	25	+ 1:10	+ 0.45	67	+ 1:52	+ 0.45	138	+ 3:03
+ 1.00	43	+ 1:43	+ 1.00	25	+ 1:25	+ 1.00	69	+ 2:09	+ 1.00	140	+ 3:20
+ 1.15	43	+ 1:58	+ 1.15	25	+ 1:40	+ 1.15	69	+ 2:24	+ 1.15	138	+ 3:33
+ 1.30	43	+ 2:13	+ 1.30	25	+ 1:55	+ 1.30	70	+ 2:40	+ 1.30	136	+ 3:46
+ 1.45	43	+ 2:28	+ 1.45	25	+ 2:10	+ 1.45	70	+ 2:55	+ 1.45	134	+ 3:59
+ 2.00	43	+ 2:43	+ 2.00	25	+ 2:25	+ 2.00	70	+ 3:10	+ 2.00	132	+ 4:12
+ 2.15	43	+ 2:58	+ 2.15	25	+ 2:40	+ 2.15	69	+ 3:24	+ 2.15	129	+ 4:24
+ 2.30	43	+ 3:13	+ 2.30	25	+ 2:55	+ 2.30	68	+ 3:38	+ 2.30	126	+ 4:36
+ 2.45	43	+ 3:28	+ 2.45	25	+ 3:10	+ 2.45	67	+ 3:52	+ 2.45	123	+ 4:48
+ 3.00	43	+ 3:43	+ 3.00	26	+ 3:26	+ 3.00	66	+ 4:06	+ 3.00	120	+ 5:00
+ 3.15	43	+ 3:58	+ 3.15	25	+ 3:40	+ 3.15	65	+ 4:20	+ 3.15	118	+ 5:13
+ 3.30	43	+ 4:13	+ 3.30	25	+ 3:55	+ 3.30	63	+ 4:33	+ 3.30	115	+ 5:25
+ 3.45	43	+ 4:28	+ 3.45	25	+ 4:10	+ 3.45	62	+ 4:47	+ 3.45	113	+ 5:38
+ 4.00	43	+ 4:43	+ 4.00	25	+ 4:25	+ 4.00	60	+ 5:00	+ 4.00	110	+ 5:50
+ 4.15	43	+ 4:58	+ 4.15	25	+ 4:40	+ 4.15	59	+ 5:14	+ 4.15	108	- 5:57
+ 4.30	43	+ 5:13	+ 4.30	25	+ 4:55	+ 4.30	58	+ 5:28	+ 4.30	105	- 5:45
+ 4.45	43	+ 5:28	+ 4.45	25	+ 5:10	+ 4.45	57	+ 5:42	+ 4.45	103	- 5:32
+ 5.00	43	+ 5:43	+ 5.00	25	+ 5:25	+ 5.00	56	+ 5:56	+ 5.00	101	- 5:19
+ 5.15	43	+ 5:58	+ 5.15	25	+ 5:40	+ 5.15	55	- 5:50	+ 5.15	99	- 5:06
+ 5.30	43	- 5:47	+ 5.30	25	+ 5:55	+ 5.30	54	- 5:36	+ 5.30	97	- 4:53
+ 5.45	43	- 5:32	+ 5.45	25	- 5:50	+ 5.45	53	- 5:22	+ 5.45	96	- 4:39
+ 6.00	43	- 5:17	+ 6.00	25	- 5:35	+ 6.00	53	- 5:07	+ 6.00	94	- 4:26

NORTH BOUND

Table A - Ramsgate to Blackwater via SW Sunk

Neaps — All times relate to HW Sheerness — **Time to cover Sectors (in minutes) at 6.0 Kts**

NORTH BOUND

	A1 Ramsgate to North Foreland			A2 North Foreland to East Margate			A3 East Margate to Outer Fisherman			A4 Outer to Inner Fisherman	
Time	Duration	Time at End of Sector	Time	Duration	Time at End of Sector	Time	Duration	Time at End of Sector	Time	Duration	Time at End of Sector
- 6.00	**55**	**- 5:05**	**- 6.00**	**34**	**- 5:26**	**- 6.00**	**66**	**- 4:54**	**- 6.00**	**40**	**- 5:20**
- 5.45	55	- 4:50	- 5.45	34	- 5:11	- 5.45	65	- 4:40	- 5.45	40	- 5:05
- 5.30	56	- 4:34	- 5.30	34	- 4:56	- 5.30	65	- 4:25	- 5.30	39	- 4:51
- 5.15	56	- 4:19	- 5.15	34	- 4:41	- 5.15	65	- 4:10	- 5.15	38	- 4:37
- 5.00	**55**	**- 4:05**	**- 5.00**	**34**	**- 4:26**	**- 5.00**	**65**	**- 3:55**	**- 5.00**	**38**	**- 4:22**
- 4.45	55	- 3:50	- 4.45	34	- 4:11	- 4.45	64	- 3:41	- 4.45	37	- 4:08
- 4.30	55	- 3:35	- 4.30	33	- 3:57	- 4.30	64	- 3:26	- 4.30	37	- 3:53
- 4.15	54	- 3:21	- 4.15	33	- 3:42	- 4.15	63	- 3:12	- 4.15	36	- 3:39
- 4.00	**52**	**- 3:08**	**- 4.00**	**33**	**- 3:27**	**- 4.00**	**62**	**- 2:58**	**- 4.00**	**36**	**- 3:24**
- 3.45	51	- 2:54	- 3.45	32	- 3:13	- 3.45	62	- 2:43	- 3.45	36	- 3:09
- 3.30	49	- 2:41	- 3.30	32	- 2:58	- 3.30	61	- 2:29	- 3.30	35	- 2:55
- 3.15	47	- 2:28	- 3.15	31	- 2:44	- 3.15	61	- 2:14	- 3.15	35	- 2:40
- 3.00	**46**	**- 2:14**	**- 3.00**	**30**	**- 2:30**	**- 3.00**	**60**	**- 2:00**	**- 3.00**	**34**	**- 2:26**
- 2.45	44	- 2:01	- 2.45	29	- 2:16	- 2.45	60	- 1:45	- 2.45	34	- 2:11
- 2.30	42	- 1:48	- 2.30	29	- 2:01	- 2.30	60	- 1:30	- 2.30	33	- 1:57
- 2.15	41	- 1:34	- 2.15	28	- 1:47	- 2.15	60	- 1:15	- 2.15	33	- 1:42
- 2.00	**40**	**- 1:20**	**- 2.00**	**27**	**- 1:33**	**- 2.00**	**60**	**- 1:00**	**- 2.00**	**32**	**- 1:28**
- 1.45	40	- 1:05	- 1.45	26	- 1:19	- 1.45	60	- 0:45	- 1.45	33	- 1:12
- 1.30	39	- 0:51	- 1.30	26	- 1:04	- 1.30	60	- 0:30	- 1.30	33	- 0:57
- 1.15	39	- 0:36	- 1.15	26	- 0:49	- 1.15	61	- 0:14	- 1.15	33	- 0:42
- 1.00	**39**	**- 0:21**	**- 1.00**	**25**	**- 0:35**	**- 1.00**	**61**	**+ 0:01**	**- 1.00**	**34**	**- 0:26**
- 0.45	39	- 0:06	- 0.45	25	- 0:20	- 0.45	62	+ 0:17	- 0.45	35	- 0:10
- 0.30	39	+ 0:09	- 0.30	26	- 0:04	- 0.30	62	+ 0:32	- 0.30	36	+ 0:06
- 0.15	39	+ 0:24	- 0.15	26	+ 0:11	- 0.15	63	+ 0:48	- 0.15	37	+ 0:22
HW	**40**	**+ 0:40**	**HW**	**26**	**+ 0:26**	**HW**	**64**	**+ 1:04**	**HW**	**38**	**+ 0:38**
+ 0.15	40	+ 0:55	+ 0.15	26	+ 0:41	+ 0.15	64	+ 1:19	+ 0.15	39	+ 0:54
+ 0.30	41	+ 1:11	+ 0.30	27	+ 0:57	+ 0.30	65	+ 1:35	+ 0.30	40	+ 1:10
+ 0.45	41	+ 1:26	+ 0.45	27	+ 1:12	+ 0.45	66	+ 1:51	+ 0.45	41	+ 1:26
+ 1.00	**42**	**+ 1:42**	**+ 1.00**	**27**	**+ 1:27**	**+ 1.00**	**66**	**+ 2:06**	**+ 1.00**	**42**	**+ 1:42**
+ 1.15	43	+ 1:58	+ 1.15	28	+ 1:43	+ 1.15	67	+ 2:22	+ 1.15	42	+ 1:57
+ 1.30	44	+ 2:14	+ 1.30	29	+ 1:59	+ 1.30	67	+ 2:37	+ 1.30	43	+ 2:13
+ 1.45	45	+ 2:30	+ 1.45	30	+ 2:15	+ 1.45	68	+ 2:53	+ 1.45	43	+ 2:28
+ 2.00	**46**	**+ 2:46**	**+ 2.00**	**30**	**+ 2:30**	**+ 2.00**	**68**	**+ 3:08**	**+ 2.00**	**44**	**+ 2:44**
+ 2.15	46	+ 3:01	+ 2.15	31	+ 2:46	+ 2.15	68	+ 3:23	+ 2.15	44	+ 2:59
+ 2.30	47	+ 3:17	+ 2.30	31	+ 3:01	+ 2.30	68	+ 3:38	+ 2.30	44	+ 3:14
+ 2.45	48	+ 3:33	+ 2.45	32	+ 3:17	+ 2.45	68	+ 3:53	+ 2.45	45	+ 3:30
+ 3.00	**49**	**+ 3:49**	**+ 3.00**	**32**	**+ 3:32**	**+ 3.00**	**68**	**+ 4:08**	**+ 3.00**	**45**	**+ 3:45**
+ 3.15	50	+ 4:05	+ 3.15	33	+ 3:48	+ 3.15	68	+ 4:23	+ 3.15	45	+ 4:00
+ 3.30	50	+ 4:20	+ 3.30	33	+ 4:03	+ 3.30	68	+ 4:38	+ 3.30	45	+ 4:15
+ 3.45	51	+ 4:36	+ 3.45	33	+ 4:18	+ 3.45	68	+ 4:53	+ 3.45	45	+ 4:30
+ 4.00	**51**	**+ 4:51**	**+ 4.00**	**33**	**+ 4:33**	**+ 4.00**	**68**	**+ 5:08**	**+ 4.00**	**45**	**+ 4:45**
+ 4.15	52	+ 5:07	+ 4.15	33	+ 4:48	+ 4.15	67	+ 5:22	+ 4.15	45	+ 5:00
+ 4.30	52	+ 5:22	+ 4.30	33	+ 5:03	+ 4.30	67	+ 5:37	+ 4.30	45	+ 5:15
+ 4.45	52	+ 5:37	+ 4.45	33	+ 5:18	+ 4.45	67	+ 5:52	+ 4.45	45	+ 5:30
+ 5.00	**53**	**+ 5:53**	**+ 5.00**	**34**	**+ 5:34**	**+ 5.00**	**66**	**- 5:54**	**+ 5.00**	**44**	**+ 5:44**
+ 5.15	53	- 5:52	+ 5.15	34	+ 5:49	+ 5.15	66	- 5:39	+ 5.15	44	+ 5:59
+ 5.30	53	- 5:37	+ 5.30	34	- 5:56	+ 5.30	66	- 5:24	+ 5.30	43	- 5:47
+ 5.45	54	- 5:21	+ 5.45	34	- 5:41	+ 5.45	65	- 5:10	+ 5.45	43	- 5:32
+ 6.00	**54**	**- 5:06**	**+ 6.00**	**34**	**- 5:26**	**+ 6.00**	**65**	**- 4:55**	**+ 6.00**	**42**	**- 5:18**

	A5 Inner Fisherman to SW Sunk			A6 SW Sunk to East Barrow Sands			A7 East Barrow to Swin Spitway			A8 Swin Spitway to Blackwater	
Time	Duration	Time at End of Sector	Time	Duration	Time at End of Sector	Time	Duration	Time at End of Sector	Time	Duration	Time at End of Sector
- 6.00	**35**	**- 5:25**	**- 6.00**	**21**	**- 5:39**	**- 6.00**	**43**	**- 5:17**	**- 6.00**	**77**	**- 4:43**
- 5.45	36	- 5:09	- 5.45	22	- 5:23	- 5.45	43	- 5:02	- 5.45	76	- 4:29
- 5.30	36	- 4:54	- 5.30	22	- 5:08	- 5.30	43	- 4:47	- 5.30	75	- 4:15
- 5.15	36	- 4:39	- 5.15	22	- 4:53	- 5.15	42	- 4:33	- 5.15	74	- 4:01
- 5.00	**37**	**- 4:23**	**- 5.00**	**22**	**- 4:38**	**- 5.00**	**42**	**- 4:18**	**- 5.00**	**73**	**- 3:47**
- 4.45	37	- 4:08	- 4.45	22	- 4:23	- 4.45	42	- 4:03	- 4.45	73	- 3:32
- 4.30	37	- 3:53	- 4.30	23	- 4:07	- 4.30	42	- 3:48	- 4.30	73	- 3:17
- 4.15	37	- 3:38	- 4.15	23	- 3:52	- 4.15	42	- 3:33	- 4.15	73	- 3:02
- 4.00	**37**	**- 3:23**	**- 4.00**	**23**	**- 3:37**	**- 4.00**	**42**	**- 3:18**	**- 4.00**	**72**	**- 2:48**
- 3.45	36	- 3:09	- 3.45	22	- 3:23	- 3.45	42	- 3:03	- 3.45	72	- 2:33
- 3.30	36	- 2:54	- 3.30	22	- 3:08	- 3.30	42	- 2:48	- 3.30	72	- 2:18
- 3.15	36	- 2:39	- 3.15	22	- 2:53	- 3.15	42	- 2:33	- 3.15	72	- 2:03
- 3.00	**35**	**- 2:25**	**- 3.00**	**22**	**- 2:38**	**- 3.00**	**42**	**- 2:18**	**- 3.00**	**72**	**- 1:48**
- 2.45	35	- 2:10	- 2.45	21	- 2:24	- 2.45	42	- 2:03	- 2.45	73	- 1:32
- 2.30	35	- 1:55	- 2.30	21	- 2:09	- 2.30	42	- 1:48	- 2.30	74	- 1:16
- 2.15	34	- 1:41	- 2.15	21	- 1:54	- 2.15	42	- 1:33	- 2.15	74	- 1:01
- 2.00	**34**	**- 1:26**	**- 2.00**	**21**	**- 1:39**	**- 2.00**	**42**	**- 1:18**	**- 2.00**	**75**	**- 0:45**
- 1.45	34	- 1:11	- 1.45	21	- 1:24	- 1.45	43	- 1:02	- 1.45	78	- 0:27
- 1.30	34	- 0:56	- 1.30	20	- 1:10	- 1.30	43	- 0:47	- 1.30	80	- 0:10
- 1.15	34	- 0:41	- 1.15	20	- 0:55	- 1.15	44	- 0:31	- 1.15	82	+ 0:07
- 1.00	**34**	**- 0:26**	**- 1.00**	**20**	**- 0:40**	**- 1.00**	**44**	**- 0:16**	**- 1.00**	**85**	**+ 0:25**
- 0.45	34	- 0:11	- 0.45	20	- 0:25	- 0.45	45	HW	- 0.45	88	+ 0:43
- 0.30	34	+ 0:04	- 0.30	20	- 0:10	- 0.30	46	+ 0:16	- 0.30	92	+ 1:02
- 0.15	34	+ 0:19	- 0.15	20	+ 0:05	- 0.15	47	+ 0:32	- 0.15	95	+ 1:20
HW	**34**	**+ 0:34**	**HW**	**20**	**+ 0:20**	**HW**	**48**	**+ 0:48**	**HW**	**98**	**+ 1:38**
+ 0.15	34	+ 0:49	+ 0.15	20	+ 0:35	+ 0.15	49	+ 1:04	+ 0.15	100	+ 1:55
+ 0.30	34	+ 1:04	+ 0.30	20	+ 0:50	+ 0.30	49	+ 1:19	+ 0.30	101	+ 2:11
+ 0.45	34	+ 1:19	+ 0.45	20	+ 1:05	+ 0.45	50	+ 1:35	+ 0.45	102	+ 2:27
+ 1.00	**34**	**+ 1:34**	**+ 1.00**	**20**	**+ 1:20**	**+ 1.00**	**51**	**+ 1:51**	**+ 1.00**	**104**	**+ 2:44**
+ 1.15	34	+ 1:49	+ 1.15	20	+ 1:35	+ 1.15	51	+ 2:06	+ 1.15	103	+ 2:58
+ 1.30	34	+ 2:04	+ 1.30	20	+ 1:50	+ 1.30	51	+ 2:21	+ 1.30	103	+ 3:13
+ 1.45	35	+ 2:20	+ 1.45	20	+ 2:05	+ 1.45	51	+ 2:36	+ 1.45	102	+ 3:27
+ 2.00	**35**	**+ 2:35**	**+ 2.00**	**20**	**+ 2:20**	**+ 2.00**	**52**	**+ 2:52**	**+ 2.00**	**102**	**+ 3:42**
+ 2.15	34	+ 2:49	+ 2.15	20	+ 2:35	+ 2.15	51	+ 3:06	+ 2.15	100	+ 3:55
+ 2.30	34	+ 3:04	+ 2.30	21	+ 2:51	+ 2.30	51	+ 3:21	+ 2.30	99	+ 4:09
+ 2.45	34	+ 3:19	+ 2.45	21	+ 3:06	+ 2.45	51	+ 3:36	+ 2.45	97	+ 4:22
+ 3.00	**34**	**+ 3:34**	**+ 3.00**	**21**	**+ 3:21**	**+ 3.00**	**50**	**+ 3:50**	**+ 3.00**	**95**	**+ 4:35**
+ 3.15	34	+ 3:49	+ 3.15	21	+ 3:36	+ 3.15	50	+ 4:05	+ 3.15	94	+ 4:49
+ 3.30	35	+ 4:05	+ 3.30	21	+ 3:51	+ 3.30	49	+ 4:19	+ 3.30	93	+ 5:03
+ 3.45	35	+ 4:20	+ 3.45	21	+ 4:06	+ 3.45	49	+ 4:34	+ 3.45	92	+ 5:17
+ 4.00	**35**	**+ 4:35**	**+ 4.00**	**21**	**+ 4:21**	**+ 4.00**	**48**	**+ 4:48**	**+ 4.00**	**90**	**+ 5:30**
+ 4.15	35	+ 4:50	+ 4.15	21	+ 4:36	+ 4.15	48	+ 5:03	+ 4.15	89	+ 5:44
+ 4.30	35	+ 5:05	+ 4.30	21	+ 4:51	+ 4.30	47	+ 5:17	+ 4.30	87	+ 5:57
+ 4.45	35	+ 5:20	+ 4.45	21	+ 5:06	+ 4.45	47	+ 5:32	+ 4.45	86	- 5:49
+ 5.00	**35**	**+ 5:35**	**+ 5.00**	**21**	**+ 5:21**	**+ 5.00**	**46**	**+ 5:46**	**+ 5.00**	**84**	**- 5:36**
+ 5.15	35	+ 5:50	+ 5.15	21	+ 5:36	+ 5.15	46	- 5:59	+ 5.15	83	- 5:22
+ 5.30	35	- 5:55	+ 5.30	21	+ 5:51	+ 5.30	45	- 5:45	+ 5.30	83	- 5:07
+ 5.45	35	- 5:40	+ 5.45	21	- 5:54	+ 5.45	45	- 5:30	+ 5.45	82	- 4:53
+ 6.00	**35**	**- 5:25**	**+ 6.00**	**21**	**- 5:39**	**+ 6.00**	**44**	**- 5:16**	**+ 6.00**	**81**	**- 4:39**

A - 6 Kts　Table A - Ramsgate to Blackwater via SW Sunk　6 Kts - A

Time to cover Sectors (in minutes) at 6.0 kts — All times relate to HW Sheerness — **Springs**

	A1			A2			A3			A4	
	Ramsgate to North Foreland			North Foreland to East Margate			East Margate to Outer Fisherman			Outer to Inner Fisherman	
Time	Duration	Time at End of Sector	Time	Duration	Time at End of Sector	Time	Duration	Time at End of Sector	Time	Duration	Time at End of Sector
- 6.00	62	- 4:58	- 6.00	37	- 5:23	- 6.00	67	- 4:53	- 6.00	41	- 5:19
- 5.45	62	- 4:43	- 5.45	37	- 5:08	- 5.45	66	- 4:39	- 5.45	40	- 5:05
- 5.30	63	- 4:27	- 5.30	37	- 4:53	- 5.30	66	- 4:24	- 5.30	39	- 4:51
- 5.15	63	- 4:12	- 5.15	37	- 4:38	- 5.15	66	- 4:09	- 5.15	38	- 4:37
- 5.00	63	- 3:57	- 5.00	37	- 4:23	- 5.00	66	- 3:54	- 5.00	37	- 4:23
- 4.45	62	- 3:43	- 4.45	37	- 4:08	- 4.45	65	- 3:40	- 4.45	36	- 4:09
- 4.30	62	- 3:28	- 4.30	36	- 3:54	- 4.30	64	- 3:26	- 4.30	36	- 3:54
- 4.15	59	- 3:16	- 4.15	36	- 3:39	- 4.15	63	- 3:12	- 4.15	35	- 3:40
- 4.00	57	- 3:03	- 4.00	35	- 3:25	- 4.00	62	- 2:58	- 4.00	34	- 3:26
- 3.45	54	- 2:51	- 3.45	34	- 3:11	- 3.45	61	- 2:44	- 3.45	34	- 3:11
- 3.30	51	- 2:39	- 3.30	33	- 2:57	- 3.30	60	- 2:30	- 3.30	33	- 2:57
- 3.15	48	- 2:27	- 3.15	32	- 2:43	- 3.15	60	- 2:15	- 3.15	33	- 2:42
- 3.00	45	- 2:15	- 3.00	30	- 2:30	- 3.00	59	- 2:01	- 3.00	32	- 2:28
- 2.45	42	- 2:03	- 2.45	29	- 2:16	- 2.45	59	- 1:46	- 2.45	31	- 2:14
- 2.30	39	- 1:51	- 2.30	27	- 2:03	- 2.30	58	- 1:32	- 2.30	31	- 1:59
- 2.15	38	- 1:37	- 2.15	26	- 1:49	- 2.15	58	- 1:17	- 2.15	30	- 1:45
- 2.00	36	- 1:24	- 2.00	25	- 1:35	- 2.00	58	- 1:02	- 2.00	29	- 1:31
- 1.45	35	- 1:10	- 1.45	24	- 1:21	- 1.45	58	- 0:47	- 1.45	30	- 1:15
- 1.30	34	- 0:56	- 1.30	23	- 1:07	- 1.30	59	- 0:31	- 1.30	30	- 1:00
- 1.15	34	- 0:41	- 1.15	22	- 0:53	- 1.15	59	- 0:16	- 1.15	30	- 0:45
- 1.00	34	- 0:26	- 1.00	22	- 0:38	- 1.00	60	HW	- 1.00	31	- 0:29
- 0.45	34	- 0:11	- 0.45	22	- 0:23	- 0.45	61	+ 0:16	- 0.45	32	- 0:13
- 0.30	34	+ 0:04	- 0.30	22	- 0:08	- 0.30	62	+ 0:32	- 0.30	34	+ 0:04
- 0.15	35	+ 0:20	- 0.15	22	+ 0:07	- 0.15	63	+ 0:48	- 0.15	36	+ 0:21
HW	36	+ 0:36	HW	22	+ 0:22	HW	63	+ 1:03	HW	37	+ 0:37
+ 0.15	36	+ 0:51	+ 0.15	23	+ 0:38	+ 0.15	65	+ 1:20	+ 0.15	39	+ 0:54
+ 0.30	37	+ 1:07	+ 0.30	24	+ 0:54	+ 0.30	66	+ 1:36	+ 0.30	41	+ 1:11
+ 0.45	38	+ 1:23	+ 0.45	25	+ 1:10	+ 0.45	67	+ 1:52	+ 0.45	43	+ 1:28
+ 1.00	39	+ 1:39	+ 1.00	26	+ 1:26	+ 1.00	68	+ 2:08	+ 1.00	44	+ 1:44
+ 1.15	40	+ 1:55	+ 1.15	27	+ 1:42	+ 1.15	69	+ 2:24	+ 1.15	45	+ 2:00
+ 1.30	42	+ 2:12	+ 1.30	28	+ 1:58	+ 1.30	70	+ 2:40	+ 1.30	46	+ 2:16
+ 1.45	43	+ 2:28	+ 1.45	29	+ 2:14	+ 1.45	71	+ 2:56	+ 1.45	47	+ 2:32
+ 2.00	45	+ 2:45	+ 2.00	30	+ 2:30	+ 2.00	72	+ 3:12	+ 2.00	47	+ 2:47
+ 2.15	46	+ 3:01	+ 2.15	32	+ 2:47	+ 2.15	72	+ 3:27	+ 2.15	48	+ 3:03
+ 2.30	48	+ 3:18	+ 2.30	33	+ 3:03	+ 2.30	72	+ 3:42	+ 2.30	48	+ 3:18
+ 2.45	49	+ 3:34	+ 2.45	34	+ 3:19	+ 2.45	72	+ 3:57	+ 2.45	49	+ 3:34
+ 3.00	50	+ 3:50	+ 3.00	35	+ 3:35	+ 3.00	72	+ 4:12	+ 3.00	49	+ 3:49
+ 3.15	51	+ 4:06	+ 3.15	35	+ 3:50	+ 3.15	71	+ 4:26	+ 3.15	49	+ 4:04
+ 3.30	52	+ 4:22	+ 3.30	35	+ 4:05	+ 3.30	71	+ 4:41	+ 3.30	49	+ 4:19
+ 3.45	53	+ 4:38	+ 3.45	36	+ 4:21	+ 3.45	70	+ 4:55	+ 3.45	50	+ 4:35
+ 4.00	53	+ 4:53	+ 4.00	36	+ 4:36	+ 4.00	70	+ 5:10	+ 4.00	50	+ 4:50
+ 4.15	53	+ 5:08	+ 4.15	36	+ 4:51	+ 4.15	69	+ 5:24	+ 4.15	49	+ 5:04
+ 4.30	54	+ 5:24	+ 4.30	36	+ 5:06	+ 4.30	69	+ 5:39	+ 4.30	49	+ 5:19
+ 4.45	55	+ 5:40	+ 4.45	37	+ 5:22	+ 4.45	68	+ 5:53	+ 4.45	49	+ 5:34
+ 5.00	56	+ 5:56	+ 5.00	37	+ 5:37	+ 5.00	67	- 5:53	+ 5.00	48	+ 5:48
+ 5.15	57	- 5:48	+ 5.15	37	+ 5:52	+ 5.15	67	- 5:38	+ 5.15	47	- 5:58
+ 5.30	58	- 5:32	+ 5.30	37	- 5:53	+ 5.30	66	- 5:24	+ 5.30	46	- 5:44
+ 5.45	60	- 5:15	+ 5.45	37	- 5:38	+ 5.45	66	- 5:09	+ 5.45	45	- 5:30
+ 6.00	61	- 4:59	+ 6.00	38	- 5:22	+ 6.00	66	- 4:54	+ 6.00	44	- 5:16

	A5			A6			A7			A8	
	Inner Fisherman to SW Sunk			SW Sunk to East Barrow Sands			East Barrow to Swin Spitway			Swin Spitway to Blackwater	
Time	Duration	Time at End of Sector	Time	Duration	Time at End of Sector	Time	Duration	Time at End of Sector	Time	Duration	Time at End of Sector
- 6.00	36	- 5:24	- 6.00	22	- 5:38	- 6.00	42	- 5:18	- 6.00	74	- 4:46
- 5.45	37	- 5:08	- 5.45	22	- 5:23	- 5.45	42	- 5:03	- 5.45	73	- 4:32
- 5.30	37	- 4:53	- 5.30	23	- 5:07	- 5.30	42	- 4:48	- 5.30	72	- 4:18
- 5.15	38	- 4:37	- 5.15	23	- 4:52	- 5.15	41	- 4:34	- 5.15	70	- 4:05
- 5.00	38	- 4:22	- 5.00	24	- 4:36	- 5.00	41	- 4:19	- 5.00	69	- 3:51
- 4.45	38	- 4:07	- 4.45	24	- 4:21	- 4.45	41	- 4:04	- 4.45	69	- 3:36
- 4.30	39	- 3:51	- 4.30	24	- 4:06	- 4.30	41	- 3:49	- 4.30	68	- 3:22
- 4.15	39	- 3:36	- 4.15	24	- 3:51	- 4.15	40	- 3:35	- 4.15	67	- 3:08
- 4.00	39	- 3:21	- 4.00	24	- 3:36	- 4.00	40	- 3:20	- 4.00	67	- 2:53
- 3.45	38	- 3:07	- 3.45	24	- 3:21	- 3.45	40	- 3:05	- 3.45	67	- 2:38
- 3.30	38	- 2:52	- 3.30	23	- 3:07	- 3.30	40	- 2:50	- 3.30	66	- 2:24
- 3.15	37	- 2:38	- 3.15	23	- 2:52	- 3.15	40	- 2:35	- 3.15	66	- 2:09
- 3.00	37	- 2:23	- 3.00	23	- 2:37	- 3.00	40	- 2:20	- 3.00	66	- 1:54
- 2.45	36	- 2:09	- 2.45	22	- 2:23	- 2.45	40	- 2:05	- 2.45	67	- 1:38
- 2.30	35	- 1:55	- 2.30	22	- 2:08	- 2.30	40	- 1:50	- 2.30	69	- 1:21
- 2.15	35	- 1:40	- 2.15	21	- 1:54	- 2.15	41	- 1:34	- 2.15	70	- 1:05
- 2.00	34	- 1:26	- 2.00	21	- 1:39	- 2.00	41	- 1:19	- 2.00	71	- 0:49
- 1.45	34	- 1:11	- 1.45	21	- 1:24	- 1.45	42	- 1:03	- 1.45	75	- 0:30
- 1.30	33	- 0:57	- 1.30	21	- 1:09	- 1.30	42	- 0:48	- 1.30	79	- 0:11
- 1.15	33	- 0:42	- 1.15	20	- 0:55	- 1.15	43	- 0:32	- 1.15	82	+ 0:07
- 1.00	33	- 0:27	- 1.00	20	- 0:40	- 1.00	44	- 0:16	- 1.00	86	+ 0:26
- 0.45	33	- 0:12	- 0.45	20	- 0:25	- 0.45	45	HW	- 0.45	91	+ 0:46
- 0.30	33	+ 0:03	- 0.30	20	- 0:10	- 0.30	47	+ 0:17	- 0.30	96	+ 1:06
- 0.15	33	+ 0:18	- 0.15	20	+ 0:05	- 0.15	48	+ 0:33	- 0.15	101	+ 1:26
HW	34	+ 0:34	HW	20	+ 0:20	HW	49	+ 0:49	HW	105	+ 1:45
+ 0.15	34	+ 0:49	+ 0.15	20	+ 0:35	+ 0.15	51	+ 1:06	+ 0.15	107	+ 2:02
+ 0.30	34	+ 1:04	+ 0.30	20	+ 0:50	+ 0.30	52	+ 1:22	+ 0.30	108	+ 2:18
+ 0.45	35	+ 1:20	+ 0.45	20	+ 1:05	+ 0.45	54	+ 1:39	+ 0.45	110	+ 2:35
+ 1.00	35	+ 1:35	+ 1.00	21	+ 1:21	+ 1.00	55	+ 1:55	+ 1.00	112	+ 2:52
+ 1.15	35	+ 1:50	+ 1.15	21	+ 1:36	+ 1.15	55	+ 2:10	+ 1.15	110	+ 3:05
+ 1.30	35	+ 2:05	+ 1.30	21	+ 1:51	+ 1.30	55	+ 2:25	+ 1.30	109	+ 3:19
+ 1.45	35	+ 2:20	+ 1.45	21	+ 2:06	+ 1.45	56	+ 2:41	+ 1.45	108	+ 3:33
+ 2.00	35	+ 2:35	+ 2.00	21	+ 2:21	+ 2.00	56	+ 2:56	+ 2.00	107	+ 3:47
+ 2.15	35	+ 2:50	+ 2.15	21	+ 2:36	+ 2.15	55	+ 3:10	+ 2.15	105	+ 4:00
+ 2.30	35	+ 3:05	+ 2.30	21	+ 2:51	+ 2.30	55	+ 3:25	+ 2.30	103	+ 4:13
+ 2.45	35	+ 3:20	+ 2.45	21	+ 3:06	+ 2.45	54	+ 3:39	+ 2.45	101	+ 4:26
+ 3.00	35	+ 3:35	+ 3.00	21	+ 3:21	+ 3.00	54	+ 3:54	+ 3.00	99	+ 4:39
+ 3.15	35	+ 3:50	+ 3.15	21	+ 3:36	+ 3.15	53	+ 4:08	+ 3.15	97	+ 4:52
+ 3.30	35	+ 4:05	+ 3.30	21	+ 3:51	+ 3.30	52	+ 4:22	+ 3.30	95	+ 5:05
+ 3.45	35	+ 4:20	+ 3.45	21	+ 4:06	+ 3.45	51	+ 4:36	+ 3.45	94	+ 5:19
+ 4.00	35	+ 4:35	+ 4.00	21	+ 4:21	+ 4.00	50	+ 4:50	+ 4.00	92	+ 5:32
+ 4.15	35	+ 4:50	+ 4.15	21	+ 4:36	+ 4.15	49	+ 5:04	+ 4.15	90	+ 5:45
+ 4.30	35	+ 5:05	+ 4.30	21	+ 4:51	+ 4.30	48	+ 5:18	+ 4.30	88	+ 5:58
+ 4.45	35	+ 5:20	+ 4.45	21	+ 5:06	+ 4.45	47	+ 5:32	+ 4.45	87	- 5:48
+ 5.00	35	+ 5:35	+ 5.00	21	+ 5:21	+ 5.00	47	+ 5:47	+ 5.00	85	- 5:35
+ 5.15	35	+ 5:50	+ 5.15	21	+ 5:36	+ 5.15	46	- 5:59	+ 5.15	83	- 5:22
+ 5.30	35	- 5:55	+ 5.30	21	+ 5:51	+ 5.30	45	- 5:45	+ 5.30	82	- 5:08
+ 5.45	35	- 5:40	+ 5.45	21	- 5:54	+ 5.45	45	- 5:30	+ 5.45	81	- 4:54
+ 6.00	35	- 5:25	+ 6.00	21	- 5:39	+ 6.00	44	- 5:16	+ 6.00	79	- 4:41

NORTH BOUND

A - 7 Kts   Table A - Ramsgate to Blackwater via the SW Sunk   7 Kts - A

Neaps | All times relate to HW Sheerness | **Time to cover Sectors (in minutes) at 7.0 Kts**

NORTH BOUND

Time	A1 Ramsgate to North Foreland Duration	A1 Time at End of Sector	Time	A2 North Foreland to East Margate Duration	A2 Time at End of Sector	Time	A3 East Margate to Outer Fisherman Duration	A3 Time at End of Sector	Time	A4 Outer to Inner Fisherman Duration	A4 Time at End of Sector
- 6.00	46	- 5:14	- 6.00	29	- 5:31	- 6.00	56	- 5:04	- 6.00	35	- 5:25
- 5.45	46	- 4:59	- 5.45	29	- 5:16	- 5.45	56	- 4:49	- 5.45	34	- 5:11
- 5.30	47	- 4:43	- 5.30	29	- 5:01	- 5.30	56	- 4:34	- 5.30	33	- 4:57
- 5.15	47	- 4:28	- 5.15	29	- 4:46	- 5.15	56	- 4:19	- 5.15	33	- 4:42
- 5.00	46	- 4:14	- 5.00	29	- 4:31	- 5.00	55	- 4:05	- 5.00	32	- 4:28
- 4.45	46	- 3:59	- 4.45	29	- 4:16	- 4.45	55	- 3:50	- 4.45	32	- 4:13
- 4.30	46	- 3:44	- 4.30	28	- 4:02	- 4.30	55	- 3:35	- 4.30	32	- 3:58
- 4.15	45	- 3:30	- 4.15	28	- 3:47	- 4.15	54	- 3:21	- 4.15	32	- 3:43
- 4.00	45	- 3:15	- 4.00	28	- 3:32	- 4.00	54	- 3:06	- 4.00	31	- 3:29
- 3.45	44	- 3:01	- 3.45	27	- 3:18	- 3.45	53	- 2:52	- 3.45	31	- 3:14
- 3.30	43	- 2:47	- 3.30	27	- 3:03	- 3.30	53	- 2:37	- 3.30	31	- 2:59
- 3.15	41	- 2:34	- 3.15	26	- 2:49	- 3.15	52	- 2:23	- 3.15	30	- 2:45
- 3.00	40	- 2:20	- 3.00	26	- 2:34	- 3.00	52	- 2:08	- 3.00	30	- 2:30
- 2.45	38	- 2:07	- 2.45	25	- 2:20	- 2.45	52	- 1:53	- 2.45	30	- 2:15
- 2.30	37	- 1:53	- 2.30	24	- 2:06	- 2.30	52	- 1:38	- 2.30	29	- 2:01
- 2.15	36	- 1:39	- 2.15	24	- 1:51	- 2.15	52	- 1:23	- 2.15	29	- 1:46
- 2.00	36	- 1:24	- 2.00	23	- 1:37	- 2.00	51	- 1:09	- 2.00	28	- 1:32
- 1.45	35	- 1:10	- 1.45	23	- 1:22	- 1.45	52	- 0:53	- 1.45	28	- 1:17
- 1.30	34	- 0:56	- 1.30	22	- 1:08	- 1.30	52	- 0:38	- 1.30	29	- 1:01
- 1.15	34	- 0:41	- 1.15	22	- 0:53	- 1.15	52	- 0:23	- 1.15	29	- 0:46
- 1.00	34	- 0:26	- 1.00	22	- 0:38	- 1.00	52	- 0:08	- 1.00	29	- 0:31
- 0.45	34	- 0:11	- 0.45	22	- 0:23	- 0.45	53	+ 0:08	- 0.45	30	- 0:15
- 0.30	34	+ 0:04	- 0.30	22	- 0:08	- 0.30	53	+ 0:23	- 0.30	30	HW
- 0.15	34	+ 0:19	- 0.15	22	+ 0:07	- 0.15	54	+ 0:39	- 0.15	31	+ 0:16
HW	35	+ 0:35	HW	22	+ 0:22	HW	54	+ 0:54	HW	32	+ 0:32
+ 0.15	35	+ 0:50	+ 0.15	22	+ 0:37	+ 0.15	55	+ 1:10	+ 0.15	33	+ 0:48
+ 0.30	35	+ 1:05	+ 0.30	23	+ 0:53	+ 0.30	55	+ 1:25	+ 0.30	34	+ 1:04
+ 0.45	36	+ 1:21	+ 0.45	23	+ 1:08	+ 0.45	56	+ 1:41	+ 0.45	34	+ 1:19
+ 1.00	36	+ 1:36	+ 1.00	23	+ 1:23	+ 1.00	56	+ 1:56	+ 1.00	35	+ 1:35
+ 1.15	37	+ 1:52	+ 1.15	24	+ 1:39	+ 1.15	57	+ 2:12	+ 1.15	36	+ 1:51
+ 1.30	38	+ 2:08	+ 1.30	25	+ 1:55	+ 1.30	57	+ 2:27	+ 1.30	36	+ 2:06
+ 1.45	38	+ 2:23	+ 1.45	25	+ 2:10	+ 1.45	57	+ 2:42	+ 1.45	36	+ 2:21
+ 2.00	39	+ 2:39	+ 2.00	26	+ 2:26	+ 2.00	58	+ 2:58	+ 2.00	37	+ 2:37
+ 2.15	40	+ 2:55	+ 2.15	26	+ 2:41	+ 2.15	58	+ 3:13	+ 2.15	37	+ 2:52
+ 2.30	40	+ 3:10	+ 2.30	27	+ 2:57	+ 2.30	58	+ 3:28	+ 2.30	37	+ 3:07
+ 2.45	41	+ 3:26	+ 2.45	27	+ 3:12	+ 2.45	58	+ 3:43	+ 2.45	37	+ 3:22
+ 3.00	41	+ 3:41	+ 3.00	27	+ 3:27	+ 3.00	58	+ 3:58	+ 3.00	38	+ 3:38
+ 3.15	42	+ 3:57	+ 3.15	28	+ 3:43	+ 3.15	58	+ 4:13	+ 3.15	38	+ 3:53
+ 3.30	43	+ 4:13	+ 3.30	28	+ 3:58	+ 3.30	58	+ 4:28	+ 3.30	38	+ 4:08
+ 3.45	43	+ 4:28	+ 3.45	28	+ 4:13	+ 3.45	58	+ 4:43	+ 3.45	38	+ 4:23
+ 4.00	43	+ 4:43	+ 4.00	28	+ 4:28	+ 4.00	58	+ 4:58	+ 4.00	38	+ 4:38
+ 4.15	44	+ 4:59	+ 4.15	28	+ 4:43	+ 4.15	57	+ 5:12	+ 4.15	38	+ 4:53
+ 4.30	44	+ 5:14	+ 4.30	28	+ 4:58	+ 4.30	57	+ 5:27	+ 4.30	38	+ 5:08
+ 4.45	44	+ 5:29	+ 4.45	28	+ 5:13	+ 4.45	57	+ 5:42	+ 4.45	38	+ 5:23
+ 5.00	44	+ 5:44	+ 5.00	28	+ 5:28	+ 5.00	56	+ 5:56	+ 5.00	38	+ 5:38
+ 5.15	44	+ 5:59	+ 5.15	28	+ 5:43	+ 5.15	56	- 5:49	+ 5.15	37	+ 5:52
+ 5.30	45	- 5:45	+ 5.30	29	+ 5:59	+ 5.30	56	- 5:34	+ 5.30	37	- 5:53
+ 5.45	45	- 5:30	+ 5.45	29	- 5:46	+ 5.45	56	- 5:19	+ 5.45	36	- 5:39
+ 6.00	45	- 5:15	+ 6.00	29	- 5:31	+ 6.00	56	- 5:04	+ 6.00	36	- 5:24

Time	A5 Inner Fisherman to SW Sunk Duration	A5 Time at End of Sector	Time	A6 SW Sunk to East Barrow Sands Duration	A6 Time at End of Sector	Time	A7 East Barrow to Swin Spitway Duration	A7 Time at End of Sector	Time	A8 Swin Spitway to Blackwater Duration	A8 Time at End of Sector
- 6.00	30	- 5:30	- 6.00	18	- 5:42	- 6.00	37	- 5:23	- 6.00	67	- 4:53
- 5.45	30	- 5:15	- 5.45	18	- 5:27	- 5.45	37	- 5:08	- 5.45	66	- 4:39
- 5.30	31	- 4:59	- 5.30	19	- 5:11	- 5.30	37	- 4:53	- 5.30	66	- 4:24
- 5.15	31	- 4:44	- 5.15	19	- 4:56	- 5.15	37	- 4:38	- 5.15	65	- 4:10
- 5.00	31	- 4:29	- 5.00	19	- 4:41	- 5.00	36	- 4:24	- 5.00	64	- 3:56
- 4.45	31	- 4:14	- 4.45	19	- 4:26	- 4.45	36	- 4:09	- 4.45	64	- 3:41
- 4.30	31	- 3:59	- 4.30	19	- 4:11	- 4.30	36	- 3:54	- 4.30	64	- 3:26
- 4.15	31	- 3:44	- 4.15	19	- 3:56	- 4.15	36	- 3:39	- 4.15	64	- 3:11
- 4.00	31	- 3:29	- 4.00	19	- 3:41	- 4.00	36	- 3:24	- 4.00	63	- 2:57
- 3.45	31	- 3:14	- 3.45	19	- 3:26	- 3.45	36	- 3:09	- 3.45	63	- 2:42
- 3.30	31	- 2:59	- 3.30	19	- 3:11	- 3.30	36	- 2:54	- 3.30	63	- 2:27
- 3.15	30	- 2:45	- 3.15	19	- 2:56	- 3.15	36	- 2:39	- 3.15	63	- 2:12
- 3.00	30	- 2:30	- 3.00	19	- 2:41	- 3.00	36	- 2:24	- 3.00	63	- 1:57
- 2.45	30	- 2:15	- 2.45	18	- 2:27	- 2.45	36	- 2:09	- 2.45	64	- 1:41
- 2.30	30	- 2:00	- 2.30	18	- 2:12	- 2.30	36	- 1:54	- 2.30	64	- 1:26
- 2.15	29	- 1:46	- 2.15	18	- 1:57	- 2.15	37	- 1:38	- 2.15	65	- 1:10
- 2.00	29	- 1:31	- 2.00	18	- 1:42	- 2.00	37	- 1:23	- 2.00	65	- 0:55
- 1.45	29	- 1:16	- 1.45	18	- 1:27	- 1.45	37	- 1:08	- 1.45	67	- 0:38
- 1.30	29	- 1:01	- 1.30	17	- 1:13	- 1.30	37	- 0:53	- 1.30	69	- 0:21
- 1.15	29	- 0:46	- 1.15	17	- 0:58	- 1.15	37	- 0:38	- 1.15	70	- 0:05
- 1.00	29	- 0:31	- 1.00	17	- 0:43	- 1.00	38	- 0:22	- 1.00	72	+ 0:12
- 0.45	29	- 0:16	- 0.45	17	- 0:28	- 0.45	38	- 0:07	- 0.45	74	+ 0:29
- 0.30	29	- 0:01	- 0.30	17	- 0:13	- 0.30	39	+ 0:09	- 0.30	76	+ 0:46
- 0.15	29	+ 0:14	- 0.15	17	+ 0:02	- 0.15	39	+ 0:24	- 0.15	78	+ 1:03
HW	29	+ 0:29	HW	17	+ 0:17	HW	39	+ 0:39	HW	80	+ 1:20
+ 0.15	29	+ 0:44	+ 0.15	17	+ 0:32	+ 0.15	40	+ 0:55	+ 0.15	81	+ 1:36
+ 0.30	29	+ 0:59	+ 0.30	17	+ 0:47	+ 0.30	41	+ 1:11	+ 0.30	81	+ 1:51
+ 0.45	29	+ 1:14	+ 0.45	17	+ 1:02	+ 0.45	42	+ 1:27	+ 0.45	82	+ 2:07
+ 1.00	29	+ 1:29	+ 1.00	17	+ 1:17	+ 1.00	43	+ 1:43	+ 1.00	83	+ 2:23
+ 1.15	29	+ 1:44	+ 1.15	17	+ 1:32	+ 1.15	43	+ 1:58	+ 1.15	83	+ 2:38
+ 1.30	29	+ 1:59	+ 1.30	17	+ 1:47	+ 1.30	43	+ 2:13	+ 1.30	83	+ 2:53
+ 1.45	29	+ 2:14	+ 1.45	17	+ 2:02	+ 1.45	43	+ 2:28	+ 1.45	82	+ 3:07
+ 2.00	29	+ 2:29	+ 2.00	17	+ 2:17	+ 2.00	43	+ 2:43	+ 2.00	82	+ 3:22
+ 2.15	29	+ 2:44	+ 2.15	17	+ 2:32	+ 2.15	43	+ 2:58	+ 2.15	81	+ 3:36
+ 2.30	29	+ 2:59	+ 2.30	18	+ 2:48	+ 2.30	43	+ 3:13	+ 2.30	80	+ 3:50
+ 2.45	29	+ 3:14	+ 2.45	18	+ 3:03	+ 2.45	43	+ 3:28	+ 2.45	80	+ 4:05
+ 3.00	29	+ 3:29	+ 3.00	18	+ 3:18	+ 3.00	43	+ 3:43	+ 3.00	79	+ 4:19
+ 3.15	29	+ 3:44	+ 3.15	18	+ 3:33	+ 3.15	42	+ 3:57	+ 3.15	78	+ 4:33
+ 3.30	29	+ 3:59	+ 3.30	18	+ 3:48	+ 3.30	42	+ 4:12	+ 3.30	77	+ 4:47
+ 3.45	29	+ 4:14	+ 3.45	18	+ 4:03	+ 3.45	41	+ 4:26	+ 3.45	76	+ 5:01
+ 4.00	30	+ 4:30	+ 4.00	18	+ 4:18	+ 4.00	41	+ 4:41	+ 4.00	76	+ 5:16
+ 4.15	30	+ 4:45	+ 4.15	18	+ 4:33	+ 4.15	41	+ 4:56	+ 4.15	75	+ 5:30
+ 4.30	30	+ 5:00	+ 4.30	18	+ 4:48	+ 4.30	40	+ 5:10	+ 4.30	74	+ 5:44
+ 4.45	30	+ 5:15	+ 4.45	18	+ 5:03	+ 4.45	40	+ 5:25	+ 4.45	73	+ 5:58
+ 5.00	30	+ 5:30	+ 5.00	18	+ 5:18	+ 5.00	39	+ 5:39	+ 5.00	72	- 5:48
+ 5.15	30	+ 5:45	+ 5.15	18	+ 5:33	+ 5.15	39	+ 5:54	+ 5.15	72	- 5:33
+ 5.30	30	- 6:00	+ 5.30	18	+ 5:48	+ 5.30	39	- 5:51	+ 5.30	71	- 5:19
+ 5.45	30	- 5:45	+ 5.45	18	- 5:57	+ 5.45	39	- 5:36	+ 5.45	70	- 5:05
+ 6.00	30	- 5:30	+ 6.00	18	- 5:42	+ 6.00	38	- 5:22	+ 6.00	70	- 4:50

A - 7 Kts

Table A - Ramsgate to Blackwater via the SW Sunk

7 Kts - A

Time to cover Sectors (in minutes) at 7.0 kts

All times relate to HW Sheerness

Springs

NORTH BOUND

A1 – Ramsgate to North Foreland

Time	Duration	Time at End of Sector
- 6.00	51	- 5:09
- 5.45	51	- 4:54
- 5.30	52	- 4:38
- 5.15	52	- 4:23
- 5.00	52	- 4:08
- 4.45	52	- 3:53
- 4.30	52	- 3:38
- 4.15	50	- 3:25
- 4.00	48	- 3:12
- 3.45	46	- 2:59
- 3.30	44	- 2:46
- 3.15	42	- 2:33
- 3.00	40	- 2:20
- 2.45	37	- 2:08
- 2.30	35	- 1:55
- 2.15	34	- 1:41
- 2.00	33	- 1:27
- 1.45	32	- 1:13
- 1.30	30	- 1:00
- 1.15	31	- 0:44
- 1.00	31	- 0:29
- 0.45	31	- 0:14
- 0.30	31	+ 0:01
- 0.15	31	+ 0:16
HW	31	+ 0:31
+ 0.15	32	+ 0:47
+ 0.30	32	+ 1:02
+ 0.45	33	+ 1:18
+ 1.00	34	+ 1:34
+ 1.15	35	+ 1:50
+ 1.30	36	+ 2:06
+ 1.45	37	+ 2:22
+ 2.00	38	+ 2:38
+ 2.15	39	+ 2:54
+ 2.30	40	+ 3:10
+ 2.45	41	+ 3:26
+ 3.00	42	+ 3:42
+ 3.15	43	+ 3:58
+ 3.30	44	+ 4:14
+ 3.45	44	+ 4:29
+ 4.00	44	+ 4:44
+ 4.15	45	+ 5:00
+ 4.30	45	+ 5:15
+ 4.45	46	+ 5:31
+ 5.00	47	+ 5:47
+ 5.15	47	- 5:58
+ 5.30	48	- 5:42
+ 5.45	49	- 5:26
+ 6.00	50	- 5:10

A2 – North Foreland to East Margate

Time	Duration	Time at End of Sector
- 6.00	31	- 5:29
- 5.45	31	- 5:14
- 5.30	31	- 4:59
- 5.15	31	- 4:44
- 5.00	31	- 4:29
- 4.45	31	- 4:14
- 4.30	30	- 4:00
- 4.15	30	- 3:45
- 4.00	30	- 3:30
- 3.45	29	- 3:16
- 3.30	28	- 3:02
- 3.15	27	- 2:48
- 3.00	26	- 2:34
- 2.45	25	- 2:20
- 2.30	24	- 2:06
- 2.15	22	- 1:53
- 2.00	21	- 1:39
- 1.45	20	- 1:25
- 1.30	20	- 1:10
- 1.15	19	- 0:56
- 1.00	18	- 0:42
- 0.45	19	- 0:26
- 0.30	19	- 0:11
- 0.15	19	+ 0:04
HW	19	+ 0:19
+ 0.15	20	+ 0:35
+ 0.30	21	+ 0:51
+ 0.45	21	+ 1:06
+ 1.00	22	+ 1:22
+ 1.15	23	+ 1:38
+ 1.30	24	+ 1:54
+ 1.45	25	+ 2:10
+ 2.00	26	+ 2:26
+ 2.15	27	+ 2:42
+ 2.30	27	+ 2:57
+ 2.45	28	+ 3:13
+ 3.00	29	+ 3:29
+ 3.15	29	+ 3:44
+ 3.30	30	+ 4:00
+ 3.45	30	+ 4:15
+ 4.00	30	+ 4:30
+ 4.15	30	+ 4:45
+ 4.30	30	+ 5:00
+ 4.45	30	+ 5:15
+ 5.00	30	+ 5:30
+ 5.15	31	+ 5:46
+ 5.30	31	- 5:59
+ 5.45	31	- 5:44
+ 6.00	31	- 5:29

A3 – East Margate to Outer Fisherman

Time	Duration	Time at End of Sector
- 6.00	57	- 5:03
- 5.45	56	- 4:49
- 5.30	56	- 4:34
- 5.15	56	- 4:19
- 5.00	56	- 4:04
- 4.45	55	- 3:50
- 4.30	55	- 3:35
- 4.15	54	- 3:21
- 4.00	53	- 3:07
- 3.45	53	- 2:52
- 3.30	52	- 2:38
- 3.15	52	- 2:23
- 3.00	51	- 2:09
- 2.45	51	- 1:54
- 2.30	51	- 1:39
- 2.15	50	- 1:25
- 2.00	50	- 1:10
- 1.45	50	- 0:55
- 1.30	51	- 0:39
- 1.15	51	- 0:24
- 1.00	51	- 0:09
- 0.45	52	+ 0:07
- 0.30	53	+ 0:23
- 0.15	53	+ 0:38
HW	54	+ 0:54
+ 0.15	55	+ 1:10
+ 0.30	56	+ 1:26
+ 0.45	57	+ 1:42
+ 1.00	57	+ 1:57
+ 1.15	58	+ 2:13
+ 1.30	59	+ 2:29
+ 1.45	59	+ 2:44
+ 2.00	60	+ 3:00
+ 2.15	60	+ 3:15
+ 2.30	60	+ 3:30
+ 2.45	60	+ 3:45
+ 3.00	60	+ 4:00
+ 3.15	60	+ 4:15
+ 3.30	60	+ 4:30
+ 3.45	59	+ 4:44
+ 4.00	59	+ 4:59
+ 4.15	59	+ 5:14
+ 4.30	58	+ 5:28
+ 4.45	58	+ 5:43
+ 5.00	57	+ 5:57
+ 5.15	57	- 5:48
+ 5.30	57	- 5:33
+ 5.45	56	- 5:19
+ 6.00	56	- 5:04

A4 – Outer to Inner Fisherman

Time	Duration	Time at End of Sector
- 6.00	35	- 5:25
- 5.45	35	- 5:10
- 5.30	34	- 4:56
- 5.15	33	- 4:42
- 5.00	32	- 4:28
- 4.45	32	- 4:13
- 4.30	31	- 3:59
- 4.15	31	- 3:44
- 4.00	30	- 3:30
- 3.45	30	- 3:15
- 3.30	29	- 3:01
- 3.15	29	- 2:46
- 3.00	28	- 2:32
- 2.45	27	- 2:18
- 2.30	27	- 2:03
- 2.15	26	- 1:49
- 2.00	25	- 1:35
- 1.45	25	- 1:20
- 1.30	26	- 1:04
- 1.15	26	- 0:49
- 1.00	26	- 0:34
- 0.45	28	- 0:17
- 0.30	29	- 0:01
- 0.15	30	+ 0:15
HW	31	+ 0:31
+ 0.15	33	+ 0:48
+ 0.30	34	+ 1:04
+ 0.45	36	+ 1:21
+ 1.00	37	+ 1:37
+ 1.15	38	+ 1:53
+ 1.30	38	+ 2:08
+ 1.45	39	+ 2:24
+ 2.00	39	+ 2:39
+ 2.15	40	+ 2:55
+ 2.30	40	+ 3:10
+ 2.45	40	+ 3:25
+ 3.00	41	+ 3:41
+ 3.15	41	+ 3:56
+ 3.30	41	+ 4:11
+ 3.45	41	+ 4:26
+ 4.00	41	+ 4:41
+ 4.15	41	+ 4:56
+ 4.30	41	+ 5:11
+ 4.45	41	+ 5:26
+ 5.00	41	+ 5:41
+ 5.15	40	+ 5:55
+ 5.30	39	- 5:51
+ 5.45	38	- 5:37
+ 6.00	37	- 5:23

A5 – Inner Fisherman to SW Sunk

Time	Duration	Time at End of Sector
- 6.00	30	- 5:30
- 5.45	31	- 5:14
- 5.30	31	- 4:59
- 5.15	32	- 4:43
- 5.00	32	- 4:28
- 4.45	32	- 4:13
- 4.30	32	- 3:58
- 4.15	32	- 3:43
- 4.00	32	- 3:28
- 3.45	32	- 3:13
- 3.30	32	- 2:58
- 3.15	31	- 2:44
- 3.00	31	- 2:29
- 2.45	31	- 2:14
- 2.30	30	- 2:00
- 2.15	30	- 1:45
- 2.00	29	- 1:31
- 1.45	29	- 1:16
- 1.30	29	- 1:01
- 1.15	29	- 0:46
- 1.00	28	- 0:32
- 0.45	28	- 0:17
- 0.30	28	- 0:02
- 0.15	29	+ 0:14
HW	29	+ 0:29
+ 0.15	29	+ 0:44
+ 0.30	29	+ 0:59
+ 0.45	29	+ 1:14
+ 1.00	30	+ 1:30
+ 1.15	30	+ 1:45
+ 1.30	30	+ 2:00
+ 1.45	30	+ 2:15
+ 2.00	30	+ 2:30
+ 2.15	30	+ 2:45
+ 2.30	30	+ 3:00
+ 2.45	30	+ 3:15
+ 3.00	30	+ 3:30
+ 3.15	30	+ 3:45
+ 3.30	30	+ 4:00
+ 3.45	30	+ 4:15
+ 4.00	30	+ 4:30
+ 4.15	30	+ 4:45
+ 4.30	30	+ 5:00
+ 4.45	30	+ 5:15
+ 5.00	30	+ 5:30
+ 5.15	30	+ 5:45
+ 5.30	30	- 6:00
+ 5.45	30	- 5:45
+ 6.00	30	- 5:30

A6 – SW Sunk to East Barrow Sands

Time	Duration	Time at End of Sector
- 6.00	19	- 5:41
- 5.45	19	- 5:26
- 5.30	19	- 5:11
- 5.15	20	- 4:55
- 5.00	20	- 4:40
- 4.45	20	- 4:25
- 4.30	20	- 4:10
- 4.15	21	- 3:54
- 4.00	21	- 3:39
- 3.45	20	- 3:25
- 3.30	20	- 3:10
- 3.15	20	- 2:55
- 3.00	19	- 2:41
- 2.45	19	- 2:26
- 2.30	19	- 2:11
- 2.15	18	- 1:57
- 2.00	18	- 1:42
- 1.45	18	- 1:27
- 1.30	18	- 1:12
- 1.15	17	- 0:58
- 1.00	17	- 0:43
- 0.45	17	- 0:28
- 0.30	17	- 0:13
- 0.15	17	+ 0:02
HW	17	+ 0:17
+ 0.15	17	+ 0:32
+ 0.30	17	+ 0:47
+ 0.45	17	+ 1:02
+ 1.00	18	+ 1:18
+ 1.15	18	+ 1:33
+ 1.30	18	+ 1:48
+ 1.45	18	+ 2:03
+ 2.00	18	+ 2:18
+ 2.15	18	+ 2:33
+ 2.30	18	+ 2:48
+ 2.45	18	+ 3:03
+ 3.00	18	+ 3:18
+ 3.15	18	+ 3:33
+ 3.30	18	+ 3:48
+ 3.45	18	+ 4:03
+ 4.00	18	+ 4:18
+ 4.15	18	+ 4:33
+ 4.30	18	+ 4:48
+ 4.45	18	+ 5:03
+ 5.00	18	+ 5:18
+ 5.15	18	+ 5:33
+ 5.30	18	+ 5:48
+ 5.45	18	- 5:57
+ 6.00	18	- 5:42

A7 – East Barrow to Swin Spitway

Time	Duration	Time at End of Sector
- 6.00	37	- 5:23
- 5.45	36	- 5:09
- 5.30	36	- 4:54
- 5.15	36	- 4:39
- 5.00	35	- 4:25
- 4.45	35	- 4:10
- 4.30	35	- 3:55
- 4.15	35	- 3:40
- 4.00	35	- 3:25
- 3.45	35	- 3:10
- 3.30	35	- 2:55
- 3.15	35	- 2:40
- 3.00	35	- 2:25
- 2.45	35	- 2:10
- 2.30	35	- 1:55
- 2.15	35	- 1:40
- 2.00	35	- 1:25
- 1.45	36	- 1:09
- 1.30	36	- 0:54
- 1.15	37	- 0:38
- 1.00	37	- 0:23
- 0.45	38	- 0:07
- 0.30	38	+ 0:08
- 0.15	39	+ 0:24
HW	40	+ 0:40
+ 0.15	41	+ 0:56
+ 0.30	43	+ 1:13
+ 0.45	44	+ 1:29
+ 1.00	46	+ 1:46
+ 1.15	46	+ 2:01
+ 1.30	46	+ 2:16
+ 1.45	46	+ 2:31
+ 2.00	47	+ 2:47
+ 2.15	46	+ 3:01
+ 2.30	46	+ 3:16
+ 2.45	45	+ 3:30
+ 3.00	45	+ 3:45
+ 3.15	44	+ 3:59
+ 3.30	44	+ 4:14
+ 3.45	43	+ 4:28
+ 4.00	42	+ 4:42
+ 4.15	42	+ 4:57
+ 4.30	41	+ 5:11
+ 4.45	40	+ 5:25
+ 5.00	40	+ 5:40
+ 5.15	39	+ 5:54
+ 5.30	39	- 5:51
+ 5.45	39	- 5:36
+ 6.00	38	- 5:22

A8 – Swin Spitway to Blackwater

Time	Duration	Time at End of Sector
- 6.00	65	- 4:55
- 5.45	64	- 4:41
- 5.30	63	- 4:27
- 5.15	62	- 4:13
- 5.00	61	- 3:59
- 4.45	61	- 3:44
- 4.30	60	- 3:30
- 4.15	60	- 3:15
- 4.00	59	- 3:01
- 3.45	59	- 2:46
- 3.30	59	- 2:31
- 3.15	59	- 2:16
- 3.00	59	- 2:01
- 2.45	60	- 1:45
- 2.30	60	- 1:30
- 2.15	61	- 1:14
- 2.00	62	- 0:58
- 1.45	65	- 0:40
- 1.30	67	- 0:23
- 1.15	70	- 0:05
- 1.00	73	+ 0:13
- 0.45	75	+ 0:30
- 0.30	78	+ 0:48
- 0.15	81	+ 1:06
HW	84	+ 1:24
+ 0.15	86	+ 1:41
+ 0.30	88	+ 1:58
+ 0.45	91	+ 2:16
+ 1.00	93	+ 2:33
+ 1.15	92	+ 2:47
+ 1.30	91	+ 3:01
+ 1.45	90	+ 3:15
+ 2.00	90	+ 3:30
+ 2.15	88	+ 3:43
+ 2.30	86	+ 3:56
+ 2.45	84	+ 4:09
+ 3.00	82	+ 4:22
+ 3.15	81	+ 4:36
+ 3.30	80	+ 4:50
+ 3.45	79	+ 5:04
+ 4.00	78	+ 5:18
+ 4.15	77	+ 5:32
+ 4.30	75	+ 5:45
+ 4.45	74	+ 5:59
+ 5.00	73	- 5:47
+ 5.15	72	- 5:33
+ 5.30	71	- 5:19
+ 5.45	70	- 5:05
+ 6.00	69	- 4:51

Table B - Ramsgate to Essex Rivers via Fisherman's and Foulger's Gats

Neaps — All times relate to HW Sheerness — **Time to cover Sectors (in minutes) at 4.0 Kts**

NORTH BOUND

	B1 North Foreland to Tongue			B2 Tongue to Long Sand Outer			B3 Long Sand Outer to Black Deep			B4 Black Deep to NE Middle	
Time	Duration	Time at End of Sector	Time	Duration	Time at End of Sector	Time	Duration	Time at End of Sector	Time	Duration	Time at End of Sector
- 6.00	123	- 3:57	- 6.00	77	- 4:43	- 6.00	128	- 3:52	- 6.00	69	- 4:51
- 5.45	121	- 3:44	- 5.45	77	- 4:28	- 5.45	127	- 3:38	- 5.45	69	- 4:36
- 5.30	120	- 3:30	- 5.30	78	- 4:12	- 5.30	126	- 3:24	- 5.30	68	- 4:22
- 5.15	119	- 3:16	- 5.15	78	- 3:57	- 5.15	124	- 3:11	- 5.15	67	- 4:08
- 5.00	117	- 3:03	- 5.00	78	- 3:42	- 5.00	123	- 2:57	- 5.00	66	- 3:54
- 4.45	115	- 2:50	- 4.45	77	- 3:28	- 4.45	121	- 2:44	- 4.45	66	- 3:39
- 4.30	112	- 2:38	- 4.30	75	- 3:15	- 4.30	118	- 2:32	- 4.30	66	- 3:24
- 4.15	109	- 2:26	- 4.15	74	- 3:01	- 4.15	115	- 2:20	- 4.15	65	- 3:10
- 4.00	107	- 2:13	- 4.00	73	- 2:47	- 4.00	113	- 2:07	- 4.00	65	- 2:55
- 3.45	103	- 2:02	- 3.45	71	- 2:34	- 3.45	110	- 1:55	- 3.45	66	- 2:39
- 3.30	99	- 1:51	- 3.30	69	- 2:21	- 3.30	107	- 1:43	- 3.30	66	- 2:24
- 3.15	96	- 1:39	- 3.15	67	- 2:08	- 3.15	104	- 1:31	- 3.15	67	- 2:08
- 3.00	92	- 1:28	- 3.00	65	- 1:55	- 3.00	101	- 1:19	- 3.00	67	- 1:53
- 2.45	89	- 1:16	- 2.45	63	- 1:42	- 2.45	98	- 1:07	- 2.45	68	- 1:37
- 2.30	86	- 1:04	- 2.30	61	- 1:29	- 2.30	95	- 0:55	- 2.30	69	- 1:21
- 2.15	83	- 0:52	- 2.15	59	- 1:16	- 2.15	93	- 0:42	- 2.15	70	- 1:05
- 2.00	80	- 0:40	- 2.00	57	- 1:03	- 2.00	90	- 0:30	- 2.00	71	- 0:49
- 1.45	79	- 0:26	- 1.45	56	- 0:49	- 1.45	90	- 0:15	- 1.45	74	- 0:31
- 1.30	79	- 0:11	- 1.30	54	- 0:36	- 1.30	90	HW	- 1.30	76	- 0:14
- 1.15	78	+ 0:03	- 1.15	53	- 0:22	- 1.15	90	+ 0:15	- 1.15	78	+ 0:03
- 1.00	78	+ 0:18	- 1.00	52	- 0:08	- 1.00	90	+ 0:30	- 1.00	81	+ 0:21
- 0.45	78	+ 0:33	- 0.45	51	+ 0:06	- 0.45	91	+ 0:46	- 0.45	84	+ 0:39
- 0.30	79	+ 0:49	- 0.30	50	+ 0:20	- 0.30	93	+ 1:03	- 0.30	88	+ 0:58
- 0.15	80	+ 1:05	- 0.15	49	+ 0:34	- 0.15	94	+ 1:19	- 0.15	91	+ 1:16
HW	81	+ 1:21	HW	49	+ 0:49	HW	96	+ 1:36	HW	95	+ 1:35
+ 0.15	83	+ 1:38	+ 0.15	49	+ 1:04	+ 0.15	98	+ 1:53	+ 0.15	97	+ 1:52
+ 0.30	86	+ 1:56	+ 0.30	49	+ 1:19	+ 0.30	100	+ 2:10	+ 0.30	100	+ 2:10
+ 0.45	88	+ 2:13	+ 0.45	49	+ 1:34	+ 0.45	102	+ 2:27	+ 0.45	103	+ 2:28
+ 1.00	90	+ 2:30	+ 1.00	49	+ 1:49	+ 1.00	104	+ 2:44	+ 1.00	106	+ 2:46
+ 1.15	93	+ 2:48	+ 1.15	49	+ 2:04	+ 1.15	105	+ 3:00	+ 1.15	106	+ 3:01
+ 1.30	96	+ 3:06	+ 1.30	50	+ 2:20	+ 1.30	107	+ 3:17	+ 1.30	106	+ 3:16
+ 1.45	98	+ 3:23	+ 1.45	50	+ 2:35	+ 1.45	108	+ 3:33	+ 1.45	107	+ 3:32
+ 2.00	101	+ 3:41	+ 2.00	51	+ 2:51	+ 2.00	110	+ 3:50	+ 2.00	107	+ 3:47
+ 2.15	103	+ 3:58	+ 2.15	52	+ 3:07	+ 2.15	111	+ 4:06	+ 2.15	105	+ 4:00
+ 2.30	106	+ 4:16	+ 2.30	53	+ 3:23	+ 2.30	112	+ 4:22	+ 2.30	103	+ 4:13
+ 2.45	108	+ 4:33	+ 2.45	53	+ 3:38	+ 2.45	113	+ 4:38	+ 2.45	101	+ 4:26
+ 3.00	111	+ 4:51	+ 3.00	54	+ 3:54	+ 3.00	114	+ 4:54	+ 3.00	99	+ 4:39
+ 3.15	112	+ 5:07	+ 3.15	55	+ 4:10	+ 3.15	115	+ 5:10	+ 3.15	97	+ 4:52
+ 3.30	113	+ 5:23	+ 3.30	57	+ 4:27	+ 3.30	116	+ 5:26	+ 3.30	95	+ 5:05
+ 3.45	114	+ 5:39	+ 3.45	58	+ 4:43	+ 3.45	117	+ 5:42	+ 3.45	92	+ 5:17
+ 4.00	116	+ 5:56	+ 4.00	59	+ 4:59	+ 4.00	118	+ 5:58	+ 4.00	90	+ 5:30
+ 4.15	117	- 5:48	+ 4.15	60	+ 5:15	+ 4.15	121	- 5:44	+ 4.15	87	+ 5:42
+ 4.30	118	- 5:32	+ 4.30	62	+ 5:32	+ 4.30	124	- 5:26	+ 4.30	85	+ 5:55
+ 4.45	119	- 5:16	+ 4.45	64	+ 5:49	+ 4.45	126	- 5:09	+ 4.45	82	- 5:53
+ 5.00	120	- 5:00	+ 5.00	65	- 5:55	+ 5.00	129	- 4:51	+ 5.00	79	- 5:41
+ 5.15	121	- 4:44	+ 5.15	65	- 5:40	+ 5.15	128	- 4:37	+ 5.15	78	- 5:27
+ 5.30	121	- 4:29	+ 5.30	65	- 5:25	+ 5.30	126	- 4:24	+ 5.30	77	- 5:13
+ 5.45	122	- 4:13	+ 5.45	65	- 5:10	+ 5.45	125	- 4:10	+ 5.45	76	- 4:59
+ 6.00	123	- 3:57	+ 6.00	64	- 4:56	+ 6.00	123	- 3:57	+ 6.00	74	- 4:46

Via Foulger's Gat and Little Sunk

	B5 NE Middle to Mid-Point Spitway			B6 Outer Fisherman to Blk Deep No 8			B7 Blk Deep No 8 to Barrow Deep			B8 Barrow Deep to Mid-Spitway	
Time	Duration	Time at End of Sector	Time	Duration	Time at End of Sector	Time	Duration	Time at End of Sector	Time	Duration	Time at End of Sector
- 6.00	66	- 4:54	- 6.00	56	- 5:04	- 6.00	69	- 4:51	- 6.00	103	- 4:17
- 5.45	65	- 4:40	- 5.45	55	- 4:50	- 5.45	70	- 4:35	- 5.45	102	- 4:03
- 5.30	63	- 4:27	- 5.30	54	- 4:36	- 5.30	71	- 4:19	- 5.30	102	- 3:48
- 5.15	62	- 4:13	- 5.15	52	- 4:23	- 5.15	72	- 4:03	- 5.15	101	- 3:34
- 5.00	61	- 3:59	- 5.00	51	- 4:09	- 5.00	73	- 3:47	- 5.00	100	- 3:20
- 4.45	61	- 3:44	- 4.45	50	- 3:55	- 4.45	73	- 3:32	- 4.45	100	- 3:05
- 4.30	61	- 3:29	- 4.30	49	- 3:41	- 4.30	73	- 3:17	- 4.30	100	- 2:50
- 4.15	61	- 3:14	- 4.15	49	- 3:26	- 4.15	73	- 3:02	- 4.15	99	- 2:36
- 4.00	60	- 3:00	- 4.00	48	- 3:12	- 4.00	73	- 2:47	- 4.00	99	- 2:21
- 3.45	61	- 2:44	- 3.45	47	- 2:58	- 3.45	72	- 2:33	- 3.45	100	- 2:05
- 3.30	61	- 2:29	- 3.30	45	- 2:45	- 3.30	71	- 2:19	- 3.30	100	- 1:50
- 3.15	62	- 2:13	- 3.15	44	- 2:31	- 3.15	70	- 2:05	- 3.15	101	- 1:34
- 3.00	62	- 1:58	- 3.00	43	- 2:17	- 3.00	69	- 1:51	- 3.00	101	- 1:19
- 2.45	64	- 1:41	- 2.45	43	- 2:02	- 2.45	67	- 1:38	- 2.45	103	- 1:02
- 2.30	65	- 1:25	- 2.30	42	- 1:48	- 2.30	66	- 1:24	- 2.30	104	- 0:46
- 2.15	67	- 1:08	- 2.15	42	- 1:33	- 2.15	65	- 1:10	- 2.15	106	- 0:29
- 2.00	68	- 0:52	- 2.00	41	- 1:19	- 2.00	63	- 0:57	- 2.00	107	- 0:13
- 1.45	71	- 0:34	- 1.45	42	- 1:03	- 1.45	62	- 0:43	- 1.45	111	+ 0:06
- 1.30	73	- 0:17	- 1.30	42	- 0:48	- 1.30	62	- 0:28	- 1.30	115	+ 0:25
- 1.15	76	+ 0:01	- 1.15	43	- 0:32	- 1.15	61	- 0:14	- 1.15	118	+ 0:43
- 1.00	78	+ 0:18	- 1.00	44	- 0:16	- 1.00	60	HW	- 1.00	122	+ 1:02
- 0.45	82	+ 0:37	- 0.45	46	+ 0:01	- 0.45	59	+ 0:14	- 0.45	126	+ 1:21
- 0.30	87	+ 0:57	- 0.30	48	+ 0:18	- 0.30	59	+ 0:29	- 0.30	130	+ 1:40
- 0.15	91	+ 1:16	- 0.15	49	+ 0:34	- 0.15	59	+ 0:44	- 0.15	134	+ 1:59
HW	95	+ 1:35	HW	51	+ 0:51	HW	59	+ 0:59	HW	138	+ 2:18
+ 0.15	99	+ 1:54	+ 0.15	53	+ 1:08	+ 0.15	59	+ 1:14	+ 0.15	141	+ 2:36
+ 0.30	102	+ 2:12	+ 0.30	55	+ 1:25	+ 0.30	59	+ 1:29	+ 0.30	144	+ 2:54
+ 0.45	105	+ 2:30	+ 0.45	57	+ 1:42	+ 0.45	59	+ 1:44	+ 0.45	147	+ 3:12
+ 1.00	108	+ 2:48	+ 1.00	59	+ 1:59	+ 1.00	59	+ 1:59	+ 1.00	150	+ 3:30
+ 1.15	108	+ 3:03	+ 1.15	60	+ 2:15	+ 1.15	59	+ 2:14	+ 1.15	149	+ 3:44
+ 1.30	108	+ 3:18	+ 1.30	61	+ 2:31	+ 1.30	59	+ 2:29	+ 1.30	148	+ 3:58
+ 1.45	108	+ 3:33	+ 1.45	62	+ 2:47	+ 1.45	59	+ 2:44	+ 1.45	147	+ 4:12
+ 2.00	108	+ 3:48	+ 2.00	63	+ 3:03	+ 2.00	59	+ 2:59	+ 2.00	146	+ 4:26
+ 2.15	106	+ 4:01	+ 2.15	64	+ 3:19	+ 2.15	59	+ 3:14	+ 2.15	144	+ 4:39
+ 2.30	104	+ 4:14	+ 2.30	64	+ 3:34	+ 2.30	59	+ 3:29	+ 2.30	141	+ 4:51
+ 2.45	102	+ 4:27	+ 2.45	65	+ 3:50	+ 2.45	59	+ 3:44	+ 2.45	139	+ 5:04
+ 3.00	99	+ 4:39	+ 3.00	66	+ 4:06	+ 3.00	60	+ 4:00	+ 3.00	137	+ 5:17
+ 3.15	97	+ 4:52	+ 3.15	66	+ 4:21	+ 3.15	60	+ 4:15	+ 3.15	134	+ 5:29
+ 3.30	95	+ 5:05	+ 3.30	66	+ 4:36	+ 3.30	60	+ 4:30	+ 3.30	131	+ 5:41
+ 3.45	92	+ 5:17	+ 3.45	66	+ 4:51	+ 3.45	61	+ 4:46	+ 3.45	128	+ 5:53
+ 4.00	90	+ 5:30	+ 4.00	67	+ 5:07	+ 4.00	61	+ 5:01	+ 4.00	125	- 5:55
+ 4.15	87	+ 5:42	+ 4.15	66	+ 5:21	+ 4.15	62	+ 5:17	+ 4.15	123	- 5:42
+ 4.30	84	+ 5:54	+ 4.30	66	+ 5:36	+ 4.30	62	+ 5:32	+ 4.30	120	- 5:30
+ 4.45	81	- 5:54	+ 4.45	65	+ 5:50	+ 4.45	63	+ 5:48	+ 4.45	118	- 5:17
+ 5.00	79	- 5:41	+ 5.00	64	- 5:56	+ 5.00	63	- 5:57	+ 5.00	116	- 5:04
+ 5.15	77	- 5:28	+ 5.15	63	- 5:42	+ 5.15	64	- 5:41	+ 5.15	114	- 4:51
+ 5.30	76	- 5:14	+ 5.30	62	- 5:28	+ 5.30	64	- 5:26	+ 5.30	112	- 4:38
+ 5.45	75	- 5:00	+ 5.45	61	- 5:14	+ 5.45	65	- 5:10	+ 5.45	110	- 4:25
+ 6.00	74	- 4:46	+ 6.00	60	- 5:00	+ 6.00	65	- 4:55	+ 6.00	108	- 4:12

Via Fisherman's Gat and Middle Sunk

B - 4 Kts

Table B - Ramsgate to Essex Rivers via Fisherman's and Foulger's Gats

4 Kts - B

Time to cover Sectors (in minutes) at 4.0 kts — All times relate to HW Sheerness — **Springs**

NORTH BOUND

Time	B1 North Foreland to Tongue: Duration	B1 Time at End of Sector	Time	B2 Tongue to Long Sand Outer: Duration	B2 Time at End of Sector	Time	B3 Long Sand Outer to Black Deep: Duration	B3 Time at End of Sector	Time	B4 Black Deep to NE Middle: Duration	B4 Time at End of Sector
- 6.00	136	- 3:44	- 6.00	102	- 4:18	- 6.00	148	- 3:32	- 6.00	66	- 4:54
- 5.45	134	- 3:31	- 5.45	102	- 4:03	- 5.45	145	- 3:20	- 5.45	65	- 4:40
- 5.30	132	- 3:18	- 5.30	101	- 3:49	- 5.30	143	- 3:07	- 5.30	64	- 4:26
- 5.15	129	- 3:06	- 5.15	101	- 3:34	- 5.15	141	- 2:54	- 5.15	63	- 4:12
- 5.00	127	- 2:53	- 5.00	100	- 3:20	- 5.00	139	- 2:41	- 5.00	62	- 3:58
- 4.45	123	- 2:42	- 4.45	96	- 3:09	- 4.45	134	- 2:31	- 4.45	62	- 3:43
- 4.30	118	- 2:32	- 4.30	92	- 2:58	- 4.30	129	- 2:21	- 4.30	62	- 3:28
- 4.15	113	- 2:22	- 4.15	87	- 2:48	- 4.15	125	- 2:10	- 4.15	61	- 3:14
- 4.00	108	- 2:12	- 4.00	83	- 2:37	- 4.00	120	- 2:00	- 4.00	61	- 2:59
- 3.45	103	- 2:02	- 3.45	79	- 2:26	- 3.45	115	- 1:50	- 3.45	61	- 2:44
- 3.30	98	- 1:52	- 3.30	76	- 2:14	- 3.30	110	- 1:40	- 3.30	62	- 2:28
- 3.15	93	- 1:42	- 3.15	72	- 2:03	- 3.15	105	- 1:30	- 3.15	62	- 2:13
- 3.00	88	- 1:32	- 3.00	69	- 1:51	- 3.00	100	- 1:20	- 3.00	62	- 1:58
- 2.45	83	- 1:22	- 2.45	66	- 1:39	- 2.45	96	- 1:09	- 2.45	64	- 1:41
- 2.30	79	- 1:11	- 2.30	63	- 1:27	- 2.30	92	- 0:58	- 2.30	65	- 1:25
- 2.15	74	- 1:01	- 2.15	59	- 1:16	- 2.15	88	- 0:47	- 2.15	67	- 1:08
- 2.00	70	- 0:50	- 2.00	56	- 1:04	- 2.00	85	- 0:35	- 2.00	68	- 0:52
- 1.45	69	- 0:36	- 1.45	54	- 0:51	- 1.45	84	- 0:21	- 1.45	72	- 0:33
- 1.30	67	- 0:23	- 1.30	52	- 0:38	- 1.30	83	- 0:07	- 1.30	75	- 0:15
- 1.15	66	- 0:09	- 1.15	50	- 0:25	- 1.15	83	+ 0:08	- 1.15	78	+ 0:03
- 1.00	64	+ 0:04	- 1.00	48	- 0:12	- 1.00	82	+ 0:22	- 1.00	82	+ 0:22
- 0.45	66	+ 0:21	- 0.45	48	+ 0:03	- 0.45	85	+ 0:40	- 0.45	87	+ 0:42
- 0.30	68	+ 0:38	- 0.30	47	+ 0:17	- 0.30	88	+ 0:58	- 0.30	93	+ 1:03
- 0.15	70	+ 0:55	- 0.15	46	+ 0:31	- 0.15	90	+ 1:15	- 0.15	98	+ 1:23
HW	71	+ 1:11	HW	45	+ 0:45	HW	93	+ 1:33	HW	104	+ 1:44
+ 0.15	75	+ 1:30	+ 0.15	45	+ 1:00	+ 0.15	96	+ 1:51	+ 0.15	107	+ 2:02
+ 0.30	79	+ 1:49	+ 0.30	45	+ 1:15	+ 0.30	99	+ 2:09	+ 0.30	111	+ 2:21
+ 0.45	83	+ 2:08	+ 0.45	45	+ 1:30	+ 0.45	103	+ 2:28	+ 0.45	114	+ 2:39
+ 1.00	87	+ 2:27	+ 1.00	45	+ 1:45	+ 1.00	106	+ 2:46	+ 1.00	118	+ 2:58
+ 1.15	92	+ 2:47	+ 1.15	46	+ 2:01	+ 1.15	108	+ 3:03	+ 1.15	118	+ 3:13
+ 1.30	97	+ 3:07	+ 1.30	46	+ 2:16	+ 1.30	111	+ 3:21	+ 1.30	117	+ 3:27
+ 1.45	103	+ 3:28	+ 1.45	47	+ 2:32	+ 1.45	113	+ 3:38	+ 1.45	117	+ 3:42
+ 2.00	108	+ 3:48	+ 2.00	48	+ 2:48	+ 2.00	115	+ 3:55	+ 2.00	117	+ 3:57
+ 2.15	111	+ 4:06	+ 2.15	49	+ 3:04	+ 2.15	117	+ 4:12	+ 2.15	114	+ 4:09
+ 2.30	114	+ 4:24	+ 2.30	50	+ 3:20	+ 2.30	118	+ 4:28	+ 2.30	111	+ 4:21
+ 2.45	117	+ 4:42	+ 2.45	51	+ 3:36	+ 2.45	120	+ 4:45	+ 2.45	108	+ 4:33
+ 3.00	121	+ 5:01	+ 3.00	52	+ 3:52	+ 3.00	121	+ 5:01	+ 3.00	105	+ 4:45
+ 3.15	122	+ 5:17	+ 3.15	54	+ 4:09	+ 3.15	123	+ 5:18	+ 3.15	102	+ 4:57
+ 3.30	124	+ 5:34	+ 3.30	55	+ 4:25	+ 3.30	124	+ 5:34	+ 3.30	99	+ 5:09
+ 3.45	125	+ 5:50	+ 3.45	57	+ 4:42	+ 3.45	125	+ 5:50	+ 3.45	96	+ 5:21
+ 4.00	127	- 5:53	+ 4.00	58	+ 4:58	+ 4.00	127	- 5:53	+ 4.00	92	+ 5:32
+ 4.15	128	- 5:37	+ 4.15	61	+ 5:16	+ 4.15	132	- 5:33	+ 4.15	89	+ 5:44
+ 4.30	130	- 5:20	+ 4.30	63	+ 5:33	+ 4.30	138	- 5:12	+ 4.30	86	+ 5:56
+ 4.45	131	- 5:04	+ 4.45	66	+ 5:51	+ 4.45	143	- 4:52	+ 4.45	83	- 5:52
+ 5.00	133	- 4:47	+ 5.00	68	- 5:52	+ 5.00	148	- 4:32	+ 5.00	80	- 5:40
+ 5.15	133	- 4:32	+ 5.15	71	- 5:34	+ 5.15	145	- 4:20	+ 5.15	78	- 5:27
+ 5.30	134	- 4:16	+ 5.30	74	- 5:16	+ 5.30	141	- 4:09	+ 5.30	76	- 5:14
+ 5.45	135	- 4:00	+ 5.45	77	- 4:58	+ 5.45	137	- 3:58	+ 5.45	74	- 5:01
+ 6.00	136	- 3:44	+ 6.00	80	- 4:40	+ 6.00	134	- 3:46	+ 6.00	72	- 4:48

Via Foulger's Gat and Little Sunk

Time	B5 NE Middle to Mid-Point Spitway: Duration	B5 Time at End of Sector	Time	B6 Outer Fisherman to Blk Deep No 8: Duration	B6 Time at End of Sector	Time	B7 Blk Deep No 8 to Barrow Deep: Duration	B7 Time at End of Sector	Time	B8 Barrow Deep to Mid-Spitway: Duration	B8 Time at End of Sector
- 6.00	61	- 4:59	- 6.00	58	- 5:02	- 6.00	73	- 4:47	- 6.00	101	- 4:19
- 5.45	60	- 4:45	- 5.45	56	- 4:49	- 5.45	75	- 4:30	- 5.45	100	- 4:05
- 5.30	58	- 4:32	- 5.30	54	- 4:36	- 5.30	77	- 4:13	- 5.30	99	- 3:51
- 5.15	56	- 4:19	- 5.15	52	- 4:23	- 5.15	79	- 3:56	- 5.15	98	- 3:37
- 5.00	55	- 4:05	- 5.00	50	- 4:10	- 5.00	81	- 3:39	- 5.00	97	- 3:23
- 4.45	55	- 3:50	- 4.45	49	- 3:56	- 4.45	82	- 3:23	- 4.45	97	- 3:08
- 4.30	54	- 3:36	- 4.30	47	- 3:43	- 4.30	82	- 3:08	- 4.30	97	- 2:53
- 4.15	54	- 3:21	- 4.15	46	- 3:29	- 4.15	82	- 2:53	- 4.15	96	- 2:39
- 4.00	54	- 3:06	- 4.00	45	- 3:15	- 4.00	83	- 2:37	- 4.00	96	- 2:24
- 3.45	54	- 2:51	- 3.45	43	- 3:02	- 3.45	81	- 2:24	- 3.45	96	- 2:09
- 3.30	55	- 2:35	- 3.30	42	- 2:48	- 3.30	79	- 2:11	- 3.30	97	- 1:53
- 3.15	55	- 2:20	- 3.15	40	- 2:35	- 3.15	77	- 1:58	- 3.15	97	- 1:38
- 3.00	56	- 2:04	- 3.00	39	- 2:21	- 3.00	75	- 1:45	- 3.00	97	- 1:23
- 2.45	58	- 1:47	- 2.45	38	- 2:07	- 2.45	73	- 1:32	- 2.45	100	- 1:05
- 2.30	60	- 1:30	- 2.30	37	- 1:53	- 2.30	70	- 1:20	- 2.30	102	- 0:48
- 2.15	62	- 1:13	- 2.15	37	- 1:38	- 2.15	67	- 1:08	- 2.15	104	- 0:31
- 2.00	64	- 0:56	- 2.00	36	- 1:24	- 2.00	65	- 0:55	- 2.00	107	- 0:13
- 1.45	67	- 0:38	- 1.45	37	- 1:08	- 1.45	63	- 0:42	- 1.45	112	+ 0:07
- 1.30	71	- 0:19	- 1.30	38	- 0:52	- 1.30	62	- 0:28	- 1.30	117	+ 0:27
- 1.15	74	- 0:01	- 1.15	38	- 0:37	- 1.15	60	- 0:15	- 1.15	122	+ 0:47
- 1.00	78	+ 0:18	- 1.00	39	- 0:21	- 1.00	59	- 0:01	- 1.00	127	+ 1:07
- 0.45	85	+ 0:40	- 0.45	42	- 0:03	- 0.45	59	+ 0:14	- 0.45	135	+ 1:30
- 0.30	92	+ 1:02	- 0.30	45	+ 0:15	- 0.30	59	+ 0:29	- 0.30	143	+ 1:53
- 0.15	99	+ 1:24	- 0.15	48	+ 0:33	- 0.15	59	+ 0:44	- 0.15	151	+ 2:16
HW	106	+ 1:46	HW	51	+ 0:51	HW	58	+ 0:58	HW	158	+ 2:38
+ 0.15	111	+ 2:06	+ 0.15	54	+ 1:09	+ 0.15	59	+ 1:14	+ 0.15	161	+ 2:56
+ 0.30	115	+ 2:25	+ 0.30	57	+ 1:27	+ 0.30	59	+ 1:29	+ 0.30	163	+ 3:13
+ 0.45	120	+ 2:45	+ 0.45	61	+ 1:46	+ 0.45	60	+ 1:45	+ 0.45	165	+ 3:30
+ 1.00	124	+ 3:04	+ 1.00	64	+ 2:04	+ 1.00	60	+ 2:00	+ 1.00	168	+ 3:48
+ 1.15	123	+ 3:18	+ 1.15	65	+ 2:20	+ 1.15	60	+ 2:15	+ 1.15	166	+ 4:01
+ 1.30	122	+ 3:32	+ 1.30	67	+ 2:37	+ 1.30	60	+ 2:30	+ 1.30	164	+ 4:14
+ 1.45	121	+ 3:46	+ 1.45	69	+ 2:54	+ 1.45	60	+ 2:45	+ 1.45	162	+ 4:27
+ 2.00	120	+ 4:00	+ 2.00	70	+ 3:10	+ 2.00	60	+ 3:00	+ 2.00	160	+ 4:40
+ 2.15	117	+ 4:12	+ 2.15	71	+ 3:26	+ 2.15	60	+ 3:15	+ 2.15	156	+ 4:51
+ 2.30	113	+ 4:23	+ 2.30	72	+ 3:42	+ 2.30	60	+ 3:30	+ 2.30	152	+ 5:02
+ 2.45	110	+ 4:35	+ 2.45	73	+ 3:58	+ 2.45	60	+ 3:45	+ 2.45	148	+ 5:13
+ 3.00	106	+ 4:46	+ 3.00	74	+ 4:14	+ 3.00	60	+ 4:00	+ 3.00	144	+ 5:24
+ 3.15	103	+ 4:58	+ 3.15	75	+ 4:30	+ 3.15	60	+ 4:15	+ 3.15	140	+ 5:35
+ 3.30	99	+ 5:09	+ 3.30	75	+ 4:45	+ 3.30	61	+ 4:31	+ 3.30	135	+ 5:45
+ 3.45	96	+ 5:21	+ 3.45	76	+ 5:01	+ 3.45	61	+ 4:46	+ 3.45	131	+ 5:56
+ 4.00	92	+ 5:32	+ 4.00	76	+ 5:16	+ 4.00	61	+ 5:01	+ 4.00	127	- 5:53
+ 4.15	89	+ 5:44	+ 4.15	75	+ 5:30	+ 4.15	62	+ 5:17	+ 4.15	124	- 5:41
+ 4.30	86	+ 5:56	+ 4.30	74	+ 5:44	+ 4.30	63	+ 5:33	+ 4.30	121	- 5:29
+ 4.45	83	- 5:52	+ 4.45	73	+ 5:58	+ 4.45	63	+ 5:48	+ 4.45	117	- 5:18
+ 5.00	80	- 5:40	+ 5.00	72	- 5:48	+ 5.00	64	- 5:56	+ 5.00	114	- 5:06
+ 5.15	78	- 5:27	+ 5.15	70	- 5:35	+ 5.15	65	- 5:40	+ 5.15	112	- 4:53
+ 5.30	76	- 5:14	+ 5.30	68	- 5:22	+ 5.30	65	- 5:25	+ 5.30	110	- 4:40
+ 5.45	74	- 5:01	+ 5.45	67	- 5:08	+ 5.45	66	- 5:09	+ 5.45	108	- 4:27
+ 6.00	72	- 4:48	+ 6.00	65	- 4:55	+ 6.00	67	- 4:53	+ 6.00	106	- 4:14

Via Fisherman's Gat and Middle Sunk

B - 5 Kts Table B - Ramsgate to Essex Rivers via Fisherman's and Foulger's Gats 5 Kts - B

Neaps — All times relate to HW Sheerness — **Time to cover Sectors (in minutes) at 5.0 Kts**

NORTH BOUND

	B1			B2			B3			B4			B5			B6			B7			B8	
	North Foreland to Tongue			Tongue to Long Sand Outer			Long Sand Outer to Black Deep			Black Deep to NE Middle			NE Middle to Mid-Point Spitway			Outer Fisherman to Blk Deep No 8			Blk Deep No 8 to Barrow Deep			Barrow Deep to Mid-Spitway	
Time	Duration	Time at End of Sector	Time	Duration	Time at End of Sector	Time	Duration	Time at End of Sector	Time	Duration	Time at End of Sector	Time	Duration	Time at End of Sector	Time	Duration	Time at End of Sector	Time	Duration	Time at End of Sector	Time	Duration	Time at End of Sector
- 6.00	95	- 4:25	- 6.00	58	- 5:02	- 6.00	99	- 4:21	- 6.00	57	- 5:03	- 6.00	55	- 5:05	- 6.00	45	- 5:15	- 6.00	53	- 5:07	- 6.00	85	- 4:35
- 5.45	95	- 4:10	- 5.45	59	- 4:46	- 5.45	99	- 4:06	- 5.45	56	- 4:49	- 5.45	54	- 4:51	- 5.45	44	- 5:01	- 5.45	54	- 4:51	- 5.45	84	- 4:21
- 5.30	94	- 3:56	- 5.30	59	- 4:31	- 5.30	98	- 3:52	- 5.30	56	- 4:34	- 5.30	53	- 4:37	- 5.30	43	- 4:47	- 5.30	55	- 4:35	- 5.30	83	- 4:07
- 5.15	93	- 3:42	- 5.15	59	- 4:16	- 5.15	98	- 3:37	- 5.15	55	- 4:20	- 5.15	52	- 4:23	- 5.15	42	- 4:33	- 5.15	56	- 4:19	- 5.15	83	- 3:52
- 5.00	93	- 3:27	- 5.00	60	- 4:00	- 5.00	98	- 3:22	- 5.00	55	- 4:05	- 5.00	51	- 4:09	- 5.00	41	- 4:19	- 5.00	56	- 4:04	- 5.00	82	- 3:38
- 4.45	90	- 3:15	- 4.45	59	- 3:46	- 4.45	96	- 3:09	- 4.45	54	- 3:51	- 4.45	51	- 3:54	- 4.45	41	- 4:04	- 4.45	56	- 3:49	- 4.45	82	- 3:23
- 4.30	88	- 3:02	- 4.30	58	- 3:32	- 4.30	95	- 2:55	- 4.30	54	- 3:36	- 4.30	51	- 3:39	- 4.30	40	- 3:50	- 4.30	56	- 3:34	- 4.30	82	- 3:08
- 4.15	86	- 2:49	- 4.15	57	- 3:18	- 4.15	94	- 2:41	- 4.15	54	- 3:21	- 4.15	51	- 3:24	- 4.15	40	- 3:35	- 4.15	56	- 3:19	- 4.15	81	- 2:54
- 4.00	83	- 2:37	- 4.00	56	- 3:04	- 4.00	92	- 2:28	- 4.00	54	- 3:06	- 4.00	51	- 3:09	- 4.00	39	- 3:21	- 4.00	56	- 3:04	- 4.00	81	- 2:39
- 3.45	81	- 2:24	- 3.45	55	- 2:50	- 3.45	90	- 2:15	- 3.45	54	- 2:51	- 3.45	51	- 2:54	- 3.45	39	- 3:06	- 3.45	56	- 2:49	- 3.45	82	- 2:23
- 3.30	79	- 2:11	- 3.30	54	- 2:36	- 3.30	88	- 2:02	- 3.30	55	- 2:35	- 3.30	51	- 2:39	- 3.30	38	- 2:52	- 3.30	55	- 2:35	- 3.30	82	- 2:08
- 3.15	76	- 1:59	- 3.15	53	- 2:22	- 3.15	85	- 1:50	- 3.15	55	- 2:20	- 3.15	52	- 2:23	- 3.15	37	- 2:38	- 3.15	54	- 2:21	- 3.15	82	- 1:53
- 3.00	74	- 1:46	- 3.00	52	- 2:08	- 3.00	83	- 1:37	- 3.00	55	- 2:05	- 3.00	52	- 2:08	- 3.00	37	- 2:23	- 3.00	54	- 2:06	- 3.00	83	- 1:37
- 2.45	72	- 1:33	- 2.45	51	- 1:54	- 2.45	81	- 1:24	- 2.45	56	- 1:49	- 2.45	53	- 1:52	- 2.45	36	- 2:09	- 2.45	53	- 1:52	- 2.45	84	- 1:21
- 2.30	70	- 1:20	- 2.30	49	- 1:41	- 2.30	79	- 1:11	- 2.30	57	- 1:33	- 2.30	54	- 1:36	- 2.30	36	- 1:54	- 2.30	52	- 1:38	- 2.30	85	- 1:05
- 2.15	69	- 1:06	- 2.15	48	- 1:27	- 2.15	77	- 0:58	- 2.15	57	- 1:18	- 2.15	55	- 1:20	- 2.15	35	- 1:40	- 2.15	51	- 1:24	- 2.15	85	- 0:50
- 2.00	67	- 0:53	- 2.00	47	- 1:13	- 2.00	75	- 0:45	- 2.00	58	- 1:02	- 2.00	55	- 1:05	- 2.00	34	- 1:26	- 2.00	51	- 1:09	- 2.00	86	- 0:34
- 1.45	66	- 0:39	- 1.45	46	- 0:59	- 1.45	75	- 0:30	- 1.45	59	- 0:46	- 1.45	57	- 0:48	- 1.45	35	- 1:10	- 1.45	50	- 0:55	- 1.45	88	- 0:17
- 1.30	66	- 0:24	- 1.30	45	- 0:45	- 1.30	74	- 0:16	- 1.30	61	- 0:29	- 1.30	58	- 0:32	- 1.30	35	- 0:55	- 1.30	49	- 0:41	- 1.30	90	- 0:00
- 1.15	66	- 0:09	- 1.15	44	- 0:31	- 1.15	74	- 0:01	- 1.15	62	- 0:13	- 1.15	60	- 0:15	- 1.15	36	- 0:39	- 1.15	49	- 0:26	- 1.15	92	+ 0:17
- 1.00	65	+ 0:05	- 1.00	43	- 0:17	- 1.00	73	+ 0:13	- 1.00	63	+ 0:03	- 1.00	61	+ 0:01	- 1.00	36	- 0:24	- 1.00	48	- 0:12	- 1.00	94	+ 0:34
- 0.45	66	+ 0:21	- 0.45	42	- 0:03	- 0.45	74	+ 0:29	- 0.45	65	+ 0:20	- 0.45	63	+ 0:18	- 0.45	37	- 0:08	- 0.45	48	+ 0:03	- 0.45	97	+ 0:52
- 0.30	66	+ 0:36	- 0.30	42	+ 0:12	- 0.30	75	+ 0:45	- 0.30	67	+ 0:37	- 0.30	65	+ 0:35	- 0.30	38	+ 0:08	- 0.30	48	+ 0:18	- 0.30	100	+ 1:10
- 0.15	67	+ 0:52	- 0.15	41	+ 0:26	- 0.15	76	+ 1:01	- 0.15	68	+ 0:53	- 0.15	67	+ 0:52	- 0.15	39	+ 0:24	- 0.15	47	+ 0:32	- 0.15	102	+ 1:27
HW	67	+ 1:07	HW	41	+ 0:41	HW	77	+ 1:17	HW	70	+ 1:10	HW	69	+ 1:09	HW	40	+ 0:40	HW	47	+ 0:47	HW	105	+ 1:45
+ 0.15	68	+ 1:23	+ 0.15	41	+ 0:56	+ 0.15	78	+ 1:33	+ 0.15	71	+ 1:26	+ 0.15	71	+ 1:26	+ 0.15	42	+ 0:57	+ 0.15	47	+ 1:02	+ 0.15	107	+ 2:02
+ 0.30	70	+ 1:40	+ 0.30	40	+ 1:10	+ 0.30	79	+ 1:49	+ 0.30	72	+ 1:42	+ 0.30	72	+ 1:42	+ 0.30	43	+ 1:13	+ 0.30	47	+ 1:17	+ 0.30	109	+ 2:19
+ 0.45	71	+ 1:56	+ 0.45	40	+ 1:25	+ 0.45	80	+ 2:05	+ 0.45	73	+ 1:58	+ 0.45	74	+ 1:59	+ 0.45	45	+ 1:30	+ 0.45	47	+ 1:32	+ 0.45	111	+ 2:36
+ 1.00	72	+ 2:12	+ 1.00	40	+ 1:40	+ 1.00	82	+ 2:22	+ 1.00	75	+ 2:15	+ 1.00	76	+ 2:16	+ 1.00	46	+ 1:46	+ 1.00	47	+ 1:47	+ 1.00	112	+ 2:52
+ 1.15	74	+ 2:29	+ 1.15	41	+ 1:56	+ 1.15	83	+ 2:38	+ 1.15	75	+ 2:30	+ 1.15	76	+ 2:31	+ 1.15	47	+ 2:02	+ 1.15	47	+ 2:02	+ 1.15	113	+ 3:08
+ 1.30	76	+ 2:46	+ 1.30	41	+ 2:11	+ 1.30	84	+ 2:54	+ 1.30	75	+ 2:45	+ 1.30	76	+ 2:46	+ 1.30	47	+ 2:17	+ 1.30	47	+ 2:17	+ 1.30	113	+ 3:23
+ 1.45	77	+ 3:02	+ 1.45	41	+ 2:26	+ 1.45	85	+ 3:10	+ 1.45	76	+ 3:01	+ 1.45	76	+ 3:01	+ 1.45	48	+ 2:33	+ 1.45	47	+ 2:32	+ 1.45	113	+ 3:38
+ 2.00	79	+ 3:19	+ 2.00	41	+ 2:41	+ 2.00	85	+ 3:25	+ 2.00	76	+ 3:16	+ 2.00	76	+ 3:16	+ 2.00	49	+ 2:49	+ 2.00	47	+ 2:47	+ 2.00	113	+ 3:53
+ 2.15	80	+ 3:35	+ 2.15	42	+ 2:57	+ 2.15	86	+ 3:41	+ 2.15	75	+ 3:30	+ 2.15	75	+ 3:30	+ 2.15	49	+ 3:04	+ 2.15	47	+ 3:02	+ 2.15	112	+ 4:07
+ 2.30	81	+ 3:51	+ 2.30	43	+ 3:13	+ 2.30	87	+ 3:57	+ 2.30	75	+ 3:45	+ 2.30	74	+ 3:44	+ 2.30	49	+ 3:19	+ 2.30	47	+ 3:17	+ 2.30	110	+ 4:20
+ 2.45	82	+ 4:07	+ 2.45	43	+ 3:28	+ 2.45	87	+ 4:12	+ 2.45	74	+ 3:59	+ 2.45	73	+ 3:58	+ 2.45	50	+ 3:35	+ 2.45	47	+ 3:32	+ 2.45	109	+ 4:34
+ 3.00	83	+ 4:23	+ 3.00	44	+ 3:44	+ 3.00	88	+ 4:28	+ 3.00	73	+ 4:13	+ 3.00	73	+ 4:13	+ 3.00	50	+ 3:50	+ 3.00	48	+ 3:48	+ 3.00	108	+ 4:48
+ 3.15	84	+ 4:39	+ 3.15	45	+ 4:00	+ 3.15	88	+ 4:43	+ 3.15	72	+ 4:27	+ 3.15	71	+ 4:26	+ 3.15	50	+ 4:05	+ 3.15	48	+ 4:03	+ 3.15	106	+ 5:01
+ 3.30	85	+ 4:55	+ 3.30	45	+ 4:15	+ 3.30	89	+ 4:59	+ 3.30	71	+ 4:41	+ 3.30	70	+ 4:40	+ 3.30	51	+ 4:21	+ 3.30	48	+ 4:18	+ 3.30	104	+ 5:14
+ 3.45	85	+ 5:10	+ 3.45	46	+ 4:31	+ 3.45	89	+ 5:14	+ 3.45	70	+ 4:55	+ 3.45	69	+ 4:54	+ 3.45	51	+ 4:36	+ 3.45	48	+ 4:33	+ 3.45	102	+ 5:27
+ 4.00	86	+ 5:26	+ 4.00	47	+ 4:47	+ 4.00	90	+ 5:30	+ 4.00	69	+ 5:09	+ 4.00	68	+ 5:08	+ 4.00	51	+ 4:51	+ 4.00	49	+ 4:49	+ 4.00	100	+ 5:40
+ 4.15	87	+ 5:42	+ 4.15	48	+ 5:03	+ 4.15	91	+ 5:46	+ 4.15	67	+ 5:22	+ 4.15	67	+ 5:22	+ 4.15	51	+ 5:06	+ 4.15	49	+ 5:04	+ 4.15	99	+ 5:54
+ 4.30	89	+ 5:59	+ 4.30	49	+ 5:19	+ 4.30	92	- 5:58	+ 4.30	66	+ 5:36	+ 4.30	66	+ 5:36	+ 4.30	51	+ 5:21	+ 4.30	49	+ 5:19	+ 4.30	97	- 5:53
+ 4.45	91	- 5:44	+ 4.45	50	+ 5:35	+ 4.45	93	- 5:42	+ 4.45	65	+ 5:50	+ 4.45	64	+ 5:49	+ 4.45	50	+ 5:35	+ 4.45	50	+ 5:35	+ 4.45	95	- 5:40
+ 5.00	93	- 5:27	+ 5.00	51	+ 5:51	+ 5.00	94	- 5:26	+ 5.00	64	- 5:56	+ 5.00	63	- 5:57	+ 5.00	50	+ 5:50	+ 5.00	50	+ 5:50	+ 5.00	93	- 5:27
+ 5.15	93	- 5:12	+ 5.15	52	- 5:53	+ 5.15	95	- 5:10	+ 5.15	63	- 5:42	+ 5.15	62	- 5:43	+ 5.15	49	- 5:56	+ 5.15	50	- 5:55	+ 5.15	92	- 5:13
+ 5.30	93	- 4:57	+ 5.30	53	- 5:37	+ 5.30	97	- 4:53	+ 5.30	62	- 5:28	+ 5.30	61	- 5:29	+ 5.30	49	- 5:41	+ 5.30	51	- 5:39	+ 5.30	91	- 4:59
+ 5.45	94	- 4:41	+ 5.45	54	- 5:21	+ 5.45	98	- 4:37	+ 5.45	61	- 5:14	+ 5.45	60	- 5:15	+ 5.45	48	- 5:27	+ 5.45	51	- 5:24	+ 5.45	90	- 4:45
+ 6.00	94	- 4:26	+ 6.00	55	- 5:05	+ 6.00	99	- 4:21	+ 6.00	60	- 5:00	+ 6.00	60	- 5:00	+ 6.00	47	- 5:13	+ 6.00	51	- 5:09	+ 6.00	89	- 4:31

Via Foulger's Gat and Little Sunk

Via Fisherman's Gat and Middle Sunk

Table B - Ramsgate to Essex Rivers via Fisherman's and Foulger's Gats

Time to cover Sectors (in minutes) at 5.0 kts — All times relate to HW Sheerness — **Springs**

NORTH BOUND

Time	B1 North Foreland to Tongue Duration	B1 Time at End of Sector	Time	B2 Tongue to Long Sand Outer Duration	B2 Time at End of Sector	Time	B3 Long Sand Outer to Black Deep Duration	B3 Time at End of Sector	Time	B4 Black Deep to NE Middle Duration	B4 Time at End of Sector
-6.00	103	-4:17	-6.00	66	-4:54	-6.00	112	-4:08	-6.00	55	-5:05
-5.45	102	-4:03	-5.45	66	-4:39	-5.45	111	-3:54	-5.45	54	-4:51
-5.30	101	-3:49	-5.30	67	-4:23	-5.30	111	-3:39	-5.30	53	-4:37
-5.15	100	-3:35	-5.15	67	-4:08	-5.15	110	-3:25	-5.15	53	-4:22
-5.00	100	-3:20	-5.00	68	-3:52	-5.00	109	-3:11	-5.00	52	-4:08
-4.45	97	-3:08	-4.45	67	-3:38	-4.45	107	-2:58	-4.45	52	-3:53
-4.30	94	-2:56	-4.30	65	-3:25	-4.30	104	-2:46	-4.30	51	-3:39
-4.15	91	-2:44	-4.15	64	-3:11	-4.15	102	-2:33	-4.15	51	-3:24
-4.00	89	-2:31	-4.00	63	-2:57	-4.00	99	-2:21	-4.00	51	-3:09
-3.45	85	-2:20	-3.45	61	-2:44	-3.45	95	-2:10	-3.45	51	-2:54
-3.30	80	-2:10	-3.30	59	-2:31	-3.30	91	-1:59	-3.30	51	-2:39
-3.15	76	-1:59	-3.15	57	-2:18	-3.15	87	-1:48	-3.15	52	-2:23
-3.00	72	-1:48	-3.00	55	-2:05	-3.00	83	-1:37	-3.00	52	-2:08
-2.45	69	-1:36	-2.45	52	-1:53	-2.45	80	-1:25	-2.45	53	-1:52
-2.30	66	-1:24	-2.30	50	-1:40	-2.30	77	-1:13	-2.30	54	-1:36
-2.15	63	-1:12	-2.15	48	-1:27	-2.15	74	-1:01	-2.15	55	-1:20
-2.00	60	-1:00	-2.00	46	-1:14	-2.00	71	-0:49	-2.00	56	-1:04
-1.45	59	-0:46	-1.45	45	-1:00	-1.45	71	-0:34	-1.45	58	-0:47
-1.30	59	-0:31	-1.30	44	-0:46	-1.30	70	-0:20	-1.30	60	-0:30
-1.15	58	-0:17	-1.15	42	-0:33	-1.15	69	-0:06	-1.15	62	-0:13
-1.00	57	-0:03	-1.00	41	-0:19	-1.00	68	+0:08	-1.00	64	+0:04
-0.45	58	+0:13	-0.45	40	-0:05	-0.45	69	+0:24	-0.45	66	+0:21
-0.30	59	+0:29	-0.30	40	+0:10	-0.30	71	+0:41	-0.30	69	+0:39
-0.15	59	+0:44	-0.15	39	+0:24	-0.15	72	+0:57	-0.15	71	+0:56
HW	60	+1:00	HW	38	+0:38	HW	74	+1:14	HW	74	+1:14
+0.15	63	+1:18	+0.15	38	+0:53	+0.15	76	+1:31	+0.15	76	+1:31
+0.30	65	+1:35	+0.30	38	+1:08	+0.30	78	+1:48	+0.30	78	+1:48
+0.45	67	+1:52	+0.45	38	+1:23	+0.45	80	+2:05	+0.45	80	+2:05
+1.00	70	+2:10	+1.00	38	+1:38	+1.00	83	+2:23	+1.00	81	+2:21
+1.15	73	+2:28	+1.15	38	+1:53	+1.15	84	+2:39	+1.15	82	+2:37
+1.30	75	+2:45	+1.30	38	+2:08	+1.30	85	+2:55	+1.30	82	+2:52
+1.45	78	+3:03	+1.45	39	+2:24	+1.45	86	+3:11	+1.45	83	+3:08
+2.00	81	+3:21	+2.00	39	+2:39	+2.00	88	+3:28	+2.00	83	+3:23
+2.15	84	+3:39	+2.15	40	+2:55	+2.15	88	+3:43	+2.15	82	+3:37
+2.30	86	+3:56	+2.30	41	+3:11	+2.30	89	+3:59	+2.30	81	+3:51
+2.45	89	+4:14	+2.45	41	+3:26	+2.45	90	+4:15	+2.45	80	+4:05
+3.00	91	+4:31	+3.00	42	+3:42	+3.00	91	+4:31	+3.00	79	+4:19
+3.15	92	+4:47	+3.15	43	+3:58	+3.15	91	+4:46	+3.15	77	+4:32
+3.30	93	+5:03	+3.30	44	+4:14	+3.30	92	+5:02	+3.30	75	+4:45
+3.45	94	+5:19	+3.45	45	+4:30	+3.45	93	+5:18	+3.45	74	+4:59
+4.00	96	+5:36	+4.00	46	+4:46	+4.00	94	+5:34	+4.00	72	+5:12
+4.15	97	+5:52	+4.15	48	+5:03	+4.15	95	+5:50	+4.15	70	+5:25
+4.30	98	-5:52	+4.30	49	+5:19	+4.30	97	-5:53	+4.30	68	+5:38
+4.45	99	-5:36	+4.45	50	+5:35	+4.45	98	-5:37	+4.45	66	+5:51
+5.00	100	-5:20	+5.00	52	+5:52	+5.00	100	-5:20	+5.00	64	-5:56
+5.15	101	-5:04	+5.15	54	-5:51	+5.15	102	-5:03	+5.15	63	-5:42
+5.30	101	-4:49	+5.30	56	-5:34	+5.30	104	-4:46	+5.30	62	-5:28
+5.45	102	-4:33	+5.45	58	-5:17	+5.45	107	-4:28	+5.45	60	-5:15
+6.00	102	-4:18	+6.00	60	-5:00	+6.00	109	-4:11	+6.00	59	-5:01

Via Foulger's Gat and Little Sunk

Time	B5 NE Middle to Mid-Point Spitway Duration	B5 Time at End of Sector	Time	B6 Outer Fisherman to Blk Deep No 8 Duration	B6 Time at End of Sector	Time	B7 Blk Deep No 8 to Barrow Deep Duration	B7 Time at End of Sector	Time	B8 Barrow Deep to Mid-Spitway Duration	B8 Time at End of Sector
-6.00	52	-5:08	-6.00	46	-5:14	-6.00	56	-5:04	-6.00	82	-4:38
-5.45	51	-4:54	-5.45	45	-5:00	-5.45	57	-4:48	-5.45	81	-4:24
-5.30	50	-4:40	-5.30	44	-4:46	-5.30	58	-4:32	-5.30	81	-4:09
-5.15	48	-4:27	-5.15	42	-4:33	-5.15	60	-4:15	-5.15	80	-3:55
-5.00	47	-4:13	-5.00	41	-4:19	-5.00	61	-3:59	-5.00	79	-3:41
-4.45	47	-3:58	-4.45	40	-4:05	-4.45	61	-3:44	-4.45	79	-3:26
-4.30	47	-3:43	-4.30	39	-3:51	-4.30	61	-3:29	-4.30	78	-3:12
-4.15	47	-3:28	-4.15	38	-3:37	-4.15	62	-3:13	-4.15	78	-2:57
-4.00	46	-3:14	-4.00	37	-3:23	-4.00	62	-2:58	-4.00	78	-2:42
-3.45	47	-2:58	-3.45	37	-3:08	-3.45	61	-2:44	-3.45	78	-2:27
-3.30	47	-2:43	-3.30	36	-2:54	-3.30	60	-2:30	-3.30	78	-2:12
-3.15	47	-2:28	-3.15	35	-2:40	-3.15	59	-2:16	-3.15	78	-1:57
-3.00	48	-2:12	-3.00	34	-2:26	-3.00	58	-2:02	-3.00	78	-1:42
-2.45	49	-1:56	-2.45	33	-2:12	-2.45	56	-1:49	-2.45	80	-1:25
-2.30	50	-1:40	-2.30	33	-1:57	-2.30	55	-1:35	-2.30	81	-1:09
-2.15	51	-1:24	-2.15	32	-1:43	-2.15	53	-1:22	-2.15	82	-0:53
-2.00	52	-1:08	-2.00	31	-1:29	-2.00	52	-1:08	-2.00	84	-0:36
-1.45	54	-0:51	-1.45	31	-1:14	-1.45	51	-0:54	-1.45	87	-0:18
-1.30	57	-0:33	-1.30	32	-0:58	-1.30	50	-0:40	-1.30	90	HW
-1.15	59	-0:16	-1.15	32	-0:43	-1.15	49	-0:26	-1.15	93	+0:18
-1.00	61	+0:01	-1.00	32	-0:28	-1.00	48	-0:12	-1.00	97	+0:37
-0.45	64	+0:19	-0.45	34	-0:11	-0.45	47	+0:02	-0.45	100	+0:55
-0.30	67	+0:37	-0.30	36	+0:06	-0.30	47	+0:17	-0.30	104	+1:14
-0.15	71	+0:56	-0.15	38	+0:23	-0.15	47	+0:32	-0.15	108	+1:33
HW	74	+1:14	HW	39	+0:39	HW	47	+0:47	HW	112	+1:52
+0.15	78	+1:33	+0.15	42	+0:57	+0.15	47	+1:02	+0.15	114	+2:09
+0.30	83	+1:53	+0.30	44	+1:14	+0.30	47	+1:17	+0.30	116	+2:26
+0.45	87	+2:12	+0.45	46	+1:31	+0.45	47	+1:32	+0.45	119	+2:44
+1.00	92	+2:32	+1.00	49	+1:49	+1.00	47	+1:47	+1.00	121	+3:01
+1.15	92	+2:47	+1.15	50	+2:05	+1.15	47	+2:02	+1.15	121	+3:16
+1.30	92	+3:02	+1.30	51	+2:21	+1.30	47	+2:17	+1.30	121	+3:31
+1.45	91	+3:16	+1.45	52	+2:37	+1.45	47	+2:32	+1.45	120	+3:45
+2.00	91	+3:31	+2.00	53	+2:53	+2.00	47	+2:47	+2.00	120	+4:00
+2.15	88	+3:43	+2.15	54	+3:09	+2.15	47	+3:02	+2.15	118	+4:13
+2.30	85	+3:55	+2.30	54	+3:24	+2.30	47	+3:17	+2.30	116	+4:26
+2.45	82	+4:07	+2.45	55	+3:40	+2.45	47	+3:32	+2.45	114	+4:39
+3.00	79	+4:19	+3.00	56	+3:56	+3.00	47	+3:47	+3.00	112	+4:52
+3.15	77	+4:32	+3.15	56	+4:11	+3.15	48	+4:03	+3.15	110	+5:05
+3.30	75	+4:45	+3.30	56	+4:26	+3.30	48	+4:18	+3.30	107	+5:17
+3.45	73	+4:58	+3.45	57	+4:42	+3.45	48	+4:33	+3.45	105	+5:30
+4.00	72	+5:12	+4.00	57	+4:57	+4.00	49	+4:49	+4.00	102	+5:42
+4.15	70	+5:25	+4.15	57	+5:12	+4.15	49	+5:04	+4.15	100	+5:55
+4.30	68	+5:38	+4.30	56	+5:26	+4.30	50	+5:20	+4.30	97	-5:53
+4.45	66	+5:51	+4.45	56	+5:41	+4.45	50	+5:35	+4.45	95	-5:40
+5.00	64	-5:56	+5.00	55	+5:55	+5.00	50	+5:50	+5.00	93	-5:27
+5.15	63	-5:42	+5.15	54	-5:51	+5.15	51	-5:54	+5.15	91	-5:14
+5.30	61	-5:29	+5.30	53	-5:37	+5.30	51	-5:39	+5.30	90	-5:00
+5.45	60	-5:15	+5.45	51	-5:24	+5.45	52	-5:23	+5.45	88	-4:47
+6.00	59	-5:01	+6.00	50	-5:10	+6.00	52	-5:08	+6.00	87	-4:33

Via Fisherman's Gat and Middle Sunk

Table B - Ramsgate to Essex Rivers via Fisherman's and Foulger's Gats

Neaps — All times relate to HW Sheerness — **Time to cover Sectors (in minutes) at 6.0 Kts**

NORTH BOUND

	B1			B2			B3			B4			B5			B6			B7			B8	
	North Foreland to Tongue			Tongue to Long Sand Outer			Long Sand Outer to Black Deep			Black Deep to NE Middle			NE Middle to Mid-Point Spitway			Outer Fisherman to Blk Deep No 8			Blk Deep No 8 to Barrow Deep			Barrow Deep to Mid-Spitway	
Time	Duration	Time at End of Sector	Time	Duration	Time at End of Sector	Time	Duration	Time at End of Sector	Time	Duration	Time at End of Sector	Time	Duration	Time at End of Sector	Time	Duration	Time at End of Sector	Time	Duration	Time at End of Sector	Time	Duration	Time at End of Sector
- 6.00	**74**	**- 4:46**	**- 6.00**	**47**	**- 5:13**	**- 6.00**	**81**	**- 4:39**	**- 6.00**	**49**	**- 5:11**	**- 6.00**	**47**	**- 5:13**	**- 6.00**	**37**	**- 5:23**	**- 6.00**	**44**	**- 5:16**	**- 6.00**	**72**	**- 4:48**
- 5.45	73	- 4:32	- 5.45	47	- 4:58	- 5.45	81	- 4:24	- 5.45	48	- 4:57	- 5.45	46	- 4:59	- 5.45	37	- 5:08	- 5.45	44	- 5:01	- 5.45	71	- 4:34
- 5.30	73	- 4:17	- 5.30	47	- 4:43	- 5.30	80	- 4:10	- 5.30	48	- 4:42	- 5.30	46	- 4:44	- 5.30	36	- 4:54	- 5.30	45	- 4:45	- 5.30	71	- 4:19
- 5.15	73	- 4:02	- 5.15	48	- 4:27	- 5.15	80	- 3:55	- 5.15	47	- 4:28	- 5.15	45	- 4:30	- 5.15	35	- 4:40	- 5.15	45	- 4:30	- 5.15	70	- 4:05
- 5.00	**73**	**- 3:47**	**- 5.00**	**48**	**- 4:12**	**- 5.00**	**80**	**- 3:40**	**- 5.00**	**47**	**- 4:13**	**- 5.00**	**44**	**- 4:16**	**- 5.00**	**35**	**- 4:25**	**- 5.00**	**46**	**- 4:14**	**- 5.00**	**69**	**- 3:51**
- 4.45	72	- 3:33	- 4.45	47	- 3:58	- 4.45	79	- 3:26	- 4.45	46	- 3:59	- 4.45	44	- 4:01	- 4.45	34	- 4:11	- 4.45	46	- 3:59	- 4.45	69	- 3:36
- 4.30	71	- 3:19	- 4.30	47	- 3:43	- 4.30	78	- 3:12	- 4.30	46	- 3:44	- 4.30	44	- 3:46	- 4.30	34	- 3:56	- 4.30	46	- 3:44	- 4.30	69	- 3:21
- 4.15	70	- 3:05	- 4.15	46	- 3:29	- 4.15	78	- 2:57	- 4.15	46	- 3:29	- 4.15	44	- 3:31	- 4.15	34	- 3:41	- 4.15	46	- 3:29	- 4.15	69	- 3:06
- 4.00	**69**	**- 2:51**	**- 4.00**	**46**	**- 3:14**	**- 4.00**	**77**	**- 2:43**	**- 4.00**	**46**	**- 3:14**	**- 4.00**	**44**	**- 3:16**	**- 4.00**	**33**	**- 3:27**	**- 4.00**	**46**	**- 3:14**	**- 4.00**	**69**	**- 2:51**
- 3.45	67	- 2:38	- 3.45	45	- 3:00	- 3.45	76	- 2:29	- 3.45	46	- 2:59	- 3.45	44	- 3:01	- 3.45	33	- 3:12	- 3.45	45	- 3:00	- 3.45	69	- 2:36
- 3.30	66	- 2:24	- 3.30	44	- 2:46	- 3.30	74	- 2:16	- 3.30	46	- 2:44	- 3.30	44	- 2:46	- 3.30	33	- 2:57	- 3.30	45	- 2:45	- 3.30	69	- 2:21
- 3.15	64	- 2:11	- 3.15	44	- 2:31	- 3.15	72	- 2:03	- 3.15	47	- 2:28	- 3.15	44	- 2:31	- 3.15	32	- 2:43	- 3.15	45	- 2:30	- 3.15	70	- 2:05
- 3.00	**63**	**- 1:57**	**- 3.00**	**43**	**- 2:17**	**- 3.00**	**71**	**- 1:49**	**- 3.00**	**47**	**- 2:13**	**- 3.00**	**44**	**- 2:16**	**- 3.00**	**32**	**- 2:28**	**- 3.00**	**44**	**- 2:16**	**- 3.00**	**70**	**- 1:50**
- 2.45	61	- 1:44	- 2.45	42	- 2:03	- 2.45	69	- 1:36	- 2.45	47	- 1:58	- 2.45	45	- 2:00	- 2.45	31	- 2:14	- 2.45	44	- 2:01	- 2.45	71	- 1:34
- 2.30	60	- 1:30	- 2.30	41	- 1:49	- 2.30	67	- 1:23	- 2.30	48	- 1:42	- 2.30	45	- 1:45	- 2.30	31	- 1:59	- 2.30	43	- 1:47	- 2.30	71	- 1:19
- 2.15	59	- 1:16	- 2.15	40	- 1:35	- 2.15	65	- 1:10	- 2.15	48	- 1:27	- 2.15	46	- 1:29	- 2.15	30	- 1:45	- 2.15	43	- 1:32	- 2.15	72	- 1:03
- 2.00	**57**	**- 1:03**	**- 2.00**	**39**	**- 1:21**	**- 2.00**	**63**	**- 0:57**	**- 2.00**	**49**	**- 1:11**	**- 2.00**	**47**	**- 1:13**	**- 2.00**	**30**	**- 1:30**	**- 2.00**	**42**	**- 1:18**	**- 2.00**	**72**	**- 0:48**
- 1.45	57	- 0:48	- 1.45	39	- 1:06	- 1.45	63	- 0:42	- 1.45	49	- 0:56	- 1.45	48	- 0:57	- 1.45	30	- 1:15	- 1.45	42	- 1:03	- 1.45	74	- 0:31
- 1.30	57	- 0:33	- 1.30	38	- 0:52	- 1.30	62	- 0:28	- 1.30	50	- 0:40	- 1.30	49	- 0:41	- 1.30	30	- 1:00	- 1.30	41	- 0:49	- 1.30	75	- 0:15
- 1.15	56	- 0:19	- 1.15	37	- 0:38	- 1.15	62	- 0:13	- 1.15	51	- 0:24	- 1.15	50	- 0:25	- 1.15	30	- 0:45	- 1.15	41	- 0:34	- 1.15	77	+ 0:02
- 1.00	**56**	**- 0:04**	**- 1.00**	**37**	**- 0:23**	**- 1.00**	**61**	**+ 0:01**	**- 1.00**	**52**	**- 0:08**	**- 1.00**	**51**	**- 0:09**	**- 1.00**	**30**	**- 0:30**	**- 1.00**	**40**	**- 0:20**	**- 1.00**	**78**	**+ 0:18**
- 0.45	56	+ 0:11	- 0.45	36	- 0:09	- 0.45	62	+ 0:17	- 0.45	53	+ 0:08	- 0.45	52	+ 0:07	- 0.45	31	- 0:14	- 0.45	40	- 0:05	- 0.45	79	+ 0:34
- 0.30	57	+ 0:27	- 0.30	36	+ 0:06	- 0.30	63	+ 0:33	- 0.30	55	+ 0:25	- 0.30	53	+ 0:23	- 0.30	32	+ 0:02	- 0.30	40	+ 0:10	- 0.30	81	+ 0:51
- 0.15	57	+ 0:42	- 0.15	35	+ 0:20	- 0.15	63	+ 0:48	- 0.15	56	+ 0:41	- 0.15	55	+ 0:40	- 0.15	32	+ 0:17	- 0.15	40	+ 0:25	- 0.15	82	+ 1:07
HW	**57**	**+ 0:57**	**HW**	**35**	**+ 0:35**	**HW**	**64**	**+ 1:04**	**HW**	**57**	**+ 0:57**	**HW**	**56**	**+ 0:56**	**HW**	**33**	**+ 0:33**	**HW**	**39**	**+ 0:39**	**HW**	**84**	**+ 1:24**
+ 0.15	58	+ 1:13	+ 0.15	35	+ 0:50	+ 0.15	65	+ 1:20	+ 0.15	58	+ 1:13	+ 0.15	57	+ 1:12	+ 0.15	34	+ 0:49	+ 0.15	39	+ 0:54	+ 0.15	85	+ 1:40
+ 0.30	59	+ 1:29	+ 0.30	35	+ 1:05	+ 0.30	66	+ 1:36	+ 0.30	59	+ 1:29	+ 0.30	58	+ 1:28	+ 0.30	35	+ 1:05	+ 0.30	39	+ 1:09	+ 0.30	87	+ 1:57
+ 0.45	60	+ 1:45	+ 0.45	34	+ 1:19	+ 0.45	67	+ 1:52	+ 0.45	59	+ 1:44	+ 0.45	60	+ 1:45	+ 0.45	36	+ 1:21	+ 0.45	39	+ 1:24	+ 0.45	89	+ 2:14
+ 1.00	**61**	**+ 2:01**	**+ 1.00**	**34**	**+ 1:34**	**+ 1.00**	**68**	**+ 2:08**	**+ 1.00**	**60**	**+ 2:00**	**+ 1.00**	**61**	**+ 2:01**	**+ 1.00**	**37**	**+ 1:37**	**+ 1.00**	**39**	**+ 1:39**	**+ 1.00**	**91**	**+ 2:31**
+ 1.15	62	+ 2:17	+ 1.15	35	+ 1:50	+ 1.15	69	+ 2:24	+ 1.15	60	+ 2:15	+ 1.15	61	+ 2:16	+ 1.15	38	+ 1:53	+ 1.15	39	+ 1:54	+ 1.15	91	+ 2:46
+ 1.30	63	+ 2:33	+ 1.30	35	+ 2:05	+ 1.30	69	+ 2:39	+ 1.30	61	+ 2:31	+ 1.30	61	+ 2:31	+ 1.30	38	+ 2:08	+ 1.30	39	+ 2:09	+ 1.30	91	+ 3:01
+ 1.45	64	+ 2:49	+ 1.45	35	+ 2:20	+ 1.45	70	+ 2:55	+ 1.45	61	+ 2:46	+ 1.45	61	+ 2:46	+ 1.45	39	+ 2:24	+ 1.45	39	+ 2:24	+ 1.45	92	+ 3:17
+ 2.00	**65**	**+ 3:05**	**+ 2.00**	**35**	**+ 2:35**	**+ 2.00**	**71**	**+ 3:11**	**+ 2.00**	**61**	**+ 3:01**	**+ 2.00**	**61**	**+ 3:01**	**+ 2.00**	**39**	**+ 2:39**	**+ 2.00**	**39**	**+ 2:39**	**+ 2.00**	**92**	**+ 3:32**
+ 2.15	66	+ 3:21	+ 2.15	35	+ 2:50	+ 2.15	71	+ 3:26	+ 2.15	61	+ 3:16	+ 2.15	61	+ 3:16	+ 2.15	40	+ 2:55	+ 2.15	39	+ 2:54	+ 2.15	90	+ 3:45
+ 2.30	67	+ 3:37	+ 2.30	36	+ 3:06	+ 2.30	72	+ 3:42	+ 2.30	61	+ 3:31	+ 2.30	60	+ 3:30	+ 2.30	40	+ 3:10	+ 2.30	39	+ 3:09	+ 2.30	89	+ 3:59
+ 2.45	68	+ 3:53	+ 2.45	36	+ 3:21	+ 2.45	72	+ 3:57	+ 2.45	60	+ 3:45	+ 2.45	60	+ 3:45	+ 2.45	40	+ 3:25	+ 2.45	40	+ 3:25	+ 2.45	87	+ 4:12
+ 3.00	**68**	**+ 4:08**	**+ 3.00**	**37**	**+ 3:37**	**+ 3.00**	**72**	**+ 4:12**	**+ 3.00**	**60**	**+ 4:00**	**+ 3.00**	**59**	**+ 3:59**	**+ 3.00**	**41**	**+ 3:41**	**+ 3.00**	**40**	**+ 3:40**	**+ 3.00**	**86**	**+ 4:26**
+ 3.15	69	+ 4:24	+ 3.15	37	+ 3:52	+ 3.15	73	+ 4:28	+ 3.15	59	+ 4:14	+ 3.15	58	+ 4:13	+ 3.15	41	+ 3:56	+ 3.15	40	+ 3:55	+ 3.15	85	+ 4:40
+ 3.30	69	+ 4:39	+ 3.30	38	+ 4:08	+ 3.30	73	+ 4:43	+ 3.30	58	+ 4:28	+ 3.30	58	+ 4:28	+ 3.30	41	+ 4:11	+ 3.30	40	+ 4:10	+ 3.30	84	+ 4:54
+ 3.45	70	+ 4:55	+ 3.45	38	+ 4:23	+ 3.45	74	+ 4:59	+ 3.45	57	+ 4:42	+ 3.45	57	+ 4:42	+ 3.45	41	+ 4:26	+ 3.45	40	+ 4:25	+ 3.45	83	+ 5:08
+ 4.00	**70**	**+ 5:10**	**+ 4.00**	**39**	**+ 4:39**	**+ 4.00**	**74**	**+ 5:14**	**+ 4.00**	**57**	**+ 4:57**	**+ 4.00**	**56**	**+ 4:56**	**+ 4.00**	**41**	**+ 4:41**	**+ 4.00**	**40**	**+ 4:40**	**+ 4.00**	**82**	**+ 5:22**
+ 4.15	71	+ 5:26	+ 4.15	39	+ 4:54	+ 4.15	75	+ 5:30	+ 4.15	56	+ 5:11	+ 4.15	55	+ 5:10	+ 4.15	41	+ 4:56	+ 4.15	41	+ 4:56	+ 4.15	81	+ 5:36
+ 4.30	71	+ 5:41	+ 4.30	40	+ 5:10	+ 4.30	76	+ 5:46	+ 4.30	55	+ 5:25	+ 4.30	54	+ 5:24	+ 4.30	41	+ 5:11	+ 4.30	41	+ 5:11	+ 4.30	79	+ 5:49
+ 4.45	72	+ 5:57	+ 4.45	41	+ 5:26	+ 4.45	77	- 5:58	+ 4.45	54	+ 5:39	+ 4.45	54	+ 5:39	+ 4.45	41	+ 5:26	+ 4.45	41	+ 5:26	+ 4.45	78	- 5:57
+ 5.00	**72**	**- 5:48**	**+ 5.00**	**41**	**+ 5:41**	**+ 5.00**	**78**	**- 5:42**	**+ 5.00**	**53**	**+ 5:53**	**+ 5.00**	**53**	**+ 5:53**	**+ 5.00**	**41**	**+ 5:41**	**+ 5.00**	**41**	**+ 5:41**	**+ 5.00**	**77**	**- 5:43**
+ 5.15	72	- 5:33	+ 5.15	42	+ 5:57	+ 5.15	79	- 5:26	+ 5.15	52	- 5:53	+ 5.15	52	- 5:53	+ 5.15	40	+ 5:55	+ 5.15	42	+ 5:57	+ 5.15	77	- 5:28
+ 5.30	73	- 5:17	+ 5.30	43	- 5:47	+ 5.30	79	- 5:11	+ 5.30	52	- 5:38	+ 5.30	51	- 5:39	+ 5.30	40	- 5:50	+ 5.30	42	- 5:48	+ 5.30	76	- 5:14
+ 5.45	73	- 5:02	+ 5.45	44	- 5:31	+ 5.45	80	- 4:55	+ 5.45	51	- 5:24	+ 5.45	51	- 5:24	+ 5.45	39	- 5:36	+ 5.45	42	- 5:33	+ 5.45	75	- 5:00
+ 6.00	**73**	**- 4:47**	**+ 6.00**	**45**	**- 5:15**	**+ 6.00**	**81**	**- 4:39**	**+ 6.00**	**51**	**- 5:09**	**+ 6.00**	**50**	**- 5:10**	**+ 6.00**	**39**	**- 5:21**	**+ 6.00**	**42**	**- 5:18**	**+ 6.00**	**75**	**- 4:45**

B1–B5: Via Foulger's Gat and Little Sunk

B6–B8: Via Fisherman's Gat and Middle Sunk

B - 6 Kts

Table B - Ramsgate to Essex Rivers via Fisherman's and Foulger's Gats

6 Kts - B

Time to cover Sectors (in minutes) at 6.0 kts | All times relate to HW Sheerness | **Springs**

	B1		B2		B3		B4		B5		B6		B7		B8	
	North Foreland to Tongue		Tongue to Long Sand Outer		Long Sand Outer to Black Deep		Black Deep to NE Middle		NE Middle to Mid-Point Spitway		Outer Fisherman to Blk Deep No 8		Blk Deep No 8 to Barrow Deep		Barrow Deep to Mid-Spitway	
Time	Duration	Time at End of Sector	Duration	Time at End of Sector	Duration	Time at End of Sector	Duration	Time at End of Sector	Duration	Time at End of Sector	Duration	Time at End of Sector	Duration	Time at End of Sector	Duration	Time at End of Sector
- 6.00	80	- 4:40	52	- 5:08	90	- 4:30	47	- 5:13	45	- 5:15	39	- 5:21	45	- 5:15	70	- 4:50
- 5.45	80	- 4:25	52	- 4:53	90	- 4:15	46	- 4:59	44	- 5:01	38	- 5:07	46	- 4:59	69	- 4:36
- 5.30	79	- 4:11	53	- 4:37	89	- 4:01	46	- 4:44	43	- 4:47	37	- 4:53	47	- 4:43	68	- 4:22
- 5.15	79	- 3:56	53	- 4:22	89	- 3:46	45	- 4:30	42	- 4:33	36	- 4:39	48	- 4:27	68	- 4:07
- 5.00	79	- 3:41	54	- 4:06	89	- 3:31	45	- 4:15	41	- 4:19	35	- 4:25	49	- 4:11	67	- 3:53
- 4.45	77	- 3:28	53	- 3:52	87	- 3:18	44	- 4:01	41	- 4:04	34	- 4:11	49	- 3:56	67	- 3:38
- 4.30	76	- 3:14	52	- 3:38	86	- 3:04	44	- 3:46	41	- 3:49	33	- 3:57	49	- 3:41	67	- 3:23
- 4.15	74	- 3:01	51	- 3:24	85	- 2:50	44	- 3:31	41	- 3:34	33	- 3:42	49	- 3:26	66	- 3:09
- 4.00	73	- 2:47	51	- 3:09	83	- 2:37	44	- 3:16	40	- 3:20	32	- 3:28	49	- 3:11	66	- 2:54
- 3.45	70	- 2:35	49	- 2:56	80	- 2:25	44	- 3:01	41	- 3:04	32	- 3:13	49	- 2:56	66	- 2:39
- 3.30	67	- 2:23	48	- 2:42	78	- 2:12	44	- 2:46	41	- 2:49	31	- 2:59	48	- 2:42	67	- 2:23
- 3.15	64	- 2:11	46	- 2:29	75	- 2:00	44	- 2:31	41	- 2:34	31	- 2:44	48	- 2:27	67	- 2:08
- 3.00	62	- 1:58	45	- 2:15	72	- 1:48	44	- 2:16	41	- 2:19	30	- 2:30	47	- 2:13	67	- 1:53
- 2.45	59	- 1:46	44	- 2:01	69	- 1:36	45	- 2:00	42	- 2:03	29	- 2:16	46	- 1:59	68	- 1:37
- 2.30	57	- 1:33	42	- 1:48	66	- 1:24	46	- 1:44	43	- 1:47	28	- 2:02	45	- 1:45	69	- 1:21
- 2.15	55	- 1:20	41	- 1:34	63	- 1:12	46	- 1:29	43	- 1:32	27	- 1:48	44	- 1:31	70	- 1:05
- 2.00	53	- 1:07	39	- 1:21	60	- 1:00	47	- 1:13	44	- 1:16	26	- 1:34	43	- 1:17	71	- 0:49
- 1.45	52	- 0:53	38	- 1:07	59	- 0:46	48	- 0:57	46	- 0:59	27	- 1:18	42	- 1:03	73	- 0:32
- 1.30	52	- 0:38	37	- 0:53	59	- 0:31	49	- 0:41	47	- 0:43	27	- 1:03	41	- 0:49	74	- 0:16
- 1.15	51	- 0:24	36	- 0:39	58	- 0:17	51	- 0:24	49	- 0:26	27	- 0:48	41	- 0:34	76	+ 0:01
- 1.00	50	- 0:10	35	- 0:25	57	- 0:03	52	- 0:08	50	- 0:10	27	- 0:33	40	- 0:20	78	+ 0:18
- 0.45	51	+ 0:06	35	- 0:10	58	+ 0:13	54	+ 0:09	52	+ 0:07	29	- 0:16	40	- 0:05	81	+ 0:36
- 0.30	51	+ 0:21	34	+ 0:04	60	+ 0:30	56	+ 0:26	55	+ 0:25	30	HW	40	+ 0:10	83	+ 0:53
- 0.15	52	+ 0:37	34	+ 0:19	61	+ 0:46	58	+ 0:43	57	+ 0:42	31	+ 0:16	39	+ 0:24	85	+ 1:10
HW	52	+ 0:52	33	+ 0:33	62	+ 1:02	59	+ 0:59	59	+ 0:59	32	+ 0:32	39	+ 0:39	87	+ 1:27
+ 0.15	54	+ 1:09	33	+ 0:48	63	+ 1:18	61	+ 1:16	61	+ 1:16	34	+ 0:49	39	+ 0:54	89	+ 1:44
+ 0.30	55	+ 1:25	33	+ 1:03	65	+ 1:35	62	+ 1:32	63	+ 1:33	36	+ 1:06	39	+ 1:09	92	+ 2:02
+ 0.45	57	+ 1:42	33	+ 1:18	67	+ 1:52	63	+ 1:48	65	+ 1:50	37	+ 1:22	39	+ 1:24	94	+ 2:19
+ 1.00	58	+ 1:58	32	+ 1:32	68	+ 2:08	65	+ 2:05	67	+ 2:07	39	+ 1:39	39	+ 1:39	96	+ 2:36
+ 1.15	60	+ 2:15	33	+ 1:48	69	+ 2:24	65	+ 2:20	67	+ 2:22	40	+ 1:55	39	+ 1:54	96	+ 2:51
+ 1.30	62	+ 2:32	33	+ 2:03	70	+ 2:40	65	+ 2:35	67	+ 2:37	41	+ 2:11	39	+ 2:09	96	+ 3:06
+ 1.45	64	+ 2:49	33	+ 2:18	71	+ 2:56	66	+ 2:51	68	+ 2:53	42	+ 2:27	39	+ 2:24	96	+ 3:21
+ 2.00	66	+ 3:06	33	+ 2:33	72	+ 3:12	66	+ 3:06	68	+ 3:08	42	+ 2:42	39	+ 2:39	97	+ 3:37
+ 2.15	68	+ 3:23	34	+ 2:49	73	+ 3:28	66	+ 3:21	67	+ 3:22	43	+ 2:58	39	+ 2:54	95	+ 3:50
+ 2.30	69	+ 3:39	34	+ 3:04	73	+ 3:43	65	+ 3:35	66	+ 3:36	43	+ 3:13	39	+ 3:09	94	+ 4:04
+ 2.45	71	+ 3:56	35	+ 3:20	74	+ 3:59	64	+ 3:49	65	+ 3:50	44	+ 3:29	39	+ 3:24	93	+ 4:18
+ 3.00	72	+ 4:12	35	+ 3:35	74	+ 4:14	64	+ 4:04	64	+ 4:04	44	+ 3:44	39	+ 3:39	92	+ 4:32
+ 3.15	73	+ 4:28	36	+ 3:51	75	+ 4:30	63	+ 4:18	63	+ 4:18	45	+ 4:00	40	+ 3:55	90	+ 4:45
+ 3.30	74	+ 4:44	37	+ 4:07	76	+ 4:46	61	+ 4:31	61	+ 4:31	45	+ 4:15	40	+ 4:10	88	+ 4:58
+ 3.45	74	+ 4:59	38	+ 4:23	77	+ 5:02	60	+ 4:45	60	+ 4:45	45	+ 4:30	40	+ 4:25	86	+ 5:11
+ 4.00	75	+ 5:15	38	+ 4:38	77	+ 5:17	59	+ 4:59	59	+ 4:59	45	+ 4:45	40	+ 4:40	85	+ 5:25
+ 4.15	76	+ 5:31	39	+ 4:54	79	+ 5:34	58	+ 5:13	57	+ 5:12	45	+ 5:00	41	+ 4:56	83	+ 5:38
+ 4.30	76	+ 5:46	40	+ 5:10	80	+ 5:50	56	+ 5:26	56	+ 5:26	45	+ 5:15	41	+ 5:11	81	+ 5:51
+ 4.45	77	- 5:58	41	+ 5:26	82	- 5:53	55	+ 5:40	55	+ 5:40	45	+ 5:30	41	+ 5:26	79	- 5:56
+ 5.00	78	- 5:42	42	+ 5:42	83	- 5:37	54	+ 5:54	54	+ 5:54	45	+ 5:45	42	+ 5:42	78	- 5:42
+ 5.15	78	- 5:27	43	+ 5:58	84	- 5:21	53	- 5:52	52	- 5:53	44	+ 5:59	42	+ 5:57	77	- 5:28
+ 5.30	78	- 5:12	45	- 5:45	86	- 5:04	52	- 5:38	51	- 5:39	43	- 5:47	42	- 5:48	76	- 5:14
+ 5.45	79	- 4:56	46	- 5:29	87	- 4:48	51	- 5:24	50	- 5:25	42	- 5:33	43	- 5:32	74	- 5:01
+ 6.00	79	- 4:41	48	- 5:12	88	- 4:32	50	- 5:10	49	- 5:11	41	- 5:19	43	- 5:17	73	- 4:47

B1–B4: Via Foulger's Gat and Little Sunk

B5–B8: Via Fisherman's Gat and Middle Sunk

NORTH BOUND

Table B - Ramsgate to Essex Rivers via Fisherman's and Foulger's Gats

Neaps — All times relate to HW Sheerness — **Time to cover Sectors (in minutes) at 7.0 Kts**

NORTH BOUND

Time	B1 North Foreland to Tongue Duration	B1 Time at End of Sector	Time	B2 Tongue to Long Sand Outer Duration	B2 Time at End of Sector	Time	B3 Long Sand Outer to Black Deep Duration	B3 Time at End of Sector	Time	B4 Black Deep to NE Middle Duration	B4 Time at End of Sector
- 6.00	**62**	**- 4:58**	**- 6.00**	**39**	**- 5:21**	**- 6.00**	**69**	**- 4:51**	**- 6.00**	**42**	**- 5:18**
- 5.45	62	- 4:43	- 5.45	39	- 5:06	- 5.45	69	- 4:36	- 5.45	42	- 5:03
- 5.30	62	- 4:28	- 5.30	40	- 4:50	- 5.30	68	- 4:22	- 5.30	41	- 4:49
- 5.15	62	- 4:13	- 5.15	40	- 4:35	- 5.15	68	- 4:07	- 5.15	41	- 4:34
- 5.00	**61**	**- 3:59**	**- 5.00**	**40**	**- 4:20**	**- 5.00**	**68**	**- 3:52**	**- 5.00**	**41**	**- 4:19**
- 4.45	61	- 3:44	- 4.45	40	- 4:05	- 4.45	68	- 3:37	- 4.45	40	- 4:05
- 4.30	60	- 3:30	- 4.30	39	- 3:51	- 4.30	67	- 3:23	- 4.30	40	- 3:50
- 4.15	59	- 3:16	- 4.15	39	- 3:36	- 4.15	67	- 3:08	- 4.15	40	- 3:35
- 4.00	**59**	**- 3:01**	**- 4.00**	**39**	**- 3:21**	**- 4.00**	**66**	**- 2:54**	**- 4.00**	**40**	**- 3:20**
- 3.45	58	- 2:47	- 3.45	38	- 3:07	- 3.45	65	- 2:40	- 3.45	40	- 3:05
- 3.30	57	- 2:33	- 3.30	38	- 2:52	- 3.30	64	- 2:26	- 3.30	40	- 2:50
- 3.15	55	- 2:20	- 3.15	37	- 2:38	- 3.15	62	- 2:13	- 3.15	40	- 2:35
- 3.00	**54**	**- 2:06**	**- 3.00**	**37**	**- 2:23**	**- 3.00**	**61**	**- 1:59**	**- 3.00**	**41**	**- 2:19**
- 2.45	53	- 1:52	- 2.45	36	- 2:09	- 2.45	59	- 1:46	- 2.45	41	- 2:04
- 2.30	52	- 1:38	- 2.30	35	- 1:55	- 2.30	58	- 1:32	- 2.30	41	- 1:49
- 2.15	51	- 1:24	- 2.15	35	- 1:40	- 2.15	56	- 1:19	- 2.15	42	- 1:33
- 2.00	**50**	**- 1:10**	**- 2.00**	**34**	**- 1:26**	**- 2.00**	**55**	**- 1:05**	**- 2.00**	**42**	**- 1:18**
- 1.45	50	- 0:55	- 1.45	33	- 1:12	- 1.45	54	- 0:51	- 1.45	42	- 1:03
- 1.30	50	- 0:40	- 1.30	33	- 0:57	- 1.30	54	- 0:36	- 1.30	43	- 0:47
- 1.15	49	- 0:26	- 1.15	32	- 0:43	- 1.15	53	- 0:22	- 1.15	44	- 0:31
- 1.00	**49**	**- 0:11**	**- 1.00**	**32**	**- 0:28**	**- 1.00**	**53**	**- 0:07**	**- 1.00**	**44**	**- 0:16**
- 0.45	49	+ 0:04	- 0.45	32	- 0:13	- 0.45	53	+ 0:08	- 0.45	45	HW
- 0.30	49	+ 0:19	- 0.30	31	+ 0:01	- 0.30	54	+ 0:24	- 0.30	46	+ 0:16
- 0.15	50	+ 0:35	- 0.15	31	+ 0:16	- 0.15	54	+ 0:39	- 0.15	47	+ 0:32
HW	**50**	**+ 0:50**	**HW**	**30**	**+ 0:30**	**HW**	**55**	**+ 0:55**	**HW**	**48**	**+ 0:48**
+ 0.15	50	+ 1:05	+ 0.15	30	+ 0:45	+ 0.15	56	+ 1:11	+ 0.15	49	+ 1:04
+ 0.30	51	+ 1:21	+ 0.30	30	+ 1:00	+ 0.30	56	+ 1:26	+ 0.30	49	+ 1:19
+ 0.45	52	+ 1:37	+ 0.45	30	+ 1:15	+ 0.45	57	+ 1:42	+ 0.45	50	+ 1:35
+ 1.00	**52**	**+ 1:52**	**+ 1.00**	**30**	**+ 1:30**	**+ 1.00**	**58**	**+ 1:58**	**+ 1.00**	**50**	**+ 1:50**
+ 1.15	53	+ 2:08	+ 1.15	30	+ 1:45	+ 1.15	58	+ 2:13	+ 1.15	51	+ 2:06
+ 1.30	54	+ 2:24	+ 1.30	30	+ 2:00	+ 1.30	59	+ 2:29	+ 1.30	51	+ 2:21
+ 1.45	55	+ 2:40	+ 1.45	30	+ 2:15	+ 1.45	59	+ 2:44	+ 1.45	51	+ 2:36
+ 2.00	**56**	**+ 2:56**	**+ 2.00**	**30**	**+ 2:30**	**+ 2.00**	**60**	**+ 3:00**	**+ 2.00**	**51**	**+ 2:51**
+ 2.15	56	+ 3:11	+ 2.15	31	+ 2:46	+ 2.15	60	+ 3:15	+ 2.15	51	+ 3:06
+ 2.30	57	+ 3:27	+ 2.30	31	+ 3:01	+ 2.30	61	+ 3:31	+ 2.30	51	+ 3:21
+ 2.45	57	+ 3:42	+ 2.45	31	+ 3:16	+ 2.45	61	+ 3:46	+ 2.45	51	+ 3:36
+ 3.00	**58**	**+ 3:58**	**+ 3.00**	**31**	**+ 3:31**	**+ 3.00**	**61**	**+ 4:01**	**+ 3.00**	**50**	**+ 3:50**
+ 3.15	58	+ 4:13	+ 3.15	32	+ 3:47	+ 3.15	62	+ 4:17	+ 3.15	50	+ 4:05
+ 3.30	59	+ 4:29	+ 3.30	32	+ 4:02	+ 3.30	62	+ 4:32	+ 3.30	49	+ 4:19
+ 3.45	59	+ 4:44	+ 3.45	33	+ 4:18	+ 3.45	62	+ 4:47	+ 3.45	49	+ 4:34
+ 4.00	**59**	**+ 4:59**	**+ 4.00**	**33**	**+ 4:33**	**+ 4.00**	**63**	**+ 5:03**	**+ 4.00**	**48**	**+ 4:48**
+ 4.15	60	+ 5:15	+ 4.15	34	+ 4:49	+ 4.15	63	+ 5:18	+ 4.15	47	+ 5:02
+ 4.30	60	+ 5:30	+ 4.30	34	+ 5:04	+ 4.30	64	+ 5:34	+ 4.30	47	+ 5:17
+ 4.45	60	+ 5:45	+ 4.45	34	+ 5:19	+ 4.45	65	+ 5:50	+ 4.45	46	+ 5:31
+ 5.00	**61**	**- 5:59**	**+ 5.00**	**35**	**+ 5:35**	**+ 5.00**	**66**	**- 5:54**	**+ 5.00**	**46**	**+ 5:46**
+ 5.15	61	- 5:44	+ 5.15	35	+ 5:50	+ 5.15	66	- 5:39	+ 5.15	45	- 6:00
+ 5.30	61	- 5:29	+ 5.30	36	- 5:54	+ 5.30	67	- 5:23	+ 5.30	45	- 5:45
+ 5.45	61	- 5:14	+ 5.45	37	- 5:38	+ 5.45	68	- 5:07	+ 5.45	44	- 5:31
+ 6.00	**62**	**- 4:58**	**+ 6.00**	**37**	**- 5:23**	**+ 6.00**	**69**	**- 4:51**	**+ 6.00**	**44**	**- 5:16**

Via Foulger's Gat and Little Sunk

Time	B5 NE Middle to Mid-Point Spitway Duration	B5 Time at End of Sector	Time	B6 Outer Fisherman to Blk Deep No 8 Duration	B6 Time at End of Sector	Time	B7 Blk Deep No 8 to Barrow Deep Duration	B7 Time at End of Sector	Time	B8 Barrow Deep to Mid-Spitway Duration	B8 Time at End of Sector
- 6.00	**41**	**- 5:19**	**- 6.00**	**32**	**- 5:28**	**- 6.00**	**37**	**- 5:23**	**- 6.00**	**62**	**- 4:58**
- 5.45	41	- 5:04	- 5.45	31	- 5:14	- 5.45	37	- 5:08	- 5.45	62	- 4:43
- 5.30	40	- 4:50	- 5.30	31	- 4:59	- 5.30	38	- 4:52	- 5.30	61	- 4:29
- 5.15	39	- 4:36	- 5.15	30	- 4:45	- 5.15	38	- 4:37	- 5.15	61	- 4:14
- 5.00	**39**	**- 4:21**	**- 5.00**	**30**	**- 4:30**	**- 5.00**	**38**	**- 4:22**	**- 5.00**	**60**	**- 4:00**
- 4.45	39	- 4:06	- 4.45	30	- 4:15	- 4.45	38	- 4:07	- 4.45	60	- 3:45
- 4.30	38	- 3:52	- 4.30	29	- 4:01	- 4.30	39	- 3:51	- 4.30	60	- 3:30
- 4.15	38	- 3:37	- 4.15	29	- 3:46	- 4.15	39	- 3:36	- 4.15	60	- 3:15
- 4.00	**38**	**- 3:22**	**- 4.00**	**29**	**- 3:31**	**- 4.00**	**39**	**- 3:21**	**- 4.00**	**60**	**- 3:00**
- 3.45	38	- 3:07	- 3.45	28	- 3:17	- 3.45	38	- 3:07	- 3.45	60	- 2:45
- 3.30	38	- 2:52	- 3.30	28	- 3:02	- 3.30	38	- 2:52	- 3.30	60	- 2:30
- 3.15	39	- 2:36	- 3.15	28	- 2:47	- 3.15	38	- 2:37	- 3.15	60	- 2:15
- 3.00	**39**	**- 2:21**	**- 3.00**	**28**	**- 2:32**	**- 3.00**	**38**	**- 2:22**	**- 3.00**	**61**	**- 1:59**
- 2.45	39	- 2:06	- 2.45	27	- 2:18	- 2.45	37	- 2:08	- 2.45	61	- 1:44
- 2.30	39	- 1:51	- 2.30	26	- 2:04	- 2.30	37	- 1:53	- 2.30	62	- 1:28
- 2.15	40	- 1:35	- 2.15	26	- 1:49	- 2.15	36	- 1:39	- 2.15	62	- 1:13
- 2.00	**40**	**- 1:20**	**- 2.00**	**25**	**- 1:35**	**- 2.00**	**36**	**- 1:24**	**- 2.00**	**62**	**- 0:58**
- 1.45	41	- 1:04	- 1.45	25	- 1:20	- 1.45	36	- 1:09	- 1.45	63	- 0:42
- 1.30	42	- 0:48	- 1.30	26	- 1:04	- 1.30	35	- 0:55	- 1.30	64	- 0:26
- 1.15	42	- 0:33	- 1.15	26	- 0:49	- 1.15	35	- 0:40	- 1.15	65	- 0:10
- 1.00	**43**	**- 0:17**	**- 1.00**	**26**	**- 0:34**	**- 1.00**	**35**	**- 0:25**	**- 1.00**	**66**	**+ 0:06**
- 0.45	44	- 0:01	- 0.45	26	- 0:19	- 0.45	35	- 0:10	- 0.45	67	+ 0:22
- 0.30	45	+ 0:15	- 0.30	27	- 0:03	- 0.30	34	+ 0:04	- 0.30	68	+ 0:38
- 0.15	46	+ 0:31	- 0.15	28	+ 0:13	- 0.15	34	+ 0:19	- 0.15	69	+ 0:54
HW	**47**	**+ 0:47**	**HW**	**28**	**+ 0:28**	**HW**	**34**	**+ 0:34**	**HW**	**70**	**+ 1:10**
+ 0.15	48	+ 1:03	+ 0.15	29	+ 0:44	+ 0.15	34	+ 0:49	+ 0.15	71	+ 1:26
+ 0.30	49	+ 1:19	+ 0.30	30	+ 1:00	+ 0.30	34	+ 1:04	+ 0.30	72	+ 1:42
+ 0.45	50	+ 1:35	+ 0.45	31	+ 1:16	+ 0.45	34	+ 1:19	+ 0.45	73	+ 1:58
+ 1.00	**51**	**+ 1:51**	**+ 1.00**	**32**	**+ 1:32**	**+ 1.00**	**34**	**+ 1:34**	**+ 1.00**	**73**	**+ 2:13**
+ 1.15	51	+ 2:06	+ 1.15	32	+ 1:47	+ 1.15	34	+ 1:49	+ 1.15	73	+ 2:28
+ 1.30	51	+ 2:21	+ 1.30	32	+ 2:02	+ 1.30	34	+ 2:04	+ 1.30	74	+ 2:44
+ 1.45	51	+ 2:36	+ 1.45	33	+ 2:18	+ 1.45	34	+ 2:19	+ 1.45	74	+ 2:59
+ 2.00	**51**	**+ 2:51**	**+ 2.00**	**33**	**+ 2:33**	**+ 2.00**	**34**	**+ 2:34**	**+ 2.00**	**74**	**+ 3:14**
+ 2.15	51	+ 3:06	+ 2.15	33	+ 2:48	+ 2.15	34	+ 2:49	+ 2.15	74	+ 3:29
+ 2.30	51	+ 3:21	+ 2.30	34	+ 3:04	+ 2.30	34	+ 3:04	+ 2.30	73	+ 3:43
+ 2.45	50	+ 3:35	+ 2.45	34	+ 3:19	+ 2.45	34	+ 3:19	+ 2.45	73	+ 3:58
+ 3.00	**50**	**+ 3:50**	**+ 3.00**	**34**	**+ 3:34**	**+ 3.00**	**34**	**+ 3:34**	**+ 3.00**	**73**	**+ 4:13**
+ 3.15	49	+ 4:04	+ 3.15	34	+ 3:49	+ 3.15	34	+ 3:49	+ 3.15	72	+ 4:27
+ 3.30	49	+ 4:19	+ 3.30	34	+ 4:04	+ 3.30	34	+ 4:04	+ 3.30	71	+ 4:41
+ 3.45	48	+ 4:33	+ 3.45	34	+ 4:19	+ 3.45	34	+ 4:19	+ 3.45	70	+ 4:55
+ 4.00	**47**	**+ 4:47**	**+ 4.00**	**35**	**+ 4:35**	**+ 4.00**	**35**	**+ 4:35**	**+ 4.00**	**70**	**+ 5:10**
+ 4.15	47	+ 5:02	+ 4.15	35	+ 4:50	+ 4.15	35	+ 4:50	+ 4.15	69	+ 5:24
+ 4.30	46	+ 5:16	+ 4.30	34	+ 5:04	+ 4.30	35	+ 5:05	+ 4.30	68	+ 5:38
+ 4.45	46	+ 5:31	+ 4.45	34	+ 5:19	+ 4.45	35	+ 5:20	+ 4.45	67	+ 5:52
+ 5.00	**45**	**+ 5:45**	**+ 5.00**	**34**	**+ 5:34**	**+ 5.00**	**35**	**+ 5:35**	**+ 5.00**	**66**	**- 5:54**
+ 5.15	45	- 6:00	+ 5.15	34	+ 5:49	+ 5.15	35	+ 5:50	+ 5.15	66	- 5:39
+ 5.30	44	- 5:46	+ 5.30	34	- 5:56	+ 5.30	36	- 5:54	+ 5.30	65	- 5:25
+ 5.45	44	- 5:31	+ 5.45	33	- 5:42	+ 5.45	36	- 5:39	+ 5.45	65	- 5:10
+ 6.00	**43**	**- 5:17**	**+ 6.00**	**33**	**- 5:27**	**+ 6.00**	**36**	**- 5:24**	**+ 6.00**	**64**	**- 4:56**

Via Fisherman's Gat and Middle Sunk

Table B - Ramsgate to Essex Rivers via Fisherman's and Foulger's Gats

Time to cover Sectors (in minutes) at 7.0 kts — All times relate to HW Sheerness — **Springs**

	B1 North Foreland to Tongue			B2 Tongue to Long Sand Outer			B3 Long Sand Outer to Black Deep			B4 Black Deep to NE Middle	
Time	Duration	Time at End of Sector	Time	Duration	Time at End of Sector	Time	Duration	Time at End of Sector	Time	Duration	Time at End of Sector
- 6.00	66	- 4:54	- 6.00	42	- 5:18	- 6.00	75	- 4:45	- 6.00	41	- 5:19
- 5.45	66	- 4:39	- 5.45	43	- 5:02	- 5.45	75	- 4:30	- 5.45	41	- 5:04
- 5.30	66	- 4:24	- 5.30	43	- 4:47	- 5.30	74	- 4:16	- 5.30	40	- 4:50
- 5.15	66	- 4:09	- 5.15	44	- 4:31	- 5.15	74	- 4:01	- 5.15	40	- 4:35
- 5.00	66	- 3:54	- 5.00	44	- 4:16	- 5.00	74	- 3:46	- 5.00	39	- 4:21
- 4.45	65	- 3:40	- 4.45	44	- 4:01	- 4.45	74	- 3:31	- 4.45	39	- 4:06
- 4.30	64	- 3:26	- 4.30	43	- 3:47	- 4.30	73	- 3:17	- 4.30	39	- 3:51
- 4.15	63	- 3:12	- 4.15	43	- 3:32	- 4.15	72	- 3:03	- 4.15	39	- 3:36
- 4.00	62	- 2:58	- 4.00	42	- 3:18	- 4.00	71	- 2:49	- 4.00	38	- 3:22
- 3.45	60	- 2:45	- 3.45	41	- 3:04	- 3.45	69	- 2:36	- 3.45	38	- 3:07
- 3.30	58	- 2:32	- 3.30	40	- 2:50	- 3.30	67	- 2:23	- 3.30	39	- 2:51
- 3.15	56	- 2:19	- 3.15	39	- 2:36	- 3.15	65	- 2:10	- 3.15	39	- 2:36
- 3.00	54	- 2:06	- 3.00	38	- 2:22	- 3.00	64	- 1:56	- 3.00	39	- 2:21
- 2.45	52	- 1:53	- 2.45	37	- 2:08	- 2.45	61	- 1:44	- 2.45	39	- 2:06
- 2.30	50	- 1:40	- 2.30	36	- 1:54	- 2.30	58	- 1:32	- 2.30	40	- 1:50
- 2.15	49	- 1:26	- 2.15	35	- 1:40	- 2.15	55	- 1:20	- 2.15	40	- 1:35
- 2.00	47	- 1:13	- 2.00	34	- 1:26	- 2.00	53	- 1:07	- 2.00	40	- 1:20
- 1.45	46	- 0:59	- 1.45	33	- 1:12	- 1.45	52	- 0:53	- 1.45	41	- 1:04
- 1.30	46	- 0:44	- 1.30	33	- 0:57	- 1.30	51	- 0:39	- 1.30	42	- 0:48
- 1.15	45	- 0:30	- 1.15	32	- 0:43	- 1.15	50	- 0:25	- 1.15	43	- 0:32
- 1.00	45	- 0:15	- 1.00	31	- 0:29	- 1.00	49	- 0:11	- 1.00	44	- 0:16
- 0.45	45	HW	- 0.45	31	- 0:14	- 0.45	50	+ 0:05	- 0.45	45	HW
- 0.30	45	+ 0:15	- 0.30	30	HW	- 0.30	51	+ 0:21	- 0.30	47	+ 0:17
- 0.15	46	+ 0:31	- 0.15	30	+ 0:15	- 0.15	52	+ 0:37	- 0.15	48	+ 0:33
HW	46	+ 0:46	HW	29	+ 0:29	HW	53	+ 0:53	HW	50	+ 0:50
+ 0.15	47	+ 1:02	+ 0.15	29	+ 0:44	+ 0.15	54	+ 1:09	+ 0.15	51	+ 1:06
+ 0.30	48	+ 1:18	+ 0.30	29	+ 0:59	+ 0.30	55	+ 1:25	+ 0.30	52	+ 1:22
+ 0.45	49	+ 1:34	+ 0.45	28	+ 1:13	+ 0.45	57	+ 1:42	+ 0.45	53	+ 1:38
+ 1.00	50	+ 1:50	+ 1.00	28	+ 1:28	+ 1.00	58	+ 1:58	+ 1.00	54	+ 1:54
+ 1.15	52	+ 2:07	+ 1.15	28	+ 1:43	+ 1.15	59	+ 2:14	+ 1.15	54	+ 2:09
+ 1.30	53	+ 2:23	+ 1.30	29	+ 1:59	+ 1.30	59	+ 2:29	+ 1.30	54	+ 2:24
+ 1.45	55	+ 2:40	+ 1.45	29	+ 2:14	+ 1.45	60	+ 2:45	+ 1.45	55	+ 2:40
+ 2.00	56	+ 2:56	+ 2.00	29	+ 2:29	+ 2.00	61	+ 3:01	+ 2.00	55	+ 2:55
+ 2.15	57	+ 3:12	+ 2.15	29	+ 2:44	+ 2.15	61	+ 3:16	+ 2.15	54	+ 3:09
+ 2.30	58	+ 3:28	+ 2.30	30	+ 3:00	+ 2.30	62	+ 3:32	+ 2.30	54	+ 3:24
+ 2.45	59	+ 3:44	+ 2.45	30	+ 3:15	+ 2.45	62	+ 3:47	+ 2.45	54	+ 3:39
+ 3.00	61	+ 4:01	+ 3.00	30	+ 3:30	+ 3.00	63	+ 4:03	+ 3.00	53	+ 3:53
+ 3.15	61	+ 4:16	+ 3.15	31	+ 3:46	+ 3.15	63	+ 4:18	+ 3.15	52	+ 4:07
+ 3.30	62	+ 4:32	+ 3.30	32	+ 4:02	+ 3.30	64	+ 4:34	+ 3.30	52	+ 4:22
+ 3.45	62	+ 4:47	+ 3.45	32	+ 4:17	+ 3.45	64	+ 4:49	+ 3.45	51	+ 4:36
+ 4.00	63	+ 5:03	+ 4.00	33	+ 4:33	+ 4.00	65	+ 5:05	+ 4.00	50	+ 4:50
+ 4.15	63	+ 5:18	+ 4.15	33	+ 4:48	+ 4.15	66	+ 5:21	+ 4.15	49	+ 5:04
+ 4.30	64	+ 5:34	+ 4.30	34	+ 5:04	+ 4.30	67	+ 5:37	+ 4.30	48	+ 5:18
+ 4.45	64	+ 5:49	+ 4.45	34	+ 5:19	+ 4.45	68	+ 5:53	+ 4.45	47	+ 5:32
+ 5.00	65	- 5:55	+ 5.00	35	+ 5:35	+ 5.00	69	- 5:51	+ 5.00	46	+ 5:46
+ 5.15	65	- 5:40	+ 5.15	36	+ 5:51	+ 5.15	70	- 5:35	+ 5.15	45	- 6:00
+ 5.30	65	- 5:25	+ 5.30	37	- 5:53	+ 5.30	71	- 5:19	+ 5.30	45	- 5:45
+ 5.45	66	- 5:09	+ 5.45	39	- 5:36	+ 5.45	72	- 5:03	+ 5.45	44	- 5:31
+ 6.00	66	- 4:54	+ 6.00	40	- 5:20	+ 6.00	74	- 4:46	+ 6.00	43	- 5:17

Via Foulger's Gat and Middle Sunk

	B5 NE Middle to Mid-Point Spitway			B6 Outer Fisherman to Blk Deep No 8			B7 Blk Deep No 8 to Barrow Deep			B8 Barrow Deep to Mid-Spitway	
Time	Duration	Time at End of Sector	Time	Duration	Time at End of Sector	Time	Duration	Time at End of Sector	Time	Duration	Time at End of Sector
- 6.00	40	- 5:20	- 6.00	33	- 5:27	- 6.00	38	- 5:22	- 6.00	61	- 4:59
- 5.45	39	- 5:06	- 5.45	32	- 5:13	- 5.45	38	- 5:07	- 5.45	60	- 4:45
- 5.30	38	- 4:52	- 5.30	31	- 4:59	- 5.30	39	- 4:51	- 5.30	60	- 4:30
- 5.15	37	- 4:38	- 5.15	31	- 4:44	- 5.15	40	- 4:35	- 5.15	59	- 4:16
- 5.00	37	- 4:23	- 5.00	30	- 4:30	- 5.00	41	- 4:19	- 5.00	58	- 4:02
- 4.45	36	- 4:09	- 4.45	29	- 4:16	- 4.45	41	- 4:04	- 4.45	58	- 3:47
- 4.30	36	- 3:54	- 4.30	29	- 4:01	- 4.30	41	- 3:49	- 4.30	58	- 3:32
- 4.15	36	- 3:39	- 4.15	28	- 3:47	- 4.15	41	- 3:34	- 4.15	58	- 3:17
- 4.00	36	- 3:24	- 4.00	28	- 3:32	- 4.00	41	- 3:19	- 4.00	58	- 3:02
- 3.45	36	- 3:09	- 3.45	27	- 3:18	- 3.45	41	- 3:04	- 3.45	58	- 2:47
- 3.30	36	- 2:54	- 3.30	27	- 3:03	- 3.30	40	- 2:50	- 3.30	58	- 2:32
- 3.15	36	- 2:39	- 3.15	26	- 2:49	- 3.15	40	- 2:35	- 3.15	58	- 2:17
- 3.00	36	- 2:24	- 3.00	26	- 2:34	- 3.00	39	- 2:21	- 3.00	58	- 2:02
- 2.45	37	- 2:08	- 2.45	25	- 2:20	- 2.45	39	- 2:06	- 2.45	59	- 1:46
- 2.30	37	- 1:53	- 2.30	24	- 2:06	- 2.30	38	- 1:52	- 2.30	60	- 1:30
- 2.15	38	- 1:37	- 2.15	23	- 1:52	- 2.15	37	- 1:38	- 2.15	60	- 1:15
- 2.00	38	- 1:22	- 2.00	23	- 1:37	- 2.00	36	- 1:24	- 2.00	61	- 0:59
- 1.45	39	- 1:06	- 1.45	23	- 1:22	- 1.45	36	- 1:09	- 1.45	62	- 0:43
- 1.30	40	- 0:50	- 1.30	23	- 1:07	- 1.30	36	- 0:54	- 1.30	64	- 0:26
- 1.15	41	- 0:34	- 1.15	23	- 0:52	- 1.15	35	- 0:40	- 1.15	65	- 0:10
- 1.00	43	- 0:17	- 1.00	23	- 0:37	- 1.00	35	- 0:25	- 1.00	66	+ 0:06
- 0.45	44	- 0:01	- 0.45	24	- 0:21	- 0.45	34	- 0:11	- 0.45	68	+ 0:23
- 0.30	46	+ 0:16	- 0.30	25	- 0:05	- 0.30	34	+ 0:04	- 0.30	70	+ 0:40
- 0.15	47	+ 0:32	- 0.15	26	+ 0:11	- 0.15	34	+ 0:19	- 0.15	71	+ 0:56
HW	49	+ 0:49	HW	27	+ 0:27	HW	33	+ 0:33	HW	73	+ 1:13
+ 0.15	50	+ 1:05	+ 0.15	29	+ 0:44	+ 0.15	33	+ 0:48	+ 0.15	74	+ 1:29
+ 0.30	52	+ 1:22	+ 0.30	30	+ 1:00	+ 0.30	33	+ 1:03	+ 0.30	75	+ 1:45
+ 0.45	53	+ 1:38	+ 0.45	31	+ 1:16	+ 0.45	34	+ 1:19	+ 0.45	76	+ 2:01
+ 1.00	55	+ 1:55	+ 1.00	33	+ 1:33	+ 1.00	34	+ 1:34	+ 1.00	77	+ 2:17
+ 1.15	55	+ 2:10	+ 1.15	33	+ 1:48	+ 1.15	34	+ 1:49	+ 1.15	78	+ 2:33
+ 1.30	56	+ 2:26	+ 1.30	34	+ 2:04	+ 1.30	34	+ 2:04	+ 1.30	78	+ 2:48
+ 1.45	56	+ 2:41	+ 1.45	35	+ 2:20	+ 1.45	34	+ 2:19	+ 1.45	78	+ 3:03
+ 2.00	56	+ 2:56	+ 2.00	35	+ 2:35	+ 2.00	34	+ 2:34	+ 2.00	78	+ 3:18
+ 2.15	56	+ 3:11	+ 2.15	36	+ 2:51	+ 2.15	34	+ 2:49	+ 2.15	78	+ 3:33
+ 2.30	55	+ 3:25	+ 2.30	36	+ 3:06	+ 2.30	34	+ 3:04	+ 2.30	77	+ 3:47
+ 2.45	54	+ 3:39	+ 2.45	36	+ 3:21	+ 2.45	34	+ 3:19	+ 2.45	77	+ 4:02
+ 3.00	54	+ 3:54	+ 3.00	37	+ 3:37	+ 3.00	34	+ 3:34	+ 3.00	76	+ 4:16
+ 3.15	53	+ 4:08	+ 3.15	37	+ 3:52	+ 3.15	34	+ 3:49	+ 3.15	75	+ 4:30
+ 3.30	52	+ 4:22	+ 3.30	37	+ 4:07	+ 3.30	34	+ 4:04	+ 3.30	74	+ 4:44
+ 3.45	51	+ 4:36	+ 3.45	37	+ 4:22	+ 3.45	34	+ 4:19	+ 3.45	73	+ 4:58
+ 4.00	50	+ 4:50	+ 4.00	38	+ 4:38	+ 4.00	34	+ 4:34	+ 4.00	72	+ 5:12
+ 4.15	49	+ 5:04	+ 4.15	38	+ 4:53	+ 4.15	35	+ 4:50	+ 4.15	70	+ 5:25
+ 4.30	48	+ 5:18	+ 4.30	38	+ 5:08	+ 4.30	35	+ 5:05	+ 4.30	69	+ 5:39
+ 4.45	47	+ 5:32	+ 4.45	37	+ 5:22	+ 4.45	35	+ 5:20	+ 4.45	68	+ 5:53
+ 5.00	46	+ 5:46	+ 5.00	37	+ 5:37	+ 5.00	35	+ 5:35	+ 5.00	67	- 5:53
+ 5.15	45	- 6:00	+ 5.15	37	+ 5:52	+ 5.15	36	+ 5:51	+ 5.15	66	- 5:39
+ 5.30	44	- 5:46	+ 5.30	36	- 5:54	+ 5.30	36	- 5:54	+ 5.30	65	- 5:25
+ 5.45	44	- 5:31	+ 5.45	35	- 5:40	+ 5.45	36	- 5:39	+ 5.45	64	- 5:11
+ 6.00	43	- 5:17	+ 6.00	34	- 5:26	+ 6.00	36	- 5:24	+ 6.00	63	- 4:57

Via Fisherman's Gat and Middle Sunk

NORTH BOUND

C - 4 Kts

Table C - North Foreland to Spitway via Princes Channel

4 Kts - C

Neaps — All times relate to HW Sheerness — **Time to cover Sectors (in minutes) at 4.0 kts**

NORTH & WEST

	C1			C2			C3			C4			C5			C6			C7			C8	
	North Foreland to Margate Sand			Margate Sand to Princes South			Princes South to Princes No 6			Princes No 6 to SW Barrow			SW Barrow to Maplin Edge			Maplin Edge to NE Maplin			NE Maplin to Whitaker Spit			Whitaker Spit to Mid-Spitway	
Time	Duration	Time at End of Sector	Time	Duration	Time at End of Sector	Time	Duration	Time at End of Sector	Time	Duration	Time at End of Sector	Time	Duration	Time at End of Sector	Time	Duration	Time at End of Sector	Time	Duration	Time at End of Sector	Time	Duration	Time at End of Sector
- 6.00	70	- 4:50	- 6.00	86	- 4:34	- 6.00	102	- 4:18	- 6.00	64	- 4:56	- 6.00	61	- 4:59	- 6.00	42	- 5:18	- 6.00	71	- 4:49	- 6.00	25	- 5:35
- 5.45	76	- 4:29	- 5.45	84	- 4:21	- 5.45	99	- 4:06	- 5.45	63	- 4:42	- 5.45	60	- 4:45	- 5.45	43	- 5:02	- 5.45	73	- 4:32	- 5.45	26	- 5:19
- 5.30	82	- 4:08	- 5.30	83	- 4:07	- 5.30	96	- 3:54	- 5.30	62	- 4:28	- 5.30	59	- 4:31	- 5.30	45	- 4:45	- 5.30	76	- 4:14	- 5.30	26	- 5:04
- 5.15	88	- 3:47	- 5.15	82	- 3:53	- 5.15	93	- 3:42	- 5.15	62	- 4:13	- 5.15	58	- 4:17	- 5.15	46	- 4:29	- 5.15	78	- 3:57	- 5.15	27	- 4:48
- 5.00	94	- 3:26	- 5.00	80	- 3:40	- 5.00	89	- 3:31	- 5.00	61	- 3:59	- 5.00	57	- 4:03	- 5.00	47	- 4:13	- 5.00	80	- 3:40	- 5.00	27	- 4:33
- 4.45	94	- 3:11	- 4.45	80	- 3:25	- 4.45	87	- 3:18	- 4.45	60	- 3:45	- 4.45	56	- 3:49	- 4.45	48	- 3:57	- 4.45	82	- 3:23	- 4.45	27	- 4:18
- 4.30	94	- 2:56	- 4.30	79	- 3:11	- 4.30	85	- 3:05	- 4.30	58	- 3:32	- 4.30	55	- 3:35	- 4.30	48	- 3:42	- 4.30	85	- 3:05	- 4.30	27	- 4:03
- 4.15	94	- 2:41	- 4.15	79	- 2:56	- 4.15	82	- 2:53	- 4.15	57	- 3:18	- 4.15	54	- 3:21	- 4.15	48	- 3:27	- 4.15	88	- 2:47	- 4.15	28	- 3:47
- 4.00	94	- 2:26	- 4.00	78	- 2:42	- 4.00	80	- 2:40	- 4.00	55	- 3:05	- 4.00	54	- 3:06	- 4.00	48	- 3:12	- 4.00	91	- 2:29	- 4.00	28	- 3:32
- 3.45	90	- 2:15	- 3.45	78	- 2:27	- 3.45	79	- 2:26	- 3.45	54	- 2:51	- 3.45	53	- 2:52	- 3.45	48	- 2:57	- 3.45	87	- 2:18	- 3.45	28	- 3:17
- 3.30	85	- 2:05	- 3.30	78	- 2:12	- 3.30	78	- 2:12	- 3.30	52	- 2:38	- 3.30	52	- 2:38	- 3.30	48	- 2:42	- 3.30	84	- 2:06	- 3.30	28	- 3:02
- 3.15	81	- 1:54	- 3.15	77	- 1:58	- 3.15	77	- 1:58	- 3.15	50	- 2:25	- 3.15	52	- 2:23	- 3.15	47	- 2:28	- 3.15	81	- 1:54	- 3.15	27	- 2:48
- 3.00	76	- 1:44	- 3.00	77	- 1:43	- 3.00	75	- 1:45	- 3.00	49	- 2:11	- 3.00	51	- 2:09	- 3.00	47	- 2:13	- 3.00	78	- 1:42	- 3.00	27	- 2:33
- 2.45	75	- 1:30	- 2.45	77	- 1:28	- 2.45	76	- 1:29	- 2.45	47	- 1:58	- 2.45	51	- 1:54	- 2.45	46	- 1:59	- 2.45	76	- 1:29	- 2.45	27	- 2:18
- 2.30	74	- 1:16	- 2.30	77	- 1:13	- 2.30	76	- 1:14	- 2.30	46	- 1:44	- 2.30	52	- 1:38	- 2.30	46	- 1:44	- 2.30	75	- 1:15	- 2.30	26	- 2:04
- 2.15	73	- 1:02	- 2.15	77	- 0:58	- 2.15	77	- 0:58	- 2.15	45	- 1:30	- 2.15	52	- 1:23	- 2.15	45	- 1:30	- 2.15	74	- 1:01	- 2.15	26	- 1:49
- 2.00	72	- 0:48	- 2.00	77	- 0:43	- 2.00	77	- 0:43	- 2.00	44	- 1:16	- 2.00	52	- 1:08	- 2.00	44	- 1:16	- 2.00	72	- 0:48	- 2.00	26	- 1:34
- 1.45	70	- 0:35	- 1.45	78	- 0:27	- 1.45	80	- 0:25	- 1.45	44	- 1:01	- 1.45	54	- 0:51	- 1.45	43	- 1:02	- 1.45	70	- 0:35	- 1.45	25	- 1:20
- 1.30	68	- 0:22	- 1.30	79	- 0:11	- 1.30	83	- 0:07	- 1.30	44	- 0:46	- 1.30	55	- 0:35	- 1.30	42	- 0:48	- 1.30	68	- 0:22	- 1.30	25	- 1:05
- 1.15	66	- 0:09	- 1.15	81	+ 0:06	- 1.15	86	+ 0:11	- 1.15	44	- 0:31	- 1.15	57	- 0:18	- 1.15	41	- 0:34	- 1.15	65	- 0:10	- 1.15	25	- 0:50
- 1.00	64	+ 0:04	- 1.00	82	+ 0:22	- 1.00	89	+ 0:29	- 1.00	44	- 0:16	- 1.00	58	- 0:02	- 1.00	40	- 0:20	- 1.00	63	+ 0:03	- 1.00	24	- 0:36
- 0.45	62	+ 0:17	- 0.45	84	+ 0:39	- 0.45	98	+ 0:53	- 0.45	45	HW	- 0.45	61	+ 0:16	- 0.45	39	- 0:06	- 0.45	61	+ 0:16	- 0.45	24	- 0:21
- 0.30	59	+ 0:29	- 0.30	86	+ 0:56	- 0.30	107	+ 1:17	- 0.30	45	+ 0:15	- 0.30	63	+ 0:33	- 0.30	38	+ 0:08	- 0.30	58	+ 0:28	- 0.30	24	- 0:06
- 0.15	57	+ 0:42	- 0.15	89	+ 1:14	- 0.15	116	+ 1:41	- 0.15	46	+ 0:31	- 0.15	65	+ 0:50	- 0.15	38	+ 0:23	- 0.15	56	+ 0:41	- 0.15	24	+ 0:09
HW	54	+ 0:54	HW	91	+ 1:31	HW	125	+ 2:05	HW	47	+ 0:47	HW	68	+ 1:08	HW	37	+ 0:37	HW	54	+ 0:54	HW	25	+ 0:25
+ 0.15	51	+ 1:06	+ 0.15	95	+ 1:50	+ 0.15	134	+ 2:29	+ 0.15	49	+ 1:04	+ 0.15	71	+ 1:26	+ 0.15	36	+ 0:51	+ 0.15	53	+ 1:08	+ 0.15	25	+ 0:40
+ 0.30	49	+ 1:19	+ 0.30	98	+ 2:08	+ 0.30	144	+ 2:54	+ 0.30	51	+ 1:21	+ 0.30	74	+ 1:44	+ 0.30	36	+ 1:06	+ 0.30	52	+ 1:22	+ 0.30	25	+ 0:55
+ 0.45	46	+ 1:31	+ 0.45	101	+ 2:26	+ 0.45	154	+ 3:19	+ 0.45	53	+ 1:38	+ 0.45	77	+ 2:02	+ 0.45	35	+ 1:20	+ 0.45	51	+ 1:36	+ 0.45	26	+ 1:11
+ 1.00	43	+ 1:43	+ 1.00	104	+ 2:44	+ 1.00	163	+ 3:43	+ 1.00	54	+ 1:54	+ 1.00	81	+ 2:21	+ 1.00	34	+ 1:34	+ 1.00	50	+ 1:50	+ 1.00	26	+ 1:26
+ 1.15	42	+ 1:57	+ 1.15	105	+ 3:00	+ 1.15	164	+ 3:59	+ 1.15	56	+ 2:11	+ 1.15	85	+ 2:40	+ 1.15	34	+ 1:49	+ 1.15	50	+ 2:05	+ 1.15	26	+ 1:41
+ 1.30	41	+ 2:11	+ 1.30	106	+ 3:16	+ 1.30	165	+ 4:15	+ 1.30	58	+ 2:28	+ 1.30	88	+ 2:58	+ 1.30	34	+ 2:04	+ 1.30	50	+ 2:20	+ 1.30	26	+ 1:56
+ 1.45	40	+ 2:25	+ 1.45	107	+ 3:32	+ 1.45	167	+ 4:32	+ 1.45	60	+ 2:45	+ 1.45	92	+ 3:17	+ 1.45	34	+ 2:19	+ 1.45	50	+ 2:35	+ 1.45	26	+ 2:11
+ 2.00	39	+ 2:39	+ 2.00	108	+ 3:48	+ 2.00	168	+ 4:48	+ 2.00	62	+ 3:02	+ 2.00	96	+ 3:36	+ 2.00	33	+ 2:33	+ 2.00	50	+ 2:50	+ 2.00	26	+ 2:26
+ 2.15	39	+ 2:54	+ 2.15	107	+ 4:02	+ 2.15	164	+ 4:59	+ 2.15	63	+ 3:18	+ 2.15	95	+ 3:50	+ 2.15	33	+ 2:48	+ 2.15	50	+ 3:05	+ 2.15	26	+ 2:41
+ 2.30	40	+ 3:10	+ 2.30	106	+ 4:16	+ 2.30	161	+ 5:11	+ 2.30	63	+ 3:33	+ 2.30	95	+ 4:05	+ 2.30	33	+ 3:03	+ 2.30	51	+ 3:21	+ 2.30	26	+ 2:56
+ 2.45	41	+ 3:26	+ 2.45	105	+ 4:30	+ 2.45	158	+ 5:23	+ 2.45	64	+ 3:49	+ 2.45	94	+ 4:19	+ 2.45	33	+ 3:18	+ 2.45	51	+ 3:36	+ 2.45	26	+ 3:11
+ 3.00	42	+ 3:42	+ 3.00	104	+ 4:44	+ 3.00	154	+ 5:34	+ 3.00	65	+ 4:05	+ 3.00	93	+ 4:33	+ 3.00	33	+ 3:33	+ 3.00	52	+ 3:52	+ 3.00	26	+ 3:26
+ 3.15	43	+ 3:58	+ 3.15	102	+ 4:57	+ 3.15	151	+ 5:46	+ 3.15	65	+ 4:20	+ 3.15	89	+ 4:44	+ 3.15	33	+ 3:48	+ 3.15	52	+ 4:07	+ 3.15	26	+ 3:41
+ 3.30	44	+ 4:14	+ 3.30	101	+ 5:11	+ 3.30	147	+ 5:57	+ 3.30	65	+ 4:35	+ 3.30	85	+ 4:55	+ 3.30	33	+ 4:03	+ 3.30	53	+ 4:23	+ 3.30	26	+ 3:56
+ 3.45	45	+ 4:30	+ 3.45	99	+ 5:24	+ 3.45	143	- 5:52	+ 3.45	65	+ 4:50	+ 3.45	81	+ 5:06	+ 3.45	34	+ 4:19	+ 3.45	54	+ 4:39	+ 3.45	26	+ 4:11
+ 4.00	46	+ 4:46	+ 4.00	97	+ 5:37	+ 4.00	140	- 5:40	+ 4.00	65	+ 5:05	+ 4.00	77	+ 5:17	+ 4.00	34	+ 4:34	+ 4.00	55	+ 4:55	+ 4.00	25	+ 4:25
+ 4.15	48	+ 5:03	+ 4.15	96	+ 5:51	+ 4.15	136	- 5:29	+ 4.15	65	+ 5:20	+ 4.15	75	+ 5:30	+ 4.15	35	+ 4:50	+ 4.15	56	+ 5:11	+ 4.15	25	+ 4:40
+ 4.30	49	+ 5:19	+ 4.30	95	- 5:55	+ 4.30	133	- 5:17	+ 4.30	65	+ 5:35	+ 4.30	73	+ 5:43	+ 4.30	36	+ 5:06	+ 4.30	57	+ 5:27	+ 4.30	25	+ 4:55
+ 4.45	51	+ 5:36	+ 4.45	94	- 5:41	+ 4.45	130	- 5:05	+ 4.45	65	+ 5:50	+ 4.45	71	+ 5:56	+ 4.45	36	+ 5:21	+ 4.45	59	+ 5:44	+ 4.45	25	+ 5:10
+ 5.00	53	+ 5:53	+ 5.00	93	- 5:27	+ 5.00	126	- 4:54	+ 5.00	65	- 5:55	+ 5.00	69	- 5:51	+ 5.00	37	+ 5:37	+ 5.00	60	- 6:00	+ 5.00	25	+ 5:25
+ 5.15	55	- 5:50	+ 5.15	92	- 5:13	+ 5.15	123	- 4:42	+ 5.15	65	- 5:40	+ 5.15	68	- 5:37	+ 5.15	38	+ 5:53	+ 5.15	61	- 5:44	+ 5.15	25	+ 5:40
+ 5.30	57	- 5:33	+ 5.30	91	- 4:59	+ 5.30	119	- 4:31	+ 5.30	65	- 5:25	+ 5.30	67	- 5:23	+ 5.30	39	- 5:51	+ 5.30	62	- 5:28	+ 5.30	25	+ 5:55
+ 5.45	59	- 5:16	+ 5.45	91	- 4:44	+ 5.45	116	- 4:19	+ 5.45	65	- 5:10	+ 5.45	65	- 5:10	+ 5.45	39	- 5:36	+ 5.45	63	- 5:12	+ 5.45	25	- 5:50
+ 6.00	62	- 4:58	+ 6.00	90	- 4:30	+ 6.00	112	- 4:08	+ 6.00	65	- 4:55	+ 6.00	64	- 4:56	+ 6.00	40	- 5:20	+ 6.00	65	- 4:55	+ 6.00	25	- 5:35

Table C - North Foreland to Spitway via Princes Channel

Time to cover Sectors (in minutes) at 4.0 kts | All times relate to HW Sheerness | **Springs**

	C1 North Foreland to Margate Sand			C2 Margate Sand to Princes South			C3 Princes South to Princes No 6			C4 Princes No 6 to SW Barrow			C5 SW Barrow to Maplin Edge			C6 Maplin Edge to NE Maplin			C7 NE Maplin to Whitaker Spit			C8 Whitaker Spit to Mid-Spitway	
Time	*Duration*	*Time at End of Sector*	*Time*	*Duration*	*Time at End of Sector*	*Time*	*Duration*	*Time at End of Sector*	*Time*	*Duration*	*Time at End of Sector*	*Time*	*Duration*	*Time at End of Sector*	*Time*	*Duration*	*Time at End of Sector*	*Time*	*Duration*	*Time at End of Sector*	*Time*	*Duration*	*Time at End of Sector*
- 6.00	**76**	**- 4:44**	**- 6.00**	**86**	**- 4:34**	**- 6.00**	**96**	**- 4:24**	**- 6.00**	**73**	**- 4:47**	**- 6.00**	**60**	**- 5:00**	**- 6.00**	**44**	**- 5:16**	**- 6.00**	**77**	**- 4:43**	**- 6.00**	**25**	**- 5:35**
- 5.45	85	- 4:20	- 5.45	85	- 4:20	- 5.45	92	- 4:13	- 5.45	71	- 4:34	- 5.45	58	- 4:47	- 5.45	46	- 4:59	- 5.45	84	- 4:21	- 5.45	26	- 5:19
- 5.30	94	- 3:56	- 5.30	83	- 4:07	- 5.30	87	- 4:03	- 5.30	70	- 4:20	- 5.30	57	- 4:33	- 5.30	48	- 4:42	- 5.30	90	- 4:00	- 5.30	27	- 5:03
- 5.15	103	- 3:32	- 5.15	81	- 3:54	- 5.15	83	- 3:52	- 5.15	69	- 4:06	- 5.15	56	- 4:19	- 5.15	50	- 4:25	- 5.15	97	- 3:38	- 5.15	28	- 4:47
- 5.00	**112**	**- 3:08**	**- 5.00**	**80**	**- 3:40**	**- 5.00**	**78**	**- 3:42**	**- 5.00**	**68**	**- 3:52**	**- 5.00**	**54**	**- 4:06**	**- 5.00**	**53**	**- 4:07**	**- 5.00**	**104**	**- 3:16**	**- 5.00**	**29**	**- 4:31**
- 4.45	111	- 2:54	- 4.45	79	- 3:26	- 4.45	76	- 3:29	- 4.45	65	- 3:40	- 4.45	53	- 3:52	- 4.45	53	- 3:52	- 4.45	104	- 3:01	- 4.45	29	- 4:16
- 4.30	110	- 2:40	- 4.30	79	- 3:11	- 4.30	74	- 3:16	- 4.30	62	- 3:28	- 4.30	52	- 3:38	- 4.30	54	- 3:36	- 4.30	104	- 2:46	- 4.30	30	- 4:00
- 4.15	108	- 2:27	- 4.15	78	- 2:57	- 4.15	72	- 3:03	- 4.15	60	- 3:15	- 4.15	51	- 3:24	- 4.15	54	- 3:21	- 4.15	104	- 2:31	- 4.15	30	- 3:45
- 4.00	**107**	**- 2:13**	**- 4.00**	**77**	**- 2:43**	**- 4.00**	**70**	**- 2:50**	**- 4.00**	**57**	**- 3:03**	**- 4.00**	**50**	**- 3:10**	**- 4.00**	**55**	**- 3:05**	**- 4.00**	**104**	**- 2:16**	**- 4.00**	**31**	**- 3:29**
- 3.45	104	- 2:01	- 3.45	76	- 2:29	- 3.45	69	- 2:36	- 3.45	54	- 2:51	- 3.45	49	- 2:56	- 3.45	54	- 2:51	- 3.45	101	- 2:04	- 3.45	31	- 3:14
- 3.30	101	- 1:49	- 3.30	76	- 2:14	- 3.30	68	- 2:22	- 3.30	51	- 2:39	- 3.30	48	- 2:42	- 3.30	53	- 2:37	- 3.30	99	- 1:51	- 3.30	30	- 3:00
- 3.15	98	- 1:37	- 3.15	75	- 2:00	- 3.15	67	- 2:08	- 3.15	49	- 2:26	- 3.15	48	- 2:27	- 3.15	53	- 2:22	- 3.15	97	- 1:38	- 3.15	30	- 2:45
- 3.00	**95**	**- 1:25**	**- 3.00**	**74**	**- 1:46**	**- 3.00**	**66**	**- 1:54**	**- 3.00**	**46**	**- 2:14**	**- 3.00**	**47**	**- 2:13**	**- 3.00**	**52**	**- 2:08**	**- 3.00**	**94**	**- 1:26**	**- 3.00**	**29**	**- 2:31**
- 2.45	91	- 1:14	- 2.45	74	- 1:31	- 2.45	67	- 1:38	- 2.45	44	- 2:01	- 2.45	47	- 1:58	- 2.45	51	- 1:54	- 2.45	90	- 1:15	- 2.45	29	- 2:16
- 2.30	87	- 1:03	- 2.30	74	- 1:16	- 2.30	67	- 1:23	- 2.30	42	- 1:48	- 2.30	47	- 1:43	- 2.30	50	- 1:40	- 2.30	87	- 1:03	- 2.30	28	- 2:02
- 2.15	83	- 0:52	- 2.15	74	- 1:01	- 2.15	67	- 1:08	- 2.15	40	- 1:35	- 2.15	47	- 1:28	- 2.15	49	- 1:26	- 2.15	83	- 0:52	- 2.15	27	- 1:48
- 2.00	**80**	**- 0:40**	**- 2.00**	**74**	**- 0:46**	**- 2.00**	**68**	**- 0:52**	**- 2.00**	**39**	**- 1:21**	**- 2.00**	**47**	**- 1:13**	**- 2.00**	**47**	**- 1:13**	**- 2.00**	**79**	**- 0:41**	**- 2.00**	**27**	**- 1:33**
- 1.45	77	- 0:28	- 1.45	76	- 0:29	- 1.45	72	- 0:33	- 1.45	38	- 1:07	- 1.45	49	- 0:56	- 1.45	46	- 0:59	- 1.45	75	- 0:30	- 1.45	26	- 1:19
- 1.30	74	- 0:16	- 1.30	77	- 0:13	- 1.30	75	- 0:15	- 1.30	38	- 0:52	- 1.30	51	- 0:39	- 1.30	44	- 0:46	- 1.30	71	- 0:19	- 1.30	25	- 1:05
- 1.15	70	- 0:05	- 1.15	79	+ 0:04	- 1.15	79	+ 0:04	- 1.15	38	- 0:37	- 1.15	53	- 0:22	- 1.15	42	- 0:33	- 1.15	68	- 0:07	- 1.15	25	- 0:50
- 1.00	**67**	**+ 0:07**	**- 1.00**	**80**	**+ 0:20**	**- 1.00**	**83**	**+ 0:23**	**- 1.00**	**38**	**- 0:22**	**- 1.00**	**55**	**- 0:05**	**- 1.00**	**40**	**- 0:20**	**- 1.00**	**64**	**+ 0:04**	**- 1.00**	**24**	**- 0:36**
- 0.45	63	+ 0:18	- 0.45	85	+ 0:40	- 0.45	107	+ 1:02	- 0.45	39	- 0:06	- 0.45	59	+ 0:14	- 0.45	39	- 0:06	- 0.45	60	+ 0:15	- 0.45	24	- 0:21
- 0.30	60	+ 0:30	- 0.30	89	+ 0:59	- 0.30	130	+ 1:40	- 0.30	40	+ 0:10	- 0.30	63	+ 0:33	- 0.30	38	+ 0:08	- 0.30	57	+ 0:27	- 0.30	24	- 0:06
- 0.15	56	+ 0:41	- 0.15	93	+ 1:18	- 0.15	153	+ 2:18	- 0.15	42	+ 0:27	- 0.15	67	+ 0:52	- 0.15	37	+ 0:22	- 0.15	54	+ 0:39	- 0.15	24	+ 0:09
HW	**52**	**+ 0:52**	**HW**	**97**	**+ 1:37**	**HW**	**177**	**+ 2:57**	**HW**	**43**	**+ 0:43**	**HW**	**71**	**+ 1:11**	**HW**	**37**	**+ 0:37**	**HW**	**51**	**+ 0:51**	**HW**	**24**	**+ 0:24**
+ 0.15	48	+ 1:03	+ 0.15	103	+ 1:58	+ 0.15	190	+ 3:25	+ 0.15	46	+ 1:01	+ 0.15	78	+ 1:33	+ 0.15	36	+ 0:51	+ 0.15	49	+ 1:04	+ 0.15	25	+ 0:40
+ 0.30	44	+ 1:14	+ 0.30	108	+ 2:18	+ 0.30	203	+ 3:53	+ 0.30	49	+ 1:19	+ 0.30	84	+ 1:54	+ 0.30	35	+ 1:05	+ 0.30	48	+ 1:18	+ 0.30	26	+ 0:56
+ 0.45	41	+ 1:26	+ 0.45	114	+ 2:39	+ 0.45	216	+ 4:21	+ 0.45	53	+ 1:38	+ 0.45	91	+ 2:16	+ 0.45	34	+ 1:19	+ 0.45	47	+ 1:32	+ 0.45	27	+ 1:12
+ 1.00	**56**	**+ 1:56**	**+ 1.00**	**120**	**+ 3:00**	**+ 1.00**	**229**	**+ 4:49**	**+ 1.00**	**56**	**+ 1:56**	**+ 1.00**	**98**	**+ 2:38**	**+ 1.00**	**33**	**+ 1:33**	**+ 1.00**	**45**	**+ 1:45**	**+ 1.00**	**28**	**+ 1:28**
+ 1.15	36	+ 1:51	+ 1.15	120	+ 3:15	+ 1.15	226	+ 5:01	+ 1.15	60	+ 2:15	+ 1.15	102	+ 2:57	+ 1.15	32	+ 1:47	+ 1.15	45	+ 2:00	+ 1.15	28	+ 1:43
+ 1.30	35	+ 2:05	+ 1.30	120	+ 3:30	+ 1.30	223	+ 5:13	+ 1.30	64	+ 2:34	+ 1.30	106	+ 3:16	+ 1.30	32	+ 2:02	+ 1.30	45	+ 2:15	+ 1.30	28	+ 1:58
+ 1.45	34	+ 2:19	+ 1.45	120	+ 3:45	+ 1.45	220	+ 5:25	+ 1.45	68	+ 2:53	+ 1.45	109	+ 3:34	+ 1.45	32	+ 2:17	+ 1.45	45	+ 2:30	+ 1.45	28	+ 2:13
+ 2.00	**33**	**+ 2:33**	**+ 2.00**	**121**	**+ 4:01**	**+ 2.00**	**218**	**+ 5:38**	**+ 2.00**	**72**	**+ 3:12**	**+ 2.00**	**113**	**+ 3:53**	**+ 2.00**	**32**	**+ 2:32**	**+ 2.00**	**44**	**+ 2:44**	**+ 2.00**	**28**	**+ 2:28**
+ 2.15	34	+ 2:49	+ 2.15	118	+ 4:13	+ 2.15	210	+ 5:45	+ 2.15	74	+ 3:29	+ 2.15	110	+ 4:05	+ 2.15	32	+ 2:47	+ 2.15	45	+ 3:00	+ 2.15	28	+ 2:43
+ 2.30	34	+ 3:04	+ 2.30	116	+ 4:26	+ 2.30	202	+ 5:52	+ 2.30	75	+ 3:45	+ 2.30	107	+ 4:17	+ 2.30	31	+ 3:01	+ 2.30	46	+ 3:16	+ 2.30	28	+ 2:58
+ 2.45	35	+ 3:20	+ 2.45	113	+ 4:38	+ 2.45	194	+ 5:59	+ 2.45	77	+ 4:02	+ 2.45	105	+ 4:30	+ 2.45	31	+ 3:16	+ 2.45	46	+ 3:31	+ 2.45	28	+ 3:13
+ 3.00	**36**	**+ 3:36**	**+ 3.00**	**110**	**+ 4:50**	**+ 3.00**	**187**	**- 5:53**	**+ 3.00**	**79**	**+ 4:19**	**+ 3.00**	**102**	**+ 4:42**	**+ 3.00**	**31**	**+ 3:31**	**+ 3.00**	**47**	**+ 3:47**	**+ 3.00**	**28**	**+ 3:28**
+ 3.15	37	+ 3:52	+ 3.15	108	+ 5:03	+ 3.15	180	- 5:45	+ 3.15	78	+ 4:33	+ 3.15	98	+ 4:53	+ 3.15	31	+ 3:46	+ 3.15	48	+ 4:03	+ 3.15	27	+ 3:42
+ 3.30	38	+ 4:08	+ 3.30	105	+ 5:15	+ 3.30	173	- 5:37	+ 3.30	78	+ 4:48	+ 3.30	94	+ 5:04	+ 3.30	32	+ 4:02	+ 3.30	49	+ 4:19	+ 3.30	27	+ 3:57
+ 3.45	40	+ 4:25	+ 3.45	103	+ 5:28	+ 3.45	166	- 5:29	+ 3.45	77	+ 5:02	+ 3.45	89	+ 5:14	+ 3.45	32	+ 4:17	+ 3.45	50	+ 4:35	+ 3.45	26	+ 4:11
+ 4.00	**41**	**+ 4:41**	**+ 4.00**	**101**	**+ 5:41**	**+ 4.00**	**159**	**- 5:21**	**+ 4.00**	**77**	**+ 5:17**	**+ 4.00**	**85**	**+ 5:25**	**+ 4.00**	**32**	**+ 4:32**	**+ 4.00**	**51**	**+ 4:51**	**+ 4.00**	**26**	**+ 4:26**
+ 4.15	43	+ 4:58	+ 4.15	99	+ 5:54	+ 4.15	153	- 5:12	+ 4.15	77	+ 5:32	+ 4.15	82	+ 5:37	+ 4.15	33	+ 4:48	+ 4.15	53	+ 5:08	+ 4.15	26	+ 4:41
+ 4.30	46	+ 5:16	+ 4.30	97	- 5:53	+ 4.30	147	- 5:03	+ 4.30	77	+ 5:47	+ 4.30	78	+ 5:48	+ 4.30	34	+ 5:04	+ 4.30	55	+ 5:25	+ 4.30	25	+ 4:55
+ 4.45	48	+ 5:33	+ 4.45	96	- 5:39	+ 4.45	141	- 4:54	+ 4.45	76	- 5:59	+ 4.45	74	+ 5:59	+ 4.45	35	+ 5:20	+ 4.45	57	+ 5:42	+ 4.45	25	+ 5:10
+ 5.00	**50**	**+ 5:50**	**+ 5.00**	**94**	**- 5:26**	**+ 5.00**	**135**	**- 4:45**	**+ 5.00**	**76**	**- 5:44**	**+ 5.00**	**71**	**- 5:49**	**+ 5.00**	**36**	**+ 5:36**	**+ 5.00**	**59**	**+ 5:59**	**+ 5.00**	**25**	**+ 5:25**
+ 5.15	53	- 5:52	+ 5.15	93	- 5:12	+ 5.15	130	- 4:35	+ 5.15	76	- 5:29	+ 5.15	69	- 5:36	+ 5.15	38	+ 5:53	+ 5.15	60	- 5:45	+ 5.15	25	+ 5:40
+ 5.30	57	- 5:33	+ 5.30	93	- 4:57	+ 5.30	124	- 4:26	+ 5.30	76	- 5:14	+ 5.30	68	- 5:22	+ 5.30	39	- 5:51	+ 5.30	62	- 5:28	+ 5.30	25	+ 5:55
+ 5.45	60	- 5:15	+ 5.45	92	- 4:43	+ 5.45	119	- 4:16	+ 5.45	76	- 4:59	+ 5.45	66	- 5:09	+ 5.45	40	- 5:35	+ 5.45	64	- 5:11	+ 5.45	25	- 5:50
+ 6.00	**64**	**- 4:56**	**+ 6.00**	**91**	**- 4:29**	**+ 6.00**	**114**	**- 4:06**	**+ 6.00**	**75**	**- 4:45**	**+ 6.00**	**64**	**- 4:56**	**+ 6.00**	**41**	**- 5:19**	**+ 6.00**	**65**	**- 4:55**	**+ 6.00**	**25**	**- 5:35**

Table C - North Foreland to Spitway via Princes Channel

Neaps | All times relate to HW Sheerness | **Time to cover Sectors (in minutes) at 5.0 kts**

NORTH & WEST

Time	C1 North Foreland to Margate Sand: Duration	C1: Time at End of Sector	Time	C2 Margate Sand to Princes South: Duration	C2: Time at End of Sector	Time	C3 Princes South to Princes No 6: Duration	C3: Time at End of Sector	Time	C4 Princes No 6 to SW Barrow: Duration	C4: Time at End of Sector
- 6.00	53	- 5:07	- 6.00	69	- 4:51	- 6.00	52	- 5:08	- 6.00	49	- 5:11
- 5.45	55	- 4:50	- 5.45	68	- 4:37	- 5.45	58	- 4:47	- 5.45	49	- 4:56
- 5.30	57	- 4:33	- 5.30	67	- 4:23	- 5.30	63	- 4:27	- 5.30	48	- 4:42
- 5.15	58	- 4:17	- 5.15	66	- 4:09	- 5.15	69	- 4:06	- 5.15	48	- 4:27
- 5.00	60	- 4:00	- 5.00	65	- 3:55	- 5.00	74	- 3:46	- 5.00	48	- 4:12
- 4.45	60	- 3:45	- 4.45	65	- 3:40	- 4.45	72	- 3:33	- 4.45	47	- 3:58
- 4.30	61	- 3:29	- 4.30	64	- 3:26	- 4.30	71	- 3:19	- 4.30	46	- 3:44
- 4.15	61	- 3:14	- 4.15	64	- 3:11	- 4.15	69	- 3:06	- 4.15	45	- 3:30
- 4.00	62	- 2:58	- 4.00	63	- 2:57	- 4.00	67	- 2:53	- 4.00	45	- 3:15
- 3.45	61	- 2:44	- 3.45	63	- 2:42	- 3.45	67	- 2:38	- 3.45	43	- 3:02
- 3.30	60	- 2:30	- 3.30	63	- 2:27	- 3.30	66	- 2:24	- 3.30	42	- 2:48
- 3.15	59	- 2:16	- 3.15	63	- 2:12	- 3.15	65	- 2:10	- 3.15	41	- 2:34
- 3.00	58	- 2:02	- 3.00	63	- 1:57	- 3.00	64	- 1:56	- 3.00	40	- 2:20
- 2.45	58	- 1:47	- 2.45	63	- 1:42	- 2.45	64	- 1:41	- 2.45	39	- 2:06
- 2.30	57	- 1:33	- 2.30	63	- 1:27	- 2.30	64	- 1:26	- 2.30	38	- 1:52
- 2.15	56	- 1:19	- 2.15	63	- 1:12	- 2.15	65	- 1:10	- 2.15	37	- 1:38
- 2.00	55	- 1:05	- 2.00	63	- 0:57	- 2.00	65	- 0:55	- 2.00	36	- 1:24
- 1.45	54	- 0:51	- 1.45	63	- 0:42	- 1.45	67	- 0:38	- 1.45	36	- 1:09
- 1.30	53	- 0:37	- 1.30	64	- 0:26	- 1.30	69	- 0:21	- 1.30	36	- 0:54
- 1.15	52	- 0:23	- 1.15	65	- 0:10	- 1.15	71	- 0:04	- 1.15	36	- 0:39
- 1.00	51	- 0:09	- 1.00	65	+ 0:05	- 1.00	73	+ 0:13	- 1.00	36	- 0:24
- 0.45	50	+ 0:05	- 0.45	67	+ 0:22	- 0.45	77	+ 0:32	- 0.45	36	- 0:09
- 0.30	48	+ 0:18	- 0.30	68	+ 0:38	- 0.30	81	+ 0:51	- 0.30	37	+ 0:07
- 0.15	46	+ 0:31	- 0.15	70	+ 0:55	- 0.15	86	+ 1:11	- 0.15	38	+ 0:23
HW	45	+ 0:45	HW	71	+ 1:11	HW	90	+ 1:30	HW	38	+ 0:38
+ 0.15	43	+ 0:58	+ 0.15	73	+ 1:28	+ 0.15	97	+ 1:52	+ 0.15	39	+ 0:54
+ 0.30	41	+ 1:11	+ 0.30	74	+ 1:44	+ 0.30	104	+ 2:14	+ 0.30	40	+ 1:10
+ 0.45	40	+ 1:25	+ 0.45	76	+ 2:01	+ 0.45	111	+ 2:36	+ 0.45	41	+ 1:26
+ 1.00	38	+ 1:38	+ 1.00	78	+ 2:18	+ 1.00	118	+ 2:58	+ 1.00	43	+ 1:43
+ 1.15	37	+ 1:52	+ 1.15	78	+ 2:33	+ 1.15	119	+ 3:14	+ 1.15	44	+ 1:59
+ 1.30	36	+ 2:06	+ 1.30	79	+ 2:49	+ 1.30	121	+ 3:31	+ 1.30	45	+ 2:15
+ 1.45	35	+ 2:20	+ 1.45	79	+ 3:04	+ 1.45	123	+ 3:48	+ 1.45	46	+ 2:31
+ 2.00	34	+ 2:34	+ 2.00	80	+ 3:20	+ 2.00	125	+ 4:05	+ 2.00	47	+ 2:47
+ 2.15	34	+ 2:49	+ 2.15	79	+ 3:34	+ 2.15	123	+ 4:18	+ 2.15	48	+ 3:03
+ 2.30	34	+ 3:04	+ 2.30	78	+ 3:48	+ 2.30	121	+ 4:31	+ 2.30	48	+ 3:18
+ 2.45	35	+ 3:20	+ 2.45	78	+ 4:03	+ 2.45	119	+ 4:44	+ 2.45	49	+ 3:34
+ 3.00	35	+ 3:35	+ 3.00	77	+ 4:17	+ 3.00	117	+ 4:57	+ 3.00	50	+ 3:50
+ 3.15	36	+ 3:51	+ 3.15	76	+ 4:31	+ 3.15	115	+ 5:10	+ 3.15	50	+ 4:05
+ 3.30	37	+ 4:07	+ 3.30	76	+ 4:46	+ 3.30	113	+ 5:23	+ 3.30	50	+ 4:20
+ 3.45	38	+ 4:23	+ 3.45	75	+ 5:00	+ 3.45	111	+ 5:36	+ 3.45	50	+ 4:35
+ 4.00	38	+ 4:38	+ 4.00	74	+ 5:14	+ 4.00	109	+ 5:49	+ 4.00	50	+ 4:50
+ 4.15	39	+ 4:54	+ 4.15	74	+ 5:29	+ 4.15	106	- 5:59	+ 4.15	50	+ 5:05
+ 4.30	40	+ 5:10	+ 4.30	73	+ 5:43	+ 4.30	104	- 5:46	+ 4.30	50	+ 5:20
+ 4.45	41	+ 5:26	+ 4.45	73	+ 5:58	+ 4.45	102	- 5:33	+ 4.45	50	+ 5:35
+ 5.00	42	+ 5:42	+ 5.00	72	- 5:48	+ 5.00	100	- 5:20	+ 5.00	50	+ 5:50
+ 5.15	43	+ 5:58	+ 5.15	72	- 5:33	+ 5.15	98	- 5:07	+ 5.15	50	- 5:55
+ 5.30	45	- 5:45	+ 5.30	72	- 5:18	+ 5.30	95	- 4:55	+ 5.30	50	- 5:40
+ 5.45	47	- 5:28	+ 5.45	71	- 5:04	+ 5.45	93	- 4:42	+ 5.45	50	- 5:25
+ 6.00	48	- 5:12	+ 6.00	71	- 4:49	+ 6.00	91	- 4:29	+ 6.00	50	- 5:10

Time	C5 SW Barrow to Maplin Edge: Duration	C5: Time at End of Sector	Time	C6 Maplin Edge to NE Maplin: Duration	C6: Time at End of Sector	Time	C7 NE Maplin to Whitaker Spit: Duration	C7: Time at End of Sector	Time	C8 Whitaker Spit to Mid-Spitway: Duration	C8: Time at End of Sector
- 6.00	49	- 5:11	- 6.00	32	- 5:28	- 6.00	55	- 5:05	- 6.00	20	- 5:40
- 5.45	49	- 4:56	- 5.45	33	- 5:12	- 5.45	56	- 4:49	- 5.45	20	- 5:25
- 5.30	48	- 4:42	- 5.30	34	- 4:56	- 5.30	58	- 4:32	- 5.30	21	- 5:09
- 5.15	47	- 4:28	- 5.15	35	- 4:40	- 5.15	59	- 4:16	- 5.15	21	- 4:54
- 5.00	47	- 4:13	- 5.00	36	- 4:24	- 5.00	61	- 3:59	- 5.00	22	- 4:38
- 4.45	46	- 3:59	- 4.45	36	- 4:09	- 4.45	61	- 3:44	- 4.45	22	- 4:23
- 4.30	46	- 3:44	- 4.30	37	- 3:53	- 4.30	61	- 3:29	- 4.30	22	- 4:08
- 4.15	45	- 3:30	- 4.15	37	- 3:38	- 4.15	61	- 3:14	- 4.15	22	- 3:53
- 4.00	44	- 3:16	- 4.00	37	- 3:23	- 4.00	62	- 2:58	- 4.00	22	- 3:38
- 3.45	44	- 3:01	- 3.45	37	- 3:08	- 3.45	61	- 2:44	- 3.45	22	- 3:23
- 3.30	44	- 2:46	- 3.30	37	- 2:53	- 3.30	61	- 2:29	- 3.30	22	- 3:08
- 3.15	43	- 2:32	- 3.15	36	- 2:39	- 3.15	60	- 2:15	- 3.15	22	- 2:53
- 3.00	43	- 2:17	- 3.00	36	- 2:24	- 3.00	60	- 2:00	- 3.00	22	- 2:38
- 2.45	43	- 2:02	- 2.45	36	- 2:09	- 2.45	59	- 1:46	- 2.45	21	- 2:24
- 2.30	43	- 1:47	- 2.30	36	- 1:54	- 2.30	58	- 1:32	- 2.30	21	- 2:09
- 2.15	43	- 1:32	- 2.15	35	- 1:40	- 2.15	57	- 1:18	- 2.15	21	- 1:54
- 2.00	43	- 1:17	- 2.00	35	- 1:25	- 2.00	57	- 1:03	- 2.00	20	- 1:40
- 1.45	44	- 1:01	- 1.45	34	- 1:11	- 1.45	55	- 0:50	- 1.45	20	- 1:25
- 1.30	45	- 0:45	- 1.30	33	- 0:57	- 1.30	54	- 0:36	- 1.30	20	- 1:10
- 1.15	46	- 0:29	- 1.15	33	- 0:42	- 1.15	52	- 0:23	- 1.15	20	- 0:55
- 1.00	47	- 0:13	- 1.00	32	- 0:28	- 1.00	51	- 0:09	- 1.00	19	- 0:41
- 0.45	48	+ 0:03	- 0.45	31	- 0:14	- 0.45	50	+ 0:05	- 0.45	19	- 0:26
- 0.30	50	+ 0:20	- 0.30	31	+ 0:01	- 0.30	48	+ 0:18	- 0.30	19	- 0:11
- 0.15	51	+ 0:36	- 0.15	31	+ 0:16	- 0.15	47	+ 0:32	- 0.15	19	+ 0:04
HW	53	+ 0:53	HW	31	+ 0:31	HW	45	+ 0:45	HW	20	+ 0:20
+ 0.15	54	+ 1:09	+ 0.15	30	+ 0:45	+ 0.15	44	+ 0:59	+ 0.15	20	+ 0:35
+ 0.30	56	+ 1:26	+ 0.30	29	+ 0:59	+ 0.30	43	+ 1:13	+ 0.30	20	+ 0:50
+ 0.45	58	+ 1:43	+ 0.45	28	+ 1:13	+ 0.45	43	+ 1:28	+ 0.45	21	+ 1:06
+ 1.00	60	+ 2:00	+ 1.00	28	+ 1:28	+ 1.00	42	+ 1:42	+ 1.00	21	+ 1:21
+ 1.15	62	+ 2:17	+ 1.15	28	+ 1:43	+ 1.15	42	+ 1:57	+ 1.15	21	+ 1:36
+ 1.30	63	+ 2:33	+ 1.30	27	+ 1:57	+ 1.30	42	+ 2:12	+ 1.30	21	+ 1:51
+ 1.45	65	+ 2:50	+ 1.45	27	+ 2:12	+ 1.45	42	+ 2:27	+ 1.45	21	+ 2:06
+ 2.00	66	+ 3:06	+ 2.00	27	+ 2:27	+ 2.00	41	+ 2:41	+ 2.00	21	+ 2:21
+ 2.15	66	+ 3:21	+ 2.15	27	+ 2:42	+ 2.15	42	+ 2:57	+ 2.15	21	+ 2:36
+ 2.30	66	+ 3:36	+ 2.30	27	+ 2:57	+ 2.30	42	+ 3:12	+ 2.30	21	+ 2:51
+ 2.45	65	+ 3:50	+ 2.45	27	+ 3:12	+ 2.45	42	+ 3:27	+ 2.45	21	+ 3:06
+ 3.00	65	+ 4:05	+ 3.00	26	+ 3:26	+ 3.00	43	+ 3:43	+ 3.00	21	+ 3:21
+ 3.15	64	+ 4:19	+ 3.15	27	+ 3:42	+ 3.15	43	+ 3:58	+ 3.15	21	+ 3:36
+ 3.30	62	+ 4:32	+ 3.30	27	+ 3:57	+ 3.30	44	+ 4:14	+ 3.30	21	+ 3:51
+ 3.45	61	+ 4:46	+ 3.45	27	+ 4:12	+ 3.45	44	+ 4:29	+ 3.45	20	+ 4:05
+ 4.00	60	+ 5:00	+ 4.00	27	+ 4:27	+ 4.00	44	+ 4:44	+ 4.00	20	+ 4:20
+ 4.15	58	+ 5:13	+ 4.15	28	+ 4:43	+ 4.15	45	+ 5:00	+ 4.15	20	+ 4:35
+ 4.30	57	+ 5:27	+ 4.30	28	+ 4:58	+ 4.30	46	+ 5:16	+ 4.30	20	+ 4:50
+ 4.45	56	+ 5:41	+ 4.45	29	+ 5:14	+ 4.45	47	+ 5:32	+ 4.45	20	+ 5:05
+ 5.00	55	+ 5:55	+ 5.00	29	+ 5:29	+ 5.00	48	+ 5:48	+ 5.00	20	+ 5:20
+ 5.15	54	- 5:51	+ 5.15	30	+ 5:45	+ 5.15	49	- 5:56	+ 5.15	20	+ 5:35
+ 5.30	53	- 5:37	+ 5.30	31	- 5:59	+ 5.30	49	- 5:41	+ 5.30	20	+ 5:50
+ 5.45	52	- 5:23	+ 5.45	31	- 5:44	+ 5.45	50	- 5:25	+ 5.45	20	- 5:55
+ 6.00	52	- 5:08	+ 6.00	32	- 5:28	+ 6.00	51	- 5:09	+ 6.00	20	- 5:40

Table C - North Foreland to Spitway via Princes Channel

5 Kts - C

Time to cover Sectors (in minutes) at 5.0 kts | All times relate to HW Sheerness | **Springs**

	C1			C2			C3			C4			C5			C6			C7			C8	
	North Foreland to Margate Sand			Margate Sand to Princes South			Princes South to Princes No 6			Princes No 6 to SW Barrow			SW Barrow to Maplin Edge			Maplin Edge to NE Maplin			NE Maplin to Whitaker Spit			Whitaker Spit to Mid-Spitway	
Time	*Duration*	*Time at End of Sector*	*Time*	*Duration*	*Time at End of Sector*	*Time*	*Duration*	*Time at End of Sector*	*Time*	*Duration*	*Time at End of Sector*	*Time*	*Duration*	*Time at End of Sector*	*Time*	*Duration*	*Time at End of Sector*	*Time*	*Duration*	*Time at End of Sector*	*Time*	*Duration*	*Time at End of Sector*
- 6.00	**57**	**- 5:03**	**- 6.00**	**69**	**- 4:51**	**- 6.00**	**80**	**- 4:40**	**- 6.00**	**54**	**- 5:06**	**- 6.00**	**49**	**- 5:11**	**- 6.00**	**33**	**- 5:27**	**- 6.00**	**58**	**- 5:02**	**- 6.00**	**20**	**- 5:40**
- 5.45	60	- 4:45	- 5.45	68	- 4:37	- 5.45	77	- 4:28	- 5.45	54	- 4:51	- 5.45	48	- 4:57	- 5.45	35	- 5:10	- 5.45	60	- 4:45	- 5.45	21	- 5:24
- 5.30	63	- 4:27	- 5.30	67	- 4:23	- 5.30	73	- 4:17	- 5.30	53	- 4:37	- 5.30	47	- 4:43	- 5.30	36	- 4:54	- 5.30	63	- 4:27	- 5.30	22	- 5:08
- 5.15	66	- 4:09	- 5.15	65	- 4:10	- 5.15	70	- 4:05	- 5.15	52	- 4:23	- 5.15	46	- 4:29	- 5.15	38	- 4:37	- 5.15	66	- 4:09	- 5.15	22	- 4:53
- 5.00	**69**	**- 3:51**	**- 5.00**	**64**	**- 3:56**	**- 5.00**	**66**	**- 3:54**	**- 5.00**	**52**	**- 4:08**	**- 5.00**	**45**	**- 4:15**	**- 5.00**	**39**	**- 4:21**	**- 5.00**	**68**	**- 3:52**	**- 5.00**	**23**	**- 4:37**
- 4.45	69	- 3:36	- 4.45	64	- 3:41	- 4.45	65	- 3:40	- 4.45	50	- 3:55	- 4.45	44	- 4:01	- 4.45	40	- 4:05	- 4.45	69	- 3:36	- 4.45	23	- 4:22
- 4.30	70	- 3:20	- 4.30	63	- 3:27	- 4.30	63	- 3:27	- 4.30	49	- 3:41	- 4.30	43	- 3:47	- 4.30	40	- 3:50	- 4.30	69	- 3:21	- 4.30	24	- 4:06
- 4.15	71	- 3:04	- 4.15	63	- 3:12	- 4.15	62	- 3:13	- 4.15	47	- 3:28	- 4.15	43	- 3:32	- 4.15	41	- 3:34	- 4.15	70	- 3:05	- 4.15	24	- 3:51
- 4.00	**71**	**- 2:49**	**- 4.00**	**62**	**- 2:58**	**- 4.00**	**60**	**- 3:00**	**- 4.00**	**46**	**- 3:14**	**- 4.00**	**42**	**- 3:18**	**- 4.00**	**41**	**- 3:19**	**- 4.00**	**70**	**- 2:50**	**- 4.00**	**24**	**- 3:36**
- 3.45	70	- 2:35	- 3.45	62	- 2:43	- 3.45	60	- 2:45	- 3.45	44	- 3:01	- 3.45	41	- 3:04	- 3.45	41	- 3:04	- 3.45	69	- 2:36	- 3.45	24	- 3:21
- 3.30	68	- 2:22	- 3.30	61	- 2:29	- 3.30	59	- 2:31	- 3.30	42	- 2:48	- 3.30	41	- 2:49	- 3.30	40	- 2:50	- 3.30	69	- 2:21	- 3.30	24	- 3:06
- 3.15	67	- 2:08	- 3.15	61	- 2:14	- 3.15	58	- 2:17	- 3.15	40	- 2:35	- 3.15	40	- 2:35	- 3.15	40	- 2:35	- 3.15	68	- 2:07	- 3.15	24	- 2:51
- 3.00	**65**	**- 1:55**	**- 3.00**	**61**	**- 1:59**	**- 3.00**	**57**	**- 2:03**	**- 3.00**	**39**	**- 2:21**	**- 3.00**	**39**	**- 2:21**	**- 3.00**	**40**	**- 2:20**	**- 3.00**	**67**	**- 1:53**	**- 3.00**	**23**	**- 2:37**
- 2.45	64	- 1:41	- 2.45	61	- 1:44	- 2.45	58	- 1:47	- 2.45	37	- 2:08	- 2.45	39	- 2:06	- 2.45	39	- 2:06	- 2.45	65	- 1:40	- 2.45	23	- 2:22
- 2.30	63	- 1:27	- 2.30	61	- 1:29	- 2.30	58	- 1:32	- 2.30	36	- 1:54	- 2.30	39	- 1:51	- 2.30	38	- 1:52	- 2.30	64	- 1:26	- 2.30	22	- 2:08
- 2.15	62	- 1:13	- 2.15	60	- 1:15	- 2.15	58	- 1:17	- 2.15	34	- 1:41	- 2.15	39	- 1:36	- 2.15	38	- 1:37	- 2.15	62	- 1:13	- 2.15	22	- 1:53
- 2.00	**61**	**- 0:59**	**- 2.00**	**60**	**- 1:00**	**- 2.00**	**58**	**- 1:02**	**- 2.00**	**33**	**- 1:27**	**- 2.00**	**39**	**- 1:21**	**- 2.00**	**37**	**- 1:23**	**- 2.00**	**61**	**- 0:59**	**- 2.00**	**21**	**- 1:39**
- 1.45	59	- 0:46	- 1.45	61	- 0:44	- 1.45	60	- 0:45	- 1.45	33	- 1:12	- 1.45	41	- 1:04	- 1.45	36	- 1:09	- 1.45	59	- 0:46	- 1.45	21	- 1:24
- 1.30	57	- 0:33	- 1.30	62	- 0:28	- 1.30	63	- 0:27	- 1.30	32	- 0:58	- 1.30	42	- 0:48	- 1.30	35	- 0:55	- 1.30	56	- 0:34	- 1.30	20	- 1:10
- 1.15	55	- 0:20	- 1.15	63	- 0:12	- 1.15	65	- 0:10	- 1.15	32	- 0:43	- 1.15	43	- 0:32	- 1.15	33	- 0:42	- 1.15	54	- 0:21	- 1.15	20	- 0:55
- 1.00	**53**	**- 0:07**	**- 1.00**	**64**	**+ 0:04**	**- 1.00**	**68**	**+ 0:08**	**- 1.00**	**32**	**- 0:28**	**- 1.00**	**44**	**- 0:16**	**- 1.00**	**32**	**- 0:28**	**- 1.00**	**52**	**- 0:08**	**- 1.00**	**19**	**- 0:41**
- 0.45	51	+ 0:06	- 0.45	67	+ 0:22	- 0.45	78	+ 0:33	- 0.45	32	- 0:13	- 0.45	47	+ 0:02	- 0.45	32	- 0:13	- 0.45	50	+ 0:05	- 0.45	19	- 0:26
- 0.30	49	+ 0:19	- 0.30	69	+ 0:39	- 0.30	87	+ 0:57	- 0.30	33	+ 0:03	- 0.30	49	+ 0:19	- 0.30	31	+ 0:01	- 0.30	48	+ 0:18	- 0.30	19	- 0:11
- 0.15	46	+ 0:31	- 0.15	71	+ 0:56	- 0.15	97	+ 1:22	- 0.15	34	+ 0:19	- 0.15	51	+ 0:36	- 0.15	31	+ 0:16	- 0.15	45	+ 0:30	- 0.15	19	+ 0:04
HW	**44**	**+ 0:44**	**HW**	**73**	**+ 1:13**	**HW**	**107**	**+ 1:47**	**HW**	**35**	**+ 0:35**	**HW**	**54**	**+ 0:54**	**HW**	**30**	**+ 0:30**	**HW**	**43**	**+ 0:43**	**HW**	**19**	**+ 0:19**
+ 0.15	41	+ 0:56	+ 0.15	77	+ 1:32	+ 0.15	118	+ 2:13	+ 0.15	37	+ 0:52	+ 0.15	57	+ 1:12	+ 0.15	29	+ 0:44	+ 0.15	42	+ 0:57	+ 0.15	20	+ 0:35
+ 0.30	39	+ 1:09	+ 0.30	80	+ 1:50	+ 0.30	130	+ 2:40	+ 0.30	39	+ 1:09	+ 0.30	61	+ 1:31	+ 0.30	28	+ 0:58	+ 0.30	41	+ 1:11	+ 0.30	21	+ 0:51
+ 0.45	37	+ 1:22	+ 0.45	83	+ 2:08	+ 0.45	141	+ 3:06	+ 0.45	41	+ 1:26	+ 0.45	64	+ 1:49	+ 0.45	27	+ 1:12	+ 0.45	40	+ 1:25	+ 0.45	21	+ 1:06
+ 1.00	**43**	**+ 1:43**	**+ 1.00**	**86**	**+ 2:26**	**+ 1.00**	**152**	**+ 3:32**	**+ 1.00**	**43**	**+ 1:43**	**+ 1.00**	**68**	**+ 2:08**	**+ 1.00**	**26**	**+ 1:26**	**+ 1.00**	**39**	**+ 1:39**	**+ 1.00**	**22**	**+ 1:22**
+ 1.15	33	+ 1:48	+ 1.15	87	+ 2:42	+ 1.15	153	+ 3:48	+ 1.15	45	+ 2:00	+ 1.15	71	+ 2:26	+ 1.15	26	+ 1:41	+ 1.15	39	+ 1:54	+ 1.15	22	+ 1:37
+ 1.30	32	+ 2:02	+ 1.30	88	+ 2:58	+ 1.30	153	+ 4:03	+ 1.30	48	+ 2:18	+ 1.30	74	+ 2:44	+ 1.30	26	+ 1:56	+ 1.30	38	+ 2:08	+ 1.30	22	+ 1:52
+ 1.45	31	+ 2:16	+ 1.45	89	+ 3:14	+ 1.45	153	+ 4:18	+ 1.45	50	+ 2:35	+ 1.45	76	+ 3:01	+ 1.45	26	+ 2:11	+ 1.45	38	+ 2:23	+ 1.45	23	+ 2:08
+ 2.00	**30**	**+ 2:30**	**+ 2.00**	**90**	**+ 3:30**	**+ 2.00**	**154**	**+ 4:34**	**+ 2.00**	**52**	**+ 2:52**	**+ 2.00**	**79**	**+ 3:19**	**+ 2.00**	**26**	**+ 2:26**	**+ 2.00**	**38**	**+ 2:38**	**+ 2.00**	**23**	**+ 2:23**
+ 2.15	30	+ 2:45	+ 2.15	89	+ 3:44	+ 2.15	150	+ 4:45	+ 2.15	54	+ 3:09	+ 2.15	78	+ 3:33	+ 2.15	26	+ 2:41	+ 2.15	38	+ 2:53	+ 2.15	23	+ 2:38
+ 2.30	30	+ 3:00	+ 2.30	87	+ 3:57	+ 2.30	147	+ 4:57	+ 2.30	55	+ 3:25	+ 2.30	77	+ 3:47	+ 2.30	25	+ 2:55	+ 2.30	39	+ 3:09	+ 2.30	22	+ 2:52
+ 2.45	31	+ 3:16	+ 2.45	86	+ 4:11	+ 2.45	144	+ 5:09	+ 2.45	56	+ 3:41	+ 2.45	76	+ 4:01	+ 2.45	25	+ 3:10	+ 2.45	39	+ 3:24	+ 2.45	22	+ 3:07
+ 3.00	**31**	**+ 3:31**	**+ 3.00**	**84**	**+ 4:24**	**+ 3.00**	**140**	**+ 5:20**	**+ 3.00**	**57**	**+ 3:57**	**+ 3.00**	**75**	**+ 4:15**	**+ 3.00**	**25**	**+ 3:25**	**+ 3.00**	**39**	**+ 3:39**	**+ 3.00**	**22**	**+ 3:22**
+ 3.15	32	+ 3:47	+ 3.15	83	+ 4:38	+ 3.15	135	+ 5:30	+ 3.15	57	+ 4:12	+ 3.15	72	+ 4:27	+ 3.15	25	+ 3:40	+ 3.15	40	+ 3:55	+ 3.15	22	+ 3:37
+ 3.30	33	+ 4:03	+ 3.30	81	+ 4:51	+ 3.30	131	+ 5:41	+ 3.30	57	+ 4:27	+ 3.30	70	+ 4:40	+ 3.30	25	+ 3:55	+ 3.30	41	+ 4:11	+ 3.30	21	+ 3:51
+ 3.45	34	+ 4:19	+ 3.45	80	+ 5:05	+ 3.45	126	+ 5:51	+ 3.45	57	+ 4:42	+ 3.45	67	+ 4:52	+ 3.45	26	+ 4:11	+ 3.45	41	+ 4:26	+ 3.45	21	+ 4:06
+ 4.00	**35**	**+ 4:35**	**+ 4.00**	**78**	**+ 5:18**	**+ 4.00**	**121**	**- 5:59**	**+ 4.00**	**57**	**+ 4:57**	**+ 4.00**	**65**	**+ 5:05**	**+ 4.00**	**26**	**+ 4:26**	**+ 4.00**	**42**	**+ 4:42**	**+ 4.00**	**21**	**+ 4:21**
+ 4.15	36	+ 4:51	+ 4.15	77	+ 5:32	+ 4.15	117	- 5:48	+ 4.15	57	+ 5:12	+ 4.15	63	+ 5:18	+ 4.15	27	+ 4:42	+ 4.15	43	+ 4:58	+ 4.15	20	+ 4:35
+ 4.30	37	+ 5:07	+ 4.30	76	+ 5:46	+ 4.30	113	- 5:37	+ 4.30	57	+ 5:27	+ 4.30	61	+ 5:31	+ 4.30	27	+ 4:57	+ 4.30	44	+ 5:14	+ 4.30	20	+ 4:50
+ 4.45	38	+ 5:23	+ 4.45	75	- 6:00	+ 4.45	109	- 5:26	+ 4.45	57	+ 5:42	+ 4.45	58	+ 5:43	+ 4.45	28	+ 5:13	+ 4.45	45	+ 5:30	+ 4.45	20	+ 5:05
+ 5.00	**40**	**+ 5:40**	**+ 5.00**	**74**	**- 5:46**	**+ 5.00**	**105**	**- 5:15**	**+ 5.00**	**56**	**+ 5:56**	**+ 5.00**	**56**	**+ 5:56**	**+ 5.00**	**29**	**+ 5:29**	**+ 5.00**	**47**	**+ 5:47**	**+ 5.00**	**20**	**+ 5:20**
+ 5.15	42	+ 5:57	+ 5.15	74	- 5:31	+ 5.15	102	- 5:03	+ 5.15	56	- 5:49	+ 5.15	55	- 5:50	+ 5.15	30	+ 5:45	+ 5.15	48	- 5:57	+ 5.15	20	+ 5:35
+ 5.30	44	- 5:46	+ 5.30	73	- 5:17	+ 5.30	99	- 4:51	+ 5.30	56	- 5:34	+ 5.30	54	- 5:36	+ 5.30	30	- 6:00	+ 5.30	49	- 5:41	+ 5.30	20	+ 5:50
+ 5.45	47	- 5:28	+ 5.45	73	- 5:02	+ 5.45	96	- 4:39	+ 5.45	56	- 5:19	+ 5.45	53	- 5:22	+ 5.45	31	- 5:44	+ 5.45	50	- 5:25	+ 5.45	20	- 5:55
+ 6.00	**49**	**- 5:11**	**+ 6.00**	**72**	**- 4:48**	**+ 6.00**	**94**	**- 4:26**	**+ 6.00**	**56**	**- 5:04**	**+ 6.00**	**51**	**- 5:09**	**+ 6.00**	**32**	**- 5:28**	**+ 6.00**	**51**	**- 5:09**	**+ 6.00**	**20**	**- 5:40**

NORTH & WEST

Table C - North Foreland to Spitway via Princes Channel

Neaps — All times relate to HW Sheerness — **Time to cover Sectors (in minutes) at 6.0 kts**

NORTH & WEST

Time	C1 North Foreland to Margate Sand: Duration	C1: Time at End of Sector	Time	C2 Margate Sand to Princes South: Duration	C2: Time at End of Sector	Time	C3 Princes South to Princes No 6: Duration	C3: Time at End of Sector	Time	C4 Princes No 6 to SW Barrow: Duration	C4: Time at End of Sector	Time	C5 SW Barrow to Maplin Edge: Duration	C5: Time at End of Sector	Time	C6 Maplin Edge to NE Maplin: Duration	C6: Time at End of Sector	Time	C7 NE Maplin to Whitaker Spit: Duration	C7: Time at End of Sector	Time	C8 Whitaker Spit to Mid-Spitway: Duration	C8: Time at End of Sector
- 6.00	43	- 5:17	- 6.00	57	- 5:03	- 6.00	69	- 4:51	- 6.00	40	- 5:20	- 6.00	42	- 5:18	- 6.00	27	- 5:33	- 6.00	44	- 5:16	- 6.00	17	- 5:43
- 5.45	44	- 5:01	- 5.45	57	- 4:48	- 5.45	68	- 4:37	- 5.45	40	- 5:05	- 5.45	41	- 5:04	- 5.45	27	- 5:18	- 5.45	45	- 5:00	- 5.45	17	- 5:28
- 5.30	45	- 4:45	- 5.30	56	- 4:34	- 5.30	66	- 4:24	- 5.30	40	- 4:50	- 5.30	41	- 4:49	- 5.30	28	- 5:02	- 5.30	47	- 4:43	- 5.30	17	- 5:13
- 5.15	46	- 4:29	- 5.15	55	- 4:20	- 5.15	65	- 4:10	- 5.15	40	- 4:35	- 5.15	40	- 4:35	- 5.15	29	- 4:46	- 5.15	48	- 4:27	- 5.15	18	- 4:57
- 5.00	48	- 4:12	- 5.00	55	- 4:05	- 5.00	63	- 3:57	- 5.00	39	- 4:21	- 5.00	40	- 4:20	- 5.00	29	- 4:31	- 5.00	49	- 4:11	- 5.00	18	- 4:42
- 4.45	48	- 3:57	- 4.45	54	- 3:51	- 4.45	62	- 3:43	- 4.45	39	- 4:06	- 4.45	39	- 4:06	- 4.45	29	- 4:16	- 4.45	49	- 3:56	- 4.45	18	- 4:27
- 4.30	49	- 3:41	- 4.30	54	- 3:36	- 4.30	61	- 3:29	- 4.30	38	- 3:52	- 4.30	39	- 3:51	- 4.30	30	- 4:00	- 4.30	49	- 3:41	- 4.30	18	- 4:12
- 4.15	49	- 3:26	- 4.15	54	- 3:21	- 4.15	59	- 3:16	- 4.15	38	- 3:37	- 4.15	38	- 3:37	- 4.15	30	- 3:45	- 4.15	49	- 3:26	- 4.15	18	- 3:57
- 4.00	49	- 3:11	- 4.00	53	- 3:07	- 4.00	58	- 3:02	- 4.00	37	- 3:23	- 4.00	38	- 3:22	- 4.00	30	- 3:30	- 4.00	50	- 3:10	- 4.00	18	- 3:42
- 3.45	49	- 2:56	- 3.45	53	- 2:52	- 3.45	58	- 2:47	- 3.45	37	- 3:08	- 3.45	38	- 3:07	- 3.45	30	- 3:15	- 3.45	49	- 2:56	- 3.45	18	- 3:27
- 3.30	48	- 2:42	- 3.30	53	- 2:37	- 3.30	57	- 2:33	- 3.30	36	- 2:54	- 3.30	37	- 2:53	- 3.30	30	- 3:00	- 3.30	49	- 2:41	- 3.30	18	- 3:12
- 3.15	48	- 2:27	- 3.15	53	- 2:22	- 3.15	56	- 2:19	- 3.15	35	- 2:40	- 3.15	37	- 2:38	- 3.15	30	- 2:45	- 3.15	49	- 2:26	- 3.15	18	- 2:57
- 3.00	47	- 2:13	- 3.00	53	- 2:07	- 3.00	55	- 2:05	- 3.00	34	- 2:26	- 3.00	36	- 2:24	- 3.00	29	- 2:31	- 3.00	48	- 2:12	- 3.00	18	- 2:42
- 2.45	47	- 1:58	- 2.45	53	- 1:52	- 2.45	56	- 1:49	- 2.45	34	- 2:11	- 2.45	36	- 2:09	- 2.45	29	- 2:16	- 2.45	48	- 1:57	- 2.45	18	- 2:27
- 2.30	46	- 1:44	- 2.30	53	- 1:37	- 2.30	56	- 1:34	- 2.30	33	- 1:57	- 2.30	36	- 1:54	- 2.30	29	- 2:01	- 2.30	47	- 1:43	- 2.30	17	- 2:13
- 2.15	46	- 1:29	- 2.15	53	- 1:22	- 2.15	56	- 1:19	- 2.15	32	- 1:43	- 2.15	36	- 1:39	- 2.15	29	- 1:46	- 2.15	47	- 1:28	- 2.15	17	- 1:58
- 2.00	45	- 1:15	- 2.00	53	- 1:07	- 2.00	56	- 1:04	- 2.00	31	- 1:29	- 2.00	36	- 1:24	- 2.00	29	- 1:31	- 2.00	46	- 1:14	- 2.00	17	- 1:43
- 1.45	44	- 1:01	- 1.45	53	- 0:52	- 1.45	57	- 0:48	- 1.45	31	- 1:14	- 1.45	37	- 1:08	- 1.45	28	- 1:17	- 1.45	46	- 0:59	- 1.45	17	- 1:28
- 1.30	44	- 0:46	- 1.30	54	- 0:36	- 1.30	58	- 0:32	- 1.30	31	- 0:59	- 1.30	38	- 0:52	- 1.30	28	- 1:02	- 1.30	45	- 0:45	- 1.30	16	- 1:14
- 1.15	43	- 0:32	- 1.15	54	- 0:21	- 1.15	60	- 0:15	- 1.15	31	- 0:44	- 1.15	38	- 0:37	- 1.15	27	- 0:48	- 1.15	44	- 0:31	- 1.15	16	- 0:59
- 1.00	42	- 0:18	- 1.00	55	- 0:05	- 1.00	61	+ 0:01	- 1.00	31	- 0:29	- 1.00	39	- 0:21	- 1.00	26	- 0:34	- 1.00	43	- 0:17	- 1.00	16	- 0:44
- 0.45	41	- 0:04	- 0.45	56	+ 0:11	- 0.45	64	+ 0:19	- 0.45	31	- 0:14	- 0.45	40	- 0:05	- 0.45	26	- 0:19	- 0.45	42	- 0:03	- 0.45	16	- 0:29
- 0.30	40	+ 0:10	- 0.30	57	+ 0:27	- 0.30	67	+ 0:37	- 0.30	31	+ 0:01	- 0.30	41	+ 0:11	- 0.30	26	- 0:04	- 0.30	41	+ 0:11	- 0.30	16	- 0:14
- 0.15	39	+ 0:24	- 0.15	58	+ 0:43	- 0.15	70	+ 0:55	- 0.15	32	+ 0:17	- 0.15	42	+ 0:27	- 0.15	26	+ 0:11	- 0.15	40	+ 0:25	- 0.15	16	+ 0:01
HW	38	+ 0:38	HW	58	+ 0:58	HW	73	+ 1:13	HW	32	+ 0:32	HW	43	+ 0:43	HW	25	+ 0:25	HW	39	+ 0:39	HW	16	+ 0:16
+ 0.15	37	+ 0:52	+ 0.15	60	+ 1:15	+ 0.15	78	+ 1:33	+ 0.15	33	+ 0:48	+ 0.15	44	+ 0:59	+ 0.15	25	+ 0:40	+ 0.15	38	+ 0:53	+ 0.15	16	+ 0:31
+ 0.30	36	+ 1:06	+ 0.30	61	+ 1:31	+ 0.30	82	+ 1:52	+ 0.30	34	+ 1:04	+ 0.30	45	+ 1:15	+ 0.30	24	+ 0:54	+ 0.30	37	+ 1:07	+ 0.30	17	+ 0:47
+ 0.45	35	+ 1:20	+ 0.45	62	+ 1:47	+ 0.45	87	+ 2:12	+ 0.45	34	+ 1:19	+ 0.45	47	+ 1:32	+ 0.45	24	+ 1:09	+ 0.45	37	+ 1:22	+ 0.45	17	+ 1:02
+ 1.00	34	+ 1:34	+ 1.00	63	+ 2:03	+ 1.00	91	+ 2:31	+ 1.00	35	+ 1:35	+ 1.00	48	+ 1:48	+ 1.00	23	+ 1:23	+ 1.00	36	+ 1:36	+ 1.00	17	+ 1:17
+ 1.15	33	+ 1:48	+ 1.15	63	+ 2:18	+ 1.15	93	+ 2:48	+ 1.15	36	+ 1:51	+ 1.15	49	+ 2:04	+ 1.15	23	+ 1:38	+ 1.15	36	+ 1:51	+ 1.15	17	+ 1:32
+ 1.30	32	+ 2:02	+ 1.30	64	+ 2:34	+ 1.30	95	+ 3:05	+ 1.30	37	+ 2:07	+ 1.30	50	+ 2:20	+ 1.30	23	+ 1:53	+ 1.30	36	+ 2:06	+ 1.30	17	+ 1:47
+ 1.45	31	+ 2:16	+ 1.45	64	+ 2:49	+ 1.45	97	+ 3:22	+ 1.45	38	+ 2:23	+ 1.45	51	+ 2:36	+ 1.45	23	+ 2:08	+ 1.45	36	+ 2:21	+ 1.45	17	+ 2:02
+ 2.00	30	+ 2:30	+ 2.00	64	+ 3:04	+ 2.00	99	+ 3:39	+ 2.00	39	+ 2:39	+ 2.00	52	+ 2:52	+ 2.00	23	+ 2:23	+ 2.00	35	+ 2:35	+ 2.00	17	+ 2:17
+ 2.15	30	+ 2:45	+ 2.15	64	+ 3:19	+ 2.15	98	+ 3:53	+ 2.15	39	+ 2:54	+ 2.15	52	+ 3:07	+ 2.15	22	+ 2:37	+ 2.15	36	+ 2:51	+ 2.15	17	+ 2:32
+ 2.30	30	+ 3:00	+ 2.30	64	+ 3:34	+ 2.30	96	+ 4:06	+ 2.30	39	+ 3:09	+ 2.30	52	+ 3:22	+ 2.30	22	+ 2:52	+ 2.30	36	+ 3:06	+ 2.30	17	+ 2:47
+ 2.45	30	+ 3:15	+ 2.45	63	+ 3:48	+ 2.45	95	+ 4:20	+ 2.45	40	+ 3:25	+ 2.45	52	+ 3:37	+ 2.45	22	+ 3:07	+ 2.45	36	+ 3:21	+ 2.45	17	+ 3:02
+ 3.00	30	+ 3:30	+ 3.00	63	+ 4:03	+ 3.00	94	+ 4:34	+ 3.00	40	+ 3:40	+ 3.00	52	+ 3:52	+ 3.00	22	+ 3:22	+ 3.00	36	+ 3:36	+ 3.00	17	+ 3:17
+ 3.15	31	+ 3:46	+ 3.15	62	+ 4:17	+ 3.15	91	+ 4:46	+ 3.15	40	+ 3:55	+ 3.15	51	+ 4:06	+ 3.15	22	+ 3:37	+ 3.15	37	+ 3:52	+ 3.15	17	+ 3:32
+ 3.30	32	+ 4:02	+ 3.30	62	+ 4:32	+ 3.30	89	+ 4:59	+ 3.30	41	+ 4:11	+ 3.30	50	+ 4:20	+ 3.30	22	+ 3:52	+ 3.30	37	+ 4:07	+ 3.30	17	+ 3:47
+ 3.45	32	+ 4:17	+ 3.45	62	+ 4:47	+ 3.45	86	+ 5:11	+ 3.45	41	+ 4:26	+ 3.45	50	+ 4:35	+ 3.45	23	+ 4:08	+ 3.45	37	+ 4:22	+ 3.45	17	+ 4:02
+ 4.00	33	+ 4:33	+ 4.00	61	+ 5:01	+ 4.00	83	+ 5:23	+ 4.00	41	+ 4:41	+ 4.00	49	+ 4:49	+ 4.00	23	+ 4:23	+ 4.00	37	+ 4:37	+ 4.00	17	+ 4:17
+ 4.15	33	+ 4:48	+ 4.15	61	+ 5:16	+ 4.15	82	+ 5:37	+ 4.15	41	+ 4:56	+ 4.15	48	+ 5:03	+ 4.15	23	+ 4:38	+ 4.15	38	+ 4:53	+ 4.15	17	+ 4:32
+ 4.30	34	+ 5:04	+ 4.30	60	+ 5:30	+ 4.30	81	+ 5:51	+ 4.30	41	+ 5:11	+ 4.30	47	+ 5:17	+ 4.30	24	+ 4:54	+ 4.30	39	+ 5:09	+ 4.30	17	+ 4:47
+ 4.45	34	+ 5:19	+ 4.45	60	+ 5:45	+ 4.45	79	- 5:56	+ 4.45	41	+ 5:26	+ 4.45	46	+ 5:31	+ 4.45	24	+ 5:09	+ 4.45	39	+ 5:24	+ 4.45	16	+ 5:01
+ 5.00	35	+ 5:35	+ 5.00	60	- 6:00	+ 5.00	78	- 5:42	+ 5.00	41	+ 5:41	+ 5.00	45	+ 5:45	+ 5.00	24	+ 5:24	+ 5.00	40	+ 5:40	+ 5.00	16	+ 5:16
+ 5.15	36	+ 5:51	+ 5.15	59	- 5:46	+ 5.15	77	- 5:28	+ 5.15	41	+ 5:56	+ 5.15	45	- 6:00	+ 5.15	25	+ 5:40	+ 5.15	40	+ 5:55	+ 5.15	16	+ 5:31
+ 5.30	37	- 5:53	+ 5.30	59	- 5:31	+ 5.30	76	- 5:14	+ 5.30	41	- 5:49	+ 5.30	44	- 5:46	+ 5.30	25	+ 5:55	+ 5.30	41	- 5:49	+ 5.30	16	+ 5:46
+ 5.45	38	- 5:37	+ 5.45	59	- 5:16	+ 5.45	74	- 5:01	+ 5.45	41	- 5:34	+ 5.45	44	- 5:31	+ 5.45	26	- 5:49	+ 5.45	42	- 5:33	+ 5.45	16	- 5:59
+ 6.00	40	- 5:20	+ 6.00	59	- 5:01	+ 6.00	73	- 4:47	+ 6.00	41	- 5:19	+ 6.00	43	- 5:17	+ 6.00	26	- 5:34	+ 6.00	42	- 5:18	+ 6.00	16	- 5:44

Table C - North Foreland to Spitway via Princes Channel

Time to cover Sectors (in minutes) at 6.0 kts | All times relate to HW Sheerness | **Springs**

	C1 North Foreland to Margate Sand			C2 Margate Sand to Princes South			C3 Princes South to Princes No 6			C4 Princes No 6 to SW Barrow			C5 SW Barrow to Maplin Edge			C6 Maplin Edge to NE Maplin			C7 NE Maplin to Whitaker Spit			C8 Whitaker Spit to Mid-Spitway	
Time	Duration	Time at End of Sector	Time	Duration	Time at End of Sector	Time	Duration	Time at End of Sector	Time	Duration	Time at End of Sector	Time	Duration	Time at End of Sector	Time	Duration	Time at End of Sector	Time	Duration	Time at End of Sector	Time	Duration	Time at End of Sector
- 6.00	**45**	**- 5:15**	**- 6.00**	**57**	**- 5:03**	**- 6.00**	**68**	**- 4:52**	**- 6.00**	**44**	**- 5:16**	**- 6.00**	**41**	**- 5:19**	**- 6.00**	**27**	**- 5:33**	**- 6.00**	**46**	**- 5:14**	**- 6.00**	**17**	**- 5:43**
- 5.45	47	- 4:58	- 5.45	57	- 4:48	- 5.45	66	- 4:39	- 5.45	43	- 5:02	- 5.45	40	- 5:05	- 5.45	28	- 5:17	- 5.45	48	- 4:57	- 5.45	17	- 5:28
- 5.30	49	- 4:41	- 5.30	56	- 4:34	- 5.30	63	- 4:27	- 5.30	43	- 4:47	- 5.30	40	- 4:50	- 5.30	29	- 5:01	- 5.30	50	- 4:40	- 5.30	18	- 5:12
- 5.15	51	- 4:24	- 5.15	55	- 4:20	- 5.15	60	- 4:15	- 5.15	42	- 4:33	- 5.15	39	- 4:36	- 5.15	30	- 4:45	- 5.15	52	- 4:23	- 5.15	18	- 4:57
- 5.00	**54**	**- 4:06**	**- 5.00**	**54**	**- 4:06**	**- 5.00**	**58**	**- 4:02**	**- 5.00**	**42**	**- 4:18**	**- 5.00**	**38**	**- 4:22**	**- 5.00**	**31**	**- 4:29**	**- 5.00**	**54**	**- 4:06**	**- 5.00**	**19**	**- 4:41**
- 4.45	54	- 3:51	- 4.45	54	- 3:51	- 4.45	57	- 3:48	- 4.45	41	- 4:04	- 4.45	38	- 4:07	- 4.45	32	- 4:13	- 4.45	54	- 3:51	- 4.45	19	- 4:26
- 4.30	55	- 3:35	- 4.30	53	- 3:37	- 4.30	55	- 3:35	- 4.30	40	- 3:50	- 4.30	37	- 3:53	- 4.30	32	- 3:58	- 4.30	55	- 3:35	- 4.30	20	- 4:10
- 4.15	56	- 3:19	- 4.15	53	- 3:22	- 4.15	54	- 3:21	- 4.15	39	- 3:36	- 4.15	37	- 3:38	- 4.15	32	- 3:43	- 4.15	55	- 3:20	- 4.15	20	- 3:55
- 4.00	**56**	**- 3:04**	**- 4.00**	**52**	**- 3:08**	**- 4.00**	**53**	**- 3:07**	**- 4.00**	**39**	**- 3:21**	**- 4.00**	**36**	**- 3:24**	**- 4.00**	**33**	**- 3:27**	**- 4.00**	**56**	**- 3:04**	**- 4.00**	**20**	**- 3:40**
- 3.45	55	- 2:50	- 3.45	52	- 2:53	- 3.45	52	- 2:53	- 3.45	37	- 3:08	- 3.45	36	- 3:09	- 3.45	33	- 3:12	- 3.45	55	- 2:50	- 3.45	20	- 3:25
- 3.30	54	- 2:36	- 3.30	52	- 2:38	- 3.30	52	- 2:38	- 3.30	36	- 2:54	- 3.30	35	- 2:55	- 3.30	32	- 2:58	- 3.30	55	- 2:35	- 3.30	20	- 3:10
- 3.15	53	- 2:22	- 3.15	52	- 2:23	- 3.15	51	- 2:24	- 3.15	35	- 2:40	- 3.15	35	- 2:40	- 3.15	32	- 2:43	- 3.15	54	- 2:21	- 3.15	20	- 2:55
- 3.00	**52**	**- 2:08**	**- 3.00**	**51**	**- 2:09**	**- 3.00**	**51**	**- 2:09**	**- 3.00**	**33**	**- 2:27**	**- 3.00**	**34**	**- 2:26**	**- 3.00**	**32**	**- 2:28**	**- 3.00**	**54**	**- 2:06**	**- 3.00**	**19**	**- 2:41**
- 2.45	51	- 1:54	- 2.45	51	- 1:54	- 2.45	51	- 1:54	- 2.45	32	- 2:13	- 2.45	34	- 2:11	- 2.45	32	- 2:13	- 2.45	53	- 1:52	- 2.45	19	- 2:26
- 2.30	50	- 1:40	- 2.30	51	- 1:39	- 2.30	50	- 1:40	- 2.30	31	- 1:59	- 2.30	34	- 1:56	- 2.30	31	- 1:59	- 2.30	52	- 1:38	- 2.30	18	- 2:12
- 2.15	50	- 1:25	- 2.15	51	- 1:24	- 2.15	50	- 1:25	- 2.15	30	- 1:45	- 2.15	34	- 1:41	- 2.15	31	- 1:44	- 2.15	51	- 1:24	- 2.15	18	- 1:57
- 2.00	**49**	**- 1:11**	**- 2.00**	**51**	**- 1:09**	**- 2.00**	**50**	**- 1:10**	**- 2.00**	**28**	**- 1:32**	**- 2.00**	**34**	**- 1:26**	**- 2.00**	**30**	**- 1:30**	**- 2.00**	**50**	**- 1:10**	**- 2.00**	**18**	**- 1:42**
- 1.45	48	- 0:57	- 1.45	52	- 0:53	- 1.45	52	- 0:53	- 1.45	28	- 1:17	- 1.45	34	- 1:11	- 1.45	30	- 1:15	- 1.45	48	- 0:57	- 1.45	17	- 1:28
- 1.30	47	- 0:43	- 1.30	52	- 0:38	- 1.30	54	- 0:36	- 1.30	28	- 1:02	- 1.30	35	- 0:55	- 1.30	29	- 1:01	- 1.30	47	- 0:43	- 1.30	17	- 1:13
- 1.15	45	- 0:30	- 1.15	53	- 0:22	- 1.15	56	- 0:19	- 1.15	27	- 0:48	- 1.15	36	- 0:39	- 1.15	28	- 0:47	- 1.15	45	- 0:30	- 1.15	16	- 0:59
- 1.00	**44**	**- 0:16**	**- 1.00**	**54**	**- 0:06**	**- 1.00**	**58**	**- 0:02**	**- 1.00**	**27**	**- 0:33**	**- 1.00**	**37**	**- 0:23**	**- 1.00**	**27**	**- 0:33**	**- 1.00**	**44**	**- 0:16**	**- 1.00**	**16**	**- 0:44**
- 0.45	43	- 0:02	- 0.45	55	+ 0:10	- 0.45	63	+ 0:18	- 0.45	27	- 0:18	- 0.45	39	- 0:06	- 0.45	26	- 0:19	- 0.45	42	- 0:03	- 0.45	16	- 0:29
- 0.30	41	+ 0:11	- 0.30	57	+ 0:27	- 0.30	68	+ 0:38	- 0.30	28	- 0:02	- 0.30	40	+ 0:10	- 0.30	26	- 0:04	- 0.30	41	+ 0:11	- 0.30	16	- 0:14
- 0.15	39	+ 0:24	- 0.15	58	+ 0:43	- 0.15	74	+ 0:59	- 0.15	29	+ 0:14	- 0.15	42	+ 0:27	- 0.15	26	+ 0:11	- 0.15	39	+ 0:24	- 0.15	16	+ 0:01
HW	**38**	**+ 0:38**	**HW**	**60**	**+ 1:00**	**HW**	**79**	**+ 1:19**	**HW**	**29**	**+ 0:29**	**HW**	**43**	**+ 0:43**	**HW**	**25**	**+ 0:25**	**HW**	**37**	**+ 0:37**	**HW**	**16**	**+ 0:16**
+ 0.15	36	+ 0:51	+ 0.15	62	+ 1:17	+ 0.15	87	+ 1:42	+ 0.15	30	+ 0:45	+ 0.15	46	+ 1:01	+ 0.15	24	+ 0:39	+ 0.15	37	+ 0:52	+ 0.15	17	+ 0:32
+ 0.30	35	+ 1:05	+ 0.30	64	+ 1:34	+ 0.30	95	+ 2:05	+ 0.30	32	+ 1:02	+ 0.30	48	+ 1:18	+ 0.30	24	+ 0:54	+ 0.30	36	+ 1:06	+ 0.30	17	+ 0:47
+ 0.45	33	+ 1:18	+ 0.45	65	+ 1:50	+ 0.45	102	+ 2:27	+ 0.45	33	+ 1:18	+ 0.45	50	+ 1:35	+ 0.45	23	+ 1:08	+ 0.45	35	+ 1:20	+ 0.45	18	+ 1:03
+ 1.00	**34**	**+ 1:34**	**+ 1.00**	**67**	**+ 2:07**	**+ 1.00**	**110**	**+ 2:50**	**+ 1.00**	**34**	**+ 1:34**	**+ 1.00**	**52**	**+ 1:52**	**+ 1.00**	**22**	**+ 1:22**	**+ 1.00**	**34**	**+ 1:34**	**+ 1.00**	**18**	**+ 1:18**
+ 1.15	30	+ 1:45	+ 1.15	68	+ 2:23	+ 1.15	111	+ 3:06	+ 1.15	36	+ 1:51	+ 1.15	54	+ 2:09	+ 1.15	22	+ 1:37	+ 1.15	34	+ 1:49	+ 1.15	18	+ 1:33
+ 1.30	29	+ 1:59	+ 1.30	69	+ 2:39	+ 1.30	112	+ 3:22	+ 1.30	38	+ 2:08	+ 1.30	56	+ 2:26	+ 1.30	22	+ 1:52	+ 1.30	33	+ 2:03	+ 1.30	19	+ 1:49
+ 1.45	27	+ 2:12	+ 1.45	70	+ 2:55	+ 1.45	114	+ 3:39	+ 1.45	40	+ 2:25	+ 1.45	58	+ 2:43	+ 1.45	22	+ 2:07	+ 1.45	33	+ 2:18	+ 1.45	19	+ 2:04
+ 2.00	**25**	**+ 2:25**	**+ 2.00**	**71**	**+ 3:11**	**+ 2.00**	**115**	**+ 3:55**	**+ 2.00**	**41**	**+ 2:41**	**+ 2.00**	**60**	**+ 3:00**	**+ 2.00**	**21**	**+ 2:21**	**+ 2.00**	**33**	**+ 2:33**	**+ 2.00**	**19**	**+ 2:19**
+ 2.15	26	+ 2:41	+ 2.15	70	+ 3:25	+ 2.15	113	+ 4:08	+ 2.15	42	+ 2:57	+ 2.15	59	+ 3:14	+ 2.15	21	+ 2:36	+ 2.15	33	+ 2:48	+ 2.15	19	+ 2:34
+ 2.30	26	+ 2:56	+ 2.30	69	+ 3:39	+ 2.30	111	+ 4:21	+ 2.30	43	+ 3:13	+ 2.30	59	+ 3:29	+ 2.30	21	+ 2:51	+ 2.30	33	+ 3:03	+ 2.30	19	+ 2:49
+ 2.45	26	+ 3:11	+ 2.45	68	+ 3:53	+ 2.45	109	+ 4:34	+ 2.45	44	+ 3:29	+ 2.45	59	+ 3:44	+ 2.45	21	+ 3:06	+ 2.45	33	+ 3:18	+ 2.45	18	+ 3:03
+ 3.00	**26**	**+ 3:26**	**+ 3.00**	**67**	**+ 4:07**	**+ 3.00**	**107**	**+ 4:47**	**+ 3.00**	**45**	**+ 3:45**	**+ 3.00**	**58**	**+ 3:58**	**+ 3.00**	**21**	**+ 3:21**	**+ 3.00**	**34**	**+ 3:34**	**+ 3.00**	**18**	**+ 3:18**
+ 3.15	27	+ 3:42	+ 3.15	67	+ 4:22	+ 3.15	105	+ 5:00	+ 3.15	45	+ 4:00	+ 3.15	57	+ 4:12	+ 3.15	21	+ 3:36	+ 3.15	34	+ 3:49	+ 3.15	18	+ 3:33
+ 3.30	28	+ 3:58	+ 3.30	66	+ 4:36	+ 3.30	103	+ 5:13	+ 3.30	45	+ 4:15	+ 3.30	55	+ 4:25	+ 3.30	21	+ 3:51	+ 3.30	35	+ 4:05	+ 3.30	18	+ 3:48
+ 3.45	29	+ 4:14	+ 3.45	65	+ 4:50	+ 3.45	100	+ 5:25	+ 3.45	45	+ 4:30	+ 3.45	54	+ 4:39	+ 3.45	21	+ 4:06	+ 3.45	35	+ 4:20	+ 3.45	17	+ 4:02
+ 4.00	**30**	**+ 4:30**	**+ 4.00**	**64**	**+ 5:04**	**+ 4.00**	**98**	**+ 5:38**	**+ 4.00**	**45**	**+ 4:45**	**+ 4.00**	**52**	**+ 4:52**	**+ 4.00**	**21**	**+ 4:21**	**+ 4.00**	**35**	**+ 4:35**	**+ 4.00**	**17**	**+ 4:17**
+ 4.15	31	+ 4:46	+ 4.15	63	+ 5:18	+ 4.15	95	+ 5:50	+ 4.15	45	+ 5:00	+ 4.15	51	+ 5:06	+ 4.15	22	+ 4:37	+ 4.15	36	+ 4:51	+ 4.15	17	+ 4:32
+ 4.30	32	+ 5:02	+ 4.30	62	+ 5:32	+ 4.30	92	- 5:58	+ 4.30	45	+ 5:15	+ 4.30	49	+ 5:19	+ 4.30	23	+ 4:53	+ 4.30	37	+ 5:07	+ 4.30	17	+ 4:47
+ 4.45	32	+ 5:17	+ 4.45	62	+ 5:47	+ 4.45	88	- 5:47	+ 4.45	45	+ 5:30	+ 4.45	48	+ 5:33	+ 4.45	23	+ 5:08	+ 4.45	38	+ 5:23	+ 4.45	16	+ 5:01
+ 5.00	**33**	**+ 5:33**	**+ 5.00**	**61**	**- 5:59**	**+ 5.00**	**85**	**- 5:35**	**+ 5.00**	**45**	**+ 5:45**	**+ 5.00**	**47**	**+ 5:47**	**+ 5.00**	**24**	**+ 5:24**	**+ 5.00**	**39**	**+ 5:39**	**+ 5.00**	**16**	**+ 5:16**
+ 5.15	35	+ 5:50	+ 5.15	61	- 5:44	+ 5.15	83	- 5:22	+ 5.15	45	- 6:00	+ 5.15	46	- 5:59	+ 5.15	25	+ 5:40	+ 5.15	40	+ 5:55	+ 5.15	16	+ 5:31
+ 5.30	36	- 5:54	+ 5.30	60	- 5:30	+ 5.30	81	- 5:09	+ 5.30	45	- 5:45	+ 5.30	45	- 5:45	+ 5.30	25	+ 5:55	+ 5.30	40	- 5:50	+ 5.30	16	+ 5:46
+ 5.45	38	- 5:37	+ 5.45	60	- 5:15	+ 5.45	79	- 4:56	+ 5.45	45	- 5:30	+ 5.45	44	- 5:31	+ 5.45	26	- 5:49	+ 5.45	41	- 5:34	+ 5.45	16	- 5:59
+ 6.00	**40**	**- 5:20**	**+ 6.00**	**60**	**- 5:00**	**+ 6.00**	**77**	**- 4:43**	**+ 6.00**	**45**	**- 5:15**	**+ 6.00**	**43**	**- 5:17**	**+ 6.00**	**27**	**- 5:33**	**+ 6.00**	**42**	**- 5:18**	**+ 6.00**	**16**	**- 5:44**

NORTH & WEST

Table C - North Foreland to Spitway via Princes Channel

Neaps — All times relate to HW Sheerness — **Time to cover Sectors (in minutes) at 7.0 kts**

NORTH & WEST

	C1			C2			C3			C4			C5			C6			C7			C8	
	North Foreland to Margate Sand			Margate Sand to Princes South			Princes South to Princes No 6			Princes No 6 to SW Barrow			SW Barrow to Maplin Edge			Maplin Edge to NE Maplin			NE Maplin to Whitaker Spit			Whitaker Spit to Mid-Spitway	
Time	Duration	Time at End of Sector	Time	Duration	Time at End of Sector	Time	Duration	Time at End of Sector	Time	Duration	Time at End of Sector	Time	Duration	Time at End of Sector	Time	Duration	Time at End of Sector	Time	Duration	Time at End of Sector	Time	Duration	Time at End of Sector
- 6.00	**36**	**- 5:24**	**- 6.00**	**49**	**- 5:11**	**- 6.00**	**59**	**- 5:01**	**- 6.00**	**34**	**- 5:26**	**- 6.00**	**36**	**- 5:24**	**- 6.00**	**23**	**- 5:37**	**- 6.00**	**37**	**- 5:23**	**- 6.00**	**14**	**- 5:46**
- 5.45	37	- 5:08	- 5.45	49	- 4:56	- 5.45	58	- 4:47	- 5.45	34	- 5:11	- 5.45	35	- 5:10	- 5.45	23	- 5:22	- 5.45	38	- 5:07	- 5.45	14	- 5:31
- 5.30	38	- 4:52	- 5.30	48	- 4:42	- 5.30	57	- 4:33	- 5.30	34	- 4:56	- 5.30	35	- 4:55	- 5.30	24	- 5:06	- 5.30	39	- 4:51	- 5.30	15	- 5:15
- 5.15	39	- 4:36	- 5.15	48	- 4:27	- 5.15	56	- 4:19	- 5.15	34	- 4:41	- 5.15	35	- 4:40	- 5.15	24	- 4:51	- 5.15	40	- 4:35	- 5.15	15	- 5:00
- 5.00	**40**	**- 4:20**	**- 5.00**	**47**	**- 4:13**	**- 5.00**	**55**	**- 4:05**	**- 5.00**	**33**	**- 4:27**	**- 5.00**	**34**	**- 4:26**	**- 5.00**	**25**	**- 4:35**	**- 5.00**	**41**	**- 4:19**	**- 5.00**	**15**	**- 4:45**
- 4.45	40	- 4:05	- 4.45	47	- 3:58	- 4.45	54	- 3:51	- 4.45	33	- 4:12	- 4.45	34	- 4:11	- 4.45	25	- 4:20	- 4.45	41	- 4:04	- 4.45	15	- 4:30
- 4.30	41	- 3:49	- 4.30	47	- 3:43	- 4.30	53	- 3:37	- 4.30	33	- 3:57	- 4.30	34	- 3:56	- 4.30	25	- 4:05	- 4.30	41	- 3:49	- 4.30	15	- 4:15
- 4.15	41	- 3:34	- 4.15	46	- 3:29	- 4.15	52	- 3:23	- 4.15	32	- 3:43	- 4.15	33	- 3:42	- 4.15	25	- 3:50	- 4.15	41	- 3:34	- 4.15	16	- 3:59
- 4.00	**41**	**- 3:19**	**- 4.00**	**46**	**- 3:14**	**- 4.00**	**51**	**- 3:09**	**- 4.00**	**32**	**- 3:28**	**- 4.00**	**33**	**- 3:27**	**- 4.00**	**26**	**- 3:34**	**- 4.00**	**41**	**- 3:19**	**- 4.00**	**16**	**- 3:44**
- 3.45	41	- 3:04	- 3.45	46	- 2:59	- 3.45	51	- 2:54	- 3.45	32	- 3:13	- 3.45	33	- 3:12	- 3.45	26	- 3:19	- 3.45	41	- 3:04	- 3.45	16	- 3:29
- 3.30	40	- 2:50	- 3.30	46	- 2:44	- 3.30	50	- 2:40	- 3.30	31	- 2:59	- 3.30	32	- 2:58	- 3.30	25	- 3:05	- 3.30	41	- 2:49	- 3.30	16	- 3:14
- 3.15	40	- 2:35	- 3.15	46	- 2:29	- 3.15	50	- 2:25	- 3.15	30	- 2:45	- 3.15	32	- 2:43	- 3.15	25	- 2:50	- 3.15	41	- 2:34	- 3.15	15	- 3:00
- 3.00	**40**	**- 2:20**	**- 3.00**	**46**	**- 2:14**	**- 3.00**	**49**	**- 2:11**	**- 3.00**	**30**	**- 2:30**	**- 3.00**	**32**	**- 2:28**	**- 3.00**	**25**	**- 2:35**	**- 3.00**	**41**	**- 2:19**	**- 3.00**	**15**	**- 2:45**
- 2.45	39	- 2:06	- 2.45	46	- 1:59	- 2.45	49	- 1:56	- 2.45	29	- 2:16	- 2.45	32	- 2:13	- 2.45	25	- 2:20	- 2.45	40	- 2:05	- 2.45	15	- 2:30
- 2.30	39	- 1:51	- 2.30	46	- 1:44	- 2.30	49	- 1:41	- 2.30	28	- 2:02	- 2.30	32	- 1:58	- 2.30	25	- 2:05	- 2.30	40	- 1:50	- 2.30	15	- 2:15
- 2.15	38	- 1:37	- 2.15	46	- 1:29	- 2.15	49	- 1:26	- 2.15	28	- 1:47	- 2.15	32	- 1:43	- 2.15	25	- 1:50	- 2.15	40	- 1:35	- 2.15	15	- 2:00
- 2.00	**38**	**- 1:22**	**- 2.00**	**46**	**- 1:14**	**- 2.00**	**49**	**- 1:11**	**- 2.00**	**27**	**- 1:33**	**- 2.00**	**32**	**- 1:28**	**- 2.00**	**25**	**- 1:35**	**- 2.00**	**39**	**- 1:21**	**- 2.00**	**14**	**- 1:46**
- 1.45	38	- 1:07	- 1.45	46	- 0:59	- 1.45	50	- 0:55	- 1.45	27	- 1:18	- 1.45	32	- 1:13	- 1.45	24	- 1:21	- 1.45	39	- 1:06	- 1.45	14	- 1:31
- 1.30	37	- 0:53	- 1.30	46	- 0:44	- 1.30	51	- 0:39	- 1.30	27	- 1:03	- 1.30	32	- 0:58	- 1.30	24	- 1:06	- 1.30	38	- 0:52	- 1.30	14	- 1:16
- 1.15	37	- 0:38	- 1.15	47	- 0:28	- 1.15	52	- 0:23	- 1.15	27	- 0:48	- 1.15	33	- 0:42	- 1.15	23	- 0:52	- 1.15	38	- 0:37	- 1.15	14	- 1:01
- 1.00	**36**	**- 0:24**	**- 1.00**	**47**	**- 0:13**	**- 1.00**	**53**	**- 0:07**	**- 1.00**	**26**	**- 0:34**	**- 1.00**	**33**	**- 0:27**	**- 1.00**	**23**	**- 0:37**	**- 1.00**	**37**	**- 0:23**	**- 1.00**	**14**	**- 0:46**
- 0.45	35	- 0:10	- 0.45	48	+ 0:03	- 0.45	55	+ 0:10	- 0.45	27	- 0:18	- 0.45	34	- 0:11	- 0.45	22	- 0:23	- 0.45	36	- 0:09	- 0.45	14	- 0:31
- 0.30	35	+ 0:05	- 0.30	48	+ 0:18	- 0.30	57	+ 0:27	- 0.30	27	- 0:03	- 0.30	35	+ 0:05	- 0.30	22	- 0:08	- 0.30	35	+ 0:05	- 0.30	14	- 0:16
- 0.15	34	+ 0:19	- 0.15	49	+ 0:34	- 0.15	59	+ 0:44	- 0.15	27	+ 0:12	- 0.15	36	+ 0:21	- 0.15	22	+ 0:07	- 0.15	34	+ 0:19	- 0.15	14	- 0:01
HW	**33**	**+ 0:33**	**HW**	**50**	**+ 0:50**	**HW**	**62**	**+ 1:02**	**HW**	**28**	**+ 0:28**	**HW**	**36**	**+ 0:36**	**HW**	**22**	**+ 0:22**	**HW**	**34**	**+ 0:34**	**HW**	**14**	**+ 0:14**
+ 0.15	32	+ 0:47	+ 0.15	50	+ 1:05	+ 0.15	64	+ 1:19	+ 0.15	28	+ 0:43	+ 0.15	37	+ 0:52	+ 0.15	21	+ 0:36	+ 0.15	33	+ 0:48	+ 0.15	14	+ 0:29
+ 0.30	32	+ 1:02	+ 0.30	51	+ 1:21	+ 0.30	66	+ 1:36	+ 0.30	29	+ 0:59	+ 0.30	38	+ 1:08	+ 0.30	21	+ 0:51	+ 0.30	33	+ 1:03	+ 0.30	14	+ 0:44
+ 0.45	31	+ 1:16	+ 0.45	52	+ 1:37	+ 0.45	69	+ 1:54	+ 0.45	29	+ 1:14	+ 0.45	39	+ 1:24	+ 0.45	20	+ 1:05	+ 0.45	32	+ 1:17	+ 0.45	15	+ 1:00
+ 1.00	**30**	**+ 1:30**	**+ 1.00**	**53**	**+ 1:53**	**+ 1.00**	**71**	**+ 2:11**	**+ 1.00**	**30**	**+ 1:30**	**+ 1.00**	**40**	**+ 1:40**	**+ 1.00**	**20**	**+ 1:20**	**+ 1.00**	**32**	**+ 1:32**	**+ 1.00**	**15**	**+ 1:15**
+ 1.15	29	+ 1:44	+ 1.15	53	+ 2:08	+ 1.15	72	+ 2:27	+ 1.15	30	+ 1:45	+ 1.15	41	+ 1:56	+ 1.15	20	+ 1:35	+ 1.15	31	+ 1:46	+ 1.15	15	+ 1:30
+ 1.30	28	+ 1:58	+ 1.30	53	+ 2:23	+ 1.30	73	+ 2:43	+ 1.30	31	+ 2:01	+ 1.30	41	+ 2:11	+ 1.30	19	+ 1:49	+ 1.30	31	+ 2:01	+ 1.30	15	+ 1:45
+ 1.45	27	+ 2:12	+ 1.45	54	+ 2:39	+ 1.45	74	+ 2:59	+ 1.45	32	+ 2:17	+ 1.45	42	+ 2:27	+ 1.45	19	+ 2:04	+ 1.45	31	+ 2:16	+ 1.45	15	+ 2:00
+ 2.00	**25**	**+ 2:25**	**+ 2.00**	**54**	**+ 2:54**	**+ 2.00**	**75**	**+ 3:15**	**+ 2.00**	**32**	**+ 2:32**	**+ 2.00**	**43**	**+ 2:43**	**+ 2.00**	**19**	**+ 2:19**	**+ 2.00**	**31**	**+ 2:31**	**+ 2.00**	**15**	**+ 2:15**
+ 2.15	26	+ 2:41	+ 2.15	54	+ 3:09	+ 2.15	75	+ 3:30	+ 2.15	33	+ 2:48	+ 2.15	43	+ 2:58	+ 2.15	19	+ 2:34	+ 2.15	31	+ 2:46	+ 2.15	15	+ 2:30
+ 2.30	26	+ 2:56	+ 2.30	54	+ 3:24	+ 2.30	74	+ 3:44	+ 2.30	33	+ 3:03	+ 2.30	43	+ 3:13	+ 2.30	19	+ 2:49	+ 2.30	31	+ 3:01	+ 2.30	15	+ 2:45
+ 2.45	26	+ 3:11	+ 2.45	53	+ 3:38	+ 2.45	74	+ 3:59	+ 2.45	34	+ 3:19	+ 2.45	43	+ 3:28	+ 2.45	19	+ 3:04	+ 2.45	31	+ 3:16	+ 2.45	15	+ 3:00
+ 3.00	**26**	**+ 3:26**	**+ 3.00**	**53**	**+ 3:53**	**+ 3.00**	**73**	**+ 4:13**	**+ 3.00**	**34**	**+ 3:34**	**+ 3.00**	**43**	**+ 3:43**	**+ 3.00**	**19**	**+ 3:19**	**+ 3.00**	**32**	**+ 3:32**	**+ 3.00**	**15**	**+ 3:15**
+ 3.15	27	+ 3:42	+ 3.15	53	+ 4:08	+ 3.15	72	+ 4:27	+ 3.15	34	+ 3:49	+ 3.15	43	+ 3:58	+ 3.15	19	+ 3:34	+ 3.15	32	+ 3:47	+ 3.15	15	+ 3:30
+ 3.30	27	+ 3:57	+ 3.30	52	+ 4:22	+ 3.30	72	+ 4:42	+ 3.30	34	+ 4:04	+ 3.30	42	+ 4:12	+ 3.30	19	+ 3:49	+ 3.30	32	+ 4:02	+ 3.30	15	+ 3:45
+ 3.45	28	+ 4:13	+ 3.45	52	+ 4:37	+ 3.45	71	+ 4:56	+ 3.45	34	+ 4:19	+ 3.45	42	+ 4:27	+ 3.45	19	+ 4:04	+ 3.45	32	+ 4:17	+ 3.45	14	+ 3:59
+ 4.00	**29**	**+ 4:29**	**+ 4.00**	**52**	**+ 4:52**	**+ 4.00**	**70**	**+ 5:10**	**+ 4.00**	**34**	**+ 4:34**	**+ 4.00**	**41**	**+ 4:41**	**+ 4.00**	**19**	**+ 4:19**	**+ 4.00**	**32**	**+ 4:32**	**+ 4.00**	**14**	**+ 4:14**
+ 4.15	29	+ 4:44	+ 4.15	52	+ 5:07	+ 4.15	69	+ 5:24	+ 4.15	34	+ 4:49	+ 4.15	41	+ 4:56	+ 4.15	20	+ 4:35	+ 4.15	33	+ 4:48	+ 4.15	14	+ 4:29
+ 4.30	29	+ 4:59	+ 4.30	51	+ 5:21	+ 4.30	68	+ 5:38	+ 4.30	34	+ 5:04	+ 4.30	40	+ 5:10	+ 4.30	20	+ 4:50	+ 4.30	33	+ 5:03	+ 4.30	14	+ 4:44
+ 4.45	29	+ 5:14	+ 4.45	51	+ 5:36	+ 4.45	67	+ 5:52	+ 4.45	34	+ 5:19	+ 4.45	39	+ 5:24	+ 4.45	20	+ 5:05	+ 4.45	34	+ 5:19	+ 4.45	14	+ 4:59
+ 5.00	**30**	**+ 5:30**	**+ 5.00**	**51**	**+ 5:51**	**+ 5.00**	**66**	**- 5:54**	**+ 5.00**	**34**	**+ 5:34**	**+ 5.00**	**39**	**+ 5:39**	**+ 5.00**	**21**	**+ 5:21**	**+ 5.00**	**34**	**+ 5:34**	**+ 5.00**	**14**	**+ 5:14**
+ 5.15	31	+ 5:46	+ 5.15	51	- 5:54	+ 5.15	65	- 5:40	+ 5.15	34	- 5:49	+ 5.15	38	+ 5:53	+ 5.15	21	+ 5:36	+ 5.15	34	+ 5:49	+ 5.15	14	+ 5:29
+ 5.30	32	- 5:58	+ 5.30	50	- 5:40	+ 5.30	64	- 5:26	+ 5.30	34	- 5:56	+ 5.30	38	- 5:52	+ 5.30	22	+ 5:52	+ 5.30	35	- 5:55	+ 5.30	14	+ 5:44
+ 5.45	33	- 5:42	+ 5.45	50	- 5:25	+ 5.45	63	- 5:12	+ 5.45	34	- 5:41	+ 5.45	37	- 5:38	+ 5.45	22	- 5:53	+ 5.45	35	- 5:40	+ 5.45	14	+ 5:59
+ 6.00	**34**	**- 5:26**	**+ 6.00**	**50**	**- 5:10**	**+ 6.00**	**62**	**- 4:58**	**+ 6.00**	**34**	**- 5:26**	**+ 6.00**	**37**	**- 5:23**	**+ 6.00**	**22**	**- 5:38**	**+ 6.00**	**36**	**- 5:24**	**+ 6.00**	**14**	**- 5:46**

Table C - North Foreland to Spitway via Princes Channel

Time to cover Sectors (in minutes) at 7.0 kts — All times relate to HW Sheerness — **Springs**

	C1 North Foreland to Margate Sand			C2 Margate Sand to Princes South			C3 Princes South to Princes No 6			C4 Princes No 6 to SW Barrow	
Time	Duration	Time at End of Sector	Time	Duration	Time at End of Sector	Time	Duration	Time at End of Sector	Time	Duration	Time at End of Sector
- 6.00	**37**	**- 5:23**	**- 6.00**	**49**	**- 5:11**	**- 6.00**	**59**	**- 5:01**	**- 6.00**	**36**	**- 5:24**
- 5.45	39	- 5:06	- 5.45	49	- 4:56	- 5.45	57	- 4:48	- 5.45	36	- 5:09
- 5.30	40	- 4:50	- 5.30	48	- 4:42	- 5.30	55	- 4:35	- 5.30	36	- 4:54
- 5.15	42	- 4:33	- 5.15	47	- 4:28	- 5.15	53	- 4:22	- 5.15	35	- 4:40
- 5.00	**44**	**- 4:16**	**- 5.00**	**47**	**- 4:13**	**- 5.00**	**51**	**- 4:09**	**- 5.00**	**35**	**- 4:25**
- 4.45	44	- 4:01	- 4.45	46	- 3:59	- 4.45	50	- 3:55	- 4.45	35	- 4:10
- 4.30	45	- 3:45	- 4.30	46	- 3:44	- 4.30	49	- 3:41	- 4.30	34	- 3:56
- 4.15	46	- 3:29	- 4.15	45	- 3:30	- 4.15	48	- 3:27	- 4.15	34	- 3:41
- 4.00	**46**	**- 3:14**	**- 4.00**	**45**	**- 3:15**	**- 4.00**	**47**	**- 3:13**	**- 4.00**	**33**	**- 3:27**
- 3.45	46	- 2:59	- 3.45	45	- 3:00	- 3.45	46	- 2:59	- 3.45	32	- 3:13
- 3.30	45	- 2:45	- 3.30	45	- 2:45	- 3.30	46	- 2:44	- 3.30	31	- 2:59
- 3.15	44	- 2:31	- 3.15	45	- 2:30	- 3.15	46	- 2:29	- 3.15	30	- 2:45
- 3.00	**43**	**- 2:17**	**- 3.00**	**45**	**- 2:15**	**- 3.00**	**45**	**- 2:15**	**- 3.00**	**29**	**- 2:31**
- 2.45	43	- 2:02	- 2.45	44	- 2:01	- 2.45	45	- 2:00	- 2.45	28	- 2:17
- 2.30	42	- 1:48	- 2.30	44	- 1:46	- 2.30	45	- 1:45	- 2.30	27	- 2:03
- 2.15	42	- 1:33	- 2.15	44	- 1:31	- 2.15	45	- 1:30	- 2.15	26	- 1:49
- 2.00	**41**	**- 1:19**	**- 2.00**	**44**	**- 1:16**	**- 2.00**	**45**	**- 1:15**	**- 2.00**	**24**	**- 1:36**
- 1.45	40	- 1:05	- 1.45	45	- 1:00	- 1.45	46	- 0:59	- 1.45	24	- 1:21
- 1.30	39	- 0:51	- 1.30	45	- 0:45	- 1.30	47	- 0:43	- 1.30	24	- 1:06
- 1.15	39	- 0:36	- 1.15	46	- 0:29	- 1.15	49	- 0:26	- 1.15	23	- 0:52
- 1.00	**38**	**- 0:22**	**- 1.00**	**46**	**- 0:14**	**- 1.00**	**50**	**- 0:10**	**- 1.00**	**23**	**- 0:37**
- 0.45	36	- 0:09	- 0.45	47	+ 0:02	- 0.45	54	+ 0:09	- 0.45	23	- 0:22
- 0.30	35	+ 0:05	- 0.30	48	+ 0:18	- 0.30	57	+ 0:27	- 0.30	24	- 0:06
- 0.15	34	+ 0:19	- 0.15	49	+ 0:34	- 0.15	61	+ 0:46	- 0.15	24	+ 0:09
HW	**33**	**+ 0:33**	**HW**	**50**	**+ 0:50**	**HW**	**65**	**+ 1:05**	**HW**	**25**	**+ 0:25**
+ 0.15	32	+ 0:47	+ 0.15	52	+ 1:07	+ 0.15	70	+ 1:25	+ 0.15	26	+ 0:41
+ 0.30	31	+ 1:01	+ 0.30	53	+ 1:23	+ 0.30	75	+ 1:45	+ 0.30	27	+ 0:57
+ 0.45	30	+ 1:15	+ 0.45	54	+ 1:39	+ 0.45	81	+ 2:06	+ 0.45	28	+ 1:13
+ 1.00	**29**	**+ 1:29**	**+ 1.00**	**56**	**+ 1:56**	**+ 1.00**	**86**	**+ 2:26**	**+ 1.00**	**29**	**+ 1:29**
+ 1.15	27	+ 1:42	+ 1.15	56	+ 2:11	+ 1.15	87	+ 2:42	+ 1.15	30	+ 1:45
+ 1.30	25	+ 1:55	+ 1.30	57	+ 2:27	+ 1.30	89	+ 2:59	+ 1.30	32	+ 2:02
+ 1.45	23	+ 2:08	+ 1.45	57	+ 2:42	+ 1.45	90	+ 3:15	+ 1.45	33	+ 2:18
+ 2.00	**22**	**+ 2:22**	**+ 2.00**	**58**	**+ 2:58**	**+ 2.00**	**91**	**+ 3:31**	**+ 2.00**	**34**	**+ 2:34**
+ 2.15	22	+ 2:37	+ 2.15	58	+ 3:13	+ 2.15	90	+ 3:45	+ 2.15	35	+ 2:50
+ 2.30	22	+ 2:52	+ 2.30	57	+ 3:27	+ 2.30	89	+ 3:59	+ 2.30	36	+ 3:06
+ 2.45	22	+ 3:07	+ 2.45	57	+ 3:42	+ 2.45	88	+ 4:13	+ 2.45	36	+ 3:21
+ 3.00	**22**	**+ 3:22**	**+ 3.00**	**56**	**+ 3:56**	**+ 3.00**	**87**	**+ 4:27**	**+ 3.00**	**37**	**+ 3:37**
+ 3.15	23	+ 3:38	+ 3.15	56	+ 4:11	+ 3.15	85	+ 4:40	+ 3.15	37	+ 3:52
+ 3.30	24	+ 3:54	+ 3.30	55	+ 4:25	+ 3.30	84	+ 4:54	+ 3.30	37	+ 4:07
+ 3.45	25	+ 4:10	+ 3.45	54	+ 4:39	+ 3.45	82	+ 5:07	+ 3.45	37	+ 4:22
+ 4.00	**26**	**+ 4:26**	**+ 4.00**	**54**	**+ 4:54**	**+ 4.00**	**81**	**+ 5:21**	**+ 4.00**	**37**	**+ 4:37**
+ 4.15	27	+ 4:42	+ 4.15	53	+ 5:08	+ 4.15	79	+ 5:34	+ 4.15	37	+ 4:52
+ 4.30	27	+ 4:57	+ 4.30	53	+ 5:23	+ 4.30	76	+ 5:46	+ 4.30	37	+ 5:07
+ 4.45	27	+ 5:12	+ 4.45	52	+ 5:37	+ 4.45	74	+ 5:59	+ 4.45	37	+ 5:22
+ 5.00	**28**	**+ 5:28**	**+ 5.00**	**52**	**+ 5:52**	**+ 5.00**	**71**	**- 5:49**	**+ 5.00**	**37**	**+ 5:37**
+ 5.15	29	+ 5:44	+ 5.15	52	- 5:53	+ 5.15	70	- 5:35	+ 5.15	37	+ 5:52
+ 5.30	31	- 5:59	+ 5.30	51	- 5:39	+ 5.30	68	- 5:22	+ 5.30	37	- 5:53
+ 5.45	32	- 5:43	+ 5.45	51	- 5:24	+ 5.45	67	- 5:08	+ 5.45	37	- 5:38
+ 6.00	**34**	**- 5:26**	**+ 6.00**	**51**	**- 5:09**	**+ 6.00**	**65**	**- 4:55**	**+ 6.00**	**37**	**- 5:23**

	C5 SW Barrow to Maplin Edge			C6 Maplin Edge to NE Maplin			C7 NE Maplin to Whitaker Spit			C8 Whitaker Spit to Mid-Spitway	
Time	Duration	Time at End of Sector	Time	Duration	Time at End of Sector	Time	Duration	Time at End of Sector	Time	Duration	Time at End of Sector
- 6.00	**36**	**- 5:24**	**- 6.00**	**23**	**- 5:37**	**- 6.00**	**38**	**- 5:22**	**- 6.00**	**14**	**- 5:46**
- 5.45	35	- 5:10	- 5.45	24	- 5:21	- 5.45	40	- 5:05	- 5.45	15	- 5:30
- 5.30	35	- 4:55	- 5.30	25	- 5:05	- 5.30	41	- 4:49	- 5.30	15	- 5:15
- 5.15	34	- 4:41	- 5.15	26	- 4:49	- 5.15	43	- 4:32	- 5.15	16	- 4:59
- 5.00	**33**	**- 4:27**	**- 5.00**	**26**	**- 4:34**	**- 5.00**	**44**	**- 4:16**	**- 5.00**	**16**	**- 4:44**
- 4.45	33	- 4:12	- 4.45	27	- 4:18	- 4.45	45	- 4:00	- 4.45	17	- 4:28
- 4.30	33	- 3:57	- 4.30	27	- 4:03	- 4.30	45	- 3:45	- 4.30	17	- 4:13
- 4.15	32	- 3:43	- 4.15	27	- 3:48	- 4.15	45	- 3:30	- 4.15	17	- 3:58
- 4.00	**32**	**- 3:28**	**- 4.00**	**28**	**- 3:32**	**- 4.00**	**46**	**- 3:14**	**- 4.00**	**17**	**- 3:43**
- 3.45	31	- 3:14	- 3.45	27	- 3:18	- 3.45	45	- 3:00	- 3.45	17	- 3:28
- 3.30	31	- 2:59	- 3.30	27	- 3:03	- 3.30	45	- 2:45	- 3.30	17	- 3:13
- 3.15	31	- 2:44	- 3.15	27	- 2:48	- 3.15	45	- 2:30	- 3.15	17	- 2:58
- 3.00	**30**	**- 2:30**	**- 3.00**	**27**	**- 2:33**	**- 3.00**	**45**	**- 2:15**	**- 3.00**	**16**	**- 2:44**
- 2.45	30	- 2:15	- 2.45	27	- 2:18	- 2.45	44	- 2:01	- 2.45	16	- 2:29
- 2.30	30	- 2:00	- 2.30	26	- 2:04	- 2.30	43	- 1:47	- 2.30	16	- 2:14
- 2.15	30	- 1:45	- 2.15	26	- 1:49	- 2.15	42	- 1:33	- 2.15	15	- 2:00
- 2.00	**29**	**- 1:31**	**- 2.00**	**26**	**- 1:34**	**- 2.00**	**42**	**- 1:18**	**- 2.00**	**15**	**- 1:45**
- 1.45	30	- 1:15	- 1.45	25	- 1:20	- 1.45	41	- 1:04	- 1.45	15	- 1:30
- 1.30	31	- 0:59	- 1.30	24	- 1:06	- 1.30	40	- 0:50	- 1.30	14	- 1:16
- 1.15	31	- 0:44	- 1.15	24	- 0:51	- 1.15	39	- 0:36	- 1.15	14	- 1:01
- 1.00	**32**	**- 0:28**	**- 1.00**	**23**	**- 0:37**	**- 1.00**	**38**	**- 0:22**	**- 1.00**	**13**	**- 0:47**
- 0.45	33	- 0:12	- 0.45	23	- 0:22	- 0.45	37	- 0:08	- 0.45	13	- 0:32
- 0.30	34	+ 0:04	- 0.30	22	- 0:08	- 0.30	35	+ 0:05	- 0.30	14	- 0:16
- 0.15	35	+ 0:20	- 0.15	22	+ 0:07	- 0.15	34	+ 0:19	- 0.15	14	- 0:01
HW	**36**	**+ 0:36**	**HW**	**22**	**+ 0:22**	**HW**	**33**	**+ 0:33**	**HW**	**14**	**+ 0:14**
+ 0.15	38	+ 0:53	+ 0.15	21	+ 0:36	+ 0.15	32	+ 0:47	+ 0.15	14	+ 0:29
+ 0.30	39	+ 1:09	+ 0.30	20	+ 0:50	+ 0.30	32	+ 1:02	+ 0.30	15	+ 0:45
+ 0.45	41	+ 1:26	+ 0.45	19	+ 1:04	+ 0.45	31	+ 1:16	+ 0.45	15	+ 1:00
+ 1.00	**43**	**+ 1:43**	**+ 1.00**	**19**	**+ 1:19**	**+ 1.00**	**30**	**+ 1:30**	**+ 1.00**	**16**	**+ 1:16**
+ 1.15	44	+ 1:59	+ 1.15	19	+ 1:34	+ 1.15	30	+ 1:45	+ 1.15	16	+ 1:31
+ 1.30	45	+ 2:15	+ 1.30	19	+ 1:49	+ 1.30	30	+ 2:00	+ 1.30	16	+ 1:46
+ 1.45	46	+ 2:31	+ 1.45	18	+ 2:03	+ 1.45	30	+ 2:15	+ 1.45	16	+ 2:01
+ 2.00	**48**	**+ 2:48**	**+ 2.00**	**18**	**+ 2:18**	**+ 2.00**	**30**	**+ 2:30**	**+ 2.00**	**16**	**+ 2:16**
+ 2.15	48	+ 3:03	+ 2.15	18	+ 2:33	+ 2.15	30	+ 2:45	+ 2.15	16	+ 2:31
+ 2.30	48	+ 3:18	+ 2.30	18	+ 2:48	+ 2.30	30	+ 3:00	+ 2.30	16	+ 2:46
+ 2.45	48	+ 3:33	+ 2.45	18	+ 3:03	+ 2.45	30	+ 3:15	+ 2.45	16	+ 3:01
+ 3.00	**48**	**+ 3:48**	**+ 3.00**	**18**	**+ 3:18**	**+ 3.00**	**30**	**+ 3:30**	**+ 3.00**	**16**	**+ 3:16**
+ 3.15	47	+ 4:02	+ 3.15	18	+ 3:33	+ 3.15	30	+ 3:45	+ 3.15	15	+ 3:30
+ 3.30	46	+ 4:16	+ 3.30	18	+ 3:48	+ 3.30	30	+ 4:00	+ 3.30	15	+ 3:45
+ 3.45	45	+ 4:30	+ 3.45	18	+ 4:03	+ 3.45	30	+ 4:15	+ 3.45	15	+ 4:00
+ 4.00	**44**	**+ 4:44**	**+ 4.00**	**18**	**+ 4:18**	**+ 4.00**	**31**	**+ 4:31**	**+ 4.00**	**15**	**+ 4:15**
+ 4.15	43	+ 4:58	+ 4.15	19	+ 4:34	+ 4.15	31	+ 4:46	+ 4.15	14	+ 4:29
+ 4.30	42	+ 5:12	+ 4.30	19	+ 4:49	+ 4.30	32	+ 5:02	+ 4.30	14	+ 4:44
+ 4.45	41	+ 5:26	+ 4.45	20	+ 5:05	+ 4.45	32	+ 5:17	+ 4.45	14	+ 4:59
+ 5.00	**40**	**+ 5:40**	**+ 5.00**	**20**	**+ 5:20**	**+ 5.00**	**33**	**+ 5:33**	**+ 5.00**	**14**	**+ 5:14**
+ 5.15	39	+ 5:54	+ 5.15	21	+ 5:36	+ 5.15	34	+ 5:49	+ 5.15	14	+ 5:29
+ 5.30	38	- 5:52	+ 5.30	22	+ 5:52	+ 5.30	34	- 5:56	+ 5.30	14	+ 5:44
+ 5.45	38	- 5:37	+ 5.45	22	- 5:53	+ 5.45	35	- 5:40	+ 5.45	14	+ 5:59
+ 6.00	**37**	**- 5:23**	**+ 6.00**	**23**	**- 5:37**	**+ 6.00**	**36**	**- 5:24**	**+ 6.00**	**14**	**- 5:46**

NORTH & WEST

Table D - North Edinburgh, Crouch and Colne

Neaps — All times relate to HW Sheerness — **Time to cover Sectors (in minutes) at 4.0 Kts**

NORTH BOUND

	D1 East Margate to North Edinburgh			D2 North Edinburgh to NW Long Sand			D3 NW Long Sand to SW Sunk			D4 Barrow Sands to Whitaker Spit			D5 Barrow Deep to Whitaker Spit			D6 Black Deep to Whitaker Spit			D7 Whitaker Spit to Crouch Landfall			D8 Spitway to Colne Landfall
Time	Duration	Time at End of Sector	Time	Duration	Time at End of Sector	Time	Duration	Time at End of Sector	Time	Duration	Time at End of Sector	Time	Duration	Time at End of Sector	Time	Duration	Time at End of Sector	Time	Duration	Time at End of Sector	Time	Duration	Time at End of Sector
- 6.00	**105**	**- 4:15**	**- 6.00**	**46**	**- 5:14**	**- 6.00**	**71**	**- 4:49**	**- 6.00**	**45**	**- 5:15**	**- 6.00**	**89**	**- 4:31**	**- 6.00**	**122**	**- 3:58**	**- 6.00**	**54**	**- 5:06**	**- 6.00**	**57**	**- 5:03**
- 5.45	104	- 4:01	- 5.45	45	- 5:00	- 5.45	76	- 4:29	- 5.45	44	- 5:01	- 5.45	88	- 4:17	- 5.45	121	- 3:44	- 5.45	53	- 4:52	- 5.45	56	- 4:49
- 5.30	103	- 3:47	- 5.30	43	- 4:47	- 5.30	82	- 4:08	- 5.30	43	- 4:47	- 5.30	87	- 4:03	- 5.30	119	- 3:31	- 5.30	51	- 4:39	- 5.30	55	- 4:35
- 5.15	101	- 3:34	- 5.15	42	- 4:33	- 5.15	87	- 3:48	- 5.15	42	- 4:33	- 5.15	85	- 3:50	- 5.15	118	- 3:17	- 5.15	50	- 4:25	- 5.15	55	- 4:20
- 5.00	**100**	**- 3:20**	**- 5.00**	**40**	**- 4:20**	**- 5.00**	**92**	**- 3:28**	**- 5.00**	**41**	**- 4:19**	**- 5.00**	**84**	**- 3:36**	**- 5.00**	**117**	**- 3:03**	**- 5.00**	**48**	**- 4:12**	**- 5.00**	**54**	**- 4:06**
- 4.45	99	- 3:06	- 4.45	40	- 4:05	- 4.45	92	- 3:13	- 4.45	41	- 4:04	- 4.45	84	- 3:21	- 4.45	118	- 2:47	- 4.45	48	- 3:57	- 4.45	53	- 3:52
- 4.30	97	- 2:53	- 4.30	39	- 3:51	- 4.30	92	- 2:58	- 4.30	41	- 3:49	- 4.30	84	- 3:06	- 4.30	118	- 2:32	- 4.30	48	- 3:42	- 4.30	53	- 3:37
- 4.15	95	- 2:40	- 4.15	38	- 3:37	- 4.15	93	- 2:42	- 4.15	41	- 3:34	- 4.15	84	- 2:51	- 4.15	118	- 2:17	- 4.15	48	- 3:27	- 4.15	53	- 3:22
- 4.00	**94**	**- 2:26**	**- 4.00**	**38**	**- 3:22**	**- 4.00**	**93**	**- 2:27**	**- 4.00**	**41**	**- 3:19**	**- 4.00**	**84**	**- 2:36**	**- 4.00**	**119**	**- 2:01**	**- 4.00**	**48**	**- 3:12**	**- 4.00**	**52**	**- 3:08**
- 3.45	93	- 2:12	- 3.45	37	- 3:08	- 3.45	88	- 2:17	- 3.45	41	- 3:04	- 3.45	85	- 2:20	- 3.45	120	- 1:45	- 3.45	48	- 2:57	- 3.45	52	- 2:53
- 3.30	92	- 1:58	- 3.30	37	- 2:53	- 3.30	84	- 2:06	- 3.30	41	- 2:49	- 3.30	86	- 2:04	- 3.30	122	- 1:28	- 3.30	49	- 2:41	- 3.30	52	- 2:38
- 3.15	90	- 1:45	- 3.15	37	- 2:38	- 3.15	80	- 1:55	- 3.15	41	- 2:34	- 3.15	86	- 1:49	- 3.15	124	- 1:11	- 3.15	49	- 2:26	- 3.15	52	- 2:23
- 3.00	**89**	**- 1:31**	**- 3.00**	**37**	**- 2:23**	**- 3.00**	**76**	**- 1:44**	**- 3.00**	**41**	**- 2:19**	**- 3.00**	**87**	**- 1:33**	**- 3.00**	**125**	**- 0:55**	**- 3.00**	**49**	**- 2:11**	**- 3.00**	**52**	**- 2:08**
- 2.45	89	- 1:16	- 2.45	37	- 2:08	- 2.45	73	- 1:32	- 2.45	42	- 2:03	- 2.45	89	- 1:16	- 2.45	129	- 0:36	- 2.45	50	- 1:55	- 2.45	52	- 1:53
- 2.30	90	- 1:00	- 2.30	37	- 1:53	- 2.30	71	- 1:19	- 2.30	43	- 1:47	- 2.30	90	- 1:00	- 2.30	132	- 0:18	- 2.30	51	- 1:39	- 2.30	53	- 1:37
- 2.15	90	- 0:45	- 2.15	37	- 1:38	- 2.15	68	- 1:07	- 2.15	43	- 1:32	- 2.15	91	- 0:44	- 2.15	136	+ 0:01	- 2.15	52	- 1:23	- 2.15	53	- 1:22
- 2.00	**90**	**- 0:30**	**- 2.00**	**36**	**- 1:24**	**- 2.00**	**65**	**- 0:55**	**- 2.00**	**44**	**- 1:16**	**- 2.00**	**92**	**- 0:28**	**- 2.00**	**140**	**+ 0:20**	**- 2.00**	**53**	**- 1:07**	**- 2.00**	**54**	**- 1:06**
- 1.45	92	- 0:13	- 1.45	37	- 1:08	- 1.45	63	- 0:42	- 1.45	45	- 1:00	- 1.45	97	- 0:08	- 1.45	146	+ 0:41	- 1.45	55	- 0:50	- 1.45	56	- 0:49
- 1.30	94	+ 0:04	- 1.30	37	- 0:53	- 1.30	61	- 0:29	- 1.30	46	- 0:44	- 1.30	101	+ 0:11	- 1.30	153	+ 1:03	- 1.30	57	- 0:33	- 1.30	59	- 0:31
- 1.15	96	+ 0:21	- 1.15	38	- 0:37	- 1.15	58	- 0:17	- 1.15	48	- 0:27	- 1.15	105	+ 0:30	- 1.15	159	+ 1:24	- 1.15	59	- 0:16	- 1.15	61	- 0:14
- 1.00	**98**	**+ 0:38**	**- 1.00**	**38**	**- 0:22**	**- 1.00**	**56**	**- 0:04**	**- 1.00**	**49**	**- 0:11**	**- 1.00**	**109**	**+ 0:49**	**- 1.00**	**166**	**+ 1:46**	**- 1.00**	**61**	**+ 0:01**	**- 1.00**	**63**	**+ 0:03**
- 0.45	102	+ 0:57	- 0.45	39	- 0:06	- 0.45	54	+ 0:09	- 0.45	51	+ 0:06	- 0.45	113	+ 1:08	- 0.45	171	+ 2:06	- 0.45	65	+ 0:20	- 0.45	66	+ 0:21
- 0.30	105	+ 1:15	- 0.30	40	+ 0:10	- 0.30	53	+ 0:23	- 0.30	53	+ 0:23	- 0.30	118	+ 1:28	- 0.30	177	+ 2:27	- 0.30	68	+ 0:38	- 0.30	69	+ 0:39
- 0.15	109	+ 1:34	- 0.15	41	+ 0:26	- 0.15	52	+ 0:37	- 0.15	55	+ 0:40	- 0.15	122	+ 1:47	- 0.15	182	+ 2:47	- 0.15	71	+ 0:56	- 0.15	72	+ 0:57
HW	**113**	**+ 1:53**	**HW**	**42**	**+ 0:42**	**HW**	**51**	**+ 0:51**	**HW**	**56**	**+ 0:56**	**HW**	**127**	**+ 2:07**	**HW**	**188**	**+ 3:08**	**HW**	**74**	**+ 1:14**	**HW**	**76**	**+ 1:16**
+ 0.15	116	+ 2:11	+ 0.15	44	+ 0:59	+ 0.15	50	+ 1:05	+ 0.15	58	+ 1:13	+ 0.15	129	+ 2:24	+ 0.15	190	+ 3:25	+ 0.15	79	+ 1:34	+ 0.15	79	+ 1:34
+ 0.30	119	+ 2:29	+ 0.30	47	+ 1:17	+ 0.30	49	+ 1:19	+ 0.30	60	+ 1:30	+ 0.30	132	+ 2:42	+ 0.30	192	+ 3:42	+ 0.30	85	+ 1:55	+ 0.30	83	+ 1:53
+ 0.45	123	+ 2:48	+ 0.45	49	+ 1:34	+ 0.45	48	+ 1:33	+ 0.45	62	+ 1:47	+ 0.45	135	+ 3:00	+ 0.45	193	+ 3:58	+ 0.45	90	+ 2:15	+ 0.45	86	+ 2:11
+ 1.00	**126**	**+ 3:06**	**+ 1.00**	**52**	**+ 1:52**	**+ 1.00**	**48**	**+ 1:48**	**+ 1.00**	**64**	**+ 2:04**	**+ 1.00**	**138**	**+ 3:18**	**+ 1.00**	**195**	**+ 4:15**	**+ 1.00**	**95**	**+ 2:35**	**+ 1.00**	**90**	**+ 2:30**
+ 1.15	128	+ 3:23	+ 1.15	55	+ 2:10	+ 1.15	47	+ 2:02	+ 1.15	64	+ 2:19	+ 1.15	137	+ 3:32	+ 1.15	193	+ 4:28	+ 1.15	95	+ 2:50	+ 1.15	88	+ 2:43
+ 1.30	129	+ 3:39	+ 1.30	58	+ 2:28	+ 1.30	47	+ 2:17	+ 1.30	64	+ 2:34	+ 1.30	137	+ 3:47	+ 1.30	192	+ 4:42	+ 1.30	96	+ 3:06	+ 1.30	85	+ 2:55
+ 1.45	131	+ 3:56	+ 1.45	61	+ 2:46	+ 1.45	46	+ 2:31	+ 1.45	64	+ 2:49	+ 1.45	137	+ 4:02	+ 1.45	190	+ 4:55	+ 1.45	96	+ 3:21	+ 1.45	83	+ 3:08
+ 2.00	**133**	**+ 4:13**	**+ 2.00**	**64**	**+ 3:04**	**+ 2.00**	**46**	**+ 2:46**	**+ 2.00**	**64**	**+ 3:04**	**+ 2.00**	**137**	**+ 4:17**	**+ 2.00**	**188**	**+ 5:08**	**+ 2.00**	**96**	**+ 3:36**	**+ 2.00**	**80**	**+ 3:20**
+ 2.15	132	+ 4:27	+ 2.15	71	+ 3:26	+ 2.15	46	+ 3:01	+ 2.15	64	+ 3:19	+ 2.15	134	+ 4:29	+ 2.15	184	+ 5:19	+ 2.15	95	+ 3:50	+ 2.15	79	+ 3:34
+ 2.30	131	+ 4:41	+ 2.30	78	+ 3:48	+ 2.30	46	+ 3:16	+ 2.30	63	+ 3:33	+ 2.30	132	+ 4:42	+ 2.30	180	+ 5:30	+ 2.30	93	+ 4:03	+ 2.30	78	+ 3:48
+ 2.45	131	+ 4:56	+ 2.45	85	+ 4:10	+ 2.45	46	+ 3:31	+ 2.45	62	+ 3:47	+ 2.45	129	+ 4:54	+ 2.45	176	+ 5:41	+ 2.45	92	+ 4:17	+ 2.45	76	+ 4:01
+ 3.00	**130**	**+ 5:10**	**+ 3.00**	**92**	**+ 4:32**	**+ 3.00**	**46**	**+ 3:46**	**+ 3.00**	**61**	**+ 4:01**	**+ 3.00**	**126**	**+ 5:06**	**+ 3.00**	**172**	**+ 5:52**	**+ 3.00**	**90**	**+ 4:30**	**+ 3.00**	**75**	**+ 4:15**
+ 3.15	128	+ 5:23	+ 3.15	87	+ 4:42	+ 3.15	47	+ 4:02	+ 3.15	60	+ 4:15	+ 3.15	123	+ 5:18	+ 3.15	168	- 5:57	+ 3.15	87	+ 4:42	+ 3.15	74	+ 4:29
+ 3.30	126	+ 5:36	+ 3.30	81	+ 4:51	+ 3.30	48	+ 4:18	+ 3.30	59	+ 4:29	+ 3.30	120	+ 5:30	+ 3.30	164	- 5:46	+ 3.30	83	+ 4:53	+ 3.30	72	+ 4:42
+ 3.45	124	+ 5:49	+ 3.45	76	+ 5:01	+ 3.45	49	+ 4:34	+ 3.45	58	+ 4:43	+ 3.45	117	+ 5:42	+ 3.45	160	- 5:35	+ 3.45	79	+ 5:04	+ 3.45	71	+ 4:56
+ 4.00	**122**	**- 5:58**	**+ 4.00**	**70**	**+ 5:10**	**+ 4.00**	**51**	**+ 4:51**	**+ 4.00**	**56**	**+ 4:56**	**+ 4.00**	**114**	**+ 5:54**	**+ 4.00**	**156**	**- 5:24**	**+ 4.00**	**75**	**+ 5:15**	**+ 4.00**	**70**	**+ 5:10**
+ 4.15	120	- 5:45	+ 4.15	68	+ 5:23	+ 4.15	52	+ 5:07	+ 4.15	55	+ 5:10	+ 4.15	111	- 5:54	+ 4.15	153	- 5:12	+ 4.15	73	+ 5:28	+ 4.15	69	+ 5:24
+ 4.30	117	- 5:33	+ 4.30	65	+ 5:35	+ 4.30	54	+ 5:24	+ 4.30	54	+ 5:24	+ 4.30	109	- 5:41	+ 4.30	149	- 5:01	+ 4.30	71	+ 5:41	+ 4.30	68	+ 5:38
+ 4.45	115	- 5:20	+ 4.45	63	+ 5:48	+ 4.45	55	+ 5:40	+ 4.45	53	+ 5:38	+ 4.45	106	- 5:29	+ 4.45	146	- 4:49	+ 4.45	69	+ 5:54	+ 4.45	66	+ 5:51
+ 5.00	**112**	**- 5:08**	**+ 5.00**	**61**	**- 5:59**	**+ 5.00**	**57**	**+ 5:57**	**+ 5.00**	**52**	**+ 5:52**	**+ 5.00**	**103**	**- 5:17**	**+ 5.00**	**143**	**- 4:37**	**+ 5.00**	**67**	**- 5:53**	**+ 5.00**	**65**	**- 5:55**
+ 5.15	111	- 4:54	+ 5.15	59	- 5:46	+ 5.15	58	- 5:47	+ 5.15	51	- 5:54	+ 5.15	102	- 5:03	+ 5.15	140	- 4:25	+ 5.15	66	- 5:39	+ 5.15	64	- 5:41
+ 5.30	110	- 4:40	+ 5.30	57	- 5:33	+ 5.30	60	- 5:30	+ 5.30	50	- 5:40	+ 5.30	100	- 4:50	+ 5.30	137	- 4:13	+ 5.30	65	- 5:25	+ 5.30	63	- 5:27
+ 5.45	109	- 4:26	+ 5.45	55	- 5:20	+ 5.45	61	- 5:14	+ 5.45	49	- 5:26	+ 5.45	98	- 4:37	+ 5.45	134	- 4:01	+ 5.45	63	- 5:12	+ 5.45	62	- 5:13
+ 6.00	**108**	**- 4:12**	**+ 6.00**	**53**	**- 5:07**	**+ 6.00**	**62**	**- 4:58**	**+ 6.00**	**48**	**- 5:12**	**+ 6.00**	**96**	**- 4:24**	**+ 6.00**	**130**	**- 3:50**	**+ 6.00**	**62**	**- 4:58**	**+ 6.00**	**61**	**- 4:59**

River Colne

Table D - North Edinburgh, Crouch and Colne

Time to cover Sectors (in minutes) at 4.0 kts — All times relate to HW Sheerness — **Springs**

Time	D1 East Margate to North Edinburgh Duration	D1 Time at End of Sector	Time	D2 North Edinburgh to NW Long Sand Duration	D2 Time at End of Sector	Time	D3 NW Long Sand to SW Sunk Duration	D3 Time at End of Sector	Time	D4 Barrow Sands to Whitaker Spit Duration	D4 Time at End of Sector	Time	D5 Barrow Deep to Whitaker Spit Duration	D5 Time at End of Sector	Time	D6 Black Deep to Whitaker Spit Duration	D6 Time at End of Sector	Time	D7 Whitaker Spit to Crouch Landfall Duration	D7 Time at End of Sector	Time	D8 Spitway to Colne Landfall Duration	D8 Time at End of Sector
- 6.00	105	- 4:15	- 6.00	46	- 5:14	- 6.00	91	- 4:29	- 6.00	43	- 5:17	- 6.00	84	- 4:36	- 6.00	115	- 4:05	- 6.00	49	- 5:11	- 6.00	54	- 5:06
- 5.45	103	- 4:02	- 5.45	44	- 5:01	- 5.45	96	- 4:09	- 5.45	42	- 5:03	- 5.45	82	- 4:23	- 5.45	114	- 3:51	- 5.45	47	- 4:58	- 5.45	53	- 4:52
- 5.30	102	- 3:48	- 5.30	41	- 4:49	- 5.30	101	- 3:49	- 5.30	41	- 4:49	- 5.30	81	- 4:09	- 5.30	113	- 3:37	- 5.30	45	- 4:45	- 5.30	52	- 4:38
- 5.15	100	- 3:35	- 5.15	39	- 4:36	- 5.15	105	- 3:30	- 5.15	40	- 4:35	- 5.15	80	- 3:55	- 5.15	112	- 3:23	- 5.15	43	- 4:32	- 5.15	51	- 4:24
- 5.00	98	- 3:22	- 5.00	37	- 4:23	- 5.00	110	- 3:10	- 5.00	39	- 4:21	- 5.00	79	- 3:41	- 5.00	110	- 3:10	- 5.00	41	- 4:19	- 5.00	50	- 4:10
- 4.45	96	- 3:09	- 4.45	36	- 4:09	- 4.45	109	- 2:56	- 4.45	39	- 4:06	- 4.45	78	- 3:27	- 4.45	111	- 2:54	- 4.45	41	- 4:04	- 4.45	49	- 3:56
- 4.30	94	- 2:56	- 4.30	36	- 3:54	- 4.30	108	- 2:42	- 4.30	38	- 3:52	- 4.30	78	- 3:12	- 4.30	111	- 2:39	- 4.30	41	- 3:49	- 4.30	49	- 3:41
- 4.15	92	- 2:43	- 4.15	35	- 3:40	- 4.15	107	- 2:28	- 4.15	38	- 3:37	- 4.15	78	- 2:57	- 4.15	111	- 2:24	- 4.15	41	- 3:34	- 4.15	48	- 3:27
- 4.00	90	- 2:30	- 4.00	34	- 3:26	- 4.00	106	- 2:14	- 4.00	38	- 3:22	- 4.00	77	- 2:43	- 4.00	112	- 2:08	- 4.00	41	- 3:19	- 4.00	48	- 3:12
- 3.45	88	- 2:17	- 3.45	34	- 3:11	- 3.45	103	- 2:02	- 3.45	38	- 3:07	- 3.45	78	- 2:27	- 3.45	114	- 1:51	- 3.45	41	- 3:04	- 3.45	47	- 2:58
- 3.30	86	- 2:04	- 3.30	34	- 2:56	- 3.30	99	- 1:51	- 3.30	38	- 2:52	- 3.30	79	- 2:11	- 3.30	116	- 1:34	- 3.30	42	- 2:48	- 3.30	47	- 2:43
- 3.15	84	- 1:51	- 3.15	33	- 2:42	- 3.15	95	- 1:40	- 3.15	38	- 2:37	- 3.15	79	- 1:56	- 3.15	118	- 1:17	- 3.15	42	- 2:33	- 3.15	47	- 2:28
- 3.00	82	- 1:38	- 3.00	33	- 2:27	- 3.00	91	- 1:29	- 3.00	38	- 2:22	- 3.00	80	- 1:40	- 3.00	120	- 1:00	- 3.00	43	- 2:17	- 3.00	46	- 2:14
- 2.45	83	- 1:22	- 2.45	33	- 2:12	- 2.45	86	- 1:19	- 2.45	39	- 2:06	- 2.45	83	- 1:22	- 2.45	125	- 0:40	- 2.45	44	- 2:01	- 2.45	47	- 1:58
- 2.30	84	- 1:06	- 2.30	32	- 1:58	- 2.30	80	- 1:10	- 2.30	39	- 1:51	- 2.30	86	- 1:04	- 2.30	130	- 0:20	- 2.30	46	- 1:44	- 2.30	48	- 1:42
- 2.15	84	- 0:51	- 2.15	32	- 1:43	- 2.15	74	- 1:01	- 2.15	40	- 1:35	- 2.15	88	- 0:47	- 2.15	135	HW	- 2.15	47	- 1:28	- 2.15	49	- 1:26
- 2.00	85	- 0:35	- 2.00	32	- 1:28	- 2.00	68	- 0:52	- 2.00	41	- 1:19	- 2.00	91	- 0:29	- 2.00	140	+ 0:20	- 2.00	48	- 1:12	- 2.00	50	- 1:10
- 1.45	88	- 0:17	- 1.45	32	- 1:13	- 1.45	65	- 0:40	- 1.45	42	- 1:03	- 1.45	97	- 0:08	- 1.45	150	+ 0:45	- 1.45	51	- 0:54	- 1.45	53	- 0:52
- 1.30	91	+ 0:01	- 1.30	33	- 0:57	- 1.30	61	- 0:29	- 1.30	44	- 0:46	- 1.30	102	+ 0:12	- 1.30	160	+ 1:10	- 1.30	54	- 0:36	- 1.30	56	- 0:34
- 1.15	94	+ 0:19	- 1.15	33	- 0:42	- 1.15	57	- 0:18	- 1.15	46	- 0:29	- 1.15	108	+ 0:33	- 1.15	170	+ 1:35	- 1.15	57	- 0:18	- 1.15	60	- 0:15
- 1.00	97	+ 0:37	- 1.00	34	- 0:26	- 1.00	53	- 0:07	- 1.00	48	- 0:12	- 1.00	114	+ 0:54	- 1.00	180	+ 2:00	- 1.00	60	HW	- 1.00	63	+ 0:03
- 0.45	102	+ 0:57	- 0.45	35	- 0:10	- 0.45	52	+ 0:07	- 0.45	51	+ 0:06	- 0.45	123	+ 1:18	- 0.45	190	+ 2:25	- 0.45	65	+ 0:20	- 0.45	70	+ 0:25
- 0.30	108	+ 1:18	- 0.30	36	+ 0:06	- 0.30	50	+ 0:20	- 0.30	54	+ 0:24	- 0.30	132	+ 1:42	- 0.30	200	+ 2:50	- 0.30	69	+ 0:39	- 0.30	77	+ 0:47
- 0.15	113	+ 1:38	- 0.15	38	+ 0:23	- 0.15	48	+ 0:33	- 0.15	57	+ 0:42	- 0.15	141	+ 2:06	- 0.15	210	+ 3:15	- 0.15	74	+ 0:59	- 0.15	84	+ 1:09
HW	118	+ 1:58	HW	39	+ 0:39	HW	47	+ 0:47	HW	60	+ 1:00	HW	150	+ 2:30	HW	220	+ 3:40	HW	79	+ 1:19	HW	90	+ 1:30
+ 0.15	124	+ 2:19	+ 0.15	43	+ 0:58	+ 0.15	46	+ 1:01	+ 0.15	63	+ 1:18	+ 0.15	152	+ 2:47	+ 0.15	221	+ 3:56	+ 0.15	87	+ 1:42	+ 0.15	93	+ 1:48
+ 0.30	129	+ 2:39	+ 0.30	47	+ 1:17	+ 0.30	46	+ 1:16	+ 0.30	66	+ 1:36	+ 0.30	155	+ 3:05	+ 0.30	221	+ 4:11	+ 0.30	95	+ 2:05	+ 0.30	96	+ 2:06
+ 0.45	134	+ 2:59	+ 0.45	50	+ 1:35	+ 0.45	45	+ 1:30	+ 0.45	70	+ 1:55	+ 0.45	158	+ 3:23	+ 0.45	221	+ 4:26	+ 0.45	103	+ 2:28	+ 0.45	99	+ 2:24
+ 1.00	139	+ 3:19	+ 1.00	54	+ 1:54	+ 1.00	44	+ 1:44	+ 1.00	73	+ 2:13	+ 1.00	160	+ 3:40	+ 1.00	221	+ 4:41	+ 1.00	111	+ 2:51	+ 1.00	102	+ 2:42
+ 1.15	142	+ 3:37	+ 1.15	65	+ 2:20	+ 1.15	44	+ 1:59	+ 1.15	73	+ 2:28	+ 1.15	159	+ 3:54	+ 1.15	217	+ 4:52	+ 1.15	111	+ 3:06	+ 1.15	100	+ 2:55
+ 1.30	145	+ 3:55	+ 1.30	77	+ 2:47	+ 1.30	43	+ 2:13	+ 1.30	74	+ 2:44	+ 1.30	157	+ 4:07	+ 1.30	212	+ 5:02	+ 1.30	111	+ 3:21	+ 1.30	98	+ 3:08
+ 1.45	147	+ 4:12	+ 1.45	88	+ 3:13	+ 1.45	42	+ 2:27	+ 1.45	74	+ 2:59	+ 1.45	155	+ 4:20	+ 1.45	208	+ 5:13	+ 1.45	111	+ 3:36	+ 1.45	97	+ 3:22
+ 2.00	150	+ 4:30	+ 2.00	99	+ 3:39	+ 2.00	41	+ 2:41	+ 2.00	75	+ 3:15	+ 2.00	153	+ 4:33	+ 2.00	203	+ 5:23	+ 2.00	111	+ 3:51	+ 2.00	95	+ 3:35
+ 2.15	147	+ 4:42	+ 2.15	103	+ 3:58	+ 2.15	41	+ 2:56	+ 2.15	73	+ 3:28	+ 2.15	148	+ 4:43	+ 2.15	197	+ 5:32	+ 2.15	108	+ 4:03	+ 2.15	92	+ 3:47
+ 2.30	143	+ 4:53	+ 2.30	106	+ 4:16	+ 2.30	41	+ 3:11	+ 2.30	72	+ 3:42	+ 2.30	143	+ 4:53	+ 2.30	191	+ 5:41	+ 2.30	105	+ 4:15	+ 2.30	88	+ 3:58
+ 2.45	140	+ 5:05	+ 2.45	109	+ 4:34	+ 2.45	41	+ 3:26	+ 2.45	70	+ 3:55	+ 2.45	139	+ 5:04	+ 2.45	185	+ 5:50	+ 2.45	102	+ 4:27	+ 2.45	85	+ 4:10
+ 3.00	137	+ 5:17	+ 3.00	113	+ 4:53	+ 3.00	41	+ 3:41	+ 3.00	69	+ 4:09	+ 3.00	134	+ 5:14	+ 3.00	179	+ 5:59	+ 3.00	100	+ 4:40	+ 3.00	81	+ 4:21
+ 3.15	133	+ 5:28	+ 3.15	109	+ 5:04	+ 3.15	43	+ 3:58	+ 3.15	67	+ 4:22	+ 3.15	129	+ 5:24	+ 3.15	174	- 5:51	+ 3.15	95	+ 4:50	+ 3.15	80	+ 4:35
+ 3.30	130	+ 5:40	+ 3.30	105	+ 5:15	+ 3.30	44	+ 4:14	+ 3.30	64	+ 4:34	+ 3.30	125	+ 5:35	+ 3.30	168	- 5:42	+ 3.30	91	+ 5:01	+ 3.30	78	+ 4:48
+ 3.45	127	+ 5:52	+ 3.45	102	+ 5:27	+ 3.45	45	+ 4:30	+ 3.45	62	+ 4:47	+ 3.45	121	+ 5:46	+ 3.45	163	- 5:32	+ 3.45	87	+ 5:12	+ 3.45	76	+ 5:01
+ 4.00	123	- 5:57	+ 4.00	98	+ 5:38	+ 4.00	46	+ 4:46	+ 4.00	60	+ 5:00	+ 4.00	116	+ 5:56	+ 4.00	157	- 5:23	+ 4.00	83	+ 5:23	+ 4.00	74	+ 5:14
+ 4.15	121	- 5:44	+ 4.15	91	+ 5:46	+ 4.15	49	+ 5:04	+ 4.15	58	+ 5:13	+ 4.15	113	- 5:52	+ 4.15	153	- 5:12	+ 4.15	79	+ 5:34	+ 4.15	72	+ 5:27
+ 4.30	118	- 5:32	+ 4.30	83	+ 5:53	+ 4.30	51	+ 5:21	+ 4.30	57	+ 5:27	+ 4.30	109	- 5:41	+ 4.30	148	- 5:02	+ 4.30	76	+ 5:46	+ 4.30	70	+ 5:40
+ 4.45	116	- 5:19	+ 4.45	76	- 5:59	+ 4.45	54	+ 5:39	+ 4.45	55	+ 5:40	+ 4.45	106	- 5:29	+ 4.45	144	- 4:51	+ 4.45	73	+ 5:58	+ 4.45	68	+ 5:53
+ 5.00	114	- 5:06	+ 5.00	69	- 5:51	+ 5.00	56	+ 5:56	+ 5.00	53	+ 5:53	+ 5.00	102	- 5:18	+ 5.00	139	- 4:41	+ 5.00	70	- 5:50	+ 5.00	66	- 5:54
+ 5.15	112	- 4:53	+ 5.15	66	- 5:39	+ 5.15	58	- 5:47	+ 5.15	51	- 5:54	+ 5.15	100	- 5:05	+ 5.15	136	- 4:29	+ 5.15	68	- 5:37	+ 5.15	64	- 5:41
+ 5.30	111	- 4:39	+ 5.30	62	- 5:28	+ 5.30	60	- 5:30	+ 5.30	50	- 5:40	+ 5.30	98	- 4:52	+ 5.30	132	- 4:18	+ 5.30	65	- 5:25	+ 5.30	63	- 5:27
+ 5.45	110	- 4:25	+ 5.45	59	- 5:16	+ 5.45	62	- 5:13	+ 5.45	48	- 5:27	+ 5.45	95	- 4:40	+ 5.45	128	- 4:07	+ 5.45	63	- 5:12	+ 5.45	61	- 5:14
+ 6.00	109	- 4:11	+ 6.00	56	- 5:04	+ 6.00	65	- 4:55	+ 6.00	47	- 5:13	+ 6.00	93	- 4:27	+ 6.00	125	- 3:55	+ 6.00	61	- 4:59	+ 6.00	60	- 5:00

River Colne

NORTH BOUND

Table D - North Edinburgh, Crouch and Colne

Neaps

All times relate to HW Sheerness

Time to cover Sectors (in minutes) at 5.0 Kts

NORTH BOUND

	D1			D2			D3			D4			D5			D6			D7			D8	
	East Margate to North Edinburgh			North Edinburgh to NW Long Sand			NW Long Sand to SW Sunk			Barrow Sands to Whitaker Spit			Barrow Deep to Whitaker Spit			Black Deep to Whitaker Spit			Whitaker Spit to Crouch Landfall			Spitway to Colne Landfall	
Time	Duration	Time at End of Sector	Time	Duration	Time at End of Sector	Time	Duration	Time at End of Sector	Time	Duration	Time at End of Sector	Time	Duration	Time at End of Sector	Time	Duration	Time at End of Sector	Time	Duration	Time at End of Sector	Time	Duration	Time at End of Sector
- 6.00	85	- 4:35	- 6.00	38	- 5:22	- 6.00	54	- 5:06	- 6.00	37	- 5:23	- 6.00	73	- 4:47	- 6.00	102	- 4:18	- 6.00	46	- 5:14	- 6.00	47	- 5:13
- 5.45	84	- 4:21	- 5.45	37	- 5:08	- 5.45	55	- 4:50	- 5.45	37	- 5:08	- 5.45	73	- 4:32	- 5.45	101	- 4:04	- 5.45	44	- 5:01	- 5.45	46	- 4:59
- 5.30	83	- 4:07	- 5.30	36	- 4:54	- 5.30	57	- 4:33	- 5.30	36	- 4:54	- 5.30	72	- 4:18	- 5.30	100	- 3:50	- 5.30	43	- 4:47	- 5.30	46	- 4:44
- 5.15	82	- 3:53	- 5.15	35	- 4:40	- 5.15	59	- 4:16	- 5.15	35	- 4:40	- 5.15	71	- 4:04	- 5.15	99	- 3:36	- 5.15	42	- 4:33	- 5.15	45	- 4:30
- 5.00	81	- 3:39	- 5.00	34	- 4:26	- 5.00	60	- 4:00	- 5.00	34	- 4:26	- 5.00	70	- 3:50	- 5.00	98	- 3:22	- 5.00	41	- 4:19	- 5.00	45	- 4:15
- 4.45	80	- 3:25	- 4.45	33	- 4:12	- 4.45	60	- 3:45	- 4.45	34	- 4:11	- 4.45	70	- 3:35	- 4.45	98	- 3:07	- 4.45	41	- 4:04	- 4.45	44	- 4:01
- 4.30	79	- 3:11	- 4.30	33	- 3:57	- 4.30	61	- 3:29	- 4.30	34	- 3:56	- 4.30	70	- 3:20	- 4.30	98	- 2:52	- 4.30	41	- 3:49	- 4.30	44	- 3:46
- 4.15	78	- 2:57	- 4.15	32	- 3:43	- 4.15	61	- 3:14	- 4.15	34	- 3:41	- 4.15	70	- 3:05	- 4.15	98	- 2:37	- 4.15	41	- 3:34	- 4.15	44	- 3:31
- 4.00	77	- 2:43	- 4.00	32	- 3:28	- 4.00	61	- 2:59	- 4.00	34	- 3:26	- 4.00	70	- 2:50	- 4.00	98	- 2:22	- 4.00	40	- 3:20	- 4.00	44	- 3:16
- 3.45	76	- 2:29	- 3.45	32	- 3:13	- 3.45	60	- 2:45	- 3.45	34	- 3:11	- 3.45	70	- 2:35	- 3.45	99	- 2:06	- 3.45	41	- 3:04	- 3.45	44	- 3:01
- 3.30	75	- 2:15	- 3.30	32	- 2:58	- 3.30	60	- 2:30	- 3.30	34	- 2:56	- 3.30	71	- 2:19	- 3.30	100	- 1:50	- 3.30	41	- 2:49	- 3.30	43	- 2:47
- 3.15	75	- 2:00	- 3.15	32	- 2:43	- 3.15	59	- 2:16	- 3.15	34	- 2:41	- 3.15	71	- 2:04	- 3.15	101	- 1:34	- 3.15	41	- 2:34	- 3.15	43	- 2:32
- 3.00	74	- 1:46	- 3.00	31	- 2:29	- 3.00	58	- 2:02	- 3.00	34	- 2:26	- 3.00	72	- 1:48	- 3.00	102	- 1:18	- 3.00	41	- 2:19	- 3.00	43	- 2:17
- 2.45	74	- 1:31	- 2.45	31	- 2:14	- 2.45	57	- 1:48	- 2.45	34	- 2:11	- 2.45	73	- 1:32	- 2.45	104	- 1:01	- 2.45	42	- 2:03	- 2.45	44	- 2:01
- 2.30	74	- 1:16	- 2.30	31	- 1:59	- 2.30	55	- 1:35	- 2.30	35	- 1:55	- 2.30	74	- 1:16	- 2.30	105	- 0:45	- 2.30	43	- 1:47	- 2.30	44	- 1:46
- 2.15	75	- 1:00	- 2.15	31	- 1:44	- 2.15	54	- 1:21	- 2.15	35	- 1:40	- 2.15	75	- 1:00	- 2.15	107	- 0:28	- 2.15	43	- 1:32	- 2.15	44	- 1:31
- 2.00	75	- 0:45	- 2.00	31	- 1:29	- 2.00	52	- 1:08	- 2.00	35	- 1:25	- 2.00	76	- 0:44	- 2.00	109	- 0:11	- 2.00	44	- 1:16	- 2.00	44	- 1:16
- 1.45	76	- 0:29	- 1.45	31	- 1:14	- 1.45	51	- 0:54	- 1.45	36	- 1:09	- 1.45	78	- 0:27	- 1.45	113	+ 0:08	- 1.45	45	- 1:00	- 1.45	45	- 1:00
- 1.30	77	- 0:13	- 1.30	31	- 0:59	- 1.30	49	- 0:41	- 1.30	37	- 0:53	- 1.30	80	- 0:10	- 1.30	117	+ 0:27	- 1.30	46	- 0:44	- 1.30	47	- 0:43
- 1.15	78	+ 0:03	- 1.15	31	- 0:44	- 1.15	47	- 0:28	- 1.15	38	- 0:37	- 1.15	82	+ 0:07	- 1.15	121	+ 0:46	- 1.15	47	- 0:28	- 1.15	48	- 0:27
- 1.00	80	+ 0:20	- 1.00	31	- 0:29	- 1.00	46	- 0:14	- 1.00	39	- 0:21	- 1.00	84	+ 0:24	- 1.00	125	+ 1:05	- 1.00	48	- 0:12	- 1.00	49	- 0:11
- 0.45	82	+ 0:37	- 0.45	32	- 0:13	- 0.45	45	HW	- 0.45	40	- 0:05	- 0.45	87	+ 0:42	- 0.45	128	+ 1:23	- 0.45	50	+ 0:05	- 0.45	52	+ 0:07
- 0.30	84	+ 0:54	- 0.30	32	+ 0:02	- 0.30	44	+ 0:14	- 0.30	41	+ 0:11	- 0.30	90	+ 1:00	- 0.30	132	+ 1:42	- 0.30	52	+ 0:22	- 0.30	54	+ 0:24
- 0.15	86	+ 1:11	- 0.15	33	+ 0:18	- 0.15	43	+ 0:28	- 0.15	42	+ 0:27	- 0.15	93	+ 1:18	- 0.15	136	+ 2:01	- 0.15	55	+ 0:40	- 0.15	56	+ 0:41
HW	88	+ 1:28	HW	34	+ 0:34	HW	42	+ 0:42	HW	43	+ 0:43	HW	96	+ 1:36	HW	139	+ 2:19	HW	57	+ 0:57	HW	58	+ 0:58
+ 0.15	90	+ 1:45	+ 0.15	35	+ 0:50	+ 0.15	41	+ 0:56	+ 0.15	45	+ 1:00	+ 0.15	98	+ 1:53	+ 0.15	142	+ 2:37	+ 0.15	58	+ 1:13	+ 0.15	59	+ 1:14
+ 0.30	92	+ 2:02	+ 0.30	37	+ 1:07	+ 0.30	41	+ 1:11	+ 0.30	46	+ 1:16	+ 0.30	100	+ 2:10	+ 0.30	145	+ 2:55	+ 0.30	60	+ 1:30	+ 0.30	60	+ 1:30
+ 0.45	94	+ 2:19	+ 0.45	38	+ 1:23	+ 0.45	40	+ 1:25	+ 0.45	47	+ 1:32	+ 0.45	102	+ 2:27	+ 0.45	148	+ 3:13	+ 0.45	62	+ 1:47	+ 0.45	61	+ 1:46
+ 1.00	97	+ 2:37	+ 1.00	40	+ 1:40	+ 1.00	40	+ 1:40	+ 1.00	48	+ 1:48	+ 1.00	104	+ 2:44	+ 1.00	150	+ 3:30	+ 1.00	64	+ 2:04	+ 1.00	62	+ 2:02
+ 1.15	98	+ 2:53	+ 1.15	42	+ 1:57	+ 1.15	40	+ 1:55	+ 1.15	49	+ 2:04	+ 1.15	105	+ 3:00	+ 1.15	149	+ 3:44	+ 1.15	64	+ 2:19	+ 1.15	62	+ 2:17
+ 1.30	99	+ 3:09	+ 1.30	44	+ 2:14	+ 1.30	39	+ 2:09	+ 1.30	49	+ 2:19	+ 1.30	105	+ 3:15	+ 1.30	148	+ 3:58	+ 1.30	64	+ 2:34	+ 1.30	62	+ 2:32
+ 1.45	101	+ 3:26	+ 1.45	46	+ 2:31	+ 1.45	39	+ 2:24	+ 1.45	49	+ 2:34	+ 1.45	105	+ 3:30	+ 1.45	147	+ 4:12	+ 1.45	64	+ 2:49	+ 1.45	62	+ 2:47
+ 2.00	102	+ 3:42	+ 2.00	48	+ 2:48	+ 2.00	39	+ 2:39	+ 2.00	49	+ 2:49	+ 2.00	105	+ 3:45	+ 2.00	146	+ 4:26	+ 2.00	65	+ 3:05	+ 2.00	62	+ 3:02
+ 2.15	102	+ 3:57	+ 2.15	49	+ 3:04	+ 2.15	39	+ 2:54	+ 2.15	49	+ 3:04	+ 2.15	104	+ 3:59	+ 2.15	144	+ 4:39	+ 2.15	64	+ 3:19	+ 2.15	61	+ 3:16
+ 2.30	102	+ 4:12	+ 2.30	51	+ 3:21	+ 2.30	39	+ 3:09	+ 2.30	48	+ 3:18	+ 2.30	102	+ 4:12	+ 2.30	142	+ 4:52	+ 2.30	63	+ 3:33	+ 2.30	60	+ 3:30
+ 2.45	101	+ 4:26	+ 2.45	52	+ 3:37	+ 2.45	39	+ 3:24	+ 2.45	48	+ 3:33	+ 2.45	101	+ 4:26	+ 2.45	139	+ 5:04	+ 2.45	63	+ 3:48	+ 2.45	59	+ 3:44
+ 3.00	101	+ 4:41	+ 3.00	54	+ 3:54	+ 3.00	39	+ 3:39	+ 3.00	47	+ 3:47	+ 3.00	99	+ 4:39	+ 3.00	137	+ 5:17	+ 3.00	62	+ 4:02	+ 3.00	59	+ 3:59
+ 3.15	100	+ 4:55	+ 3.15	53	+ 4:08	+ 3.15	39	+ 3:54	+ 3.15	47	+ 4:02	+ 3.15	97	+ 4:52	+ 3.15	134	+ 5:29	+ 3.15	61	+ 4:16	+ 3.15	58	+ 4:13
+ 3.30	99	+ 5:09	+ 3.30	53	+ 4:23	+ 3.30	40	+ 4:10	+ 3.30	46	+ 4:16	+ 3.30	95	+ 5:05	+ 3.30	131	+ 5:41	+ 3.30	60	+ 4:30	+ 3.30	57	+ 4:27
+ 3.45	98	+ 5:23	+ 3.45	53	+ 4:38	+ 3.45	41	+ 4:26	+ 3.45	45	+ 4:30	+ 3.45	94	+ 5:19	+ 3.45	129	+ 5:54	+ 3.45	60	+ 4:45	+ 3.45	56	+ 4:41
+ 4.00	97	+ 5:37	+ 4.00	53	+ 4:53	+ 4.00	41	+ 4:41	+ 4.00	44	+ 4:44	+ 4.00	92	+ 5:32	+ 4.00	126	- 5:54	+ 4.00	59	+ 4:59	+ 4.00	55	+ 4:55
+ 4.15	95	+ 5:50	+ 4.15	51	+ 5:06	+ 4.15	42	+ 4:57	+ 4.15	44	+ 4:59	+ 4.15	89	+ 5:44	+ 4.15	123	- 5:42	+ 4.15	57	+ 5:12	+ 4.15	54	+ 5:09
+ 4.30	93	- 5:57	+ 4.30	50	+ 5:20	+ 4.30	43	+ 5:13	+ 4.30	43	+ 5:13	+ 4.30	87	+ 5:57	+ 4.30	121	- 5:29	+ 4.30	56	+ 5:26	+ 4.30	54	+ 5:24
+ 4.45	91	- 5:44	+ 4.45	49	+ 5:34	+ 4.45	44	+ 5:29	+ 4.45	42	+ 5:27	+ 4.45	85	- 5:50	+ 4.45	119	- 5:16	+ 4.45	55	+ 5:40	+ 4.45	53	+ 5:38
+ 5.00	89	- 5:31	+ 5.00	47	+ 5:47	+ 5.00	45	+ 5:45	+ 5.00	42	+ 5:42	+ 5.00	83	- 5:37	+ 5.00	116	- 5:04	+ 5.00	54	+ 5:54	+ 5.00	52	+ 5:52
+ 5.15	88	- 5:17	+ 5.15	46	- 5:59	+ 5.15	46	- 5:59	+ 5.15	41	+ 5:56	+ 5.15	82	- 5:23	+ 5.15	114	- 4:51	+ 5.15	53	- 5:52	+ 5.15	52	- 5:53
+ 5.30	88	- 5:02	+ 5.30	44	- 5:46	+ 5.30	47	- 5:43	+ 5.30	40	- 5:50	+ 5.30	80	- 5:10	+ 5.30	112	- 4:38	+ 5.30	52	- 5:38	+ 5.30	51	- 5:39
+ 5.45	87	- 4:48	+ 5.45	43	- 5:32	+ 5.45	48	- 5:27	+ 5.45	40	- 5:35	+ 5.45	79	- 4:56	+ 5.45	110	- 4:25	+ 5.45	51	- 5:24	+ 5.45	50	- 5:25
+ 6.00	86	- 4:34	+ 6.00	42	- 5:18	+ 6.00	49	- 5:11	+ 6.00	39	- 5:21	+ 6.00	78	- 4:42	+ 6.00	108	- 4:12	+ 6.00	50	- 5:10	+ 6.00	49	- 5:11

River Colne

Table D - North Edinburgh, Crouch and Colne

Time to cover Sectors (in minutes) at 5.0 kts — All times relate to HW Sheerness — **Springs**

NORTH BOUND

Time	D1 East Margate to North Edinburgh: Duration	D1: Time at End of Sector	Time	D2 North Edinburgh to NW Long Sand: Duration	D2: Time at End of Sector	Time	D3 NW Long Sand to SW Sunk: Duration	D3: Time at End of Sector	Time	D4 Barrow Sands to Whitaker Spit: Duration	D4: Time at End of Sector
- 6.00	**85**	**- 4:35**	**- 6.00**	**38**	**- 5:22**	**- 6.00**	**58**	**- 5:02**	**- 6.00**	**36**	**- 5:24**
- 5.45	84	- 4:21	- 5.45	37	- 5:08	- 5.45	61	- 4:44	- 5.45	35	- 5:10
- 5.30	82	- 4:08	- 5.30	35	- 4:55	- 5.30	64	- 4:26	- 5.30	34	- 4:56
- 5.15	81	- 3:54	- 5.15	34	- 4:41	- 5.15	67	- 4:08	- 5.15	33	- 4:42
- 5.00	**80**	**- 3:40**	**- 5.00**	**32**	**- 4:28**	**- 5.00**	**70**	**- 3:50**	**- 5.00**	**33**	**- 4:27**
- 4.45	78	- 3:27	- 4.45	31	- 4:14	- 4.45	70	- 3:35	- 4.45	32	- 4:13
- 4.30	77	- 3:13	- 4.30	31	- 3:59	- 4.30	70	- 3:20	- 4.30	32	- 3:58
- 4.15	75	- 3:00	- 4.15	30	- 3:45	- 4.15	70	- 3:05	- 4.15	32	- 3:43
- 4.00	**73**	**- 2:47**	**- 4.00**	**29**	**- 3:31**	**- 4.00**	**71**	**- 2:49**	**- 4.00**	**32**	**- 3:28**
- 3.45	72	- 2:33	- 3.45	29	- 3:16	- 3.45	69	- 2:36	- 3.45	32	- 3:13
- 3.30	71	- 2:19	- 3.30	29	- 3:01	- 3.30	68	- 2:22	- 3.30	32	- 2:58
- 3.15	70	- 2:05	- 3.15	29	- 2:46	- 3.15	67	- 2:08	- 3.15	32	- 2:43
- 3.00	**69**	**- 1:51**	**- 3.00**	**29**	**- 2:31**	**- 3.00**	**65**	**- 1:55**	**- 3.00**	**32**	**- 2:28**
- 2.45	70	- 1:35	- 2.45	28	- 2:17	- 2.45	63	- 1:42	- 2.45	32	- 2:13
- 2.30	70	- 1:20	- 2.30	28	- 2:02	- 2.30	60	- 1:30	- 2.30	33	- 1:57
- 2.15	70	- 1:05	- 2.15	27	- 1:48	- 2.15	57	- 1:18	- 2.15	33	- 1:42
- 2.00	**71**	**- 0:49**	**- 2.00**	**27**	**- 1:33**	**- 2.00**	**55**	**- 1:05**	**- 2.00**	**33**	**- 1:27**
- 1.45	72	- 0:33	- 1.45	27	- 1:18	- 1.45	52	- 0:53	- 1.45	34	- 1:11
- 1.30	74	- 0:16	- 1.30	27	- 1:03	- 1.30	50	- 0:40	- 1.30	35	- 0:55
- 1.15	76	+ 0:01	- 1.15	28	- 0:47	- 1.15	47	- 0:28	- 1.15	37	- 0:38
- 1.00	**77**	**+ 0:17**	**- 1.00**	**28**	**- 0:32**	**- 1.00**	**44**	**- 0:16**	**- 1.00**	**38**	**- 0:22**
- 0.45	80	+ 0:35	- 0.45	29	- 0:16	- 0.45	43	- 0:02	- 0.45	40	- 0:05
- 0.30	83	+ 0:53	- 0.30	30	HW	- 0.30	42	+ 0:12	- 0.30	41	+ 0:11
- 0.15	86	+ 1:11	- 0.15	30	+ 0:15	- 0.15	41	+ 0:26	- 0.15	43	+ 0:28
HW	**89**	**+ 1:29**	**HW**	**31**	**+ 0:31**	**HW**	**39**	**+ 0:39**	**HW**	**45**	**+ 0:45**
+ 0.15	93	+ 1:48	+ 0.15	34	+ 0:49	+ 0.15	39	+ 0:54	+ 0.15	47	+ 1:02
+ 0.30	96	+ 2:06	+ 0.30	36	+ 1:06	+ 0.30	38	+ 1:08	+ 0.30	50	+ 1:20
+ 0.45	100	+ 2:25	+ 0.45	38	+ 1:23	+ 0.45	38	+ 1:23	+ 0.45	52	+ 1:37
+ 1.00	**104**	**+ 2:44**	**+ 1.00**	**40**	**+ 1:40**	**+ 1.00**	**37**	**+ 1:37**	**+ 1.00**	**54**	**+ 1:54**
+ 1.15	105	+ 3:00	+ 1.15	44	+ 1:59	+ 1.15	37	+ 1:52	+ 1.15	54	+ 2:09
+ 1.30	107	+ 3:17	+ 1.30	47	+ 2:17	+ 1.30	37	+ 2:07	+ 1.30	55	+ 2:25
+ 1.45	108	+ 3:33	+ 1.45	51	+ 2:36	+ 1.45	36	+ 2:21	+ 1.45	55	+ 2:40
+ 2.00	**110**	**+ 3:50**	**+ 2.00**	**55**	**+ 2:55**	**+ 2.00**	**36**	**+ 2:36**	**+ 2.00**	**56**	**+ 2:56**
+ 2.15	109	+ 4:04	+ 2.15	57	+ 3:12	+ 2.15	36	+ 2:51	+ 2.15	55	+ 3:10
+ 2.30	108	+ 4:18	+ 2.30	60	+ 3:30	+ 2.30	35	+ 3:05	+ 2.30	54	+ 3:24
+ 2.45	107	+ 4:32	+ 2.45	62	+ 3:47	+ 2.45	35	+ 3:20	+ 2.45	53	+ 3:38
+ 3.00	**106**	**+ 4:46**	**+ 3.00**	**65**	**+ 4:05**	**+ 3.00**	**35**	**+ 3:35**	**+ 3.00**	**52**	**+ 3:52**
+ 3.15	104	+ 4:59	+ 3.15	65	+ 4:20	+ 3.15	36	+ 3:51	+ 3.15	51	+ 4:06
+ 3.30	102	+ 5:12	+ 3.30	64	+ 4:34	+ 3.30	37	+ 4:07	+ 3.30	50	+ 4:20
+ 3.45	99	+ 5:24	+ 3.45	63	+ 4:48	+ 3.45	37	+ 4:22	+ 3.45	48	+ 4:33
+ 4.00	**97**	**+ 5:37**	**+ 4.00**	**63**	**+ 5:03**	**+ 4.00**	**38**	**+ 4:38**	**+ 4.00**	**47**	**+ 4:47**
+ 4.15	96	+ 5:51	+ 4.15	60	+ 5:15	+ 4.15	40	+ 4:55	+ 4.15	46	+ 5:01
+ 4.30	94	- 5:56	+ 4.30	58	+ 5:28	+ 4.30	41	+ 5:11	+ 4.30	45	+ 5:15
+ 4.45	92	- 5:43	+ 4.45	55	+ 5:40	+ 4.45	43	+ 5:28	+ 4.45	44	+ 5:29
+ 5.00	**90**	**- 5:30**	**+ 5.00**	**53**	**+ 5:53**	**+ 5.00**	**44**	**+ 5:44**	**+ 5.00**	**42**	**+ 5:42**
+ 5.15	90	- 5:15	+ 5.15	51	- 5:54	+ 5.15	46	- 5:59	+ 5.15	41	+ 5:56
+ 5.30	89	- 5:01	+ 5.30	48	- 5:42	+ 5.30	47	- 5:43	+ 5.30	41	- 5:49
+ 5.45	88	- 4:47	+ 5.45	46	- 5:29	+ 5.45	49	- 5:26	+ 5.45	40	- 5:35
+ 6.00	**87**	**- 4:33**	**+ 6.00**	**44**	**- 5:16**	**+ 6.00**	**50**	**- 5:10**	**+ 6.00**	**39**	**- 5:21**

Time	D5 Barrow Deep to Whitaker Spit: Duration	D5: Time at End of Sector	Time	D6 Black Deep to Whitaker Spit: Duration	D6: Time at End of Sector	Time	D7 Whitaker Spit to Crouch Landfall: Duration	D7: Time at End of Sector	Time	D8 Spitway to Colne Landfall: Duration	D8: Time at End of Sector
- 6.00	**70**	**- 4:50**	**- 6.00**	**98**	**- 4:22**	**- 6.00**	**43**	**- 5:17**	**- 6.00**	**45**	**- 5:15**
- 5.45	69	- 4:36	- 5.45	97	- 4:08	- 5.45	41	- 5:04	- 5.45	45	- 5:00
- 5.30	68	- 4:22	- 5.30	96	- 3:54	- 5.30	40	- 4:50	- 5.30	44	- 4:46
- 5.15	67	- 4:08	- 5.15	95	- 3:40	- 5.15	38	- 4:37	- 5.15	43	- 4:32
- 5.00	**66**	**- 3:54**	**- 5.00**	**93**	**- 3:27**	**- 5.00**	**37**	**- 4:23**	**- 5.00**	**42**	**- 4:18**
- 4.45	66	- 3:39	- 4.45	93	- 3:12	- 4.45	37	- 4:08	- 4.45	42	- 4:03
- 4.30	65	- 3:25	- 4.30	93	- 2:57	- 4.30	36	- 3:54	- 4.30	41	- 3:49
- 4.15	65	- 3:10	- 4.15	93	- 2:42	- 4.15	36	- 3:39	- 4.15	41	- 3:34
- 4.00	**65**	**- 2:55**	**- 4.00**	**93**	**- 2:27**	**- 4.00**	**36**	**- 3:24**	**- 4.00**	**41**	**- 3:19**
- 3.45	66	- 2:39	- 3.45	94	- 2:11	- 3.45	36	- 3:09	- 3.45	41	- 3:04
- 3.30	66	- 2:24	- 3.30	95	- 1:55	- 3.30	36	- 2:54	- 3.30	40	- 2:50
- 3.15	67	- 2:08	- 3.15	96	- 1:39	- 3.15	37	- 2:38	- 3.15	40	- 2:35
- 3.00	**67**	**- 1:53**	**- 3.00**	**97**	**- 1:23**	**- 3.00**	**37**	**- 2:23**	**- 3.00**	**40**	**- 2:20**
- 2.45	69	- 1:36	- 2.45	100	- 1:05	- 2.45	38	- 2:07	- 2.45	40	- 2:05
- 2.30	70	- 1:20	- 2.30	103	- 0:47	- 2.30	39	- 1:51	- 2.30	40	- 1:50
- 2.15	72	- 1:03	- 2.15	106	- 0:29	- 2.15	39	- 1:36	- 2.15	41	- 1:34
- 2.00	**73**	**- 0:47**	**- 2.00**	**109**	**- 0:11**	**- 2.00**	**40**	**- 1:20**	**- 2.00**	**41**	**- 1:19**
- 1.45	76	- 0:29	- 1.45	114	+ 0:09	- 1.45	42	- 1:03	- 1.45	43	- 1:02
- 1.30	79	- 0:11	- 1.30	119	+ 0:29	- 1.30	44	- 0:46	- 1.30	45	- 0:45
- 1.15	82	+ 0:07	- 1.15	124	+ 0:49	- 1.15	45	- 0:30	- 1.15	47	- 0:28
- 1.00	**85**	**+ 0:25**	**- 1.00**	**130**	**+ 1:10**	**- 1.00**	**47**	**- 0:13**	**- 1.00**	**49**	**- 0:11**
- 0.45	90	+ 0:45	- 0.45	136	+ 1:31	- 0.45	50	+ 0:05	- 0.45	52	+ 0:07
- 0.30	94	+ 1:04	- 0.30	143	+ 1:53	- 0.30	53	+ 0:23	- 0.30	55	+ 0:25
- 0.15	99	+ 1:24	- 0.15	150	+ 2:15	- 0.15	56	+ 0:41	- 0.15	59	+ 0:44
HW	**103**	**+ 1:43**	**HW**	**157**	**+ 2:37**	**HW**	**59**	**+ 0:59**	**HW**	**62**	**+ 1:02**
+ 0.15	106	+ 2:01	+ 0.15	159	+ 2:54	+ 0.15	62	+ 1:17	+ 0.15	64	+ 1:19
+ 0.30	108	+ 2:18	+ 0.30	161	+ 3:11	+ 0.30	65	+ 1:35	+ 0.30	65	+ 1:35
+ 0.45	111	+ 2:36	+ 0.45	163	+ 3:28	+ 0.45	69	+ 1:54	+ 0.45	67	+ 1:52
+ 1.00	**114**	**+ 2:54**	**+ 1.00**	**165**	**+ 3:45**	**+ 1.00**	**72**	**+ 2:12**	**+ 1.00**	**69**	**+ 2:09**
+ 1.15	113	+ 3:08	+ 1.15	163	+ 3:58	+ 1.15	72	+ 2:27	+ 1.15	69	+ 2:24
+ 1.30	113	+ 3:23	+ 1.30	162	+ 4:12	+ 1.30	73	+ 2:43	+ 1.30	69	+ 2:39
+ 1.45	113	+ 3:38	+ 1.45	160	+ 4:25	+ 1.45	74	+ 2:59	+ 1.45	68	+ 2:53
+ 2.00	**113**	**+ 3:53**	**+ 2.00**	**158**	**+ 4:38**	**+ 2.00**	**74**	**+ 3:14**	**+ 2.00**	**68**	**+ 3:08**
+ 2.15	111	+ 4:06	+ 2.15	155	+ 4:50	+ 2.15	73	+ 3:28	+ 2.15	67	+ 3:22
+ 2.30	109	+ 4:19	+ 2.30	151	+ 5:01	+ 2.30	72	+ 3:42	+ 2.30	65	+ 3:35
+ 2.45	106	+ 4:31	+ 2.45	147	+ 5:12	+ 2.45	71	+ 3:56	+ 2.45	64	+ 3:49
+ 3.00	**104**	**+ 4:44**	**+ 3.00**	**143**	**+ 5:23**	**+ 3.00**	**70**	**+ 4:10**	**+ 3.00**	**63**	**+ 4:03**
+ 3.15	102	+ 4:57	+ 3.15	139	+ 5:34	+ 3.15	69	+ 4:24	+ 3.15	61	+ 4:16
+ 3.30	99	+ 5:09	+ 3.30	135	+ 5:45	+ 3.30	67	+ 4:37	+ 3.30	60	+ 4:30
+ 3.45	96	+ 5:21	+ 3.45	131	+ 5:56	+ 3.45	65	+ 4:50	+ 3.45	59	+ 4:44
+ 4.00	**94**	**+ 5:34**	**+ 4.00**	**127**	**- 5:53**	**+ 4.00**	**64**	**+ 5:04**	**+ 4.00**	**58**	**+ 4:58**
+ 4.15	91	+ 5:46	+ 4.15	124	- 5:41	+ 4.15	62	+ 5:17	+ 4.15	57	+ 5:12
+ 4.30	88	+ 5:58	+ 4.30	121	- 5:29	+ 4.30	60	+ 5:30	+ 4.30	55	+ 5:25
+ 4.45	86	- 5:49	+ 4.45	118	- 5:17	+ 4.45	58	+ 5:43	+ 4.45	54	+ 5:39
+ 5.00	**83**	**- 5:37**	**+ 5.00**	**114**	**- 5:06**	**+ 5.00**	**56**	**+ 5:56**	**+ 5.00**	**53**	**+ 5:53**
+ 5.15	81	- 5:24	+ 5.15	112	- 4:53	+ 5.15	54	- 5:51	+ 5.15	52	- 5:53
+ 5.30	80	- 5:10	+ 5.30	110	- 4:40	+ 5.30	53	- 5:37	+ 5.30	51	- 5:39
+ 5.45	78	- 4:57	+ 5.45	107	- 4:28	+ 5.45	51	- 5:24	+ 5.45	50	- 5:25
+ 6.00	**76**	**- 4:44**	**+ 6.00**	**105**	**- 4:15**	**+ 6.00**	**50**	**- 5:10**	**+ 6.00**	**49**	**- 5:11**

River Colne

Table D - North Edinburgh, Crouch and Colne

Neaps — All times relate to HW Sheerness — **Time to cover Sectors (in minutes) at 6.0 Kts**

NORTH BOUND

	D1 East Margate to North Edinburgh			D2 North Edinburgh to NW Long Sand			D3 NW Long Sand to SW Sunk			D4 Barrow Sands to Whitaker Spit			D5 Barrow Deep to Whitaker Spit			D6 Black Deep to Whitaker Spit			D7 Whitaker Spit to Crouch Landfall			D8 Spitway to Colne Landfall	
Time	Duration	Time at End of Sector	Time	Duration	Time at End of Sector	Time	Duration	Time at End of Sector	Time	Duration	Time at End of Sector	Time	Duration	Time at End of Sector	Time	Duration	Time at End of Sector	Time	Duration	Time at End of Sector	Time	Duration	Time at End of Sector
- 6.00	71	- 4:49	- 6.00	32	- 5:28	- 6.00	43	- 5:17	- 6.00	32	- 5:28	- 6.00	63	- 4:57	- 6.00	87	- 4:33	- 6.00	39	- 5:21	- 6.00	40	- 5:20
- 5.45	70	- 4:35	- 5.45	31	- 5:14	- 5.45	44	- 5:01	- 5.45	31	- 5:14	- 5.45	62	- 4:43	- 5.45	86	- 4:19	- 5.45	38	- 5:07	- 5.45	39	- 5:06
- 5.30	69	- 4:21	- 5.30	31	- 4:59	- 5.30	46	- 4:44	- 5.30	31	- 4:59	- 5.30	61	- 4:29	- 5.30	85	- 4:05	- 5.30	37	- 4:53	- 5.30	39	- 4:51
- 5.15	69	- 4:06	- 5.15	30	- 4:45	- 5.15	47	- 4:28	- 5.15	30	- 4:45	- 5.15	61	- 4:14	- 5.15	84	- 3:51	- 5.15	37	- 4:38	- 5.15	39	- 4:36
- 5.00	68	- 3:52	- 5.00	29	- 4:31	- 5.00	48	- 4:12	- 5.00	29	- 4:31	- 5.00	60	- 4:00	- 5.00	84	- 3:36	- 5.00	36	- 4:24	- 5.00	38	- 4:22
- 4.45	68	- 3:37	- 4.45	28	- 4:17	- 4.45	48	- 3:57	- 4.45	29	- 4:16	- 4.45	60	- 3:45	- 4.45	84	- 3:21	- 4.45	35	- 4:10	- 4.45	38	- 4:07
- 4.30	67	- 3:23	- 4.30	28	- 4:02	- 4.30	49	- 3:41	- 4.30	29	- 4:01	- 4.30	60	- 3:30	- 4.30	84	- 3:06	- 4.30	35	- 3:55	- 4.30	38	- 3:52
- 4.15	66	- 3:09	- 4.15	27	- 3:48	- 4.15	49	- 3:26	- 4.15	29	- 3:46	- 4.15	60	- 3:15	- 4.15	84	- 2:51	- 4.15	35	- 3:40	- 4.15	38	- 3:37
- 4.00	65	- 2:55	- 4.00	27	- 3:33	- 4.00	49	- 3:11	- 4.00	29	- 3:31	- 4.00	60	- 3:00	- 4.00	84	- 2:36	- 4.00	35	- 3:25	- 4.00	37	- 3:23
- 3.45	65	- 2:40	- 3.45	27	- 3:18	- 3.45	48	- 2:57	- 3.45	29	- 3:16	- 3.45	60	- 2:45	- 3.45	84	- 2:21	- 3.45	35	- 3:10	- 3.45	37	- 3:08
- 3.30	64	- 2:26	- 3.30	27	- 3:03	- 3.30	48	- 2:42	- 3.30	29	- 3:01	- 3.30	60	- 2:30	- 3.30	85	- 2:05	- 3.30	35	- 2:55	- 3.30	37	- 2:53
- 3.15	64	- 2:11	- 3.15	27	- 2:48	- 3.15	48	- 2:27	- 3.15	29	- 2:46	- 3.15	61	- 2:14	- 3.15	86	- 1:49	- 3.15	35	- 2:40	- 3.15	37	- 2:38
- 3.00	63	- 1:57	- 3.00	27	- 2:33	- 3.00	47	- 2:13	- 3.00	29	- 2:31	- 3.00	61	- 1:59	- 3.00	87	- 1:33	- 3.00	36	- 2:24	- 3.00	37	- 2:23
- 2.45	63	- 1:42	- 2.45	26	- 2:19	- 2.45	46	- 1:59	- 2.45	29	- 2:16	- 2.45	62	- 1:43	- 2.45	87	- 1:18	- 2.45	36	- 2:09	- 2.45	37	- 2:08
- 2.30	63	- 1:27	- 2.30	26	- 2:04	- 2.30	45	- 1:45	- 2.30	29	- 2:01	- 2.30	63	- 1:27	- 2.30	88	- 1:02	- 2.30	36	- 1:54	- 2.30	37	- 1:53
- 2.15	63	- 1:12	- 2.15	26	- 1:49	- 2.15	44	- 1:31	- 2.15	29	- 1:46	- 2.15	63	- 1:12	- 2.15	89	- 0:46	- 2.15	37	- 1:38	- 2.15	37	- 1:38
- 2.00	64	- 0:56	- 2.00	26	- 1:34	- 2.00	43	- 1:17	- 2.00	30	- 1:30	- 2.00	64	- 0:56	- 2.00	90	- 0:30	- 2.00	37	- 1:23	- 2.00	37	- 1:23
- 1.45	64	- 0:41	- 1.45	26	- 1:19	- 1.45	42	- 1:03	- 1.45	30	- 1:15	- 1.45	65	- 0:40	- 1.45	93	- 0:12	- 1.45	38	- 1:07	- 1.45	38	- 1:07
- 1.30	65	- 0:25	- 1.30	26	- 1:04	- 1.30	41	- 0:49	- 1.30	31	- 0:59	- 1.30	67	- 0:23	- 1.30	95	+ 0:05	- 1.30	38	- 0:52	- 1.30	39	- 0:51
- 1.15	66	- 0:09	- 1.15	26	- 0:49	- 1.15	40	- 0:35	- 1.15	31	- 0:44	- 1.15	68	- 0:07	- 1.15	98	+ 0:23	- 1.15	39	- 0:36	- 1.15	40	- 0:35
- 1.00	67	+ 0:07	- 1.00	26	- 0:34	- 1.00	39	- 0:21	- 1.00	32	- 0:28	- 1.00	69	+ 0:09	- 1.00	101	+ 0:41	- 1.00	40	- 0:20	- 1.00	41	- 0:19
- 0.45	68	+ 0:23	- 0.45	27	- 0:18	- 0.45	38	- 0:07	- 0.45	33	- 0:12	- 0.45	71	+ 0:26	- 0.45	104	+ 0:59	- 0.45	41	- 0:04	- 0.45	42	- 0:03
- 0.30	69	+ 0:39	- 0.30	27	- 0:03	- 0.30	37	+ 0:07	- 0.30	33	+ 0:03	- 0.30	73	+ 0:43	- 0.30	106	+ 1:16	- 0.30	43	+ 0:13	- 0.30	44	+ 0:14
- 0.15	71	+ 0:56	- 0.15	27	+ 0:12	- 0.15	37	+ 0:22	- 0.15	34	+ 0:19	- 0.15	74	+ 0:59	- 0.15	109	+ 1:34	- 0.15	44	+ 0:29	- 0.15	45	+ 0:30
HW	72	+ 1:12	HW	28	+ 0:28	HW	36	+ 0:36	HW	35	+ 0:35	HW	76	+ 1:16	HW	112	+ 1:52	HW	46	+ 0:46	HW	47	+ 0:47
+ 0.15	73	+ 1:28	+ 0.15	29	+ 0:44	+ 0.15	36	+ 0:51	+ 0.15	36	+ 0:51	+ 0.15	77	+ 1:32	+ 0.15	114	+ 2:09	+ 0.15	47	+ 1:02	+ 0.15	48	+ 1:03
+ 0.30	75	+ 1:45	+ 0.30	30	+ 1:00	+ 0.30	35	+ 1:05	+ 0.30	37	+ 1:07	+ 0.30	78	+ 1:48	+ 0.30	115	+ 2:25	+ 0.30	48	+ 1:18	+ 0.30	48	+ 1:18
+ 0.45	76	+ 2:01	+ 0.45	31	+ 1:16	+ 0.45	35	+ 1:20	+ 0.45	38	+ 1:23	+ 0.45	79	+ 2:04	+ 0.45	117	+ 2:42	+ 0.45	50	+ 1:35	+ 0.45	49	+ 1:34
+ 1.00	77	+ 2:17	+ 1.00	32	+ 1:32	+ 1.00	34	+ 1:34	+ 1.00	39	+ 1:39	+ 1.00	80	+ 2:20	+ 1.00	119	+ 2:59	+ 1.00	51	+ 1:51	+ 1.00	50	+ 1:50
+ 1.15	78	+ 2:33	+ 1.15	33	+ 1:48	+ 1.15	34	+ 1:49	+ 1.15	39	+ 1:54	+ 1.15	80	+ 2:35	+ 1.15	119	+ 3:14	+ 1.15	51	+ 2:06	+ 1.15	50	+ 2:05
+ 1.30	78	+ 2:48	+ 1.30	35	+ 2:05	+ 1.30	34	+ 2:04	+ 1.30	39	+ 2:09	+ 1.30	80	+ 2:50	+ 1.30	119	+ 3:29	+ 1.30	51	+ 2:21	+ 1.30	50	+ 2:20
+ 1.45	79	+ 3:04	+ 1.45	36	+ 2:21	+ 1.45	34	+ 2:19	+ 1.45	39	+ 2:24	+ 1.45	80	+ 3:05	+ 1.45	119	+ 3:44	+ 1.45	52	+ 2:37	+ 1.45	50	+ 2:35
+ 2.00	80	+ 3:20	+ 2.00	38	+ 2:38	+ 2.00	33	+ 2:33	+ 2.00	40	+ 2:40	+ 2.00	81	+ 3:21	+ 2.00	119	+ 3:59	+ 2.00	52	+ 2:52	+ 2.00	50	+ 2:50
+ 2.15	79	+ 3:34	+ 2.15	39	+ 2:54	+ 2.15	33	+ 2:48	+ 2.15	39	+ 2:54	+ 2.15	80	+ 3:35	+ 2.15	117	+ 4:12	+ 2.15	52	+ 3:07	+ 2.15	50	+ 3:05
+ 2.30	79	+ 3:49	+ 2.30	40	+ 3:10	+ 2.30	33	+ 3:03	+ 2.30	39	+ 3:09	+ 2.30	80	+ 3:50	+ 2.30	116	+ 4:26	+ 2.30	51	+ 3:21	+ 2.30	49	+ 3:19
+ 2.45	79	+ 4:04	+ 2.45	41	+ 3:26	+ 2.45	33	+ 3:18	+ 2.45	39	+ 3:24	+ 2.45	79	+ 4:04	+ 2.45	114	+ 4:39	+ 2.45	51	+ 3:36	+ 2.45	48	+ 3:33
+ 3.00	79	+ 4:19	+ 3.00	42	+ 3:42	+ 3.00	33	+ 3:33	+ 3.00	39	+ 3:39	+ 3.00	78	+ 4:18	+ 3.00	113	+ 4:53	+ 3.00	50	+ 3:50	+ 3.00	48	+ 3:48
+ 3.15	79	+ 4:34	+ 3.15	42	+ 3:57	+ 3.15	33	+ 3:48	+ 3.15	38	+ 3:53	+ 3.15	77	+ 4:32	+ 3.15	111	+ 5:06	+ 3.15	50	+ 4:05	+ 3.15	47	+ 4:02
+ 3.30	78	+ 4:48	+ 3.30	42	+ 4:12	+ 3.30	34	+ 4:04	+ 3.30	38	+ 4:08	+ 3.30	76	+ 4:46	+ 3.30	109	+ 5:19	+ 3.30	49	+ 4:19	+ 3.30	47	+ 4:17
+ 3.45	78	+ 5:03	+ 3.45	42	+ 4:27	+ 3.45	34	+ 4:19	+ 3.45	37	+ 4:22	+ 3.45	75	+ 5:00	+ 3.45	107	+ 5:32	+ 3.45	49	+ 4:34	+ 3.45	46	+ 4:31
+ 4.00	77	+ 5:17	+ 4.00	42	+ 4:42	+ 4.00	35	+ 4:35	+ 4.00	36	+ 4:36	+ 4.00	74	+ 5:14	+ 4.00	105	+ 5:45	+ 4.00	48	+ 4:48	+ 4.00	45	+ 4:45
+ 4.15	77	+ 5:32	+ 4.15	41	+ 4:56	+ 4.15	35	+ 4:50	+ 4.15	36	+ 4:51	+ 4.15	73	+ 5:28	+ 4.15	103	+ 5:58	+ 4.15	47	+ 5:02	+ 4.15	45	+ 5:00
+ 4.30	76	+ 5:46	+ 4.30	40	+ 5:10	+ 4.30	36	+ 5:06	+ 4.30	36	+ 5:06	+ 4.30	71	+ 5:41	+ 4.30	102	- 5:48	+ 4.30	46	+ 5:16	+ 4.30	45	+ 5:15
+ 4.45	75	- 6:00	+ 4.45	40	+ 5:25	+ 4.45	37	+ 5:22	+ 4.45	35	+ 5:20	+ 4.45	70	+ 5:55	+ 4.45	100	- 5:35	+ 4.45	45	+ 5:30	+ 4.45	44	+ 5:29
+ 5.00	74	- 5:46	+ 5.00	39	+ 5:39	+ 5.00	37	+ 5:37	+ 5.00	35	+ 5:35	+ 5.00	69	- 5:51	+ 5.00	98	- 5:22	+ 5.00	45	+ 5:45	+ 5.00	44	+ 5:44
+ 5.15	73	- 5:32	+ 5.15	38	+ 5:53	+ 5.15	38	+ 5:53	+ 5.15	34	+ 5:49	+ 5.15	68	- 5:37	+ 5.15	97	- 5:08	+ 5.15	44	+ 5:59	+ 5.15	43	+ 5:58
+ 5.30	73	- 5:17	+ 5.30	37	- 5:53	+ 5.30	39	- 5:51	+ 5.30	34	- 5:56	+ 5.30	67	- 5:23	+ 5.30	95	- 4:55	+ 5.30	43	- 5:47	+ 5.30	43	- 5:47
+ 5.45	72	- 5:03	+ 5.45	35	- 5:40	+ 5.45	40	- 5:35	+ 5.45	33	- 5:42	+ 5.45	67	- 5:08	+ 5.45	94	- 4:41	+ 5.45	43	- 5:32	+ 5.45	42	- 5:33
+ 6.00	72	- 4:48	+ 6.00	34	- 5:26	+ 6.00	40	- 5:20	+ 6.00	33	- 5:27	+ 6.00	66	- 4:54	+ 6.00	93	- 4:27	+ 6.00	42	- 5:18	+ 6.00	41	- 5:19

River Colne

Table D - North Edinburgh, Crouch and Colne

Time to cover Sectors (in minutes) at 6.0 kts

All times relate to HW Sheerness

Springs

NORTH BOUND

D1 – East Margate to North Edinburgh

Time	Duration	Time at End of Sector
- 6.00	71	- 4:49
- 5.45	70	- 4:35
- 5.30	69	- 4:21
- 5.15	68	- 4:07
- 5.00	67	- 3:53
- 4.45	66	- 3:39
- 4.30	65	- 3:25
- 4.15	64	- 3:11
- 4.00	63	- 2:57
- 3.45	62	- 2:43
- 3.30	61	- 2:29
- 3.15	60	- 2:15
- 3.00	60	- 2:00
- 2.45	60	- 1:45
- 2.30	60	- 1:30
- 2.15	60	- 1:15
- 2.00	61	- 0:59
- 1.45	62	- 0:43
- 1.30	63	- 0:27
- 1.15	64	- 0:11
- 1.00	65	+ 0:05
- 0.45	67	+ 0:22
- 0.30	69	+ 0:39
- 0.15	71	+ 0:56
HW	73	+ 1:13
+ 0.15	75	+ 1:30
+ 0.30	77	+ 1:47
+ 0.45	79	+ 2:04
+ 1.00	81	+ 2:21
+ 1.15	82	+ 2:37
+ 1.30	83	+ 2:53
+ 1.45	84	+ 3:09
+ 2.00	85	+ 3:25
+ 2.15	85	+ 3:40
+ 2.30	85	+ 3:55
+ 2.45	85	+ 4:10
+ 3.00	85	+ 4:25
+ 3.15	83	+ 4:38
+ 3.30	82	+ 4:52
+ 3.45	81	+ 5:06
+ 4.00	79	+ 5:19
+ 4.15	78	+ 5:33
+ 4.30	77	+ 5:47
+ 4.45	76	- 5:59
+ 5.00	75	- 5:45
+ 5.15	74	- 5:31
+ 5.30	74	- 5:16
+ 5.45	73	- 5:02
+ 6.00	72	- 4:48

D2 – North Edinburgh to NW Long Sand

Time	Duration	Time at End of Sector
- 6.00	33	- 5:27
- 5.45	31	- 5:14
- 5.30	30	- 5:00
- 5.15	29	- 4:46
- 5.00	28	- 4:32
- 4.45	27	- 4:18
- 4.30	26	- 4:04
- 4.15	25	- 3:50
- 4.00	24	- 3:36
- 3.45	24	- 3:21
- 3.30	24	- 3:06
- 3.15	24	- 2:51
- 3.00	24	- 2:36
- 2.45	24	- 2:21
- 2.30	23	- 2:07
- 2.15	23	- 1:52
- 2.00	22	- 1:38
- 1.45	22	- 1:23
- 1.30	23	- 1:07
- 1.15	23	- 0:52
- 1.00	23	- 0:37
- 0.45	24	- 0:21
- 0.30	25	- 0:05
- 0.15	25	+ 0:10
HW	26	+ 0:26
+ 0.15	28	+ 0:43
+ 0.30	29	+ 0:59
+ 0.45	31	+ 1:16
+ 1.00	32	+ 1:32
+ 1.15	35	+ 1:50
+ 1.30	37	+ 2:07
+ 1.45	40	+ 2:25
+ 2.00	42	+ 2:42
+ 2.15	44	+ 2:59
+ 2.30	46	+ 3:16
+ 2.45	48	+ 3:33
+ 3.00	50	+ 3:50
+ 3.15	50	+ 4:05
+ 3.30	50	+ 4:20
+ 3.45	50	+ 4:35
+ 4.00	49	+ 4:49
+ 4.15	48	+ 5:03
+ 4.30	46	+ 5:16
+ 4.45	45	+ 5:30
+ 5.00	43	+ 5:43
+ 5.15	41	+ 5:56
+ 5.30	39	- 5:51
+ 5.45	38	- 5:37
+ 6.00	36	- 5:24

D3 – NW Long Sand to SW Sunk

Time	Duration	Time at End of Sector
- 6.00	46	- 5:14
- 5.45	48	- 4:57
- 5.30	50	- 4:40
- 5.15	53	- 4:22
- 5.00	55	- 4:05
- 4.45	55	- 3:50
- 4.30	55	- 3:35
- 4.15	55	- 3:20
- 4.00	56	- 3:04
- 3.45	55	- 2:50
- 3.30	54	- 2:36
- 3.15	53	- 2:22
- 3.00	52	- 2:08
- 2.45	51	- 1:54
- 2.30	49	- 1:41
- 2.15	47	- 1:28
- 2.00	45	- 1:15
- 1.45	44	- 1:01
- 1.30	42	- 0:48
- 1.15	40	- 0:35
- 1.00	38	- 0:22
- 0.45	37	- 0:08
- 0.30	36	+ 0:06
- 0.15	35	+ 0:20
HW	34	+ 0:34
+ 0.15	34	+ 0:49
+ 0.30	33	+ 1:03
+ 0.45	33	+ 1:18
+ 1.00	32	+ 1:32
+ 1.15	32	+ 1:47
+ 1.30	32	+ 2:02
+ 1.45	32	+ 2:17
+ 2.00	31	+ 2:31
+ 2.15	31	+ 2:46
+ 2.30	31	+ 3:01
+ 2.45	31	+ 3:16
+ 3.00	30	+ 3:30
+ 3.15	31	+ 3:46
+ 3.30	31	+ 4:01
+ 3.45	32	+ 4:17
+ 4.00	32	+ 4:32
+ 4.15	33	+ 4:48
+ 4.30	34	+ 5:04
+ 4.45	35	+ 5:20
+ 5.00	37	+ 5:37
+ 5.15	38	+ 5:53
+ 5.30	39	- 5:51
+ 5.45	40	- 5:35
+ 6.00	41	- 5:19

D4 – Barrow Sands to Whitaker Spit

Time	Duration	Time at End of Sector
- 6.00	31	- 5:29
- 5.45	30	- 5:15
- 5.30	29	- 5:01
- 5.15	29	- 4:46
- 5.00	28	- 4:32
- 4.45	28	- 4:17
- 4.30	27	- 4:03
- 4.15	27	- 3:48
- 4.00	27	- 3:33
- 3.45	27	- 3:18
- 3.30	27	- 3:03
- 3.15	27	- 2:48
- 3.00	27	- 2:33
- 2.45	27	- 2:18
- 2.30	27	- 2:03
- 2.15	28	- 1:47
- 2.00	28	- 1:32
- 1.45	29	- 1:16
- 1.30	29	- 1:01
- 1.15	30	- 0:45
- 1.00	31	- 0:29
- 0.45	32	- 0:13
- 0.30	34	+ 0:04
- 0.15	35	+ 0:20
HW	36	+ 0:36
+ 0.15	38	+ 0:53
+ 0.30	39	+ 1:09
+ 0.45	41	+ 1:26
+ 1.00	42	+ 1:42
+ 1.15	43	+ 1:58
+ 1.30	43	+ 2:13
+ 1.45	44	+ 2:29
+ 2.00	44	+ 2:44
+ 2.15	44	+ 2:59
+ 2.30	43	+ 3:13
+ 2.45	43	+ 3:28
+ 3.00	42	+ 3:42
+ 3.15	41	+ 3:56
+ 3.30	40	+ 4:10
+ 3.45	39	+ 4:24
+ 4.00	38	+ 4:38
+ 4.15	38	+ 4:53
+ 4.30	37	+ 5:07
+ 4.45	36	+ 5:21
+ 5.00	35	+ 5:35
+ 5.15	35	+ 5:50
+ 5.30	34	- 5:56
+ 5.45	33	- 5:42
+ 6.00	33	- 5:27

D5 – Barrow Deep to Whitaker Spit

Time	Duration	Time at End of Sector
- 6.00	60	- 5:00
- 5.45	59	- 4:46
- 5.30	58	- 4:32
- 5.15	58	- 4:17
- 5.00	57	- 4:03
- 4.45	57	- 3:48
- 4.30	57	- 3:33
- 4.15	56	- 3:19
- 4.00	56	- 3:04
- 3.45	57	- 2:48
- 3.30	57	- 2:33
- 3.15	57	- 2:18
- 3.00	58	- 2:02
- 2.45	59	- 1:46
- 2.30	60	- 1:30
- 2.15	61	- 1:14
- 2.00	62	- 0:58
- 1.45	64	- 0:41
- 1.30	66	- 0:24
- 1.15	68	- 0:07
- 1.00	70	+ 0:10
- 0.45	72	+ 0:27
- 0.30	75	+ 0:45
- 0.15	77	+ 1:02
HW	79	+ 1:19
+ 0.15	82	+ 1:37
+ 0.30	85	+ 1:55
+ 0.45	87	+ 2:12
+ 1.00	90	+ 2:30
+ 1.15	90	+ 2:45
+ 1.30	90	+ 3:00
+ 1.45	90	+ 3:15
+ 2.00	90	+ 3:30
+ 2.15	89	+ 3:44
+ 2.30	87	+ 3:57
+ 2.45	85	+ 4:10
+ 3.00	83	+ 4:23
+ 3.15	82	+ 4:37
+ 3.30	80	+ 4:50
+ 3.45	78	+ 5:03
+ 4.00	77	+ 5:17
+ 4.15	75	+ 5:30
+ 4.30	73	+ 5:43
+ 4.45	71	+ 5:56
+ 5.00	70	- 5:50
+ 5.15	68	- 5:37
+ 5.30	67	- 5:23
+ 5.45	66	- 5:09
+ 6.00	64	- 4:56

D6 – Black Deep to Whitaker Spit

Time	Duration	Time at End of Sector
- 6.00	83	- 4:37
- 5.45	82	- 4:23
- 5.30	81	- 4:09
- 5.15	79	- 3:56
- 5.00	78	- 3:42
- 4.45	78	- 3:27
- 4.30	78	- 3:12
- 4.15	78	- 2:57
- 4.00	78	- 2:42
- 3.45	79	- 2:26
- 3.30	80	- 2:10
- 3.15	81	- 1:54
- 3.00	81	- 1:39
- 2.45	83	- 1:22
- 2.30	85	- 1:05
- 2.15	87	- 0:48
- 2.00	89	- 0:31
- 1.45	92	- 0:13
- 1.30	96	+ 0:06
- 1.15	100	+ 0:25
- 1.00	104	+ 0:44
- 0.45	107	+ 1:02
- 0.30	111	+ 1:21
- 0.15	115	+ 1:40
HW	119	+ 1:59
+ 0.15	121	+ 2:16
+ 0.30	123	+ 2:33
+ 0.45	125	+ 2:50
+ 1.00	127	+ 3:07
+ 1.15	127	+ 3:22
+ 1.30	127	+ 3:37
+ 1.45	126	+ 3:51
+ 2.00	126	+ 4:06
+ 2.15	124	+ 4:19
+ 2.30	122	+ 4:32
+ 2.45	120	+ 4:45
+ 3.00	117	+ 4:57
+ 3.15	115	+ 5:10
+ 3.30	112	+ 5:22
+ 3.45	109	+ 5:34
+ 4.00	107	+ 5:47
+ 4.15	104	+ 5:59
+ 4.30	102	- 5:48
+ 4.45	100	- 5:35
+ 5.00	97	- 5:23
+ 5.15	95	- 5:10
+ 5.30	94	- 4:56
+ 5.45	92	- 4:43
+ 6.00	91	- 4:29

D7 – Whitaker Spit to Crouch Landfall

Time	Duration	Time at End of Sector
- 6.00	38	- 5:22
- 5.45	37	- 5:08
- 5.30	35	- 4:55
- 5.15	34	- 4:41
- 5.00	33	- 4:27
- 4.45	32	- 4:13
- 4.30	32	- 3:58
- 4.15	32	- 3:43
- 4.00	32	- 3:28
- 3.45	32	- 3:13
- 3.30	32	- 2:58
- 3.15	32	- 2:43
- 3.00	32	- 2:28
- 2.45	33	- 2:12
- 2.30	33	- 1:57
- 2.15	34	- 1:41
- 2.00	34	- 1:26
- 1.45	35	- 1:10
- 1.30	36	- 0:54
- 1.15	38	- 0:37
- 1.00	39	- 0:21
- 0.45	41	- 0:04
- 0.30	43	+ 0:13
- 0.15	45	+ 0:30
HW	47	+ 0:47
+ 0.15	49	+ 1:04
+ 0.30	52	+ 1:22
+ 0.45	54	+ 1:39
+ 1.00	56	+ 1:56
+ 1.15	57	+ 2:12
+ 1.30	58	+ 2:28
+ 1.45	58	+ 2:43
+ 2.00	59	+ 2:59
+ 2.15	58	+ 3:13
+ 2.30	57	+ 3:27
+ 2.45	57	+ 3:42
+ 3.00	56	+ 3:56
+ 3.15	55	+ 4:10
+ 3.30	54	+ 4:24
+ 3.45	53	+ 4:38
+ 4.00	52	+ 4:52
+ 4.15	50	+ 5:05
+ 4.30	49	+ 5:19
+ 4.45	48	+ 5:33
+ 5.00	46	+ 5:46
+ 5.15	45	- 6:00
+ 5.30	44	- 5:46
+ 5.45	43	- 5:32
+ 6.00	42	- 5:18

D8 – Spitway to Colne Landfall

Time	Duration	Time at End of Sector
- 6.00	39	- 5:21
- 5.45	38	- 5:07
- 5.30	38	- 4:52
- 5.15	37	- 4:38
- 5.00	37	- 4:23
- 4.45	36	- 4:09
- 4.30	36	- 3:54
- 4.15	36	- 3:39
- 4.00	35	- 3:25
- 3.45	35	- 3:10
- 3.30	35	- 2:55
- 3.15	35	- 2:40
- 3.00	35	- 2:25
- 2.45	35	- 2:10
- 2.30	35	- 1:55
- 2.15	35	- 1:40
- 2.00	35	- 1:25
- 1.45	36	- 1:09
- 1.30	37	- 0:53
- 1.15	39	- 0:36
- 1.00	40	- 0:20
- 0.45	42	- 0:03
- 0.30	45	+ 0:15
- 0.15	47	+ 0:32
HW	49	+ 0:49
+ 0.15	51	+ 1:06
+ 0.30	52	+ 1:22
+ 0.45	53	+ 1:38
+ 1.00	55	+ 1:55
+ 1.15	55	+ 2:10
+ 1.30	55	+ 2:25
+ 1.45	55	+ 2:40
+ 2.00	55	+ 2:55
+ 2.15	54	+ 3:09
+ 2.30	53	+ 3:23
+ 2.45	52	+ 3:37
+ 3.00	51	+ 3:51
+ 3.15	50	+ 4:05
+ 3.30	49	+ 4:19
+ 3.45	48	+ 4:33
+ 4.00	47	+ 4:47
+ 4.15	47	+ 5:02
+ 4.30	46	+ 5:16
+ 4.45	45	+ 5:30
+ 5.00	44	+ 5:44
+ 5.15	43	+ 5:58
+ 5.30	43	- 5:47
+ 5.45	42	- 5:33
+ 6.00	41	- 5:19

River Colne

Table D - North Edinburgh, Crouch and Colne

Neaps — All times relate to HW Sheerness — **Time to cover Sectors (in minutes) at 7.0 Kts**

NORTH BOUND

	D1 East Margate to North Edinburgh			D2 North Edinburgh to NW Long Sand			D3 NW Long Sand to SW Sunk			D4 Barrow Sands to Whitaker Spit			D5 Barrow Deep to Whitaker Spit			D6 Black Deep to Whitaker Spit			D7 Whitaker Spit to Crouch Landfall			D8 Spitway to Colne Landfall	
Time	Duration	Time at End of Sector	Time	Duration	Time at End of Sector	Time	Duration	Time at End of Sector	Time	Duration	Time at End of Sector	Time	Duration	Time at End of Sector	Time	Duration	Time at End of Sector	Time	Duration	Time at End of Sector	Time	Duration	Time at End of Sector
- 6.00	60	- 5:00	- 6.00	28	- 5:32	- 6.00	36	- 5:24	- 6.00	27	- 5:33	- 6.00	54	- 5:06	- 6.00	76	- 4:44	- 6.00	34	- 5:26	- 6.00	35	- 5:25
- 5.45	60	- 4:45	- 5.45	27	- 5:18	- 5.45	37	- 5:08	- 5.45	27	- 5:18	- 5.45	54	- 4:51	- 5.45	75	- 4:30	- 5.45	34	- 5:11	- 5.45	34	- 5:11
- 5.30	60	- 4:30	- 5.30	26	- 5:04	- 5.30	38	- 4:52	- 5.30	26	- 5:04	- 5.30	53	- 4:37	- 5.30	75	- 4:15	- 5.30	33	- 4:57	- 5.30	34	- 4:56
- 5.15	59	- 4:16	- 5.15	26	- 4:49	- 5.15	39	- 4:36	- 5.15	26	- 4:49	- 5.15	53	- 4:22	- 5.15	74	- 4:01	- 5.15	32	- 4:43	- 5.15	34	- 4:41
- 5.00	59	- 4:01	- 5.00	25	- 4:35	- 5.00	40	- 4:20	- 5.00	25	- 4:35	- 5.00	52	- 4:08	- 5.00	73	- 3:47	- 5.00	31	- 4:29	- 5.00	33	- 4:27
- 4.45	58	- 3:47	- 4.45	24	- 4:21	- 4.45	40	- 4:05	- 4.45	25	- 4:20	- 4.45	52	- 3:53	- 4.45	73	- 3:32	- 4.45	31	- 4:14	- 4.45	33	- 4:12
- 4.30	58	- 3:32	- 4.30	24	- 4:06	- 4.30	40	- 3:50	- 4.30	25	- 4:05	- 4.30	52	- 3:38	- 4.30	73	- 3:17	- 4.30	31	- 3:59	- 4.30	33	- 3:57
- 4.15	57	- 3:18	- 4.15	23	- 3:52	- 4.15	40	- 3:35	- 4.15	25	- 3:50	- 4.15	52	- 3:23	- 4.15	73	- 3:02	- 4.15	31	- 3:44	- 4.15	33	- 3:42
- 4.00	57	- 3:03	- 4.00	23	- 3:37	- 4.00	41	- 3:19	- 4.00	25	- 3:35	- 4.00	52	- 3:08	- 4.00	73	- 2:47	- 4.00	31	- 3:29	- 4.00	33	- 3:27
- 3.45	56	- 2:49	- 3.45	23	- 3:22	- 3.45	40	- 3:05	- 3.45	25	- 3:20	- 3.45	52	- 2:53	- 3.45	74	- 2:31	- 3.45	31	- 3:14	- 3.45	32	- 3:13
- 3.30	56	- 2:34	- 3.30	23	- 3:07	- 3.30	40	- 2:50	- 3.30	25	- 3:05	- 3.30	53	- 2:37	- 3.30	74	- 2:16	- 3.30	31	- 2:59	- 3.30	32	- 2:58
- 3.15	55	- 2:20	- 3.15	23	- 2:52	- 3.15	40	- 2:35	- 3.15	25	- 2:50	- 3.15	53	- 2:22	- 3.15	75	- 2:00	- 3.15	31	- 2:44	- 3.15	32	- 2:43
- 3.00	55	- 2:05	- 3.00	23	- 2:37	- 3.00	40	- 2:20	- 3.00	25	- 2:35	- 3.00	53	- 2:07	- 3.00	75	- 1:45	- 3.00	31	- 2:29	- 3.00	32	- 2:28
- 2.45	55	- 1:50	- 2.45	23	- 2:22	- 2.45	39	- 2:06	- 2.45	25	- 2:20	- 2.45	54	- 1:51	- 2.45	76	- 1:29	- 2.45	31	- 2:14	- 2.45	32	- 2:13
- 2.30	55	- 1:35	- 2.30	22	- 2:08	- 2.30	38	- 1:52	- 2.30	25	- 2:05	- 2.30	54	- 1:36	- 2.30	77	- 1:13	- 2.30	32	- 1:58	- 2.30	32	- 1:58
- 2.15	55	- 1:20	- 2.15	22	- 1:53	- 2.15	38	- 1:37	- 2.15	25	- 1:50	- 2.15	55	- 1:20	- 2.15	78	- 0:57	- 2.15	32	- 1:43	- 2.15	32	- 1:43
- 2.00	55	- 1:05	- 2.00	22	- 1:38	- 2.00	37	- 1:23	- 2.00	25	- 1:35	- 2.00	55	- 1:05	- 2.00	79	- 0:41	- 2.00	32	- 1:28	- 2.00	32	- 1:28
- 1.45	56	- 0:49	- 1.45	22	- 1:23	- 1.45	36	- 1:09	- 1.45	26	- 1:19	- 1.45	56	- 0:49	- 1.45	80	- 0:25	- 1.45	32	- 1:13	- 1.45	33	- 1:12
- 1.30	56	- 0:34	- 1.30	22	- 1:08	- 1.30	35	- 0:55	- 1.30	26	- 1:04	- 1.30	57	- 0:33	- 1.30	82	- 0:08	- 1.30	33	- 0:57	- 1.30	33	- 0:57
- 1.15	57	- 0:18	- 1.15	22	- 0:53	- 1.15	34	- 0:41	- 1.15	27	- 0:48	- 1.15	58	- 0:17	- 1.15	84	+ 0:09	- 1.15	34	- 0:41	- 1.15	34	- 0:41
- 1.00	57	- 0:03	- 1.00	23	- 0:37	- 1.00	33	- 0:27	- 1.00	27	- 0:33	- 1.00	59	- 0:01	- 1.00	85	+ 0:25	- 1.00	34	- 0:26	- 1.00	34	- 0:26
- 0.45	58	+ 0:13	- 0.45	23	- 0:22	- 0.45	33	- 0:12	- 0.45	28	- 0:17	- 0.45	60	+ 0:15	- 0.45	87	+ 0:42	- 0.45	35	- 0:10	- 0.45	36	- 0:09
- 0.30	59	+ 0:29	- 0.30	23	- 0:07	- 0.30	32	+ 0:02	- 0.30	28	- 0:02	- 0.30	61	+ 0:31	- 0.30	89	+ 0:59	- 0.30	36	+ 0:06	- 0.30	37	+ 0:07
- 0.15	60	+ 0:45	- 0.15	23	+ 0:08	- 0.15	32	+ 0:17	- 0.15	29	+ 0:14	- 0.15	62	+ 0:47	- 0.15	91	+ 1:16	- 0.15	37	+ 0:22	- 0.15	38	+ 0:23
HW	61	+ 1:01	HW	24	+ 0:24	HW	31	+ 0:31	HW	29	+ 0:29	HW	64	+ 1:04	HW	93	+ 1:33	HW	38	+ 0:38	HW	39	+ 0:39
+ 0.15	62	+ 1:17	+ 0.15	25	+ 0:40	+ 0.15	31	+ 0:46	+ 0.15	30	+ 0:45	+ 0.15	64	+ 1:19	+ 0.15	95	+ 1:50	+ 0.15	39	+ 0:54	+ 0.15	40	+ 0:55
+ 0.30	63	+ 1:33	+ 0.30	25	+ 0:55	+ 0.30	31	+ 1:01	+ 0.30	31	+ 1:01	+ 0.30	65	+ 1:35	+ 0.30	96	+ 2:06	+ 0.30	40	+ 1:10	+ 0.30	40	+ 1:10
+ 0.45	64	+ 1:49	+ 0.45	26	+ 1:11	+ 0.45	30	+ 1:15	+ 0.45	32	+ 1:17	+ 0.45	66	+ 1:51	+ 0.45	98	+ 2:23	+ 0.45	41	+ 1:26	+ 0.45	41	+ 1:26
+ 1.00	65	+ 2:05	+ 1.00	27	+ 1:27	+ 1.00	30	+ 1:30	+ 1.00	32	+ 1:32	+ 1.00	67	+ 2:07	+ 1.00	99	+ 2:39	+ 1.00	42	+ 1:42	+ 1.00	42	+ 1:42
+ 1.15	65	+ 2:20	+ 1.15	28	+ 1:43	+ 1.15	30	+ 1:45	+ 1.15	33	+ 1:48	+ 1.15	67	+ 2:22	+ 1.15	100	+ 2:55	+ 1.15	43	+ 1:58	+ 1.15	42	+ 1:57
+ 1.30	66	+ 2:36	+ 1.30	29	+ 1:59	+ 1.30	30	+ 2:00	+ 1.30	33	+ 2:03	+ 1.30	67	+ 2:37	+ 1.30	100	+ 3:10	+ 1.30	43	+ 2:13	+ 1.30	42	+ 2:12
+ 1.45	66	+ 2:51	+ 1.45	30	+ 2:15	+ 1.45	30	+ 2:15	+ 1.45	33	+ 2:18	+ 1.45	67	+ 2:52	+ 1.45	100	+ 3:25	+ 1.45	43	+ 2:28	+ 1.45	42	+ 2:27
+ 2.00	67	+ 3:07	+ 2.00	31	+ 2:31	+ 2.00	29	+ 2:29	+ 2.00	33	+ 2:33	+ 2.00	68	+ 3:08	+ 2.00	100	+ 3:40	+ 2.00	43	+ 2:43	+ 2.00	42	+ 2:42
+ 2.15	67	+ 3:22	+ 2.15	32	+ 2:47	+ 2.15	29	+ 2:44	+ 2.15	33	+ 2:48	+ 2.15	67	+ 3:22	+ 2.15	99	+ 3:54	+ 2.15	43	+ 2:58	+ 2.15	42	+ 2:57
+ 2.30	67	+ 3:37	+ 2.30	33	+ 3:03	+ 2.30	29	+ 2:59	+ 2.30	33	+ 3:03	+ 2.30	67	+ 3:37	+ 2.30	98	+ 4:08	+ 2.30	43	+ 3:13	+ 2.30	41	+ 3:11
+ 2.45	67	+ 3:52	+ 2.45	34	+ 3:19	+ 2.45	29	+ 3:14	+ 2.45	33	+ 3:18	+ 2.45	66	+ 3:51	+ 2.45	97	+ 4:22	+ 2.45	42	+ 3:27	+ 2.45	41	+ 3:26
+ 3.00	67	+ 4:07	+ 3.00	35	+ 3:35	+ 3.00	29	+ 3:29	+ 3.00	33	+ 3:33	+ 3.00	66	+ 4:06	+ 3.00	96	+ 4:36	+ 3.00	42	+ 3:42	+ 3.00	41	+ 3:41
+ 3.15	67	+ 4:22	+ 3.15	35	+ 3:50	+ 3.15	29	+ 3:44	+ 3.15	32	+ 3:47	+ 3.15	65	+ 4:20	+ 3.15	95	+ 4:50	+ 3.15	42	+ 3:57	+ 3.15	40	+ 3:55
+ 3.30	66	+ 4:36	+ 3.30	35	+ 4:05	+ 3.30	29	+ 3:59	+ 3.30	32	+ 4:02	+ 3.30	64	+ 4:34	+ 3.30	93	+ 5:03	+ 3.30	41	+ 4:11	+ 3.30	40	+ 4:10
+ 3.45	66	+ 4:51	+ 3.45	35	+ 4:20	+ 3.45	30	+ 4:15	+ 3.45	31	+ 4:16	+ 3.45	64	+ 4:49	+ 3.45	92	+ 5:17	+ 3.45	41	+ 4:26	+ 3.45	39	+ 4:24
+ 4.00	66	+ 5:06	+ 4.00	35	+ 4:35	+ 4.00	30	+ 4:30	+ 4.00	31	+ 4:31	+ 4.00	63	+ 5:03	+ 4.00	90	+ 5:30	+ 4.00	41	+ 4:41	+ 4.00	39	+ 4:39
+ 4.15	65	+ 5:20	+ 4.15	35	+ 4:50	+ 4.15	30	+ 4:45	+ 4.15	31	+ 4:46	+ 4.15	62	+ 5:17	+ 4.15	89	+ 5:44	+ 4.15	40	+ 4:55	+ 4.15	38	+ 4:53
+ 4.30	64	+ 5:34	+ 4.30	34	+ 5:04	+ 4.30	31	+ 5:01	+ 4.30	30	+ 5:00	+ 4.30	61	+ 5:31	+ 4.30	87	+ 5:57	+ 4.30	39	+ 5:09	+ 4.30	38	+ 5:08
+ 4.45	64	+ 5:49	+ 4.45	33	+ 5:18	+ 4.45	31	+ 5:16	+ 4.45	30	+ 5:15	+ 4.45	60	+ 5:45	+ 4.45	85	- 5:50	+ 4.45	39	+ 5:24	+ 4.45	38	+ 5:23
+ 5.00	63	- 5:57	+ 5.00	33	+ 5:33	+ 5.00	32	+ 5:32	+ 5.00	30	+ 5:30	+ 5.00	59	+ 5:59	+ 5.00	84	- 5:36	+ 5.00	38	+ 5:38	+ 5.00	37	+ 5:37
+ 5.15	63	- 5:42	+ 5.15	32	+ 5:47	+ 5.15	32	+ 5:47	+ 5.15	29	+ 5:44	+ 5.15	59	- 5:46	+ 5.15	83	- 5:22	+ 5.15	38	+ 5:53	+ 5.15	37	+ 5:52
+ 5.30	62	- 5:28	+ 5.30	31	- 5:59	+ 5.30	33	- 5:57	+ 5.30	29	+ 5:59	+ 5.30	58	- 5:32	+ 5.30	82	- 5:08	+ 5.30	37	- 5:53	+ 5.30	37	- 5:53
+ 5.45	62	- 5:13	+ 5.45	30	- 5:45	+ 5.45	34	- 5:41	+ 5.45	28	- 5:47	+ 5.45	57	- 5:18	+ 5.45	81	- 4:54	+ 5.45	36	- 5:39	+ 5.45	36	- 5:39
+ 6.00	61	- 4:59	+ 6.00	29	- 5:31	+ 6.00	34	- 5:26	+ 6.00	28	- 5:32	+ 6.00	57	- 5:03	+ 6.00	80	- 4:40	+ 6.00	36	- 5:24	+ 6.00	36	- 5:24

River Colne

Table D - North Edinburgh, Crouch and Colne

Time to cover Sectors (in minutes) at 7.0 kts — All times relate to HW Sheerness — **Springs**

Time	D1 East Margate to North Edinburgh — Duration	D1 Time at End of Sector	Time	D2 North Edinburgh to NW Long Sand — Duration	D2 Time at End of Sector	Time	D3 NW Long Sand to SW Sunk — Duration	D3 Time at End of Sector	Time	D4 Barrow Sands to Whitaker Spit — Duration	D4 Time at End of Sector	Time	D5 Barrow Deep to Whitaker Spit — Duration	D5 Time at End of Sector	Time	D6 Black Deep to Whitaker Spit — Duration	D6 Time at End of Sector	Time	D7 Whitaker Spit to Crouch Landfall — Duration	D7 Time at End of Sector	Time	D8 Spitway to Colne Landfall — Duration	D8 Time at End of Sector
- 6.00	61	- 4:59	- 6.00	28	- 5:32	- 6.00	38	- 5:22	- 6.00	27	- 5:33	- 6.00	53	- 5:07	- 6.00	73	- 4:47	- 6.00	34	- 5:26	- 6.00	34	- 5:26
- 5.45	60	- 4:45	- 5.45	27	- 5:18	- 5.45	39	- 5:06	- 5.45	26	- 5:19	- 5.45	52	- 4:53	- 5.45	72	- 4:33	- 5.45	33	- 5:12	- 5.45	34	- 5:11
- 5.30	59	- 4:31	- 5.30	26	- 5:04	- 5.30	41	- 4:49	- 5.30	25	- 5:05	- 5.30	51	- 4:39	- 5.30	71	- 4:19	- 5.30	31	- 4:59	- 5.30	33	- 4:57
- 5.15	59	- 4:16	- 5.15	25	- 4:50	- 5.15	43	- 4:32	- 5.15	25	- 4:50	- 5.15	51	- 4:24	- 5.15	70	- 4:05	- 5.15	30	- 4:45	- 5.15	33	- 4:42
- 5.00	58	- 4:02	- 5.00	24	- 4:36	- 5.00	45	- 4:15	- 5.00	24	- 4:36	- 5.00	50	- 4:10	- 5.00	69	- 3:51	- 5.00	29	- 4:31	- 5.00	32	- 4:28
- 4.45	57	- 3:48	- 4.45	23	- 4:22	- 4.45	45	- 4:00	- 4.45	24	- 4:21	- 4.45	50	- 3:55	- 4.45	69	- 3:36	- 4.45	29	- 4:16	- 4.45	32	- 4:13
- 4.30	56	- 3:34	- 4.30	22	- 4:08	- 4.30	45	- 3:45	- 4.30	23	- 4:07	- 4.30	50	- 3:40	- 4.30	69	- 3:21	- 4.30	29	- 4:01	- 4.30	32	- 3:58
- 4.15	56	- 3:19	- 4.15	21	- 3:54	- 4.15	45	- 3:30	- 4.15	23	- 3:52	- 4.15	50	- 3:25	- 4.15	69	- 3:06	- 4.15	28	- 3:47	- 4.15	31	- 3:44
- 4.00	55	- 3:05	- 4.00	21	- 3:39	- 4.00	46	- 3:14	- 4.00	23	- 3:37	- 4.00	49	- 3:11	- 4.00	69	- 2:51	- 4.00	28	- 3:32	- 4.00	31	- 3:29
- 3.45	54	- 2:51	- 3.45	21	- 3:24	- 3.45	45	- 3:00	- 3.45	23	- 3:22	- 3.45	50	- 2:55	- 3.45	70	- 2:35	- 3.45	28	- 3:17	- 3.45	31	- 3:14
- 3.30	54	- 2:36	- 3.30	21	- 3:09	- 3.30	45	- 2:45	- 3.30	23	- 3:07	- 3.30	50	- 2:40	- 3.30	70	- 2:20	- 3.30	28	- 3:02	- 3.30	31	- 2:59
- 3.15	53	- 2:22	- 3.15	21	- 2:54	- 3.15	44	- 2:31	- 3.15	23	- 2:52	- 3.15	50	- 2:25	- 3.15	71	- 2:04	- 3.15	28	- 2:47	- 3.15	31	- 2:44
- 3.00	52	- 2:08	- 3.00	21	- 2:39	- 3.00	44	- 2:16	- 3.00	23	- 2:37	- 3.00	51	- 2:09	- 3.00	71	- 1:49	- 3.00	28	- 2:32	- 3.00	31	- 2:29
- 2.45	53	- 1:52	- 2.45	20	- 2:25	- 2.45	42	- 2:03	- 2.45	23	- 2:22	- 2.45	51	- 1:54	- 2.45	73	- 1:32	- 2.45	29	- 2:16	- 2.45	31	- 2:14
- 2.30	53	- 1:37	- 2.30	20	- 2:10	- 2.30	41	- 1:49	- 2.30	23	- 2:07	- 2.30	52	- 1:38	- 2.30	74	- 1:16	- 2.30	29	- 2:01	- 2.30	31	- 1:59
- 2.15	53	- 1:22	- 2.15	19	- 1:56	- 2.15	40	- 1:35	- 2.15	24	- 1:51	- 2.15	53	- 1:22	- 2.15	75	- 1:00	- 2.15	30	- 1:45	- 2.15	30	- 1:45
- 2.00	53	- 1:07	- 2.00	19	- 1:41	- 2.00	39	- 1:21	- 2.00	24	- 1:36	- 2.00	53	- 1:07	- 2.00	77	- 0:43	- 2.00	30	- 1:30	- 2.00	30	- 1:30
- 1.45	54	- 0:51	- 1.45	19	- 1:26	- 1.45	37	- 1:08	- 1.45	24	- 1:21	- 1.45	55	- 0:50	- 1.45	79	- 0:26	- 1.45	31	- 1:14	- 1.45	31	- 1:14
- 1.30	54	- 0:36	- 1.30	19	- 1:11	- 1.30	36	- 0:54	- 1.30	25	- 1:05	- 1.30	56	- 0:34	- 1.30	81	- 0:09	- 1.30	31	- 0:59	- 1.30	32	- 0:58
- 1.15	55	- 0:20	- 1.15	20	- 0:55	- 1.15	35	- 0:40	- 1.15	26	- 0:49	- 1.15	58	- 0:17	- 1.15	84	+ 2:39	- 1.15	32	- 0:43	- 1.15	33	- 0:42
- 1.00	56	- 0:04	- 1.00	20	- 0:40	- 1.00	33	- 0:27	- 1.00	26	- 0:34	- 1.00	59	- 0:01	- 1.00	86	+ 0:26	- 1.00	33	- 0:27	- 1.00	34	- 0:26
- 0.45	57	+ 0:12	- 0.45	20	- 0:25	- 0.45	32	- 0:13	- 0.45	27	- 0:18	- 0.45	61	+ 1:46	- 0.45	89	+ 0:44	- 0.45	34	- 0:11	- 0.45	35	- 0:10
- 0.30	59	+ 0:29	- 0.30	21	- 0:09	- 0.30	32	+ 0:02	- 0.30	28	- 0:02	- 0.30	63	+ 0:33	- 0.30	92	+ 1:02	- 0.30	36	+ 0:06	- 0.30	37	+ 0:07
- 0.15	60	+ 0:45	- 0.15	22	+ 0:07	- 0.15	31	+ 0:16	- 0.15	29	+ 0:44	- 0.15	64	+ 0:49	- 0.15	95	+ 1:20	- 0.15	37	+ 0:22	- 0.15	39	+ 0:24
HW	61	+ 1:01	HW	22	+ 0:22	HW	30	+ 0:30	HW	30	+ 0:30	HW	66	+ 1:06	HW	98	+ 1:38	HW	39	+ 0:39	HW	41	+ 0:41
+ 0.15	63	+ 1:18	+ 0.15	23	+ 0:38	+ 0.15	30	+ 0:45	+ 0.15	31	+ 0:46	+ 0.15	67	+ 1:22	+ 0.15	100	+ 1:55	+ 0.15	41	+ 0:56	+ 0.15	42	+ 0:57
+ 0.30	65	+ 1:35	+ 0.30	25	+ 0:55	+ 0.30	29	+ 0:59	+ 0.30	32	+ 1:02	+ 0.30	69	+ 1:39	+ 0.30	102	+ 2:12	+ 0.30	43	+ 1:13	+ 0.30	43	+ 1:13
+ 0.45	66	+ 1:51	+ 0.45	26	+ 1:11	+ 0.45	29	+ 1:14	+ 0.45	34	+ 1:19	+ 0.45	70	+ 1:55	+ 0.45	104	+ 2:29	+ 0.45	44	+ 1:29	+ 0.45	44	+ 1:29
+ 1.00	68	+ 2:08	+ 1.00	27	+ 1:27	+ 1.00	29	+ 1:29	+ 1.00	35	+ 1:35	+ 1.00	71	+ 2:11	+ 1.00	105	+ 2:45	+ 1.00	46	+ 1:46	+ 1.00	45	+ 1:45
+ 1.15	68	+ 2:23	+ 1.15	29	+ 1:44	+ 1.15	28	+ 1:43	+ 1.15	35	+ 1:50	+ 1.15	71	+ 2:26	+ 1.15	105	+ 3:00	+ 1.15	47	+ 2:02	+ 1.15	45	+ 2:00
+ 1.30	69	+ 2:39	+ 1.30	31	+ 2:01	+ 1.30	28	+ 1:58	+ 1.30	36	+ 2:06	+ 1.30	72	+ 2:42	+ 1.30	105	+ 3:15	+ 1.30	47	+ 2:17	+ 1.30	45	+ 2:15
+ 1.45	70	+ 2:55	+ 1.45	32	+ 2:17	+ 1.45	28	+ 2:13	+ 1.45	36	+ 2:21	+ 1.45	72	+ 2:57	+ 1.45	105	+ 3:30	+ 1.45	48	+ 2:33	+ 1.45	45	+ 2:30
+ 2.00	71	+ 3:11	+ 2.00	34	+ 2:34	+ 2.00	27	+ 2:27	+ 2.00	37	+ 2:37	+ 2.00	72	+ 3:12	+ 2.00	105	+ 3:45	+ 2.00	48	+ 2:48	+ 2.00	45	+ 2:45
+ 2.15	71	+ 3:26	+ 2.15	36	+ 2:51	+ 2.15	27	+ 2:42	+ 2.15	36	+ 2:51	+ 2.15	72	+ 3:27	+ 2.15	104	+ 3:59	+ 2.15	48	+ 3:03	+ 2.15	45	+ 3:00
+ 2.30	71	+ 3:41	+ 2.30	38	+ 3:08	+ 2.30	27	+ 2:57	+ 2.30	36	+ 3:06	+ 2.30	71	+ 3:41	+ 2.30	102	+ 4:12	+ 2.30	47	+ 3:17	+ 2.30	44	+ 3:14
+ 2.45	71	+ 3:56	+ 2.45	39	+ 3:24	+ 2.45	26	+ 3:11	+ 2.45	36	+ 3:21	+ 2.45	70	+ 3:55	+ 2.45	101	+ 4:26	+ 2.45	47	+ 3:32	+ 2.45	43	+ 3:28
+ 3.00	71	+ 4:11	+ 3.00	41	+ 3:41	+ 3.00	26	+ 3:26	+ 3.00	35	+ 3:35	+ 3.00	70	+ 4:10	+ 3.00	99	+ 4:39	+ 3.00	47	+ 3:47	+ 3.00	43	+ 3:43
+ 3.15	70	+ 4:25	+ 3.15	41	+ 3:56	+ 3.15	27	+ 3:42	+ 3.15	35	+ 3:50	+ 3.15	69	+ 4:24	+ 3.15	98	+ 4:53	+ 3.15	46	+ 4:01	+ 3.15	42	+ 3:57
+ 3.30	69	+ 4:39	+ 3.30	41	+ 4:11	+ 3.30	27	+ 3:57	+ 3.30	34	+ 4:04	+ 3.30	67	+ 4:37	+ 3.30	96	+ 5:06	+ 3.30	45	+ 4:15	+ 3.30	41	+ 4:11
+ 3.45	68	+ 4:53	+ 3.45	41	+ 4:26	+ 3.45	27	+ 4:12	+ 3.45	33	+ 4:18	+ 3.45	66	+ 4:51	+ 3.45	94	+ 5:19	+ 3.45	44	+ 4:29	+ 3.45	41	+ 4:26
+ 4.00	67	+ 5:07	+ 4.00	40	+ 4:40	+ 4.00	28	+ 4:28	+ 4.00	33	+ 4:33	+ 4.00	65	+ 5:05	+ 4.00	92	+ 5:32	+ 4.00	43	+ 4:43	+ 4.00	40	+ 4:40
+ 4.15	66	+ 5:21	+ 4.15	39	+ 4:54	+ 4.15	29	+ 4:44	+ 4.15	32	+ 4:47	+ 4.15	64	+ 5:19	+ 4.15	90	+ 5:45	+ 4.15	42	+ 4:57	+ 4.15	40	+ 4:55
+ 4.30	65	+ 5:35	+ 4.30	38	+ 5:08	+ 4.30	29	+ 4:59	+ 4.30	31	+ 5:01	+ 4.30	62	+ 5:32	+ 4.30	88	+ 5:58	+ 4.30	41	+ 5:11	+ 4.30	39	+ 5:09
+ 4.45	65	+ 5:50	+ 4.45	37	+ 5:22	+ 4.45	30	+ 5:15	+ 4.45	31	+ 5:16	+ 4.45	61	+ 5:46	+ 4.45	86	- 5:49	+ 4.45	40	+ 5:25	+ 4.45	39	+ 5:24
+ 5.00	64	- 5:56	+ 5.00	36	+ 5:36	+ 5.00	31	+ 5:31	+ 5.00	30	+ 5:30	+ 5.00	60	- 6:00	+ 5.00	84	- 5:36	+ 5.00	39	+ 5:39	+ 5.00	38	+ 5:38
+ 5.15	63	- 5:42	+ 5.15	35	+ 5:50	+ 5.15	32	+ 5:47	+ 5.15	30	+ 5:45	+ 5.15	59	- 5:46	+ 5.15	83	- 5:22	+ 5.15	39	+ 5:54	+ 5.15	37	+ 5:52
+ 5.30	63	- 5:27	+ 5.30	33	- 5:57	+ 5.30	33	- 5:57	+ 5.30	29	+ 5:59	+ 5.30	58	- 5:32	+ 5.30	81	- 5:09	+ 5.30	38	- 5:52	+ 5.30	37	- 5:53
+ 5.45	62	- 5:13	+ 5.45	32	- 5:43	+ 5.45	34	- 5:41	+ 5.45	29	- 5:46	+ 5.45	57	- 5:18	+ 5.45	80	- 4:55	+ 5.45	37	- 5:38	+ 5.45	36	- 5:39
+ 6.00	62	- 4:58	+ 6.00	31	- 5:29	+ 6.00	35	- 5:25	+ 6.00	28	- 5:32	+ 6.00	56	- 5:04	+ 6.00	78	- 4:42	+ 6.00	36	- 5:24	+ 6.00	35	- 5:25

River Colne

NORTH BOUND

Table E - Ramsgate to Swale and Medway via Copperas Channel

Neaps — All times relate to HW Sheerness — **Time to cover Sectors (in minutes) at 4.0 kts**

W E S T B O U N D

	Medway / Swale			Medway / Swale			Medway / Swale			Ignore for Medway / Swale			Medway			Medway			Medway	
	E1 Ramsgate to North Foreland			**E2** North Foreland to SE Margate			**E3** SE Margate to Copperas			**E4** Copperas to Swale Landfall			**E5** Copperas to Kentish Flats			**E6** Kentish Flats to Spile			**E7** Spile to Medway Channel	
Time	*Duration*	*Time at End of Sector*	*Time*	*Duration*	*Time at End of Sector*	*Time*	*Duration*	*Time at End of Sector*	*Time*	*Duration*	*Time at End of Sector*	*Time*	*Duration*	*Time at End of Sector*	*Time*	*Duration*	*Time at End of Sector*	*Time*	*Duration*	*Time at End of Sector*
- 6.00	**99**	**- 4:21**	**- 6.00**	**65**	**- 4:55**	**- 6.00**	**77**	**- 4:43**	**- 6.00**	**74**	**- 4:46**	**- 6.00**	**74**	**- 4:46**	**- 6.00**	**63**	**- 4:57**	**- 6.00**	**69**	**- 4:51**
- 5.45	100	- 4:05	- 5.45	64	- 4:41	- 5.45	76	- 4:29	- 5.45	73	- 4:32	- 5.45	73	- 4:32	- 5.45	63	- 4:42	- 5.45	69	- 4:36
- 5.30	101	- 3:49	- 5.30	63	- 4:27	- 5.30	75	- 4:15	- 5.30	71	- 4:19	- 5.30	73	- 4:17	- 5.30	62	- 4:28	- 5.30	69	- 4:21
- 5.15	100	- 3:35	- 5.15	62	- 4:13	- 5.15	74	- 4:01	- 5.15	70	- 4:05	- 5.15	72	- 4:03	- 5.15	62	- 4:13	- 5.15	69	- 4:06
- 5.00	**98**	**- 3:22**	**- 5.00**	**60**	**- 4:00**	**- 5.00**	**72**	**- 3:48**	**- 5.00**	**69**	**- 3:51**	**- 5.00**	**71**	**- 3:49**	**- 5.00**	**62**	**- 3:58**	**- 5.00**	**68**	**- 3:52**
- 4.45	97	- 3:08	- 4.45	60	- 3:45	- 4.45	72	- 3:33	- 4.45	69	- 3:36	- 4.45	71	- 3:34	- 4.45	62	- 3:43	- 4.45	69	- 3:36
- 4.30	95	- 2:55	- 4.30	59	- 3:31	- 4.30	71	- 3:19	- 4.30	68	- 3:22	- 4.30	71	- 3:19	- 4.30	62	- 3:28	- 4.30	69	- 3:21
- 4.15	89	- 2:46	- 4.15	59	- 3:16	- 4.15	70	- 3:05	- 4.15	68	- 3:07	- 4.15	70	- 3:05	- 4.15	62	- 3:13	- 4.15	69	- 3:06
- 4.00	**84**	**- 2:36**	**- 4.00**	**58**	**- 3:02**	**- 4.00**	**70**	**- 2:50**	**- 4.00**	**68**	**- 2:52**	**- 4.00**	**70**	**- 2:50**	**- 4.00**	**63**	**- 2:57**	**- 4.00**	**70**	**- 2:50**
- 3.45	78	- 2:27	- 3.45	58	- 2:47	- 3.45	69	- 2:36	- 3.45	67	- 2:38	- 3.45	70	- 2:35	- 3.45	63	- 2:42	- 3.45	70	- 2:35
- 3.30	72	- 2:18	- 3.30	57	- 2:33	- 3.30	68	- 2:22	- 3.30	67	- 2:23	- 3.30	70	- 2:20	- 3.30	63	- 2:27	- 3.30	70	- 2:20
- 3.15	68	- 2:07	- 3.15	57	- 2:18	- 3.15	68	- 2:07	- 3.15	67	- 2:08	- 3.15	70	- 2:05	- 3.15	63	- 2:12	- 3.15	70	- 2:05
- 3.00	**64**	**- 1:56**	**- 3.00**	**56**	**- 2:04**	**- 3.00**	**67**	**- 1:53**	**- 3.00**	**67**	**- 1:53**	**- 3.00**	**70**	**- 1:50**	**- 3.00**	**64**	**- 1:56**	**- 3.00**	**70**	**- 1:50**
- 2.45	60	- 1:45	- 2.45	57	- 1:48	- 2.45	68	- 1:37	- 2.45	68	- 1:37	- 2.45	71	- 1:34	- 2.45	64	- 1:41	- 2.45	70	- 1:35
- 2.30	56	- 1:34	- 2.30	58	- 1:32	- 2.30	69	- 1:21	- 2.30	69	- 1:21	- 2.30	72	- 1:18	- 2.30	64	- 1:26	- 2.30	70	- 1:20
- 2.15	55	- 1:20	- 2.15	58	- 1:17	- 2.15	70	- 1:05	- 2.15	70	- 1:05	- 2.15	72	- 1:03	- 2.15	64	- 1:11	- 2.15	71	- 1:04
- 2.00	**54**	**- 1:06**	**- 2.00**	**59**	**- 1:01**	**- 2.00**	**71**	**- 0:49**	**- 2.00**	**70**	**- 0:50**	**- 2.00**	**73**	**- 0:47**	**- 2.00**	**64**	**- 0:56**	**- 2.00**	**71**	**- 0:49**
- 1.45	53	- 0:52	- 1.45	61	- 0:44	- 1.45	74	- 0:31	- 1.45	73	- 0:32	- 1.45	74	- 0:31	- 1.45	65	- 0:40	- 1.45	72	- 0:33
- 1.30	52	- 0:38	- 1.30	64	- 0:26	- 1.30	77	- 0:13	- 1.30	75	- 0:15	- 1.30	76	- 0:14	- 1.30	66	- 0:24	- 1.30	73	- 0:17
- 1.15	52	- 0:23	- 1.15	66	- 0:09	- 1.15	80	+ 0:05	- 1.15	78	+ 0:03	- 1.15	78	+ 0:03	- 1.15	67	- 0:08	- 1.15	75	HW
- 1.00	**53**	**- 0:07**	**- 1.00**	**68**	**+ 0:08**	**- 1.00**	**83**	**+ 0:23**	**- 1.00**	**80**	**+ 0:20**	**- 1.00**	**79**	**+ 0:19**	**- 1.00**	**69**	**+ 0:09**	**- 1.00**	**76**	**+ 0:16**
- 0.45	53	+ 0:08	- 0.45	72	+ 0:27	- 0.45	88	+ 0:43	- 0.45	85	+ 0:40	- 0.45	81	+ 0:36	- 0.45	71	+ 0:26	- 0.45	78	+ 0:33
- 0.30	54	+ 0:24	- 0.30	75	+ 0:45	- 0.30	94	+ 1:04	- 0.30	90	+ 1:00	- 0.30	84	+ 0:54	- 0.30	73	+ 0:43	- 0.30	81	+ 0:51
- 0.15	55	+ 0:40	- 0.15	79	+ 1:04	- 0.15	99	+ 1:24	- 0.15	95	+ 1:20	- 0.15	86	+ 1:11	- 0.15	75	+ 1:00	- 0.15	83	+ 1:08
HW	**56**	**+ 0:56**	**HW**	**82**	**+ 1:22**	**HW**	**104**	**+ 1:44**	**HW**	**100**	**+ 1:40**	**HW**	**88**	**+ 1:28**	**HW**	**78**	**+ 1:18**	**HW**	**86**	**+ 1:26**
+ 0.15	57	+ 1:12	+ 0.15	87	+ 1:42	+ 0.15	108	+ 2:03	+ 0.15	104	+ 1:59	+ 0.15	91	+ 1:46	+ 0.15	78	+ 1:33	+ 0.15	88	+ 1:43
+ 0.30	58	+ 1:28	+ 0.30	92	+ 2:02	+ 0.30	113	+ 2:23	+ 0.30	107	+ 2:17	+ 0.30	93	+ 2:03	+ 0.30	81	+ 1:51	+ 0.30	91	+ 2:01
+ 0.45	60	+ 1:45	+ 0.45	98	+ 2:23	+ 0.45	117	+ 2:42	+ 0.45	111	+ 2:36	+ 0.45	96	+ 2:21	+ 0.45	84	+ 2:09	+ 0.45	94	+ 2:19
+ 1.00	**62**	**+ 2:02**	**+ 1.00**	**103**	**+ 2:43**	**+ 1.00**	**121**	**+ 3:01**	**+ 1.00**	**114**	**+ 2:54**	**+ 1.00**	**98**	**+ 2:38**	**+ 1.00**	**87**	**+ 2:27**	**+ 1.00**	**97**	**+ 2:37**
+ 1.15	64	+ 2:19	+ 1.15	102	+ 2:57	+ 1.15	121	+ 3:16	+ 1.15	115	+ 3:10	+ 1.15	98	+ 2:53	+ 1.15	90	+ 2:45	+ 1.15	96	+ 2:51
+ 1.30	66	+ 2:36	+ 1.30	102	+ 3:12	+ 1.30	120	+ 3:30	+ 1.30	115	+ 3:25	+ 1.30	98	+ 3:08	+ 1.30	88	+ 2:58	+ 1.30	94	+ 3:04
+ 1.45	67	+ 2:52	+ 1.45	102	+ 3:27	+ 1.45	120	+ 3:45	+ 1.45	115	+ 3:40	+ 1.45	97	+ 3:22	+ 1.45	85	+ 3:10	+ 1.45	93	+ 3:18
+ 2.00	**69**	**+ 3:09**	**+ 2.00**	**102**	**+ 3:42**	**+ 2.00**	**119**	**+ 3:59**	**+ 2.00**	**115**	**+ 3:55**	**+ 2.00**	**97**	**+ 3:37**	**+ 2.00**	**83**	**+ 3:23**	**+ 2.00**	**92**	**+ 3:32**
+ 2.15	71	+ 3:26	+ 2.15	100	+ 3:55	+ 2.15	117	+ 4:12	+ 2.15	113	+ 4:08	+ 2.15	96	+ 3:51	+ 2.15	80	+ 3:35	+ 2.15	89	+ 3:44
+ 2.30	73	+ 3:43	+ 2.30	98	+ 4:08	+ 2.30	115	+ 4:25	+ 2.30	111	+ 4:21	+ 2.30	95	+ 4:05	+ 2.30	79	+ 3:49	+ 2.30	86	+ 3:56
+ 2.45	75	+ 4:00	+ 2.45	96	+ 4:21	+ 2.45	113	+ 4:38	+ 2.45	109	+ 4:34	+ 2.45	93	+ 4:18	+ 2.45	77	+ 4:02	+ 2.45	83	+ 4:08
+ 3.00	**76**	**+ 4:16**	**+ 3.00**	**94**	**+ 4:34**	**+ 3.00**	**111**	**+ 4:51**	**+ 3.00**	**107**	**+ 4:47**	**+ 3.00**	**92**	**+ 4:32**	**+ 3.00**	**75**	**+ 4:15**	**+ 3.00**	**80**	**+ 4:20**
+ 3.15	78	+ 4:33	+ 3.15	92	+ 4:47	+ 3.15	109	+ 5:04	+ 3.15	104	+ 4:59	+ 3.15	90	+ 4:45	+ 3.15	74	+ 4:29	+ 3.15	79	+ 4:34
+ 3.30	79	+ 4:49	+ 3.30	89	+ 4:59	+ 3.30	107	+ 5:17	+ 3.30	102	+ 5:12	+ 3.30	88	+ 4:58	+ 3.30	72	+ 4:42	+ 3.30	77	+ 4:47
+ 3.45	80	+ 5:05	+ 3.45	86	+ 5:11	+ 3.45	105	+ 5:30	+ 3.45	100	+ 5:25	+ 3.45	87	+ 5:12	+ 3.45	71	+ 4:56	+ 3.45	76	+ 5:01
+ 4.00	**81**	**+ 5:21**	**+ 4.00**	**83**	**+ 5:23**	**+ 4.00**	**103**	**+ 5:43**	**+ 4.00**	**98**	**+ 5:38**	**+ 4.00**	**85**	**+ 5:25**	**+ 4.00**	**69**	**+ 5:09**	**+ 4.00**	**74**	**+ 5:14**
+ 4.15	82	+ 5:37	+ 4.15	82	+ 5:37	+ 4.15	100	+ 5:55	+ 4.15	96	+ 5:51	+ 4.15	84	+ 5:39	+ 4.15	68	+ 5:23	+ 4.15	74	+ 5:29
+ 4.30	83	+ 5:53	+ 4.30	80	+ 5:50	+ 4.30	98	- 5:52	+ 4.30	95	- 5:55	+ 4.30	83	+ 5:53	+ 4.30	67	+ 5:37	+ 4.30	73	+ 5:43
+ 4.45	85	- 5:50	+ 4.45	79	- 5:56	+ 4.45	96	- 5:39	+ 4.45	93	- 5:42	+ 4.45	81	- 5:54	+ 4.45	67	+ 5:52	+ 4.45	72	+ 5:57
+ 5.00	**87**	**- 5:33**	**+ 5.00**	**77**	**- 5:43**	**+ 5.00**	**94**	**- 5:26**	**+ 5.00**	**91**	**- 5:29**	**+ 5.00**	**80**	**- 5:40**	**+ 5.00**	**66**	**- 5:54**	**+ 5.00**	**72**	**- 5:48**
+ 5.15	88	- 5:17	+ 5.15	76	- 5:29	+ 5.15	92	- 5:13	+ 5.15	94	- 5:11	+ 5.15	79	- 5:26	+ 5.15	65	- 5:40	+ 5.15	72	- 5:33
+ 5.30	90	- 5:00	+ 5.30	75	- 5:15	+ 5.30	90	- 5:00	+ 5.30	96	- 4:54	+ 5.30	79	- 5:11	+ 5.30	65	- 5:25	+ 5.30	72	- 5:18
+ 5.45	96	- 4:39	+ 5.45	74	- 5:01	+ 5.45	89	- 4:46	+ 5.45	98	- 4:37	+ 5.45	78	- 4:57	+ 5.45	65	- 5:10	+ 5.45	72	- 5:03
+ 6.00	**97**	**- 4:23**	**+ 6.00**	**72**	**- 4:48**	**+ 6.00**	**87**	**- 4:33**	**+ 6.00**	**101**	**- 4:19**	**+ 6.00**	**77**	**- 4:43**	**+ 6.00**	**65**	**- 4:55**	**+ 6.00**	**72**	**- 4:48**

Table E - Ramsgate to Swale and Medway via Copperas Channel

Time to cover Sectors (in minutes) at 4.0 kts — All times relate to HW Sheerness — **Springs**

Medway (E1–E3) | Ignore for Medway (E4) | Medway (E5–E7)

Swale (E1–E4)

Time	E1 Ramsgate to North Foreland Duration	E1 Time at End of Sector	Time	E2 North Foreland to SE Margate Duration	E2 Time at End of Sector	Time	E3 SE Margate to Copperas Duration	E3 Time at End of Sector	Time	E4 Copperas to Swale Landfall Duration	E4 Time at End of Sector	Time	E5 Copperas to Kentish Flats Duration	E5 Time at End of Sector	Time	E6 Kentish Flats to Spile Duration	E6 Time at End of Sector	Time	E7 Spile to Medway Channel Duration	E7 Time at End of Sector
- 6.00	115	- 4:05	- 6.00	62	- 4:58	- 6.00	73	- 4:47	- 6.00	68	- 4:52	- 6.00	72	- 4:48	- 6.00	60	- 5:00	- 6.00	66	- 4:54
- 5.45	117	- 3:48	- 5.45	60	- 4:45	- 5.45	71	- 4:34	- 5.45	66	- 4:39	- 5.45	71	- 4:34	- 5.45	60	- 4:45	- 5.45	66	- 4:39
- 5.30	118	- 3:32	- 5.30	58	- 4:32	- 5.30	69	- 4:21	- 5.30	64	- 4:26	- 5.30	70	- 4:20	- 5.30	59	- 4:31	- 5.30	66	- 4:24
- 5.15	114	- 3:21	- 5.15	57	- 4:18	- 5.15	67	- 4:08	- 5.15	63	- 4:12	- 5.15	69	- 4:06	- 5.15	59	- 4:16	- 5.15	65	- 4:10
- 5.00	110	- 3:10	- 5.00	55	- 4:05	- 5.00	65	- 3:55	- 5.00	61	- 3:59	- 5.00	68	- 3:52	- 5.00	58	- 4:02	- 5.00	65	- 3:55
- 4.45	106	- 2:59	- 4.45	54	- 3:51	- 4.45	64	- 3:41	- 4.45	61	- 3:44	- 4.45	67	- 3:38	- 4.45	59	- 3:46	- 4.45	65	- 3:40
- 4.30	102	- 2:48	- 4.30	53	- 3:37	- 4.30	63	- 3:27	- 4.30	60	- 3:30	- 4.30	67	- 3:23	- 4.30	59	- 3:31	- 4.30	66	- 3:24
- 4.15	95	- 2:40	- 4.15	53	- 3:22	- 4.15	62	- 3:13	- 4.15	60	- 3:15	- 4.15	66	- 3:09	- 4.15	59	- 3:16	- 4.15	66	- 3:09
- 4.00	88	- 2:32	- 4.00	52	- 3:08	- 4.00	61	- 2:59	- 4.00	60	- 3:00	- 4.00	66	- 2:54	- 4.00	60	- 3:00	- 4.00	66	- 2:54
- 3.45	80	- 2:25	- 3.45	51	- 2:54	- 3.45	61	- 2:44	- 3.45	60	- 2:45	- 3.45	66	- 2:39	- 3.45	60	- 2:45	- 3.45	67	- 2:38
- 3.30	73	- 2:17	- 3.30	51	- 2:39	- 3.30	60	- 2:30	- 3.30	60	- 2:30	- 3.30	66	- 2:24	- 3.30	60	- 2:30	- 3.30	67	- 2:23
- 3.15	66	- 2:09	- 3.15	50	- 2:25	- 3.15	59	- 2:16	- 3.15	60	- 2:15	- 3.15	66	- 2:09	- 3.15	61	- 2:14	- 3.15	67	- 2:08
- 3.00	60	- 2:00	- 3.00	49	- 2:11	- 3.00	58	- 2:02	- 3.00	59	- 2:01	- 3.00	66	- 1:54	- 3.00	61	- 1:59	- 3.00	68	- 1:52
- 2.45	53	- 1:52	- 2.45	50	- 1:55	- 2.45	59	- 1:46	- 2.45	60	- 1:45	- 2.45	66	- 1:39	- 2.45	61	- 1:44	- 2.45	68	- 1:37
- 2.30	47	- 1:43	- 2.30	51	- 1:39	- 2.30	61	- 1:29	- 2.30	61	- 1:29	- 2.30	67	- 1:23	- 2.30	62	- 1:28	- 2.30	68	- 1:22
- 2.15	45	- 1:30	- 2.15	52	- 1:23	- 2.15	62	- 1:13	- 2.15	62	- 1:13	- 2.15	68	- 1:07	- 2.15	62	- 1:13	- 2.15	69	- 1:06
- 2.00	44	- 1:16	- 2.00	53	- 1:07	- 2.00	64	- 0:56	- 2.00	63	- 0:57	- 2.00	68	- 0:52	- 2.00	62	- 0:58	- 2.00	69	- 0:51
- 1.45	43	- 1:02	- 1.45	56	- 0:49	- 1.45	68	- 0:37	- 1.45	67	- 0:38	- 1.45	70	- 0:35	- 1.45	64	- 0:41	- 1.45	71	- 0:34
- 1.30	42	- 0:48	- 1.30	59	- 0:31	- 1.30	72	- 0:18	- 1.30	71	- 0:19	- 1.30	73	- 0:17	- 1.30	66	- 0:24	- 1.30	73	- 0:17
- 1.15	42	- 0:33	- 1.15	62	- 0:13	- 1.15	76	+ 0:01	- 1.15	74	- 0:01	- 1.15	75	+ 0:00	- 1.15	67	- 0:08	- 1.15	74	- 0:01
- 1.00	43	- 0:17	- 1.00	65	+ 0:05	- 1.00	80	+ 0:20	- 1.00	78	+ 0:18	- 1.00	77	+ 0:17	- 1.00	69	+ 0:09	- 1.00	76	+ 0:16
- 0.45	44	- 0:01	- 0.45	73	+ 0:28	- 0.45	89	+ 0:44	- 0.45	86	+ 0:41	- 0.45	81	+ 0:36	- 0.45	74	+ 0:29	- 0.45	82	+ 0:37
- 0.30	44	+ 0:14	- 0.30	80	+ 0:50	- 0.30	98	+ 1:08	- 0.30	94	+ 1:04	- 0.30	86	+ 0:56	- 0.30	79	+ 0:49	- 0.30	87	+ 0:57
- 0.15	46	+ 0:31	- 0.15	88	+ 1:13	- 0.15	108	+ 1:33	- 0.15	102	+ 1:27	- 0.15	90	+ 1:15	- 0.15	84	+ 1:09	- 0.15	93	+ 1:18
HW	48	+ 0:48	HW	95	+ 1:35	HW	117	+ 1:57	HW	110	+ 1:50	HW	95	+ 1:35	HW	90	+ 1:30	HW	98	+ 1:38
+ 0.15	49	+ 1:04	+ 0.15	100	+ 1:55	+ 0.15	122	+ 2:17	+ 0.15	116	+ 2:11	+ 0.15	97	+ 1:52	+ 0.15	92	+ 1:47	+ 0.15	100	+ 1:55
+ 0.30	51	+ 1:21	+ 0.30	106	+ 2:16	+ 0.30	127	+ 2:37	+ 0.30	121	+ 2:31	+ 0.30	100	+ 2:10	+ 0.30	94	+ 2:04	+ 0.30	102	+ 2:12
+ 0.45	54	+ 1:39	+ 0.45	111	+ 2:36	+ 0.45	132	+ 2:57	+ 0.45	126	+ 2:51	+ 0.45	103	+ 2:28	+ 0.45	96	+ 2:21	+ 0.45	104	+ 2:29
+ 1.00	56	+ 1:56	+ 1.00	116	+ 2:56	+ 1.00	137	+ 3:17	+ 1.00	131	+ 3:11	+ 1.00	106	+ 2:46	+ 1.00	99	+ 2:39	+ 1.00	105	+ 2:45
+ 1.15	59	+ 2:14	+ 1.15	116	+ 3:11	+ 1.15	136	+ 3:31	+ 1.15	130	+ 3:25	+ 1.15	106	+ 3:01	+ 1.15	96	+ 2:51	+ 1.15	103	+ 2:58
+ 1.30	62	+ 2:32	+ 1.30	115	+ 3:25	+ 1.30	135	+ 3:45	+ 1.30	129	+ 3:39	+ 1.30	105	+ 3:15	+ 1.30	94	+ 3:04	+ 1.30	100	+ 3:10
+ 1.45	65	+ 2:50	+ 1.45	114	+ 3:39	+ 1.45	134	+ 3:59	+ 1.45	128	+ 3:53	+ 1.45	104	+ 3:29	+ 1.45	92	+ 3:17	+ 1.45	98	+ 3:23
+ 2.00	69	+ 3:09	+ 2.00	114	+ 3:54	+ 2.00	133	+ 4:13	+ 2.00	127	+ 4:07	+ 2.00	104	+ 3:44	+ 2.00	90	+ 3:30	+ 2.00	96	+ 3:36
+ 2.15	72	+ 3:27	+ 2.15	111	+ 4:06	+ 2.15	129	+ 4:24	+ 2.15	124	+ 4:19	+ 2.15	102	+ 3:57	+ 2.15	86	+ 3:41	+ 2.15	92	+ 3:47
+ 2.30	75	+ 3:45	+ 2.30	108	+ 4:18	+ 2.30	126	+ 4:36	+ 2.30	120	+ 4:30	+ 2.30	100	+ 4:10	+ 2.30	83	+ 3:53	+ 2.30	89	+ 3:59
+ 2.45	77	+ 4:02	+ 2.45	104	+ 4:29	+ 2.45	122	+ 4:47	+ 2.45	117	+ 4:42	+ 2.45	98	+ 4:23	+ 2.45	80	+ 4:05	+ 2.45	86	+ 4:11
+ 3.00	79	+ 4:19	+ 3.00	101	+ 4:41	+ 3.00	119	+ 4:59	+ 3.00	114	+ 4:54	+ 3.00	96	+ 4:36	+ 3.00	77	+ 4:17	+ 3.00	83	+ 4:23
+ 3.15	80	+ 4:35	+ 3.15	99	+ 4:54	+ 3.15	116	+ 5:11	+ 3.15	111	+ 5:06	+ 3.15	94	+ 4:49	+ 3.15	74	+ 4:29	+ 3.15	81	+ 4:36
+ 3.30	82	+ 4:52	+ 3.30	96	+ 5:06	+ 3.30	112	+ 5:22	+ 3.30	107	+ 5:17	+ 3.30	92	+ 5:02	+ 3.30	72	+ 4:42	+ 3.30	78	+ 4:48
+ 3.45	85	+ 5:10	+ 3.45	93	+ 5:18	+ 3.45	109	+ 5:34	+ 3.45	104	+ 5:29	+ 3.45	90	+ 5:15	+ 3.45	70	+ 4:55	+ 3.45	76	+ 5:01
+ 4.00	88	+ 5:28	+ 4.00	90	+ 5:30	+ 4.00	106	+ 5:46	+ 4.00	101	+ 5:41	+ 4.00	88	+ 5:28	+ 4.00	68	+ 5:08	+ 4.00	74	+ 5:14
+ 4.15	91	+ 5:46	+ 4.15	88	+ 5:43	+ 4.15	103	+ 5:58	+ 4.15	97	+ 5:52	+ 4.15	86	+ 5:41	+ 4.15	67	+ 5:22	+ 4.15	73	+ 5:28
+ 4.30	94	- 5:56	+ 4.30	85	+ 5:55	+ 4.30	101	- 5:49	+ 4.30	94	- 5:56	+ 4.30	84	+ 5:54	+ 4.30	66	+ 5:36	+ 4.30	72	+ 5:42
+ 4.45	96	- 5:39	+ 4.45	82	- 5:53	+ 4.45	98	- 5:37	+ 4.45	91	- 5:44	+ 4.45	83	- 5:52	+ 4.45	65	+ 5:50	+ 4.45	71	+ 5:56
+ 5.00	98	- 5:22	+ 5.00	80	- 5:40	+ 5.00	95	- 5:25	+ 5.00	88	- 5:32	+ 5.00	81	- 5:39	+ 5.00	64	- 5:56	+ 5.00	70	- 5:50
+ 5.15	101	- 5:04	+ 5.15	78	- 5:27	+ 5.15	93	- 5:12	+ 5.15	86	- 5:19	+ 5.15	80	- 5:25	+ 5.15	64	- 5:41	+ 5.15	70	- 5:35
+ 5.30	98	- 4:52	+ 5.30	76	- 5:14	+ 5.30	91	- 4:59	+ 5.30	84	- 5:06	+ 5.30	78	- 5:12	+ 5.30	64	- 5:26	+ 5.30	70	- 5:20
+ 5.45	112	- 4:23	+ 5.45	75	- 5:00	+ 5.45	90	- 4:45	+ 5.45	82	- 4:53	+ 5.45	77	- 4:58	+ 5.45	64	- 5:11	+ 5.45	70	- 5:05
+ 6.00	114	- 4:06	+ 6.00	73	- 4:47	+ 6.00	88	- 4:32	+ 6.00	80	- 4:40	+ 6.00	76	- 4:44	+ 6.00	64	- 4:56	+ 6.00	70	- 4:50

WEST BOUND

Table E - Ramsgate to Swale and Medway via Copperas Channel

Neaps — All times relate to HW Sheerness — **Time to cover Sectors (in minutes) at 5.0 kts**

Medway: E1–E7 (E4: Ignore for Medway). Swale: E1–E4.

WEST BOUND

	E1 Ramsgate to North Foreland			E2 North Foreland to SE Margate			E3 SE Margate to Copperas			E4 Copperas to Swale Landfall			E5 Copperas to Kentish Flats			E6 Kentish Flats to Spile			E7 Spile to Medway Channel	
Time	*Duration*	*Time at End of Sector*	*Time*	*Duration*	*Time at End of Sector*	*Time*	*Duration*	*Time at End of Sector*	*Time*	*Duration*	*Time at End of Sector*	*Time*	*Duration*	*Time at End of Sector*	*Time*	*Duration*	*Time at End of Sector*	*Time*	*Duration*	*Time at End of Sector*
- 6.00	68	- 4:52	- 6.00	54	- 5:06	- 6.00	64	- 4:56	- 6.00	61	- 4:59	- 6.00	60	- 5:00	- 6.00	51	- 5:09	- 6.00	57	- 5:03
- 5.45	69	- 4:36	- 5.45	53	- 4:52	- 5.45	63	- 4:42	- 5.45	60	- 4:45	- 5.45	60	- 4:45	- 5.45	51	- 4:54	- 5.45	56	- 4:49
- 5.30	69	- 4:21	- 5.30	52	- 4:38	- 5.30	62	- 4:28	- 5.30	59	- 4:31	- 5.30	59	- 4:31	- 5.30	51	- 4:39	- 5.30	56	- 4:34
- 5.15	69	- 4:06	- 5.15	51	- 4:24	- 5.15	61	- 4:14	- 5.15	59	- 4:16	- 5.15	59	- 4:16	- 5.15	51	- 4:24	- 5.15	56	- 4:19
- 5.00	69	- 3:51	- 5.00	50	- 4:10	- 5.00	60	- 4:00	- 5.00	58	- 4:02	- 5.00	58	- 4:02	- 5.00	50	- 4:10	- 5.00	56	- 4:04
- 4.45	68	- 3:37	- 4.45	50	- 3:55	- 4.45	60	- 3:45	- 4.45	57	- 3:48	- 4.45	58	- 3:47	- 4.45	50	- 3:55	- 4.45	56	- 3:49
- 4.30	68	- 3:22	- 4.30	50	- 3:40	- 4.30	59	- 3:31	- 4.30	57	- 3:33	- 4.30	58	- 3:32	- 4.30	51	- 3:39	- 4.30	56	- 3:34
- 4.15	66	- 3:09	- 4.15	49	- 3:26	- 4.15	59	- 3:16	- 4.15	57	- 3:18	- 4.15	58	- 3:17	- 4.15	51	- 3:24	- 4.15	56	- 3:19
- 4.00	63	- 2:57	- 4.00	49	- 3:11	- 4.00	59	- 3:01	- 4.00	57	- 3:03	- 4.00	58	- 3:02	- 4.00	51	- 3:09	- 4.00	56	- 3:04
- 3.45	61	- 2:44	- 3.45	49	- 2:56	- 3.45	58	- 2:47	- 3.45	56	- 2:49	- 3.45	58	- 2:47	- 3.45	51	- 2:54	- 3.45	56	- 2:49
- 3.30	58	- 2:32	- 3.30	48	- 2:42	- 3.30	58	- 2:32	- 3.30	56	- 2:34	- 3.30	58	- 2:32	- 3.30	51	- 2:39	- 3.30	57	- 2:33
- 3.15	56	- 2:19	- 3.15	48	- 2:27	- 3.15	57	- 2:18	- 3.15	56	- 2:19	- 3.15	58	- 2:17	- 3.15	51	- 2:24	- 3.15	57	- 2:18
- 3.00	53	- 2:07	- 3.00	48	- 2:12	- 3.00	57	- 2:03	- 3.00	56	- 2:04	- 3.00	58	- 2:02	- 3.00	52	- 2:08	- 3.00	57	- 2:03
- 2.45	51	- 1:54	- 2.45	48	- 1:57	- 2.45	57	- 1:48	- 2.45	57	- 1:48	- 2.45	58	- 1:47	- 2.45	52	- 1:53	- 2.45	57	- 1:48
- 2.30	48	- 1:42	- 2.30	48	- 1:42	- 2.30	58	- 1:32	- 2.30	57	- 1:33	- 2.30	58	- 1:32	- 2.30	52	- 1:38	- 2.30	57	- 1:33
- 2.15	47	- 1:28	- 2.15	48	- 1:27	- 2.15	58	- 1:17	- 2.15	58	- 1:17	- 2.15	59	- 1:16	- 2.15	52	- 1:23	- 2.15	57	- 1:18
- 2.00	46	- 1:14	- 2.00	49	- 1:11	- 2.00	59	- 1:01	- 2.00	58	- 1:02	- 2.00	59	- 1:01	- 2.00	52	- 1:08	- 2.00	57	- 1:03
- 1.45	46	- 0:59	- 1.45	50	- 0:55	- 1.45	61	- 0:44	- 1.45	60	- 0:45	- 1.45	60	- 0:45	- 1.45	52	- 0:53	- 1.45	58	- 0:47
- 1.30	45	- 0:45	- 1.30	51	- 0:39	- 1.30	63	- 0:27	- 1.30	61	- 0:29	- 1.30	61	- 0:29	- 1.30	53	- 0:37	- 1.30	59	- 0:31
- 1.15	45	- 0:30	- 1.15	53	- 0:22	- 1.15	64	- 0:11	- 1.15	62	- 0:13	- 1.15	62	- 0:13	- 1.15	54	- 0:21	- 1.15	59	- 0:16
- 1.00	45	- 0:15	- 1.00	54	- 0:06	- 1.00	66	+ 0:06	- 1.00	64	+ 0:04	- 1.00	63	+ 0:03	- 1.00	54	- 0:06	- 1.00	60	HW
- 0.45	45	HW	- 0.45	56	+ 0:11	- 0.45	69	+ 0:24	- 0.45	66	+ 0:21	- 0.45	64	+ 0:19	- 0.45	56	+ 0:11	- 0.45	61	+ 0:16
- 0.30	45	+ 0:15	- 0.30	59	+ 0:29	- 0.30	72	+ 0:42	- 0.30	69	+ 0:39	- 0.30	66	+ 0:36	- 0.30	57	+ 0:27	- 0.30	63	+ 0:33
- 0.15	46	+ 0:31	- 0.15	61	+ 0:46	- 0.15	74	+ 0:59	- 0.15	72	+ 0:57	- 0.15	67	+ 0:52	- 0.15	59	+ 0:44	- 0.15	65	+ 0:50
HW	47	+ 0:47	HW	63	+ 1:03	HW	77	+ 1:17	HW	74	+ 1:14	HW	68	+ 1:08	HW	60	+ 1:00	HW	66	+ 1:06
+ 0.15	47	+ 1:02	+ 0.15	65	+ 1:20	+ 0.15	81	+ 1:36	+ 0.15	76	+ 1:31	+ 0.15	70	+ 1:25	+ 0.15	60	+ 1:15	+ 0.15	67	+ 1:22
+ 0.30	48	+ 1:18	+ 0.30	67	+ 1:37	+ 0.30	85	+ 1:55	+ 0.30	78	+ 1:48	+ 0.30	71	+ 1:41	+ 0.30	61	+ 1:31	+ 0.30	68	+ 1:38
+ 0.45	49	+ 1:34	+ 0.45	69	+ 1:54	+ 0.45	89	+ 2:14	+ 0.45	80	+ 2:05	+ 0.45	72	+ 1:57	+ 0.45	62	+ 1:47	+ 0.45	69	+ 1:54
+ 1.00	50	+ 1:50	+ 1.00	71	+ 2:11	+ 1.00	92	+ 2:32	+ 1.00	81	+ 2:21	+ 1.00	73	+ 2:13	+ 1.00	63	+ 2:03	+ 1.00	70	+ 2:10
+ 1.15	51	+ 2:06	+ 1.15	71	+ 2:26	+ 1.15	92	+ 2:47	+ 1.15	82	+ 2:37	+ 1.15	73	+ 2:28	+ 1.15	64	+ 2:19	+ 1.15	69	+ 2:24
+ 1.30	53	+ 2:23	+ 1.30	71	+ 2:41	+ 1.30	92	+ 3:02	+ 1.30	82	+ 2:52	+ 1.30	73	+ 2:43	+ 1.30	64	+ 2:34	+ 1.30	69	+ 2:39
+ 1.45	54	+ 2:39	+ 1.45	71	+ 2:56	+ 1.45	92	+ 3:17	+ 1.45	82	+ 3:07	+ 1.45	73	+ 2:58	+ 1.45	63	+ 2:48	+ 1.45	68	+ 2:53
+ 2.00	55	+ 2:55	+ 2.00	71	+ 3:11	+ 2.00	92	+ 3:32	+ 2.00	82	+ 3:22	+ 2.00	72	+ 3:12	+ 2.00	63	+ 3:03	+ 2.00	68	+ 3:08
+ 2.15	56	+ 3:11	+ 2.15	71	+ 3:26	+ 2.15	89	+ 3:44	+ 2.15	81	+ 3:36	+ 2.15	72	+ 3:27	+ 2.15	62	+ 3:17	+ 2.15	67	+ 3:22
+ 2.30	58	+ 3:28	+ 2.30	70	+ 3:40	+ 2.30	87	+ 3:57	+ 2.30	80	+ 3:50	+ 2.30	71	+ 3:41	+ 2.30	61	+ 3:31	+ 2.30	66	+ 3:36
+ 2.45	59	+ 3:44	+ 2.45	69	+ 3:54	+ 2.45	84	+ 4:09	+ 2.45	79	+ 4:04	+ 2.45	70	+ 3:55	+ 2.45	60	+ 3:45	+ 2.45	65	+ 3:50
+ 3.00	60	+ 4:00	+ 3.00	68	+ 4:08	+ 3.00	82	+ 4:22	+ 3.00	79	+ 4:19	+ 3.00	70	+ 4:10	+ 3.00	59	+ 3:59	+ 3.00	64	+ 4:04
+ 3.15	61	+ 4:16	+ 3.15	67	+ 4:22	+ 3.15	81	+ 4:36	+ 3.15	78	+ 4:33	+ 3.15	69	+ 4:24	+ 3.15	58	+ 4:13	+ 3.15	63	+ 4:18
+ 3.30	62	+ 4:32	+ 3.30	66	+ 4:36	+ 3.30	80	+ 4:50	+ 3.30	77	+ 4:47	+ 3.30	68	+ 4:38	+ 3.30	57	+ 4:27	+ 3.30	62	+ 4:32
+ 3.45	62	+ 4:47	+ 3.45	66	+ 4:51	+ 3.45	79	+ 5:04	+ 3.45	75	+ 5:00	+ 3.45	68	+ 4:53	+ 3.45	57	+ 4:42	+ 3.45	61	+ 4:46
+ 4.00	63	+ 5:03	+ 4.00	65	+ 5:05	+ 4.00	78	+ 5:18	+ 4.00	74	+ 5:14	+ 4.00	67	+ 5:07	+ 4.00	56	+ 4:56	+ 4.00	60	+ 5:00
+ 4.15	64	+ 5:19	+ 4.15	64	+ 5:19	+ 4.15	77	+ 5:32	+ 4.15	73	+ 5:28	+ 4.15	67	+ 5:22	+ 4.15	55	+ 5:10	+ 4.15	59	+ 5:14
+ 4.30	64	+ 5:34	+ 4.30	63	+ 5:33	+ 4.30	76	+ 5:46	+ 4.30	72	+ 5:42	+ 4.30	66	+ 5:36	+ 4.30	54	+ 5:24	+ 4.30	59	+ 5:29
+ 4.45	64	+ 5:49	+ 4.45	62	+ 5:47	+ 4.45	74	+ 5:59	+ 4.45	70	+ 5:55	+ 4.45	65	+ 5:50	+ 4.45	54	+ 5:39	+ 4.45	58	+ 5:43
+ 5.00	65	- 5:55	+ 5.00	61	- 5:59	+ 5.00	73	- 5:47	+ 5.00	69	- 5:51	+ 5.00	64	- 5:56	+ 5.00	53	+ 5:53	+ 5.00	58	+ 5:58
+ 5.15	65	- 5:40	+ 5.15	60	- 5:45	+ 5.15	72	- 5:33	+ 5.15	68	- 5:37	+ 5.15	64	- 5:41	+ 5.15	53	- 5:52	+ 5.15	58	- 5:47
+ 5.30	65	- 5:25	+ 5.30	60	- 5:30	+ 5.30	72	- 5:18	+ 5.30	67	- 5:23	+ 5.30	63	- 5:27	+ 5.30	53	- 5:37	+ 5.30	58	- 5:32
+ 5.45	67	- 5:08	+ 5.45	59	- 5:16	+ 5.45	71	- 5:04	+ 5.45	66	- 5:09	+ 5.45	63	- 5:12	+ 5.45	53	- 5:22	+ 5.45	58	- 5:17
+ 6.00	67	- 4:53	+ 6.00	58	- 5:02	+ 6.00	70	- 4:50	+ 6.00	65	- 4:55	+ 6.00	62	- 4:58	+ 6.00	53	- 5:07	+ 6.00	58	- 5:02

Table E - Ramsgate to Swale and Medway via Copperas Channel

Time to cover Sectors (in minutes) at 5.0 kts — All times relate to HW Sheerness — **Springs**

Medway (E1–E3) | Ignore for Medway (E4) | Medway (E5–E7)

Swale (E1–E4)

	E1 Ramsgate to North Foreland			E2 North Foreland to SE Margate			E3 SE Margate to Copperas			E4 Copperas to Swale Landfall			E5 Copperas to Kentish Flats			E6 Kentish Flats to Spile			E7 Spile to Medway Channel	
Time	Duration	Time at End of Sector	Time	Duration	Time at End of Sector	Time	Duration	Time at End of Sector	Time	Duration	Time at End of Sector	Time	Duration	Time at End of Sector	Time	Duration	Time at End of Sector	Time	Duration	Time at End of Sector
- 6.00	**78**	**- 4:42**	**- 6.00**	**52**	**- 5:08**	**- 6.00**	**62**	**- 4:58**	**- 6.00**	**58**	**- 5:02**	**- 6.00**	**59**	**- 5:01**	**- 6.00**	**50**	**- 5:10**	**- 6.00**	**55**	**- 5:05**
- 5.45	79	- 4:26	- 5.45	51	- 4:54	- 5.45	60	- 4:45	- 5.45	56	- 4:49	- 5.45	58	- 4:47	- 5.45	49	- 4:56	- 5.45	54	- 4:51
- 5.30	80	- 4:10	- 5.30	49	- 4:41	- 5.30	59	- 4:31	- 5.30	55	- 4:35	- 5.30	58	- 4:32	- 5.30	49	- 4:41	- 5.30	54	- 4:36
- 5.15	79	- 3:56	- 5.15	48	- 4:27	- 5.15	57	- 4:18	- 5.15	54	- 4:21	- 5.15	57	- 4:18	- 5.15	49	- 4:26	- 5.15	54	- 4:21
- 5.00	**79**	**- 3:41**	**- 5.00**	**47**	**- 4:13**	**- 5.00**	**56**	**- 4:04**	**- 5.00**	**53**	**- 4:07**	**- 5.00**	**56**	**- 4:04**	**- 5.00**	**48**	**- 4:12**	**- 5.00**	**53**	**- 4:07**
- 4.45	78	- 3:27	- 4.45	46	- 3:59	- 4.45	55	- 3:50	- 4.45	52	- 3:53	- 4.45	56	- 3:49	- 4.45	48	- 3:57	- 4.45	54	- 3:51
- 4.30	78	- 3:12	- 4.30	46	- 3:44	- 4.30	54	- 3:36	- 4.30	52	- 3:38	- 4.30	55	- 3:35	- 4.30	48	- 3:42	- 4.30	54	- 3:36
- 4.15	73	- 3:02	- 4.15	45	- 3:30	- 4.15	54	- 3:21	- 4.15	52	- 3:23	- 4.15	55	- 3:20	- 4.15	49	- 3:26	- 4.15	54	- 3:21
- 4.00	**69**	**- 2:51**	**- 4.00**	**45**	**- 3:15**	**- 4.00**	**53**	**- 3:07**	**- 4.00**	**52**	**- 3:08**	**- 4.00**	**55**	**- 3:05**	**- 4.00**	**49**	**- 3:11**	**- 4.00**	**54**	**- 3:06**
- 3.45	65	- 2:40	- 3.45	44	- 3:01	- 3.45	53	- 2:52	- 3.45	51	- 2:54	- 3.45	55	- 2:50	- 3.45	49	- 2:56	- 3.45	54	- 2:51
- 3.30	60	- 2:30	- 3.30	44	- 2:46	- 3.30	52	- 2:38	- 3.30	51	- 2:39	- 3.30	55	- 2:35	- 3.30	49	- 2:41	- 3.30	55	- 2:35
- 3.15	56	- 2:19	- 3.15	44	- 2:31	- 3.15	52	- 2:23	- 3.15	51	- 2:24	- 3.15	55	- 2:20	- 3.15	49	- 2:26	- 3.15	55	- 2:20
- 3.00	**52**	**- 2:08**	**- 3.00**	**43**	**- 2:17**	**- 3.00**	**51**	**- 2:09**	**- 3.00**	**51**	**- 2:09**	**- 3.00**	**55**	**- 2:05**	**- 3.00**	**50**	**- 2:10**	**- 3.00**	**55**	**- 2:05**
- 2.45	47	- 1:58	- 2.45	43	- 2:02	- 2.45	52	- 1:53	- 2.45	52	- 1:53	- 2.45	55	- 1:50	- 2.45	50	- 1:55	- 2.45	55	- 1:50
- 2.30	43	- 1:47	- 2.30	44	- 1:46	- 2.30	52	- 1:38	- 2.30	52	- 1:38	- 2.30	55	- 1:35	- 2.30	50	- 1:40	- 2.30	55	- 1:35
- 2.15	42	- 1:33	- 2.15	44	- 1:31	- 2.15	53	- 1:22	- 2.15	53	- 1:22	- 2.15	56	- 1:19	- 2.15	50	- 1:25	- 2.15	56	- 1:19
- 2.00	**40**	**- 1:20**	**- 2.00**	**44**	**- 1:16**	**- 2.00**	**54**	**- 1:06**	**- 2.00**	**53**	**- 1:07**	**- 2.00**	**56**	**- 1:04**	**- 2.00**	**51**	**- 1:09**	**- 2.00**	**56**	**- 1:04**
- 1.45	39	- 1:06	- 1.45	46	- 0:59	- 1.45	56	- 0:49	- 1.45	55	- 0:50	- 1.45	57	- 0:48	- 1.45	51	- 0:54	- 1.45	57	- 0:48
- 1.30	38	- 0:52	- 1.30	48	- 0:42	- 1.30	59	- 0:31	- 1.30	58	- 0:32	- 1.30	59	- 0:31	- 1.30	52	- 0:38	- 1.30	58	- 0:32
- 1.15	38	- 0:37	- 1.15	50	- 0:25	- 1.15	61	- 0:14	- 1.15	60	- 0:15	- 1.15	60	- 0:15	- 1.15	53	- 0:22	- 1.15	59	- 0:16
- 1.00	**38**	**- 0:22**	**- 1.00**	**52**	**- 0:08**	**- 1.00**	**64**	**+ 0:04**	**- 1.00**	**62**	**+ 0:02**	**- 1.00**	**61**	**+ 0:01**	**- 1.00**	**54**	**- 0:06**	**- 1.00**	**60**	**HW**
- 0.45	39	- 0:06	- 0.45	56	+ 0:11	- 0.45	68	+ 0:23	- 0.45	66	+ 0:21	- 0.45	64	+ 0:19	- 0.45	56	+ 0:11	- 0.45	63	+ 0:18
- 0.30	39	+ 0:09	- 0.30	59	+ 0:29	- 0.30	73	+ 0:43	- 0.30	70	+ 0:40	- 0.30	66	+ 0:36	- 0.30	59	+ 0:29	- 0.30	65	+ 0:35
- 0.15	40	+ 0:25	- 0.15	63	+ 0:48	- 0.15	77	+ 1:02	- 0.15	74	+ 0:59	- 0.15	68	+ 0:53	- 0.15	61	+ 0:46	- 0.15	67	+ 0:52
HW	**41**	**+ 0:41**	**HW**	**66**	**+ 1:06**	**HW**	**81**	**+ 1:21**	**HW**	**78**	**+ 1:18**	**HW**	**70**	**+ 1:10**	**HW**	**63**	**+ 1:03**	**HW**	**70**	**+ 1:10**
+ 0.15	42	+ 0:57	+ 0.15	69	+ 1:24	+ 0.15	86	+ 1:41	+ 0.15	83	+ 1:38	+ 0.15	72	+ 1:27	+ 0.15	65	+ 1:20	+ 0.15	72	+ 1:27
+ 0.30	43	+ 1:13	+ 0.30	72	+ 1:42	+ 0.30	92	+ 2:02	+ 0.30	88	+ 1:58	+ 0.30	74	+ 1:44	+ 0.30	67	+ 1:37	+ 0.30	73	+ 1:43
+ 0.45	45	+ 1:30	+ 0.45	76	+ 2:01	+ 0.45	97	+ 2:22	+ 0.45	93	+ 2:18	+ 0.45	76	+ 2:01	+ 0.45	69	+ 1:54	+ 0.45	75	+ 2:00
+ 1.00	**46**	**+ 1:46**	**+ 1.00**	**79**	**+ 2:19**	**+ 1.00**	**102**	**+ 2:42**	**+ 1.00**	**98**	**+ 2:38**	**+ 1.00**	**78**	**+ 2:18**	**+ 1.00**	**70**	**+ 2:10**	**+ 1.00**	**77**	**+ 2:17**
+ 1.15	48	+ 2:03	+ 1.15	79	+ 2:34	+ 1.15	101	+ 2:56	+ 1.15	97	+ 2:52	+ 1.15	78	+ 2:33	+ 1.15	70	+ 2:25	+ 1.15	76	+ 2:31
+ 1.30	50	+ 2:20	+ 1.30	79	+ 2:49	+ 1.30	101	+ 3:11	+ 1.30	97	+ 3:07	+ 1.30	78	+ 2:48	+ 1.30	69	+ 2:39	+ 1.30	75	+ 2:45
+ 1.45	52	+ 2:37	+ 1.45	80	+ 3:05	+ 1.45	101	+ 3:26	+ 1.45	97	+ 3:22	+ 1.45	78	+ 3:03	+ 1.45	68	+ 2:53	+ 1.45	74	+ 2:59
+ 2.00	**54**	**+ 2:54**	**+ 2.00**	**80**	**+ 3:20**	**+ 2.00**	**101**	**+ 3:41**	**+ 2.00**	**96**	**+ 3:36**	**+ 2.00**	**78**	**+ 3:18**	**+ 2.00**	**67**	**+ 3:07**	**+ 2.00**	**73**	**+ 3:13**
+ 2.15	56	+ 3:11	+ 2.15	79	+ 3:34	+ 2.15	98	+ 3:53	+ 2.15	94	+ 3:49	+ 2.15	77	+ 3:32	+ 2.15	66	+ 3:21	+ 2.15	71	+ 3:26
+ 2.30	59	+ 3:29	+ 2.30	77	+ 3:47	+ 2.30	96	+ 4:06	+ 2.30	91	+ 4:01	+ 2.30	76	+ 3:46	+ 2.30	64	+ 3:34	+ 2.30	69	+ 3:39
+ 2.45	60	+ 3:45	+ 2.45	76	+ 4:01	+ 2.45	94	+ 4:19	+ 2.45	88	+ 4:13	+ 2.45	75	+ 4:00	+ 2.45	62	+ 3:47	+ 2.45	67	+ 3:52
+ 3.00	**61**	**+ 4:01**	**+ 3.00**	**75**	**+ 4:15**	**+ 3.00**	**92**	**+ 4:32**	**+ 3.00**	**86**	**+ 4:26**	**+ 3.00**	**74**	**+ 4:14**	**+ 3.00**	**60**	**+ 4:00**	**+ 3.00**	**66**	**+ 4:06**
+ 3.15	62	+ 4:17	+ 3.15	73	+ 4:28	+ 3.15	89	+ 4:44	+ 3.15	84	+ 4:39	+ 3.15	73	+ 4:28	+ 3.15	59	+ 4:14	+ 3.15	64	+ 4:19
+ 3.30	64	+ 4:34	+ 3.30	72	+ 4:42	+ 3.30	87	+ 4:57	+ 3.30	82	+ 4:52	+ 3.30	72	+ 4:42	+ 3.30	58	+ 4:28	+ 3.30	63	+ 4:33
+ 3.45	65	+ 4:50	+ 3.45	70	+ 4:55	+ 3.45	85	+ 5:10	+ 3.45	80	+ 5:05	+ 3.45	71	+ 4:56	+ 3.45	56	+ 4:41	+ 3.45	61	+ 4:46
+ 4.00	**65**	**+ 5:05**	**+ 4.00**	**69**	**+ 5:09**	**+ 4.00**	**82**	**+ 5:22**	**+ 4.00**	**79**	**+ 5:19**	**+ 4.00**	**70**	**+ 5:10**	**+ 4.00**	**55**	**+ 4:55**	**+ 4.00**	**60**	**+ 5:00**
+ 4.15	66	+ 5:21	+ 4.15	67	+ 5:22	+ 4.15	80	+ 5:35	+ 4.15	76	+ 5:31	+ 4.15	68	+ 5:23	+ 4.15	54	+ 5:09	+ 4.15	59	+ 5:14
+ 4.30	67	+ 5:37	+ 4.30	66	+ 5:36	+ 4.30	79	+ 5:49	+ 4.30	74	+ 5:44	+ 4.30	67	+ 5:37	+ 4.30	53	+ 5:23	+ 4.30	58	+ 5:28
+ 4.45	69	+ 5:54	+ 4.45	64	+ 5:49	+ 4.45	77	- 5:58	+ 4.45	72	+ 5:57	+ 4.45	66	+ 5:51	+ 4.45	53	+ 5:38	+ 4.45	58	+ 5:43
+ 5.00	**70**	**- 5:50**	**+ 5.00**	**63**	**- 5:57**	**+ 5.00**	**75**	**- 5:45**	**+ 5.00**	**70**	**- 5:50**	**+ 5.00**	**65**	**- 5:55**	**+ 5.00**	**52**	**+ 5:52**	**+ 5.00**	**57**	**+ 5:57**
+ 5.15	71	- 5:34	+ 5.15	62	- 5:43	+ 5.15	74	- 5:31	+ 5.15	69	- 5:36	+ 5.15	64	- 5:41	+ 5.15	52	- 5:53	+ 5.15	57	- 5:48
+ 5.30	72	- 5:18	+ 5.30	61	- 5:29	+ 5.30	73	- 5:17	+ 5.30	67	- 5:23	+ 5.30	63	- 5:27	+ 5.30	52	- 5:38	+ 5.30	57	- 5:33
+ 5.45	76	- 4:59	+ 5.45	60	- 5:15	+ 5.45	72	- 5:03	+ 5.45	66	- 5:09	+ 5.45	62	- 5:13	+ 5.45	52	- 5:23	+ 5.45	57	- 5:18
+ 6.00	**77**	**- 4:43**	**+ 6.00**	**59**	**- 5:01**	**+ 6.00**	**70**	**- 4:50**	**+ 6.00**	**65**	**- 4:55**	**+ 6.00**	**62**	**- 4:58**	**+ 6.00**	**52**	**- 5:08**	**+ 6.00**	**57**	**- 5:03**

WEST BOUND

Table E - Ramsgate to Swale and Medway via Copperas Channel

Neaps — All times relate to HW Sheerness — **Time to cover Sectors (in minutes) at 6.0 kts**

WEST BOUND

	Medway								Ignore for Medway			Medway								
	Swale																			
	E1			E2			E3			E4			E5			E6			E7	
	Ramsgate to North Foreland			North Foreland to SE Margate			SE Margate to Copperas			Copperas to Swale Landfall			Copperas to Kentish Flats			Kentish Flats to Spile			Spile to Medway Channel	
Time	Duration	Time at End of Sector	Time	Duration	Time at End of Sector	Time	Duration	Time at End of Sector	Time	Duration	Time at End of Sector	Time	Duration	Time at End of Sector	Time	Duration	Time at End of Sector	Time	Duration	Time at End of Sector
- 6.00	55	- 5:05	- 6.00	46	- 5:14	- 6.00	55	- 5:05	- 6.00	52	- 5:08	- 6.00	51	- 5:09	- 6.00	43	- 5:17	- 6.00	48	- 5:12
- 5.45	55	- 4:50	- 5.45	45	- 5:00	- 5.45	54	- 4:51	- 5.45	51	- 4:54	- 5.45	50	- 4:55	- 5.45	43	- 5:02	- 5.45	48	- 4:57
- 5.30	56	- 4:34	- 5.30	44	- 4:46	- 5.30	53	- 4:37	- 5.30	51	- 4:39	- 5.30	50	- 4:40	- 5.30	43	- 4:47	- 5.30	47	- 4:43
- 5.15	56	- 4:19	- 5.15	44	- 4:31	- 5.15	52	- 4:23	- 5.15	50	- 4:25	- 5.15	50	- 4:25	- 5.15	43	- 4:32	- 5.15	47	- 4:28
- 5.00	55	- 4:05	- 5.00	43	- 4:17	- 5.00	52	- 4:08	- 5.00	49	- 4:11	- 5.00	49	- 4:11	- 5.00	42	- 4:18	- 5.00	47	- 4:13
- 4.45	55	- 3:50	- 4.45	43	- 4:02	- 4.45	51	- 3:54	- 4.45	49	- 3:56	- 4.45	49	- 3:56	- 4.45	42	- 4:03	- 4.45	47	- 3:58
- 4.30	55	- 3:35	- 4.30	42	- 3:48	- 4.30	51	- 3:39	- 4.30	49	- 3:41	- 4.30	49	- 3:41	- 4.30	43	- 3:47	- 4.30	47	- 3:43
- 4.15	54	- 3:21	- 4.15	42	- 3:33	- 4.15	51	- 3:24	- 4.15	49	- 3:26	- 4.15	49	- 3:26	- 4.15	43	- 3:32	- 4.15	47	- 3:28
- 4.00	52	- 3:08	- 4.00	42	- 3:18	- 4.00	50	- 3:10	- 4.00	48	- 3:12	- 4.00	49	- 3:11	- 4.00	43	- 3:17	- 4.00	47	- 3:13
- 3.45	51	- 2:54	- 3.45	42	- 3:03	- 3.45	50	- 2:55	- 3.45	48	- 2:57	- 3.45	49	- 2:56	- 3.45	43	- 3:02	- 3.45	47	- 2:58
- 3.30	49	- 2:41	- 3.30	42	- 2:48	- 3.30	50	- 2:40	- 3.30	48	- 2:42	- 3.30	49	- 2:41	- 3.30	43	- 2:47	- 3.30	47	- 2:43
- 3.15	47	- 2:28	- 3.15	41	- 2:34	- 3.15	49	- 2:26	- 3.15	48	- 2:27	- 3.15	49	- 2:26	- 3.15	43	- 2:32	- 3.15	48	- 2:27
- 3.00	46	- 2:14	- 3.00	41	- 2:19	- 3.00	49	- 2:11	- 3.00	48	- 2:12	- 3.00	49	- 2:11	- 3.00	43	- 2:17	- 3.00	48	- 2:12
- 2.45	44	- 2:01	- 2.45	41	- 2:04	- 2.45	49	- 1:56	- 2.45	49	- 1:56	- 2.45	49	- 1:56	- 2.45	43	- 2:02	- 2.45	48	- 1:57
- 2.30	42	- 1:48	- 2.30	41	- 1:49	- 2.30	50	- 1:40	- 2.30	49	- 1:41	- 2.30	49	- 1:41	- 2.30	43	- 1:47	- 2.30	48	- 1:42
- 2.15	41	- 1:34	- 2.15	41	- 1:34	- 2.15	50	- 1:25	- 2.15	49	- 1:26	- 2.15	49	- 1:26	- 2.15	43	- 1:32	- 2.15	48	- 1:27
- 2.00	40	- 1:20	- 2.00	41	- 1:19	- 2.00	50	- 1:10	- 2.00	49	- 1:11	- 2.00	50	- 1:10	- 2.00	43	- 1:17	- 2.00	48	- 1:12
- 1.45	40	- 1:05	- 1.45	42	- 1:03	- 1.45	51	- 0:54	- 1.45	50	- 0:55	- 1.45	50	- 0:55	- 1.45	44	- 1:01	- 1.45	48	- 0:57
- 1.30	39	- 0:51	- 1.30	43	- 0:47	- 1.30	53	- 0:37	- 1.30	51	- 0:39	- 1.30	51	- 0:39	- 1.30	44	- 0:46	- 1.30	49	- 0:41
- 1.15	39	- 0:36	- 1.15	44	- 0:31	- 1.15	54	- 0:21	- 1.15	52	- 0:23	- 1.15	52	- 0:23	- 1.15	44	- 0:31	- 1.15	49	- 0:26
- 1.00	39	- 0:21	- 1.00	45	- 0:15	- 1.00	55	- 0:05	- 1.00	53	- 0:07	- 1.00	52	- 0:08	- 1.00	45	- 0:15	- 1.00	50	- 0:10
- 0.45	39	- 0:06	- 0.45	47	+ 0:02	- 0.45	57	+ 0:12	- 0.45	55	+ 0:10	- 0.45	53	+ 0:08	- 0.45	46	+ 0:01	- 0.45	51	+ 0:06
- 0.30	39	+ 0:09	- 0.30	48	+ 0:18	- 0.30	59	+ 0:29	- 0.30	57	+ 0:27	- 0.30	54	+ 0:24	- 0.30	47	+ 0:17	- 0.30	52	+ 0:22
- 0.15	39	+ 0:24	- 0.15	50	+ 0:35	- 0.15	61	+ 0:46	- 0.15	58	+ 0:43	- 0.15	55	+ 0:40	- 0.15	48	+ 0:33	- 0.15	53	+ 0:38
HW	40	+ 0:40	HW	51	+ 0:51	HW	63	+ 1:03	HW	60	+ 1:00	HW	56	+ 0:56	HW	49	+ 0:49	HW	54	+ 0:54
+ 0.15	40	+ 0:55	+ 0.15	53	+ 1:08	+ 0.15	64	+ 1:19	+ 0.15	61	+ 1:16	+ 0.15	57	+ 1:12	+ 0.15	49	+ 1:04	+ 0.15	54	+ 1:09
+ 0.30	41	+ 1:11	+ 0.30	54	+ 1:24	+ 0.30	66	+ 1:36	+ 0.30	63	+ 1:33	+ 0.30	58	+ 1:28	+ 0.30	49	+ 1:19	+ 0.30	55	+ 1:25
+ 0.45	41	+ 1:26	+ 0.45	55	+ 1:40	+ 0.45	67	+ 1:52	+ 0.45	64	+ 1:49	+ 0.45	58	+ 1:43	+ 0.45	50	+ 1:35	+ 0.45	56	+ 1:41
+ 1.00	42	+ 1:42	+ 1.00	57	+ 1:57	+ 1.00	69	+ 2:09	+ 1.00	66	+ 2:06	+ 1.00	59	+ 1:59	+ 1.00	51	+ 1:51	+ 1.00	57	+ 1:57
+ 1.15	43	+ 1:58	+ 1.15	57	+ 2:12	+ 1.15	69	+ 2:24	+ 1.15	66	+ 2:21	+ 1.15	59	+ 2:14	+ 1.15	52	+ 2:07	+ 1.15	57	+ 2:12
+ 1.30	44	+ 2:14	+ 1.30	57	+ 2:27	+ 1.30	69	+ 2:39	+ 1.30	66	+ 2:36	+ 1.30	59	+ 2:29	+ 1.30	52	+ 2:22	+ 1.30	56	+ 2:26
+ 1.45	45	+ 2:30	+ 1.45	58	+ 2:43	+ 1.45	69	+ 2:54	+ 1.45	66	+ 2:51	+ 1.45	59	+ 2:44	+ 1.45	52	+ 2:37	+ 1.45	56	+ 2:41
+ 2.00	46	+ 2:46	+ 2.00	58	+ 2:58	+ 2.00	69	+ 3:09	+ 2.00	66	+ 3:06	+ 2.00	59	+ 2:59	+ 2.00	51	+ 2:51	+ 2.00	56	+ 2:56
+ 2.15	46	+ 3:01	+ 2.15	57	+ 3:12	+ 2.15	69	+ 3:24	+ 2.15	66	+ 3:21	+ 2.15	59	+ 3:14	+ 2.15	51	+ 3:06	+ 2.15	55	+ 3:10
+ 2.30	47	+ 3:17	+ 2.30	57	+ 3:27	+ 2.30	68	+ 3:38	+ 2.30	65	+ 3:35	+ 2.30	58	+ 3:28	+ 2.30	50	+ 3:20	+ 2.30	54	+ 3:24
+ 2.45	48	+ 3:33	+ 2.45	56	+ 3:41	+ 2.45	67	+ 3:52	+ 2.45	65	+ 3:50	+ 2.45	58	+ 3:43	+ 2.45	50	+ 3:35	+ 2.45	53	+ 3:38
+ 3.00	49	+ 3:49	+ 3.00	55	+ 3:55	+ 3.00	66	+ 4:06	+ 3.00	64	+ 4:04	+ 3.00	57	+ 3:57	+ 3.00	49	+ 3:49	+ 3.00	53	+ 3:53
+ 3.15	50	+ 4:05	+ 3.15	55	+ 4:10	+ 3.15	66	+ 4:21	+ 3.15	63	+ 4:18	+ 3.15	57	+ 4:12	+ 3.15	48	+ 4:03	+ 3.15	52	+ 4:07
+ 3.30	50	+ 4:20	+ 3.30	54	+ 4:24	+ 3.30	65	+ 4:35	+ 3.30	63	+ 4:33	+ 3.30	56	+ 4:26	+ 3.30	48	+ 4:18	+ 3.30	51	+ 4:21
+ 3.45	51	+ 4:36	+ 3.45	54	+ 4:39	+ 3.45	64	+ 4:49	+ 3.45	62	+ 4:47	+ 3.45	56	+ 4:41	+ 3.45	47	+ 4:32	+ 3.45	51	+ 4:36
+ 4.00	51	+ 4:51	+ 4.00	53	+ 4:53	+ 4.00	64	+ 5:04	+ 4.00	61	+ 5:01	+ 4.00	56	+ 4:56	+ 4.00	46	+ 4:46	+ 4.00	50	+ 4:50
+ 4.15	52	+ 5:07	+ 4.15	53	+ 5:08	+ 4.15	63	+ 5:18	+ 4.15	60	+ 5:15	+ 4.15	55	+ 5:10	+ 4.15	46	+ 5:01	+ 4.15	50	+ 5:05
+ 4.30	52	+ 5:22	+ 4.30	52	+ 5:22	+ 4.30	62	+ 5:32	+ 4.30	59	+ 5:29	+ 4.30	55	+ 5:25	+ 4.30	45	+ 5:15	+ 4.30	49	+ 5:19
+ 4.45	52	+ 5:37	+ 4.45	51	+ 5:36	+ 4.45	62	+ 5:47	+ 4.45	58	+ 5:43	+ 4.45	54	+ 5:39	+ 4.45	45	+ 5:30	+ 4.45	49	+ 5:34
+ 5.00	53	+ 5:53	+ 5.00	51	+ 5:51	+ 5.00	61	- 5:59	+ 5.00	57	+ 5:57	+ 5.00	54	+ 5:54	+ 5.00	45	+ 5:45	+ 5.00	49	+ 5:49
+ 5.15	53	- 5:52	+ 5.15	50	- 5:55	+ 5.15	60	- 5:45	+ 5.15	57	- 5:48	+ 5.15	53	- 5:52	+ 5.15	44	+ 5:59	+ 5.15	49	- 5:56
+ 5.30	53	- 5:37	+ 5.30	50	- 5:40	+ 5.30	59	- 5:31	+ 5.30	56	- 5:34	+ 5.30	53	- 5:37	+ 5.30	44	- 5:46	+ 5.30	48	- 5:42
+ 5.45	54	- 5:21	+ 5.45	49	- 5:26	+ 5.45	59	- 5:16	+ 5.45	55	- 5:20	+ 5.45	52	- 5:23	+ 5.45	44	- 5:31	+ 5.45	48	- 5:27
+ 6.00	54	- 5:06	+ 6.00	48	- 5:12	+ 6.00	58	- 5:02	+ 6.00	55	- 5:05	+ 6.00	52	- 5:08	+ 6.00	44	- 5:16	+ 6.00	48	- 5:12

Table E - Ramsgate to Swale and Medway via Copperas Channel

Time to cover Sectors (in minutes) at 6.0 kts — All times relate to HW Sheerness — **Springs**

	Medway								Ignore for Medway			Medway								
	Swale																			
	E1			E2			E3			E4			E5			E6			E7	
	Ramsgate to North Foreland			North Foreland to SE Margate			SE Margate to Copperas			Copperas to Swale Landfall			Copperas to Kentish Flats			Kentish Flats to Spile			Spile to Medway Channel	
Time	*Duration*	*Time at End of Sector*	*Time*	*Duration*	*Time at End of Sector*	*Time*	*Duration*	*Time at End of Sector*	*Time*	*Duration*	*Time at End of Sector*	*Time*	*Duration*	*Time at End of Sector*	*Time*	*Duration*	*Time at End of Sector*	*Time*	*Duration*	*Time at End of Sector*
- 6.00	**62**	**- 4:58**	**- 6.00**	**45**	**- 5:15**	**- 6.00**	**53**	**- 5:07**	**- 6.00**	**50**	**- 5:10**	**- 6.00**	**50**	**- 5:10**	**- 6.00**	**42**	**- 5:18**	**- 6.00**	**47**	**- 5:13**
- 5.45	62	- 4:43	- 5.45	44	- 5:01	- 5.45	52	- 4:53	- 5.45	49	- 4:56	- 5.45	49	- 4:56	- 5.45	42	- 5:03	- 5.45	46	- 4:59
- 5.30	63	- 4:27	- 5.30	43	- 4:47	- 5.30	51	- 4:39	- 5.30	48	- 4:42	- 5.30	49	- 4:41	- 5.30	42	- 4:48	- 5.30	46	- 4:44
- 5.15	63	- 4:12	- 5.15	42	- 4:33	- 5.15	50	- 4:25	- 5.15	47	- 4:28	- 5.15	48	- 4:27	- 5.15	41	- 4:34	- 5.15	46	- 4:29
- 5.00	**63**	**- 3:57**	**- 5.00**	**41**	**- 4:19**	**- 5.00**	**48**	**- 4:12**	**- 5.00**	**46**	**- 4:14**	**- 5.00**	**48**	**- 4:12**	**- 5.00**	**41**	**- 4:19**	**- 5.00**	**45**	**- 4:15**
- 4.45	62	- 3:43	- 4.45	40	- 4:05	- 4.45	48	- 3:57	- 4.45	46	- 3:59	- 4.45	48	- 3:57	- 4.45	41	- 4:04	- 4.45	45	- 4:00
- 4.30	62	- 3:28	- 4.30	40	- 3:50	- 4.30	48	- 3:42	- 4.30	45	- 3:45	- 4.30	47	- 3:43	- 4.30	41	- 3:49	- 4.30	46	- 3:44
- 4.15	59	- 3:16	- 4.15	40	- 3:35	- 4.15	47	- 3:28	- 4.15	45	- 3:30	- 4.15	47	- 3:28	- 4.15	41	- 3:34	- 4.15	46	- 3:29
- 4.00	**57**	**- 3:03**	**- 4.00**	**39**	**- 3:21**	**- 4.00**	**47**	**- 3:13**	**- 4.00**	**45**	**- 3:15**	**- 4.00**	**47**	**- 3:13**	**- 4.00**	**41**	**- 3:19**	**- 4.00**	**46**	**- 3:14**
- 3.45	54	- 2:51	- 3.45	39	- 3:06	- 3.45	46	- 2:59	- 3.45	45	- 3:00	- 3.45	47	- 2:58	- 3.45	41	- 3:04	- 3.45	46	- 2:59
- 3.30	51	- 2:39	- 3.30	39	- 2:51	- 3.30	46	- 2:44	- 3.30	45	- 2:45	- 3.30	47	- 2:43	- 3.30	42	- 2:48	- 3.30	46	- 2:44
- 3.15	48	- 2:27	- 3.15	38	- 2:37	- 3.15	46	- 2:29	- 3.15	45	- 2:30	- 3.15	47	- 2:28	- 3.15	42	- 2:33	- 3.15	46	- 2:29
- 3.00	**45**	**- 2:15**	**- 3.00**	**38**	**- 2:22**	**- 3.00**	**45**	**- 2:15**	**- 3.00**	**45**	**- 2:15**	**- 3.00**	**47**	**- 2:13**	**- 3.00**	**42**	**- 2:18**	**- 3.00**	**46**	**- 2:14**
- 2.45	42	- 2:03	- 2.45	38	- 2:07	- 2.45	46	- 1:59	- 2.45	45	- 2:00	- 2.45	47	- 1:58	- 2.45	42	- 2:03	- 2.45	47	- 1:58
- 2.30	39	- 1:51	- 2.30	38	- 1:52	- 2.30	46	- 1:44	- 2.30	45	- 1:45	- 2.30	47	- 1:43	- 2.30	42	- 1:48	- 2.30	47	- 1:43
- 2.15	38	- 1:37	- 2.15	38	- 1:37	- 2.15	46	- 1:29	- 2.15	46	- 1:29	- 2.15	47	- 1:28	- 2.15	42	- 1:33	- 2.15	47	- 1:28
- 2.00	**36**	**- 1:24**	**- 2.00**	**38**	**- 1:22**	**- 2.00**	**46**	**- 1:14**	**- 2.00**	**46**	**- 1:14**	**- 2.00**	**48**	**- 1:12**	**- 2.00**	**42**	**- 1:18**	**- 2.00**	**47**	**- 1:13**
- 1.45	35	- 1:10	- 1.45	39	- 1:06	- 1.45	48	- 0:57	- 1.45	47	- 0:58	- 1.45	48	- 0:57	- 1.45	43	- 1:02	- 1.45	48	- 0:57
- 1.30	34	- 0:56	- 1.30	41	- 0:49	- 1.30	50	- 0:40	- 1.30	49	- 0:41	- 1.30	49	- 0:41	- 1.30	44	- 0:46	- 1.30	48	- 0:42
- 1.15	34	- 0:41	- 1.15	42	- 0:33	- 1.15	51	- 0:24	- 1.15	50	- 0:25	- 1.15	50	- 0:25	- 1.15	44	- 0:31	- 1.15	49	- 0:26
- 1.00	**34**	**- 0:26**	**- 1.00**	**43**	**- 0:17**	**- 1.00**	**53**	**- 0:07**	**- 1.00**	**51**	**- 0:09**	**- 1.00**	**51**	**- 0:09**	**- 1.00**	**45**	**- 0:15**	**- 1.00**	**49**	**- 0:11**
- 0.45	34	- 0:11	- 0.45	46	+ 0:01	- 0.45	56	+ 0:11	- 0.45	54	+ 0:09	- 0.45	52	+ 0:07	- 0.45	46	+ 0:01	- 0.45	51	+ 0:06
- 0.30	34	+ 0:04	- 0.30	48	+ 0:18	- 0.30	59	+ 0:29	- 0.30	57	+ 0:27	- 0.30	54	+ 0:24	- 0.30	48	+ 0:18	- 0.30	53	+ 0:23
- 0.15	35	+ 0:20	- 0.15	50	+ 0:35	- 0.15	62	+ 0:47	- 0.15	59	+ 0:44	- 0.15	55	+ 0:40	- 0.15	49	+ 0:34	- 0.15	54	+ 0:39
HW	**36**	**+ 0:36**	**HW**	**53**	**+ 0:53**	**HW**	**65**	**+ 1:05**	**HW**	**62**	**+ 1:02**	**HW**	**57**	**+ 0:57**	**HW**	**51**	**+ 0:51**	**HW**	**56**	**+ 0:56**
+ 0.15	36	+ 0:51	+ 0.15	55	+ 1:10	+ 0.15	67	+ 1:22	+ 0.15	65	+ 1:20	+ 0.15	58	+ 1:13	+ 0.15	52	+ 1:07	+ 0.15	57	+ 1:12
+ 0.30	37	+ 1:07	+ 0.30	57	+ 1:27	+ 0.30	70	+ 1:40	+ 0.30	67	+ 1:37	+ 0.30	60	+ 1:30	+ 0.30	54	+ 1:24	+ 0.30	59	+ 1:29
+ 0.45	38	+ 1:23	+ 0.45	60	+ 1:45	+ 0.45	73	+ 1:58	+ 0.45	69	+ 1:54	+ 0.45	61	+ 1:46	+ 0.45	55	+ 1:40	+ 0.45	60	+ 1:45
+ 1.00	**39**	**+ 1:39**	**+ 1.00**	**62**	**+ 2:02**	**+ 1.00**	**75**	**+ 2:15**	**+ 1.00**	**72**	**+ 2:12**	**+ 1.00**	**62**	**+ 2:02**	**+ 1.00**	**56**	**+ 1:56**	**+ 1.00**	**61**	**+ 2:01**
+ 1.15	40	+ 1:55	+ 1.15	63	+ 2:18	+ 1.15	75	+ 2:30	+ 1.15	72	+ 2:27	+ 1.15	63	+ 2:18	+ 1.15	56	+ 2:11	+ 1.15	61	+ 2:16
+ 1.30	42	+ 2:12	+ 1.30	63	+ 2:33	+ 1.30	76	+ 2:46	+ 1.30	72	+ 2:42	+ 1.30	63	+ 2:33	+ 1.30	55	+ 2:25	+ 1.30	60	+ 2:30
+ 1.45	43	+ 2:28	+ 1.45	63	+ 2:48	+ 1.45	76	+ 3:01	+ 1.45	73	+ 2:58	+ 1.45	63	+ 2:48	+ 1.45	55	+ 2:40	+ 1.45	60	+ 2:45
+ 2.00	**45**	**+ 2:45**	**+ 2.00**	**64**	**+ 3:04**	**+ 2.00**	**76**	**+ 3:16**	**+ 2.00**	**73**	**+ 3:13**	**+ 2.00**	**63**	**+ 3:03**	**+ 2.00**	**55**	**+ 2:55**	**+ 2.00**	**59**	**+ 2:59**
+ 2.15	46	+ 3:01	+ 2.15	63	+ 3:18	+ 2.15	75	+ 3:30	+ 2.15	72	+ 3:27	+ 2.15	62	+ 3:17	+ 2.15	53	+ 3:08	+ 2.15	58	+ 3:13
+ 2.30	48	+ 3:18	+ 2.30	62	+ 3:32	+ 2.30	74	+ 3:44	+ 2.30	71	+ 3:41	+ 2.30	62	+ 3:32	+ 2.30	52	+ 3:22	+ 2.30	57	+ 3:27
+ 2.45	49	+ 3:34	+ 2.45	61	+ 3:46	+ 2.45	73	+ 3:58	+ 2.45	70	+ 3:55	+ 2.45	61	+ 3:46	+ 2.45	51	+ 3:36	+ 2.45	55	+ 3:40
+ 3.00	**50**	**+ 3:50**	**+ 3.00**	**60**	**+ 4:00**	**+ 3.00**	**72**	**+ 4:12**	**+ 3.00**	**69**	**+ 4:09**	**+ 3.00**	**60**	**+ 4:00**	**+ 3.00**	**50**	**+ 3:50**	**+ 3.00**	**54**	**+ 3:54**
+ 3.15	51	+ 4:06	+ 3.15	59	+ 4:14	+ 3.15	71	+ 4:26	+ 3.15	68	+ 4:23	+ 3.15	60	+ 4:15	+ 3.15	49	+ 4:04	+ 3.15	53	+ 4:08
+ 3.30	52	+ 4:22	+ 3.30	58	+ 4:28	+ 3.30	69	+ 4:39	+ 3.30	67	+ 4:37	+ 3.30	59	+ 4:29	+ 3.30	48	+ 4:18	+ 3.30	52	+ 4:22
+ 3.45	53	+ 4:38	+ 3.45	57	+ 4:42	+ 3.45	68	+ 4:53	+ 3.45	65	+ 4:50	+ 3.45	58	+ 4:43	+ 3.45	47	+ 4:32	+ 3.45	51	+ 4:36
+ 4.00	**53**	**+ 4:53**	**+ 4.00**	**56**	**+ 4:56**	**+ 4.00**	**67**	**+ 5:07**	**+ 4.00**	**64**	**+ 5:04**	**+ 4.00**	**57**	**+ 4:57**	**+ 4.00**	**46**	**+ 4:46**	**+ 4.00**	**50**	**+ 4:50**
+ 4.15	53	+ 5:08	+ 4.15	55	+ 5:10	+ 4.15	66	+ 5:21	+ 4.15	63	+ 5:18	+ 4.15	57	+ 5:12	+ 4.15	45	+ 5:00	+ 4.15	49	+ 5:04
+ 4.30	54	+ 5:24	+ 4.30	54	+ 5:24	+ 4.30	65	+ 5:35	+ 4.30	61	+ 5:31	+ 4.30	56	+ 5:26	+ 4.30	45	+ 5:15	+ 4.30	49	+ 5:19
+ 4.45	55	+ 5:40	+ 4.45	53	+ 5:38	+ 4.45	64	+ 5:49	+ 4.45	60	+ 5:45	+ 4.45	55	+ 5:40	+ 4.45	44	+ 5:29	+ 4.45	48	+ 5:33
+ 5.00	**56**	**+ 5:56**	**+ 5.00**	**52**	**+ 5:52**	**+ 5.00**	**62**	**- 5:58**	**+ 5.00**	**58**	**+ 5:58**	**+ 5.00**	**54**	**+ 5:54**	**+ 5.00**	**44**	**+ 5:44**	**+ 5.00**	**48**	**+ 5:48**
+ 5.15	57	- 5:48	+ 5.15	51	- 5:54	+ 5.15	61	- 5:44	+ 5.15	57	- 5:48	+ 5.15	53	- 5:52	+ 5.15	44	+ 5:59	+ 5.15	48	- 5:57
+ 5.30	58	- 5:32	+ 5.30	50	- 5:40	+ 5.30	60	- 5:30	+ 5.30	56	- 5:34	+ 5.30	53	- 5:37	+ 5.30	43	- 5:47	+ 5.30	48	- 5:42
+ 5.45	60	- 5:15	+ 5.45	50	- 5:25	+ 5.45	60	- 5:15	+ 5.45	55	- 5:20	+ 5.45	52	- 5:23	+ 5.45	43	- 5:32	+ 5.45	48	- 5:27
+ 6.00	61	**- 4:59**	**+ 6.00**	49	**- 5:11**	**+ 6.00**	59	**- 5:01**	**+ 6.00**	54	**- 5:06**	**+ 6.00**	52	**- 5:08**	**+ 6.00**	**43**	**- 5:17**	**+ 6.00**	48	**- 5:12**

WEST BOUND

Table E - Ramsgate to Swale and Medway via Copperas Channel

Neaps — All times relate to HW Sheerness — **Time to cover Sectors (in minutes) at 7.0 kts**

Medway (E1–E3, E5–E7) — Ignore for Medway (E4) — Swale (E1–E4)

WEST BOUND

Time	E1 Ramsgate to North Foreland Duration	E1 Time at End of Sector	Time	E2 North Foreland to SE Margate Duration	E2 Time at End of Sector	Time	E3 SE Margate to Copperas Duration	E3 Time at End of Sector	Time	E4 Copperas to Swale Landfall Duration	E4 Time at End of Sector	Time	E5 Copperas to Kentish Flats Duration	E5 Time at End of Sector	Time	E6 Kentish Flats to Spile Duration	E6 Time at End of Sector	Time	E7 Spile to Medway Channel Duration	E7 Time at End of Sector
- 6.00	46	- 5:14	- 6.00	40	- 5:20	- 6.00	47	- 5:13	- 6.00	45	- 5:15	- 6.00	44	- 5:16	- 6.00	38	- 5:22	- 6.00	41	- 5:19
- 5.45	46	- 4:59	- 5.45	39	- 5:06	- 5.45	47	- 4:58	- 5.45	45	- 5:00	- 5.45	44	- 5:01	- 5.45	37	- 5:08	- 5.45	41	- 5:04
- 5.30	47	- 4:43	- 5.30	38	- 4:52	- 5.30	46	- 4:44	- 5.30	44	- 4:46	- 5.30	43	- 4:47	- 5.30	37	- 4:53	- 5.30	41	- 4:49
- 5.15	47	- 4:28	- 5.15	38	- 4:37	- 5.15	46	- 4:29	- 5.15	44	- 4:31	- 5.15	43	- 4:32	- 5.15	37	- 4:38	- 5.15	41	- 4:34
- 5.00	46	- 4:14	- 5.00	37	- 4:23	- 5.00	45	- 4:15	- 5.00	43	- 4:17	- 5.00	43	- 4:17	- 5.00	37	- 4:23	- 5.00	40	- 4:20
- 4.45	46	- 3:59	- 4.45	37	- 4:08	- 4.45	45	- 4:00	- 4.45	43	- 4:02	- 4.45	43	- 4:02	- 4.45	37	- 4:08	- 4.45	40	- 4:05
- 4.30	46	- 3:44	- 4.30	37	- 3:53	- 4.30	45	- 3:45	- 4.30	43	- 3:47	- 4.30	43	- 3:47	- 4.30	37	- 3:53	- 4.30	41	- 3:49
- 4.15	45	- 3:30	- 4.15	37	- 3:38	- 4.15	44	- 3:31	- 4.15	42	- 3:33	- 4.15	42	- 3:33	- 4.15	37	- 3:38	- 4.15	41	- 3:34
- 4.00	45	- 3:15	- 4.00	37	- 3:23	- 4.00	44	- 3:16	- 4.00	42	- 3:18	- 4.00	42	- 3:18	- 4.00	37	- 3:23	- 4.00	41	- 3:19
- 3.45	44	- 3:01	- 3.45	36	- 3:09	- 3.45	44	- 3:01	- 3.45	42	- 3:03	- 3.45	42	- 3:03	- 3.45	37	- 3:08	- 3.45	41	- 3:04
- 3.30	43	- 2:47	- 3.30	36	- 2:54	- 3.30	44	- 2:46	- 3.30	42	- 2:48	- 3.30	42	- 2:48	- 3.30	37	- 2:53	- 3.30	41	- 2:49
- 3.15	41	- 2:34	- 3.15	36	- 2:39	- 3.15	43	- 2:32	- 3.15	42	- 2:33	- 3.15	42	- 2:33	- 3.15	37	- 2:38	- 3.15	41	- 2:34
- 3.00	40	- 2:20	- 3.00	36	- 2:24	- 3.00	43	- 2:17	- 3.00	42	- 2:18	- 3.00	42	- 2:18	- 3.00	37	- 2:23	- 3.00	41	- 2:19
- 2.45	38	- 2:07	- 2.45	36	- 2:09	- 2.45	43	- 2:02	- 2.45	42	- 2:03	- 2.45	42	- 2:03	- 2.45	37	- 2:08	- 2.45	41	- 2:04
- 2.30	37	- 1:53	- 2.30	36	- 1:54	- 2.30	43	- 1:47	- 2.30	42	- 1:48	- 2.30	42	- 1:48	- 2.30	37	- 1:53	- 2.30	41	- 1:49
- 2.15	36	- 1:39	- 2.15	36	- 1:39	- 2.15	44	- 1:31	- 2.15	42	- 1:33	- 2.15	43	- 1:32	- 2.15	37	- 1:38	- 2.15	41	- 1:34
- 2.00	36	- 1:24	- 2.00	36	- 1:24	- 2.00	44	- 1:16	- 2.00	43	- 1:17	- 2.00	43	- 1:17	- 2.00	37	- 1:23	- 2.00	41	- 1:19
- 1.45	35	- 1:10	- 1.45	37	- 1:08	- 1.45	44	- 1:01	- 1.45	43	- 1:02	- 1.45	43	- 1:02	- 1.45	38	- 1:07	- 1.45	41	- 1:04
- 1.30	34	- 0:56	- 1.30	37	- 0:53	- 1.30	45	- 0:45	- 1.30	44	- 0:46	- 1.30	44	- 0:46	- 1.30	38	- 0:52	- 1.30	42	- 0:48
- 1.15	34	- 0:41	- 1.15	38	- 0:37	- 1.15	46	- 0:29	- 1.15	45	- 0:30	- 1.15	44	- 0:31	- 1.15	38	- 0:37	- 1.15	42	- 0:33
- 1.00	34	- 0:26	- 1.00	38	- 0:22	- 1.00	47	- 0:13	- 1.00	45	- 0:15	- 1.00	45	- 0:15	- 1.00	38	- 0:22	- 1.00	42	- 0:18
- 0.45	34	- 0:11	- 0.45	40	- 0:05	- 0.45	48	+ 0:03	- 0.45	47	+ 0:02	- 0.45	45	HW	- 0.45	39	- 0:06	- 0.45	43	- 0:02
- 0.30	34	+ 0:04	- 0.30	41	+ 0:11	- 0.30	50	+ 0:20	- 0.30	48	+ 0:18	- 0.30	46	+ 0:16	- 0.30	40	+ 0:10	- 0.30	44	+ 0:14
- 0.15	34	+ 0:19	- 0.15	42	+ 0:27	- 0.15	51	+ 0:36	- 0.15	49	+ 0:34	- 0.15	47	+ 0:32	- 0.15	40	+ 0:25	- 0.15	44	+ 0:29
HW	35	+ 0:35	HW	43	+ 0:43	HW	52	+ 0:52	HW	51	+ 0:51	HW	47	+ 0:47	HW	41	+ 0:41	HW	45	+ 0:45
+ 0.15	35	+ 0:50	+ 0.15	44	+ 0:59	+ 0.15	54	+ 1:09	+ 0.15	52	+ 1:07	+ 0.15	48	+ 1:03	+ 0.15	41	+ 0:56	+ 0.15	46	+ 1:01
+ 0.30	35	+ 1:05	+ 0.30	46	+ 1:16	+ 0.30	55	+ 1:25	+ 0.30	53	+ 1:23	+ 0.30	49	+ 1:19	+ 0.30	42	+ 1:12	+ 0.30	46	+ 1:16
+ 0.45	36	+ 1:21	+ 0.45	47	+ 1:32	+ 0.45	56	+ 1:41	+ 0.45	54	+ 1:39	+ 0.45	49	+ 1:34	+ 0.45	42	+ 1:27	+ 0.45	47	+ 1:32
+ 1.00	36	+ 1:36	+ 1.00	48	+ 1:48	+ 1.00	57	+ 1:57	+ 1.00	55	+ 1:55	+ 1.00	50	+ 1:50	+ 1.00	43	+ 1:43	+ 1.00	48	+ 1:48
+ 1.15	37	+ 1:52	+ 1.15	48	+ 2:03	+ 1.15	58	+ 2:13	+ 1.15	55	+ 2:10	+ 1.15	50	+ 2:05	+ 1.15	44	+ 1:59	+ 1.15	48	+ 2:03
+ 1.30	38	+ 2:08	+ 1.30	48	+ 2:18	+ 1.30	58	+ 2:28	+ 1.30	55	+ 2:25	+ 1.30	50	+ 2:20	+ 1.30	44	+ 2:14	+ 1.30	47	+ 2:17
+ 1.45	38	+ 2:23	+ 1.45	48	+ 2:33	+ 1.45	58	+ 2:43	+ 1.45	55	+ 2:40	+ 1.45	50	+ 2:35	+ 1.45	43	+ 2:28	+ 1.45	47	+ 2:32
+ 2.00	39	+ 2:39	+ 2.00	49	+ 2:49	+ 2.00	58	+ 2:58	+ 2.00	55	+ 2:55	+ 2.00	50	+ 2:50	+ 2.00	43	+ 2:43	+ 2.00	47	+ 2:47
+ 2.15	40	+ 2:55	+ 2.15	48	+ 3:03	+ 2.15	58	+ 3:13	+ 2.15	55	+ 3:10	+ 2.15	50	+ 3:05	+ 2.15	43	+ 2:58	+ 2.15	47	+ 3:02
+ 2.30	40	+ 3:10	+ 2.30	48	+ 3:18	+ 2.30	57	+ 3:27	+ 2.30	55	+ 3:25	+ 2.30	49	+ 3:19	+ 2.30	43	+ 3:13	+ 2.30	46	+ 3:16
+ 2.45	41	+ 3:26	+ 2.45	47	+ 3:32	+ 2.45	57	+ 3:42	+ 2.45	54	+ 3:39	+ 2.45	49	+ 3:34	+ 2.45	42	+ 3:27	+ 2.45	46	+ 3:31
+ 3.00	41	+ 3:41	+ 3.00	47	+ 3:47	+ 3.00	56	+ 3:56	+ 3.00	54	+ 3:54	+ 3.00	49	+ 3:49	+ 3.00	42	+ 3:42	+ 3.00	45	+ 3:45
+ 3.15	42	+ 3:57	+ 3.15	46	+ 4:01	+ 3.15	56	+ 4:11	+ 3.15	53	+ 4:08	+ 3.15	48	+ 4:03	+ 3.15	41	+ 3:56	+ 3.15	44	+ 3:59
+ 3.30	43	+ 4:13	+ 3.30	46	+ 4:16	+ 3.30	55	+ 4:25	+ 3.30	53	+ 4:23	+ 3.30	48	+ 4:18	+ 3.30	41	+ 4:11	+ 3.30	44	+ 4:14
+ 3.45	43	+ 4:28	+ 3.45	46	+ 4:31	+ 3.45	55	+ 4:40	+ 3.45	52	+ 4:37	+ 3.45	48	+ 4:33	+ 3.45	40	+ 4:25	+ 3.45	43	+ 4:28
+ 4.00	43	+ 4:43	+ 4.00	45	+ 4:45	+ 4.00	54	+ 4:54	+ 4.00	52	+ 4:52	+ 4.00	47	+ 4:47	+ 4.00	40	+ 4:40	+ 4.00	43	+ 4:43
+ 4.15	44	+ 4:59	+ 4.15	45	+ 5:00	+ 4.15	54	+ 5:09	+ 4.15	51	+ 5:06	+ 4.15	47	+ 5:02	+ 4.15	39	+ 4:54	+ 4.15	43	+ 4:58
+ 4.30	44	+ 5:14	+ 4.30	44	+ 5:14	+ 4.30	53	+ 5:23	+ 4.30	51	+ 5:21	+ 4.30	47	+ 5:17	+ 4.30	39	+ 5:09	+ 4.30	42	+ 5:12
+ 4.45	44	+ 5:29	+ 4.45	44	+ 5:29	+ 4.45	52	+ 5:37	+ 4.45	50	+ 5:35	+ 4.45	46	+ 5:31	+ 4.45	39	+ 5:24	+ 4.45	42	+ 5:27
+ 5.00	44	+ 5:44	+ 5.00	43	+ 5:43	+ 5.00	52	+ 5:52	+ 5.00	49	+ 5:49	+ 5.00	46	+ 5:46	+ 5.00	38	+ 5:38	+ 5.00	42	+ 5:42
+ 5.15	44	+ 5:59	+ 5.15	43	+ 5:58	+ 5.15	51	- 5:54	+ 5.15	49	- 5:56	+ 5.15	46	- 5:59	+ 5.15	38	+ 5:53	+ 5.15	42	+ 5:57
+ 5.30	45	- 5:45	+ 5.30	42	- 5:48	+ 5.30	51	- 5:39	+ 5.30	48	- 5:42	+ 5.30	45	- 5:45	+ 5.30	38	- 5:52	+ 5.30	42	- 5:48
+ 5.45	45	- 5:30	+ 5.45	42	- 5:33	+ 5.45	50	- 5:25	+ 5.45	48	- 5:27	+ 5.45	45	- 5:30	+ 5.45	38	- 5:37	+ 5.45	42	- 5:33
+ 6.00	45	- 5:15	+ 6.00	41	- 5:19	+ 6.00	50	- 5:10	+ 6.00	47	- 5:13	+ 6.00	45	- 5:15	+ 6.00	38	- 5:22	+ 6.00	42	- 5:18

Table E - Ramsgate to Swale and Medway via Copperas Channel

Time to cover Sectors (in minutes) at 7.0 kts — All times relate to HW Sheerness — **Springs**

Medway / Swale (E1–E3); Ignore for Medway (E4); Medway (E5–E7)

WEST BOUND

Time	E1 Ramsgate to North Foreland: Duration	Time at End of Sector	Time	E2 North Foreland to SE Margate: Duration	Time at End of Sector	Time	E3 SE Margate to Copperas: Duration	Time at End of Sector	Time	E4 Copperas to Swale Landfall: Duration	Time at End of Sector
- 6.00	**51**	**- 5:09**	**- 6.00**	**39**	**- 5:21**	**- 6.00**	**47**	**- 5:13**	**- 6.00**	**44**	**- 5:16**
- 5.45	51	- 4:54	- 5.45	38	- 5:07	- 5.45	46	- 4:59	- 5.45	43	- 5:02
- 5.30	52	- 4:38	- 5.30	38	- 4:52	- 5.30	45	- 4:45	- 5.30	42	- 4:48
- 5.15	52	- 4:23	- 5.15	37	- 4:38	- 5.15	44	- 4:31	- 5.15	41	- 4:34
- 5.00	**52**	**- 4:08**	**- 5.00**	**36**	**- 4:24**	**- 5.00**	**43**	**- 4:17**	**- 5.00**	**41**	**- 4:19**
- 4.45	52	- 3:53	- 4.45	36	- 4:09	- 4.45	42	- 4:03	- 4.45	40	- 4:05
- 4.30	52	- 3:38	- 4.30	35	- 3:55	- 4.30	42	- 3:48	- 4.30	40	- 3:50
- 4.15	50	- 3:25	- 4.15	35	- 3:40	- 4.15	42	- 3:33	- 4.15	40	- 3:35
- 4.00	**48**	**- 3:12**	**- 4.00**	**35**	**- 3:25**	**- 4.00**	**41**	**- 3:19**	**- 4.00**	**39**	**- 3:21**
- 3.45	46	- 2:59	- 3.45	34	- 3:11	- 3.45	41	- 3:04	- 3.45	39	- 3:06
- 3.30	44	- 2:46	- 3.30	34	- 2:56	- 3.30	41	- 2:49	- 3.30	39	- 2:51
- 3.15	42	- 2:33	- 3.15	34	- 2:41	- 3.15	41	- 2:34	- 3.15	39	- 2:36
- 3.00	**40**	**- 2:20**	**- 3.00**	**34**	**- 2:26**	**- 3.00**	**40**	**- 2:20**	**- 3.00**	**39**	**- 2:21**
- 2.45	37	- 2:08	- 2.45	34	- 2:11	- 2.45	40	- 2:05	- 2.45	39	- 2:06
- 2.30	35	- 1:55	- 2.30	34	- 1:56	- 2.30	41	- 1:49	- 2.30	40	- 1:50
- 2.15	34	- 1:41	- 2.15	34	- 1:41	- 2.15	41	- 1:34	- 2.15	40	- 1:35
- 2.00	**33**	**- 1:27**	**- 2.00**	**33**	**- 1:27**	**- 2.00**	**41**	**- 1:19**	**- 2.00**	**40**	**- 1:20**
- 1.45	32	- 1:13	- 1.45	34	- 1:11	- 1.45	42	- 1:03	- 1.45	41	- 1:04
- 1.30	30	- 1:00	- 1.30	35	- 0:55	- 1.30	43	- 0:47	- 1.30	42	- 0:48
- 1.15	31	- 0:44	- 1.15	36	- 0:39	- 1.15	44	- 0:31	- 1.15	43	- 0:32
- 1.00	**31**	**- 0:29**	**- 1.00**	**37**	**- 0:23**	**- 1.00**	**45**	**- 0:15**	**- 1.00**	**44**	**- 0:16**
- 0.45	31	- 0:14	- 0.45	39	- 0:06	- 0.45	48	+ 0:03	- 0.45	46	+ 0:01
- 0.30	31	+ 0:01	- 0.30	40	+ 0:10	- 0.30	50	+ 0:20	- 0.30	48	+ 0:18
- 0.15	31	+ 0:16	- 0.15	42	+ 0:27	- 0.15	52	+ 0:37	- 0.15	50	+ 0:35
HW	**31**	**+ 0:31**	**HW**	**44**	**+ 0:44**	**HW**	**54**	**+ 0:54**	**HW**	**52**	**+ 0:52**
+ 0.15	32	+ 0:47	+ 0.15	46	+ 1:01	+ 0.15	56	+ 1:11	+ 0.15	54	+ 1:09
+ 0.30	32	+ 1:02	+ 0.30	48	+ 1:18	+ 0.30	58	+ 1:28	+ 0.30	56	+ 1:26
+ 0.45	33	+ 1:18	+ 0.45	50	+ 1:35	+ 0.45	60	+ 1:45	+ 0.45	57	+ 1:42
+ 1.00	**34**	**+ 1:34**	**+ 1.00**	**52**	**+ 1:52**	**+ 1.00**	**62**	**+ 2:02**	**+ 1.00**	**59**	**+ 1:59**
+ 1.15	35	+ 1:50	+ 1.15	52	+ 2:07	+ 1.15	62	+ 2:17	+ 1.15	59	+ 2:14
+ 1.30	36	+ 2:06	+ 1.30	53	+ 2:23	+ 1.30	63	+ 2:33	+ 1.30	60	+ 2:30
+ 1.45	37	+ 2:22	+ 1.45	53	+ 2:38	+ 1.45	63	+ 2:48	+ 1.45	60	+ 2:45
+ 2.00	**38**	**+ 2:38**	**+ 2.00**	**53**	**+ 2:53**	**+ 2.00**	**63**	**+ 3:03**	**+ 2.00**	**61**	**+ 3:01**
+ 2.15	39	+ 2:54	+ 2.15	53	+ 3:08	+ 2.15	62	+ 3:17	+ 2.15	60	+ 3:15
+ 2.30	40	+ 3:10	+ 2.30	52	+ 3:22	+ 2.30	62	+ 3:32	+ 2.30	59	+ 3:29
+ 2.45	41	+ 3:26	+ 2.45	52	+ 3:37	+ 2.45	61	+ 3:46	+ 2.45	58	+ 3:43
+ 3.00	**42**	**+ 3:42**	**+ 3.00**	**51**	**+ 3:51**	**+ 3.00**	**60**	**+ 4:00**	**+ 3.00**	**58**	**+ 3:58**
+ 3.15	43	+ 3:58	+ 3.15	50	+ 4:05	+ 3.15	59	+ 4:14	+ 3.15	57	+ 4:12
+ 3.30	44	+ 4:14	+ 3.30	49	+ 4:19	+ 3.30	58	+ 4:28	+ 3.30	56	+ 4:26
+ 3.45	44	+ 4:29	+ 3.45	48	+ 4:33	+ 3.45	57	+ 4:42	+ 3.45	55	+ 4:40
+ 4.00	**44**	**+ 4:44**	**+ 4.00**	**47**	**+ 4:47**	**+ 4.00**	**56**	**+ 4:56**	**+ 4.00**	**54**	**+ 4:54**
+ 4.15	45	+ 5:00	+ 4.15	46	+ 5:01	+ 4.15	56	+ 5:11	+ 4.15	53	+ 5:08
+ 4.30	45	+ 5:15	+ 4.30	46	+ 5:16	+ 4.30	55	+ 5:25	+ 4.30	52	+ 5:22
+ 4.45	46	+ 5:31	+ 4.45	45	+ 5:30	+ 4.45	54	+ 5:39	+ 4.45	51	+ 5:36
+ 5.00	**47**	**+ 5:47**	**+ 5.00**	**44**	**+ 5:44**	**+ 5.00**	**53**	**+ 5:53**	**+ 5.00**	**50**	**+ 5:50**
+ 5.15	47	- 5:58	+ 5.15	44	+ 5:59	+ 5.15	52	- 5:53	+ 5.15	49	- 5:56
+ 5.30	48	- 5:42	+ 5.30	43	- 5:47	+ 5.30	52	- 5:38	+ 5.30	48	- 5:42
+ 5.45	49	- 5:26	+ 5.45	42	- 5:33	+ 5.45	51	- 5:24	+ 5.45	48	- 5:27
+ 6.00	50	**- 5:10**	**+ 6.00**	42	**- 5:18**	**+ 6.00**	50	**- 5:10**	**+ 6.00**	47	**- 5:13**

Time	E5 Copperas to Kentish Flats: Duration	Time at End of Sector	Time	E6 Kentish Flats to Spile: Duration	Time at End of Sector	Time	E7 Spile to Medway Channel: Duration	Time at End of Sector
- 6.00	**43**	**- 5:17**	**- 6.00**	**37**	**- 5:23**	**- 6.00**	**40**	**- 5:20**
- 5.45	43	- 5:02	- 5.45	37	- 5:08	- 5.45	40	- 5:05
- 5.30	43	- 4:47	- 5.30	36	- 4:54	- 5.30	40	- 4:50
- 5.15	42	- 4:33	- 5.15	36	- 4:39	- 5.15	40	- 4:35
- 5.00	**42**	**- 4:18**	**- 5.00**	**35**	**- 4:25**	**- 5.00**	**39**	**- 4:21**
- 4.45	42	- 4:03	- 4.45	36	- 4:09	- 4.45	39	- 4:06
- 4.30	41	- 3:49	- 4.30	36	- 3:54	- 4.30	39	- 3:51
- 4.15	41	- 3:34	- 4.15	36	- 3:39	- 4.15	40	- 3:35
- 4.00	**41**	**- 3:19**	**- 4.00**	**36**	**- 3:24**	**- 4.00**	**40**	**- 3:20**
- 3.45	41	- 3:04	- 3.45	36	- 3:09	- 3.45	40	- 3:05
- 3.30	41	- 2:49	- 3.30	36	- 2:54	- 3.30	40	- 2:50
- 3.15	41	- 2:34	- 3.15	36	- 2:39	- 3.15	40	- 2:35
- 3.00	**41**	**- 2:19**	**- 3.00**	**36**	**- 2:24**	**- 3.00**	**40**	**- 2:20**
- 2.45	41	- 2:04	- 2.45	36	- 2:09	- 2.45	40	- 2:05
- 2.30	41	- 1:49	- 2.30	36	- 1:54	- 2.30	40	- 1:50
- 2.15	41	- 1:34	- 2.15	37	- 1:38	- 2.15	40	- 1:35
- 2.00	**41**	**- 1:19**	**- 2.00**	**37**	**- 1:23**	**- 2.00**	**41**	**- 1:19**
- 1.45	42	- 1:03	- 1.45	37	- 1:08	- 1.45	41	- 1:04
- 1.30	42	- 0:48	- 1.30	37	- 0:53	- 1.30	41	- 0:49
- 1.15	43	- 0:32	- 1.15	38	- 0:37	- 1.15	42	- 0:33
- 1.00	**43**	**- 0:17**	**- 1.00**	**38**	**- 0:22**	**- 1.00**	**42**	**- 0:18**
- 0.45	44	- 0:01	- 0.45	39	- 0:06	- 0.45	43	- 0:02
- 0.30	46	+ 0:16	- 0.30	40	+ 0:10	- 0.30	44	+ 0:14
- 0.15	47	+ 0:32	- 0.15	41	+ 0:26	- 0.15	45	+ 0:30
HW	**48**	**+ 0:48**	**HW**	**42**	**+ 0:42**	**HW**	**47**	**+ 0:47**
+ 0.15	49	+ 1:04	+ 0.15	43	+ 0:58	+ 0.15	48	+ 1:03
+ 0.30	50	+ 1:20	+ 0.30	45	+ 1:15	+ 0.30	49	+ 1:19
+ 0.45	51	+ 1:36	+ 0.45	46	+ 1:31	+ 0.45	50	+ 1:35
+ 1.00	**52**	**+ 1:52**	**+ 1.00**	**47**	**+ 1:47**	**+ 1.00**	**51**	**+ 1:51**
+ 1.15	52	+ 2:07	+ 1.15	47	+ 2:02	+ 1.15	51	+ 2:06
+ 1.30	53	+ 2:23	+ 1.30	46	+ 2:16	+ 1.30	50	+ 2:20
+ 1.45	53	+ 2:38	+ 1.45	46	+ 2:31	+ 1.45	50	+ 2:35
+ 2.00	**53**	**+ 2:53**	**+ 2.00**	**46**	**+ 2:46**	**+ 2.00**	**50**	**+ 2:50**
+ 2.15	52	+ 3:07	+ 2.15	45	+ 3:00	+ 2.15	49	+ 3:04
+ 2.30	52	+ 3:22	+ 2.30	44	+ 3:14	+ 2.30	48	+ 3:18
+ 2.45	51	+ 3:36	+ 2.45	43	+ 3:28	+ 2.45	47	+ 3:32
+ 3.00	**51**	**+ 3:51**	**+ 3.00**	**42**	**+ 3:42**	**+ 3.00**	**46**	**+ 3:46**
+ 3.15	50	+ 4:05	+ 3.15	42	+ 3:57	+ 3.15	45	+ 4:00
+ 3.30	50	+ 4:20	+ 3.30	41	+ 4:11	+ 3.30	45	+ 4:15
+ 3.45	49	+ 4:34	+ 3.45	40	+ 4:25	+ 3.45	44	+ 4:29
+ 4.00	**49**	**+ 4:49**	**+ 4.00**	**39**	**+ 4:39**	**+ 4.00**	**43**	**+ 4:43**
+ 4.15	48	+ 5:03	+ 4.15	39	+ 4:54	+ 4.15	43	+ 4:58
+ 4.30	48	+ 5:18	+ 4.30	39	+ 5:09	+ 4.30	42	+ 5:12
+ 4.45	47	+ 5:32	+ 4.45	38	+ 5:23	+ 4.45	42	+ 5:27
+ 5.00	**46**	**+ 5:46**	**+ 5.00**	**38**	**+ 5:38**	**+ 5.00**	**41**	**+ 5:41**
+ 5.15	46	- 5:59	+ 5.15	38	+ 5:53	+ 5.15	41	+ 5:56
+ 5.30	45	- 5:45	+ 5.30	37	- 5:53	+ 5.30	41	- 5:49
+ 5.45	45	- 5:30	+ 5.45	37	- 5:38	+ 5.45	41	- 5:34
+ 6.00	45	**- 5:15**	**+ 6.00**	**37**	**- 5:23**	**+ 6.00**	41	**- 5:19**

Table F - Queens Channel and Swale Northwards

Neaps — All times relate to HW Sheerness — **Time to cover Sectors (in minutes) at 4.0 Kts**

NORTH & WEST

	The Queens Channel														Swale Northwards								
	F1			F2			F3			F4			F5			F6			F7			F8	
	Margate Sand to Wedge			Wedge to Woolpack			Woolpack to Swale Landfall			Wedge to Spaniard			Spaniard to Spile			Swale Landfall to Spaniard			Spaniard to Red Sand			Red Sand to SW Barrow	
Time	Duration	Time at End of Sector	Time	Duration	Time at End of Sector	Time	Duration	Time at End of Sector	Time	Duration	Time at End of Sector	Time	Duration	Time at End of Sector	Time	Duration	Time at End of Sector	Time	Duration	Time at End of Sector	Time	Duration	Time at End of Sector
- 6.00	**67**	**- 4:53**	**- 6.00**	**114**	**- 4:06**	**- 6.00**	**76**	**- 4:44**	**- 6.00**	**56**	**- 5:04**	**- 6.00**	**67**	**- 4:53**	**- 6.00**	**33**	**- 5:27**	**- 6.00**	**76**	**- 4:44**	**- 6.00**	**35**	**- 5:25**
- 5.45	66	- 4:39	- 5.45	112	- 3:53	- 5.45	76	- 4:29	- 5.45	55	- 4:50	- 5.45	66	- 4:39	- 5.45	32	- 5:13	- 5.45	75	- 4:30	- 5.45	36	- 5:09
- 5.30	66	- 4:24	- 5.30	109	- 3:41	- 5.30	75	- 4:15	- 5.30	54	- 4:36	- 5.30	64	- 4:26	- 5.30	31	- 4:59	- 5.30	74	- 4:16	- 5.30	37	- 4:53
- 5.15	65	- 4:10	- 5.15	107	- 3:28	- 5.15	75	- 4:00	- 5.15	53	- 4:22	- 5.15	63	- 4:12	- 5.15	29	- 4:46	- 5.15	73	- 4:02	- 5.15	37	- 4:38
- 5.00	**65**	**- 3:55**	**- 5.00**	**105**	**- 3:15**	**- 5.00**	**74**	**- 3:46**	**- 5.00**	**52**	**- 4:08**	**- 5.00**	**62**	**- 3:58**	**- 5.00**	**28**	**- 4:32**	**- 5.00**	**73**	**- 3:47**	**- 5.00**	**38**	**- 4:22**
- 4.45	65	- 3:40	- 4.45	103	- 3:02	- 4.45	74	- 3:31	- 4.45	51	- 3:54	- 4.45	61	- 3:44	- 4.45	28	- 4:17	- 4.45	73	- 3:32	- 4.45	38	- 4:07
- 4.30	65	- 3:25	- 4.30	102	- 2:48	- 4.30	75	- 3:15	- 4.30	50	- 3:40	- 4.30	60	- 3:30	- 4.30	28	- 4:02	- 4.30	72	- 3:18	- 4.30	38	- 3:52
- 4.15	65	- 3:10	- 4.15	100	- 2:35	- 4.15	75	- 3:00	- 4.15	49	- 3:26	- 4.15	59	- 3:16	- 4.15	28	- 3:47	- 4.15	72	- 3:03	- 4.15	39	- 3:36
- 4.00	**65**	**- 2:55**	**- 4.00**	**98**	**- 2:22**	**- 4.00**	**75**	**- 2:45**	**- 4.00**	**48**	**- 3:12**	**- 4.00**	**58**	**- 3:02**	**- 4.00**	**28**	**- 3:32**	**- 4.00**	**72**	**- 2:48**	**- 4.00**	**39**	**- 3:21**
- 3.45	65	- 2:40	- 3.45	97	- 2:08	- 3.45	76	- 2:29	- 3.45	48	- 2:57	- 3.45	58	- 2:47	- 3.45	28	- 3:17	- 3.45	72	- 2:33	- 3.45	39	- 3:06
- 3.30	64	- 2:26	- 3.30	97	- 1:53	- 3.30	76	- 2:14	- 3.30	47	- 2:43	- 3.30	57	- 2:33	- 3.30	27	- 3:03	- 3.30	72	- 2:18	- 3.30	39	- 2:51
- 3.15	64	- 2:11	- 3.15	96	- 1:39	- 3.15	76	- 1:59	- 3.15	47	- 2:28	- 3.15	57	- 2:18	- 3.15	27	- 2:48	- 3.15	72	- 2:03	- 3.15	38	- 2:37
- 3.00	**64**	**- 1:56**	**- 3.00**	**95**	**- 1:25**	**- 3.00**	**76**	**- 1:44**	**- 3.00**	**46**	**- 2:14**	**- 3.00**	**56**	**- 2:04**	**- 3.00**	**27**	**- 2:33**	**- 3.00**	**72**	**- 1:48**	**- 3.00**	**38**	**- 2:22**
- 2.45	64	- 1:41	- 2.45	97	- 1:08	- 2.45	77	- 1:28	- 2.45	46	- 1:59	- 2.45	57	- 1:48	- 2.45	27	- 2:18	- 2.45	73	- 1:32	- 2.45	38	- 2:07
- 2.30	64	- 1:26	- 2.30	98	- 0:52	- 2.30	77	- 1:13	- 2.30	46	- 1:44	- 2.30	57	- 1:33	- 2.30	27	- 2:03	- 2.30	73	- 1:17	- 2.30	38	- 1:52
- 2.15	64	- 1:11	- 2.15	100	- 0:35	- 2.15	77	- 0:58	- 2.15	47	- 1:28	- 2.15	58	- 1:17	- 2.15	27	- 1:48	- 2.15	74	- 1:01	- 2.15	38	- 1:37
- 2.00	**64**	**- 0:56**	**- 2.00**	**101**	**- 0:19**	**- 2.00**	**77**	**- 0:43**	**- 2.00**	**47**	**- 1:13**	**- 2.00**	**58**	**- 1:02**	**- 2.00**	**28**	**- 1:32**	**- 2.00**	**75**	**- 0:45**	**- 2.00**	**38**	**- 1:22**
- 1.45	64	- 0:41	- 1.45	106	+ 0:01	- 1.45	79	- 0:26	- 1.45	48	- 0:57	- 1.45	60	- 0:45	- 1.45	28	- 1:17	- 1.45	77	- 0:28	- 1.45	37	- 1:08
- 1.30	65	- 0:25	- 1.30	111	+ 0:21	- 1.30	81	- 0:09	- 1.30	50	- 0:40	- 1.30	62	- 0:28	- 1.30	28	- 1:02	- 1.30	78	- 0:12	- 1.30	37	- 0:53
- 1.15	65	- 0:10	- 1.15	116	+ 0:41	- 1.15	82	+ 0:07	- 1.15	52	- 0:23	- 1.15	64	- 0:11	- 1.15	28	- 0:47	- 1.15	80	+ 0:05	- 1.15	36	- 0:39
- 1.00	**65**	**+ 0:05**	**- 1.00**	**121**	**+ 1:01**	**- 1.00**	**84**	**+ 0:24**	**- 1.00**	**53**	**- 0:07**	**- 1.00**	**66**	**+ 0:06**	**- 1.00**	**28**	**- 0:32**	**- 1.00**	**82**	**+ 0:22**	**- 1.00**	**35**	**- 0:25**
- 0.45	66	+ 0:21	- 0.45	130	+ 1:25	- 0.45	88	+ 0:43	- 0.45	56	+ 0:11	- 0.45	69	+ 0:24	- 0.45	28	- 0:17	- 0.45	85	+ 0:40	- 0.45	35	- 0:10
- 0.30	67	+ 0:37	- 0.30	138	+ 1:48	- 0.30	92	+ 1:02	- 0.30	58	+ 0:28	- 0.30	73	+ 0:43	- 0.30	28	- 0:02	- 0.30	88	+ 0:58	- 0.30	34	+ 0:04
- 0.15	67	+ 0:52	- 0.15	147	+ 2:12	- 0.15	96	+ 1:21	- 0.15	61	+ 0:46	- 0.15	76	+ 1:01	- 0.15	29	+ 0:14	- 0.15	90	+ 1:15	- 0.15	33	+ 0:18
HW	**68**	**+ 1:08**	**HW**	**155**	**+ 2:35**	**HW**	**100**	**+ 1:40**	**HW**	**63**	**+ 1:03**	**HW**	**80**	**+ 1:20**	**HW**	**29**	**+ 0:29**	**HW**	**93**	**+ 1:33**	**HW**	**33**	**+ 0:33**
+ 0.15	69	+ 1:24	+ 0.15	163	+ 2:58	+ 0.15	102	+ 1:57	+ 0.15	67	+ 1:22	+ 0.15	86	+ 1:41	+ 0.15	30	+ 0:45	+ 0.15	96	+ 1:51	+ 0.15	32	+ 0:47
+ 0.30	71	+ 1:41	+ 0.30	170	+ 3:20	+ 0.30	104	+ 2:14	+ 0.30	71	+ 1:41	+ 0.30	92	+ 2:02	+ 0.30	30	+ 1:00	+ 0.30	98	+ 2:08	+ 0.30	32	+ 1:02
+ 0.45	72	+ 1:57	+ 0.45	177	+ 3:42	+ 0.45	107	+ 2:32	+ 0.45	75	+ 2:00	+ 0.45	98	+ 2:23	+ 0.45	31	+ 1:16	+ 0.45	101	+ 2:26	+ 0.45	31	+ 1:16
+ 1.00	**73**	**+ 2:13**	**+ 1.00**	**185**	**+ 4:05**	**+ 1.00**	**109**	**+ 2:49**	**+ 1.00**	**78**	**+ 2:18**	**+ 1.00**	**104**	**+ 2:44**	**+ 1.00**	**31**	**+ 1:31**	**+ 1.00**	**104**	**+ 2:44**	**+ 1.00**	**30**	**+ 1:30**
+ 1.15	74	+ 2:29	+ 1.15	185	+ 4:20	+ 1.15	107	+ 3:02	+ 1.15	83	+ 2:38	+ 1.15	107	+ 3:02	+ 1.15	31	+ 1:46	+ 1.15	103	+ 2:58	+ 1.15	30	+ 1:45
+ 1.30	75	+ 2:45	+ 1.30	185	+ 4:35	+ 1.30	106	+ 3:16	+ 1.30	87	+ 2:57	+ 1.30	110	+ 3:20	+ 1.30	31	+ 2:01	+ 1.30	103	+ 3:13	+ 1.30	30	+ 2:00
+ 1.45	76	+ 3:01	+ 1.45	185	+ 4:50	+ 1.45	104	+ 3:29	+ 1.45	91	+ 3:16	+ 1.45	112	+ 3:37	+ 1.45	32	+ 2:17	+ 1.45	102	+ 3:27	+ 1.45	29	+ 2:14
+ 2.00	**77**	**+ 3:17**	**+ 2.00**	**185**	**+ 5:05**	**+ 2.00**	**103**	**+ 3:43**	**+ 2.00**	**95**	**+ 3:35**	**+ 2.00**	**115**	**+ 3:55**	**+ 2.00**	**32**	**+ 2:32**	**+ 2.00**	**102**	**+ 3:42**	**+ 2.00**	**29**	**+ 2:29**
+ 2.15	77	+ 3:32	+ 2.15	181	+ 5:16	+ 2.15	100	+ 3:55	+ 2.15	94	+ 3:49	+ 2.15	113	+ 4:08	+ 2.15	31	+ 2:46	+ 2.15	101	+ 3:56	+ 2.15	29	+ 2:44
+ 2.30	77	+ 3:47	+ 2.30	178	+ 5:28	+ 2.30	98	+ 4:08	+ 2.30	94	+ 4:04	+ 2.30	112	+ 4:22	+ 2.30	31	+ 3:01	+ 2.30	99	+ 4:09	+ 2.30	30	+ 3:00
+ 2.45	77	+ 4:02	+ 2.45	174	+ 5:39	+ 2.45	95	+ 4:20	+ 2.45	93	+ 4:18	+ 2.45	110	+ 4:35	+ 2.45	31	+ 3:16	+ 2.45	98	+ 4:23	+ 2.45	30	+ 3:15
+ 3.00	**77**	**+ 4:17**	**+ 3.00**	**170**	**+ 5:50**	**+ 3.00**	**92**	**+ 4:32**	**+ 3.00**	**92**	**+ 4:32**	**+ 3.00**	**109**	**+ 4:49**	**+ 3.00**	**31**	**+ 3:31**	**+ 3.00**	**97**	**+ 4:37**	**+ 3.00**	**30**	**+ 3:30**
+ 3.15	76	+ 4:31	+ 3.15	165	- 6:00	+ 3.15	90	+ 4:45	+ 3.15	87	+ 4:42	+ 3.15	105	+ 5:00	+ 3.15	30	+ 3:45	+ 3.15	95	+ 4:50	+ 3.15	30	+ 3:45
+ 3.30	75	+ 4:45	+ 3.30	161	- 5:49	+ 3.30	88	+ 4:58	+ 3.30	83	+ 4:53	+ 3.30	102	+ 5:12	+ 3.30	30	+ 4:00	+ 3.30	94	+ 5:04	+ 3.30	31	+ 4:01
+ 3.45	75	+ 5:00	+ 3.45	156	- 5:39	+ 3.45	86	+ 5:11	+ 3.45	79	+ 5:04	+ 3.45	98	+ 5:23	+ 3.45	30	+ 4:15	+ 3.45	92	+ 5:17	+ 3.45	31	+ 4:16
+ 4.00	**74**	**+ 5:14**	**+ 4.00**	**151**	**- 5:29**	**+ 4.00**	**83**	**+ 5:23**	**+ 4.00**	**74**	**+ 5:14**	**+ 4.00**	**95**	**+ 5:35**	**+ 4.00**	**30**	**+ 4:30**	**+ 4.00**	**91**	**+ 5:31**	**+ 4.00**	**31**	**+ 4:31**
+ 4.15	73	+ 5:28	+ 4.15	147	- 5:18	+ 4.15	82	+ 5:37	+ 4.15	72	+ 5:27	+ 4.15	91	+ 5:46	+ 4.15	30	+ 4:45	+ 4.15	89	+ 5:44	+ 4.15	31	+ 4:46
+ 4.30	72	+ 5:42	+ 4.30	143	- 5:07	+ 4.30	82	+ 5:52	+ 4.30	70	+ 5:40	+ 4.30	87	+ 5:57	+ 4.30	29	+ 4:59	+ 4.30	87	+ 5:57	+ 4.30	32	+ 5:02
+ 4.45	72	+ 5:57	+ 4.45	139	- 4:56	+ 4.45	81	- 5:54	+ 4.45	67	+ 5:52	+ 4.45	83	- 5:52	+ 4.45	29	+ 5:14	+ 4.45	85	- 5:50	+ 4.45	32	+ 5:17
+ 5.00	**71**	**- 5:49**	**+ 5.00**	**135**	**- 4:45**	**+ 5.00**	**80**	**- 5:40**	**+ 5.00**	**65**	**- 5:55**	**+ 5.00**	**79**	**- 5:41**	**+ 5.00**	**29**	**+ 5:29**	**+ 5.00**	**84**	**- 5:36**	**+ 5.00**	**32**	**+ 5:32**
+ 5.15	70	- 5:35	+ 5.15	132	- 4:33	+ 5.15	80	- 5:25	+ 5.15	64	- 5:41	+ 5.15	77	- 5:28	+ 5.15	29	+ 5:44	+ 5.15	83	- 5:22	+ 5.15	33	+ 5:48
+ 5.30	70	- 5:20	+ 5.30	129	- 4:21	+ 5.30	80	- 5:10	+ 5.30	62	- 5:28	+ 5.30	75	- 5:15	+ 5.30	29	+ 5:59	+ 5.30	82	- 5:08	+ 5.30	33	- 5:57
+ 5.45	69	- 5:06	+ 5.45	126	- 4:09	+ 5.45	80	- 4:55	+ 5.45	61	- 5:14	+ 5.45	74	- 5:01	+ 5.45	28	- 5:47	+ 5.45	81	- 4:54	+ 5.45	33	- 5:42
+ 6.00	**68**	**- 4:52**	**+ 6.00**	**123**	**- 3:57**	**+ 6.00**	**79**	**- 4:41**	**+ 6.00**	**60**	**- 5:00**	**+ 6.00**	**72**	**- 4:48**	**+ 6.00**	**28**	**- 5:32**	**+ 6.00**	**80**	**- 4:40**	**+ 6.00**	**34**	**- 5:26**

The Queens Channel Swale Northwards

Table F - Queens Channel and Swale Northwards

Time to cover Sectors (in minutes) at 4.0 kts — All times relate to HW Sheerness — **Springs**

The Queens Channel

Time	F1 Margate Sand to Wedge: Duration	F1 Time at End of Sector	F2 Wedge to Woolpack: Duration	F2 Time at End of Sector	F3 Woolpack to Swale Landfall: Duration	F3 Time at End of Sector	F4 Wedge to Spaniard: Duration	F4 Time at End of Sector	F5 Spaniard to Spile: Duration	F5 Time at End of Sector
- 6.00	66	- 4:54	109	- 4:11	73	- 4:47	54	- 5:06	64	- 4:56
- 5.45	66	- 4:39	106	- 3:59	72	- 4:33	53	- 4:52	62	- 4:43
- 5.30	66	- 4:24	104	- 3:46	71	- 4:19	51	- 4:39	61	- 4:29
- 5.15	65	- 4:10	101	- 3:34	71	- 4:04	50	- 4:25	59	- 4:16
- 5.00	65	- 3:55	99	- 3:21	70	- 3:50	48	- 4:12	57	- 4:03
- 4.45	65	- 3:40	97	- 3:08	70	- 3:35	47	- 3:58	56	- 3:49
- 4.30	64	- 3:26	95	- 2:55	71	- 3:19	46	- 3:44	55	- 3:35
- 4.15	64	- 3:11	93	- 2:42	71	- 3:04	45	- 3:30	54	- 3:21
- 4.00	64	- 2:56	91	- 2:29	71	- 2:49	44	- 3:16	53	- 3:07
- 3.45	64	- 2:41	90	- 2:15	72	- 2:33	43	- 3:02	52	- 2:53
- 3.30	64	- 2:26	89	- 2:01	72	- 2:18	43	- 2:47	51	- 2:39
- 3.15	64	- 2:11	88	- 1:47	73	- 2:02	42	- 2:33	51	- 2:24
- 3.00	64	- 1:56	87	- 1:33	73	- 1:47	41	- 2:19	50	- 2:10
- 2.45	64	- 1:41	89	- 1:16	73	- 1:32	41	- 2:04	51	- 1:54
- 2.30	63	- 1:27	91	- 0:59	74	- 1:16	41	- 1:49	51	- 1:39
- 2.15	63	- 1:12	92	- 0:43	75	- 1:00	41	- 1:34	51	- 1:24
- 2.00	63	- 0:57	94	- 0:26	75	- 0:45	41	- 1:19	52	- 1:08
- 1.45	63	- 0:42	101	- 0:04	77	- 0:28	43	- 1:02	54	- 0:51
- 1.30	64	- 0:26	109	+ 0:19	80	- 0:10	45	- 0:45	57	- 0:33
- 1.15	64	- 0:11	116	+ 0:41	82	+ 0:07	47	- 0:28	59	- 0:16
- 1.00	64	+ 0:04	123	+ 1:03	84	+ 0:24	49	- 0:11	62	+ 0:02
- 0.45	65	+ 0:20	140	+ 1:35	92	+ 0:47	54	+ 0:09	68	+ 0:23
- 0.30	66	+ 0:36	156	+ 2:06	99	+ 1:09	58	+ 0:28	73	+ 0:43
- 0.15	67	+ 0:52	172	+ 2:37	106	+ 1:31	62	+ 0:47	79	+ 1:04
HW	68	+ 1:08	189	+ 3:09	113	+ 1:53	67	+ 1:07	85	+ 1:25
+ 0.15	70	+ 1:25	197	+ 3:32	115	+ 2:10	74	+ 1:29	96	+ 1:51
+ 0.30	73	+ 1:43	205	+ 3:55	116	+ 2:26	82	+ 1:52	107	+ 2:17
+ 0.45	75	+ 2:00	213	+ 4:18	118	+ 2:43	90	+ 2:15	118	+ 2:43
+ 1.00	77	+ 2:17	221	+ 4:41	120	+ 3:00	98	+ 2:38	128	+ 3:08
+ 1.15	78	+ 2:33	218	+ 4:53	117	+ 3:12	102	+ 2:57	131	+ 3:26
+ 1.30	80	+ 2:50	216	+ 5:06	114	+ 3:24	106	+ 3:16	133	+ 3:43
+ 1.45	82	+ 3:07	213	+ 5:18	111	+ 3:36	110	+ 3:35	135	+ 4:00
+ 2.00	84	+ 3:24	211	+ 5:31	108	+ 3:48	114	+ 3:54	138	+ 4:18
+ 2.15	84	+ 3:39	204	+ 5:39	104	+ 3:59	111	+ 4:06	133	+ 4:28
+ 2.30	84	+ 3:54	197	+ 5:47	101	+ 4:11	107	+ 4:17	129	+ 4:39
+ 2.45	84	+ 4:09	190	+ 5:55	98	+ 4:23	104	+ 4:29	125	+ 4:50
+ 3.00	83	+ 4:23	183	- 5:57	94	+ 4:34	101	+ 4:41	120	+ 5:00
+ 3.15	82	+ 4:37	176	- 5:49	92	+ 4:47	97	+ 4:52	115	+ 5:10
+ 3.30	81	+ 4:51	169	- 5:41	89	+ 4:59	92	+ 5:02	110	+ 5:20
+ 3.45	80	+ 5:05	162	- 5:33	86	+ 5:11	88	+ 5:13	104	+ 5:29
+ 4.00	78	+ 5:18	155	- 5:25	83	+ 5:23	83	+ 5:23	99	+ 5:39
+ 4.15	77	+ 5:32	151	- 5:14	82	+ 5:37	79	+ 5:34	95	+ 5:50
+ 4.30	75	+ 5:45	147	- 5:03	81	+ 5:51	75	+ 5:45	90	- 6:00
+ 4.45	74	+ 5:59	143	- 4:52	80	- 5:55	71	+ 5:56	85	- 5:50
+ 5.00	73	- 5:47	139	- 4:41	79	- 5:41	67	- 5:53	81	- 5:39
+ 5.15	72	- 5:33	134	- 4:31	78	- 5:27	65	- 5:40	78	- 5:27
+ 5.30	71	- 5:19	130	- 4:20	78	- 5:12	63	- 5:27	76	- 5:14
+ 5.45	70	- 5:05	126	- 4:09	78	- 4:57	61	- 5:14	74	- 5:01
+ 6.00	69	- 4:51	121	- 3:59	78	- 4:42	59	- 5:01	71	- 4:49

Swale Northwards

Time	F6 Swale Landfall to Spaniard: Duration	F6 Time at End of Sector	F7 Spaniard to Red Sand: Duration	F7 Time at End of Sector	F8 Red Sand to SW Barrow: Duration	F8 Time at End of Sector
- 6.00	32	- 5:28	73	- 4:47	36	- 5:24
- 5.45	31	- 5:14	72	- 4:33	37	- 5:08
- 5.30	30	- 5:00	71	- 4:19	38	- 4:52
- 5.15	29	- 4:46	70	- 4:05	39	- 4:36
- 5.00	28	- 4:32	69	- 3:51	40	- 4:20
- 4.45	28	- 4:17	69	- 3:36	41	- 4:04
- 4.30	28	- 4:02	68	- 3:22	41	- 3:49
- 4.15	28	- 3:47	68	- 3:07	41	- 3:34
- 4.00	27	- 3:33	67	- 2:53	42	- 3:18
- 3.45	27	- 3:18	67	- 2:38	41	- 3:04
- 3.30	27	- 3:03	67	- 2:23	41	- 2:49
- 3.15	27	- 2:48	67	- 2:08	41	- 2:34
- 3.00	27	- 2:33	67	- 1:53	41	- 2:19
- 2.45	27	- 2:18	68	- 1:37	41	- 2:04
- 2.30	27	- 2:03	69	- 1:21	41	- 1:49
- 2.15	27	- 1:48	69	- 1:06	41	- 1:34
- 2.00	27	- 1:33	70	- 0:50	41	- 1:19
- 1.45	27	- 1:18	72	- 0:33	40	- 1:05
- 1.30	27	- 1:03	75	- 0:15	39	- 0:51
- 1.15	27	- 0:48	77	+ 0:02	38	- 0:37
- 1.00	27	- 0:33	79	+ 0:19	37	- 0:23
- 0.45	27	- 0:18	85	+ 0:40	36	- 0:09
- 0.30	28	- 0:02	90	+ 1:00	35	+ 0:05
- 0.15	29	+ 0:14	95	+ 1:20	34	+ 0:19
HW	29	+ 0:29	100	+ 1:40	33	+ 0:33
+ 0.15	30	+ 0:45	104	+ 1:59	32	+ 0:47
+ 0.30	31	+ 1:01	107	+ 2:17	31	+ 1:01
+ 0.45	32	+ 1:17	110	+ 2:35	30	+ 1:15
+ 1.00	33	+ 1:33	113	+ 2:53	29	+ 1:29
+ 1.15	33	+ 1:48	113	+ 3:08	28	+ 1:43
+ 1.30	33	+ 2:03	112	+ 3:22	28	+ 1:58
+ 1.45	34	+ 2:19	111	+ 3:36	28	+ 2:13
+ 2.00	34	+ 2:34	110	+ 3:50	27	+ 2:27
+ 2.15	33	+ 2:48	108	+ 4:03	27	+ 2:42
+ 2.30	33	+ 3:03	106	+ 4:16	27	+ 2:57
+ 2.45	33	+ 3:18	104	+ 4:29	28	+ 3:13
+ 3.00	32	+ 3:32	102	+ 4:42	28	+ 3:28
+ 3.15	32	+ 3:47	99	+ 4:54	28	+ 3:43
+ 3.30	32	+ 4:02	97	+ 5:07	29	+ 3:59
+ 3.45	31	+ 4:16	95	+ 5:20	29	+ 4:14
+ 4.00	31	+ 4:31	92	+ 5:32	29	+ 4:29
+ 4.15	30	+ 4:45	90	+ 5:45	30	+ 4:45
+ 4.30	30	+ 5:00	88	+ 5:58	31	+ 5:01
+ 4.45	30	+ 5:15	86	- 5:49	31	+ 5:16
+ 5.00	29	+ 5:29	84	- 5:36	32	+ 5:32
+ 5.15	29	+ 5:44	83	- 5:22	32	+ 5:47
+ 5.30	29	+ 5:59	82	- 5:08	33	- 5:57
+ 5.45	28	- 5:47	80	- 4:55	33	- 5:42
+ 6.00	28	- 5:32	79	- 4:41	34	- 5:26

The Queens Channel — Swale Northwards

NORTH & WEST

Table F - Queens Channel and Swale Northwards

Neaps — All times relate to HW Sheerness — **Time to cover Sectors (in minutes) at 5.0 Kts**

NORTH & WEST

The Queens Channel

Time	F1 Margate Sand to Wedge: Duration	F1 Time at End of Sector	F2 Wedge to Woolpack: Duration	F2 Time at End of Sector	F3 Woolpack to Swale Landfall: Duration	F3 Time at End of Sector	F4 Wedge to Spaniard: Duration	F4 Time at End of Sector	F5 Spaniard to Spile: Duration	F5 Time at End of Sector
- 6.00	**53**	**- 5:07**	**94**	**- 4:26**	**62**	**- 4:58**	**46**	**- 5:14**	**55**	**- 5:05**
- 5.45	53	- 4:52	93	- 4:12	62	- 4:43	45	- 5:00	54	- 4:51
- 5.30	53	- 4:37	92	- 3:58	61	- 4:29	44	- 4:46	53	- 4:37
- 5.15	53	- 4:22	91	- 3:44	61	- 4:14	43	- 4:32	52	- 4:23
- 5.00	**52**	**- 4:08**	**89**	**- 3:31**	**61**	**- 3:59**	**43**	**- 4:17**	**51**	**- 4:09**
- 4.45	52	- 3:53	88	- 3:17	61	- 3:44	42	- 4:03	51	- 3:54
- 4.30	52	- 3:38	87	- 3:03	61	- 3:29	41	- 3:49	50	- 3:40
- 4.15	52	- 3:23	86	- 2:49	61	- 3:14	41	- 3:34	49	- 3:26
- 4.00	**52**	**- 3:08**	**85**	**- 2:35**	**61**	**- 2:59**	**40**	**- 3:20**	**49**	**- 3:11**
- 3.45	52	- 2:53	84	- 2:21	61	- 2:44	40	- 3:05	48	- 2:57
- 3.30	52	- 2:38	83	- 2:07	62	- 2:28	39	- 2:51	48	- 2:42
- 3.15	52	- 2:23	83	- 1:52	62	- 2:13	39	- 2:36	48	- 2:27
- 3.00	**52**	**- 2:08**	**82**	**- 1:38**	**62**	**- 1:58**	**39**	**- 2:21**	**47**	**- 2:13**
- 2.45	52	- 1:53	83	- 1:22	62	- 1:43	39	- 2:06	47	- 1:58
- 2.30	52	- 1:38	84	- 1:06	62	- 1:28	39	- 1:51	48	- 1:42
- 2.15	52	- 1:23	85	- 0:50	62	- 1:13	39	- 1:36	48	- 1:27
- 2.00	**52**	**- 1:08**	**86**	**- 0:34**	**63**	**- 0:57**	**39**	**- 1:21**	**48**	**- 1:12**
- 1.45	52	- 0:53	88	- 0:17	64	- 0:41	40	- 1:05	49	- 0:56
- 1.30	52	- 0:38	89	- 0:01	64	- 0:26	41	- 0:49	51	- 0:39
- 1.15	52	- 0:23	91	+ 0:16	65	- 0:10	42	- 0:33	52	- 0:23
- 1.00	**52**	**- 0:08**	**93**	**+ 0:33**	**66**	**+ 0:06**	**43**	**- 0:17**	**53**	**- 0:07**
- 0.45	53	+ 0:08	98	+ 0:53	68	+ 0:23	44	- 0:01	55	+ 0:10
- 0.30	53	+ 0:23	103	+ 1:13	71	+ 0:41	46	+ 0:16	57	+ 0:27
- 0.15	54	+ 0:39	109	+ 1:34	73	+ 0:58	47	+ 0:32	59	+ 0:44
HW	**54**	**+ 0:54**	**114**	**+ 1:54**	**75**	**+ 1:15**	**49**	**+ 0:49**	**61**	**+ 1:01**
+ 0.15	55	+ 1:10	120	+ 2:15	76	+ 1:31	51	+ 1:06	64	+ 1:19
+ 0.30	56	+ 1:26	125	+ 2:35	78	+ 1:48	53	+ 1:23	67	+ 1:37
+ 0.45	56	+ 1:41	131	+ 2:56	79	+ 2:04	56	+ 1:41	70	+ 1:55
+ 1.00	**57**	**+ 1:57**	**136**	**+ 3:16**	**80**	**+ 2:20**	**58**	**+ 1:58**	**73**	**+ 2:13**
+ 1.15	58	+ 2:13	137	+ 3:32	79	+ 2:34	59	+ 2:14	75	+ 2:30
+ 1.30	58	+ 2:28	139	+ 3:49	79	+ 2:49	61	+ 2:31	76	+ 2:46
+ 1.45	59	+ 2:44	140	+ 4:05	78	+ 3:03	63	+ 2:48	78	+ 3:03
+ 2.00	**60**	**+ 3:00**	**142**	**+ 4:22**	**77**	**+ 3:17**	**64**	**+ 3:04**	**80**	**+ 3:20**
+ 2.15	60	+ 3:15	140	+ 4:35	76	+ 3:31	64	+ 3:19	79	+ 3:34
+ 2.30	60	+ 3:30	138	+ 4:48	74	+ 3:44	64	+ 3:34	79	+ 3:49
+ 2.45	60	+ 3:45	136	+ 5:01	73	+ 3:58	64	+ 3:49	78	+ 4:03
+ 3.00	**60**	**+ 4:00**	**134**	**+ 5:14**	**71**	**+ 4:11**	**63**	**+ 4:03**	**78**	**+ 4:18**
+ 3.15	59	+ 4:14	131	+ 5:26	70	+ 4:25	62	+ 4:17	76	+ 4:31
+ 3.30	59	+ 4:29	127	+ 5:37	69	+ 4:39	60	+ 4:30	74	+ 4:44
+ 3.45	59	+ 4:44	124	+ 5:49	68	+ 4:53	59	+ 4:44	72	+ 4:57
+ 4.00	**58**	**+ 4:58**	**120**	**- 6:00**	**67**	**+ 5:07**	**57**	**+ 4:57**	**70**	**+ 5:10**
+ 4.15	58	+ 5:13	118	- 5:47	66	+ 5:21	56	+ 5:11	68	+ 5:23
+ 4.30	57	+ 5:27	115	- 5:35	66	+ 5:36	55	+ 5:25	66	+ 5:36
+ 4.45	57	+ 5:42	112	- 5:23	65	+ 5:50	53	+ 5:38	65	+ 5:50
+ 5.00	**56**	**+ 5:56**	**110**	**- 5:10**	**65**	**- 5:55**	**52**	**+ 5:52**	**63**	**- 5:57**
+ 5.15	56	- 5:49	107	- 4:58	64	- 5:41	51	- 5:54	62	- 5:43
+ 5.30	55	- 5:35	105	- 4:45	64	- 5:26	50	- 5:40	60	- 5:30
+ 5.45	55	- 5:20	103	- 4:32	64	- 5:11	49	- 5:26	59	- 5:16
+ 6.00	**55**	**- 5:05**	**101**	**- 4:19**	**64**	**- 4:56**	**48**	**- 5:12**	**58**	**- 5:02**

Swale Northwards

Time	F6 Swale Landfall to Spaniard: Duration	F6 Time at End of Sector	F7 Spaniard to Red Sand: Duration	F7 Time at End of Sector	F8 Red Sand to SW Barrow: Duration	F8 Time at End of Sector
- 6.00	**26**	**- 5:34**	**62**	**- 4:58**	**28**	**- 5:32**
- 5.45	25	- 5:20	61	- 4:44	28	- 5:17
- 5.30	24	- 5:06	61	- 4:29	29	- 5:01
- 5.15	23	- 4:52	60	- 4:15	29	- 4:46
- 5.00	**23**	**- 4:37**	**60**	**- 4:00**	**30**	**- 4:30**
- 4.45	22	- 4:23	59	- 3:46	30	- 4:15
- 4.30	22	- 4:08	59	- 3:31	30	- 4:00
- 4.15	22	- 3:53	59	- 3:16	30	- 3:45
- 4.00	**22**	**- 3:38**	**59**	**- 3:01**	**30**	**- 3:30**
- 3.45	22	- 3:23	59	- 2:46	30	- 3:15
- 3.30	22	- 3:08	59	- 2:31	30	- 3:00
- 3.15	22	- 2:53	59	- 2:16	30	- 2:45
- 3.00	**22**	**- 2:38**	**59**	**- 2:01**	**30**	**- 2:30**
- 2.45	22	- 2:23	59	- 1:46	30	- 2:15
- 2.30	22	- 2:08	60	- 1:30	30	- 2:00
- 2.15	22	- 1:53	60	- 1:15	30	- 1:45
- 2.00	**22**	**- 1:38**	**61**	**- 0:59**	**30**	**- 1:30**
- 1.45	22	- 1:23	62	- 0:43	30	- 1:15
- 1.30	22	- 1:08	63	- 0:27	29	- 1:01
- 1.15	22	- 0:53	64	- 0:11	29	- 0:46
- 1.00	**22**	**- 0:38**	**65**	**+ 0:05**	**28**	**- 0:32**
- 0.45	22	- 0:23	67	+ 0:22	28	- 0:17
- 0.30	23	- 0:07	68	+ 0:38	27	- 0:03
- 0.15	23	+ 0:08	70	+ 0:55	27	+ 0:12
HW	**23**	**+ 0:23**	**72**	**+ 1:12**	**26**	**+ 0:26**
+ 0.15	24	+ 0:39	73	+ 1:28	26	+ 0:41
+ 0.30	24	+ 0:54	75	+ 1:45	25	+ 0:55
+ 0.45	24	+ 1:09	76	+ 2:01	25	+ 1:10
+ 1.00	**25**	**+ 1:25**	**77**	**+ 2:17**	**24**	**+ 1:24**
+ 1.15	25	+ 1:40	77	+ 2:32	24	+ 1:39
+ 1.30	25	+ 1:55	77	+ 2:47	24	+ 1:54
+ 1.45	25	+ 2:10	77	+ 3:02	23	+ 2:08
+ 2.00	**25**	**+ 2:25**	**77**	**+ 3:17**	**23**	**+ 2:23**
+ 2.15	25	+ 2:40	76	+ 3:31	23	+ 2:38
+ 2.30	25	+ 2:55	75	+ 3:45	24	+ 2:54
+ 2.45	25	+ 3:10	74	+ 3:59	24	+ 3:09
+ 3.00	**24**	**+ 3:24**	**73**	**+ 4:13**	**24**	**+ 3:24**
+ 3.15	24	+ 3:39	72	+ 4:27	24	+ 3:39
+ 3.30	24	+ 3:54	72	+ 4:42	24	+ 3:54
+ 3.45	24	+ 4:09	71	+ 4:56	25	+ 4:10
+ 4.00	**24**	**+ 4:24**	**70**	**+ 5:10**	**25**	**+ 4:25**
+ 4.15	24	+ 4:39	69	+ 5:24	25	+ 4:40
+ 4.30	23	+ 4:53	69	+ 5:39	25	+ 4:55
+ 4.45	23	+ 5:08	68	+ 5:53	26	+ 5:11
+ 5.00	**23**	**+ 5:23**	**67**	**- 5:53**	**26**	**+ 5:26**
+ 5.15	23	+ 5:38	66	- 5:39	26	+ 5:41
+ 5.30	23	+ 5:53	66	- 5:24	26	+ 5:56
+ 5.45	23	- 5:52	65	- 5:10	27	- 5:48
+ 6.00	**22**	**- 5:38**	**64**	**- 4:56**	**27**	**- 5:33**

Table F - Queens Channel and Swale Northwards

Time to cover Sectors (in minutes) at 5.0 kts — All times relate to HW Sheerness — **Springs**

NORTH & WEST

The Queens Channel

	F1		F2		F3		F4		F5	
	Margate Sand to Wedge		Wedge to Woolpack		Woolpack to Swale Landfall		Wedge to Spaniard		Spaniard to Spile	
Time	Duration	Time at End of Sector	Duration	Time at End of Sector	Duration	Time at End of Sector	Duration	Time at End of Sector	Duration	Time at End of Sector
- 6.00	54	- 5:06	91	- 4:29	60	- 5:00	45	- 5:15	53	- 5:07
- 5.45	53	- 4:52	89	- 4:16	60	- 4:45	44	- 5:01	52	- 4:53
- 5.30	53	- 4:37	87	- 4:03	59	- 4:31	42	- 4:48	51	- 4:39
- 5.15	52	- 4:23	85	- 3:50	58	- 4:17	41	- 4:34	49	- 4:26
- 5.00	52	- 4:08	83	- 3:37	58	- 4:02	40	- 4:20	48	- 4:12
- 4.45	52	- 3:53	82	- 3:23	58	- 3:47	40	- 4:05	47	- 3:58
- 4.30	52	- 3:38	81	- 3:09	58	- 3:32	39	- 3:51	47	- 3:43
- 4.15	52	- 3:23	79	- 2:56	58	- 3:17	38	- 3:37	46	- 3:29
- 4.00	51	- 3:09	78	- 2:42	58	- 3:02	37	- 3:23	45	- 3:15
- 3.45	51	- 2:54	77	- 2:28	59	- 2:46	37	- 3:08	44	- 3:01
- 3.30	51	- 2:39	76	- 2:14	59	- 2:31	36	- 2:54	44	- 2:46
- 3.15	51	- 2:24	75	- 2:00	59	- 2:16	36	- 2:39	43	- 2:32
- 3.00	51	- 2:09	74	- 1:46	60	- 2:00	35	- 2:25	43	- 2:17
- 2.45	51	- 1:54	75	- 1:30	60	- 1:45	35	- 2:10	43	- 2:02
- 2.30	51	- 1:39	76	- 1:14	60	- 1:30	35	- 1:55	43	- 1:47
- 2.15	51	- 1:24	77	- 0:58	61	- 1:14	35	- 1:40	43	- 1:32
- 2.00	51	- 1:09	78	- 0:42	61	- 0:59	35	- 1:25	43	- 1:17
- 1.45	51	- 0:54	82	- 0:23	62	- 0:43	36	- 1:09	45	- 1:00
- 1.30	51	- 0:39	85	- 0:05	64	- 0:26	37	- 0:53	47	- 0:43
- 1.15	51	- 0:24	89	+ 0:14	65	- 0:10	38	- 0:37	48	- 0:27
- 1.00	52	- 0:08	92	+ 0:32	66	+ 0:06	40	- 0:20	50	- 0:10
- 0.45	52	+ 0:07	101	+ 0:56	70	+ 0:25	42	- 0:03	53	+ 0:08
- 0.30	53	+ 0:23	109	+ 1:19	74	+ 0:44	45	+ 0:15	57	+ 0:27
- 0.15	53	+ 0:38	118	+ 1:43	78	+ 1:03	48	+ 0:33	60	+ 0:45
HW	54	+ 0:54	126	+ 2:06	82	+ 1:22	50	+ 0:50	64	+ 1:04
+ 0.15	55	+ 1:10	134	+ 2:29	84	+ 1:39	54	+ 1:09	69	+ 1:24
+ 0.30	57	+ 1:27	142	+ 2:52	86	+ 1:56	58	+ 1:28	74	+ 1:44
+ 0.45	58	+ 1:43	150	+ 3:15	89	+ 2:14	62	+ 1:47	79	+ 2:04
+ 1.00	59	+ 1:59	158	+ 3:38	91	+ 2:31	66	+ 2:06	85	+ 2:25
+ 1.15	60	+ 2:15	159	+ 3:54	89	+ 2:44	69	+ 2:24	88	+ 2:43
+ 1.30	61	+ 2:31	159	+ 4:09	87	+ 2:57	73	+ 2:43	91	+ 3:01
+ 1.45	63	+ 2:48	159	+ 4:24	86	+ 3:11	76	+ 3:01	94	+ 3:19
+ 2.00	64	+ 3:04	160	+ 4:40	84	+ 3:24	79	+ 3:19	97	+ 3:37
+ 2.15	64	+ 3:19	156	+ 4:51	82	+ 3:37	77	+ 3:32	96	+ 3:51
+ 2.30	64	+ 3:34	152	+ 5:02	79	+ 3:49	76	+ 3:46	94	+ 4:04
+ 2.45	64	+ 3:49	148	+ 5:13	77	+ 4:02	75	+ 4:00	92	+ 4:17
+ 3.00	64	+ 4:04	144	+ 5:24	74	+ 4:14	74	+ 4:14	91	+ 4:31
+ 3.15	63	+ 4:18	139	+ 5:34	73	+ 4:28	71	+ 4:26	87	+ 4:42
+ 3.30	62	+ 4:32	134	+ 5:44	71	+ 4:41	69	+ 4:39	84	+ 4:54
+ 3.45	62	+ 4:47	129	+ 5:54	69	+ 4:54	66	+ 4:51	80	+ 5:05
+ 4.00	61	+ 5:01	124	- 5:56	67	+ 5:07	63	+ 5:03	77	+ 5:17
+ 4.15	60	+ 5:15	120	- 5:45	66	+ 5:21	61	+ 5:16	74	+ 5:29
+ 4.30	59	+ 5:29	116	- 5:34	65	+ 5:35	58	+ 5:28	71	+ 5:41
+ 4.45	58	+ 5:43	112	- 5:23	65	+ 5:50	56	+ 5:41	68	+ 5:53
+ 5.00	57	+ 5:57	108	- 5:12	64	- 5:56	53	+ 5:53	64	- 5:56
+ 5.15	57	- 5:48	106	- 4:59	63	- 5:42	52	- 5:53	63	- 5:42
+ 5.30	56	- 5:34	104	- 4:46	63	- 5:27	51	- 5:39	61	- 5:29
+ 5.45	56	- 5:19	102	- 4:33	63	- 5:12	49	- 5:26	59	- 5:16
+ 6.00	55	- 5:05	99	- 4:21	63	- 4:57	48	- 5:12	58	- 5:02

Swale Northwards

	F6		F7		F8	
	Swale Landfall to Spaniard		Spaniard to Red Sand		Red Sand to SW Barrow	
Time	Duration	Time at End of Sector	Duration	Time at End of Sector	Duration	Time at End of Sector
- 6.00	26	- 5:34	60	- 5:00	28	- 5:32
- 5.45	25	- 5:20	59	- 4:46	29	- 5:16
- 5.30	24	- 5:06	59	- 4:31	30	- 5:00
- 5.15	23	- 4:52	58	- 4:17	30	- 4:45
- 5.00	23	- 4:37	57	- 4:03	31	- 4:29
- 4.45	22	- 4:23	57	- 3:48	31	- 4:14
- 4.30	22	- 4:08	57	- 3:33	31	- 3:59
- 4.15	22	- 3:53	56	- 3:19	32	- 3:43
- 4.00	22	- 3:38	56	- 3:04	32	- 3:28
- 3.45	22	- 3:23	56	- 2:49	32	- 3:13
- 3.30	22	- 3:08	56	- 2:34	32	- 2:58
- 3.15	21	- 2:54	56	- 2:19	32	- 2:43
- 3.00	21	- 2:39	56	- 2:04	32	- 2:28
- 2.45	21	- 2:24	56	- 1:49	32	- 2:13
- 2.30	22	- 2:08	57	- 1:33	32	- 1:58
- 2.15	22	- 1:53	57	- 1:18	32	- 1:43
- 2.00	22	- 1:38	57	- 1:03	32	- 1:28
- 1.45	22	- 1:23	59	- 0:46	31	- 1:14
- 1.30	22	- 1:08	60	- 0:30	31	- 0:59
- 1.15	21	- 0:54	62	- 0:13	30	- 0:45
- 1.00	21	- 0:39	63	+ 0:03	30	- 0:30
- 0.45	22	- 0:23	66	+ 0:21	29	- 0:16
- 0.30	22	- 0:08	69	+ 0:39	28	- 0:02
- 0.15	23	+ 0:08	72	+ 0:57	27	+ 0:12
HW	23	+ 0:23	75	+ 1:15	26	+ 0:26
+ 0.15	24	+ 0:39	77	+ 1:32	26	+ 0:41
+ 0.30	24	+ 0:54	80	+ 1:50	25	+ 0:55
+ 0.45	25	+ 1:10	82	+ 2:07	24	+ 1:09
+ 1.00	26	+ 1:26	85	+ 2:25	23	+ 1:23
+ 1.15	26	+ 1:41	85	+ 2:40	23	+ 1:38
+ 1.30	26	+ 1:56	84	+ 2:54	22	+ 1:52
+ 1.45	26	+ 2:11	84	+ 3:09	22	+ 2:07
+ 2.00	27	+ 2:27	84	+ 3:24	22	+ 2:22
+ 2.15	26	+ 2:41	83	+ 3:38	22	+ 2:37
+ 2.30	26	+ 2:56	82	+ 3:52	22	+ 2:52
+ 2.45	26	+ 3:11	80	+ 4:05	22	+ 3:07
+ 3.00	25	+ 3:25	79	+ 4:19	22	+ 3:22
+ 3.15	25	+ 3:40	77	+ 4:32	22	+ 3:37
+ 3.30	25	+ 3:55	76	+ 4:46	23	+ 3:53
+ 3.45	25	+ 4:10	74	+ 4:59	23	+ 4:08
+ 4.00	25	+ 4:25	73	+ 5:13	23	+ 4:23
+ 4.15	24	+ 4:39	72	+ 5:27	24	+ 4:39
+ 4.30	24	+ 4:54	70	+ 5:40	24	+ 4:54
+ 4.45	24	+ 5:09	69	+ 5:54	25	+ 5:10
+ 5.00	23	+ 5:23	68	- 5:52	25	+ 5:25
+ 5.15	23	+ 5:38	67	- 5:38	26	+ 5:41
+ 5.30	23	+ 5:53	66	- 5:24	26	+ 5:56
+ 5.45	23	- 5:52	65	- 5:10	26	- 5:49
+ 6.00	22	- 5:38	64	- 4:56	27	- 5:33

The Queens Channel — Swale Northwards

F - 6 Kts — Table F - Queens Channel and Swale Northwards — 6 Kts - F

Neaps — All times relate to HW Sheerness — **Time to cover Sectors (in minutes) at 6.0 Kts**

NORTH & WEST

The Queens Channel

Time	F1 Margate Sand to Wedge: Duration	F1: Time at End of Sector	Time	F2 Wedge to Woolpack: Duration	F2: Time at End of Sector	Time	F3 Woolpack to Swale Landfall: Duration	F3: Time at End of Sector	Time	F4 Wedge to Spaniard: Duration	F4: Time at End of Sector	Time	F5 Spaniard to Spile: Duration	F5: Time at End of Sector
- 6.00	45	- 5:15	- 6.00	80	- 4:40	- 6.00	53	- 5:07	- 6.00	38	- 5:22	- 6.00	46	- 5:14
- 5.45	44	- 5:01	- 5.45	79	- 4:26	- 5.45	52	- 4:53	- 5.45	38	- 5:07	- 5.45	46	- 4:59
- 5.30	44	- 4:46	- 5.30	78	- 4:12	- 5.30	52	- 4:38	- 5.30	37	- 4:53	- 5.30	45	- 4:45
- 5.15	44	- 4:31	- 5.15	77	- 3:58	- 5.15	52	- 4:23	- 5.15	37	- 4:38	- 5.15	44	- 4:31
- 5.00	44	- 4:16	- 5.00	76	- 3:44	- 5.00	51	- 4:09	- 5.00	36	- 4:24	- 5.00	44	- 4:16
- 4.45	44	- 4:01	- 4.45	75	- 3:30	- 4.45	51	- 3:54	- 4.45	36	- 4:09	- 4.45	43	- 4:02
- 4.30	44	- 3:46	- 4.30	75	- 3:15	- 4.30	51	- 3:39	- 4.30	35	- 3:55	- 4.30	43	- 3:47
- 4.15	44	- 3:31	- 4.15	74	- 3:01	- 4.15	51	- 3:24	- 4.15	35	- 3:40	- 4.15	42	- 3:33
- 4.00	43	- 3:17	- 4.00	73	- 2:47	- 4.00	52	- 3:08	- 4.00	35	- 3:25	- 4.00	42	- 3:18
- 3.45	43	- 3:02	- 3.45	72	- 2:33	- 3.45	52	- 2:53	- 3.45	34	- 3:11	- 3.45	42	- 3:03
- 3.30	43	- 2:47	- 3.30	72	- 2:18	- 3.30	52	- 2:38	- 3.30	34	- 2:56	- 3.30	41	- 2:49
- 3.15	43	- 2:32	- 3.15	71	- 2:04	- 3.15	52	- 2:23	- 3.15	34	- 2:41	- 3.15	41	- 2:34
- 3.00	43	- 2:17	- 3.00	71	- 1:49	- 3.00	52	- 2:08	- 3.00	33	- 2:27	- 3.00	41	- 2:19
- 2.45	43	- 2:02	- 2.45	72	- 1:33	- 2.45	52	- 1:53	- 2.45	33	- 2:12	- 2.45	41	- 2:04
- 2.30	43	- 1:47	- 2.30	72	- 1:18	- 2.30	52	- 1:38	- 2.30	33	- 1:57	- 2.30	41	- 1:49
- 2.15	43	- 1:32	- 2.15	73	- 1:02	- 2.15	52	- 1:23	- 2.15	33	- 1:42	- 2.15	41	- 1:34
- 2.00	43	- 1:17	- 2.00	73	- 0:47	- 2.00	53	- 1:07	- 2.00	33	- 1:27	- 2.00	41	- 1:19
- 1.45	43	- 1:02	- 1.45	75	- 0:30	- 1.45	53	- 0:52	- 1.45	34	- 1:11	- 1.45	42	- 1:03
- 1.30	43	- 0:47	- 1.30	77	- 0:13	- 1.30	54	- 0:36	- 1.30	34	- 0:56	- 1.30	43	- 0:47
- 1.15	44	- 0:31	- 1.15	79	+ 0:04	- 1.15	54	- 0:21	- 1.15	35	- 0:40	- 1.15	44	- 0:31
- 1.00	44	- 0:16	- 1.00	80	+ 0:20	- 1.00	55	- 0:05	- 1.00	36	- 0:24	- 1.00	44	- 0:16
- 0.45	44	- 0:01	- 0.45	83	+ 0:38	- 0.45	56	+ 0:11	- 0.45	37	- 0:08	- 0.45	46	+ 0:01
- 0.30	44	+ 0:14	- 0.30	85	+ 0:55	- 0.30	58	+ 0:28	- 0.30	38	+ 0:08	- 0.30	47	+ 0:17
- 0.15	45	+ 0:30	- 0.15	88	+ 1:13	- 0.15	59	+ 0:44	- 0.15	39	+ 0:24	- 0.15	49	+ 0:34
HW	45	+ 0:45	HW	90	+ 1:30	HW	60	+ 1:00	HW	40	+ 0:40	HW	50	+ 0:50
+ 0.15	45	+ 1:00	+ 0.15	94	+ 1:49	+ 0.15	61	+ 1:16	+ 0.15	41	+ 0:56	+ 0.15	52	+ 1:07
+ 0.30	46	+ 1:16	+ 0.30	98	+ 2:08	+ 0.30	62	+ 1:32	+ 0.30	43	+ 1:13	+ 0.30	54	+ 1:24
+ 0.45	46	+ 1:31	+ 0.45	102	+ 2:27	+ 0.45	63	+ 1:48	+ 0.45	44	+ 1:29	+ 0.45	56	+ 1:41
+ 1.00	47	+ 1:47	+ 1.00	106	+ 2:46	+ 1.00	64	+ 2:04	+ 1.00	46	+ 1:46	+ 1.00	57	+ 1:57
+ 1.15	47	+ 2:02	+ 1.15	108	+ 3:03	+ 1.15	64	+ 2:19	+ 1.15	47	+ 2:02	+ 1.15	59	+ 2:14
+ 1.30	48	+ 2:18	+ 1.30	110	+ 3:20	+ 1.30	64	+ 2:34	+ 1.30	48	+ 2:18	+ 1.30	60	+ 2:30
+ 1.45	48	+ 2:33	+ 1.45	111	+ 3:36	+ 1.45	63	+ 2:48	+ 1.45	49	+ 2:34	+ 1.45	61	+ 2:46
+ 2.00	49	+ 2:49	+ 2.00	113	+ 3:53	+ 2.00	63	+ 3:03	+ 2.00	50	+ 2:50	+ 2.00	63	+ 3:03
+ 2.15	49	+ 3:04	+ 2.15	112	+ 4:07	+ 2.15	62	+ 3:17	+ 2.15	50	+ 3:05	+ 2.15	62	+ 3:17
+ 2.30	49	+ 3:19	+ 2.30	111	+ 4:21	+ 2.30	61	+ 3:31	+ 2.30	50	+ 3:20	+ 2.30	62	+ 3:32
+ 2.45	49	+ 3:34	+ 2.45	110	+ 4:35	+ 2.45	60	+ 3:45	+ 2.45	50	+ 3:35	+ 2.45	62	+ 3:47
+ 3.00	49	+ 3:49	+ 3.00	109	+ 4:49	+ 3.00	59	+ 3:59	+ 3.00	50	+ 3:50	+ 3.00	62	+ 4:02
+ 3.15	49	+ 4:04	+ 3.15	107	+ 5:02	+ 3.15	58	+ 4:13	+ 3.15	49	+ 4:04	+ 3.15	61	+ 4:16
+ 3.30	48	+ 4:18	+ 3.30	104	+ 5:14	+ 3.30	57	+ 4:27	+ 3.30	49	+ 4:19	+ 3.30	59	+ 4:29
+ 3.45	48	+ 4:33	+ 3.45	102	+ 5:27	+ 3.45	57	+ 4:42	+ 3.45	48	+ 4:33	+ 3.45	58	+ 4:43
+ 4.00	48	+ 4:48	+ 4.00	100	+ 5:40	+ 4.00	56	+ 4:56	+ 4.00	47	+ 4:47	+ 4.00	57	+ 4:57
+ 4.15	48	+ 5:03	+ 4.15	98	+ 5:53	+ 4.15	55	+ 5:10	+ 4.15	46	+ 5:01	+ 4.15	56	+ 5:11
+ 4.30	47	+ 5:17	+ 4.30	95	- 5:55	+ 4.30	55	+ 5:25	+ 4.30	45	+ 5:15	+ 4.30	55	+ 5:25
+ 4.45	47	+ 5:32	+ 4.45	93	- 5:42	+ 4.45	54	+ 5:39	+ 4.45	44	+ 5:29	+ 4.45	53	+ 5:38
+ 5.00	47	+ 5:47	+ 5.00	91	- 5:29	+ 5.00	54	+ 5:54	+ 5.00	43	+ 5:43	+ 5.00	52	+ 5:52
+ 5.15	46	- 5:59	+ 5.15	89	- 5:16	+ 5.15	54	- 5:51	+ 5.15	42	+ 5:57	+ 5.15	51	- 5:54
+ 5.30	46	- 5:44	+ 5.30	88	- 5:02	+ 5.30	54	- 5:36	+ 5.30	41	- 5:49	+ 5.30	50	- 5:40
+ 5.45	46	- 5:29	+ 5.45	86	- 4:49	+ 5.45	54	- 5:21	+ 5.45	41	- 5:34	+ 5.45	49	- 5:26
+ 6.00	45	- 5:15	+ 6.00	85	- 4:35	+ 6.00	54	- 5:06	+ 6.00	40	- 5:20	+ 6.00	49	- 5:11

The Queens Channel

Swale Northwards

Time	F6 Swale Landfall to Spaniard: Duration	F6: Time at End of Sector	Time	F7 Spaniard to Red Sand: Duration	F7: Time at End of Sector	Time	F8 Red Sand to SW Barrow: Duration	F8: Time at End of Sector
- 6.00	22	- 5:38	- 6.00	52	- 5:08	- 6.00	23	- 5:37
- 5.45	21	- 5:24	- 5.45	52	- 4:53	- 5.45	23	- 5:22
- 5.30	20	- 5:10	- 5.30	51	- 4:39	- 5.30	24	- 5:06
- 5.15	19	- 4:56	- 5.15	51	- 4:24	- 5.15	24	- 4:51
- 5.00	19	- 4:41	- 5.00	51	- 4:09	- 5.00	25	- 4:35
- 4.45	19	- 4:26	- 4.45	50	- 3:55	- 4.45	25	- 4:20
- 4.30	19	- 4:11	- 4.30	50	- 3:40	- 4.30	25	- 4:05
- 4.15	18	- 3:57	- 4.15	50	- 3:25	- 4.15	25	- 3:50
- 4.00	18	- 3:42	- 4.00	50	- 3:10	- 4.00	25	- 3:35
- 3.45	18	- 3:27	- 3.45	50	- 2:55	- 3.45	25	- 3:20
- 3.30	18	- 3:12	- 3.30	50	- 2:40	- 3.30	25	- 3:05
- 3.15	18	- 2:57	- 3.15	50	- 2:25	- 3.15	25	- 2:50
- 3.00	18	- 2:42	- 3.00	50	- 2:10	- 3.00	25	- 2:35
- 2.45	18	- 2:27	- 2.45	50	- 1:55	- 2.45	25	- 2:20
- 2.30	18	- 2:12	- 2.30	50	- 1:40	- 2.30	25	- 2:05
- 2.15	18	- 1:57	- 2.15	51	- 1:24	- 2.15	25	- 1:50
- 2.00	18	- 1:42	- 2.00	51	- 1:09	- 2.00	25	- 1:35
- 1.45	18	- 1:27	- 1.45	52	- 0:53	- 1.45	24	- 1:21
- 1.30	18	- 1:12	- 1.30	52	- 0:38	- 1.30	24	- 1:06
- 1.15	18	- 0:57	- 1.15	53	- 0:22	- 1.15	24	- 0:51
- 1.00	18	- 0:42	- 1.00	54	- 0:06	- 1.00	23	- 0:37
- 0.45	19	- 0:26	- 0.45	55	+ 0:10	- 0.45	23	- 0:22
- 0.30	19	- 0:11	- 0.30	56	+ 0:26	- 0.30	23	- 0:07
- 0.15	19	+ 0:04	- 0.15	57	+ 0:42	- 0.15	22	+ 0:07
HW	19	+ 0:19	HW	58	+ 0:58	HW	22	+ 0:22
+ 0.15	20	+ 0:35	+ 0.15	59	+ 1:14	+ 0.15	21	+ 0:36
+ 0.30	20	+ 0:50	+ 0.30	60	+ 1:30	+ 0.30	21	+ 0:51
+ 0.45	20	+ 1:05	+ 0.45	61	+ 1:46	+ 0.45	21	+ 1:06
+ 1.00	20	+ 1:20	+ 1.00	62	+ 2:02	+ 1.00	20	+ 1:20
+ 1.15	21	+ 1:36	+ 1.15	62	+ 2:17	+ 1.15	20	+ 1:35
+ 1.30	21	+ 1:51	+ 1.30	62	+ 2:32	+ 1.30	20	+ 1:50
+ 1.45	21	+ 2:06	+ 1.45	62	+ 2:47	+ 1.45	19	+ 2:04
+ 2.00	21	+ 2:21	+ 2.00	62	+ 3:02	+ 2.00	19	+ 2:19
+ 2.15	21	+ 2:36	+ 2.15	62	+ 3:17	+ 2.15	19	+ 2:34
+ 2.30	21	+ 2:51	+ 2.30	61	+ 3:31	+ 2.30	20	+ 2:50
+ 2.45	20	+ 3:05	+ 2.45	61	+ 3:46	+ 2.45	20	+ 3:05
+ 3.00	20	+ 3:20	+ 3.00	60	+ 4:00	+ 3.00	20	+ 3:20
+ 3.15	20	+ 3:35	+ 3.15	59	+ 4:14	+ 3.15	20	+ 3:35
+ 3.30	20	+ 3:50	+ 3.30	59	+ 4:29	+ 3.30	20	+ 3:50
+ 3.45	20	+ 4:05	+ 3.45	58	+ 4:43	+ 3.45	20	+ 4:05
+ 4.00	20	+ 4:20	+ 4.00	58	+ 4:58	+ 4.00	21	+ 4:21
+ 4.15	20	+ 4:35	+ 4.15	57	+ 5:12	+ 4.15	21	+ 4:36
+ 4.30	19	+ 4:49	+ 4.30	57	+ 5:27	+ 4.30	21	+ 4:51
+ 4.45	19	+ 5:04	+ 4.45	56	+ 5:41	+ 4.45	21	+ 5:06
+ 5.00	19	+ 5:19	+ 5.00	56	+ 5:56	+ 5.00	21	+ 5:21
+ 5.15	19	+ 5:34	+ 5.15	55	- 5:50	+ 5.15	22	+ 5:37
+ 5.30	19	+ 5:49	+ 5.30	55	- 5:35	+ 5.30	22	+ 5:52
+ 5.45	19	- 5:56	+ 5.45	54	- 5:21	+ 5.45	22	- 5:53
+ 6.00	19	- 5:41	+ 6.00	54	- 5:06	+ 6.00	22	- 5:38

Swale Northwards

F - 6 Kts | Table F - Queens Channel and Swale Northwards | 6 Kts - F

Time to cover Sectors (in minutes) at 6.0 kts — All times relate to HW Sheerness — **Springs**

NORTH & WEST

	The Queens Channel										Swale Northwards					
	F1 Margate Sand to Wedge		F2 Wedge to Woolpack		F3 Woolpack to Swale Landfall		F4 Wedge to Spaniard		F5 Spaniard to Spile		F6 Swale Landfall to Spaniard		F7 Spaniard to Red Sand		F8 Red Sand to SW Barrow	
Time	Duration	Time at End of Sector	Duration	Time at End of Sector	Duration	Time at End of Sector	Duration	Time at End of Sector	Duration	Time at End of Sector	Duration	Time at End of Sector	Duration	Time at End of Sector	Duration	Time at End of Sector
- 6.00	45	- 5:15	78	- 4:42	51	- 5:09	38	- 5:22	45	- 5:15	21	- 5:39	51	- 5:09	23	- 5:37
- 5.45	44	- 5:01	77	- 4:28	51	- 4:54	37	- 5:08	44	- 5:01	21	- 5:24	51	- 4:54	24	- 5:21
- 5.30	44	- 4:46	75	- 4:15	50	- 4:40	36	- 4:54	43	- 4:47	20	- 5:10	50	- 4:40	24	- 5:06
- 5.15	44	- 4:31	74	- 4:01	50	- 4:25	36	- 4:39	43	- 4:32	19	- 4:56	49	- 4:26	25	- 4:50
- 5.00	43	- 4:17	72	- 3:48	49	- 4:11	35	- 4:25	42	- 4:18	19	- 4:41	49	- 4:11	26	- 4:34
- 4.45	43	- 4:02	71	- 3:34	49	- 3:56	34	- 4:11	41	- 4:04	19	- 4:26	49	- 3:56	26	- 4:19
- 4.30	43	- 3:47	70	- 3:20	49	- 3:41	34	- 3:56	40	- 3:50	18	- 4:12	48	- 3:42	26	- 4:04
- 4.15	43	- 3:32	69	- 3:06	49	- 3:26	33	- 3:42	40	- 3:35	18	- 3:57	48	- 3:27	26	- 3:49
- 4.00	43	- 3:17	68	- 2:52	49	- 3:11	32	- 3:28	39	- 3:21	18	- 3:42	48	- 3:12	26	- 3:34
- 3.45	43	- 3:02	67	- 2:38	50	- 2:55	32	- 3:13	39	- 3:06	18	- 3:27	48	- 2:57	26	- 3:19
- 3.30	43	- 2:47	66	- 2:24	50	- 2:40	32	- 2:58	38	- 2:52	18	- 3:12	48	- 2:42	26	- 3:04
- 3.15	43	- 2:32	66	- 2:09	50	- 2:25	31	- 2:44	38	- 2:37	18	- 2:57	48	- 2:27	26	- 2:49
- 3.00	43	- 2:17	65	- 1:55	50	- 2:10	31	- 2:29	37	- 2:23	18	- 2:42	48	- 2:12	26	- 2:34
- 2.45	43	- 2:02	66	- 1:39	51	- 1:54	31	- 2:14	37	- 2:08	18	- 2:27	48	- 1:57	26	- 2:19
- 2.30	43	- 1:47	66	- 1:24	51	- 1:39	30	- 2:00	37	- 1:53	18	- 2:12	48	- 1:42	26	- 2:04
- 2.15	43	- 1:32	67	- 1:08	51	- 1:24	30	- 1:45	37	- 1:38	18	- 1:57	48	- 1:27	26	- 1:49
- 2.00	43	- 1:17	68	- 0:52	51	- 1:09	30	- 1:30	37	- 1:23	18	- 1:42	49	- 1:11	26	- 1:34
- 1.45	43	- 1:02	70	- 0:35	52	- 0:53	31	- 1:14	39	- 1:06	18	- 1:27	50	- 0:55	26	- 1:19
- 1.30	43	- 0:47	72	- 0:18	53	- 0:37	32	- 0:58	40	- 0:50	18	- 1:12	50	- 0:40	25	- 1:05
- 1.15	43	- 0:32	75	HW	54	- 0:21	32	- 0:43	41	- 0:34	18	- 0:57	51	- 0:24	25	- 0:50
- 1.00	43	- 0:17	77	+ 0:17	55	- 0:05	33	- 0:27	42	- 0:18	18	- 0:42	52	- 0:08	25	- 0:35
- 0.45	44	- 0:01	82	+ 0:37	57	+ 0:12	35	- 0:10	44	- 0:01	18	- 0:27	54	+ 0:09	24	- 0:21
- 0.30	44	+ 0:14	87	+ 0:57	60	+ 0:30	37	+ 0:07	46	+ 0:16	19	- 0:11	56	+ 0:26	23	- 0:07
- 0.15	44	+ 0:29	91	+ 1:16	62	+ 0:47	38	+ 0:23	49	+ 0:34	19	+ 0:04	58	+ 0:43	23	+ 0:08
HW	45	+ 0:45	96	+ 1:36	64	+ 1:04	40	+ 0:40	51	+ 0:51	19	+ 0:19	60	+ 1:00	22	+ 0:22
+ 0.15	46	+ 1:01	102	+ 1:57	66	+ 1:21	43	+ 0:58	54	+ 1:09	20	+ 0:35	62	+ 1:17	21	+ 0:36
+ 0.30	46	+ 1:16	107	+ 2:17	68	+ 1:38	45	+ 1:15	58	+ 1:28	20	+ 0:50	64	+ 1:34	21	+ 0:51
+ 0.45	47	+ 1:32	113	+ 2:38	70	+ 1:55	48	+ 1:33	61	+ 1:46	21	+ 1:06	65	+ 1:50	20	+ 1:05
+ 1.00	48	+ 1:48	118	+ 2:58	71	+ 2:11	51	+ 1:51	64	+ 2:04	21	+ 1:21	67	+ 2:07	19	+ 1:19
+ 1.15	49	+ 2:04	120	+ 3:15	70	+ 2:25	53	+ 2:08	67	+ 2:22	22	+ 1:37	67	+ 2:22	19	+ 1:34
+ 1.30	50	+ 2:20	122	+ 3:32	69	+ 2:39	55	+ 2:25	69	+ 2:39	22	+ 1:52	67	+ 2:37	18	+ 1:48
+ 1.45	50	+ 2:35	123	+ 3:48	68	+ 2:53	57	+ 2:42	71	+ 2:56	22	+ 2:07	67	+ 2:52	18	+ 2:03
+ 2.00	51	+ 2:51	125	+ 4:05	68	+ 3:08	58	+ 2:58	73	+ 3:13	22	+ 2:22	67	+ 3:07	18	+ 2:18
+ 2.15	51	+ 3:06	123	+ 4:18	66	+ 3:21	58	+ 3:13	72	+ 3:27	22	+ 2:37	66	+ 3:21	18	+ 2:33
+ 2.30	51	+ 3:21	121	+ 4:31	64	+ 3:34	58	+ 3:28	72	+ 3:42	22	+ 2:52	66	+ 3:36	18	+ 2:48
+ 2.45	52	+ 3:37	118	+ 4:43	63	+ 3:48	58	+ 3:43	71	+ 3:56	21	+ 3:06	65	+ 3:50	18	+ 3:03
+ 3.00	52	+ 3:52	116	+ 4:56	61	+ 4:01	57	+ 3:57	70	+ 4:10	21	+ 3:21	64	+ 4:04	18	+ 3:18
+ 3.15	51	+ 4:06	113	+ 5:08	60	+ 4:15	56	+ 4:11	68	+ 4:23	21	+ 3:36	63	+ 4:18	19	+ 3:34
+ 3.30	51	+ 4:21	109	+ 5:19	59	+ 4:29	54	+ 4:24	66	+ 4:36	21	+ 3:51	62	+ 4:32	19	+ 3:49
+ 3.45	50	+ 4:35	106	+ 5:31	57	+ 4:42	52	+ 4:37	64	+ 4:49	21	+ 4:06	61	+ 4:46	19	+ 4:04
+ 4.00	50	+ 4:50	103	+ 5:43	56	+ 4:56	51	+ 4:51	62	+ 5:02	20	+ 4:20	60	+ 5:00	19	+ 4:19
+ 4.15	49	+ 5:04	100	+ 5:55	56	+ 5:11	49	+ 5:04	60	+ 5:15	20	+ 4:35	59	+ 5:14	20	+ 4:35
+ 4.30	49	+ 5:19	97	- 5:53	55	+ 5:25	47	+ 5:17	58	+ 5:28	20	+ 4:50	58	+ 5:28	20	+ 4:50
+ 4.45	48	+ 5:33	94	- 5:41	54	+ 5:39	46	+ 5:31	56	+ 5:41	20	+ 5:05	57	+ 5:42	21	+ 5:06
+ 5.00	48	+ 5:48	91	- 5:29	53	+ 5:53	44	+ 5:44	54	+ 5:54	19	+ 5:19	56	+ 5:56	21	+ 5:21
+ 5.15	47	- 5:58	89	- 5:16	53	- 5:52	43	+ 5:58	52	- 5:53	19	+ 5:34	56	- 5:49	21	+ 5:36
+ 5.30	47	- 5:43	88	- 5:02	53	- 5:37	42	- 5:48	51	- 5:39	19	+ 5:49	55	- 5:35	22	+ 5:52
+ 5.45	46	- 5:29	86	- 4:49	53	- 5:22	41	- 5:34	50	- 5:25	19	- 5:56	54	- 5:21	22	- 5:53
+ 6.00	46	- 5:14	84	- 4:36	53	- 5:07	40	- 5:20	48	- 5:12	19	- 5:41	54	- 5:06	22	- 5:38

The Queens Channel — Swale Northwards

F - 7 Kts

Table F - Queens Channel and Swale Northwards

7 Kts - F

Neaps — All times relate to HW Sheerness — **Time to cover Sectors (in minutes) at 7.0 Kts**

NORTH & WEST

The Queens Channel

Time	F1 Margate Sand to Wedge Duration	F1 Time at End of Sector	Time	F2 Wedge to Woolpack Duration	F2 Time at End of Sector	Time	F3 Woolpack to Swale Landfall Duration	F3 Time at End of Sector	Time	F4 Wedge to Spaniard Duration	F4 Time at End of Sector	Time	F5 Spaniard to Spile Duration	F5 Time at End of Sector
- 6.00	38	- 5:22	- 6.00	70	- 4:50	- 6.00	45	- 5:15	- 6.00	33	- 5:27	- 6.00	40	- 5:20
- 5.45	38	- 5:07	- 5.45	69	- 4:36	- 5.45	45	- 5:00	- 5.45	33	- 5:12	- 5.45	40	- 5:05
- 5.30	38	- 4:52	- 5.30	68	- 4:22	- 5.30	45	- 4:45	- 5.30	32	- 4:58	- 5.30	39	- 4:51
- 5.15	38	- 4:37	- 5.15	67	- 4:08	- 5.15	45	- 4:30	- 5.15	32	- 4:43	- 5.15	39	- 4:36
- 5.00	38	- 4:22	- 5.00	66	- 3:54	- 5.00	44	- 4:16	- 5.00	32	- 4:28	- 5.00	38	- 4:22
- 4.45	38	- 4:07	- 4.45	66	- 3:39	- 4.45	44	- 4:01	- 4.45	31	- 4:14	- 4.45	38	- 4:07
- 4.30	37	- 3:53	- 4.30	65	- 3:25	- 4.30	44	- 3:46	- 4.30	31	- 3:59	- 4.30	37	- 3:53
- 4.15	37	- 3:38	- 4.15	65	- 3:10	- 4.15	44	- 3:31	- 4.15	31	- 3:44	- 4.15	37	- 3:38
- 4.00	37	- 3:23	- 4.00	64	- 2:56	- 4.00	44	- 3:16	- 4.00	30	- 3:30	- 4.00	37	- 3:23
- 3.45	37	- 3:08	- 3.45	63	- 2:42	- 3.45	45	- 3:00	- 3.45	30	- 3:15	- 3.45	36	- 3:09
- 3.30	37	- 2:53	- 3.30	63	- 2:27	- 3.30	45	- 2:45	- 3.30	30	- 3:00	- 3.30	36	- 2:54
- 3.15	37	- 2:38	- 3.15	63	- 2:12	- 3.15	45	- 2:30	- 3.15	29	- 2:46	- 3.15	36	- 2:39
- 3.00	37	- 2:23	- 3.00	62	- 1:58	- 3.00	45	- 2:15	- 3.00	29	- 2:31	- 3.00	36	- 2:24
- 2.45	37	- 2:08	- 2.45	63	- 1:42	- 2.45	45	- 2:00	- 2.45	29	- 2:16	- 2.45	36	- 2:09
- 2.30	37	- 1:53	- 2.30	63	- 1:27	- 2.30	45	- 1:45	- 2.30	29	- 2:01	- 2.30	36	- 1:54
- 2.15	37	- 1:38	- 2.15	64	- 1:11	- 2.15	45	- 1:30	- 2.15	29	- 1:46	- 2.15	36	- 1:39
- 2.00	37	- 1:23	- 2.00	64	- 0:56	- 2.00	45	- 1:15	- 2.00	29	- 1:31	- 2.00	36	- 1:24
- 1.45	37	- 1:08	- 1.45	65	- 0:40	- 1.45	46	- 0:59	- 1.45	29	- 1:16	- 1.45	36	- 1:09
- 1.30	37	- 0:53	- 1.30	66	- 0:24	- 1.30	46	- 0:44	- 1.30	30	- 1:00	- 1.30	37	- 0:53
- 1.15	37	- 0:38	- 1.15	68	- 0:07	- 1.15	46	- 0:29	- 1.15	30	- 0:45	- 1.15	38	- 0:37
- 1.00	37	- 0:23	- 1.00	69	+ 0:09	- 1.00	47	- 0:13	- 1.00	31	- 0:29	- 1.00	38	- 0:22
- 0.45	38	- 0:07	- 0.45	71	+ 0:26	- 0.45	48	+ 0:03	- 0.45	31	- 0:14	- 0.45	39	- 0:06
- 0.30	38	+ 0:08	- 0.30	73	+ 0:43	- 0.30	49	+ 0:19	- 0.30	32	+ 0:02	- 0.30	40	+ 0:10
- 0.15	38	+ 0:23	- 0.15	75	+ 1:00	- 0.15	50	+ 0:35	- 0.15	33	+ 0:18	- 0.15	41	+ 0:26
HW	38	+ 0:38	HW	77	+ 1:17	HW	51	+ 0:51	HW	34	+ 0:34	HW	42	+ 0:42
+ 0.15	39	+ 0:54	+ 0.15	79	+ 1:34	+ 0.15	51	+ 1:06	+ 0.15	35	+ 0:50	+ 0.15	43	+ 0:58
+ 0.30	39	+ 1:09	+ 0.30	81	+ 1:51	+ 0.30	52	+ 1:22	+ 0.30	36	+ 1:06	+ 0.30	45	+ 1:15
+ 0.45	39	+ 1:24	+ 0.45	83	+ 2:08	+ 0.45	53	+ 1:38	+ 0.45	37	+ 1:22	+ 0.45	46	+ 1:31
+ 1.00	40	+ 1:40	+ 1.00	85	+ 2:25	+ 1.00	54	+ 1:54	+ 1.00	38	+ 1:38	+ 1.00	47	+ 1:47
+ 1.15	40	+ 1:55	+ 1.15	87	+ 2:42	+ 1.15	54	+ 2:09	+ 1.15	39	+ 1:54	+ 1.15	48	+ 2:03
+ 1.30	40	+ 2:10	+ 1.30	90	+ 3:00	+ 1.30	53	+ 2:23	+ 1.30	40	+ 2:10	+ 1.30	49	+ 2:19
+ 1.45	41	+ 2:26	+ 1.45	92	+ 3:17	+ 1.45	53	+ 2:38	+ 1.45	40	+ 2:25	+ 1.45	50	+ 2:35
+ 2.00	41	+ 2:41	+ 2.00	94	+ 3:34	+ 2.00	53	+ 2:53	+ 2.00	41	+ 2:41	+ 2.00	51	+ 2:51
+ 2.15	41	+ 2:56	+ 2.15	93	+ 3:48	+ 2.15	52	+ 3:07	+ 2.15	41	+ 2:56	+ 2.15	51	+ 3:06
+ 2.30	41	+ 3:11	+ 2.30	93	+ 4:03	+ 2.30	52	+ 3:22	+ 2.30	42	+ 3:12	+ 2.30	51	+ 3:21
+ 2.45	41	+ 3:26	+ 2.45	92	+ 4:17	+ 2.45	51	+ 3:36	+ 2.45	42	+ 3:27	+ 2.45	51	+ 3:36
+ 3.00	41	+ 3:41	+ 3.00	92	+ 4:32	+ 3.00	50	+ 3:50	+ 3.00	42	+ 3:42	+ 3.00	51	+ 3:51
+ 3.15	41	+ 3:56	+ 3.15	90	+ 4:45	+ 3.15	50	+ 4:05	+ 3.15	41	+ 3:56	+ 3.15	50	+ 4:05
+ 3.30	41	+ 4:11	+ 3.30	87	+ 4:57	+ 3.30	49	+ 4:19	+ 3.30	41	+ 4:11	+ 3.30	50	+ 4:20
+ 3.45	41	+ 4:26	+ 3.45	85	+ 5:10	+ 3.45	49	+ 4:34	+ 3.45	40	+ 4:25	+ 3.45	49	+ 4:34
+ 4.00	41	+ 4:41	+ 4.00	83	+ 5:23	+ 4.00	48	+ 4:48	+ 4.00	39	+ 4:39	+ 4.00	48	+ 4:48
+ 4.15	40	+ 4:55	+ 4.15	81	+ 5:36	+ 4.15	48	+ 5:03	+ 4.15	39	+ 4:54	+ 4.15	47	+ 5:02
+ 4.30	40	+ 5:10	+ 4.30	80	+ 5:50	+ 4.30	47	+ 5:17	+ 4.30	38	+ 5:08	+ 4.30	46	+ 5:16
+ 4.45	40	+ 5:25	+ 4.45	78	- 5:57	+ 4.45	47	+ 5:32	+ 4.45	37	+ 5:22	+ 4.45	45	+ 5:30
+ 5.00	40	+ 5:40	+ 5.00	76	- 5:44	+ 5.00	46	+ 5:46	+ 5.00	37	+ 5:37	+ 5.00	44	+ 5:44
+ 5.15	40	+ 5:55	+ 5.15	76	- 5:29	+ 5.15	46	- 5:59	+ 5.15	36	+ 5:51	+ 5.15	44	+ 5:59
+ 5.30	39	+ 5:51	+ 5.30	75	- 5:15	+ 5.30	46	- 5:44	+ 5.30	35	- 5:55	+ 5.30	43	- 5:47
+ 5.45	39	- 5:36	+ 5.45	74	- 5:01	+ 5.45	46	- 5:29	+ 5.45	35	- 5:40	+ 5.45	42	- 5:33
+ 6.00	39	- 5:21	+ 6.00	73	- 4:47	+ 6.00	46	- 5:14	+ 6.00	34	- 5:26	+ 6.00	42	- 5:18

Swale Northwards

Time	F6 Swale Landfall to Spaniard Duration	F6 Time at End of Sector	Time	F7 Spaniard to Red Sand Duration	F7 Time at End of Sector	Time	F8 Red Sand to SW Barrow Duration	F8 Time at End of Sector
- 6.00	18	- 5:42	- 6.00	45	- 5:15	- 6.00	20	- 5:40
- 5.45	18	- 5:27	- 5.45	45	- 5:00	- 5.45	20	- 5:25
- 5.30	17	- 5:13	- 5.30	44	- 4:46	- 5.30	20	- 5:10
- 5.15	17	- 4:58	- 5.15	44	- 4:31	- 5.15	21	- 4:54
- 5.00	16	- 4:44	- 5.00	44	- 4:16	- 5.00	21	- 4:39
- 4.45	16	- 4:29	- 4.45	44	- 4:01	- 4.45	21	- 4:24
- 4.30	16	- 4:14	- 4.30	44	- 3:46	- 4.30	21	- 4:09
- 4.15	16	- 3:59	- 4.15	43	- 3:32	- 4.15	21	- 3:54
- 4.00	16	- 3:44	- 4.00	43	- 3:17	- 4.00	21	- 3:39
- 3.45	16	- 3:29	- 3.45	43	- 3:02	- 3.45	21	- 3:24
- 3.30	15	- 3:15	- 3.30	43	- 2:47	- 3.30	21	- 3:09
- 3.15	15	- 3:00	- 3.15	43	- 2:32	- 3.15	21	- 2:54
- 3.00	15	- 2:45	- 3.00	43	- 2:17	- 3.00	21	- 2:39
- 2.45	15	- 2:30	- 2.45	43	- 2:02	- 2.45	21	- 2:24
- 2.30	15	- 2:15	- 2.30	44	- 1:46	- 2.30	21	- 2:09
- 2.15	15	- 2:00	- 2.15	44	- 1:31	- 2.15	21	- 1:54
- 2.00	16	- 1:44	- 2.00	44	- 1:16	- 2.00	21	- 1:39
- 1.45	16	- 1:29	- 1.45	44	- 1:01	- 1.45	21	- 1:24
- 1.30	16	- 1:14	- 1.30	45	- 0:45	- 1.30	21	- 1:09
- 1.15	16	- 0:59	- 1.15	45	- 0:30	- 1.15	20	- 0:55
- 1.00	16	- 0:44	- 1.00	46	- 0:14	- 1.00	20	- 0:40
- 0.45	16	- 0:29	- 0.45	47	+ 0:02	- 0.45	20	- 0:25
- 0.30	16	- 0:14	- 0.30	48	+ 0:18	- 0.30	19	- 0:11
- 0.15	16	+ 0:01	- 0.15	48	+ 0:33	- 0.15	19	+ 0:04
HW	16	+ 0:16	HW	49	+ 0:49	HW	19	+ 0:19
+ 0.15	17	+ 0:32	+ 0.15	50	+ 1:05	+ 0.15	18	+ 0:33
+ 0.30	17	+ 0:47	+ 0.30	51	+ 1:21	+ 0.30	18	+ 0:48
+ 0.45	17	+ 1:02	+ 0.45	51	+ 1:36	+ 0.45	18	+ 1:03
+ 1.00	17	+ 1:17	+ 1.00	52	+ 1:52	+ 1.00	17	+ 1:17
+ 1.15	18	+ 1:33	+ 1.15	52	+ 2:07	+ 1.15	17	+ 1:32
+ 1.30	18	+ 1:48	+ 1.30	52	+ 2:22	+ 1.30	17	+ 1:47
+ 1.45	18	+ 2:03	+ 1.45	52	+ 2:37	+ 1.45	17	+ 2:02
+ 2.00	18	+ 2:18	+ 2.00	52	+ 2:52	+ 2.00	16	+ 2:16
+ 2.15	18	+ 2:33	+ 2.15	52	+ 3:07	+ 2.15	17	+ 2:32
+ 2.30	18	+ 2:48	+ 2.30	52	+ 3:22	+ 2.30	17	+ 2:47
+ 2.45	17	+ 3:02	+ 2.45	51	+ 3:36	+ 2.45	17	+ 3:02
+ 3.00	17	+ 3:17	+ 3.00	51	+ 3:51	+ 3.00	17	+ 3:17
+ 3.15	17	+ 3:32	+ 3.15	50	+ 4:05	+ 3.15	17	+ 3:32
+ 3.30	17	+ 3:47	+ 3.30	50	+ 4:20	+ 3.30	17	+ 3:47
+ 3.45	17	+ 4:02	+ 3.45	50	+ 4:35	+ 3.45	17	+ 4:02
+ 4.00	17	+ 4:17	+ 4.00	49	+ 4:49	+ 4.00	18	+ 4:18
+ 4.15	17	+ 4:32	+ 4.15	49	+ 5:04	+ 4.15	18	+ 4:33
+ 4.30	17	+ 4:47	+ 4.30	49	+ 5:19	+ 4.30	18	+ 4:48
+ 4.45	17	+ 5:02	+ 4.45	48	+ 5:33	+ 4.45	18	+ 5:03
+ 5.00	16	+ 5:16	+ 5.00	48	+ 5:48	+ 5.00	18	+ 5:18
+ 5.15	16	+ 5:31	+ 5.15	47	- 5:58	+ 5.15	18	+ 5:33
+ 5.30	16	+ 5:46	+ 5.30	47	- 5:43	+ 5.30	19	+ 5:49
+ 5.45	16	- 5:59	+ 5.45	47	- 5:28	+ 5.45	19	- 5:56
+ 6.00	16	- 5:44	+ 6.00	46	- 5:14	+ 6.00	19	- 5:41

The Queens Channel

Swale Northwards

Table F - Queens Channel and Swale Northwards

Time to cover Sectors (in minutes) at 7.0 kts — All times relate to HW Sheerness — **Springs**

The Queens Channel

Time	F1 Margate Sand to Wedge: Duration	F1 Time at End of Sector	Time	F2 Wedge to Woolpack: Duration	F2 Time at End of Sector	Time	F3 Woolpack to Swale Landfall: Duration	F3 Time at End of Sector	Time	F4 Wedge to Spaniard: Duration	F4 Time at End of Sector	Time	F5 Spaniard to Spile: Duration	F5 Time at End of Sector
- 6.00	39	- 5:21	- 6.00	68	- 4:52	- 6.00	44	- 5:16	- 6.00	33	- 5:27	- 6.00	40	- 5:20
- 5.45	38	- 5:07	- 5.45	67	- 4:38	- 5.45	44	- 5:01	- 5.45	32	- 5:13	- 5.45	39	- 5:06
- 5.30	38	- 4:52	- 5.30	66	- 4:24	- 5.30	44	- 4:46	- 5.30	32	- 4:58	- 5.30	38	- 4:52
- 5.15	38	- 4:37	- 5.15	65	- 4:10	- 5.15	43	- 4:32	- 5.15	31	- 4:44	- 5.15	37	- 4:38
- 5.00	37	- 4:23	- 5.00	63	- 3:57	- 5.00	43	- 4:17	- 5.00	31	- 4:29	- 5.00	37	- 4:23
- 4.45	37	- 4:08	- 4.45	62	- 3:43	- 4.45	43	- 4:02	- 4.45	30	- 4:15	- 4.45	36	- 4:09
- 4.30	37	- 3:53	- 4.30	62	- 3:28	- 4.30	43	- 3:47	- 4.30	30	- 4:00	- 4.30	36	- 3:54
- 4.15	37	- 3:38	- 4.15	61	- 3:14	- 4.15	43	- 3:32	- 4.15	29	- 3:46	- 4.15	35	- 3:40
- 4.00	37	- 3:23	- 4.00	60	- 3:00	- 4.00	43	- 3:17	- 4.00	28	- 3:32	- 4.00	35	- 3:25
- 3.45	37	- 3:08	- 3.45	59	- 2:46	- 3.45	43	- 3:02	- 3.45	28	- 3:17	- 3.45	34	- 3:11
- 3.30	37	- 2:53	- 3.30	59	- 2:31	- 3.30	43	- 2:47	- 3.30	28	- 3:02	- 3.30	34	- 2:56
- 3.15	37	- 2:38	- 3.15	58	- 2:17	- 3.15	43	- 2:32	- 3.15	27	- 2:48	- 3.15	34	- 2:41
- 3.00	37	- 2:23	- 3.00	58	- 2:02	- 3.00	44	- 2:16	- 3.00	27	- 2:33	- 3.00	33	- 2:27
- 2.45	37	- 2:08	- 2.45	58	- 1:47	- 2.45	44	- 2:01	- 2.45	26	- 2:19	- 2.45	33	- 2:12
- 2.30	37	- 1:53	- 2.30	59	- 1:31	- 2.30	44	- 1:46	- 2.30	26	- 2:04	- 2.30	33	- 1:57
- 2.15	37	- 1:38	- 2.15	59	- 1:16	- 2.15	44	- 1:31	- 2.15	26	- 1:49	- 2.15	33	- 1:42
- 2.00	37	- 1:23	- 2.00	59	- 1:01	- 2.00	44	- 1:16	- 2.00	26	- 1:34	- 2.00	33	- 1:27
- 1.45	37	- 1:08	- 1.45	61	- 0:44	- 1.45	45	- 1:00	- 1.45	26	- 1:19	- 1.45	34	- 1:11
- 1.30	37	- 0:53	- 1.30	63	- 0:27	- 1.30	45	- 0:45	- 1.30	27	- 1:03	- 1.30	34	- 0:56
- 1.15	37	- 0:38	- 1.15	65	- 0:10	- 1.15	46	- 0:29	- 1.15	28	- 0:47	- 1.15	35	- 0:40
- 1.00	37	- 0:23	- 1.00	66	+ 0:06	- 1.00	47	- 0:13	- 1.00	29	- 0:31	- 1.00	36	- 0:24
- 0.45	37	- 0:08	- 0.45	70	+ 0:25	- 0.45	48	+ 0:03	- 0.45	30	- 0:15	- 0.45	38	- 0:07
- 0.30	38	+ 0:08	- 0.30	73	+ 0:43	- 0.30	50	+ 0:20	- 0.30	31	+ 0:01	- 0.30	39	+ 0:09
- 0.15	38	+ 0:23	- 0.15	76	+ 1:01	- 0.15	51	+ 0:36	- 0.15	32	+ 0:17	- 0.15	41	+ 0:26
HW	38	+ 0:38	HW	79	+ 1:19	HW	53	+ 0:53	HW	33	+ 0:33	HW	42	+ 0:42
+ 0.15	39	+ 0:54	+ 0.15	83	+ 1:38	+ 0.15	54	+ 1:09	+ 0.15	35	+ 0:50	+ 0.15	45	+ 1:00
+ 0.30	39	+ 1:09	+ 0.30	87	+ 1:57	+ 0.30	56	+ 1:26	+ 0.30	37	+ 1:07	+ 0.30	47	+ 1:17
+ 0.45	40	+ 1:25	+ 0.45	91	+ 2:16	+ 0.45	57	+ 1:42	+ 0.45	39	+ 1:24	+ 0.45	50	+ 1:35
+ 1.00	40	+ 1:40	+ 1.00	94	+ 2:34	+ 1.00	59	+ 1:59	+ 1.00	41	+ 1:41	+ 1.00	52	+ 1:52
+ 1.15	41	+ 1:56	+ 1.15	96	+ 2:51	+ 1.15	58	+ 2:13	+ 1.15	42	+ 1:57	+ 1.15	53	+ 2:08
+ 1.30	42	+ 2:12	+ 1.30	98	+ 3:08	+ 1.30	58	+ 2:28	+ 1.30	44	+ 2:14	+ 1.30	55	+ 2:25
+ 1.45	42	+ 2:27	+ 1.45	100	+ 3:25	+ 1.45	57	+ 2:42	+ 1.45	45	+ 2:30	+ 1.45	57	+ 2:42
+ 2.00	43	+ 2:43	+ 2.00	102	+ 3:42	+ 2.00	56	+ 2:56	+ 2.00	46	+ 2:46	+ 2.00	58	+ 2:58
+ 2.15	43	+ 2:58	+ 2.15	101	+ 3:56	+ 2.15	55	+ 3:10	+ 2.15	47	+ 3:02	+ 2.15	58	+ 3:13
+ 2.30	43	+ 3:13	+ 2.30	99	+ 4:09	+ 2.30	54	+ 3:24	+ 2.30	47	+ 3:17	+ 2.30	58	+ 3:28
+ 2.45	43	+ 3:28	+ 2.45	98	+ 4:23	+ 2.45	53	+ 3:38	+ 2.45	47	+ 3:32	+ 2.45	57	+ 3:42
+ 3.00	43	+ 3:43	+ 3.00	97	+ 4:37	+ 3.00	52	+ 3:52	+ 3.00	47	+ 3:47	+ 3.00	57	+ 3:57
+ 3.15	43	+ 3:58	+ 3.15	95	+ 4:50	+ 3.15	51	+ 4:06	+ 3.15	46	+ 4:01	+ 3.15	56	+ 4:11
+ 3.30	43	+ 4:13	+ 3.30	92	+ 5:02	+ 3.30	50	+ 4:20	+ 3.30	44	+ 4:14	+ 3.30	54	+ 4:24
+ 3.45	42	+ 4:27	+ 3.45	90	+ 5:15	+ 3.45	49	+ 4:34	+ 3.45	43	+ 4:28	+ 3.45	53	+ 4:38
+ 4.00	42	+ 4:42	+ 4.00	88	+ 5:28	+ 4.00	48	+ 4:48	+ 4.00	42	+ 4:42	+ 4.00	52	+ 4:52
+ 4.15	42	+ 4:57	+ 4.15	85	+ 5:40	+ 4.15	48	+ 5:03	+ 4.15	41	+ 4:56	+ 4.15	50	+ 5:05
+ 4.30	41	+ 5:11	+ 4.30	83	+ 5:53	+ 4.30	47	+ 5:17	+ 4.30	40	+ 5:10	+ 4.30	49	+ 5:19
+ 4.45	41	+ 5:26	+ 4.45	80	- 5:55	+ 4.45	47	+ 5:32	+ 4.45	39	+ 5:24	+ 4.45	47	+ 5:32
+ 5.00	41	+ 5:41	+ 5.00	78	- 5:42	+ 5.00	46	+ 5:46	+ 5.00	38	+ 5:38	+ 5.00	46	+ 5:46
+ 5.15	40	+ 5:55	+ 5.15	76	- 5:29	+ 5.15	46	- 5:59	+ 5.15	37	+ 5:52	+ 5.15	45	- 6:00
+ 5.30	40	- 5:50	+ 5.30	75	- 5:15	+ 5.30	46	- 5:44	+ 5.30	36	- 5:54	+ 5.30	44	- 5:46
+ 5.45	40	- 5:35	+ 5.45	74	- 5:01	+ 5.45	46	- 5:29	+ 5.45	35	- 5:40	+ 5.45	43	- 5:32
+ 6.00	39	- 5:21	+ 6.00	72	- 4:48	+ 6.00	45	- 5:15	+ 6.00	34	- 5:26	+ 6.00	42	- 5:18

Swale Northwards

Time	F6 Swale Landfall to Spaniard: Duration	F6 Time at End of Sector	Time	F7 Spaniard to Red Sand: Duration	F7 Time at End of Sector	Time	F8 Red Sand to SW Barrow: Duration	F8 Time at End of Sector
- 6.00	18	- 5:42	- 6.00	44	- 5:16	- 6.00	20	- 5:40
- 5.45	18	- 5:27	- 5.45	44	- 5:01	- 5.45	20	- 5:25
- 5.30	17	- 5:13	- 5.30	43	- 4:47	- 5.30	21	- 5:09
- 5.15	17	- 4:58	- 5.15	43	- 4:32	- 5.15	21	- 4:54
- 5.00	16	- 4:44	- 5.00	43	- 4:17	- 5.00	22	- 4:38
- 4.45	16	- 4:29	- 4.45	42	- 4:03	- 4.45	22	- 4:23
- 4.30	16	- 4:14	- 4.30	42	- 3:48	- 4.30	22	- 4:08
- 4.15	16	- 3:59	- 4.15	42	- 3:33	- 4.15	22	- 3:53
- 4.00	15	- 3:45	- 4.00	42	- 3:18	- 4.00	22	- 3:38
- 3.45	15	- 3:30	- 3.45	42	- 3:03	- 3.45	22	- 3:23
- 3.30	15	- 3:15	- 3.30	42	- 2:48	- 3.30	22	- 3:08
- 3.15	15	- 3:00	- 3.15	42	- 2:33	- 3.15	22	- 2:53
- 3.00	15	- 2:45	- 3.00	42	- 2:18	- 3.00	22	- 2:38
- 2.45	15	- 2:30	- 2.45	42	- 2:03	- 2.45	22	- 2:23
- 2.30	15	- 2:15	- 2.30	42	- 1:48	- 2.30	22	- 2:08
- 2.15	15	- 2:00	- 2.15	42	- 1:33	- 2.15	22	- 1:53
- 2.00	15	- 1:45	- 2.00	42	- 1:18	- 2.00	22	- 1:38
- 1.45	15	- 1:30	- 1.45	43	- 1:02	- 1.45	22	- 1:23
- 1.30	15	- 1:15	- 1.30	43	- 0:47	- 1.30	22	- 1:08
- 1.15	15	- 1:00	- 1.15	44	- 0:31	- 1.15	21	- 0:54
- 1.00	15	- 0:45	- 1.00	45	- 0:15	- 1.00	21	- 0:39
- 0.45	15	- 0:30	- 0.45	46	+ 0:01	- 0.45	20	- 0:25
- 0.30	16	- 0:14	- 0.30	47	+ 0:17	- 0.30	20	- 0:10
- 0.15	16	+ 0:01	- 0.15	49	+ 0:34	- 0.15	19	+ 0:04
HW	16	+ 0:16	HW	50	+ 0:50	HW	19	+ 0:19
+ 0.15	17	+ 0:32	+ 0.15	51	+ 1:06	+ 0.15	18	+ 0:33
+ 0.30	17	+ 0:47	+ 0.30	53	+ 1:23	+ 0.30	18	+ 0:48
+ 0.45	18	+ 1:03	+ 0.45	54	+ 1:39	+ 0.45	17	+ 1:02
+ 1.00	18	+ 1:18	+ 1.00	55	+ 1:55	+ 1.00	16	+ 1:16
+ 1.15	18	+ 1:33	+ 1.15	56	+ 2:11	+ 1.15	16	+ 1:31
+ 1.30	19	+ 1:49	+ 1.30	56	+ 2:26	+ 1.30	16	+ 1:46
+ 1.45	19	+ 2:04	+ 1.45	56	+ 2:41	+ 1.45	16	+ 2:01
+ 2.00	19	+ 2:19	+ 2.00	56	+ 2:56	+ 2.00	15	+ 2:15
+ 2.15	19	+ 2:34	+ 2.15	55	+ 3:10	+ 2.15	15	+ 2:30
+ 2.30	18	+ 2:48	+ 2.30	55	+ 3:25	+ 2.30	15	+ 2:45
+ 2.45	18	+ 3:03	+ 2.45	54	+ 3:39	+ 2.45	16	+ 3:01
+ 3.00	18	+ 3:18	+ 3.00	54	+ 3:54	+ 3.00	16	+ 3:16
+ 3.15	18	+ 3:33	+ 3.15	53	+ 4:08	+ 3.15	16	+ 3:31
+ 3.30	18	+ 3:48	+ 3.30	52	+ 4:22	+ 3.30	16	+ 3:46
+ 3.45	18	+ 4:03	+ 3.45	52	+ 4:37	+ 3.45	16	+ 4:01
+ 4.00	17	+ 4:17	+ 4.00	51	+ 4:51	+ 4.00	17	+ 4:17
+ 4.15	17	+ 4:32	+ 4.15	50	+ 5:05	+ 4.15	17	+ 4:32
+ 4.30	17	+ 4:47	+ 4.30	50	+ 5:20	+ 4.30	17	+ 4:47
+ 4.45	17	+ 5:02	+ 4.45	49	+ 5:34	+ 4.45	18	+ 5:03
+ 5.00	17	+ 5:17	+ 5.00	48	+ 5:48	+ 5.00	18	+ 5:18
+ 5.15	16	+ 5:31	+ 5.15	48	- 5:57	+ 5.15	18	+ 5:33
+ 5.30	16	+ 5:46	+ 5.30	47	- 5:43	+ 5.30	18	+ 5:48
+ 5.45	16	- 5:59	+ 5.45	47	- 5:28	+ 5.45	19	- 5:56
+ 6.00	16	- 5:44	+ 6.00	46	- 5:14	+ 6.00	19	- 5:41

The Queens Channel — Swale Northwards

NORTH & WEST

Table G - Medway, Sea Reach and Black Deep Connections

Neaps — All times relate to HW Sheerness — **Time to cover Sectors (in minutes) at 4.0 Kts**

NORTH BOUND

	G1 Princes No 6 to Red Sand Tower			G2 Red Sand Tower to Medway			G3 Red Sand Tower to Sea Reach			G4 Medway to Sea Reach			G5 Medway to SW Barrow			G6 Sea Reach to SW Barrow			G7 Blk Deep No 8 to Black Deep			G8 Blk Deep No 8 to Long Sand Inner	
Time	Duration	Time at End of Sector	Time	Duration	Time at End of Sector	Time	Duration	Time at End of Sector	Time	Duration	Time at End of Sector	Time	Duration	Time at End of Sector	Time	Duration	Time at End of Sector	Time	Duration	Time at End of Sector	Time	Duration	Time at End of Sector
- 6.00	68	- 4:52	- 6.00	95	- 4:25	- 6.00	62	- 4:58	- 6.00	49	- 5:11	- 6.00	138	- 3:42	- 6.00	80	- 4:40	- 6.00	124	- 3:56	- 6.00	64	- 4:56
- 5.45	67	- 4:38	- 5.45	93	- 4:12	- 5.45	60	- 4:45	- 5.45	51	- 4:54	- 5.45	143	- 3:22	- 5.45	84	- 4:21	- 5.45	126	- 3:39	- 5.45	66	- 4:39
- 5.30	65	- 4:25	- 5.30	90	- 4:00	- 5.30	58	- 4:32	- 5.30	52	- 4:38	- 5.30	148	- 3:02	- 5.30	87	- 4:03	- 5.30	128	- 3:22	- 5.30	68	- 4:22
- 5.15	63	- 4:12	- 5.15	88	- 3:47	- 5.15	57	- 4:18	- 5.15	54	- 4:21	- 5.15	153	- 2:42	- 5.15	91	- 3:44	- 5.15	130	- 3:05	- 5.15	70	- 4:05
- 5.00	62	- 3:58	- 5.00	86	- 3:34	- 5.00	55	- 4:05	- 5.00	55	- 4:05	- 5.00	158	- 2:22	- 5.00	94	- 3:26	- 5.00	132	- 2:48	- 5.00	72	- 3:48
- 4.45	61	- 3:44	- 4.45	85	- 3:20	- 4.45	54	- 3:51	- 4.45	57	- 3:48	- 4.45	159	- 2:06	- 4.45	96	- 3:09	- 4.45	130	- 2:35	- 4.45	73	- 3:32
- 4.30	61	- 3:29	- 4.30	84	- 3:06	- 4.30	54	- 3:36	- 4.30	58	- 3:32	- 4.30	159	- 1:51	- 4.30	98	- 2:52	- 4.30	128	- 2:22	- 4.30	74	- 3:16
- 4.15	60	- 3:15	- 4.15	84	- 2:51	- 4.15	53	- 3:22	- 4.15	59	- 3:16	- 4.15	160	- 1:35	- 4.15	99	- 2:36	- 4.15	126	- 2:09	- 4.15	75	- 3:00
- 4.00	59	- 3:01	- 4.00	83	- 2:37	- 4.00	52	- 3:08	- 4.00	61	- 2:59	- 4.00	161	- 1:19	- 4.00	101	- 2:19	- 4.00	123	- 1:57	- 4.00	76	- 2:44
- 3.45	59	- 2:46	- 3.45	83	- 2:22	- 3.45	52	- 2:53	- 3.45	61	- 2:44	- 3.45	160	- 1:05	- 3.45	101	- 2:04	- 3.45	118	- 1:47	- 3.45	75	- 2:30
- 3.30	59	- 2:31	- 3.30	83	- 2:07	- 3.30	52	- 2:38	- 3.30	61	- 2:29	- 3.30	158	- 0:52	- 3.30	100	- 1:50	- 3.30	112	- 1:38	- 3.30	74	- 2:16
- 3.15	59	- 2:16	- 3.15	83	- 1:52	- 3.15	52	- 2:23	- 3.15	61	- 2:14	- 3.15	157	- 0:38	- 3.15	100	- 1:35	- 3.15	107	- 1:28	- 3.15	74	- 2:01
- 3.00	58	- 2:02	- 3.00	83	- 1:37	- 3.00	52	- 2:08	- 3.00	61	- 1:59	- 3.00	155	- 0:25	- 3.00	100	- 1:20	- 3.00	102	- 1:18	- 3.00	73	- 1:47
- 2.45	59	- 1:46	- 2.45	84	- 1:21	- 2.45	52	- 1:53	- 2.45	60	- 1:45	- 2.45	152	- 0:13	- 2.45	98	- 1:07	- 2.45	96	- 1:09	- 2.45	71	- 1:34
- 2.30	59	- 1:31	- 2.30	84	- 1:06	- 2.30	52	- 1:38	- 2.30	59	- 1:31	- 2.30	149	- 0:01	- 2.30	96	- 0:54	- 2.30	90	- 1:00	- 2.30	68	- 1:22
- 2.15	60	- 1:15	- 2.15	85	- 0:50	- 2.15	53	- 1:22	- 2.15	58	- 1:17	- 2.15	146	+ 0:11	- 2.15	95	- 0:40	- 2.15	84	- 0:51	- 2.15	66	- 1:09
- 2.00	60	- 1:00	- 2.00	85	- 0:35	- 2.00	53	- 1:07	- 2.00	57	- 1:03	- 2.00	143	+ 0:23	- 2.00	93	- 0:27	- 2.00	78	- 0:42	- 2.00	64	- 0:56
- 1.45	63	- 0:42	- 1.45	87	- 0:18	- 1.45	54	- 0:51	- 1.45	56	- 0:49	- 1.45	140	+ 0:35	- 1.45	90	- 0:15	- 1.45	75	- 0:30	- 1.45	61	- 0:44
- 1.30	65	- 0:25	- 1.30	89	- 0:01	- 1.30	55	- 0:35	- 1.30	55	- 0:35	- 1.30	136	+ 0:46	- 1.30	87	- 0:03	- 1.30	73	- 0:17	- 1.30	58	- 0:32
- 1.15	67	- 0:08	- 1.15	90	+ 0:15	- 1.15	56	- 0:19	- 1.15	54	- 0:21	- 1.15	132	+ 0:57	- 1.15	84	+ 0:09	- 1.15	70	- 0:05	- 1.15	55	- 0:20
- 1.00	70	+ 0:10	- 1.00	92	+ 0:32	- 1.00	57	- 0:03	- 1.00	52	- 0:08	- 1.00	128	+ 1:08	- 1.00	80	+ 0:20	- 1.00	67	+ 0:07	- 1.00	53	- 0:07
- 0.45	74	+ 0:29	- 0.45	99	+ 0:54	- 0.45	60	+ 0:15	- 0.45	51	+ 0:06	- 0.45	125	+ 1:20	- 0.45	78	+ 0:33	- 0.45	66	+ 0:21	- 0.45	50	+ 0:05
- 0.30	78	+ 0:48	- 0.30	105	+ 1:15	- 0.30	62	+ 0:32	- 0.30	50	+ 0:20	- 0.30	121	+ 1:31	- 0.30	76	+ 0:46	- 0.30	64	+ 0:34	- 0.30	48	+ 0:18
- 0.15	83	+ 1:08	- 0.15	112	+ 1:37	- 0.15	64	+ 0:49	- 0.15	49	+ 0:34	- 0.15	117	+ 1:42	- 0.15	74	+ 0:59	- 0.15	62	+ 0:47	- 0.15	46	+ 0:31
HW	87	+ 1:27	HW	118	+ 1:58	HW	67	+ 1:07	HW	48	+ 0:48	HW	113	+ 1:53	HW	72	+ 1:12	HW	60	+ 1:00	HW	44	+ 0:44
+ 0.15	94	+ 1:49	+ 0.15	128	+ 2:23	+ 0.15	72	+ 1:27	+ 0.15	47	+ 1:02	+ 0.15	110	+ 2:05	+ 0.15	70	+ 1:25	+ 0.15	59	+ 1:14	+ 0.15	43	+ 0:58
+ 0.30	100	+ 2:10	+ 0.30	138	+ 2:48	+ 0.30	77	+ 1:47	+ 0.30	46	+ 1:16	+ 0.30	107	+ 2:17	+ 0.30	68	+ 1:38	+ 0.30	58	+ 1:28	+ 0.30	42	+ 1:12
+ 0.45	106	+ 2:31	+ 0.45	148	+ 3:13	+ 0.45	82	+ 2:07	+ 0.45	45	+ 1:30	+ 0.45	104	+ 2:29	+ 0.45	66	+ 1:51	+ 0.45	57	+ 1:42	+ 0.45	41	+ 1:26
+ 1.00	112	+ 2:52	+ 1.00	158	+ 3:38	+ 1.00	87	+ 2:27	+ 1.00	44	+ 1:44	+ 1.00	102	+ 2:42	+ 1.00	64	+ 2:04	+ 1.00	56	+ 1:56	+ 1.00	40	+ 1:40
+ 1.15	112	+ 3:07	+ 1.15	160	+ 3:55	+ 1.15	93	+ 2:48	+ 1.15	43	+ 1:58	+ 1.15	100	+ 2:55	+ 1.15	63	+ 2:18	+ 1.15	57	+ 2:12	+ 1.15	40	+ 1:55
+ 1.30	112	+ 3:22	+ 1.30	162	+ 4:12	+ 1.30	98	+ 3:08	+ 1.30	43	+ 2:13	+ 1.30	98	+ 3:08	+ 1.30	62	+ 2:32	+ 1.30	58	+ 2:28	+ 1.30	40	+ 2:10
+ 1.45	112	+ 3:37	+ 1.45	165	+ 4:30	+ 1.45	104	+ 3:29	+ 1.45	42	+ 2:27	+ 1.45	97	+ 3:22	+ 1.45	60	+ 2:45	+ 1.45	58	+ 2:43	+ 1.45	40	+ 2:25
+ 2.00	112	+ 3:52	+ 2.00	167	+ 4:47	+ 2.00	109	+ 3:49	+ 2.00	41	+ 2:41	+ 2.00	95	+ 3:35	+ 2.00	59	+ 2:59	+ 2.00	59	+ 2:59	+ 2.00	40	+ 2:40
+ 2.15	110	+ 4:05	+ 2.15	163	+ 4:58	+ 2.15	107	+ 4:02	+ 2.15	41	+ 2:56	+ 2.15	95	+ 3:50	+ 2.15	59	+ 3:14	+ 2.15	60	+ 3:15	+ 2.15	41	+ 2:56
+ 2.30	108	+ 4:18	+ 2.30	160	+ 5:10	+ 2.30	106	+ 4:16	+ 2.30	41	+ 3:11	+ 2.30	96	+ 4:06	+ 2.30	59	+ 3:29	+ 2.30	61	+ 3:31	+ 2.30	41	+ 3:11
+ 2.45	106	+ 4:31	+ 2.45	156	+ 5:21	+ 2.45	104	+ 4:29	+ 2.45	41	+ 3:26	+ 2.45	96	+ 4:21	+ 2.45	59	+ 3:44	+ 2.45	62	+ 3:47	+ 2.45	42	+ 3:27
+ 3.00	104	+ 4:44	+ 3.00	153	+ 5:33	+ 3.00	102	+ 4:42	+ 3.00	41	+ 3:41	+ 3.00	96	+ 4:36	+ 3.00	59	+ 3:59	+ 3.00	63	+ 4:03	+ 3.00	43	+ 3:43
+ 3.15	101	+ 4:56	+ 3.15	148	+ 5:43	+ 3.15	97	+ 4:52	+ 3.15	42	+ 3:57	+ 3.15	98	+ 4:53	+ 3.15	60	+ 4:15	+ 3.15	65	+ 4:20	+ 3.15	44	+ 3:59
+ 3.30	98	+ 5:08	+ 3.30	143	+ 5:53	+ 3.30	93	+ 5:03	+ 3.30	42	+ 4:12	+ 3.30	100	+ 5:10	+ 3.30	61	+ 4:31	+ 3.30	67	+ 4:37	+ 3.30	45	+ 4:15
+ 3.45	94	+ 5:19	+ 3.45	138	- 5:57	+ 3.45	88	+ 5:13	+ 3.45	42	+ 4:27	+ 3.45	101	+ 5:26	+ 3.45	62	+ 4:47	+ 3.45	68	+ 4:53	+ 3.45	46	+ 4:31
+ 4.00	91	+ 5:31	+ 4.00	133	- 5:47	+ 4.00	83	+ 5:23	+ 4.00	43	+ 4:43	+ 4.00	103	+ 5:43	+ 4.00	62	+ 5:02	+ 4.00	70	+ 5:10	+ 4.00	47	+ 4:47
+ 4.15	89	+ 5:44	+ 4.15	129	- 5:36	+ 4.15	80	+ 5:35	+ 4.15	43	+ 4:58	+ 4.15	105	- 6:00	+ 4.15	64	+ 5:19	+ 4.15	74	+ 5:29	+ 4.15	48	+ 5:03
+ 4.30	86	+ 5:56	+ 4.30	125	- 5:25	+ 4.30	78	+ 5:48	+ 4.30	44	+ 5:14	+ 4.30	108	- 5:42	+ 4.30	65	+ 5:35	+ 4.30	78	+ 5:48	+ 4.30	50	+ 5:20
+ 4.45	84	- 5:51	+ 4.45	121	- 5:14	+ 4.45	75	- 6:00	+ 4.45	44	+ 5:29	+ 4.45	110	- 5:25	+ 4.45	66	+ 5:51	+ 4.45	82	- 5:53	+ 4.45	51	+ 5:36
+ 5.00	82	- 5:38	+ 5.00	117	- 5:03	+ 5.00	72	- 5:48	+ 5.00	45	+ 5:45	+ 5.00	112	- 5:08	+ 5.00	68	- 5:52	+ 5.00	86	- 5:34	+ 5.00	53	+ 5:53
+ 5.15	80	- 5:25	+ 5.15	114	- 4:51	+ 5.15	71	- 5:34	+ 5.15	45	- 6:00	+ 5.15	115	- 4:50	+ 5.15	69	- 5:36	+ 5.15	91	- 5:14	+ 5.15	54	- 5:51
+ 5.30	79	- 5:11	+ 5.30	111	- 4:39	+ 5.30	70	- 5:20	+ 5.30	46	- 5:44	+ 5.30	117	- 4:33	+ 5.30	70	- 5:20	+ 5.30	97	- 4:53	+ 5.30	56	- 5:34
+ 5.45	77	- 4:58	+ 5.45	109	- 4:26	+ 5.45	69	- 5:06	+ 5.45	47	- 5:28	+ 5.45	120	- 4:15	+ 5.45	71	- 5:04	+ 5.45	102	- 4:33	+ 5.45	57	- 5:18
+ 6.00	75	- 4:45	+ 6.00	106	- 4:14	+ 6.00	68	- 4:52	+ 6.00	47	- 5:13	+ 6.00	122	- 3:58	+ 6.00	72	- 4:48	+ 6.00	108	- 4:12	+ 6.00	59	- 5:01

Black Deep Connections

Table G - Medway, Sea Reach and Black Deep Connections

Time to cover Sectors (in minutes) at 4.0 kts — All times relate to HW Sheerness — **Springs**

	G1 Princes No 6 to Red Sand Tower			G2 Red Sand Tower to Medway			G3 Red Sand Tower to Sea Reach			G4 Medway to Sea Reach			G5 Medway to SW Barrow			G6 Sea Reach to SW Barrow			G7 Blk Deep No 8 to Black Deep			G8 Blk Deep No 8 to Long Sand Inner
Time	Duration	Time at End of Sector	Time	Duration	Time at End of Sector	Time	Duration	Time at End of Sector	Time	Duration	Time at End of Sector	Time	Duration	Time at End of Sector	Time	Duration	Time at End of Sector	Time	Duration	Time at End of Sector	Time	Duration	Time at End of Sector
- 6.00	64	- 4:56	- 6.00	92	- 4:28	- 6.00	61	- 4:59	- 6.00	50	- 5:10	- 6.00	154	- 3:26	- 6.00	84	- 4:36	- 6.00	175	- 3:05	- 6.00	70	- 4:50
- 5.45	62	- 4:43	- 5.45	88	- 4:17	- 5.45	58	- 4:47	- 5.45	53	- 4:52	- 5.45	159	- 3:06	- 5.45	89	- 4:16	- 5.45	175	- 2:50	- 5.45	77	- 4:28
- 5.30	60	- 4:30	- 5.30	85	- 4:05	- 5.30	56	- 4:34	- 5.30	55	- 4:35	- 5.30	165	- 2:45	- 5.30	94	- 3:56	- 5.30	174	- 2:36	- 5.30	84	- 4:06
- 5.15	57	- 4:18	- 5.15	82	- 3:53	- 5.15	54	- 4:21	- 5.15	58	- 4:17	- 5.15	171	- 2:24	- 5.15	99	- 3:36	- 5.15	174	- 2:21	- 5.15	91	- 3:44
- 5.00	55	- 4:05	- 5.00	78	- 3:42	- 5.00	51	- 4:09	- 5.00	61	- 3:59	- 5.00	176	- 2:04	- 5.00	105	- 3:15	- 5.00	173	- 2:07	- 5.00	98	- 3:22
- 4.45	55	- 3:50	- 4.45	77	- 3:28	- 4.45	50	- 3:55	- 4.45	64	- 3:41	- 4.45	177	- 1:48	- 4.45	107	- 2:58	- 4.45	165	- 2:00	- 4.45	100	- 3:05
- 4.30	54	- 3:36	- 4.30	76	- 3:14	- 4.30	49	- 3:41	- 4.30	67	- 3:23	- 4.30	178	- 1:32	- 4.30	110	- 2:40	- 4.30	156	- 1:54	- 4.30	102	- 2:48
- 4.15	53	- 3:22	- 4.15	75	- 3:00	- 4.15	48	- 3:27	- 4.15	70	- 3:05	- 4.15	179	- 1:16	- 4.15	112	- 2:23	- 4.15	148	- 1:47	- 4.15	104	- 2:31
- 4.00	53	- 3:07	- 4.00	74	- 2:46	- 4.00	47	- 3:13	- 4.00	73	- 2:47	- 4.00	180	- 1:00	- 4.00	114	- 2:06	- 4.00	140	- 1:40	- 4.00	105	- 2:15
- 3.45	53	- 2:52	- 3.45	74	- 2:31	- 3.45	47	- 2:58	- 3.45	73	- 2:32	- 3.45	177	- 0:48	- 3.45	113	- 1:52	- 3.45	131	- 1:34	- 3.45	102	- 2:03
- 3.30	52	- 2:38	- 3.30	75	- 2:15	- 3.30	47	- 2:43	- 3.30	73	- 2:17	- 3.30	174	- 0:36	- 3.30	112	- 1:38	- 3.30	122	- 1:28	- 3.30	99	- 1:51
- 3.15	52	- 2:23	- 3.15	75	- 2:00	- 3.15	47	- 2:28	- 3.15	73	- 2:02	- 3.15	171	- 0:24	- 3.15	111	- 1:24	- 3.15	113	- 1:22	- 3.15	96	- 1:39
- 3.00	52	- 2:08	- 3.00	75	- 1:45	- 3.00	47	- 2:13	- 3.00	73	- 1:47	- 3.00	168	- 0:12	- 3.00	110	- 1:10	- 3.00	105	- 1:15	- 3.00	92	- 1:28
- 2.45	53	- 1:52	- 2.45	76	- 1:29	- 2.45	47	- 1:58	- 2.45	71	- 1:34	- 2.45	163	- 0:02	- 2.45	107	- 0:58	- 2.45	98	- 1:07	- 2.45	87	- 1:18
- 2.30	53	- 1:37	- 2.30	77	- 1:13	- 2.30	48	- 1:42	- 2.30	69	- 1:21	- 2.30	159	+ 0:09	- 2.30	104	- 0:46	- 2.30	91	- 0:59	- 2.30	81	- 1:09
- 2.15	54	- 1:21	- 2.15	77	- 0:58	- 2.15	48	- 1:27	- 2.15	66	- 1:09	- 2.15	154	+ 0:19	- 2.15	101	- 0:34	- 2.15	84	- 0:51	- 2.15	76	- 0:59
- 2.00	55	- 1:05	- 2.00	78	- 0:42	- 2.00	49	- 1:11	- 2.00	64	- 0:56	- 2.00	150	+ 0:30	- 2.00	98	- 0:22	- 2.00	78	- 0:42	- 2.00	70	- 0:50
- 1.45	58	- 0:47	- 1.45	81	- 0:24	- 1.45	50	- 0:55	- 1.45	62	- 0:43	- 1.45	144	+ 0:39	- 1.45	94	- 0:11	- 1.45	74	- 0:31	- 1.45	65	- 0:40
- 1.30	62	- 0:28	- 1.30	84	- 0:06	- 1.30	51	- 0:39	- 1.30	59	- 0:31	- 1.30	139	+ 0:49	- 1.30	91	+ 0:01	- 1.30	70	- 0:20	- 1.30	61	- 0:29
- 1.15	65	- 0:10	- 1.15	86	+ 0:11	- 1.15	53	- 0:22	- 1.15	57	- 0:18	- 1.15	133	+ 0:58	- 1.15	88	+ 0:13	- 1.15	66	- 0:09	- 1.15	56	- 0:19
- 1.00	69	+ 0:09	- 1.00	89	+ 0:29	- 1.00	54	- 0:06	- 1.00	54	- 0:06	- 1.00	127	+ 1:07	- 1.00	84	+ 0:24	- 1.00	62	+ 0:02	- 1.00	52	- 0:08
- 0.45	79	+ 0:34	- 0.45	100	+ 0:55	- 0.45	57	+ 0:12	- 0.45	53	+ 0:08	- 0.45	123	+ 1:18	- 0.45	81	+ 0:36	- 0.45	59	+ 0:14	- 0.45	49	+ 0:04
- 0.30	90	+ 1:00	- 0.30	112	+ 1:22	- 0.30	60	+ 0:30	- 0.30	51	+ 0:21	- 0.30	118	+ 1:28	- 0.30	77	+ 0:47	- 0.30	57	+ 0:27	- 0.30	46	+ 0:16
- 0.15	100	+ 1:25	- 0.15	123	+ 1:48	- 0.15	64	+ 0:49	- 0.15	49	+ 0:34	- 0.15	113	+ 1:38	- 0.15	74	+ 0:59	- 0.15	54	+ 0:39	- 0.15	43	+ 0:28
HW	110	+ 1:50	HW	135	+ 2:15	HW	67	+ 1:07	HW	48	+ 0:48	HW	108	+ 1:48	HW	71	+ 1:11	HW	51	+ 0:51	HW	40	+ 0:40
+ 0.15	119	+ 2:14	+ 0.15	152	+ 2:47	+ 0.15	79	+ 1:34	+ 0.15	46	+ 1:01	+ 0.15	105	+ 2:00	+ 0.15	68	+ 1:23	+ 0.15	50	+ 1:05	+ 0.15	39	+ 0:54
+ 0.30	127	+ 2:37	+ 0.30	169	+ 3:19	+ 0.30	91	+ 2:01	+ 0.30	45	+ 1:15	+ 0.30	102	+ 2:12	+ 0.30	65	+ 1:35	+ 0.30	49	+ 1:19	+ 0.30	38	+ 1:08
+ 0.45	136	+ 3:01	+ 0.45	186	+ 3:51	+ 0.45	102	+ 2:27	+ 0.45	44	+ 1:29	+ 0.45	98	+ 2:23	+ 0.45	63	+ 1:48	+ 0.45	48	+ 1:33	+ 0.45	37	+ 1:22
+ 1.00	144	+ 3:24	+ 1.00	204	+ 4:24	+ 1.00	114	+ 2:54	+ 1.00	42	+ 1:42	+ 1.00	95	+ 2:35	+ 1.00	60	+ 2:00	+ 1.00	47	+ 1:47	+ 1.00	36	+ 1:36
+ 1.15	141	+ 3:36	+ 1.15	202	+ 4:37	+ 1.15	120	+ 3:15	+ 1.15	41	+ 1:56	+ 1.15	91	+ 2:46	+ 1.15	58	+ 2:13	+ 1.15	48	+ 2:03	+ 1.15	36	+ 1:51
+ 1.30	138	+ 3:48	+ 1.30	201	+ 4:51	+ 1.30	126	+ 3:36	+ 1.30	41	+ 2:11	+ 1.30	87	+ 2:57	+ 1.30	57	+ 2:27	+ 1.30	48	+ 2:18	+ 1.30	36	+ 2:06
+ 1.45	135	+ 4:00	+ 1.45	200	+ 5:05	+ 1.45	132	+ 3:57	+ 1.45	40	+ 2:25	+ 1.45	83	+ 3:08	+ 1.45	55	+ 2:40	+ 1.45	49	+ 2:34	+ 1.45	36	+ 2:21
+ 2.00	132	+ 4:12	+ 2.00	198	+ 5:18	+ 2.00	138	+ 4:18	+ 2.00	39	+ 2:39	+ 2.00	79	+ 3:19	+ 2.00	54	+ 2:54	+ 2.00	50	+ 2:50	+ 2.00	36	+ 2:36
+ 2.15	127	+ 4:22	+ 2.15	191	+ 5:26	+ 2.15	133	+ 4:28	+ 2.15	39	+ 2:54	+ 2.15	82	+ 3:37	+ 2.15	54	+ 3:09	+ 2.15	51	+ 3:06	+ 2.15	36	+ 2:51
+ 2.30	121	+ 4:31	+ 2.30	183	+ 5:33	+ 2.30	127	+ 4:37	+ 2.30	39	+ 3:09	+ 2.30	85	+ 3:55	+ 2.30	54	+ 3:24	+ 2.30	53	+ 3:23	+ 2.30	37	+ 3:07
+ 2.45	116	+ 4:41	+ 2.45	176	+ 5:41	+ 2.45	122	+ 4:47	+ 2.45	39	+ 3:24	+ 2.45	87	+ 4:12	+ 2.45	53	+ 3:38	+ 2.45	54	+ 3:39	+ 2.45	37	+ 3:22
+ 3.00	111	+ 4:51	+ 3.00	168	+ 5:48	+ 3.00	117	+ 4:57	+ 3.00	39	+ 3:39	+ 3.00	90	+ 4:30	+ 3.00	53	+ 3:53	+ 3.00	55	+ 3:55	+ 3.00	38	+ 3:38
+ 3.15	107	+ 5:02	+ 3.15	161	+ 5:56	+ 3.15	111	+ 5:06	+ 3.15	39	+ 3:54	+ 3.15	92	+ 4:47	+ 3.15	54	+ 4:09	+ 3.15	58	+ 4:13	+ 3.15	39	+ 3:54
+ 3.30	102	+ 5:12	+ 3.30	153	- 5:57	+ 3.30	105	+ 5:15	+ 3.30	40	+ 4:10	+ 3.30	94	+ 5:04	+ 3.30	55	+ 4:25	+ 3.30	60	+ 4:30	+ 3.30	40	+ 4:10
+ 3.45	98	+ 5:23	+ 3.45	145	- 5:50	+ 3.45	100	+ 5:25	+ 3.45	40	+ 4:25	+ 3.45	97	+ 5:22	+ 3.45	56	+ 4:41	+ 3.45	62	+ 4:47	+ 3.45	42	+ 4:27
+ 4.00	94	+ 5:34	+ 4.00	138	- 5:42	+ 4.00	94	+ 5:34	+ 4.00	41	+ 4:41	+ 4.00	99	+ 5:39	+ 4.00	57	+ 4:57	+ 4.00	65	+ 5:05	+ 4.00	43	+ 4:43
+ 4.15	92	+ 5:47	+ 4.15	133	- 5:32	+ 4.15	89	+ 5:44	+ 4.15	41	+ 4:56	+ 4.15	102	+ 5:57	+ 4.15	59	+ 5:14	+ 4.15	72	+ 5:27	+ 4.15	45	+ 5:00
+ 4.30	89	+ 5:59	+ 4.30	128	- 5:22	+ 4.30	84	+ 5:54	+ 4.30	42	+ 5:12	+ 4.30	105	- 5:45	+ 4.30	61	+ 5:31	+ 4.30	79	+ 5:49	+ 4.30	47	+ 5:17
+ 4.45	86	- 5:49	+ 4.45	123	- 5:12	+ 4.45	80	- 5:55	+ 4.45	43	+ 5:28	+ 4.45	108	- 5:27	+ 4.45	63	+ 5:48	+ 4.45	86	- 5:49	+ 4.45	49	+ 5:34
+ 5.00	83	- 5:37	+ 5.00	118	- 5:02	+ 5.00	75	- 5:45	+ 5.00	44	+ 5:44	+ 5.00	111	- 5:09	+ 5.00	65	- 5:55	+ 5.00	93	- 5:27	+ 5.00	52	+ 5:52
+ 5.15	82	- 5:23	+ 5.15	115	- 4:50	+ 5.15	73	- 5:32	+ 5.15	44	+ 5:59	+ 5.15	115	- 4:50	+ 5.15	66	- 5:39	+ 5.15	101	- 5:04	+ 5.15	54	- 5:51
+ 5.30	80	- 5:10	+ 5.30	112	- 4:38	+ 5.30	72	- 5:18	+ 5.30	45	- 5:45	+ 5.30	118	- 4:32	+ 5.30	68	- 5:22	+ 5.30	109	- 4:41	+ 5.30	56	- 5:34
+ 5.45	78	- 4:57	+ 5.45	109	- 4:26	+ 5.45	70	- 5:05	+ 5.45	46	- 5:29	+ 5.45	121	- 4:14	+ 5.45	69	- 5:06	+ 5.45	117	- 4:18	+ 5.45	58	- 5:17
+ 6.00	76	- 4:44	+ 6.00	106	- 4:14	+ 6.00	69	- 4:51	+ 6.00	47	- 5:13	+ 6.00	124	- 3:56	+ 6.00	71	- 4:49	+ 6.00	125	- 3:55	+ 6.00	61	- 4:59

Black Deep Connections

NORTH BOUND

Table G - Medway, Sea Reach and Black Deep Connections

Neaps — All times relate to HW Sheerness — **Time to cover Sectors (in minutes) at 5.0 Kts**

NORTH BOUND

Time	G1 Princes No 6 to Red Sand Tower: Duration	G1 Time at End of Sector	G2 Red Sand Tower to Medway: Duration	G2 Time at End of Sector	G3 Red Sand Tower to Sea Reach: Duration	G3 Time at End of Sector	G4 Medway to Sea Reach: Duration	G4 Time at End of Sector	G5 Medway to SW Barrow: Duration	G5 Time at End of Sector	G6 Sea Reach to SW Barrow: Duration	G6 Time at End of Sector	G7 Blk Deep No 8 to Black Deep: Duration	G7 Time at End of Sector	G8 Blk Deep No 8 to Long Sand Inner: Duration	G8 Time at End of Sector
- 6.00	56	- 5:04	78	- 4:42	50	- 5:10	39	- 5:21	105	- 4:15	62	- 4:58	91	- 4:29	49	- 5:11
- 5.45	54	- 4:51	77	- 4:28	49	- 4:56	40	- 5:05	108	- 3:57	64	- 4:41	93	- 4:12	50	- 4:55
- 5.30	53	- 4:37	75	- 4:15	48	- 4:42	40	- 4:50	112	- 3:38	66	- 4:24	95	- 3:55	52	- 4:38
- 5.15	52	- 4:23	73	- 4:02	47	- 4:28	41	- 4:34	115	- 3:20	67	- 4:08	97	- 3:38	53	- 4:22
- 5.00	51	- 4:09	71	- 3:49	46	- 4:14	42	- 4:18	118	- 3:02	69	- 3:51	99	- 3:21	55	- 4:05
- 4.45	51	- 3:54	71	- 3:34	45	- 4:00	43	- 4:02	119	- 2:46	70	- 3:35	99	- 3:06	55	- 3:50
- 4.30	50	- 3:40	70	- 3:20	45	- 3:45	44	- 3:46	120	- 2:30	71	- 3:19	98	- 2:52	56	- 3:34
- 4.15	50	- 3:25	70	- 3:05	44	- 3:31	45	- 3:30	121	- 2:14	72	- 3:03	98	- 2:37	56	- 3:19
- 4.00	49	- 3:11	69	- 2:51	43	- 3:17	46	- 3:14	122	- 1:58	73	- 2:47	97	- 2:23	57	- 3:03
- 3.45	49	- 2:56	69	- 2:36	43	- 3:02	46	- 2:59	122	- 1:43	73	- 2:32	92	- 2:13	57	- 2:48
- 3.30	49	- 2:41	69	- 2:21	43	- 2:47	46	- 2:44	121	- 1:29	73	- 2:17	87	- 2:03	56	- 2:34
- 3.15	49	- 2:26	69	- 2:06	43	- 2:32	46	- 2:29	121	- 1:14	73	- 2:02	81	- 1:54	56	- 2:19
- 3.00	49	- 2:11	69	- 1:51	43	- 2:17	46	- 2:14	120	- 1:00	72	- 1:48	76	- 1:44	56	- 2:04
- 2.45	49	- 1:56	70	- 1:35	43	- 2:02	46	- 1:59	119	- 0:46	72	- 1:33	73	- 1:32	54	- 1:51
- 2.30	49	- 1:41	70	- 1:20	43	- 1:47	45	- 1:45	117	- 0:33	71	- 1:19	70	- 1:20	53	- 1:37
- 2.15	49	- 1:26	70	- 1:05	44	- 1:31	45	- 1:30	115	- 0:20	70	- 1:05	66	- 1:09	52	- 1:23
- 2.00	49	- 1:11	71	- 0:49	44	- 1:16	44	- 1:16	114	- 0:06	69	- 0:51	63	- 0:57	50	- 1:10
- 1.45	51	- 0:54	72	- 0:33	44	- 1:01	44	- 1:01	111	+ 0:06	68	- 0:37	62	- 0:43	49	- 0:56
- 1.30	52	- 0:38	74	- 0:16	45	- 0:45	43	- 0:47	109	+ 0:19	66	- 0:24	60	- 0:30	47	- 0:43
- 1.15	54	- 0:21	75	HW	46	- 0:29	42	- 0:33	106	+ 0:31	65	- 0:10	58	- 0:17	45	- 0:30
- 1.00	55	- 0:05	76	+ 0:16	46	- 0:14	42	- 0:18	104	+ 0:44	64	+ 0:04	56	- 0:04	43	- 0:17
- 0.45	58	+ 0:13	79	+ 0:34	48	+ 0:03	41	- 0:04	102	+ 0:57	62	+ 0:17	55	+ 0:10	42	- 0:03
- 0.30	60	+ 0:30	82	+ 0:52	49	+ 0:19	40	+ 0:10	99	+ 1:09	61	+ 0:31	54	+ 0:24	40	+ 0:10
- 0.15	63	+ 0:48	85	+ 1:10	51	+ 0:36	39	+ 0:24	97	+ 1:22	60	+ 0:45	53	+ 0:38	39	+ 0:24
HW	66	+ 1:06	87	+ 1:27	52	+ 0:52	38	+ 0:38	95	+ 1:35	58	+ 0:58	52	+ 0:52	37	+ 0:37
+ 0.15	68	+ 1:23	94	+ 1:49	55	+ 1:10	38	+ 0:53	92	+ 1:47	57	+ 1:12	51	+ 1:06	37	+ 0:52
+ 0.30	71	+ 1:41	100	+ 2:10	58	+ 1:28	37	+ 1:07	90	+ 2:00	56	+ 1:26	50	+ 1:20	36	+ 1:06
+ 0.45	74	+ 1:59	106	+ 2:31	61	+ 1:46	37	+ 1:22	87	+ 2:12	54	+ 1:39	50	+ 1:35	35	+ 1:20
+ 1.00	76	+ 2:16	112	+ 2:52	63	+ 2:03	36	+ 1:36	85	+ 2:25	53	+ 1:53	49	+ 1:49	34	+ 1:34
+ 1.15	77	+ 2:32	115	+ 3:10	66	+ 2:21	35	+ 1:50	83	+ 2:38	52	+ 2:07	49	+ 2:04	34	+ 1:49
+ 1.30	77	+ 2:47	119	+ 3:29	68	+ 2:38	35	+ 2:05	82	+ 2:52	51	+ 2:21	49	+ 2:19	34	+ 2:04
+ 1.45	77	+ 3:02	122	+ 3:47	71	+ 2:56	34	+ 2:19	81	+ 3:06	50	+ 2:35	50	+ 2:35	34	+ 2:19
+ 2.00	77	+ 3:17	125	+ 4:05	74	+ 3:14	34	+ 2:34	79	+ 3:19	49	+ 2:49	50	+ 2:50	34	+ 2:34
+ 2.15	76	+ 3:31	123	+ 4:18	73	+ 3:28	34	+ 2:49	80	+ 3:35	49	+ 3:04	51	+ 3:06	35	+ 2:50
+ 2.30	75	+ 3:45	121	+ 4:31	72	+ 3:42	34	+ 3:04	80	+ 3:50	49	+ 3:19	51	+ 3:21	35	+ 3:05
+ 2.45	74	+ 3:59	119	+ 4:44	72	+ 3:57	34	+ 3:19	80	+ 4:05	49	+ 3:34	52	+ 3:37	35	+ 3:20
+ 3.00	73	+ 4:13	117	+ 4:57	71	+ 4:11	34	+ 3:34	81	+ 4:21	49	+ 3:49	53	+ 3:53	35	+ 3:35
+ 3.15	72	+ 4:27	114	+ 5:09	69	+ 4:24	34	+ 3:49	82	+ 4:37	50	+ 4:05	54	+ 4:09	36	+ 3:51
+ 3.30	71	+ 4:41	111	+ 5:21	67	+ 4:37	34	+ 4:04	83	+ 4:53	50	+ 4:20	55	+ 4:25	37	+ 4:07
+ 3.45	70	+ 4:55	108	+ 5:33	66	+ 4:51	34	+ 4:19	84	+ 5:09	51	+ 4:36	56	+ 4:41	37	+ 4:22
+ 4.00	68	+ 5:08	105	+ 5:45	64	+ 5:04	35	+ 4:35	85	+ 5:25	51	+ 4:51	57	+ 4:57	38	+ 4:38
+ 4.15	67	+ 5:22	102	+ 5:57	62	+ 5:17	35	+ 4:50	87	+ 5:42	52	+ 5:07	59	+ 5:14	39	+ 4:54
+ 4.30	66	+ 5:36	99	- 5:51	61	+ 5:31	35	+ 5:05	88	+ 5:58	53	+ 5:23	62	+ 5:32	40	+ 5:10
+ 4.45	65	+ 5:50	96	- 5:39	59	+ 5:44	36	+ 5:21	89	- 5:46	54	+ 5:39	64	+ 5:49	41	+ 5:26
+ 5.00	64	- 5:56	93	- 5:27	57	+ 5:57	36	+ 5:36	90	- 5:30	54	+ 5:54	66	- 5:54	42	+ 5:42
+ 5.15	63	- 5:42	92	- 5:13	56	- 5:49	36	+ 5:51	92	- 5:13	55	- 5:50	68	- 5:37	43	+ 5:58
+ 5.30	62	- 5:28	90	- 5:00	56	- 5:34	37	- 5:53	93	- 4:57	56	- 5:34	71	- 5:19	44	- 5:46
+ 5.45	61	- 5:14	88	- 4:47	55	- 5:20	37	- 5:38	94	- 4:41	57	- 5:18	73	- 5:02	45	- 5:30
+ 6.00	60	- 5:00	87	- 4:33	54	- 5:06	38	- 5:22	95	- 4:25	58	- 5:02	75	- 4:45	46	- 5:14

Black Deep Connections (G7, G8)

Table G - Medway, Sea Reach and Black Deep Connections

Time to cover Sectors (in minutes) at 5.0 kts — All times relate to HW Sheerness — **Springs**

Time	G1 Princes No 6 to Red Sand Tower: Duration	G1 Time at End of Sector	G2 Red Sand Tower to Medway: Duration	G2 Time at End of Sector	G3 Red Sand Tower to Sea Reach: Duration	G3 Time at End of Sector	G4 Medway to Sea Reach: Duration	G4 Time at End of Sector	G5 Medway to SW Barrow: Duration	G5 Time at End of Sector	G6 Sea Reach to SW Barrow: Duration	G6 Time at End of Sector	G7 Blk Deep No 8 to Black Deep: Duration	G7 Time at End of Sector	G8 Blk Deep No 8 to Long Sand Inner: Duration	G8 Time at End of Sector
- 6.00	53	- 5:07	76	- 4:44	50	- 5:10	39	- 5:21	111	- 4:09	64	- 4:56	108	- 4:12	52	- 5:08
- 5.45	51	- 4:54	74	- 4:31	48	- 4:57	40	- 5:05	115	- 3:50	67	- 4:38	110	- 3:55	55	- 4:50
- 5.30	50	- 4:40	71	- 4:19	47	- 4:43	42	- 4:48	118	- 3:32	70	- 4:20	113	- 3:37	57	- 4:33
- 5.15	48	- 4:27	69	- 4:06	45	- 4:30	43	- 4:32	122	- 3:13	73	- 4:02	115	- 3:20	59	- 4:16
- 5.00	47	- 4:13	66	- 3:54	43	- 4:17	45	- 4:15	126	- 2:54	76	- 3:44	117	- 3:03	61	- 3:59
- 4.45	46	- 3:59	66	- 3:39	42	- 4:03	46	- 3:59	128	- 2:37	77	- 3:28	115	- 2:50	63	- 3:42
- 4.30	46	- 3:44	65	- 3:25	42	- 3:48	48	- 3:42	129	- 2:21	79	- 3:11	113	- 2:37	64	- 3:26
- 4.15	45	- 3:30	64	- 3:11	41	- 3:34	50	- 3:25	131	- 2:04	81	- 2:54	110	- 2:25	65	- 3:10
- 4.00	45	- 3:15	63	- 2:57	40	- 3:20	52	- 3:08	132	- 1:48	82	- 2:38	108	- 2:12	66	- 2:54
- 3.45	44	- 3:01	63	- 2:42	40	- 3:05	52	- 2:53	131	- 1:34	82	- 2:23	102	- 2:03	65	- 2:40
- 3.30	44	- 2:46	63	- 2:27	40	- 2:50	52	- 2:38	130	- 1:20	82	- 2:08	96	- 1:54	65	- 2:25
- 3.15	44	- 2:31	63	- 2:12	40	- 2:35	53	- 2:22	130	- 1:05	82	- 1:53	90	- 1:45	64	- 2:11
- 3.00	44	- 2:16	64	- 1:56	40	- 2:20	53	- 2:07	129	- 0:51	82	- 1:38	84	- 1:36	64	- 1:56
- 2.45	44	- 2:01	64	- 1:41	40	- 2:05	52	- 1:53	126	- 0:39	81	- 1:24	79	- 1:26	61	- 1:44
- 2.30	45	- 1:45	65	- 1:25	40	- 1:50	51	- 1:39	123	- 0:27	79	- 1:11	74	- 1:16	59	- 1:31
- 2.15	45	- 1:30	65	- 1:10	40	- 1:35	50	- 1:25	120	- 0:15	77	- 0:58	69	- 1:06	57	- 1:18
- 2.00	45	- 1:15	66	- 0:54	41	- 1:19	49	- 1:11	118	- 0:02	75	- 0:45	64	- 0:56	54	- 1:06
- 1.45	48	- 0:57	67	- 0:38	41	- 1:04	47	- 0:58	114	+ 0:09	73	- 0:32	61	- 0:44	52	- 0:53
- 1.30	50	- 0:40	69	- 0:21	42	- 0:48	46	- 0:44	111	+ 0:21	71	- 0:19	58	- 0:32	49	- 0:41
- 1.15	52	- 0:23	71	- 0:04	43	- 0:32	44	- 0:31	108	+ 0:33	68	- 0:07	56	- 0:19	46	- 0:29
- 1.00	54	- 0:06	73	+ 0:13	44	- 0:16	43	- 0:17	104	+ 0:44	66	+ 0:06	53	- 0:07	44	- 0:16
- 0.45	59	+ 0:14	77	+ 0:32	46	+ 0:01	42	- 0:03	101	+ 0:56	64	+ 0:19	51	+ 0:06	41	- 0:04
- 0.30	64	+ 0:34	81	+ 0:51	48	+ 0:18	41	+ 0:11	98	+ 1:08	62	+ 0:32	50	+ 0:20	39	+ 0:09
- 0.15	69	+ 0:54	85	+ 1:10	50	+ 0:35	40	+ 0:25	95	+ 1:20	60	+ 0:45	48	+ 0:33	37	+ 0:22
HW	74	+ 1:14	89	+ 1:29	52	+ 0:52	39	+ 0:39	92	+ 1:32	58	+ 0:58	46	+ 0:46	35	+ 0:35
+ 0.15	80	+ 1:35	100	+ 1:55	57	+ 1:12	38	+ 0:53	89	+ 1:44	56	+ 1:11	45	+ 1:00	34	+ 0:49
+ 0.30	85	+ 1:55	112	+ 2:22	62	+ 1:32	37	+ 1:07	85	+ 1:55	54	+ 1:24	44	+ 1:14	33	+ 1:03
+ 0.45	91	+ 2:16	124	+ 2:49	68	+ 1:53	36	+ 1:21	81	+ 2:06	52	+ 1:37	44	+ 1:29	32	+ 1:17
+ 1.00	96	+ 2:36	135	+ 3:15	73	+ 2:13	35	+ 1:35	78	+ 2:18	50	+ 1:50	43	+ 1:43	32	+ 1:32
+ 1.15	96	+ 2:51	139	+ 3:34	78	+ 2:33	34	+ 1:49	76	+ 2:31	49	+ 2:04	43	+ 1:58	31	+ 1:46
+ 1.30	96	+ 3:06	142	+ 3:52	83	+ 2:53	34	+ 2:04	74	+ 2:44	48	+ 2:18	43	+ 2:13	31	+ 2:01
+ 1.45	96	+ 3:21	145	+ 4:10	88	+ 3:13	33	+ 2:18	72	+ 2:57	47	+ 2:32	44	+ 2:29	31	+ 2:16
+ 2.00	96	+ 3:36	148	+ 4:28	93	+ 3:33	32	+ 2:32	70	+ 3:10	46	+ 2:46	44	+ 2:44	31	+ 2:31
+ 2.15	93	+ 3:48	144	+ 4:39	92	+ 3:47	32	+ 2:47	71	+ 3:26	45	+ 3:00	45	+ 3:00	31	+ 2:46
+ 2.30	90	+ 4:00	139	+ 4:49	90	+ 4:00	32	+ 3:02	71	+ 3:41	45	+ 3:15	46	+ 3:16	32	+ 3:02
+ 2.45	87	+ 4:12	135	+ 5:00	89	+ 4:14	32	+ 3:17	72	+ 3:57	45	+ 3:30	47	+ 3:32	32	+ 3:17
+ 3.00	83	+ 4:23	130	+ 5:10	87	+ 4:27	32	+ 3:32	72	+ 4:12	45	+ 3:45	48	+ 3:48	32	+ 3:32
+ 3.15	81	+ 4:36	125	+ 5:20	83	+ 4:38	32	+ 3:47	74	+ 4:29	46	+ 4:01	49	+ 4:04	33	+ 3:48
+ 3.30	78	+ 4:48	119	+ 5:29	79	+ 4:49	32	+ 4:02	76	+ 4:46	46	+ 4:16	50	+ 4:20	34	+ 4:04
+ 3.45	75	+ 5:00	114	+ 5:39	75	+ 5:00	33	+ 4:18	78	+ 5:03	47	+ 4:32	52	+ 4:37	34	+ 4:19
+ 4.00	72	+ 5:12	109	+ 5:49	71	+ 5:11	33	+ 4:33	79	+ 5:19	48	+ 4:48	53	+ 4:53	35	+ 4:35
+ 4.15	70	+ 5:25	105	- 6:00	68	+ 5:23	33	+ 4:48	82	+ 5:37	49	+ 5:04	57	+ 5:12	36	+ 4:51
+ 4.30	69	+ 5:39	101	- 5:49	65	+ 5:35	34	+ 5:04	84	+ 5:54	50	+ 5:20	60	+ 5:30	38	+ 5:08
+ 4.45	67	+ 5:52	97	- 5:38	62	+ 5:47	35	+ 5:20	87	- 5:48	51	+ 5:36	64	+ 5:49	39	+ 5:24
+ 5.00	65	- 5:55	93	- 5:27	59	+ 5:59	35	+ 5:35	89	- 5:31	52	+ 5:52	67	- 5:53	41	+ 5:41
+ 5.15	64	- 5:41	92	- 5:13	58	- 5:47	36	+ 5:51	91	- 5:14	53	- 5:52	71	- 5:34	42	+ 5:57
+ 5.30	63	- 5:27	90	- 5:00	57	- 5:33	36	- 5:54	92	- 4:58	55	- 5:35	75	- 5:15	44	- 5:46
+ 5.45	62	- 5:13	89	- 4:46	56	- 5:19	37	- 5:38	94	- 4:41	56	- 5:19	79	- 4:56	45	- 5:30
+ 6.00	60	- 5:00	88	- 4:32	54	- 5:06	37	- 5:23	96	- 4:24	57	- 5:03	83	- 4:37	47	- 5:13

Black Deep Connections (G7, G8)

NORTH BOUND

Table G - Medway, Sea Reach and Black Deep Connections

Neaps — All times relate to HW Sheerness — **Time to cover Sectors (in minutes) at 6.0 Kts**

NORTH BOUND

	G1			G2			G3			G4	
	Princes No 6 to Red Sand Tower			Red Sand Tower to Medway			Red Sand Tower to Sea Reach			Medway to Sea Reach	
Time	Duration	Time at End of Sector	Time	Duration	Time at End of Sector	Time	Duration	Time at End of Sector	Time	Duration	Time at End of Sector
-6.00	47	-5:13	-6.00	67	-4:53	-6.00	43	-5:17	-6.00	32	-5:28
-5.45	46	-4:59	-5.45	65	-4:40	-5.45	42	-5:03	-5.45	32	-5:13
-5.30	45	-4:45	-5.30	64	-4:26	-5.30	41	-4:49	-5.30	33	-4:57
-5.15	45	-4:30	-5.15	63	-4:12	-5.15	40	-4:35	-5.15	33	-4:42
-5.00	44	-4:16	-5.00	61	-3:59	-5.00	39	-4:21	-5.00	34	-4:26
-4.45	43	-4:02	-4.45	61	-3:44	-4.45	39	-4:06	-4.45	35	-4:10
-4.30	43	-3:47	-4.30	60	-3:30	-4.30	38	-3:52	-4.30	35	-3:55
-4.15	42	-3:33	-4.15	60	-3:15	-4.15	38	-3:37	-4.15	36	-3:39
-4.00	42	-3:18	-4.00	60	-3:00	-4.00	37	-3:23	-4.00	37	-3:23
-3.45	42	-3:03	-3.45	60	-2:45	-3.45	37	-3:08	-3.45	37	-3:08
-3.30	42	-2:48	-3.30	60	-2:30	-3.30	37	-2:53	-3.30	37	-2:53
-3.15	42	-2:33	-3.15	60	-2:15	-3.15	37	-2:38	-3.15	37	-2:38
-3.00	42	-2:18	-3.00	60	-2:00	-3.00	37	-2:23	-3.00	37	-2:23
-2.45	42	-2:03	-2.45	60	-1:45	-2.45	37	-2:08	-2.45	37	-2:08
-2.30	42	-1:48	-2.30	60	-1:30	-2.30	37	-1:53	-2.30	37	-1:53
-2.15	42	-1:33	-2.15	60	-1:15	-2.15	37	-1:38	-2.15	36	-1:39
-2.00	42	-1:18	-2.00	60	-1:00	-2.00	37	-1:23	-2.00	36	-1:24
-1.45	43	-1:02	-1.45	61	-0:44	-1.45	38	-1:07	-1.45	36	-1:09
-1.30	44	-0:46	-1.30	62	-0:28	-1.30	38	-0:52	-1.30	35	-0:55
-1.15	45	-0:30	-1.15	63	-0:12	-1.15	38	-0:37	-1.15	35	-0:40
-1.00	46	-0:14	-1.00	64	+0:04	-1.00	39	-0:21	-1.00	34	-0:26
-0.45	47	+0:02	-0.45	66	+0:21	-0.45	40	-0:05	-0.45	34	-0:11
-0.30	49	+0:19	-0.30	68	+0:38	-0.30	41	+0:11	-0.30	33	+0:03
-0.15	51	+0:36	-0.15	70	+0:55	-0.15	42	+0:27	-0.15	33	+0:18
HW	52	+0:52	HW	72	+1:12	HW	43	+0:43	HW	32	+0:32
+0.15	54	+1:09	+0.15	75	+1:30	+0.15	45	+1:00	+0.15	32	+0:47
+0.30	56	+1:26	+0.30	79	+1:49	+0.30	46	+1:16	+0.30	31	+1:01
+0.45	58	+1:43	+0.45	82	+2:07	+0.45	48	+1:33	+0.45	31	+1:16
+1.00	60	+2:00	+1.00	86	+2:26	+1.00	50	+1:50	+1.00	30	+1:30
+1.15	60	+2:15	+1.15	89	+2:44	+1.15	52	+2:07	+1.15	30	+1:45
+1.30	60	+2:30	+1.30	92	+3:02	+1.30	53	+2:23	+1.30	30	+2:00
+1.45	61	+2:46	+1.45	96	+3:21	+1.45	55	+2:40	+1.45	29	+2:14
+2.00	61	+3:01	+2.00	99	+3:39	+2.00	57	+2:57	+2.00	29	+2:29
+2.15	60	+3:15	+2.15	98	+3:53	+2.15	57	+3:12	+2.15	28	+2:43
+2.30	60	+3:30	+2.30	97	+4:07	+2.30	57	+3:27	+2.30	28	+2:58
+2.45	59	+3:44	+2.45	96	+4:21	+2.45	56	+3:41	+2.45	28	+3:13
+3.00	59	+3:59	+3.00	95	+4:35	+3.00	56	+3:56	+3.00	28	+3:28
+3.15	58	+4:13	+3.15	92	+4:47	+3.15	55	+4:10	+3.15	28	+3:43
+3.30	57	+4:27	+3.30	89	+4:59	+3.30	54	+4:24	+3.30	29	+3:59
+3.45	56	+4:41	+3.45	86	+5:11	+3.45	53	+4:38	+3.45	29	+4:14
+4.00	56	+4:56	+4.00	83	+5:23	+4.00	52	+4:52	+4.00	29	+4:29
+4.15	55	+5:10	+4.15	81	+5:36	+4.15	51	+5:06	+4.15	29	+4:44
+4.30	54	+5:24	+4.30	79	+5:49	+4.30	50	+5:20	+4.30	29	+4:59
+4.45	53	+5:38	+4.45	77	-5:58	+4.45	48	+5:33	+4.45	30	+5:15
+5.00	52	+5:52	+5.00	76	-5:44	+5.00	47	+5:47	+5.00	30	+5:30
+5.15	52	-5:53	+5.15	75	-5:30	+5.15	47	-5:58	+5.15	30	+5:45
+5.30	51	-5:39	+5.30	74	-5:16	+5.30	46	-5:44	+5.30	31	-5:59
+5.45	51	-5:24	+5.45	73	-5:02	+5.45	45	-5:30	+5.45	31	-5:44
+6.00	50	-5:10	+6.00	72	-4:48	+6.00	45	-5:15	+6.00	31	-5:29

	G5			G6			G7			G8	
	Medway to SW Barrow			Sea Reach to SW Barrow			Blk Deep No 8 to Black Deep			Blk Deep No 8 to Long Sand Inner	
Time	Duration	Time at End of Sector	Time	Duration	Time at End of Sector	Time	Duration	Time at End of Sector	Time	Duration	Time at End of Sector
-6.00	85	-4:35	-6.00	51	-5:09	-6.00	65	-4:55	-6.00	40	-5:20
-5.45	87	-4:18	-5.45	52	-4:53	-5.45	66	-4:39	-5.45	41	-5:04
-5.30	90	-4:00	-5.30	53	-4:37	-5.30	67	-4:23	-5.30	42	-4:48
-5.15	92	-3:43	-5.15	54	-4:21	-5.15	68	-4:07	-5.15	43	-4:32
-5.00	95	-3:25	-5.00	55	-4:05	-5.00	68	-3:52	-5.00	44	-4:16
-4.45	96	-3:09	-4.45	56	-3:49	-4.45	68	-3:37	-4.45	44	-4:01
-4.30	97	-2:53	-4.30	57	-3:33	-4.30	68	-3:22	-4.30	44	-3:46
-4.15	98	-2:37	-4.15	57	-3:18	-4.15	68	-3:07	-4.15	45	-3:30
-4.00	99	-2:21	-4.00	58	-3:02	-4.00	68	-2:52	-4.00	45	-3:15
-3.45	99	-2:06	-3.45	58	-2:47	-3.45	67	-2:38	-3.45	45	-3:00
-3.30	98	-1:52	-3.30	58	-2:32	-3.30	65	-2:25	-3.30	45	-2:45
-3.15	98	-1:37	-3.15	58	-2:17	-3.15	64	-2:11	-3.15	45	-2:30
-3.00	98	-1:22	-3.00	58	-2:02	-3.00	62	-1:58	-3.00	45	-2:15
-2.45	97	-1:08	-2.45	58	-1:47	-2.45	60	-1:45	-2.45	44	-2:01
-2.30	96	-0:54	-2.30	57	-1:33	-2.30	58	-1:32	-2.30	43	-1:47
-2.15	95	-0:40	-2.15	57	-1:18	-2.15	56	-1:19	-2.15	42	-1:33
-2.00	94	-0:26	-2.00	56	-1:04	-2.00	53	-1:07	-2.00	41	-1:19
-1.45	92	-0:13	-1.45	55	-0:50	-1.45	52	-0:53	-1.45	40	-1:05
-1.30	90	HW	-1.30	54	-0:36	-1.30	51	-0:39	-1.30	39	-0:51
-1.15	88	+0:13	-1.15	53	-0:22	-1.15	49	-0:26	-1.15	38	-0:37
-1.00	86	+0:26	-1.00	53	-0:07	-1.00	48	-0:12	-1.00	37	-0:23
-0.45	84	+0:39	-0.45	52	+0:07	-0.45	47	+0:02	-0.45	36	-0:09
-0.30	83	+0:53	-0.30	51	+0:21	-0.30	47	+0:17	-0.30	35	+0:05
-0.15	81	+1:06	-0.15	50	+0:35	-0.15	46	+0:31	-0.15	33	+0:18
HW	80	+1:20	HW	49	+0:49	HW	45	+0:45	HW	32	+0:32
+0.15	78	+1:33	+0.15	48	+1:03	+0.15	44	+0:59	+0.15	32	+0:47
+0.30	76	+1:46	+0.30	47	+1:17	+0.30	44	+1:14	+0.30	31	+1:01
+0.45	74	+1:59	+0.45	46	+1:31	+0.45	43	+1:28	+0.45	31	+1:16
+1.00	73	+2:13	+1.00	45	+1:45	+1.00	43	+1:43	+1.00	30	+1:30
+1.15	72	+2:27	+1.15	45	+2:00	+1.15	43	+1:58	+1.15	30	+1:45
+1.30	71	+2:41	+1.30	44	+2:14	+1.30	43	+2:13	+1.30	30	+2:00
+1.45	70	+2:55	+1.45	43	+2:28	+1.45	43	+2:28	+1.45	30	+2:15
+2.00	69	+3:09	+2.00	42	+2:42	+2.00	43	+2:43	+2.00	30	+2:30
+2.15	69	+3:24	+2.15	42	+2:57	+2.15	44	+2:59	+2.15	30	+2:45
+2.30	69	+3:39	+2.30	42	+3:12	+2.30	44	+3:14	+2.30	30	+3:00
+2.45	69	+3:54	+2.45	42	+3:27	+2.45	45	+3:30	+2.45	30	+3:15
+3.00	69	+4:09	+3.00	42	+3:42	+3.00	45	+3:45	+3.00	30	+3:30
+3.15	70	+4:25	+3.15	42	+3:57	+3.15	46	+4:01	+3.15	31	+3:46
+3.30	71	+4:41	+3.30	43	+4:13	+3.30	47	+4:17	+3.30	31	+4:01
+3.45	72	+4:57	+3.45	43	+4:28	+3.45	47	+4:32	+3.45	31	+4:16
+4.00	72	+5:12	+4.00	43	+4:43	+4.00	48	+4:48	+4.00	32	+4:32
+4.15	74	+5:29	+4.15	44	+4:59	+4.15	49	+5:04	+4.15	33	+4:48
+4.30	75	+5:45	+4.30	44	+5:14	+4.30	51	+5:21	+4.30	33	+5:03
+4.45	76	-5:59	+4.45	45	+5:30	+4.45	52	+5:37	+4.45	34	+5:19
+5.00	77	-5:43	+5.00	46	+5:46	+5.00	54	+5:54	+5.00	35	+5:35
+5.15	78	-5:27	+5.15	46	-5:59	+5.15	56	-5:49	+5.15	35	+5:50
+5.30	78	-5:12	+5.30	47	-5:43	+5.30	57	-5:33	+5.30	36	-5:54
+5.45	79	-4:56	+5.45	47	-5:28	+5.45	59	-5:16	+5.45	37	-5:38
+6.00	80	-4:40	+6.00	48	-5:12	+6.00	61	-4:59	+6.00	38	-5:22

Black Deep Connections

Table G - Medway, Sea Reach and Black Deep Connections

Time to cover Sectors (in minutes) at 6.0 kts — All times relate to HW Sheerness — **Springs**

	G1		G2		G3		G4		G5		G6		G7		G8	
	Princes No 6 to Red Sand Tower		Red Sand Tower to Medway		Red Sand Tower to Sea Reach		Medway to Sea Reach		Medway to SW Barrow		Sea Reach to SW Barrow		Blk Deep No 8 to Black Deep		Blk Deep No 8 to Long Sand Inner	
Time	Duration	Time at End of Sector	Duration	Time at End of Sector	Duration	Time at End of Sector	Duration	Time at End of Sector	Duration	Time at End of Sector	Duration	Time at End of Sector	Duration	Time at End of Sector	Duration	Time at End of Sector
- 6.00	45	- 5:15	65	- 4:55	43	- 5:17	32	- 5:28	88	- 4:32	51	- 5:09	73	- 4:47	41	- 5:19
- 5.45	44	- 5:01	63	- 4:42	41	- 5:04	33	- 5:12	91	- 4:14	53	- 4:52	78	- 4:27	43	- 5:02
- 5.30	43	- 4:47	62	- 4:28	40	- 4:50	34	- 4:56	94	- 3:56	55	- 4:35	82	- 4:08	45	- 4:45
- 5.15	42	- 4:33	60	- 4:15	39	- 4:36	34	- 4:41	97	- 3:38	57	- 4:18	87	- 3:48	47	- 4:28
- 5.00	40	- 4:20	58	- 4:02	37	- 4:23	35	- 4:25	100	- 3:20	59	- 4:01	91	- 3:29	48	- 4:12
- 4.45	40	- 4:05	57	- 3:48	37	- 4:08	36	- 4:09	101	- 3:04	61	- 3:44	88	- 3:17	49	- 3:56
- 4.30	39	- 3:51	56	- 3:34	36	- 3:54	38	- 3:52	103	- 2:47	62	- 3:28	85	- 3:05	50	- 3:40
- 4.15	39	- 3:36	56	- 3:19	35	- 3:40	39	- 3:36	104	- 2:31	63	- 3:12	82	- 2:53	51	- 3:24
- 4.00	39	- 3:21	55	- 3:05	34	- 3:26	40	- 3:20	105	- 2:15	64	- 2:56	79	- 2:41	52	- 3:08
- 3.45	38	- 3:07	55	- 2:50	34	- 3:11	41	- 3:04	105	- 2:00	64	- 2:41	76	- 2:29	51	- 2:54
- 3.30	38	- 2:52	55	- 2:35	34	- 2:56	41	- 2:49	105	- 1:45	64	- 2:26	74	- 2:16	51	- 2:39
- 3.15	38	- 2:37	55	- 2:20	34	- 2:41	41	- 2:34	105	- 1:30	64	- 2:11	71	- 2:04	51	- 2:24
- 3.00	38	- 2:22	55	- 2:05	34	- 2:26	41	- 2:19	104	- 1:16	64	- 1:56	68	- 1:52	51	- 2:09
- 2.45	38	- 2:07	56	- 1:49	34	- 2:11	41	- 2:04	102	- 1:03	63	- 1:42	65	- 1:40	49	- 1:56
- 2.30	38	- 1:52	56	- 1:34	35	- 1:55	40	- 1:50	101	- 0:49	62	- 1:28	61	- 1:29	47	- 1:43
- 2.15	39	- 1:36	56	- 1:19	35	- 1:40	40	- 1:35	99	- 0:36	61	- 1:14	58	- 1:17	46	- 1:29
- 2.00	39	- 1:21	57	- 1:03	35	- 1:25	39	- 1:21	97	- 0:23	60	- 1:00	54	- 1:06	44	- 1:16
- 1.45	40	- 1:05	58	- 0:47	35	- 1:10	38	- 1:07	95	- 0:10	59	- 0:46	52	- 0:53	43	- 1:02
- 1.30	42	- 0:48	59	- 0:31	36	- 0:54	37	- 0:53	93	+ 0:03	57	- 0:33	50	- 0:40	41	- 0:49
- 1.15	43	- 0:32	60	- 0:15	36	- 0:39	36	- 0:39	90	+ 0:15	56	- 0:19	48	- 0:27	39	- 0:36
- 1.00	44	- 0:16	61	+ 0:01	37	- 0:23	36	- 0:24	88	+ 0:28	55	- 0:05	46	- 0:14	37	- 0:23
- 0.45	48	+ 0:03	64	+ 0:19	38	- 0:07	35	- 0:10	86	+ 0:41	53	+ 0:08	45	HW	36	- 0:09
- 0.30	51	+ 0:21	67	+ 0:37	40	+ 0:10	34	+ 0:04	83	+ 0:53	52	+ 0:22	44	+ 0:14	34	+ 0:04
- 0.15	54	+ 0:39	69	+ 0:54	41	+ 0:26	33	+ 0:18	81	+ 1:06	50	+ 0:35	43	+ 0:28	33	+ 0:18
HW	57	+ 0:57	72	+ 1:12	42	+ 0:42	32	+ 0:32	78	+ 1:18	49	+ 0:49	41	+ 0:41	31	+ 0:31
+ 0.15	60	+ 1:15	79	+ 1:34	45	+ 1:00	32	+ 0:47	76	+ 1:31	47	+ 1:02	41	+ 0:56	30	+ 0:45
+ 0.30	64	+ 1:34	85	+ 1:55	48	+ 1:18	31	+ 1:01	73	+ 1:43	46	+ 1:16	40	+ 1:10	29	+ 0:59
+ 0.45	68	+ 1:53	91	+ 2:16	51	+ 1:36	31	+ 1:16	71	+ 1:56	45	+ 1:30	39	+ 1:24	28	+ 1:13
+ 1.00	71	+ 2:11	98	+ 2:38	54	+ 1:54	30	+ 1:30	68	+ 2:08	43	+ 1:43	39	+ 1:39	27	+ 1:27
+ 1.15	72	+ 2:27	101	+ 2:56	58	+ 2:13	29	+ 1:44	67	+ 2:22	42	+ 1:57	39	+ 1:54	27	+ 1:42
+ 1.30	72	+ 2:42	105	+ 3:15	61	+ 2:31	28	+ 1:58	65	+ 2:35	41	+ 2:11	39	+ 2:09	27	+ 1:57
+ 1.45	73	+ 2:58	109	+ 3:34	65	+ 2:50	28	+ 2:13	64	+ 2:49	40	+ 2:25	39	+ 2:24	27	+ 2:12
+ 2.00	73	+ 3:13	112	+ 3:52	68	+ 3:08	27	+ 2:27	63	+ 3:03	40	+ 2:40	39	+ 2:39	26	+ 2:26
+ 2.15	71	+ 3:26	110	+ 4:05	68	+ 3:23	27	+ 2:42	63	+ 3:18	39	+ 2:54	40	+ 2:55	27	+ 2:42
+ 2.30	69	+ 3:39	108	+ 4:18	67	+ 3:37	27	+ 2:57	63	+ 3:33	39	+ 3:09	40	+ 3:10	27	+ 2:57
+ 2.45	67	+ 3:52	106	+ 4:31	67	+ 3:52	27	+ 3:12	63	+ 3:48	39	+ 3:24	41	+ 3:26	27	+ 3:12
+ 3.00	66	+ 4:06	104	+ 4:44	66	+ 4:06	27	+ 3:27	63	+ 4:03	39	+ 3:39	41	+ 3:41	28	+ 3:28
+ 3.15	64	+ 4:19	100	+ 4:55	64	+ 4:19	27	+ 3:42	65	+ 4:20	39	+ 3:54	42	+ 3:57	28	+ 3:43
+ 3.30	62	+ 4:32	97	+ 5:07	62	+ 4:32	27	+ 3:57	66	+ 4:36	40	+ 4:10	43	+ 4:13	29	+ 3:59
+ 3.45	60	+ 4:45	93	+ 5:18	59	+ 4:44	27	+ 4:12	67	+ 4:52	40	+ 4:25	44	+ 4:29	29	+ 4:14
+ 4.00	58	+ 4:58	90	+ 5:30	57	+ 4:57	28	+ 4:28	68	+ 5:08	41	+ 4:41	45	+ 4:45	30	+ 4:30
+ 4.15	57	+ 5:12	87	+ 5:42	55	+ 5:10	28	+ 4:43	70	+ 5:25	41	+ 4:56	47	+ 5:02	31	+ 4:46
+ 4.30	56	+ 5:26	84	+ 5:54	53	+ 5:23	28	+ 4:58	71	+ 5:41	42	+ 5:12	50	+ 5:20	32	+ 5:02
+ 4.45	55	+ 5:40	80	- 5:55	51	+ 5:36	29	+ 5:14	73	+ 5:58	43	+ 5:28	52	+ 5:37	32	+ 5:17
+ 5.00	54	+ 5:54	77	- 5:43	49	+ 5:49	29	+ 5:29	75	- 5:45	44	+ 5:44	54	+ 5:54	33	+ 5:33
+ 5.15	53	- 5:52	76	- 5:29	48	- 5:57	30	+ 5:45	76	- 5:29	45	- 6:00	57	- 5:48	35	+ 5:50
+ 5.30	52	- 5:38	75	- 5:15	47	- 5:43	30	- 6:00	77	- 5:13	46	- 5:44	60	- 5:30	36	- 5:54
+ 5.45	51	- 5:24	74	- 5:01	46	- 5:29	31	- 5:44	78	- 4:57	46	- 5:29	63	- 5:12	37	- 5:38
+ 6.00	50	- 5:10	73	- 4:47	45	- 5:15	31	- 5:29	79	- 4:41	47	- 5:13	66	- 4:54	38	- 5:22

Black Deep Connections

NORTH BOUND

G - 7 Kts Table G - Medway, Sea Reach and Black Deep Connections 7 Kts - G

Neaps — All times relate to HW Sheerness — **Time to cover Sectors (in minutes) at 7.0 Kts**

NORTH BOUND

	G1 Princes No 6 to Red Sand Tower			G2 Red Sand Tower to Medway			G3 Red Sand Tower to Sea Reach			G4 Medway to Sea Reach	
Time	Duration	Time at End of Sector	Time	Duration	Time at End of Sector	Time	Duration	Time at End of Sector	Time	Duration	Time at End of Sector
- 6.00	40	- 5:20	- 6.00	58	- 5:02	- 6.00	37	- 5:23	- 6.00	27	- 5:33
- 5.45	40	- 5:05	- 5.45	57	- 4:48	- 5.45	36	- 5:09	- 5.45	27	- 5:18
- 5.30	39	- 4:51	- 5.30	56	- 4:34	- 5.30	36	- 4:54	- 5.30	28	- 5:02
- 5.15	39	- 4:36	- 5.15	55	- 4:20	- 5.15	35	- 4:40	- 5.15	28	- 4:47
- 5.00	38	- 4:22	- 5.00	54	- 4:06	- 5.00	34	- 4:26	- 5.00	28	- 4:32
- 4.45	38	- 4:07	- 4.45	53	- 3:52	- 4.45	34	- 4:11	- 4.45	29	- 4:16
- 4.30	37	- 3:53	- 4.30	53	- 3:37	- 4.30	33	- 3:57	- 4.30	30	- 4:00
- 4.15	37	- 3:38	- 4.15	52	- 3:23	- 4.15	33	- 3:42	- 4.15	30	- 3:45
- 4.00	36	- 3:24	- 4.00	52	- 3:08	- 4.00	32	- 3:28	- 4.00	31	- 3:29
- 3.45	36	- 3:09	- 3.45	52	- 2:53	- 3.45	32	- 3:13	- 3.45	31	- 3:14
- 3.30	36	- 2:54	- 3.30	52	- 2:38	- 3.30	32	- 2:58	- 3.30	31	- 2:59
- 3.15	36	- 2:39	- 3.15	52	- 2:23	- 3.15	32	- 2:43	- 3.15	31	- 2:44
- 3.00	36	- 2:24	- 3.00	52	- 2:08	- 3.00	32	- 2:28	- 3.00	31	- 2:29
- 2.45	36	- 2:09	- 2.45	52	- 1:53	- 2.45	32	- 2:13	- 2.45	31	- 2:14
- 2.30	36	- 1:54	- 2.30	52	- 1:38	- 2.30	32	- 1:58	- 2.30	31	- 1:59
- 2.15	36	- 1:39	- 2.15	53	- 1:22	- 2.15	32	- 1:43	- 2.15	31	- 1:44
- 2.00	36	- 1:24	- 2.00	53	- 1:07	- 2.00	32	- 1:28	- 2.00	31	- 1:29
- 1.45	37	- 1:08	- 1.45	53	- 0:52	- 1.45	33	- 1:12	- 1.45	30	- 1:15
- 1.30	38	- 0:52	- 1.30	54	- 0:36	- 1.30	33	- 0:57	- 1.30	30	- 1:00
- 1.15	38	- 0:37	- 1.15	55	- 0:20	- 1.15	33	- 0:42	- 1.15	30	- 0:45
- 1.00	39	- 0:21	- 1.00	55	- 0:05	- 1.00	33	- 0:27	- 1.00	29	- 0:31
- 0.45	40	- 0:05	- 0.45	57	+ 0:12	- 0.45	34	- 0:11	- 0.45	29	- 0:16
- 0.30	41	+ 0:11	- 0.30	58	+ 0:28	- 0.30	35	+ 0:05	- 0.30	29	- 0:01
- 0.15	42	+ 0:27	- 0.15	59	+ 0:44	- 0.15	36	+ 0:21	- 0.15	28	+ 0:13
HW	44	+ 0:44	HW	61	+ 1:01	HW	36	+ 0:36	HW	28	+ 0:28
+ 0.15	45	+ 1:00	+ 0.15	63	+ 1:18	+ 0.15	37	+ 0:52	+ 0.15	27	+ 0:42
+ 0.30	46	+ 1:16	+ 0.30	65	+ 1:35	+ 0.30	39	+ 1:09	+ 0.30	27	+ 0:57
+ 0.45	48	+ 1:33	+ 0.45	68	+ 1:53	+ 0.45	40	+ 1:25	+ 0.45	27	+ 1:12
+ 1.00	49	+ 1:49	+ 1.00	70	+ 2:10	+ 1.00	41	+ 1:41	+ 1.00	26	+ 1:26
+ 1.15	49	+ 2:04	+ 1.15	72	+ 2:27	+ 1.15	42	+ 1:57	+ 1.15	26	+ 1:41
+ 1.30	50	+ 2:20	+ 1.30	74	+ 2:44	+ 1.30	44	+ 2:14	+ 1.30	25	+ 1:55
+ 1.45	50	+ 2:35	+ 1.45	75	+ 3:00	+ 1.45	45	+ 2:30	+ 1.45	25	+ 2:10
+ 2.00	50	+ 2:50	+ 2.00	77	+ 3:17	+ 2.00	47	+ 2:47	+ 2.00	24	+ 2:24
+ 2.15	50	+ 3:05	+ 2.15	77	+ 3:32	+ 2.15	46	+ 3:01	+ 2.15	24	+ 2:39
+ 2.30	50	+ 3:20	+ 2.30	76	+ 3:46	+ 2.30	46	+ 3:16	+ 2.30	24	+ 2:54
+ 2.45	49	+ 3:34	+ 2.45	76	+ 4:01	+ 2.45	46	+ 3:31	+ 2.45	24	+ 3:09
+ 3.00	49	+ 3:49	+ 3.00	75	+ 4:15	+ 3.00	46	+ 3:46	+ 3.00	24	+ 3:24
+ 3.15	48	+ 4:03	+ 3.15	74	+ 4:29	+ 3.15	46	+ 4:01	+ 3.15	24	+ 3:39
+ 3.30	48	+ 4:18	+ 3.30	72	+ 4:42	+ 3.30	45	+ 4:15	+ 3.30	24	+ 3:54
+ 3.45	47	+ 4:32	+ 3.45	71	+ 4:56	+ 3.45	44	+ 4:29	+ 3.45	25	+ 4:10
+ 4.00	47	+ 4:47	+ 4.00	69	+ 5:09	+ 4.00	43	+ 4:43	+ 4.00	25	+ 4:25
+ 4.15	46	+ 5:01	+ 4.15	68	+ 5:23	+ 4.15	43	+ 4:58	+ 4.15	25	+ 4:40
+ 4.30	46	+ 5:16	+ 4.30	67	+ 5:37	+ 4.30	42	+ 5:12	+ 4.30	25	+ 4:55
+ 4.45	45	+ 5:30	+ 4.45	66	+ 5:51	+ 4.45	41	+ 5:26	+ 4.45	25	+ 5:10
+ 5.00	44	+ 5:44	+ 5.00	64	- 5:56	+ 5.00	40	+ 5:40	+ 5.00	26	+ 5:26
+ 5.15	44	+ 5:59	+ 5.15	64	- 5:41	+ 5.15	40	+ 5:55	+ 5.15	26	+ 5:41
+ 5.30	44	- 5:46	+ 5.30	63	- 5:27	+ 5.30	39	- 5:51	+ 5.30	26	+ 5:56
+ 5.45	43	- 5:32	+ 5.45	62	- 5:13	+ 5.45	39	- 5:36	+ 5.45	27	- 5:48
+ 6.00	43	- 5:17	+ 6.00	62	- 4:58	+ 6.00	38	- 5:22	+ 6.00	27	- 5:33

	G5 Medway to SW Barrow			G6 Sea Reach to SW Barrow			G7 Blk Deep No 8 to Black Deep			G8 Blk Deep No 8 to Long Sand Inner	
Time	Duration	Time at End of Sector	Time	Duration	Time at End of Sector	Time	Duration	Time at End of Sector	Time	Duration	Time at End of Sector
- 6.00	72	- 4:48	- 6.00	43	- 5:17	- 6.00	54	- 5:06	- 6.00	33	- 5:27
- 5.45	73	- 4:32	- 5.45	44	- 5:01	- 5.45	54	- 4:51	- 5.45	34	- 5:11
- 5.30	75	- 4:15	- 5.30	45	- 4:45	- 5.30	55	- 4:35	- 5.30	35	- 4:55
- 5.15	76	- 3:59	- 5.15	45	- 4:30	- 5.15	56	- 4:19	- 5.15	35	- 4:40
- 5.00	77	- 3:43	- 5.00	46	- 4:14	- 5.00	57	- 4:03	- 5.00	36	- 4:24
- 4.45	78	- 3:27	- 4.45	47	- 3:58	- 4.45	57	- 3:48	- 4.45	37	- 4:08
- 4.30	78	- 3:12	- 4.30	47	- 3:43	- 4.30	57	- 3:33	- 4.30	37	- 3:53
- 4.15	79	- 2:56	- 4.15	48	- 3:27	- 4.15	57	- 3:18	- 4.15	37	- 3:38
- 4.00	80	- 2:40	- 4.00	48	- 3:12	- 4.00	57	- 3:03	- 4.00	38	- 3:22
- 3.45	80	- 2:25	- 3.45	48	- 2:57	- 3.45	56	- 2:49	- 3.45	38	- 3:07
- 3.30	79	- 2:11	- 3.30	49	- 2:41	- 3.30	55	- 2:35	- 3.30	38	- 2:52
- 3.15	79	- 1:56	- 3.15	49	- 2:26	- 3.15	54	- 2:21	- 3.15	38	- 2:37
- 3.00	79	- 1:41	- 3.00	49	- 2:11	- 3.00	53	- 2:07	- 3.00	38	- 2:22
- 2.45	79	- 1:26	- 2.45	48	- 1:57	- 2.45	51	- 1:54	- 2.45	37	- 2:08
- 2.30	78	- 1:12	- 2.30	48	- 1:42	- 2.30	49	- 1:41	- 2.30	36	- 1:54
- 2.15	78	- 0:57	- 2.15	48	- 1:27	- 2.15	48	- 1:27	- 2.15	36	- 1:39
- 2.00	77	- 0:43	- 2.00	47	- 1:13	- 2.00	46	- 1:14	- 2.00	35	- 1:25
- 1.45	76	- 0:29	- 1.45	47	- 0:58	- 1.45	45	- 1:00	- 1.45	34	- 1:11
- 1.30	75	- 0:15	- 1.30	46	- 0:44	- 1.30	44	- 0:46	- 1.30	34	- 0:56
- 1.15	74	- 0:01	- 1.15	45	- 0:30	- 1.15	43	- 0:32	- 1.15	33	- 0:42
- 1.00	73	+ 0:13	- 1.00	45	- 0:15	- 1.00	42	- 0:18	- 1.00	32	- 0:28
- 0.45	72	+ 0:27	- 0.45	44	- 0:01	- 0.45	41	- 0:04	- 0.45	31	- 0:14
- 0.30	71	+ 0:41	- 0.30	44	+ 0:14	- 0.30	41	+ 0:11	- 0.30	30	HW
- 0.15	70	+ 0:55	- 0.15	43	+ 0:28	- 0.15	40	+ 0:25	- 0.15	29	+ 0:14
HW	69	+ 1:09	HW	42	+ 0:42	HW	40	+ 0:40	HW	28	+ 0:28
+ 0.15	67	+ 1:22	+ 0.15	41	+ 0:56	+ 0.15	39	+ 0:54	+ 0.15	28	+ 0:43
+ 0.30	66	+ 1:36	+ 0.30	41	+ 1:11	+ 0.30	39	+ 1:09	+ 0.30	27	+ 0:57
+ 0.45	65	+ 1:50	+ 0.45	40	+ 1:25	+ 0.45	38	+ 1:23	+ 0.45	26	+ 1:11
+ 1.00	64	+ 2:04	+ 1.00	39	+ 1:39	+ 1.00	38	+ 1:38	+ 1.00	26	+ 1:26
+ 1.15	63	+ 2:18	+ 1.15	39	+ 1:54	+ 1.15	38	+ 1:53	+ 1.15	26	+ 1:41
+ 1.30	62	+ 2:32	+ 1.30	38	+ 2:08	+ 1.30	38	+ 2:08	+ 1.30	25	+ 1:55
+ 1.45	61	+ 2:46	+ 1.45	38	+ 2:23	+ 1.45	38	+ 2:23	+ 1.45	25	+ 2:10
+ 2.00	60	+ 3:00	+ 2.00	37	+ 2:37	+ 2.00	38	+ 2:38	+ 2.00	25	+ 2:25
+ 2.15	61	+ 3:16	+ 2.15	37	+ 2:52	+ 2.15	38	+ 2:53	+ 2.15	25	+ 2:40
+ 2.30	61	+ 3:31	+ 2.30	37	+ 3:07	+ 2.30	39	+ 3:09	+ 2.30	26	+ 2:56
+ 2.45	61	+ 3:46	+ 2.45	37	+ 3:22	+ 2.45	39	+ 3:24	+ 2.45	26	+ 3:11
+ 3.00	61	+ 4:01	+ 3.00	36	+ 3:36	+ 3.00	40	+ 3:40	+ 3.00	26	+ 3:26
+ 3.15	61	+ 4:16	+ 3.15	37	+ 3:52	+ 3.15	40	+ 3:55	+ 3.15	26	+ 3:41
+ 3.30	62	+ 4:32	+ 3.30	37	+ 4:07	+ 3.30	40	+ 4:10	+ 3.30	27	+ 3:57
+ 3.45	62	+ 4:47	+ 3.45	37	+ 4:22	+ 3.45	41	+ 4:26	+ 3.45	27	+ 4:12
+ 4.00	63	+ 5:03	+ 4.00	38	+ 4:38	+ 4.00	41	+ 4:41	+ 4.00	27	+ 4:27
+ 4.15	64	+ 5:19	+ 4.15	38	+ 4:53	+ 4.15	42	+ 4:57	+ 4.15	28	+ 4:43
+ 4.30	65	+ 5:35	+ 4.30	38	+ 5:08	+ 4.30	43	+ 5:13	+ 4.30	28	+ 4:58
+ 4.45	65	+ 5:50	+ 4.45	39	+ 5:24	+ 4.45	44	+ 5:29	+ 4.45	29	+ 5:14
+ 5.00	66	- 5:54	+ 5.00	39	+ 5:39	+ 5.00	45	+ 5:45	+ 5.00	29	+ 5:29
+ 5.15	67	- 5:38	+ 5.15	40	+ 5:55	+ 5.15	47	- 5:58	+ 5.15	30	+ 5:45
+ 5.30	67	- 5:23	+ 5.30	40	- 5:50	+ 5.30	48	- 5:42	+ 5.30	31	- 5:59
+ 5.45	68	- 5:07	+ 5.45	41	- 5:34	+ 5.45	49	- 5:26	+ 5.45	31	- 5:44
+ 6.00	68	- 4:52	+ 6.00	41	- 5:19	+ 6.00	51	- 5:09	+ 6.00	32	- 5:28

Black Deep Connections

Table G - Medway, Sea Reach and Black Deep Connections

Time to cover Sectors (in minutes) at 7.0 kts — All times relate to HW Sheerness — **Springs**

NORTH BOUND

Time	G1 Princes No 6 to Red Sand Tower: Duration	G1: Time at End of Sector	Time	G2 Red Sand Tower to Medway: Duration	G2: Time at End of Sector
- 6.00	40	- 5:20	- 6.00	57	- 5:03
- 5.45	39	- 5:06	- 5.45	56	- 4:49
- 5.30	38	- 4:52	- 5.30	54	- 4:36
- 5.15	36	- 4:39	- 5.15	53	- 4:22
- 5.00	35	- 4:25	- 5.00	51	- 4:09
- 4.45	35	- 4:10	- 4.45	50	- 3:55
- 4.30	35	- 3:55	- 4.30	50	- 3:40
- 4.15	34	- 3:41	- 4.15	49	- 3:26
- 4.00	34	- 3:26	- 4.00	48	- 3:12
- 3.45	34	- 3:11	- 3.45	49	- 2:56
- 3.30	34	- 2:56	- 3.30	49	- 2:41
- 3.15	34	- 2:41	- 3.15	49	- 2:26
- 3.00	34	- 2:26	- 3.00	49	- 2:11
- 2.45	34	- 2:11	- 2.45	49	- 1:56
- 2.30	34	- 1:56	- 2.30	49	- 1:41
- 2.15	34	- 1:41	- 2.15	49	- 1:26
- 2.00	34	- 1:26	- 2.00	50	- 1:10
- 1.45	35	- 1:10	- 1.45	51	- 0:54
- 1.30	36	- 0:54	- 1.30	51	- 0:39
- 1.15	37	- 0:38	- 1.15	52	- 0:23
- 1.00	38	- 0:22	- 1.00	53	- 0:07
- 0.45	40	- 0:05	- 0.45	55	+ 0:10
- 0.30	42	+ 0:12	- 0.30	57	+ 0:27
- 0.15	44	+ 0:29	- 0.15	59	+ 0:44
HW	46	+ 0:46	HW	61	+ 1:01
+ 0.15	49	+ 1:04	+ 0.15	65	+ 1:20
+ 0.30	51	+ 1:21	+ 0.30	69	+ 1:39
+ 0.45	54	+ 1:39	+ 0.45	73	+ 1:58
+ 1.00	56	+ 1:56	+ 1.00	77	+ 2:17
+ 1.15	57	+ 2:12	+ 1.15	80	+ 2:35
+ 1.30	57	+ 2:27	+ 1.30	84	+ 2:54
+ 1.45	58	+ 2:43	+ 1.45	87	+ 3:12
+ 2.00	59	+ 2:59	+ 2.00	90	+ 3:30
+ 2.15	57	+ 3:12	+ 2.15	89	+ 3:44
+ 2.30	56	+ 3:26	+ 2.30	88	+ 3:58
+ 2.45	55	+ 3:40	+ 2.45	87	+ 4:12
+ 3.00	54	+ 3:54	+ 3.00	86	+ 4:26
+ 3.15	53	+ 4:08	+ 3.15	83	+ 4:38
+ 3.30	51	+ 4:21	+ 3.30	80	+ 4:50
+ 3.45	50	+ 4:35	+ 3.45	78	+ 5:03
+ 4.00	49	+ 4:49	+ 4.00	75	+ 5:15
+ 4.15	48	+ 5:03	+ 4.15	73	+ 5:28
+ 4.30	47	+ 5:17	+ 4.30	70	+ 5:40
+ 4.45	46	+ 5:31	+ 4.45	68	+ 5:53
+ 5.00	45	+ 5:45	+ 5.00	66	- 5:54
+ 5.15	45	- 6:00	+ 5.15	65	- 5:40
+ 5.30	44	- 5:46	+ 5.30	64	- 5:26
+ 5.45	43	- 5:32	+ 5.45	63	- 5:12
+ 6.00	43	- 5:17	+ 6.00	62	- 4:58

Time	G3 Red Sand Tower to Sea Reach: Duration	G3: Time at End of Sector	Time	G4 Medway to Sea Reach: Duration	G4: Time at End of Sector
- 6.00	37	- 5:23	- 6.00	27	- 5:33
- 5.45	36	- 5:09	- 5.45	28	- 5:17
- 5.30	35	- 4:55	- 5.30	28	- 5:02
- 5.15	34	- 4:41	- 5.15	29	- 4:46
- 5.00	33	- 4:27	- 5.00	29	- 4:31
- 4.45	32	- 4:13	- 4.45	30	- 4:15
- 4.30	32	- 3:58	- 4.30	31	- 3:59
- 4.15	31	- 3:44	- 4.15	32	- 3:43
- 4.00	30	- 3:30	- 4.00	33	- 3:27
- 3.45	30	- 3:15	- 3.45	33	- 3:12
- 3.30	30	- 3:00	- 3.30	33	- 2:57
- 3.15	30	- 2:45	- 3.15	34	- 2:41
- 3.00	30	- 2:30	- 3.00	34	- 2:26
- 2.45	30	- 2:15	- 2.45	34	- 2:11
- 2.30	30	- 2:00	- 2.30	33	- 1:57
- 2.15	31	- 1:44	- 2.15	33	- 1:42
- 2.00	31	- 1:29	- 2.00	33	- 1:27
- 1.45	31	- 1:14	- 1.45	32	- 1:13
- 1.30	31	- 0:59	- 1.30	32	- 0:58
- 1.15	32	- 0:43	- 1.15	31	- 0:44
- 1.00	32	- 0:28	- 1.00	30	- 0:30
- 0.45	33	- 0:12	- 0.45	30	- 0:15
- 0.30	34	+ 0:04	- 0.30	29	- 0:01
- 0.15	35	+ 0:20	- 0.15	28	+ 0:13
HW	36	+ 0:36	HW	28	+ 0:28
+ 0.15	38	+ 0:53	+ 0.15	27	+ 0:42
+ 0.30	40	+ 1:10	+ 0.30	27	+ 0:57
+ 0.45	41	+ 1:26	+ 0.45	26	+ 1:11
+ 1.00	43	+ 1:43	+ 1.00	26	+ 1:26
+ 1.15	46	+ 2:01	+ 1.15	25	+ 1:40
+ 1.30	48	+ 2:18	+ 1.30	24	+ 1:54
+ 1.45	51	+ 2:36	+ 1.45	24	+ 2:09
+ 2.00	54	+ 2:54	+ 2.00	23	+ 2:23
+ 2.15	53	+ 3:08	+ 2.15	23	+ 2:38
+ 2.30	53	+ 3:23	+ 2.30	23	+ 2:53
+ 2.45	53	+ 3:38	+ 2.45	23	+ 3:08
+ 3.00	53	+ 3:53	+ 3.00	23	+ 3:23
+ 3.15	52	+ 4:07	+ 3.15	23	+ 3:38
+ 3.30	50	+ 4:20	+ 3.30	23	+ 3:53
+ 3.45	49	+ 4:34	+ 3.45	23	+ 4:08
+ 4.00	47	+ 4:47	+ 4.00	24	+ 4:24
+ 4.15	46	+ 5:01	+ 4.15	24	+ 4:39
+ 4.30	45	+ 5:15	+ 4.30	24	+ 4:54
+ 4.45	43	+ 5:28	+ 4.45	25	+ 5:10
+ 5.00	42	+ 5:42	+ 5.00	25	+ 5:25
+ 5.15	41	+ 5:56	+ 5.15	25	+ 5:40
+ 5.30	40	- 5:50	+ 5.30	26	+ 5:56
+ 5.45	39	- 5:36	+ 5.45	26	- 5:49
+ 6.00	38	- 5:22	+ 6.00	27	- 5:33

Time	G5 Medway to SW Barrow: Duration	G5: Time at End of Sector	Time	G6 Sea Reach to SW Barrow: Duration	G6: Time at End of Sector
- 6.00	74	- 4:46	- 6.00	43	- 5:17
- 5.45	75	- 4:30	- 5.45	45	- 5:00
- 5.30	77	- 4:13	- 5.30	46	- 4:44
- 5.15	79	- 3:56	- 5.15	47	- 4:28
- 5.00	81	- 3:39	- 5.00	49	- 4:11
- 4.45	82	- 3:23	- 4.45	50	- 3:55
- 4.30	83	- 3:07	- 4.30	51	- 3:39
- 4.15	84	- 2:51	- 4.15	51	- 3:24
- 4.00	85	- 2:35	- 4.00	52	- 3:08
- 3.45	85	- 2:20	- 3.45	52	- 2:53
- 3.30	85	- 2:05	- 3.30	53	- 2:37
- 3.15	85	- 1:50	- 3.15	53	- 2:22
- 3.00	85	- 1:35	- 3.00	53	- 2:07
- 2.45	84	- 1:21	- 2.45	52	- 1:53
- 2.30	83	- 1:07	- 2.30	52	- 1:38
- 2.15	82	- 0:53	- 2.15	51	- 1:24
- 2.00	81	- 0:39	- 2.00	50	- 1:10
- 1.45	80	- 0:25	- 1.45	49	- 0:56
- 1.30	78	- 0:12	- 1.30	48	- 0:42
- 1.15	77	+ 0:02	- 1.15	47	- 0:28
- 1.00	75	+ 0:15	- 1.00	46	- 0:14
- 0.45	73	+ 0:28	- 0.45	45	HW
- 0.30	71	+ 0:41	- 0.30	44	+ 0:14
- 0.15	70	+ 0:55	- 0.15	43	+ 0:28
HW	68	+ 1:08	HW	42	+ 0:42
+ 0.15	66	+ 1:21	+ 0.15	41	+ 0:56
+ 0.30	64	+ 1:34	+ 0.30	40	+ 1:10
+ 0.45	62	+ 1:47	+ 0.45	39	+ 1:24
+ 1.00	60	+ 2:00	+ 1.00	38	+ 1:38
+ 1.15	59	+ 2:14	+ 1.15	37	+ 1:52
+ 1.30	58	+ 2:28	+ 1.30	37	+ 2:07
+ 1.45	57	+ 2:42	+ 1.45	36	+ 2:21
+ 2.00	56	+ 2:56	+ 2.00	35	+ 2:35
+ 2.15	56	+ 3:11	+ 2.15	35	+ 2:50
+ 2.30	56	+ 3:26	+ 2.30	34	+ 3:04
+ 2.45	56	+ 3:41	+ 2.45	34	+ 3:19
+ 3.00	56	+ 3:56	+ 3.00	34	+ 3:34
+ 3.15	57	+ 4:12	+ 3.15	34	+ 3:49
+ 3.30	58	+ 4:28	+ 3.30	35	+ 4:05
+ 3.45	59	+ 4:44	+ 3.45	35	+ 4:20
+ 4.00	60	+ 5:00	+ 4.00	35	+ 4:35
+ 4.15	61	+ 5:16	+ 4.15	36	+ 4:51
+ 4.30	62	+ 5:32	+ 4.30	37	+ 5:07
+ 4.45	63	+ 5:48	+ 4.45	37	+ 5:22
+ 5.00	64	- 5:56	+ 5.00	38	+ 5:38
+ 5.15	65	- 5:40	+ 5.15	39	+ 5:54
+ 5.30	66	- 5:24	+ 5.30	39	- 5:51
+ 5.45	67	- 5:08	+ 5.45	40	- 5:35
+ 6.00	68	- 4:52	+ 6.00	41	- 5:19

Black Deep Connections

Time	G7 Blk Deep No 8 to Black Deep: Duration	G7: Time at End of Sector	Time	G8 Blk Deep No 8 to Long Sand Inner: Duration	G8: Time at End of Sector
- 6.00	60	- 5:00	- 6.00	34	- 5:26
- 5.45	61	- 4:44	- 5.45	36	- 5:09
- 5.30	62	- 4:28	- 5.30	37	- 4:53
- 5.15	64	- 4:11	- 5.15	38	- 4:37
- 5.00	65	- 3:55	- 5.00	39	- 4:21
- 4.45	65	- 3:40	- 4.45	40	- 4:05
- 4.30	65	- 3:25	- 4.30	41	- 3:49
- 4.15	65	- 3:10	- 4.15	42	- 3:33
- 4.00	65	- 2:55	- 4.00	42	- 3:18
- 3.45	63	- 2:42	- 3.45	42	- 3:03
- 3.30	61	- 2:29	- 3.30	42	- 2:48
- 3.15	59	- 2:16	- 3.15	42	- 2:33
- 3.00	57	- 2:03	- 3.00	42	- 2:18
- 2.45	55	- 1:50	- 2.45	41	- 2:04
- 2.30	52	- 1:38	- 2.30	40	- 1:50
- 2.15	49	- 1:26	- 2.15	39	- 1:36
- 2.00	47	- 1:13	- 2.00	37	- 1:23
- 1.45	45	- 1:00	- 1.45	36	- 1:09
- 1.30	44	- 0:46	- 1.30	35	- 0:55
- 1.15	42	- 0:33	- 1.15	34	- 0:41
- 1.00	41	- 0:19	- 1.00	33	- 0:27
- 0.45	40	- 0:05	- 0.45	31	- 0:14
- 0.30	39	+ 0:09	- 0.30	30	HW
- 0.15	38	+ 0:23	- 0.15	28	+ 0:13
HW	37	+ 0:37	HW	27	+ 0:27
+ 0.15	37	+ 0:52	+ 0.15	26	+ 0:41
+ 0.30	36	+ 1:06	+ 0.30	25	+ 0:55
+ 0.45	35	+ 1:20	+ 0.45	24	+ 1:09
+ 1.00	35	+ 1:35	+ 1.00	23	+ 1:23
+ 1.15	35	+ 1:50	+ 1.15	23	+ 1:38
+ 1.30	35	+ 2:05	+ 1.30	23	+ 1:53
+ 1.45	35	+ 2:20	+ 1.45	23	+ 2:08
+ 2.00	35	+ 2:35	+ 2.00	22	+ 2:22
+ 2.15	35	+ 2:50	+ 2.15	23	+ 2:38
+ 2.30	36	+ 3:06	+ 2.30	23	+ 2:53
+ 2.45	36	+ 3:21	+ 2.45	23	+ 3:08
+ 3.00	37	+ 3:37	+ 3.00	24	+ 3:24
+ 3.15	37	+ 3:52	+ 3.15	24	+ 3:39
+ 3.30	38	+ 4:08	+ 3.30	25	+ 3:55
+ 3.45	38	+ 4:23	+ 3.45	25	+ 4:10
+ 4.00	39	+ 4:39	+ 4.00	25	+ 4:25
+ 4.15	40	+ 4:55	+ 4.15	26	+ 4:41
+ 4.30	42	+ 5:12	+ 4.30	27	+ 4:57
+ 4.45	44	+ 5:29	+ 4.45	28	+ 5:13
+ 5.00	45	+ 5:45	+ 5.00	28	+ 5:28
+ 5.15	48	- 5:57	+ 5.15	29	+ 5:44
+ 5.30	50	- 5:40	+ 5.30	30	- 6:00
+ 5.45	52	- 5:23	+ 5.45	31	- 5:44
+ 6.00	55	- 5:05	+ 6.00	32	- 5:28

Table H - Foulger's Gat to Harwich and Sunk Head Connections

Neaps — All times relate to HW Sheerness — **Time to cover Sectors (in minutes) at 4.0 Kts**

NORTH BOUND

	H1			H2			H3			H4			H5			H6			H7			H8	
	Long Sand Outer to Inner			Black Deep to Barrow No 2			Barrow No 2 to Goldmer Gat			Goldmer Gat to The Naze			The Naze to Harwich			Long Sand Inner to Sunk Head			Sunk Head to Goldmer Gat			Sunk Head to NE Gunfleet	
Time	Duration	Time at End of Sector	Time	Duration	Time at End of Sector	Time	Duration	Time at End of Sector	Time	Duration	Time at End of Sector	Time	Duration	Time at End of Sector	Time	Duration	Time at End of Sector	Time	Duration	Time at End of Sector	Time	Duration	Time at End of Sector
- 6.00	77	- 4:43	- 6.00	23	- 5:37	- 6.00	140	- 3:40	- 6.00	74	- 4:46	- 6.00	62	- 4:58	- 6.00	165	- 3:15	- 6.00	75	- 4:45	- 6.00	94	- 4:26
- 5.45	76	- 4:29	- 5.45	24	- 5:21	- 5.45	145	- 3:20	- 5.45	74	- 4:31	- 5.45	63	- 4:42	- 5.45	165	- 3:00	- 5.45	76	- 4:29	- 5.45	95	- 4:10
- 5.30	75	- 4:15	- 5.30	25	- 5:05	- 5.30	149	- 3:01	- 5.30	74	- 4:16	- 5.30	63	- 4:27	- 5.30	166	- 2:44	- 5.30	76	- 4:14	- 5.30	97	- 3:53
- 5.15	74	- 4:01	- 5.15	26	- 4:49	- 5.15	153	- 2:42	- 5.15	74	- 4:01	- 5.15	63	- 4:12	- 5.15	166	- 2:29	- 5.15	77	- 3:58	- 5.15	99	- 3:36
- 5.00	73	- 3:47	- 5.00	27	- 4:33	- 5.00	158	- 2:22	- 5.00	74	- 3:46	- 5.00	63	- 3:57	- 5.00	167	- 2:13	- 5.00	77	- 3:43	- 5.00	101	- 3:19
- 4.45	72	- 3:33	- 4.45	27	- 4:18	- 4.45	155	- 2:10	- 4.45	73	- 3:32	- 4.45	63	- 3:42	- 4.45	162	- 2:03	- 4.45	76	- 3:29	- 4.45	99	- 3:06
- 4.30	71	- 3:19	- 4.30	27	- 4:03	- 4.30	152	- 1:58	- 4.30	73	- 3:17	- 4.30	62	- 3:28	- 4.30	158	- 1:52	- 4.30	75	- 3:15	- 4.30	98	- 2:52
- 4.15	71	- 3:04	- 4.15	27	- 3:48	- 4.15	150	- 1:45	- 4.15	72	- 3:03	- 4.15	62	- 3:13	- 4.15	153	- 1:42	- 4.15	74	- 3:01	- 4.15	97	- 2:38
- 4.00	70	- 2:50	- 4.00	27	- 3:33	- 4.00	147	- 1:33	- 4.00	72	- 2:48	- 4.00	61	- 2:59	- 4.00	149	- 1:31	- 4.00	73	- 2:47	- 4.00	95	- 2:25
- 3.45	68	- 2:37	- 3.45	27	- 3:18	- 3.45	143	- 1:22	- 3.45	71	- 2:34	- 3.45	60	- 2:45	- 3.45	142	- 1:23	- 3.45	71	- 2:34	- 3.45	92	- 2:13
- 3.30	67	- 2:23	- 3.30	26	- 3:04	- 3.30	139	- 1:11	- 3.30	71	- 2:19	- 3.30	58	- 2:32	- 3.30	135	- 1:15	- 3.30	69	- 2:21	- 3.30	88	- 2:02
- 3.15	66	- 2:09	- 3.15	26	- 2:49	- 3.15	135	- 1:00	- 3.15	70	- 2:05	- 3.15	57	- 2:18	- 3.15	128	- 1:07	- 3.15	67	- 2:08	- 3.15	84	- 1:51
- 3.00	64	- 1:56	- 3.00	25	- 2:35	- 3.00	130	- 0:50	- 3.00	70	- 1:50	- 3.00	56	- 2:04	- 3.00	122	- 0:58	- 3.00	65	- 1:55	- 3.00	81	- 1:39
- 2.45	63	- 1:42	- 2.45	24	- 2:21	- 2.45	125	- 0:40	- 2.45	70	- 1:35	- 2.45	54	- 1:51	- 2.45	116	- 0:49	- 2.45	64	- 1:41	- 2.45	79	- 1:26
- 2.30	62	- 1:28	- 2.30	22	- 2:08	- 2.30	120	- 0:30	- 2.30	70	- 1:20	- 2.30	52	- 1:38	- 2.30	110	- 0:40	- 2.30	62	- 1:28	- 2.30	76	- 1:14
- 2.15	60	- 1:15	- 2.15	21	- 1:54	- 2.15	115	- 0:20	- 2.15	70	- 1:05	- 2.15	50	- 1:25	- 2.15	105	- 0:30	- 2.15	61	- 1:14	- 2.15	74	- 1:01
- 2.00	59	- 1:01	- 2.00	20	- 1:40	- 2.00	110	- 0:10	- 2.00	70	- 0:50	- 2.00	49	- 1:11	- 2.00	99	- 0:21	- 2.00	60	- 1:00	- 2.00	72	- 0:48
- 1.45	59	- 0:46	- 1.45	19	- 1:26	- 1.45	107	+ 0:02	- 1.45	71	- 0:34	- 1.45	47	- 0:58	- 1.45	96	- 0:09	- 1.45	60	- 0:45	- 1.45	70	- 0:35
- 1.30	59	- 0:31	- 1.30	18	- 1:12	- 1.30	103	+ 0:13	- 1.30	72	- 0:18	- 1.30	46	- 0:44	- 1.30	92	+ 0:02	- 1.30	60	- 0:30	- 1.30	68	- 0:22
- 1.15	60	- 0:15	- 1.15	17	- 0:58	- 1.15	99	+ 0:24	- 1.15	74	- 0:01	- 1.15	45	- 0:30	- 1.15	89	+ 0:14	- 1.15	60	- 0:15	- 1.15	66	- 0:09
- 1.00	60	HW	- 1.00	16	- 0:44	- 1.00	95	+ 0:35	- 1.00	75	+ 0:15	- 1.00	44	- 0:16	- 1.00	85	+ 0:25	- 1.00	60	HW	- 1.00	64	+ 0:04
- 0.45	62	+ 0:17	- 0.45	16	- 0:29	- 0.45	92	+ 0:47	- 0.45	79	+ 0:34	- 0.45	43	- 0:02	- 0.45	83	+ 0:38	- 0.45	61	+ 0:16	- 0.45	63	+ 0:18
- 0.30	63	+ 0:33	- 0.30	17	- 0:13	- 0.30	89	+ 0:59	- 0.30	83	+ 0:53	- 0.30	43	+ 0:13	- 0.30	81	+ 0:51	- 0.30	62	+ 0:32	- 0.30	62	+ 0:32
- 0.15	65	+ 0:50	- 0.15	17	+ 0:02	- 0.15	86	+ 1:11	- 0.15	88	+ 1:13	- 0.15	42	+ 0:27	- 0.15	79	+ 1:04	- 0.15	64	+ 0:49	- 0.15	60	+ 0:45
HW	67	+ 1:07	HW	17	+ 0:17	HW	83	+ 1:23	HW	92	+ 1:32	HW	42	+ 0:42	HW	77	+ 1:17	HW	65	+ 1:05	HW	59	+ 0:59
+ 0.15	69	+ 1:24	+ 0.15	17	+ 0:32	+ 0.15	81	+ 1:36	+ 0.15	94	+ 1:49	+ 0.15	42	+ 0:57	+ 0.15	75	+ 1:30	+ 0.15	66	+ 1:21	+ 0.15	58	+ 1:13
+ 0.30	71	+ 1:41	+ 0.30	18	+ 0:48	+ 0.30	80	+ 1:50	+ 0.30	97	+ 2:07	+ 0.30	41	+ 1:11	+ 0.30	74	+ 1:44	+ 0.30	67	+ 1:37	+ 0.30	58	+ 1:28
+ 0.45	73	+ 1:58	+ 0.45	18	+ 1:03	+ 0.45	78	+ 2:03	+ 0.45	100	+ 2:25	+ 0.45	41	+ 1:26	+ 0.45	73	+ 1:58	+ 0.45	69	+ 1:54	+ 0.45	58	+ 1:43
+ 1.00	75	+ 2:15	+ 1.00	19	+ 1:19	+ 1.00	77	+ 2:17	+ 1.00	103	+ 2:43	+ 1.00	41	+ 1:41	+ 1.00	72	+ 2:12	+ 1.00	70	+ 2:10	+ 1.00	57	+ 1:57
+ 1.15	77	+ 2:32	+ 1.15	19	+ 1:34	+ 1.15	77	+ 2:32	+ 1.15	102	+ 2:57	+ 1.15	41	+ 1:56	+ 1.15	73	+ 2:28	+ 1.15	70	+ 2:25	+ 1.15	58	+ 2:13
+ 1.30	78	+ 2:48	+ 1.30	19	+ 1:49	+ 1.30	77	+ 2:47	+ 1.30	101	+ 3:11	+ 1.30	41	+ 2:11	+ 1.30	74	+ 2:44	+ 1.30	70	+ 2:40	+ 1.30	58	+ 2:28
+ 1.45	79	+ 3:04	+ 1.45	19	+ 2:04	+ 1.45	77	+ 3:02	+ 1.45	100	+ 3:25	+ 1.45	41	+ 2:26	+ 1.45	75	+ 3:00	+ 1.45	70	+ 2:55	+ 1.45	58	+ 2:43
+ 2.00	80	+ 3:20	+ 2.00	19	+ 2:19	+ 2.00	77	+ 3:17	+ 2.00	99	+ 3:39	+ 2.00	41	+ 2:41	+ 2.00	76	+ 3:16	+ 2.00	71	+ 3:11	+ 2.00	59	+ 2:59
+ 2.15	81	+ 3:36	+ 2.15	19	+ 2:34	+ 2.15	78	+ 3:33	+ 2.15	97	+ 3:52	+ 2.15	42	+ 2:57	+ 2.15	78	+ 3:33	+ 2.15	70	+ 3:25	+ 2.15	59	+ 3:14
+ 2.30	81	+ 3:51	+ 2.30	18	+ 2:48	+ 2.30	80	+ 3:50	+ 2.30	95	+ 4:05	+ 2.30	43	+ 3:13	+ 2.30	79	+ 3:49	+ 2.30	70	+ 3:40	+ 2.30	60	+ 3:30
+ 2.45	82	+ 4:07	+ 2.45	18	+ 3:03	+ 2.45	81	+ 4:06	+ 2.45	93	+ 4:18	+ 2.45	44	+ 3:29	+ 2.45	80	+ 4:05	+ 2.45	69	+ 3:54	+ 2.45	61	+ 3:46
+ 3.00	82	+ 4:22	+ 3.00	18	+ 3:18	+ 3.00	82	+ 4:22	+ 3.00	91	+ 4:31	+ 3.00	45	+ 3:45	+ 3.00	82	+ 4:22	+ 3.00	69	+ 4:09	+ 3.00	62	+ 4:02
+ 3.15	82	+ 4:37	+ 3.15	18	+ 3:33	+ 3.15	84	+ 4:39	+ 3.15	88	+ 4:43	+ 3.15	46	+ 4:01	+ 3.15	84	+ 4:39	+ 3.15	69	+ 4:24	+ 3.15	62	+ 4:17
+ 3.30	82	+ 4:52	+ 3.30	18	+ 3:48	+ 3.30	86	+ 4:56	+ 3.30	86	+ 4:56	+ 3.30	47	+ 4:17	+ 3.30	87	+ 4:57	+ 3.30	68	+ 4:38	+ 3.30	63	+ 4:33
+ 3.45	83	+ 5:08	+ 3.45	18	+ 4:03	+ 3.45	88	+ 5:13	+ 3.45	84	+ 5:09	+ 3.45	48	+ 4:33	+ 3.45	89	+ 5:14	+ 3.45	68	+ 4:53	+ 3.45	64	+ 4:49
+ 4.00	83	+ 5:23	+ 4.00	18	+ 4:18	+ 4.00	90	+ 5:30	+ 4.00	81	+ 5:21	+ 4.00	50	+ 4:50	+ 4.00	91	+ 5:31	+ 4.00	68	+ 5:08	+ 4.00	65	+ 5:05
+ 4.15	82	+ 5:37	+ 4.15	18	+ 4:33	+ 4.15	94	+ 5:49	+ 4.15	80	+ 5:35	+ 4.15	50	+ 5:05	+ 4.15	97	+ 5:52	+ 4.15	68	+ 5:23	+ 4.15	67	+ 5:22
+ 4.30	82	+ 5:52	+ 4.30	18	+ 4:48	+ 4.30	98	- 5:52	+ 4.30	78	+ 5:48	+ 4.30	51	+ 5:21	+ 4.30	103	- 5:47	+ 4.30	69	+ 5:39	+ 4.30	68	+ 5:38
+ 4.45	81	- 5:54	+ 4.45	18	+ 5:03	+ 4.45	101	- 5:34	+ 4.45	77	- 5:58	+ 4.45	52	+ 5:37	+ 4.45	108	- 5:27	+ 4.45	69	+ 5:54	+ 4.45	70	+ 5:55
+ 5.00	81	- 5:39	+ 5.00	18	+ 5:18	+ 5.00	105	- 5:15	+ 5.00	76	- 5:44	+ 5.00	53	+ 5:53	+ 5.00	114	- 5:06	+ 5.00	69	- 5:51	+ 5.00	72	- 5:48
+ 5.15	80	- 5:25	+ 5.15	19	+ 5:34	+ 5.15	109	- 4:56	+ 5.15	75	- 5:30	+ 5.15	54	- 5:51	+ 5.15	120	- 4:45	+ 5.15	70	- 5:35	+ 5.15	74	- 5:31
+ 5.30	78	- 5:12	+ 5.30	20	+ 5:50	+ 5.30	114	- 4:36	+ 5.30	75	- 5:15	+ 5.30	55	- 5:35	+ 5.30	126	- 4:24	+ 5.30	70	- 5:20	+ 5.30	75	- 5:15
+ 5.45	77	- 4:58	+ 5.45	21	- 5:54	+ 5.45	118	- 4:17	+ 5.45	74	- 5:01	+ 5.45	56	- 5:19	+ 5.45	133	- 4:02	+ 5.45	71	- 5:04	+ 5.45	77	- 4:58
+ 6.00	76	- 4:44	+ 6.00	22	- 5:38	+ 6.00	122	- 3:58	+ 6.00	73	- 4:47	+ 6.00	57	- 5:03	+ 6.00	139	- 3:41	+ 6.00	72	- 4:48	+ 6.00	79	- 4:41

Sunk Head connections

Table H - Foulger's Gat to Harwich and Sunk Head Connections

Time to cover Sectors (in minutes) at 4.0 kts — All times relate to HW Sheerness — **Springs**

NORTH BOUND

	H1 Long Sand Outer to Inner			H2 Black Deep to Barrow No 2			H3 Barrow No 2 to Goldmer Gat			H4 Goldmer Gat to The Naze	
Time	Duration	Time at End of Sector	Time	Duration	Time at End of Sector	Time	Duration	Time at End of Sector	Time	Duration	Time at End of Sector
- 6.00	82	- 4:38	- 6.00	27	- 5:33	- 6.00	179	- 3:01	- 6.00	75	- 4:45
- 5.45	81	- 4:24	- 5.45	28	- 5:17	- 5.45	182	- 2:43	- 5.45	75	- 4:30
- 5.30	79	- 4:11	- 5.30	30	- 5:00	- 5.30	184	- 2:26	- 5.30	76	- 4:14
- 5.15	78	- 3:57	- 5.15	32	- 4:43	- 5.15	186	- 2:09	- 5.15	76	- 3:59
- 5.00	77	- 3:43	- 5.00	34	- 4:26	- 5.00	189	- 1:51	- 5.00	77	- 3:43
- 4.45	75	- 3:30	- 4.45	34	- 4:11	- 4.45	184	- 1:41	- 4.45	76	- 3:29
- 4.30	74	- 3:16	- 4.30	35	- 3:55	- 4.30	179	- 1:31	- 4.30	75	- 3:15
- 4.15	73	- 3:02	- 4.15	35	- 3:40	- 4.15	174	- 1:21	- 4.15	75	- 3:00
- 4.00	71	- 2:49	- 4.00	36	- 3:24	- 4.00	168	- 1:12	- 4.00	74	- 2:46
- 3.45	69	- 2:36	- 3.45	34	- 3:11	- 3.45	161	- 1:04	- 3.45	73	- 2:32
- 3.30	67	- 2:23	- 3.30	33	- 2:57	- 3.30	153	- 0:57	- 3.30	72	- 2:18
- 3.15	65	- 2:10	- 3.15	31	- 2:44	- 3.15	145	- 0:50	- 3.15	71	- 2:04
- 3.00	63	- 1:57	- 3.00	30	- 2:30	- 3.00	138	- 0:42	- 3.00	69	- 1:51
- 2.45	61	- 1:44	- 2.45	28	- 2:17	- 2.45	131	- 0:34	- 2.45	69	- 1:36
- 2.30	59	- 1:31	- 2.30	25	- 2:05	- 2.30	124	- 0:26	- 2.30	68	- 1:22
- 2.15	57	- 1:18	- 2.15	23	- 1:52	- 2.15	117	- 0:18	- 2.15	67	- 1:08
- 2.00	55	- 1:05	- 2.00	20	- 1:40	- 2.00	110	- 0:10	- 2.00	67	- 0:53
- 1.45	55	- 0:50	- 1.45	19	- 1:26	- 1.45	106	+ 0:01	- 1.45	69	- 0:36
- 1.30	55	- 0:35	- 1.30	17	- 1:13	- 1.30	101	+ 0:11	- 1.30	71	- 0:19
- 1.15	55	- 0:20	- 1.15	16	- 0:59	- 1.15	97	+ 0:22	- 1.15	73	- 0:02
- 1.00	55	- 0:05	- 1.00	15	- 0:45	- 1.00	92	+ 0:32	- 1.00	75	+ 0:15
- 0.45	58	+ 0:13	- 0.45	15	- 0:30	- 0.45	88	+ 0:43	- 0.45	83	+ 0:38
- 0.30	61	+ 0:31	- 0.30	16	- 0:14	- 0.30	84	+ 0:54	- 0.30	91	+ 1:01
- 0.15	64	+ 0:49	- 0.15	16	+ 0:01	- 0.15	79	+ 1:04	- 0.15	98	+ 1:23
HW	67	+ 1:07	HW	16	+ 0:16	HW	75	+ 1:15	HW	106	+ 1:46
+ 0.15	70	+ 1:25	+ 0.15	17	+ 0:32	+ 0.15	74	+ 1:29	+ 0.15	109	+ 2:04
+ 0.30	73	+ 1:43	+ 0.30	18	+ 0:48	+ 0.30	72	+ 1:42	+ 0.30	111	+ 2:21
+ 0.45	77	+ 2:02	+ 0.45	19	+ 1:04	+ 0.45	71	+ 1:56	+ 0.45	114	+ 2:39
+ 1.00	80	+ 2:20	+ 1.00	20	+ 1:20	+ 1.00	69	+ 2:09	+ 1.00	117	+ 2:57
+ 1.15	82	+ 2:37	+ 1.15	20	+ 1:35	+ 1.15	69	+ 2:24	+ 1.15	115	+ 3:10
+ 1.30	84	+ 2:54	+ 1.30	21	+ 1:51	+ 1.30	69	+ 2:39	+ 1.30	112	+ 3:22
+ 1.45	86	+ 3:11	+ 1.45	21	+ 2:06	+ 1.45	69	+ 2:54	+ 1.45	110	+ 3:35
+ 2.00	88	+ 3:28	+ 2.00	21	+ 2:21	+ 2.00	69	+ 3:09	+ 2.00	108	+ 3:48
+ 2.15	89	+ 3:44	+ 2.15	20	+ 2:35	+ 2.15	71	+ 3:26	+ 2.15	105	+ 4:00
+ 2.30	89	+ 3:59	+ 2.30	20	+ 2:50	+ 2.30	72	+ 3:42	+ 2.30	102	+ 4:12
+ 2.45	90	+ 4:15	+ 2.45	19	+ 3:04	+ 2.45	73	+ 3:58	+ 2.45	99	+ 4:24
+ 3.00	91	+ 4:31	+ 3.00	18	+ 3:18	+ 3.00	75	+ 4:15	+ 3.00	96	+ 4:36
+ 3.15	91	+ 4:46	+ 3.15	18	+ 3:33	+ 3.15	78	+ 4:33	+ 3.15	93	+ 4:48
+ 3.30	91	+ 5:01	+ 3.30	18	+ 3:48	+ 3.30	81	+ 4:51	+ 3.30	91	+ 5:01
+ 3.45	92	+ 5:17	+ 3.45	18	+ 4:03	+ 3.45	83	+ 5:08	+ 3.45	88	+ 5:13
+ 4.00	92	+ 5:32	+ 4.00	18	+ 4:18	+ 4.00	86	+ 5:26	+ 4.00	85	+ 5:25
+ 4.15	91	+ 5:46	+ 4.15	18	+ 4:33	+ 4.15	92	+ 5:47	+ 4.15	83	+ 5:38
+ 4.30	90	- 6:00	+ 4.30	18	+ 4:48	+ 4.30	98	- 5:52	+ 4.30	81	+ 5:51
+ 4.45	89	- 5:46	+ 4.45	18	+ 5:03	+ 4.45	104	- 5:31	+ 4.45	78	- 5:57
+ 5.00	88	- 5:32	+ 5.00	18	+ 5:18	+ 5.00	109	- 5:11	+ 5.00	76	- 5:44
+ 5.15	85	- 5:20	+ 5.15	19	+ 5:34	+ 5.15	115	- 4:50	+ 5.15	75	- 5:30
+ 5.30	82	- 5:08	+ 5.30	21	+ 5:51	+ 5.30	121	- 4:29	+ 5.30	75	- 5:15
+ 5.45	79	- 4:56	+ 5.45	22	- 5:53	+ 5.45	126	- 4:09	+ 5.45	74	- 5:01
+ 6.00	76	- 4:44	+ 6.00	24	- 5:36	+ 6.00	132	- 3:48	+ 6.00	73	- 4:47

	H5 The Naze to Harwich			H6 Long Sand Inner to Sunk Head			H7 Sunk Head to Goldmer Gat			H8 Sunk Head to NE Gunfleet	
Time	Duration	Time at End of Sector	Time	Duration	Time at End of Sector	Time	Duration	Time at End of Sector	Time	Duration	Time at End of Sector
- 6.00	70	- 4:50	- 6.00	224	- 2:16	- 6.00	95	- 4:25	- 6.00	108	- 4:12
- 5.45	70	- 4:35	- 5.45	218	- 2:07	- 5.45	96	- 4:09	- 5.45	109	- 3:56
- 5.30	70	- 4:20	- 5.30	212	- 1:58	- 5.30	96	- 3:54	- 5.30	110	- 3:40
- 5.15	71	- 4:04	- 5.15	206	- 1:49	- 5.15	97	- 3:38	- 5.15	111	- 3:24
- 5.00	71	- 3:49	- 5.00	200	- 1:40	- 5.00	97	- 3:23	- 5.00	113	- 3:07
- 4.45	70	- 3:35	- 4.45	191	- 1:34	- 4.45	93	- 3:12	- 4.45	111	- 2:54
- 4.30	69	- 3:21	- 4.30	181	- 1:29	- 4.30	89	- 3:01	- 4.30	109	- 2:41
- 4.15	68	- 3:07	- 4.15	172	- 1:23	- 4.15	85	- 2:50	- 4.15	107	- 2:28
- 4.00	67	- 2:53	- 4.00	163	- 1:17	- 4.00	81	- 2:39	- 4.00	105	- 2:15
- 3.45	65	- 2:40	- 3.45	153	- 1:12	- 3.45	77	- 2:28	- 3.45	101	- 2:04
- 3.30	63	- 2:27	- 3.30	143	- 1:07	- 3.30	74	- 2:16	- 3.30	98	- 1:52
- 3.15	61	- 2:14	- 3.15	134	- 1:01	- 3.15	71	- 2:04	- 3.15	94	- 1:41
- 3.00	58	- 2:02	- 3.00	124	- 0:56	- 3.00	67	- 1:53	- 3.00	90	- 1:30
- 2.45	56	- 1:49	- 2.45	117	- 0:48	- 2.45	65	- 1:40	- 2.45	86	- 1:19
- 2.30	53	- 1:37	- 2.30	110	- 0:40	- 2.30	63	- 1:27	- 2.30	82	- 1:08
- 2.15	51	- 1:24	- 2.15	103	- 0:32	- 2.15	60	- 1:15	- 2.15	78	- 0:57
- 2.00	48	- 1:12	- 2.00	96	- 0:24	- 2.00	58	- 1:02	- 2.00	74	- 0:46
- 1.45	46	- 0:59	- 1.45	91	- 0:14	- 1.45	58	- 0:47	- 1.45	71	- 0:34
- 1.30	44	- 0:46	- 1.30	87	- 0:03	- 1.30	58	- 0:32	- 1.30	68	- 0:22
- 1.15	43	- 0:32	- 1.15	82	+ 0:07	- 1.15	58	- 0:17	- 1.15	66	- 0:09
- 1.00	41	- 0:19	- 1.00	77	+ 0:17	- 1.00	58	- 0:02	- 1.00	63	+ 0:03
- 0.45	40	- 0:05	- 0.45	74	+ 0:29	- 0.45	61	+ 0:16	- 0.45	61	+ 0:16
- 0.30	39	+ 0:09	- 0.30	71	+ 0:41	- 0.30	63	+ 0:33	- 0.30	59	+ 0:29
- 0.15	38	+ 0:23	- 0.15	67	+ 0:52	- 0.15	65	+ 0:50	- 0.15	58	+ 0:43
HW	38	+ 0:38	HW	64	+ 1:04	HW	68	+ 1:08	HW	56	+ 0:56
+ 0.15	38	+ 0:53	+ 0.15	63	+ 1:18	+ 0.15	71	+ 1:26	+ 0.15	55	+ 1:10
+ 0.30	37	+ 1:07	+ 0.30	61	+ 1:31	+ 0.30	73	+ 1:43	+ 0.30	55	+ 1:25
+ 0.45	37	+ 1:22	+ 0.45	60	+ 1:45	+ 0.45	76	+ 2:01	+ 0.45	54	+ 1:39
+ 1.00	37	+ 1:37	+ 1.00	59	+ 1:59	+ 1.00	79	+ 2:19	+ 1.00	54	+ 1:54
+ 1.15	37	+ 1:52	+ 1.15	60	+ 2:15	+ 1.15	79	+ 2:34	+ 1.15	54	+ 2:09
+ 1.30	37	+ 2:07	+ 1.30	61	+ 2:31	+ 1.30	80	+ 2:50	+ 1.30	55	+ 2:25
+ 1.45	37	+ 2:22	+ 1.45	63	+ 2:48	+ 1.45	80	+ 3:05	+ 1.45	55	+ 2:40
+ 2.00	38	+ 2:38	+ 2.00	64	+ 3:04	+ 2.00	80	+ 3:20	+ 2.00	55	+ 2:55
+ 2.15	39	+ 2:54	+ 2.15	66	+ 3:21	+ 2.15	78	+ 3:33	+ 2.15	56	+ 3:11
+ 2.30	40	+ 3:10	+ 2.30	67	+ 3:37	+ 2.30	77	+ 3:47	+ 2.30	57	+ 3:27
+ 2.45	41	+ 3:26	+ 2.45	69	+ 3:54	+ 2.45	75	+ 4:00	+ 2.45	58	+ 3:43
+ 3.00	42	+ 3:42	+ 3.00	71	+ 4:11	+ 3.00	74	+ 4:14	+ 3.00	59	+ 3:59
+ 3.15	44	+ 3:59	+ 3.15	74	+ 4:29	+ 3.15	73	+ 4:28	+ 3.15	60	+ 4:15
+ 3.30	46	+ 4:16	+ 3.30	78	+ 4:48	+ 3.30	72	+ 4:42	+ 3.30	61	+ 4:31
+ 3.45	47	+ 4:32	+ 3.45	81	+ 5:06	+ 3.45	71	+ 4:56	+ 3.45	63	+ 4:48
+ 4.00	49	+ 4:49	+ 4.00	85	+ 5:25	+ 4.00	70	+ 5:10	+ 4.00	64	+ 5:04
+ 4.15	51	+ 5:06	+ 4.15	95	+ 5:50	+ 4.15	71	+ 5:26	+ 4.15	66	+ 5:21
+ 4.30	52	+ 5:22	+ 4.30	105	- 5:45	+ 4.30	71	+ 5:41	+ 4.30	69	+ 5:39
+ 4.45	53	+ 5:38	+ 4.45	115	- 5:20	+ 4.45	71	+ 5:56	+ 4.45	71	+ 5:56
+ 5.00	55	+ 5:55	+ 5.00	125	- 4:55	+ 5.00	72	- 5:48	+ 5.00	74	- 5:46
+ 5.15	56	- 5:49	+ 5.15	140	- 4:25	+ 5.15	73	- 5:32	+ 5.15	77	- 5:28
+ 5.30	58	- 5:32	+ 5.30	155	- 3:55	+ 5.30	74	- 5:16	+ 5.30	79	- 5:11
+ 5.45	60	- 5:15	+ 5.45	169	- 3:26	+ 5.45	75	- 5:00	+ 5.45	82	- 4:53
+ 6.00	61	- 4:59	+ 6.00	184	- 2:56	+ 6.00	76	- 4:44	+ 6.00	85	- 4:35

Sunk Head connections

Table H - Foulger's Gat to Harwich and Sunk Head Connections

Neaps — All times relate to HW Sheerness — **Time to cover Sectors (in minutes) at 5.0 Kts**

NORTH BOUND

Time	H1 Long Sand Outer to Inner: Duration	H1 Time at End of Sector	Time	H2 Black Deep to Barrow No 2: Duration	H2 Time at End of Sector	Time	H3 Barrow No 2 to Goldmer Gat: Duration	H3 Time at End of Sector	Time	H4 Goldmer Gat to The Naze: Duration	H4 Time at End of Sector
- 6.00	61	- 4:59	- 6.00	19	- 5:41	- 6.00	105	- 4:15	- 6.00	59	- 5:01
- 5.45	60	- 4:45	- 5.45	19	- 5:26	- 5.45	107	- 3:58	- 5.45	59	- 4:46
- 5.30	60	- 4:30	- 5.30	20	- 5:10	- 5.30	110	- 3:40	- 5.30	59	- 4:31
- 5.15	59	- 4:16	- 5.15	21	- 4:54	- 5.15	112	- 3:23	- 5.15	59	- 4:16
- 5.00	59	- 4:01	- 5.00	21	- 4:39	- 5.00	115	- 3:05	- 5.00	58	- 4:02
- 4.45	58	- 3:47	- 4.45	21	- 4:24	- 4.45	114	- 2:51	- 4.45	58	- 3:47
- 4.30	58	- 3:32	- 4.30	21	- 4:09	- 4.30	114	- 2:36	- 4.30	58	- 3:32
- 4.15	57	- 3:18	- 4.15	22	- 3:53	- 4.15	113	- 2:22	- 4.15	58	- 3:17
- 4.00	56	- 3:04	- 4.00	22	- 3:38	- 4.00	113	- 2:07	- 4.00	57	- 3:03
- 3.45	56	- 2:49	- 3.45	21	- 3:24	- 3.45	110	- 1:55	- 3.45	57	- 2:48
- 3.30	55	- 2:35	- 3.30	21	- 3:09	- 3.30	108	- 1:42	- 3.30	57	- 2:33
- 3.15	54	- 2:21	- 3.15	21	- 2:54	- 3.15	106	- 1:29	- 3.15	57	- 2:18
- 3.00	53	- 2:07	- 3.00	20	- 2:40	- 3.00	103	- 1:17	- 3.00	56	- 2:04
- 2.45	52	- 1:53	- 2.45	19	- 2:26	- 2.45	100	- 1:05	- 2.45	56	- 1:49
- 2.30	51	- 1:39	- 2.30	18	- 2:12	- 2.30	97	- 0:53	- 2.30	56	- 1:34
- 2.15	50	- 1:25	- 2.15	17	- 1:58	- 2.15	93	- 0:42	- 2.15	56	- 1:19
- 2.00	49	- 1:11	- 2.00	16	- 1:44	- 2.00	90	- 0:30	- 2.00	56	- 1:04
- 1.45	49	- 0:56	- 1.45	15	- 1:30	- 1.45	87	- 0:18	- 1.45	57	- 0:48
- 1.30	49	- 0:41	- 1.30	14	- 1:16	- 1.30	84	- 0:06	- 1.30	58	- 0:32
- 1.15	49	- 0:26	- 1.15	13	- 1:02	- 1.15	81	+ 0:06	- 1.15	59	- 0:16
- 1.00	49	- 0:11	- 1.00	13	- 0:47	- 1.00	78	+ 0:18	- 1.00	59	- 0:01
- 0.45	50	+ 0:05	- 0.45	13	- 0:32	- 0.45	76	+ 0:31	- 0.45	61	+ 0:16
- 0.30	51	+ 0:21	- 0.30	13	- 0:17	- 0.30	74	+ 0:44	- 0.30	63	+ 0:33
- 0.15	52	+ 0:37	- 0.15	13	- 0:02	- 0.15	72	+ 0:57	- 0.15	65	+ 0:50
HW	53	+ 0:53	HW	13	+ 0:13	HW	70	+ 1:10	HW	66	+ 1:06
+ 0.15	55	+ 1:10	+ 0.15	14	+ 0:29	+ 0.15	69	+ 1:24	+ 0.15	67	+ 1:22
+ 0.30	56	+ 1:26	+ 0.30	14	+ 0:44	+ 0.30	67	+ 1:37	+ 0.30	69	+ 1:39
+ 0.45	58	+ 1:43	+ 0.45	14	+ 0:59	+ 0.45	66	+ 1:51	+ 0.45	70	+ 1:55
+ 1.00	59	+ 1:59	+ 1.00	15	+ 1:15	+ 1.00	65	+ 2:05	+ 1.00	71	+ 2:11
+ 1.15	60	+ 2:15	+ 1.15	15	+ 1:30	+ 1.15	65	+ 2:20	+ 1.15	71	+ 2:26
+ 1.30	60	+ 2:30	+ 1.30	15	+ 1:45	+ 1.30	65	+ 2:35	+ 1.30	70	+ 2:40
+ 1.45	61	+ 2:46	+ 1.45	15	+ 2:00	+ 1.45	65	+ 2:50	+ 1.45	70	+ 2:55
+ 2.00	62	+ 3:02	+ 2.00	15	+ 2:15	+ 2.00	65	+ 3:05	+ 2.00	70	+ 3:10
+ 2.15	62	+ 3:17	+ 2.15	15	+ 2:30	+ 2.15	66	+ 3:21	+ 2.15	69	+ 3:24
+ 2.30	63	+ 3:33	+ 2.30	15	+ 2:45	+ 2.30	67	+ 3:37	+ 2.30	69	+ 3:39
+ 2.45	63	+ 3:48	+ 2.45	14	+ 2:59	+ 2.45	68	+ 3:53	+ 2.45	68	+ 3:53
+ 3.00	63	+ 4:03	+ 3.00	14	+ 3:14	+ 3.00	68	+ 4:08	+ 3.00	67	+ 4:07
+ 3.15	63	+ 4:18	+ 3.15	14	+ 3:29	+ 3.15	70	+ 4:25	+ 3.15	66	+ 4:21
+ 3.30	63	+ 4:33	+ 3.30	14	+ 3:44	+ 3.30	72	+ 4:42	+ 3.30	66	+ 4:36
+ 3.45	63	+ 4:48	+ 3.45	14	+ 3:59	+ 3.45	73	+ 4:58	+ 3.45	65	+ 4:50
+ 4.00	63	+ 5:03	+ 4.00	14	+ 4:14	+ 4.00	75	+ 5:15	+ 4.00	64	+ 5:04
+ 4.15	63	+ 5:18	+ 4.15	14	+ 4:29	+ 4.15	77	+ 5:32	+ 4.15	63	+ 5:18
+ 4.30	63	+ 5:33	+ 4.30	14	+ 4:44	+ 4.30	79	+ 5:49	+ 4.30	62	+ 5:32
+ 4.45	63	+ 5:48	+ 4.45	14	+ 4:59	+ 4.45	81	- 5:54	+ 4.45	62	+ 5:47
+ 5.00	62	- 5:58	+ 5.00	15	+ 5:15	+ 5.00	83	- 5:37	+ 5.00	61	- 5:59
+ 5.15	62	- 5:43	+ 5.15	15	+ 5:30	+ 5.15	85	- 5:20	+ 5.15	60	- 5:45
+ 5.30	62	- 5:28	+ 5.30	16	+ 5:46	+ 5.30	88	- 5:02	+ 5.30	60	- 5:30
+ 5.45	61	- 5:14	+ 5.45	17	- 5:58	+ 5.45	90	- 4:45	+ 5.45	59	- 5:16
+ 6.00	61	- 4:59	+ 6.00	17	- 5:43	+ 6.00	92	- 4:28	+ 6.00	59	- 5:01

Time	H5 The Naze to Harwich: Duration	H5 Time at End of Sector	Time	H6 Long Sand Inner to Sunk Head: Duration	H6 Time at End of Sector	Time	H7 Sunk Head to Goldmer Gat: Duration	H7 Time at End of Sector	Time	H8 Sunk Head to NE Gunfleet: Duration	H8 Time at End of Sector
- 6.00	48	- 5:12	- 6.00	116	- 4:04	- 6.00	58	- 5:02	- 6.00	65	- 4:55
- 5.45	48	- 4:57	- 5.45	117	- 3:48	- 5.45	58	- 4:47	- 5.45	66	- 4:39
- 5.30	48	- 4:42	- 5.30	119	- 3:31	- 5.30	58	- 4:32	- 5.30	67	- 4:23
- 5.15	48	- 4:27	- 5.15	121	- 3:14	- 5.15	59	- 4:16	- 5.15	68	- 4:07
- 5.00	48	- 4:12	- 5.00	123	- 2:57	- 5.00	59	- 4:01	- 5.00	68	- 3:52
- 4.45	48	- 3:57	- 4.45	121	- 2:44	- 4.45	58	- 3:47	- 4.45	68	- 3:37
- 4.30	48	- 3:42	- 4.30	119	- 2:31	- 4.30	58	- 3:32	- 4.30	68	- 3:22
- 4.15	48	- 3:27	- 4.15	118	- 2:17	- 4.15	57	- 3:18	- 4.15	67	- 3:08
- 4.00	48	- 3:12	- 4.00	116	- 2:04	- 4.00	56	- 3:04	- 4.00	67	- 2:53
- 3.45	47	- 2:58	- 3.45	112	- 1:53	- 3.45	55	- 2:50	- 3.45	66	- 2:39
- 3.30	46	- 2:44	- 3.30	108	- 1:42	- 3.30	54	- 2:36	- 3.30	65	- 2:25
- 3.15	45	- 2:30	- 3.15	104	- 1:31	- 3.15	53	- 2:22	- 3.15	64	- 2:11
- 3.00	44	- 2:16	- 3.00	99	- 1:21	- 3.00	52	- 2:08	- 3.00	63	- 1:57
- 2.45	43	- 2:02	- 2.45	94	- 1:11	- 2.45	51	- 1:54	- 2.45	62	- 1:43
- 2.30	42	- 1:48	- 2.30	90	- 1:00	- 2.30	50	- 1:40	- 2.30	60	- 1:30
- 2.15	41	- 1:34	- 2.15	85	- 0:50	- 2.15	49	- 1:26	- 2.15	59	- 1:16
- 2.00	40	- 1:20	- 2.00	80	- 0:40	- 2.00	49	- 1:11	- 2.00	58	- 1:02
- 1.45	39	- 1:06	- 1.45	78	- 0:27	- 1.45	49	- 0:56	- 1.45	56	- 0:49
- 1.30	38	- 0:52	- 1.30	76	- 0:14	- 1.30	48	- 0:42	- 1.30	55	- 0:35
- 1.15	37	- 0:38	- 1.15	73	- 0:02	- 1.15	48	- 0:27	- 1.15	54	- 0:21
- 1.00	36	- 0:24	- 1.00	71	+ 0:11	- 1.00	48	- 0:12	- 1.00	53	- 0:07
- 0.45	36	- 0:09	- 0.45	70	+ 0:25	- 0.45	49	+ 0:04	- 0.45	52	+ 0:07
- 0.30	36	+ 0:06	- 0.30	69	+ 0:39	- 0.30	50	+ 0:20	- 0.30	51	+ 0:21
- 0.15	35	+ 0:20	- 0.15	67	+ 0:52	- 0.15	50	+ 0:35	- 0.15	50	+ 0:35
HW	35	+ 0:35	HW	66	+ 1:06	HW	51	+ 0:51	HW	49	+ 0:49
+ 0.15	35	+ 0:50	+ 0.15	65	+ 1:20	+ 0.15	52	+ 1:07	+ 0.15	48	+ 1:03
+ 0.30	35	+ 1:05	+ 0.30	64	+ 1:34	+ 0.30	52	+ 1:22	+ 0.30	48	+ 1:18
+ 0.45	34	+ 1:19	+ 0.45	63	+ 1:48	+ 0.45	53	+ 1:38	+ 0.45	48	+ 1:33
+ 1.00	34	+ 1:34	+ 1.00	62	+ 2:02	+ 1.00	54	+ 1:54	+ 1.00	47	+ 1:47
+ 1.15	34	+ 1:49	+ 1.15	63	+ 2:18	+ 1.15	54	+ 2:09	+ 1.15	47	+ 2:02
+ 1.30	34	+ 2:04	+ 1.30	64	+ 2:34	+ 1.30	54	+ 2:24	+ 1.30	48	+ 2:18
+ 1.45	34	+ 2:19	+ 1.45	64	+ 2:49	+ 1.45	54	+ 2:39	+ 1.45	48	+ 2:33
+ 2.00	34	+ 2:34	+ 2.00	65	+ 3:05	+ 2.00	55	+ 2:55	+ 2.00	48	+ 2:48
+ 2.15	35	+ 2:50	+ 2.15	66	+ 3:21	+ 2.15	54	+ 3:09	+ 2.15	48	+ 3:03
+ 2.30	35	+ 3:05	+ 2.30	67	+ 3:37	+ 2.30	54	+ 3:24	+ 2.30	49	+ 3:19
+ 2.45	36	+ 3:21	+ 2.45	67	+ 3:52	+ 2.45	54	+ 3:39	+ 2.45	49	+ 3:34
+ 3.00	36	+ 3:36	+ 3.00	68	+ 4:08	+ 3.00	54	+ 3:54	+ 3.00	50	+ 3:50
+ 3.15	37	+ 3:52	+ 3.15	70	+ 4:25	+ 3.15	54	+ 4:09	+ 3.15	50	+ 4:05
+ 3.30	38	+ 4:08	+ 3.30	71	+ 4:41	+ 3.30	54	+ 4:24	+ 3.30	51	+ 4:21
+ 3.45	39	+ 4:24	+ 3.45	73	+ 4:58	+ 3.45	54	+ 4:39	+ 3.45	52	+ 4:37
+ 4.00	39	+ 4:39	+ 4.00	74	+ 5:14	+ 4.00	54	+ 4:54	+ 4.00	52	+ 4:52
+ 4.15	40	+ 4:55	+ 4.15	77	+ 5:32	+ 4.15	54	+ 5:09	+ 4.15	53	+ 5:08
+ 4.30	40	+ 5:10	+ 4.30	81	+ 5:51	+ 4.30	54	+ 5:24	+ 4.30	54	+ 5:24
+ 4.45	41	+ 5:26	+ 4.45	84	- 5:51	+ 4.45	54	+ 5:39	+ 4.45	55	+ 5:40
+ 5.00	42	+ 5:42	+ 5.00	87	- 5:33	+ 5.00	54	+ 5:54	+ 5.00	56	+ 5:56
+ 5.15	42	+ 5:57	+ 5.15	91	- 5:14	+ 5.15	55	- 5:50	+ 5.15	58	- 5:47
+ 5.30	43	- 5:47	+ 5.30	95	- 4:55	+ 5.30	55	- 5:35	+ 5.30	59	- 5:31
+ 5.45	43	- 5:32	+ 5.45	99	- 4:36	+ 5.45	55	- 5:20	+ 5.45	60	- 5:15
+ 6.00	44	- 5:16	+ 6.00	103	- 4:17	+ 6.00	56	- 5:04	+ 6.00	61	- 4:59

Sunk Head connections

Table H - Foulger's Gat to Harwich and Sunk Head Connections

Time to cover Sectors (in minutes) at 5.0 kts — All times relate to HW Sheerness — Springs

	H1 Long Sand Outer to Inner			H2 Black Deep to Barrow No 2			H3 Barrow No 2 to Goldmer Gat			H4 Goldmer Gat to The Naze			H5 The Naze to Harwich			H6 Long Sand Inner to Sunk Head			H7 Sunk Head to Goldmer Gat			H8 Sunk Head to NE Gunfleet	
Time	Duration	Time at End of Sector	Time	Duration	Time at End of Sector	Time	Duration	Time at End of Sector	Time	Duration	Time at End of Sector	Time	Duration	Time at End of Sector	Time	Duration	Time at End of Sector	Time	Duration	Time at End of Sector	Time	Duration	Time at End of Sector
- 6.00	65	- 4:55	- 6.00	21	- 5:39	- 6.00	116	- 4:04	- 6.00	59	- 5:01	- 6.00	52	- 5:08	- 6.00	152	- 3:28	- 6.00	62	- 4:58	- 6.00	71	- 4:49
- 5.45	64	- 4:41	- 5.45	22	- 5:23	- 5.45	120	- 3:45	- 5.45	59	- 4:46	- 5.45	53	- 4:52	- 5.45	153	- 3:12	- 5.45	63	- 4:42	- 5.45	72	- 4:33
- 5.30	63	- 4:27	- 5.30	23	- 5:07	- 5.30	123	- 3:27	- 5.30	59	- 4:31	- 5.30	53	- 4:37	- 5.30	153	- 2:57	- 5.30	64	- 4:26	- 5.30	74	- 4:16
- 5.15	62	- 4:13	- 5.15	25	- 4:50	- 5.15	127	- 3:08	- 5.15	59	- 4:16	- 5.15	53	- 4:22	- 5.15	154	- 2:41	- 5.15	65	- 4:10	- 5.15	75	- 4:00
- 5.00	62	- 3:58	- 5.00	26	- 4:34	- 5.00	131	- 2:49	- 5.00	59	- 4:01	- 5.00	53	- 4:07	- 5.00	154	- 2:26	- 5.00	66	- 3:54	- 5.00	76	- 3:44
- 4.45	61	- 3:44	- 4.45	26	- 4:19	- 4.45	129	- 2:36	- 4.45	59	- 3:46	- 4.45	53	- 3:52	- 4.45	148	- 2:17	- 4.45	65	- 3:40	- 4.45	76	- 3:29
- 4.30	60	- 3:30	- 4.30	26	- 4:04	- 4.30	128	- 2:22	- 4.30	59	- 3:31	- 4.30	52	- 3:38	- 4.30	141	- 2:09	- 4.30	63	- 3:27	- 4.30	75	- 3:15
- 4.15	59	- 3:16	- 4.15	26	- 3:49	- 4.15	127	- 2:08	- 4.15	58	- 3:17	- 4.15	52	- 3:23	- 4.15	135	- 2:00	- 4.15	62	- 3:13	- 4.15	75	- 3:00
- 4.00	58	- 3:02	- 4.00	27	- 3:33	- 4.00	126	- 1:54	- 4.00	58	- 3:02	- 4.00	51	- 3:09	- 4.00	128	- 1:52	- 4.00	61	- 2:59	- 4.00	74	- 2:46
- 3.45	57	- 2:48	- 3.45	26	- 3:19	- 3.45	121	- 1:44	- 3.45	57	- 2:48	- 3.45	50	- 2:55	- 3.45	122	- 1:43	- 3.45	59	- 2:46	- 3.45	73	- 2:32
- 3.30	55	- 2:35	- 3.30	25	- 3:05	- 3.30	117	- 1:33	- 3.30	57	- 2:33	- 3.30	49	- 2:41	- 3.30	115	- 1:35	- 3.30	57	- 2:33	- 3.30	71	- 2:19
- 3.15	54	- 2:21	- 3.15	25	- 2:50	- 3.15	113	- 1:22	- 3.15	56	- 2:19	- 3.15	47	- 2:28	- 3.15	108	- 1:27	- 3.15	55	- 2:20	- 3.15	69	- 2:06
- 3.00	53	- 2:07	- 3.00	24	- 2:36	- 3.00	108	- 1:12	- 3.00	56	- 2:04	- 3.00	46	- 2:14	- 3.00	102	- 1:18	- 3.00	53	- 2:07	- 3.00	68	- 1:52
- 2.45	51	- 1:54	- 2.45	22	- 2:23	- 2.45	104	- 1:01	- 2.45	55	- 1:50	- 2.45	45	- 2:00	- 2.45	96	- 1:09	- 2.45	52	- 1:53	- 2.45	66	- 1:39
- 2.30	49	- 1:41	- 2.30	20	- 2:10	- 2.30	100	- 0:50	- 2.30	55	- 1:35	- 2.30	43	- 1:47	- 2.30	91	- 0:59	- 2.30	50	- 1:40	- 2.30	63	- 1:27
- 2.15	47	- 1:28	- 2.15	18	- 1:57	- 2.15	95	- 0:40	- 2.15	55	- 1:20	- 2.15	41	- 1:34	- 2.15	85	- 0:50	- 2.15	49	- 1:26	- 2.15	61	- 1:14
- 2.00	46	- 1:14	- 2.00	16	- 1:44	- 2.00	91	- 0:29	- 2.00	55	- 1:05	- 2.00	40	- 1:20	- 2.00	79	- 0:41	- 2.00	48	- 1:12	- 2.00	59	- 1:01
- 1.45	46	- 0:59	- 1.45	15	- 1:30	- 1.45	87	- 0:18	- 1.45	56	- 0:49	- 1.45	39	- 1:06	- 1.45	76	- 0:29	- 1.45	47	- 0:58	- 1.45	57	- 0:48
- 1.30	46	- 0:44	- 1.30	14	- 1:16	- 1.30	83	- 0:07	- 1.30	57	- 0:33	- 1.30	37	- 0:53	- 1.30	73	- 0:17	- 1.30	47	- 0:43	- 1.30	55	- 0:35
- 1.15	46	- 0:29	- 1.15	13	- 1:02	- 1.15	80	+ 0:05	- 1.15	58	- 0:17	- 1.15	36	- 0:39	- 1.15	70	- 0:05	- 1.15	47	- 0:28	- 1.15	54	- 0:21
- 1.00	45	- 0:15	- 1.00	12	- 0:48	- 1.00	76	+ 0:16	- 1.00	59	- 0:01	- 1.00	35	- 0:25	- 1.00	67	+ 0:07	- 1.00	47	- 0:13	- 1.00	52	- 0:08
- 0.45	47	+ 0:02	- 0.45	12	- 0:33	- 0.45	73	+ 0:28	- 0.45	62	+ 0:17	- 0.45	34	- 0:11	- 0.45	64	+ 0:19	- 0.45	48	+ 0:03	- 0.45	51	+ 0:06
- 0.30	49	+ 0:19	- 0.30	12	- 0:18	- 0.30	70	+ 0:40	- 0.30	65	+ 0:35	- 0.30	33	+ 0:03	- 0.30	62	+ 0:32	- 0.30	49	+ 0:19	- 0.30	49	+ 0:19
- 0.15	51	+ 0:36	- 0.15	13	- 0:02	- 0.15	67	+ 0:52	- 0.15	68	+ 0:53	- 0.15	33	+ 0:18	- 0.15	60	+ 0:45	- 0.15	51	+ 0:36	- 0.15	48	+ 0:33
HW	53	+ 0:53	HW	13	+ 0:13	HW	65	+ 1:05	HW	70	+ 1:10	HW	32	+ 0:32	HW	58	+ 0:58	HW	52	+ 0:52	HW	47	+ 0:47
+ 0.15	55	+ 1:10	+ 0.15	14	+ 0:29	+ 0.15	63	+ 1:18	+ 0.15	73	+ 1:28	+ 0.15	32	+ 0:47	+ 0.15	57	+ 1:12	+ 0.15	53	+ 1:08	+ 0.15	46	+ 1:01
+ 0.30	57	+ 1:27	+ 0.30	14	+ 0:44	+ 0.30	62	+ 1:32	+ 0.30	75	+ 1:45	+ 0.30	32	+ 1:02	+ 0.30	56	+ 1:26	+ 0.30	55	+ 1:25	+ 0.30	46	+ 1:16
+ 0.45	60	+ 1:45	+ 0.45	15	+ 1:00	+ 0.45	61	+ 1:46	+ 0.45	77	+ 2:02	+ 0.45	32	+ 1:17	+ 0.45	55	+ 1:40	+ 0.45	57	+ 1:42	+ 0.45	45	+ 1:30
+ 1.00	62	+ 2:02	+ 1.00	16	+ 1:16	+ 1.00	59	+ 1:59	+ 1.00	79	+ 2:19	+ 1.00	32	+ 1:32	+ 1.00	54	+ 1:54	+ 1.00	58	+ 1:58	+ 1.00	45	+ 1:45
+ 1.15	63	+ 2:18	+ 1.15	16	+ 1:31	+ 1.15	59	+ 2:14	+ 1.15	79	+ 2:34	+ 1.15	32	+ 1:47	+ 1.15	55	+ 2:10	+ 1.15	59	+ 2:14	+ 1.15	45	+ 2:00
+ 1.30	64	+ 2:34	+ 1.30	16	+ 1:46	+ 1.30	59	+ 2:29	+ 1.30	78	+ 2:48	+ 1.30	32	+ 2:02	+ 1.30	55	+ 2:25	+ 1.30	59	+ 2:29	+ 1.30	45	+ 2:15
+ 1.45	65	+ 2:50	+ 1.45	17	+ 2:02	+ 1.45	59	+ 2:44	+ 1.45	77	+ 3:02	+ 1.45	32	+ 2:17	+ 1.45	56	+ 2:41	+ 1.45	59	+ 2:44	+ 1.45	45	+ 2:30
+ 2.00	67	+ 3:07	+ 2.00	17	+ 2:17	+ 2.00	59	+ 2:59	+ 2.00	77	+ 3:17	+ 2.00	32	+ 2:32	+ 2.00	57	+ 2:57	+ 2.00	59	+ 2:59	+ 2.00	45	+ 2:45
+ 2.15	67	+ 3:22	+ 2.15	16	+ 2:31	+ 2.15	60	+ 3:15	+ 2.15	76	+ 3:31	+ 2.15	32	+ 2:47	+ 2.15	58	+ 3:13	+ 2.15	59	+ 3:14	+ 2.15	46	+ 3:01
+ 2.30	68	+ 3:38	+ 2.30	16	+ 2:46	+ 2.30	61	+ 3:31	+ 2.30	74	+ 3:44	+ 2.30	33	+ 3:03	+ 2.30	59	+ 3:29	+ 2.30	58	+ 3:28	+ 2.30	47	+ 3:17
+ 2.45	68	+ 3:53	+ 2.45	15	+ 3:00	+ 2.45	62	+ 3:47	+ 2.45	73	+ 3:58	+ 2.45	34	+ 3:19	+ 2.45	60	+ 3:45	+ 2.45	57	+ 3:42	+ 2.45	47	+ 3:32
+ 3.00	68	+ 4:08	+ 3.00	14	+ 3:14	+ 3.00	63	+ 4:03	+ 3.00	72	+ 4:12	+ 3.00	34	+ 3:34	+ 3.00	61	+ 4:01	+ 3.00	57	+ 3:57	+ 3.00	48	+ 3:48
+ 3.15	68	+ 4:23	+ 3.15	14	+ 3:29	+ 3.15	65	+ 4:20	+ 3.15	71	+ 4:26	+ 3.15	35	+ 3:50	+ 3.15	63	+ 4:18	+ 3.15	56	+ 4:11	+ 3.15	49	+ 4:04
+ 3.30	68	+ 4:38	+ 3.30	14	+ 3:44	+ 3.30	67	+ 4:37	+ 3.30	69	+ 4:39	+ 3.30	37	+ 4:07	+ 3.30	65	+ 4:35	+ 3.30	56	+ 4:26	+ 3.30	50	+ 4:20
+ 3.45	68	+ 4:53	+ 3.45	14	+ 3:59	+ 3.45	69	+ 4:54	+ 3.45	68	+ 4:53	+ 3.45	38	+ 4:23	+ 3.45	67	+ 4:52	+ 3.45	55	+ 4:40	+ 3.45	50	+ 4:35
+ 4.00	68	+ 5:08	+ 4.00	14	+ 4:14	+ 4.00	71	+ 5:11	+ 4.00	67	+ 5:07	+ 4.00	39	+ 4:39	+ 4.00	69	+ 5:09	+ 4.00	55	+ 4:55	+ 4.00	51	+ 4:51
+ 4.15	68	+ 5:23	+ 4.15	14	+ 4:29	+ 4.15	74	+ 5:29	+ 4.15	65	+ 5:20	+ 4.15	40	+ 4:55	+ 4.15	75	+ 5:30	+ 4.15	55	+ 5:10	+ 4.15	53	+ 5:08
+ 4.30	68	+ 5:38	+ 4.30	14	+ 4:44	+ 4.30	77	+ 5:47	+ 4.30	64	+ 5:34	+ 4.30	41	+ 5:11	+ 4.30	81	+ 5:51	+ 4.30	55	+ 5:25	+ 4.30	54	+ 5:24
+ 4.45	67	+ 5:52	+ 4.45	14	+ 4:59	+ 4.45	80	- 5:55	+ 4.45	63	+ 5:48	+ 4.45	42	+ 5:27	+ 4.45	87	- 5:48	+ 4.45	56	+ 5:41	+ 4.45	56	+ 5:41
+ 5.00	67	- 5:53	+ 5.00	14	+ 5:14	+ 5.00	84	- 5:36	+ 5.00	61	- 5:59	+ 5.00	43	+ 5:43	+ 5.00	93	- 5:27	+ 5.00	56	+ 5:56	+ 5.00	57	+ 5:57
+ 5.15	66	- 5:39	+ 5.15	15	+ 5:30	+ 5.15	86	- 5:19	+ 5.15	61	- 5:44	+ 5.15	44	+ 5:59	+ 5.15	98	- 5:07	+ 5.15	56	- 5:49	+ 5.15	59	- 5:46
+ 5.30	64	- 5:26	+ 5.30	17	+ 5:47	+ 5.30	88	- 5:02	+ 5.30	60	- 5:30	+ 5.30	45	- 5:45	+ 5.30	104	- 4:46	+ 5.30	57	- 5:33	+ 5.30	61	- 5:29
+ 5.45	63	- 5:12	+ 5.45	18	- 5:57	+ 5.45	91	- 4:44	+ 5.45	59	- 5:16	+ 5.45	46	- 5:29	+ 5.45	110	- 4:25	+ 5.45	58	- 5:17	+ 5.45	63	- 5:12
+ 6.00	62	- 4:58	+ 6.00	19	- 5:41	+ 6.00	93	- 4:27	+ 6.00	58	- 5:02	+ 6.00	46	- 5:14	+ 6.00	116	- 4:04	+ 6.00	58	- 5:02	+ 6.00	65	- 4:55

Sunk Head connections

NORTH BOUND

Table H - Foulger's Gat to Harwich and Sunk Head Connections

Neaps | All times relate to HW Sheerness | **Time to cover Sectors (in minutes) at 6.0 Kts**

NORTH BOUND

H1 – Long Sand Outer to Inner

Time	Duration	Time at End of Sector
- 6.00	51	- 5:09
- 5.45	50	- 4:55
- 5.30	50	- 4:40
- 5.15	49	- 4:26
- 5.00	49	- 4:11
- 4.45	49	- 3:56
- 4.30	48	- 3:42
- 4.15	48	- 3:27
- 4.00	47	- 3:13
- 3.45	47	- 2:58
- 3.30	46	- 2:44
- 3.15	45	- 2:30
- 3.00	45	- 2:15
- 2.45	44	- 2:01
- 2.30	43	- 1:47
- 2.15	42	- 1:33
- 2.00	41	- 1:19
- 1.45	41	- 1:04
- 1.30	41	- 0:49
- 1.15	41	- 0:34
- 1.00	41	- 0:19
- 0.45	42	- 0:03
- 0.30	43	+ 0:13
- 0.15	44	+ 0:29
HW	44	+ 0:44
+ 0.15	46	+ 1:01
+ 0.30	47	+ 1:17
+ 0.45	48	+ 1:33
+ 1.00	49	+ 1:49
+ 1.15	49	+ 2:04
+ 1.30	50	+ 2:20
+ 1.45	50	+ 2:35
+ 2.00	51	+ 2:51
+ 2.15	51	+ 3:06
+ 2.30	52	+ 3:22
+ 2.45	52	+ 3:37
+ 3.00	52	+ 3:52
+ 3.15	52	+ 4:07
+ 3.30	52	+ 4:22
+ 3.45	52	+ 4:37
+ 4.00	52	+ 4:52
+ 4.15	52	+ 5:07
+ 4.30	52	+ 5:22
+ 4.45	52	+ 5:37
+ 5.00	52	+ 5:52
+ 5.15	51	- 5:54
+ 5.30	51	- 5:39
+ 5.45	51	- 5:24
+ 6.00	50	- 5:10

H2 – Black Deep to Barrow No 2

Time	Duration	Time at End of Sector
- 6.00	15	- 5:45
- 5.45	16	- 5:29
- 5.30	17	- 5:13
- 5.15	17	- 4:58
- 5.00	18	- 4:42
- 4.45	18	- 4:27
- 4.30	18	- 4:12
- 4.15	18	- 3:57
- 4.00	18	- 3:42
- 3.45	18	- 3:27
- 3.30	17	- 3:13
- 3.15	17	- 2:58
- 3.00	17	- 2:43
- 2.45	16	- 2:29
- 2.30	15	- 2:15
- 2.15	14	- 2:01
- 2.00	13	- 1:47
- 1.45	12	- 1:33
- 1.30	12	- 1:18
- 1.15	11	- 1:04
- 1.00	11	- 0:49
- 0.45	11	- 0:34
- 0.30	11	- 0:19
- 0.15	11	- 0:04
HW	11	+ 0:11
+ 0.15	11	+ 0:26
+ 0.30	12	+ 0:42
+ 0.45	12	+ 0:57
+ 1.00	12	+ 1:12
+ 1.15	12	+ 1:27
+ 1.30	12	+ 1:42
+ 1.45	13	+ 1:58
+ 2.00	13	+ 2:13
+ 2.15	12	+ 2:27
+ 2.30	12	+ 2:42
+ 2.45	12	+ 2:57
+ 3.00	12	+ 3:12
+ 3.15	12	+ 3:27
+ 3.30	12	+ 3:42
+ 3.45	12	+ 3:57
+ 4.00	12	+ 4:12
+ 4.15	12	+ 4:27
+ 4.30	12	+ 4:42
+ 4.45	12	+ 4:57
+ 5.00	12	+ 5:12
+ 5.15	13	+ 5:28
+ 5.30	13	+ 5:43
+ 5.45	14	+ 5:59
+ 6.00	14	- 5:46

H3 – Barrow No 2 to Goldmer Gat

Time	Duration	Time at End of Sector
- 6.00	79	- 4:41
- 5.45	82	- 4:23
- 5.30	85	- 4:05
- 5.15	89	- 3:46
- 5.00	92	- 3:28
- 4.45	92	- 3:13
- 4.30	92	- 2:58
- 4.15	91	- 2:44
- 4.00	91	- 2:29
- 3.45	89	- 2:16
- 3.30	86	- 2:04
- 3.15	83	- 1:52
- 3.00	80	- 1:40
- 2.45	78	- 1:27
- 2.30	76	- 1:14
- 2.15	75	- 1:00
- 2.00	73	- 0:47
- 1.45	71	- 0:34
- 1.30	69	- 0:21
- 1.15	67	- 0:08
- 1.00	66	+ 0:06
- 0.45	64	+ 0:19
- 0.30	63	+ 0:33
- 0.15	61	+ 0:46
HW	60	+ 1:00
+ 0.15	59	+ 1:14
+ 0.30	58	+ 1:28
+ 0.45	57	+ 1:42
+ 1.00	57	+ 1:57
+ 1.15	56	+ 2:11
+ 1.30	56	+ 2:26
+ 1.45	56	+ 2:41
+ 2.00	56	+ 2:56
+ 2.15	57	+ 3:12
+ 2.30	57	+ 3:27
+ 2.45	58	+ 3:43
+ 3.00	58	+ 3:58
+ 3.15	59	+ 4:14
+ 3.30	61	+ 4:31
+ 3.45	62	+ 4:47
+ 4.00	63	+ 5:03
+ 4.15	64	+ 5:19
+ 4.30	66	+ 5:36
+ 4.45	67	+ 5:52
+ 5.00	69	- 5:51
+ 5.15	70	- 5:35
+ 5.30	71	- 5:19
+ 5.45	72	- 5:03
+ 6.00	73	- 4:47

H4 – Goldmer Gat to The Naze

Time	Duration	Time at End of Sector
- 6.00	49	- 5:11
- 5.45	49	- 4:56
- 5.30	49	- 4:41
- 5.15	49	- 4:26
- 5.00	49	- 4:11
- 4.45	48	- 3:57
- 4.30	48	- 3:42
- 4.15	48	- 3:27
- 4.00	48	- 3:12
- 3.45	48	- 2:57
- 3.30	48	- 2:42
- 3.15	48	- 2:27
- 3.00	47	- 2:13
- 2.45	47	- 1:58
- 2.30	47	- 1:43
- 2.15	47	- 1:28
- 2.00	47	- 1:13
- 1.45	48	- 0:57
- 1.30	48	- 0:42
- 1.15	49	- 0:26
- 1.00	49	- 0:11
- 0.45	50	+ 0:05
- 0.30	51	+ 0:21
- 0.15	53	+ 0:38
HW	54	+ 0:54
+ 0.15	55	+ 1:10
+ 0.30	55	+ 1:25
+ 0.45	56	+ 1:41
+ 1.00	57	+ 1:57
+ 1.15	57	+ 2:12
+ 1.30	57	+ 2:27
+ 1.45	57	+ 2:42
+ 2.00	57	+ 2:57
+ 2.15	56	+ 3:11
+ 2.30	56	+ 3:26
+ 2.45	55	+ 3:40
+ 3.00	55	+ 3:55
+ 3.15	55	+ 4:10
+ 3.30	54	+ 4:24
+ 3.45	53	+ 4:38
+ 4.00	53	+ 4:53
+ 4.15	52	+ 5:07
+ 4.30	52	+ 5:22
+ 4.45	51	+ 5:36
+ 5.00	51	+ 5:51
+ 5.15	50	- 5:55
+ 5.30	50	- 5:40
+ 5.45	50	- 5:25
+ 6.00	49	- 5:11

H5 – The Naze to Harwich

Time	Duration	Time at End of Sector
- 6.00	39	- 5:21
- 5.45	39	- 5:06
- 5.30	39	- 4:51
- 5.15	39	- 4:36
- 5.00	39	- 4:21
- 4.45	39	- 4:06
- 4.30	39	- 3:51
- 4.15	39	- 3:36
- 4.00	39	- 3:21
- 3.45	38	- 3:07
- 3.30	38	- 2:52
- 3.15	37	- 2:38
- 3.00	37	- 2:23
- 2.45	36	- 2:09
- 2.30	35	- 1:55
- 2.15	34	- 1:41
- 2.00	34	- 1:26
- 1.45	33	- 1:12
- 1.30	32	- 0:58
- 1.15	32	- 0:43
- 1.00	31	- 0:29
- 0.45	31	- 0:14
- 0.30	30	HW
- 0.15	30	+ 0:15
HW	30	+ 0:30
+ 0.15	30	+ 0:45
+ 0.30	30	+ 1:00
+ 0.45	30	+ 1:15
+ 1.00	29	+ 1:29
+ 1.15	29	+ 1:44
+ 1.30	29	+ 1:59
+ 1.45	29	+ 2:14
+ 2.00	29	+ 2:29
+ 2.15	29	+ 2:44
+ 2.30	30	+ 3:00
+ 2.45	30	+ 3:15
+ 3.00	30	+ 3:30
+ 3.15	31	+ 3:46
+ 3.30	31	+ 4:01
+ 3.45	32	+ 4:17
+ 4.00	33	+ 4:33
+ 4.15	33	+ 4:48
+ 4.30	33	+ 5:03
+ 4.45	34	+ 5:19
+ 5.00	34	+ 5:34
+ 5.15	35	+ 5:50
+ 5.30	35	- 5:55
+ 5.45	35	- 5:40
+ 6.00	36	- 5:24

Sunk Head connections

H6 – Long Sand Inner to Sunk Head

Time	Duration	Time at End of Sector
- 6.00	91	- 4:29
- 5.45	93	- 4:12
- 5.30	94	- 3:56
- 5.15	96	- 3:39
- 5.00	98	- 3:22
- 4.45	97	- 3:08
- 4.30	96	- 2:54
- 4.15	96	- 2:39
- 4.00	95	- 2:25
- 3.45	91	- 2:14
- 3.30	87	- 2:03
- 3.15	83	- 1:52
- 3.00	78	- 1:42
- 2.45	76	- 1:29
- 2.30	73	- 1:17
- 2.15	70	- 1:05
- 2.00	67	- 0:53
- 1.45	66	- 0:39
- 1.30	64	- 0:26
- 1.15	63	- 0:12
- 1.00	61	+ 0:01
- 0.45	60	+ 0:15
- 0.30	59	+ 0:29
- 0.15	58	+ 0:43
HW	57	+ 0:57
+ 0.15	57	+ 1:12
+ 0.30	56	+ 1:26
+ 0.45	55	+ 1:40
+ 1.00	55	+ 1:55
+ 1.15	55	+ 2:10
+ 1.30	55	+ 2:25
+ 1.45	56	+ 2:41
+ 2.00	56	+ 2:56
+ 2.15	57	+ 3:12
+ 2.30	57	+ 3:27
+ 2.45	58	+ 3:43
+ 3.00	59	+ 3:59
+ 3.15	59	+ 4:14
+ 3.30	60	+ 4:30
+ 3.45	61	+ 4:46
+ 4.00	62	+ 5:02
+ 4.15	64	+ 5:19
+ 4.30	67	+ 5:37
+ 4.45	69	+ 5:54
+ 5.00	71	- 5:49
+ 5.15	73	- 5:32
+ 5.30	75	- 5:15
+ 5.45	77	- 4:58
+ 6.00	78	- 4:42

H7 – Sunk Head to Goldmer Gat

Time	Duration	Time at End of Sector
- 6.00	47	- 5:13
- 5.45	47	- 4:58
- 5.30	47	- 4:43
- 5.15	47	- 4:28
- 5.00	48	- 4:12
- 4.45	47	- 3:58
- 4.30	47	- 3:43
- 4.15	47	- 3:28
- 4.00	46	- 3:14
- 3.45	45	- 3:00
- 3.30	45	- 2:45
- 3.15	44	- 2:31
- 3.00	43	- 2:17
- 2.45	43	- 2:02
- 2.30	42	- 1:48
- 2.15	42	- 1:33
- 2.00	41	- 1:19
- 1.45	41	- 1:04
- 1.30	41	- 0:49
- 1.15	41	- 0:34
- 1.00	40	- 0:20
- 0.45	41	- 0:04
- 0.30	41	+ 0:11
- 0.15	42	+ 0:27
HW	42	+ 0:42
+ 0.15	42	+ 0:57
+ 0.30	43	+ 1:13
+ 0.45	44	+ 1:29
+ 1.00	44	+ 1:44
+ 1.15	44	+ 1:59
+ 1.30	44	+ 2:14
+ 1.45	44	+ 2:29
+ 2.00	45	+ 2:45
+ 2.15	45	+ 3:00
+ 2.30	44	+ 3:14
+ 2.45	44	+ 3:29
+ 3.00	44	+ 3:44
+ 3.15	44	+ 3:59
+ 3.30	44	+ 4:14
+ 3.45	44	+ 4:29
+ 4.00	44	+ 4:44
+ 4.15	44	+ 4:59
+ 4.30	44	+ 5:14
+ 4.45	45	+ 5:30
+ 5.00	45	+ 5:45
+ 5.15	45	- 6:00
+ 5.30	45	- 5:45
+ 5.45	45	- 5:30
+ 6.00	46	- 5:14

H8 – Sunk Head to NE Gunfleet

Time	Duration	Time at End of Sector
- 6.00	52	- 5:08
- 5.45	53	- 4:52
- 5.30	54	- 4:36
- 5.15	54	- 4:21
- 5.00	55	- 4:05
- 4.45	55	- 3:50
- 4.30	55	- 3:35
- 4.15	54	- 3:21
- 4.00	54	- 3:06
- 3.45	54	- 2:51
- 3.30	53	- 2:37
- 3.15	52	- 2:23
- 3.00	52	- 2:08
- 2.45	51	- 1:54
- 2.30	50	- 1:40
- 2.15	49	- 1:26
- 2.00	48	- 1:12
- 1.45	47	- 0:58
- 1.30	46	- 0:44
- 1.15	45	- 0:30
- 1.00	45	- 0:15
- 0.45	44	- 0:01
- 0.30	43	+ 0:13
- 0.15	42	+ 0:27
HW	42	+ 0:42
+ 0.15	41	+ 0:56
+ 0.30	41	+ 1:11
+ 0.45	41	+ 1:26
+ 1.00	40	+ 1:40
+ 1.15	40	+ 1:55
+ 1.30	40	+ 2:10
+ 1.45	41	+ 2:26
+ 2.00	41	+ 2:41
+ 2.15	41	+ 2:56
+ 2.30	41	+ 3:11
+ 2.45	42	+ 3:27
+ 3.00	42	+ 3:42
+ 3.15	42	+ 3:57
+ 3.30	43	+ 4:13
+ 3.45	43	+ 4:28
+ 4.00	44	+ 4:44
+ 4.15	44	+ 4:59
+ 4.30	45	+ 5:15
+ 4.45	46	+ 5:31
+ 5.00	46	+ 5:46
+ 5.15	47	- 5:58
+ 5.30	48	- 5:42
+ 5.45	49	- 5:26
+ 6.00	50	- 5:10

Table H - Foulger's Gat to Harwich and Sunk Head Connections

Time to cover Sectors (in minutes) at 6.0 kts — All times relate to HW Sheerness — Springs

Time	H1 Long Sand Outer to Inner		H2 Black Deep to Barrow No 2		H3 Barrow No 2 to Goldmer Gat		H4 Goldmer Gat to The Naze		H5 The Naze to Harwich		H6 Long Sand Inner to Sunk Head		H7 Sunk Head to Goldmer Gat		H8 Sunk Head to NE Gunfleet	
	Duration	Time at End of Sector	Duration	Time at End of Sector	Duration	Time at End of Sector	Duration	Time at End of Sector	Duration	Time at End of Sector	Duration	Time at End of Sector	Duration	Time at End of Sector	Duration	Time at End of Sector
- 6.00	54	- 5:06	18	- 5:42	90	- 4:30	49	- 5:11	42	- 5:18	105	- 4:15	50	- 5:10	56	- 5:04
- 5.45	53	- 4:52	18	- 5:27	93	- 4:12	49	- 4:56	42	- 5:03	106	- 3:59	50	- 4:55	57	- 4:48
- 5.30	53	- 4:37	19	- 5:11	96	- 3:54	49	- 4:41	42	- 4:48	108	- 3:42	51	- 4:39	58	- 4:32
- 5.15	52	- 4:23	20	- 4:55	99	- 3:36	49	- 4:26	42	- 4:33	110	- 3:25	51	- 4:24	59	- 4:16
- 5.00	51	- 4:09	21	- 4:39	102	- 3:18	49	- 4:11	43	- 4:17	112	- 3:08	52	- 4:08	60	- 4:00
- 4.45	51	- 3:54	22	- 4:23	102	- 3:03	49	- 3:56	42	- 4:03	110	- 2:55	51	- 3:54	60	- 3:45
- 4.30	50	- 3:40	22	- 4:08	101	- 2:49	48	- 3:42	42	- 3:48	108	- 2:42	51	- 3:39	60	- 3:30
- 4.15	49	- 3:26	22	- 3:53	101	- 2:34	48	- 3:27	42	- 3:33	106	- 2:29	50	- 3:25	59	- 3:16
- 4.00	49	- 3:11	22	- 3:38	100	- 2:20	48	- 3:12	41	- 3:19	105	- 2:15	49	- 3:11	59	- 3:01
- 3.45	48	- 2:57	22	- 3:23	97	- 2:08	48	- 2:57	41	- 3:04	100	- 2:05	48	- 2:57	58	- 2:47
- 3.30	47	- 2:43	21	- 3:09	94	- 1:56	47	- 2:43	40	- 2:50	95	- 1:55	47	- 2:43	57	- 2:33
- 3.15	46	- 2:29	20	- 2:55	90	- 1:45	47	- 2:28	39	- 2:36	90	- 1:45	45	- 2:30	56	- 2:19
- 3.00	44	- 2:16	20	- 2:40	87	- 1:33	47	- 2:13	38	- 2:22	85	- 1:35	44	- 2:16	55	- 2:05
- 2.45	43	- 2:02	18	- 2:27	84	- 1:21	47	- 1:58	37	- 2:08	80	- 1:25	43	- 2:02	54	- 1:51
- 2.30	42	- 1:48	16	- 2:14	81	- 1:09	46	- 1:44	36	- 1:54	76	- 1:14	42	- 1:48	52	- 1:38
- 2.15	40	- 1:35	15	- 2:00	78	- 0:57	46	- 1:29	35	- 1:40	72	- 1:03	41	- 1:34	51	- 1:24
- 2.00	39	- 1:21	13	- 1:47	75	- 0:45	46	- 1:14	34	- 1:26	67	- 0:53	40	- 1:20	49	- 1:11
- 1.45	38	- 1:07	12	- 1:33	73	- 0:32	47	- 0:58	33	- 1:12	65	- 0:40	40	- 1:05	48	- 0:57
- 1.30	38	- 0:52	11	- 1:19	70	- 0:20	47	- 0:43	32	- 0:58	63	- 0:27	40	- 0:50	47	- 0:43
- 1.15	38	- 0:37	11	- 1:04	67	- 0:08	48	- 0:27	31	- 0:44	60	- 0:15	40	- 0:35	45	- 0:30
- 1.00	38	- 0:22	10	- 0:50	65	+ 0:05	49	- 0:11	30	- 0:30	58	- 0:02	39	- 0:21	44	- 0:16
- 0.45	40	- 0:05	10	- 0:35	63	+ 0:18	50	+ 0:05	29	- 0:16	56	+ 0:11	40	- 0:05	43	- 0:02
- 0.30	41	+ 0:11	10	- 0:20	61	+ 0:31	52	+ 0:22	29	- 0:01	55	+ 0:25	41	+ 0:11	42	+ 0:12
- 0.15	43	+ 0:28	11	- 0:04	59	+ 0:44	54	+ 0:39	28	+ 0:13	53	+ 0:38	41	+ 0:26	41	+ 0:26
HW	44	+ 0:44	11	+ 0:11	57	+ 0:57	56	+ 0:56	27	+ 0:27	52	+ 0:52	42	+ 0:42	40	+ 0:40
+ 0.15	46	+ 1:01	11	+ 0:26	56	+ 1:11	58	+ 1:13	27	+ 0:42	51	+ 1:06	43	+ 0:58	40	+ 0:55
+ 0.30	47	+ 1:17	12	+ 0:42	54	+ 1:24	59	+ 1:29	27	+ 0:57	50	+ 1:20	44	+ 1:14	39	+ 1:09
+ 0.45	49	+ 1:34	13	+ 0:58	53	+ 1:38	61	+ 1:46	27	+ 1:12	50	+ 1:35	45	+ 1:30	39	+ 1:24
+ 1.00	51	+ 1:51	13	+ 1:13	52	+ 1:52	62	+ 2:02	27	+ 1:27	49	+ 1:49	46	+ 1:46	38	+ 1:38
+ 1.15	52	+ 2:07	13	+ 1:28	52	+ 2:07	62	+ 2:17	27	+ 1:42	49	+ 2:04	47	+ 2:02	38	+ 1:53
+ 1.30	53	+ 2:23	14	+ 1:44	52	+ 2:22	62	+ 2:32	27	+ 1:57	50	+ 2:20	47	+ 2:17	38	+ 2:08
+ 1.45	54	+ 2:39	14	+ 1:59	52	+ 2:37	62	+ 2:47	27	+ 2:12	50	+ 2:35	47	+ 2:32	38	+ 2:23
+ 2.00	55	+ 2:55	14	+ 2:14	52	+ 2:52	61	+ 3:01	27	+ 2:27	50	+ 2:50	47	+ 2:47	39	+ 2:39
+ 2.15	55	+ 3:10	13	+ 2:28	52	+ 3:07	61	+ 3:16	27	+ 2:42	51	+ 3:06	47	+ 3:02	39	+ 2:54
+ 2.30	55	+ 3:25	13	+ 2:43	53	+ 3:23	60	+ 3:30	28	+ 2:58	52	+ 3:22	47	+ 3:17	39	+ 3:09
+ 2.45	56	+ 3:41	12	+ 2:57	54	+ 3:39	59	+ 3:44	28	+ 3:13	53	+ 3:38	46	+ 3:31	40	+ 3:25
+ 3.00	56	+ 3:56	12	+ 3:12	55	+ 3:55	58	+ 3:58	29	+ 3:29	53	+ 3:53	46	+ 3:46	40	+ 3:40
+ 3.15	56	+ 4:11	12	+ 3:27	56	+ 4:11	57	+ 4:12	30	+ 3:45	55	+ 4:10	46	+ 4:01	41	+ 3:56
+ 3.30	56	+ 4:26	12	+ 3:42	57	+ 4:27	56	+ 4:26	30	+ 4:00	56	+ 4:26	46	+ 4:16	42	+ 4:12
+ 3.45	56	+ 4:41	12	+ 3:57	58	+ 4:43	56	+ 4:41	31	+ 4:16	58	+ 4:43	45	+ 4:30	42	+ 4:27
+ 4.00	56	+ 4:56	12	+ 4:12	60	+ 5:00	55	+ 4:55	32	+ 4:32	59	+ 4:59	45	+ 4:45	43	+ 4:43
+ 4.15	56	+ 5:11	12	+ 4:27	62	+ 5:17	54	+ 5:09	33	+ 4:48	62	+ 5:17	45	+ 5:00	44	+ 4:59
+ 4.30	55	+ 5:25	12	+ 4:42	64	+ 5:34	53	+ 5:23	33	+ 5:03	65	+ 5:35	45	+ 5:15	45	+ 5:15
+ 4.45	55	+ 5:40	12	+ 4:57	66	+ 5:51	52	+ 5:37	34	+ 5:19	69	+ 5:54	45	+ 5:30	46	+ 5:31
+ 5.00	55	+ 5:55	12	+ 5:12	69	- 5:51	51	+ 5:51	35	+ 5:35	72	- 5:48	46	+ 5:46	47	+ 5:47
+ 5.15	54	- 5:51	13	+ 5:28	71	- 5:34	51	- 5:54	35	+ 5:50	75	- 5:30	46	- 5:59	48	- 5:57
+ 5.30	53	- 5:37	14	+ 5:44	72	- 5:18	50	- 5:40	36	- 5:54	79	- 5:11	46	- 5:44	49	- 5:41
+ 5.45	53	- 5:22	15	- 6:00	74	- 5:01	49	- 5:26	37	- 5:38	82	- 4:53	47	- 5:28	51	- 5:24
+ 6.00	52	- 5:08	16	- 5:44	76	- 4:44	49	- 5:11	37	- 5:23	85	- 4:35	47	- 5:13	52	- 5:08

Sunk Head connections (H6–H8)

NORTH BOUND

Table H - Foulger's Gat to Harwich and Sunk Head Connections

Neaps — All times relate to HW Sheerness — **Time to cover Sectors (in minutes) at 7.0 Kts**

NORTH BOUND

Time	H1 Long Sand Outer to Inner: Duration	H1 Time at End of Sector	Time	H2 Black Deep to Barrow No 2: Duration	H2 Time at End of Sector	Time	H3 Barrow No 2 to Goldmer Gat: Duration	H3 Time at End of Sector	Time	H4 Goldmer Gat to The Naze: Duration	H4 Time at End of Sector
- 6.00	43	- 5:17	- 6.00	13	- 5:47	- 6.00	66	- 4:54	- 6.00	42	- 5:18
- 5.45	43	- 5:02	- 5.45	14	- 5:31	- 5.45	67	- 4:38	- 5.45	42	- 5:03
- 5.30	43	- 4:47	- 5.30	14	- 5:16	- 5.30	68	- 4:22	- 5.30	42	- 4:48
- 5.15	42	- 4:33	- 5.15	15	- 5:00	- 5.15	69	- 4:06	- 5.15	42	- 4:33
- 5.00	42	- 4:18	- 5.00	15	- 4:45	- 5.00	70	- 3:50	- 5.00	42	- 4:18
- 4.45	42	- 4:03	- 4.45	15	- 4:30	- 4.45	70	- 3:35	- 4.45	42	- 4:03
- 4.30	41	- 3:49	- 4.30	15	- 4:15	- 4.30	70	- 3:20	- 4.30	41	- 3:49
- 4.15	41	- 3:34	- 4.15	15	- 4:00	- 4.15	70	- 3:05	- 4.15	41	- 3:34
- 4.00	41	- 3:19	- 4.00	15	- 3:45	- 4.00	70	- 2:50	- 4.00	41	- 3:19
- 3.45	40	- 3:05	- 3.45	15	- 3:30	- 3.45	70	- 2:35	- 3.45	41	- 3:04
- 3.30	40	- 2:50	- 3.30	15	- 3:15	- 3.30	69	- 2:21	- 3.30	41	- 2:49
- 3.15	39	- 2:36	- 3.15	15	- 3:00	- 3.15	68	- 2:07	- 3.15	41	- 2:34
- 3.00	39	- 2:21	- 3.00	14	- 2:46	- 3.00	67	- 1:53	- 3.00	41	- 2:19
- 2.45	38	- 2:07	- 2.45	13	- 2:32	- 2.45	66	- 1:39	- 2.45	41	- 2:04
- 2.30	37	- 1:53	- 2.30	13	- 2:17	- 2.30	65	- 1:25	- 2.30	41	- 1:49
- 2.15	36	- 1:39	- 2.15	12	- 2:03	- 2.15	63	- 1:12	- 2.15	41	- 1:34
- 2.00	35	- 1:25	- 2.00	11	- 1:49	- 2.00	62	- 0:58	- 2.00	41	- 1:19
- 1.45	35	- 1:10	- 1.45	10	- 1:35	- 1.45	61	- 0:44	- 1.45	41	- 1:04
- 1.30	35	- 0:55	- 1.30	10	- 1:20	- 1.30	59	- 0:31	- 1.30	41	- 0:49
- 1.15	35	- 0:40	- 1.15	9	- 1:06	- 1.15	58	- 0:17	- 1.15	42	- 0:33
- 1.00	35	- 0:25	- 1.00	9	- 0:51	- 1.00	57	- 0:03	- 1.00	42	- 0:18
- 0.45	36	- 0:09	- 0.45	9	- 0:36	- 0.45	56	+ 0:11	- 0.45	43	- 0:02
- 0.30	37	+ 0:07	- 0.30	9	- 0:21	- 0.30	55	+ 0:25	- 0.30	43	+ 0:13
- 0.15	37	+ 0:22	- 0.15	9	- 0:06	- 0.15	54	+ 0:39	- 0.15	44	+ 0:29
HW	38	+ 0:38	HW	9	+ 0:09	HW	53	+ 0:53	HW	45	+ 0:45
+ 0.15	39	+ 0:54	+ 0.15	10	+ 0:25	+ 0.15	52	+ 1:07	+ 0.15	46	+ 1:01
+ 0.30	40	+ 1:10	+ 0.30	10	+ 0:40	+ 0.30	51	+ 1:21	+ 0.30	46	+ 1:16
+ 0.45	41	+ 1:26	+ 0.45	10	+ 0:55	+ 0.45	51	+ 1:36	+ 0.45	47	+ 1:32
+ 1.00	42	+ 1:42	+ 1.00	10	+ 1:10	+ 1.00	50	+ 1:50	+ 1.00	48	+ 1:48
+ 1.15	42	+ 1:57	+ 1.15	10	+ 1:25	+ 1.15	50	+ 2:05	+ 1.15	48	+ 2:03
+ 1.30	42	+ 2:12	+ 1.30	11	+ 1:41	+ 1.30	50	+ 2:20	+ 1.30	48	+ 2:18
+ 1.45	43	+ 2:28	+ 1.45	11	+ 1:56	+ 1.45	49	+ 2:34	+ 1.45	48	+ 2:33
+ 2.00	43	+ 2:43	+ 2.00	11	+ 2:11	+ 2.00	49	+ 2:49	+ 2.00	48	+ 2:48
+ 2.15	43	+ 2:58	+ 2.15	11	+ 2:26	+ 2.15	50	+ 3:05	+ 2.15	47	+ 3:02
+ 2.30	44	+ 3:14	+ 2.30	10	+ 2:40	+ 2.30	50	+ 3:20	+ 2.30	47	+ 3:17
+ 2.45	44	+ 3:29	+ 2.45	10	+ 2:55	+ 2.45	51	+ 3:36	+ 2.45	47	+ 3:32
+ 3.00	44	+ 3:44	+ 3.00	10	+ 3:10	+ 3.00	51	+ 3:51	+ 3.00	47	+ 3:47
+ 3.15	44	+ 3:59	+ 3.15	10	+ 3:25	+ 3.15	52	+ 4:07	+ 3.15	46	+ 4:01
+ 3.30	44	+ 4:14	+ 3.30	10	+ 3:40	+ 3.30	52	+ 4:22	+ 3.30	46	+ 4:16
+ 3.45	44	+ 4:29	+ 3.45	10	+ 3:55	+ 3.45	53	+ 4:38	+ 3.45	45	+ 4:30
+ 4.00	44	+ 4:44	+ 4.00	10	+ 4:10	+ 4.00	54	+ 4:54	+ 4.00	45	+ 4:45
+ 4.15	44	+ 4:59	+ 4.15	10	+ 4:25	+ 4.15	55	+ 5:10	+ 4.15	45	+ 5:00
+ 4.30	44	+ 5:14	+ 4.30	10	+ 4:40	+ 4.30	56	+ 5:26	+ 4.30	44	+ 5:14
+ 4.45	44	+ 5:29	+ 4.45	10	+ 4:55	+ 4.45	57	+ 5:42	+ 4.45	44	+ 5:29
+ 5.00	44	+ 5:44	+ 5.00	10	+ 5:10	+ 5.00	58	+ 5:58	+ 5.00	44	+ 5:44
+ 5.15	44	+ 5:59	+ 5.15	11	+ 5:26	+ 5.15	59	- 5:46	+ 5.15	43	+ 5:58
+ 5.30	43	- 5:47	+ 5.30	11	+ 5:41	+ 5.30	60	- 5:30	+ 5.30	43	- 5:47
+ 5.45	43	- 5:32	+ 5.45	12	+ 5:57	+ 5.45	61	- 5:14	+ 5.45	43	- 5:32
+ 6.00	43	- 5:17	+ 6.00	12	- 5:48	+ 6.00	62	- 4:58	+ 6.00	42	- 5:18

Time	H5 The Naze to Harwich: Duration	H5 Time at End of Sector	Time	H6 Long Sand Inner to Sunk Head: Duration	H6 Time at End of Sector	Time	H7 Sunk Head to Goldmer Gat: Duration	H7 Time at End of Sector	Time	H8 Sunk Head to NE Gunfleet: Duration	H8 Time at End of Sector
- 6.00	32	- 5:28	- 6.00	71	- 4:49	- 6.00	39	- 5:21	- 6.00	44	- 5:16
- 5.45	32	- 5:13	- 5.45	72	- 4:33	- 5.45	40	- 5:05	- 5.45	44	- 5:01
- 5.30	33	- 4:57	- 5.30	72	- 4:18	- 5.30	40	- 4:50	- 5.30	45	- 4:45
- 5.15	33	- 4:42	- 5.15	73	- 4:02	- 5.15	40	- 4:35	- 5.15	45	- 4:30
- 5.00	33	- 4:27	- 5.00	74	- 3:46	- 5.00	40	- 4:20	- 5.00	46	- 4:14
- 4.45	33	- 4:12	- 4.45	74	- 3:31	- 4.45	40	- 4:05	- 4.45	46	- 3:59
- 4.30	33	- 3:57	- 4.30	74	- 3:16	- 4.30	40	- 3:50	- 4.30	46	- 3:44
- 4.15	33	- 3:42	- 4.15	74	- 3:01	- 4.15	39	- 3:36	- 4.15	46	- 3:29
- 4.00	33	- 3:27	- 4.00	73	- 2:47	- 4.00	39	- 3:21	- 4.00	45	- 3:15
- 3.45	32	- 3:13	- 3.45	72	- 2:33	- 3.45	39	- 3:06	- 3.45	45	- 3:00
- 3.30	32	- 2:58	- 3.30	70	- 2:20	- 3.30	38	- 2:52	- 3.30	45	- 2:45
- 3.15	32	- 2:43	- 3.15	68	- 2:07	- 3.15	38	- 2:37	- 3.15	44	- 2:31
- 3.00	31	- 2:29	- 3.00	67	- 1:53	- 3.00	37	- 2:23	- 3.00	44	- 2:16
- 2.45	31	- 2:14	- 2.45	65	- 1:40	- 2.45	37	- 2:08	- 2.45	43	- 2:02
- 2.30	30	- 2:00	- 2.30	62	- 1:28	- 2.30	36	- 1:54	- 2.30	42	- 1:48
- 2.15	30	- 1:45	- 2.15	60	- 1:15	- 2.15	36	- 1:39	- 2.15	42	- 1:33
- 2.00	29	- 1:31	- 2.00	58	- 1:02	- 2.00	35	- 1:25	- 2.00	41	- 1:19
- 1.45	28	- 1:17	- 1.45	57	- 0:48	- 1.45	35	- 1:10	- 1.45	40	- 1:05
- 1.30	28	- 1:02	- 1.30	55	- 0:35	- 1.30	35	- 0:55	- 1.30	40	- 0:50
- 1.15	27	- 0:48	- 1.15	54	- 0:21	- 1.15	35	- 0:40	- 1.15	39	- 0:36
- 1.00	27	- 0:33	- 1.00	53	- 0:07	- 1.00	35	- 0:25	- 1.00	39	- 0:21
- 0.45	26	- 0:19	- 0.45	52	+ 0:07	- 0.45	35	- 0:10	- 0.45	38	- 0:07
- 0.30	26	- 0:04	- 0.30	51	+ 0:21	- 0.30	35	+ 0:05	- 0.30	37	+ 0:07
- 0.15	26	+ 0:11	- 0.15	51	+ 0:36	- 0.15	35	+ 0:20	- 0.15	37	+ 0:22
HW	25	+ 0:25	HW	50	+ 0:50	HW	36	+ 0:36	HW	36	+ 0:36
+ 0.15	25	+ 0:40	+ 0.15	49	+ 1:04	+ 0.15	36	+ 0:51	+ 0.15	36	+ 0:51
+ 0.30	25	+ 0:55	+ 0.30	49	+ 1:19	+ 0.30	36	+ 1:06	+ 0.30	36	+ 1:06
+ 0.45	25	+ 1:10	+ 0.45	48	+ 1:33	+ 0.45	37	+ 1:22	+ 0.45	35	+ 1:20
+ 1.00	25	+ 1:25	+ 1.00	48	+ 1:48	+ 1.00	37	+ 1:37	+ 1.00	35	+ 1:35
+ 1.15	25	+ 1:40	+ 1.15	48	+ 2:03	+ 1.15	37	+ 1:52	+ 1.15	35	+ 1:50
+ 1.30	25	+ 1:55	+ 1.30	48	+ 2:18	+ 1.30	38	+ 2:08	+ 1.30	35	+ 2:05
+ 1.45	25	+ 2:10	+ 1.45	48	+ 2:33	+ 1.45	38	+ 2:23	+ 1.45	35	+ 2:20
+ 2.00	25	+ 2:25	+ 2.00	49	+ 2:49	+ 2.00	38	+ 2:38	+ 2.00	35	+ 2:35
+ 2.15	25	+ 2:40	+ 2.15	49	+ 3:04	+ 2.15	38	+ 2:53	+ 2.15	35	+ 2:50
+ 2.30	25	+ 2:55	+ 2.30	50	+ 3:20	+ 2.30	38	+ 3:08	+ 2.30	36	+ 3:06
+ 2.45	26	+ 3:11	+ 2.45	50	+ 3:35	+ 2.45	38	+ 3:23	+ 2.45	36	+ 3:21
+ 3.00	26	+ 3:26	+ 3.00	51	+ 3:51	+ 3.00	38	+ 3:38	+ 3.00	36	+ 3:36
+ 3.15	26	+ 3:41	+ 3.15	51	+ 4:06	+ 3.15	38	+ 3:53	+ 3.15	36	+ 3:51
+ 3.30	27	+ 3:57	+ 3.30	52	+ 4:22	+ 3.30	38	+ 4:08	+ 3.30	37	+ 4:07
+ 3.45	27	+ 4:12	+ 3.45	53	+ 4:38	+ 3.45	38	+ 4:23	+ 3.45	37	+ 4:22
+ 4.00	28	+ 4:28	+ 4.00	54	+ 4:54	+ 4.00	38	+ 4:38	+ 4.00	37	+ 4:37
+ 4.15	28	+ 4:43	+ 4.15	55	+ 5:10	+ 4.15	38	+ 4:53	+ 4.15	38	+ 4:53
+ 4.30	28	+ 4:58	+ 4.30	57	+ 5:27	+ 4.30	38	+ 5:08	+ 4.30	38	+ 5:08
+ 4.45	29	+ 5:14	+ 4.45	58	+ 5:43	+ 4.45	38	+ 5:23	+ 4.45	39	+ 5:24
+ 5.00	29	+ 5:29	+ 5.00	60	- 6:00	+ 5.00	38	+ 5:38	+ 5.00	39	+ 5:39
+ 5.15	29	+ 5:44	+ 5.15	62	- 5:43	+ 5.15	38	+ 5:53	+ 5.15	40	+ 5:55
+ 5.30	30	- 6:00	+ 5.30	63	- 5:27	+ 5.30	38	- 5:52	+ 5.30	41	- 5:49
+ 5.45	30	- 5:45	+ 5.45	65	- 5:10	+ 5.45	38	- 5:37	+ 5.45	41	- 5:34
+ 6.00	30	- 5:30	+ 6.00	66	- 4:54	+ 6.00	39	- 5:21	+ 6.00	42	- 5:18

Sunk Head connections (H6–H8)

Table H - Foulger's Gat to Harwich and Sunk Head Connections

Time to cover Sectors (in minutes) at 7.0 kts — All times relate to HW Sheerness — **Springs**

NORTH BOUND

Time	H1 Long Sand Outer to Inner Duration	H1 Time at End of Sector	Time	H2 Black Deep to Barrow No 2 Duration	H2 Time at End of Sector	Time	H3 Barrow No 2 to Goldmer Gat Duration	H3 Time at End of Sector	Time	H4 Goldmer Gat to The Naze Duration	H4 Time at End of Sector	Time	H5 The Naze to Harwich Duration	H5 Time at End of Sector	Time	H6 Long Sand Inner to Sunk Head Duration	H6 Time at End of Sector	Time	H7 Sunk Head to Goldmer Gat Duration	H7 Time at End of Sector	Time	H8 Sunk Head to NE Gunfleet Duration	H8 Time at End of Sector
- 6.00	**46**	**- 5:14**	**- 6.00**	**15**	**- 5:45**	**- 6.00**	**70**	**- 4:50**	**- 6.00**	**42**	**- 5:18**	**- 6.00**	**35**	**- 5:25**	**- 6.00**	**79**	**- 4:41**	**- 6.00**	**41**	**- 5:19**	**- 6.00**	**46**	**- 5:14**
- 5.45	45	- 5:00	- 5.45	16	- 5:29	- 5.45	72	- 4:33	- 5.45	42	- 5:03	- 5.45	35	- 5:10	- 5.45	82	- 4:23	- 5.45	42	- 5:03	- 5.45	47	- 4:58
- 5.30	45	- 4:45	- 5.30	17	- 5:13	- 5.30	74	- 4:16	- 5.30	42	- 4:48	- 5.30	35	- 4:55	- 5.30	85	- 4:05	- 5.30	42	- 4:48	- 5.30	48	- 4:42
- 5.15	45	- 4:30	- 5.15	17	- 4:58	- 5.15	75	- 4:00	- 5.15	42	- 4:33	- 5.15	35	- 4:40	- 5.15	88	- 3:47	- 5.15	43	- 4:32	- 5.15	49	- 4:26
- 5.00	**44**	**- 4:16**	**- 5.00**	**18**	**- 4:42**	**- 5.00**	**77**	**- 3:43**	**- 5.00**	**42**	**- 4:18**	**- 5.00**	**35**	**- 4:25**	**- 5.00**	**91**	**- 3:29**	**- 5.00**	**43**	**- 4:17**	**- 5.00**	**50**	**- 4:10**
- 4.45	44	- 4:01	- 4.45	18	- 4:27	- 4.45	77	- 3:28	- 4.45	42	- 4:03	- 4.45	35	- 4:10	- 4.45	89	- 3:16	- 4.45	43	- 4:02	- 4.45	50	- 3:55
- 4.30	43	- 3:47	- 4.30	19	- 4:11	- 4.30	78	- 3:12	- 4.30	41	- 3:49	- 4.30	35	- 3:55	- 4.30	88	- 3:02	- 4.30	42	- 3:48	- 4.30	49	- 3:41
- 4.15	42	- 3:33	- 4.15	19	- 3:56	- 4.15	78	- 2:57	- 4.15	41	- 3:34	- 4.15	35	- 3:40	- 4.15	86	- 2:49	- 4.15	42	- 3:33	- 4.15	49	- 3:26
- 4.00	**42**	**- 3:18**	**- 4.00**	**19**	**- 3:41**	**- 4.00**	**78**	**- 2:42**	**- 4.00**	**41**	**- 3:19**	**- 4.00**	**35**	**- 3:25**	**- 4.00**	**84**	**- 2:36**	**- 4.00**	**41**	**- 3:19**	**- 4.00**	**49**	**- 3:11**
- 3.45	41	- 3:04	- 3.45	18	- 3:27	- 3.45	77	- 2:28	- 3.45	41	- 3:04	- 3.45	34	- 3:11	- 3.45	81	- 2:24	- 3.45	40	- 3:05	- 3.45	48	- 2:57
- 3.30	40	- 2:50	- 3.30	18	- 3:12	- 3.30	75	- 2:15	- 3.30	41	- 2:49	- 3.30	34	- 2:56	- 3.30	78	- 2:12	- 3.30	40	- 2:50	- 3.30	48	- 2:42
- 3.15	39	- 2:36	- 3.15	17	- 2:58	- 3.15	74	- 2:01	- 3.15	40	- 2:35	- 3.15	33	- 2:42	- 3.15	75	- 2:00	- 3.15	39	- 2:36	- 3.15	47	- 2:28
- 3.00	**38**	**- 2:22**	**- 3.00**	**17**	**- 2:43**	**- 3.00**	**73**	**- 1:47**	**- 3.00**	**40**	**- 2:20**	**- 3.00**	**33**	**- 2:27**	**- 3.00**	**72**	**- 1:48**	**- 3.00**	**38**	**- 2:22**	**- 3.00**	**46**	**- 2:14**
- 2.45	37	- 2:08	- 2.45	15	- 2:30	- 2.45	70	- 1:35	- 2.45	40	- 2:05	- 2.45	32	- 2:13	- 2.45	69	- 1:36	- 2.45	37	- 2:08	- 2.45	45	- 2:00
- 2.30	36	- 1:54	- 2.30	14	- 2:16	- 2.30	68	- 1:22	- 2.30	40	- 1:50	- 2.30	31	- 1:59	- 2.30	65	- 1:25	- 2.30	36	- 1:54	- 2.30	44	- 1:46
- 2.15	34	- 1:41	- 2.15	13	- 2:02	- 2.15	66	- 1:09	- 2.15	40	- 1:35	- 2.15	30	- 1:45	- 2.15	62	- 1:13	- 2.15	36	- 1:39	- 2.15	43	- 1:32
- 2.00	**33**	**- 1:27**	**- 2.00**	**11**	**- 1:49**	**- 2.00**	**64**	**- 0:56**	**- 2.00**	**40**	**- 1:20**	**- 2.00**	**30**	**- 1:30**	**- 2.00**	**58**	**- 1:02**	**- 2.00**	**35**	**- 1:25**	**- 2.00**	**42**	**- 1:18**
- 1.45	33	- 1:12	- 1.45	10	- 1:35	- 1.45	62	- 0:43	- 1.45	40	- 1:05	- 1.45	29	- 1:16	- 1.45	56	- 0:49	- 1.45	35	- 1:10	- 1.45	41	- 1:04
- 1.30	33	- 0:57	- 1.30	10	- 1:20	- 1.30	60	- 0:30	- 1.30	41	- 0:49	- 1.30	28	- 1:02	- 1.30	54	- 0:36	- 1.30	34	- 0:56	- 1.30	40	- 0:50
- 1.15	33	- 0:42	- 1.15	9	- 1:06	- 1.15	58	- 0:17	- 1.15	41	- 0:34	- 1.15	27	- 0:48	- 1.15	52	- 0:23	- 1.15	34	- 0:41	- 1.15	39	- 0:36
- 1.00	**33**	**- 0:27**	**- 1.00**	**8**	**- 0:52**	**- 1.00**	**56**	**- 0:04**	**- 1.00**	**41**	**- 0:19**	**- 1.00**	**26**	**- 0:34**	**- 1.00**	**50**	**+ 1:50**	**- 1.00**	**34**	**- 0:26**	**- 1.00**	**38**	**- 0:22**
- 0.45	34	- 0:11	- 0.45	9	- 0:36	- 0.45	55	+ 0:10	- 0.45	43	- 0:02	- 0.45	25	- 0:20	- 0.45	49	+ 1:34	- 0.45	34	- 0:11	- 0.45	38	- 0:07
- 0.30	35	+ 0:05	- 0.30	9	- 0:21	- 0.30	53	+ 0:23	- 0.30	44	+ 0:14	- 0.30	25	- 0:05	- 0.30	48	+ 1:18	- 0.30	35	+ 0:05	- 0.30	37	+ 0:07
- 0.15	36	+ 0:21	- 0.15	9	- 0:06	- 0.15	52	+ 0:37	- 0.15	45	+ 0:30	- 0.15	24	+ 0:09	- 0.15	47	+ 0:32	- 0.15	35	+ 0:20	- 0.15	36	+ 0:21
HW	**38**	**+ 0:38**	**HW**	**9**	**+ 0:09**	**HW**	**50**	**+ 0:50**	**HW**	**46**	**+ 0:46**	**HW**	**23**	**+ 0:23**	**HW**	**46**	**+ 0:46**	**HW**	**35**	**+ 0:35**	**HW**	**35**	**+ 0:35**
+ 0.15	39	+ 0:54	+ 0.15	10	+ 0:25	+ 0.15	49	+ 1:04	+ 0.15	48	+ 1:03	+ 0.15	23	+ 0:38	+ 0.15	45	+ 1:00	+ 0.15	36	+ 0:51	+ 0.15	35	+ 0:50
+ 0.30	40	+ 1:10	+ 0.30	10	+ 0:40	+ 0.30	48	+ 1:18	+ 0.30	49	+ 1:19	+ 0.30	23	+ 0:53	+ 0.30	44	+ 1:14	+ 0.30	37	+ 1:07	+ 0.30	34	+ 1:04
+ 0.45	42	+ 1:27	+ 0.45	11	+ 0:56	+ 0.45	48	+ 1:33	+ 0.45	50	+ 1:35	+ 0.45	23	+ 1:08	+ 0.45	44	+ 1:29	+ 0.45	38	+ 1:23	+ 0.45	34	+ 1:19
+ 1.00	**43**	**+ 1:43**	**+ 1.00**	**11**	**+ 1:11**	**+ 1.00**	**47**	**+ 1:47**	**+ 1.00**	**51**	**+ 1:51**	**+ 1.00**	**23**	**+ 1:23**	**+ 1.00**	**43**	**+ 1:43**	**+ 1.00**	**39**	**+ 1:39**	**+ 1.00**	**33**	**+ 1:33**
+ 1.15	44	+ 1:59	+ 1.15	11	+ 1:26	+ 1.15	46	+ 2:01	+ 1.15	51	+ 2:06	+ 1.15	23	+ 1:38	+ 1.15	43	+ 1:58	+ 1.15	39	+ 1:54	+ 1.15	34	+ 1:49
+ 1.30	45	+ 2:15	+ 1.30	12	+ 1:42	+ 1.30	46	+ 2:16	+ 1.30	51	+ 2:21	+ 1.30	23	+ 1:53	+ 1.30	44	+ 2:14	+ 1.30	39	+ 2:09	+ 1.30	34	+ 2:04
+ 1.45	45	+ 2:30	+ 1.45	12	+ 1:57	+ 1.45	46	+ 2:31	+ 1.45	51	+ 2:36	+ 1.45	23	+ 2:08	+ 1.45	44	+ 2:29	+ 1.45	39	+ 2:24	+ 1.45	34	+ 2:19
+ 2.00	**46**	**+ 2:46**	**+ 2.00**	**12**	**+ 2:12**	**+ 2.00**	**46**	**+ 2:46**	**+ 2.00**	**51**	**+ 2:51**	**+ 2.00**	**23**	**+ 2:23**	**+ 2.00**	**44**	**+ 2:44**	**+ 2.00**	**39**	**+ 2:39**	**+ 2.00**	**34**	**+ 2:34**
+ 2.15	46	+ 3:01	+ 2.15	11	+ 2:26	+ 2.15	46	+ 3:01	+ 2.15	50	+ 3:05	+ 2.15	23	+ 2:38	+ 2.15	45	+ 3:00	+ 2.15	39	+ 2:54	+ 2.15	34	+ 2:49
+ 2.30	47	+ 3:17	+ 2.30	11	+ 2:41	+ 2.30	47	+ 3:17	+ 2.30	50	+ 3:20	+ 2.30	24	+ 2:54	+ 2.30	45	+ 3:15	+ 2.30	39	+ 3:09	+ 2.30	34	+ 3:04
+ 2.45	47	+ 3:32	+ 2.45	11	+ 2:56	+ 2.45	47	+ 3:32	+ 2.45	49	+ 3:34	+ 2.45	24	+ 3:09	+ 2.45	46	+ 3:31	+ 2.45	39	+ 3:24	+ 2.45	35	+ 3:20
+ 3.00	**47**	**+ 3:47**	**+ 3.00**	**10**	**+ 3:10**	**+ 3.00**	**48**	**+ 3:48**	**+ 3.00**	**49**	**+ 3:49**	**+ 3.00**	**25**	**+ 3:25**	**+ 3.00**	**47**	**+ 3:47**	**+ 3.00**	**39**	**+ 3:39**	**+ 3.00**	**35**	**+ 3:35**
+ 3.15	47	+ 4:02	+ 3.15	10	+ 3:25	+ 3.15	49	+ 4:04	+ 3.15	48	+ 4:03	+ 3.15	25	+ 3:40	+ 3.15	48	+ 4:03	+ 3.15	39	+ 3:54	+ 3.15	35	+ 3:50
+ 3.30	47	+ 4:17	+ 3.30	10	+ 3:40	+ 3.30	50	+ 4:20	+ 3.30	48	+ 4:18	+ 3.30	26	+ 3:56	+ 3.30	49	+ 4:19	+ 3.30	38	+ 4:08	+ 3.30	36	+ 4:06
+ 3.45	47	+ 4:32	+ 3.45	10	+ 3:55	+ 3.45	51	+ 4:36	+ 3.45	47	+ 4:32	+ 3.45	27	+ 4:12	+ 3.45	50	+ 4:35	+ 3.45	38	+ 4:23	+ 3.45	36	+ 4:21
+ 4.00	**47**	**+ 4:47**	**+ 4.00**	**10**	**+ 4:10**	**+ 4.00**	**52**	**+ 4:52**	**+ 4.00**	**46**	**+ 4:46**	**+ 4.00**	**27**	**+ 4:27**	**+ 4.00**	**51**	**+ 4:51**	**+ 4.00**	**38**	**+ 4:38**	**+ 4.00**	**37**	**+ 4:37**
+ 4.15	47	+ 5:02	+ 4.15	10	+ 4:25	+ 4.15	53	+ 5:08	+ 4.15	46	+ 5:01	+ 4.15	28	+ 4:43	+ 4.15	53	+ 5:08	+ 4.15	38	+ 4:53	+ 4.15	37	+ 4:52
+ 4.30	47	+ 5:17	+ 4.30	10	+ 4:40	+ 4.30	55	+ 5:25	+ 4.30	45	+ 5:15	+ 4.30	28	+ 4:58	+ 4.30	56	+ 5:26	+ 4.30	38	+ 5:08	+ 4.30	38	+ 5:08
+ 4.45	47	+ 5:32	+ 4.45	10	+ 4:55	+ 4.45	56	+ 5:41	+ 4.45	45	+ 5:30	+ 4.45	29	+ 5:14	+ 4.45	58	+ 5:43	+ 4.45	38	+ 5:23	+ 4.45	39	+ 5:24
+ 5.00	**47**	**+ 5:47**	**+ 5.00**	**10**	**+ 5:10**	**+ 5.00**	**58**	**+ 5:58**	**+ 5.00**	**44**	**+ 5:44**	**+ 5.00**	**29**	**+ 5:29**	**+ 5.00**	**60**	**- 6:00**	**+ 5.00**	**38**	**+ 5:38**	**+ 5.00**	**39**	**+ 5:39**
+ 5.15	46	- 5:59	+ 5.15	11	+ 5:26	+ 5.15	60	- 5:45	+ 5.15	43	+ 5:58	+ 5.15	30	+ 5:45	+ 5.15	63	- 5:42	+ 5.15	39	+ 5:54	+ 5.15	40	+ 5:55
+ 5.30	46	- 5:44	+ 5.30	12	+ 5:42	+ 5.30	61	- 5:29	+ 5.30	43	- 5:47	+ 5.30	30	- 6:00	+ 5.30	65	- 5:25	+ 5.30	39	- 5:51	+ 5.30	42	- 5:48
+ 5.45	45	- 5:30	+ 5.45	13	+ 5:58	+ 5.45	63	- 5:12	+ 5.45	42	- 5:33	+ 5.45	31	- 5:44	+ 5.45	68	- 5:07	+ 5.45	39	- 5:36	+ 5.45	43	- 5:32
+ 6.00	**45**	**- 5:15**	**+ 6.00**	**13**	**- 5:47**	**+ 6.00**	**64**	**- 4:56**	**+ 6.00**	**42**	**- 5:18**	**+ 6.00**	**31**	**- 5:29**	**+ 6.00**	**71**	**- 4:49**	**+ 6.00**	**40**	**- 5:20**	**+ 6.00**	**44**	**- 5:16**

Sunk Head connections (H6–H8)

Table I - Barrow Deep and Deben

Neaps — All times relate to HW Sheerness — **Time to cover Sectors (in minutes) at 4.0 Kts**

NORTH BOUND

Time	I1 Red Sand to Barrow No 10 Duration	I1 Time at End of Sector	Time	I2 Medway to North Oaze PHM Duration	I2 Time at End of Sector	Time	I3 North Oaze PHM to Barrow No 10 Duration	I3 Time at End of Sector	Time	I4 Barrow No 10 to Barrow No 4 Duration	I4 Time at End of Sector
- 6.00	**115**	**- 4:05**	**- 6.00**	**103**	**- 4:17**	**- 6.00**	**137**	**- 3:43**	**- 6.00**	**169**	**- 3:11**
- 5.45	119	- 3:46	- 5.45	107	- 3:58	- 5.45	146	- 3:19	- 5.45	172	- 2:53
- 5.30	123	- 3:27	- 5.30	111	- 3:39	- 5.30	154	- 2:56	- 5.30	175	- 2:35
- 5.15	127	- 3:08	- 5.15	115	- 3:20	- 5.15	163	- 2:32	- 5.15	178	- 2:17
- 5.00	**131**	**- 2:49**	**- 5.00**	**119**	**- 3:01**	**- 5.00**	**171**	**- 2:09**	**- 5.00**	**180**	**- 2:00**
- 4.45	131	- 2:34	- 4.45	121	- 2:44	- 4.45	172	- 1:53	- 4.45	179	- 1:46
- 4.30	131	- 2:19	- 4.30	122	- 2:28	- 4.30	172	- 1:38	- 4.30	178	- 1:32
- 4.15	131	- 2:04	- 4.15	124	- 2:11	- 4.15	172	- 1:23	- 4.15	177	- 1:18
- 4.00	**131**	**- 1:49**	**- 4.00**	**125**	**- 1:55**	**- 4.00**	**173**	**- 1:07**	**- 4.00**	**176**	**- 1:04**
- 3.45	129	- 1:36	- 3.45	125	- 1:40	- 3.45	169	- 0:56	- 3.45	172	- 0:53
- 3.30	127	- 1:23	- 3.30	124	- 1:26	- 3.30	165	- 0:45	- 3.30	169	- 0:41
- 3.15	125	- 1:10	- 3.15	124	- 1:11	- 3.15	162	- 0:33	- 3.15	165	- 0:30
- 3.00	**122**	**- 0:58**	**- 3.00**	**123**	**- 0:57**	**- 3.00**	**158**	**- 0:22**	**- 3.00**	**161**	**- 0:19**
- 2.45	120	- 0:45	- 2.45	121	- 0:44	- 2.45	153	- 0:12	- 2.45	157	- 0:08
- 2.30	117	- 0:33	- 2.30	119	- 0:31	- 2.30	147	- 0:03	- 2.30	152	+ 0:02
- 2.15	115	- 0:20	- 2.15	117	- 0:18	- 2.15	142	+ 0:07	- 2.15	147	+ 0:12
- 2.00	**112**	**- 0:08**	**- 2.00**	**115**	**- 0:05**	**- 2.00**	**136**	**+ 0:16**	**- 2.00**	**143**	**+ 0:23**
- 1.45	109	+ 0:04	- 1.45	112	+ 0:07	- 1.45	130	+ 0:25	- 1.45	138	+ 0:33
- 1.30	106	+ 0:16	- 1.30	109	+ 0:19	- 1.30	124	+ 0:34	- 1.30	133	+ 0:43
- 1.15	103	+ 0:28	- 1.15	106	+ 0:31	- 1.15	118	+ 0:43	- 1.15	128	+ 0:53
- 1.00	**101**	**+ 0:41**	**- 1.00**	**103**	**+ 0:43**	**- 1.00**	**112**	**+ 0:52**	**- 1.00**	**122**	**+ 1:02**
- 0.45	97	+ 0:52	- 0.45	100	+ 0:55	- 0.45	107	+ 1:02	- 0.45	118	+ 1:13
- 0.30	94	+ 1:04	- 0.30	97	+ 1:07	- 0.30	103	+ 1:13	- 0.30	114	+ 1:24
- 0.15	90	+ 1:15	- 0.15	94	+ 1:19	- 0.15	98	+ 1:23	- 0.15	110	+ 1:35
HW	**87**	**+ 1:27**	**HW**	**91**	**+ 1:31**	**HW**	**93**	**+ 1:33**	**HW**	**106**	**+ 1:46**
+ 0.15	84	+ 1:39	+ 0.15	88	+ 1:43	+ 0.15	89	+ 1:44	+ 0.15	103	+ 1:58
+ 0.30	81	+ 1:51	+ 0.30	85	+ 1:55	+ 0.30	85	+ 1:55	+ 0.30	101	+ 2:11
+ 0.45	79	+ 2:04	+ 0.45	81	+ 2:06	+ 0.45	80	+ 2:05	+ 0.45	98	+ 2:23
+ 1.00	**76**	**+ 2:16**	**+ 1.00**	**78**	**+ 2:18**	**+ 1.00**	**76**	**+ 2:16**	**+ 1.00**	**96**	**+ 2:36**
+ 1.15	76	+ 2:31	+ 1.15	76	+ 2:31	+ 1.15	75	+ 2:30	+ 1.15	95	+ 2:50
+ 1.30	75	+ 2:45	+ 1.30	75	+ 2:45	+ 1.30	74	+ 2:44	+ 1.30	94	+ 3:04
+ 1.45	75	+ 3:00	+ 1.45	73	+ 2:58	+ 1.45	73	+ 2:58	+ 1.45	94	+ 3:19
+ 2.00	**75**	**+ 3:15**	**+ 2.00**	**71**	**+ 3:11**	**+ 2.00**	**73**	**+ 3:13**	**+ 2.00**	**93**	**+ 3:33**
+ 2.15	75	+ 3:30	+ 2.15	72	+ 3:27	+ 2.15	73	+ 3:28	+ 2.15	94	+ 3:49
+ 2.30	76	+ 3:46	+ 2.30	72	+ 3:42	+ 2.30	74	+ 3:44	+ 2.30	95	+ 4:05
+ 2.45	77	+ 4:02	+ 2.45	73	+ 3:58	+ 2.45	74	+ 3:59	+ 2.45	96	+ 4:21
+ 3.00	**78**	**+ 4:18**	**+ 3.00**	**73**	**+ 4:13**	**+ 3.00**	**75**	**+ 4:15**	**+ 3.00**	**97**	**+ 4:37**
+ 3.15	79	+ 4:34	+ 3.15	75	+ 4:30	+ 3.15	77	+ 4:32	+ 3.15	100	+ 4:55
+ 3.30	81	+ 4:51	+ 3.30	76	+ 4:46	+ 3.30	80	+ 4:50	+ 3.30	102	+ 5:12
+ 3.45	82	+ 5:07	+ 3.45	77	+ 5:02	+ 3.45	83	+ 5:08	+ 3.45	105	+ 5:30
+ 4.00	**83**	**+ 5:23**	**+ 4.00**	**79**	**+ 5:19**	**+ 4.00**	**85**	**+ 5:25**	**+ 4.00**	**107**	**+ 5:47**
+ 4.15	85	+ 5:40	+ 4.15	81	+ 5:36	+ 4.15	88	+ 5:43	+ 4.15	110	- 5:55
+ 4.30	87	+ 5:57	+ 4.30	83	+ 5:53	+ 4.30	91	- 5:59	+ 4.30	114	- 5:36
+ 4.45	88	- 5:47	+ 4.45	85	- 5:50	+ 4.45	93	- 5:42	+ 4.45	117	- 5:18
+ 5.00	**90**	**- 5:30**	**+ 5.00**	**87**	**- 5:33**	**+ 5.00**	**96**	**- 5:24**	**+ 5.00**	**121**	**- 4:59**
+ 5.15	92	- 5:13	+ 5.15	88	- 5:17	+ 5.15	99	- 5:06	+ 5.15	126	- 4:39
+ 5.30	94	- 4:56	+ 5.30	88	- 5:02	+ 5.30	103	- 4:47	+ 5.30	131	- 4:19
+ 5.45	97	- 4:38	+ 5.45	89	- 4:46	+ 5.45	106	- 4:29	+ 5.45	136	- 3:59
+ 6.00	**99**	**- 4:21**	**+ 6.00**	**90**	**- 4:30**	**+ 6.00**	**110**	**- 4:10**	**+ 6.00**	**141**	**- 3:39**

Time	I5 Barrow No 4 to Gunfleet Spit Duration	I5 Time at End of Sector	Time	I6 Gunfleet Spit to Goldmer Gat Duration	I6 Time at End of Sector	Time	I7 Goldmer Gat to Cork Sand Duration	I7 Time at End of Sector	Time	I8 Cork Sand to Deben Landfall Duration	I8 Time at End of Sector
- 6.00	**124**	**- 3:56**	**- 6.00**	**79**	**- 4:41**	**- 6.00**	**131**	**- 3:49**	**- 6.00**	**47**	**- 5:13**
- 5.45	127	- 3:38	- 5.45	85	- 4:20	- 5.45	132	- 3:33	- 5.45	47	- 4:58
- 5.30	129	- 3:21	- 5.30	92	- 3:58	- 5.30	132	- 3:18	- 5.30	47	- 4:43
- 5.15	132	- 3:03	- 5.15	98	- 3:37	- 5.15	133	- 3:02	- 5.15	47	- 4:28
- 5.00	**134**	**- 2:46**	**- 5.00**	**104**	**- 3:16**	**- 5.00**	**134**	**- 2:46**	**- 5.00**	**47**	**- 4:13**
- 4.45	133	- 2:32	- 4.45	104	- 3:01	- 4.45	132	- 2:33	- 4.45	47	- 3:58
- 4.30	131	- 2:19	- 4.30	104	- 2:46	- 4.30	130	- 2:20	- 4.30	47	- 3:43
- 4.15	130	- 2:05	- 4.15	103	- 2:32	- 4.15	128	- 2:07	- 4.15	47	- 3:28
- 4.00	**129**	**- 1:51**	**- 4.00**	**103**	**- 2:17**	**- 4.00**	**127**	**- 1:53**	**- 4.00**	**47**	**- 3:13**
- 3.45	126	- 1:39	- 3.45	100	- 2:05	- 3.45	123	- 1:42	- 3.45	46	- 2:59
- 3.30	123	- 1:27	- 3.30	98	- 1:52	- 3.30	119	- 1:31	- 3.30	45	- 2:45
- 3.15	120	- 1:15	- 3.15	95	- 1:40	- 3.15	115	- 1:20	- 3.15	45	- 2:30
- 3.00	**116**	**- 1:04**	**- 3.00**	**92**	**- 1:28**	**- 3.00**	**112**	**- 1:08**	**- 3.00**	**44**	**- 2:16**
- 2.45	113	- 0:52	- 2.45	87	- 1:18	- 2.45	107	- 0:58	- 2.45	44	- 2:01
- 2.30	110	- 0:40	- 2.30	82	- 1:08	- 2.30	103	- 0:47	- 2.30	43	- 1:47
- 2.15	106	- 0:29	- 2.15	77	- 0:58	- 2.15	99	- 0:36	- 2.15	43	- 1:32
- 2.00	**103**	**- 0:17**	**- 2.00**	**72**	**- 0:48**	**- 2.00**	**94**	**- 0:26**	**- 2.00**	**42**	**- 1:18**
- 1.45	99	- 0:06	- 1.45	69	- 0:36	- 1.45	91	- 0:14	- 1.45	42	- 1:03
- 1.30	96	+ 0:06	- 1.30	66	- 0:24	- 1.30	87	- 0:03	- 1.30	42	- 0:48
- 1.15	92	+ 0:17	- 1.15	63	- 0:12	- 1.15	83	+ 0:08	- 1.15	41	- 0:34
- 1.00	**88**	**+ 0:28**	**- 1.00**	**60**	**HW**	**- 1.00**	**80**	**+ 0:20**	**- 1.00**	**41**	**- 0:19**
- 0.45	85	+ 0:40	- 0.45	58	+ 0:13	- 0.45	78	+ 0:33	- 0.45	41	- 0:04
- 0.30	82	+ 0:52	- 0.30	55	+ 0:25	- 0.30	76	+ 0:46	- 0.30	41	+ 0:11
- 0.15	79	+ 1:04	- 0.15	53	+ 0:38	- 0.15	74	+ 0:59	- 0.15	41	+ 0:26
HW	**76**	**+ 1:16**	**HW**	**51**	**+ 0:51**	**HW**	**72**	**+ 1:12**	**HW**	**41**	**+ 0:41**
+ 0.15	75	+ 1:30	+ 0.15	49	+ 1:04	+ 0.15	71	+ 1:26	+ 0.15	41	+ 0:56
+ 0.30	73	+ 1:43	+ 0.30	48	+ 1:18	+ 0.30	71	+ 1:41	+ 0.30	41	+ 1:11
+ 0.45	71	+ 1:56	+ 0.45	47	+ 1:32	+ 0.45	71	+ 1:56	+ 0.45	41	+ 1:26
+ 1.00	**70**	**+ 2:10**	**+ 1.00**	**45**	**+ 1:45**	**+ 1.00**	**71**	**+ 2:11**	**+ 1.00**	**41**	**+ 1:41**
+ 1.15	70	+ 2:25	+ 1.15	45	+ 2:00	+ 1.15	72	+ 2:27	+ 1.15	41	+ 1:56
+ 1.30	70	+ 2:40	+ 1.30	45	+ 2:15	+ 1.30	74	+ 2:44	+ 1.30	41	+ 2:11
+ 1.45	70	+ 2:55	+ 1.45	44	+ 2:29	+ 1.45	75	+ 3:00	+ 1.45	41	+ 2:26
+ 2.00	**70**	**+ 3:10**	**+ 2.00**	**44**	**+ 2:44**	**+ 2.00**	**77**	**+ 3:17**	**+ 2.00**	**41**	**+ 2:41**
+ 2.15	71	+ 3:26	+ 2.15	45	+ 3:00	+ 2.15	79	+ 3:34	+ 2.15	41	+ 2:56
+ 2.30	73	+ 3:43	+ 2.30	46	+ 3:16	+ 2.30	81	+ 3:51	+ 2.30	41	+ 3:11
+ 2.45	74	+ 3:59	+ 2.45	47	+ 3:32	+ 2.45	83	+ 4:08	+ 2.45	42	+ 3:27
+ 3.00	**76**	**+ 4:16**	**+ 3.00**	**47**	**+ 3:47**	**+ 3.00**	**85**	**+ 4:25**	**+ 3.00**	**42**	**+ 3:42**
+ 3.15	78	+ 4:33	+ 3.15	49	+ 4:04	+ 3.15	87	+ 4:42	+ 3.15	42	+ 3:57
+ 3.30	80	+ 4:50	+ 3.30	51	+ 4:21	+ 3.30	89	+ 4:59	+ 3.30	42	+ 4:12
+ 3.45	83	+ 5:08	+ 3.45	52	+ 4:37	+ 3.45	90	+ 5:15	+ 3.45	42	+ 4:27
+ 4.00	**85**	**+ 5:25**	**+ 4.00**	**54**	**+ 4:54**	**+ 4.00**	**92**	**+ 5:32**	**+ 4.00**	**42**	**+ 4:42**
+ 4.15	87	+ 5:42	+ 4.15	56	+ 5:11	+ 4.15	95	+ 5:50	+ 4.15	42	+ 4:57
+ 4.30	90	- 6:00	+ 4.30	58	+ 5:28	+ 4.30	97	- 5:53	+ 4.30	43	+ 5:13
+ 4.45	92	- 5:43	+ 4.45	60	+ 5:45	+ 4.45	100	- 5:35	+ 4.45	43	+ 5:28
+ 5.00	**95**	**- 5:25**	**+ 5.00**	**62**	**- 5:58**	**+ 5.00**	**103**	**- 5:17**	**+ 5.00**	**43**	**+ 5:43**
+ 5.15	98	- 5:07	+ 5.15	64	- 5:41	+ 5.15	107	- 4:58	+ 5.15	44	+ 5:59
+ 5.30	101	- 4:49	+ 5.30	66	- 5:24	+ 5.30	110	- 4:40	+ 5.30	44	- 5:46
+ 5.45	104	- 4:31	+ 5.45	68	- 5:07	+ 5.45	114	- 4:21	+ 5.45	45	- 5:30
+ 6.00	**107**	**- 4:13**	**+ 6.00**	**70**	**- 4:50**	**+ 6.00**	**118**	**- 4:02**	**+ 6.00**	**45**	**- 5:15**

Table I - Barrow Deep and Deben

Time to cover Sectors (in minutes) at 4.0 kts

All times relate to HW Sheerness

Springs

I1 — Red Sand to Barrow No 10

Time	Duration	Time at End of Sector
- 6.00	126	- 3:54
- 5.45	134	- 3:31
- 5.30	142	- 3:08
- 5.15	149	- 2:46
- 5.00	157	- 2:23
- 4.45	155	- 2:10
- 4.30	154	- 1:56
- 4.15	152	- 1:43
- 4.00	151	- 1:29
- 3.45	146	- 1:19
- 3.30	141	- 1:09
- 3.15	136	- 0:59
- 3.00	132	- 0:48
- 2.45	128	- 0:37
- 2.30	124	- 0:26
- 2.15	120	- 0:15
- 2.00	116	- 0:04
- 1.45	112	+ 0:07
- 1.30	108	+ 0:18
- 1.15	104	+ 0:29
- 1.00	100	+ 0:40
- 0.45	95	+ 0:50
- 0.30	91	+ 1:01
- 0.15	86	+ 1:11
HW	82	+ 1:22
+ 0.15	78	+ 1:33
+ 0.30	75	+ 1:45
+ 0.45	71	+ 1:56
+ 1.00	68	+ 2:08
+ 1.15	67	+ 2:22
+ 1.30	67	+ 2:37
+ 1.45	66	+ 2:51
+ 2.00	65	+ 3:05
+ 2.15	67	+ 3:22
+ 2.30	68	+ 3:38
+ 2.45	69	+ 3:54
+ 3.00	70	+ 4:10
+ 3.15	72	+ 4:27
+ 3.30	74	+ 4:44
+ 3.45	76	+ 5:01
+ 4.00	78	+ 5:18
+ 4.15	80	+ 5:35
+ 4.30	83	+ 5:53
+ 4.45	86	- 5:49
+ 5.00	89	- 5:31
+ 5.15	92	- 5:13
+ 5.30	95	- 4:55
+ 5.45	98	- 4:37
+ 6.00	101	- 4:19

I2 — Medway to North Oaze PHM

Time	Duration	Time at End of Sector
- 6.00	110	- 4:10
- 5.45	116	- 3:49
- 5.30	121	- 3:29
- 5.15	126	- 3:09
- 5.00	131	- 2:49
- 4.45	133	- 2:32
- 4.30	135	- 2:15
- 4.15	137	- 1:58
- 4.00	139	- 1:41
- 3.45	138	- 1:27
- 3.30	137	- 1:13
- 3.15	136	- 0:59
- 3.00	134	- 0:46
- 2.45	131	- 0:34
- 2.30	127	- 0:23
- 2.15	124	- 0:11
- 2.00	120	HW
- 1.45	116	+ 0:11
- 1.30	112	+ 0:22
- 1.15	107	+ 0:32
- 1.00	103	+ 0:43
- 0.45	99	+ 0:54
- 0.30	95	+ 1:05
- 0.15	92	+ 1:17
HW	88	+ 1:28
+ 0.15	83	+ 1:38
+ 0.30	79	+ 1:49
+ 0.45	74	+ 1:59
+ 1.00	69	+ 2:09
+ 1.15	67	+ 2:22
+ 1.30	65	+ 2:35
+ 1.45	63	+ 2:48
+ 2.00	61	+ 3:01
+ 2.15	61	+ 3:16
+ 2.30	62	+ 3:32
+ 2.45	63	+ 3:48
+ 3.00	63	+ 4:03
+ 3.15	65	+ 4:20
+ 3.30	67	+ 4:37
+ 3.45	69	+ 4:54
+ 4.00	71	+ 5:11
+ 4.15	74	+ 5:29
+ 4.30	77	+ 5:47
+ 4.45	80	- 5:55
+ 5.00	83	- 5:37
+ 5.15	85	- 5:20
+ 5.30	87	- 5:03
+ 5.45	89	- 4:46
+ 6.00	91	- 4:29

I3 — North Oaze PHM to Barrow No 10

Time	Duration	Time at End of Sector
- 6.00	178	- 3:02
- 5.45	190	- 2:35
- 5.30	202	- 2:08
- 5.15	214	- 1:41
- 5.00	226	- 1:14
- 4.45	223	- 1:02
- 4.30	219	- 0:51
- 4.15	215	- 0:40
- 4.00	212	- 0:28
- 3.45	203	- 0:22
- 3.30	194	- 0:16
- 3.15	186	- 0:09
- 3.00	177	- 0:03
- 2.45	169	+ 0:04
- 2.30	160	+ 0:10
- 2.15	152	+ 0:17
- 2.00	144	+ 0:24
- 1.45	135	+ 0:30
- 1.30	126	+ 0:36
- 1.15	117	+ 0:42
- 1.00	108	+ 0:48
- 0.45	102	+ 0:57
- 0.30	95	+ 1:05
- 0.15	88	+ 1:13
HW	82	+ 1:22
+ 0.15	76	+ 1:31
+ 0.30	70	+ 1:40
+ 0.45	65	+ 1:50
+ 1.00	59	+ 1:59
+ 1.15	58	+ 2:13
+ 1.30	57	+ 2:27
+ 1.45	56	+ 2:41
+ 2.00	55	+ 2:55
+ 2.15	56	+ 3:11
+ 2.30	58	+ 3:28
+ 2.45	59	+ 3:44
+ 3.00	60	+ 4:00
+ 3.15	64	+ 4:19
+ 3.30	68	+ 4:38
+ 3.45	71	+ 4:56
+ 4.00	75	+ 5:15
+ 4.15	80	+ 5:35
+ 4.30	84	+ 5:54
+ 4.45	89	- 5:46
+ 5.00	93	- 5:27
+ 5.15	98	- 5:07
+ 5.30	103	- 4:47
+ 5.45	108	- 4:27
+ 6.00	112	- 4:08

I4 — Barrow No 10 to Barrow No 4

Time	Duration	Time at End of Sector
- 6.00	211	- 2:29
- 5.45	213	- 2:12
- 5.30	215	- 1:55
- 5.15	216	- 1:39
- 5.00	218	- 1:22
- 4.45	213	- 1:12
- 4.30	208	- 1:02
- 4.15	203	- 0:52
- 4.00	198	- 0:42
- 3.45	192	- 0:33
- 3.30	185	- 0:25
- 3.15	179	- 0:16
- 3.00	172	- 0:08
- 2.45	165	HW
- 2.30	159	+ 0:09
- 2.15	152	+ 0:17
- 2.00	145	+ 0:25
- 1.45	138	+ 0:33
- 1.30	131	+ 0:41
- 1.15	124	+ 0:49
- 1.00	117	+ 0:57
- 0.45	113	+ 1:08
- 0.30	108	+ 1:18
- 0.15	104	+ 1:29
HW	99	+ 1:39
+ 0.15	97	+ 1:52
+ 0.30	94	+ 2:04
+ 0.45	92	+ 2:17
+ 1.00	90	+ 2:30
+ 1.15	86	+ 2:41
+ 1.30	83	+ 2:53
+ 1.45	79	+ 3:04
+ 2.00	76	+ 3:16
+ 2.15	80	+ 3:35
+ 2.30	83	+ 3:53
+ 2.45	87	+ 4:12
+ 3.00	91	+ 4:31
+ 3.15	94	+ 4:49
+ 3.30	97	+ 5:07
+ 3.45	100	+ 5:25
+ 4.00	103	+ 5:43
+ 4.15	108	- 5:57
+ 4.30	113	- 5:37
+ 4.45	117	- 5:18
+ 5.00	122	- 4:58
+ 5.15	132	- 4:33
+ 5.30	141	- 4:09
+ 5.45	150	- 3:45
+ 6.00	159	- 3:21

I5 — Barrow No 4 to Gunfleet Spit

Time	Duration	Time at End of Sector
- 6.00	152	- 3:28
- 5.45	154	- 3:11
- 5.30	155	- 2:55
- 5.15	157	- 2:38
- 5.00	158	- 2:22
- 4.45	154	- 2:11
- 4.30	150	- 2:00
- 4.15	146	- 1:49
- 4.00	141	- 1:39
- 3.45	137	- 1:28
- 3.30	132	- 1:18
- 3.15	127	- 1:08
- 3.00	123	- 0:57
- 2.45	118	- 0:47
- 2.30	113	- 0:37
- 2.15	108	- 0:27
- 2.00	103	- 0:17
- 1.45	99	- 0:06
- 1.30	94	+ 0:04
- 1.15	90	+ 0:15
- 1.00	85	+ 0:25
- 0.45	81	+ 0:36
- 0.30	77	+ 0:47
- 0.15	73	+ 0:58
HW	68	+ 1:08
+ 0.15	66	+ 1:21
+ 0.30	64	+ 1:34
+ 0.45	62	+ 1:47
+ 1.00	60	+ 2:00
+ 1.15	61	+ 2:16
+ 1.30	61	+ 2:31
+ 1.45	61	+ 2:46
+ 2.00	61	+ 3:01
+ 2.15	63	+ 3:18
+ 2.30	65	+ 3:35
+ 2.45	67	+ 3:52
+ 3.00	69	+ 4:09
+ 3.15	71	+ 4:26
+ 3.30	74	+ 4:44
+ 3.45	77	+ 5:02
+ 4.00	80	+ 5:20
+ 4.15	84	+ 5:39
+ 4.30	88	+ 5:58
+ 4.45	93	- 5:42
+ 5.00	97	- 5:23
+ 5.15	101	- 5:04
+ 5.30	106	- 4:44
+ 5.45	111	- 4:24
+ 6.00	115	- 4:05

I6 — Gunfleet Spit to Goldmer Gat

Time	Duration	Time at End of Sector
- 6.00	102	- 4:18
- 5.45	108	- 3:57
- 5.30	113	- 3:37
- 5.15	119	- 3:16
- 5.00	124	- 2:56
- 4.45	123	- 2:42
- 4.30	122	- 2:28
- 4.15	121	- 2:14
- 4.00	120	- 2:00
- 3.45	115	- 1:50
- 3.30	110	- 1:40
- 3.15	105	- 1:30
- 3.00	100	- 1:20
- 2.45	94	- 1:11
- 2.30	88	- 1:02
- 2.15	82	- 0:53
- 2.00	76	- 0:44
- 1.45	72	- 0:33
- 1.30	68	- 0:22
- 1.15	63	- 0:12
- 1.00	59	- 0:01
- 0.45	56	+ 0:11
- 0.30	52	+ 0:22
- 0.15	49	+ 0:34
HW	46	+ 0:46
+ 0.15	44	+ 0:59
+ 0.30	43	+ 1:13
+ 0.45	41	+ 1:26
+ 1.00	40	+ 1:40
+ 1.15	39	+ 1:54
+ 1.30	39	+ 2:09
+ 1.45	39	+ 2:24
+ 2.00	39	+ 2:39
+ 2.15	39	+ 2:54
+ 2.30	40	+ 3:10
+ 2.45	41	+ 3:26
+ 3.00	42	+ 3:42
+ 3.15	44	+ 3:59
+ 3.30	46	+ 4:16
+ 3.45	47	+ 4:32
+ 4.00	49	+ 4:49
+ 4.15	52	+ 5:07
+ 4.30	55	+ 5:25
+ 4.45	59	+ 5:44
+ 5.00	62	- 5:58
+ 5.15	65	- 5:40
+ 5.30	68	- 5:22
+ 5.45	72	- 5:03
+ 6.00	75	- 4:45

I7 — Goldmer Gat to Cork Sand

Time	Duration	Time at End of Sector
- 6.00	159	- 3:21
- 5.45	159	- 3:06
- 5.30	159	- 2:51
- 5.15	159	- 2:36
- 5.00	159	- 2:21
- 4.45	154	- 2:11
- 4.30	148	- 2:02
- 4.15	143	- 1:52
- 4.00	138	- 1:42
- 3.45	132	- 1:33
- 3.30	126	- 1:24
- 3.15	120	- 1:15
- 3.00	114	- 1:06
- 2.45	108	- 0:57
- 2.30	103	- 0:47
- 2.15	98	- 0:37
- 2.00	93	- 0:27
- 1.45	88	- 0:17
- 1.30	83	- 0:07
- 1.15	78	+ 0:03
- 1.00	73	+ 0:13
- 0.45	70	+ 0:25
- 0.30	68	+ 0:38
- 0.15	65	+ 0:50
HW	62	+ 1:02
+ 0.15	62	+ 1:17
+ 0.30	62	+ 1:32
+ 0.45	61	+ 1:46
+ 1.00	61	+ 2:01
+ 1.15	63	+ 2:18
+ 1.30	65	+ 2:35
+ 1.45	67	+ 2:52
+ 2.00	69	+ 3:09
+ 2.15	72	+ 3:27
+ 2.30	74	+ 3:44
+ 2.45	77	+ 4:02
+ 3.00	80	+ 4:20
+ 3.15	83	+ 4:38
+ 3.30	86	+ 4:56
+ 3.45	89	+ 5:14
+ 4.00	92	+ 5:32
+ 4.15	93	+ 5:48
+ 4.30	95	- 5:55
+ 4.45	96	- 5:39
+ 5.00	98	- 5:22
+ 5.15	100	- 5:05
+ 5.30	102	- 4:48
+ 5.45	104	- 4:31
+ 6.00	107	- 4:13

I8 — Cork Sand to Deben Landfall

Time	Duration	Time at End of Sector
- 6.00	50	- 5:10
- 5.45	50	- 4:55
- 5.30	51	- 4:39
- 5.15	51	- 4:24
- 5.00	51	- 4:09
- 4.45	51	- 3:54
- 4.30	50	- 3:40
- 4.15	50	- 3:25
- 4.00	49	- 3:11
- 3.45	48	- 2:57
- 3.30	47	- 2:43
- 3.15	46	- 2:29
- 3.00	45	- 2:15
- 2.45	45	- 2:00
- 2.30	44	- 1:46
- 2.15	43	- 1:32
- 2.00	42	- 1:18
- 1.45	42	- 1:03
- 1.30	41	- 0:49
- 1.15	41	- 0:34
- 1.00	40	- 0:20
- 0.45	40	- 0:05
- 0.30	40	+ 0:10
- 0.15	40	+ 0:25
HW	40	+ 0:40
+ 0.15	40	+ 0:55
+ 0.30	41	+ 1:11
+ 0.45	41	+ 1:26
+ 1.00	41	+ 1:41
+ 1.15	41	+ 1:56
+ 1.30	41	+ 2:11
+ 1.45	41	+ 2:26
+ 2.00	41	+ 2:41
+ 2.15	41	+ 2:56
+ 2.30	41	+ 3:11
+ 2.45	41	+ 3:26
+ 3.00	41	+ 3:41
+ 3.15	41	+ 3:56
+ 3.30	42	+ 4:12
+ 3.45	42	+ 4:27
+ 4.00	42	+ 4:42
+ 4.15	42	+ 4:57
+ 4.30	43	+ 5:13
+ 4.45	43	+ 5:28
+ 5.00	43	+ 5:43
+ 5.15	44	+ 5:59
+ 5.30	45	- 5:45
+ 5.45	45	- 5:30
+ 6.00	46	- 5:14

NORTH BOUND

Table I - Barrow Deep and Deben

Neaps — All times relate to HW Sheerness — **Time to cover Sectors (in minutes) at 5.0 Kts**

NORTH BOUND

Time	I1 Red Sand to Barrow No 10: Duration	I1: Time at End of Sector	Time	I2 Medway to North Oaze PHM: Duration	I2: Time at End of Sector	Time	I3 North Oaze PHM to Barrow No 10: Duration	I3: Time at End of Sector	Time	I4 Barrow No 10 to Barrow No 4: Duration	I4: Time at End of Sector
- 6.00	85	- 4:35	- 6.00	79	- 4:41	- 6.00	102	- 4:18	- 6.00	123	- 3:57
- 5.45	89	- 4:16	- 5.45	82	- 4:23	- 5.45	107	- 3:58	- 5.45	126	- 3:39
- 5.30	92	- 3:58	- 5.30	85	- 4:05	- 5.30	112	- 3:38	- 5.30	128	- 3:22
- 5.15	96	- 3:39	- 5.15	88	- 3:47	- 5.15	117	- 3:18	- 5.15	131	- 3:04
- 5.00	99	- 3:21	- 5.00	91	- 3:29	- 5.00	122	- 2:58	- 5.00	134	- 2:46
- 4.45	100	- 3:05	- 4.45	92	- 3:13	- 4.45	123	- 2:42	- 4.45	134	- 2:31
- 4.30	100	- 2:50	- 4.30	93	- 2:57	- 4.30	124	- 2:26	- 4.30	134	- 2:16
- 4.15	101	- 2:34	- 4.15	95	- 2:40	- 4.15	125	- 2:10	- 4.15	134	- 2:01
- 4.00	101	- 2:19	- 4.00	96	- 2:24	- 4.00	127	- 1:53	- 4.00	134	- 1:46
- 3.45	100	- 2:05	- 3.45	96	- 2:09	- 3.45	125	- 1:40	- 3.45	132	- 1:33
- 3.30	98	- 1:52	- 3.30	96	- 1:54	- 3.30	124	- 1:26	- 3.30	130	- 1:20
- 3.15	97	- 1:38	- 3.15	96	- 1:39	- 3.15	123	- 1:12	- 3.15	129	- 1:06
- 3.00	95	- 1:25	- 3.00	96	- 1:24	- 3.00	121	- 0:59	- 3.00	127	- 0:53
- 2.45	93	- 1:12	- 2.45	94	- 1:11	- 2.45	118	- 0:47	- 2.45	124	- 0:41
- 2.30	90	- 1:00	- 2.30	93	- 0:57	- 2.30	115	- 0:35	- 2.30	121	- 0:29
- 2.15	88	- 0:47	- 2.15	92	- 0:43	- 2.15	112	- 0:23	- 2.15	118	- 0:17
- 2.00	86	- 0:34	- 2.00	91	- 0:29	- 2.00	109	- 0:11	- 2.00	115	- 0:05
- 1.45	84	- 0:21	- 1.45	88	- 0:17	- 1.45	105	HW	- 1.45	111	+ 0:06
- 1.30	83	- 0:07	- 1.30	86	- 0:04	- 1.30	101	+ 0:11	- 1.30	108	+ 0:18
- 1.15	82	+ 0:07	- 1.15	83	+ 0:08	- 1.15	97	+ 0:22	- 1.15	105	+ 0:30
- 1.00	80	+ 0:20	- 1.00	81	+ 0:21	- 1.00	94	+ 0:34	- 1.00	102	+ 0:42
- 0.45	78	+ 0:33	- 0.45	79	+ 0:34	- 0.45	89	+ 0:44	- 0.45	99	+ 0:54
- 0.30	76	+ 0:46	- 0.30	77	+ 0:47	- 0.30	85	+ 0:55	- 0.30	96	+ 1:06
- 0.15	74	+ 0:59	- 0.15	75	+ 1:00	- 0.15	81	+ 1:06	- 0.15	93	+ 1:18
HW	72	+ 1:12	HW	73	+ 1:13	HW	77	+ 1:17	HW	90	+ 1:30
+ 0.15	70	+ 1:25	+ 0.15	71	+ 1:26	+ 0.15	74	+ 1:29	+ 0.15	88	+ 1:43
+ 0.30	68	+ 1:38	+ 0.30	69	+ 1:39	+ 0.30	72	+ 1:42	+ 0.30	85	+ 1:55
+ 0.45	66	+ 1:51	+ 0.45	67	+ 1:52	+ 0.45	69	+ 1:54	+ 0.45	82	+ 2:07
+ 1.00	64	+ 2:04	+ 1.00	65	+ 2:05	+ 1.00	66	+ 2:06	+ 1.00	79	+ 2:19
+ 1.15	64	+ 2:19	+ 1.15	64	+ 2:19	+ 1.15	66	+ 2:21	+ 1.15	79	+ 2:34
+ 1.30	63	+ 2:33	+ 1.30	63	+ 2:33	+ 1.30	65	+ 2:35	+ 1.30	78	+ 2:48
+ 1.45	63	+ 2:48	+ 1.45	62	+ 2:47	+ 1.45	64	+ 2:49	+ 1.45	78	+ 3:03
+ 2.00	63	+ 3:03	+ 2.00	61	+ 3:01	+ 2.00	64	+ 3:04	+ 2.00	78	+ 3:18
+ 2.15	63	+ 3:18	+ 2.15	61	+ 3:16	+ 2.15	64	+ 3:19	+ 2.15	79	+ 3:34
+ 2.30	64	+ 3:34	+ 2.30	61	+ 3:31	+ 2.30	64	+ 3:34	+ 2.30	80	+ 3:50
+ 2.45	64	+ 3:49	+ 2.45	61	+ 3:46	+ 2.45	65	+ 3:50	+ 2.45	80	+ 4:05
+ 3.00	65	+ 4:05	+ 3.00	62	+ 4:02	+ 3.00	65	+ 4:05	+ 3.00	81	+ 4:21
+ 3.15	66	+ 4:21	+ 3.15	62	+ 4:17	+ 3.15	67	+ 4:22	+ 3.15	83	+ 4:38
+ 3.30	67	+ 4:37	+ 3.30	63	+ 4:33	+ 3.30	68	+ 4:38	+ 3.30	85	+ 4:55
+ 3.45	67	+ 4:52	+ 3.45	64	+ 4:49	+ 3.45	70	+ 4:55	+ 3.45	86	+ 5:11
+ 4.00	68	+ 5:08	+ 4.00	65	+ 5:05	+ 4.00	71	+ 5:11	+ 4.00	88	+ 5:28
+ 4.15	69	+ 5:24	+ 4.15	66	+ 5:21	+ 4.15	73	+ 5:28	+ 4.15	90	+ 5:45
+ 4.30	71	+ 5:41	+ 4.30	67	+ 5:37	+ 4.30	75	+ 5:45	+ 4.30	92	- 5:58
+ 4.45	72	+ 5:57	+ 4.45	69	+ 5:54	+ 4.45	77	- 5:58	+ 4.45	93	- 5:42
+ 5.00	73	- 5:47	+ 5.00	70	- 5:50	+ 5.00	79	- 5:41	+ 5.00	95	- 5:25
+ 5.15	74	- 5:31	+ 5.15	71	- 5:34	+ 5.15	81	- 5:24	+ 5.15	98	- 5:07
+ 5.30	76	- 5:14	+ 5.30	71	- 5:19	+ 5.30	83	- 5:07	+ 5.30	101	- 4:49
+ 5.45	77	- 4:58	+ 5.45	72	- 5:03	+ 5.45	84	- 4:51	+ 5.45	104	- 4:31
+ 6.00	78	- 4:42	+ 6.00	73	- 4:47	+ 6.00	86	- 4:34	+ 6.00	107	- 4:13

Time	I5 Barrow No 4 to Gunfleet Spit: Duration	I5: Time at End of Sector	Time	I6 Gunfleet Spit to Goldmer Gat: Duration	I6: Time at End of Sector	Time	I7 Goldmer Gat to Cork Sand: Duration	I7: Time at End of Sector	Time	I8 Cork Sand to Deben Landfall: Duration	I8: Time at End of Sector
- 6.00	94	- 4:26	- 6.00	60	- 5:00	- 6.00	100	- 4:20	- 6.00	37	- 5:23
- 5.45	96	- 4:09	- 5.45	62	- 4:43	- 5.45	100	- 4:05	- 5.45	37	- 5:08
- 5.30	98	- 3:52	- 5.30	63	- 4:27	- 5.30	101	- 3:49	- 5.30	37	- 4:53
- 5.15	100	- 3:35	- 5.15	65	- 4:10	- 5.15	101	- 3:34	- 5.15	37	- 4:38
- 5.00	102	- 3:18	- 5.00	67	- 3:53	- 5.00	102	- 3:18	- 5.00	37	- 4:23
- 4.45	101	- 3:04	- 4.45	67	- 3:38	- 4.45	101	- 3:04	- 4.45	37	- 4:08
- 4.30	101	- 2:49	- 4.30	67	- 3:23	- 4.30	101	- 2:49	- 4.30	37	- 3:53
- 4.15	100	- 2:35	- 4.15	67	- 3:08	- 4.15	100	- 2:35	- 4.15	37	- 3:38
- 4.00	100	- 2:20	- 4.00	67	- 2:53	- 4.00	99	- 2:21	- 4.00	37	- 3:23
- 3.45	98	- 2:07	- 3.45	66	- 2:39	- 3.45	97	- 2:08	- 3.45	36	- 3:09
- 3.30	96	- 1:54	- 3.30	65	- 2:25	- 3.30	95	- 1:55	- 3.30	36	- 2:54
- 3.15	94	- 1:41	- 3.15	64	- 2:11	- 3.15	93	- 1:42	- 3.15	36	- 2:39
- 3.00	92	- 1:28	- 3.00	63	- 1:57	- 3.00	90	- 1:30	- 3.00	35	- 2:25
- 2.45	89	- 1:16	- 2.45	62	- 1:43	- 2.45	87	- 1:18	- 2.45	35	- 2:10
- 2.30	87	- 1:03	- 2.30	60	- 1:30	- 2.30	83	- 1:07	- 2.30	35	- 1:55
- 2.15	84	- 0:51	- 2.15	58	- 1:17	- 2.15	79	- 0:56	- 2.15	34	- 1:41
- 2.00	81	- 0:39	- 2.00	57	- 1:03	- 2.00	76	- 0:44	- 2.00	34	- 1:26
- 1.45	79	- 0:26	- 1.45	55	- 0:50	- 1.45	74	- 0:31	- 1.45	34	- 1:11
- 1.30	77	- 0:13	- 1.30	53	- 0:37	- 1.30	71	- 0:19	- 1.30	34	- 0:56
- 1.15	74	- 0:01	- 1.15	51	- 0:24	- 1.15	69	- 0:06	- 1.15	33	- 0:42
- 1.00	72	+ 0:12	- 1.00	49	- 0:11	- 1.00	67	+ 0:07	- 1.00	33	- 0:27
- 0.45	70	+ 0:25	- 0.45	48	+ 0:03	- 0.45	66	+ 0:21	- 0.45	33	- 0:12
- 0.30	68	+ 0:38	- 0.30	46	+ 0:16	- 0.30	64	+ 0:34	- 0.30	33	+ 0:03
- 0.15	66	+ 0:51	- 0.15	45	+ 0:30	- 0.15	63	+ 0:48	- 0.15	33	+ 0:18
HW	64	+ 1:04	HW	43	+ 0:43	HW	61	+ 1:01	HW	33	+ 0:33
+ 0.15	63	+ 1:18	+ 0.15	42	+ 0:57	+ 0.15	61	+ 1:16	+ 0.15	33	+ 0:48
+ 0.30	62	+ 1:32	+ 0.30	41	+ 1:11	+ 0.30	61	+ 1:31	+ 0.30	33	+ 1:03
+ 0.45	61	+ 1:46	+ 0.45	40	+ 1:25	+ 0.45	61	+ 1:46	+ 0.45	33	+ 1:18
+ 1.00	60	+ 2:00	+ 1.00	39	+ 1:39	+ 1.00	60	+ 2:00	+ 1.00	33	+ 1:33
+ 1.15	60	+ 2:15	+ 1.15	39	+ 1:54	+ 1.15	61	+ 2:16	+ 1.15	33	+ 1:48
+ 1.30	60	+ 2:30	+ 1.30	39	+ 2:09	+ 1.30	62	+ 2:32	+ 1.30	33	+ 2:03
+ 1.45	60	+ 2:45	+ 1.45	38	+ 2:23	+ 1.45	63	+ 2:48	+ 1.45	33	+ 2:18
+ 2.00	59	+ 2:59	+ 2.00	38	+ 2:38	+ 2.00	64	+ 3:04	+ 2.00	33	+ 2:33
+ 2.15	60	+ 3:15	+ 2.15	38	+ 2:53	+ 2.15	65	+ 3:20	+ 2.15	33	+ 2:48
+ 2.30	61	+ 3:31	+ 2.30	39	+ 3:09	+ 2.30	67	+ 3:37	+ 2.30	33	+ 3:03
+ 2.45	62	+ 3:47	+ 2.45	39	+ 3:24	+ 2.45	68	+ 3:53	+ 2.45	33	+ 3:18
+ 3.00	63	+ 4:03	+ 3.00	40	+ 3:40	+ 3.00	69	+ 4:09	+ 3.00	33	+ 3:33
+ 3.15	64	+ 4:19	+ 3.15	41	+ 3:56	+ 3.15	70	+ 4:25	+ 3.15	33	+ 3:48
+ 3.30	66	+ 4:36	+ 3.30	42	+ 4:12	+ 3.30	72	+ 4:42	+ 3.30	33	+ 4:03
+ 3.45	67	+ 4:52	+ 3.45	43	+ 4:28	+ 3.45	73	+ 4:58	+ 3.45	34	+ 4:19
+ 4.00	69	+ 5:09	+ 4.00	44	+ 4:44	+ 4.00	74	+ 5:14	+ 4.00	34	+ 4:34
+ 4.15	70	+ 5:25	+ 4.15	45	+ 5:00	+ 4.15	76	+ 5:31	+ 4.15	34	+ 4:49
+ 4.30	72	+ 5:42	+ 4.30	46	+ 5:16	+ 4.30	77	+ 5:47	+ 4.30	34	+ 5:04
+ 4.45	74	+ 5:59	+ 4.45	48	+ 5:33	+ 4.45	78	- 5:57	+ 4.45	34	+ 5:19
+ 5.00	75	- 5:45	+ 5.00	49	+ 5:49	+ 5.00	79	- 5:41	+ 5.00	34	+ 5:34
+ 5.15	77	- 5:28	+ 5.15	50	- 5:55	+ 5.15	82	- 5:23	+ 5.15	35	+ 5:50
+ 5.30	78	- 5:12	+ 5.30	52	- 5:38	+ 5.30	85	- 5:05	+ 5.30	35	- 5:55
+ 5.45	80	- 4:55	+ 5.45	53	- 5:22	+ 5.45	87	- 4:48	+ 5.45	35	- 5:40
+ 6.00	81	- 4:39	+ 6.00	55	- 5:05	+ 6.00	90	- 4:30	+ 6.00	35	- 5:25

Table I - Barrow Deep and Deben

Time to cover Sectors (in minutes) at 5.0 kts — All times relate to HW Sheerness — **Springs**

	I1			I2			I3			I4			I5			I6			I7			I8	
	Red Sand to Barrow No 10			Medway to North Oaze PHM			North Oaze PHM to Barrow No 10			Barrow No 10 to Barrow No 4			Barrow No 4 to Gunfleet Spit			Gunfleet Spit to Goldmer Gat			Goldmer Gat to Cork Sand			Cork Sand to Deben Landfall	
Time	Duration	Time at End of Sector	Time	Duration	Time at End of Sector	Time	Duration	Time at End of Sector	Time	Duration	Time at End of Sector	Time	Duration	Time at End of Sector	Time	Duration	Time at End of Sector	Time	Duration	Time at End of Sector	Time	Duration	Time at End of Sector
- 6.00	**93**	**- 4:27**	**- 6.00**	**82**	**- 4:38**	**- 6.00**	**114**	**- 4:06**	**- 6.00**	**135**	**- 3:45**	**- 6.00**	**102**	**- 4:18**	**- 6.00**	**65**	**- 4:55**	**- 6.00**	**110**	**- 4:10**	**- 6.00**	**39**	**- 5:21**
- 5.45	97	- 4:08	- 5.45	86	- 4:19	- 5.45	124	- 3:41	- 5.45	141	- 3:24	- 5.45	105	- 4:00	- 5.45	71	- 4:34	- 5.45	111	- 3:54	- 5.45	39	- 5:06
- 5.30	101	- 3:49	- 5.30	90	- 4:00	- 5.30	133	- 3:17	- 5.30	146	- 3:04	- 5.30	107	- 3:43	- 5.30	77	- 4:13	- 5.30	111	- 3:39	- 5.30	39	- 4:51
- 5.15	105	- 3:30	- 5.15	93	- 3:42	- 5.15	143	- 2:52	- 5.15	152	- 2:43	- 5.15	109	- 3:26	- 5.15	84	- 3:51	- 5.15	112	- 3:23	- 5.15	39	- 4:36
- 5.00	**109**	**- 3:11**	**- 5.00**	**97**	**- 3:23**	**- 5.00**	**152**	**- 2:28**	**- 5.00**	**158**	**- 2:22**	**- 5.00**	**112**	**- 3:08**	**- 5.00**	**90**	**- 3:30**	**- 5.00**	**112**	**- 3:08**	**- 5.00**	**39**	**- 4:21**
- 4.45	109	- 2:56	- 4.45	99	- 3:06	- 4.45	153	- 2:12	- 4.45	157	- 2:08	- 4.45	111	- 2:54	- 4.45	90	- 3:15	- 4.45	111	- 2:54	- 4.45	39	- 4:06
- 4.30	110	- 2:40	- 4.30	101	- 2:49	- 4.30	154	- 1:56	- 4.30	155	- 1:55	- 4.30	110	- 2:40	- 4.30	90	- 3:00	- 4.30	110	- 2:40	- 4.30	39	- 3:51
- 4.15	110	- 2:25	- 4.15	102	- 2:33	- 4.15	155	- 1:40	- 4.15	154	- 1:41	- 4.15	109	- 2:26	- 4.15	90	- 2:45	- 4.15	109	- 2:26	- 4.15	39	- 3:36
- 4.00	**110**	**- 2:10**	**- 4.00**	**104**	**- 2:16**	**- 4.00**	**155**	**- 1:25**	**- 4.00**	**153**	**- 1:27**	**- 4.00**	**107**	**- 2:13**	**- 4.00**	**90**	**- 2:30**	**- 4.00**	**107**	**- 2:13**	**- 4.00**	**38**	**- 3:22**
- 3.45	108	- 1:57	- 3.45	104	- 2:01	- 3.45	150	- 1:15	- 3.45	148	- 1:17	- 3.45	105	- 2:00	- 3.45	85	- 2:20	- 3.45	104	- 2:01	- 3.45	38	- 3:07
- 3.30	105	- 1:45	- 3.30	104	- 1:46	- 3.30	146	- 1:04	- 3.30	144	- 1:06	- 3.30	102	- 1:48	- 3.30	81	- 2:09	- 3.30	100	- 1:50	- 3.30	37	- 2:53
- 3.15	103	- 1:32	- 3.15	103	- 1:32	- 3.15	141	- 0:54	- 3.15	140	- 0:55	- 3.15	99	- 1:36	- 3.15	76	- 1:59	- 3.15	96	- 1:39	- 3.15	37	- 2:38
- 3.00	**101**	**- 1:19**	**- 3.00**	**103**	**- 1:17**	**- 3.00**	**136**	**- 0:44**	**- 3.00**	**135**	**- 0:45**	**- 3.00**	**97**	**- 1:23**	**- 3.00**	**72**	**- 1:48**	**- 3.00**	**93**	**- 1:27**	**- 3.00**	**36**	**- 2:24**
- 2.45	99	- 1:06	- 2.45	101	- 1:04	- 2.45	131	- 0:34	- 2.45	131	- 0:34	- 2.45	93	- 1:12	- 2.45	69	- 1:36	- 2.45	88	- 1:17	- 2.45	36	- 2:09
- 2.30	96	- 0:54	- 2.30	99	- 0:51	- 2.30	125	- 0:25	- 2.30	126	- 0:24	- 2.30	90	- 1:00	- 2.30	66	- 1:24	- 2.30	84	- 1:06	- 2.30	35	- 1:55
- 2.15	94	- 0:41	- 2.15	97	- 0:38	- 2.15	120	- 0:15	- 2.15	122	- 0:13	- 2.15	87	- 0:48	- 2.15	63	- 1:12	- 2.15	80	- 0:55	- 2.15	34	- 1:41
- 2.00	**92**	**- 0:28**	**- 2.00**	**95**	**- 0:25**	**- 2.00**	**115**	**- 0:05**	**- 2.00**	**117**	**- 0:03**	**- 2.00**	**84**	**- 0:36**	**- 2.00**	**60**	**- 1:00**	**- 2.00**	**76**	**- 0:44**	**- 2.00**	**34**	**- 1:26**
- 1.45	89	- 0:16	- 1.45	92	- 0:13	- 1.45	109	+ 0:04	- 1.45	113	+ 0:08	- 1.45	81	- 0:24	- 1.45	57	- 0:48	- 1.45	73	- 0:32	- 1.45	34	- 1:11
- 1.30	87	- 0:03	- 1.30	89	- 0:01	- 1.30	104	+ 0:14	- 1.30	109	+ 0:19	- 1.30	77	- 0:13	- 1.30	54	- 0:36	- 1.30	69	- 0:21	- 1.30	33	- 0:57
- 1.15	84	+ 0:09	- 1.15	86	+ 0:11	- 1.15	98	+ 0:23	- 1.15	104	+ 0:29	- 1.15	74	- 0:01	- 1.15	52	- 0:23	- 1.15	66	- 0:09	- 1.15	33	- 0:42
- 1.00	**82**	**+ 0:22**	**- 1.00**	**83**	**+ 0:23**	**- 1.00**	**93**	**+ 0:33**	**- 1.00**	**100**	**+ 0:40**	**- 1.00**	**71**	**+ 0:11**	**- 1.00**	**49**	**- 0:11**	**- 1.00**	**63**	**+ 0:03**	**- 1.00**	**33**	**- 0:27**
- 0.45	78	+ 0:33	- 0.45	81	+ 0:36	- 0.45	88	+ 0:43	- 0.45	96	+ 0:51	- 0.45	68	+ 0:23	- 0.45	47	+ 0:02	- 0.45	61	+ 0:16	- 0.45	33	- 0:12
- 0.30	75	+ 0:45	- 0.30	78	+ 0:48	- 0.30	82	+ 0:52	- 0.30	92	+ 1:02	- 0.30	65	+ 0:35	- 0.30	45	+ 0:15	- 0.30	59	+ 0:29	- 0.30	32	+ 0:02
- 0.15	72	+ 0:57	- 0.15	75	+ 1:00	- 0.15	77	+ 1:02	- 0.15	88	+ 1:13	- 0.15	62	+ 0:47	- 0.15	43	+ 0:28	- 0.15	57	+ 0:42	- 0.15	32	+ 0:17
HW	**69**	**+ 1:09**	**HW**	**72**	**+ 1:12**	**HW**	**71**	**+ 1:11**	**HW**	**83**	**+ 1:23**	**HW**	**60**	**+ 1:00**	**HW**	**40**	**+ 0:40**	**HW**	**55**	**+ 0:55**	**HW**	**32**	**+ 0:32**
+ 0.15	66	+ 1:21	+ 0.15	69	+ 1:24	+ 0.15	67	+ 1:22	+ 0.15	80	+ 1:35	+ 0.15	58	+ 1:13	+ 0.15	39	+ 0:54	+ 0.15	55	+ 1:10	+ 0.15	32	+ 0:47
+ 0.30	64	+ 1:34	+ 0.30	66	+ 1:36	+ 0.30	64	+ 1:34	+ 0.30	77	+ 1:47	+ 0.30	57	+ 1:27	+ 0.30	38	+ 1:08	+ 0.30	55	+ 1:25	+ 0.30	32	+ 1:02
+ 0.45	61	+ 1:46	+ 0.45	63	+ 1:48	+ 0.45	60	+ 1:45	+ 0.45	73	+ 1:58	+ 0.45	55	+ 1:40	+ 0.45	37	+ 1:22	+ 0.45	54	+ 1:39	+ 0.45	32	+ 1:17
+ 1.00	**59**	**+ 1:59**	**+ 1.00**	**60**	**+ 2:00**	**+ 1.00**	**56**	**+ 1:56**	**+ 1.00**	**70**	**+ 2:10**	**+ 1.00**	**54**	**+ 1:54**	**+ 1.00**	**36**	**+ 1:36**	**+ 1.00**	**54**	**+ 1:54**	**+ 1.00**	**33**	**+ 1:33**
+ 1.15	58	+ 2:13	+ 1.15	59	+ 2:14	+ 1.15	55	+ 2:10	+ 1.15	70	+ 2:25	+ 1.15	54	+ 2:09	+ 1.15	35	+ 1:50	+ 1.15	55	+ 2:10	+ 1.15	33	+ 1:48
+ 1.30	58	+ 2:28	+ 1.30	57	+ 2:27	+ 1.30	54	+ 2:24	+ 1.30	69	+ 2:39	+ 1.30	54	+ 2:24	+ 1.30	35	+ 2:05	+ 1.30	56	+ 2:26	+ 1.30	33	+ 2:03
+ 1.45	57	+ 2:42	+ 1.45	56	+ 2:41	+ 1.45	53	+ 2:38	+ 1.45	69	+ 2:54	+ 1.45	54	+ 2:39	+ 1.45	34	+ 2:19	+ 1.45	57	+ 2:42	+ 1.45	33	+ 2:18
+ 2.00	**56**	**+ 2:56**	**+ 2.00**	**54**	**+ 2:54**	**+ 2.00**	**52**	**+ 2:52**	**+ 2.00**	**68**	**+ 3:08**	**+ 2.00**	**54**	**+ 2:54**	**+ 2.00**	**34**	**+ 2:34**	**+ 2.00**	**59**	**+ 2:59**	**+ 2.00**	**33**	**+ 2:33**
+ 2.15	57	+ 3:12	+ 2.15	54	+ 3:09	+ 2.15	53	+ 3:08	+ 2.15	69	+ 3:24	+ 2.15	55	+ 3:10	+ 2.15	35	+ 2:50	+ 2.15	60	+ 3:15	+ 2.15	33	+ 2:48
+ 2.30	58	+ 3:28	+ 2.30	55	+ 3:25	+ 2.30	54	+ 3:24	+ 2.30	71	+ 3:41	+ 2.30	56	+ 3:26	+ 2.30	35	+ 3:05	+ 2.30	62	+ 3:32	+ 2.30	33	+ 3:03
+ 2.45	59	+ 3:44	+ 2.45	55	+ 3:40	+ 2.45	55	+ 3:40	+ 2.45	72	+ 3:57	+ 2.45	57	+ 3:42	+ 2.45	35	+ 3:20	+ 2.45	64	+ 3:49	+ 2.45	33	+ 3:18
+ 3.00	**59**	**+ 3:59**	**+ 3.00**	**55**	**+ 3:55**	**+ 3.00**	**55**	**+ 3:55**	**+ 3.00**	**73**	**+ 4:13**	**+ 3.00**	**58**	**+ 3:58**	**+ 3.00**	**36**	**+ 3:36**	**+ 3.00**	**66**	**+ 4:06**	**+ 3.00**	**33**	**+ 3:33**
+ 3.15	61	+ 4:16	+ 3.15	56	+ 4:11	+ 3.15	58	+ 4:13	+ 3.15	75	+ 4:30	+ 3.15	60	+ 4:15	+ 3.15	37	+ 3:52	+ 3.15	68	+ 4:23	+ 3.15	33	+ 3:48
+ 3.30	62	+ 4:32	+ 3.30	58	+ 4:28	+ 3.30	60	+ 4:30	+ 3.30	77	+ 4:47	+ 3.30	62	+ 4:32	+ 3.30	38	+ 4:08	+ 3.30	70	+ 4:40	+ 3.30	33	+ 4:03
+ 3.45	63	+ 4:48	+ 3.45	59	+ 4:44	+ 3.45	62	+ 4:47	+ 3.45	80	+ 5:05	+ 3.45	64	+ 4:49	+ 3.45	39	+ 4:24	+ 3.45	71	+ 4:56	+ 3.45	33	+ 4:18
+ 4.00	**64**	**+ 5:04**	**+ 4.00**	**60**	**+ 5:00**	**+ 4.00**	**64**	**+ 5:04**	**+ 4.00**	**82**	**+ 5:22**	**+ 4.00**	**65**	**+ 5:05**	**+ 4.00**	**40**	**+ 4:40**	**+ 4.00**	**73**	**+ 5:13**	**+ 4.00**	**33**	**+ 4:33**
+ 4.15	66	+ 5:21	+ 4.15	62	+ 5:17	+ 4.15	67	+ 5:22	+ 4.15	85	+ 5:40	+ 4.15	68	+ 5:23	+ 4.15	42	+ 4:57	+ 4.15	75	+ 5:30	+ 4.15	34	+ 4:49
+ 4.30	68	+ 5:38	+ 4.30	64	+ 5:34	+ 4.30	70	+ 5:40	+ 4.30	89	+ 5:59	+ 4.30	70	+ 5:40	+ 4.30	44	+ 5:14	+ 4.30	77	+ 5:47	+ 4.30	34	+ 5:04
+ 4.45	70	+ 5:55	+ 4.45	66	+ 5:51	+ 4.45	73	+ 5:58	+ 4.45	92	- 5:43	+ 4.45	73	+ 5:58	+ 4.45	46	+ 5:31	+ 4.45	79	- 5:56	+ 4.45	34	+ 5:19
+ 5.00	**72**	**- 5:48**	**+ 5.00**	**67**	**- 5:53**	**+ 5.00**	**75**	**- 5:45**	**+ 5.00**	**95**	**- 5:25**	**+ 5.00**	**75**	**- 5:45**	**+ 5.00**	**48**	**+ 5:48**	**+ 5.00**	**80**	**- 5:40**	**+ 5.00**	**34**	**+ 5:34**
+ 5.15	73	- 5:32	+ 5.15	69	- 5:36	+ 5.15	78	- 5:27	+ 5.15	99	- 5:06	+ 5.15	78	- 5:27	+ 5.15	50	- 5:55	+ 5.15	85	- 5:20	+ 5.15	35	+ 5:50
+ 5.30	75	- 5:15	+ 5.30	70	- 5:20	+ 5.30	80	- 5:10	+ 5.30	104	- 4:46	+ 5.30	80	- 5:10	+ 5.30	53	- 5:37	+ 5.30	89	- 5:01	+ 5.30	35	- 5:55
+ 5.45	77	- 4:58	+ 5.45	71	- 5:04	+ 5.45	82	- 4:53	+ 5.45	108	- 4:27	+ 5.45	82	- 4:53	+ 5.45	55	- 5:20	+ 5.45	93	- 4:42	+ 5.45	35	- 5:40
+ 6.00	**78**	**- 4:42**	**+ 6.00**	**72**	**- 4:48**	**+ 6.00**	**85**	**- 4:35**	**+ 6.00**	**112**	**- 4:08**	**+ 6.00**	**84**	**- 4:36**	**+ 6.00**	**57**	**- 5:03**	**+ 6.00**	**98**	**- 4:22**	**+ 6.00**	**36**	**- 5:24**

NORTH BOUND

Table I - Barrow Deep and Deben

Neaps — All times relate to HW Sheerness — **Time to cover Sectors (in minutes) at 6.0 Kts**

NORTH BOUND

Time	I1 Red Sand to Barrow No 10 Duration	I1 Time at End of Sector	Time	I2 Medway to North Oaze PHM Duration	I2 Time at End of Sector	Time	I3 North Oaze PHM to Barrow No 10 Duration	I3 Time at End of Sector	Time	I4 Barrow No 10 to Barrow No 4 Duration	I4 Time at End of Sector
- 6.00	69	- 4:51	- 6.00	65	- 4:55	- 6.00	80	- 4:40	- 6.00	98	- 4:22
- 5.45	71	- 4:34	- 5.45	66	- 4:39	- 5.45	84	- 4:21	- 5.45	100	- 4:05
- 5.30	72	- 4:18	- 5.30	68	- 4:22	- 5.30	88	- 4:02	- 5.30	103	- 3:47
- 5.15	74	- 4:01	- 5.15	69	- 4:06	- 5.15	93	- 3:42	- 5.15	105	- 3:30
- 5.00	75	- 3:45	- 5.00	70	- 3:50	- 5.00	97	- 3:23	- 5.00	107	- 3:13
- 4.45	75	- 3:30	- 4.45	71	- 3:34	- 4.45	98	- 3:07	- 4.45	108	- 2:57
- 4.30	76	- 3:14	- 4.30	72	- 3:18	- 4.30	99	- 2:51	- 4.30	108	- 2:42
- 4.15	76	- 2:59	- 4.15	73	- 3:02	- 4.15	100	- 2:35	- 4.15	108	- 2:27
- 4.00	77	- 2:43	- 4.00	73	- 2:47	- 4.00	101	- 2:19	- 4.00	108	- 2:12
- 3.45	76	- 2:29	- 3.45	73	- 2:32	- 3.45	100	- 2:05	- 3.45	107	- 1:58
- 3.30	75	- 2:15	- 3.30	73	- 2:17	- 3.30	100	- 1:50	- 3.30	106	- 1:44
- 3.15	74	- 2:01	- 3.15	73	- 2:02	- 3.15	99	- 1:36	- 3.15	105	- 1:30
- 3.00	74	- 1:46	- 3.00	73	- 1:47	- 3.00	99	- 1:21	- 3.00	104	- 1:16
- 2.45	73	- 1:32	- 2.45	73	- 1:32	- 2.45	97	- 1:08	- 2.45	102	- 1:03
- 2.30	72	- 1:18	- 2.30	72	- 1:18	- 2.30	95	- 0:55	- 2.30	100	- 0:50
- 2.15	71	- 1:04	- 2.15	71	- 1:04	- 2.15	93	- 0:42	- 2.15	98	- 0:37
- 2.00	70	- 0:50	- 2.00	71	- 0:49	- 2.00	91	- 0:29	- 2.00	96	- 0:24
- 1.45	69	- 0:36	- 1.45	70	- 0:35	- 1.45	87	- 0:18	- 1.45	93	- 0:12
- 1.30	68	- 0:22	- 1.30	69	- 0:21	- 1.30	83	- 0:07	- 1.30	91	+ 0:01
- 1.15	68	- 0:07	- 1.15	68	- 0:07	- 1.15	80	+ 0:05	- 1.15	88	+ 0:13
- 1.00	67	+ 0:07	- 1.00	67	+ 0:07	- 1.00	76	+ 0:16	- 1.00	86	+ 0:26
- 0.45	65	+ 0:20	- 0.45	65	+ 0:20	- 0.45	74	+ 0:29	- 0.45	83	+ 0:38
- 0.30	64	+ 0:34	- 0.30	64	+ 0:34	- 0.30	71	+ 0:41	- 0.30	81	+ 0:51
- 0.15	62	+ 0:47	- 0.15	63	+ 0:48	- 0.15	69	+ 0:54	- 0.15	79	+ 1:04
HW	61	+ 1:01	HW	62	+ 1:02	HW	66	+ 1:06	HW	77	+ 1:17
+ 0.15	59	+ 1:14	+ 0.15	60	+ 1:15	+ 0.15	64	+ 1:19	+ 0.15	75	+ 1:30
+ 0.30	58	+ 1:28	+ 0.30	59	+ 1:29	+ 0.30	62	+ 1:32	+ 0.30	73	+ 1:43
+ 0.45	57	+ 1:42	+ 0.45	58	+ 1:43	+ 0.45	60	+ 1:45	+ 0.45	71	+ 1:56
+ 1.00	55	+ 1:55	+ 1.00	56	+ 1:56	+ 1.00	59	+ 1:59	+ 1.00	69	+ 2:09
+ 1.15	55	+ 2:10	+ 1.15	55	+ 2:10	+ 1.15	58	+ 2:13	+ 1.15	69	+ 2:24
+ 1.30	55	+ 2:25	+ 1.30	55	+ 2:25	+ 1.30	57	+ 2:27	+ 1.30	69	+ 2:39
+ 1.45	54	+ 2:39	+ 1.45	54	+ 2:39	+ 1.45	57	+ 2:42	+ 1.45	68	+ 2:53
+ 2.00	54	+ 2:54	+ 2.00	53	+ 2:53	+ 2.00	56	+ 2:56	+ 2.00	68	+ 3:08
+ 2.15	54	+ 3:09	+ 2.15	53	+ 3:08	+ 2.15	56	+ 3:11	+ 2.15	68	+ 3:23
+ 2.30	55	+ 3:25	+ 2.30	53	+ 3:23	+ 2.30	57	+ 3:27	+ 2.30	69	+ 3:39
+ 2.45	55	+ 3:40	+ 2.45	53	+ 3:38	+ 2.45	57	+ 3:42	+ 2.45	70	+ 3:55
+ 3.00	55	+ 3:55	+ 3.00	53	+ 3:53	+ 3.00	57	+ 3:57	+ 3.00	70	+ 4:10
+ 3.15	56	+ 4:11	+ 3.15	53	+ 4:08	+ 3.15	58	+ 4:13	+ 3.15	71	+ 4:26
+ 3.30	57	+ 4:27	+ 3.30	54	+ 4:24	+ 3.30	59	+ 4:29	+ 3.30	72	+ 4:42
+ 3.45	57	+ 4:42	+ 3.45	55	+ 4:40	+ 3.45	60	+ 4:45	+ 3.45	74	+ 4:59
+ 4.00	58	+ 4:58	+ 4.00	55	+ 4:55	+ 4.00	61	+ 5:01	+ 4.00	75	+ 5:15
+ 4.15	59	+ 5:14	+ 4.15	56	+ 5:11	+ 4.15	62	+ 5:17	+ 4.15	76	+ 5:31
+ 4.30	59	+ 5:29	+ 4.30	57	+ 5:27	+ 4.30	64	+ 5:34	+ 4.30	78	+ 5:48
+ 4.45	60	+ 5:45	+ 4.45	58	+ 5:43	+ 4.45	65	+ 5:50	+ 4.45	79	- 5:56
+ 5.00	61	- 5:59	+ 5.00	59	+ 5:59	+ 5.00	67	- 5:53	+ 5.00	81	- 5:39
+ 5.15	62	- 5:43	+ 5.15	59	- 5:46	+ 5.15	68	- 5:37	+ 5.15	82	- 5:23
+ 5.30	63	- 5:27	+ 5.30	60	- 5:30	+ 5.30	69	- 5:21	+ 5.30	83	- 5:07
+ 5.45	64	- 5:11	+ 5.45	60	- 5:15	+ 5.45	70	- 5:05	+ 5.45	85	- 4:50
+ 6.00	64	- 4:56	+ 6.00	61	- 4:59	+ 6.00	71	- 4:49	+ 6.00	86	- 4:34

Time	I5 Barrow No 4 to Gunfleet Spit Duration	I5 Time at End of Sector	Time	I6 Gunfleet Spit to Goldmer Gat Duration	I6 Time at End of Sector	Time	I7 Goldmer Gat to Cork Sand Duration	I7 Time at End of Sector	Time	I8 Cork Sand to Deben Landfall Duration	I8 Time at End of Sector
- 6.00	71	- 4:49	- 6.00	48	- 5:12	- 6.00	75	- 4:45	- 6.00	30	- 5:30
- 5.45	73	- 4:32	- 5.45	49	- 4:56	- 5.45	75	- 4:30	- 5.45	30	- 5:15
- 5.30	74	- 4:16	- 5.30	50	- 4:40	- 5.30	76	- 4:14	- 5.30	30	- 5:00
- 5.15	75	- 4:00	- 5.15	52	- 4:23	- 5.15	76	- 3:59	- 5.15	30	- 4:45
- 5.00	76	- 3:44	- 5.00	53	- 4:07	- 5.00	76	- 3:44	- 5.00	30	- 4:30
- 4.45	76	- 3:29	- 4.45	53	- 3:52	- 4.45	76	- 3:29	- 4.45	30	- 4:15
- 4.30	76	- 3:14	- 4.30	53	- 3:37	- 4.30	76	- 3:14	- 4.30	30	- 4:00
- 4.15	76	- 2:59	- 4.15	54	- 3:21	- 4.15	76	- 2:59	- 4.15	30	- 3:45
- 4.00	76	- 2:44	- 4.00	54	- 3:06	- 4.00	76	- 2:44	- 4.00	30	- 3:30
- 3.45	75	- 2:30	- 3.45	53	- 2:52	- 3.45	75	- 2:30	- 3.45	30	- 3:15
- 3.30	74	- 2:16	- 3.30	53	- 2:37	- 3.30	73	- 2:17	- 3.30	30	- 3:00
- 3.15	73	- 2:02	- 3.15	52	- 2:23	- 3.15	72	- 2:03	- 3.15	30	- 2:45
- 3.00	72	- 1:48	- 3.00	51	- 2:09	- 3.00	71	- 1:49	- 3.00	29	- 2:31
- 2.45	71	- 1:34	- 2.45	50	- 1:55	- 2.45	69	- 1:36	- 2.45	29	- 2:16
- 2.30	69	- 1:21	- 2.30	49	- 1:41	- 2.30	67	- 1:23	- 2.30	29	- 2:01
- 2.15	68	- 1:07	- 2.15	48	- 1:27	- 2.15	66	- 1:09	- 2.15	29	- 1:46
- 2.00	67	- 0:53	- 2.00	47	- 1:13	- 2.00	64	- 0:56	- 2.00	28	- 1:32
- 1.45	66	- 0:39	- 1.45	45	- 1:00	- 1.45	62	- 0:43	- 1.45	28	- 1:17
- 1.30	64	- 0:26	- 1.30	44	- 0:46	- 1.30	61	- 0:29	- 1.30	28	- 1:02
- 1.15	63	- 0:12	- 1.15	43	- 0:32	- 1.15	59	- 0:16	- 1.15	28	- 0:47
- 1.00	61	+ 0:01	- 1.00	42	- 0:18	- 1.00	57	- 0:03	- 1.00	28	- 0:32
- 0.45	60	+ 0:15	- 0.45	41	- 0:04	- 0.45	56	+ 0:11	- 0.45	28	- 0:17
- 0.30	58	+ 0:28	- 0.30	39	+ 0:09	- 0.30	55	+ 0:25	- 0.30	27	- 0:03
- 0.15	57	+ 0:42	- 0.15	38	+ 0:23	- 0.15	54	+ 0:39	- 0.15	27	+ 0:12
HW	55	+ 0:55	HW	37	+ 0:37	HW	53	+ 0:53	HW	27	+ 0:27
+ 0.15	55	+ 1:10	+ 0.15	37	+ 0:52	+ 0.15	53	+ 1:08	+ 0.15	27	+ 0:42
+ 0.30	54	+ 1:24	+ 0.30	36	+ 1:06	+ 0.30	53	+ 1:23	+ 0.30	27	+ 0:57
+ 0.45	53	+ 1:38	+ 0.45	35	+ 1:20	+ 0.45	53	+ 1:38	+ 0.45	27	+ 1:12
+ 1.00	52	+ 1:52	+ 1.00	34	+ 1:34	+ 1.00	52	+ 1:52	+ 1.00	27	+ 1:27
+ 1.15	52	+ 2:07	+ 1.15	34	+ 1:49	+ 1.15	53	+ 2:08	+ 1.15	27	+ 1:42
+ 1.30	52	+ 2:22	+ 1.30	34	+ 2:04	+ 1.30	54	+ 2:24	+ 1.30	27	+ 1:57
+ 1.45	52	+ 2:37	+ 1.45	33	+ 2:18	+ 1.45	54	+ 2:39	+ 1.45	27	+ 2:12
+ 2.00	52	+ 2:52	+ 2.00	33	+ 2:33	+ 2.00	55	+ 2:55	+ 2.00	28	+ 2:28
+ 2.15	52	+ 3:07	+ 2.15	33	+ 2:48	+ 2.15	56	+ 3:11	+ 2.15	28	+ 2:43
+ 2.30	53	+ 3:23	+ 2.30	34	+ 3:04	+ 2.30	56	+ 3:26	+ 2.30	28	+ 2:58
+ 2.45	53	+ 3:38	+ 2.45	34	+ 3:19	+ 2.45	57	+ 3:42	+ 2.45	28	+ 3:13
+ 3.00	54	+ 3:54	+ 3.00	34	+ 3:34	+ 3.00	58	+ 3:58	+ 3.00	28	+ 3:28
+ 3.15	55	+ 4:10	+ 3.15	35	+ 3:50	+ 3.15	59	+ 4:14	+ 3.15	28	+ 3:43
+ 3.30	56	+ 4:26	+ 3.30	35	+ 4:05	+ 3.30	60	+ 4:30	+ 3.30	28	+ 3:58
+ 3.45	57	+ 4:42	+ 3.45	36	+ 4:21	+ 3.45	61	+ 4:46	+ 3.45	28	+ 4:13
+ 4.00	58	+ 4:58	+ 4.00	37	+ 4:37	+ 4.00	62	+ 5:02	+ 4.00	28	+ 4:28
+ 4.15	59	+ 5:14	+ 4.15	38	+ 4:53	+ 4.15	63	+ 5:18	+ 4.15	28	+ 4:43
+ 4.30	60	+ 5:30	+ 4.30	39	+ 5:09	+ 4.30	64	+ 5:34	+ 4.30	28	+ 4:58
+ 4.45	61	+ 5:46	+ 4.45	39	+ 5:24	+ 4.45	65	+ 5:50	+ 4.45	28	+ 5:13
+ 5.00	62	- 5:58	+ 5.00	40	+ 5:40	+ 5.00	65	- 5:55	+ 5.00	28	+ 5:28
+ 5.15	63	- 5:42	+ 5.15	41	+ 5:56	+ 5.15	67	- 5:38	+ 5.15	29	+ 5:44
+ 5.30	64	- 5:26	+ 5.30	42	- 5:48	+ 5.30	68	- 5:22	+ 5.30	29	+ 5:59
+ 5.45	65	- 5:10	+ 5.45	44	- 5:31	+ 5.45	69	- 5:06	+ 5.45	29	- 5:46
+ 6.00	66	- 4:54	+ 6.00	45	- 5:15	+ 6.00	71	- 4:49	+ 6.00	29	- 5:31

Table I - Barrow Deep and Deben

Time to cover Sectors (in minutes) at 6.0 kts — All times relate to HW Sheerness — **Springs**

	I1			I2			I3			I4			I5			I6			I7			I8	
	Red Sand to Barrow No 10			Medway to North Oaze PHM			North Oaze PHM to Barrow No 10			Barrow No 10 to Barrow No 4			Barrow No 4 to Gunfleet Spit			Gunfleet Spit to Goldmer Gat			Goldmer Gat to Cork Sand			Cork Sand to Deben Landfall	
Time	Duration	Time at End of Sector	Time	Duration	Time at End of Sector	Time	Duration	Time at End of Sector	Time	Duration	Time at End of Sector	Time	Duration	Time at End of Sector	Time	Duration	Time at End of Sector	Time	Duration	Time at End of Sector	Time	Duration	Time at End of Sector
- 6.00	**72**	**- 4:48**	**- 6.00**	**66**	**- 4:54**	**- 6.00**	**84**	**- 4:36**	**- 6.00**	**106**	**- 4:14**	**- 6.00**	**76**	**- 4:44**	**- 6.00**	**51**	**- 5:09**	**- 6.00**	**82**	**- 4:38**	**- 6.00**	**31**	**- 5:29**
- 5.45	74	- 4:31	- 5.45	68	- 4:37	- 5.45	90	- 4:15	- 5.45	109	- 3:56	- 5.45	78	- 4:27	- 5.45	53	- 4:52	- 5.45	83	- 4:22	- 5.45	31	- 5:14
- 5.30	76	- 4:14	- 5.30	70	- 4:20	- 5.30	96	- 3:54	- 5.30	112	- 3:38	- 5.30	80	- 4:10	- 5.30	55	- 4:35	- 5.30	83	- 4:07	- 5.30	32	- 4:58
- 5.15	79	- 3:56	- 5.15	72	- 4:03	- 5.15	102	- 3:33	- 5.15	115	- 3:20	- 5.15	81	- 3:54	- 5.15	57	- 4:18	- 5.15	84	- 3:51	- 5.15	32	- 4:43
- 5.00	**81**	**- 3:39**	**- 5.00**	**75**	**- 3:45**	**- 5.00**	**109**	**- 3:11**	**- 5.00**	**118**	**- 3:02**	**- 5.00**	**83**	**- 3:37**	**- 5.00**	**59**	**- 4:01**	**- 5.00**	**84**	**- 3:36**	**- 5.00**	**32**	**- 4:28**
- 4.45	82	- 3:23	- 4.45	76	- 3:29	- 4.45	110	- 2:55	- 4.45	118	- 2:47	- 4.45	83	- 3:22	- 4.45	60	- 3:45	- 4.45	84	- 3:21	- 4.45	32	- 4:13
- 4.30	82	- 3:08	- 4.30	77	- 3:13	- 4.30	111	- 2:39	- 4.30	118	- 2:32	- 4.30	83	- 3:07	- 4.30	61	- 3:29	- 4.30	84	- 3:06	- 4.30	32	- 3:58
- 4.15	83	- 2:52	- 4.15	78	- 2:57	- 4.15	112	- 2:23	- 4.15	118	- 2:17	- 4.15	83	- 2:52	- 4.15	61	- 3:14	- 4.15	83	- 2:52	- 4.15	31	- 3:44
- 4.00	**84**	**- 2:36**	**- 4.00**	**79**	**- 2:41**	**- 4.00**	**113**	**- 2:07**	**- 4.00**	**118**	**- 2:02**	**- 4.00**	**82**	**- 2:38**	**- 4.00**	**62**	**- 2:58**	**- 4.00**	**83**	**- 2:37**	**- 4.00**	**31**	**- 3:29**
- 3.45	83	- 2:22	- 3.45	79	- 2:26	- 3.45	112	- 1:53	- 3.45	116	- 1:49	- 3.45	81	- 2:24	- 3.45	61	- 2:44	- 3.45	81	- 2:24	- 3.45	31	- 3:14
- 3.30	82	- 2:08	- 3.30	79	- 2:11	- 3.30	111	- 1:39	- 3.30	114	- 1:36	- 3.30	80	- 2:10	- 3.30	60	- 2:30	- 3.30	79	- 2:11	- 3.30	31	- 2:59
- 3.15	80	- 1:55	- 3.15	79	- 1:56	- 3.15	110	- 1:25	- 3.15	112	- 1:23	- 3.15	78	- 1:57	- 3.15	58	- 2:17	- 3.15	77	- 1:58	- 3.15	30	- 2:45
- 3.00	**79**	**- 1:41**	**- 3.00**	**79**	**- 1:41**	**- 3.00**	**109**	**- 1:11**	**- 3.00**	**110**	**- 1:10**	**- 3.00**	**77**	**- 1:43**	**- 3.00**	**57**	**- 2:03**	**- 3.00**	**75**	**- 1:45**	**- 3.00**	**30**	**- 2:30**
- 2.45	78	- 1:27	- 2.45	78	- 1:27	- 2.45	105	- 1:00	- 2.45	107	- 0:58	- 2.45	75	- 1:30	- 2.45	55	- 1:50	- 2.45	73	- 1:32	- 2.45	30	- 2:15
- 2.30	77	- 1:13	- 2.30	77	- 1:13	- 2.30	102	- 0:48	- 2.30	104	- 0:46	- 2.30	73	- 1:17	- 2.30	53	- 1:37	- 2.30	70	- 1:20	- 2.30	29	- 2:01
- 2.15	75	- 1:00	- 2.15	76	- 0:59	- 2.15	99	- 0:36	- 2.15	101	- 0:34	- 2.15	71	- 1:04	- 2.15	51	- 1:24	- 2.15	67	- 1:08	- 2.15	29	- 1:46
- 2.00	**74**	**- 0:46**	**- 2.00**	**75**	**- 0:45**	**- 2.00**	**96**	**- 0:24**	**- 2.00**	**98**	**- 0:22**	**- 2.00**	**69**	**- 0:51**	**- 2.00**	**49**	**- 1:11**	**- 2.00**	**64**	**- 0:56**	**- 2.00**	**28**	**- 1:32**
- 1.45	72	- 0:33	- 1.45	74	- 0:31	- 1.45	91	- 0:14	- 1.45	95	- 0:10	- 1.45	67	- 0:38	- 1.45	47	- 0:58	- 1.45	62	- 0:43	- 1.45	28	- 1:17
- 1.30	71	- 0:19	- 1.30	72	- 0:18	- 1.30	87	- 0:03	- 1.30	92	+ 0:02	- 1.30	65	- 0:25	- 1.30	46	- 0:44	- 1.30	59	- 0:31	- 1.30	28	- 1:02
- 1.15	69	- 0:06	- 1.15	70	- 0:05	- 1.15	83	+ 0:08	- 1.15	89	+ 0:14	- 1.15	63	- 0:12	- 1.15	44	- 0:31	- 1.15	57	- 0:18	- 1.15	28	- 0:47
- 1.00	**68**	**+ 0:08**	**- 1.00**	**69**	**+ 0:09**	**- 1.00**	**79**	**+ 0:19**	**- 1.00**	**86**	**+ 0:26**	**- 1.00**	**60**	**HW**	**- 1.00**	**42**	**- 0:18**	**- 1.00**	**55**	**- 0:05**	**- 1.00**	**27**	**- 0:33**
- 0.45	66	+ 0:21	- 0.45	67	+ 0:22	- 0.45	75	+ 0:30	- 0.45	83	+ 0:38	- 0.45	58	+ 0:13	- 0.45	40	- 0:05	- 0.45	53	+ 0:08	- 0.45	27	- 0:18
- 0.30	63	+ 0:33	- 0.30	65	+ 0:35	- 0.30	71	+ 0:41	- 0.30	79	+ 0:49	- 0.30	56	+ 0:26	- 0.30	39	+ 0:09	- 0.30	52	+ 0:22	- 0.30	27	- 0:03
- 0.15	61	+ 0:46	- 0.15	63	+ 0:48	- 0.15	67	+ 0:52	- 0.15	76	+ 1:01	- 0.15	54	+ 0:39	- 0.15	37	+ 0:22	- 0.15	51	+ 0:36	- 0.15	27	+ 0:12
HW	**59**	**+ 0:59**	**HW**	**61**	**+ 1:01**	**HW**	**63**	**+ 1:03**	**HW**	**73**	**+ 1:13**	**HW**	**52**	**+ 0:52**	**HW**	**36**	**+ 0:36**	**HW**	**49**	**+ 0:49**	**HW**	**27**	**+ 0:27**
+ 0.15	57	+ 1:12	+ 0.15	59	+ 1:14	+ 0.15	60	+ 1:15	+ 0.15	70	+ 1:25	+ 0.15	51	+ 1:06	+ 0.15	35	+ 0:50	+ 0.15	49	+ 1:04	+ 0.15	27	+ 0:42
+ 0.30	55	+ 1:25	+ 0.30	57	+ 1:27	+ 0.30	57	+ 1:27	+ 0.30	68	+ 1:38	+ 0.30	50	+ 1:20	+ 0.30	34	+ 1:04	+ 0.30	49	+ 1:19	+ 0.30	27	+ 0:57
+ 0.45	53	+ 1:38	+ 0.45	55	+ 1:40	+ 0.45	54	+ 1:39	+ 0.45	66	+ 1:51	+ 0.45	49	+ 1:34	+ 0.45	33	+ 1:18	+ 0.45	48	+ 1:33	+ 0.45	27	+ 1:12
+ 1.00	**52**	**+ 1:52**	**+ 1.00**	**53**	**+ 1:53**	**+ 1.00**	**52**	**+ 1:52**	**+ 1.00**	**63**	**+ 2:03**	**+ 1.00**	**48**	**+ 1:48**	**+ 1.00**	**32**	**+ 1:32**	**+ 1.00**	**48**	**+ 1:48**	**+ 1.00**	**27**	**+ 1:27**
+ 1.15	51	+ 2:06	+ 1.15	52	+ 2:07	+ 1.15	51	+ 2:06	+ 1.15	63	+ 2:18	+ 1.15	48	+ 2:03	+ 1.15	31	+ 1:46	+ 1.15	49	+ 2:04	+ 1.15	27	+ 1:42
+ 1.30	51	+ 2:21	+ 1.30	51	+ 2:21	+ 1.30	50	+ 2:20	+ 1.30	62	+ 2:32	+ 1.30	48	+ 2:18	+ 1.30	31	+ 2:01	+ 1.30	49	+ 2:19	+ 1.30	27	+ 1:57
+ 1.45	50	+ 2:35	+ 1.45	49	+ 2:34	+ 1.45	49	+ 2:34	+ 1.45	62	+ 2:47	+ 1.45	48	+ 2:33	+ 1.45	31	+ 2:16	+ 1.45	50	+ 2:35	+ 1.45	27	+ 2:12
+ 2.00	**49**	**+ 2:49**	**+ 2.00**	**48**	**+ 2:48**	**+ 2.00**	**48**	**+ 2:48**	**+ 2.00**	**61**	**+ 3:01**	**+ 2.00**	**47**	**+ 2:47**	**+ 2.00**	**30**	**+ 2:30**	**+ 2.00**	**51**	**+ 2:51**	**+ 2.00**	**27**	**+ 2:27**
+ 2.15	50	+ 3:05	+ 2.15	48	+ 3:03	+ 2.15	49	+ 3:04	+ 2.15	62	+ 3:17	+ 2.15	48	+ 3:03	+ 2.15	30	+ 2:45	+ 2.15	52	+ 3:07	+ 2.15	27	+ 2:42
+ 2.30	50	+ 3:20	+ 2.30	48	+ 3:18	+ 2.30	49	+ 3:19	+ 2.30	63	+ 3:33	+ 2.30	49	+ 3:19	+ 2.30	31	+ 3:01	+ 2.30	53	+ 3:23	+ 2.30	27	+ 2:57
+ 2.45	51	+ 3:36	+ 2.45	48	+ 3:33	+ 2.45	50	+ 3:35	+ 2.45	64	+ 3:49	+ 2.45	50	+ 3:35	+ 2.45	31	+ 3:16	+ 2.45	54	+ 3:39	+ 2.45	27	+ 3:12
+ 3.00	**51**	**+ 3:51**	**+ 3.00**	**48**	**+ 3:48**	**+ 3.00**	**50**	**+ 3:50**	**+ 3.00**	**64**	**+ 4:04**	**+ 3.00**	**50**	**+ 3:50**	**+ 3.00**	**31**	**+ 3:31**	**+ 3.00**	**56**	**+ 3:56**	**+ 3.00**	**27**	**+ 3:27**
+ 3.15	52	+ 4:07	+ 3.15	49	+ 4:04	+ 3.15	52	+ 4:07	+ 3.15	66	+ 4:21	+ 3.15	52	+ 4:07	+ 3.15	32	+ 3:47	+ 3.15	57	+ 4:12	+ 3.15	27	+ 3:42
+ 3.30	53	+ 4:23	+ 3.30	50	+ 4:20	+ 3.30	53	+ 4:23	+ 3.30	67	+ 4:37	+ 3.30	53	+ 4:23	+ 3.30	33	+ 4:03	+ 3.30	58	+ 4:28	+ 3.30	28	+ 3:58
+ 3.45	54	+ 4:39	+ 3.45	51	+ 4:36	+ 3.45	54	+ 4:39	+ 3.45	69	+ 4:54	+ 3.45	54	+ 4:39	+ 3.45	34	+ 4:19	+ 3.45	60	+ 4:45	+ 3.45	28	+ 4:13
+ 4.00	**55**	**+ 4:55**	**+ 4.00**	**52**	**+ 4:52**	**+ 4.00**	**56**	**+ 4:56**	**+ 4.00**	**70**	**+ 5:10**	**+ 4.00**	**55**	**+ 4:55**	**+ 4.00**	**34**	**+ 4:34**	**+ 4.00**	**61**	**+ 5:01**	**+ 4.00**	**28**	**+ 4:28**
+ 4.15	56	+ 5:11	+ 4.15	53	+ 5:08	+ 4.15	58	+ 5:13	+ 4.15	72	+ 5:27	+ 4.15	57	+ 5:12	+ 4.15	36	+ 4:51	+ 4.15	62	+ 5:17	+ 4.15	28	+ 4:43
+ 4.30	57	+ 5:27	+ 4.30	54	+ 5:24	+ 4.30	60	+ 5:30	+ 4.30	75	+ 5:45	+ 4.30	59	+ 5:29	+ 4.30	37	+ 5:07	+ 4.30	64	+ 5:34	+ 4.30	28	+ 4:58
+ 4.45	59	+ 5:44	+ 4.45	55	+ 5:40	+ 4.45	62	+ 5:47	+ 4.45	77	- 5:58	+ 4.45	60	+ 5:45	+ 4.45	38	+ 5:23	+ 4.45	65	+ 5:50	+ 4.45	28	+ 5:13
+ 5.00	**60**	**- 6:00**	**+ 5.00**	**57**	**+ 5:57**	**+ 5.00**	**64**	**- 5:56**	**+ 5.00**	**79**	**- 5:41**	**+ 5.00**	**62**	**- 5:58**	**+ 5.00**	**39**	**+ 5:39**	**+ 5.00**	**66**	**- 5:54**	**+ 5.00**	**28**	**+ 5:28**
+ 5.15	61	- 5:44	+ 5.15	58	- 5:47	+ 5.15	65	- 5:40	+ 5.15	79	- 5:26	+ 5.15	64	- 5:41	+ 5.15	41	+ 5:56	+ 5.15	68	- 5:37	+ 5.15	29	+ 5:44
+ 5.30	62	- 5:28	+ 5.30	59	- 5:31	+ 5.30	67	- 5:23	+ 5.30	79	- 5:11	+ 5.30	65	- 5:25	+ 5.30	43	- 5:47	+ 5.30	70	- 5:20	+ 5.30	29	+ 5:59
+ 5.45	63	- 5:12	+ 5.45	60	- 5:15	+ 5.45	69	- 5:06	+ 5.45	79	- 4:56	+ 5.45	67	- 5:08	+ 5.45	45	- 5:30	+ 5.45	72	- 5:03	+ 5.45	29	- 5:46
+ 6.00	**65**	**- 4:55**	**+ 6.00**	**61**	**- 4:59**	**+ 6.00**	**70**	**- 4:50**	**+ 6.00**	**79**	**- 4:41**	**+ 6.00**	**69**	**- 4:51**	**+ 6.00**	**46**	**- 5:14**	**+ 6.00**	**74**	**- 4:46**	**+ 6.00**	**29**	**- 5:31**

NORTH BOUND

Table I - Barrow Deep and Deben

Neaps — All times relate to HW Sheerness — **Time to cover Sectors (in minutes) at 7.0 Kts**

NORTH BOUND

Time	I1 Red Sand to Barrow No 10		Time	I2 Medway to North Oaze PHM		Time	I3 North Oaze PHM to Barrow No 10		Time	I4 Barrow No 10 to Barrow No 4	
	Duration	Time at End of Sector		Duration	Time at End of Sector		Duration	Time at End of Sector		Duration	Time at End of Sector
- 6.00	58	- 5:02	- 6.00	55	- 5:05	- 6.00	68	- 4:52	- 6.00	81	- 4:39
- 5.45	59	- 4:46	- 5.45	56	- 4:49	- 5.45	70	- 4:35	- 5.45	82	- 4:23
- 5.30	60	- 4:30	- 5.30	57	- 4:33	- 5.30	71	- 4:19	- 5.30	84	- 4:06
- 5.15	61	- 4:14	- 5.15	58	- 4:17	- 5.15	73	- 4:02	- 5.15	85	- 3:50
- 5.00	63	- 3:57	- 5.00	59	- 4:01	- 5.00	75	- 3:45	- 5.00	86	- 3:34
- 4.45	63	- 3:42	- 4.45	60	- 3:45	- 4.45	76	- 3:29	- 4.45	87	- 3:18
- 4.30	63	- 3:27	- 4.30	60	- 3:30	- 4.30	77	- 3:13	- 4.30	89	- 3:01
- 4.15	64	- 3:11	- 4.15	61	- 3:14	- 4.15	77	- 2:58	- 4.15	90	- 2:45
- 4.00	64	- 2:56	- 4.00	61	- 2:59	- 4.00	78	- 2:42	- 4.00	91	- 2:29
- 3.45	64	- 2:41	- 3.45	61	- 2:44	- 3.45	78	- 2:27	- 3.45	89	- 2:16
- 3.30	63	- 2:27	- 3.30	61	- 2:29	- 3.30	78	- 2:12	- 3.30	88	- 2:02
- 3.15	62	- 2:13	- 3.15	61	- 2:14	- 3.15	77	- 1:58	- 3.15	86	- 1:49
- 3.00	62	- 1:58	- 3.00	61	- 1:59	- 3.00	77	- 1:43	- 3.00	85	- 1:35
- 2.45	61	- 1:44	- 2.45	61	- 1:44	- 2.45	76	- 1:29	- 2.45	83	- 1:22
- 2.30	61	- 1:29	- 2.30	61	- 1:29	- 2.30	75	- 1:15	- 2.30	82	- 1:08
- 2.15	60	- 1:15	- 2.15	60	- 1:15	- 2.15	74	- 1:01	- 2.15	81	- 0:54
- 2.00	60	- 1:00	- 2.00	60	- 1:00	- 2.00	73	- 0:47	- 2.00	80	- 0:40
- 1.45	59	- 0:46	- 1.45	59	- 0:46	- 1.45	71	- 0:34	- 1.45	78	- 0:27
- 1.30	58	- 0:32	- 1.30	58	- 0:32	- 1.30	69	- 0:21	- 1.30	76	- 0:14
- 1.15	58	- 0:17	- 1.15	58	- 0:17	- 1.15	67	- 0:08	- 1.15	75	HW
- 1.00	57	- 0:03	- 1.00	57	- 0:03	- 1.00	65	+ 0:05	- 1.00	73	+ 0:13
- 0.45	56	+ 0:11	- 0.45	56	+ 0:11	- 0.45	63	+ 0:18	- 0.45	71	+ 0:26
- 0.30	55	+ 0:25	- 0.30	55	+ 0:25	- 0.30	61	+ 0:31	- 0.30	70	+ 0:40
- 0.15	54	+ 0:39	- 0.15	54	+ 0:39	- 0.15	59	+ 0:44	- 0.15	68	+ 0:53
HW	53	+ 0:53	HW	53	+ 0:53	HW	57	+ 0:57	HW	66	+ 1:06
+ 0.15	52	+ 1:07	+ 0.15	52	+ 1:07	+ 0.15	56	+ 1:11	+ 0.15	65	+ 1:20
+ 0.30	51	+ 1:21	+ 0.30	51	+ 1:21	+ 0.30	54	+ 1:24	+ 0.30	63	+ 1:33
+ 0.45	50	+ 1:35	+ 0.45	50	+ 1:35	+ 0.45	53	+ 1:38	+ 0.45	62	+ 1:47
+ 1.00	49	+ 1:49	+ 1.00	49	+ 1:49	+ 1.00	51	+ 1:51	+ 1.00	60	+ 2:00
+ 1.15	48	+ 2:03	+ 1.15	49	+ 2:04	+ 1.15	51	+ 2:06	+ 1.15	60	+ 2:15
+ 1.30	48	+ 2:18	+ 1.30	48	+ 2:18	+ 1.30	50	+ 2:20	+ 1.30	60	+ 2:30
+ 1.45	48	+ 2:33	+ 1.45	47	+ 2:32	+ 1.45	50	+ 2:35	+ 1.45	59	+ 2:44
+ 2.00	47	+ 2:47	+ 2.00	47	+ 2:47	+ 2.00	49	+ 2:49	+ 2.00	59	+ 2:59
+ 2.15	48	+ 3:03	+ 2.15	46	+ 3:01	+ 2.15	49	+ 3:04	+ 2.15	59	+ 3:14
+ 2.30	48	+ 3:18	+ 2.30	46	+ 3:16	+ 2.30	49	+ 3:19	+ 2.30	60	+ 3:30
+ 2.45	48	+ 3:33	+ 2.45	46	+ 3:31	+ 2.45	50	+ 3:35	+ 2.45	60	+ 3:45
+ 3.00	48	+ 3:48	+ 3.00	46	+ 3:46	+ 3.00	50	+ 3:50	+ 3.00	61	+ 4:01
+ 3.15	49	+ 4:04	+ 3.15	47	+ 4:02	+ 3.15	50	+ 4:05	+ 3.15	62	+ 4:17
+ 3.30	49	+ 4:19	+ 3.30	47	+ 4:17	+ 3.30	51	+ 4:21	+ 3.30	63	+ 4:33
+ 3.45	50	+ 4:35	+ 3.45	48	+ 4:33	+ 3.45	52	+ 4:37	+ 3.45	63	+ 4:48
+ 4.00	50	+ 4:50	+ 4.00	48	+ 4:48	+ 4.00	53	+ 4:53	+ 4.00	64	+ 5:04
+ 4.15	51	+ 5:06	+ 4.15	49	+ 5:04	+ 4.15	54	+ 5:09	+ 4.15	65	+ 5:20
+ 4.30	51	+ 5:21	+ 4.30	49	+ 5:19	+ 4.30	55	+ 5:25	+ 4.30	67	+ 5:37
+ 4.45	52	+ 5:37	+ 4.45	50	+ 5:35	+ 4.45	56	+ 5:41	+ 4.45	68	+ 5:53
+ 5.00	52	+ 5:52	+ 5.00	50	+ 5:50	+ 5.00	57	+ 5:57	+ 5.00	69	- 5:51
+ 5.15	53	- 5:52	+ 5.15	51	- 5:54	+ 5.15	58	- 5:47	+ 5.15	70	- 5:35
+ 5.30	54	- 5:36	+ 5.30	51	- 5:39	+ 5.30	59	- 5:31	+ 5.30	71	- 5:19
+ 5.45	54	- 5:21	+ 5.45	52	- 5:23	+ 5.45	60	- 5:15	+ 5.45	73	- 5:02
+ 6.00	55	- 5:05	+ 6.00	52	- 5:08	+ 6.00	61	- 4:59	+ 6.00	74	- 4:46

Time	I5 Barrow No 4 to Gunfleet Spit		Time	I6 Gunfleet Spit to Goldmer Gat		Time	I7 Goldmer Gat to Cork Sand		Time	I8 Cork Sand to Deben Landfall	
	Duration	Time at End of Sector		Duration	Time at End of Sector		Duration	Time at End of Sector		Duration	Time at End of Sector
- 6.00	60	- 5:00	- 6.00	40	- 5:20	- 6.00	63	- 4:57	- 6.00	26	- 5:34
- 5.45	61	- 4:44	- 5.45	41	- 5:04	- 5.45	63	- 4:42	- 5.45	26	- 5:19
- 5.30	61	- 4:29	- 5.30	42	- 4:48	- 5.30	63	- 4:27	- 5.30	26	- 5:04
- 5.15	62	- 4:13	- 5.15	43	- 4:32	- 5.15	64	- 4:11	- 5.15	26	- 4:49
- 5.00	63	- 3:57	- 5.00	44	- 4:16	- 5.00	64	- 3:56	- 5.00	26	- 4:34
- 4.45	63	- 3:42	- 4.45	44	- 4:01	- 4.45	64	- 3:41	- 4.45	26	- 4:19
- 4.30	63	- 3:27	- 4.30	44	- 3:46	- 4.30	64	- 3:26	- 4.30	26	- 4:04
- 4.15	63	- 3:12	- 4.15	45	- 3:30	- 4.15	64	- 3:11	- 4.15	26	- 3:49
- 4.00	63	- 2:57	- 4.00	45	- 3:15	- 4.00	63	- 2:57	- 4.00	26	- 3:34
- 3.45	63	- 2:42	- 3.45	44	- 3:01	- 3.45	63	- 2:42	- 3.45	26	- 3:19
- 3.30	62	- 2:28	- 3.30	44	- 2:46	- 3.30	62	- 2:28	- 3.30	25	- 3:05
- 3.15	61	- 2:14	- 3.15	43	- 2:32	- 3.15	61	- 2:14	- 3.15	25	- 2:50
- 3.00	61	- 1:59	- 3.00	43	- 2:17	- 3.00	60	- 2:00	- 3.00	25	- 2:35
- 2.45	60	- 1:45	- 2.45	42	- 2:03	- 2.45	59	- 1:46	- 2.45	25	- 2:20
- 2.30	59	- 1:31	- 2.30	41	- 1:49	- 2.30	58	- 1:32	- 2.30	25	- 2:05
- 2.15	58	- 1:17	- 2.15	41	- 1:34	- 2.15	56	- 1:19	- 2.15	24	- 1:51
- 2.00	57	- 1:03	- 2.00	40	- 1:20	- 2.00	55	- 1:05	- 2.00	24	- 1:36
- 1.45	56	- 0:49	- 1.45	39	- 1:06	- 1.45	54	- 0:51	- 1.45	24	- 1:21
- 1.30	55	- 0:35	- 1.30	38	- 0:52	- 1.30	53	- 0:37	- 1.30	24	- 1:06
- 1.15	54	- 0:21	- 1.15	37	- 0:38	- 1.15	51	- 0:24	- 1.15	24	- 0:51
- 1.00	53	- 0:07	- 1.00	36	- 0:24	- 1.00	50	- 0:10	- 1.00	24	- 0:36
- 0.45	52	+ 0:07	- 0.45	35	- 0:10	- 0.45	50	+ 0:05	- 0.45	24	- 0:21
- 0.30	51	+ 0:21	- 0.30	34	+ 0:04	- 0.30	49	+ 0:19	- 0.30	23	- 0:07
- 0.15	50	+ 0:35	- 0.15	34	+ 0:19	- 0.15	48	+ 0:33	- 0.15	23	+ 0:08
HW	49	+ 0:49	HW	33	+ 0:33	HW	47	+ 0:47	HW	23	+ 0:23
+ 0.15	48	+ 1:03	+ 0.15	32	+ 0:47	+ 0.15	47	+ 1:02	+ 0.15	23	+ 0:38
+ 0.30	47	+ 1:17	+ 0.30	32	+ 1:02	+ 0.30	47	+ 1:17	+ 0.30	23	+ 0:53
+ 0.45	47	+ 1:32	+ 0.45	31	+ 1:16	+ 0.45	46	+ 1:31	+ 0.45	23	+ 1:08
+ 1.00	46	+ 1:46	+ 1.00	31	+ 1:31	+ 1.00	46	+ 1:46	+ 1.00	23	+ 1:23
+ 1.15	46	+ 2:01	+ 1.15	30	+ 1:45	+ 1.15	47	+ 2:02	+ 1.15	23	+ 1:38
+ 1.30	46	+ 2:16	+ 1.30	30	+ 2:00	+ 1.30	47	+ 2:17	+ 1.30	23	+ 1:53
+ 1.45	46	+ 2:31	+ 1.45	29	+ 2:14	+ 1.45	47	+ 2:32	+ 1.45	23	+ 2:08
+ 2.00	45	+ 2:45	+ 2.00	29	+ 2:29	+ 2.00	48	+ 2:48	+ 2.00	24	+ 2:24
+ 2.15	46	+ 3:01	+ 2.15	29	+ 2:44	+ 2.15	48	+ 3:03	+ 2.15	24	+ 2:39
+ 2.30	46	+ 3:16	+ 2.30	29	+ 2:59	+ 2.30	49	+ 3:19	+ 2.30	24	+ 2:54
+ 2.45	46	+ 3:31	+ 2.45	30	+ 3:15	+ 2.45	50	+ 3:35	+ 2.45	24	+ 3:09
+ 3.00	47	+ 3:47	+ 3.00	30	+ 3:30	+ 3.00	50	+ 3:50	+ 3.00	24	+ 3:24
+ 3.15	48	+ 4:03	+ 3.15	30	+ 3:45	+ 3.15	51	+ 4:06	+ 3.15	24	+ 3:39
+ 3.30	48	+ 4:18	+ 3.30	31	+ 4:01	+ 3.30	52	+ 4:22	+ 3.30	24	+ 3:54
+ 3.45	49	+ 4:34	+ 3.45	31	+ 4:16	+ 3.45	52	+ 4:37	+ 3.45	24	+ 4:09
+ 4.00	50	+ 4:50	+ 4.00	32	+ 4:32	+ 4.00	53	+ 4:53	+ 4.00	24	+ 4:24
+ 4.15	51	+ 5:06	+ 4.15	32	+ 4:47	+ 4.15	54	+ 5:09	+ 4.15	24	+ 4:39
+ 4.30	51	+ 5:21	+ 4.30	33	+ 5:03	+ 4.30	54	+ 5:24	+ 4.30	24	+ 4:54
+ 4.45	52	+ 5:37	+ 4.45	34	+ 5:19	+ 4.45	55	+ 5:40	+ 4.45	24	+ 5:09
+ 5.00	53	+ 5:53	+ 5.00	34	+ 5:34	+ 5.00	56	+ 5:56	+ 5.00	24	+ 5:24
+ 5.15	54	- 5:51	+ 5.15	35	+ 5:50	+ 5.15	57	- 5:48	+ 5.15	24	+ 5:39
+ 5.30	55	- 5:35	+ 5.30	36	- 5:54	+ 5.30	57	- 5:33	+ 5.30	25	+ 5:55
+ 5.45	55	- 5:20	+ 5.45	37	- 5:38	+ 5.45	58	- 5:17	+ 5.45	25	- 5:50
+ 6.00	56	- 5:04	+ 6.00	38	- 5:22	+ 6.00	59	- 5:01	+ 6.00	25	- 5:35

Table I - Barrow Deep and Deben

Time to cover Sectors (in minutes) at 7.0 kts — All times relate to HW Sheerness — **Springs**

Time	I1 Red Sand to Barrow No 10 Duration	I1 Time at End of Sector	Time	I2 Medway to North Oaze PHM Duration	I2 Time at End of Sector	Time	I3 North Oaze PHM to Barrow No 10 Duration	I3 Time at End of Sector	Time	I4 Barrow No 10 to Barrow No 4 Duration	I4 Time at End of Sector
- 6.00	60	- 5:00	- 6.00	56	- 5:04	- 6.00	70	- 4:50	- 6.00	84	- 4:36
- 5.45	62	- 4:43	- 5.45	57	- 4:48	- 5.45	73	- 4:32	- 5.45	87	- 4:18
- 5.30	63	- 4:27	- 5.30	59	- 4:31	- 5.30	76	- 4:14	- 5.30	90	- 4:00
- 5.15	65	- 4:10	- 5.15	60	- 4:15	- 5.15	79	- 3:56	- 5.15	94	- 3:41
- 5.00	67	- 3:53	- 5.00	62	- 3:58	- 5.00	82	- 3:38	- 5.00	97	- 3:23
- 4.45	67	- 3:38	- 4.45	63	- 3:42	- 4.45	84	- 3:21	- 4.45	97	- 3:08
- 4.30	68	- 3:22	- 4.30	64	- 3:26	- 4.30	87	- 3:03	- 4.30	97	- 2:53
- 4.15	69	- 3:06	- 4.15	65	- 3:10	- 4.15	89	- 2:46	- 4.15	98	- 2:37
- 4.00	69	- 2:51	- 4.00	65	- 2:55	- 4.00	92	- 2:28	- 4.00	98	- 2:22
- 3.45	68	- 2:37	- 3.45	66	- 2:39	- 3.45	92	- 2:13	- 3.45	96	- 2:09
- 3.30	68	- 2:22	- 3.30	66	- 2:24	- 3.30	91	- 1:59	- 3.30	95	- 1:55
- 3.15	67	- 2:08	- 3.15	66	- 2:09	- 3.15	91	- 1:44	- 3.15	94	- 1:41
- 3.00	66	- 1:54	- 3.00	66	- 1:54	- 3.00	90	- 1:30	- 3.00	93	- 1:27
- 2.45	65	- 1:40	- 2.45	65	- 1:40	- 2.45	88	- 1:17	- 2.45	90	- 1:15
- 2.30	64	- 1:26	- 2.30	65	- 1:25	- 2.30	85	- 1:05	- 2.30	88	- 1:02
- 2.15	63	- 1:12	- 2.15	64	- 1:11	- 2.15	82	- 0:53	- 2.15	86	- 0:49
- 2.00	62	- 0:58	- 2.00	63	- 0:57	- 2.00	80	- 0:40	- 2.00	84	- 0:36
- 1.45	61	- 0:44	- 1.45	62	- 0:43	- 1.45	77	- 0:28	- 1.45	81	- 0:24
- 1.30	60	- 0:30	- 1.30	61	- 0:29	- 1.30	74	- 0:16	- 1.30	79	- 0:11
- 1.15	59	- 0:16	- 1.15	60	- 0:15	- 1.15	70	- 0:05	- 1.15	76	+ 0:01
- 1.00	58	- 0:02	- 1.00	58	- 0:02	- 1.00	67	+ 0:07	- 1.00	74	+ 0:14
- 0.45	56	+ 0:11	- 0.45	57	+ 0:12	- 0.45	64	+ 0:19	- 0.45	71	+ 0:26
- 0.30	55	+ 0:25	- 0.30	56	+ 0:26	- 0.30	61	+ 0:31	- 0.30	68	+ 0:38
- 0.15	53	+ 0:38	- 0.15	54	+ 0:39	- 0.15	58	+ 0:43	- 0.15	66	+ 0:51
HW	52	+ 0:52	HW	53	+ 0:53	HW	55	+ 0:55	HW	63	+ 1:03
+ 0.15	50	+ 1:05	+ 0.15	51	+ 1:06	+ 0.15	52	+ 1:07	+ 0.15	61	+ 1:16
+ 0.30	49	+ 1:19	+ 0.30	50	+ 1:20	+ 0.30	50	+ 1:20	+ 0.30	59	+ 1:29
+ 0.45	47	+ 1:32	+ 0.45	48	+ 1:33	+ 0.45	48	+ 1:33	+ 0.45	57	+ 1:42
+ 1.00	46	+ 1:46	+ 1.00	47	+ 1:47	+ 1.00	46	+ 1:46	+ 1.00	55	+ 1:55
+ 1.15	45	+ 2:00	+ 1.15	46	+ 2:01	+ 1.15	45	+ 2:00	+ 1.15	55	+ 2:10
+ 1.30	45	+ 2:15	+ 1.30	45	+ 2:15	+ 1.30	44	+ 2:14	+ 1.30	55	+ 2:25
+ 1.45	44	+ 2:29	+ 1.45	44	+ 2:29	+ 1.45	44	+ 2:29	+ 1.45	54	+ 2:39
+ 2.00	44	+ 2:44	+ 2.00	43	+ 2:43	+ 2.00	43	+ 2:43	+ 2.00	54	+ 2:54
+ 2.15	44	+ 2:59	+ 2.15	43	+ 2:58	+ 2.15	43	+ 2:58	+ 2.15	54	+ 3:09
+ 2.30	45	+ 3:15	+ 2.30	43	+ 3:13	+ 2.30	44	+ 3:14	+ 2.30	55	+ 3:25
+ 2.45	45	+ 3:30	+ 2.45	43	+ 3:28	+ 2.45	44	+ 3:29	+ 2.45	55	+ 3:40
+ 3.00	45	+ 3:45	+ 3.00	43	+ 3:43	+ 3.00	44	+ 3:44	+ 3.00	56	+ 3:56
+ 3.15	46	+ 4:01	+ 3.15	43	+ 3:58	+ 3.15	46	+ 4:01	+ 3.15	57	+ 4:12
+ 3.30	46	+ 4:16	+ 3.30	44	+ 4:14	+ 3.30	47	+ 4:17	+ 3.30	59	+ 4:29
+ 3.45	47	+ 4:32	+ 3.45	45	+ 4:30	+ 3.45	48	+ 4:33	+ 3.45	60	+ 4:45
+ 4.00	48	+ 4:48	+ 4.00	45	+ 4:45	+ 4.00	49	+ 4:49	+ 4.00	61	+ 5:01
+ 4.15	49	+ 5:04	+ 4.15	46	+ 5:01	+ 4.15	51	+ 5:06	+ 4.15	63	+ 5:18
+ 4.30	49	+ 5:19	+ 4.30	47	+ 5:17	+ 4.30	52	+ 5:22	+ 4.30	65	+ 5:35
+ 4.45	50	+ 5:35	+ 4.45	48	+ 5:33	+ 4.45	54	+ 5:39	+ 4.45	66	+ 5:51
+ 5.00	51	+ 5:51	+ 5.00	49	+ 5:49	+ 5.00	55	+ 5:55	+ 5.00	68	- 5:52
+ 5.15	52	- 5:53	+ 5.15	50	- 5:55	+ 5.15	56	- 5:49	+ 5.15	70	- 5:35
+ 5.30	53	- 5:37	+ 5.30	50	- 5:40	+ 5.30	58	- 5:32	+ 5.30	71	- 5:19
+ 5.45	54	- 5:21	+ 5.45	51	- 5:24	+ 5.45	59	- 5:16	+ 5.45	73	- 5:02
+ 6.00	55	- 5:05	+ 6.00	52	- 5:08	+ 6.00	60	- 5:00	+ 6.00	75	- 4:45

Time	I5 Barrow No 4 to Gunfleet Spit Duration	I5 Time at End of Sector	Time	I6 Gunfleet Spit to Goldmer Gat Duration	I6 Time at End of Sector	Time	I7 Goldmer Gat to Cork Sand Duration	I7 Time at End of Sector	Time	I8 Cork Sand to Deben Landfall Duration	I8 Time at End of Sector
- 6.00	63	- 4:57	- 6.00	42	- 5:18	- 6.00	68	- 4:52	- 6.00	27	- 5:33
- 5.45	64	- 4:41	- 5.45	44	- 5:01	- 5.45	68	- 4:37	- 5.45	27	- 5:18
- 5.30	66	- 4:24	- 5.30	45	- 4:45	- 5.30	69	- 4:21	- 5.30	27	- 5:03
- 5.15	67	- 4:08	- 5.15	47	- 4:28	- 5.15	69	- 4:06	- 5.15	27	- 4:48
- 5.00	68	- 3:52	- 5.00	48	- 4:12	- 5.00	69	- 3:51	- 5.00	27	- 4:33
- 4.45	68	- 3:37	- 4.45	49	- 3:56	- 4.45	69	- 3:36	- 4.45	27	- 4:18
- 4.30	68	- 3:22	- 4.30	49	- 3:41	- 4.30	69	- 3:21	- 4.30	27	- 4:03
- 4.15	68	- 3:07	- 4.15	50	- 3:25	- 4.15	69	- 3:06	- 4.15	27	- 3:48
- 4.00	68	- 2:52	- 4.00	51	- 3:09	- 4.00	69	- 2:51	- 4.00	27	- 3:33
- 3.45	67	- 2:38	- 3.45	50	- 2:55	- 3.45	68	- 2:37	- 3.45	26	- 3:19
- 3.30	66	- 2:24	- 3.30	49	- 2:41	- 3.30	66	- 2:24	- 3.30	26	- 3:04
- 3.15	65	- 2:10	- 3.15	48	- 2:27	- 3.15	65	- 2:10	- 3.15	26	- 2:49
- 3.00	64	- 1:56	- 3.00	48	- 2:12	- 3.00	64	- 1:56	- 3.00	26	- 2:34
- 2.45	63	- 1:42	- 2.45	46	- 1:59	- 2.45	62	- 1:43	- 2.45	25	- 2:20
- 2.30	62	- 1:28	- 2.30	45	- 1:45	- 2.30	60	- 1:30	- 2.30	25	- 2:05
- 2.15	60	- 1:15	- 2.15	43	- 1:32	- 2.15	57	- 1:18	- 2.15	25	- 1:50
- 2.00	59	- 1:01	- 2.00	42	- 1:18	- 2.00	55	- 1:05	- 2.00	24	- 1:36
- 1.45	57	- 0:48	- 1.45	40	- 1:05	- 1.45	54	- 0:51	- 1.45	24	- 1:21
- 1.30	56	- 0:34	- 1.30	39	- 0:51	- 1.30	52	- 0:38	- 1.30	24	- 1:06
- 1.15	54	- 0:21	- 1.15	38	- 0:37	- 1.15	50	- 0:25	- 1.15	24	- 0:51
- 1.00	52	- 0:08	- 1.00	36	- 0:24	- 1.00	49	- 0:11	- 1.00	23	- 0:37
- 0.45	51	+ 0:06	- 0.45	35	- 0:10	- 0.45	47	+ 0:02	- 0.45	23	- 0:22
- 0.30	49	+ 0:19	- 0.30	34	+ 0:04	- 0.30	46	+ 0:16	- 0.30	23	- 0:07
- 0.15	48	+ 0:33	- 0.15	33	+ 0:18	- 0.15	45	+ 0:30	- 0.15	23	+ 0:08
HW	46	+ 0:46	HW	32	+ 0:32	HW	44	+ 0:44	HW	23	+ 0:23
+ 0.15	46	+ 1:01	+ 0.15	31	+ 0:46	+ 0.15	44	+ 0:59	+ 0.15	23	+ 0:38
+ 0.30	45	+ 1:15	+ 0.30	30	+ 1:00	+ 0.30	43	+ 1:13	+ 0.30	23	+ 0:53
+ 0.45	44	+ 1:29	+ 0.45	29	+ 1:14	+ 0.45	43	+ 1:28	+ 0.45	23	+ 1:08
+ 1.00	43	+ 1:43	+ 1.00	28	+ 1:28	+ 1.00	43	+ 1:43	+ 1.00	23	+ 1:23
+ 1.15	43	+ 1:58	+ 1.15	28	+ 1:43	+ 1.15	43	+ 1:58	+ 1.15	23	+ 1:38
+ 1.30	43	+ 2:13	+ 1.30	27	+ 1:57	+ 1.30	44	+ 2:14	+ 1.30	23	+ 1:53
+ 1.45	42	+ 2:27	+ 1.45	27	+ 2:12	+ 1.45	44	+ 2:29	+ 1.45	23	+ 2:08
+ 2.00	42	+ 2:42	+ 2.00	26	+ 2:26	+ 2.00	45	+ 2:45	+ 2.00	23	+ 2:23
+ 2.15	43	+ 2:58	+ 2.15	26	+ 2:41	+ 2.15	46	+ 3:01	+ 2.15	23	+ 2:38
+ 2.30	43	+ 3:13	+ 2.30	27	+ 2:57	+ 2.30	46	+ 3:16	+ 2.30	23	+ 2:53
+ 2.45	44	+ 3:29	+ 2.45	27	+ 3:12	+ 2.45	47	+ 3:32	+ 2.45	23	+ 3:08
+ 3.00	44	+ 3:44	+ 3.00	27	+ 3:27	+ 3.00	48	+ 3:48	+ 3.00	23	+ 3:23
+ 3.15	45	+ 4:00	+ 3.15	28	+ 3:43	+ 3.15	49	+ 4:04	+ 3.15	23	+ 3:38
+ 3.30	46	+ 4:16	+ 3.30	28	+ 3:58	+ 3.30	50	+ 4:20	+ 3.30	24	+ 3:54
+ 3.45	47	+ 4:32	+ 3.45	29	+ 4:14	+ 3.45	51	+ 4:36	+ 3.45	24	+ 4:09
+ 4.00	48	+ 4:48	+ 4.00	30	+ 4:30	+ 4.00	52	+ 4:52	+ 4.00	24	+ 4:24
+ 4.15	49	+ 5:04	+ 4.15	31	+ 4:46	+ 4.15	53	+ 5:08	+ 4.15	24	+ 4:39
+ 4.30	50	+ 5:20	+ 4.30	32	+ 5:02	+ 4.30	54	+ 5:24	+ 4.30	24	+ 4:54
+ 4.45	51	+ 5:36	+ 4.45	32	+ 5:17	+ 4.45	55	+ 5:40	+ 4.45	24	+ 5:09
+ 5.00	53	+ 5:53	+ 5.00	33	+ 5:33	+ 5.00	56	+ 5:56	+ 5.00	24	+ 5:24
+ 5.15	54	- 5:51	+ 5.15	35	+ 5:50	+ 5.15	57	- 5:48	+ 5.15	24	+ 5:39
+ 5.30	55	- 5:35	+ 5.30	36	- 5:54	+ 5.30	59	- 5:31	+ 5.30	25	+ 5:55
+ 5.45	56	- 5:19	+ 5.45	37	- 5:38	+ 5.45	60	- 5:15	+ 5.45	25	- 5:50
+ 6.00	58	- 5:02	+ 6.00	39	- 5:21	+ 6.00	62	- 4:58	+ 6.00	25	- 5:35

NORTH BOUND

Table J - Essex to Suffolk Rivers Sea Reach to North Oaze

Neaps | All times relate to HW Sheerness | **Time to cover Sectors (in minutes) at 4.0 Kts**

NORTH BOUND

	J1		J2		J3		J4		J5		J6		J7		J8	
	Spitway to the Naze		Blackwater to Colne		Colne to Holland-on-Sea		Holland-on-Sea to the Naze		The Naze to Deben Landfall		NE Gunfleet to Cork Sand Bcn		Sea Reach No 1 to North Oaze		Crouch to Spitway	
Time	Duration	Time at End of Sector	Duration	Time at End of Sector	Duration	Time at End of Sector	Duration	Time at End of Sector	Duration	Time at End of Sector	Duration	Time at End of Sector	Duration	Time at End of Sector	Duration	Time at End of Sector
- 6.00	**242**	**- 1:58**	**72**	**- 4:48**	**164**	**- 3:16**	**112**	**- 4:08**	**122**	**- 3:58**	**115**	**- 4:05**	**50**	**- 5:10**	**75**	**- 4:45**
- 5.45	243	- 1:42	73	- 4:32	167	- 2:58	115	- 3:50	122	- 3:43	115	- 3:50	52	- 4:53	81	- 4:24
- 5.30	243	- 1:27	74	- 4:16	170	- 2:40	119	- 3:31	122	- 3:28	116	- 3:34	53	- 4:37	86	- 4:04
- 5.15	243	- 1:12	76	- 3:59	173	- 2:22	122	- 3:13	122	- 3:13	116	- 3:19	55	- 4:20	91	- 3:44
- 5.00	**244**	**- 0:56**	**77**	**- 3:43**	**176**	**- 2:04**	**126**	**- 2:54**	**122**	**- 2:58**	**117**	**- 3:03**	**57**	**- 4:03**	**96**	**- 3:24**
- 4.45	240	- 0:45	78	- 3:27	176	- 1:49	124	- 2:41	120	- 2:45	115	- 2:50	58	- 3:47	96	- 3:09
- 4.30	236	- 0:34	78	- 3:12	175	- 1:35	123	- 2:27	119	- 2:31	114	- 2:36	59	- 3:31	96	- 2:54
- 4.15	233	- 0:22	79	- 2:56	174	- 1:21	121	- 2:14	117	- 2:18	113	- 2:22	60	- 3:15	96	- 2:39
- 4.00	**229**	**- 0:11**	**80**	**- 2:40**	**173**	**- 1:07**	**120**	**- 2:00**	**116**	**- 2:04**	**111**	**- 2:09**	**61**	**- 2:59**	**96**	**- 2:24**
- 3.45	224	- 0:01	80	- 2:25	170	- 0:55	116	- 1:49	113	- 1:52	108	- 1:57	61	- 2:44	95	- 2:10
- 3.30	219	+ 0:09	80	- 2:10	166	- 0:44	113	- 1:37	111	- 1:39	105	- 1:45	61	- 2:29	94	- 1:56
- 3.15	214	+ 0:19	80	- 1:55	163	- 0:32	109	- 1:26	109	- 1:26	101	- 1:34	61	- 2:14	93	- 1:42
- 3.00	**208**	**+ 0:28**	**80**	**- 1:40**	**159**	**- 0:21**	**106**	**- 1:14**	**107**	**- 1:13**	**98**	**- 1:22**	**62**	**- 1:58**	**91**	**- 1:29**
- 2.45	202	+ 0:37	79	- 1:26	154	- 0:11	100	- 1:05	104	- 1:01	97	- 1:08	61	- 1:44	88	- 1:17
- 2.30	195	+ 0:45	78	- 1:12	149	- 0:01	95	- 0:55	102	- 0:48	96	- 0:54	60	- 1:30	84	- 1:06
- 2.15	188	+ 0:53	77	- 0:58	144	+ 0:09	90	- 0:45	99	- 0:36	96	- 0:39	60	- 1:15	80	- 0:55
- 2.00	**181**	**+ 1:01**	**76**	**- 0:44**	**139**	**+ 0:19**	**84**	**- 0:36**	**97**	**- 0:23**	**95**	**- 0:25**	**59**	**- 1:01**	**77**	**- 0:43**
- 1.45	176	+ 1:11	72	- 0:33	133	+ 0:28	81	- 0:24	94	- 0:11	89	- 0:16	58	- 0:47	74	- 0:31
- 1.30	171	+ 1:21	69	- 0:21	127	+ 0:37	77	- 0:13	91	+ 0:01	84	- 0:06	56	- 0:34	71	- 0:19
- 1.15	166	+ 1:31	66	- 0:09	120	+ 0:45	74	- 0:01	88	+ 0:13	78	+ 0:03	55	- 0:20	68	- 0:07
- 1.00	**161**	**+ 1:41**	**63**	**+ 0:03**	**114**	**+ 0:54**	**70**	**+ 0:10**	**86**	**+ 0:26**	**73**	**+ 0:13**	**54**	**- 0:06**	**66**	**+ 0:06**
- 0.45	156	+ 1:51	61	+ 0:16	110	+ 1:05	67	+ 0:22	84	+ 0:39	72	+ 0:27	53	+ 0:08	63	+ 0:18
- 0.30	151	+ 2:01	58	+ 0:28	106	+ 1:16	64	+ 0:34	82	+ 0:52	70	+ 0:40	51	+ 0:21	60	+ 0:30
- 0.15	147	+ 2:12	55	+ 0:40	102	+ 1:27	61	+ 0:46	80	+ 1:05	68	+ 0:53	50	+ 0:35	58	+ 0:43
HW	**142**	**+ 2:22**	**53**	**+ 0:53**	**98**	**+ 1:38**	**58**	**+ 0:58**	**79**	**+ 1:19**	**67**	**+ 1:07**	**48**	**+ 0:48**	**55**	**+ 0:55**
+ 0.15	141	+ 2:36	52	+ 1:07	96	+ 1:51	57	+ 1:12	79	+ 1:34	67	+ 1:22	47	+ 1:02	54	+ 1:09
+ 0.30	141	+ 2:51	51	+ 1:21	94	+ 2:04	57	+ 1:27	79	+ 1:49	66	+ 1:36	45	+ 1:15	52	+ 1:22
+ 0.45	140	+ 3:05	50	+ 1:35	92	+ 2:17	56	+ 1:41	80	+ 2:05	66	+ 1:51	44	+ 1:29	51	+ 1:36
+ 1.00	**140**	**+ 3:20**	**49**	**+ 1:49**	**90**	**+ 2:30**	**55**	**+ 1:55**	**80**	**+ 2:20**	**66**	**+ 2:06**	**42**	**+ 1:42**	**49**	**+ 1:49**
+ 1.15	142	+ 3:37	49	+ 2:04	90	+ 2:45	56	+ 2:11	81	+ 2:36	67	+ 2:22	41	+ 1:56	49	+ 2:04
+ 1.30	145	+ 3:55	49	+ 2:19	90	+ 3:00	57	+ 2:27	82	+ 2:52	68	+ 2:38	40	+ 2:10	49	+ 2:19
+ 1.45	147	+ 4:12	50	+ 2:35	91	+ 3:16	58	+ 2:43	83	+ 3:08	69	+ 2:54	39	+ 2:24	49	+ 2:34
+ 2.00	**150**	**+ 4:30**	**50**	**+ 2:50**	**91**	**+ 3:31**	**59**	**+ 2:59**	**84**	**+ 3:24**	**70**	**+ 3:10**	**38**	**+ 2:38**	**49**	**+ 2:49**
+ 2.15	152	+ 4:47	51	+ 3:06	93	+ 3:48	60	+ 3:15	85	+ 3:40	71	+ 3:26	38	+ 2:53	50	+ 3:05
+ 2.30	155	+ 5:05	52	+ 3:22	95	+ 4:05	61	+ 3:31	86	+ 3:56	73	+ 3:43	38	+ 3:08	50	+ 3:20
+ 2.45	157	+ 5:22	53	+ 3:38	97	+ 4:22	62	+ 3:47	88	+ 4:13	75	+ 4:00	38	+ 3:23	51	+ 3:36
+ 3.00	**160**	**+ 5:40**	**54**	**+ 3:54**	**99**	**+ 4:39**	**63**	**+ 4:03**	**89**	**+ 4:29**	**76**	**+ 4:16**	**38**	**+ 3:38**	**52**	**+ 3:52**
+ 3.15	164	+ 5:59	55	+ 4:10	101	+ 4:56	65	+ 4:20	90	+ 4:45	78	+ 4:33	38	+ 3:53	53	+ 4:08
+ 3.30	167	- 5:43	56	+ 4:26	103	+ 5:13	66	+ 4:36	92	+ 5:02	79	+ 4:49	39	+ 4:09	54	+ 4:24
+ 3.45	171	- 5:24	57	+ 4:42	106	+ 5:31	68	+ 4:53	94	+ 5:19	81	+ 5:06	39	+ 4:24	55	+ 4:40
+ 4.00	**174**	**- 5:06**	**58**	**+ 4:58**	**108**	**+ 5:48**	**69**	**+ 5:09**	**95**	**+ 5:35**	**82**	**+ 5:22**	**40**	**+ 4:40**	**55**	**+ 4:55**
+ 4.15	180	- 4:45	59	+ 5:14	111	- 5:54	72	+ 5:27	97	+ 5:52	84	+ 5:39	41	+ 4:56	57	+ 5:12
+ 4.30	185	- 4:25	60	+ 5:30	114	- 5:36	74	+ 5:44	100	- 5:50	85	+ 5:55	42	+ 5:12	59	+ 5:29
+ 4.45	190	- 4:05	61	+ 5:46	118	- 5:17	77	- 5:58	102	- 5:33	87	- 5:48	42	+ 5:27	61	+ 5:46
+ 5.00	**196**	**- 3:44**	**62**	**- 5:58**	**121**	**- 4:59**	**79**	**- 5:41**	**104**	**- 5:16**	**88**	**- 5:32**	**43**	**+ 5:43**	**62**	**- 5:58**
+ 5.15	203	- 3:22	64	- 5:41	126	- 4:39	82	- 5:23	106	- 4:59	91	- 5:14	44	+ 5:59	64	- 5:41
+ 5.30	211	- 2:59	65	- 5:25	130	- 4:20	86	- 5:04	109	- 4:41	93	- 4:57	45	- 5:45	65	- 5:25
+ 5.45	219	- 2:36	66	- 5:09	135	- 4:00	89	- 4:46	111	- 4:24	96	- 4:39	46	- 5:29	66	- 5:09
+ 6.00	**226**	**- 2:14**	**67**	**- 4:53**	**139**	**- 3:41**	**92**	**- 4:28**	**114**	**- 4:06**	**98**	**- 4:22**	**46**	**- 5:14**	**68**	**- 4:52**

Table J - Essex to Suffolk Rivers Sea Reach to North Oaze

Time to cover Sectors (in minutes) at 4.0 kts — All times relate to HW Sheerness — **Springs**

NORTH BOUND

Time	J1 Spitway to the Naze: Duration	J1 Time at End of Sector	Time	J2 Blackwater to Colne: Duration	J2 Time at End of Sector	Time	J3 Colne to Holland-on-Sea: Duration	J3 Time at End of Sector	Time	J4 Holland-on-Sea to the Naze: Duration	J4 Time at End of Sector
- 6.00	**282**	**- 1:18**	**- 6.00**	**75**	**- 4:45**	**- 6.00**	**189**	**- 2:51**	**- 6.00**	**150**	**- 3:30**
- 5.45	279	- 1:06	- 5.45	79	- 4:26	- 5.45	195	- 2:30	- 5.45	153	- 3:12
- 5.30	277	- 0:53	- 5.30	83	- 4:07	- 5.30	200	- 2:10	- 5.30	155	- 2:55
- 5.15	274	- 0:41	- 5.15	86	- 3:49	- 5.15	206	- 1:49	- 5.15	158	- 2:37
- 5.00	**272**	**- 0:28**	**- 5.00**	**90**	**- 3:30**	**- 5.00**	**211**	**- 1:29**	**- 5.00**	**161**	**- 2:19**
- 4.45	264	- 0:21	- 4.45	92	- 3:13	- 4.45	206	- 1:19	- 4.45	155	- 2:10
- 4.30	257	- 0:13	- 4.30	93	- 2:57	- 4.30	202	- 1:08	- 4.30	150	- 2:00
- 4.15	250	- 0:05	- 4.15	95	- 2:40	- 4.15	197	- 0:58	- 4.15	144	- 1:51
- 4.00	**242**	**+ 0:02**	**- 4.00**	**96**	**- 2:24**	**- 4.00**	**192**	**- 0:48**	**- 4.00**	**138**	**- 1:42**
- 3.45	235	+ 0:10	- 3.45	96	- 2:09	- 3.45	186	- 0:39	- 3.45	132	- 1:33
- 3.30	228	+ 0:18	- 3.30	96	- 1:54	- 3.30	180	- 0:30	- 3.30	125	- 1:25
- 3.15	220	+ 0:25	- 3.15	96	- 1:39	- 3.15	174	- 0:21	- 3.15	119	- 1:16
- 3.00	**213**	**+ 0:33**	**- 3.00**	**96**	**- 1:24**	**- 3.00**	**168**	**- 0:12**	**- 3.00**	**113**	**- 1:07**
- 2.45	204	+ 0:39	- 2.45	93	- 1:12	- 2.45	161	- 0:04	- 2.45	106	- 0:59
- 2.30	195	+ 0:45	- 2.30	89	- 1:01	- 2.30	154	+ 0:04	- 2.30	100	- 0:50
- 2.15	185	+ 0:50	- 2.15	86	- 0:49	- 2.15	146	+ 0:11	- 2.15	94	- 0:41
- 2.00	**176**	**+ 0:56**	**- 2.00**	**82**	**- 0:38**	**- 2.00**	**139**	**+ 0:19**	**- 2.00**	**88**	**- 0:32**
- 1.45	171	+ 1:06	- 1.45	77	- 0:28	- 1.45	132	+ 0:27	- 1.45	82	- 0:23
- 1.30	165	+ 1:15	- 1.30	72	- 0:18	- 1.30	124	+ 0:34	- 1.30	77	- 0:13
- 1.15	159	+ 1:24	- 1.15	67	- 0:08	- 1.15	116	+ 0:41	- 1.15	71	- 0:04
- 1.00	**153**	**+ 1:33**	**- 1.00**	**62**	**+ 0:02**	**- 1.00**	**109**	**+ 0:49**	**- 1.00**	**66**	**+ 0:06**
- 0.45	148	+ 1:43	- 0.45	58	+ 0:13	- 0.45	105	+ 1:00	- 0.45	62	+ 0:17
- 0.30	142	+ 1:52	- 0.30	55	+ 0:25	- 0.30	100	+ 1:10	- 0.30	58	+ 0:28
- 0.15	136	+ 2:01	- 0.15	51	+ 0:36	- 0.15	96	+ 1:21	- 0.15	55	+ 0:40
HW	**131**	**+ 2:11**	**HW**	**47**	**+ 0:47**	**HW**	**92**	**+ 1:32**	**HW**	**51**	**+ 0:51**
+ 0.15	131	+ 2:26	+ 0.15	46	+ 1:01	+ 0.15	89	+ 1:44	+ 0.15	50	+ 1:05
+ 0.30	130	+ 2:40	+ 0.30	45	+ 1:15	+ 0.30	86	+ 1:56	+ 0.30	50	+ 1:20
+ 0.45	130	+ 2:55	+ 0.45	44	+ 1:29	+ 0.45	82	+ 2:07	+ 0.45	49	+ 1:34
+ 1.00	**130**	**+ 3:10**	**+ 1.00**	**43**	**+ 1:43**	**+ 1.00**	**79**	**+ 2:19**	**+ 1.00**	**48**	**+ 1:48**
+ 1.15	132	+ 3:27	+ 1.15	43	+ 1:58	+ 1.15	76	+ 2:31	+ 1.15	49	+ 2:04
+ 1.30	135	+ 3:45	+ 1.30	43	+ 2:13	+ 1.30	73	+ 2:43	+ 1.30	50	+ 2:20
+ 1.45	137	+ 4:02	+ 1.45	44	+ 2:29	+ 1.45	69	+ 2:54	+ 1.45	51	+ 2:36
+ 2.00	**140**	**+ 4:20**	**+ 2.00**	**44**	**+ 2:44**	**+ 2.00**	**66**	**+ 3:06**	**+ 2.00**	**52**	**+ 2:52**
+ 2.15	143	+ 4:38	+ 2.15	45	+ 3:00	+ 2.15	73	+ 3:28	+ 2.15	53	+ 3:08
+ 2.30	147	+ 4:57	+ 2.30	47	+ 3:17	+ 2.30	80	+ 3:50	+ 2.30	54	+ 3:24
+ 2.45	150	+ 5:15	+ 2.45	48	+ 3:33	+ 2.45	87	+ 4:12	+ 2.45	55	+ 3:40
+ 3.00	**154**	**+ 5:34**	**+ 3.00**	**49**	**+ 3:49**	**+ 3.00**	**94**	**+ 4:34**	**+ 3.00**	**57**	**+ 3:57**
+ 3.15	159	+ 5:54	+ 3.15	50	+ 4:05	+ 3.15	97	+ 4:52	+ 3.15	59	+ 4:14
+ 3.30	164	- 5:46	+ 3.30	52	+ 4:22	+ 3.30	99	+ 5:09	+ 3.30	61	+ 4:31
+ 3.45	169	- 5:26	+ 3.45	53	+ 4:38	+ 3.45	102	+ 5:27	+ 3.45	63	+ 4:48
+ 4.00	**175**	**- 5:05**	**+ 4.00**	**54**	**+ 4:54**	**+ 4.00**	**105**	**+ 5:45**	**+ 4.00**	**65**	**+ 5:05**
+ 4.15	185	- 4:40	+ 4.15	56	+ 5:11	+ 4.15	109	- 5:56	+ 4.15	69	+ 5:24
+ 4.30	195	- 4:15	+ 4.30	58	+ 5:28	+ 4.30	114	- 5:36	+ 4.30	72	+ 5:42
+ 4.45	205	- 3:50	+ 4.45	60	+ 5:45	+ 4.45	118	- 5:17	+ 4.45	76	- 5:59
+ 5.00	**215**	**- 3:25**	**+ 5.00**	**62**	**- 5:58**	**+ 5.00**	**123**	**- 4:57**	**+ 5.00**	**79**	**- 5:41**
+ 5.15	225	- 3:00	+ 5.15	63	- 5:42	+ 5.15	132	- 4:33	+ 5.15	84	- 5:21
+ 5.30	235	- 2:35	+ 5.30	65	- 5:25	+ 5.30	140	- 4:10	+ 5.30	89	- 5:01
+ 5.45	245	- 2:10	+ 5.45	67	- 5:08	+ 5.45	149	- 3:46	+ 5.45	94	- 4:41
+ 6.00	**255**	**- 1:45**	**+ 6.00**	**69**	**- 4:51**	**+ 6.00**	**157**	**- 3:23**	**+ 6.00**	**98**	**- 4:22**

Time	J5 The Naze to Deben Landfall: Duration	J5 Time at End of Sector	Time	J6 NE Gunfleet to Cork Sand Bcn: Duration	J6 Time at End of Sector	Time	J7 Sea Reach No 1 to North Oaze: Duration	J7 Time at End of Sector	Time	J8 Crouch to Spitway: Duration	J8 Time at End of Sector
- 6.00	**134**	**- 3:46**	**- 6.00**	**129**	**- 3:51**	**- 6.00**	**51**	**- 5:09**	**- 6.00**	**91**	**- 4:29**
- 5.45	133	- 3:32	- 5.45	130	- 3:35	- 5.45	54	- 4:51	- 5.45	96	- 4:09
- 5.30	132	- 3:18	- 5.30	130	- 3:20	- 5.30	57	- 4:33	- 5.30	101	- 3:49
- 5.15	132	- 3:03	- 5.15	131	- 3:04	- 5.15	59	- 4:16	- 5.15	106	- 3:29
- 5.00	**131**	**- 2:49**	**- 5.00**	**131**	**- 2:49**	**- 5.00**	**62**	**- 3:58**	**- 5.00**	**111**	**- 3:09**
- 4.45	128	- 2:37	- 4.45	129	- 2:36	- 4.45	64	- 3:41	- 4.45	111	- 2:54
- 4.30	126	- 2:24	- 4.30	126	- 2:24	- 4.30	65	- 3:25	- 4.30	111	- 2:39
- 4.15	124	- 2:11	- 4.15	123	- 2:12	- 4.15	67	- 3:08	- 4.15	111	- 2:24
- 4.00	**121**	**- 1:59**	**- 4.00**	**121**	**- 1:59**	**- 4.00**	**68**	**- 2:52**	**- 4.00**	**111**	**- 2:09**
- 3.45	118	- 1:47	- 3.45	116	- 1:49	- 3.45	69	- 2:36	- 3.45	108	- 1:57
- 3.30	115	- 1:35	- 3.30	110	- 1:40	- 3.30	69	- 2:21	- 3.30	106	- 1:44
- 3.15	112	- 1:23	- 3.15	105	- 1:30	- 3.15	69	- 2:06	- 3.15	103	- 1:32
- 3.00	**109**	**- 1:11**	**- 3.00**	**100**	**- 1:20**	**- 3.00**	**70**	**- 1:50**	**- 3.00**	**100**	**- 1:20**
- 2.45	105	- 1:00	- 2.45	99	- 1:06	- 2.45	69	- 1:36	- 2.45	96	- 1:09
- 2.30	102	- 0:48	- 2.30	98	- 0:52	- 2.30	68	- 1:22	- 2.30	92	- 0:58
- 2.15	99	- 0:36	- 2.15	97	- 0:38	- 2.15	66	- 1:09	- 2.15	88	- 0:47
- 2.00	**95**	**- 0:25**	**- 2.00**	**95**	**- 0:25**	**- 2.00**	**65**	**- 0:55**	**- 2.00**	**84**	**- 0:36**
- 1.45	91	- 0:14	- 1.45	89	- 0:16	- 1.45	63	- 0:42	- 1.45	80	- 0:25
- 1.30	87	- 0:03	- 1.30	82	- 0:08	- 1.30	61	- 0:29	- 1.30	75	- 0:15
- 1.15	83	+ 0:08	- 1.15	75	HW	- 1.15	59	- 0:16	- 1.15	71	- 0:04
- 1.00	**79**	**+ 0:19**	**- 1.00**	**69**	**+ 0:09**	**- 1.00**	**57**	**- 0:03**	**- 1.00**	**67**	**+ 0:07**
- 0.45	77	+ 0:32	- 0.45	67	+ 0:22	- 0.45	55	+ 0:10	- 0.45	63	+ 0:18
- 0.30	75	+ 0:45	- 0.30	65	+ 0:35	- 0.30	53	+ 0:23	- 0.30	59	+ 0:29
- 0.15	73	+ 0:58	- 0.15	63	+ 0:48	- 0.15	50	+ 0:35	- 0.15	55	+ 0:40
HW	**72**	**+ 1:12**	**HW**	**61**	**+ 1:01**	**HW**	**48**	**+ 0:48**	**HW**	**51**	**+ 0:51**
+ 0.15	72	+ 1:27	+ 0.15	60	+ 1:15	+ 0.15	46	+ 1:01	+ 0.15	49	+ 1:04
+ 0.30	72	+ 1:42	+ 0.30	60	+ 1:30	+ 0.30	44	+ 1:14	+ 0.30	47	+ 1:17
+ 0.45	73	+ 1:58	+ 0.45	59	+ 1:44	+ 0.45	42	+ 1:27	+ 0.45	45	+ 1:30
+ 1.00	**73**	**+ 2:13**	**+ 1.00**	**59**	**+ 1:59**	**+ 1.00**	**39**	**+ 1:39**	**+ 1.00**	**43**	**+ 1:43**
+ 1.15	74	+ 2:29	+ 1.15	60	+ 2:15	+ 1.15	38	+ 1:53	+ 1.15	43	+ 1:58
+ 1.30	75	+ 2:45	+ 1.30	61	+ 2:31	+ 1.30	37	+ 2:07	+ 1.30	43	+ 2:13
+ 1.45	77	+ 3:02	+ 1.45	63	+ 2:48	+ 1.45	36	+ 2:21	+ 1.45	43	+ 2:28
+ 2.00	**78**	**+ 3:18**	**+ 2.00**	**64**	**+ 3:04**	**+ 2.00**	**34**	**+ 2:34**	**+ 2.00**	**42**	**+ 2:42**
+ 2.15	79	+ 3:34	+ 2.15	66	+ 3:21	+ 2.15	34	+ 2:49	+ 2.15	43	+ 2:58
+ 2.30	81	+ 3:51	+ 2.30	68	+ 3:38	+ 2.30	34	+ 3:04	+ 2.30	44	+ 3:14
+ 2.45	83	+ 4:08	+ 2.45	70	+ 3:55	+ 2.45	34	+ 3:19	+ 2.45	45	+ 3:30
+ 3.00	**84**	**+ 4:24**	**+ 3.00**	**72**	**+ 4:12**	**+ 3.00**	**34**	**+ 3:34**	**+ 3.00**	**45**	**+ 3:45**
+ 3.15	87	+ 4:42	+ 3.15	74	+ 4:29	+ 3.15	34	+ 3:49	+ 3.15	47	+ 4:02
+ 3.30	90	+ 5:00	+ 3.30	77	+ 4:47	+ 3.30	35	+ 4:05	+ 3.30	48	+ 4:18
+ 3.45	93	+ 5:18	+ 3.45	79	+ 5:04	+ 3.45	36	+ 4:21	+ 3.45	49	+ 4:34
+ 4.00	**95**	**+ 5:35**	**+ 4.00**	**81**	**+ 5:21**	**+ 4.00**	**36**	**+ 4:36**	**+ 4.00**	**51**	**+ 4:51**
+ 4.15	98	+ 5:53	+ 4.15	83	+ 5:38	+ 4.15	37	+ 4:52	+ 4.15	53	+ 5:08
+ 4.30	101	- 5:49	+ 4.30	85	+ 5:55	+ 4.30	39	+ 5:09	+ 4.30	56	+ 5:26
+ 4.45	104	- 5:31	+ 4.45	87	- 5:48	+ 4.45	40	+ 5:25	+ 4.45	59	+ 5:44
+ 5.00	**107**	**- 5:13**	**+ 5.00**	**90**	**- 5:30**	**+ 5.00**	**41**	**+ 5:41**	**+ 5.00**	**61**	**- 5:59**
+ 5.15	111	- 4:54	+ 5.15	96	- 5:09	+ 5.15	42	+ 5:57	+ 5.15	63	- 5:42
+ 5.30	116	- 4:34	+ 5.30	102	- 4:48	+ 5.30	43	- 5:47	+ 5.30	65	- 5:25
+ 5.45	120	- 4:15	+ 5.45	108	- 4:27	+ 5.45	45	- 5:30	+ 5.45	67	- 5:08
+ 6.00	**124**	**- 3:56**	**+ 6.00**	**114**	**- 4:06**	**+ 6.00**	**46**	**- 5:14**	**+ 6.00**	**69**	**- 4:51**

Table J - Essex to Suffolk Rivers Sea Reach to North Oaze

Neaps

All times relate to HW Sheerness

Time to cover Sectors (in minutes) at 5.0 Kts

NORTH BOUND

J1	Spitway to the Naze		J2	Blackwater to Colne	
Time	Duration	Time at End of Sector	Time	Duration	Time at End of Sector
- 6.00	181	- 2:59	- 6.00	56	- 5:04
- 5.45	183	- 2:42	- 5.45	56	- 4:49
- 5.30	184	- 2:26	- 5.30	57	- 4:33
- 5.15	186	- 2:09	- 5.15	58	- 4:17
- 5.00	187	- 1:53	- 5.00	59	- 4:01
- 4.45	186	- 1:39	- 4.45	60	- 3:45
- 4.30	185	- 1:25	- 4.30	60	- 3:30
- 4.15	183	- 1:12	- 4.15	61	- 3:14
- 4.00	182	- 0:58	- 4.00	61	- 2:59
- 3.45	179	- 0:46	- 3.45	61	- 2:44
- 3.30	175	- 0:35	- 3.30	61	- 2:29
- 3.15	172	- 0:23	- 3.15	61	- 2:14
- 3.00	169	- 0:11	- 3.00	61	- 1:59
- 2.45	165	HW	- 2.45	61	- 1:44
- 2.30	161	+ 0:11	- 2.30	60	- 1:30
- 2.15	157	+ 0:22	- 2.15	60	- 1:15
- 2.00	153	+ 0:33	- 2.00	59	- 1:01
- 1.45	148	+ 0:43	- 1.45	57	- 0:48
- 1.30	143	+ 0:53	- 1.30	55	- 0:35
- 1.15	138	+ 1:03	- 1.15	53	- 0:22
- 1.00	133	+ 1:13	- 1.00	52	- 0:08
- 0.45	130	+ 1:25	- 0.45	50	+ 0:05
- 0.30	127	+ 1:37	- 0.30	48	+ 0:18
- 0.15	124	+ 1:49	- 0.15	46	+ 0:31
HW	120	+ 2:00	HW	44	+ 0:44
+ 0.15	120	+ 2:15	+ 0.15	44	+ 0:59
+ 0.30	119	+ 2:29	+ 0.30	43	+ 1:13
+ 0.45	118	+ 2:43	+ 0.45	42	+ 1:27
+ 1.00	117	+ 2:57	+ 1.00	42	+ 1:42
+ 1.15	118	+ 3:13	+ 1.15	42	+ 1:57
+ 1.30	119	+ 3:29	+ 1.30	42	+ 2:12
+ 1.45	121	+ 3:46	+ 1.45	42	+ 2:27
+ 2.00	122	+ 4:02	+ 2.00	42	+ 2:42
+ 2.15	124	+ 4:19	+ 2.15	42	+ 2:57
+ 2.30	125	+ 4:35	+ 2.30	43	+ 3:13
+ 2.45	127	+ 4:52	+ 2.45	43	+ 3:28
+ 3.00	129	+ 5:09	+ 3.00	44	+ 3:44
+ 3.15	131	+ 5:26	+ 3.15	45	+ 4:00
+ 3.30	133	+ 5:43	+ 3.30	45	+ 4:15
+ 3.45	135	- 6:00	+ 3.45	46	+ 4:31
+ 4.00	137	- 5:43	+ 4.00	47	+ 4:47
+ 4.15	140	- 5:25	+ 4.15	48	+ 5:03
+ 4.30	143	- 5:07	+ 4.30	48	+ 5:18
+ 4.45	145	- 4:50	+ 4.45	49	+ 5:34
+ 5.00	148	- 4:32	+ 5.00	50	+ 5:50
+ 5.15	153	- 4:12	+ 5.15	50	- 5:55
+ 5.30	158	- 3:52	+ 5.30	51	- 5:39
+ 5.45	163	- 3:32	+ 5.45	52	- 5:23
+ 6.00	168	- 3:12	+ 6.00	53	- 5:07

J3	Colne to Holland-on-Sea		J4	Holland-on-Sea to the Naze	
Time	Duration	Time at End of Sector	Time	Duration	Time at End of Sector
- 6.00	111	- 4:09	- 6.00	77	- 4:43
- 5.45	113	- 3:52	- 5.45	81	- 4:24
- 5.30	115	- 3:35	- 5.30	85	- 4:05
- 5.15	117	- 3:18	- 5.15	90	- 3:45
- 5.00	119	- 3:01	- 5.00	94	- 3:26
- 4.45	120	- 2:45	- 4.45	94	- 3:11
- 4.30	120	- 2:30	- 4.30	93	- 2:57
- 4.15	121	- 2:14	- 4.15	92	- 2:43
- 4.00	122	- 1:58	- 4.00	92	- 2:28
- 3.45	121	- 1:44	- 3.45	88	- 2:17
- 3.30	121	- 1:29	- 3.30	84	- 2:06
- 3.15	121	- 1:14	- 3.15	81	- 1:54
- 3.00	120	- 1:00	- 3.00	77	- 1:43
- 2.45	118	- 0:47	- 2.45	74	- 1:31
- 2.30	115	- 0:35	- 2.30	72	- 1:18
- 2.15	113	- 0:22	- 2.15	70	- 1:05
- 2.00	110	- 0:10	- 2.00	67	- 0:53
- 1.45	107	+ 0:02	- 1.45	65	- 0:40
- 1.30	103	+ 0:13	- 1.30	63	- 0:27
- 1.15	99	+ 0:24	- 1.15	61	- 0:14
- 1.00	96	+ 0:36	- 1.00	58	- 0:02
- 0.45	93	+ 0:48	- 0.45	56	+ 0:11
- 0.30	90	+ 1:00	- 0.30	54	+ 0:24
- 0.15	88	+ 1:13	- 0.15	52	+ 0:37
HW	85	+ 1:25	HW	50	+ 0:50
+ 0.15	84	+ 1:39	+ 0.15	50	+ 1:05
+ 0.30	84	+ 1:54	+ 0.30	49	+ 1:19
+ 0.45	83	+ 2:08	+ 0.45	48	+ 1:33
+ 1.00	82	+ 2:22	+ 1.00	48	+ 1:48
+ 1.15	83	+ 2:38	+ 1.15	48	+ 2:03
+ 1.30	83	+ 2:53	+ 1.30	49	+ 2:19
+ 1.45	83	+ 3:08	+ 1.45	49	+ 2:34
+ 2.00	84	+ 3:24	+ 2.00	49	+ 2:49
+ 2.15	85	+ 3:40	+ 2.15	50	+ 3:05
+ 2.30	86	+ 3:56	+ 2.30	51	+ 3:21
+ 2.45	88	+ 4:13	+ 2.45	52	+ 3:37
+ 3.00	89	+ 4:29	+ 3.00	52	+ 3:52
+ 3.15	90	+ 4:45	+ 3.15	53	+ 4:08
+ 3.30	90	+ 5:00	+ 3.30	54	+ 4:24
+ 3.45	91	+ 5:16	+ 3.45	55	+ 4:40
+ 4.00	92	+ 5:32	+ 4.00	56	+ 4:56
+ 4.15	93	+ 5:48	+ 4.15	58	+ 5:13
+ 4.30	95	- 5:55	+ 4.30	59	+ 5:29
+ 4.45	96	- 5:39	+ 4.45	61	+ 5:46
+ 5.00	98	- 5:22	+ 5.00	63	- 5:57
+ 5.15	100	- 5:05	+ 5.15	64	- 5:41
+ 5.30	102	- 4:48	+ 5.30	66	- 5:24
+ 5.45	104	- 4:31	+ 5.45	67	- 5:08
+ 6.00	106	- 4:14	+ 6.00	69	- 4:51

J5	The Naze to Deben Landfall		J6	NE Gunfleet to Cork Sand Bcn	
Time	Duration	Time at End of Sector	Time	Duration	Time at End of Sector
- 6.00	94	- 4:26	- 6.00	81	- 4:39
- 5.45	94	- 4:11	- 5.45	81	- 4:24
- 5.30	94	- 3:56	- 5.30	82	- 4:08
- 5.15	94	- 3:41	- 5.15	82	- 3:53
- 5.00	95	- 3:25	- 5.00	83	- 3:37
- 4.45	94	- 3:11	- 4.45	82	- 3:23
- 4.30	93	- 2:57	- 4.30	82	- 3:08
- 4.15	92	- 2:43	- 4.15	82	- 2:53
- 4.00	91	- 2:29	- 4.00	81	- 2:39
- 3.45	89	- 2:16	- 3.45	80	- 2:25
- 3.30	87	- 2:03	- 3.30	78	- 2:12
- 3.15	86	- 1:49	- 3.15	76	- 1:59
- 3.00	84	- 1:36	- 3.00	75	- 1:45
- 2.45	82	- 1:23	- 2.45	73	- 1:32
- 2.30	81	- 1:09	- 2.30	71	- 1:19
- 2.15	79	- 0:56	- 2.15	69	- 1:06
- 2.00	78	- 0:42	- 2.00	67	- 0:53
- 1.45	76	- 0:29	- 1.45	65	- 0:40
- 1.30	74	- 0:16	- 1.30	64	- 0:26
- 1.15	73	- 0:02	- 1.15	62	- 0:13
- 1.00	71	+ 0:11	- 1.00	61	+ 0:01
- 0.45	70	+ 0:25	- 0.45	60	+ 0:15
- 0.30	68	+ 0:38	- 0.30	58	+ 0:28
- 0.15	67	+ 0:52	- 0.15	57	+ 0:42
HW	66	+ 1:06	HW	56	+ 0:56
+ 0.15	66	+ 1:21	+ 0.15	56	+ 1:11
+ 0.30	66	+ 1:36	+ 0.30	56	+ 1:26
+ 0.45	66	+ 1:51	+ 0.45	56	+ 1:41
+ 1.00	66	+ 2:06	+ 1.00	55	+ 1:55
+ 1.15	67	+ 2:22	+ 1.15	56	+ 2:11
+ 1.30	68	+ 2:38	+ 1.30	56	+ 2:26
+ 1.45	68	+ 2:53	+ 1.45	57	+ 2:42
+ 2.00	69	+ 3:09	+ 2.00	58	+ 2:58
+ 2.15	70	+ 3:25	+ 2.15	59	+ 3:14
+ 2.30	70	+ 3:40	+ 2.30	60	+ 3:30
+ 2.45	71	+ 3:56	+ 2.45	61	+ 3:46
+ 3.00	72	+ 4:12	+ 3.00	62	+ 4:02
+ 3.15	73	+ 4:28	+ 3.15	63	+ 4:18
+ 3.30	74	+ 4:44	+ 3.30	64	+ 4:34
+ 3.45	75	+ 5:00	+ 3.45	65	+ 4:50
+ 4.00	77	+ 5:17	+ 4.00	66	+ 5:06
+ 4.15	78	+ 5:33	+ 4.15	67	+ 5:22
+ 4.30	79	+ 5:49	+ 4.30	68	+ 5:38
+ 4.45	80	- 5:55	+ 4.45	69	+ 5:54
+ 5.00	81	- 5:39	+ 5.00	70	- 5:50
+ 5.15	82	- 5:23	+ 5.15	71	- 5:34
+ 5.30	83	- 5:07	+ 5.30	73	- 5:17
+ 5.45	85	- 4:50	+ 5.45	74	- 5:01
+ 6.00	86	- 4:34	+ 6.00	76	- 4:44

J7	Sea Reach No 1 to North Oaze		J8	Crouch to Spitway	
Time	Duration	Time at End of Sector	Time	Duration	Time at End of Sector
- 6.00	39	- 5:21	- 6.00	58	- 5:02
- 5.45	40	- 5:05	- 5.45	59	- 4:46
- 5.30	41	- 4:49	- 5.30	61	- 4:29
- 5.15	42	- 4:33	- 5.15	63	- 4:12
- 5.00	44	- 4:16	- 5.00	64	- 3:56
- 4.45	44	- 4:01	- 4.45	65	- 3:40
- 4.30	45	- 3:45	- 4.30	65	- 3:25
- 4.15	46	- 3:29	- 4.15	65	- 3:10
- 4.00	47	- 3:13	- 4.00	65	- 2:55
- 3.45	47	- 2:58	- 3.45	65	- 2:40
- 3.30	47	- 2:43	- 3.30	64	- 2:26
- 3.15	47	- 2:28	- 3.15	64	- 2:11
- 3.00	47	- 2:13	- 3.00	63	- 1:57
- 2.45	47	- 1:58	- 2.45	62	- 1:43
- 2.30	46	- 1:44	- 2.30	62	- 1:28
- 2.15	46	- 1:29	- 2.15	61	- 1:14
- 2.00	46	- 1:14	- 2.00	60	- 1:00
- 1.45	45	- 1:00	- 1.45	58	- 0:47
- 1.30	44	- 0:46	- 1.30	57	- 0:33
- 1.15	43	- 0:32	- 1.15	55	- 0:20
- 1.00	43	- 0:17	- 1.00	53	- 0:07
- 0.45	42	- 0:03	- 0.45	52	+ 0:07
- 0.30	41	+ 0:11	- 0.30	50	+ 0:20
- 0.15	40	+ 0:25	- 0.15	48	+ 0:33
HW	39	+ 0:39	HW	46	+ 0:46
+ 0.15	38	+ 0:53	+ 0.15	45	+ 1:00
+ 0.30	37	+ 1:07	+ 0.30	44	+ 1:14
+ 0.45	36	+ 1:21	+ 0.45	43	+ 1:28
+ 1.00	36	+ 1:36	+ 1.00	42	+ 1:42
+ 1.15	35	+ 1:50	+ 1.15	42	+ 1:57
+ 1.30	34	+ 2:04	+ 1.30	42	+ 2:12
+ 1.45	33	+ 2:18	+ 1.45	42	+ 2:27
+ 2.00	32	+ 2:32	+ 2.00	42	+ 2:42
+ 2.15	32	+ 2:47	+ 2.15	42	+ 2:57
+ 2.30	32	+ 3:02	+ 2.30	42	+ 3:12
+ 2.45	32	+ 3:17	+ 2.45	43	+ 3:28
+ 3.00	32	+ 3:32	+ 3.00	43	+ 3:43
+ 3.15	32	+ 3:47	+ 3.15	44	+ 3:59
+ 3.30	32	+ 4:02	+ 3.30	44	+ 4:14
+ 3.45	33	+ 4:18	+ 3.45	45	+ 4:30
+ 4.00	33	+ 4:33	+ 4.00	45	+ 4:45
+ 4.15	33	+ 4:48	+ 4.15	46	+ 5:01
+ 4.30	34	+ 5:04	+ 4.30	47	+ 5:17
+ 4.45	34	+ 5:19	+ 4.45	48	+ 5:33
+ 5.00	35	+ 5:35	+ 5.00	49	+ 5:49
+ 5.15	35	+ 5:50	+ 5.15	50	- 5:55
+ 5.30	36	- 5:54	+ 5.30	51	- 5:39
+ 5.45	37	- 5:38	+ 5.45	52	- 5:23
+ 6.00	37	- 5:23	+ 6.00	53	- 5:07

Table J - Essex to Suffolk Rivers Sea Reach to North Oaze

Time to cover Sectors (in minutes) at 5.0 kts — All times relate to HW Sheerness — **Springs**

	J1 Spitway to the Naze			J2 Blackwater to Colne			J3 Colne to Holland-on-Sea			J4 Holland-on-Sea to the Naze			J5 The Naze to Deben Landfall			J6 NE Gunfleet to Cork Sand Bcn			J7 Sea Reach No 1 to North Oaze			J8 Crouch to Spitway	
Time	Duration	Time at End of Sector	Time	Duration	Time at End of Sector	Time	Duration	Time at End of Sector	Time	Duration	Time at End of Sector	Time	Duration	Time at End of Sector	Time	Duration	Time at End of Sector	Time	Duration	Time at End of Sector	Time	Duration	Time at End of Sector
- 6.00	201	- 2:39	- 6.00	58	- 5:02	- 6.00	117	- 4:03	- 6.00	94	- 4:26	- 6.00	101	- 4:19	- 6.00	90	- 4:30	- 6.00	39	- 5:21	- 6.00	61	- 4:59
- 5.45	203	- 2:22	- 5.45	59	- 4:46	- 5.45	120	- 3:45	- 5.45	97	- 4:08	- 5.45	101	- 4:04	- 5.45	92	- 4:13	- 5.45	41	- 5:04	- 5.45	64	- 4:41
- 5.30	206	- 2:04	- 5.30	61	- 4:29	- 5.30	122	- 3:28	- 5.30	100	- 3:50	- 5.30	101	- 3:49	- 5.30	94	- 3:56	- 5.30	43	- 4:47	- 5.30	67	- 4:23
- 5.15	208	- 1:47	- 5.15	62	- 4:13	- 5.15	125	- 3:10	- 5.15	103	- 3:32	- 5.15	101	- 3:34	- 5.15	96	- 3:39	- 5.15	45	- 4:30	- 5.15	70	- 4:05
- 5.00	210	- 1:30	- 5.00	63	- 3:57	- 5.00	127	- 2:53	- 5.00	106	- 3:14	- 5.00	100	- 3:20	- 5.00	98	- 3:22	- 5.00	47	- 4:13	- 5.00	73	- 3:47
- 4.45	206	- 1:19	- 4.45	64	- 3:41	- 4.45	129	- 2:36	- 4.45	106	- 2:59	- 4.45	99	- 3:06	- 4.45	97	- 3:08	- 4.45	48	- 3:57	- 4.45	73	- 3:32
- 4.30	203	- 1:07	- 4.30	65	- 3:25	- 4.30	130	- 2:20	- 4.30	105	- 2:45	- 4.30	98	- 2:52	- 4.30	96	- 2:54	- 4.30	49	- 3:41	- 4.30	74	- 3:16
- 4.15	199	- 0:56	- 4.15	66	- 3:09	- 4.15	131	- 2:04	- 4.15	104	- 2:31	- 4.15	96	- 2:39	- 4.15	95	- 2:40	- 4.15	50	- 3:25	- 4.15	74	- 3:01
- 4.00	195	- 0:45	- 4.00	67	- 2:53	- 4.00	132	- 1:48	- 4.00	103	- 2:17	- 4.00	95	- 2:25	- 4.00	94	- 2:26	- 4.00	51	- 3:09	- 4.00	75	- 2:45
- 3.45	190	- 0:35	- 3.45	67	- 2:38	- 3.45	131	- 1:34	- 3.45	100	- 2:05	- 3.45	93	- 2:12	- 3.45	95	- 2:10	- 3.45	51	- 2:54	- 3.45	74	- 2:31
- 3.30	185	- 0:25	- 3.30	67	- 2:23	- 3.30	130	- 1:20	- 3.30	97	- 1:53	- 3.30	91	- 1:59	- 3.30	96	- 1:54	- 3.30	52	- 2:38	- 3.30	73	- 2:17
- 3.15	180	- 0:15	- 3.15	67	- 2:08	- 3.15	129	- 1:06	- 3.15	93	- 1:42	- 3.15	89	- 1:46	- 3.15	97	- 1:38	- 3.15	52	- 2:23	- 3.15	72	- 2:03
- 3.00	174	- 0:06	- 3.00	68	- 1:52	- 3.00	128	- 0:52	- 3.00	90	- 1:30	- 3.00	87	- 1:33	- 3.00	98	- 1:22	- 3.00	52	- 2:08	- 3.00	71	- 1:49
- 2.45	169	+ 0:04	- 2.45	67	- 1:38	- 2.45	124	- 0:41	- 2.45	85	- 1:20	- 2.45	85	- 1:20	- 2.45	90	- 1:15	- 2.45	52	- 1:53	- 2.45	70	- 1:35
- 2.30	164	+ 0:14	- 2.30	66	- 1:24	- 2.30	120	- 0:30	- 2.30	80	- 1:10	- 2.30	83	- 1:07	- 2.30	82	- 1:08	- 2.30	51	- 1:39	- 2.30	68	- 1:22
- 2.15	158	+ 0:23	- 2.15	64	- 1:11	- 2.15	115	- 0:20	- 2.15	75	- 1:00	- 2.15	80	- 0:55	- 2.15	74	- 1:01	- 2.15	51	- 1:24	- 2.15	66	- 1:09
- 2.00	153	+ 0:33	- 2.00	63	- 0:57	- 2.00	111	- 0:09	- 2.00	70	- 0:50	- 2.00	78	- 0:42	- 2.00	67	- 0:53	- 2.00	50	- 1:10	- 2.00	65	- 0:55
- 1.45	146	+ 0:41	- 1.45	60	- 0:45	- 1.45	106	+ 0:01	- 1.45	66	- 0:39	- 1.45	75	- 0:30	- 1.45	64	- 0:41	- 1.45	49	- 0:56	- 1.45	62	- 0:43
- 1.30	139	+ 0:49	- 1.30	57	- 0:33	- 1.30	102	+ 0:12	- 1.30	63	- 0:27	- 1.30	73	- 0:17	- 1.30	62	- 0:28	- 1.30	47	- 0:43	- 1.30	60	- 0:30
- 1.15	133	+ 0:58	- 1.15	54	- 0:21	- 1.15	97	+ 0:22	- 1.15	59	- 0:16	- 1.15	70	- 0:05	- 1.15	60	- 0:15	- 1.15	46	- 0:29	- 1.15	57	- 0:18
- 1.00	126	+ 1:06	- 1.00	51	- 0:09	- 1.00	92	+ 0:32	- 1.00	56	- 0:04	- 1.00	67	+ 0:07	- 1.00	58	- 0:02	- 1.00	45	- 0:15	- 1.00	54	- 0:06
- 0.45	123	+ 1:18	- 0.45	49	+ 0:04	- 0.45	89	+ 0:44	- 0.45	53	+ 0:08	- 0.45	66	+ 0:21	- 0.45	56	+ 0:11	- 0.45	43	- 0:02	- 0.45	52	+ 0:07
- 0.30	120	+ 1:30	- 0.30	46	+ 0:16	- 0.30	86	+ 0:56	- 0.30	51	+ 0:21	- 0.30	64	+ 0:34	- 0.30	55	+ 0:25	- 0.30	42	+ 0:12	- 0.30	49	+ 0:19
- 0.15	117	+ 1:42	- 0.15	44	+ 0:29	- 0.15	82	+ 1:07	- 0.15	48	+ 0:33	- 0.15	63	+ 0:48	- 0.15	54	+ 0:39	- 0.15	41	+ 0:26	- 0.15	47	+ 0:32
HW	113	+ 1:53	HW	41	+ 0:41	HW	79	+ 1:19	HW	46	+ 0:46	HW	61	+ 1:01	HW	52	+ 0:52	HW	39	+ 0:39	HW	44	+ 0:44
+ 0.15	113	+ 2:08	+ 0.15	40	+ 0:55	+ 0.15	78	+ 1:33	+ 0.15	45	+ 1:00	+ 0.15	61	+ 1:16	+ 0.15	52	+ 1:07	+ 0.15	38	+ 0:53	+ 0.15	42	+ 0:57
+ 0.30	112	+ 2:22	+ 0.30	40	+ 1:10	+ 0.30	77	+ 1:47	+ 0.30	44	+ 1:14	+ 0.30	62	+ 1:32	+ 0.30	51	+ 1:21	+ 0.30	37	+ 1:07	+ 0.30	41	+ 1:11
+ 0.45	111	+ 2:36	+ 0.45	39	+ 1:24	+ 0.45	76	+ 2:01	+ 0.45	43	+ 1:28	+ 0.45	62	+ 1:47	+ 0.45	51	+ 1:36	+ 0.45	35	+ 1:20	+ 0.45	40	+ 1:25
+ 1.00	110	+ 2:50	+ 1.00	38	+ 1:38	+ 1.00	75	+ 2:15	+ 1.00	42	+ 1:42	+ 1.00	62	+ 2:02	+ 1.00	51	+ 1:51	+ 1.00	34	+ 1:34	+ 1.00	38	+ 1:38
+ 1.15	112	+ 3:07	+ 1.15	38	+ 1:53	+ 1.15	76	+ 2:31	+ 1.15	43	+ 1:58	+ 1.15	63	+ 2:18	+ 1.15	51	+ 2:06	+ 1.15	33	+ 1:48	+ 1.15	38	+ 1:53
+ 1.30	113	+ 3:23	+ 1.30	38	+ 2:08	+ 1.30	76	+ 2:46	+ 1.30	44	+ 2:14	+ 1.30	63	+ 2:33	+ 1.30	52	+ 2:22	+ 1.30	32	+ 2:02	+ 1.30	38	+ 2:08
+ 1.45	115	+ 3:40	+ 1.45	38	+ 2:23	+ 1.45	77	+ 3:02	+ 1.45	44	+ 2:29	+ 1.45	64	+ 2:49	+ 1.45	53	+ 2:38	+ 1.45	31	+ 2:16	+ 1.45	37	+ 2:22
+ 2.00	116	+ 3:56	+ 2.00	38	+ 2:38	+ 2.00	78	+ 3:18	+ 2.00	45	+ 2:45	+ 2.00	65	+ 3:05	+ 2.00	54	+ 2:54	+ 2.00	30	+ 2:30	+ 2.00	37	+ 2:37
+ 2.15	118	+ 4:13	+ 2.15	39	+ 2:54	+ 2.15	79	+ 3:34	+ 2.15	46	+ 3:01	+ 2.15	66	+ 3:21	+ 2.15	55	+ 3:10	+ 2.15	30	+ 2:45	+ 2.15	38	+ 2:53
+ 2.30	120	+ 4:30	+ 2.30	39	+ 3:09	+ 2.30	81	+ 3:51	+ 2.30	46	+ 3:16	+ 2.30	67	+ 3:37	+ 2.30	56	+ 3:26	+ 2.30	29	+ 2:59	+ 2.30	38	+ 3:08
+ 2.45	122	+ 4:47	+ 2.45	40	+ 3:25	+ 2.45	83	+ 4:08	+ 2.45	47	+ 3:32	+ 2.45	68	+ 3:53	+ 2.45	58	+ 3:43	+ 2.45	29	+ 3:14	+ 2.45	38	+ 3:23
+ 3.00	125	+ 5:05	+ 3.00	41	+ 3:41	+ 3.00	84	+ 4:24	+ 3.00	48	+ 3:48	+ 3.00	69	+ 4:09	+ 3.00	59	+ 3:59	+ 3.00	29	+ 3:29	+ 3.00	39	+ 3:39
+ 3.15	127	+ 5:22	+ 3.15	42	+ 3:57	+ 3.15	86	+ 4:41	+ 3.15	49	+ 4:04	+ 3.15	71	+ 4:26	+ 3.15	60	+ 4:15	+ 3.15	29	+ 3:44	+ 3.15	40	+ 3:55
+ 3.30	130	+ 5:40	+ 3.30	43	+ 4:13	+ 3.30	87	+ 4:57	+ 3.30	51	+ 4:21	+ 3.30	72	+ 4:42	+ 3.30	62	+ 4:32	+ 3.30	29	+ 3:59	+ 3.30	40	+ 4:10
+ 3.45	133	+ 5:58	+ 3.45	44	+ 4:29	+ 3.45	88	+ 5:13	+ 3.45	52	+ 4:37	+ 3.45	74	+ 4:59	+ 3.45	63	+ 4:48	+ 3.45	30	+ 4:15	+ 3.45	41	+ 4:26
+ 4.00	136	- 5:44	+ 4.00	45	+ 4:45	+ 4.00	89	+ 5:29	+ 4.00	53	+ 4:53	+ 4.00	76	+ 5:16	+ 4.00	65	+ 5:05	+ 4.00	30	+ 4:30	+ 4.00	42	+ 4:42
+ 4.15	141	- 5:24	+ 4.15	46	+ 5:01	+ 4.15	91	+ 5:46	+ 4.15	55	+ 5:10	+ 4.15	77	+ 5:32	+ 4.15	66	+ 5:21	+ 4.15	31	+ 4:46	+ 4.15	43	+ 4:58
+ 4.30	145	- 5:05	+ 4.30	47	+ 5:17	+ 4.30	94	- 5:56	+ 4.30	58	+ 5:28	+ 4.30	79	+ 5:49	+ 4.30	68	+ 5:38	+ 4.30	32	+ 5:02	+ 4.30	45	+ 5:15
+ 4.45	149	- 4:46	+ 4.45	48	+ 5:33	+ 4.45	96	- 5:39	+ 4.45	60	+ 5:45	+ 4.45	80	- 5:55	+ 4.45	69	+ 5:54	+ 4.45	32	+ 5:17	+ 4.45	46	+ 5:31
+ 5.00	153	- 4:27	+ 5.00	49	+ 5:49	+ 5.00	99	- 5:21	+ 5.00	62	- 5:58	+ 5.00	82	- 5:38	+ 5.00	70	- 5:50	+ 5.00	33	+ 5:33	+ 5.00	48	+ 5:48
+ 5.15	160	- 4:05	+ 5.15	50	- 5:55	+ 5.15	101	- 5:04	+ 5.15	64	- 5:41	+ 5.15	85	- 5:20	+ 5.15	73	- 5:32	+ 5.15	34	+ 5:49	+ 5.15	49	- 5:56
+ 5.30	167	- 3:43	+ 5.30	51	- 5:39	+ 5.30	103	- 4:47	+ 5.30	67	- 5:23	+ 5.30	87	- 5:03	+ 5.30	75	- 5:15	+ 5.30	35	- 5:55	+ 5.30	51	- 5:39
+ 5.45	174	- 3:21	+ 5.45	53	- 5:22	+ 5.45	105	- 4:30	+ 5.45	69	- 5:06	+ 5.45	90	- 4:45	+ 5.45	78	- 4:57	+ 5.45	36	- 5:39	+ 5.45	52	- 5:23
+ 6.00	181	- 2:59	+ 6.00	54	- 5:06	+ 6.00	107	- 4:13	+ 6.00	72	- 4:48	+ 6.00	93	- 4:27	+ 6.00	80	- 4:40	+ 6.00	37	- 5:23	+ 6.00	53	- 5:07

NORTH BOUND

Table J - Essex to Suffolk Rivers Sea Reach to North Oaze

Neaps — All times relate to HW Sheerness — **Time to cover Sectors (in minutes) at 6.0 Kts**

NORTH BOUND

Time	J1 Spitway to the Naze Duration	J1 Time at End of Sector	Time	J2 Blackwater to Colne Duration	J2 Time at End of Sector	Time	J3 Colne to Holland-on-Sea Duration	J3 Time at End of Sector	Time	J4 Holland-on-Sea to the Naze Duration	J4 Time at End of Sector
- 6.00	144	- 3:36	- 6.00	45	- 5:15	- 6.00	87	- 4:33	- 6.00	61	- 4:59
- 5.45	146	- 3:19	- 5.45	46	- 4:59	- 5.45	89	- 4:16	- 5.45	63	- 4:42
- 5.30	148	- 3:02	- 5.30	47	- 4:43	- 5.30	91	- 3:59	- 5.30	64	- 4:26
- 5.15	150	- 2:45	- 5.15	47	- 4:28	- 5.15	93	- 3:42	- 5.15	65	- 4:10
- 5.00	152	- 2:28	- 5.00	48	- 4:12	- 5.00	94	- 3:26	- 5.00	66	- 3:54
- 4.45	151	- 2:14	- 4.45	48	- 3:57	- 4.45	95	- 3:10	- 4.45	66	- 3:39
- 4.30	151	- 1:59	- 4.30	49	- 3:41	- 4.30	95	- 2:55	- 4.30	66	- 3:24
- 4.15	150	- 1:45	- 4.15	49	- 3:26	- 4.15	96	- 2:39	- 4.15	66	- 3:09
- 4.00	150	- 1:30	- 4.00	49	- 3:11	- 4.00	96	- 2:24	- 4.00	66	- 2:54
- 3.45	147	- 1:18	- 3.45	49	- 2:56	- 3.45	96	- 2:09	- 3.45	65	- 2:40
- 3.30	145	- 1:05	- 3.30	49	- 2:41	- 3.30	96	- 1:54	- 3.30	64	- 2:26
- 3.15	143	- 0:52	- 3.15	49	- 2:26	- 3.15	96	- 1:39	- 3.15	63	- 2:12
- 3.00	141	- 0:39	- 3.00	49	- 2:11	- 3.00	95	- 1:25	- 3.00	62	- 1:58
- 2.45	138	- 0:27	- 2.45	49	- 1:56	- 2.45	94	- 1:11	- 2.45	61	- 1:44
- 2.30	135	- 0:15	- 2.30	49	- 1:41	- 2.30	93	- 0:57	- 2.30	59	- 1:31
- 2.15	132	- 0:03	- 2.15	49	- 1:26	- 2.15	92	- 0:43	- 2.15	58	- 1:17
- 2.00	129	+ 0:09	- 2.00	48	- 1:12	- 2.00	91	- 0:29	- 2.00	56	- 1:04
- 1.45	126	+ 0:21	- 1.45	47	- 0:58	- 1.45	88	- 0:17	- 1.45	54	- 0:51
- 1.30	122	+ 0:32	- 1.30	46	- 0:44	- 1.30	85	- 0:05	- 1.30	53	- 0:37
- 1.15	119	+ 0:44	- 1.15	45	- 0:30	- 1.15	82	+ 0:07	- 1.15	51	- 0:24
- 1.00	115	+ 0:55	- 1.00	44	- 0:16	- 1.00	79	+ 0:19	- 1.00	50	- 0:10
- 0.45	112	+ 1:07	- 0.45	42	- 0:03	- 0.45	78	+ 0:33	- 0.45	48	+ 0:03
- 0.30	110	+ 1:20	- 0.30	41	+ 0:11	- 0.30	76	+ 0:46	- 0.30	47	+ 0:17
- 0.15	107	+ 1:32	- 0.15	40	+ 0:25	- 0.15	74	+ 0:59	- 0.15	46	+ 0:31
HW	104	+ 1:44	HW	38	+ 0:38	HW	73	+ 1:13	HW	44	+ 0:44
+ 0.15	103	+ 1:58	+ 0.15	38	+ 0:53	+ 0.15	72	+ 1:27	+ 0.15	44	+ 0:59
+ 0.30	102	+ 2:12	+ 0.30	37	+ 1:07	+ 0.30	72	+ 1:42	+ 0.30	43	+ 1:13
+ 0.45	101	+ 2:26	+ 0.45	37	+ 1:22	+ 0.45	71	+ 1:56	+ 0.45	42	+ 1:27
+ 1.00	100	+ 2:40	+ 1.00	36	+ 1:36	+ 1.00	71	+ 2:11	+ 1.00	41	+ 1:41
+ 1.15	101	+ 2:56	+ 1.15	36	+ 1:51	+ 1.15	71	+ 2:26	+ 1.15	42	+ 1:57
+ 1.30	102	+ 3:12	+ 1.30	36	+ 2:06	+ 1.30	71	+ 2:41	+ 1.30	42	+ 2:12
+ 1.45	102	+ 3:27	+ 1.45	36	+ 2:21	+ 1.45	71	+ 2:56	+ 1.45	42	+ 2:27
+ 2.00	103	+ 3:43	+ 2.00	36	+ 2:36	+ 2.00	72	+ 3:12	+ 2.00	43	+ 2:43
+ 2.15	104	+ 3:59	+ 2.15	36	+ 2:51	+ 2.15	72	+ 3:27	+ 2.15	43	+ 2:58
+ 2.30	106	+ 4:16	+ 2.30	37	+ 3:07	+ 2.30	73	+ 3:43	+ 2.30	44	+ 3:14
+ 2.45	107	+ 4:32	+ 2.45	37	+ 3:22	+ 2.45	74	+ 3:59	+ 2.45	44	+ 3:29
+ 3.00	109	+ 4:49	+ 3.00	37	+ 3:37	+ 3.00	75	+ 4:15	+ 3.00	45	+ 3:45
+ 3.15	110	+ 5:05	+ 3.15	38	+ 3:53	+ 3.15	76	+ 4:31	+ 3.15	45	+ 4:00
+ 3.30	111	+ 5:21	+ 3.30	38	+ 4:08	+ 3.30	76	+ 4:46	+ 3.30	46	+ 4:16
+ 3.45	113	+ 5:38	+ 3.45	39	+ 4:24	+ 3.45	77	+ 5:02	+ 3.45	47	+ 4:32
+ 4.00	114	+ 5:54	+ 4.00	39	+ 4:39	+ 4.00	78	+ 5:18	+ 4.00	47	+ 4:47
+ 4.15	116	- 5:49	+ 4.15	40	+ 4:55	+ 4.15	79	+ 5:34	+ 4.15	48	+ 5:03
+ 4.30	118	- 5:32	+ 4.30	40	+ 5:10	+ 4.30	80	+ 5:50	+ 4.30	49	+ 5:19
+ 4.45	120	- 5:15	+ 4.45	41	+ 5:26	+ 4.45	80	- 5:55	+ 4.45	51	+ 5:36
+ 5.00	122	- 4:58	+ 5.00	41	+ 5:41	+ 5.00	81	- 5:39	+ 5.00	52	+ 5:52
+ 5.15	125	- 4:40	+ 5.15	42	+ 5:57	+ 5.15	82	- 5:23	+ 5.15	53	- 5:52
+ 5.30	127	- 4:23	+ 5.30	42	- 5:48	+ 5.30	83	- 5:07	+ 5.30	54	- 5:36
+ 5.45	130	- 4:05	+ 5.45	43	- 5:32	+ 5.45	84	- 4:51	+ 5.45	55	- 5:20
+ 6.00	133	- 3:47	+ 6.00	44	- 5:16	+ 6.00	85	- 4:35	+ 6.00	56	- 5:04

Time	J5 The Naze to Deben Landfall Duration	J5 Time at End of Sector	Time	J6 NE Gunfleet to Cork Sand Bcn Duration	J6 Time at End of Sector	Time	J7 Sea Reach No 1 to North Oaze Duration	J7 Time at End of Sector	Time	J8 Crouch to Spitway Duration	J8 Time at End of Sector
- 6.00	73	- 4:47	- 6.00	65	- 4:55	- 6.00	32	- 5:28	- 6.00	47	- 5:13
- 5.45	73	- 4:32	- 5.45	66	- 4:39	- 5.45	33	- 5:12	- 5.45	48	- 4:57
- 5.30	73	- 4:17	- 5.30	66	- 4:24	- 5.30	34	- 4:56	- 5.30	49	- 4:41
- 5.15	73	- 4:02	- 5.15	66	- 4:09	- 5.15	34	- 4:41	- 5.15	50	- 4:25
- 5.00	73	- 3:47	- 5.00	67	- 3:53	- 5.00	35	- 4:25	- 5.00	52	- 4:08
- 4.45	73	- 3:32	- 4.45	66	- 3:39	- 4.45	36	- 4:09	- 4.45	52	- 3:53
- 4.30	73	- 3:17	- 4.30	66	- 3:24	- 4.30	36	- 3:54	- 4.30	52	- 3:38
- 4.15	72	- 3:03	- 4.15	66	- 3:09	- 4.15	37	- 3:38	- 4.15	52	- 3:23
- 4.00	72	- 2:48	- 4.00	66	- 2:54	- 4.00	38	- 3:22	- 4.00	53	- 3:07
- 3.45	71	- 2:34	- 3.45	65	- 2:40	- 3.45	38	- 3:07	- 3.45	52	- 2:53
- 3.30	70	- 2:20	- 3.30	64	- 2:26	- 3.30	38	- 2:52	- 3.30	52	- 2:38
- 3.15	70	- 2:05	- 3.15	63	- 2:12	- 3.15	38	- 2:37	- 3.15	52	- 2:23
- 3.00	69	- 1:51	- 3.00	62	- 1:58	- 3.00	38	- 2:22	- 3.00	51	- 2:09
- 2.45	68	- 1:37	- 2.45	60	- 1:45	- 2.45	38	- 2:07	- 2.45	51	- 1:54
- 2.30	67	- 1:23	- 2.30	59	- 1:31	- 2.30	38	- 1:52	- 2.30	50	- 1:40
- 2.15	66	- 1:09	- 2.15	57	- 1:18	- 2.15	37	- 1:38	- 2.15	50	- 1:25
- 2.00	65	- 0:55	- 2.00	56	- 1:04	- 2.00	37	- 1:23	- 2.00	49	- 1:11
- 1.45	64	- 0:41	- 1.45	55	- 0:50	- 1.45	37	- 1:08	- 1.45	48	- 0:57
- 1.30	63	- 0:27	- 1.30	54	- 0:36	- 1.30	36	- 0:54	- 1.30	47	- 0:43
- 1.15	61	- 0:14	- 1.15	53	- 0:22	- 1.15	36	- 0:39	- 1.15	46	- 0:29
- 1.00	60	HW	- 1.00	52	- 0:08	- 1.00	35	- 0:25	- 1.00	45	- 0:15
- 0.45	59	+ 0:14	- 0.45	51	+ 0:06	- 0.45	35	- 0:10	- 0.45	44	- 0:01
- 0.30	58	+ 0:28	- 0.30	50	+ 0:20	- 0.30	34	+ 0:04	- 0.30	42	+ 0:12
- 0.15	58	+ 0:43	- 0.15	49	+ 0:34	- 0.15	34	+ 0:19	- 0.15	41	+ 0:26
HW	57	+ 0:57	HW	49	+ 0:49	HW	33	+ 0:33	HW	40	+ 0:40
+ 0.15	57	+ 1:12	+ 0.15	48	+ 1:03	+ 0.15	32	+ 0:47	+ 0.15	39	+ 0:54
+ 0.30	57	+ 1:27	+ 0.30	48	+ 1:18	+ 0.30	32	+ 1:02	+ 0.30	38	+ 1:08
+ 0.45	57	+ 1:42	+ 0.45	48	+ 1:33	+ 0.45	31	+ 1:16	+ 0.45	37	+ 1:22
+ 1.00	57	+ 1:57	+ 1.00	48	+ 1:48	+ 1.00	30	+ 1:30	+ 1.00	37	+ 1:37
+ 1.15	57	+ 2:12	+ 1.15	48	+ 2:03	+ 1.15	30	+ 1:45	+ 1.15	36	+ 1:51
+ 1.30	57	+ 2:27	+ 1.30	48	+ 2:18	+ 1.30	29	+ 1:59	+ 1.30	36	+ 2:06
+ 1.45	58	+ 2:43	+ 1.45	49	+ 2:34	+ 1.45	28	+ 2:13	+ 1.45	36	+ 2:21
+ 2.00	58	+ 2:58	+ 2.00	49	+ 2:49	+ 2.00	28	+ 2:28	+ 2.00	36	+ 2:36
+ 2.15	59	+ 3:14	+ 2.15	50	+ 3:05	+ 2.15	27	+ 2:42	+ 2.15	36	+ 2:51
+ 2.30	59	+ 3:29	+ 2.30	50	+ 3:20	+ 2.30	27	+ 2:57	+ 2.30	36	+ 3:06
+ 2.45	60	+ 3:45	+ 2.45	51	+ 3:36	+ 2.45	27	+ 3:12	+ 2.45	37	+ 3:22
+ 3.00	60	+ 4:00	+ 3.00	52	+ 3:52	+ 3.00	27	+ 3:27	+ 3.00	37	+ 3:37
+ 3.15	61	+ 4:16	+ 3.15	53	+ 4:08	+ 3.15	27	+ 3:42	+ 3.15	37	+ 3:52
+ 3.30	62	+ 4:32	+ 3.30	53	+ 4:23	+ 3.30	27	+ 3:57	+ 3.30	38	+ 4:08
+ 3.45	63	+ 4:48	+ 3.45	54	+ 4:39	+ 3.45	27	+ 4:12	+ 3.45	38	+ 4:23
+ 4.00	64	+ 5:04	+ 4.00	55	+ 4:55	+ 4.00	28	+ 4:28	+ 4.00	38	+ 4:38
+ 4.15	64	+ 5:19	+ 4.15	55	+ 5:10	+ 4.15	28	+ 4:43	+ 4.15	39	+ 4:54
+ 4.30	65	+ 5:35	+ 4.30	56	+ 5:26	+ 4.30	28	+ 4:58	+ 4.30	40	+ 5:10
+ 4.45	66	+ 5:51	+ 4.45	57	+ 5:42	+ 4.45	29	+ 5:14	+ 4.45	40	+ 5:25
+ 5.00	67	- 5:53	+ 5.00	57	+ 5:57	+ 5.00	29	+ 5:29	+ 5.00	41	+ 5:41
+ 5.15	67	- 5:38	+ 5.15	58	- 5:47	+ 5.15	30	+ 5:45	+ 5.15	42	+ 5:57
+ 5.30	68	- 5:22	+ 5.30	59	- 5:31	+ 5.30	30	- 6:00	+ 5.30	42	- 5:48
+ 5.45	69	- 5:06	+ 5.45	60	- 5:15	+ 5.45	31	- 5:44	+ 5.45	43	- 5:32
+ 6.00	70	- 4:50	+ 6.00	61	- 4:59	+ 6.00	31	- 5:29	+ 6.00	44	- 5:16

Table J - Essex to Suffolk Rivers Sea Reach to North Oaze

Time to cover Sectors (in minutes) at 6.0 kts — All times relate to HW Sheerness — **Springs**

Time	J1 Spitway to the Naze Duration	J1 Time at End of Sector	Time	J2 Blackwater to Colne Duration	J2 Time at End of Sector	Time	J3 Colne to Holland-on-Sea Duration	J3 Time at End of Sector	Time	J4 Holland-on-Sea to the Naze Duration	J4 Time at End of Sector
- 6.00	159	- 3:21	- 6.00	47	- 5:13	- 6.00	91	- 4:29	- 6.00	66	- 4:54
- 5.45	160	- 3:05	- 5.45	48	- 4:57	- 5.45	93	- 4:12	- 5.45	68	- 4:37
- 5.30	162	- 2:48	- 5.30	49	- 4:41	- 5.30	95	- 3:55	- 5.30	70	- 4:20
- 5.15	163	- 2:32	- 5.15	50	- 4:25	- 5.15	97	- 3:38	- 5.15	72	- 4:03
- 5.00	164	- 2:16	- 5.00	51	- 4:09	- 5.00	99	- 3:21	- 5.00	74	- 3:46
- 4.45	163	- 2:02	- 4.45	51	- 3:54	- 4.45	100	- 3:05	- 4.45	74	- 3:31
- 4.30	162	- 1:48	- 4.30	52	- 3:38	- 4.30	101	- 2:49	- 4.30	74	- 3:16
- 4.15	160	- 1:35	- 4.15	53	- 3:22	- 4.15	101	- 2:34	- 4.15	75	- 3:00
- 4.00	159	- 1:21	- 4.00	53	- 3:07	- 4.00	102	- 2:18	- 4.00	75	- 2:45
- 3.45	156	- 1:09	- 3.45	54	- 2:51	- 3.45	102	- 2:03	- 3.45	73	- 2:32
- 3.30	153	- 0:57	- 3.30	54	- 2:36	- 3.30	101	- 1:49	- 3.30	72	- 2:18
- 3.15	150	- 0:45	- 3.15	54	- 2:21	- 3.15	101	- 1:34	- 3.15	70	- 2:05
- 3.00	147	- 0:33	- 3.00	54	- 2:06	- 3.00	100	- 1:20	- 3.00	69	- 1:51
- 2.45	142	- 0:23	- 2.45	53	- 1:52	- 2.45	98	- 1:07	- 2.45	66	- 1:39
- 2.30	138	- 0:12	- 2.30	53	- 1:37	- 2.30	96	- 0:54	- 2.30	64	- 1:26
- 2.15	134	- 0:01	- 2.15	52	- 1:23	- 2.15	94	- 0:41	- 2.15	61	- 1:14
- 2.00	129	+ 0:09	- 2.00	52	- 1:08	- 2.00	92	- 0:28	- 2.00	58	- 1:02
- 1.45	125	+ 0:20	- 1.45	50	- 0:55	- 1.45	88	- 0:17	- 1.45	56	- 0:49
- 1.30	120	+ 0:30	- 1.30	48	- 0:42	- 1.30	85	- 0:05	- 1.30	53	- 0:37
- 1.15	116	+ 0:41	- 1.15	46	- 0:29	- 1.15	81	+ 0:06	- 1.15	51	- 0:24
- 1.00	111	+ 0:51	- 1.00	44	- 0:16	- 1.00	77	+ 0:17	- 1.00	48	- 0:12
- 0.45	108	+ 1:03	- 0.45	42	- 0:03	- 0.45	75	+ 0:30	- 0.45	46	+ 0:01
- 0.30	106	+ 1:16	- 0.30	40	+ 0:10	- 0.30	73	+ 0:43	- 0.30	45	+ 0:15
- 0.15	103	+ 1:28	- 0.15	38	+ 0:23	- 0.15	71	+ 0:56	- 0.15	43	+ 0:28
HW	100	+ 1:40	HW	36	+ 0:36	HW	69	+ 1:09	HW	41	+ 0:41
+ 0.15	99	+ 1:54	+ 0.15	36	+ 0:51	+ 0.15	68	+ 1:23	+ 0.15	40	+ 0:55
+ 0.30	98	+ 2:08	+ 0.30	35	+ 1:05	+ 0.30	67	+ 1:37	+ 0.30	39	+ 1:09
+ 0.45	97	+ 2:22	+ 0.45	34	+ 1:19	+ 0.45	66	+ 1:51	+ 0.45	39	+ 1:24
+ 1.00	96	+ 2:36	+ 1.00	33	+ 1:33	+ 1.00	65	+ 2:05	+ 1.00	38	+ 1:38
+ 1.15	97	+ 2:52	+ 1.15	33	+ 1:48	+ 1.15	66	+ 2:21	+ 1.15	38	+ 1:53
+ 1.30	97	+ 3:07	+ 1.30	33	+ 2:03	+ 1.30	66	+ 2:36	+ 1.30	38	+ 2:08
+ 1.45	98	+ 3:23	+ 1.45	33	+ 2:18	+ 1.45	67	+ 2:52	+ 1.45	39	+ 2:24
+ 2.00	99	+ 3:39	+ 2.00	33	+ 2:33	+ 2.00	67	+ 3:07	+ 2.00	39	+ 2:39
+ 2.15	101	+ 3:56	+ 2.15	33	+ 2:48	+ 2.15	68	+ 3:23	+ 2.15	40	+ 2:55
+ 2.30	102	+ 4:12	+ 2.30	34	+ 3:04	+ 2.30	69	+ 3:39	+ 2.30	40	+ 3:10
+ 2.45	104	+ 4:29	+ 2.45	35	+ 3:20	+ 2.45	71	+ 3:56	+ 2.45	41	+ 3:26
+ 3.00	105	+ 4:45	+ 3.00	35	+ 3:35	+ 3.00	72	+ 4:12	+ 3.00	42	+ 3:42
+ 3.15	107	+ 5:02	+ 3.15	36	+ 3:51	+ 3.15	73	+ 4:28	+ 3.15	42	+ 3:57
+ 3.30	109	+ 5:19	+ 3.30	36	+ 4:06	+ 3.30	73	+ 4:43	+ 3.30	43	+ 4:13
+ 3.45	111	+ 5:36	+ 3.45	37	+ 4:22	+ 3.45	74	+ 4:59	+ 3.45	44	+ 4:29
+ 4.00	113	+ 5:53	+ 4.00	38	+ 4:38	+ 4.00	75	+ 5:15	+ 4.00	45	+ 4:45
+ 4.15	116	- 5:49	+ 4.15	38	+ 4:53	+ 4.15	77	+ 5:32	+ 4.15	47	+ 5:02
+ 4.30	118	- 5:32	+ 4.30	39	+ 5:09	+ 4.30	78	+ 5:48	+ 4.30	48	+ 5:18
+ 4.45	121	- 5:14	+ 4.45	40	+ 5:25	+ 4.45	80	- 5:55	+ 4.45	50	+ 5:35
+ 5.00	124	- 4:56	+ 5.00	40	+ 5:40	+ 5.00	81	- 5:39	+ 5.00	51	+ 5:51
+ 5.15	127	- 4:38	+ 5.15	41	+ 5:56	+ 5.15	82	- 5:23	+ 5.15	53	- 5:52
+ 5.30	131	- 4:19	+ 5.30	42	- 5:48	+ 5.30	84	- 5:06	+ 5.30	54	- 5:36
+ 5.45	135	- 4:00	+ 5.45	43	- 5:32	+ 5.45	85	- 4:50	+ 5.45	56	- 5:19
+ 6.00	138	- 3:42	+ 6.00	44	- 5:16	+ 6.00	86	- 4:34	+ 6.00	58	- 5:02

Time	J5 The Naze to Deben Landfall Duration	J5 Time at End of Sector	Time	J6 NE Gunfleet to Cork Sand Bcn Duration	J6 Time at End of Sector	Time	J7 Sea Reach No 1 to North Oaze Duration	J7 Time at End of Sector	Time	J8 Crouch to Spitway Duration	J8 Time at End of Sector
- 6.00	78	- 4:42	- 6.00	71	- 4:49	- 6.00	32	- 5:28	- 6.00	49	- 5:11
- 5.45	78	- 4:27	- 5.45	72	- 4:33	- 5.45	33	- 5:12	- 5.45	51	- 4:54
- 5.30	78	- 4:12	- 5.30	72	- 4:18	- 5.30	35	- 4:55	- 5.30	53	- 4:37
- 5.15	79	- 3:56	- 5.15	73	- 4:02	- 5.15	36	- 4:39	- 5.15	55	- 4:20
- 5.00	79	- 3:41	- 5.00	73	- 3:47	- 5.00	37	- 4:23	- 5.00	58	- 4:02
- 4.45	78	- 3:27	- 4.45	73	- 3:32	- 4.45	38	- 4:07	- 4.45	58	- 3:47
- 4.30	77	- 3:13	- 4.30	73	- 3:17	- 4.30	39	- 3:51	- 4.30	58	- 3:32
- 4.15	77	- 2:58	- 4.15	72	- 3:03	- 4.15	40	- 3:35	- 4.15	59	- 3:16
- 4.00	76	- 2:44	- 4.00	72	- 2:48	- 4.00	41	- 3:19	- 4.00	59	- 3:01
- 3.45	75	- 2:30	- 3.45	70	- 2:35	- 3.45	41	- 3:04	- 3.45	59	- 2:46
- 3.30	74	- 2:16	- 3.30	69	- 2:21	- 3.30	41	- 2:49	- 3.30	58	- 2:32
- 3.15	73	- 2:02	- 3.15	67	- 2:08	- 3.15	41	- 2:34	- 3.15	58	- 2:17
- 3.00	71	- 1:49	- 3.00	65	- 1:55	- 3.00	42	- 2:18	- 3.00	57	- 2:03
- 2.45	70	- 1:35	- 2.45	63	- 1:42	- 2.45	41	- 2:04	- 2.45	56	- 1:49
- 2.30	68	- 1:22	- 2.30	61	- 1:29	- 2.30	41	- 1:49	- 2.30	55	- 1:35
- 2.15	67	- 1:08	- 2.15	58	- 1:17	- 2.15	41	- 1:34	- 2.15	54	- 1:21
- 2.00	65	- 0:55	- 2.00	56	- 1:04	- 2.00	40	- 1:20	- 2.00	53	- 1:07
- 1.45	64	- 0:41	- 1.45	55	- 0:50	- 1.45	40	- 1:05	- 1.45	51	- 0:54
- 1.30	62	- 0:28	- 1.30	53	- 0:37	- 1.30	39	- 0:51	- 1.30	49	- 0:41
- 1.15	60	- 0:15	- 1.15	51	- 0:24	- 1.15	38	- 0:37	- 1.15	48	- 0:27
- 1.00	58	- 0:02	- 1.00	50	- 0:10	- 1.00	37	- 0:23	- 1.00	46	- 0:14
- 0.45	57	+ 0:12	- 0.45	49	+ 0:04	- 0.45	36	- 0:09	- 0.45	44	- 0:01
- 0.30	56	+ 0:26	- 0.30	48	+ 0:18	- 0.30	35	+ 0:05	- 0.30	42	+ 0:12
- 0.15	55	+ 0:40	- 0.15	47	+ 0:32	- 0.15	34	+ 0:19	- 0.15	40	+ 0:25
HW	53	+ 0:53	HW	46	+ 0:46	HW	33	+ 0:33	HW	38	+ 0:38
+ 0.15	53	+ 1:08	+ 0.15	45	+ 1:00	+ 0.15	32	+ 0:47	+ 0.15	37	+ 0:52
+ 0.30	53	+ 1:23	+ 0.30	45	+ 1:15	+ 0.30	31	+ 1:01	+ 0.30	36	+ 1:06
+ 0.45	53	+ 1:38	+ 0.45	45	+ 1:30	+ 0.45	31	+ 1:16	+ 0.45	35	+ 1:20
+ 1.00	53	+ 1:53	+ 1.00	44	+ 1:44	+ 1.00	30	+ 1:30	+ 1.00	34	+ 1:34
+ 1.15	54	+ 2:09	+ 1.15	45	+ 2:00	+ 1.15	29	+ 1:44	+ 1.15	34	+ 1:49
+ 1.30	54	+ 2:24	+ 1.30	45	+ 2:15	+ 1.30	27	+ 1:57	+ 1.30	33	+ 2:03
+ 1.45	55	+ 2:40	+ 1.45	46	+ 2:31	+ 1.45	26	+ 2:11	+ 1.45	33	+ 2:18
+ 2.00	55	+ 2:55	+ 2.00	46	+ 2:46	+ 2.00	25	+ 2:25	+ 2.00	33	+ 2:33
+ 2.15	56	+ 3:11	+ 2.15	47	+ 3:02	+ 2.15	25	+ 2:40	+ 2.15	33	+ 2:48
+ 2.30	57	+ 3:27	+ 2.30	48	+ 3:18	+ 2.30	24	+ 2:54	+ 2.30	33	+ 3:03
+ 2.45	58	+ 3:43	+ 2.45	49	+ 3:34	+ 2.45	24	+ 3:09	+ 2.45	33	+ 3:18
+ 3.00	58	+ 3:58	+ 3.00	50	+ 3:50	+ 3.00	24	+ 3:24	+ 3.00	34	+ 3:34
+ 3.15	59	+ 4:14	+ 3.15	51	+ 4:06	+ 3.15	24	+ 3:39	+ 3.15	34	+ 3:49
+ 3.30	61	+ 4:31	+ 3.30	52	+ 4:22	+ 3.30	24	+ 3:54	+ 3.30	35	+ 4:05
+ 3.45	62	+ 4:47	+ 3.45	53	+ 4:38	+ 3.45	25	+ 4:10	+ 3.45	35	+ 4:20
+ 4.00	63	+ 5:03	+ 4.00	54	+ 4:54	+ 4.00	25	+ 4:25	+ 4.00	36	+ 4:36
+ 4.15	64	+ 5:19	+ 4.15	55	+ 5:10	+ 4.15	26	+ 4:41	+ 4.15	37	+ 4:52
+ 4.30	65	+ 5:35	+ 4.30	56	+ 5:26	+ 4.30	26	+ 4:56	+ 4.30	38	+ 5:08
+ 4.45	66	+ 5:51	+ 4.45	57	+ 5:42	+ 4.45	27	+ 5:12	+ 4.45	39	+ 5:24
+ 5.00	67	- 5:53	+ 5.00	58	+ 5:58	+ 5.00	28	+ 5:28	+ 5.00	40	+ 5:40
+ 5.15	69	- 5:36	+ 5.15	59	- 5:46	+ 5.15	28	+ 5:43	+ 5.15	41	+ 5:56
+ 5.30	70	- 5:20	+ 5.30	61	- 5:29	+ 5.30	29	+ 5:59	+ 5.30	42	- 5:48
+ 5.45	72	- 5:03	+ 5.45	63	- 5:12	+ 5.45	30	- 5:45	+ 5.45	43	- 5:32
+ 6.00	73	- 4:47	+ 6.00	64	- 4:56	+ 6.00	31	- 5:29	+ 6.00	44	- 5:16

NORTH BOUND

Table J - Essex to Suffolk Rivers Sea Reach to North Oaze

Neaps — All times relate to HW Sheerness — **Time to cover Sectors (in minutes) at 7.0 Kts**

NORTH BOUND

	J1			J2			J3			J4	
	Spitway to the Naze			Blackwater to Colne			Colne to Holland-on-Sea			Holland-on-Sea to the Naze	
Time	Duration	Time at End of Sector	Time	Duration	Time at End of Sector	Time	Duration	Time at End of Sector	Time	Duration	Time at End of Sector
- 6.00	120	- 4:00	- 6.00	38	- 5:22	- 6.00	74	- 4:46	- 6.00	51	- 5:09
- 5.45	121	- 3:44	- 5.45	39	- 5:06	- 5.45	75	- 4:30	- 5.45	52	- 4:53
- 5.30	122	- 3:28	- 5.30	39	- 4:51	- 5.30	76	- 4:14	- 5.30	53	- 4:37
- 5.15	124	- 3:11	- 5.15	40	- 4:35	- 5.15	76	- 3:59	- 5.15	54	- 4:21
- 5.00	125	- 2:55	- 5.00	40	- 4:20	- 5.00	77	- 3:43	- 5.00	55	- 4:05
- 4.45	125	- 2:40	- 4.45	40	- 4:05	- 4.45	77	- 3:28	- 4.45	55	- 3:50
- 4.30	125	- 2:25	- 4.30	41	- 3:49	- 4.30	78	- 3:12	- 4.30	55	- 3:35
- 4.15	125	- 2:10	- 4.15	41	- 3:34	- 4.15	78	- 2:57	- 4.15	55	- 3:20
- 4.00	124	- 1:56	- 4.00	41	- 3:19	- 4.00	79	- 2:41	- 4.00	55	- 3:05
- 3.45	123	- 1:42	- 3.45	41	- 3:04	- 3.45	78	- 2:27	- 3.45	54	- 2:51
- 3.30	122	- 1:28	- 3.30	41	- 2:49	- 3.30	78	- 2:12	- 3.30	54	- 2:36
- 3.15	121	- 1:14	- 3.15	41	- 2:34	- 3.15	78	- 1:57	- 3.15	53	- 2:22
- 3.00	120	- 1:00	- 3.00	41	- 2:19	- 3.00	78	- 1:42	- 3.00	52	- 2:08
- 2.45	118	- 0:47	- 2.45	41	- 2:04	- 2.45	77	- 1:28	- 2.45	51	- 1:54
- 2.30	116	- 0:34	- 2.30	41	- 1:49	- 2.30	77	- 1:13	- 2.30	50	- 1:40
- 2.15	114	- 0:21	- 2.15	41	- 1:34	- 2.15	76	- 0:59	- 2.15	49	- 1:26
- 2.00	112	- 0:08	- 2.00	41	- 1:19	- 2.00	75	- 0:45	- 2.00	48	- 1:12
- 1.45	109	+ 0:04	- 1.45	40	- 1:05	- 1.45	74	- 0:31	- 1.45	47	- 0:58
- 1.30	107	+ 0:17	- 1.30	39	- 0:51	- 1.30	72	- 0:18	- 1.30	46	- 0:44
- 1.15	104	+ 0:29	- 1.15	39	- 0:36	- 1.15	70	- 0:05	- 1.15	44	- 0:31
- 1.00	101	+ 0:41	- 1.00	38	- 0:22	- 1.00	69	+ 0:09	- 1.00	43	- 0:17
- 0.45	99	+ 0:54	- 0.45	37	- 0:08	- 0.45	67	+ 0:22	- 0.45	42	- 0:03
- 0.30	97	+ 1:07	- 0.30	36	+ 0:06	- 0.30	66	+ 0:36	- 0.30	41	+ 0:11
- 0.15	94	+ 1:19	- 0.15	35	+ 0:20	- 0.15	65	+ 0:50	- 0.15	40	+ 0:25
HW	92	+ 1:32	HW	34	+ 0:34	HW	64	+ 1:04	HW	39	+ 0:39
+ 0.15	91	+ 1:46	+ 0.15	33	+ 0:48	+ 0.15	63	+ 1:18	+ 0.15	39	+ 0:54
+ 0.30	90	+ 2:00	+ 0.30	33	+ 1:03	+ 0.30	63	+ 1:33	+ 0.30	38	+ 1:08
+ 0.45	89	+ 2:14	+ 0.45	32	+ 1:17	+ 0.45	62	+ 1:47	+ 0.45	37	+ 1:22
+ 1.00	88	+ 2:28	+ 1.00	32	+ 1:32	+ 1.00	62	+ 2:02	+ 1.00	37	+ 1:37
+ 1.15	88	+ 2:43	+ 1.15	32	+ 1:47	+ 1.15	62	+ 2:17	+ 1.15	37	+ 1:52
+ 1.30	89	+ 2:59	+ 1.30	31	+ 2:01	+ 1.30	62	+ 2:32	+ 1.30	37	+ 2:07
+ 1.45	90	+ 3:15	+ 1.45	31	+ 2:16	+ 1.45	62	+ 2:47	+ 1.45	37	+ 2:22
+ 2.00	90	+ 3:30	+ 2.00	31	+ 2:31	+ 2.00	62	+ 3:02	+ 2.00	37	+ 2:37
+ 2.15	91	+ 3:46	+ 2.15	32	+ 2:47	+ 2.15	63	+ 3:18	+ 2.15	38	+ 2:53
+ 2.30	92	+ 4:02	+ 2.30	32	+ 3:02	+ 2.30	64	+ 3:34	+ 2.30	38	+ 3:08
+ 2.45	93	+ 4:18	+ 2.45	32	+ 3:17	+ 2.45	64	+ 3:49	+ 2.45	39	+ 3:24
+ 3.00	94	+ 4:34	+ 3.00	32	+ 3:32	+ 3.00	65	+ 4:05	+ 3.00	39	+ 3:39
+ 3.15	95	+ 4:50	+ 3.15	33	+ 3:48	+ 3.15	65	+ 4:20	+ 3.15	39	+ 3:54
+ 3.30	96	+ 5:06	+ 3.30	33	+ 4:03	+ 3.30	66	+ 4:36	+ 3.30	40	+ 4:10
+ 3.45	96	+ 5:21	+ 3.45	34	+ 4:19	+ 3.45	66	+ 4:51	+ 3.45	40	+ 4:25
+ 4.00	97	+ 5:37	+ 4.00	34	+ 4:34	+ 4.00	67	+ 5:07	+ 4.00	41	+ 4:41
+ 4.15	99	+ 5:54	+ 4.15	34	+ 4:49	+ 4.15	68	+ 5:23	+ 4.15	42	+ 4:57
+ 4.30	100	- 5:50	+ 4.30	34	+ 5:04	+ 4.30	68	+ 5:38	+ 4.30	42	+ 5:12
+ 4.45	102	- 5:33	+ 4.45	35	+ 5:20	+ 4.45	69	+ 5:54	+ 4.45	43	+ 5:28
+ 5.00	103	- 5:17	+ 5.00	35	+ 5:35	+ 5.00	70	- 5:50	+ 5.00	44	+ 5:44
+ 5.15	105	- 5:00	+ 5.15	36	+ 5:51	+ 5.15	70	- 5:35	+ 5.15	45	- 6:00
+ 5.30	107	- 4:43	+ 5.30	36	- 5:54	+ 5.30	71	- 5:19	+ 5.30	46	- 5:44
+ 5.45	109	- 4:26	+ 5.45	36	- 5:39	+ 5.45	71	- 5:04	+ 5.45	47	- 5:28
+ 6.00	111	- 4:09	+ 6.00	37	- 5:23	+ 6.00	72	- 4:48	+ 6.00	47	- 5:13

	J5			J6			J7			J8	
	The Naze to Deben Landfall			NE Gunfleet to Cork Sand Bcn			Sea Reach No 1 to North Oaze			Crouch to Spitway	
Time	Duration	Time at End of Sector	Time	Duration	Time at End of Sector	Time	Duration	Time at End of Sector	Time	Duration	Time at End of Sector
- 6.00	61	- 4:59	- 6.00	55	- 5:05	- 6.00	27	- 5:33	- 6.00	39	- 5:21
- 5.45	61	- 4:44	- 5.45	56	- 4:49	- 5.45	28	- 5:17	- 5.45	40	- 5:05
- 5.30	61	- 4:29	- 5.30	56	- 4:34	- 5.30	28	- 5:02	- 5.30	41	- 4:49
- 5.15	62	- 4:13	- 5.15	56	- 4:19	- 5.15	29	- 4:46	- 5.15	42	- 4:33
- 5.00	62	- 3:58	- 5.00	56	- 4:04	- 5.00	30	- 4:30	- 5.00	43	- 4:17
- 4.45	61	- 3:44	- 4.45	56	- 3:49	- 4.45	30	- 4:15	- 4.45	43	- 4:02
- 4.30	61	- 3:29	- 4.30	56	- 3:34	- 4.30	30	- 4:00	- 4.30	43	- 3:47
- 4.15	61	- 3:14	- 4.15	56	- 3:19	- 4.15	31	- 3:44	- 4.15	44	- 3:31
- 4.00	61	- 2:59	- 4.00	56	- 3:04	- 4.00	31	- 3:29	- 4.00	44	- 3:16
- 3.45	60	- 2:45	- 3.45	55	- 2:50	- 3.45	32	- 3:13	- 3.45	44	- 3:01
- 3.30	60	- 2:30	- 3.30	54	- 2:36	- 3.30	32	- 2:58	- 3.30	43	- 2:47
- 3.15	59	- 2:16	- 3.15	53	- 2:22	- 3.15	32	- 2:43	- 3.15	43	- 2:32
- 3.00	59	- 2:01	- 3.00	53	- 2:07	- 3.00	32	- 2:28	- 3.00	43	- 2:17
- 2.45	58	- 1:47	- 2.45	52	- 1:53	- 2.45	32	- 2:13	- 2.45	43	- 2:02
- 2.30	57	- 1:33	- 2.30	50	- 1:40	- 2.30	32	- 1:58	- 2.30	42	- 1:48
- 2.15	57	- 1:18	- 2.15	49	- 1:26	- 2.15	32	- 1:43	- 2.15	42	- 1:33
- 2.00	56	- 1:04	- 2.00	48	- 1:12	- 2.00	31	- 1:29	- 2.00	41	- 1:19
- 1.45	55	- 0:50	- 1.45	47	- 0:58	- 1.45	31	- 1:14	- 1.45	41	- 1:04
- 1.30	54	- 0:36	- 1.30	46	- 0:44	- 1.30	31	- 0:59	- 1.30	40	- 0:50
- 1.15	53	- 0:22	- 1.15	46	- 0:29	- 1.15	30	- 0:45	- 1.15	39	- 0:36
- 1.00	52	- 0:08	- 1.00	45	- 0:15	- 1.00	30	- 0:30	- 1.00	39	- 0:21
- 0.45	52	+ 0:07	- 0.45	44	- 0:01	- 0.45	30	- 0:15	- 0.45	38	- 0:07
- 0.30	51	+ 0:21	- 0.30	44	+ 0:14	- 0.30	29	- 0:01	- 0.30	37	+ 0:07
- 0.15	50	+ 0:35	- 0.15	43	+ 0:28	- 0.15	29	+ 0:14	- 0.15	36	+ 0:21
HW	50	+ 0:50	HW	42	+ 0:42	HW	28	+ 0:28	HW	35	+ 0:35
+ 0.15	50	+ 1:05	+ 0.15	42	+ 0:57	+ 0.15	28	+ 0:43	+ 0.15	34	+ 0:49
+ 0.30	49	+ 1:19	+ 0.30	42	+ 1:12	+ 0.30	27	+ 0:57	+ 0.30	34	+ 1:04
+ 0.45	49	+ 1:34	+ 0.45	42	+ 1:27	+ 0.45	27	+ 1:12	+ 0.45	33	+ 1:18
+ 1.00	49	+ 1:49	+ 1.00	41	+ 1:41	+ 1.00	26	+ 1:26	+ 1.00	32	+ 1:32
+ 1.15	50	+ 2:05	+ 1.15	42	+ 1:57	+ 1.15	26	+ 1:41	+ 1.15	32	+ 1:47
+ 1.30	50	+ 2:20	+ 1.30	42	+ 2:12	+ 1.30	25	+ 1:55	+ 1.30	32	+ 2:02
+ 1.45	50	+ 2:35	+ 1.45	42	+ 2:27	+ 1.45	24	+ 2:09	+ 1.45	32	+ 2:17
+ 2.00	51	+ 2:51	+ 2.00	42	+ 2:42	+ 2.00	24	+ 2:24	+ 2.00	31	+ 2:31
+ 2.15	51	+ 3:06	+ 2.15	43	+ 2:58	+ 2.15	23	+ 2:38	+ 2.15	32	+ 2:47
+ 2.30	51	+ 3:21	+ 2.30	43	+ 3:13	+ 2.30	23	+ 2:53	+ 2.30	32	+ 3:02
+ 2.45	52	+ 3:37	+ 2.45	44	+ 3:29	+ 2.45	23	+ 3:08	+ 2.45	32	+ 3:17
+ 3.00	52	+ 3:52	+ 3.00	45	+ 3:45	+ 3.00	23	+ 3:23	+ 3.00	32	+ 3:32
+ 3.15	53	+ 4:08	+ 3.15	45	+ 4:00	+ 3.15	23	+ 3:38	+ 3.15	32	+ 3:47
+ 3.30	53	+ 4:23	+ 3.30	46	+ 4:16	+ 3.30	23	+ 3:53	+ 3.30	33	+ 4:03
+ 3.45	54	+ 4:39	+ 3.45	46	+ 4:31	+ 3.45	23	+ 4:08	+ 3.45	33	+ 4:18
+ 4.00	54	+ 4:54	+ 4.00	47	+ 4:47	+ 4.00	24	+ 4:24	+ 4.00	33	+ 4:33
+ 4.15	55	+ 5:10	+ 4.15	47	+ 5:02	+ 4.15	24	+ 4:39	+ 4.15	34	+ 4:49
+ 4.30	56	+ 5:26	+ 4.30	48	+ 5:18	+ 4.30	24	+ 4:54	+ 4.30	34	+ 5:04
+ 4.45	56	+ 5:41	+ 4.45	48	+ 5:33	+ 4.45	25	+ 5:10	+ 4.45	35	+ 5:20
+ 5.00	57	+ 5:57	+ 5.00	49	+ 5:49	+ 5.00	25	+ 5:25	+ 5.00	35	+ 5:35
+ 5.15	57	- 5:48	+ 5.15	50	- 5:55	+ 5.15	25	+ 5:40	+ 5.15	36	+ 5:51
+ 5.30	58	- 5:32	+ 5.30	50	- 5:40	+ 5.30	26	+ 5:56	+ 5.30	36	- 5:54
+ 5.45	58	- 5:17	+ 5.45	51	- 5:24	+ 5.45	26	- 5:49	+ 5.45	37	- 5:38
+ 6.00	59	- 5:01	+ 6.00	52	- 5:08	+ 6.00	27	- 5:33	+ 6.00	37	- 5:23

Table J - Essex to Suffolk Rivers Sea Reach to North Oaze

Time to cover Sectors (in minutes) at 7.0 kts — All times relate to HW Sheerness — **Springs**

NORTH BOUND

	J1 Spitway to the Naze			J2 Blackwater to Colne			J3 Colne to Holland-on-Sea			J4 Holland-on-Sea to the Naze	
Time	Duration	Time at End of Sector	Time	Duration	Time at End of Sector	Time	Duration	Time at End of Sector	Time	Duration	Time at End of Sector
- 6.00	127	- 3:53	- 6.00	39	- 5:21	- 6.00	76	- 4:44	- 6.00	54	- 5:06
- 5.45	129	- 3:36	- 5.45	40	- 5:05	- 5.45	77	- 4:28	- 5.45	56	- 4:49
- 5.30	130	- 3:20	- 5.30	41	- 4:49	- 5.30	78	- 4:12	- 5.30	57	- 4:33
- 5.15	132	- 3:03	- 5.15	41	- 4:34	- 5.15	79	- 3:56	- 5.15	59	- 4:16
- 5.00	133	- 2:47	- 5.00	42	- 4:18	- 5.00	81	- 3:39	- 5.00	61	- 3:59
- 4.45	132	- 2:33	- 4.45	43	- 4:02	- 4.45	81	- 3:24	- 4.45	61	- 3:44
- 4.30	132	- 2:18	- 4.30	43	- 3:47	- 4.30	82	- 3:08	- 4.30	61	- 3:29
- 4.15	131	- 2:04	- 4.15	44	- 3:31	- 4.15	83	- 2:52	- 4.15	61	- 3:14
- 4.00	131	- 1:49	- 4.00	44	- 3:16	- 4.00	83	- 2:37	- 4.00	61	- 2:59
- 3.45	129	- 1:36	- 3.45	44	- 3:01	- 3.45	83	- 2:22	- 3.45	60	- 2:45
- 3.30	127	- 1:23	- 3.30	45	- 2:45	- 3.30	83	- 2:07	- 3.30	59	- 2:31
- 3.15	126	- 1:09	- 3.15	45	- 2:30	- 3.15	83	- 1:52	- 3.15	58	- 2:17
- 3.00	124	- 0:56	- 3.00	45	- 2:15	- 3.00	83	- 1:37	- 3.00	58	- 2:02
- 2.45	121	- 0:44	- 2.45	44	- 2:01	- 2.45	81	- 1:24	- 2.45	56	- 1:49
- 2.30	118	- 0:32	- 2.30	44	- 1:46	- 2.30	80	- 1:10	- 2.30	54	- 1:36
- 2.15	115	- 0:20	- 2.15	44	- 1:31	- 2.15	79	- 0:56	- 2.15	52	- 1:23
- 2.00	112	- 0:08	- 2.00	43	- 1:17	- 2.00	78	- 0:42	- 2.00	50	- 1:10
- 1.45	109	+ 0:04	- 1.45	42	- 1:03	- 1.45	75	- 0:30	- 1.45	48	- 0:57
- 1.30	106	+ 0:16	- 1.30	41	- 0:49	- 1.30	73	- 0:17	- 1.30	46	- 0:44
- 1.15	102	+ 0:27	- 1.15	40	- 0:35	- 1.15	70	- 0:05	- 1.15	44	- 0:31
- 1.00	99	+ 0:39	- 1.00	38	- 0:22	- 1.00	68	+ 0:08	- 1.00	42	- 0:18
- 0.45	96	+ 0:51	- 0.45	37	- 0:08	- 0.45	66	+ 0:21	- 0.45	41	- 0:04
- 0.30	92	+ 1:02	- 0.30	35	+ 0:05	- 0.30	64	+ 0:34	- 0.30	40	+ 0:10
- 0.15	89	+ 1:14	- 0.15	34	+ 0:19	- 0.15	62	+ 0:47	- 0.15	38	+ 0:23
HW	86	+ 1:26	HW	32	+ 0:32	HW	61	+ 1:01	HW	37	+ 0:37
+ 0.15	85	+ 1:40	+ 0.15	32	+ 0:47	+ 0.15	60	+ 1:15	+ 0.15	36	+ 0:51
+ 0.30	84	+ 1:54	+ 0.30	31	+ 1:01	+ 0.30	59	+ 1:29	+ 0.30	35	+ 1:05
+ 0.45	83	+ 2:08	+ 0.45	30	+ 1:15	+ 0.45	59	+ 1:44	+ 0.45	35	+ 1:20
+ 1.00	82	+ 2:22	+ 1.00	30	+ 1:30	+ 1.00	58	+ 1:58	+ 1.00	34	+ 1:34
+ 1.15	82	+ 2:37	+ 1.15	30	+ 1:45	+ 1.15	58	+ 2:13	+ 1.15	34	+ 1:49
+ 1.30	83	+ 2:53	+ 1.30	29	+ 1:59	+ 1.30	59	+ 2:29	+ 1.30	34	+ 2:04
+ 1.45	84	+ 3:09	+ 1.45	29	+ 2:14	+ 1.45	59	+ 2:44	+ 1.45	34	+ 2:19
+ 2.00	85	+ 3:25	+ 2.00	29	+ 2:29	+ 2.00	59	+ 2:59	+ 2.00	35	+ 2:35
+ 2.15	86	+ 3:41	+ 2.15	29	+ 2:44	+ 2.15	60	+ 3:15	+ 2.15	35	+ 2:50
+ 2.30	88	+ 3:58	+ 2.30	30	+ 3:00	+ 2.30	61	+ 3:31	+ 2.30	36	+ 3:06
+ 2.45	90	+ 4:15	+ 2.45	30	+ 3:15	+ 2.45	62	+ 3:47	+ 2.45	36	+ 3:21
+ 3.00	91	+ 4:31	+ 3.00	31	+ 3:31	+ 3.00	62	+ 4:02	+ 3.00	37	+ 3:37
+ 3.15	93	+ 4:48	+ 3.15	31	+ 3:46	+ 3.15	63	+ 4:18	+ 3.15	37	+ 3:52
+ 3.30	94	+ 5:04	+ 3.30	32	+ 4:02	+ 3.30	64	+ 4:34	+ 3.30	38	+ 4:08
+ 3.45	95	+ 5:20	+ 3.45	32	+ 4:17	+ 3.45	64	+ 4:49	+ 3.45	38	+ 4:23
+ 4.00	96	+ 5:36	+ 4.00	33	+ 4:33	+ 4.00	65	+ 5:05	+ 4.00	39	+ 4:39
+ 4.15	98	+ 5:53	+ 4.15	33	+ 4:48	+ 4.15	66	+ 5:21	+ 4.15	40	+ 4:55
+ 4.30	100	- 5:50	+ 4.30	33	+ 5:03	+ 4.30	67	+ 5:37	+ 4.30	41	+ 5:11
+ 4.45	102	- 5:33	+ 4.45	34	+ 5:19	+ 4.45	68	+ 5:53	+ 4.45	42	+ 5:27
+ 5.00	104	- 5:16	+ 5.00	34	+ 5:34	+ 5.00	69	- 5:51	+ 5.00	43	+ 5:43
+ 5.15	107	- 4:58	+ 5.15	35	+ 5:50	+ 5.15	70	- 5:35	+ 5.15	45	- 6:00
+ 5.30	109	- 4:41	+ 5.30	36	- 5:54	+ 5.30	71	- 5:19	+ 5.30	46	- 5:44
+ 5.45	112	- 4:23	+ 5.45	37	- 5:38	+ 5.45	72	- 5:03	+ 5.45	47	- 5:28
+ 6.00	114	- 4:06	+ 6.00	37	- 5:23	+ 6.00	73	- 4:47	+ 6.00	49	- 5:11

	J5 The Naze to Deben Landfall			J6 NE Gunfleet to Cork Sand Bcn			J7 Sea Reach No 1 to North Oaze			J8 Crouch to Spitway	
Time	Duration	Time at End of Sector	Time	Duration	Time at End of Sector	Time	Duration	Time at End of Sector	Time	Duration	Time at End of Sector
- 6.00	65	- 4:55	- 6.00	59	- 5:01	- 6.00	27	- 5:33	- 6.00	40	- 5:20
- 5.45	65	- 4:40	- 5.45	59	- 4:46	- 5.45	28	- 5:17	- 5.45	42	- 5:03
- 5.30	65	- 4:25	- 5.30	60	- 4:30	- 5.30	29	- 5:01	- 5.30	44	- 4:46
- 5.15	66	- 4:09	- 5.15	60	- 4:15	- 5.15	30	- 4:45	- 5.15	46	- 4:29
- 5.00	66	- 3:54	- 5.00	60	- 4:00	- 5.00	31	- 4:29	- 5.00	47	- 4:13
- 4.45	65	- 3:40	- 4.45	60	- 3:45	- 4.45	32	- 4:13	- 4.45	48	- 3:57
- 4.30	65	- 3:25	- 4.30	60	- 3:30	- 4.30	32	- 3:58	- 4.30	48	- 3:42
- 4.15	64	- 3:11	- 4.15	60	- 3:15	- 4.15	33	- 3:42	- 4.15	48	- 3:27
- 4.00	64	- 2:56	- 4.00	60	- 3:00	- 4.00	34	- 3:26	- 4.00	49	- 3:11
- 3.45	63	- 2:42	- 3.45	59	- 2:46	- 3.45	34	- 3:11	- 3.45	48	- 2:57
- 3.30	62	- 2:28	- 3.30	58	- 2:32	- 3.30	34	- 2:56	- 3.30	48	- 2:42
- 3.15	61	- 2:14	- 3.15	56	- 2:19	- 3.15	34	- 2:41	- 3.15	48	- 2:27
- 3.00	61	- 1:59	- 3.00	55	- 2:05	- 3.00	35	- 2:25	- 3.00	47	- 2:13
- 2.45	59	- 1:46	- 2.45	54	- 1:51	- 2.45	34	- 2:11	- 2.45	47	- 1:58
- 2.30	58	- 1:32	- 2.30	52	- 1:38	- 2.30	34	- 1:56	- 2.30	46	- 1:44
- 2.15	57	- 1:18	- 2.15	50	- 1:25	- 2.15	34	- 1:41	- 2.15	45	- 1:30
- 2.00	56	- 1:04	- 2.00	48	- 1:12	- 2.00	34	- 1:26	- 2.00	44	- 1:16
- 1.45	55	- 0:50	- 1.45	47	- 0:58	- 1.45	33	- 1:12	- 1.45	43	- 1:02
- 1.30	54	- 0:36	- 1.30	46	- 0:44	- 1.30	33	- 0:57	- 1.30	42	- 0:48
- 1.15	52	- 0:23	- 1.15	45	- 0:30	- 1.15	32	- 0:43	- 1.15	41	- 0:34
- 1.00	51	- 0:09	- 1.00	43	- 0:17	- 1.00	31	- 0:29	- 1.00	40	- 0:20
- 0.45	50	+ 0:05	- 0.45	43	- 0:02	- 0.45	31	- 0:14	- 0.45	38	- 0:07
- 0.30	49	+ 0:19	- 0.30	42	+ 0:12	- 0.30	30	HW	- 0.30	37	+ 0:07
- 0.15	48	+ 0:33	- 0.15	41	+ 0:26	- 0.15	29	+ 0:14	- 0.15	35	+ 0:20
HW	47	+ 0:47	HW	40	+ 0:40	HW	29	+ 0:29	HW	34	+ 0:34
+ 0.15	47	+ 1:02	+ 0.15	40	+ 0:55	+ 0.15	28	+ 0:43	+ 0.15	33	+ 0:48
+ 0.30	47	+ 1:17	+ 0.30	39	+ 1:09	+ 0.30	27	+ 0:57	+ 0.30	32	+ 1:02
+ 0.45	47	+ 1:32	+ 0.45	39	+ 1:24	+ 0.45	26	+ 1:11	+ 0.45	31	+ 1:16
+ 1.00	47	+ 1:47	+ 1.00	39	+ 1:39	+ 1.00	25	+ 1:25	+ 1.00	30	+ 1:30
+ 1.15	47	+ 2:02	+ 1.15	39	+ 1:54	+ 1.15	24	+ 1:39	+ 1.15	30	+ 1:45
+ 1.30	48	+ 2:18	+ 1.30	39	+ 2:09	+ 1.30	23	+ 1:53	+ 1.30	30	+ 2:00
+ 1.45	48	+ 2:33	+ 1.45	40	+ 2:25	+ 1.45	22	+ 2:07	+ 1.45	29	+ 2:14
+ 2.00	48	+ 2:48	+ 2.00	40	+ 2:40	+ 2.00	22	+ 2:22	+ 2.00	29	+ 2:29
+ 2.15	49	+ 3:04	+ 2.15	41	+ 2:56	+ 2.15	21	+ 2:36	+ 2.15	29	+ 2:44
+ 2.30	49	+ 3:19	+ 2.30	41	+ 3:11	+ 2.30	21	+ 2:51	+ 2.30	29	+ 2:59
+ 2.45	50	+ 3:35	+ 2.45	42	+ 3:27	+ 2.45	21	+ 3:06	+ 2.45	30	+ 3:15
+ 3.00	50	+ 3:50	+ 3.00	43	+ 3:43	+ 3.00	20	+ 3:20	+ 3.00	30	+ 3:30
+ 3.15	51	+ 4:06	+ 3.15	44	+ 3:59	+ 3.15	21	+ 3:36	+ 3.15	30	+ 3:45
+ 3.30	52	+ 4:22	+ 3.30	45	+ 4:15	+ 3.30	21	+ 3:51	+ 3.30	30	+ 4:00
+ 3.45	53	+ 4:38	+ 3.45	45	+ 4:30	+ 3.45	21	+ 4:06	+ 3.45	31	+ 4:16
+ 4.00	54	+ 4:54	+ 4.00	46	+ 4:46	+ 4.00	22	+ 4:22	+ 4.00	31	+ 4:31
+ 4.15	54	+ 5:09	+ 4.15	47	+ 5:02	+ 4.15	22	+ 4:37	+ 4.15	32	+ 4:47
+ 4.30	55	+ 5:25	+ 4.30	48	+ 5:18	+ 4.30	23	+ 4:53	+ 4.30	33	+ 5:03
+ 4.45	56	+ 5:41	+ 4.45	48	+ 5:33	+ 4.45	23	+ 5:08	+ 4.45	33	+ 5:18
+ 5.00	57	+ 5:57	+ 5.00	49	+ 5:49	+ 5.00	24	+ 5:24	+ 5.00	34	+ 5:34
+ 5.15	58	- 5:47	+ 5.15	50	- 5:55	+ 5.15	24	+ 5:39	+ 5.15	35	+ 5:50
+ 5.30	59	- 5:31	+ 5.30	51	- 5:39	+ 5.30	25	+ 5:55	+ 5.30	36	- 5:54
+ 5.45	60	- 5:15	+ 5.45	52	- 5:23	+ 5.45	26	- 5:49	+ 5.45	37	- 5:38
+ 6.00	61	- 4:59	+ 6.00	53	- 5:07	+ 6.00	26	- 5:34	+ 6.00	37	- 5:23

Table K - Ramsgate to Harwich - Outside Route

Neaps — All times relate to HW Sheerness — **Time to cover Sectors (in minutes) at 4.0 Kts**

NORTH BOUND

Time	K1 Ramsgate to North Foreland: Duration	K1 Time at End of Sector	Time	K2 North Foreland to Thanet: Duration	K2 Time at End of Sector	Time	K3 Thanet to South Knock: Duration	K3 Time at End of Sector	Time	K4 South Knock to Kentish Knock: Duration	K4 Time at End of Sector
- 6.00	99	- 4:21	- 6.00	130	- 3:50	- 6.00	115	- 4:05	- 6.00	121	- 3:59
- 5.45	100	- 4:05	- 5.45	132	- 3:33	- 5.45	117	- 3:48	- 5.45	122	- 3:43
- 5.30	101	- 3:49	- 5.30	134	- 3:16	- 5.30	120	- 3:30	- 5.30	123	- 3:27
- 5.15	100	- 3:35	- 5.15	132	- 3:03	- 5.15	120	- 3:15	- 5.15	124	- 3:11
- 5.00	98	- 3:22	- 5.00	130	- 2:50	- 5.00	120	- 3:00	- 5.00	125	- 2:55
- 4.45	97	- 3:08	- 4.45	128	- 2:37	- 4.45	120	- 2:45	- 4.45	123	- 2:42
- 4.30	95	- 2:55	- 4.30	127	- 2:23	- 4.30	121	- 2:29	- 4.30	120	- 2:30
- 4.15	89	- 2:46	- 4.15	123	- 2:12	- 4.15	118	- 2:17	- 4.15	118	- 2:17
- 4.00	84	- 2:36	- 4.00	119	- 2:01	- 4.00	116	- 2:04	- 4.00	116	- 2:04
- 3.45	78	- 2:27	- 3.45	115	- 1:50	- 3.45	114	- 1:51	- 3.45	112	- 1:53
- 3.30	72	- 2:18	- 3.30	111	- 1:39	- 3.30	112	- 1:38	- 3.30	108	- 1:42
- 3.15	68	- 2:07	- 3.15	107	- 1:28	- 3.15	109	- 1:26	- 3.15	105	- 1:30
- 3.00	64	- 1:56	- 3.00	104	- 1:16	- 3.00	106	- 1:14	- 3.00	101	- 1:19
- 2.45	60	- 1:45	- 2.45	100	- 1:05	- 2.45	103	- 1:02	- 2.45	96	- 1:09
- 2.30	56	- 1:34	- 2.30	97	- 0:53	- 2.30	100	- 0:50	- 2.30	92	- 0:58
- 2.15	55	- 1:20	- 2.15	95	- 0:40	- 2.15	98	- 0:37	- 2.15	88	- 0:47
- 2.00	54	- 1:06	- 2.00	93	- 0:27	- 2.00	95	- 0:25	- 2.00	83	- 0:37
- 1.45	53	- 0:52	- 1.45	91	- 0:14	- 1.45	93	- 0:12	- 1.45	81	- 0:24
- 1.30	52	- 0:38	- 1.30	89	- 0:01	- 1.30	90	HW	- 1.30	78	- 0:12
- 1.15	52	- 0:23	- 1.15	87	+ 0:12	- 1.15	88	+ 0:13	- 1.15	75	HW
- 1.00	53	- 0:07	- 1.00	86	+ 0:26	- 1.00	85	+ 0:25	- 1.00	72	+ 0:12
- 0.45	53	+ 0:08	- 0.45	84	+ 0:39	- 0.45	83	+ 0:38	- 0.45	70	+ 0:25
- 0.30	54	+ 0:24	- 0.30	83	+ 0:53	- 0.30	80	+ 0:50	- 0.30	69	+ 0:39
- 0.15	55	+ 0:40	- 0.15	83	+ 1:08	- 0.15	80	+ 1:05	- 0.15	67	+ 0:52
HW	56	+ 0:56	HW	83	+ 1:23	HW	79	+ 1:19	HW	66	+ 1:06
+ 0.15	57	+ 1:12	+ 0.15	84	+ 1:39	+ 0.15	79	+ 1:34	+ 0.15	66	+ 1:21
+ 0.30	58	+ 1:28	+ 0.30	84	+ 1:54	+ 0.30	78	+ 1:48	+ 0.30	65	+ 1:35
+ 0.45	60	+ 1:45	+ 0.45	85	+ 2:10	+ 0.45	79	+ 2:04	+ 0.45	65	+ 1:50
+ 1.00	62	+ 2:02	+ 1.00	86	+ 2:26	+ 1.00	80	+ 2:20	+ 1.00	65	+ 2:05
+ 1.15	64	+ 2:19	+ 1.15	87	+ 2:42	+ 1.15	81	+ 2:36	+ 1.15	65	+ 2:20
+ 1.30	66	+ 2:36	+ 1.30	87	+ 2:57	+ 1.30	81	+ 2:51	+ 1.30	65	+ 2:35
+ 1.45	67	+ 2:52	+ 1.45	89	+ 3:14	+ 1.45	83	+ 3:08	+ 1.45	65	+ 2:50
+ 2.00	69	+ 3:09	+ 2.00	90	+ 3:30	+ 2.00	84	+ 3:24	+ 2.00	66	+ 3:06
+ 2.15	71	+ 3:26	+ 2.15	91	+ 3:46	+ 2.15	86	+ 3:41	+ 2.15	67	+ 3:22
+ 2.30	73	+ 3:43	+ 2.30	92	+ 4:02	+ 2.30	87	+ 3:57	+ 2.30	68	+ 3:38
+ 2.45	75	+ 4:00	+ 2.45	93	+ 4:18	+ 2.45	88	+ 4:13	+ 2.45	69	+ 3:54
+ 3.00	76	+ 4:16	+ 3.00	94	+ 4:34	+ 3.00	89	+ 4:29	+ 3.00	70	+ 4:10
+ 3.15	78	+ 4:33	+ 3.15	95	+ 4:50	+ 3.15	90	+ 4:45	+ 3.15	73	+ 4:28
+ 3.30	79	+ 4:49	+ 3.30	96	+ 5:06	+ 3.30	91	+ 5:01	+ 3.30	75	+ 4:45
+ 3.45	80	+ 5:05	+ 3.45	98	+ 5:23	+ 3.45	93	+ 5:18	+ 3.45	77	+ 5:02
+ 4.00	81	+ 5:21	+ 4.00	100	+ 5:40	+ 4.00	95	+ 5:35	+ 4.00	80	+ 5:20
+ 4.15	82	+ 5:37	+ 4.15	101	+ 5:56	+ 4.15	96	+ 5:51	+ 4.15	83	+ 5:38
+ 4.30	83	+ 5:53	+ 4.30	103	- 5:47	+ 4.30	98	- 5:52	+ 4.30	87	+ 5:57
+ 4.45	85	- 5:50	+ 4.45	105	- 5:30	+ 4.45	99	- 5:36	+ 4.45	90	- 5:45
+ 5.00	87	- 5:33	+ 5.00	108	- 5:12	+ 5.00	100	- 5:20	+ 5.00	94	- 5:26
+ 5.15	88	- 5:17	+ 5.15	110	- 4:55	+ 5.15	101	- 5:04	+ 5.15	97	- 5:08
+ 5.30	90	- 5:00	+ 5.30	112	- 4:38	+ 5.30	102	- 4:48	+ 5.30	100	- 4:50
+ 5.45	96	- 4:39	+ 5.45	126	- 4:09	+ 5.45	110	- 4:25	+ 5.45	103	- 4:32
+ 6.00	97	- 4:23	+ 6.00	128	- 3:52	+ 6.00	112	- 4:08	+ 6.00	107	- 4:13

Time	K5 Kentish Knock to Long Sand Hd: Duration	K5 Time at End of Sector	Time	K6 Long Sand Hd to S. Threshold: Duration	K6 Time at End of Sector	Time	K7 S. Threshold to Cork Sand B'cn: Duration	K7 Time at End of Sector	Time	K8 Cork Sand B'cn to Harwich: Duration	K8 Time at End of Sector
- 6.00	140	- 3:40	- 6.00	98	- 4:22	- 6.00	102	- 4:18	- 6.00	120	- 4:00
- 5.45	141	- 3:24	- 5.45	98	- 4:07	- 5.45	102	- 4:03	- 5.45	121	- 3:44
- 5.30	141	- 3:09	- 5.30	99	- 3:51	- 5.30	103	- 3:47	- 5.30	121	- 3:29
- 5.15	141	- 2:54	- 5.15	100	- 3:35	- 5.15	103	- 3:32	- 5.15	121	- 3:14
- 5.00	141	- 2:39	- 5.00	101	- 3:19	- 5.00	103	- 3:17	- 5.00	122	- 2:58
- 4.45	138	- 2:27	- 4.45	100	- 3:05	- 4.45	102	- 3:03	- 4.45	120	- 2:45
- 4.30	135	- 2:15	- 4.30	99	- 2:51	- 4.30	101	- 2:49	- 4.30	119	- 2:31
- 4.15	131	- 2:04	- 4.15	99	- 2:36	- 4.15	100	- 2:35	- 4.15	117	- 2:18
- 4.00	128	- 1:52	- 4.00	98	- 2:22	- 4.00	98	- 2:22	- 4.00	116	- 2:04
- 3.45	123	- 1:42	- 3.45	97	- 2:08	- 3.45	95	- 2:10	- 3.45	113	- 1:52
- 3.30	118	- 1:32	- 3.30	95	- 1:55	- 3.30	92	- 1:58	- 3.30	109	- 1:41
- 3.15	113	- 1:22	- 3.15	94	- 1:41	- 3.15	89	- 1:46	- 3.15	106	- 1:29
- 3.00	108	- 1:12	- 3.00	92	- 1:28	- 3.00	86	- 1:34	- 3.00	103	- 1:17
- 2.45	104	- 1:01	- 2.45	91	- 1:14	- 2.45	84	- 1:21	- 2.45	99	- 1:06
- 2.30	100	- 0:50	- 2.30	89	- 1:01	- 2.30	83	- 1:07	- 2.30	96	- 0:54
- 2.15	96	- 0:39	- 2.15	88	- 0:47	- 2.15	82	- 0:53	- 2.15	92	- 0:43
- 2.00	92	- 0:28	- 2.00	87	- 0:33	- 2.00	81	- 0:39	- 2.00	88	- 0:32
- 1.45	88	- 0:17	- 1.45	85	- 0:20	- 1.45	78	- 0:27	- 1.45	86	- 0:19
- 1.30	84	- 0:06	- 1.30	83	- 0:07	- 1.30	76	- 0:14	- 1.30	84	- 0:06
- 1.15	80	+ 0:05	- 1.15	81	+ 0:06	- 1.15	73	- 0:02	- 1.15	81	+ 0:06
- 1.00	77	+ 0:17	- 1.00	79	+ 0:19	- 1.00	71	+ 0:11	- 1.00	79	+ 0:19
- 0.45	75	+ 0:30	- 0.45	77	+ 0:32	- 0.45	69	+ 0:24	- 0.45	79	+ 0:34
- 0.30	74	+ 0:44	- 0.30	74	+ 0:44	- 0.30	68	+ 0:38	- 0.30	79	+ 0:49
- 0.15	73	+ 0:58	- 0.15	71	+ 0:56	- 0.15	66	+ 0:51	- 0.15	78	+ 1:03
HW	71	+ 1:11	HW	68	+ 1:08	HW	65	+ 1:05	HW	78	+ 1:18
+ 0.15	73	+ 1:28	+ 0.15	67	+ 1:22	+ 0.15	65	+ 1:20	+ 0.15	77	+ 1:32
+ 0.30	74	+ 1:44	+ 0.30	65	+ 1:35	+ 0.30	65	+ 1:35	+ 0.30	77	+ 1:47
+ 0.45	75	+ 2:00	+ 0.45	64	+ 1:49	+ 0.45	65	+ 1:50	+ 0.45	76	+ 2:01
+ 1.00	77	+ 2:17	+ 1.00	62	+ 2:02	+ 1.00	65	+ 2:05	+ 1.00	75	+ 2:15
+ 1.15	79	+ 2:34	+ 1.15	63	+ 2:18	+ 1.15	66	+ 2:21	+ 1.15	76	+ 2:31
+ 1.30	81	+ 2:51	+ 1.30	63	+ 2:33	+ 1.30	67	+ 2:37	+ 1.30	77	+ 2:47
+ 1.45	83	+ 3:08	+ 1.45	63	+ 2:48	+ 1.45	68	+ 2:53	+ 1.45	78	+ 3:03
+ 2.00	85	+ 3:25	+ 2.00	64	+ 3:04	+ 2.00	69	+ 3:09	+ 2.00	79	+ 3:19
+ 2.15	87	+ 3:42	+ 2.15	65	+ 3:20	+ 2.15	70	+ 3:25	+ 2.15	80	+ 3:35
+ 2.30	89	+ 3:59	+ 2.30	67	+ 3:37	+ 2.30	72	+ 3:42	+ 2.30	82	+ 3:52
+ 2.45	90	+ 4:15	+ 2.45	69	+ 3:54	+ 2.45	73	+ 3:58	+ 2.45	83	+ 4:08
+ 3.00	92	+ 4:32	+ 3.00	71	+ 4:11	+ 3.00	75	+ 4:15	+ 3.00	84	+ 4:24
+ 3.15	94	+ 4:49	+ 3.15	73	+ 4:28	+ 3.15	77	+ 4:32	+ 3.15	85	+ 4:40
+ 3.30	97	+ 5:07	+ 3.30	75	+ 4:45	+ 3.30	78	+ 4:48	+ 3.30	87	+ 4:57
+ 3.45	99	+ 5:24	+ 3.45	77	+ 5:02	+ 3.45	80	+ 5:05	+ 3.45	88	+ 5:13
+ 4.00	102	+ 5:42	+ 4.00	79	+ 5:19	+ 4.00	82	+ 5:22	+ 4.00	89	+ 5:29
+ 4.15	105	- 6:00	+ 4.15	81	+ 5:36	+ 4.15	83	+ 5:38	+ 4.15	91	+ 5:46
+ 4.30	109	- 5:41	+ 4.30	83	+ 5:53	+ 4.30	84	+ 5:54	+ 4.30	92	- 5:58
+ 4.45	112	- 5:23	+ 4.45	85	- 5:50	+ 4.45	85	- 5:50	+ 4.45	93	- 5:42
+ 5.00	116	- 5:04	+ 5.00	88	- 5:32	+ 5.00	87	- 5:33	+ 5.00	95	- 5:25
+ 5.15	119	- 4:46	+ 5.15	89	- 5:16	+ 5.15	88	- 5:17	+ 5.15	98	- 5:07
+ 5.30	122	- 4:28	+ 5.30	90	- 5:00	+ 5.30	90	- 5:00	+ 5.30	101	- 4:49
+ 5.45	125	- 4:10	+ 5.45	91	- 4:44	+ 5.45	92	- 4:43	+ 5.45	105	- 4:30
+ 6.00	129	- 3:51	+ 6.00	92	- 4:28	+ 6.00	94	- 4:26	+ 6.00	108	- 4:12

Table K - Ramsgate to Harwich - Outside Route

Time to cover Sectors (in minutes) at 4.0 kts — All times relate to HW Sheerness — Springs

NORTHBOUND

	K1			K2			K3			K4	
	Ramsgate to North Foreland			North Foreland to Thanet			Thanet to South Knock			South Knock to Kentish Knock	
Time	Duration	Time at End of Sector	Time	Duration	Time at End of Sector	Time	Duration	Time at End of Sector	Time	Duration	Time at End of Sector
- 6.00	115	- 4:05	- 6.00	159	- 3:21	- 6.00	131	- 3:49	- 6.00	151	- 3:29
- 5.45	117	- 3:48	- 5.45	160	- 3:05	- 5.45	135	- 3:30	- 5.45	148	- 3:17
- 5.30	118	- 3:32	- 5.30	161	- 2:49	- 5.30	140	- 3:10	- 5.30	145	- 3:05
- 5.15	114	- 3:21	- 5.15	155	- 2:40	- 5.15	138	- 2:57	- 5.15	143	- 2:52
- 5.00	110	- 3:10	- 5.00	149	- 2:31	- 5.00	137	- 2:43	- 5.00	140	- 2:40
- 4.45	106	- 2:59	- 4.45	143	- 2:22	- 4.45	136	- 2:29	- 4.45	137	- 2:28
- 4.30	102	- 2:48	- 4.30	138	- 2:12	- 4.30	134	- 2:16	- 4.30	133	- 2:17
- 4.15	95	- 2:40	- 4.15	131	- 2:04	- 4.15	129	- 2:06	- 4.15	129	- 2:06
- 4.00	88	- 2:32	- 4.00	124	- 1:56	- 4.00	125	- 1:55	- 4.00	125	- 1:55
- 3.45	80	- 2:25	- 3.45	117	- 1:48	- 3.45	120	- 1:45	- 3.45	120	- 1:45
- 3.30	73	- 2:17	- 3.30	111	- 1:39	- 3.30	115	- 1:35	- 3.30	114	- 1:36
- 3.15	66	- 2:09	- 3.15	107	- 1:28	- 3.15	111	- 1:24	- 3.15	108	- 1:27
- 3.00	60	- 2:00	- 3.00	102	- 1:18	- 3.00	106	- 1:14	- 3.00	103	- 1:17
- 2.45	53	- 1:52	- 2.45	98	- 1:07	- 2.45	102	- 1:03	- 2.45	98	- 1:07
- 2.30	47	- 1:43	- 2.30	94	- 0:56	- 2.30	98	- 0:52	- 2.30	92	- 0:58
- 2.15	45	- 1:30	- 2.15	90	- 0:45	- 2.15	93	- 0:42	- 2.15	87	- 0:48
- 2.00	44	- 1:16	- 2.00	87	- 0:33	- 2.00	89	- 0:31	- 2.00	82	- 0:38
- 1.45	43	- 1:02	- 1.45	83	- 0:22	- 1.45	85	- 0:20	- 1.45	78	- 0:27
- 1.30	42	- 0:48	- 1.30	80	- 0:10	- 1.30	81	- 0:09	- 1.30	74	- 0:16
- 1.15	42	- 0:33	- 1.15	78	+ 0:03	- 1.15	76	+ 0:01	- 1.15	70	- 0:05
- 1.00	43	- 0:17	- 1.00	76	+ 0:16	- 1.00	72	+ 0:12	- 1.00	65	+ 0:05
- 0.45	44	- 0:01	- 0.45	73	+ 0:28	- 0.45	68	+ 0:23	- 0.45	64	+ 0:19
- 0.30	44	+ 0:14	- 0.30	71	+ 0:41	- 0.30	64	+ 0:34	- 0.30	62	+ 0:32
- 0.15	46	+ 0:31	- 0.15	73	+ 0:58	- 0.15	63	+ 0:48	- 0.15	60	+ 0:45
HW	48	+ 0:48	HW	71	+ 1:11	HW	63	+ 1:03	HW	58	+ 0:58
+ 0.15	49	+ 1:04	+ 0.15	71	+ 1:26	+ 0.15	62	+ 1:17	+ 0.15	58	+ 1:13
+ 0.30	51	+ 1:21	+ 0.30	71	+ 1:41	+ 0.30	62	+ 1:32	+ 0.30	57	+ 1:27
+ 0.45	54	+ 1:39	+ 0.45	73	+ 1:58	+ 0.45	63	+ 1:48	+ 0.45	57	+ 1:42
+ 1.00	56	+ 1:56	+ 1.00	74	+ 2:14	+ 1.00	64	+ 2:04	+ 1.00	56	+ 1:56
+ 1.15	59	+ 2:14	+ 1.15	75	+ 2:30	+ 1.15	65	+ 2:20	+ 1.15	57	+ 2:12
+ 1.30	62	+ 2:32	+ 1.30	76	+ 2:46	+ 1.30	67	+ 2:37	+ 1.30	57	+ 2:27
+ 1.45	65	+ 2:50	+ 1.45	78	+ 3:03	+ 1.45	69	+ 2:54	+ 1.45	58	+ 2:43
+ 2.00	69	+ 3:09	+ 2.00	80	+ 3:20	+ 2.00	72	+ 3:12	+ 2.00	58	+ 2:58
+ 2.15	72	+ 3:27	+ 2.15	82	+ 3:37	+ 2.15	74	+ 3:29	+ 2.15	60	+ 3:15
+ 2.30	75	+ 3:45	+ 2.30	84	+ 3:54	+ 2.30	77	+ 3:47	+ 2.30	61	+ 3:31
+ 2.45	77	+ 4:02	+ 2.45	87	+ 4:12	+ 2.45	80	+ 4:05	+ 2.45	63	+ 3:48
+ 3.00	79	+ 4:19	+ 3.00	90	+ 4:30	+ 3.00	83	+ 4:23	+ 3.00	64	+ 4:04
+ 3.15	80	+ 4:35	+ 3.15	93	+ 4:48	+ 3.15	87	+ 4:42	+ 3.15	68	+ 4:23
+ 3.30	82	+ 4:52	+ 3.30	96	+ 5:06	+ 3.30	90	+ 5:00	+ 3.30	71	+ 4:41
+ 3.45	85	+ 5:10	+ 3.45	98	+ 5:23	+ 3.45	92	+ 5:17	+ 3.45	74	+ 4:59
+ 4.00	88	+ 5:28	+ 4.00	101	+ 5:41	+ 4.00	94	+ 5:34	+ 4.00	78	+ 5:18
+ 4.15	91	+ 5:46	+ 4.15	103	+ 5:58	+ 4.15	96	+ 5:51	+ 4.15	83	+ 5:38
+ 4.30	94	- 5:56	+ 4.30	106	- 5:44	+ 4.30	98	- 5:52	+ 4.30	88	+ 5:58
+ 4.45	96	- 5:39	+ 4.45	110	- 5:25	+ 4.45	100	- 5:35	+ 4.45	94	- 5:41
+ 5.00	98	- 5:22	+ 5.00	115	- 5:05	+ 5.00	102	- 5:18	+ 5.00	99	- 5:21
+ 5.15	101	- 5:04	+ 5.15	119	- 4:46	+ 5.15	104	- 5:01	+ 5.15	104	- 5:01
+ 5.30	103	- 4:47	+ 5.30	123	- 4:27	+ 5.30	102	- 4:48	+ 5.30	109	- 4:41
+ 5.45	112	- 4:23	+ 5.45	158	- 3:37	+ 5.45	122	- 4:13	+ 5.45	114	- 4:21
+ 6.00	114	- 4:06	+ 6.00	158	- 3:22	+ 6.00	126	- 3:54	+ 6.00	119	- 4:01

	K5			K6			K7			K8	
	Kentish Knock to Long Sand Hd			Long Sand Hd to S. Threshold			S. Threshold to Cork Sand B'cn			Cork Sand B'cn to Harwich	
Time	Duration	Time at End of Sector	Time	Duration	Time at End of Sector	Time	Duration	Time at End of Sector	Time	Duration	Time at End of Sector
- 6.00	176	- 3:04	- 6.00	105	- 4:15	- 6.00	111	- 4:09	- 6.00	138	- 3:42
- 5.45	173	- 2:52	- 5.45	106	- 3:59	- 5.45	112	- 3:53	- 5.45	138	- 3:27
- 5.30	170	- 2:40	- 5.30	107	- 3:43	- 5.30	112	- 3:38	- 5.30	138	- 3:12
- 5.15	167	- 2:28	- 5.15	108	- 3:27	- 5.15	112	- 3:23	- 5.15	138	- 2:57
- 5.00	165	- 2:15	- 5.00	109	- 3:11	- 5.00	112	- 3:08	- 5.00	138	- 2:42
- 4.45	158	- 2:07	- 4.45	107	- 2:58	- 4.45	110	- 2:55	- 4.45	136	- 2:29
- 4.30	150	- 2:00	- 4.30	105	- 2:45	- 4.30	108	- 2:42	- 4.30	133	- 2:17
- 4.15	143	- 1:52	- 4.15	104	- 2:31	- 4.15	105	- 2:30	- 4.15	130	- 2:05
- 4.00	136	- 1:44	- 4.00	102	- 2:18	- 4.00	103	- 2:17	- 4.00	127	- 1:53
- 3.45	129	- 1:36	- 3.45	100	- 2:05	- 3.45	99	- 2:06	- 3.45	122	- 1:43
- 3.30	122	- 1:28	- 3.30	97	- 1:53	- 3.30	95	- 1:55	- 3.30	116	- 1:34
- 3.15	115	- 1:20	- 3.15	95	- 1:40	- 3.15	92	- 1:43	- 3.15	111	- 1:24
- 3.00	108	- 1:12	- 3.00	92	- 1:28	- 3.00	88	- 1:32	- 3.00	105	- 1:15
- 2.45	104	- 1:01	- 2.45	91	- 1:14	- 2.45	86	- 1:19	- 2.45	101	- 1:04
- 2.30	99	- 0:51	- 2.30	89	- 1:01	- 2.30	84	- 1:06	- 2.30	96	- 0:54
- 2.15	95	- 0:40	- 2.15	87	- 0:48	- 2.15	82	- 0:53	- 2.15	92	- 0:43
- 2.00	90	- 0:30	- 2.00	86	- 0:34	- 2.00	80	- 0:40	- 2.00	87	- 0:33
- 1.45	85	- 0:20	- 1.45	83	- 0:22	- 1.45	76	- 0:29	- 1.45	84	- 0:21
- 1.30	79	- 0:11	- 1.30	80	- 0:10	- 1.30	72	- 0:18	- 1.30	82	- 0:08
- 1.15	74	- 0:01	- 1.15	77	+ 0:02	- 1.15	69	- 0:06	- 1.15	79	+ 0:04
- 1.00	69	+ 0:09	- 1.00	75	+ 0:15	- 1.00	65	+ 0:05	- 1.00	76	+ 0:16
- 0.45	67	+ 0:22	- 0.45	71	+ 0:26	- 0.45	63	+ 0:18	- 0.45	75	+ 0:30
- 0.30	65	+ 0:35	- 0.30	67	+ 0:37	- 0.30	61	+ 0:31	- 0.30	75	+ 0:45
- 0.15	64	+ 0:49	- 0.15	62	+ 0:47	- 0.15	59	+ 0:44	- 0.15	75	+ 1:00
HW	62	+ 1:02	HW	58	+ 0:58	HW	57	+ 0:57	HW	75	+ 1:15
+ 0.15	64	+ 1:19	+ 0.15	56	+ 1:11	+ 0.15	57	+ 1:12	+ 0.15	74	+ 1:29
+ 0.30	66	+ 1:36	+ 0.30	55	+ 1:25	+ 0.30	58	+ 1:28	+ 0.30	72	+ 1:42
+ 0.45	68	+ 1:53	+ 0.45	53	+ 1:38	+ 0.45	58	+ 1:43	+ 0.45	71	+ 1:56
+ 1.00	69	+ 2:09	+ 1.00	51	+ 1:51	+ 1.00	58	+ 1:58	+ 1.00	70	+ 2:10
+ 1.15	72	+ 2:27	+ 1.15	51	+ 2:06	+ 1.15	59	+ 2:14	+ 1.15	71	+ 2:26
+ 1.30	75	+ 2:45	+ 1.30	52	+ 2:22	+ 1.30	60	+ 2:30	+ 1.30	73	+ 2:43
+ 1.45	78	+ 3:03	+ 1.45	53	+ 2:38	+ 1.45	61	+ 2:46	+ 1.45	74	+ 2:59
+ 2.00	81	+ 3:21	+ 2.00	53	+ 2:53	+ 2.00	62	+ 3:02	+ 2.00	76	+ 3:16
+ 2.15	83	+ 3:38	+ 2.15	56	+ 3:11	+ 2.15	64	+ 3:19	+ 2.15	77	+ 3:32
+ 2.30	86	+ 3:56	+ 2.30	58	+ 3:28	+ 2.30	66	+ 3:36	+ 2.30	78	+ 3:48
+ 2.45	89	+ 4:14	+ 2.45	60	+ 3:45	+ 2.45	68	+ 3:53	+ 2.45	80	+ 4:05
+ 3.00	91	+ 4:31	+ 3.00	63	+ 4:03	+ 3.00	70	+ 4:10	+ 3.00	81	+ 4:21
+ 3.15	95	+ 4:50	+ 3.15	66	+ 4:21	+ 3.15	73	+ 4:28	+ 3.15	83	+ 4:38
+ 3.30	98	+ 5:08	+ 3.30	69	+ 4:39	+ 3.30	75	+ 4:45	+ 3.30	85	+ 4:55
+ 3.45	102	+ 5:27	+ 3.45	72	+ 4:57	+ 3.45	78	+ 5:03	+ 3.45	87	+ 5:12
+ 4.00	105	+ 5:45	+ 4.00	75	+ 5:15	+ 4.00	80	+ 5:20	+ 4.00	89	+ 5:29
+ 4.15	110	- 5:55	+ 4.15	78	+ 5:33	+ 4.15	82	+ 5:37	+ 4.15	91	+ 5:46
+ 4.30	115	- 5:35	+ 4.30	81	+ 5:51	+ 4.30	84	+ 5:54	+ 4.30	93	- 5:57
+ 4.45	120	- 5:15	+ 4.45	84	- 5:51	+ 4.45	86	- 5:49	+ 4.45	95	- 5:40
+ 5.00	125	- 4:55	+ 5.00	88	- 5:32	+ 5.00	87	- 5:33	+ 5.00	97	- 5:23
+ 5.15	133	- 4:32	+ 5.15	90	- 5:15	+ 5.15	91	- 5:14	+ 5.15	103	- 5:02
+ 5.30	142	- 4:08	+ 5.30	91	- 4:59	+ 5.30	94	- 4:56	+ 5.30	108	- 4:42
+ 5.45	151	- 3:44	+ 5.45	93	- 4:42	+ 5.45	97	- 4:38	+ 5.45	114	- 4:21
+ 6.00	160	- 3:20	+ 6.00	95	- 4:25	+ 6.00	100	- 4:20	+ 6.00	120	- 4:00

Table K - Ramsgate to Harwich - Outside Route

Neaps — All times relate to HW Sheerness — **Time to cover Sectors (in minutes) at 5.0 Kts**

NORTH BOUND

	K1			K2			K3			K4			K5			K6			K7			K8	
	Ramsgate to North Foreland			North Foreland to Thanet			Thanet to South Knock			South Knock to Kentish Knock			Kentish Knock to Long Sand Hd			Long Sand Hd to S. Threshold			S. Threshold to Cork Sand B'cn			Cork Sand B'cn to Harwich	
Time	Duration	Time at End of Sector	Time	Duration	Time at End of Sector	Time	Duration	Time at End of Sector	Time	Duration	Time at End of Sector	Time	Duration	Time at End of Sector	Time	Duration	Time at End of Sector	Time	Duration	Time at End of Sector	Time	Duration	Time at End of Sector
- 6.00	68	- 4:52	- 6.00	99	- 4:21	- 6.00	88	- 4:32	- 6.00	90	- 4:30	- 6.00	106	- 4:14	- 6.00	74	- 4:46	- 6.00	75	- 4:45	- 6.00	85	- 4:35
- 5.45	69	- 4:36	- 5.45	101	- 4:04	- 5.45	90	- 4:15	- 5.45	91	- 4:14	- 5.45	106	- 3:59	- 5.45	75	- 4:30	- 5.45	75	- 4:30	- 5.45	87	- 4:18
- 5.30	69	- 4:21	- 5.30	103	- 3:47	- 5.30	93	- 3:57	- 5.30	93	- 3:57	- 5.30	107	- 3:43	- 5.30	75	- 4:15	- 5.30	76	- 4:14	- 5.30	89	- 4:01
- 5.15	69	- 4:06	- 5.15	103	- 3:32	- 5.15	93	- 3:42	- 5.15	94	- 3:41	- 5.15	107	- 3:28	- 5.15	75	- 4:00	- 5.15	76	- 3:59	- 5.15	91	- 3:44
- 5.00	69	- 3:51	- 5.00	102	- 3:18	- 5.00	93	- 3:27	- 5.00	95	- 3:25	- 5.00	108	- 3:12	- 5.00	76	- 3:44	- 5.00	76	- 3:44	- 5.00	93	- 3:27
- 4.45	68	- 3:37	- 4.45	101	- 3:04	- 4.45	94	- 3:11	- 4.45	94	- 3:11	- 4.45	106	- 2:59	- 4.45	75	- 3:30	- 4.45	76	- 3:29	- 4.45	91	- 3:14
- 4.30	68	- 3:22	- 4.30	101	- 2:49	- 4.30	94	- 2:56	- 4.30	93	- 2:57	- 4.30	105	- 2:45	- 4.30	75	- 3:15	- 4.30	75	- 3:15	- 4.30	89	- 3:01
- 4.15	66	- 3:09	- 4.15	98	- 2:37	- 4.15	92	- 2:43	- 4.15	92	- 2:43	- 4.15	103	- 2:32	- 4.15	75	- 3:00	- 4.15	75	- 3:00	- 4.15	87	- 2:48
- 4.00	63	- 2:57	- 4.00	95	- 2:25	- 4.00	90	- 2:30	- 4.00	90	- 2:30	- 4.00	101	- 2:19	- 4.00	74	- 2:46	- 4.00	74	- 2:46	- 4.00	85	- 2:35
- 3.45	61	- 2:44	- 3.45	92	- 2:13	- 3.45	87	- 2:18	- 3.45	87	- 2:18	- 3.45	97	- 2:08	- 3.45	74	- 2:31	- 3.45	73	- 2:32	- 3.45	83	- 2:22
- 3.30	58	- 2:32	- 3.30	90	- 2:00	- 3.30	85	- 2:05	- 3.30	84	- 2:06	- 3.30	93	- 1:57	- 3.30	73	- 2:17	- 3.30	71	- 2:19	- 3.30	82	- 2:08
- 3.15	56	- 2:19	- 3.15	87	- 1:48	- 3.15	84	- 1:51	- 3.15	80	- 1:55	- 3.15	89	- 1:46	- 3.15	72	- 2:03	- 3.15	70	- 2:05	- 3.15	80	- 1:55
- 3.00	53	- 2:07	- 3.00	84	- 1:36	- 3.00	82	- 1:38	- 3.00	77	- 1:43	- 3.00	85	- 1:35	- 3.00	72	- 1:48	- 3.00	69	- 1:51	- 3.00	79	- 1:41
- 2.45	51	- 1:54	- 2.45	81	- 1:24	- 2.45	81	- 1:24	- 2.45	75	- 1:30	- 2.45	83	- 1:22	- 2.45	71	- 1:34	- 2.45	68	- 1:37	- 2.45	77	- 1:28
- 2.30	48	- 1:42	- 2.30	78	- 1:12	- 2.30	80	- 1:10	- 2.30	72	- 1:18	- 2.30	80	- 1:10	- 2.30	71	- 1:19	- 2.30	67	- 1:23	- 2.30	75	- 1:15
- 2.15	47	- 1:28	- 2.15	77	- 0:58	- 2.15	78	- 0:57	- 2.15	70	- 1:05	- 2.15	77	- 0:58	- 2.15	70	- 1:05	- 2.15	66	- 1:09	- 2.15	73	- 1:02
- 2.00	46	- 1:14	- 2.00	76	- 0:44	- 2.00	77	- 0:43	- 2.00	68	- 0:52	- 2.00	75	- 0:45	- 2.00	70	- 0:50	- 2.00	65	- 0:55	- 2.00	71	- 0:49
- 1.45	46	- 0:59	- 1.45	74	- 0:31	- 1.45	75	- 0:30	- 1.45	66	- 0:39	- 1.45	72	- 0:33	- 1.45	69	- 0:36	- 1.45	64	- 0:41	- 1.45	70	- 0:35
- 1.30	45	- 0:45	- 1.30	73	- 0:17	- 1.30	74	- 0:16	- 1.30	64	- 0:26	- 1.30	70	- 0:20	- 1.30	67	- 0:23	- 1.30	62	- 0:28	- 1.30	69	- 0:21
- 1.15	45	- 0:30	- 1.15	72	- 0:03	- 1.15	72	- 0:03	- 1.15	62	- 0:13	- 1.15	68	- 0:07	- 1.15	66	- 0:09	- 1.15	61	- 0:14	- 1.15	67	- 0:08
- 1.00	45	- 0:15	- 1.00	71	+ 0:11	- 1.00	71	+ 0:11	- 1.00	60	HW	- 1.00	65	+ 0:05	- 1.00	65	+ 0:05	- 1.00	60	HW	- 1.00	66	+ 0:06
- 0.45	45	HW	- 0.45	70	+ 0:25	- 0.45	69	+ 0:24	- 0.45	59	+ 0:14	- 0.45	64	+ 0:19	- 0.45	64	+ 0:19	- 0.45	58	+ 0:13	- 0.45	66	+ 0:21
- 0.30	45	+ 0:15	- 0.30	69	+ 0:39	- 0.30	68	+ 0:38	- 0.30	58	+ 0:28	- 0.30	63	+ 0:33	- 0.30	62	+ 0:32	- 0.30	57	+ 0:27	- 0.30	66	+ 0:36
- 0.15	46	+ 0:31	- 0.15	69	+ 0:54	- 0.15	69	+ 0:54	- 0.15	57	+ 0:42	- 0.15	62	+ 0:47	- 0.15	60	+ 0:45	- 0.15	56	+ 0:41	- 0.15	66	+ 0:51
HW	47	+ 0:47	HW	69	+ 1:09	HW	67	+ 1:07	HW	56	+ 0:56	HW	61	+ 1:01	HW	58	+ 0:58	HW	55	+ 0:55	HW	66	+ 1:06
+ 0.15	47	+ 1:02	+ 0.15	69	+ 1:24	+ 0.15	66	+ 1:21	+ 0.15	55	+ 1:10	+ 0.15	62	+ 1:17	+ 0.15	57	+ 1:12	+ 0.15	55	+ 1:10	+ 0.15	65	+ 1:20
+ 0.30	48	+ 1:18	+ 0.30	69	+ 1:39	+ 0.30	66	+ 1:36	+ 0.30	55	+ 1:25	+ 0.30	63	+ 1:33	+ 0.30	56	+ 1:26	+ 0.30	55	+ 1:25	+ 0.30	64	+ 1:34
+ 0.45	49	+ 1:34	+ 0.45	70	+ 1:55	+ 0.45	66	+ 1:51	+ 0.45	55	+ 1:40	+ 0.45	63	+ 1:48	+ 0.45	55	+ 1:40	+ 0.45	55	+ 1:40	+ 0.45	64	+ 1:49
+ 1.00	50	+ 1:50	+ 1.00	71	+ 2:11	+ 1.00	67	+ 2:07	+ 1.00	54	+ 1:54	+ 1.00	64	+ 2:04	+ 1.00	54	+ 1:54	+ 1.00	55	+ 1:55	+ 1.00	63	+ 2:03
+ 1.15	51	+ 2:06	+ 1.15	71	+ 2:26	+ 1.15	67	+ 2:22	+ 1.15	55	+ 2:10	+ 1.15	65	+ 2:20	+ 1.15	54	+ 2:09	+ 1.15	55	+ 2:10	+ 1.15	64	+ 2:19
+ 1.30	53	+ 2:23	+ 1.30	72	+ 2:42	+ 1.30	68	+ 2:38	+ 1.30	55	+ 2:25	+ 1.30	67	+ 2:37	+ 1.30	54	+ 2:24	+ 1.30	56	+ 2:26	+ 1.30	64	+ 2:34
+ 1.45	54	+ 2:39	+ 1.45	72	+ 2:57	+ 1.45	68	+ 2:53	+ 1.45	55	+ 2:40	+ 1.45	68	+ 2:53	+ 1.45	54	+ 2:39	+ 1.45	56	+ 2:41	+ 1.45	65	+ 2:50
+ 2.00	55	+ 2:55	+ 2.00	73	+ 3:13	+ 2.00	69	+ 3:09	+ 2.00	55	+ 2:55	+ 2.00	69	+ 3:09	+ 2.00	54	+ 2:54	+ 2.00	57	+ 2:57	+ 2.00	65	+ 3:05
+ 2.15	56	+ 3:11	+ 2.15	74	+ 3:29	+ 2.15	70	+ 3:25	+ 2.15	56	+ 3:11	+ 2.15	71	+ 3:26	+ 2.15	56	+ 3:11	+ 2.15	58	+ 3:13	+ 2.15	66	+ 3:21
+ 2.30	58	+ 3:28	+ 2.30	75	+ 3:45	+ 2.30	71	+ 3:41	+ 2.30	57	+ 3:27	+ 2.30	72	+ 3:42	+ 2.30	57	+ 3:27	+ 2.30	59	+ 3:29	+ 2.30	67	+ 3:37
+ 2.45	59	+ 3:44	+ 2.45	76	+ 4:01	+ 2.45	72	+ 3:57	+ 2.45	57	+ 3:42	+ 2.45	73	+ 3:58	+ 2.45	58	+ 3:43	+ 2.45	60	+ 3:45	+ 2.45	67	+ 3:52
+ 3.00	60	+ 4:00	+ 3.00	77	+ 4:17	+ 3.00	73	+ 4:13	+ 3.00	58	+ 3:58	+ 3.00	74	+ 4:14	+ 3.00	59	+ 3:59	+ 3.00	61	+ 4:01	+ 3.00	68	+ 4:08
+ 3.15	61	+ 4:16	+ 3.15	77	+ 4:32	+ 3.15	75	+ 4:30	+ 3.15	59	+ 4:14	+ 3.15	76	+ 4:31	+ 3.15	60	+ 4:15	+ 3.15	62	+ 4:17	+ 3.15	69	+ 4:24
+ 3.30	62	+ 4:32	+ 3.30	78	+ 4:48	+ 3.30	76	+ 4:46	+ 3.30	61	+ 4:31	+ 3.30	77	+ 4:47	+ 3.30	61	+ 4:31	+ 3.30	63	+ 4:33	+ 3.30	70	+ 4:40
+ 3.45	62	+ 4:47	+ 3.45	79	+ 5:04	+ 3.45	76	+ 5:01	+ 3.45	62	+ 4:47	+ 3.45	78	+ 5:03	+ 3.45	63	+ 4:48	+ 3.45	64	+ 4:49	+ 3.45	71	+ 4:56
+ 4.00	63	+ 5:03	+ 4.00	80	+ 5:20	+ 4.00	77	+ 5:17	+ 4.00	64	+ 5:04	+ 4.00	80	+ 5:20	+ 4.00	64	+ 5:04	+ 4.00	65	+ 5:05	+ 4.00	71	+ 5:11
+ 4.15	64	+ 5:19	+ 4.15	81	+ 5:36	+ 4.15	78	+ 5:33	+ 4.15	66	+ 5:21	+ 4.15	81	+ 5:36	+ 4.15	65	+ 5:20	+ 4.15	66	+ 5:21	+ 4.15	72	+ 5:27
+ 4.30	64	+ 5:34	+ 4.30	81	+ 5:51	+ 4.30	78	+ 5:48	+ 4.30	68	+ 5:38	+ 4.30	83	+ 5:53	+ 4.30	67	+ 5:37	+ 4.30	67	+ 5:37	+ 4.30	73	+ 5:43
+ 4.45	64	+ 5:49	+ 4.45	82	- 5:53	+ 4.45	79	- 5:56	+ 4.45	70	+ 5:55	+ 4.45	85	- 5:50	+ 4.45	68	+ 5:53	+ 4.45	68	+ 5:53	+ 4.45	74	+ 5:59
+ 5.00	65	- 5:55	+ 5.00	83	- 5:37	+ 5.00	80	- 5:40	+ 5.00	71	- 5:49	+ 5.00	87	- 5:33	+ 5.00	69	- 5:51	+ 5.00	69	- 5:51	+ 5.00	75	- 5:45
+ 5.15	65	- 5:40	+ 5.15	84	- 5:21	+ 5.15	80	- 5:25	+ 5.15	73	- 5:32	+ 5.15	89	- 5:16	+ 5.15	70	- 5:35	+ 5.15	70	- 5:35	+ 5.15	76	- 5:29
+ 5.30	65	- 5:25	+ 5.30	86	- 5:04	+ 5.30	81	- 5:09	+ 5.30	74	- 5:16	+ 5.30	92	- 4:58	+ 5.30	71	- 5:19	+ 5.30	70	- 5:20	+ 5.30	77	- 5:13
+ 5.45	67	- 5:08	+ 5.45	95	- 4:40	+ 5.45	83	- 4:52	+ 5.45	76	- 4:59	+ 5.45	94	- 4:41	+ 5.45	72	- 5:03	+ 5.45	71	- 5:04	+ 5.45	79	- 4:56
+ 6.00	67	- 4:53	+ 6.00	97	- 4:23	+ 6.00	86	- 4:34	+ 6.00	77	- 4:43	+ 6.00	96	- 4:24	+ 6.00	72	- 4:48	+ 6.00	72	- 4:48	+ 6.00	80	- 4:40

Table K - Ramsgate to Harwich - Outside Route

Time to cover Sectors (in minutes) at 5.0 kts — All times relate to HW Sheerness — Springs

Time	K1 Ramsgate to North Foreland		Time	K2 North Foreland to Thanet		Time	K3 Thanet to South Knock		Time	K4 South Knock to Kentish Knock		Time	K5 Kentish Knock to Long Sand Hd		Time	K6 Long Sand Hd to S. Threshold		Time	K7 S. Threshold to Cork Sand B'cn		Time	K8 Cork Sand B'cn to Harwich	
	Duration	Time at End of Sector		Duration	Time at End of Sector		Duration	Time at End of Sector		Duration	Time at End of Sector		Duration	Time at End of Sector		Duration	Time at End of Sector		Duration	Time at End of Sector		Duration	Time at End of Sector
- 6.00	78	- 4:42	- 6.00	112	- 4:08	- 6.00	97	- 4:23	- 6.00	100	- 4:20	- 6.00	119	- 4:01	- 6.00	78	- 4:42	- 6.00	81	- 4:39	- 6.00	102	- 4:18
- 5.45	79	- 4:26	- 5.45	114	- 3:51	- 5.45	101	- 4:04	- 5.45	101	- 4:04	- 5.45	119	- 3:46	- 5.45	78	- 4:27	- 5.45	81	- 4:24	- 5.45	102	- 4:03
- 5.30	80	- 4:10	- 5.30	117	- 3:33	- 5.30	104	- 3:46	- 5.30	102	- 3:48	- 5.30	120	- 3:30	- 5.30	79	- 4:11	- 5.30	82	- 4:08	- 5.30	103	- 3:47
- 5.15	79	- 3:56	- 5.15	115	- 3:20	- 5.15	104	- 3:31	- 5.15	103	- 3:32	- 5.15	120	- 3:15	- 5.15	80	- 3:55	- 5.15	82	- 3:53	- 5.15	103	- 3:32
- 5.00	79	- 3:41	- 5.00	113	- 3:07	- 5.00	103	- 3:17	- 5.00	104	- 3:16	- 5.00	121	- 2:59	- 5.00	80	- 3:40	- 5.00	82	- 3:38	- 5.00	103	- 3:17
- 4.45	78	- 3:27	- 4.45	111	- 2:54	- 4.45	103	- 3:02	- 4.45	102	- 3:03	- 4.45	117	- 2:48	- 4.45	80	- 3:25	- 4.45	82	- 3:23	- 4.45	102	- 3:03
- 4.30	78	- 3:12	- 4.30	109	- 2:41	- 4.30	103	- 2:47	- 4.30	100	- 2:50	- 4.30	114	- 2:36	- 4.30	79	- 3:11	- 4.30	81	- 3:09	- 4.30	101	- 2:49
- 4.15	73	- 3:02	- 4.15	105	- 2:30	- 4.15	100	- 2:35	- 4.15	99	- 2:36	- 4.15	110	- 2:25	- 4.15	79	- 2:56	- 4.15	80	- 2:55	- 4.15	100	- 2:35
- 4.00	69	- 2:51	- 4.00	100	- 2:20	- 4.00	97	- 2:23	- 4.00	97	- 2:23	- 4.00	107	- 2:13	- 4.00	78	- 2:42	- 4.00	79	- 2:41	- 4.00	99	- 2:21
- 3.45	65	- 2:40	- 3.45	95	- 2:10	- 3.45	95	- 2:10	- 3.45	93	- 2:12	- 3.45	102	- 2:03	- 3.45	77	- 2:28	- 3.45	77	- 2:28	- 3.45	95	- 2:10
- 3.30	60	- 2:30	- 3.30	90	- 2:00	- 3.30	92	- 1:58	- 3.30	89	- 2:01	- 3.30	98	- 1:52	- 3.30	76	- 2:14	- 3.30	75	- 2:15	- 3.30	91	- 1:59
- 3.15	56	- 2:19	- 3.15	87	- 1:48	- 3.15	89	- 1:46	- 3.15	85	- 1:50	- 3.15	93	- 1:42	- 3.15	74	- 2:01	- 3.15	72	- 2:03	- 3.15	87	- 1:48
- 3.00	52	- 2:08	- 3.00	83	- 1:37	- 3.00	86	- 1:34	- 3.00	82	- 1:38	- 3.00	89	- 1:31	- 3.00	73	- 1:47	- 3.00	70	- 1:50	- 3.00	83	- 1:37
- 2.45	47	- 1:58	- 2.45	80	- 1:25	- 2.45	83	- 1:22	- 2.45	78	- 1:27	- 2.45	85	- 1:20	- 2.45	72	- 1:33	- 2.45	69	- 1:36	- 2.45	80	- 1:25
- 2.30	43	- 1:47	- 2.30	77	- 1:13	- 2.30	80	- 1:10	- 2.30	74	- 1:16	- 2.30	81	- 1:09	- 2.30	71	- 1:19	- 2.30	67	- 1:23	- 2.30	77	- 1:13
- 2.15	42	- 1:33	- 2.15	75	- 1:00	- 2.15	77	- 0:58	- 2.15	71	- 1:04	- 2.15	77	- 0:58	- 2.15	70	- 1:05	- 2.15	66	- 1:09	- 2.15	74	- 1:01
- 2.00	40	- 1:20	- 2.00	72	- 0:48	- 2.00	74	- 0:46	- 2.00	67	- 0:53	- 2.00	73	- 0:47	- 2.00	69	- 0:51	- 2.00	65	- 0:55	- 2.00	71	- 0:49
- 1.45	39	- 1:06	- 1.45	70	- 0:35	- 1.45	71	- 0:34	- 1.45	64	- 0:41	- 1.45	70	- 0:35	- 1.45	67	- 0:38	- 1.45	62	- 0:43	- 1.45	69	- 0:36
- 1.30	38	- 0:52	- 1.30	68	- 0:22	- 1.30	68	- 0:22	- 1.30	62	- 0:28	- 1.30	67	- 0:23	- 1.30	66	- 0:24	- 1.30	60	- 0:30	- 1.30	67	- 0:23
- 1.15	38	- 0:37	- 1.15	66	- 0:09	- 1.15	66	- 0:09	- 1.15	59	- 0:16	- 1.15	64	- 0:11	- 1.15	64	- 0:11	- 1.15	58	- 0:17	- 1.15	66	- 0:09
- 1.00	38	- 0:22	- 1.00	65	+ 0:05	- 1.00	63	+ 0:03	- 1.00	56	- 0:04	- 1.00	60	HW	- 1.00	63	+ 0:03	- 1.00	56	- 0:04	- 1.00	64	+ 0:04
- 0.45	39	- 0:06	- 0.45	63	+ 0:18	- 0.45	60	+ 0:15	- 0.45	55	+ 0:10	- 0.45	59	+ 0:14	- 0.45	60	+ 0:15	- 0.45	55	+ 0:10	- 0.45	64	+ 0:19
- 0.30	39	+ 0:09	- 0.30	62	+ 0:32	- 0.30	57	+ 0:27	- 0.30	53	+ 0:23	- 0.30	58	+ 0:28	- 0.30	57	+ 0:27	- 0.30	53	+ 0:23	- 0.30	64	+ 0:34
- 0.15	40	+ 0:25	- 0.15	62	+ 0:47	- 0.15	57	+ 0:42	- 0.15	52	+ 0:37	- 0.15	56	+ 0:41	- 0.15	55	+ 0:40	- 0.15	52	+ 0:37	- 0.15	64	+ 0:49
HW	41	+ 0:41	HW	62	+ 1:02	HW	56	+ 0:56	HW	51	+ 0:51	HW	55	+ 0:55	HW	52	+ 0:52	HW	50	+ 0:50	HW	64	+ 1:04
+ 0.15	42	+ 0:57	+ 0.15	62	+ 1:17	+ 0.15	56	+ 1:11	+ 0.15	50	+ 1:05	+ 0.15	56	+ 1:11	+ 0.15	51	+ 1:06	+ 0.15	50	+ 1:05	+ 0.15	63	+ 1:18
+ 0.30	43	+ 1:13	+ 0.30	62	+ 1:32	+ 0.30	55	+ 1:25	+ 0.30	50	+ 1:20	+ 0.30	57	+ 1:27	+ 0.30	50	+ 1:20	+ 0.30	50	+ 1:20	+ 0.30	62	+ 1:32
+ 0.45	45	+ 1:30	+ 0.45	62	+ 1:47	+ 0.45	56	+ 1:41	+ 0.45	49	+ 1:34	+ 0.45	58	+ 1:43	+ 0.45	48	+ 1:33	+ 0.45	50	+ 1:35	+ 0.45	61	+ 1:46
+ 1.00	46	+ 1:46	+ 1.00	63	+ 2:03	+ 1.00	57	+ 1:57	+ 1.00	49	+ 1:49	+ 1.00	59	+ 1:59	+ 1.00	47	+ 1:47	+ 1.00	50	+ 1:50	+ 1.00	60	+ 2:00
+ 1.15	48	+ 2:03	+ 1.15	64	+ 2:19	+ 1.15	57	+ 2:12	+ 1.15	49	+ 2:04	+ 1.15	60	+ 2:15	+ 1.15	47	+ 2:02	+ 1.15	50	+ 2:05	+ 1.15	61	+ 2:16
+ 1.30	50	+ 2:20	+ 1.30	64	+ 2:34	+ 1.30	58	+ 2:28	+ 1.30	50	+ 2:20	+ 1.30	62	+ 2:32	+ 1.30	47	+ 2:17	+ 1.30	51	+ 2:21	+ 1.30	62	+ 2:32
+ 1.45	52	+ 2:37	+ 1.45	66	+ 2:51	+ 1.45	59	+ 2:44	+ 1.45	50	+ 2:35	+ 1.45	64	+ 2:49	+ 1.45	47	+ 2:32	+ 1.45	52	+ 2:37	+ 1.45	62	+ 2:47
+ 2.00	54	+ 2:54	+ 2.00	67	+ 3:07	+ 2.00	61	+ 3:01	+ 2.00	50	+ 2:50	+ 2.00	66	+ 3:06	+ 2.00	48	+ 2:48	+ 2.00	53	+ 2:53	+ 2.00	63	+ 3:03
+ 2.15	56	+ 3:11	+ 2.15	68	+ 3:23	+ 2.15	63	+ 3:18	+ 2.15	51	+ 3:06	+ 2.15	68	+ 3:23	+ 2.15	49	+ 3:04	+ 2.15	54	+ 3:09	+ 2.15	64	+ 3:19
+ 2.30	59	+ 3:29	+ 2.30	69	+ 3:39	+ 2.30	64	+ 3:34	+ 2.30	52	+ 3:22	+ 2.30	70	+ 3:40	+ 2.30	50	+ 3:20	+ 2.30	55	+ 3:25	+ 2.30	65	+ 3:35
+ 2.45	60	+ 3:45	+ 2.45	71	+ 3:56	+ 2.45	66	+ 3:51	+ 2.45	53	+ 3:38	+ 2.45	71	+ 3:56	+ 2.45	52	+ 3:37	+ 2.45	56	+ 3:41	+ 2.45	65	+ 3:50
+ 3.00	61	+ 4:01	+ 3.00	73	+ 4:13	+ 3.00	68	+ 4:08	+ 3.00	54	+ 3:54	+ 3.00	73	+ 4:13	+ 3.00	53	+ 3:53	+ 3.00	58	+ 3:58	+ 3.00	66	+ 4:06
+ 3.15	62	+ 4:17	+ 3.15	75	+ 4:30	+ 3.15	70	+ 4:25	+ 3.15	56	+ 4:11	+ 3.15	75	+ 4:30	+ 3.15	55	+ 4:10	+ 3.15	59	+ 4:14	+ 3.15	68	+ 4:23
+ 3.30	64	+ 4:34	+ 3.30	76	+ 4:46	+ 3.30	72	+ 4:42	+ 3.30	58	+ 4:28	+ 3.30	77	+ 4:47	+ 3.30	57	+ 4:27	+ 3.30	61	+ 4:31	+ 3.30	69	+ 4:39
+ 3.45	65	+ 4:50	+ 3.45	78	+ 5:03	+ 3.45	74	+ 4:59	+ 3.45	60	+ 4:45	+ 3.45	79	+ 5:04	+ 3.45	59	+ 4:44	+ 3.45	63	+ 4:48	+ 3.45	70	+ 4:55
+ 4.00	65	+ 5:05	+ 4.00	79	+ 5:19	+ 4.00	75	+ 5:15	+ 4.00	62	+ 5:02	+ 4.00	81	+ 5:21	+ 4.00	61	+ 5:01	+ 4.00	64	+ 5:04	+ 4.00	71	+ 5:11
+ 4.15	66	+ 5:21	+ 4.15	81	+ 5:36	+ 4.15	77	+ 5:32	+ 4.15	65	+ 5:20	+ 4.15	84	+ 5:39	+ 4.15	63	+ 5:18	+ 4.15	65	+ 5:20	+ 4.15	73	+ 5:28
+ 4.30	67	+ 5:37	+ 4.30	82	+ 5:52	+ 4.30	78	+ 5:48	+ 4.30	68	+ 5:38	+ 4.30	87	+ 5:57	+ 4.30	65	+ 5:35	+ 4.30	67	+ 5:37	+ 4.30	74	+ 5:44
+ 4.45	69	+ 5:54	+ 4.45	84	- 5:51	+ 4.45	79	- 5:56	+ 4.45	71	+ 5:56	+ 4.45	90	- 5:45	+ 4.45	67	+ 5:52	+ 4.45	68	+ 5:53	+ 4.45	75	- 6:00
+ 5.00	70	- 5:50	+ 5.00	86	- 5:34	+ 5.00	80	- 5:40	+ 5.00	73	- 5:47	+ 5.00	93	- 5:27	+ 5.00	69	- 5:51	+ 5.00	69	- 5:51	+ 5.00	76	- 5:44
+ 5.15	71	- 5:34	+ 5.15	88	- 5:17	+ 5.15	81	- 5:24	+ 5.15	76	- 5:29	+ 5.15	96	- 5:09	+ 5.15	70	- 5:35	+ 5.15	70	- 5:35	+ 5.15	78	- 5:27
+ 5.30	72	- 5:18	+ 5.30	90	- 5:00	+ 5.30	82	- 5:08	+ 5.30	78	- 5:12	+ 5.30	99	- 4:51	+ 5.30	72	- 5:18	+ 5.30	72	- 5:18	+ 5.30	80	- 5:10
+ 5.45	76	- 4:59	+ 5.45	106	- 4:29	+ 5.45	90	- 4:45	+ 5.45	80	- 4:55	+ 5.45	102	- 4:33	+ 5.45	73	- 5:02	+ 5.45	73	- 5:02	+ 5.45	82	- 4:53
+ 6.00	77	- 4:43	+ 6.00	109	- 4:11	+ 6.00	94	- 4:26	+ 6.00	83	- 4:37	+ 6.00	105	- 4:15	+ 6.00	74	- 4:46	+ 6.00	75	- 4:45	+ 6.00	84	- 4:36

NORTH BOUND

Table K - Ramsgate to Harwich - Outside Route

Neaps — All times relate to HW Sheerness — **Time to cover Sectors (in minutes) at 6.0 Kts**

NORTH BOUND

	K1			K2			K3			K4			K5			K6			K7			K8	
	Ramsgate to North Foreland			North Foreland to Thanet			Thanet to South Knock			South Knock to Kentish Knock			Kentish Knock to Long Sand Hd			Long Sand Hd to S. Threshold			S. Threshold to Cork Sand B'cn			Cork Sand B'cn to Harwich	
Time	Duration	Time at End of Sector	Time	Duration	Time at End of Sector	Time	Duration	Time at End of Sector	Time	Duration	Time at End of Sector	Time	Duration	Time at End of Sector	Time	Duration	Time at End of Sector	Time	Duration	Time at End of Sector	Time	Duration	Time at End of Sector
- 6.00	**55**	**- 5:05**	**- 6.00**	**76**	**- 4:44**	**- 6.00**	**70**	**- 4:50**	**- 6.00**	**66**	**- 4:54**	**- 6.00**	**78**	**- 4:42**	**- 6.00**	**61**	**- 4:59**	**- 6.00**	**61**	**- 4:59**	**- 6.00**	**69**	**- 4:51**
- 5.45	55	- 4:50	- 5.45	77	- 4:28	- 5.45	71	- 4:34	- 5.45	67	- 4:38	- 5.45	79	- 4:26	- 5.45	61	- 4:44	- 5.45	61	- 4:44	- 5.45	69	- 4:36
- 5.30	56	- 4:34	- 5.30	78	- 4:12	- 5.30	72	- 4:18	- 5.30	68	- 4:22	- 5.30	79	- 4:11	- 5.30	62	- 4:28	- 5.30	62	- 4:28	- 5.30	69	- 4:21
- 5.15	56	- 4:19	- 5.15	78	- 3:57	- 5.15	72	- 4:03	- 5.15	69	- 4:06	- 5.15	80	- 3:55	- 5.15	62	- 4:13	- 5.15	62	- 4:13	- 5.15	69	- 4:06
- 5.00	**55**	**- 4:05**	**- 5.00**	**78**	**- 3:42**	**- 5.00**	**72**	**- 3:48**	**- 5.00**	**69**	**- 3:51**	**- 5.00**	**80**	**- 3:40**	**- 5.00**	**62**	**- 3:58**	**- 5.00**	**62**	**- 3:58**	**- 5.00**	**69**	**- 3:51**
- 4.45	55	- 3:50	- 4.45	78	- 3:27	- 4.45	72	- 3:33	- 4.45	69	- 3:36	- 4.45	80	- 3:25	- 4.45	62	- 3:43	- 4.45	62	- 3:43	- 4.45	69	- 3:36
- 4.30	55	- 3:35	- 4.30	78	- 3:12	- 4.30	72	- 3:18	- 4.30	68	- 3:22	- 4.30	79	- 3:11	- 4.30	62	- 3:28	- 4.30	61	- 3:29	- 4.30	69	- 3:21
- 4.15	54	- 3:21	- 4.15	76	- 2:59	- 4.15	72	- 3:03	- 4.15	68	- 3:07	- 4.15	78	- 2:57	- 4.15	61	- 3:14	- 4.15	61	- 3:14	- 4.15	69	- 3:06
- 4.00	**52**	**- 3:08**	**- 4.00**	**74**	**- 2:46**	**- 4.00**	**71**	**- 2:49**	**- 4.00**	**68**	**- 2:52**	**- 4.00**	**77**	**- 2:43**	**- 4.00**	**61**	**- 2:59**	**- 4.00**	**61**	**- 2:59**	**- 4.00**	**69**	**- 2:51**
- 3.45	51	- 2:54	- 3.45	73	- 2:32	- 3.45	71	- 2:34	- 3.45	67	- 2:38	- 3.45	76	- 2:29	- 3.45	61	- 2:44	- 3.45	60	- 2:45	- 3.45	68	- 2:37
- 3.30	49	- 2:41	- 3.30	71	- 2:19	- 3.30	70	- 2:20	- 3.30	65	- 2:25	- 3.30	74	- 2:16	- 3.30	60	- 2:30	- 3.30	59	- 2:31	- 3.30	67	- 2:23
- 3.15	47	- 2:28	- 3.15	70	- 2:05	- 3.15	69	- 2:06	- 3.15	64	- 2:11	- 3.15	72	- 2:03	- 3.15	60	- 2:15	- 3.15	58	- 2:17	- 3.15	66	- 2:09
- 3.00	**46**	**- 2:14**	**- 3.00**	**68**	**- 1:52**	**- 3.00**	**68**	**- 1:52**	**- 3.00**	**63**	**- 1:57**	**- 3.00**	**71**	**- 1:49**	**- 3.00**	**59**	**- 2:01**	**- 3.00**	**57**	**- 2:03**	**- 3.00**	**65**	**- 1:55**
- 2.45	44	- 2:01	- 2.45	67	- 1:38	- 2.45	68	- 1:37	- 2.45	61	- 1:44	- 2.45	69	- 1:36	- 2.45	59	- 1:46	- 2.45	57	- 1:48	- 2.45	64	- 1:41
- 2.30	42	- 1:48	- 2.30	66	- 1:24	- 2.30	67	- 1:23	- 2.30	60	- 1:30	- 2.30	67	- 1:23	- 2.30	59	- 1:31	- 2.30	56	- 1:34	- 2.30	62	- 1:28
- 2.15	41	- 1:34	- 2.15	65	- 1:10	- 2.15	66	- 1:09	- 2.15	58	- 1:17	- 2.15	65	- 1:10	- 2.15	58	- 1:17	- 2.15	55	- 1:20	- 2.15	61	- 1:14
- 2.00	**40**	**- 1:20**	**- 2.00**	**64**	**- 0:56**	**- 2.00**	**65**	**- 0:55**	**- 2.00**	**57**	**- 1:03**	**- 2.00**	**63**	**- 0:57**	**- 2.00**	**58**	**- 1:02**	**- 2.00**	**55**	**- 1:05**	**- 2.00**	**60**	**- 1:00**
- 1.45	40	- 1:05	- 1.45	63	- 0:42	- 1.45	63	- 0:42	- 1.45	55	- 0:50	- 1.45	62	- 0:43	- 1.45	57	- 0:48	- 1.45	54	- 0:51	- 1.45	59	- 0:46
- 1.30	39	- 0:51	- 1.30	62	- 0:28	- 1.30	62	- 0:28	- 1.30	54	- 0:36	- 1.30	60	- 0:30	- 1.30	57	- 0:33	- 1.30	53	- 0:37	- 1.30	58	- 0:32
- 1.15	39	- 0:36	- 1.15	61	- 0:14	- 1.15	61	- 0:14	- 1.15	53	- 0:22	- 1.15	58	- 0:17	- 1.15	56	- 0:19	- 1.15	52	- 0:23	- 1.15	57	- 0:18
- 1.00	**39**	**- 0:21**	**- 1.00**	**61**	**+ 0:01**	**- 1.00**	**60**	**HW**	**- 1.00**	**51**	**- 0:09**	**- 1.00**	**57**	**- 0:03**	**- 1.00**	**55**	**- 0:05**	**- 1.00**	**51**	**- 0:09**	**- 1.00**	**56**	**- 0:04**
- 0.45	39	- 0:06	- 0.45	60	+ 0:15	- 0.45	59	+ 0:14	- 0.45	50	+ 0:05	- 0.45	56	+ 0:11	- 0.45	54	+ 0:09	- 0.45	50	+ 0:05	- 0.45	56	+ 0:11
- 0.30	39	+ 0:09	- 0.30	59	+ 0:29	- 0.30	58	+ 0:28	- 0.30	50	+ 0:20	- 0.30	55	+ 0:25	- 0.30	53	+ 0:23	- 0.30	49	+ 0:19	- 0.30	56	+ 0:26
- 0.15	39	+ 0:24	- 0.15	59	+ 0:44	- 0.15	58	+ 0:43	- 0.15	49	+ 0:34	- 0.15	54	+ 0:39	- 0.15	52	+ 0:37	- 0.15	48	+ 0:33	- 0.15	56	+ 0:41
HW	**40**	**+ 0:40**	**HW**	**59**	**+ 0:59**	**HW**	**57**	**+ 0:57**	**HW**	**48**	**+ 0:48**	**HW**	**53**	**+ 0:53**	**HW**	**51**	**+ 0:51**	**HW**	**48**	**+ 0:48**	**HW**	**56**	**+ 0:56**
+ 0.15	40	+ 0:55	+ 0.15	59	+ 1:14	+ 0.15	57	+ 1:12	+ 0.15	48	+ 1:03	+ 0.15	54	+ 1:09	+ 0.15	50	+ 1:05	+ 0.15	47	+ 1:02	+ 0.15	56	+ 1:11
+ 0.30	41	+ 1:11	+ 0.30	59	+ 1:29	+ 0.30	57	+ 1:27	+ 0.30	48	+ 1:18	+ 0.30	54	+ 1:24	+ 0.30	49	+ 1:19	+ 0.30	47	+ 1:17	+ 0.30	55	+ 1:25
+ 0.45	41	+ 1:26	+ 0.45	60	+ 1:45	+ 0.45	57	+ 1:42	+ 0.45	47	+ 1:32	+ 0.45	54	+ 1:39	+ 0.45	48	+ 1:33	+ 0.45	47	+ 1:32	+ 0.45	55	+ 1:40
+ 1.00	**42**	**+ 1:42**	**+ 1.00**	**60**	**+ 2:00**	**+ 1.00**	**57**	**+ 1:57**	**+ 1.00**	**47**	**+ 1:47**	**+ 1.00**	**55**	**+ 1:55**	**+ 1.00**	**48**	**+ 1:48**	**+ 1.00**	**47**	**+ 1:47**	**+ 1.00**	**54**	**+ 1:54**
+ 1.15	43	+ 1:58	+ 1.15	60	+ 2:15	+ 1.15	57	+ 2:12	+ 1.15	47	+ 2:02	+ 1.15	56	+ 2:11	+ 1.15	47	+ 2:02	+ 1.15	47	+ 2:02	+ 1.15	55	+ 2:10
+ 1.30	44	+ 2:14	+ 1.30	61	+ 2:31	+ 1.30	58	+ 2:28	+ 1.30	47	+ 2:17	+ 1.30	57	+ 2:27	+ 1.30	47	+ 2:17	+ 1.30	48	+ 2:18	+ 1.30	55	+ 2:25
+ 1.45	45	+ 2:30	+ 1.45	61	+ 2:46	+ 1.45	58	+ 2:43	+ 1.45	47	+ 2:32	+ 1.45	58	+ 2:43	+ 1.45	47	+ 2:32	+ 1.45	48	+ 2:33	+ 1.45	55	+ 2:40
+ 2.00	**46**	**+ 2:46**	**+ 2.00**	**62**	**+ 3:02**	**+ 2.00**	**59**	**+ 2:59**	**+ 2.00**	**47**	**+ 2:47**	**+ 2.00**	**59**	**+ 2:59**	**+ 2.00**	**47**	**+ 2:47**	**+ 2.00**	**49**	**+ 2:49**	**+ 2.00**	**55**	**+ 2:55**
+ 2.15	46	+ 3:01	+ 2.15	62	+ 3:17	+ 2.15	60	+ 3:15	+ 2.15	48	+ 3:03	+ 2.15	59	+ 3:14	+ 2.15	48	+ 3:03	+ 2.15	49	+ 3:04	+ 2.15	56	+ 3:11
+ 2.30	47	+ 3:17	+ 2.30	63	+ 3:33	+ 2.30	60	+ 3:30	+ 2.30	48	+ 3:18	+ 2.30	60	+ 3:30	+ 2.30	49	+ 3:19	+ 2.30	50	+ 3:20	+ 2.30	56	+ 3:26
+ 2.45	48	+ 3:33	+ 2.45	63	+ 3:48	+ 2.45	61	+ 3:46	+ 2.45	49	+ 3:34	+ 2.45	61	+ 3:46	+ 2.45	49	+ 3:34	+ 2.45	51	+ 3:36	+ 2.45	57	+ 3:42
+ 3.00	**49**	**+ 3:49**	**+ 3.00**	**64**	**+ 4:04**	**+ 3.00**	**62**	**+ 4:02**	**+ 3.00**	**49**	**+ 3:49**	**+ 3.00**	**62**	**+ 4:02**	**+ 3.00**	**50**	**+ 3:50**	**+ 3.00**	**51**	**+ 3:51**	**+ 3.00**	**57**	**+ 3:57**
+ 3.15	50	+ 4:05	+ 3.15	65	+ 4:20	+ 3.15	62	+ 4:17	+ 3.15	50	+ 4:05	+ 3.15	63	+ 4:18	+ 3.15	51	+ 4:06	+ 3.15	52	+ 4:07	+ 3.15	58	+ 4:13
+ 3.30	50	+ 4:20	+ 3.30	65	+ 4:35	+ 3.30	63	+ 4:33	+ 3.30	51	+ 4:21	+ 3.30	64	+ 4:34	+ 3.30	52	+ 4:22	+ 3.30	53	+ 4:23	+ 3.30	58	+ 4:28
+ 3.45	51	+ 4:36	+ 3.45	66	+ 4:51	+ 3.45	64	+ 4:49	+ 3.45	52	+ 4:37	+ 3.45	65	+ 4:50	+ 3.45	53	+ 4:38	+ 3.45	54	+ 4:39	+ 3.45	59	+ 4:44
+ 4.00	**51**	**+ 4:51**	**+ 4.00**	**66**	**+ 5:06**	**+ 4.00**	**64**	**+ 5:04**	**+ 4.00**	**53**	**+ 4:53**	**+ 4.00**	**66**	**+ 5:06**	**+ 4.00**	**54**	**+ 4:54**	**+ 4.00**	**54**	**+ 4:54**	**+ 4.00**	**59**	**+ 4:59**
+ 4.15	52	+ 5:07	+ 4.15	67	+ 5:22	+ 4.15	65	+ 5:20	+ 4.15	54	+ 5:09	+ 4.15	67	+ 5:22	+ 4.15	55	+ 5:10	+ 4.15	55	+ 5:10	+ 4.15	60	+ 5:15
+ 4.30	52	+ 5:22	+ 4.30	67	+ 5:37	+ 4.30	65	+ 5:35	+ 4.30	56	+ 5:26	+ 4.30	68	+ 5:38	+ 4.30	56	+ 5:26	+ 4.30	56	+ 5:26	+ 4.30	61	+ 5:31
+ 4.45	52	+ 5:37	+ 4.45	68	+ 5:53	+ 4.45	66	+ 5:51	+ 4.45	57	+ 5:42	+ 4.45	69	+ 5:54	+ 4.45	57	+ 5:42	+ 4.45	56	+ 5:41	+ 4.45	61	+ 5:46
+ 5.00	**53**	**+ 5:53**	**+ 5.00**	**69**	**- 5:51**	**+ 5.00**	**66**	**- 5:54**	**+ 5.00**	**58**	**+ 5:58**	**+ 5.00**	**71**	**- 5:49**	**+ 5.00**	**58**	**+ 5:58**	**+ 5.00**	**57**	**+ 5:57**	**+ 5.00**	**62**	**- 5:58**
+ 5.15	53	- 5:52	+ 5.15	69	- 5:36	+ 5.15	66	- 5:39	+ 5.15	59	- 5:46	+ 5.15	72	- 5:33	+ 5.15	58	- 5:47	+ 5.15	57	- 5:48	+ 5.15	62	- 5:43
+ 5.30	53	- 5:37	+ 5.30	70	- 5:20	+ 5.30	67	- 5:23	+ 5.30	60	- 5:30	+ 5.30	73	- 5:17	+ 5.30	59	- 5:31	+ 5.30	58	- 5:32	+ 5.30	63	- 5:27
+ 5.45	54	- 5:21	+ 5.45	74	- 5:01	+ 5.45	69	- 5:06	+ 5.45	62	- 5:13	+ 5.45	74	- 5:01	+ 5.45	59	- 5:16	+ 5.45	58	- 5:17	+ 5.45	64	- 5:11
+ 6.00	**54**	**- 5:06**	**+ 6.00**	**75**	**- 4:45**	**+ 6.00**	**69**	**- 4:51**	**+ 6.00**	**63**	**- 4:57**	**+ 6.00**	**75**	**- 4:45**	**+ 6.00**	**60**	**- 5:00**	**+ 6.00**	**59**	**- 5:01**	**+ 6.00**	**65**	**- 4:55**

Table K - Ramsgate to Harwich - Outside Route

Time to cover Sectors (in minutes) at 6.0 kts — All times relate to HW Sheerness — **Springs**

	K1			K2			K3			K4	
	Ramsgate to North Foreland			North Foreland to Thanet			Thanet to South Knock			South Knock to Kentish Knock	
Time	Duration	Time at End of Sector	Time	Duration	Time at End of Sector	Time	Duration	Time at End of Sector	Time	Duration	Time at End of Sector
- 6.00	62	- 4:58	- 6.00	86	- 4:34	- 6.00	75	- 4:45	- 6.00	72	- 4:48
- 5.45	62	- 4:43	- 5.45	89	- 4:16	- 5.45	77	- 4:28	- 5.45	73	- 4:32
- 5.30	63	- 4:27	- 5.30	92	- 3:58	- 5.30	79	- 4:11	- 5.30	74	- 4:16
- 5.15	63	- 4:12	- 5.15	92	- 3:43	- 5.15	79	- 3:56	- 5.15	75	- 4:00
- 5.00	63	- 3:57	- 5.00	92	- 3:28	- 5.00	80	- 3:40	- 5.00	76	- 3:44
- 4.45	62	- 3:43	- 4.45	91	- 3:14	- 4.45	80	- 3:25	- 4.45	75	- 3:30
- 4.30	62	- 3:28	- 4.30	91	- 2:59	- 4.30	80	- 3:10	- 4.30	75	- 3:15
- 4.15	59	- 3:16	- 4.15	87	- 2:48	- 4.15	79	- 2:56	- 4.15	74	- 3:01
- 4.00	57	- 3:03	- 4.00	83	- 2:37	- 4.00	78	- 2:42	- 4.00	74	- 2:46
- 3.45	54	- 2:51	- 3.45	79	- 2:26	- 3.45	76	- 2:29	- 3.45	72	- 2:33
- 3.30	51	- 2:39	- 3.30	75	- 2:15	- 3.30	75	- 2:15	- 3.30	70	- 2:20
- 3.15	48	- 2:27	- 3.15	72	- 2:03	- 3.15	73	- 2:02	- 3.15	68	- 2:07
- 3.00	45	- 2:15	- 3.00	70	- 1:50	- 3.00	71	- 1:49	- 3.00	67	- 1:53
- 2.45	42	- 2:03	- 2.45	67	- 1:38	- 2.45	69	- 1:36	- 2.45	64	- 1:41
- 2.30	39	- 1:51	- 2.30	65	- 1:25	- 2.30	67	- 1:23	- 2.30	62	- 1:28
- 2.15	38	- 1:37	- 2.15	63	- 1:12	- 2.15	65	- 1:10	- 2.15	59	- 1:16
- 2.00	36	- 1:24	- 2.00	62	- 0:58	- 2.00	63	- 0:57	- 2.00	57	- 1:03
- 1.45	35	- 1:10	- 1.45	60	- 0:45	- 1.45	61	- 0:44	- 1.45	55	- 0:50
- 1.30	34	- 0:56	- 1.30	58	- 0:32	- 1.30	59	- 0:31	- 1.30	53	- 0:37
- 1.15	34	- 0:41	- 1.15	57	- 0:18	- 1.15	57	- 0:18	- 1.15	51	- 0:24
- 1.00	34	- 0:26	- 1.00	56	- 0:04	- 1.00	55	- 0:05	- 1.00	49	- 0:11
- 0.45	34	- 0:11	- 0.45	55	+ 0:10	- 0.45	53	+ 0:08	- 0.45	48	+ 0:03
- 0.30	34	+ 0:04	- 0.30	54	+ 0:24	- 0.30	51	+ 0:21	- 0.30	47	+ 0:17
- 0.15	35	+ 0:20	- 0.15	55	+ 0:40	- 0.15	51	+ 0:36	- 0.15	46	+ 0:31
HW	36	+ 0:36	HW	54	+ 0:54	HW	50	+ 0:50	HW	45	+ 0:45
+ 0.15	36	+ 0:51	+ 0.15	54	+ 1:09	+ 0.15	50	+ 1:05	+ 0.15	44	+ 0:59
+ 0.30	37	+ 1:07	+ 0.30	54	+ 1:24	+ 0.30	49	+ 1:19	+ 0.30	44	+ 1:14
+ 0.45	38	+ 1:23	+ 0.45	54	+ 1:39	+ 0.45	50	+ 1:35	+ 0.45	44	+ 1:29
+ 1.00	39	+ 1:39	+ 1.00	55	+ 1:55	+ 1.00	50	+ 1:50	+ 1.00	43	+ 1:43
+ 1.15	40	+ 1:55	+ 1.15	55	+ 2:10	+ 1.15	50	+ 2:05	+ 1.15	43	+ 1:58
+ 1.30	42	+ 2:12	+ 1.30	56	+ 2:26	+ 1.30	51	+ 2:21	+ 1.30	43	+ 2:13
+ 1.45	43	+ 2:28	+ 1.45	56	+ 2:41	+ 1.45	52	+ 2:37	+ 1.45	44	+ 2:29
+ 2.00	45	+ 2:45	+ 2.00	57	+ 2:57	+ 2.00	53	+ 2:53	+ 2.00	44	+ 2:44
+ 2.15	46	+ 3:01	+ 2.15	58	+ 3:13	+ 2.15	54	+ 3:09	+ 2.15	44	+ 2:59
+ 2.30	48	+ 3:18	+ 2.30	59	+ 3:29	+ 2.30	55	+ 3:25	+ 2.30	45	+ 3:15
+ 2.45	49	+ 3:34	+ 2.45	60	+ 3:45	+ 2.45	56	+ 3:41	+ 2.45	46	+ 3:31
+ 3.00	50	+ 3:50	+ 3.00	61	+ 4:01	+ 3.00	58	+ 3:58	+ 3.00	46	+ 3:46
+ 3.15	51	+ 4:06	+ 3.15	63	+ 4:18	+ 3.15	59	+ 4:14	+ 3.15	48	+ 4:03
+ 3.30	52	+ 4:22	+ 3.30	64	+ 4:34	+ 3.30	61	+ 4:31	+ 3.30	49	+ 4:19
+ 3.45	53	+ 4:38	+ 3.45	65	+ 4:50	+ 3.45	62	+ 4:47	+ 3.45	50	+ 4:35
+ 4.00	53	+ 4:53	+ 4.00	66	+ 5:06	+ 4.00	63	+ 5:03	+ 4.00	52	+ 4:52
+ 4.15	53	+ 5:08	+ 4.15	67	+ 5:22	+ 4.15	64	+ 5:19	+ 4.15	54	+ 5:09
+ 4.30	54	+ 5:24	+ 4.30	68	+ 5:38	+ 4.30	65	+ 5:35	+ 4.30	56	+ 5:26
+ 4.45	55	+ 5:40	+ 4.45	69	+ 5:54	+ 4.45	65	+ 5:50	+ 4.45	58	+ 5:43
+ 5.00	56	+ 5:56	+ 5.00	70	- 5:50	+ 5.00	66	- 5:54	+ 5.00	59	+ 5:59
+ 5.15	57	- 5:48	+ 5.15	72	- 5:33	+ 5.15	67	- 5:38	+ 5.15	61	- 5:44
+ 5.30	58	- 5:32	+ 5.30	73	- 5:17	+ 5.30	68	- 5:22	+ 5.30	63	- 5:27
+ 5.45	60	- 5:15	+ 5.45	80	- 4:55	+ 5.45	72	- 5:03	+ 5.45	65	- 5:10
+ 6.00	61	- 4:59	+ 6.00	83	- 4:37	+ 6.00	73	- 4:47	+ 6.00	66	- 4:54

	K5			K6			K7			K8	
	Kentish Knock to Long Sand Hd			Long Sand Hd to S. Threshold			S. Threshold to Cork Sand B'cn			Cork Sand B'cn to Harwich	
Time	Duration	Time at End of Sector	Time	Duration	Time at End of Sector	Time	Duration	Time at End of Sector	Time	Duration	Time at End of Sector
- 6.00	93	- 4:27	- 6.00	63	- 4:57	- 6.00	65	- 4:55	- 6.00	76	- 4:44
- 5.45	94	- 4:11	- 5.45	63	- 4:42	- 5.45	65	- 4:40	- 5.45	76	- 4:29
- 5.30	94	- 3:56	- 5.30	64	- 4:26	- 5.30	66	- 4:24	- 5.30	77	- 4:13
- 5.15	95	- 3:40	- 5.15	64	- 4:11	- 5.15	66	- 4:09	- 5.15	77	- 3:58
- 5.00	96	- 3:24	- 5.00	65	- 3:55	- 5.00	66	- 3:54	- 5.00	77	- 3:43
- 4.45	93	- 3:12	- 4.45	64	- 3:41	- 4.45	66	- 3:39	- 4.45	77	- 3:28
- 4.30	90	- 3:00	- 4.30	64	- 3:26	- 4.30	65	- 3:25	- 4.30	77	- 3:13
- 4.15	88	- 2:47	- 4.15	64	- 3:11	- 4.15	65	- 3:10	- 4.15	76	- 2:59
- 4.00	85	- 2:35	- 4.00	64	- 2:56	- 4.00	64	- 2:56	- 4.00	76	- 2:44
- 3.45	82	- 2:23	- 3.45	63	- 2:42	- 3.45	63	- 2:42	- 3.45	74	- 2:31
- 3.30	79	- 2:11	- 3.30	62	- 2:28	- 3.30	61	- 2:29	- 3.30	72	- 2:18
- 3.15	76	- 1:59	- 3.15	61	- 2:14	- 3.15	60	- 2:15	- 3.15	70	- 2:05
- 3.00	73	- 1:47	- 3.00	60	- 2:00	- 3.00	58	- 2:02	- 3.00	68	- 1:52
- 2.45	71	- 1:34	- 2.45	60	- 1:45	- 2.45	57	- 1:48	- 2.45	66	- 1:39
- 2.30	68	- 1:22	- 2.30	59	- 1:31	- 2.30	56	- 1:34	- 2.30	64	- 1:26
- 2.15	65	- 1:10	- 2.15	58	- 1:17	- 2.15	55	- 1:20	- 2.15	62	- 1:13
- 2.00	62	- 0:58	- 2.00	58	- 1:02	- 2.00	54	- 1:06	- 2.00	60	- 1:00
- 1.45	60	- 0:45	- 1.45	57	- 0:48	- 1.45	53	- 0:52	- 1.45	59	- 0:46
- 1.30	58	- 0:32	- 1.30	56	- 0:34	- 1.30	52	- 0:38	- 1.30	57	- 0:33
- 1.15	56	- 0:19	- 1.15	55	- 0:20	- 1.15	50	- 0:25	- 1.15	56	- 0:19
- 1.00	53	- 0:07	- 1.00	54	- 0:06	- 1.00	49	- 0:11	- 1.00	55	- 0:05
- 0.45	52	+ 0:07	- 0.45	52	+ 0:07	- 0.45	48	+ 0:03	- 0.45	55	+ 0:10
- 0.30	51	+ 0:21	- 0.30	50	+ 0:20	- 0.30	47	+ 0:17	- 0.30	55	+ 0:25
- 0.15	50	+ 0:35	- 0.15	49	+ 0:34	- 0.15	45	+ 0:30	- 0.15	55	+ 0:40
HW	49	+ 0:49	HW	47	+ 0:47	HW	44	+ 0:44	HW	56	+ 0:56
+ 0.15	49	+ 1:04	+ 0.15	46	+ 1:01	+ 0.15	44	+ 0:59	+ 0.15	55	+ 1:10
+ 0.30	50	+ 1:20	+ 0.30	45	+ 1:15	+ 0.30	44	+ 1:14	+ 0.30	54	+ 1:24
+ 0.45	50	+ 1:35	+ 0.45	43	+ 1:28	+ 0.45	44	+ 1:29	+ 0.45	53	+ 1:38
+ 1.00	51	+ 1:51	+ 1.00	42	+ 1:42	+ 1.00	44	+ 1:44	+ 1.00	52	+ 1:52
+ 1.15	52	+ 2:07	+ 1.15	42	+ 1:57	+ 1.15	44	+ 1:59	+ 1.15	53	+ 2:08
+ 1.30	53	+ 2:23	+ 1.30	42	+ 2:12	+ 1.30	44	+ 2:14	+ 1.30	53	+ 2:23
+ 1.45	55	+ 2:40	+ 1.45	42	+ 2:27	+ 1.45	45	+ 2:30	+ 1.45	54	+ 2:39
+ 2.00	56	+ 2:56	+ 2.00	42	+ 2:42	+ 2.00	45	+ 2:45	+ 2.00	54	+ 2:54
+ 2.15	57	+ 3:12	+ 2.15	43	+ 2:58	+ 2.15	46	+ 3:01	+ 2.15	54	+ 3:09
+ 2.30	58	+ 3:28	+ 2.30	44	+ 3:14	+ 2.30	47	+ 3:17	+ 2.30	55	+ 3:25
+ 2.45	60	+ 3:45	+ 2.45	45	+ 3:30	+ 2.45	48	+ 3:33	+ 2.45	55	+ 3:40
+ 3.00	61	+ 4:01	+ 3.00	46	+ 3:46	+ 3.00	49	+ 3:49	+ 3.00	56	+ 3:56
+ 3.15	62	+ 4:17	+ 3.15	47	+ 4:02	+ 3.15	50	+ 4:05	+ 3.15	57	+ 4:12
+ 3.30	64	+ 4:34	+ 3.30	49	+ 4:19	+ 3.30	51	+ 4:21	+ 3.30	58	+ 4:28
+ 3.45	65	+ 4:50	+ 3.45	50	+ 4:35	+ 3.45	52	+ 4:37	+ 3.45	59	+ 4:44
+ 4.00	66	+ 5:06	+ 4.00	52	+ 4:52	+ 4.00	53	+ 4:53	+ 4.00	59	+ 4:59
+ 4.15	68	+ 5:23	+ 4.15	53	+ 5:08	+ 4.15	54	+ 5:09	+ 4.15	60	+ 5:15
+ 4.30	70	+ 5:40	+ 4.30	55	+ 5:25	+ 4.30	55	+ 5:25	+ 4.30	61	+ 5:31
+ 4.45	71	+ 5:56	+ 4.45	56	+ 5:41	+ 4.45	56	+ 5:41	+ 4.45	62	+ 5:47
+ 5.00	73	- 5:47	+ 5.00	57	+ 5:57	+ 5.00	57	+ 5:57	+ 5.00	62	- 5:58
+ 5.15	75	- 5:30	+ 5.15	58	- 5:47	+ 5.15	58	- 5:47	+ 5.15	64	- 5:41
+ 5.30	76	- 5:14	+ 5.30	59	- 5:31	+ 5.30	59	- 5:31	+ 5.30	65	- 5:25
+ 5.45	78	- 4:57	+ 5.45	60	- 5:15	+ 5.45	60	- 5:15	+ 5.45	66	- 5:09
+ 6.00	80	- 4:40	+ 6.00	61	- 4:59	+ 6.00	61	- 4:59	+ 6.00	68	- 4:52

NORTH BOUND

Table K - Ramsgate to Harwich - Outside Route

Neaps — All times relate to HW Sheerness — **Time to cover Sectors (in minutes) at 7.0 Kts**

NORTH BOUND

	K1 Ramsgate to North Foreland			K2 North Foreland to Thanet			K3 Thanet to South Knock			K4 South Knock to Kentish Knock			K5 Kentish Knock to Long Sand Hd			K6 Long Sand Hd to S. Threshold			K7 S. Threshold to Cork Sand B'cn			K8 Cork Sand B'cn to Harwich
Time	Duration	Time at End of Sector	Time	Duration	Time at End of Sector	Time	Duration	Time at End of Sector	Time	Duration	Time at End of Sector	Time	Duration	Time at End of Sector	Time	Duration	Time at End of Sector	Time	Duration	Time at End of Sector	Time	Duration	Time at End of Sector
- 6.00	**46**	**- 5:14**	**- 6.00**	**64**	**- 4:56**	**- 6.00**	**59**	**- 5:01**	**- 6.00**	**55**	**- 5:05**	**- 6.00**	**65**	**- 4:55**	**- 6.00**	**52**	**- 5:08**	**- 6.00**	**52**	**- 5:08**	**- 6.00**	**58**	**- 5:02**
- 5.45	46	- 4:59	- 5.45	64	- 4:41	- 5.45	60	- 4:45	- 5.45	56	- 4:49	- 5.45	66	- 4:39	- 5.45	52	- 4:53	- 5.45	52	- 4:53	- 5.45	58	- 4:47
- 5.30	47	- 4:43	- 5.30	65	- 4:25	- 5.30	60	- 4:30	- 5.30	56	- 4:34	- 5.30	66	- 4:24	- 5.30	52	- 4:38	- 5.30	52	- 4:38	- 5.30	58	- 4:32
- 5.15	47	- 4:28	- 5.15	65	- 4:10	- 5.15	61	- 4:14	- 5.15	57	- 4:18	- 5.15	67	- 4:08	- 5.15	53	- 4:22	- 5.15	52	- 4:23	- 5.15	58	- 4:17
- 5.00	**46**	**- 4:14**	**- 5.00**	**65**	**- 3:55**	**- 5.00**	**61**	**- 3:59**	**- 5.00**	**58**	**- 4:02**	**- 5.00**	**67**	**- 3:53**	**- 5.00**	**53**	**- 4:07**	**- 5.00**	**52**	**- 4:08**	**- 5.00**	**58**	**- 4:02**
- 4.45	46	- 3:59	- 4.45	65	- 3:40	- 4.45	61	- 3:44	- 4.45	57	- 3:48	- 4.45	67	- 3:38	- 4.45	53	- 3:52	- 4.45	52	- 3:53	- 4.45	58	- 3:47
- 4.30	46	- 3:44	- 4.30	65	- 3:25	- 4.30	61	- 3:29	- 4.30	57	- 3:33	- 4.30	66	- 3:24	- 4.30	52	- 3:38	- 4.30	52	- 3:38	- 4.30	58	- 3:32
- 4.15	45	- 3:30	- 4.15	64	- 3:11	- 4.15	61	- 3:14	- 4.15	57	- 3:18	- 4.15	65	- 3:10	- 4.15	52	- 3:23	- 4.15	52	- 3:23	- 4.15	58	- 3:17
- 4.00	**45**	**- 3:15**	**- 4.00**	**63**	**- 2:57**	**- 4.00**	**60**	**- 3:00**	**- 4.00**	**57**	**- 3:03**	**- 4.00**	**65**	**- 2:55**	**- 4.00**	**52**	**- 3:08**	**- 4.00**	**52**	**- 3:08**	**- 4.00**	**58**	**- 3:02**
- 3.45	44	- 3:01	- 3.45	62	- 2:43	- 3.45	60	- 2:45	- 3.45	56	- 2:49	- 3.45	64	- 2:41	- 3.45	52	- 2:53	- 3.45	51	- 2:54	- 3.45	57	- 2:48
- 3.30	43	- 2:47	- 3.30	61	- 2:29	- 3.30	60	- 2:30	- 3.30	55	- 2:35	- 3.30	63	- 2:27	- 3.30	51	- 2:39	- 3.30	50	- 2:40	- 3.30	56	- 2:34
- 3.15	41	- 2:34	- 3.15	60	- 2:15	- 3.15	59	- 2:16	- 3.15	54	- 2:21	- 3.15	61	- 2:14	- 3.15	51	- 2:24	- 3.15	50	- 2:25	- 3.15	56	- 2:19
- 3.00	**40**	**- 2:20**	**- 3.00**	**59**	**- 2:01**	**- 3.00**	**58**	**- 2:02**	**- 3.00**	**53**	**- 2:07**	**- 3.00**	**60**	**- 2:00**	**- 3.00**	**51**	**- 2:09**	**- 3.00**	**49**	**- 2:11**	**- 3.00**	**55**	**- 2:05**
- 2.45	38	- 2:07	- 2.45	58	- 1:47	- 2.45	58	- 1:47	- 2.45	52	- 1:53	- 2.45	59	- 1:46	- 2.45	51	- 1:54	- 2.45	49	- 1:56	- 2.45	54	- 1:51
- 2.30	37	- 1:53	- 2.30	57	- 1:33	- 2.30	57	- 1:33	- 2.30	51	- 1:39	- 2.30	57	- 1:33	- 2.30	50	- 1:40	- 2.30	48	- 1:42	- 2.30	53	- 1:37
- 2.15	36	- 1:39	- 2.15	56	- 1:19	- 2.15	56	- 1:19	- 2.15	50	- 1:25	- 2.15	56	- 1:19	- 2.15	50	- 1:25	- 2.15	47	- 1:28	- 2.15	53	- 1:22
- 2.00	**36**	**- 1:24**	**- 2.00**	**55**	**- 1:05**	**- 2.00**	**56**	**- 1:04**	**- 2.00**	**49**	**- 1:11**	**- 2.00**	**55**	**- 1:05**	**- 2.00**	**50**	**- 1:10**	**- 2.00**	**47**	**- 1:13**	**- 2.00**	**52**	**- 1:08**
- 1.45	35	- 1:10	- 1.45	55	- 0:50	- 1.45	55	- 0:50	- 1.45	48	- 0:57	- 1.45	53	- 0:52	- 1.45	49	- 0:56	- 1.45	46	- 0:59	- 1.45	51	- 0:54
- 1.30	34	- 0:56	- 1.30	54	- 0:36	- 1.30	54	- 0:36	- 1.30	47	- 0:43	- 1.30	52	- 0:38	- 1.30	49	- 0:41	- 1.30	46	- 0:44	- 1.30	50	- 0:40
- 1.15	34	- 0:41	- 1.15	53	- 0:22	- 1.15	53	- 0:22	- 1.15	46	- 0:29	- 1.15	51	- 0:24	- 1.15	48	- 0:27	- 1.15	45	- 0:30	- 1.15	50	- 0:25
- 1.00	**34**	**- 0:26**	**- 1.00**	**53**	**- 0:07**	**- 1.00**	**53**	**- 0:07**	**- 1.00**	**45**	**- 0:15**	**- 1.00**	**50**	**- 0:10**	**- 1.00**	**48**	**- 0:12**	**- 1.00**	**45**	**- 0:15**	**- 1.00**	**49**	**- 0:11**
- 0.45	34	- 0:11	- 0.45	52	+ 0:07	- 0.45	52	+ 0:07	- 0.45	44	- 0:01	- 0.45	49	+ 0:04	- 0.45	47	+ 0:02	- 0.45	44	- 0:01	- 0.45	49	+ 0:04
- 0.30	34	+ 0:04	- 0.30	52	+ 0:22	- 0.30	51	+ 0:21	- 0.30	43	+ 0:13	- 0.30	49	+ 0:19	- 0.30	46	+ 0:16	- 0.30	43	+ 0:13	- 0.30	49	+ 0:19
- 0.15	34	+ 0:19	- 0.15	52	+ 0:37	- 0.15	51	+ 0:36	- 0.15	43	+ 0:28	- 0.15	48	+ 0:33	- 0.15	45	+ 0:30	- 0.15	43	+ 0:28	- 0.15	49	+ 0:34
HW	**35**	**+ 0:35**	**HW**	**52**	**+ 0:52**	**HW**	**50**	**+ 0:50**	**HW**	**42**	**+ 0:42**	**HW**	**47**	**+ 0:47**	**HW**	**44**	**+ 0:44**	**HW**	**42**	**+ 0:42**	**HW**	**49**	**+ 0:49**
+ 0.15	35	+ 0:50	+ 0.15	52	+ 1:07	+ 0.15	50	+ 1:05	+ 0.15	42	+ 0:57	+ 0.15	47	+ 1:02	+ 0.15	44	+ 0:59	+ 0.15	42	+ 0:57	+ 0.15	49	+ 1:04
+ 0.30	35	+ 1:05	+ 0.30	52	+ 1:22	+ 0.30	50	+ 1:20	+ 0.30	42	+ 1:12	+ 0.30	47	+ 1:17	+ 0.30	43	+ 1:13	+ 0.30	42	+ 1:12	+ 0.30	48	+ 1:18
+ 0.45	36	+ 1:21	+ 0.45	52	+ 1:37	+ 0.45	50	+ 1:35	+ 0.45	41	+ 1:26	+ 0.45	48	+ 1:33	+ 0.45	42	+ 1:27	+ 0.45	41	+ 1:26	+ 0.45	48	+ 1:33
+ 1.00	**36**	**+ 1:36**	**+ 1.00**	**52**	**+ 1:52**	**+ 1.00**	**50**	**+ 1:50**	**+ 1.00**	**41**	**+ 1:41**	**+ 1.00**	**48**	**+ 1:48**	**+ 1.00**	**42**	**+ 1:42**	**+ 1.00**	**41**	**+ 1:41**	**+ 1.00**	**48**	**+ 1:48**
+ 1.15	37	+ 1:52	+ 1.15	52	+ 2:07	+ 1.15	50	+ 2:05	+ 1.15	41	+ 1:56	+ 1.15	49	+ 2:04	+ 1.15	42	+ 1:57	+ 1.15	42	+ 1:57	+ 1.15	48	+ 2:03
+ 1.30	38	+ 2:08	+ 1.30	53	+ 2:23	+ 1.30	50	+ 2:20	+ 1.30	41	+ 2:11	+ 1.30	49	+ 2:19	+ 1.30	41	+ 2:11	+ 1.30	42	+ 2:12	+ 1.30	48	+ 2:18
+ 1.45	38	+ 2:23	+ 1.45	53	+ 2:38	+ 1.45	51	+ 2:36	+ 1.45	41	+ 2:26	+ 1.45	50	+ 2:35	+ 1.45	41	+ 2:26	+ 1.45	42	+ 2:27	+ 1.45	48	+ 2:33
+ 2.00	**39**	**+ 2:39**	**+ 2.00**	**53**	**+ 2:53**	**+ 2.00**	**51**	**+ 2:51**	**+ 2.00**	**42**	**+ 2:42**	**+ 2.00**	**51**	**+ 2:51**	**+ 2.00**	**41**	**+ 2:41**	**+ 2.00**	**42**	**+ 2:42**	**+ 2.00**	**48**	**+ 2:48**
+ 2.15	40	+ 2:55	+ 2.15	54	+ 3:09	+ 2.15	52	+ 3:07	+ 2.15	42	+ 2:57	+ 2.15	51	+ 3:06	+ 2.15	42	+ 2:57	+ 2.15	43	+ 2:58	+ 2.15	48	+ 3:03
+ 2.30	40	+ 3:10	+ 2.30	54	+ 3:24	+ 2.30	52	+ 3:22	+ 2.30	42	+ 3:12	+ 2.30	52	+ 3:22	+ 2.30	42	+ 3:12	+ 2.30	43	+ 3:13	+ 2.30	49	+ 3:19
+ 2.45	41	+ 3:26	+ 2.45	55	+ 3:40	+ 2.45	53	+ 3:38	+ 2.45	42	+ 3:27	+ 2.45	53	+ 3:38	+ 2.45	43	+ 3:28	+ 2.45	44	+ 3:29	+ 2.45	49	+ 3:34
+ 3.00	**41**	**+ 3:41**	**+ 3.00**	**55**	**+ 3:55**	**+ 3.00**	**53**	**+ 3:53**	**+ 3.00**	**43**	**+ 3:43**	**+ 3.00**	**53**	**+ 3:53**	**+ 3.00**	**43**	**+ 3:43**	**+ 3.00**	**44**	**+ 3:44**	**+ 3.00**	**49**	**+ 3:49**
+ 3.15	42	+ 3:57	+ 3.15	56	+ 4:11	+ 3.15	54	+ 4:09	+ 3.15	43	+ 3:58	+ 3.15	54	+ 4:09	+ 3.15	44	+ 3:59	+ 3.15	45	+ 4:00	+ 3.15	50	+ 4:05
+ 3.30	43	+ 4:13	+ 3.30	56	+ 4:26	+ 3.30	54	+ 4:24	+ 3.30	44	+ 4:14	+ 3.30	55	+ 4:25	+ 3.30	45	+ 4:15	+ 3.30	45	+ 4:15	+ 3.30	50	+ 4:20
+ 3.45	43	+ 4:28	+ 3.45	56	+ 4:41	+ 3.45	55	+ 4:40	+ 3.45	45	+ 4:30	+ 3.45	55	+ 4:40	+ 3.45	46	+ 4:31	+ 3.45	46	+ 4:31	+ 3.45	50	+ 4:35
+ 4.00	**43**	**+ 4:43**	**+ 4.00**	**57**	**+ 4:57**	**+ 4.00**	**55**	**+ 4:55**	**+ 4.00**	**45**	**+ 4:45**	**+ 4.00**	**56**	**+ 4:56**	**+ 4.00**	**46**	**+ 4:46**	**+ 4.00**	**47**	**+ 4:47**	**+ 4.00**	**51**	**+ 4:51**
+ 4.15	44	+ 4:59	+ 4.15	57	+ 5:12	+ 4.15	55	+ 5:10	+ 4.15	46	+ 5:01	+ 4.15	57	+ 5:12	+ 4.15	47	+ 5:02	+ 4.15	47	+ 5:02	+ 4.15	51	+ 5:06
+ 4.30	44	+ 5:14	+ 4.30	58	+ 5:28	+ 4.30	56	+ 5:26	+ 4.30	47	+ 5:17	+ 4.30	58	+ 5:28	+ 4.30	48	+ 5:18	+ 4.30	48	+ 5:18	+ 4.30	52	+ 5:22
+ 4.45	44	+ 5:29	+ 4.45	58	+ 5:43	+ 4.45	56	+ 5:41	+ 4.45	48	+ 5:33	+ 4.45	59	+ 5:44	+ 4.45	49	+ 5:34	+ 4.45	48	+ 5:33	+ 4.45	52	+ 5:37
+ 5.00	**44**	**+ 5:44**	**+ 5.00**	**59**	**+ 5:59**	**+ 5.00**	**56**	**+ 5:56**	**+ 5.00**	**49**	**+ 5:49**	**+ 5.00**	**59**	**+ 5:59**	**+ 5.00**	**49**	**+ 5:49**	**+ 5.00**	**48**	**+ 5:48**	**+ 5.00**	**52**	**+ 5:52**
+ 5.15	44	+ 5:59	+ 5.15	59	- 5:46	+ 5.15	57	- 5:48	+ 5.15	50	+ 6:05	+ 5.15	60	- 5:45	+ 5.15	50	- 5:55	+ 5.15	49	- 5:56	+ 5.15	53	- 5:52
+ 5.30	45	- 5:45	+ 5.30	59	- 5:31	+ 5.30	57	- 5:33	+ 5.30	51	- 5:39	+ 5.30	61	- 5:29	+ 5.30	50	- 5:40	+ 5.30	49	- 5:41	+ 5.30	54	- 5:36
+ 5.45	45	- 5:30	+ 5.45	62	- 5:13	+ 5.45	58	- 5:17	+ 5.45	52	- 5:23	+ 5.45	62	- 5:13	+ 5.45	51	- 5:24	+ 5.45	50	- 5:25	+ 5.45	54	- 5:21
+ 6.00	**45**	**- 5:15**	**+ 6.00**	**63**	**- 4:57**	**+ 6.00**	**59**	**- 5:01**	**+ 6.00**	**53**	**- 5:07**	**+ 6.00**	**63**	**- 4:57**	**+ 6.00**	**51**	**- 5:09**	**+ 6.00**	**50**	**- 5:10**	**+ 6.00**	**55**	**- 5:05**

Table K - Ramsgate to Harwich - Outside Route

Time to cover Sectors (in minutes) at 7.0 kts — All times relate to HW Sheerness — **Springs**

	K1 Ramsgate to North Foreland			K2 North Foreland to Thanet			K3 Thanet to South Knock			K4 South Knock to Kentish Knock			K5 Kentish Knock to Long Sand Hd			K6 Long Sand Hd to S. Threshold			K7 S. Threshold to Cork Sand B'cn			K8 Cork Sand B'cn to Harwich	
Time	Duration	Time at End of Sector	Time	Duration	Time at End of Sector	Time	Duration	Time at End of Sector	Time	Duration	Time at End of Sector	Time	Duration	Time at End of Sector	Time	Duration	Time at End of Sector	Time	Duration	Time at End of Sector	Time	Duration	Time at End of Sector
- 6.00	51	- 5:09	- 6.00	69	- 4:51	- 6.00	63	- 4:57	- 6.00	59	- 5:01	- 6.00	71	- 4:49	- 6.00	53	- 5:07	- 6.00	54	- 5:06	- 6.00	63	- 4:57
- 5.45	51	- 4:54	- 5.45	71	- 4:34	- 5.45	64	- 4:41	- 5.45	60	- 4:45	- 5.45	72	- 4:33	- 5.45	54	- 4:51	- 5.45	54	- 4:51	- 5.45	63	- 4:42
- 5.30	52	- 4:38	- 5.30	72	- 4:18	- 5.30	65	- 4:25	- 5.30	61	- 4:29	- 5.30	72	- 4:18	- 5.30	54	- 4:36	- 5.30	55	- 4:35	- 5.30	64	- 4:26
- 5.15	52	- 4:23	- 5.15	72	- 4:03	- 5.15	66	- 4:09	- 5.15	62	- 4:13	- 5.15	73	- 4:02	- 5.15	54	- 4:21	- 5.15	55	- 4:20	- 5.15	64	- 4:11
- 5.00	52	- 4:08	- 5.00	72	- 3:48	- 5.00	66	- 3:54	- 5.00	63	- 3:57	- 5.00	74	- 3:46	- 5.00	55	- 4:05	- 5.00	55	- 4:05	- 5.00	64	- 3:56
- 4.45	52	- 3:53	- 4.45	72	- 3:33	- 4.45	67	- 3:38	- 4.45	62	- 3:43	- 4.45	73	- 3:32	- 4.45	55	- 3:50	- 4.45	55	- 3:50	- 4.45	64	- 3:41
- 4.30	52	- 3:38	- 4.30	73	- 3:17	- 4.30	67	- 3:23	- 4.30	62	- 3:28	- 4.30	72	- 3:18	- 4.30	54	- 3:36	- 4.30	55	- 3:35	- 4.30	63	- 3:27
- 4.15	50	- 3:25	- 4.15	70	- 3:05	- 4.15	66	- 3:09	- 4.15	62	- 3:13	- 4.15	71	- 3:04	- 4.15	54	- 3:21	- 4.15	54	- 3:21	- 4.15	63	- 3:12
- 4.00	48	- 3:12	- 4.00	68	- 2:52	- 4.00	65	- 2:55	- 4.00	61	- 2:59	- 4.00	70	- 2:50	- 4.00	54	- 3:06	- 4.00	54	- 3:06	- 4.00	63	- 2:57
- 3.45	46	- 2:59	- 3.45	66	- 2:39	- 3.45	64	- 2:41	- 3.45	60	- 2:45	- 3.45	68	- 2:37	- 3.45	53	- 2:52	- 3.45	53	- 2:52	- 3.45	62	- 2:43
- 3.30	44	- 2:46	- 3.30	64	- 2:26	- 3.30	63	- 2:27	- 3.30	59	- 2:31	- 3.30	66	- 2:24	- 3.30	53	- 2:37	- 3.30	52	- 2:38	- 3.30	60	- 2:30
- 3.15	42	- 2:33	- 3.15	62	- 2:13	- 3.15	62	- 2:13	- 3.15	57	- 2:18	- 3.15	64	- 2:11	- 3.15	52	- 2:23	- 3.15	51	- 2:24	- 3.15	59	- 2:16
- 3.00	40	- 2:20	- 3.00	60	- 2:00	- 3.00	61	- 1:59	- 3.00	56	- 2:04	- 3.00	62	- 1:58	- 3.00	52	- 2:08	- 3.00	50	- 2:10	- 3.00	58	- 2:02
- 2.45	37	- 2:08	- 2.45	58	- 1:47	- 2.45	59	- 1:46	- 2.45	54	- 1:51	- 2.45	60	- 1:45	- 2.45	51	- 1:54	- 2.45	49	- 1:56	- 2.45	56	- 1:49
- 2.30	35	- 1:55	- 2.30	56	- 1:34	- 2.30	58	- 1:32	- 2.30	53	- 1:37	- 2.30	58	- 1:32	- 2.30	51	- 1:39	- 2.30	48	- 1:42	- 2.30	55	- 1:35
- 2.15	34	- 1:41	- 2.15	55	- 1:20	- 2.15	56	- 1:19	- 2.15	51	- 1:24	- 2.15	56	- 1:19	- 2.15	50	- 1:25	- 2.15	47	- 1:28	- 2.15	53	- 1:22
- 2.00	33	- 1:27	- 2.00	54	- 1:06	- 2.00	55	- 1:05	- 2.00	49	- 1:11	- 2.00	54	- 1:06	- 2.00	49	- 1:11	- 2.00	47	- 1:13	- 2.00	52	- 1:08
- 1.45	32	- 1:13	- 1.45	53	- 0:52	- 1.45	53	- 0:52	- 1.45	48	- 0:57	- 1.45	53	- 0:52	- 1.45	49	- 0:56	- 1.45	46	- 0:59	- 1.45	51	- 0:54
- 1.30	30	- 1:00	- 1.30	51	- 0:39	- 1.30	52	- 0:38	- 1.30	46	- 0:44	- 1.30	51	- 0:39	- 1.30	48	- 0:42	- 1.30	45	- 0:45	- 1.30	50	- 0:40
- 1.15	31	- 0:44	- 1.15	51	- 0:24	- 1.15	50	- 0:25	- 1.15	45	- 0:30	- 1.15	49	- 0:26	- 1.15	47	- 0:28	- 1.15	44	- 0:31	- 1.15	49	- 0:26
- 1.00	31	- 0:29	- 1.00	50	- 0:10	- 1.00	49	- 0:11	- 1.00	43	- 0:17	- 1.00	48	- 0:12	- 1.00	47	+ 1:47	- 1.00	44	- 0:16	- 1.00	48	- 0:12
- 0.45	31	- 0:14	- 0.45	49	+ 0:04	- 0.45	48	+ 0:03	- 0.45	42	- 0:03	- 0.45	47	+ 0:02	- 0.45	45	+ 1:30	- 0.45	43	- 0:02	- 0.45	49	+ 0:04
- 0.30	31	+ 0:01	- 0.30	48	+ 0:18	- 0.30	46	+ 0:16	- 0.30	41	+ 0:11	- 0.30	46	+ 0:16	- 0.30	44	+ 1:14	- 0.30	41	+ 0:11	- 0.30	49	+ 0:19
- 0.15	31	+ 0:16	- 0.15	48	+ 0:33	- 0.15	48	+ 0:33	- 0.15	40	+ 0:25	- 0.15	45	+ 0:30	- 0.15	43	+ 0:28	- 0.15	40	+ 0:25	- 0.15	49	+ 0:34
HW	31	+ 0:31	HW	48	+ 0:48	HW	45	+ 0:45	HW	40	+ 0:40	HW	44	+ 0:44	HW	41	+ 0:41	HW	39	+ 0:39	HW	49	+ 0:49
+ 0.15	32	+ 0:47	+ 0.15	48	+ 1:03	+ 0.15	45	+ 1:00	+ 0.15	39	+ 0:54	+ 0.15	44	+ 0:59	+ 0.15	40	+ 0:55	+ 0.15	39	+ 0:54	+ 0.15	48	+ 1:03
+ 0.30	32	+ 1:02	+ 0.30	47	+ 1:17	+ 0.30	44	+ 1:14	+ 0.30	39	+ 1:09	+ 0.30	44	+ 1:14	+ 0.30	40	+ 1:10	+ 0.30	39	+ 1:09	+ 0.30	48	+ 1:18
+ 0.45	33	+ 1:18	+ 0.45	48	+ 1:33	+ 0.45	44	+ 1:29	+ 0.45	39	+ 1:24	+ 0.45	44	+ 1:29	+ 0.45	39	+ 1:24	+ 0.45	39	+ 1:24	+ 0.45	47	+ 1:32
+ 1.00	34	+ 1:34	+ 1.00	48	+ 1:48	+ 1.00	45	+ 1:45	+ 1.00	38	+ 1:38	+ 1.00	45	+ 1:45	+ 1.00	38	+ 1:38	+ 1.00	39	+ 1:39	+ 1.00	46	+ 1:46
+ 1.15	35	+ 1:50	+ 1.15	48	+ 2:03	+ 1.15	45	+ 2:00	+ 1.15	39	+ 1:54	+ 1.15	46	+ 2:01	+ 1.15	38	+ 1:53	+ 1.15	39	+ 1:54	+ 1.15	46	+ 2:01
+ 1.30	36	+ 2:06	+ 1.30	49	+ 2:19	+ 1.30	45	+ 2:15	+ 1.30	39	+ 2:09	+ 1.30	47	+ 2:17	+ 1.30	38	+ 2:08	+ 1.30	39	+ 2:09	+ 1.30	47	+ 2:17
+ 1.45	37	+ 2:22	+ 1.45	49	+ 2:34	+ 1.45	46	+ 2:31	+ 1.45	39	+ 2:24	+ 1.45	48	+ 2:33	+ 1.45	38	+ 2:23	+ 1.45	40	+ 2:25	+ 1.45	47	+ 2:32
+ 2.00	38	+ 2:38	+ 2.00	50	+ 2:50	+ 2.00	47	+ 2:47	+ 2.00	39	+ 2:39	+ 2.00	49	+ 2:49	+ 2.00	38	+ 2:38	+ 2.00	40	+ 2:40	+ 2.00	47	+ 2:47
+ 2.15	39	+ 2:54	+ 2.15	51	+ 3:06	+ 2.15	47	+ 3:02	+ 2.15	39	+ 2:54	+ 2.15	49	+ 3:04	+ 2.15	38	+ 2:53	+ 2.15	40	+ 2:55	+ 2.15	47	+ 3:02
+ 2.30	40	+ 3:10	+ 2.30	51	+ 3:21	+ 2.30	48	+ 3:18	+ 2.30	39	+ 3:09	+ 2.30	50	+ 3:20	+ 2.30	39	+ 3:09	+ 2.30	41	+ 3:11	+ 2.30	48	+ 3:18
+ 2.45	41	+ 3:26	+ 2.45	52	+ 3:37	+ 2.45	49	+ 3:34	+ 2.45	40	+ 3:25	+ 2.45	51	+ 3:36	+ 2.45	40	+ 3:25	+ 2.45	42	+ 3:27	+ 2.45	48	+ 3:33
+ 3.00	42	+ 3:42	+ 3.00	53	+ 3:53	+ 3.00	50	+ 3:50	+ 3.00	40	+ 3:40	+ 3.00	52	+ 3:52	+ 3.00	40	+ 3:40	+ 3.00	42	+ 3:42	+ 3.00	48	+ 3:48
+ 3.15	43	+ 3:58	+ 3.15	54	+ 4:09	+ 3.15	51	+ 4:06	+ 3.15	41	+ 3:56	+ 3.15	53	+ 4:08	+ 3.15	41	+ 3:56	+ 3.15	43	+ 3:58	+ 3.15	49	+ 4:04
+ 3.30	44	+ 4:14	+ 3.30	55	+ 4:25	+ 3.30	52	+ 4:22	+ 3.30	42	+ 4:12	+ 3.30	54	+ 4:24	+ 3.30	42	+ 4:12	+ 3.30	44	+ 4:14	+ 3.30	50	+ 4:20
+ 3.45	44	+ 4:29	+ 3.45	55	+ 4:40	+ 3.45	53	+ 4:38	+ 3.45	43	+ 4:28	+ 3.45	55	+ 4:40	+ 3.45	44	+ 4:29	+ 3.45	45	+ 4:30	+ 3.45	50	+ 4:35
+ 4.00	44	+ 4:44	+ 4.00	56	+ 4:56	+ 4.00	54	+ 4:54	+ 4.00	44	+ 4:44	+ 4.00	56	+ 4:56	+ 4.00	45	+ 4:45	+ 4.00	46	+ 4:46	+ 4.00	51	+ 4:51
+ 4.15	45	+ 5:00	+ 4.15	57	+ 5:12	+ 4.15	55	+ 5:10	+ 4.15	46	+ 5:01	+ 4.15	57	+ 5:12	+ 4.15	46	+ 5:01	+ 4.15	46	+ 5:01	+ 4.15	51	+ 5:06
+ 4.30	45	+ 5:15	+ 4.30	58	+ 5:28	+ 4.30	55	+ 5:25	+ 4.30	47	+ 5:17	+ 4.30	59	+ 5:29	+ 4.30	47	+ 5:17	+ 4.30	47	+ 5:17	+ 4.30	52	+ 5:22
+ 4.45	46	+ 5:31	+ 4.45	59	+ 5:44	+ 4.45	56	+ 5:41	+ 4.45	48	+ 5:33	+ 4.45	60	+ 5:45	+ 4.45	48	+ 5:33	+ 4.45	48	+ 5:33	+ 4.45	52	+ 5:37
+ 5.00	47	+ 5:47	+ 5.00	60	- 6:00	+ 5.00	56	+ 5:56	+ 5.00	50	+ 5:50	+ 5.00	61	- 5:59	+ 5.00	49	+ 5:49	+ 5.00	49	+ 5:49	+ 5.00	53	+ 5:53
+ 5.15	47	- 5:58	+ 5.15	60	- 5:45	+ 5.15	57	- 5:48	+ 5.15	51	+ 6:06	+ 5.15	63	- 5:42	+ 5.15	50	- 5:55	+ 5.15	49	- 5:56	+ 5.15	54	- 5:51
+ 5.30	47	- 5:43	+ 5.30	61	- 5:29	+ 5.30	57	- 5:33	+ 5.30	53	- 5:37	+ 5.30	64	- 5:26	+ 5.30	50	- 5:40	+ 5.30	50	- 5:40	+ 5.30	55	- 5:35
+ 5.45	49	- 5:26	+ 5.45	67	- 5:08	+ 5.45	60	- 5:15	+ 5.45	54	- 5:21	+ 5.45	65	- 5:10	+ 5.45	51	- 5:24	+ 5.45	50	- 5:25	+ 5.45	55	- 5:20
+ 6.00	50	- 5:10	+ 6.00	68	- 4:52	+ 6.00	62	- 4:58	+ 6.00	55	- 5:05	+ 6.00	66	- 4:54	+ 6.00	52	- 5:08	+ 6.00	51	- 5:09	+ 6.00	56	- 5:04

NORTH BOUND

A - 4 Kts

Table A - Blackwater to Ramsgate via SW Sunk

4 Kts - A

Neaps — All times relate to HW Sheerness — **Time to cover Sectors (in minutes) at 4.0 Kts**

SOUTH BOUND

	A8 Blackwater to Swin Spitway		A7 Spitway to East Barrow Sands		A6 East Barrow to SW Sunk		A5 SW Sunk to Inner Fisherman	
Time	Duration	Time at End of Sector	Duration	Time at End of Sector	Duration	Time at End of Sector	Duration	Time at End of Sector
- 6.00	**151**	**- 3:29**	**76**	**- 4:44**	**30**	**- 5:30**	**50**	**- 5:10**
- 5.45	153	- 3:12	78	- 4:27	30	- 5:15	50	- 4:55
- 5.30	156	- 2:54	79	- 4:11	30	- 5:00	50	- 4:40
- 5.15	158	- 2:37	80	- 3:55	30	- 4:45	50	- 4:25
- 5.00	**161**	**- 2:19**	**82**	**- 3:38**	**30**	**- 4:30**	**50**	**- 4:10**
- 4.45	161	- 2:04	84	- 3:21	30	- 4:15	51	- 3:54
- 4.30	162	- 1:48	86	- 3:04	30	- 4:00	51	- 3:39
- 4.15	163	- 1:32	88	- 2:47	31	- 3:44	52	- 3:23
- 4.00	**163**	**- 1:17**	**90**	**- 2:30**	**31**	**- 3:29**	**52**	**- 3:08**
- 3.45	162	- 1:03	88	- 2:17	31	- 3:14	53	- 2:52
- 3.30	160	- 0:50	86	- 2:04	31	- 2:59	54	- 2:36
- 3.15	158	- 0:37	83	- 1:52	31	- 2:44	54	- 2:21
- 3.00	**156**	**- 0:24**	**81**	**- 1:39**	**31**	**- 2:29**	**55**	**- 2:05**
- 2.45	152	- 0:13	80	- 1:25	31	- 2:14	55	- 1:50
- 2.30	147	- 0:03	78	- 1:12	32	- 1:58	55	- 1:35
- 2.15	143	+ 0:08	77	- 0:58	32	- 1:43	55	- 1:20
- 2.00	**138**	**+ 0:18**	**76**	**- 0:44**	**32**	**- 1:28**	**55**	**- 1:05**
- 1.45	133	+ 0:28	74	- 0:31	32	- 1:13	55	- 0:50
- 1.30	127	+ 0:37	73	- 0:17	32	- 0:58	55	- 0:35
- 1.15	122	+ 0:47	71	- 0:04	32	- 0:43	54	- 0:21
- 1.00	**116**	**+ 0:56**	**69**	**+ 0:09**	**32**	**- 0:28**	**54**	**- 0:06**
- 0.45	113	+ 1:08	68	+ 0:23	32	- 0:13	54	+ 0:09
- 0.30	109	+ 1:19	66	+ 0:36	32	+ 0:02	55	+ 0:25
- 0.15	105	+ 1:30	64	+ 0:49	32	+ 0:17	55	+ 0:40
HW	**102**	**+ 1:42**	**63**	**+ 1:03**	**32**	**+ 0:32**	**55**	**+ 0:55**
+ 0.15	101	+ 1:56	62	+ 1:17	33	+ 0:48	55	+ 1:10
+ 0.30	99	+ 2:09	61	+ 1:31	33	+ 1:03	56	+ 1:26
+ 0.45	98	+ 2:23	60	+ 1:45	33	+ 1:18	56	+ 1:41
+ 1.00	**97**	**+ 2:37**	**60**	**+ 2:00**	**34**	**+ 1:34**	**56**	**+ 1:56**
+ 1.15	97	+ 2:52	60	+ 2:15	34	+ 1:49	56	+ 2:11
+ 1.30	98	+ 3:08	60	+ 2:30	34	+ 2:04	56	+ 2:26
+ 1.45	99	+ 3:24	60	+ 2:45	34	+ 2:19	56	+ 2:41
+ 2.00	**99**	**+ 3:39**	**60**	**+ 3:00**	**35**	**+ 2:35**	**56**	**+ 2:56**
+ 2.15	101	+ 3:56	60	+ 3:15	34	+ 2:49	56	+ 3:11
+ 2.30	103	+ 4:13	61	+ 3:31	34	+ 3:04	55	+ 3:25
+ 2.45	106	+ 4:31	61	+ 3:46	34	+ 3:19	55	+ 3:40
+ 3.00	**108**	**+ 4:48**	**61**	**+ 4:01**	**34**	**+ 3:34**	**55**	**+ 3:55**
+ 3.15	110	+ 5:05	62	+ 4:17	33	+ 3:48	54	+ 4:09
+ 3.30	112	+ 5:22	63	+ 4:33	33	+ 4:03	53	+ 4:23
+ 3.45	114	+ 5:39	64	+ 4:49	32	+ 4:17	53	+ 4:38
+ 4.00	**116**	**+ 5:56**	**64**	**+ 5:04**	**32**	**+ 4:32**	**52**	**+ 4:52**
+ 4.15	119	- 5:46	65	+ 5:20	32	+ 4:47	52	+ 5:07
+ 4.30	121	- 5:29	66	+ 5:36	31	+ 5:01	52	+ 5:22
+ 4.45	124	- 5:11	67	+ 5:52	31	+ 5:16	51	+ 5:36
+ 5.00	**126**	**- 4:54**	**68**	**- 5:52**	**31**	**+ 5:31**	**51**	**+ 5:51**
+ 5.15	129	- 4:36	69	- 5:36	31	+ 5:46	51	- 5:54
+ 5.30	132	- 4:18	69	- 5:21	31	- 5:59	51	- 5:39
+ 5.45	135	- 4:00	70	- 5:05	31	- 5:44	51	- 5:24
+ 6.00	**138**	**- 3:42**	**71**	**- 4:49**	**31**	**- 5:29**	**50**	**- 5:10**

	A4 Inner to Outer Fisherman		A3 Outer Fisherman to East Margate		A2 East Margate to North Foreland		A1 North Foreland to Ramsgate	
Time	Duration	Time at End of Sector	Duration	Time at End of Sector	Duration	Time at End of Sector	Duration	Time at End of Sector
- 6.00	**57**	**- 5:03**	**94**	**- 4:26**	**39**	**- 5:21**	**56**	**- 5:04**
- 5.45	59	- 4:46	96	- 4:09	39	- 5:06	55	- 4:50
- 5.30	60	- 4:30	97	- 3:53	39	- 4:51	55	- 4:35
- 5.15	61	- 4:14	98	- 3:37	39	- 4:36	55	- 4:20
- 5.00	**63**	**- 3:57**	**100**	**- 3:20**	**40**	**- 4:20**	**56**	**- 4:04**
- 4.45	64	- 3:41	102	- 3:03	40	- 4:05	56	- 3:49
- 4.30	65	- 3:25	104	- 2:46	41	- 3:49	57	- 3:33
- 4.15	66	- 3:09	107	- 2:28	42	- 3:33	60	- 3:15
- 4.00	**67**	**- 2:53**	**109**	**- 2:11**	**43**	**- 3:17**	**63**	**- 2:57**
- 3.45	69	- 2:36	110	- 1:55	44	- 3:01	66	- 2:39
- 3.30	70	- 2:20	112	- 1:38	46	- 2:44	69	- 2:21
- 3.15	72	- 2:03	113	- 1:22	48	- 2:27	74	- 2:01
- 3.00	**74**	**- 1:46**	**114**	**- 1:06**	**50**	**- 2:10**	**80**	**- 1:40**
- 2.45	75	- 1:30	114	- 0:51	52	- 1:53	86	- 1:19
- 2.30	75	- 1:15	113	- 0:37	54	- 1:36	91	- 0:59
- 2.15	76	- 0:59	112	- 0:23	56	- 1:19	95	- 0:40
- 2.00	**77**	**- 0:43**	**112**	**- 0:08**	**58**	**- 1:02**	**98**	**- 0:22**
- 1.45	75	- 0:30	110	+ 0:05	58	- 0:47	102	- 0:03
- 1.30	73	- 0:17	108	+ 0:18	58	- 0:32	105	+ 0:15
- 1.15	71	- 0:04	106	+ 0:31	59	- 0:16	105	+ 0:30
- 1.00	**69**	**+ 0:09**	**104**	**+ 0:44**	**59**	**- 0:01**	**104**	**+ 0:44**
- 0.45	67	+ 0:22	103	+ 0:58	58	+ 0:13	104	+ 0:59
- 0.30	64	+ 0:34	101	+ 1:11	58	+ 0:28	104	+ 1:14
- 0.15	61	+ 0:46	100	+ 1:25	57	+ 0:42	101	+ 1:26
HW	**59**	**+ 0:59**	**98**	**+ 1:38**	**56**	**+ 0:56**	**99**	**+ 1:39**
+ 0.15	57	+ 1:12	97	+ 1:52	55	+ 1:10	96	+ 1:51
+ 0.30	55	+ 1:25	96	+ 2:06	54	+ 1:24	94	+ 2:04
+ 0.45	53	+ 1:38	95	+ 2:20	52	+ 1:37	90	+ 2:15
+ 1.00	**51**	**+ 1:51**	**94**	**+ 2:34**	**51**	**+ 1:51**	**85**	**+ 2:25**
+ 1.15	51	+ 2:06	94	+ 2:49	50	+ 2:05	81	+ 2:36
+ 1.30	50	+ 2:20	93	+ 3:03	49	+ 2:19	77	+ 2:47
+ 1.45	49	+ 2:34	93	+ 3:18	47	+ 2:32	74	+ 2:59
+ 2.00	**49**	**+ 2:49**	**92**	**+ 3:32**	**46**	**+ 2:46**	**72**	**+ 3:12**
+ 2.15	48	+ 3:03	92	+ 3:47	45	+ 3:00	70	+ 3:25
+ 2.30	48	+ 3:18	92	+ 4:02	44	+ 3:14	68	+ 3:38
+ 2.45	48	+ 3:33	92	+ 4:17	43	+ 3:28	67	+ 3:52
+ 3.00	**47**	**+ 3:47**	**91**	**+ 4:31**	**42**	**+ 3:42**	**66**	**+ 4:06**
+ 3.15	47	+ 4:02	91	+ 4:46	42	+ 3:57	64	+ 4:19
+ 3.30	47	+ 4:17	91	+ 5:01	41	+ 4:11	63	+ 4:33
+ 3.45	47	+ 4:32	91	+ 5:16	41	+ 4:26	62	+ 4:47
+ 4.00	**47**	**+ 4:47**	**90**	**+ 5:30**	**41**	**+ 4:41**	**61**	**+ 5:01**
+ 4.15	47	+ 5:02	91	+ 5:46	40	+ 4:55	61	+ 5:16
+ 4.30	48	+ 5:18	91	- 5:59	40	+ 5:10	60	+ 5:30
+ 4.45	49	+ 5:34	92	- 5:43	40	+ 5:25	60	+ 5:45
+ 5.00	**49**	**+ 5:49**	**92**	**- 5:28**	**39**	**+ 5:39**	**60**	**- 6:00**
+ 5.15	50	- 5:55	93	- 5:12	39	+ 5:54	60	- 5:45
+ 5.30	51	- 5:39	93	- 4:57	39	- 5:51	59	- 5:31
+ 5.45	52	- 5:23	93	- 4:42	39	- 5:36	57	- 5:18
+ 6.00	**53**	**- 5:07**	**93**	**- 4:27**	**39**	**- 5:21**	**57**	**- 5:03**

Table A - Blackwater to Ramsgate via SW Sunk

Time to cover Sectors (in minutes) at 4.0 kts — All times relate to HW Sheerness — **Springs**

	A8 Blackwater to Swin Spitway			A7 Spitway to East Barrow Sands			A6 East Barrow to SW Sunk			A5 SW Sunk to Inner Fisherman			A4 Inner to Outer Fisherman			A3 Outer Fisherman to East Margate			A2 East Margate to North Foreland			A1 North Foreland to Ramsgate	
Time	Duration	Time at End of Sector	Time	Duration	Time at End of Sector	Time	Duration	Time at End of Sector	Time	Duration	Time at End of Sector	Time	Duration	Time at End of Sector	Time	Duration	Time at End of Sector	Time	Duration	Time at End of Sector	Time	Duration	Time at End of Sector
- 6.00	**165**	**- 3:15**	**- 6.00**	**81**	**- 4:39**	**- 6.00**	**30**	**- 5:30**	**- 6.00**	**49**	**- 5:11**	**- 6.00**	**57**	**- 5:03**	**- 6.00**	**95**	**- 4:25**	**- 6.00**	**35**	**- 5:25**	**- 6.00**	**47**	**- 5:13**
- 5.45	169	- 2:56	- 5.45	86	- 4:19	- 5.45	30	- 5:15	- 5.45	50	- 4:55	- 5.45	59	- 4:46	- 5.45	97	- 4:08	- 5.45	35	- 5:10	- 5.45	47	- 4:58
- 5.30	172	- 2:38	- 5.30	90	- 4:00	- 5.30	30	- 5:00	- 5.30	50	- 4:40	- 5.30	61	- 4:29	- 5.30	100	- 3:50	- 5.30	36	- 4:54	- 5.30	46	- 4:44
- 5.15	176	- 2:19	- 5.15	94	- 3:41	- 5.15	31	- 4:44	- 5.15	50	- 4:25	- 5.15	63	- 4:12	- 5.15	102	- 3:33	- 5.15	36	- 4:39	- 5.15	47	- 4:28
- 5.00	**180**	**- 2:00**	**- 5.00**	**99**	**- 3:21**	**- 5.00**	**31**	**- 4:29**	**- 5.00**	**51**	**- 4:09**	**- 5.00**	**66**	**- 3:54**	**- 5.00**	**105**	**- 3:15**	**- 5.00**	**36**	**- 4:24**	**- 5.00**	**47**	**- 4:13**
- 4.45	180	- 1:45	- 4.45	99	- 3:06	- 4.45	31	- 4:14	- 4.45	52	- 3:53	- 4.45	68	- 3:37	- 4.45	108	- 2:57	- 4.45	37	- 4:08	- 4.45	48	- 3:57
- 4.30	181	- 1:29	- 4.30	99	- 2:51	- 4.30	31	- 3:59	- 4.30	53	- 3:37	- 4.30	70	- 3:20	- 4.30	111	- 2:39	- 4.30	38	- 3:52	- 4.30	49	- 3:41
- 4.15	181	- 1:14	- 4.15	99	- 2:36	- 4.15	32	- 3:43	- 4.15	54	- 3:21	- 4.15	72	- 3:03	- 4.15	115	- 2:20	- 4.15	40	- 3:35	- 4.15	53	- 3:22
- 4.00	**181**	**- 0:59**	**- 4.00**	**99**	**- 2:21**	**- 4.00**	**32**	**- 3:28**	**- 4.00**	**55**	**- 3:05**	**- 4.00**	**74**	**- 2:46**	**- 4.00**	**118**	**- 2:02**	**- 4.00**	**41**	**- 3:19**	**- 4.00**	**57**	**- 3:03**
- 3.45	177	- 0:48	- 3.45	98	- 2:07	- 3.45	32	- 3:13	- 3.45	56	- 2:49	- 3.45	78	- 2:27	- 3.45	119	- 1:46	- 3.45	44	- 3:01	- 3.45	62	- 2:43
- 3.30	173	- 0:37	- 3.30	96	- 1:54	- 3.30	32	- 2:58	- 3.30	57	- 2:33	- 3.30	83	- 2:07	- 3.30	120	- 1:30	- 3.30	47	- 2:43	- 3.30	66	- 2:24
- 3.15	169	- 0:26	- 3.15	95	- 1:40	- 3.15	32	- 2:43	- 3.15	59	- 2:16	- 3.15	88	- 1:47	- 3.15	121	- 1:14	- 3.15	50	- 2:25	- 3.15	78	- 1:57
- 3.00	**165**	**- 0:15**	**- 3.00**	**93**	**- 1:27**	**- 3.00**	**32**	**- 2:28**	**- 3.00**	**60**	**- 2:00**	**- 3.00**	**93**	**- 1:27**	**- 3.00**	**122**	**- 0:58**	**- 3.00**	**54**	**- 2:06**	**- 3.00**	**90**	**- 1:30**
- 2.45	158	- 0:07	- 2.45	90	- 1:15	- 2.45	32	- 2:13	- 2.45	59	- 1:46	- 2.45	94	- 1:11	- 2.45	121	- 0:44	- 2.45	57	- 1:48	- 2.45	101	- 1:04
- 2.30	151	+ 0:01	- 2.30	87	- 1:03	- 2.30	32	- 1:58	- 2.30	59	- 1:31	- 2.30	94	- 0:56	- 2.30	119	- 0:31	- 2.30	61	- 1:29	- 2.30	113	- 0:37
- 2.15	144	+ 0:09	- 2.15	84	- 0:51	- 2.15	32	- 1:43	- 2.15	58	- 1:17	- 2.15	95	- 0:40	- 2.15	117	- 0:18	- 2.15	65	- 1:10	- 2.15	117	- 0:18
- 2.00	**137**	**+ 0:17**	**- 2.00**	**81**	**- 0:39**	**- 2.00**	**33**	**- 1:27**	**- 2.00**	**58**	**- 1:02**	**- 2.00**	**95**	**- 0:25**	**- 2.00**	**116**	**- 0:04**	**- 2.00**	**69**	**- 0:51**	**- 2.00**	**121**	**+ 0:01**
- 1.45	130	+ 0:25	- 1.45	78	- 0:27	- 1.45	32	- 1:13	- 1.45	58	- 0:47	- 1.45	90	- 0:15	- 1.45	113	+ 0:08	- 1.45	69	- 0:36	- 1.45	125	+ 0:20
- 1.30	123	+ 0:33	- 1.30	75	- 0:15	- 1.30	32	- 0:58	- 1.30	57	- 0:33	- 1.30	86	- 0:04	- 1.30	111	+ 0:21	- 1.30	70	- 0:20	- 1.30	128	+ 0:38
- 1.15	117	+ 0:42	- 1.15	73	- 0:02	- 1.15	32	- 0:43	- 1.15	57	- 0:18	- 1.15	81	+ 0:06	- 1.15	108	+ 0:33	- 1.15	71	- 0:04	- 1.15	126	+ 0:51
- 1.00	**110**	**+ 0:50**	**- 1.00**	**70**	**+ 0:10**	**- 1.00**	**32**	**- 0:28**	**- 1.00**	**56**	**- 0:04**	**- 1.00**	**76**	**+ 0:16**	**- 1.00**	**106**	**+ 0:46**	**- 1.00**	**71**	**+ 0:11**	**- 1.00**	**124**	**+ 1:04**
- 0.45	106	+ 1:01	- 0.45	68	+ 0:23	- 0.45	32	- 0:13	- 0.45	56	+ 0:11	- 0.45	72	+ 0:27	- 0.45	104	+ 0:59	- 0.45	70	+ 0:25	- 0.45	122	+ 1:17
- 0.30	102	+ 1:12	- 0.30	65	+ 0:35	- 0.30	32	+ 0:02	- 0.30	57	+ 0:27	- 0.30	67	+ 0:37	- 0.30	102	+ 1:12	- 0.30	68	+ 0:38	- 0.30	120	+ 1:30
- 0.15	99	+ 1:24	- 0.15	63	+ 0:48	- 0.15	33	+ 0:18	- 0.15	57	+ 0:42	- 0.15	63	+ 0:48	- 0.15	101	+ 1:26	- 0.15	67	+ 0:52	- 0.15	115	+ 1:40
HW	**95**	**+ 1:35**	**HW**	**61**	**+ 1:01**	**HW**	**33**	**+ 0:33**	**HW**	**58**	**+ 0:58**	**HW**	**58**	**+ 0:58**	**HW**	**99**	**+ 1:39**	**HW**	**65**	**+ 1:05**	**HW**	**111**	**+ 1:51**
+ 0.15	94	+ 1:49	+ 0.15	60	+ 1:15	+ 0.15	34	+ 0:49	+ 0.15	59	+ 1:14	+ 0.15	56	+ 1:11	+ 0.15	98	+ 1:53	+ 0.15	63	+ 1:18	+ 0.15	106	+ 2:01
+ 0.30	93	+ 2:03	+ 0.30	59	+ 1:29	+ 0.30	34	+ 1:04	+ 0.30	59	+ 1:29	+ 0.30	53	+ 1:23	+ 0.30	97	+ 2:07	+ 0.30	60	+ 1:30	+ 0.30	101	+ 2:11
+ 0.45	91	+ 2:16	+ 0.45	58	+ 1:43	+ 0.45	35	+ 1:20	+ 0.45	60	+ 1:45	+ 0.45	51	+ 1:36	+ 0.45	96	+ 2:21	+ 0.45	58	+ 1:43	+ 0.45	96	+ 2:21
+ 1.00	**90**	**+ 2:30**	**+ 1.00**	**57**	**+ 1:57**	**+ 1.00**	**36**	**+ 1:36**	**+ 1.00**	**61**	**+ 2:01**	**+ 1.00**	**48**	**+ 1:48**	**+ 1.00**	**95**	**+ 2:35**	**+ 1.00**	**56**	**+ 1:56**	**+ 1.00**	**91**	**+ 2:31**
+ 1.15	91	+ 2:46	+ 1.15	57	+ 2:12	+ 1.15	37	+ 1:52	+ 1.15	61	+ 2:16	+ 1.15	47	+ 2:02	+ 1.15	94	+ 2:49	+ 1.15	54	+ 2:09	+ 1.15	86	+ 2:41
+ 1.30	92	+ 3:02	+ 1.30	57	+ 2:27	+ 1.30	37	+ 2:07	+ 1.30	61	+ 2:31	+ 1.30	46	+ 2:16	+ 1.30	94	+ 3:04	+ 1.30	52	+ 2:22	+ 1.30	81	+ 2:51
+ 1.45	93	+ 3:18	+ 1.45	57	+ 2:42	+ 1.45	37	+ 2:22	+ 1.45	61	+ 2:46	+ 1.45	45	+ 2:30	+ 1.45	93	+ 3:18	+ 1.45	49	+ 2:34	+ 1.45	78	+ 3:03
+ 2.00	**94**	**+ 3:34**	**+ 2.00**	**57**	**+ 2:57**	**+ 2.00**	**38**	**+ 2:38**	**+ 2.00**	**61**	**+ 3:01**	**+ 2.00**	**44**	**+ 2:44**	**+ 2.00**	**92**	**+ 3:32**	**+ 2.00**	**47**	**+ 2:47**	**+ 2.00**	**74**	**+ 3:14**
+ 2.15	96	+ 3:51	+ 2.15	57	+ 3:12	+ 2.15	37	+ 2:52	+ 2.15	60	+ 3:15	+ 2.15	43	+ 2:58	+ 2.15	92	+ 3:47	+ 2.15	46	+ 3:01	+ 2.15	70	+ 3:25
+ 2.30	98	+ 4:08	+ 2.30	58	+ 3:28	+ 2.30	37	+ 3:07	+ 2.30	59	+ 3:29	+ 2.30	43	+ 3:13	+ 2.30	92	+ 4:02	+ 2.30	44	+ 3:14	+ 2.30	66	+ 3:36
+ 2.45	101	+ 4:26	+ 2.45	58	+ 3:43	+ 2.45	36	+ 3:21	+ 2.45	59	+ 3:44	+ 2.45	42	+ 3:27	+ 2.45	91	+ 4:16	+ 2.45	42	+ 3:27	+ 2.45	65	+ 3:50
+ 3.00	**103**	**+ 4:43**	**+ 3.00**	**59**	**+ 3:59**	**+ 3.00**	**36**	**+ 3:36**	**+ 3.00**	**58**	**+ 3:58**	**+ 3.00**	**42**	**+ 3:42**	**+ 3.00**	**91**	**+ 4:31**	**+ 3.00**	**41**	**+ 3:41**	**+ 3.00**	**63**	**+ 4:03**
+ 3.15	106	+ 5:01	+ 3.15	60	+ 4:15	+ 3.15	35	+ 3:50	+ 3.15	57	+ 4:12	+ 3.15	42	+ 3:57	+ 3.15	90	+ 4:45	+ 3.15	40	+ 3:55	+ 3.15	62	+ 4:17
+ 3.30	108	+ 5:18	+ 3.30	61	+ 4:31	+ 3.30	34	+ 4:04	+ 3.30	56	+ 4:26	+ 3.30	42	+ 4:12	+ 3.30	90	+ 5:00	+ 3.30	39	+ 4:09	+ 3.30	61	+ 4:31
+ 3.45	111	+ 5:36	+ 3.45	62	+ 4:47	+ 3.45	34	+ 4:19	+ 3.45	55	+ 4:40	+ 3.45	41	+ 4:26	+ 3.45	89	+ 5:14	+ 3.45	38	+ 4:23	+ 3.45	60	+ 4:45
+ 4.00	**114**	**+ 5:54**	**+ 4.00**	**63**	**+ 5:03**	**+ 4.00**	**33**	**+ 4:33**	**+ 4.00**	**53**	**+ 4:53**	**+ 4.00**	**41**	**+ 4:41**	**+ 4.00**	**89**	**+ 5:29**	**+ 4.00**	**37**	**+ 4:37**	**+ 4.00**	**58**	**+ 4:58**
+ 4.15	117	- 5:48	+ 4.15	64	+ 5:19	+ 4.15	33	+ 4:48	+ 4.15	53	+ 5:08	+ 4.15	42	+ 4:57	+ 4.15	89	+ 5:44	+ 4.15	37	+ 4:52	+ 4.15	57	+ 5:12
+ 4.30	121	- 5:29	+ 4.30	65	+ 5:35	+ 4.30	32	+ 5:02	+ 4.30	52	+ 5:22	+ 4.30	43	+ 5:13	+ 4.30	90	- 6:00	+ 4.30	36	+ 5:06	+ 4.30	56	+ 5:26
+ 4.45	125	- 5:10	+ 4.45	66	+ 5:51	+ 4.45	32	+ 5:17	+ 4.45	51	+ 5:36	+ 4.45	43	+ 5:28	+ 4.45	91	- 5:44	+ 4.45	36	+ 5:21	+ 4.45	55	+ 5:40
+ 5.00	**128**	**- 4:52**	**+ 5.00**	**68**	**- 5:52**	**+ 5.00**	**31**	**+ 5:31**	**+ 5.00**	**51**	**+ 5:51**	**+ 5.00**	**44**	**+ 5:44**	**+ 5.00**	**91**	**- 5:29**	**+ 5.00**	**36**	**+ 5:36**	**+ 5.00**	**54**	**+ 5:54**
+ 5.15	132	- 4:33	+ 5.15	69	- 5:36	+ 5.15	31	+ 5:46	+ 5.15	50	- 5:55	+ 5.15	46	- 5:59	+ 5.15	92	- 5:13	+ 5.15	35	+ 5:50	+ 5.15	53	- 5:52
+ 5.30	135	- 4:15	+ 5.30	70	- 5:20	+ 5.30	31	- 5:59	+ 5.30	50	- 5:40	+ 5.30	47	- 5:43	+ 5.30	92	- 4:58	+ 5.30	35	- 5:55	+ 5.30	52	- 5:38
+ 5.45	139	- 3:56	+ 5.45	71	- 5:04	+ 5.45	30	- 5:45	+ 5.45	50	- 5:25	+ 5.45	49	- 5:26	+ 5.45	92	- 4:43	+ 5.45	35	- 5:40	+ 5.45	49	- 5:26
+ 6.00	**143**	**- 3:37**	**+ 6.00**	**72**	**- 4:48**	**+ 6.00**	**30**	**- 5:30**	**+ 6.00**	**50**	**- 5:10**	**+ 6.00**	**50**	**- 5:10**	**+ 6.00**	**93**	**- 4:27**	**+ 6.00**	**35**	**- 5:25**	**+ 6.00**	**48**	**- 5:12**

SOUTH BOUND

Table A - Blackwater to Ramsgate via SW Sunk

Neaps — All times relate to HW Sheerness — Time to cover Sectors (in minutes) at 5.0 Kts

SOUTH BOUND

A8 — Blackwater to Swin Spitway

Time	Duration	Time at End of Sector
- 6.00	114	- 4:06
- 5.45	115	- 3:50
- 5.30	117	- 3:33
- 5.15	119	- 3:16
- 5.00	121	- 2:59
- 4.45	122	- 2:43
- 4.30	122	- 2:28
- 4.15	123	- 2:12
- 4.00	124	- 1:56
- 3.45	123	- 1:42
- 3.30	123	- 1:27
- 3.15	123	- 1:12
- 3.00	122	- 0:58
- 2.45	120	- 0:45
- 2.30	118	- 0:32
- 2.15	115	- 0:20
- 2.00	113	- 0:07
- 1.45	109	+ 0:04
- 1.30	105	+ 0:15
- 1.15	101	+ 0:26
- 1.00	98	+ 0:38
- 0.45	94	+ 0:49
- 0.30	91	+ 1:01
- 0.15	88	+ 1:13
HW	85	+ 1:25
+ 0.15	84	+ 1:39
+ 0.30	83	+ 1:53
+ 0.45	82	+ 2:07
+ 1.00	81	+ 2:21
+ 1.15	81	+ 2:36
+ 1.30	82	+ 2:52
+ 1.45	82	+ 3:07
+ 2.00	83	+ 3:23
+ 2.15	84	+ 3:39
+ 2.30	86	+ 3:56
+ 2.45	87	+ 4:12
+ 3.00	89	+ 4:29
+ 3.15	90	+ 4:45
+ 3.30	91	+ 5:01
+ 3.45	92	+ 5:17
+ 4.00	92	+ 5:32
+ 4.15	94	+ 5:49
+ 4.30	96	- 5:54
+ 4.45	98	- 5:37
+ 5.00	99	- 5:21
+ 5.15	101	- 5:04
+ 5.30	103	- 4:47
+ 5.45	105	- 4:30
+ 6.00	107	- 4:13

A7 — Spitway to East Barrow Sands

Time	Duration	Time at End of Sector
- 6.00	59	- 5:01
- 5.45	60	- 4:45
- 5.30	61	- 4:29
- 5.15	62	- 4:13
- 5.00	63	- 3:57
- 4.45	63	- 3:42
- 4.30	63	- 3:27
- 4.15	63	- 3:12
- 4.00	63	- 2:57
- 3.45	63	- 2:42
- 3.30	63	- 2:27
- 3.15	63	- 2:12
- 3.00	63	- 1:57
- 2.45	62	- 1:43
- 2.30	61	- 1:29
- 2.15	60	- 1:15
- 2.00	60	- 1:00
- 1.45	59	- 0:46
- 1.30	58	- 0:32
- 1.15	57	- 0:18
- 1.00	56	- 0:04
- 0.45	55	+ 0:10
- 0.30	53	+ 0:23
- 0.15	52	+ 0:37
HW	51	+ 0:51
+ 0.15	51	+ 1:06
+ 0.30	50	+ 1:20
+ 0.45	49	+ 1:34
+ 1.00	49	+ 1:49
+ 1.15	49	+ 2:04
+ 1.30	49	+ 2:19
+ 1.45	49	+ 2:34
+ 2.00	49	+ 2:49
+ 2.15	49	+ 3:04
+ 2.30	49	+ 3:19
+ 2.45	49	+ 3:34
+ 3.00	50	+ 3:50
+ 3.15	50	+ 4:05
+ 3.30	51	+ 4:21
+ 3.45	51	+ 4:36
+ 4.00	52	+ 4:52
+ 4.15	52	+ 5:07
+ 4.30	53	+ 5:23
+ 4.45	53	+ 5:38
+ 5.00	54	+ 5:54
+ 5.15	55	- 5:50
+ 5.30	55	- 5:35
+ 5.45	56	- 5:19
+ 6.00	56	- 5:04

A6 — East Barrow to SW Sunk

Time	Duration	Time at End of Sector
- 6.00	24	- 5:36
- 5.45	24	- 5:21
- 5.30	24	- 5:06
- 5.15	24	- 4:51
- 5.00	24	- 4:36
- 4.45	24	- 4:21
- 4.30	24	- 4:06
- 4.15	24	- 3:51
- 4.00	24	- 3:36
- 3.45	25	- 3:20
- 3.30	25	- 3:05
- 3.15	25	- 2:50
- 3.00	25	- 2:35
- 2.45	25	- 2:20
- 2.30	25	- 2:05
- 2.15	25	- 1:50
- 2.00	25	- 1:35
- 1.45	25	- 1:20
- 1.30	25	- 1:05
- 1.15	25	- 0:50
- 1.00	25	- 0:35
- 0.45	25	- 0:20
- 0.30	25	- 0:05
- 0.15	25	+ 0:10
HW	25	+ 0:25
+ 0.15	26	+ 0:41
+ 0.30	26	+ 0:56
+ 0.45	26	+ 1:11
+ 1.00	26	+ 1:26
+ 1.15	27	+ 1:42
+ 1.30	27	+ 1:57
+ 1.45	27	+ 2:12
+ 2.00	27	+ 2:27
+ 2.15	27	+ 2:42
+ 2.30	27	+ 2:57
+ 2.45	27	+ 3:12
+ 3.00	27	+ 3:27
+ 3.15	26	+ 3:41
+ 3.30	26	+ 3:56
+ 3.45	26	+ 4:11
+ 4.00	25	+ 4:25
+ 4.15	25	+ 4:40
+ 4.30	25	+ 4:55
+ 4.45	25	+ 5:10
+ 5.00	25	+ 5:25
+ 5.15	25	+ 5:40
+ 5.30	25	+ 5:55
+ 5.45	24	- 5:51
+ 6.00	24	- 5:36

A5 — SW Sunk to Inner Fisherman

Time	Duration	Time at End of Sector
- 6.00	40	- 5:20
- 5.45	40	- 5:05
- 5.30	40	- 4:50
- 5.15	40	- 4:35
- 5.00	40	- 4:20
- 4.45	40	- 4:05
- 4.30	40	- 3:50
- 4.15	41	- 3:34
- 4.00	41	- 3:19
- 3.45	41	- 3:04
- 3.30	42	- 2:48
- 3.15	42	- 2:33
- 3.00	43	- 2:17
- 2.45	43	- 2:02
- 2.30	43	- 1:47
- 2.15	43	- 1:32
- 2.00	43	- 1:17
- 1.45	43	- 1:02
- 1.30	43	- 0:47
- 1.15	43	- 0:32
- 1.00	43	- 0:17
- 0.45	43	- 0:02
- 0.30	43	+ 0:13
- 0.15	43	+ 0:28
HW	43	+ 0:43
+ 0.15	43	+ 0:58
+ 0.30	43	+ 1:13
+ 0.45	44	+ 1:29
+ 1.00	44	+ 1:44
+ 1.15	44	+ 1:59
+ 1.30	44	+ 2:14
+ 1.45	44	+ 2:29
+ 2.00	44	+ 2:44
+ 2.15	44	+ 2:59
+ 2.30	43	+ 3:13
+ 2.45	43	+ 3:28
+ 3.00	43	+ 3:43
+ 3.15	43	+ 3:58
+ 3.30	42	+ 4:12
+ 3.45	42	+ 4:27
+ 4.00	42	+ 4:42
+ 4.15	41	+ 4:56
+ 4.30	41	+ 5:11
+ 4.45	41	+ 5:26
+ 5.00	41	+ 5:41
+ 5.15	41	+ 5:56
+ 5.30	41	- 5:49
+ 5.45	41	- 5:34
+ 6.00	40	- 5:20

A4 — Inner to Outer Fisherman

Time	Duration	Time at End of Sector
- 6.00	45	- 5:15
- 5.45	46	- 4:59
- 5.30	47	- 4:43
- 5.15	48	- 4:27
- 5.00	49	- 4:11
- 4.45	50	- 3:55
- 4.30	51	- 3:39
- 4.15	51	- 3:24
- 4.00	52	- 3:08
- 3.45	53	- 2:52
- 3.30	54	- 2:36
- 3.15	55	- 2:20
- 3.00	56	- 2:04
- 2.45	57	- 1:48
- 2.30	57	- 1:33
- 2.15	58	- 1:17
- 2.00	59	- 1:01
- 1.45	58	- 0:47
- 1.30	57	- 0:33
- 1.15	55	- 0:20
- 1.00	54	- 0:06
- 0.45	53	+ 0:08
- 0.30	51	+ 0:21
- 0.15	49	+ 0:34
HW	48	+ 0:48
+ 0.15	46	+ 1:01
+ 0.30	45	+ 1:15
+ 0.45	44	+ 1:29
+ 1.00	43	+ 1:43
+ 1.15	42	+ 1:57
+ 1.30	42	+ 2:12
+ 1.45	41	+ 2:26
+ 2.00	41	+ 2:41
+ 2.15	40	+ 2:55
+ 2.30	40	+ 3:10
+ 2.45	40	+ 3:25
+ 3.00	40	+ 3:40
+ 3.15	40	+ 3:55
+ 3.30	39	+ 4:09
+ 3.45	39	+ 4:24
+ 4.00	39	+ 4:39
+ 4.15	39	+ 4:54
+ 4.30	40	+ 5:10
+ 4.45	40	+ 5:25
+ 5.00	40	+ 5:40
+ 5.15	41	+ 5:56
+ 5.30	41	- 5:49
+ 5.45	42	- 5:33
+ 6.00	43	- 5:17

A3 — Outer Fisherman to East Margate

Time	Duration	Time at End of Sector
- 6.00	76	- 4:44
- 5.45	76	- 4:29
- 5.30	77	- 4:13
- 5.15	77	- 3:58
- 5.00	78	- 3:42
- 4.45	79	- 3:26
- 4.30	80	- 3:10
- 4.15	81	- 2:54
- 4.00	82	- 2:38
- 3.45	83	- 2:22
- 3.30	84	- 2:06
- 3.15	85	- 1:50
- 3.00	85	- 1:35
- 2.45	85	- 1:20
- 2.30	85	- 1:05
- 2.15	85	- 0:50
- 2.00	85	- 0:35
- 1.45	84	- 0:21
- 1.30	83	- 0:07
- 1.15	82	+ 0:07
- 1.00	82	+ 0:22
- 0.45	81	+ 0:36
- 0.30	80	+ 0:50
- 0.15	79	+ 1:04
HW	78	+ 1:18
+ 0.15	77	+ 1:32
+ 0.30	77	+ 1:47
+ 0.45	76	+ 2:01
+ 1.00	75	+ 2:15
+ 1.15	75	+ 2:30
+ 1.30	75	+ 2:45
+ 1.45	74	+ 2:59
+ 2.00	74	+ 3:14
+ 2.15	74	+ 3:29
+ 2.30	74	+ 3:44
+ 2.45	74	+ 3:59
+ 3.00	73	+ 4:13
+ 3.15	73	+ 4:28
+ 3.30	73	+ 4:43
+ 3.45	73	+ 4:58
+ 4.00	73	+ 5:13
+ 4.15	73	+ 5:28
+ 4.30	74	+ 5:44
+ 4.45	74	+ 5:59
+ 5.00	75	- 5:45
+ 5.15	75	- 5:30
+ 5.30	75	- 5:15
+ 5.45	75	- 5:00
+ 6.00	75	- 4:45

A2 — East Margate to North Foreland

Time	Duration	Time at End of Sector
- 6.00	32	- 5:28
- 5.45	32	- 5:13
- 5.30	32	- 4:58
- 5.15	32	- 4:43
- 5.00	32	- 4:28
- 4.45	33	- 4:12
- 4.30	33	- 3:57
- 4.15	33	- 3:42
- 4.00	34	- 3:26
- 3.45	35	- 3:10
- 3.30	36	- 2:54
- 3.15	37	- 2:38
- 3.00	38	- 2:22
- 2.45	39	- 2:06
- 2.30	41	- 1:49
- 2.15	42	- 1:33
- 2.00	44	- 1:16
- 1.45	44	- 1:01
- 1.30	44	- 0:46
- 1.15	45	- 0:30
- 1.00	45	- 0:15
- 0.45	45	HW
- 0.30	44	+ 0:14
- 0.15	44	+ 0:29
HW	43	+ 0:43
+ 0.15	43	+ 0:58
+ 0.30	42	+ 1:12
+ 0.45	41	+ 1:26
+ 1.00	41	+ 1:41
+ 1.15	40	+ 1:55
+ 1.30	39	+ 2:09
+ 1.45	38	+ 2:23
+ 2.00	37	+ 2:37
+ 2.15	36	+ 2:51
+ 2.30	36	+ 3:06
+ 2.45	35	+ 3:20
+ 3.00	34	+ 3:34
+ 3.15	34	+ 3:49
+ 3.30	34	+ 4:04
+ 3.45	34	+ 4:19
+ 4.00	33	+ 4:33
+ 4.15	33	+ 4:48
+ 4.30	33	+ 5:03
+ 4.45	33	+ 5:18
+ 5.00	33	+ 5:33
+ 5.15	32	+ 5:47
+ 5.30	32	- 5:58
+ 5.45	32	- 5:43
+ 6.00	32	- 5:28

A1 — North Foreland to Ramsgate

Time	Duration	Time at End of Sector
- 6.00	47	- 5:13
- 5.45	47	- 4:58
- 5.30	46	- 4:44
- 5.15	47	- 4:28
- 5.00	47	- 4:13
- 4.45	47	- 3:58
- 4.30	47	- 3:43
- 4.15	49	- 3:26
- 4.00	51	- 3:09
- 3.45	52	- 2:53
- 3.30	54	- 2:36
- 3.15	57	- 2:18
- 3.00	59	- 2:01
- 2.45	62	- 1:43
- 2.30	65	- 1:25
- 2.15	66	- 1:09
- 2.00	67	- 0:53
- 1.45	68	- 0:37
- 1.30	70	- 0:20
- 1.15	70	- 0:05
- 1.00	70	+ 0:10
- 0.45	70	+ 0:25
- 0.30	70	+ 0:40
- 0.15	69	+ 0:54
HW	68	+ 1:08
+ 0.15	68	+ 1:23
+ 0.30	67	+ 1:37
+ 0.45	65	+ 1:50
+ 1.00	64	+ 2:04
+ 1.15	62	+ 2:17
+ 1.30	61	+ 2:31
+ 1.45	59	+ 2:44
+ 2.00	58	+ 2:58
+ 2.15	57	+ 3:12
+ 2.30	55	+ 3:25
+ 2.45	55	+ 3:40
+ 3.00	54	+ 3:54
+ 3.15	53	+ 4:08
+ 3.30	52	+ 4:22
+ 3.45	51	+ 4:36
+ 4.00	51	+ 4:51
+ 4.15	50	+ 5:05
+ 4.30	50	+ 5:20
+ 4.45	50	+ 5:35
+ 5.00	50	+ 5:50
+ 5.15	49	- 5:56
+ 5.30	49	- 5:41
+ 5.45	48	- 5:27
+ 6.00	48	- 5:12

A - 5 Kts

Table A - Blackwater to Ramsgate via SW Sunk

5 Kts - A

Time to cover Sectors (in minutes) at 5.0 kts | All times relate to HW Sheerness | Springs

Time	A8 Blackwater to Swin Spitway		Time	A7 Spitway to East Barrow Sands		Time	A6 East Barrow to SW Sunk		Time	A5 SW Sunk to Inner Fisherman	
	Duration	Time at End of Sector		Duration	Time at End of Sector		Duration	Time at End of Sector		Duration	Time at End of Sector
- 6.00	120	- 4:00	- 6.00	62	- 4:58	- 6.00	24	- 5:36	- 6.00	40	- 5:20
- 5.45	122	- 3:43	- 5.45	63	- 4:42	- 5.45	24	- 5:21	- 5.45	40	- 5:05
- 5.30	125	- 3:25	- 5.30	65	- 4:25	- 5.30	24	- 5:06	- 5.30	40	- 4:50
- 5.15	127	- 3:08	- 5.15	67	- 4:08	- 5.15	24	- 4:51	- 5.15	40	- 4:35
- 5.00	129	- 2:51	- 5.00	68	- 3:52	- 5.00	24	- 4:36	- 5.00	40	- 4:20
- 4.45	131	- 2:34	- 4.45	69	- 3:36	- 4.45	25	- 4:20	- 4.45	40	- 4:05
- 4.30	132	- 2:18	- 4.30	69	- 3:21	- 4.30	25	- 4:05	- 4.30	41	- 3:49
- 4.15	133	- 2:02	- 4.15	69	- 3:06	- 4.15	25	- 3:50	- 4.15	41	- 3:34
- 4.00	134	- 1:46	- 4.00	70	- 2:50	- 4.00	25	- 3:35	- 4.00	42	- 3:18
- 3.45	133	- 1:32	- 3.45	69	- 2:36	- 3.45	25	- 3:20	- 3.45	43	- 3:02
- 3.30	132	- 1:18	- 3.30	69	- 2:21	- 3.30	25	- 3:05	- 3.30	44	- 2:46
- 3.15	131	- 1:04	- 3.15	68	- 2:07	- 3.15	25	- 2:50	- 3.15	44	- 2:31
- 3.00	131	- 0:49	- 3.00	68	- 1:52	- 3.00	26	- 2:34	- 3.00	45	- 2:15
- 2.45	126	- 0:39	- 2.45	67	- 1:38	- 2.45	26	- 2:19	- 2.45	45	- 2:00
- 2.30	122	- 0:28	- 2.30	66	- 1:24	- 2.30	26	- 2:04	- 2.30	45	- 1:45
- 2.15	118	- 0:17	- 2.15	64	- 1:11	- 2.15	26	- 1:49	- 2.15	45	- 1:30
- 2.00	114	- 0:06	- 2.00	63	- 0:57	- 2.00	26	- 1:34	- 2.00	45	- 1:15
- 1.45	109	+ 0:04	- 1.45	61	- 0:44	- 1.45	26	- 1:19	- 1.45	45	- 1:00
- 1.30	104	+ 0:14	- 1.30	60	- 0:30	- 1.30	26	- 1:04	- 1.30	45	- 0:45
- 1.15	99	+ 0:24	- 1.15	58	- 0:17	- 1.15	25	- 0:50	- 1.15	44	- 0:31
- 1.00	95	+ 0:35	- 1.00	56	- 0:04	- 1.00	25	- 0:35	- 1.00	44	- 0:16
- 0.45	90	+ 0:45	- 0.45	55	+ 0:10	- 0.45	26	- 0:19	- 0.45	44	- 0:01
- 0.30	86	+ 0:56	- 0.30	53	+ 0:23	- 0.30	26	- 0:04	- 0.30	44	+ 0:14
- 0.15	81	+ 1:06	- 0.15	52	+ 0:37	- 0.15	26	+ 0:11	- 0.15	44	+ 0:29
HW	77	+ 1:17	HW	50	+ 0:50	HW	26	+ 0:26	HW	44	+ 0:44
+ 0.15	76	+ 1:31	+ 0.15	49	+ 1:04	+ 0.15	26	+ 0:41	+ 0.15	45	+ 1:00
+ 0.30	74	+ 1:44	+ 0.30	48	+ 1:18	+ 0.30	27	+ 0:57	+ 0.30	45	+ 1:15
+ 0.45	73	+ 1:58	+ 0.45	48	+ 1:33	+ 0.45	27	+ 1:12	+ 0.45	46	+ 1:31
+ 1.00	72	+ 2:12	+ 1.00	47	+ 1:47	+ 1.00	28	+ 1:28	+ 1.00	46	+ 1:46
+ 1.15	73	+ 2:28	+ 1.15	47	+ 2:02	+ 1.15	28	+ 1:43	+ 1.15	46	+ 2:01
+ 1.30	73	+ 2:43	+ 1.30	47	+ 2:17	+ 1.30	28	+ 1:58	+ 1.30	46	+ 2:16
+ 1.45	74	+ 2:59	+ 1.45	47	+ 2:32	+ 1.45	29	+ 2:14	+ 1.45	46	+ 2:31
+ 2.00	75	+ 3:15	+ 2.00	47	+ 2:47	+ 2.00	29	+ 2:29	+ 2.00	47	+ 2:47
+ 2.15	77	+ 3:32	+ 2.15	47	+ 3:02	+ 2.15	29	+ 2:44	+ 2.15	46	+ 3:01
+ 2.30	79	+ 3:49	+ 2.30	47	+ 3:17	+ 2.30	28	+ 2:58	+ 2.30	46	+ 3:16
+ 2.45	81	+ 4:06	+ 2.45	47	+ 3:32	+ 2.45	28	+ 3:13	+ 2.45	45	+ 3:30
+ 3.00	83	+ 4:23	+ 3.00	48	+ 3:48	+ 3.00	28	+ 3:28	+ 3.00	45	+ 3:45
+ 3.15	85	+ 4:40	+ 3.15	48	+ 4:03	+ 3.15	27	+ 3:42	+ 3.15	44	+ 3:59
+ 3.30	87	+ 4:57	+ 3.30	49	+ 4:19	+ 3.30	27	+ 3:57	+ 3.30	44	+ 4:14
+ 3.45	88	+ 5:13	+ 3.45	50	+ 4:35	+ 3.45	27	+ 4:12	+ 3.45	43	+ 4:28
+ 4.00	90	+ 5:30	+ 4.00	50	+ 4:50	+ 4.00	26	+ 4:26	+ 4.00	42	+ 4:42
+ 4.15	93	+ 5:48	+ 4.15	51	+ 5:06	+ 4.15	26	+ 4:41	+ 4.15	42	+ 4:57
+ 4.30	95	- 5:55	+ 4.30	52	+ 5:22	+ 4.30	25	+ 4:55	+ 4.30	41	+ 5:11
+ 4.45	98	- 5:37	+ 4.45	53	+ 5:38	+ 4.45	25	+ 5:10	+ 4.45	41	+ 5:26
+ 5.00	100	- 5:20	+ 5.00	54	+ 5:54	+ 5.00	25	+ 5:25	+ 5.00	41	+ 5:41
+ 5.15	103	- 5:02	+ 5.15	54	- 5:51	+ 5.15	25	+ 5:40	+ 5.15	40	+ 5:55
+ 5.30	105	- 4:45	+ 5.30	55	- 5:35	+ 5.30	24	+ 5:54	+ 5.30	40	- 5:50
+ 5.45	107	- 4:28	+ 5.45	56	- 5:19	+ 5.45	24	- 5:51	+ 5.45	40	- 5:35
+ 6.00	109	- 4:11	+ 6.00	57	- 5:03	+ 6.00	24	- 5:36	+ 6.00	40	- 5:20

Time	A4 Inner to Outer Fisherman		Time	A3 Outer Fisherman to East Margate		Time	A2 East Margate to North Foreland		Time	A1 North Foreland to Ramsgate	
	Duration	Time at End of Sector		Duration	Time at End of Sector		Duration	Time at End of Sector		Duration	Time at End of Sector
- 6.00	44	- 5:16	- 6.00	75	- 4:45	- 6.00	29	- 5:31	- 6.00	42	- 5:18
- 5.45	46	- 4:59	- 5.45	76	- 4:29	- 5.45	30	- 5:15	- 5.45	41	- 5:04
- 5.30	48	- 4:42	- 5.30	77	- 4:13	- 5.30	30	- 5:00	- 5.30	41	- 4:49
- 5.15	49	- 4:26	- 5.15	79	- 3:56	- 5.15	30	- 4:45	- 5.15	41	- 4:34
- 5.00	51	- 4:09	- 5.00	80	- 3:40	- 5.00	30	- 4:30	- 5.00	41	- 4:19
- 4.45	52	- 3:53	- 4.45	81	- 3:24	- 4.45	30	- 4:15	- 4.45	41	- 4:04
- 4.30	53	- 3:37	- 4.30	83	- 3:07	- 4.30	31	- 3:59	- 4.30	42	- 3:48
- 4.15	54	- 3:21	- 4.15	85	- 2:50	- 4.15	31	- 3:44	- 4.15	44	- 3:31
- 4.00	56	- 3:04	- 4.00	87	- 2:33	- 4.00	32	- 3:28	- 4.00	46	- 3:14
- 3.45	58	- 2:47	- 3.45	88	- 2:17	- 3.45	34	- 3:11	- 3.45	49	- 2:56
- 3.30	59	- 2:31	- 3.30	90	- 2:00	- 3.30	36	- 2:54	- 3.30	51	- 2:39
- 3.15	61	- 2:14	- 3.15	92	- 1:43	- 3.15	38	- 2:37	- 3.15	56	- 2:19
- 3.00	63	- 1:57	- 3.00	93	- 1:27	- 3.00	40	- 2:20	- 3.00	62	- 1:58
- 2.45	64	- 1:41	- 2.45	93	- 1:12	- 2.45	42	- 2:03	- 2.45	67	- 1:38
- 2.30	65	- 1:25	- 2.30	92	- 0:58	- 2.30	45	- 1:45	- 2.30	72	- 1:18
- 2.15	66	- 1:09	- 2.15	91	- 0:44	- 2.15	48	- 1:27	- 2.15	77	- 0:58
- 2.00	67	- 0:53	- 2.00	91	- 0:29	- 2.00	51	- 1:09	- 2.00	82	- 0:38
- 1.45	65	- 0:40	- 1.45	89	- 0:16	- 1.45	51	- 0:54	- 1.45	88	- 0:17
- 1.30	63	- 0:27	- 1.30	87	- 0:03	- 1.30	52	- 0:38	- 1.30	93	+ 0:03
- 1.15	61	- 0:14	- 1.15	86	+ 0:11	- 1.15	52	- 0:23	- 1.15	92	+ 0:17
- 1.00	59	- 0:01	- 1.00	84	+ 0:24	- 1.00	53	- 0:07	- 1.00	92	+ 0:32
- 0.45	56	+ 0:11	- 0.45	83	+ 0:38	- 0.45	52	+ 0:07	- 0.45	91	+ 0:46
- 0.30	54	+ 0:24	- 0.30	81	+ 0:51	- 0.30	51	+ 0:21	- 0.30	90	+ 1:00
- 0.15	51	+ 0:36	- 0.15	80	+ 1:05	- 0.15	50	+ 0:35	- 0.15	87	+ 1:12
HW	48	+ 0:48	HW	79	+ 1:19	HW	49	+ 0:49	HW	83	+ 1:23
+ 0.15	46	+ 1:01	+ 0.15	78	+ 1:33	+ 0.15	48	+ 1:03	+ 0.15	79	+ 1:34
+ 0.30	44	+ 1:14	+ 0.30	77	+ 1:47	+ 0.30	47	+ 1:17	+ 0.30	76	+ 1:46
+ 0.45	42	+ 1:27	+ 0.45	76	+ 2:01	+ 0.45	45	+ 1:30	+ 0.45	73	+ 1:58
+ 1.00	40	+ 1:40	+ 1.00	76	+ 2:16	+ 1.00	44	+ 1:44	+ 1.00	70	+ 2:10
+ 1.15	40	+ 1:55	+ 1.15	75	+ 2:30	+ 1.15	42	+ 1:57	+ 1.15	67	+ 2:22
+ 1.30	39	+ 2:09	+ 1.30	75	+ 2:45	+ 1.30	41	+ 2:11	+ 1.30	64	+ 2:34
+ 1.45	38	+ 2:23	+ 1.45	74	+ 2:59	+ 1.45	39	+ 2:24	+ 1.45	62	+ 2:47
+ 2.00	38	+ 2:38	+ 2.00	74	+ 3:14	+ 2.00	38	+ 2:38	+ 2.00	59	+ 2:59
+ 2.15	37	+ 2:52	+ 2.15	73	+ 3:28	+ 2.15	37	+ 2:52	+ 2.15	57	+ 3:12
+ 2.30	37	+ 3:07	+ 2.30	73	+ 3:43	+ 2.30	36	+ 3:06	+ 2.30	54	+ 3:24
+ 2.45	37	+ 3:22	+ 2.45	73	+ 3:58	+ 2.45	35	+ 3:20	+ 2.45	53	+ 3:38
+ 3.00	36	+ 3:36	+ 3.00	73	+ 4:13	+ 3.00	33	+ 3:33	+ 3.00	52	+ 3:52
+ 3.15	36	+ 3:51	+ 3.15	73	+ 4:28	+ 3.15	33	+ 3:48	+ 3.15	51	+ 4:06
+ 3.30	36	+ 4:06	+ 3.30	72	+ 4:42	+ 3.30	32	+ 4:02	+ 3.30	50	+ 4:20
+ 3.45	36	+ 4:21	+ 3.45	72	+ 4:57	+ 3.45	32	+ 4:17	+ 3.45	49	+ 4:34
+ 4.00	36	+ 4:36	+ 4.00	72	+ 5:12	+ 4.00	31	+ 4:31	+ 4.00	49	+ 4:49
+ 4.15	36	+ 4:51	+ 4.15	72	+ 5:27	+ 4.15	31	+ 4:46	+ 4.15	48	+ 5:03
+ 4.30	36	+ 5:06	+ 4.30	73	+ 5:43	+ 4.30	31	+ 5:01	+ 4.30	47	+ 5:17
+ 4.45	36	+ 5:21	+ 4.45	73	+ 5:58	+ 4.45	30	+ 5:15	+ 4.45	47	+ 5:32
+ 5.00	37	+ 5:37	+ 5.00	73	- 5:47	+ 5.00	30	+ 5:30	+ 5.00	46	+ 5:46
+ 5.15	38	+ 5:53	+ 5.15	74	- 5:31	+ 5.15	30	+ 5:45	+ 5.15	45	- 6:00
+ 5.30	39	- 5:51	+ 5.30	74	- 5:16	+ 5.30	30	- 6:00	+ 5.30	44	- 5:46
+ 5.45	40	- 5:35	+ 5.45	74	- 5:01	+ 5.45	30	- 5:45	+ 5.45	43	- 5:32
+ 6.00	41	- 5:19	+ 6.00	75	- 4:45	+ 6.00	29	- 5:31	+ 6.00	42	- 5:18

SOUTH BOUND

Table A - Blackwater to Ramsgate via SW Sunk

Neaps — All times relate to HW Sheerness — **Time to cover Sectors (in minutes) at 6.0 Kts**

SOUTHBOUND

Time	A8 Blackwater to Swin Spitway: Duration	A8: Time at End of Sector	Time	A7 Spitway to East Barrow Sands: Duration	A7: Time at End of Sector
- 6.00	92	- 4:28	- 6.00	48	- 5:12
- 5.45	93	- 4:12	- 5.45	49	- 4:56
- 5.30	95	- 3:55	- 5.30	49	- 4:41
- 5.15	96	- 3:39	- 5.15	50	- 4:25
- 5.00	98	- 3:22	- 5.00	51	- 4:09
- 4.45	98	- 3:07	- 4.45	51	- 3:54
- 4.30	99	- 2:51	- 4.30	51	- 3:39
- 4.15	99	- 2:36	- 4.15	51	- 3:24
- 4.00	100	- 2:20	- 4.00	51	- 3:09
- 3.45	100	- 2:05	- 3.45	51	- 2:54
- 3.30	100	- 1:50	- 3.30	51	- 2:39
- 3.15	100	- 1:35	- 3.15	51	- 2:24
- 3.00	100	- 1:20	- 3.00	51	- 2:09
- 2.45	99	- 1:06	- 2.45	51	- 1:54
- 2.30	98	- 0:52	- 2.30	50	- 1:40
- 2.15	97	- 0:38	- 2.15	50	- 1:25
- 2.00	95	- 0:25	- 2.00	49	- 1:11
- 1.45	92	- 0:13	- 1.45	48	- 0:57
- 1.30	89	- 0:01	- 1.30	48	- 0:42
- 1.15	85	+ 0:10	- 1.15	47	- 0:28
- 1.00	82	+ 0:22	- 1.00	46	- 0:14
- 0.45	80	+ 0:35	- 0.45	46	+ 0:01
- 0.30	78	+ 0:48	- 0.30	45	+ 0:15
- 0.15	75	+ 1:00	- 0.15	44	+ 0:29
HW	73	+ 1:13	HW	43	+ 0:43
+ 0.15	72	+ 1:27	+ 0.15	43	+ 0:58
+ 0.30	72	+ 1:42	+ 0.30	42	+ 1:12
+ 0.45	71	+ 1:56	+ 0.45	42	+ 1:27
+ 1.00	70	+ 2:10	+ 1.00	41	+ 1:41
+ 1.15	70	+ 2:25	+ 1.15	41	+ 1:56
+ 1.30	71	+ 2:41	+ 1.30	41	+ 2:11
+ 1.45	71	+ 2:56	+ 1.45	41	+ 2:26
+ 2.00	71	+ 3:11	+ 2.00	41	+ 2:41
+ 2.15	72	+ 3:27	+ 2.15	41	+ 2:56
+ 2.30	73	+ 3:43	+ 2.30	41	+ 3:11
+ 2.45	74	+ 3:59	+ 2.45	42	+ 3:27
+ 3.00	75	+ 4:15	+ 3.00	42	+ 3:42
+ 3.15	76	+ 4:31	+ 3.15	42	+ 3:57
+ 3.30	77	+ 4:47	+ 3.30	42	+ 4:12
+ 3.45	78	+ 5:03	+ 3.45	43	+ 4:28
+ 4.00	79	+ 5:19	+ 4.00	43	+ 4:43
+ 4.15	80	+ 5:35	+ 4.15	44	+ 4:59
+ 4.30	81	+ 5:51	+ 4.30	44	+ 5:14
+ 4.45	82	- 5:53	+ 4.45	44	+ 5:29
+ 5.00	83	- 5:37	+ 5.00	45	+ 5:45
+ 5.15	84	- 5:21	+ 5.15	45	- 6:00
+ 5.30	85	- 5:05	+ 5.30	46	- 5:44
+ 5.45	86	- 4:49	+ 5.45	46	- 5:29
+ 6.00	87	- 4:33	+ 6.00	46	- 5:14

Time	A6 East Barrow to SW Sunk: Duration	A6: Time at End of Sector	Time	A5 SW Sunk to Inner Fisherman: Duration	A5: Time at End of Sector
- 6.00	20	- 5:40	- 6.00	33	- 5:27
- 5.45	20	- 5:25	- 5.45	33	- 5:12
- 5.30	20	- 5:10	- 5.30	33	- 4:57
- 5.15	20	- 4:55	- 5.15	33	- 4:42
- 5.00	20	- 4:40	- 5.00	33	- 4:27
- 4.45	20	- 4:25	- 4.45	33	- 4:12
- 4.30	20	- 4:10	- 4.30	33	- 3:57
- 4.15	20	- 3:55	- 4.15	34	- 3:41
- 4.00	20	- 3:40	- 4.00	34	- 3:26
- 3.45	20	- 3:25	- 3.45	34	- 3:11
- 3.30	20	- 3:10	- 3.30	34	- 2:56
- 3.15	21	- 2:54	- 3.15	35	- 2:40
- 3.00	21	- 2:39	- 3.00	35	- 2:25
- 2.45	21	- 2:24	- 2.45	35	- 2:10
- 2.30	21	- 2:09	- 2.30	35	- 1:55
- 2.15	21	- 1:54	- 2.15	36	- 1:39
- 2.00	21	- 1:39	- 2.00	36	- 1:24
- 1.45	21	- 1:24	- 1.45	36	- 1:09
- 1.30	21	- 1:09	- 1.30	36	- 0:54
- 1.15	21	- 0:54	- 1.15	35	- 0:40
- 1.00	21	- 0:39	- 1.00	35	- 0:25
- 0.45	21	- 0:24	- 0.45	35	- 0:10
- 0.30	21	- 0:09	- 0.30	35	+ 0:05
- 0.15	21	+ 0:06	- 0.15	35	+ 0:20
HW	21	+ 0:21	HW	35	+ 0:35
+ 0.15	21	+ 0:36	+ 0.15	36	+ 0:51
+ 0.30	22	+ 0:52	+ 0.30	36	+ 1:06
+ 0.45	22	+ 1:07	+ 0.45	36	+ 1:21
+ 1.00	22	+ 1:22	+ 1.00	36	+ 1:36
+ 1.15	22	+ 1:37	+ 1.15	36	+ 1:51
+ 1.30	22	+ 1:52	+ 1.30	36	+ 2:06
+ 1.45	22	+ 2:07	+ 1.45	36	+ 2:21
+ 2.00	23	+ 2:23	+ 2.00	36	+ 2:36
+ 2.15	22	+ 2:37	+ 2.15	36	+ 2:51
+ 2.30	22	+ 2:52	+ 2.30	36	+ 3:06
+ 2.45	22	+ 3:07	+ 2.45	36	+ 3:21
+ 3.00	22	+ 3:22	+ 3.00	36	+ 3:36
+ 3.15	22	+ 3:37	+ 3.15	35	+ 3:50
+ 3.30	22	+ 3:52	+ 3.30	35	+ 4:05
+ 3.45	21	+ 4:06	+ 3.45	35	+ 4:20
+ 4.00	21	+ 4:21	+ 4.00	35	+ 4:35
+ 4.15	21	+ 4:36	+ 4.15	34	+ 4:49
+ 4.30	21	+ 4:51	+ 4.30	34	+ 5:04
+ 4.45	21	+ 5:06	+ 4.45	34	+ 5:19
+ 5.00	20	+ 5:20	+ 5.00	34	+ 5:34
+ 5.15	20	+ 5:35	+ 5.15	34	+ 5:49
+ 5.30	20	+ 5:50	+ 5.30	34	- 5:56
+ 5.45	20	- 5:55	+ 5.45	34	- 5:41
+ 6.00	20	- 5:40	+ 6.00	34	- 5:26

Time	A4 Inner to Outer Fisherman: Duration	A4: Time at End of Sector	Time	A3 Outer Fisherman to East Margate: Duration	A3: Time at End of Sector
- 6.00	37	- 5:23	- 6.00	63	- 4:57
- 5.45	38	- 5:07	- 5.45	63	- 4:42
- 5.30	39	- 4:51	- 5.30	64	- 4:26
- 5.15	40	- 4:35	- 5.15	64	- 4:11
- 5.00	40	- 4:20	- 5.00	64	- 3:56
- 4.45	41	- 4:04	- 4.45	65	- 3:40
- 4.30	41	- 3:49	- 4.30	66	- 3:24
- 4.15	42	- 3:33	- 4.15	67	- 3:08
- 4.00	42	- 3:18	- 4.00	67	- 2:53
- 3.45	43	- 3:02	- 3.45	68	- 2:37
- 3.30	43	- 2:47	- 3.30	68	- 2:22
- 3.15	44	- 2:31	- 3.15	69	- 2:06
- 3.00	45	- 2:15	- 3.00	70	- 1:50
- 2.45	45	- 2:00	- 2.45	70	- 1:35
- 2.30	46	- 1:44	- 2.30	70	- 1:20
- 2.15	47	- 1:28	- 2.15	70	- 1:05
- 2.00	47	- 1:13	- 2.00	70	- 0:50
- 1.45	47	- 0:58	- 1.45	69	- 0:36
- 1.30	46	- 0:44	- 1.30	69	- 0:21
- 1.15	45	- 0:30	- 1.15	68	- 0:07
- 1.00	45	- 0:15	- 1.00	67	+ 0:07
- 0.45	43	- 0:02	- 0.45	67	+ 0:22
- 0.30	42	+ 0:12	- 0.30	66	+ 0:36
- 0.15	41	+ 0:26	- 0.15	66	+ 0:51
HW	40	+ 0:40	HW	65	+ 1:05
+ 0.15	39	+ 0:54	+ 0.15	64	+ 1:19
+ 0.30	38	+ 1:08	+ 0.30	64	+ 1:34
+ 0.45	37	+ 1:22	+ 0.45	63	+ 1:48
+ 1.00	36	+ 1:36	+ 1.00	63	+ 2:03
+ 1.15	36	+ 1:51	+ 1.15	63	+ 2:18
+ 1.30	35	+ 2:05	+ 1.30	62	+ 2:32
+ 1.45	35	+ 2:20	+ 1.45	62	+ 2:47
+ 2.00	35	+ 2:35	+ 2.00	62	+ 3:02
+ 2.15	35	+ 2:50	+ 2.15	62	+ 3:17
+ 2.30	34	+ 3:04	+ 2.30	62	+ 3:32
+ 2.45	34	+ 3:19	+ 2.45	61	+ 3:46
+ 3.00	34	+ 3:34	+ 3.00	61	+ 4:01
+ 3.15	34	+ 3:49	+ 3.15	61	+ 4:16
+ 3.30	34	+ 4:04	+ 3.30	61	+ 4:31
+ 3.45	34	+ 4:19	+ 3.45	61	+ 4:46
+ 4.00	34	+ 4:34	+ 4.00	61	+ 5:01
+ 4.15	34	+ 4:49	+ 4.15	61	+ 5:16
+ 4.30	34	+ 5:04	+ 4.30	62	+ 5:32
+ 4.45	34	+ 5:19	+ 4.45	62	+ 5:47
+ 5.00	34	+ 5:34	+ 5.00	62	- 5:58
+ 5.15	34	+ 5:49	+ 5.15	62	- 5:43
+ 5.30	35	- 5:55	+ 5.30	63	- 5:27
+ 5.45	35	- 5:40	+ 5.45	63	- 5:12
+ 6.00	36	- 5:24	+ 6.00	63	- 4:57

Time	A2 East Margate to North Foreland: Duration	A2: Time at End of Sector	Time	A1 North Foreland to Ramsgate: Duration	A1: Time at End of Sector
- 6.00	27	- 5:33	- 6.00	41	- 5:19
- 5.45	27	- 5:18	- 5.45	40	- 5:05
- 5.30	27	- 5:03	- 5.30	40	- 4:50
- 5.15	27	- 4:48	- 5.15	40	- 4:35
- 5.00	27	- 4:33	- 5.00	40	- 4:20
- 4.45	27	- 4:18	- 4.45	40	- 4:05
- 4.30	28	- 4:02	- 4.30	40	- 3:50
- 4.15	28	- 3:47	- 4.15	41	- 3:34
- 4.00	28	- 3:32	- 4.00	42	- 3:18
- 3.45	29	- 3:16	- 3.45	43	- 3:02
- 3.30	29	- 3:01	- 3.30	44	- 2:46
- 3.15	30	- 2:45	- 3.15	46	- 2:29
- 3.00	31	- 2:29	- 3.00	48	- 2:12
- 2.45	32	- 2:13	- 2.45	50	- 1:55
- 2.30	33	- 1:57	- 2.30	52	- 1:38
- 2.15	34	- 1:41	- 2.15	53	- 1:22
- 2.00	35	- 1:25	- 2.00	54	- 1:06
- 1.45	35	- 1:10	- 1.45	55	- 0:50
- 1.30	36	- 0:54	- 1.30	56	- 0:34
- 1.15	36	- 0:39	- 1.15	56	- 0:19
- 1.00	36	- 0:24	- 1.00	56	- 0:04
- 0.45	36	- 0:09	- 0.45	56	+ 0:11
- 0.30	36	+ 0:06	- 0.30	56	+ 0:26
- 0.15	36	+ 0:21	- 0.15	56	+ 0:41
HW	35	+ 0:35	HW	55	+ 0:55
+ 0.15	35	+ 0:50	+ 0.15	55	+ 1:10
+ 0.30	34	+ 1:04	+ 0.30	55	+ 1:25
+ 0.45	34	+ 1:19	+ 0.45	54	+ 1:39
+ 1.00	33	+ 1:33	+ 1.00	52	+ 1:52
+ 1.15	33	+ 1:48	+ 1.15	51	+ 2:06
+ 1.30	32	+ 2:02	+ 1.30	50	+ 2:20
+ 1.45	32	+ 2:17	+ 1.45	49	+ 2:34
+ 2.00	31	+ 2:31	+ 2.00	48	+ 2:48
+ 2.15	30	+ 2:45	+ 2.15	48	+ 3:03
+ 2.30	30	+ 3:00	+ 2.30	47	+ 3:17
+ 2.45	29	+ 3:14	+ 2.45	46	+ 3:31
+ 3.00	29	+ 3:29	+ 3.00	45	+ 3:45
+ 3.15	29	+ 3:44	+ 3.15	45	+ 4:00
+ 3.30	28	+ 3:58	+ 3.30	44	+ 4:14
+ 3.45	28	+ 4:13	+ 3.45	44	+ 4:29
+ 4.00	28	+ 4:28	+ 4.00	43	+ 4:43
+ 4.15	28	+ 4:43	+ 4.15	43	+ 4:58
+ 4.30	28	+ 4:58	+ 4.30	42	+ 5:12
+ 4.45	28	+ 5:13	+ 4.45	42	+ 5:27
+ 5.00	28	+ 5:28	+ 5.00	42	+ 5:42
+ 5.15	27	+ 5:42	+ 5.15	42	+ 5:57
+ 5.30	27	+ 5:57	+ 5.30	42	- 5:48
+ 5.45	27	- 5:48	+ 5.45	41	- 5:34
+ 6.00	27	- 5:33	+ 6.00	41	- 5:19

Table A - Blackwater to Ramsgate via SW Sunk

Time to cover Sectors (in minutes) at 6.0 kts — All times relate to HW Sheerness — Springs

Time	A8 Blackwater to Swin Spitway Duration	A8 Time at End of Sector	Time	A7 Spitway to East Barrow Sands Duration	A7 Time at End of Sector	Time	A6 East Barrow to SW Sunk Duration	A6 Time at End of Sector	Time	A5 SW Sunk to Inner Fisherman Duration	A5 Time at End of Sector	Time	A4 Inner to Outer Fisherman Duration	A4 Time at End of Sector	Time	A3 Outer Fisherman to East Margate Duration	A3 Time at End of Sector	Time	A2 East Margate to North Foreland Duration	A2 Time at End of Sector	Time	A1 North Foreland to Ramsgate Duration	A1 Time at End of Sector
- 6.00	96	- 4:24	- 6.00	50	- 5:10	- 6.00	20	- 5:40	- 6.00	33	- 5:27	- 6.00	37	- 5:23	- 6.00	63	- 4:57	- 6.00	24	- 5:36	- 6.00	37	- 5:23
- 5.45	98	- 4:07	- 5.45	51	- 4:54	- 5.45	20	- 5:25	- 5.45	33	- 5:12	- 5.45	38	- 5:07	- 5.45	63	- 4:42	- 5.45	25	- 5:20	- 5.45	37	- 5:08
- 5.30	99	- 3:51	- 5.30	52	- 4:38	- 5.30	20	- 5:10	- 5.30	33	- 4:57	- 5.30	39	- 4:51	- 5.30	64	- 4:26	- 5.30	25	- 5:05	- 5.30	36	- 4:54
- 5.15	101	- 3:34	- 5.15	53	- 4:22	- 5.15	20	- 4:55	- 5.15	33	- 4:42	- 5.15	40	- 4:35	- 5.15	65	- 4:10	- 5.15	25	- 4:50	- 5.15	36	- 4:39
- 5.00	103	- 3:17	- 5.00	54	- 4:06	- 5.00	20	- 4:40	- 5.00	33	- 4:27	- 5.00	41	- 4:19	- 5.00	65	- 3:55	- 5.00	25	- 4:35	- 5.00	36	- 4:24
- 4.45	104	- 3:01	- 4.45	55	- 3:50	- 4.45	20	- 4:25	- 4.45	33	- 4:12	- 4.45	42	- 4:03	- 4.45	66	- 3:39	- 4.45	25	- 4:20	- 4.45	36	- 4:09
- 4.30	105	- 2:45	- 4.30	55	- 3:35	- 4.30	21	- 4:09	- 4.30	33	- 3:57	- 4.30	43	- 3:47	- 4.30	68	- 3:22	- 4.30	26	- 4:04	- 4.30	36	- 3:54
- 4.15	106	- 2:29	- 4.15	55	- 3:20	- 4.15	21	- 3:54	- 4.15	34	- 3:41	- 4.15	44	- 3:31	- 4.15	69	- 3:06	- 4.15	26	- 3:49	- 4.15	38	- 3:37
- 4.00	107	- 2:13	- 4.00	56	- 3:04	- 4.00	21	- 3:39	- 4.00	34	- 3:26	- 4.00	45	- 3:15	- 4.00	70	- 2:50	- 4.00	26	- 3:34	- 4.00	39	- 3:21
- 3.45	107	- 1:58	- 3.45	55	- 2:50	- 3.45	21	- 3:24	- 3.45	35	- 3:10	- 3.45	46	- 2:59	- 3.45	71	- 2:34	- 3.45	28	- 3:17	- 3.45	40	- 3:05
- 3.30	106	- 1:44	- 3.30	55	- 2:35	- 3.30	21	- 3:09	- 3.30	35	- 2:55	- 3.30	47	- 2:43	- 3.30	72	- 2:18	- 3.30	29	- 3:01	- 3.30	42	- 2:48
- 3.15	106	- 1:29	- 3.15	55	- 2:20	- 3.15	21	- 2:54	- 3.15	36	- 2:39	- 3.15	48	- 2:27	- 3.15	73	- 2:02	- 3.15	30	- 2:45	- 3.15	45	- 2:30
- 3.00	106	- 1:14	- 3.00	55	- 2:05	- 3.00	21	- 2:39	- 3.00	36	- 2:24	- 3.00	49	- 2:11	- 3.00	74	- 1:46	- 3.00	31	- 2:29	- 3.00	49	- 2:11
- 2.45	104	- 1:01	- 2.45	54	- 1:51	- 2.45	21	- 2:24	- 2.45	37	- 2:08	- 2.45	50	- 1:55	- 2.45	73	- 1:32	- 2.45	34	- 2:11	- 2.45	53	- 1:52
- 2.30	101	- 0:49	- 2.30	53	- 1:37	- 2.30	21	- 2:09	- 2.30	37	- 1:53	- 2.30	51	- 1:39	- 2.30	73	- 1:17	- 2.30	36	- 1:54	- 2.30	56	- 1:34
- 2.15	99	- 0:36	- 2.15	52	- 1:23	- 2.15	21	- 1:54	- 2.15	37	- 1:38	- 2.15	52	- 1:23	- 2.15	73	- 1:02	- 2.15	38	- 1:37	- 2.15	59	- 1:16
- 2.00	97	- 0:23	- 2.00	52	- 1:08	- 2.00	21	- 1:39	- 2.00	37	- 1:23	- 2.00	53	- 1:07	- 2.00	73	- 0:47	- 2.00	40	- 1:20	- 2.00	61	- 0:59
- 1.45	93	- 0:12	- 1.45	51	- 0:54	- 1.45	21	- 1:24	- 1.45	37	- 1:08	- 1.45	52	- 0:53	- 1.45	72	- 0:33	- 1.45	40	- 1:05	- 1.45	63	- 0:42
- 1.30	89	- 0:01	- 1.30	49	- 0:41	- 1.30	21	- 1:09	- 1.30	37	- 0:53	- 1.30	51	- 0:39	- 1.30	71	- 0:19	- 1.30	41	- 0:49	- 1.30	65	- 0:25
- 1.15	85	+ 0:10	- 1.15	48	- 0:27	- 1.15	21	- 0:54	- 1.15	36	- 0:39	- 1.15	50	- 0:25	- 1.15	70	- 0:05	- 1.15	41	- 0:34	- 1.15	65	- 0:10
- 1.00	81	+ 0:21	- 1.00	47	- 0:13	- 1.00	21	- 0:39	- 1.00	36	- 0:24	- 1.00	48	- 0:12	- 1.00	69	+ 0:09	- 1.00	42	- 0:18	- 1.00	65	+ 0:05
- 0.45	78	+ 0:33	- 0.45	46	+ 0:01	- 0.45	21	- 0:24	- 0.45	36	- 0:09	- 0.45	46	+ 0:01	- 0.45	68	+ 0:23	- 0.45	41	- 0:04	- 0.45	65	+ 0:20
- 0.30	74	+ 0:44	- 0.30	45	+ 0:15	- 0.30	21	- 0:09	- 0.30	36	+ 0:06	- 0.30	44	+ 0:14	- 0.30	67	+ 0:37	- 0.30	41	+ 0:11	- 0.30	65	+ 0:35
- 0.15	71	+ 0:56	- 0.15	44	+ 0:29	- 0.15	21	+ 0:06	- 0.15	36	+ 0:21	- 0.15	43	+ 0:28	- 0.15	66	+ 0:51	- 0.15	40	+ 0:25	- 0.15	64	+ 0:49
HW	68	+ 1:08	HW	43	+ 0:43	HW	21	+ 0:21	HW	36	+ 0:36	HW	41	+ 0:41	HW	65	+ 1:05	HW	40	+ 0:40	HW	63	+ 1:03
+ 0.15	67	+ 1:22	+ 0.15	42	+ 0:57	+ 0.15	22	+ 0:37	+ 0.15	37	+ 0:52	+ 0.15	39	+ 0:54	+ 0.15	65	+ 1:20	+ 0.15	39	+ 0:54	+ 0.15	62	+ 1:17
+ 0.30	66	+ 1:36	+ 0.30	41	+ 1:11	+ 0.30	22	+ 0:52	+ 0.30	37	+ 1:07	+ 0.30	38	+ 1:08	+ 0.30	64	+ 1:34	+ 0.30	38	+ 1:08	+ 0.30	61	+ 1:31
+ 0.45	65	+ 1:50	+ 0.45	41	+ 1:26	+ 0.45	23	+ 1:08	+ 0.45	37	+ 1:22	+ 0.45	36	+ 1:21	+ 0.45	64	+ 1:49	+ 0.45	37	+ 1:22	+ 0.45	59	+ 1:44
+ 1.00	64	+ 2:04	+ 1.00	40	+ 1:40	+ 1.00	23	+ 1:23	+ 1.00	37	+ 1:37	+ 1.00	35	+ 1:35	+ 1.00	63	+ 2:03	+ 1.00	36	+ 1:36	+ 1.00	57	+ 1:57
+ 1.15	64	+ 2:19	+ 1.15	40	+ 1:55	+ 1.15	23	+ 1:38	+ 1.15	37	+ 1:52	+ 1.15	34	+ 1:49	+ 1.15	63	+ 2:18	+ 1.15	35	+ 1:50	+ 1.15	55	+ 2:10
+ 1.30	65	+ 2:35	+ 1.30	40	+ 2:10	+ 1.30	23	+ 1:53	+ 1.30	37	+ 2:07	+ 1.30	34	+ 2:04	+ 1.30	62	+ 2:32	+ 1.30	34	+ 2:04	+ 1.30	53	+ 2:23
+ 1.45	65	+ 2:50	+ 1.45	40	+ 2:25	+ 1.45	24	+ 2:09	+ 1.45	38	+ 2:23	+ 1.45	33	+ 2:18	+ 1.45	62	+ 2:47	+ 1.45	33	+ 2:18	+ 1.45	51	+ 2:36
+ 2.00	66	+ 3:06	+ 2.00	39	+ 2:39	+ 2.00	24	+ 2:24	+ 2.00	38	+ 2:38	+ 2.00	33	+ 2:33	+ 2.00	61	+ 3:01	+ 2.00	32	+ 2:32	+ 2.00	50	+ 2:50
+ 2.15	67	+ 3:22	+ 2.15	40	+ 2:55	+ 2.15	24	+ 2:39	+ 2.15	37	+ 2:52	+ 2.15	32	+ 2:47	+ 2.15	61	+ 3:16	+ 2.15	31	+ 2:46	+ 2.15	48	+ 3:03
+ 2.30	69	+ 3:39	+ 2.30	40	+ 3:10	+ 2.30	24	+ 2:54	+ 2.30	37	+ 3:07	+ 2.30	32	+ 3:02	+ 2.30	61	+ 3:31	+ 2.30	30	+ 3:00	+ 2.30	46	+ 3:16
+ 2.45	70	+ 3:55	+ 2.45	40	+ 3:25	+ 2.45	23	+ 3:08	+ 2.45	37	+ 3:22	+ 2.45	32	+ 3:17	+ 2.45	61	+ 3:46	+ 2.45	29	+ 3:14	+ 2.45	45	+ 3:30
+ 3.00	71	+ 4:11	+ 3.00	40	+ 3:40	+ 3.00	23	+ 3:23	+ 3.00	37	+ 3:37	+ 3.00	32	+ 3:32	+ 3.00	61	+ 4:01	+ 3.00	28	+ 3:28	+ 3.00	44	+ 3:44
+ 3.15	72	+ 4:27	+ 3.15	41	+ 3:56	+ 3.15	23	+ 3:38	+ 3.15	36	+ 3:51	+ 3.15	32	+ 3:47	+ 3.15	61	+ 4:16	+ 3.15	28	+ 3:43	+ 3.15	43	+ 3:58
+ 3.30	73	+ 4:43	+ 3.30	41	+ 4:11	+ 3.30	22	+ 3:52	+ 3.30	36	+ 4:06	+ 3.30	31	+ 4:01	+ 3.30	61	+ 4:31	+ 3.30	27	+ 3:57	+ 3.30	43	+ 4:13
+ 3.45	75	+ 5:00	+ 3.45	42	+ 4:27	+ 3.45	22	+ 4:07	+ 3.45	36	+ 4:21	+ 3.45	31	+ 4:16	+ 3.45	60	+ 4:45	+ 3.45	27	+ 4:12	+ 3.45	42	+ 4:27
+ 4.00	76	+ 5:16	+ 4.00	42	+ 4:42	+ 4.00	22	+ 4:22	+ 4.00	35	+ 4:35	+ 4.00	31	+ 4:31	+ 4.00	60	+ 5:00	+ 4.00	26	+ 4:26	+ 4.00	42	+ 4:42
+ 4.15	78	+ 5:33	+ 4.15	43	+ 4:58	+ 4.15	21	+ 4:36	+ 4.15	35	+ 4:50	+ 4.15	31	+ 4:46	+ 4.15	61	+ 5:16	+ 4.15	26	+ 4:41	+ 4.15	42	+ 4:57
+ 4.30	79	+ 5:49	+ 4.30	43	+ 5:13	+ 4.30	21	+ 4:51	+ 4.30	34	+ 5:04	+ 4.30	31	+ 5:01	+ 4.30	61	+ 5:31	+ 4.30	26	+ 4:56	+ 4.30	41	+ 5:11
+ 4.45	81	- 5:54	+ 4.45	44	+ 5:29	+ 4.45	21	+ 5:06	+ 4.45	34	+ 5:19	+ 4.45	31	+ 5:16	+ 4.45	61	+ 5:46	+ 4.45	26	+ 5:11	+ 4.45	41	+ 5:26
+ 5.00	83	- 5:37	+ 5.00	44	+ 5:44	+ 5.00	21	+ 5:21	+ 5.00	34	+ 5:34	+ 5.00	31	+ 5:31	+ 5.00	61	- 5:59	+ 5.00	25	+ 5:25	+ 5.00	40	+ 5:40
+ 5.15	84	- 5:21	+ 5.15	45	- 6:00	+ 5.15	20	+ 5:35	+ 5.15	34	+ 5:49	+ 5.15	32	+ 5:47	+ 5.15	62	- 5:43	+ 5.15	25	+ 5:40	+ 5.15	39	+ 5:54
+ 5.30	85	- 5:05	+ 5.30	46	- 5:44	+ 5.30	20	+ 5:50	+ 5.30	34	- 5:56	+ 5.30	33	- 5:57	+ 5.30	62	- 5:28	+ 5.30	25	+ 5:55	+ 5.30	39	- 5:51
+ 5.45	87	- 4:48	+ 5.45	46	- 5:29	+ 5.45	20	- 5:55	+ 5.45	34	- 5:41	+ 5.45	34	- 5:41	+ 5.45	62	- 5:13	+ 5.45	25	- 5:50	+ 5.45	38	- 5:37
+ 6.00	88	- 4:32	+ 6.00	47	- 5:13	+ 6.00	20	- 5:40	+ 6.00	34	- 5:26	+ 6.00	35	- 5:25	+ 6.00	62	- 4:58	+ 6.00	24	- 5:36	+ 6.00	37	- 5:23

SOUTH BOUND

A - 7 Kts

Table A - Blackwater to Ramsgate via SW Sunk

7 Kts - A

Neaps — All times relate to HW Sheerness — **Time to cover Sectors (in minutes) at 7.0 Kts**

SOUTH BOUND

Time	A8 Blackwater to Swin Spitway Duration	A8 Time at End of Sector	Time	A7 Spitway to East Barrow Sands Duration	A7 Time at End of Sector	Time	A6 East Barrow to SW Sunk Duration	A6 Time at End of Sector	Time	A5 SW Sunk to Inner Fisherman Duration	A5 Time at End of Sector
- 6.00	77	- 4:43	- 6.00	41	- 5:19	- 6.00	17	- 5:43	- 6.00	29	- 5:31
- 5.45	77	- 4:28	- 5.45	41	- 5:04	- 5.45	17	- 5:28	- 5.45	29	- 5:16
- 5.30	78	- 4:12	- 5.30	42	- 4:48	- 5.30	17	- 5:13	- 5.30	29	- 5:01
- 5.15	79	- 3:56	- 5.15	42	- 4:33	- 5.15	17	- 4:58	- 5.15	28	- 4:47
- 5.00	80	- 3:40	- 5.00	43	- 4:17	- 5.00	17	- 4:43	- 5.00	28	- 4:32
- 4.45	80	- 3:25	- 4.45	43	- 4:02	- 4.45	17	- 4:28	- 4.45	28	- 4:17
- 4.30	80	- 3:10	- 4.30	43	- 3:47	- 4.30	17	- 4:13	- 4.30	28	- 4:02
- 4.15	81	- 2:54	- 4.15	43	- 3:32	- 4.15	17	- 3:58	- 4.15	29	- 3:46
- 4.00	81	- 2:39	- 4.00	43	- 3:17	- 4.00	17	- 3:43	- 4.00	29	- 3:31
- 3.45	81	- 2:24	- 3.45	43	- 3:02	- 3.45	17	- 3:28	- 3.45	29	- 3:16
- 3.30	81	- 2:09	- 3.30	43	- 2:47	- 3.30	17	- 3:13	- 3.30	29	- 3:01
- 3.15	81	- 1:54	- 3.15	43	- 2:32	- 3.15	18	- 2:57	- 3.15	29	- 2:46
- 3.00	81	- 1:39	- 3.00	43	- 2:17	- 3.00	18	- 2:42	- 3.00	30	- 2:30
- 2.45	81	- 1:24	- 2.45	43	- 2:02	- 2.45	18	- 2:27	- 2.45	30	- 2:15
- 2.30	80	- 1:10	- 2.30	42	- 1:48	- 2.30	18	- 2:12	- 2.30	30	- 2:00
- 2.15	79	- 0:56	- 2.15	42	- 1:33	- 2.15	18	- 1:57	- 2.15	30	- 1:45
- 2.00	79	- 0:41	- 2.00	42	- 1:18	- 2.00	18	- 1:42	- 2.00	30	- 1:30
- 1.45	77	- 0:28	- 1.45	41	- 1:04	- 1.45	18	- 1:27	- 1.45	30	- 1:15
- 1.30	75	- 0:15	- 1.30	41	- 0:49	- 1.30	18	- 1:12	- 1.30	30	- 1:00
- 1.15	73	- 0:02	- 1.15	40	- 0:35	- 1.15	18	- 0:57	- 1.15	30	- 0:45
- 1.00	71	+ 0:11	- 1.00	40	- 0:20	- 1.00	18	- 0:42	- 1.00	30	- 0:30
- 0.45	69	+ 0:24	- 0.45	39	- 0:06	- 0.45	18	- 0:27	- 0.45	30	- 0:15
- 0.30	68	+ 0:38	- 0.30	39	+ 0:09	- 0.30	18	- 0:12	- 0.30	30	HW
- 0.15	66	+ 0:51	- 0.15	38	+ 0:23	- 0.15	18	+ 0:03	- 0.15	30	+ 0:15
HW	64	+ 1:04	HW	38	+ 0:38	HW	18	+ 0:18	HW	30	+ 0:30
+ 0.15	64	+ 1:19	+ 0.15	37	+ 0:52	+ 0.15	18	+ 0:33	+ 0.15	30	+ 0:45
+ 0.30	63	+ 1:33	+ 0.30	37	+ 1:07	+ 0.30	18	+ 0:48	+ 0.30	30	+ 1:00
+ 0.45	62	+ 1:47	+ 0.45	36	+ 1:21	+ 0.45	19	+ 1:04	+ 0.45	30	+ 1:15
+ 1.00	62	+ 2:02	+ 1.00	36	+ 1:36	+ 1.00	19	+ 1:19	+ 1.00	30	+ 1:30
+ 1.15	62	+ 2:17	+ 1.15	36	+ 1:51	+ 1.15	19	+ 1:34	+ 1.15	30	+ 1:45
+ 1.30	62	+ 2:32	+ 1.30	36	+ 2:06	+ 1.30	19	+ 1:49	+ 1.30	30	+ 2:00
+ 1.45	62	+ 2:47	+ 1.45	36	+ 2:21	+ 1.45	19	+ 2:04	+ 1.45	30	+ 2:15
+ 2.00	62	+ 3:02	+ 2.00	36	+ 2:36	+ 2.00	19	+ 2:19	+ 2.00	30	+ 2:30
+ 2.15	63	+ 3:18	+ 2.15	36	+ 2:51	+ 2.15	19	+ 2:34	+ 2.15	30	+ 2:45
+ 2.30	64	+ 3:34	+ 2.30	36	+ 3:06	+ 2.30	19	+ 2:49	+ 2.30	30	+ 3:00
+ 2.45	65	+ 3:50	+ 2.45	36	+ 3:21	+ 2.45	19	+ 3:04	+ 2.45	30	+ 3:15
+ 3.00	65	+ 4:05	+ 3.00	36	+ 3:36	+ 3.00	19	+ 3:19	+ 3.00	30	+ 3:30
+ 3.15	66	+ 4:21	+ 3.15	36	+ 3:51	+ 3.15	19	+ 3:34	+ 3.15	30	+ 3:45
+ 3.30	67	+ 4:37	+ 3.30	37	+ 4:07	+ 3.30	18	+ 3:48	+ 3.30	30	+ 4:00
+ 3.45	67	+ 4:52	+ 3.45	37	+ 4:22	+ 3.45	18	+ 4:03	+ 3.45	30	+ 4:15
+ 4.00	68	+ 5:08	+ 4.00	37	+ 4:37	+ 4.00	18	+ 4:18	+ 4.00	30	+ 4:30
+ 4.15	69	+ 5:24	+ 4.15	37	+ 4:52	+ 4.15	18	+ 4:33	+ 4.15	30	+ 4:45
+ 4.30	69	+ 5:39	+ 4.30	38	+ 5:08	+ 4.30	18	+ 4:48	+ 4.30	29	+ 4:59
+ 4.45	70	+ 5:55	+ 4.45	38	+ 5:23	+ 4.45	18	+ 5:03	+ 4.45	29	+ 5:14
+ 5.00	71	- 5:49	+ 5.00	38	+ 5:38	+ 5.00	17	+ 5:17	+ 5.00	29	+ 5:29
+ 5.15	72	- 5:33	+ 5.15	39	+ 5:54	+ 5.15	17	+ 5:32	+ 5.15	29	+ 5:44
+ 5.30	72	- 5:18	+ 5.30	39	- 5:51	+ 5.30	17	+ 5:47	+ 5.30	29	+ 5:59
+ 5.45	73	- 5:02	+ 5.45	39	- 5:36	+ 5.45	17	- 5:58	+ 5.45	29	- 5:46
+ 6.00	74	- 4:46	+ 6.00	40	- 5:20	+ 6.00	17	- 5:43	+ 6.00	29	- 5:31

Time	A4 Inner to Outer Fisherman Duration	A4 Time at End of Sector	Time	A3 Outer Fisherman to East Margate Duration	A3 Time at End of Sector	Time	A2 East Margate to North Foreland Duration	A2 Time at End of Sector	Time	A1 North Foreland to Ramsgate Duration	A1 Time at End of Sector
- 6.00	32	- 5:28	- 6.00	54	- 5:06	- 6.00	23	- 5:37	- 6.00	36	- 5:24
- 5.45	32	- 5:13	- 5.45	54	- 4:51	- 5.45	23	- 5:22	- 5.45	35	- 5:10
- 5.30	33	- 4:57	- 5.30	54	- 4:36	- 5.30	23	- 5:07	- 5.30	35	- 4:55
- 5.15	34	- 4:41	- 5.15	55	- 4:20	- 5.15	23	- 4:52	- 5.15	35	- 4:40
- 5.00	34	- 4:26	- 5.00	55	- 4:05	- 5.00	23	- 4:37	- 5.00	35	- 4:25
- 4.45	34	- 4:11	- 4.45	55	- 3:50	- 4.45	23	- 4:22	- 4.45	35	- 4:10
- 4.30	35	- 3:55	- 4.30	56	- 3:34	- 4.30	24	- 4:06	- 4.30	35	- 3:55
- 4.15	35	- 3:40	- 4.15	56	- 3:19	- 4.15	24	- 3:51	- 4.15	36	- 3:39
- 4.00	36	- 3:24	- 4.00	57	- 3:03	- 4.00	24	- 3:36	- 4.00	36	- 3:24
- 3.45	36	- 3:09	- 3.45	57	- 2:48	- 3.45	25	- 3:20	- 3.45	37	- 3:08
- 3.30	36	- 2:54	- 3.30	58	- 2:32	- 3.30	25	- 3:05	- 3.30	38	- 2:52
- 3.15	37	- 2:38	- 3.15	58	- 2:17	- 3.15	26	- 2:49	- 3.15	39	- 2:36
- 3.00	37	- 2:23	- 3.00	59	- 2:01	- 3.00	26	- 2:34	- 3.00	41	- 2:19
- 2.45	38	- 2:07	- 2.45	59	- 1:46	- 2.45	27	- 2:18	- 2.45	42	- 2:03
- 2.30	38	- 1:52	- 2.30	59	- 1:31	- 2.30	28	- 2:02	- 2.30	44	- 1:46
- 2.15	39	- 1:36	- 2.15	59	- 1:16	- 2.15	28	- 1:47	- 2.15	44	- 1:31
- 2.00	40	- 1:20	- 2.00	59	- 1:01	- 2.00	29	- 1:31	- 2.00	45	- 1:15
- 1.45	39	- 1:06	- 1.45	59	- 0:46	- 1.45	30	- 1:15	- 1.45	46	- 0:59
- 1.30	39	- 0:51	- 1.30	58	- 0:32	- 1.30	30	- 1:00	- 1.30	47	- 0:43
- 1.15	38	- 0:37	- 1.15	58	- 0:17	- 1.15	30	- 0:45	- 1.15	47	- 0:28
- 1.00	38	- 0:22	- 1.00	57	- 0:03	- 1.00	31	- 0:29	- 1.00	47	- 0:13
- 0.45	37	- 0:08	- 0.45	57	+ 0:12	- 0.45	30	- 0:15	- 0.45	47	+ 0:02
- 0.30	36	+ 0:06	- 0.30	57	+ 0:27	- 0.30	30	HW	- 0.30	47	+ 0:17
- 0.15	35	+ 0:20	- 0.15	56	+ 0:41	- 0.15	30	+ 0:15	- 0.15	47	+ 0:32
HW	35	+ 0:35	HW	56	+ 0:56	HW	30	+ 0:30	HW	46	+ 0:46
+ 0.15	34	+ 0:49	+ 0.15	55	+ 1:10	+ 0.15	29	+ 0:44	+ 0.15	46	+ 1:01
+ 0.30	33	+ 1:03	+ 0.30	55	+ 1:25	+ 0.30	29	+ 0:59	+ 0.30	46	+ 1:16
+ 0.45	32	+ 1:17	+ 0.45	54	+ 1:39	+ 0.45	29	+ 1:14	+ 0.45	45	+ 1:30
+ 1.00	31	+ 1:31	+ 1.00	54	+ 1:54	+ 1.00	29	+ 1:29	+ 1.00	45	+ 1:45
+ 1.15	31	+ 1:46	+ 1.15	54	+ 2:09	+ 1.15	28	+ 1:43	+ 1.15	44	+ 1:59
+ 1.30	31	+ 2:01	+ 1.30	54	+ 2:24	+ 1.30	28	+ 1:58	+ 1.30	43	+ 2:13
+ 1.45	31	+ 2:16	+ 1.45	53	+ 2:38	+ 1.45	27	+ 2:12	+ 1.45	42	+ 2:27
+ 2.00	30	+ 2:30	+ 2.00	53	+ 2:53	+ 2.00	26	+ 2:26	+ 2.00	42	+ 2:42
+ 2.15	30	+ 2:45	+ 2.15	53	+ 3:08	+ 2.15	26	+ 2:41	+ 2.15	41	+ 2:56
+ 2.30	30	+ 3:00	+ 2.30	53	+ 3:23	+ 2.30	26	+ 2:56	+ 2.30	40	+ 3:10
+ 2.45	30	+ 3:15	+ 2.45	53	+ 3:38	+ 2.45	25	+ 3:10	+ 2.45	40	+ 3:25
+ 3.00	30	+ 3:30	+ 3.00	53	+ 3:53	+ 3.00	25	+ 3:25	+ 3.00	39	+ 3:39
+ 3.15	30	+ 3:45	+ 3.15	53	+ 4:08	+ 3.15	25	+ 3:40	+ 3.15	39	+ 3:54
+ 3.30	30	+ 4:00	+ 3.30	53	+ 4:23	+ 3.30	24	+ 3:54	+ 3.30	38	+ 4:08
+ 3.45	29	+ 4:14	+ 3.45	53	+ 4:38	+ 3.45	24	+ 4:09	+ 3.45	38	+ 4:23
+ 4.00	29	+ 4:29	+ 4.00	53	+ 4:53	+ 4.00	24	+ 4:24	+ 4.00	38	+ 4:38
+ 4.15	29	+ 4:44	+ 4.15	53	+ 5:08	+ 4.15	24	+ 4:39	+ 4.15	37	+ 4:52
+ 4.30	29	+ 4:59	+ 4.30	53	+ 5:23	+ 4.30	24	+ 4:54	+ 4.30	37	+ 5:07
+ 4.45	29	+ 5:14	+ 4.45	53	+ 5:38	+ 4.45	24	+ 5:09	+ 4.45	37	+ 5:22
+ 5.00	29	+ 5:29	+ 5.00	53	+ 5:53	+ 5.00	24	+ 5:24	+ 5.00	37	+ 5:37
+ 5.15	30	+ 5:45	+ 5.15	53	- 5:52	+ 5.15	23	+ 5:38	+ 5.15	37	+ 5:52
+ 5.30	30	- 6:00	+ 5.30	54	- 5:36	+ 5.30	23	+ 5:53	+ 5.30	37	- 5:53
+ 5.45	31	- 5:44	+ 5.45	54	- 5:21	+ 5.45	23	- 5:52	+ 5.45	36	- 5:39
+ 6.00	31	- 5:29	+ 6.00	54	- 5:06	+ 6.00	23	- 5:37	+ 6.00	36	- 5:24

A - 7 Kts   Table A - Blackwater to Ramsgate via SW Sunk   7 Kts - A

Time to cover Sectors (in minutes) at 7.0 kts — All times relate to HW Sheerness — **Springs**

SOUTH BOUND

A8 — Blackwater to Swin Spitway

Time	Duration	Time at End of Sector
- 6.00	79	- 4:41
- 5.45	80	- 4:25
- 5.30	81	- 4:09
- 5.15	83	- 3:52
- 5.00	84	- 3:36
- 4.45	84	- 3:21
- 4.30	85	- 3:05
- 4.15	86	- 2:49
- 4.00	86	- 2:34
- 3.45	86	- 2:19
- 3.30	87	- 2:03
- 3.15	87	- 1:48
- 3.00	87	- 1:33
- 2.45	86	- 1:19
- 2.30	85	- 1:05
- 2.15	84	- 0:51
- 2.00	82	- 0:38
- 1.45	79	- 0:26
- 1.30	76	- 0:14
- 1.15	73	- 0:02
- 1.00	70	+ 0:10
- 0.45	68	+ 0:23
- 0.30	65	+ 0:35
- 0.15	63	+ 0:48
HW	61	+ 1:01
+ 0.15	60	+ 1:15
+ 0.30	59	+ 1:29
+ 0.45	58	+ 1:43
+ 1.00	57	+ 1:57
+ 1.15	57	+ 2:12
+ 1.30	58	+ 2:28
+ 1.45	58	+ 2:43
+ 2.00	58	+ 2:58
+ 2.15	59	+ 3:14
+ 2.30	60	+ 3:30
+ 2.45	61	+ 3:46
+ 3.00	62	+ 4:02
+ 3.15	63	+ 4:18
+ 3.30	64	+ 4:34
+ 3.45	65	+ 4:50
+ 4.00	66	+ 5:06
+ 4.15	67	+ 5:22
+ 4.30	68	+ 5:38
+ 4.45	69	+ 5:54
+ 5.00	71	- 5:49
+ 5.15	72	- 5:33
+ 5.30	73	- 5:17
+ 5.45	74	- 5:01
+ 6.00	75	- 4:45

A7 — Spitway to East Barrow Sands

Time	Duration	Time at End of Sector
- 6.00	42	- 5:18
- 5.45	42	- 5:03
- 5.30	43	- 4:47
- 5.15	44	- 4:31
- 5.00	45	- 4:15
- 4.45	45	- 4:00
- 4.30	46	- 3:44
- 4.15	46	- 3:29
- 4.00	47	- 3:13
- 3.45	46	- 2:59
- 3.30	46	- 2:44
- 3.15	46	- 2:29
- 3.00	46	- 2:14
- 2.45	45	- 2:00
- 2.30	45	- 1:45
- 2.15	44	- 1:31
- 2.00	44	- 1:16
- 1.45	43	- 1:02
- 1.30	42	- 0:48
- 1.15	41	- 0:34
- 1.00	40	- 0:20
- 0.45	40	- 0:05
- 0.30	39	+ 0:09
- 0.15	38	+ 0:23
HW	37	+ 0:37
+ 0.15	36	+ 0:51
+ 0.30	36	+ 1:06
+ 0.45	35	+ 1:20
+ 1.00	35	+ 1:35
+ 1.15	35	+ 1:50
+ 1.30	34	+ 2:04
+ 1.45	34	+ 2:19
+ 2.00	34	+ 2:34
+ 2.15	34	+ 2:49
+ 2.30	35	+ 3:05
+ 2.45	35	+ 3:20
+ 3.00	35	+ 3:35
+ 3.15	35	+ 3:50
+ 3.30	36	+ 4:06
+ 3.45	36	+ 4:21
+ 4.00	36	+ 4:36
+ 4.15	37	+ 4:52
+ 4.30	37	+ 5:07
+ 4.45	37	+ 5:22
+ 5.00	38	+ 5:38
+ 5.15	38	+ 5:53
+ 5.30	39	- 5:51
+ 5.45	39	- 5:36
+ 6.00	40	- 5:20

A6 — East Barrow to SW Sunk

Time	Duration	Time at End of Sector
- 6.00	17	- 5:43
- 5.45	17	- 5:28
- 5.30	17	- 5:13
- 5.15	17	- 4:58
- 5.00	17	- 4:43
- 4.45	17	- 4:28
- 4.30	18	- 4:12
- 4.15	18	- 3:57
- 4.00	18	- 3:42
- 3.45	18	- 3:27
- 3.30	18	- 3:12
- 3.15	18	- 2:57
- 3.00	18	- 2:42
- 2.45	18	- 2:27
- 2.30	18	- 2:12
- 2.15	18	- 1:57
- 2.00	18	- 1:42
- 1.45	18	- 1:27
- 1.30	18	- 1:12
- 1.15	18	- 0:57
- 1.00	18	- 0:42
- 0.45	18	- 0:27
- 0.30	18	- 0:12
- 0.15	18	+ 0:03
HW	18	+ 0:18
+ 0.15	19	+ 0:34
+ 0.30	19	+ 0:49
+ 0.45	19	+ 1:04
+ 1.00	20	+ 1:20
+ 1.15	20	+ 1:35
+ 1.30	20	+ 1:50
+ 1.45	20	+ 2:05
+ 2.00	21	+ 2:21
+ 2.15	20	+ 2:35
+ 2.30	20	+ 2:50
+ 2.45	20	+ 3:05
+ 3.00	20	+ 3:20
+ 3.15	19	+ 3:34
+ 3.30	19	+ 3:49
+ 3.45	19	+ 4:04
+ 4.00	19	+ 4:19
+ 4.15	18	+ 4:33
+ 4.30	18	+ 4:48
+ 4.45	18	+ 5:03
+ 5.00	18	+ 5:18
+ 5.15	17	+ 5:32
+ 5.30	17	+ 5:47
+ 5.45	17	- 5:58
+ 6.00	17	- 5:43

A5 — SW Sunk to Inner Fisherman

Time	Duration	Time at End of Sector
- 6.00	28	- 5:32
- 5.45	28	- 5:17
- 5.30	28	- 5:02
- 5.15	28	- 4:47
- 5.00	28	- 4:32
- 4.45	28	- 4:17
- 4.30	28	- 4:02
- 4.15	29	- 3:46
- 4.00	29	- 3:31
- 3.45	29	- 3:16
- 3.30	30	- 3:00
- 3.15	30	- 2:45
- 3.00	31	- 2:29
- 2.45	31	- 2:14
- 2.30	31	- 1:59
- 2.15	31	- 1:44
- 2.00	31	- 1:29
- 1.45	31	- 1:14
- 1.30	31	- 0:59
- 1.15	31	- 0:44
- 1.00	31	- 0:29
- 0.45	31	- 0:14
- 0.30	31	+ 0:01
- 0.15	31	+ 0:16
HW	31	+ 0:31
+ 0.15	31	+ 0:46
+ 0.30	31	+ 1:01
+ 0.45	31	+ 1:16
+ 1.00	31	+ 1:31
+ 1.15	31	+ 1:46
+ 1.30	31	+ 2:01
+ 1.45	32	+ 2:17
+ 2.00	32	+ 2:32
+ 2.15	31	+ 2:46
+ 2.30	31	+ 3:01
+ 2.45	31	+ 3:16
+ 3.00	31	+ 3:31
+ 3.15	31	+ 3:46
+ 3.30	31	+ 4:01
+ 3.45	30	+ 4:15
+ 4.00	30	+ 4:30
+ 4.15	30	+ 4:45
+ 4.30	29	+ 4:59
+ 4.45	29	+ 5:14
+ 5.00	29	+ 5:29
+ 5.15	29	+ 5:44
+ 5.30	29	+ 5:59
+ 5.45	29	- 5:46
+ 6.00	29	- 5:31

A4 — Inner to Outer Fisherman

Time	Duration	Time at End of Sector
- 6.00	31	- 5:29
- 5.45	32	- 5:13
- 5.30	33	- 4:57
- 5.15	34	- 4:41
- 5.00	35	- 4:25
- 4.45	35	- 4:10
- 4.30	36	- 3:54
- 4.15	37	- 3:38
- 4.00	37	- 3:23
- 3.45	38	- 3:07
- 3.30	39	- 2:51
- 3.15	40	- 2:35
- 3.00	41	- 2:19
- 2.45	41	- 2:04
- 2.30	42	- 1:48
- 2.15	43	- 1:32
- 2.00	44	- 1:16
- 1.45	43	- 1:02
- 1.30	42	- 0:48
- 1.15	42	- 0:33
- 1.00	41	- 0:19
- 0.45	39	- 0:06
- 0.30	38	+ 0:08
- 0.15	37	+ 0:22
HW	35	+ 0:35
+ 0.15	34	+ 0:49
+ 0.30	33	+ 1:03
+ 0.45	32	+ 1:17
+ 1.00	31	+ 1:31
+ 1.15	30	+ 1:45
+ 1.30	30	+ 2:00
+ 1.45	29	+ 2:14
+ 2.00	29	+ 2:29
+ 2.15	28	+ 2:43
+ 2.30	28	+ 2:58
+ 2.45	28	+ 3:13
+ 3.00	28	+ 3:28
+ 3.15	28	+ 3:43
+ 3.30	27	+ 3:57
+ 3.45	27	+ 4:12
+ 4.00	27	+ 4:27
+ 4.15	27	+ 4:42
+ 4.30	27	+ 4:57
+ 4.45	27	+ 5:12
+ 5.00	27	+ 5:27
+ 5.15	28	+ 5:43
+ 5.30	28	+ 5:58
+ 5.45	29	- 5:46
+ 6.00	30	- 5:30

A3 — Outer Fisherman to East Margate

Time	Duration	Time at End of Sector
- 6.00	54	- 5:06
- 5.45	54	- 4:51
- 5.30	55	- 4:35
- 5.15	55	- 4:20
- 5.00	55	- 4:05
- 4.45	56	- 3:49
- 4.30	57	- 3:33
- 4.15	58	- 3:17
- 4.00	59	- 3:01
- 3.45	59	- 2:46
- 3.30	60	- 2:30
- 3.15	61	- 2:14
- 3.00	62	- 1:58
- 2.45	61	- 1:44
- 2.30	61	- 1:29
- 2.15	61	- 1:14
- 2.00	61	- 0:59
- 1.45	61	- 0:44
- 1.30	60	- 0:30
- 1.15	59	- 0:16
- 1.00	59	- 0:01
- 0.45	58	+ 0:13
- 0.30	57	+ 0:27
- 0.15	57	+ 0:42
HW	56	+ 0:56
+ 0.15	55	+ 1:10
+ 0.30	55	+ 1:25
+ 0.45	54	+ 1:39
+ 1.00	54	+ 1:54
+ 1.15	54	+ 2:09
+ 1.30	53	+ 2:23
+ 1.45	53	+ 2:38
+ 2.00	53	+ 2:53
+ 2.15	53	+ 3:08
+ 2.30	52	+ 3:22
+ 2.45	52	+ 3:37
+ 3.00	52	+ 3:52
+ 3.15	52	+ 4:07
+ 3.30	52	+ 4:22
+ 3.45	52	+ 4:37
+ 4.00	52	+ 4:52
+ 4.15	52	+ 5:07
+ 4.30	52	+ 5:22
+ 4.45	53	+ 5:38
+ 5.00	53	+ 5:53
+ 5.15	53	- 5:52
+ 5.30	53	- 5:37
+ 5.45	53	- 5:22
+ 6.00	54	- 5:06

A2 — East Margate to North Foreland

Time	Duration	Time at End of Sector
- 6.00	21	- 5:39
- 5.45	21	- 5:24
- 5.30	21	- 5:09
- 5.15	21	- 4:54
- 5.00	21	- 4:39
- 4.45	22	- 4:23
- 4.30	22	- 4:08
- 4.15	22	- 3:53
- 4.00	23	- 3:37
- 3.45	24	- 3:21
- 3.30	25	- 3:05
- 3.15	26	- 2:49
- 3.00	27	- 2:33
- 2.45	28	- 2:17
- 2.30	29	- 2:01
- 2.15	31	- 1:44
- 2.00	32	- 1:28
- 1.45	33	- 1:12
- 1.30	34	- 0:56
- 1.15	34	- 0:41
- 1.00	35	- 0:25
- 0.45	34	- 0:11
- 0.30	34	+ 0:04
- 0.15	34	+ 0:19
HW	33	+ 0:33
+ 0.15	32	+ 0:47
+ 0.30	32	+ 1:02
+ 0.45	31	+ 1:16
+ 1.00	30	+ 1:30
+ 1.15	30	+ 1:45
+ 1.30	29	+ 1:59
+ 1.45	28	+ 2:13
+ 2.00	27	+ 2:27
+ 2.15	26	+ 2:41
+ 2.30	26	+ 2:56
+ 2.45	25	+ 3:10
+ 3.00	24	+ 3:24
+ 3.15	24	+ 3:39
+ 3.30	23	+ 3:53
+ 3.45	23	+ 4:08
+ 4.00	22	+ 4:22
+ 4.15	22	+ 4:37
+ 4.30	22	+ 4:52
+ 4.45	22	+ 5:07
+ 5.00	22	+ 5:22
+ 5.15	21	+ 5:36
+ 5.30	21	+ 5:51
+ 5.45	21	- 5:54
+ 6.00	21	- 5:39

A1 — North Foreland to Ramsgate

Time	Duration	Time at End of Sector
- 6.00	33	- 5:27
- 5.45	33	- 5:12
- 5.30	32	- 4:58
- 5.15	32	- 4:43
- 5.00	32	- 4:28
- 4.45	32	- 4:13
- 4.30	32	- 3:58
- 4.15	33	- 3:42
- 4.00	34	- 3:26
- 3.45	34	- 3:11
- 3.30	35	- 2:55
- 3.15	38	- 2:37
- 3.00	41	- 2:19
- 2.45	44	- 2:01
- 2.30	46	- 1:44
- 2.15	48	- 1:27
- 2.00	50	- 1:10
- 1.45	52	- 0:53
- 1.30	54	- 0:36
- 1.15	53	- 0:22
- 1.00	53	- 0:07
- 0.45	53	+ 0:08
- 0.30	53	+ 0:23
- 0.15	53	+ 0:38
HW	52	+ 0:52
+ 0.15	51	+ 1:06
+ 0.30	51	+ 1:21
+ 0.45	49	+ 1:34
+ 1.00	48	+ 1:48
+ 1.15	47	+ 2:02
+ 1.30	45	+ 2:15
+ 1.45	44	+ 2:29
+ 2.00	43	+ 2:43
+ 2.15	41	+ 2:56
+ 2.30	40	+ 3:10
+ 2.45	39	+ 3:24
+ 3.00	39	+ 3:39
+ 3.15	38	+ 3:53
+ 3.30	37	+ 4:07
+ 3.45	37	+ 4:22
+ 4.00	37	+ 4:37
+ 4.15	36	+ 4:51
+ 4.30	36	+ 5:06
+ 4.45	36	+ 5:21
+ 5.00	35	+ 5:35
+ 5.15	35	+ 5:50
+ 5.30	34	- 5:56
+ 5.45	34	- 5:41
+ 6.00	33	- 5:27

Table B - Essex Rivers to Ramsgate via Fisherman's and Foulger's Gats

Neaps — All times relate to HW Sheerness — **Time to cover Sectors (in minutes) at 4.0 Kts**

SOUTH BOUND

Time	B8 Mid-Spitway to Barrow Deep: Duration	B8: Time at End of Sector	Time	B7 Barrow Deep to Blk Deep No 8: Duration	B7: Time at End of Sector	Time	B6 Blk Deep No 8 to Outer Fisherman: Duration	B6: Time at End of Sector	Time	B5 Mid Spitway to NE Middle: Duration	B5: Time at End of Sector
- 6.00	139	- 3:41	- 6.00	57	- 5:03	- 6.00	51	- 5:09	- 6.00	97	- 4:23
- 5.45	141	- 3:24	- 5.45	57	- 4:48	- 5.45	52	- 4:53	- 5.45	100	- 4:05
- 5.30	143	- 3:07	- 5.30	57	- 4:33	- 5.30	53	- 4:37	- 5.30	103	- 3:47
- 5.15	145	- 2:50	- 5.15	57	- 4:18	- 5.15	55	- 4:20	- 5.15	106	- 3:29
- 5.00	147	- 2:33	- 5.00	56	- 4:04	- 5.00	56	- 4:04	- 5.00	109	- 3:11
- 4.45	146	- 2:19	- 4.45	57	- 3:48	- 4.45	57	- 3:48	- 4.45	110	- 2:55
- 4.30	146	- 2:04	- 4.30	57	- 3:33	- 4.30	58	- 3:32	- 4.30	110	- 2:40
- 4.15	145	- 1:50	- 4.15	58	- 3:17	- 4.15	59	- 3:16	- 4.15	110	- 2:25
- 4.00	145	- 1:35	- 4.00	58	- 3:02	- 4.00	60	- 3:00	- 4.00	111	- 2:09
- 3.45	142	- 1:23	- 3.45	59	- 2:46	- 3.45	61	- 2:44	- 3.45	109	- 1:56
- 3.30	140	- 1:10	- 3.30	60	- 2:30	- 3.30	63	- 2:27	- 3.30	107	- 1:43
- 3.15	138	- 0:57	- 3.15	61	- 2:14	- 3.15	65	- 2:10	- 3.15	105	- 1:30
- 3.00	136	- 0:44	- 3.00	62	- 1:58	- 3.00	66	- 1:54	- 3.00	103	- 1:17
- 2.45	133	- 0:32	- 2.45	62	- 1:43	- 2.45	67	- 1:38	- 2.45	100	- 1:05
- 2.30	130	- 0:20	- 2.30	62	- 1:28	- 2.30	68	- 1:22	- 2.30	97	- 0:53
- 2.15	127	- 0:08	- 2.15	63	- 1:12	- 2.15	69	- 1:06	- 2.15	95	- 0:40
- 2.00	124	+ 0:04	- 2.00	63	- 0:57	- 2.00	70	- 0:50	- 2.00	92	- 0:28
- 1.45	121	+ 0:16	- 1.45	64	- 0:41	- 1.45	69	- 0:36	- 1.45	88	- 0:17
- 1.30	118	+ 0:28	- 1.30	64	- 0:26	- 1.30	67	- 0:23	- 1.30	84	- 0:06
- 1.15	114	+ 0:39	- 1.15	65	- 0:10	- 1.15	66	- 0:09	- 1.15	81	+ 0:06
- 1.00	111	+ 0:51	- 1.00	65	+ 0:05	- 1.00	64	+ 0:04	- 1.00	77	+ 0:17
- 0.45	109	+ 1:04	- 0.45	66	+ 0:21	- 0.45	62	+ 0:17	- 0.45	74	+ 0:29
- 0.30	107	+ 1:17	- 0.30	67	+ 0:37	- 0.30	60	+ 0:30	- 0.30	71	+ 0:41
- 0.15	105	+ 1:30	- 0.15	68	+ 0:53	- 0.15	58	+ 0:43	- 0.15	69	+ 0:54
HW	103	+ 1:43	HW	69	+ 1:09	HW	55	+ 0:55	HW	66	+ 1:06
+ 0.15	102	+ 1:57	+ 0.15	70	+ 1:25	+ 0.15	54	+ 1:09	+ 0.15	65	+ 1:20
+ 0.30	101	+ 2:11	+ 0.30	71	+ 1:41	+ 0.30	52	+ 1:22	+ 0.30	63	+ 1:33
+ 0.45	100	+ 2:25	+ 0.45	72	+ 1:57	+ 0.45	50	+ 1:35	+ 0.45	62	+ 1:47
+ 1.00	99	+ 2:39	+ 1.00	72	+ 2:12	+ 1.00	48	+ 1:48	+ 1.00	61	+ 2:01
+ 1.15	99	+ 2:54	+ 1.15	72	+ 2:27	+ 1.15	48	+ 2:03	+ 1.15	61	+ 2:16
+ 1.30	99	+ 3:09	+ 1.30	72	+ 2:42	+ 1.30	47	+ 2:17	+ 1.30	61	+ 2:31
+ 1.45	99	+ 3:24	+ 1.45	72	+ 2:57	+ 1.45	46	+ 2:31	+ 1.45	61	+ 2:46
+ 2.00	99	+ 3:39	+ 2.00	72	+ 3:12	+ 2.00	45	+ 2:45	+ 2.00	61	+ 3:01
+ 2.15	99	+ 3:54	+ 2.15	71	+ 3:26	+ 2.15	45	+ 3:00	+ 2.15	62	+ 3:17
+ 2.30	100	+ 4:10	+ 2.30	70	+ 3:40	+ 2.30	44	+ 3:14	+ 2.30	63	+ 3:33
+ 2.45	101	+ 4:26	+ 2.45	70	+ 3:55	+ 2.45	44	+ 3:29	+ 2.45	64	+ 3:49
+ 3.00	101	+ 4:41	+ 3.00	69	+ 4:09	+ 3.00	43	+ 3:43	+ 3.00	65	+ 4:05
+ 3.15	103	+ 4:58	+ 3.15	68	+ 4:23	+ 3.15	43	+ 3:58	+ 3.15	66	+ 4:21
+ 3.30	104	+ 5:14	+ 3.30	67	+ 4:37	+ 3.30	43	+ 4:13	+ 3.30	67	+ 4:37
+ 3.45	106	+ 5:31	+ 3.45	66	+ 4:51	+ 3.45	43	+ 4:28	+ 3.45	68	+ 4:53
+ 4.00	107	+ 5:47	+ 4.00	65	+ 5:05	+ 4.00	43	+ 4:43	+ 4.00	70	+ 5:10
+ 4.15	110	- 5:55	+ 4.15	64	+ 5:19	+ 4.15	43	+ 4:58	+ 4.15	71	+ 5:26
+ 4.30	112	- 5:38	+ 4.30	63	+ 5:33	+ 4.30	43	+ 5:13	+ 4.30	73	+ 5:43
+ 4.45	114	- 5:21	+ 4.45	62	+ 5:47	+ 4.45	44	+ 5:29	+ 4.45	75	- 6:00
+ 5.00	116	- 5:04	+ 5.00	61	- 5:59	+ 5.00	44	+ 5:44	+ 5.00	76	- 5:44
+ 5.15	119	- 4:46	+ 5.15	61	- 5:44	+ 5.15	45	- 6:00	+ 5.15	78	- 5:27
+ 5.30	121	- 4:29	+ 5.30	60	- 5:30	+ 5.30	46	- 5:44	+ 5.30	79	- 5:11
+ 5.45	124	- 4:11	+ 5.45	60	- 5:15	+ 5.45	46	- 5:29	+ 5.45	80	- 4:55
+ 6.00	126	- 3:54	+ 6.00	59	- 5:01	+ 6.00	47	- 5:13	+ 6.00	82	- 4:38

Via Fisherman's Gat and Middle Sunk

Time	B4 NE Middle to Black Deep: Duration	B4: Time at End of Sector	Time	B3 Black Deep to Lg Sand Outer: Duration	B3: Time at End of Sector	Time	B2 Long Sand Outer to Tongue: Duration	B2: Time at End of Sector	Time	B1 Tongue to North Foreland: Duration	B1: Time at End of Sector
- 6.00	96	- 4:24	- 6.00	99	- 4:21	- 6.00	48	- 5:12	- 6.00	81	- 4:39
- 5.45	98	- 4:07	- 5.45	99	- 4:06	- 5.45	48	- 4:57	- 5.45	81	- 4:24
- 5.30	101	- 3:49	- 5.30	100	- 3:50	- 5.30	48	- 4:42	- 5.30	82	- 4:08
- 5.15	103	- 3:32	- 5.15	100	- 3:35	- 5.15	47	- 4:28	- 5.15	83	- 3:52
- 5.00	106	- 3:14	- 5.00	100	- 3:20	- 5.00	47	- 4:13	- 5.00	84	- 3:36
- 4.45	105	- 3:00	- 4.45	101	- 3:04	- 4.45	48	- 3:57	- 4.45	86	- 3:19
- 4.30	105	- 2:45	- 4.30	102	- 2:48	- 4.30	49	- 3:41	- 4.30	88	- 3:02
- 4.15	105	- 2:30	- 4.15	103	- 2:32	- 4.15	49	- 3:26	- 4.15	90	- 2:45
- 4.00	105	- 2:15	- 4.00	103	- 2:17	- 4.00	50	- 3:10	- 4.00	93	- 2:27
- 3.45	104	- 2:01	- 3.45	105	- 2:00	- 3.45	51	- 2:54	- 3.45	97	- 2:08
- 3.30	102	- 1:48	- 3.30	107	- 1:43	- 3.30	53	- 2:37	- 3.30	102	- 1:48
- 3.15	100	- 1:35	- 3.15	109	- 1:26	- 3.15	54	- 2:21	- 3.15	107	- 1:28
- 3.00	98	- 1:22	- 3.00	111	- 1:09	- 3.00	55	- 2:05	- 3.00	112	- 1:08
- 2.45	96	- 1:09	- 2.45	113	- 0:52	- 2.45	57	- 1:48	- 2.45	116	- 0:49
- 2.30	94	- 0:56	- 2.30	115	- 0:35	- 2.30	59	- 1:31	- 2.30	120	- 0:30
- 2.15	92	- 0:43	- 2.15	117	- 0:18	- 2.15	61	- 1:14	- 2.15	125	- 0:10
- 2.00	90	- 0:30	- 2.00	119	- 0:01	- 2.00	62	- 0:58	- 2.00	129	+ 0:09
- 1.45	87	- 0:18	- 1.45	119	+ 0:14	- 1.45	64	- 0:41	- 1.45	129	+ 0:24
- 1.30	83	- 0:07	- 1.30	119	+ 0:29	- 1.30	66	- 0:24	- 1.30	130	+ 0:40
- 1.15	80	+ 0:05	- 1.15	119	+ 0:44	- 1.15	68	- 0:07	- 1.15	130	+ 0:55
- 1.00	77	+ 0:17	- 1.00	119	+ 0:59	- 1.00	70	+ 0:10	- 1.00	130	+ 1:10
- 0.45	75	+ 0:30	- 0.45	118	+ 1:13	- 0.45	71	+ 0:26	- 0.45	129	+ 1:24
- 0.30	73	+ 0:43	- 0.30	117	+ 1:27	- 0.30	73	+ 0:43	- 0.30	127	+ 1:37
- 0.15	71	+ 0:56	- 0.15	116	+ 1:41	- 0.15	75	+ 1:00	- 0.15	125	+ 1:50
HW	69	+ 1:09	HW	116	+ 1:56	HW	76	+ 1:16	HW	123	+ 2:03
+ 0.15	68	+ 1:23	+ 0.15	115	+ 2:10	+ 0.15	76	+ 1:31	+ 0.15	120	+ 2:15
+ 0.30	68	+ 1:38	+ 0.30	115	+ 2:25	+ 0.30	77	+ 1:47	+ 0.30	117	+ 2:27
+ 0.45	67	+ 1:52	+ 0.45	114	+ 2:39	+ 0.45	77	+ 2:02	+ 0.45	114	+ 2:39
+ 1.00	66	+ 2:06	+ 1.00	114	+ 2:54	+ 1.00	77	+ 2:17	+ 1.00	111	+ 2:51
+ 1.15	66	+ 2:21	+ 1.15	113	+ 3:08	+ 1.15	76	+ 2:31	+ 1.15	109	+ 3:04
+ 1.30	65	+ 2:35	+ 1.30	112	+ 3:22	+ 1.30	75	+ 2:45	+ 1.30	106	+ 3:16
+ 1.45	65	+ 2:50	+ 1.45	111	+ 3:36	+ 1.45	74	+ 2:59	+ 1.45	104	+ 3:29
+ 2.00	65	+ 3:05	+ 2.00	111	+ 3:51	+ 2.00	73	+ 3:13	+ 2.00	101	+ 3:41
+ 2.15	65	+ 3:20	+ 2.15	109	+ 4:04	+ 2.15	72	+ 3:27	+ 2.15	99	+ 3:54
+ 2.30	66	+ 3:36	+ 2.30	108	+ 4:18	+ 2.30	70	+ 3:40	+ 2.30	97	+ 4:07
+ 2.45	66	+ 3:51	+ 2.45	107	+ 4:32	+ 2.45	69	+ 3:54	+ 2.45	95	+ 4:20
+ 3.00	67	+ 4:07	+ 3.00	105	+ 4:45	+ 3.00	67	+ 4:07	+ 3.00	93	+ 4:33
+ 3.15	68	+ 4:23	+ 3.15	105	+ 5:00	+ 3.15	65	+ 4:20	+ 3.15	92	+ 4:47
+ 3.30	69	+ 4:39	+ 3.30	104	+ 5:14	+ 3.30	64	+ 4:34	+ 3.30	90	+ 5:00
+ 3.45	70	+ 4:55	+ 3.45	103	+ 5:28	+ 3.45	62	+ 4:47	+ 3.45	89	+ 5:14
+ 4.00	72	+ 5:12	+ 4.00	103	+ 5:43	+ 4.00	61	+ 5:01	+ 4.00	88	+ 5:28
+ 4.15	73	+ 5:28	+ 4.15	102	+ 5:57	+ 4.15	59	+ 5:14	+ 4.15	87	+ 5:42
+ 4.30	75	+ 5:45	+ 4.30	101	- 5:49	+ 4.30	58	+ 5:28	+ 4.30	86	+ 5:56
+ 4.45	77	- 5:58	+ 4.45	100	- 5:35	+ 4.45	56	+ 5:41	+ 4.45	84	- 5:51
+ 5.00	78	- 5:42	+ 5.00	99	- 5:21	+ 5.00	55	+ 5:55	+ 5.00	83	- 5:37
+ 5.15	80	- 5:25	+ 5.15	100	- 5:05	+ 5.15	54	- 5:51	+ 5.15	83	- 5:22
+ 5.30	81	- 5:09	+ 5.30	100	- 4:50	+ 5.30	53	- 5:37	+ 5.30	83	- 5:07
+ 5.45	82	- 4:53	+ 5.45	100	- 4:35	+ 5.45	51	- 5:24	+ 5.45	82	- 4:53
+ 6.00	84	- 4:36	+ 6.00	101	- 4:19	+ 6.00	50	- 5:10	+ 6.00	82	- 4:38

Via Foulger's Gat and Middle Sunk

Table B - Essex Rivers to Ramsgate via Fisherman's and Foulger's Gats

Time to cover Sectors (in minutes) at 4.0 kts | All times relate to HW Sheerness | **Springs**

	B8			B7			B6			B5	
	Mid-Spitway to Barrow Deep			Barrow Deep to Blk Deep No 8			Blk Deep No 8 to Outer Fisherman			Mid Spitway to NE Middle	
Time	Duration	Time at End of Sector	Time	Duration	Time at End of Sector	Time	Duration	Time at End of Sector	Time	Duration	Time at End of Sector
-6.00	159	-3:21	-6.00	56	-5:04	-6.00	49	-5:11	-6.00	108	-4:12
-5.45	161	-3:04	-5.45	56	-4:49	-5.45	51	-4:54	-5.45	112	-3:53
-5.30	163	-2:47	-5.30	56	-4:34	-5.30	53	-4:37	-5.30	117	-3:33
-5.15	164	-2:31	-5.15	55	-4:20	-5.15	56	-4:19	-5.15	121	-3:14
-5.00	166	-2:14	-5.00	55	-4:05	-5.00	58	-4:02	-5.00	126	-2:54
-4.45	164	-2:01	-4.45	56	-3:49	-4.45	60	-3:45	-4.45	125	-2:40
-4.30	162	-1:48	-4.30	57	-3:33	-4.30	61	-3:29	-4.30	125	-2:25
-4.15	160	-1:35	-4.15	58	-3:17	-4.15	63	-3:12	-4.15	125	-2:10
-4.00	158	-1:22	-4.00	59	-3:01	-4.00	65	-2:55	-4.00	124	-1:56
-3.45	154	-1:11	-3.45	60	-2:45	-3.45	68	-2:37	-3.45	121	-1:44
-3.30	150	-1:00	-3.30	62	-2:28	-3.30	71	-2:19	-3.30	118	-1:32
-3.15	146	-0:49	-3.15	63	-2:12	-3.15	73	-2:02	-3.15	115	-1:20
-3.00	142	-0:38	-3.00	64	-1:56	-3.00	76	-1:44	-3.00	112	-1:08
-2.45	138	-0:27	-2.45	64	-1:41	-2.45	80	-1:25	-2.45	107	-0:58
-2.30	133	-0:17	-2.30	65	-1:25	-2.30	84	-1:06	-2.30	103	-0:47
-2.15	129	-0:06	-2.15	65	-1:10	-2.15	87	-0:48	-2.15	99	-0:36
-2.00	124	+0:04	-2.00	65	-0:55	-2.00	91	-0:29	-2.00	94	-0:26
-1.45	120	+0:15	-1.45	66	-0:39	-1.45	86	-0:19	-1.45	90	-0:15
-1.30	117	+0:27	-1.30	66	-0:24	-1.30	82	-0:08	-1.30	85	-0:05
-1.15	113	+0:38	-1.15	67	-0:08	-1.15	77	+0:02	-1.15	81	+0:06
-1.00	109	+0:49	-1.00	67	+0:07	-1.00	72	+0:12	-1.00	77	+0:17
-0.45	107	+1:02	-0.45	69	+0:24	-0.45	68	+0:23	-0.45	73	+0:28
-0.30	105	+1:15	-0.30	71	+0:41	-0.30	64	+0:34	-0.30	69	+0:39
-0.15	102	+1:27	-0.15	73	+0:58	-0.15	60	+0:45	-0.15	65	+0:50
HW	100	+1:40	HW	74	+1:14	HW	56	+0:56	HW	61	+1:01
+0.15	99	+1:54	+0.15	76	+1:31	+0.15	54	+1:09	+0.15	59	+1:14
+0.30	98	+2:08	+0.30	77	+1:47	+0.30	51	+1:21	+0.30	57	+1:27
+0.45	97	+2:22	+0.45	79	+2:04	+0.45	49	+1:34	+0.45	55	+1:40
+1.00	97	+2:37	+1.00	80	+2:20	+1.00	46	+1:46	+1.00	54	+1:54
+1.15	96	+2:51	+1.15	80	+2:35	+1.15	45	+2:00	+1.15	54	+2:09
+1.30	96	+3:06	+1.30	80	+2:50	+1.30	44	+2:14	+1.30	54	+2:24
+1.45	96	+3:21	+1.45	80	+3:05	+1.45	42	+2:27	+1.45	54	+2:39
+2.00	96	+3:36	+2.00	80	+3:20	+2.00	41	+2:41	+2.00	54	+2:54
+2.15	96	+3:51	+2.15	79	+3:34	+2.15	41	+2:56	+2.15	55	+3:10
+2.30	97	+4:07	+2.30	77	+3:47	+2.30	40	+3:10	+2.30	56	+3:26
+2.45	97	+4:22	+2.45	76	+4:01	+2.45	40	+3:25	+2.45	57	+3:42
+3.00	98	+4:38	+3.00	75	+4:15	+3.00	39	+3:39	+3.00	59	+3:59
+3.15	100	+4:55	+3.15	73	+4:28	+3.15	39	+3:54	+3.15	60	+4:15
+3.30	102	+5:12	+3.30	71	+4:41	+3.30	38	+4:08	+3.30	62	+4:32
+3.45	104	+5:29	+3.45	69	+4:54	+3.45	38	+4:23	+3.45	64	+4:49
+4.00	105	+5:45	+4.00	67	+5:07	+4.00	38	+4:38	+4.00	66	+5:06
+4.15	109	-5:56	+4.15	66	+5:21	+4.15	38	+4:53	+4.15	68	+5:23
+4.30	112	-5:38	+4.30	64	+5:34	+4.30	39	+5:09	+4.30	71	+5:41
+4.45	115	-5:20	+4.45	63	+5:48	+4.45	39	+5:24	+4.45	73	+5:58
+5.00	118	-5:02	+5.00	61	-5:59	+5.00	39	+5:39	+5.00	75	-5:45
+5.15	122	-4:43	+5.15	61	-5:44	+5.15	41	+5:56	+5.15	77	-5:28
+5.30	126	-4:24	+5.30	60	-5:30	+5.30	42	-5:48	+5.30	79	-5:11
+5.45	129	-4:06	+5.45	59	-5:16	+5.45	43	-5:32	+5.45	82	-4:53
+6.00	133	-3:47	+6.00	58	-5:02	+6.00	44	-5:16	+6.00	84	-4:36

Via Fisherman's Gat and Middle Sunk

	B4			B3			B2			B1	
	NE Middle to Black Deep			Black Deep to Lg Sand Outer			Long Sand Outer to Tongue			Tongue to North Foreland	
Time	Duration	Time at End of Sector	Time	Duration	Time at End of Sector	Time	Duration	Time at End of Sector	Time	Duration	Time at End of Sector
-6.00	105	-4:15	-6.00	97	-4:23	-6.00	43	-5:17	-6.00	71	-4:49
-5.45	108	-3:57	-5.45	98	-4:07	-5.45	43	-5:02	-5.45	72	-4:33
-5.30	112	-3:38	-5.30	99	-3:51	-5.30	43	-4:47	-5.30	73	-4:17
-5.15	115	-3:20	-5.15	99	-3:36	-5.15	43	-4:32	-5.15	74	-4:01
-5.00	118	-3:02	-5.00	100	-3:20	-5.00	43	-4:17	-5.00	74	-3:46
-4.45	117	-2:48	-4.45	101	-3:04	-4.45	43	-4:02	-4.45	78	-3:27
-4.30	116	-2:34	-4.30	102	-2:48	-4.30	44	-3:46	-4.30	82	-3:08
-4.15	116	-2:19	-4.15	103	-2:32	-4.15	45	-3:30	-4.15	86	-2:49
-4.00	115	-2:05	-4.00	104	-2:16	-4.00	45	-3:15	-4.00	90	-2:30
-3.45	112	-1:53	-3.45	107	-1:58	-3.45	47	-2:58	-3.45	99	-2:06
-3.30	109	-1:41	-3.30	110	-1:40	-3.30	49	-2:41	-3.30	109	-1:41
-3.15	107	-1:28	-3.15	114	-1:21	-3.15	51	-2:24	-3.15	118	-1:17
-3.00	104	-1:16	-3.00	117	-1:03	-3.00	53	-2:07	-3.00	127	-0:53
-2.45	101	-1:04	-2.45	120	-0:45	-2.45	56	-1:49	-2.45	135	-0:30
-2.30	98	-0:52	-2.30	123	-0:27	-2.30	58	-1:32	-2.30	143	-0:07
-2.15	94	-0:41	-2.15	125	-0:10	-2.15	61	-1:14	-2.15	151	+0:16
-2.00	91	-0:29	-2.00	128	+0:08	-2.00	64	-0:56	-2.00	159	+0:39
-1.45	87	-0:18	-1.45	128	+0:23	-1.45	67	-0:38	-1.45	158	+0:53
-1.30	84	-0:06	-1.30	128	+0:38	-1.30	70	-0:20	-1.30	156	+1:06
-1.15	80	+0:05	-1.15	127	+0:52	-1.15	73	-0:02	-1.15	154	+1:19
-1.00	76	+0:16	-1.00	127	+1:07	-1.00	76	+0:16	-1.00	153	+1:33
-0.45	74	+0:29	-0.45	126	+1:21	-0.45	81	+0:36	-0.45	148	+1:43
-0.30	71	+0:41	-0.30	126	+1:36	-0.30	86	+0:56	-0.30	143	+1:53
-0.15	69	+0:54	-0.15	125	+1:50	-0.15	91	+1:16	-0.15	139	+2:04
HW	66	+1:06	HW	124	+2:04	HW	96	+1:36	HW	134	+2:14
+0.15	65	+1:20	+0.15	123	+2:18	+0.15	96	+1:51	+0.15	130	+2:25
+0.30	64	+1:34	+0.30	122	+2:32	+0.30	96	+2:06	+0.30	125	+2:35
+0.45	63	+1:48	+0.45	122	+2:47	+0.45	96	+2:21	+0.45	121	+2:46
+1.00	62	+2:02	+1.00	121	+3:01	+1.00	96	+2:36	+1.00	117	+2:57
+1.15	62	+2:17	+1.15	120	+3:15	+1.15	92	+2:47	+1.15	113	+3:08
+1.30	61	+2:31	+1.30	118	+3:28	+1.30	89	+2:59	+1.30	109	+3:19
+1.45	61	+2:46	+1.45	117	+3:42	+1.45	85	+3:10	+1.45	106	+3:31
+2.00	61	+3:01	+2.00	116	+3:56	+2.00	81	+3:21	+2.00	102	+3:42
+2.15	61	+3:16	+2.15	114	+4:09	+2.15	79	+3:34	+2.15	99	+3:54
+2.30	62	+3:32	+2.30	112	+4:22	+2.30	76	+3:46	+2.30	96	+4:06
+2.45	62	+3:47	+2.45	110	+4:35	+2.45	73	+3:58	+2.45	93	+4:18
+3.00	63	+4:03	+3.00	108	+4:48	+3.00	71	+4:11	+3.00	90	+4:30
+3.15	64	+4:19	+3.15	107	+5:02	+3.15	69	+4:24	+3.15	88	+4:43
+3.30	65	+4:35	+3.30	106	+5:16	+3.30	66	+4:36	+3.30	85	+4:55
+3.45	67	+4:52	+3.45	104	+5:29	+3.45	64	+4:49	+3.45	83	+5:08
+4.00	68	+5:08	+4.00	103	+5:43	+4.00	62	+5:02	+4.00	81	+5:21
+4.15	71	+5:26	+4.15	101	+5:56	+4.15	59	+5:14	+4.15	79	+5:34
+4.30	73	+5:43	+4.30	100	-5:50	+4.30	57	+5:27	+4.30	77	+5:47
+4.45	75	-6:00	+4.45	98	-5:37	+4.45	55	+5:40	+4.45	75	-6:00
+5.00	78	-5:42	+5.00	96	-5:24	+5.00	53	+5:53	+5.00	74	-5:46
+5.15	80	-5:25	+5.15	97	-5:08	+5.15	51	-5:54	+5.15	73	-5:32
+5.30	82	-5:08	+5.30	98	-4:52	+5.30	49	-5:41	+5.30	73	-5:17
+5.45	85	-4:50	+5.45	99	-4:36	+5.45	48	-5:27	+5.45	72	-5:03
+6.00	87	-4:33	+6.00	100	-4:20	+6.00	46	-5:14	+6.00	71	-4:49

Via Foulger's Gat and Middle Sunk

SOUTH BOUND

Table B - Essex Rivers to Ramsgate via Fisherman's and Foulger's Gats

Neaps — All times relate to HW Sheerness — Time to cover Sectors (in minutes) at 5.0 Kts

SOUTH BOUND

Time	B8 Mid-Spitway to Barrow Deep: Duration	B8: Time at End of Sector	B7 Barrow Deep to Blk Deep No 8: Duration	B7: Time at End of Sector	B6 Blk Deep No 8 to Outer Fisherman: Duration	B6: Time at End of Sector	B5 Mid Spitway to NE Middle: Duration	B5: Time at End of Sector
-6.00	70	-4:50	47	-5:13	40	-5:20	70	-4:50
-5.45	71	-4:34	46	-4:59	41	-5:04	71	-4:34
-5.30	73	-4:17	46	-4:44	42	-4:48	73	-4:17
-5.15	74	-4:01	46	-4:29	43	-4:32	75	-4:00
-5.00	76	-3:44	46	-4:14	44	-4:16	76	-3:44
-4.45	76	-3:29	46	-3:59	44	-4:01	76	-3:29
-4.30	76	-3:14	46	-3:44	45	-3:45	76	-3:14
-4.15	76	-2:59	46	-3:29	46	-3:29	77	-2:58
-4.00	76	-2:44	46	-3:14	46	-3:14	77	-2:43
-3.45	75	-2:30	47	-2:58	47	-2:58	76	-2:29
-3.30	73	-2:17	48	-2:42	48	-2:42	76	-2:14
-3.15	72	-2:03	48	-2:27	49	-2:26	75	-2:00
-3.00	71	-1:49	49	-2:11	50	-2:10	75	-1:45
-2.45	69	-1:36	49	-1:56	51	-1:54	73	-1:32
-2.30	68	-1:22	49	-1:41	52	-1:38	72	-1:18
-2.15	66	-1:09	50	-1:25	53	-1:22	70	-1:05
-2.00	64	-0:56	50	-1:10	53	-1:07	69	-0:51
-1.45	62	-0:43	50	-0:55	53	-0:52	67	-0:38
-1.30	60	-0:30	51	-0:39	52	-0:38	66	-0:24
-1.15	57	-0:18	51	-0:24	51	-0:24	64	-0:11
-1.00	55	-0:05	51	-0:09	50	-0:10	62	+0:02
-0.45	59	+0:14	52	+0:07	49	+0:04	60	+0:15
-0.30	64	+0:34	53	+0:23	47	+0:17	59	+0:29
-0.15	68	+0:53	53	+0:38	46	+0:31	57	+0:42
HW	73	+1:13	54	+0:54	45	+0:45	55	+0:55
+0.15	72	+1:27	54	+1:09	43	+0:58	54	+1:09
+0.30	71	+1:41	55	+1:25	42	+1:12	53	+1:23
+0.45	70	+1:55	55	+1:40	41	+1:26	52	+1:37
+1.00	70	+2:10	56	+1:56	40	+1:40	51	+1:51
+1.15	69	+2:24	56	+2:11	39	+1:54	51	+2:06
+1.30	69	+2:39	56	+2:26	39	+2:09	51	+2:21
+1.45	69	+2:54	56	+2:41	38	+2:23	51	+2:36
+2.00	69	+3:09	56	+2:56	38	+2:38	51	+2:51
+2.15	69	+3:24	55	+3:10	37	+2:52	51	+3:06
+2.30	70	+3:40	55	+3:25	37	+3:07	52	+3:22
+2.45	70	+3:55	54	+3:39	37	+3:22	53	+3:38
+3.00	71	+4:11	54	+3:54	36	+3:36	53	+3:53
+3.15	72	+4:27	53	+4:08	36	+3:51	54	+4:09
+3.30	73	+4:43	53	+4:23	36	+4:06	55	+4:25
+3.45	74	+4:59	52	+4:37	36	+4:21	56	+4:41
+4.00	75	+5:15	51	+4:51	36	+4:36	57	+4:57
+4.15	79	+5:34	51	+5:06	36	+4:51	58	+5:13
+4.30	83	+5:53	50	+5:20	36	+5:06	59	+5:29
+4.45	87	-5:48	50	+5:35	36	+5:21	60	+5:45
+5.00	91	-5:29	49	+5:49	36	+5:36	61	-5:59
+5.15	93	-5:12	49	-5:56	37	+5:52	62	-5:43
+5.30	95	-4:55	49	-5:41	37	-5:53	62	-5:28
+5.45	96	-4:39	48	-5:27	38	-5:37	63	-5:12
+6.00	98	-4:22	48	-5:12	38	-5:22	64	-4:56

Via Fisherman's Gat and Middle Sunk

Time	B4 NE Middle to Black Deep: Duration	B4: Time at End of Sector	B3 Black Deep to Lg Sand Outer: Duration	B3: Time at End of Sector	B2 Long Sand Outer to Tongue: Duration	B2: Time at End of Sector	B1 Tongue to North Foreland: Duration	B1: Time at End of Sector
-6.00	70	-4:50	79	-4:41	40	-5:20	67	-4:53
-5.45	71	-4:34	79	-4:26	40	-5:05	68	-4:37
-5.30	73	-4:17	79	-4:11	40	-4:50	68	-4:22
-5.15	74	-4:01	79	-3:56	40	-4:35	68	-4:07
-5.00	75	-3:45	79	-3:41	39	-4:21	69	-3:51
-4.45	75	-3:30	79	-3:26	40	-4:05	70	-3:35
-4.30	75	-3:15	80	-3:10	40	-3:50	71	-3:19
-4.15	75	-3:00	80	-2:55	41	-3:34	73	-3:02
-4.00	75	-2:45	80	-2:40	41	-3:19	74	-2:46
-3.45	75	-2:30	82	-2:23	42	-3:03	77	-2:28
-3.30	74	-2:16	83	-2:07	43	-2:47	79	-2:11
-3.15	73	-2:02	85	-1:50	43	-2:32	81	-1:54
-3.00	73	-1:47	86	-1:34	44	-2:16	84	-1:36
-2.45	72	-1:33	88	-1:17	45	-2:00	87	-1:18
-2.30	71	-1:19	89	-1:01	47	-1:43	91	-0:59
-2.15	69	-1:06	91	-0:44	48	-1:27	95	-0:40
-2.00	68	-0:52	93	-0:27	49	-1:11	98	-0:22
-1.45	67	-0:38	93	-0:12	50	-0:55	99	-0:06
-1.30	65	-0:25	94	+0:04	51	-0:39	99	+0:09
-1.15	64	-0:11	94	+0:19	52	-0:23	100	+0:25
-1.00	62	+0:02	94	+0:34	54	-0:06	100	+0:40
-0.45	61	+0:16	94	+0:49	55	+0:10	99	+0:54
-0.30	60	+0:30	93	+1:03	56	+0:26	99	+1:09
-0.15	58	+0:43	93	+1:18	57	+0:42	98	+1:23
HW	57	+0:57	92	+1:32	58	+0:58	97	+1:37
+0.15	56	+1:11	92	+1:47	58	+1:13	94	+1:49
+0.30	56	+1:26	91	+2:01	58	+1:28	91	+2:01
+0.45	55	+1:40	91	+2:16	58	+1:43	89	+2:14
+1.00	54	+1:54	90	+2:30	59	+1:59	86	+2:26
+1.15	54	+2:09	90	+2:45	58	+2:13	84	+2:39
+1.30	54	+2:24	89	+2:59	58	+2:28	83	+2:53
+1.45	54	+2:39	89	+3:14	57	+2:42	81	+3:06
+2.00	54	+2:54	89	+3:29	57	+2:57	79	+3:19
+2.15	54	+3:09	88	+3:43	56	+3:11	78	+3:33
+2.30	54	+3:24	87	+3:57	55	+3:25	77	+3:47
+2.45	55	+3:40	86	+4:11	54	+3:39	76	+4:01
+3.00	55	+3:55	85	+4:25	53	+3:53	75	+4:15
+3.15	56	+4:11	84	+4:39	52	+4:07	74	+4:29
+3.30	56	+4:26	84	+4:54	51	+4:21	73	+4:43
+3.45	57	+4:42	83	+5:08	50	+4:35	73	+4:58
+4.00	58	+4:58	83	+5:23	49	+4:49	72	+5:12
+4.15	59	+5:14	82	+5:37	48	+5:03	71	+5:26
+4.30	60	+5:30	82	+5:52	47	+5:17	71	+5:41
+4.45	61	+5:46	81	-5:54	46	+5:31	70	+5:55
+5.00	62	-5:58	81	-5:39	45	+5:45	69	-5:51
+5.15	63	-5:42	81	-5:24	44	+5:59	69	-5:36
+5.30	64	-5:26	81	-5:09	43	-5:47	69	-5:21
+5.45	65	-5:10	81	-4:54	43	-5:32	68	-5:07
+6.00	66	-4:54	81	-4:39	42	-5:18	68	-4:52

Via Foulger's Gat and Middle Sunk

Table B - Essex Rivers to Ramsgate via Fisherman's and Foulger's Gats

Time to cover Sectors (in minutes) at 5.0 kts

All times relate to HW Sheerness

Springs

Time	B8 Mid-Spitway to Barrow Deep — Duration	B8 Time at End of Sector	Time	B7 Barrow Deep to Blk Deep No 8 — Duration	B7 Time at End of Sector	Time	B6 Blk Deep No 8 to Outer Fisherman — Duration	B6 Time at End of Sector	Time	B5 Mid Spitway to NE Middle — Duration	B5 Time at End of Sector
- 6.00	**77**	**- 4:43**	**- 6.00**	**46**	**- 5:14**	**- 6.00**	**39**	**- 5:21**	**- 6.00**	**74**	**- 4:46**
- 5.45	79	- 4:26	- 5.45	45	- 5:00	- 5.45	40	- 5:05	- 5.45	79	- 4:26
- 5.30	81	- 4:09	- 5.30	45	- 4:45	- 5.30	42	- 4:48	- 5.30	83	- 4:07
- 5.15	83	- 3:52	- 5.15	45	- 4:30	- 5.15	43	- 4:32	- 5.15	88	- 3:47
- 5.00	**85**	**- 3:35**	**- 5.00**	**44**	**- 4:16**	**- 5.00**	**45**	**- 4:15**	**- 5.00**	**92**	**- 3:28**
- 4.45	84	- 3:21	- 4.45	45	- 4:00	- 4.45	46	- 3:59	- 4.45	92	- 3:13
- 4.30	84	- 3:06	- 4.30	45	- 3:45	- 4.30	47	- 3:43	- 4.30	92	- 2:58
- 4.15	83	- 2:52	- 4.15	46	- 3:29	- 4.15	48	- 3:27	- 4.15	93	- 2:42
- 4.00	**83**	**- 2:37**	**- 4.00**	**46**	**- 3:14**	**- 4.00**	**49**	**- 3:11**	**- 4.00**	**93**	**- 2:27**
- 3.45	81	- 2:24	- 3.45	47	- 2:58	- 3.45	51	- 2:54	- 3.45	90	- 2:15
- 3.30	79	- 2:11	- 3.30	48	- 2:42	- 3.30	53	- 2:37	- 3.30	88	- 2:02
- 3.15	77	- 1:58	- 3.15	49	- 2:26	- 3.15	54	- 2:21	- 3.15	85	- 1:50
- 3.00	**75**	**- 1:45**	**- 3.00**	**50**	**- 2:10**	**- 3.00**	**56**	**- 2:04**	**- 3.00**	**82**	**- 1:38**
- 2.45	73	- 1:32	- 2.45	50	- 1:55	- 2.45	57	- 1:48	- 2.45	80	- 1:25
- 2.30	70	- 1:20	- 2.30	50	- 1:40	- 2.30	59	- 1:31	- 2.30	78	- 1:12
- 2.15	68	- 1:07	- 2.15	51	- 1:24	- 2.15	60	- 1:15	- 2.15	76	- 0:59
- 2.00	**65**	**- 0:55**	**- 2.00**	**51**	**- 1:09**	**- 2.00**	**61**	**- 0:59**	**- 2.00**	**74**	**- 0:46**
- 1.45	62	- 0:43	- 1.45	51	- 0:54	- 1.45	60	- 0:45	- 1.45	71	- 0:34
- 1.30	60	- 0:30	- 1.30	52	- 0:38	- 1.30	58	- 0:32	- 1.30	68	- 0:22
- 1.15	57	- 0:18	- 1.15	52	- 0:23	- 1.15	57	- 0:18	- 1.15	65	- 0:10
- 1.00	**54**	**- 0:06**	**- 1.00**	**53**	**- 0:07**	**- 1.00**	**55**	**- 0:05**	**- 1.00**	**62**	**+ 0:02**
- 0.45	58	+ 0:13	- 0.45	53	+ 0:08	- 0.45	53	+ 0:08	- 0.45	60	+ 0:15
- 0.30	62	+ 0:32	- 0.30	54	+ 0:24	- 0.30	51	+ 0:21	- 0.30	57	+ 0:27
- 0.15	66	+ 0:51	- 0.15	55	+ 0:40	- 0.15	48	+ 0:33	- 0.15	55	+ 0:40
HW	**70**	**+ 1:10**	**HW**	**56**	**+ 0:56**	**HW**	**46**	**+ 0:46**	**HW**	**52**	**+ 0:52**
+ 0.15	69	+ 1:24	+ 0.15	57	+ 1:12	+ 0.15	44	+ 0:59	+ 0.15	51	+ 1:06
+ 0.30	68	+ 1:38	+ 0.30	58	+ 1:28	+ 0.30	42	+ 1:12	+ 0.30	49	+ 1:19
+ 0.45	67	+ 1:52	+ 0.45	59	+ 1:44	+ 0.45	40	+ 1:25	+ 0.45	48	+ 1:33
+ 1.00	**66**	**+ 2:06**	**+ 1.00**	**60**	**+ 2:00**	**+ 1.00**	**38**	**+ 1:38**	**+ 1.00**	**47**	**+ 1:47**
+ 1.15	66	+ 2:21	+ 1.15	60	+ 2:15	+ 1.15	38	+ 1:53	+ 1.15	46	+ 2:01
+ 1.30	66	+ 2:36	+ 1.30	60	+ 2:30	+ 1.30	37	+ 2:07	+ 1.30	46	+ 2:16
+ 1.45	66	+ 2:51	+ 1.45	60	+ 2:45	+ 1.45	36	+ 2:21	+ 1.45	46	+ 2:31
+ 2.00	**65**	**+ 3:05**	**+ 2.00**	**60**	**+ 3:00**	**+ 2.00**	**35**	**+ 2:35**	**+ 2.00**	**46**	**+ 2:46**
+ 2.15	66	+ 3:21	+ 2.15	59	+ 3:14	+ 2.15	35	+ 2:50	+ 2.15	47	+ 3:02
+ 2.30	66	+ 3:36	+ 2.30	59	+ 3:29	+ 2.30	34	+ 3:04	+ 2.30	48	+ 3:18
+ 2.45	66	+ 3:51	+ 2.45	58	+ 3:43	+ 2.45	34	+ 3:19	+ 2.45	48	+ 3:33
+ 3.00	**67**	**+ 4:07**	**+ 3.00**	**57**	**+ 3:57**	**+ 3.00**	**33**	**+ 3:33**	**+ 3.00**	**49**	**+ 3:49**
+ 3.15	68	+ 4:23	+ 3.15	56	+ 4:11	+ 3.15	33	+ 3:48	+ 3.15	50	+ 4:05
+ 3.30	69	+ 4:39	+ 3.30	55	+ 4:25	+ 3.30	33	+ 4:03	+ 3.30	51	+ 4:21
+ 3.45	71	+ 4:56	+ 3.45	54	+ 4:39	+ 3.45	33	+ 4:18	+ 3.45	53	+ 4:38
+ 4.00	**72**	**+ 5:12**	**+ 4.00**	**53**	**+ 4:53**	**+ 4.00**	**33**	**+ 4:33**	**+ 4.00**	**54**	**+ 4:54**
+ 4.15	77	+ 5:32	+ 4.15	52	+ 5:07	+ 4.15	33	+ 4:48	+ 4.15	55	+ 5:10
+ 4.30	82	+ 5:52	+ 4.30	51	+ 5:21	+ 4.30	33	+ 5:03	+ 4.30	57	+ 5:27
+ 4.45	87	- 5:48	+ 4.45	50	+ 5:35	+ 4.45	33	+ 5:18	+ 4.45	58	+ 5:43
+ 5.00	**92**	**- 5:28**	**+ 5.00**	**49**	**+ 5:49**	**+ 5.00**	**33**	**+ 5:33**	**+ 5.00**	**60**	**- 6:00**
+ 5.15	94	- 5:11	+ 5.15	49	- 5:56	+ 5.15	34	+ 5:49	+ 5.15	61	- 5:44
+ 5.30	96	- 4:54	+ 5.30	48	- 5:42	+ 5.30	35	- 5:55	+ 5.30	63	- 5:27
+ 5.45	99	- 4:36	+ 5.45	48	- 5:27	+ 5.45	35	- 5:40	+ 5.45	64	- 5:11
+ 6.00	**101**	**- 4:19**	**+ 6.00**	**47**	**- 5:13**	**+ 6.00**	**36**	**- 5:24**	**+ 6.00**	**65**	**- 4:55**

Via Fisherman's Gat and Middle Sunk

Time	B4 NE Middle to Black Deep — Duration	B4 Time at End of Sector	Time	B3 Black Deep to Lg Sand Outer — Duration	B3 Time at End of Sector	Time	B2 Long Sand Outer to Tongue — Duration	B2 Time at End of Sector	Time	B1 Tongue to North Foreland — Duration	B1 Time at End of Sector
- 6.00	**75**	**- 4:45**	**- 6.00**	**76**	**- 4:44**	**- 6.00**	**37**	**- 5:23**	**- 6.00**	**61**	**- 4:59**
- 5.45	76	- 4:29	- 5.45	76	- 4:29	- 5.45	37	- 5:08	- 5.45	61	- 4:44
- 5.30	78	- 4:12	- 5.30	77	- 4:13	- 5.30	37	- 4:53	- 5.30	62	- 4:28
- 5.15	80	- 3:55	- 5.15	77	- 3:58	- 5.15	36	- 4:39	- 5.15	62	- 4:13
- 5.00	**82**	**- 3:38**	**- 5.00**	**78**	**- 3:42**	**- 5.00**	**36**	**- 4:24**	**- 5.00**	**63**	**- 3:57**
- 4.45	82	- 3:23	- 4.45	78	- 3:27	- 4.45	37	- 4:08	- 4.45	65	- 3:40
- 4.30	82	- 3:08	- 4.30	79	- 3:11	- 4.30	37	- 3:53	- 4.30	67	- 3:23
- 4.15	82	- 2:53	- 4.15	80	- 2:55	- 4.15	37	- 3:38	- 4.15	69	- 3:06
- 4.00	**82**	**- 2:38**	**- 4.00**	**80**	**- 2:40**	**- 4.00**	**38**	**- 3:22**	**- 4.00**	**71**	**- 2:49**
- 3.45	81	- 2:24	- 3.45	82	- 2:23	- 3.45	39	- 3:06	- 3.45	77	- 2:28
- 3.30	80	- 2:10	- 3.30	84	- 2:06	- 3.30	40	- 2:50	- 3.30	82	- 2:08
- 3.15	79	- 1:56	- 3.15	86	- 1:49	- 3.15	41	- 2:34	- 3.15	87	- 1:48
- 3.00	**78**	**- 1:42**	**- 3.00**	**88**	**- 1:32**	**- 3.00**	**42**	**- 2:18**	**- 3.00**	**93**	**- 1:27**
- 2.45	77	- 1:28	- 2.45	91	- 1:14	- 2.45	44	- 2:01	- 2.45	97	- 1:08
- 2.30	75	- 1:15	- 2.30	93	- 0:57	- 2.30	46	- 1:44	- 2.30	102	- 0:48
- 2.15	73	- 1:02	- 2.15	96	- 0:39	- 2.15	48	- 1:27	- 2.15	107	- 0:28
- 2.00	**71**	**- 0:49**	**- 2.00**	**99**	**- 0:21**	**- 2.00**	**50**	**- 1:10**	**- 2.00**	**111**	**- 0:09**
- 1.45	69	- 0:36	- 1.45	99	- 0:06	- 1.45	51	- 0:54	- 1.45	112	+ 0:07
- 1.30	67	- 0:23	- 1.30	100	+ 0:10	- 1.30	53	- 0:37	- 1.30	112	+ 0:22
- 1.15	64	- 0:11	- 1.15	100	+ 0:25	- 1.15	55	- 0:20	- 1.15	113	+ 0:38
- 1.00	**62**	**+ 0:02**	**- 1.00**	**101**	**+ 0:41**	**- 1.00**	**57**	**- 0:03**	**- 1.00**	**113**	**+ 0:53**
- 0.45	60	+ 0:15	- 0.45	100	+ 0:55	- 0.45	59	+ 0:14	- 0.45	111	+ 1:06
- 0.30	58	+ 0:28	- 0.30	99	+ 1:09	- 0.30	60	+ 0:30	- 0.30	109	+ 1:19
- 0.15	57	+ 0:42	- 0.15	99	+ 1:24	- 0.15	62	+ 0:47	- 0.15	107	+ 1:32
HW	**55**	**+ 0:55**	**HW**	**98**	**+ 1:38**	**HW**	**64**	**+ 1:04**	**HW**	**105**	**+ 1:45**
+ 0.15	54	+ 1:09	+ 0.15	98	+ 1:53	+ 0.15	64	+ 1:19	+ 0.15	102	+ 1:57
+ 0.30	53	+ 1:23	+ 0.30	97	+ 2:07	+ 0.30	65	+ 1:35	+ 0.30	99	+ 2:09
+ 0.45	52	+ 1:37	+ 0.45	96	+ 2:21	+ 0.45	65	+ 1:50	+ 0.45	96	+ 2:21
+ 1.00	**52**	**+ 1:52**	**+ 1.00**	**96**	**+ 2:36**	**+ 1.00**	**65**	**+ 2:05**	**+ 1.00**	**93**	**+ 2:33**
+ 1.15	51	+ 2:06	+ 1.15	95	+ 2:50	+ 1.15	64	+ 2:19	+ 1.15	90	+ 2:45
+ 1.30	51	+ 2:21	+ 1.30	94	+ 3:04	+ 1.30	64	+ 2:34	+ 1.30	87	+ 2:57
+ 1.45	51	+ 2:36	+ 1.45	93	+ 3:18	+ 1.45	63	+ 2:48	+ 1.45	85	+ 3:10
+ 2.00	**51**	**+ 2:51**	**+ 2.00**	**92**	**+ 3:32**	**+ 2.00**	**62**	**+ 3:02**	**+ 2.00**	**82**	**+ 3:22**
+ 2.15	51	+ 3:06	+ 2.15	91	+ 3:46	+ 2.15	60	+ 3:15	+ 2.15	80	+ 3:35
+ 2.30	51	+ 3:21	+ 2.30	90	+ 4:00	+ 2.30	59	+ 3:29	+ 2.30	77	+ 3:47
+ 2.45	52	+ 3:37	+ 2.45	88	+ 4:13	+ 2.45	57	+ 3:42	+ 2.45	75	+ 4:00
+ 3.00	**52**	**+ 3:52**	**+ 3.00**	**87**	**+ 4:27**	**+ 3.00**	**55**	**+ 3:55**	**+ 3.00**	**73**	**+ 4:13**
+ 3.15	53	+ 4:08	+ 3.15	86	+ 4:41	+ 3.15	54	+ 4:09	+ 3.15	72	+ 4:27
+ 3.30	54	+ 4:24	+ 3.30	85	+ 4:55	+ 3.30	52	+ 4:22	+ 3.30	70	+ 4:40
+ 3.45	55	+ 4:40	+ 3.45	84	+ 5:09	+ 3.45	51	+ 4:36	+ 3.45	69	+ 4:54
+ 4.00	**56**	**+ 4:56**	**+ 4.00**	**83**	**+ 5:23**	**+ 4.00**	**50**	**+ 4:50**	**+ 4.00**	**67**	**+ 5:07**
+ 4.15	57	+ 5:12	+ 4.15	82	+ 5:37	+ 4.15	48	+ 5:03	+ 4.15	66	+ 5:21
+ 4.30	58	+ 5:28	+ 4.30	81	+ 5:51	+ 4.30	47	+ 5:17	+ 4.30	65	+ 5:35
+ 4.45	60	+ 5:45	+ 4.45	80	- 5:55	+ 4.45	45	+ 5:30	+ 4.45	64	+ 5:49
+ 5.00	**61**	**- 5:59**	**+ 5.00**	**80**	**- 5:40**	**+ 5.00**	**44**	**+ 5:44**	**+ 5.00**	**63**	**- 5:57**
+ 5.15	63	- 5:42	+ 5.15	80	- 5:25	+ 5.15	43	+ 5:58	+ 5.15	63	- 5:42
+ 5.30	65	- 5:25	+ 5.30	80	- 5:10	+ 5.30	42	- 5:48	+ 5.30	62	- 5:28
+ 5.45	66	- 5:09	+ 5.45	80	- 4:55	+ 5.45	40	- 5:35	+ 5.45	62	- 5:13
+ 6.00	**68**	**- 4:52**	**+ 6.00**	**80**	**- 4:40**	**+ 6.00**	**39**	**- 5:21**	**+ 6.00**	**61**	**- 4:59**

Via Foulger's Gat and Middle Sunk

SOUTH BOUND

Table B - Essex Rivers to Ramsgate via Fisherman's and Foulger's Gats

Neaps — All times relate to HW Sheerness — **Time to cover Sectors (in minutes) at 6.0 Kts**

SOUTH BOUND

Via Fisherman's Gat and Middle Sunk

Time	B8 Mid-Spitway to Barrow Deep		Time	B7 Barrow Deep to Blk Deep No 8		Time	B6 Blk Deep No 8 to Outer Fisherman	
	Duration	Time at End of Sector		Duration	Time at End of Sector		Duration	Time at End of Sector
- 6.00	84	- 4:36	- 6.00	39	- 5:21	- 6.00	33	- 5:27
- 5.45	98	- 4:07	- 5.45	39	- 5:06	- 5.45	34	- 5:11
- 5.30	112	- 3:38	- 5.30	39	- 4:51	- 5.30	35	- 4:55
- 5.15	126	- 3:09	- 5.15	39	- 4:36	- 5.15	35	- 4:40
- 5.00	140	- 2:40	- 5.00	38	- 4:22	- 5.00	36	- 4:24
- 4.45	141	- 2:24	- 4.45	38	- 4:07	- 4.45	36	- 4:09
- 4.30	141	- 2:09	- 4.30	38	- 3:52	- 4.30	37	- 3:53
- 4.15	141	- 1:54	- 4.15	39	- 3:36	- 4.15	37	- 3:38
- 4.00	141	- 1:39	- 4.00	39	- 3:21	- 4.00	38	- 3:22
- 3.45	127	- 1:38	- 3.45	39	- 3:06	- 3.45	38	- 3:07
- 3.30	113	- 1:37	- 3.30	39	- 2:51	- 3.30	39	- 2:51
- 3.15	99	- 1:36	- 3.15	40	- 2:35	- 3.15	40	- 2:35
- 3.00	85	- 1:35	- 3.00	40	- 2:20	- 3.00	40	- 2:20
- 2.45	84	- 1:21	- 2.45	41	- 2:04	- 2.45	41	- 2:04
- 2.30	84	- 1:06	- 2.30	41	- 1:49	- 2.30	42	- 1:48
- 2.15	83	- 0:52	- 2.15	41	- 1:34	- 2.15	42	- 1:33
- 2.00	82	- 0:38	- 2.00	41	- 1:19	- 2.00	43	- 1:17
- 1.45	80	- 0:25	- 1.45	42	- 1:03	- 1.45	43	- 1:02
- 1.30	79	- 0:11	- 1.30	42	- 0:48	- 1.30	42	- 0:48
- 1.15	77	+ 0:02	- 1.15	42	- 0:33	- 1.15	42	- 0:33
- 1.00	76	+ 0:16	- 1.00	42	- 0:18	- 1.00	41	- 0:19
- 0.45	75	+ 0:30	- 0.45	43	- 0:02	- 0.45	40	- 0:05
- 0.30	74	+ 0:44	- 0.30	43	+ 0:13	- 0.30	39	+ 0:09
- 0.15	73	+ 0:58	- 0.15	43	+ 0:28	- 0.15	38	+ 0:23
HW	72	+ 1:12	HW	44	+ 0:44	HW	38	+ 0:38
+ 0.15	71	+ 1:26	+ 0.15	44	+ 0:59	+ 0.15	37	+ 0:52
+ 0.30	70	+ 1:40	+ 0.30	45	+ 1:15	+ 0.30	36	+ 1:06
+ 0.45	70	+ 1:55	+ 0.45	45	+ 1:30	+ 0.45	35	+ 1:20
+ 1.00	69	+ 2:09	+ 1.00	45	+ 1:45	+ 1.00	34	+ 1:34
+ 1.15	69	+ 2:24	+ 1.15	45	+ 2:00	+ 1.15	33	+ 1:48
+ 1.30	69	+ 2:39	+ 1.30	45	+ 2:15	+ 1.30	33	+ 2:03
+ 1.45	69	+ 2:54	+ 1.45	45	+ 2:30	+ 1.45	32	+ 2:17
+ 2.00	69	+ 3:09	+ 2.00	45	+ 2:45	+ 2.00	32	+ 2:32
+ 2.15	69	+ 3:24	+ 2.15	45	+ 3:00	+ 2.15	32	+ 2:47
+ 2.30	69	+ 3:39	+ 2.30	45	+ 3:15	+ 2.30	32	+ 3:02
+ 2.45	70	+ 3:55	+ 2.45	45	+ 3:30	+ 2.45	31	+ 3:16
+ 3.00	70	+ 4:10	+ 3.00	44	+ 3:44	+ 3.00	31	+ 3:31
+ 3.15	71	+ 4:26	+ 3.15	44	+ 3:59	+ 3.15	31	+ 3:46
+ 3.30	71	+ 4:41	+ 3.30	43	+ 4:13	+ 3.30	31	+ 4:01
+ 3.45	72	+ 4:57	+ 3.45	43	+ 4:28	+ 3.45	31	+ 4:16
+ 4.00	73	+ 5:13	+ 4.00	43	+ 4:43	+ 4.00	31	+ 4:31
+ 4.15	74	+ 5:29	+ 4.15	42	+ 4:57	+ 4.15	31	+ 4:46
+ 4.30	75	+ 5:45	+ 4.30	42	+ 5:12	+ 4.30	31	+ 5:01
+ 4.45	76	- 5:59	+ 4.45	42	+ 5:27	+ 4.45	31	+ 5:16
+ 5.00	77	- 5:43	+ 5.00	41	+ 5:41	+ 5.00	31	+ 5:31
+ 5.15	77	- 5:28	+ 5.15	41	+ 5:56	+ 5.15	31	+ 5:46
+ 5.30	78	- 5:12	+ 5.30	41	- 5:49	+ 5.30	31	- 5:59
+ 5.45	79	- 4:56	+ 5.45	40	- 5:35	+ 5.45	32	- 5:43
+ 6.00	80	- 4:40	+ 6.00	40	- 5:20	+ 6.00	32	- 5:28

Via Foulger's Gat and Middle Sunk

Time	B5 Mid Spitway to NE Middle		Time	B4 NE Middle to Black Deep		Time	B3 Black Deep to Lg Sand Outer		Time	B2 Long Sand Outer to Tongue		Time	B1 Tongue to North Foreland	
	Duration	Time at End of Sector		Duration	Time at End of Sector		Duration	Time at End of Sector		Duration	Time at End of Sector		Duration	Time at End of Sector
- 6.00	56	- 5:04	- 6.00	57	- 5:03	- 6.00	65	- 4:55	- 6.00	35	- 5:25	- 6.00	58	- 5:02
- 5.45	58	- 4:47	- 5.45	58	- 4:47	- 5.45	65	- 4:40	- 5.45	34	- 5:11	- 5.45	58	- 4:47
- 5.30	59	- 4:31	- 5.30	59	- 4:31	- 5.30	65	- 4:25	- 5.30	34	- 4:56	- 5.30	58	- 4:32
- 5.15	60	- 4:15	- 5.15	59	- 4:16	- 5.15	65	- 4:10	- 5.15	34	- 4:41	- 5.15	58	- 4:17
- 5.00	61	- 3:59	- 5.00	60	- 4:00	- 5.00	65	- 3:55	- 5.00	34	- 4:26	- 5.00	58	- 4:02
- 4.45	61	- 3:44	- 4.45	60	- 3:45	- 4.45	66	- 3:39	- 4.45	34	- 4:11	- 4.45	59	- 3:46
- 4.30	61	- 3:29	- 4.30	61	- 3:29	- 4.30	66	- 3:24	- 4.30	34	- 3:56	- 4.30	60	- 3:30
- 4.15	62	- 3:13	- 4.15	61	- 3:14	- 4.15	66	- 3:09	- 4.15	34	- 3:41	- 4.15	61	- 3:14
- 4.00	62	- 2:58	- 4.00	61	- 2:59	- 4.00	66	- 2:54	- 4.00	35	- 3:25	- 4.00	62	- 2:58
- 3.45	62	- 2:43	- 3.45	60	- 2:45	- 3.45	67	- 2:38	- 3.45	35	- 3:10	- 3.45	63	- 2:42
- 3.30	61	- 2:29	- 3.30	60	- 2:30	- 3.30	68	- 2:22	- 3.30	36	- 2:54	- 3.30	65	- 2:25
- 3.15	61	- 2:14	- 3.15	60	- 2:15	- 3.15	69	- 2:06	- 3.15	36	- 2:39	- 3.15	67	- 2:08
- 3.00	60	- 2:00	- 3.00	59	- 2:01	- 3.00	70	- 1:50	- 3.00	37	- 2:23	- 3.00	68	- 1:52
- 2.45	60	- 1:45	- 2.45	59	- 1:46	- 2.45	71	- 1:34	- 2.45	38	- 2:07	- 2.45	70	- 1:35
- 2.30	59	- 1:31	- 2.30	58	- 1:32	- 2.30	73	- 1:17	- 2.30	38	- 1:52	- 2.30	71	- 1:19
- 2.15	58	- 1:17	- 2.15	57	- 1:18	- 2.15	74	- 1:01	- 2.15	39	- 1:36	- 2.15	73	- 1:02
- 2.00	57	- 1:03	- 2.00	56	- 1:04	- 2.00	76	- 0:44	- 2.00	40	- 1:20	- 2.00	74	- 0:46
- 1.45	56	- 0:49	- 1.45	55	- 0:50	- 1.45	77	- 0:28	- 1.45	41	- 1:04	- 1.45	75	- 0:30
- 1.30	55	- 0:35	- 1.30	54	- 0:36	- 1.30	77	- 0:13	- 1.30	42	- 0:48	- 1.30	75	- 0:15
- 1.15	53	- 0:22	- 1.15	53	- 0:22	- 1.15	78	+ 0:03	- 1.15	43	- 0:32	- 1.15	75	HW
- 1.00	52	- 0:08	- 1.00	52	- 0:08	- 1.00	78	+ 0:18	- 1.00	43	- 0:17	- 1.00	76	+ 0:16
- 0.45	51	+ 0:06	- 0.45	51	+ 0:06	- 0.45	78	+ 0:33	- 0.45	44	- 0:01	- 0.45	75	+ 0:30
- 0.30	50	+ 0:20	- 0.30	50	+ 0:20	- 0.30	77	+ 0:47	- 0.30	45	+ 0:15	- 0.30	75	+ 0:45
- 0.15	49	+ 0:34	- 0.15	49	+ 0:34	- 0.15	77	+ 1:02	- 0.15	46	+ 0:31	- 0.15	75	+ 1:00
HW	47	+ 0:47	HW	48	+ 0:48	HW	76	+ 1:16	HW	46	+ 0:46	HW	74	+ 1:14
+ 0.15	47	+ 1:02	+ 0.15	48	+ 1:03	+ 0.15	76	+ 1:31	+ 0.15	47	+ 1:02	+ 0.15	73	+ 1:28
+ 0.30	46	+ 1:16	+ 0.30	47	+ 1:17	+ 0.30	76	+ 1:46	+ 0.30	47	+ 1:17	+ 0.30	72	+ 1:42
+ 0.45	45	+ 1:30	+ 0.45	47	+ 1:32	+ 0.45	75	+ 2:00	+ 0.45	47	+ 1:32	+ 0.45	72	+ 1:57
+ 1.00	44	+ 1:44	+ 1.00	47	+ 1:47	+ 1.00	75	+ 2:15	+ 1.00	47	+ 1:47	+ 1.00	71	+ 2:11
+ 1.15	44	+ 1:59	+ 1.15	46	+ 2:01	+ 1.15	75	+ 2:30	+ 1.15	47	+ 2:02	+ 1.15	70	+ 2:25
+ 1.30	44	+ 2:14	+ 1.30	46	+ 2:16	+ 1.30	74	+ 2:44	+ 1.30	47	+ 2:17	+ 1.30	68	+ 2:38
+ 1.45	44	+ 2:29	+ 1.45	46	+ 2:31	+ 1.45	74	+ 2:59	+ 1.45	46	+ 2:31	+ 1.45	67	+ 2:52
+ 2.00	44	+ 2:44	+ 2.00	46	+ 2:46	+ 2.00	74	+ 3:14	+ 2.00	46	+ 2:46	+ 2.00	66	+ 3:06
+ 2.15	44	+ 2:59	+ 2.15	46	+ 3:01	+ 2.15	73	+ 3:28	+ 2.15	45	+ 3:00	+ 2.15	65	+ 3:20
+ 2.30	44	+ 3:14	+ 2.30	46	+ 3:16	+ 2.30	72	+ 3:42	+ 2.30	45	+ 3:15	+ 2.30	64	+ 3:34
+ 2.45	45	+ 3:30	+ 2.45	46	+ 3:31	+ 2.45	71	+ 3:56	+ 2.45	44	+ 3:29	+ 2.45	64	+ 3:49
+ 3.00	45	+ 3:45	+ 3.00	46	+ 3:46	+ 3.00	71	+ 4:11	+ 3.00	43	+ 3:43	+ 3.00	63	+ 4:03
+ 3.15	46	+ 4:01	+ 3.15	47	+ 4:02	+ 3.15	70	+ 4:25	+ 3.15	43	+ 3:58	+ 3.15	62	+ 4:17
+ 3.30	46	+ 4:16	+ 3.30	48	+ 4:18	+ 3.30	70	+ 4:40	+ 3.30	42	+ 4:12	+ 3.30	62	+ 4:32
+ 3.45	47	+ 4:32	+ 3.45	48	+ 4:33	+ 3.45	70	+ 4:55	+ 3.45	41	+ 4:26	+ 3.45	61	+ 4:46
+ 4.00	48	+ 4:48	+ 4.00	49	+ 4:49	+ 4.00	69	+ 5:09	+ 4.00	41	+ 4:41	+ 4.00	61	+ 5:01
+ 4.15	48	+ 5:03	+ 4.15	49	+ 5:04	+ 4.15	69	+ 5:24	+ 4.15	40	+ 4:55	+ 4.15	60	+ 5:15
+ 4.30	49	+ 5:19	+ 4.30	50	+ 5:20	+ 4.30	69	+ 5:39	+ 4.30	39	+ 5:09	+ 4.30	60	+ 5:30
+ 4.45	50	+ 5:35	+ 4.45	51	+ 5:36	+ 4.45	68	+ 5:53	+ 4.45	39	+ 5:24	+ 4.45	59	+ 5:44
+ 5.00	50	+ 5:50	+ 5.00	51	+ 5:51	+ 5.00	68	- 5:52	+ 5.00	38	+ 5:38	+ 5.00	59	+ 5:59
+ 5.15	51	- 5:54	+ 5.15	52	- 5:53	+ 5.15	67	- 5:38	+ 5.15	38	+ 5:53	+ 5.15	59	- 5:46
+ 5.30	52	- 5:38	+ 5.30	53	- 5:37	+ 5.30	67	- 5:23	+ 5.30	37	- 5:53	+ 5.30	58	- 5:32
+ 5.45	52	- 5:23	+ 5.45	53	- 5:22	+ 5.45	66	- 5:09	+ 5.45	36	- 5:39	+ 5.45	58	- 5:17
+ 6.00	53	- 5:07	+ 6.00	54	- 5:06	+ 6.00	65	- 4:55	+ 6.00	36	- 5:24	+ 6.00	58	- 5:02

Table B - Essex Rivers to Ramsgate via Fisherman's and Foulger's Gats

Time to cover Sectors (in minutes) at 6.0 kts — All times relate to HW Sheerness — **Springs**

SOUTH BOUND

	B8		B7		B6		B5		B4		B3		B2		B1	
	Mid-Spitway to Barrow Deep		Barrow Deep to Blk Deep No 8		Blk Deep No 8 to Outer Fisherman		Mid Spitway to NE Middle		NE Middle to Black Deep		Black Deep to Lg Sand Outer		Long Sand Outer to Tongue		Tongue to North Foreland	
Time	Duration	Time at End of Sector	Duration	Time at End of Sector	Duration	Time at End of Sector	Duration	Time at End of Sector	Duration	Time at End of Sector	Duration	Time at End of Sector	Duration	Time at End of Sector	Duration	Time at End of Sector
- 6.00	**88**	**- 4:32**	**39**	**- 5:21**	**32**	**- 5:28**	**59**	**- 5:01**	**60**	**- 5:00**	**63**	**- 4:57**	**32**	**- 5:28**	**53**	**- 5:07**
- 5.45	90	- 4:15	38	- 5:07	33	- 5:12	61	- 4:44	61	- 4:44	63	- 4:42	32	- 5:13	53	- 4:52
- 5.30	92	- 3:58	38	- 4:52	34	- 4:56	63	- 4:27	62	- 4:28	64	- 4:26	32	- 4:58	54	- 4:36
- 5.15	94	- 3:41	38	- 4:37	35	- 4:40	65	- 4:10	64	- 4:11	64	- 4:11	32	- 4:43	54	- 4:21
- 5.00	**96**	**- 3:24**	**37**	**- 4:23**	**36**	**- 4:24**	**67**	**- 3:53**	**65**	**- 3:55**	**64**	**- 3:56**	**31**	**- 4:29**	**54**	**- 4:06**
- 4.45	96	- 3:09	37	- 4:08	37	- 4:08	67	- 3:38	65	- 3:40	65	- 3:40	32	- 4:13	55	- 3:50
- 4.30	96	- 2:54	38	- 3:52	38	- 3:52	68	- 3:22	65	- 3:25	65	- 3:25	32	- 3:58	57	- 3:33
- 4.15	96	- 2:39	38	- 3:37	39	- 3:36	68	- 3:07	66	- 3:09	65	- 3:10	32	- 3:43	58	- 3:17
- 4.00	**96**	**- 2:24**	**38**	**- 3:22**	**40**	**- 3:20**	**68**	**- 2:52**	**66**	**- 2:54**	**66**	**- 2:54**	**32**	**- 3:28**	**59**	**- 3:01**
- 3.45	95	- 2:10	39	- 3:06	41	- 3:04	68	- 2:37	65	- 2:40	67	- 2:38	33	- 3:12	62	- 2:43
- 3.30	94	- 1:56	39	- 2:51	42	- 2:48	67	- 2:23	64	- 2:26	69	- 2:21	34	- 2:56	65	- 2:25
- 3.15	92	- 1:43	40	- 2:35	43	- 2:32	67	- 2:08	64	- 2:11	70	- 2:05	34	- 2:41	68	- 2:07
- 3.00	**91**	**- 1:29**	**40**	**- 2:20**	**44**	**- 2:16**	**66**	**- 1:54**	**63**	**- 1:57**	**71**	**- 1:49**	**35**	**- 2:25**	**71**	**- 1:49**
- 2.45	90	- 1:15	41	- 2:04	45	- 2:00	65	- 1:40	62	- 1:43	74	- 1:31	36	- 2:09	74	- 1:31
- 2.30	88	- 1:02	41	- 1:49	46	- 1:44	63	- 1:27	61	- 1:29	76	- 1:14	38	- 1:52	77	- 1:13
- 2.15	86	- 0:49	42	- 1:33	47	- 1:28	62	- 1:13	60	- 1:15	78	- 0:57	39	- 1:36	80	- 0:55
- 2.00	**84**	**- 0:36**	**42**	**- 1:18**	**48**	**- 1:12**	**60**	**- 1:00**	**59**	**- 1:01**	**80**	**- 0:40**	**40**	**- 1:20**	**82**	**- 0:38**
- 1.45	82	- 0:23	42	- 1:03	48	- 0:57	58	- 0:47	57	- 0:48	81	- 0:24	42	- 1:03	83	- 0:22
- 1.30	80	- 0:10	42	- 0:48	47	- 0:43	56	- 0:34	56	- 0:34	81	- 0:09	43	- 0:47	84	- 0:06
- 1.15	78	+ 0:03	43	- 0:32	46	- 0:29	54	- 0:21	54	- 0:21	82	+ 0:07	44	- 0:31	84	+ 0:09
- 1.00	**76**	**+ 0:16**	**43**	**- 0:17**	**45**	**- 0:15**	**53**	**- 0:07**	**52**	**- 0:08**	**83**	**+ 0:23**	**45**	**- 0:15**	**85**	**+ 0:25**
- 0.45	74	+ 0:29	44	- 0:01	43	- 0:02	51	+ 0:06	51	+ 0:06	82	+ 0:37	47	+ 0:02	84	+ 0:39
- 0.30	73	+ 0:43	44	+ 0:14	42	+ 0:12	49	+ 0:19	50	+ 0:20	82	+ 0:52	48	+ 0:18	83	+ 0:53
- 0.15	71	+ 0:56	45	+ 0:30	40	+ 0:25	47	+ 0:32	48	+ 0:33	81	+ 1:06	49	+ 0:34	82	+ 1:07
HW	**69**	**+ 1:09**	**46**	**+ 0:46**	**39**	**+ 0:39**	**45**	**+ 0:45**	**47**	**+ 0:47**	**81**	**+ 1:21**	**50**	**+ 0:50**	**81**	**+ 1:21**
+ 0.15	69	+ 1:24	46	+ 1:01	37	+ 0:52	44	+ 0:59	46	+ 1:01	80	+ 1:35	51	+ 1:06	80	+ 1:35
+ 0.30	68	+ 1:38	47	+ 1:17	36	+ 1:06	43	+ 1:13	46	+ 1:16	80	+ 1:50	51	+ 1:21	78	+ 1:48
+ 0.45	67	+ 1:52	47	+ 1:32	34	+ 1:19	42	+ 1:27	45	+ 1:30	80	+ 2:05	52	+ 1:37	77	+ 2:02
+ 1.00	**67**	**+ 2:07**	**48**	**+ 1:48**	**33**	**+ 1:33**	**41**	**+ 1:41**	**44**	**+ 1:44**	**80**	**+ 2:20**	**52**	**+ 1:52**	**75**	**+ 2:15**
+ 1.15	67	+ 2:22	48	+ 2:03	32	+ 1:47	41	+ 1:56	44	+ 1:59	79	+ 2:34	51	+ 2:06	73	+ 2:28
+ 1.30	66	+ 2:36	48	+ 2:18	32	+ 2:02	41	+ 2:11	44	+ 2:14	78	+ 2:48	51	+ 2:21	71	+ 2:41
+ 1.45	66	+ 2:51	48	+ 2:33	31	+ 2:16	40	+ 2:25	44	+ 2:29	78	+ 3:03	50	+ 2:35	69	+ 2:54
+ 2.00	**66**	**+ 3:06**	**48**	**+ 2:48**	**31**	**+ 2:31**	**40**	**+ 2:40**	**44**	**+ 2:44**	**77**	**+ 3:17**	**50**	**+ 2:50**	**68**	**+ 3:08**
+ 2.15	66	+ 3:21	48	+ 3:03	30	+ 2:45	41	+ 2:56	44	+ 2:59	76	+ 3:31	49	+ 3:04	66	+ 3:21
+ 2.30	67	+ 3:37	47	+ 3:17	30	+ 3:00	41	+ 3:11	44	+ 3:14	74	+ 3:44	48	+ 3:18	65	+ 3:35
+ 2.45	67	+ 3:52	47	+ 3:32	29	+ 3:14	42	+ 3:27	44	+ 3:29	73	+ 3:58	46	+ 3:31	63	+ 3:48
+ 3.00	**67**	**+ 4:07**	**46**	**+ 3:46**	**29**	**+ 3:29**	**42**	**+ 3:42**	**44**	**+ 3:44**	**72**	**+ 4:12**	**45**	**+ 3:45**	**62**	**+ 4:02**
+ 3.15	68	+ 4:23	46	+ 4:01	29	+ 3:44	43	+ 3:58	45	+ 4:00	71	+ 4:26	44	+ 3:59	61	+ 4:16
+ 3.30	69	+ 4:39	45	+ 4:15	29	+ 3:59	44	+ 4:14	46	+ 4:16	71	+ 4:41	43	+ 4:13	60	+ 4:30
+ 3.45	70	+ 4:55	45	+ 4:30	29	+ 4:14	45	+ 4:30	46	+ 4:31	70	+ 4:55	42	+ 4:27	59	+ 4:44
+ 4.00	**71**	**+ 5:11**	**44**	**+ 4:44**	**28**	**+ 4:28**	**46**	**+ 4:46**	**47**	**+ 4:47**	**69**	**+ 5:09**	**41**	**+ 4:41**	**58**	**+ 4:58**
+ 4.15	72	+ 5:27	43	+ 4:58	28	+ 4:43	47	+ 5:02	48	+ 5:03	69	+ 5:24	40	+ 4:55	57	+ 5:12
+ 4.30	73	+ 5:43	43	+ 5:13	28	+ 4:58	48	+ 5:18	49	+ 5:19	68	+ 5:38	40	+ 5:10	56	+ 5:26
+ 4.45	75	- 6:00	42	+ 5:27	28	+ 5:13	49	+ 5:34	50	+ 5:35	68	+ 5:53	39	+ 5:24	55	+ 5:40
+ 5.00	**76**	**- 5:44**	**41**	**+ 5:41**	**28**	**+ 5:28**	**50**	**+ 5:50**	**51**	**+ 5:51**	**67**	**- 5:53**	**38**	**+ 5:38**	**55**	**+ 5:55**
+ 5.15	77	- 5:28	41	+ 5:56	29	+ 5:44	51	- 5:54	52	- 5:53	66	- 5:39	37	+ 5:52	54	- 5:51
+ 5.30	79	- 5:11	40	- 5:50	29	+ 5:59	52	- 5:38	53	- 5:37	66	- 5:24	36	- 5:54	54	- 5:36
+ 5.45	80	- 4:55	40	- 5:35	30	- 5:45	53	- 5:22	54	- 5:21	65	- 5:10	35	- 5:40	54	- 5:21
+ 6.00	**81**	**- 4:39**	**40**	**- 5:20**	**31**	**- 5:29**	**54**	**- 5:06**	**55**	**- 5:05**	**65**	**- 4:55**	**34**	**- 5:26**	**53**	**- 5:07**

Via Fisherman's Gat and Middle Sunk (B8–B6)

Via Foulger's Gat and Middle Sunk (B5–B1)

Table B - Essex Rivers to Ramsgate via Fisherman's and Foulger's Gats

Neaps — All times relate to HW Sheerness — Time to cover Sectors (in minutes) at 7.0 Kts

SOUTH BOUND

	B8 Mid-Spitway to Barrow Deep			B7 Barrow Deep to Blk Deep No 8			B6 Blk Deep No 8 to Outer Fisherman			B5 Mid Spitway to NE Middle	
Time	Duration	Time at End of Sector	Time	Duration	Time at End of Sector	Time	Duration	Time at End of Sector	Time	Duration	Time at End of Sector
- 6.00	71	- 4:49	- 6.00	34	- 5:26	- 6.00	28	- 5:32	- 6.00	47	- 5:13
- 5.45	71	- 4:34	- 5.45	34	- 5:11	- 5.45	29	- 5:16	- 5.45	48	- 4:57
- 5.30	72	- 4:18	- 5.30	34	- 4:56	- 5.30	29	- 5:01	- 5.30	49	- 4:41
- 5.15	73	- 4:02	- 5.15	33	- 4:42	- 5.15	30	- 4:45	- 5.15	50	- 4:25
- 5.00	73	- 3:47	- 5.00	33	- 4:27	- 5.00	31	- 4:29	- 5.00	51	- 4:09
- 4.45	73	- 3:32	- 4.45	33	- 4:12	- 4.45	31	- 4:14	- 4.45	51	- 3:54
- 4.30	73	- 3:17	- 4.30	33	- 3:57	- 4.30	31	- 3:59	- 4.30	51	- 3:39
- 4.15	74	- 3:01	- 4.15	33	- 3:42	- 4.15	32	- 3:43	- 4.15	52	- 3:23
- 4.00	74	- 2:46	- 4.00	33	- 3:27	- 4.00	32	- 3:28	- 4.00	52	- 3:08
- 3.45	73	- 2:32	- 3.45	33	- 3:12	- 3.45	32	- 3:13	- 3.45	51	- 2:54
- 3.30	73	- 2:17	- 3.30	34	- 2:56	- 3.30	33	- 2:57	- 3.30	51	- 2:39
- 3.15	73	- 2:02	- 3.15	34	- 2:41	- 3.15	33	- 2:42	- 3.15	51	- 2:24
- 3.00	72	- 1:48	- 3.00	34	- 2:26	- 3.00	33	- 2:27	- 3.00	51	- 2:09
- 2.45	71	- 1:34	- 2.45	35	- 2:10	- 2.45	34	- 2:11	- 2.45	50	- 1:55
- 2.30	71	- 1:19	- 2.30	35	- 1:55	- 2.30	35	- 1:55	- 2.30	50	- 1:40
- 2.15	70	- 1:05	- 2.15	35	- 1:40	- 2.15	35	- 1:40	- 2.15	49	- 1:26
- 2.00	70	- 0:50	- 2.00	35	- 1:25	- 2.00	36	- 1:24	- 2.00	48	- 1:12
- 1.45	69	- 0:36	- 1.45	35	- 1:10	- 1.45	36	- 1:09	- 1.45	47	- 0:58
- 1.30	68	- 0:22	- 1.30	36	- 0:54	- 1.30	35	- 0:55	- 1.30	47	- 0:43
- 1.15	67	- 0:08	- 1.15	36	- 0:39	- 1.15	35	- 0:40	- 1.15	46	- 0:29
- 1.00	66	+ 0:06	- 1.00	36	- 0:24	- 1.00	35	- 0:25	- 1.00	45	- 0:15
- 0.45	65	+ 0:20	- 0.45	36	- 0:09	- 0.45	34	- 0:11	- 0.45	44	- 0:01
- 0.30	64	+ 0:34	- 0.30	36	+ 0:06	- 0.30	33	+ 0:03	- 0.30	43	+ 0:13
- 0.15	63	+ 0:48	- 0.15	37	+ 0:22	- 0.15	33	+ 0:18	- 0.15	42	+ 0:27
HW	62	+ 1:02	HW	37	+ 0:37	HW	32	+ 0:32	HW	41	+ 0:41
+ 0.15	62	+ 1:17	+ 0.15	37	+ 0:52	+ 0.15	31	+ 0:46	+ 0.15	41	+ 0:56
+ 0.30	61	+ 1:31	+ 0.30	38	+ 1:08	+ 0.30	31	+ 1:01	+ 0.30	40	+ 1:10
+ 0.45	61	+ 1:46	+ 0.45	38	+ 1:23	+ 0.45	30	+ 1:15	+ 0.45	39	+ 1:24
+ 1.00	60	+ 2:00	+ 1.00	38	+ 1:38	+ 1.00	29	+ 1:29	+ 1.00	39	+ 1:39
+ 1.15	60	+ 2:15	+ 1.15	38	+ 1:53	+ 1.15	29	+ 1:44	+ 1.15	39	+ 1:54
+ 1.30	60	+ 2:30	+ 1.30	38	+ 2:08	+ 1.30	28	+ 1:58	+ 1.30	39	+ 2:09
+ 1.45	60	+ 2:45	+ 1.45	38	+ 2:23	+ 1.45	28	+ 2:13	+ 1.45	38	+ 2:23
+ 2.00	60	+ 3:00	+ 2.00	38	+ 2:38	+ 2.00	28	+ 2:28	+ 2.00	38	+ 2:38
+ 2.15	60	+ 3:15	+ 2.15	38	+ 2:53	+ 2.15	27	+ 2:42	+ 2.15	39	+ 2:54
+ 2.30	60	+ 3:30	+ 2.30	38	+ 3:08	+ 2.30	27	+ 2:57	+ 2.30	39	+ 3:09
+ 2.45	60	+ 3:45	+ 2.45	38	+ 3:23	+ 2.45	27	+ 3:12	+ 2.45	39	+ 3:24
+ 3.00	60	+ 4:00	+ 3.00	38	+ 3:38	+ 3.00	27	+ 3:27	+ 3.00	39	+ 3:39
+ 3.15	61	+ 4:16	+ 3.15	37	+ 3:52	+ 3.15	27	+ 3:42	+ 3.15	40	+ 3:55
+ 3.30	62	+ 4:32	+ 3.30	37	+ 4:07	+ 3.30	27	+ 3:57	+ 3.30	40	+ 4:10
+ 3.45	62	+ 4:47	+ 3.45	37	+ 4:22	+ 3.45	27	+ 4:12	+ 3.45	41	+ 4:26
+ 4.00	63	+ 5:03	+ 4.00	36	+ 4:36	+ 4.00	26	+ 4:26	+ 4.00	41	+ 4:41
+ 4.15	63	+ 5:18	+ 4.15	36	+ 4:51	+ 4.15	26	+ 4:41	+ 4.15	41	+ 4:56
+ 4.30	64	+ 5:34	+ 4.30	36	+ 5:06	+ 4.30	26	+ 4:56	+ 4.30	42	+ 5:12
+ 4.45	65	+ 5:50	+ 4.45	36	+ 5:21	+ 4.45	26	+ 5:11	+ 4.45	42	+ 5:27
+ 5.00	65	- 5:55	+ 5.00	35	+ 5:35	+ 5.00	26	+ 5:26	+ 5.00	43	+ 5:43
+ 5.15	66	- 5:39	+ 5.15	35	+ 5:50	+ 5.15	27	+ 5:42	+ 5.15	43	+ 5:58
+ 5.30	67	- 5:23	+ 5.30	35	- 5:55	+ 5.30	27	+ 5:57	+ 5.30	44	- 5:46
+ 5.45	67	- 5:08	+ 5.45	35	- 5:40	+ 5.45	27	- 5:48	+ 5.45	45	- 5:30
+ 6.00	68	- 4:52	+ 6.00	35	- 5:25	+ 6.00	28	- 5:32	+ 6.00	45	- 5:15

Via Fisherman's Gat and Middle Sunk

	B4 NE Middle to Black Deep			B3 Black Deep to Lg Sand Outer			B2 Long Sand Outer to Tongue			B1 Tongue to North Foreland	
Time	Duration	Time at End of Sector	Time	Duration	Time at End of Sector	Time	Duration	Time at End of Sector	Time	Duration	Time at End of Sector
- 6.00	48	- 5:12	- 6.00	56	- 5:04	- 6.00	30	- 5:30	- 6.00	50	- 5:10
- 5.45	49	- 4:56	- 5.45	56	- 4:49	- 5.45	30	- 5:15	- 5.45	50	- 4:55
- 5.30	49	- 4:41	- 5.30	56	- 4:34	- 5.30	30	- 5:00	- 5.30	50	- 4:40
- 5.15	50	- 4:25	- 5.15	56	- 4:19	- 5.15	30	- 4:45	- 5.15	51	- 4:24
- 5.00	50	- 4:10	- 5.00	56	- 4:04	- 5.00	29	- 4:31	- 5.00	51	- 4:09
- 4.45	51	- 3:54	- 4.45	56	- 3:49	- 4.45	30	- 4:15	- 4.45	51	- 3:54
- 4.30	51	- 3:39	- 4.30	56	- 3:34	- 4.30	30	- 4:00	- 4.30	52	- 3:38
- 4.15	51	- 3:24	- 4.15	56	- 3:19	- 4.15	30	- 3:45	- 4.15	52	- 3:23
- 4.00	51	- 3:09	- 4.00	56	- 3:04	- 4.00	30	- 3:30	- 4.00	53	- 3:07
- 3.45	51	- 2:54	- 3.45	57	- 2:48	- 3.45	30	- 3:15	- 3.45	54	- 2:51
- 3.30	51	- 2:39	- 3.30	58	- 2:32	- 3.30	31	- 2:59	- 3.30	55	- 2:35
- 3.15	50	- 2:25	- 3.15	58	- 2:17	- 3.15	31	- 2:44	- 3.15	56	- 2:19
- 3.00	50	- 2:10	- 3.00	59	- 2:01	- 3.00	31	- 2:29	- 3.00	58	- 2:02
- 2.45	49	- 1:56	- 2.45	60	- 1:45	- 2.45	32	- 2:13	- 2.45	59	- 1:46
- 2.30	49	- 1:41	- 2.30	62	- 1:28	- 2.30	33	- 1:57	- 2.30	60	- 1:30
- 2.15	48	- 1:27	- 2.15	63	- 1:12	- 2.15	33	- 1:42	- 2.15	61	- 1:14
- 2.00	48	- 1:12	- 2.00	65	- 0:55	- 2.00	34	- 1:26	- 2.00	62	- 0:58
- 1.45	47	- 0:58	- 1.45	65	- 0:40	- 1.45	35	- 1:10	- 1.45	63	- 0:42
- 1.30	47	- 0:43	- 1.30	66	- 0:24	- 1.30	35	- 0:55	- 1.30	63	- 0:27
- 1.15	46	- 0:29	- 1.15	66	- 0:09	- 1.15	36	- 0:39	- 1.15	63	- 0:12
- 1.00	45	- 0:15	- 1.00	67	+ 0:07	- 1.00	36	- 0:24	- 1.00	64	+ 0:04
- 0.45	44	- 0:01	- 0.45	66	+ 0:21	- 0.45	37	- 0:08	- 0.45	63	+ 0:18
- 0.30	44	+ 0:14	- 0.30	66	+ 0:36	- 0.30	38	+ 0:08	- 0.30	63	+ 0:33
- 0.15	43	+ 0:28	- 0.15	66	+ 0:51	- 0.15	38	+ 0:23	- 0.15	63	+ 0:48
HW	42	+ 0:42	HW	66	+ 1:06	HW	39	+ 0:39	HW	63	+ 1:03
+ 0.15	42	+ 0:57	+ 0.15	65	+ 1:20	+ 0.15	39	+ 0:54	+ 0.15	62	+ 1:17
+ 0.30	41	+ 1:11	+ 0.30	65	+ 1:35	+ 0.30	39	+ 1:09	+ 0.30	61	+ 1:31
+ 0.45	41	+ 1:26	+ 0.45	65	+ 1:50	+ 0.45	39	+ 1:24	+ 0.45	61	+ 1:46
+ 1.00	41	+ 1:41	+ 1.00	64	+ 2:04	+ 1.00	40	+ 1:40	+ 1.00	60	+ 2:00
+ 1.15	40	+ 1:55	+ 1.15	64	+ 2:19	+ 1.15	39	+ 1:54	+ 1.15	59	+ 2:14
+ 1.30	40	+ 2:10	+ 1.30	64	+ 2:34	+ 1.30	39	+ 2:09	+ 1.30	58	+ 2:28
+ 1.45	40	+ 2:25	+ 1.45	64	+ 2:49	+ 1.45	39	+ 2:24	+ 1.45	57	+ 2:42
+ 2.00	40	+ 2:40	+ 2.00	63	+ 3:03	+ 2.00	39	+ 2:39	+ 2.00	57	+ 2:57
+ 2.15	40	+ 2:55	+ 2.15	63	+ 3:18	+ 2.15	38	+ 2:53	+ 2.15	56	+ 3:11
+ 2.30	40	+ 3:10	+ 2.30	62	+ 3:32	+ 2.30	38	+ 3:08	+ 2.30	55	+ 3:25
+ 2.45	40	+ 3:25	+ 2.45	61	+ 3:46	+ 2.45	37	+ 3:22	+ 2.45	55	+ 3:40
+ 3.00	40	+ 3:40	+ 3.00	61	+ 4:01	+ 3.00	37	+ 3:37	+ 3.00	54	+ 3:54
+ 3.15	41	+ 3:56	+ 3.15	60	+ 4:15	+ 3.15	36	+ 3:51	+ 3.15	54	+ 4:09
+ 3.30	41	+ 4:11	+ 3.30	60	+ 4:30	+ 3.30	36	+ 4:06	+ 3.30	53	+ 4:23
+ 3.45	41	+ 4:26	+ 3.45	60	+ 4:45	+ 3.45	35	+ 4:20	+ 3.45	53	+ 4:38
+ 4.00	42	+ 4:42	+ 4.00	59	+ 4:59	+ 4.00	35	+ 4:35	+ 4.00	53	+ 4:53
+ 4.15	42	+ 4:57	+ 4.15	59	+ 5:14	+ 4.15	34	+ 4:49	+ 4.15	52	+ 5:07
+ 4.30	43	+ 5:13	+ 4.30	59	+ 5:29	+ 4.30	34	+ 5:04	+ 4.30	52	+ 5:22
+ 4.45	43	+ 5:28	+ 4.45	58	+ 5:43	+ 4.45	34	+ 5:19	+ 4.45	52	+ 5:37
+ 5.00	44	+ 5:44	+ 5.00	58	+ 5:58	+ 5.00	33	+ 5:33	+ 5.00	51	+ 5:51
+ 5.15	44	+ 5:59	+ 5.15	58	- 5:47	+ 5.15	33	+ 5:48	+ 5.15	51	- 5:54
+ 5.30	45	- 5:45	+ 5.30	58	- 5:32	+ 5.30	32	- 5:58	+ 5.30	51	- 5:39
+ 5.45	45	- 5:30	+ 5.45	58	- 5:17	+ 5.45	32	- 5:43	+ 5.45	51	- 5:24
+ 6.00	46	- 5:14	+ 6.00	57	- 5:03	+ 6.00	31	- 5:29	+ 6.00	50	- 5:10

Via Foulger's Gat and Middle Sunk

Table B - Essex Rivers to Ramsgate via Fisherman's and Foulger's Gats

Time to cover Sectors (in minutes) at 7.0 kts | All times relate to HW Sheerness | **Springs**

	B8			B7			B6			B5			B4			B3			B2			B1	
	Mid-Spitway to Barrow Deep			Barrow Deep to Blk Deep No 8			Blk Deep No 8 to Outer Fisherman			Mid Spitway to NE Middle			NE Middle to Black Deep			Black Deep to Lg Sand Outer			Long Sand Outer to Tongue			Tongue to North Foreland	
Time	*Duration*	*Time at End of Sector*	*Time*	*Duration*	*Time at End of Sector*	*Time*	*Duration*	*Time at End of Sector*	*Time*	*Duration*	*Time at End of Sector*	*Time*	*Duration*	*Time at End of Sector*	*Time*	*Duration*	*Time at End of Sector*	*Time*	*Duration*	*Time at End of Sector*	*Time*	*Duration*	*Time at End of Sector*
- 6.00	**73**	**- 4:47**	**- 6.00**	**33**	**- 5:27**	**- 6.00**	**27**	**- 5:33**	**- 6.00**	**49**	**- 5:11**	**- 6.00**	**50**	**- 5:10**	**- 6.00**	**54**	**- 5:06**	**- 6.00**	**28**	**- 5:32**	**- 6.00**	**47**	**- 5:13**
- 5.45	74	- 4:31	- 5.45	33	- 5:12	- 5.45	28	- 5:17	- 5.45	51	- 4:54	- 5.45	51	- 4:54	- 5.45	54	- 4:51	- 5.45	28	- 5:17	- 5.45	47	- 4:58
- 5.30	75	- 4:15	- 5.30	33	- 4:57	- 5.30	29	- 5:01	- 5.30	52	- 4:38	- 5.30	52	- 4:38	- 5.30	54	- 4:36	- 5.30	28	- 5:02	- 5.30	47	- 4:43
- 5.15	76	- 3:59	- 5.15	33	- 4:42	- 5.15	30	- 4:45	- 5.15	54	- 4:21	- 5.15	53	- 4:22	- 5.15	54	- 4:21	- 5.15	28	- 4:47	- 5.15	47	- 4:28
- 5.00	**77**	**- 3:43**	**- 5.00**	**32**	**- 4:28**	**- 5.00**	**31**	**- 4:29**	**- 5.00**	**55**	**- 4:05**	**- 5.00**	**54**	**- 4:06**	**- 5.00**	**55**	**- 4:05**	**- 5.00**	**27**	**- 4:33**	**- 5.00**	**47**	**- 4:13**
- 4.45	77	- 3:28	- 4.45	32	- 4:13	- 4.45	31	- 4:14	- 4.45	55	- 3:50	- 4.45	54	- 3:51	- 4.45	55	- 3:50	- 4.45	27	- 4:18	- 4.45	48	- 3:57
- 4.30	78	- 3:12	- 4.30	32	- 3:58	- 4.30	32	- 3:58	- 4.30	56	- 3:34	- 4.30	54	- 3:36	- 4.30	55	- 3:35	- 4.30	28	- 4:02	- 4.30	49	- 3:41
- 4.15	78	- 2:57	- 4.15	32	- 3:43	- 4.15	33	- 3:42	- 4.15	56	- 3:19	- 4.15	54	- 3:21	- 4.15	55	- 3:20	- 4.15	28	- 3:47	- 4.15	50	- 3:25
- 4.00	**78**	**- 2:42**	**- 4.00**	**33**	**- 3:27**	**- 4.00**	**33**	**- 3:27**	**- 4.00**	**56**	**- 3:04**	**- 4.00**	**55**	**- 3:05**	**- 4.00**	**55**	**- 3:05**	**- 4.00**	**28**	**- 3:32**	**- 4.00**	**51**	**- 3:09**
- 3.45	77	- 2:28	- 3.45	33	- 3:12	- 3.45	34	- 3:11	- 3.45	56	- 2:49	- 3.45	54	- 2:51	- 3.45	57	- 2:48	- 3.45	28	- 3:17	- 3.45	53	- 2:52
- 3.30	77	- 2:13	- 3.30	33	- 2:57	- 3.30	35	- 2:55	- 3.30	56	- 2:34	- 3.30	54	- 2:36	- 3.30	58	- 2:32	- 3.30	29	- 3:01	- 3.30	55	- 2:35
- 3.15	76	- 1:59	- 3.15	34	- 2:41	- 3.15	36	- 2:39	- 3.15	55	- 2:20	- 3.15	53	- 2:22	- 3.15	59	- 2:16	- 3.15	29	- 2:46	- 3.15	57	- 2:18
- 3.00	**76**	**- 1:44**	**- 3.00**	**34**	**- 2:26**	**- 3.00**	**36**	**- 2:24**	**- 3.00**	**55**	**- 2:05**	**- 3.00**	**53**	**- 2:07**	**- 3.00**	**60**	**- 2:00**	**- 3.00**	**30**	**- 2:30**	**- 3.00**	**59**	**- 2:01**
- 2.45	75	- 1:30	- 2.45	35	- 2:10	- 2.45	37	- 2:08	- 2.45	54	- 1:51	- 2.45	52	- 1:53	- 2.45	62	- 1:43	- 2.45	31	- 2:14	- 2.45	61	- 1:44
- 2.30	74	- 1:16	- 2.30	35	- 1:55	- 2.30	38	- 1:52	- 2.30	53	- 1:37	- 2.30	51	- 1:39	- 2.30	64	- 1:26	- 2.30	32	- 1:58	- 2.30	64	- 1:26
- 2.15	73	- 1:02	- 2.15	35	- 1:40	- 2.15	39	- 1:36	- 2.15	52	- 1:23	- 2.15	51	- 1:24	- 2.15	66	- 1:09	- 2.15	33	- 1:42	- 2.15	66	- 1:09
- 2.00	**72**	**- 0:48**	**- 2.00**	**36**	**- 1:24**	**- 2.00**	**40**	**- 1:20**	**- 2.00**	**51**	**- 1:09**	**- 2.00**	**50**	**- 1:10**	**- 2.00**	**68**	**- 0:52**	**- 2.00**	**34**	**- 1:26**	**- 2.00**	**68**	**- 0:52**
- 1.45	70	- 0:35	- 1.45	36	- 1:09	- 1.45	40	- 1:05	- 1.45	50	- 0:55	- 1.45	49	- 0:56	- 1.45	69	- 0:36	- 1.45	35	- 1:10	- 1.45	69	- 0:36
- 1.30	68	- 0:22	- 1.30	36	- 0:54	- 1.30	39	- 0:51	- 1.30	48	- 0:42	- 1.30	48	- 0:42	- 1.30	69	- 0:21	- 1.30	36	- 0:54	- 1.30	69	- 0:21
- 1.15	67	- 0:08	- 1.15	36	- 0:39	- 1.15	39	- 0:36	- 1.15	47	- 0:28	- 1.15	46	- 0:29	- 1.15	70	- 0:05	- 1.15	37	- 0:38	- 1.15	70	- 0:05
- 1.00	**65**	**+ 0:05**	**- 1.00**	**36**	**- 0:24**	**- 1.00**	**38**	**- 0:22**	**- 1.00**	**45**	**- 0:15**	**- 1.00**	**45**	**- 0:15**	**- 1.00**	**70**	**+ 0:10**	**- 1.00**	**38**	**- 0:22**	**- 1.00**	**70**	**+ 0:10**
- 0.45	64	+ 0:19	- 0.45	37	- 0:08	- 0.45	37	- 0:08	- 0.45	44	- 0:01	- 0.45	44	- 0:01	- 0.45	70	+ 0:25	- 0.45	39	- 0:06	- 0.45	70	+ 0:25
- 0.30	63	+ 0:33	- 0.30	37	+ 0:07	- 0.30	35	+ 0:05	- 0.30	43	+ 0:13	- 0.30	43	+ 0:13	- 0.30	70	+ 0:40	- 0.30	40	+ 0:10	- 0.30	69	+ 0:39
- 0.15	62	+ 0:47	- 0.15	38	+ 0:23	- 0.15	34	+ 0:19	- 0.15	41	+ 0:26	- 0.15	42	+ 0:27	- 0.15	69	+ 0:54	- 0.15	41	+ 0:26	- 0.15	69	+ 0:54
HW	**60**	**+ 1:00**	**HW**	**38**	**+ 0:38**	**HW**	**33**	**+ 0:33**	**HW**	**40**	**+ 0:40**	**HW**	**41**	**+ 0:41**	**HW**	**69**	**+ 1:09**	**HW**	**42**	**+ 0:42**	**HW**	**68**	**+ 1:08**
+ 0.15	60	+ 1:15	+ 0.15	39	+ 0:54	+ 0.15	32	+ 0:47	+ 0.15	39	+ 0:54	+ 0.15	41	+ 0:56	+ 0.15	69	+ 1:24	+ 0.15	42	+ 0:57	+ 0.15	67	+ 1:22
+ 0.30	59	+ 1:29	+ 0.30	39	+ 1:09	+ 0.30	31	+ 1:01	+ 0.30	38	+ 1:08	+ 0.30	40	+ 1:10	+ 0.30	69	+ 1:39	+ 0.30	42	+ 1:12	+ 0.30	66	+ 1:36
+ 0.45	59	+ 1:44	+ 0.45	40	+ 1:25	+ 0.45	30	+ 1:15	+ 0.45	37	+ 1:22	+ 0.45	39	+ 1:24	+ 0.45	68	+ 1:53	+ 0.45	43	+ 1:28	+ 0.45	64	+ 1:49
+ 1.00	**58**	**+ 1:58**	**+ 1.00**	**40**	**+ 1:40**	**+ 1.00**	**29**	**+ 1:29**	**+ 1.00**	**36**	**+ 1:36**	**+ 1.00**	**39**	**+ 1:39**	**+ 1.00**	**68**	**+ 2:08**	**+ 1.00**	**43**	**+ 1:43**	**+ 1.00**	**63**	**+ 2:03**
+ 1.15	58	+ 2:13	+ 1.15	40	+ 1:55	+ 1.15	28	+ 1:43	+ 1.15	36	+ 1:51	+ 1.15	39	+ 1:54	+ 1.15	67	+ 2:22	+ 1.15	43	+ 1:58	+ 1.15	62	+ 2:17
+ 1.30	58	+ 2:28	+ 1.30	40	+ 2:10	+ 1.30	27	+ 1:57	+ 1.30	36	+ 2:06	+ 1.30	39	+ 2:09	+ 1.30	67	+ 2:37	+ 1.30	42	+ 2:12	+ 1.30	61	+ 2:31
+ 1.45	58	+ 2:43	+ 1.45	40	+ 2:25	+ 1.45	27	+ 2:12	+ 1.45	36	+ 2:21	+ 1.45	38	+ 2:23	+ 1.45	66	+ 2:51	+ 1.45	42	+ 2:27	+ 1.45	59	+ 2:44
+ 2.00	**58**	**+ 2:58**	**+ 2.00**	**40**	**+ 2:40**	**+ 2.00**	**26**	**+ 2:26**	**+ 2.00**	**36**	**+ 2:36**	**+ 2.00**	**38**	**+ 2:38**	**+ 2.00**	**65**	**+ 3:05**	**+ 2.00**	**41**	**+ 2:41**	**+ 2.00**	**58**	**+ 2:58**
+ 2.15	58	+ 3:13	+ 2.15	40	+ 2:55	+ 2.15	26	+ 2:41	+ 2.15	36	+ 2:51	+ 2.15	38	+ 2:53	+ 2.15	64	+ 3:19	+ 2.15	41	+ 2:56	+ 2.15	57	+ 3:12
+ 2.30	58	+ 3:28	+ 2.30	40	+ 3:10	+ 2.30	26	+ 2:56	+ 2.30	36	+ 3:06	+ 2.30	38	+ 3:08	+ 2.30	64	+ 3:34	+ 2.30	40	+ 3:10	+ 2.30	56	+ 3:26
+ 2.45	58	+ 3:43	+ 2.45	39	+ 3:24	+ 2.45	25	+ 3:10	+ 2.45	37	+ 3:22	+ 2.45	39	+ 3:24	+ 2.45	63	+ 3:48	+ 2.45	39	+ 3:24	+ 2.45	54	+ 3:39
+ 3.00	**58**	**+ 3:58**	**+ 3.00**	**39**	**+ 3:39**	**+ 3.00**	**25**	**+ 3:25**	**+ 3.00**	**37**	**+ 3:37**	**+ 3.00**	**39**	**+ 3:39**	**+ 3.00**	**62**	**+ 4:02**	**+ 3.00**	**38**	**+ 3:38**	**+ 3.00**	**53**	**+ 3:53**
+ 3.15	59	+ 4:14	+ 3.15	39	+ 3:54	+ 3.15	25	+ 3:40	+ 3.15	37	+ 3:52	+ 3.15	39	+ 3:54	+ 3.15	61	+ 4:16	+ 3.15	38	+ 3:53	+ 3.15	53	+ 4:08
+ 3.30	60	+ 4:30	+ 3.30	38	+ 4:08	+ 3.30	25	+ 3:55	+ 3.30	38	+ 4:08	+ 3.30	40	+ 4:10	+ 3.30	61	+ 4:31	+ 3.30	37	+ 4:07	+ 3.30	52	+ 4:22
+ 3.45	60	+ 4:45	+ 3.45	38	+ 4:23	+ 3.45	24	+ 4:09	+ 3.45	39	+ 4:24	+ 3.45	40	+ 4:25	+ 3.45	60	+ 4:45	+ 3.45	36	+ 4:21	+ 3.45	51	+ 4:36
+ 4.00	**61**	**+ 5:01**	**+ 4.00**	**37**	**+ 4:37**	**+ 4.00**	**24**	**+ 4:24**	**+ 4.00**	**39**	**+ 4:39**	**+ 4.00**	**40**	**+ 4:40**	**+ 4.00**	**59**	**+ 4:59**	**+ 4.00**	**35**	**+ 4:35**	**+ 4.00**	**50**	**+ 4:50**
+ 4.15	62	+ 5:17	+ 4.15	37	+ 4:52	+ 4.15	24	+ 4:39	+ 4.15	40	+ 4:55	+ 4.15	41	+ 4:56	+ 4.15	59	+ 5:14	+ 4.15	35	+ 4:50	+ 4.15	50	+ 5:05
+ 4.30	63	+ 5:33	+ 4.30	36	+ 5:06	+ 4.30	24	+ 4:54	+ 4.30	41	+ 5:11	+ 4.30	42	+ 5:12	+ 4.30	58	+ 5:28	+ 4.30	34	+ 5:04	+ 4.30	49	+ 5:19
+ 4.45	64	+ 5:49	+ 4.45	36	+ 5:21	+ 4.45	24	+ 5:09	+ 4.45	42	+ 5:27	+ 4.45	43	+ 5:28	+ 4.45	58	+ 5:43	+ 4.45	34	+ 5:19	+ 4.45	49	+ 5:34
+ 5.00	**65**	**- 5:55**	**+ 5.00**	**35**	**+ 5:35**	**+ 5.00**	**24**	**+ 5:24**	**+ 5.00**	**42**	**+ 5:42**	**+ 5.00**	**43**	**+ 5:43**	**+ 5.00**	**57**	**+ 5:57**	**+ 5.00**	**33**	**+ 5:33**	**+ 5.00**	**48**	**+ 5:48**
+ 5.15	66	- 5:39	+ 5.15	35	+ 5:50	+ 5.15	24	+ 5:39	+ 5.15	43	+ 5:58	+ 5.15	44	+ 5:59	+ 5.15	57	- 5:48	+ 5.15	32	+ 5:47	+ 5.15	48	- 5:57
+ 5.30	67	- 5:23	+ 5.30	35	- 5:55	+ 5.30	25	+ 5:55	+ 5.30	44	- 5:46	+ 5.30	45	- 5:45	+ 5.30	57	- 5:33	+ 5.30	32	- 5:58	+ 5.30	48	- 5:42
+ 5.45	68	- 5:07	+ 5.45	35	- 5:40	+ 5.45	26	- 5:49	+ 5.45	45	- 5:30	+ 5.45	46	- 5:29	+ 5.45	57	- 5:18	+ 5.45	31	- 5:44	+ 5.45	47	- 5:28
+ 6.00	**69**	**- 4:51**	**+ 6.00**	**34**	**- 5:26**	**+ 6.00**	**27**	**- 5:33**	**+ 6.00**	**45**	**- 5:15**	**+ 6.00**	**47**	**- 5:13**	**+ 6.00**	**57**	**- 5:03**	**+ 6.00**	**30**	**- 5:30**	**+ 6.00**	**47**	**- 5:13**

Via Fisherman's Gat and Middle Sunk (B8–B6) | Via Foulger's Gat and Middle Sunk (B5–B1)

SOUTH BOUND

Table C - Spitway to North Foreland via Princes Channel

Neaps — All times relate to HW Sheerness — Time to cover Sectors (in minutes) at 4.0 Kts

SOUTHBOUND

	C8			C7			C6			C5	
	Spitway to Whitaker Spit			Whitaker Spit to NE Maplin			NE Maplin to Maplin Edge			Maplin Edge to SW Barrow	
Time	Duration	Time at End of Sector	Time	Duration	Time at End of Sector	Time	Duration	Time at End of Sector	Time	Duration	Time at End of Sector
- 6.00	25	- 5:35	- 6.00	55	- 5:05	- 6.00	36	- 5:24	- 6.00	49	- 5:11
- 5.45	25	- 5:20	- 5.45	54	- 4:51	- 5.45	35	- 5:10	- 5.45	47	- 4:58
- 5.30	25	- 5:05	- 5.30	52	- 4:38	- 5.30	35	- 4:55	- 5.30	46	- 4:44
- 5.15	25	- 4:50	- 5.15	51	- 4:24	- 5.15	34	- 4:41	- 5.15	44	- 4:31
- 5.00	25	- 4:35	- 5.00	50	- 4:10	- 5.00	33	- 4:27	- 5.00	43	- 4:17
- 4.45	26	- 4:19	- 4.45	50	- 3:55	- 4.45	33	- 4:12	- 4.45	42	- 4:03
- 4.30	26	- 4:04	- 4.30	50	- 3:40	- 4.30	33	- 3:57	- 4.30	42	- 3:48
- 4.15	26	- 3:49	- 4.15	50	- 3:25	- 4.15	32	- 3:43	- 4.15	42	- 3:33
- 4.00	26	- 3:34	- 4.00	49	- 3:11	- 4.00	32	- 3:28	- 4.00	42	- 3:18
- 3.45	26	- 3:19	- 3.45	50	- 2:55	- 3.45	33	- 3:12	- 3.45	42	- 3:03
- 3.30	26	- 3:04	- 3.30	50	- 2:40	- 3.30	33	- 2:57	- 3.30	43	- 2:47
- 3.15	26	- 2:49	- 3.15	51	- 2:24	- 3.15	33	- 2:42	- 3.15	44	- 2:31
- 3.00	26	- 2:34	- 3.00	51	- 2:09	- 3.00	33	- 2:27	- 3.00	44	- 2:16
- 2.45	26	- 2:19	- 2.45	52	- 1:53	- 2.45	34	- 2:11	- 2.45	45	- 2:00
- 2.30	26	- 2:04	- 2.30	53	- 1:37	- 2.30	34	- 1:56	- 2.30	46	- 1:44
- 2.15	26	- 1:49	- 2.15	54	- 1:21	- 2.15	35	- 1:40	- 2.15	47	- 1:28
- 2.00	26	- 1:34	- 2.00	54	- 1:06	- 2.00	36	- 1:24	- 2.00	47	- 1:13
- 1.45	26	- 1:19	- 1.45	56	- 0:49	- 1.45	36	- 1:09	- 1.45	49	- 0:56
- 1.30	26	- 1:04	- 1.30	58	- 0:32	- 1.30	37	- 0:53	- 1.30	50	- 0:40
- 1.15	26	- 0:49	- 1.15	60	- 0:15	- 1.15	37	- 0:38	- 1.15	51	- 0:24
- 1.00	26	- 0:34	- 1.00	62	+ 0:02	- 1.00	38	- 0:22	- 1.00	52	- 0:08
- 0.45	26	- 0:19	- 0.45	64	+ 0:19	- 0.45	39	- 0:06	- 0.45	55	+ 0:10
- 0.30	26	- 0:04	- 0.30	67	+ 0:37	- 0.30	39	+ 0:09	- 0.30	57	+ 0:27
- 0.15	26	+ 0:11	- 0.15	70	+ 0:55	- 0.15	40	+ 0:25	- 0.15	59	+ 0:44
HW	26	+ 0:26	HW	73	+ 1:13	HW	41	+ 0:41	HW	62	+ 1:02
+ 0.15	26	+ 0:41	+ 0.15	77	+ 1:32	+ 0.15	42	+ 0:57	+ 0.15	70	+ 1:25
+ 0.30	26	+ 0:56	+ 0.30	81	+ 1:51	+ 0.30	43	+ 1:13	+ 0.30	78	+ 1:48
+ 0.45	26	+ 1:11	+ 0.45	85	+ 2:10	+ 0.45	45	+ 1:30	+ 0.45	86	+ 2:11
+ 1.00	26	+ 1:26	+ 1.00	90	+ 2:30	+ 1.00	46	+ 1:46	+ 1.00	94	+ 2:34
+ 1.15	26	+ 1:41	+ 1.15	90	+ 2:45	+ 1.15	47	+ 2:02	+ 1.15	98	+ 2:53
+ 1.30	26	+ 1:56	+ 1.30	90	+ 3:00	+ 1.30	47	+ 2:17	+ 1.30	101	+ 3:11
+ 1.45	27	+ 2:12	+ 1.45	90	+ 3:15	+ 1.45	47	+ 2:32	+ 1.45	104	+ 3:29
+ 2.00	27	+ 2:27	+ 2.00	90	+ 3:30	+ 2.00	48	+ 2:48	+ 2.00	107	+ 3:47
+ 2.15	27	+ 2:42	+ 2.15	87	+ 3:42	+ 2.15	48	+ 3:03	+ 2.15	104	+ 3:59
+ 2.30	27	+ 2:57	+ 2.30	84	+ 3:54	+ 2.30	48	+ 3:18	+ 2.30	101	+ 4:11
+ 2.45	27	+ 3:12	+ 2.45	81	+ 4:06	+ 2.45	48	+ 3:33	+ 2.45	97	+ 4:22
+ 3.00	26	+ 3:26	+ 3.00	77	+ 4:17	+ 3.00	48	+ 3:48	+ 3.00	94	+ 4:34
+ 3.15	26	+ 3:41	+ 3.15	76	+ 4:31	+ 3.15	47	+ 4:02	+ 3.15	89	+ 4:44
+ 3.30	26	+ 3:56	+ 3.30	75	+ 4:45	+ 3.30	47	+ 4:17	+ 3.30	84	+ 4:54
+ 3.45	26	+ 4:11	+ 3.45	73	+ 4:58	+ 3.45	46	+ 4:31	+ 3.45	79	+ 5:04
+ 4.00	26	+ 4:26	+ 4.00	72	+ 5:12	+ 4.00	45	+ 4:45	+ 4.00	73	+ 5:13
+ 4.15	26	+ 4:41	+ 4.15	70	+ 5:25	+ 4.15	44	+ 4:59	+ 4.15	71	+ 5:26
+ 4.30	26	+ 4:56	+ 4.30	69	+ 5:39	+ 4.30	43	+ 5:13	+ 4.30	69	+ 5:39
+ 4.45	26	+ 5:11	+ 4.45	67	+ 5:52	+ 4.45	42	+ 5:27	+ 4.45	66	+ 5:51
+ 5.00	26	+ 5:26	+ 5.00	65	- 5:55	+ 5.00	41	+ 5:41	+ 5.00	64	- 5:56
+ 5.15	26	+ 5:41	+ 5.15	64	- 5:41	+ 5.15	40	+ 5:55	+ 5.15	61	- 5:44
+ 5.30	26	+ 5:56	+ 5.30	63	- 5:27	+ 5.30	39	- 5:51	+ 5.30	59	- 5:31
+ 5.45	25	- 5:50	+ 5.45	62	- 5:13	+ 5.45	38	- 5:37	+ 5.45	57	- 5:18
+ 6.00	25	- 5:35	+ 6.00	61	- 4:59	+ 6.00	38	- 5:22	+ 6.00	55	- 5:05

	C4			C3			C2			C1	
	SW Barrow to Princes No 6			Princes No 6 to Princes South			Princes South to Margate Sand			Margate Sand to North Foreland	
Time	Duration	Time at End of Sector	Time	Duration	Time at End of Sector	Time	Duration	Time at End of Sector	Time	Duration	Time at End of Sector
- 6.00	89	- 4:31	- 6.00	108	- 4:12	- 6.00	69	- 4:51	- 6.00	48	- 5:12
- 5.45	92	- 4:13	- 5.45	116	- 3:49	- 5.45	70	- 4:35	- 5.45	49	- 4:56
- 5.30	96	- 3:54	- 5.30	124	- 3:26	- 5.30	72	- 4:18	- 5.30	49	- 4:41
- 5.15	99	- 3:36	- 5.15	132	- 3:03	- 5.15	74	- 4:01	- 5.15	50	- 4:25
- 5.00	103	- 3:17	- 5.00	140	- 2:40	- 5.00	76	- 3:44	- 5.00	51	- 4:09
- 4.45	104	- 3:01	- 4.45	147	- 2:18	- 4.45	78	- 3:27	- 4.45	52	- 3:53
- 4.30	106	- 2:44	- 4.30	155	- 1:55	- 4.30	80	- 3:10	- 4.30	53	- 3:37
- 4.15	107	- 2:28	- 4.15	162	- 1:33	- 4.15	82	- 2:53	- 4.15	54	- 3:21
- 4.00	108	- 2:12	- 4.00	169	- 1:11	- 4.00	84	- 2:36	- 4.00	55	- 3:05
- 3.45	108	- 1:57	- 3.45	168	- 0:57	- 3.45	87	- 2:18	- 3.45	58	- 2:47
- 3.30	107	- 1:43	- 3.30	167	- 0:43	- 3.30	90	- 2:00	- 3.30	61	- 2:29
- 3.15	107	- 1:28	- 3.15	165	- 0:30	- 3.15	92	- 1:43	- 3.15	63	- 2:12
- 3.00	106	- 1:14	- 3.00	164	- 0:16	- 3.00	95	- 1:25	- 3.00	66	- 1:54
- 2.45	105	- 1:00	- 2.45	160	- 0:05	- 2.45	92	- 1:13	- 2.45	68	- 1:37
- 2.30	104	- 0:46	- 2.30	156	+ 0:06	- 2.30	89	- 1:01	- 2.30	70	- 1:20
- 2.15	103	- 0:32	- 2.15	152	+ 0:17	- 2.15	86	- 0:49	- 2.15	72	- 1:03
- 2.00	102	- 0:18	- 2.00	148	+ 0:28	- 2.00	82	- 0:38	- 2.00	74	- 0:46
- 1.45	99	- 0:06	- 1.45	140	+ 0:35	- 1.45	80	- 0:25	- 1.45	74	- 0:31
- 1.30	97	+ 0:07	- 1.30	133	+ 0:43	- 1.30	77	- 0:13	- 1.30	73	- 0:17
- 1.15	95	+ 0:20	- 1.15	126	+ 0:51	- 1.15	74	- 0:01	- 1.15	72	- 0:03
- 1.00	93	+ 0:33	- 1.00	118	+ 0:58	- 1.00	71	+ 0:11	- 1.00	72	+ 0:12
- 0.45	90	+ 0:45	- 0.45	112	+ 1:07	- 0.45	69	+ 0:24	- 0.45	70	+ 0:25
- 0.30	88	+ 0:58	- 0.30	106	+ 1:16	- 0.30	66	+ 0:36	- 0.30	68	+ 0:38
- 0.15	85	+ 1:10	- 0.15	101	+ 1:26	- 0.15	64	+ 0:49	- 0.15	66	+ 0:51
HW	83	+ 1:23	HW	95	+ 1:35	HW	62	+ 1:02	HW	65	+ 1:05
+ 0.15	82	+ 1:37	+ 0.15	91	+ 1:46	+ 0.15	60	+ 1:15	+ 0.15	63	+ 1:18
+ 0.30	81	+ 1:51	+ 0.30	88	+ 1:58	+ 0.30	58	+ 1:28	+ 0.30	61	+ 1:31
+ 0.45	80	+ 2:05	+ 0.45	84	+ 2:09	+ 0.45	57	+ 1:42	+ 0.45	59	+ 1:44
+ 1.00	79	+ 2:19	+ 1.00	81	+ 2:21	+ 1.00	55	+ 1:55	+ 1.00	57	+ 1:57
+ 1.15	79	+ 2:34	+ 1.15	79	+ 2:34	+ 1.15	54	+ 2:09	+ 1.15	55	+ 2:10
+ 1.30	79	+ 2:49	+ 1.30	78	+ 2:48	+ 1.30	53	+ 2:23	+ 1.30	54	+ 2:24
+ 1.45	78	+ 3:03	+ 1.45	77	+ 3:02	+ 1.45	52	+ 2:37	+ 1.45	52	+ 2:37
+ 2.00	78	+ 3:18	+ 2.00	76	+ 3:16	+ 2.00	51	+ 2:51	+ 2.00	51	+ 2:51
+ 2.15	78	+ 3:33	+ 2.15	77	+ 3:32	+ 2.15	51	+ 3:06	+ 2.15	50	+ 3:05
+ 2.30	79	+ 3:49	+ 2.30	77	+ 3:47	+ 2.30	51	+ 3:21	+ 2.30	49	+ 3:19
+ 2.45	79	+ 4:04	+ 2.45	78	+ 4:03	+ 2.45	51	+ 3:36	+ 2.45	49	+ 3:34
+ 3.00	79	+ 4:19	+ 3.00	78	+ 4:18	+ 3.00	51	+ 3:51	+ 3.00	48	+ 3:48
+ 3.15	79	+ 4:34	+ 3.15	80	+ 4:35	+ 3.15	52	+ 4:07	+ 3.15	48	+ 4:03
+ 3.30	80	+ 4:50	+ 3.30	81	+ 4:51	+ 3.30	53	+ 4:23	+ 3.30	48	+ 4:18
+ 3.45	80	+ 5:05	+ 3.45	82	+ 5:07	+ 3.45	54	+ 4:39	+ 3.45	47	+ 4:32
+ 4.00	80	+ 5:20	+ 4.00	83	+ 5:23	+ 4.00	55	+ 4:55	+ 4.00	47	+ 4:47
+ 4.15	81	+ 5:36	+ 4.15	85	+ 5:40	+ 4.15	56	+ 5:11	+ 4.15	47	+ 5:02
+ 4.30	81	+ 5:51	+ 4.30	87	+ 5:57	+ 4.30	57	+ 5:27	+ 4.30	47	+ 5:17
+ 4.45	81	- 5:54	+ 4.45	88	- 5:47	+ 4.45	59	+ 5:44	+ 4.45	47	+ 5:32
+ 5.00	82	- 5:38	+ 5.00	90	- 5:30	+ 5.00	60	- 6:00	+ 5.00	47	+ 5:47
+ 5.15	82	- 5:23	+ 5.15	91	- 5:14	+ 5.15	61	- 5:44	+ 5.15	47	- 5:58
+ 5.30	82	- 5:08	+ 5.30	93	- 4:57	+ 5.30	62	- 5:28	+ 5.30	47	- 5:43
+ 5.45	83	- 4:52	+ 5.45	94	- 4:41	+ 5.45	63	- 5:12	+ 5.45	47	- 5:28
+ 6.00	83	- 4:37	+ 6.00	96	- 4:24	+ 6.00	64	- 4:56	+ 6.00	47	- 5:13

Table C - Spitway to North Foreland via Princes Channel

Time to cover Sectors (in minutes) at 4.0 kts | All times relate to HW Sheerness | **Springs**

	C8			C7			C6			C5			C4			C3			C2			C1	
	Spitway to Whitaker Spit			Whitaker Spit to NE Maplin			NE Maplin to Maplin Edge			Maplin Edge to SW Barrow			SW Barrow to Princes No 6			Princes No 6 to Princes South			Princes South to Margate Sand			Margate Sand to North Foreland	
Time	*Duration*	*Time at End of Sector*	*Time*	*Duration*	*Time at End of Sector*	*Time*	*Duration*	*Time at End of Sector*	*Time*	*Duration*	*Time at End of Sector*	*Time*	*Duration*	*Time at End of Sector*	*Time*	*Duration*	*Time at End of Sector*	*Time*	*Duration*	*Time at End of Sector*	*Time*	*Duration*	*Time at End of Sector*
- 6.00	**25**	**- 5:35**	**- 6.00**	**51**	**- 5:09**	**- 6.00**	**35**	**- 5:25**	**- 6.00**	**45**	**- 5:15**	**- 6.00**	**92**	**- 4:28**	**- 6.00**	**126**	**- 3:54**	**- 6.00**	**72**	**- 4:48**	**- 6.00**	**45**	**- 5:15**
- 5.45	26	- 5:19	- 5.45	49	- 4:56	- 5.45	34	- 5:11	- 5.45	43	- 5:02	- 5.45	98	- 4:07	- 5.45	143	- 3:22	- 5.45	75	- 4:30	- 5.45	46	- 4:59
- 5.30	26	- 5:04	- 5.30	48	- 4:42	- 5.30	33	- 4:57	- 5.30	41	- 4:49	- 5.30	103	- 3:47	- 5.30	160	- 2:50	- 5.30	79	- 4:11	- 5.30	47	- 4:43
- 5.15	26	- 4:49	- 5.15	46	- 4:29	- 5.15	32	- 4:43	- 5.15	39	- 4:36	- 5.15	109	- 3:26	- 5.15	176	- 2:19	- 5.15	82	- 3:53	- 5.15	48	- 4:27
- 5.00	**27**	**- 4:33**	**- 5.00**	**45**	**- 4:15**	**- 5.00**	**31**	**- 4:29**	**- 5.00**	**37**	**- 4:23**	**- 5.00**	**115**	**- 3:05**	**- 5.00**	**193**	**- 1:47**	**- 5.00**	**85**	**- 3:35**	**- 5.00**	**49**	**- 4:11**
- 4.45	27	- 4:18	- 4.45	44	- 4:01	- 4.45	31	- 4:14	- 4.45	37	- 4:08	- 4.45	116	- 2:49	- 4.45	198	- 1:27	- 4.45	90	- 3:15	- 4.45	51	- 3:54
- 4.30	27	- 4:03	- 4.30	44	- 3:46	- 4.30	30	- 4:00	- 4.30	36	- 3:54	- 4.30	117	- 2:33	- 4.30	204	- 1:06	- 4.30	95	- 2:55	- 4.30	53	- 3:37
- 4.15	27	- 3:48	- 4.15	44	- 3:31	- 4.15	30	- 3:45	- 4.15	36	- 3:39	- 4.15	119	- 2:16	- 4.15	209	- 0:46	- 4.15	100	- 2:35	- 4.15	55	- 3:20
- 4.00	**27**	**- 3:33**	**- 4.00**	**44**	**- 3:16**	**- 4.00**	**30**	**- 3:30**	**- 4.00**	**36**	**- 3:24**	**- 4.00**	**120**	**- 2:00**	**- 4.00**	**214**	**- 0:26**	**- 4.00**	**104**	**- 2:16**	**- 4.00**	**57**	**- 3:03**
- 3.45	27	- 3:18	- 3.45	44	- 3:01	- 3.45	30	- 3:15	- 3.45	37	- 3:08	- 3.45	119	- 1:46	- 3.45	209	- 0:16	- 3.45	106	- 1:59	- 3.45	63	- 2:42
- 3.30	27	- 3:03	- 3.30	45	- 2:45	- 3.30	31	- 2:59	- 3.30	38	- 2:52	- 3.30	118	- 1:32	- 3.30	203	- 0:07	- 3.30	107	- 1:43	- 3.30	69	- 2:21
- 3.15	27	- 2:48	- 3.15	45	- 2:30	- 3.15	31	- 2:44	- 3.15	38	- 2:37	- 3.15	116	- 1:19	- 3.15	197	+ 0:02	- 3.15	109	- 1:26	- 3.15	75	- 2:00
- 3.00	**28**	**- 2:32**	**- 3.00**	**46**	**- 2:14**	**- 3.00**	**31**	**- 2:29**	**- 3.00**	**39**	**- 2:21**	**- 3.00**	**115**	**- 1:05**	**- 3.00**	**191**	**+ 0:11**	**- 3.00**	**110**	**- 1:10**	**- 3.00**	**80**	**- 1:40**
- 2.45	27	- 2:18	- 2.45	47	- 1:58	- 2.45	32	- 2:13	- 2.45	40	- 2:05	- 2.45	112	- 0:53	- 2.45	182	+ 0:17	- 2.45	107	- 0:58	- 2.45	85	- 1:20
- 2.30	27	- 2:03	- 2.30	48	- 1:42	- 2.30	33	- 1:57	- 2.30	41	- 1:49	- 2.30	110	- 0:40	- 2.30	174	+ 0:24	- 2.30	103	- 0:47	- 2.30	90	- 1:00
- 2.15	27	- 1:48	- 2.15	49	- 1:26	- 2.15	34	- 1:41	- 2.15	42	- 1:33	- 2.15	108	- 0:27	- 2.15	165	+ 0:30	- 2.15	100	- 0:35	- 2.15	95	- 0:40
- 2.00	**27**	**- 1:33**	**- 2.00**	**51**	**- 1:09**	**- 2.00**	**35**	**- 1:25**	**- 2.00**	**43**	**- 1:17**	**- 2.00**	**105**	**- 0:15**	**- 2.00**	**157**	**+ 0:37**	**- 2.00**	**96**	**- 0:24**	**- 2.00**	**99**	**- 0:21**
- 1.45	27	- 1:18	- 1.45	53	- 0:52	- 1.45	35	- 1:10	- 1.45	44	- 1:01	- 1.45	102	- 0:03	- 1.45	147	+ 0:42	- 1.45	91	- 0:14	- 1.45	97	- 0:08
- 1.30	27	- 1:03	- 1.30	56	- 0:34	- 1.30	36	- 0:54	- 1.30	46	- 0:44	- 1.30	99	+ 0:09	- 1.30	137	+ 0:47	- 1.30	86	- 0:04	- 1.30	96	+ 0:06
- 1.15	27	- 0:48	- 1.15	58	- 0:17	- 1.15	37	- 0:38	- 1.15	48	- 0:27	- 1.15	96	+ 0:21	- 1.15	127	+ 0:52	- 1.15	81	+ 0:06	- 1.15	94	+ 0:19
- 1.00	**27**	**- 0:33**	**- 1.00**	**61**	**+ 0:01**	**- 1.00**	**38**	**- 0:22**	**- 1.00**	**50**	**- 0:10**	**- 1.00**	**93**	**+ 0:33**	**- 1.00**	**117**	**+ 0:57**	**- 1.00**	**75**	**+ 0:15**	**- 1.00**	**92**	**+ 0:32**
- 0.45	27	- 0:18	- 0.45	65	+ 0:20	- 0.45	39	- 0:06	- 0.45	53	+ 0:08	- 0.45	90	+ 0:45	- 0.45	109	+ 1:04	- 0.45	72	+ 0:27	- 0.45	88	+ 0:43
- 0.30	26	- 0:04	- 0.30	69	+ 0:39	- 0.30	40	+ 0:10	- 0.30	57	+ 0:27	- 0.30	87	+ 0:57	- 0.30	102	+ 1:12	- 0.30	68	+ 0:38	- 0.30	83	+ 0:53
- 0.15	26	+ 0:11	- 0.15	73	+ 0:58	- 0.15	41	+ 0:26	- 0.15	61	+ 0:46	- 0.15	84	+ 1:09	- 0.15	94	+ 1:19	- 0.15	64	+ 0:49	- 0.15	79	+ 1:04
HW	**26**	**+ 0:26**	**HW**	**78**	**+ 1:18**	**HW**	**42**	**+ 0:42**	**HW**	**64**	**+ 1:04**	**HW**	**82**	**+ 1:22**	**HW**	**87**	**+ 1:27**	**HW**	**60**	**+ 1:00**	**HW**	**74**	**+ 1:14**
+ 0.15	26	+ 0:41	+ 0.15	84	+ 1:39	+ 0.15	44	+ 0:59	+ 0.15	78	+ 1:33	+ 0.15	81	+ 1:36	+ 0.15	82	+ 1:37	+ 0.15	58	+ 1:13	+ 0.15	71	+ 1:26
+ 0.30	27	+ 0:57	+ 0.30	91	+ 2:01	+ 0.30	46	+ 1:16	+ 0.30	91	+ 2:01	+ 0.30	80	+ 1:50	+ 0.30	78	+ 1:48	+ 0.30	56	+ 1:26	+ 0.30	67	+ 1:37
+ 0.45	27	+ 1:12	+ 0.45	97	+ 2:22	+ 0.45	49	+ 1:34	+ 0.45	104	+ 2:29	+ 0.45	79	+ 2:04	+ 0.45	73	+ 1:58	+ 0.45	54	+ 1:39	+ 0.45	63	+ 1:48
+ 1.00	**27**	**+ 1:27**	**+ 1.00**	**104**	**+ 2:44**	**+ 1.00**	**51**	**+ 1:51**	**+ 1.00**	**117**	**+ 2:57**	**+ 1.00**	**78**	**+ 2:18**	**+ 1.00**	**69**	**+ 2:09**	**+ 1.00**	**52**	**+ 1:52**	**+ 1.00**	**59**	**+ 1:59**
+ 1.15	28	+ 1:43	+ 1.15	104	+ 2:59	+ 1.15	51	+ 2:06	+ 1.15	120	+ 3:15	+ 1.15	78	+ 2:33	+ 1.15	68	+ 2:23	+ 1.15	51	+ 2:06	+ 1.15	57	+ 2:12
+ 1.30	28	+ 1:58	+ 1.30	104	+ 3:14	+ 1.30	52	+ 2:22	+ 1.30	123	+ 3:33	+ 1.30	77	+ 2:47	+ 1.30	67	+ 2:37	+ 1.30	50	+ 2:20	+ 1.30	54	+ 2:24
+ 1.45	28	+ 2:13	+ 1.45	104	+ 3:29	+ 1.45	53	+ 2:38	+ 1.45	125	+ 3:50	+ 1.45	77	+ 3:02	+ 1.45	66	+ 2:51	+ 1.45	49	+ 2:34	+ 1.45	52	+ 2:37
+ 2.00	**29**	**+ 2:29**	**+ 2.00**	**103**	**+ 3:43**	**+ 2.00**	**53**	**+ 2:53**	**+ 2.00**	**128**	**+ 4:08**	**+ 2.00**	**77**	**+ 3:17**	**+ 2.00**	**65**	**+ 3:05**	**+ 2.00**	**47**	**+ 2:47**	**+ 2.00**	**49**	**+ 2:49**
+ 2.15	29	+ 2:44	+ 2.15	101	+ 3:56	+ 2.15	53	+ 3:08	+ 2.15	123	+ 4:18	+ 2.15	77	+ 3:32	+ 2.15	65	+ 3:20	+ 2.15	47	+ 3:02	+ 2.15	48	+ 3:03
+ 2.30	29	+ 2:59	+ 2.30	98	+ 4:08	+ 2.30	53	+ 3:23	+ 2.30	117	+ 4:27	+ 2.30	77	+ 3:47	+ 2.30	66	+ 3:36	+ 2.30	47	+ 3:17	+ 2.30	46	+ 3:16
+ 2.45	28	+ 3:13	+ 2.45	96	+ 4:21	+ 2.45	54	+ 3:39	+ 2.45	112	+ 4:37	+ 2.45	77	+ 4:02	+ 2.45	66	+ 3:51	+ 2.45	47	+ 3:32	+ 2.45	45	+ 3:30
+ 3.00	**28**	**+ 3:28**	**+ 3.00**	**93**	**+ 4:33**	**+ 3.00**	**54**	**+ 3:54**	**+ 3.00**	**106**	**+ 4:46**	**+ 3.00**	**77**	**+ 4:17**	**+ 3.00**	**67**	**+ 4:07**	**+ 3.00**	**47**	**+ 3:47**	**+ 3.00**	**44**	**+ 3:44**
+ 3.15	28	+ 3:43	+ 3.15	90	+ 4:45	+ 3.15	52	+ 4:07	+ 3.15	100	+ 4:55	+ 3.15	78	+ 4:33	+ 3.15	68	+ 4:23	+ 3.15	48	+ 4:03	+ 3.15	43	+ 3:58
+ 3.30	27	+ 3:57	+ 3.30	86	+ 4:56	+ 3.30	51	+ 4:21	+ 3.30	95	+ 5:05	+ 3.30	78	+ 4:48	+ 3.30	69	+ 4:39	+ 3.30	49	+ 4:19	+ 3.30	43	+ 4:13
+ 3.45	27	+ 4:12	+ 3.45	82	+ 5:07	+ 3.45	50	+ 4:35	+ 3.45	89	+ 5:14	+ 3.45	78	+ 5:03	+ 3.45	70	+ 4:55	+ 3.45	51	+ 4:36	+ 3.45	43	+ 4:28
+ 4.00	**27**	**+ 4:27**	**+ 4.00**	**78**	**+ 5:18**	**+ 4.00**	**48**	**+ 4:48**	**+ 4.00**	**83**	**+ 5:23**	**+ 4.00**	**79**	**+ 5:19**	**+ 4.00**	**71**	**+ 5:11**	**+ 4.00**	**52**	**+ 4:52**	**+ 4.00**	**43**	**+ 4:43**
+ 4.15	26	+ 4:41	+ 4.15	76	+ 5:31	+ 4.15	47	+ 5:02	+ 4.15	79	+ 5:34	+ 4.15	79	+ 5:34	+ 4.15	74	+ 5:29	+ 4.15	53	+ 5:08	+ 4.15	43	+ 4:58
+ 4.30	26	+ 4:56	+ 4.30	73	+ 5:43	+ 4.30	45	+ 5:15	+ 4.30	74	+ 5:44	+ 4.30	79	+ 5:49	+ 4.30	76	+ 5:46	+ 4.30	55	+ 5:25	+ 4.30	43	+ 5:13
+ 4.45	26	+ 5:11	+ 4.45	70	+ 5:55	+ 4.45	43	+ 5:28	+ 4.45	70	+ 5:55	+ 4.45	80	- 5:55	+ 4.45	79	- 5:56	+ 4.45	57	+ 5:42	+ 4.45	43	+ 5:28
+ 5.00	**26**	**+ 5:26**	**+ 5.00**	**67**	**- 5:53**	**+ 5.00**	**41**	**+ 5:41**	**+ 5.00**	**66**	**- 5:54**	**+ 5.00**	**80**	**- 5:40**	**+ 5.00**	**81**	**- 5:39**	**+ 5.00**	**58**	**+ 5:58**	**+ 5.00**	**43**	**+ 5:43**
+ 5.15	26	+ 5:41	+ 5.15	65	- 5:40	+ 5.15	40	+ 5:55	+ 5.15	63	- 5:42	+ 5.15	80	- 5:25	+ 5.15	84	- 5:21	+ 5.15	60	- 5:45	+ 5.15	43	+ 5:58
+ 5.30	26	+ 5:56	+ 5.30	63	- 5:27	+ 5.30	39	- 5:51	+ 5.30	59	- 5:31	+ 5.30	81	- 5:09	+ 5.30	86	- 5:04	+ 5.30	61	- 5:29	+ 5.30	43	- 5:47
+ 5.45	26	- 5:49	+ 5.45	62	- 5:13	+ 5.45	38	- 5:37	+ 5.45	56	- 5:19	+ 5.45	81	- 4:54	+ 5.45	89	- 4:46	+ 5.45	63	- 5:12	+ 5.45	43	- 5:32
+ 6.00	**25**	**- 5:35**	**+ 6.00**	**60**	**- 5:00**	**+ 6.00**	**37**	**- 5:23**	**+ 6.00**	**53**	**- 5:07**	**+ 6.00**	**81**	**- 4:39**	**+ 6.00**	**91**	**- 4:29**	**+ 6.00**	**64**	**- 4:56**	**+ 6.00**	**43**	**- 5:17**

SOUTH BOUND

Table C - Spitway to North Foreland via Princes Channel

Neaps — All times relate to HW Sheerness — **Time to cover Sectors (in minutes) at 5.0 Kts**

SOUTHBOUND

	C8			C7			C6			C5	
	Spitway to Whitaker Spit			Whitaker Spit to NE Maplin			NE Maplin to Maplin Edge			Maplin Edge to SW Barrow	
Time	Duration	Time at End of Sector	Time	Duration	Time at End of Sector	Time	Duration	Time at End of Sector	Time	Duration	Time at End of Sector
- 6.00	20	- 5:40	- 6.00	46	- 5:14	- 6.00	30	- 5:30	- 6.00	41	- 5:19
- 5.45	20	- 5:25	- 5.45	45	- 5:00	- 5.45	29	- 5:16	- 5.45	40	- 5:05
- 5.30	20	- 5:10	- 5.30	44	- 4:46	- 5.30	28	- 5:02	- 5.30	39	- 4:51
- 5.15	20	- 4:55	- 5.15	43	- 4:32	- 5.15	28	- 4:47	- 5.15	38	- 4:37
- 5.00	20	- 4:40	- 5.00	42	- 4:18	- 5.00	27	- 4:33	- 5.00	37	- 4:23
- 4.45	20	- 4:25	- 4.45	42	- 4:03	- 4.45	27	- 4:18	- 4.45	37	- 4:08
- 4.30	20	- 4:10	- 4.30	42	- 3:48	- 4.30	27	- 4:03	- 4.30	36	- 3:54
- 4.15	20	- 3:55	- 4.15	42	- 3:33	- 4.15	26	- 3:49	- 4.15	36	- 3:39
- 4.00	20	- 3:40	- 4.00	41	- 3:19	- 4.00	26	- 3:34	- 4.00	36	- 3:24
- 3.45	20	- 3:25	- 3.45	42	- 3:03	- 3.45	26	- 3:19	- 3.45	36	- 3:09
- 3.30	21	- 3:09	- 3.30	42	- 2:48	- 3.30	27	- 3:03	- 3.30	36	- 2:54
- 3.15	21	- 2:54	- 3.15	42	- 2:33	- 3.15	27	- 2:48	- 3.15	37	- 2:38
- 3.00	21	- 2:39	- 3.00	42	- 2:18	- 3.00	27	- 2:33	- 3.00	37	- 2:23
- 2.45	21	- 2:24	- 2.45	43	- 2:02	- 2.45	27	- 2:18	- 2.45	38	- 2:07
- 2.30	21	- 2:09	- 2.30	43	- 1:47	- 2.30	28	- 2:02	- 2.30	38	- 1:52
- 2.15	21	- 1:54	- 2.15	44	- 1:31	- 2.15	28	- 1:47	- 2.15	39	- 1:36
- 2.00	21	- 1:39	- 2.00	44	- 1:16	- 2.00	28	- 1:32	- 2.00	39	- 1:21
- 1.45	21	- 1:24	- 1.45	45	- 1:00	- 1.45	29	- 1:16	- 1.45	40	- 1:05
- 1.30	21	- 1:09	- 1.30	46	- 0:44	- 1.30	29	- 1:01	- 1.30	41	- 0:49
- 1.15	21	- 0:54	- 1.15	48	- 0:27	- 1.15	30	- 0:45	- 1.15	41	- 0:34
- 1.00	21	- 0:39	- 1.00	49	- 0:11	- 1.00	30	- 0:30	- 1.00	42	- 0:18
- 0.45	21	- 0:24	- 0.45	50	+ 0:05	- 0.45	31	- 0:14	- 0.45	44	- 0:01
- 0.30	21	- 0:09	- 0.30	52	+ 0:22	- 0.30	31	+ 0:01	- 0.30	45	+ 0:15
- 0.15	20	+ 0:05	- 0.15	54	+ 0:39	- 0.15	31	+ 0:16	- 0.15	46	+ 0:31
HW	20	+ 0:20	HW	56	+ 0:56	HW	31	+ 0:31	HW	48	+ 0:48
+ 0.15	20	+ 0:35	+ 0.15	57	+ 1:12	+ 0.15	32	+ 0:47	+ 0.15	50	+ 1:05
+ 0.30	21	+ 0:51	+ 0.30	58	+ 1:28	+ 0.30	34	+ 1:04	+ 0.30	53	+ 1:23
+ 0.45	21	+ 1:06	+ 0.45	60	+ 1:45	+ 0.45	35	+ 1:20	+ 0.45	55	+ 1:40
+ 1.00	21	+ 1:21	+ 1.00	61	+ 2:01	+ 1.00	36	+ 1:36	+ 1.00	58	+ 1:58
+ 1.15	21	+ 1:36	+ 1.15	61	+ 2:16	+ 1.15	36	+ 1:51	+ 1.15	60	+ 2:15
+ 1.30	21	+ 1:51	+ 1.30	61	+ 2:31	+ 1.30	36	+ 2:06	+ 1.30	62	+ 2:32
+ 1.45	21	+ 2:06	+ 1.45	61	+ 2:46	+ 1.45	36	+ 2:21	+ 1.45	64	+ 2:49
+ 2.00	21	+ 2:21	+ 2.00	62	+ 3:02	+ 2.00	36	+ 2:36	+ 2.00	66	+ 3:06
+ 2.15	21	+ 2:36	+ 2.15	61	+ 3:16	+ 2.15	36	+ 2:51	+ 2.15	65	+ 3:20
+ 2.30	21	+ 2:51	+ 2.30	61	+ 3:31	+ 2.30	37	+ 3:07	+ 2.30	64	+ 3:34
+ 2.45	21	+ 3:06	+ 2.45	60	+ 3:45	+ 2.45	37	+ 3:22	+ 2.45	63	+ 3:48
+ 3.00	21	+ 3:21	+ 3.00	59	+ 3:59	+ 3.00	37	+ 3:37	+ 3.00	62	+ 4:02
+ 3.15	21	+ 3:36	+ 3.15	59	+ 4:14	+ 3.15	37	+ 3:52	+ 3.15	61	+ 4:16
+ 3.30	21	+ 3:51	+ 3.30	58	+ 4:28	+ 3.30	36	+ 4:06	+ 3.30	59	+ 4:29
+ 3.45	21	+ 4:06	+ 3.45	57	+ 4:42	+ 3.45	36	+ 4:21	+ 3.45	58	+ 4:43
+ 4.00	20	+ 4:20	+ 4.00	56	+ 4:56	+ 4.00	35	+ 4:35	+ 4.00	57	+ 4:57
+ 4.15	20	+ 4:35	+ 4.15	55	+ 5:10	+ 4.15	35	+ 4:50	+ 4.15	55	+ 5:10
+ 4.30	20	+ 4:50	+ 4.30	54	+ 5:24	+ 4.30	34	+ 5:04	+ 4.30	54	+ 5:24
+ 4.45	20	+ 5:05	+ 4.45	53	+ 5:38	+ 4.45	33	+ 5:18	+ 4.45	52	+ 5:37
+ 5.00	20	+ 5:20	+ 5.00	52	+ 5:52	+ 5.00	33	+ 5:33	+ 5.00	51	+ 5:51
+ 5.15	20	+ 5:35	+ 5.15	51	- 5:54	+ 5.15	32	+ 5:47	+ 5.15	49	- 5:56
+ 5.30	20	+ 5:50	+ 5.30	50	- 5:40	+ 5.30	31	- 5:59	+ 5.30	48	- 5:42
+ 5.45	20	- 5:55	+ 5.45	50	- 5:25	+ 5.45	31	- 5:44	+ 5.45	46	- 5:29
+ 6.00	20	- 5:40	+ 6.00	49	- 5:11	+ 6.00	30	- 5:30	+ 6.00	45	- 5:15

	C4			C3			C2			C1	
	SW Barrow to Princes No 6			Princes No 6 to Princes South			Princes South to Margate Sand			Margate Sand to North Foreland	
Time	Duration	Time at End of Sector	Time	Duration	Time at End of Sector	Time	Duration	Time at End of Sector	Time	Duration	Time at End of Sector
- 6.00	70	- 4:50	- 6.00	84	- 4:36	- 6.00	54	- 5:06	- 6.00	39	- 5:21
- 5.45	72	- 4:33	- 5.45	89	- 4:16	- 5.45	55	- 4:50	- 5.45	40	- 5:05
- 5.30	73	- 4:17	- 5.30	93	- 3:57	- 5.30	56	- 4:34	- 5.30	40	- 4:50
- 5.15	75	- 4:00	- 5.15	97	- 3:38	- 5.15	57	- 4:18	- 5.15	40	- 4:35
- 5.00	77	- 3:43	- 5.00	101	- 3:19	- 5.00	58	- 4:02	- 5.00	41	- 4:19
- 4.45	77	- 3:28	- 4.45	106	- 2:59	- 4.45	59	- 3:46	- 4.45	41	- 4:04
- 4.30	78	- 3:12	- 4.30	111	- 2:39	- 4.30	60	- 3:30	- 4.30	42	- 3:48
- 4.15	79	- 2:56	- 4.15	116	- 2:19	- 4.15	61	- 3:14	- 4.15	43	- 3:32
- 4.00	79	- 2:41	- 4.00	121	- 1:59	- 4.00	62	- 2:58	- 4.00	43	- 3:17
- 3.45	79	- 2:26	- 3.45	122	- 1:43	- 3.45	63	- 2:42	- 3.45	45	- 3:00
- 3.30	79	- 2:11	- 3.30	122	- 1:28	- 3.30	64	- 2:26	- 3.30	46	- 2:44
- 3.15	79	- 1:56	- 3.15	123	- 1:12	- 3.15	65	- 2:10	- 3.15	48	- 2:27
- 3.00	79	- 1:41	- 3.00	123	- 0:57	- 3.00	66	- 1:54	- 3.00	49	- 2:11
- 2.45	78	- 1:27	- 2.45	121	- 0:44	- 2.45	65	- 1:40	- 2.45	51	- 1:54
- 2.30	78	- 1:12	- 2.30	120	- 0:30	- 2.30	65	- 1:25	- 2.30	52	- 1:38
- 2.15	78	- 0:57	- 2.15	118	- 0:17	- 2.15	64	- 1:11	- 2.15	54	- 1:21
- 2.00	77	- 0:43	- 2.00	116	- 0:04	- 2.00	63	- 0:57	- 2.00	55	- 1:05
- 1.45	76	- 0:29	- 1.45	111	+ 0:06	- 1.45	61	- 0:44	- 1.45	55	- 0:50
- 1.30	75	- 0:15	- 1.30	107	+ 0:17	- 1.30	60	- 0:30	- 1.30	55	- 0:35
- 1.15	74	- 0:01	- 1.15	102	+ 0:27	- 1.15	58	- 0:17	- 1.15	55	- 0:20
- 1.00	72	+ 0:12	- 1.00	98	+ 0:38	- 1.00	56	- 0:04	- 1.00	54	- 0:06
- 0.45	71	+ 0:26	- 0.45	93	+ 0:48	- 0.45	55	+ 0:10	- 0.45	53	+ 0:08
- 0.30	70	+ 0:40	- 0.30	88	+ 0:58	- 0.30	53	+ 0:23	- 0.30	52	+ 0:22
- 0.15	68	+ 0:53	- 0.15	83	+ 1:08	- 0.15	52	+ 0:37	- 0.15	51	+ 0:36
HW	67	+ 1:07	HW	78	+ 1:18	HW	50	+ 0:50	HW	50	+ 0:50
+ 0.15	66	+ 1:21	+ 0.15	75	+ 1:30	+ 0.15	49	+ 1:04	+ 0.15	49	+ 1:04
+ 0.30	66	+ 1:36	+ 0.30	73	+ 1:43	+ 0.30	48	+ 1:18	+ 0.30	48	+ 1:18
+ 0.45	65	+ 1:50	+ 0.45	70	+ 1:55	+ 0.45	47	+ 1:32	+ 0.45	47	+ 1:32
+ 1.00	64	+ 2:04	+ 1.00	68	+ 2:08	+ 1.00	46	+ 1:46	+ 1.00	46	+ 1:46
+ 1.15	64	+ 2:19	+ 1.15	67	+ 2:22	+ 1.15	45	+ 2:00	+ 1.15	45	+ 2:00
+ 1.30	64	+ 2:34	+ 1.30	66	+ 2:36	+ 1.30	44	+ 2:14	+ 1.30	43	+ 2:13
+ 1.45	63	+ 2:48	+ 1.45	65	+ 2:50	+ 1.45	44	+ 2:29	+ 1.45	42	+ 2:27
+ 2.00	63	+ 3:03	+ 2.00	64	+ 3:04	+ 2.00	43	+ 2:43	+ 2.00	41	+ 2:41
+ 2.15	63	+ 3:18	+ 2.15	65	+ 3:20	+ 2.15	43	+ 2:58	+ 2.15	41	+ 2:56
+ 2.30	64	+ 3:34	+ 2.30	65	+ 3:35	+ 2.30	43	+ 3:13	+ 2.30	40	+ 3:10
+ 2.45	64	+ 3:49	+ 2.45	65	+ 3:50	+ 2.45	43	+ 3:28	+ 2.45	40	+ 3:25
+ 3.00	64	+ 4:04	+ 3.00	66	+ 4:06	+ 3.00	42	+ 3:42	+ 3.00	39	+ 3:39
+ 3.15	64	+ 4:19	+ 3.15	67	+ 4:22	+ 3.15	43	+ 3:58	+ 3.15	39	+ 3:54
+ 3.30	64	+ 4:34	+ 3.30	67	+ 4:37	+ 3.30	44	+ 4:14	+ 3.30	39	+ 4:09
+ 3.45	65	+ 4:50	+ 3.45	68	+ 4:53	+ 3.45	44	+ 4:29	+ 3.45	39	+ 4:24
+ 4.00	65	+ 5:05	+ 4.00	69	+ 5:09	+ 4.00	45	+ 4:45	+ 4.00	39	+ 4:39
+ 4.15	65	+ 5:20	+ 4.15	70	+ 5:25	+ 4.15	46	+ 5:01	+ 4.15	39	+ 4:54
+ 4.30	65	+ 5:35	+ 4.30	71	+ 5:41	+ 4.30	46	+ 5:16	+ 4.30	39	+ 5:09
+ 4.45	66	+ 5:51	+ 4.45	72	+ 5:57	+ 4.45	47	+ 5:32	+ 4.45	39	+ 5:24
+ 5.00	66	- 5:54	+ 5.00	74	- 5:46	+ 5.00	48	+ 5:48	+ 5.00	39	+ 5:39
+ 5.15	66	- 5:39	+ 5.15	75	- 5:30	+ 5.15	49	- 5:56	+ 5.15	39	+ 5:54
+ 5.30	66	- 5:24	+ 5.30	76	- 5:14	+ 5.30	49	- 5:41	+ 5.30	39	- 5:51
+ 5.45	66	- 5:09	+ 5.45	77	- 4:58	+ 5.45	50	- 5:25	+ 5.45	39	- 5:36
+ 6.00	67	- 4:53	+ 6.00	78	- 4:42	+ 6.00	51	- 5:09	+ 6.00	39	- 5:21

C - 5 Kts

Table C - Spitway to North Foreland via Princes Channel

5 Kts - C

Time to cover Sectors (in minutes) at 5.0 kts — All times relate to HW Sheerness — Springs

	C8			C7			C6			C5			C4			C3			C2			C1	
	Spitway to Whitaker Spit			Whitaker Spit to NE Maplin			NE Maplin to Maplin Edge			Maplin Edge to SW Barrow			SW Barrow to Princes No 6			Princes No 6 to Princes South			Princes South to Margate Sand			Margate Sand to North Foreland	
Time	Duration	Time at End of Sector	Time	Duration	Time at End of Sector	Time	Duration	Time at End of Sector	Time	Duration	Time at End of Sector	Time	Duration	Time at End of Sector	Time	Duration	Time at End of Sector	Time	Duration	Time at End of Sector	Time	Duration	Time at End of Sector
- 6.00	20	- 5:40	- 6.00	44	- 5:16	- 6.00	29	- 5:31	- 6.00	39	- 5:21	- 6.00	71	- 4:49	- 6.00	87	- 4:33	- 6.00	55	- 5:05	- 6.00	37	- 5:23
- 5.45	20	- 5:25	- 5.45	42	- 5:03	- 5.45	28	- 5:17	- 5.45	38	- 5:07	- 5.45	74	- 4:31	- 5.45	96	- 4:09	- 5.45	57	- 4:48	- 5.45	37	- 5:08
- 5.30	21	- 5:09	- 5.30	41	- 4:49	- 5.30	27	- 5:03	- 5.30	36	- 4:54	- 5.30	77	- 4:13	- 5.30	104	- 3:46	- 5.30	59	- 4:31	- 5.30	38	- 4:52
- 5.15	21	- 4:54	- 5.15	40	- 4:35	- 5.15	26	- 4:49	- 5.15	35	- 4:40	- 5.15	80	- 3:55	- 5.15	113	- 3:22	- 5.15	61	- 4:14	- 5.15	39	- 4:36
- 5.00	21	- 4:39	- 5.00	38	- 4:22	- 5.00	25	- 4:35	- 5.00	34	- 4:26	- 5.00	83	- 3:37	- 5.00	121	- 2:59	- 5.00	63	- 3:57	- 5.00	39	- 4:21
- 4.45	21	- 4:24	- 4.45	38	- 4:07	- 4.45	25	- 4:20	- 4.45	33	- 4:12	- 4.45	84	- 3:21	- 4.45	128	- 2:37	- 4.45	65	- 3:40	- 4.45	40	- 4:05
- 4.30	21	- 4:09	- 4.30	38	- 3:52	- 4.30	25	- 4:05	- 4.30	33	- 3:57	- 4.30	86	- 3:04	- 4.30	134	- 2:16	- 4.30	67	- 3:23	- 4.30	41	- 3:49
- 4.15	22	- 3:53	- 4.15	38	- 3:37	- 4.15	24	- 3:51	- 4.15	32	- 3:43	- 4.15	87	- 2:48	- 4.15	140	- 1:55	- 4.15	69	- 3:06	- 4.15	42	- 3:33
- 4.00	22	- 3:38	- 4.00	38	- 3:22	- 4.00	24	- 3:36	- 4.00	32	- 3:28	- 4.00	88	- 2:32	- 4.00	147	- 1:33	- 4.00	72	- 2:48	- 4.00	44	- 3:16
- 3.45	22	- 3:23	- 3.45	38	- 3:07	- 3.45	24	- 3:21	- 3.45	32	- 3:13	- 3.45	88	- 2:17	- 3.45	147	- 1:18	- 3.45	74	- 2:31	- 3.45	47	- 2:58
- 3.30	22	- 3:08	- 3.30	38	- 2:52	- 3.30	25	- 3:05	- 3.30	33	- 2:57	- 3.30	87	- 2:03	- 3.30	147	- 1:03	- 3.30	75	- 2:15	- 3.30	50	- 2:40
- 3.15	22	- 2:53	- 3.15	38	- 2:37	- 3.15	25	- 2:50	- 3.15	33	- 2:42	- 3.15	87	- 1:48	- 3.15	147	- 0:48	- 3.15	77	- 1:58	- 3.15	53	- 2:22
- 3.00	22	- 2:38	- 3.00	39	- 2:21	- 3.00	25	- 2:35	- 3.00	34	- 2:26	- 3.00	87	- 1:33	- 3.00	147	- 0:33	- 3.00	79	- 1:41	- 3.00	56	- 2:04
- 2.45	22	- 2:23	- 2.45	39	- 2:06	- 2.45	26	- 2:19	- 2.45	34	- 2:11	- 2.45	86	- 1:19	- 2.45	142	- 0:23	- 2.45	77	- 1:28	- 2.45	59	- 1:46
- 2.30	22	- 2:08	- 2.30	40	- 1:50	- 2.30	26	- 2:04	- 2.30	35	- 1:55	- 2.30	85	- 1:05	- 2.30	136	- 0:14	- 2.30	76	- 1:14	- 2.30	62	- 1:28
- 2.15	22	- 1:53	- 2.15	41	- 1:34	- 2.15	27	- 1:48	- 2.15	35	- 1:40	- 2.15	83	- 0:52	- 2.15	130	- 0:05	- 2.15	74	- 1:01	- 2.15	65	- 1:10
- 2.00	22	- 1:38	- 2.00	42	- 1:18	- 2.00	28	- 1:32	- 2.00	36	- 1:24	- 2.00	82	- 0:38	- 2.00	125	+ 0:05	- 2.00	72	- 0:48	- 2.00	68	- 0:52
- 1.45	22	- 1:23	- 1.45	43	- 1:02	- 1.45	28	- 1:17	- 1.45	37	- 1:08	- 1.45	80	- 0:25	- 1.45	118	+ 0:13	- 1.45	69	- 0:36	- 1.45	68	- 0:37
- 1.30	22	- 1:08	- 1.30	45	- 0:45	- 1.30	29	- 1:01	- 1.30	38	- 0:52	- 1.30	78	- 0:12	- 1.30	112	+ 0:22	- 1.30	66	- 0:24	- 1.30	67	- 0:23
- 1.15	21	- 0:54	- 1.15	46	- 0:29	- 1.15	29	- 0:46	- 1.15	39	- 0:36	- 1.15	76	+ 0:01	- 1.15	105	+ 0:30	- 1.15	63	- 0:12	- 1.15	67	- 0:08
- 1.00	21	- 0:39	- 1.00	47	- 0:13	- 1.00	30	- 0:30	- 1.00	40	- 0:20	- 1.00	74	+ 0:14	- 1.00	99	+ 0:39	- 1.00	59	- 0:01	- 1.00	66	+ 0:06
- 0.45	21	- 0:24	- 0.45	50	+ 0:05	- 0.45	31	- 0:14	- 0.45	42	- 0:03	- 0.45	72	+ 0:27	- 0.45	92	+ 0:47	- 0.45	57	+ 0:12	- 0.45	64	+ 0:19
- 0.30	21	- 0:09	- 0.30	53	+ 0:23	- 0.30	31	+ 0:01	- 0.30	44	+ 0:14	- 0.30	70	+ 0:40	- 0.30	86	+ 0:56	- 0.30	55	+ 0:25	- 0.30	61	+ 0:31
- 0.15	21	+ 0:06	- 0.15	56	+ 0:41	- 0.15	31	+ 0:16	- 0.15	47	+ 0:32	- 0.15	68	+ 0:53	- 0.15	80	+ 1:05	- 0.15	52	+ 0:37	- 0.15	59	+ 0:44
HW	21	+ 0:21	HW	58	+ 0:58	HW	32	+ 0:32	HW	49	+ 0:49	HW	66	+ 1:06	HW	74	+ 1:14	HW	50	+ 0:50	HW	57	+ 0:57
+ 0.15	21	+ 0:36	+ 0.15	61	+ 1:16	+ 0.15	34	+ 0:49	+ 0.15	53	+ 1:08	+ 0.15	65	+ 1:20	+ 0.15	70	+ 1:25	+ 0.15	48	+ 1:03	+ 0.15	54	+ 1:09
+ 0.30	21	+ 0:51	+ 0.30	63	+ 1:33	+ 0.30	35	+ 1:05	+ 0.30	57	+ 1:27	+ 0.30	65	+ 1:35	+ 0.30	66	+ 1:36	+ 0.30	47	+ 1:17	+ 0.30	52	+ 1:22
+ 0.45	21	+ 1:06	+ 0.45	65	+ 1:50	+ 0.45	37	+ 1:22	+ 0.45	61	+ 1:46	+ 0.45	64	+ 1:49	+ 0.45	63	+ 1:48	+ 0.45	45	+ 1:30	+ 0.45	50	+ 1:35
+ 1.00	22	+ 1:22	+ 1.00	68	+ 2:08	+ 1.00	38	+ 1:38	+ 1.00	65	+ 2:05	+ 1.00	63	+ 2:03	+ 1.00	59	+ 1:59	+ 1.00	43	+ 1:43	+ 1.00	47	+ 1:47
+ 1.15	22	+ 1:37	+ 1.15	68	+ 2:23	+ 1.15	39	+ 1:54	+ 1.15	73	+ 2:28	+ 1.15	62	+ 2:17	+ 1.15	59	+ 2:14	+ 1.15	43	+ 1:58	+ 1.15	45	+ 2:00
+ 1.30	22	+ 1:52	+ 1.30	69	+ 2:39	+ 1.30	39	+ 2:09	+ 1.30	80	+ 2:50	+ 1.30	62	+ 2:32	+ 1.30	58	+ 2:28	+ 1.30	42	+ 2:12	+ 1.30	44	+ 2:14
+ 1.45	23	+ 2:08	+ 1.45	70	+ 2:55	+ 1.45	39	+ 2:24	+ 1.45	87	+ 3:12	+ 1.45	62	+ 2:47	+ 1.45	57	+ 2:42	+ 1.45	41	+ 2:26	+ 1.45	42	+ 2:27
+ 2.00	23	+ 2:23	+ 2.00	70	+ 3:10	+ 2.00	40	+ 2:40	+ 2.00	94	+ 3:34	+ 2.00	62	+ 3:02	+ 2.00	56	+ 2:56	+ 2.00	40	+ 2:40	+ 2.00	40	+ 2:40
+ 2.15	23	+ 2:38	+ 2.15	69	+ 3:24	+ 2.15	40	+ 2:55	+ 2.15	89	+ 3:44	+ 2.15	62	+ 3:17	+ 2.15	56	+ 3:11	+ 2.15	40	+ 2:55	+ 2.15	39	+ 2:54
+ 2.30	23	+ 2:53	+ 2.30	68	+ 3:38	+ 2.30	40	+ 3:10	+ 2.30	83	+ 3:53	+ 2.30	62	+ 3:32	+ 2.30	57	+ 3:27	+ 2.30	40	+ 3:10	+ 2.30	38	+ 3:08
+ 2.45	23	+ 3:08	+ 2.45	67	+ 3:52	+ 2.45	40	+ 3:25	+ 2.45	78	+ 4:03	+ 2.45	62	+ 3:47	+ 2.45	57	+ 3:42	+ 2.45	39	+ 3:24	+ 2.45	37	+ 3:22
+ 3.00	22	+ 3:22	+ 3.00	66	+ 4:06	+ 3.00	41	+ 3:41	+ 3.00	72	+ 4:12	+ 3.00	62	+ 4:02	+ 3.00	57	+ 3:57	+ 3.00	39	+ 3:39	+ 3.00	36	+ 3:36
+ 3.15	22	+ 3:37	+ 3.15	65	+ 4:20	+ 3.15	40	+ 3:55	+ 3.15	70	+ 4:25	+ 3.15	63	+ 4:18	+ 3.15	58	+ 4:13	+ 3.15	40	+ 3:55	+ 3.15	36	+ 3:51
+ 3.30	22	+ 3:52	+ 3.30	64	+ 4:34	+ 3.30	39	+ 4:09	+ 3.30	68	+ 4:38	+ 3.30	63	+ 4:33	+ 3.30	59	+ 4:29	+ 3.30	41	+ 4:11	+ 3.30	36	+ 4:06
+ 3.45	21	+ 4:06	+ 3.45	62	+ 4:47	+ 3.45	38	+ 4:23	+ 3.45	65	+ 4:50	+ 3.45	63	+ 4:48	+ 3.45	60	+ 4:45	+ 3.45	42	+ 4:27	+ 3.45	36	+ 4:21
+ 4.00	21	+ 4:21	+ 4.00	61	+ 5:01	+ 4.00	38	+ 4:38	+ 4.00	63	+ 5:03	+ 4.00	63	+ 5:03	+ 4.00	60	+ 5:00	+ 4.00	42	+ 4:42	+ 4.00	35	+ 4:35
+ 4.15	21	+ 4:36	+ 4.15	59	+ 5:14	+ 4.15	37	+ 4:52	+ 4.15	60	+ 5:15	+ 4.15	64	+ 5:19	+ 4.15	62	+ 5:17	+ 4.15	43	+ 4:58	+ 4.15	36	+ 4:51
+ 4.30	21	+ 4:51	+ 4.30	57	+ 5:27	+ 4.30	35	+ 5:05	+ 4.30	58	+ 5:28	+ 4.30	64	+ 5:34	+ 4.30	64	+ 5:34	+ 4.30	45	+ 5:15	+ 4.30	36	+ 5:06
+ 4.45	21	+ 5:06	+ 4.45	55	+ 5:40	+ 4.45	34	+ 5:19	+ 4.45	55	+ 5:40	+ 4.45	64	+ 5:49	+ 4.45	65	+ 5:50	+ 4.45	46	+ 5:31	+ 4.45	36	+ 5:21
+ 5.00	21	+ 5:21	+ 5.00	54	+ 5:54	+ 5.00	33	+ 5:33	+ 5.00	53	+ 5:53	+ 5.00	65	- 5:55	+ 5.00	67	- 5:53	+ 5.00	47	+ 5:47	+ 5.00	36	+ 5:36
+ 5.15	21	+ 5:36	+ 5.15	52	- 5:53	+ 5.15	32	+ 5:47	+ 5.15	51	- 5:54	+ 5.15	65	- 5:40	+ 5.15	71	- 5:34	+ 5.15	48	- 5:57	+ 5.15	37	+ 5:52
+ 5.30	21	+ 5:51	+ 5.30	51	- 5:39	+ 5.30	32	- 5:58	+ 5.30	48	- 5:42	+ 5.30	65	- 5:25	+ 5.30	76	- 5:14	+ 5.30	49	- 5:41	+ 5.30	38	- 5:52
+ 5.45	20	- 5:55	+ 5.45	50	- 5:25	+ 5.45	31	- 5:44	+ 5.45	46	- 5:29	+ 5.45	65	- 5:10	+ 5.45	80	- 4:55	+ 5.45	50	- 5:25	+ 5.45	38	- 5:37
+ 6.00	20	- 5:40	+ 6.00	48	- 5:12	+ 6.00	30	- 5:30	+ 6.00	44	- 5:16	+ 6.00	66	- 4:54	+ 6.00	84	- 4:36	+ 6.00	51	- 5:09	+ 6.00	39	- 5:21

SOUTH BOUND

Table C - Spitway to North Foreland via Princes Channel

Neaps — All times relate to HW Sheerness — Time to cover Sectors (in minutes) at 6.0 Kts

SOUTH BOUND

Time	C8 Spitway to Whitaker Spit		Time	C7 Whitaker Spit to NE Maplin		Time	C6 NE Maplin to Maplin Edge		Time	C5 Maplin Edge to SW Barrow		Time	C4 SW Barrow to Princes No 6		Time	C3 Princes No 6 to Princes South		Time	C2 Princes South to Margate Sand		Time	C1 Margate Sand to North Foreland	
	Duration	Time at End of Sector		Duration	Time at End of Sector		Duration	Time at End of Sector		Duration	Time at End of Sector		Duration	Time at End of Sector		Duration	Time at End of Sector		Duration	Time at End of Sector		Duration	Time at End of Sector
- 6.00	**17**	**- 5:43**	**- 6.00**	**39**	**- 5:21**	**- 6.00**	**25**	**- 5:35**	**- 6.00**	**35**	**- 5:25**	**- 6.00**	**58**	**- 5:02**	**- 6.00**	**70**	**- 4:50**	**- 6.00**	**44**	**- 5:16**	**- 6.00**	**33**	**- 5:27**
- 5.45	17	- 5:28	- 5.45	38	- 5:07	- 5.45	24	- 5:21	- 5.45	35	- 5:10	- 5.45	59	- 4:46	- 5.45	72	- 4:33	- 5.45	45	- 5:00	- 5.45	34	- 5:11
- 5.30	17	- 5:13	- 5.30	38	- 4:52	- 5.30	24	- 5:06	- 5.30	34	- 4:56	- 5.30	60	- 4:30	- 5.30	74	- 4:16	- 5.30	45	- 4:45	- 5.30	34	- 4:56
- 5.15	17	- 4:58	- 5.15	37	- 4:38	- 5.15	23	- 4:52	- 5.15	33	- 4:42	- 5.15	61	- 4:14	- 5.15	76	- 3:59	- 5.15	46	- 4:29	- 5.15	34	- 4:41
- 5.00	**17**	**- 4:43**	**- 5.00**	**36**	**- 4:24**	**- 5.00**	**22**	**- 4:38**	**- 5.00**	**32**	**- 4:28**	**- 5.00**	**62**	**- 3:58**	**- 5.00**	**78**	**- 3:42**	**- 5.00**	**47**	**- 4:13**	**- 5.00**	**34**	**- 4:26**
- 4.45	17	- 4:28	- 4.45	36	- 4:09	- 4.45	26	- 4:19	- 4.45	32	- 4:13	- 4.45	63	- 3:42	- 4.45	82	- 3:23	- 4.45	47	- 3:58	- 4.45	34	- 4:11
- 4.30	17	- 4:13	- 4.30	36	- 3:54	- 4.30	29	- 4:01	- 4.30	32	- 3:58	- 4.30	63	- 3:27	- 4.30	86	- 3:04	- 4.30	48	- 3:42	- 4.30	35	- 3:55
- 4.15	17	- 3:58	- 4.15	36	- 3:39	- 4.15	33	- 3:42	- 4.15	31	- 3:44	- 4.15	64	- 3:11	- 4.15	89	- 2:46	- 4.15	49	- 3:26	- 4.15	35	- 3:40
- 4.00	**17**	**- 3:43**	**- 4.00**	**35**	**- 3:25**	**- 4.00**	**36**	**- 3:24**	**- 4.00**	**31**	**- 3:29**	**- 4.00**	**64**	**- 2:56**	**- 4.00**	**93**	**- 2:27**	**- 4.00**	**50**	**- 3:10**	**- 4.00**	**35**	**- 3:25**
- 3.45	17	- 3:28	- 3.45	36	- 3:09	- 3.45	33	- 3:12	- 3.45	31	- 3:14	- 3.45	64	- 2:41	- 3.45	94	- 2:11	- 3.45	50	- 2:55	- 3.45	36	- 3:09
- 3.30	17	- 3:13	- 3.30	36	- 2:54	- 3.30	29	- 3:01	- 3.30	31	- 2:59	- 3.30	64	- 2:26	- 3.30	95	- 1:55	- 3.30	51	- 2:39	- 3.30	37	- 2:53
- 3.15	17	- 2:58	- 3.15	36	- 2:39	- 3.15	26	- 2:49	- 3.15	32	- 2:43	- 3.15	64	- 2:11	- 3.15	96	- 1:39	- 3.15	52	- 2:23	- 3.15	38	- 2:37
- 3.00	**17**	**- 2:43**	**- 3.00**	**36**	**- 2:24**	**- 3.00**	**22**	**- 2:38**	**- 3.00**	**32**	**- 2:28**	**- 3.00**	**64**	**- 1:56**	**- 3.00**	**97**	**- 1:23**	**- 3.00**	**52**	**- 2:08**	**- 3.00**	**39**	**- 2:21**
- 2.45	17	- 2:28	- 2.45	36	- 2:09	- 2.45	23	- 2:22	- 2.45	32	- 2:13	- 2.45	64	- 1:41	- 2.45	97	- 1:08	- 2.45	52	- 1:53	- 2.45	41	- 2:04
- 2.30	17	- 2:13	- 2.30	37	- 1:53	- 2.30	23	- 2:07	- 2.30	33	- 1:57	- 2.30	63	- 1:27	- 2.30	96	- 0:54	- 2.30	52	- 1:38	- 2.30	42	- 1:48
- 2.15	17	- 1:58	- 2.15	37	- 1:38	- 2.15	23	- 1:52	- 2.15	33	- 1:42	- 2.15	63	- 1:12	- 2.15	96	- 0:39	- 2.15	51	- 1:24	- 2.15	43	- 1:32
- 2.00	**17**	**- 1:43**	**- 2.00**	**37**	**- 1:23**	**- 2.00**	**24**	**- 1:36**	**- 2.00**	**33**	**- 1:27**	**- 2.00**	**63**	**- 0:57**	**- 2.00**	**95**	**- 0:25**	**- 2.00**	**51**	**- 1:09**	**- 2.00**	**44**	**- 1:16**
- 1.45	17	- 1:28	- 1.45	38	- 1:07	- 1.45	24	- 1:21	- 1.45	34	- 1:11	- 1.45	62	- 0:43	- 1.45	91	- 0:14	- 1.45	50	- 0:55	- 1.45	44	- 1:01
- 1.30	17	- 1:13	- 1.30	39	- 0:51	- 1.30	24	- 1:06	- 1.30	34	- 0:56	- 1.30	62	- 0:28	- 1.30	87	- 0:03	- 1.30	49	- 0:41	- 1.30	44	- 0:46
- 1.15	17	- 0:58	- 1.15	39	- 0:36	- 1.15	25	- 0:50	- 1.15	35	- 0:40	- 1.15	61	- 0:14	- 1.15	83	+ 0:08	- 1.15	48	- 0:27	- 1.15	44	- 0:31
- 1.00	**17**	**- 0:43**	**- 1.00**	**40**	**- 0:20**	**- 1.00**	**25**	**- 0:35**	**- 1.00**	**35**	**- 0:25**	**- 1.00**	**60**	**HW**	**- 1.00**	**79**	**+ 0:19**	**- 1.00**	**47**	**- 0:13**	**- 1.00**	**44**	**- 0:16**
- 0.45	17	- 0:28	- 0.45	41	- 0:04	- 0.45	25	- 0:20	- 0.45	36	- 0:09	- 0.45	59	+ 0:14	- 0.45	76	+ 0:31	- 0.45	45	HW	- 0.45	43	- 0:02
- 0.30	17	- 0:13	- 0.30	42	+ 0:12	- 0.30	26	- 0:04	- 0.30	37	+ 0:07	- 0.30	58	+ 0:28	- 0.30	73	+ 0:43	- 0.30	44	+ 0:14	- 0.30	43	+ 0:13
- 0.15	17	+ 0:02	- 0.15	44	+ 0:29	- 0.15	26	+ 0:11	- 0.15	38	+ 0:23	- 0.15	57	+ 0:42	- 0.15	69	+ 0:54	- 0.15	43	+ 0:28	- 0.15	42	+ 0:27
HW	**17**	**+ 0:17**	**HW**	**45**	**+ 0:45**	**HW**	**26**	**+ 0:26**	**HW**	**39**	**+ 0:39**	**HW**	**56**	**+ 0:56**	**HW**	**66**	**+ 1:06**	**HW**	**42**	**+ 0:42**	**HW**	**41**	**+ 0:41**
+ 0.15	17	+ 0:32	+ 0.15	46	+ 1:01	+ 0.15	27	+ 0:42	+ 0.15	40	+ 0:55	+ 0.15	56	+ 1:11	+ 0.15	64	+ 1:19	+ 0.15	42	+ 0:57	+ 0.15	40	+ 0:55
+ 0.30	17	+ 0:47	+ 0.30	47	+ 1:17	+ 0.30	27	+ 0:57	+ 0.30	42	+ 1:12	+ 0.30	55	+ 1:25	+ 0.30	62	+ 1:32	+ 0.30	41	+ 1:11	+ 0.30	40	+ 1:10
+ 0.45	17	+ 1:02	+ 0.45	48	+ 1:33	+ 0.45	28	+ 1:13	+ 0.45	44	+ 1:29	+ 0.45	55	+ 1:40	+ 0.45	61	+ 1:46	+ 0.45	40	+ 1:25	+ 0.45	39	+ 1:24
+ 1.00	**17**	**+ 1:17**	**+ 1.00**	**49**	**+ 1:49**	**+ 1.00**	**29**	**+ 1:29**	**+ 1.00**	**46**	**+ 1:46**	**+ 1.00**	**54**	**+ 1:54**	**+ 1.00**	**59**	**+ 1:59**	**+ 1.00**	**39**	**+ 1:39**	**+ 1.00**	**38**	**+ 1:38**
+ 1.15	17	+ 1:32	+ 1.15	49	+ 2:04	+ 1.15	29	+ 1:44	+ 1.15	47	+ 2:02	+ 1.15	54	+ 2:09	+ 1.15	58	+ 2:13	+ 1.15	38	+ 1:53	+ 1.15	37	+ 1:52
+ 1.30	17	+ 1:47	+ 1.30	49	+ 2:19	+ 1.30	29	+ 1:59	+ 1.30	49	+ 2:19	+ 1.30	54	+ 2:24	+ 1.30	57	+ 2:27	+ 1.30	38	+ 2:08	+ 1.30	36	+ 2:06
+ 1.45	18	+ 2:03	+ 1.45	50	+ 2:35	+ 1.45	29	+ 2:14	+ 1.45	51	+ 2:36	+ 1.45	53	+ 2:38	+ 1.45	57	+ 2:42	+ 1.45	37	+ 2:22	+ 1.45	36	+ 2:21
+ 2.00	**18**	**+ 2:18**	**+ 2.00**	**50**	**+ 2:50**	**+ 2.00**	**29**	**+ 2:29**	**+ 2.00**	**52**	**+ 2:52**	**+ 2.00**	**53**	**+ 2:53**	**+ 2.00**	**56**	**+ 2:56**	**+ 2.00**	**37**	**+ 2:37**	**+ 2.00**	**35**	**+ 2:35**
+ 2.15	18	+ 2:33	+ 2.15	49	+ 3:04	+ 2.15	29	+ 2:44	+ 2.15	52	+ 3:07	+ 2.15	53	+ 3:08	+ 2.15	56	+ 3:11	+ 2.15	37	+ 2:52	+ 2.15	35	+ 2:50
+ 2.30	18	+ 2:48	+ 2.30	49	+ 3:19	+ 2.30	30	+ 3:00	+ 2.30	51	+ 3:21	+ 2.30	53	+ 3:23	+ 2.30	56	+ 3:26	+ 2.30	36	+ 3:06	+ 2.30	34	+ 3:04
+ 2.45	18	+ 3:03	+ 2.45	49	+ 3:34	+ 2.45	30	+ 3:15	+ 2.45	51	+ 3:36	+ 2.45	53	+ 3:38	+ 2.45	56	+ 3:41	+ 2.45	36	+ 3:21	+ 2.45	34	+ 3:19
+ 3.00	**17**	**+ 3:17**	**+ 3.00**	**48**	**+ 3:48**	**+ 3.00**	**30**	**+ 3:30**	**+ 3.00**	**50**	**+ 3:50**	**+ 3.00**	**54**	**+ 3:54**	**+ 3.00**	**57**	**+ 3:57**	**+ 3.00**	**36**	**+ 3:36**	**+ 3.00**	**34**	**+ 3:34**
+ 3.15	17	+ 3:32	+ 3.15	48	+ 4:03	+ 3.15	30	+ 3:45	+ 3.15	49	+ 4:04	+ 3.15	54	+ 4:09	+ 3.15	57	+ 4:12	+ 3.15	37	+ 3:52	+ 3.15	33	+ 3:48
+ 3.30	17	+ 3:47	+ 3.30	47	+ 4:17	+ 3.30	30	+ 4:00	+ 3.30	48	+ 4:18	+ 3.30	54	+ 4:24	+ 3.30	58	+ 4:28	+ 3.30	37	+ 4:07	+ 3.30	33	+ 4:03
+ 3.45	17	+ 4:02	+ 3.45	47	+ 4:32	+ 3.45	29	+ 4:14	+ 3.45	47	+ 4:32	+ 3.45	54	+ 4:39	+ 3.45	58	+ 4:43	+ 3.45	37	+ 4:22	+ 3.45	33	+ 4:18
+ 4.00	**17**	**+ 4:17**	**+ 4.00**	**46**	**+ 4:46**	**+ 4.00**	**29**	**+ 4:29**	**+ 4.00**	**46**	**+ 4:46**	**+ 4.00**	**54**	**+ 4:54**	**+ 4.00**	**59**	**+ 4:59**	**+ 4.00**	**38**	**+ 4:38**	**+ 4.00**	**33**	**+ 4:33**
+ 4.15	17	+ 4:32	+ 4.15	46	+ 5:01	+ 4.15	29	+ 4:44	+ 4.15	45	+ 5:00	+ 4.15	55	+ 5:10	+ 4.15	60	+ 5:15	+ 4.15	38	+ 4:53	+ 4.15	33	+ 4:48
+ 4.30	17	+ 4:47	+ 4.30	45	+ 5:15	+ 4.30	28	+ 4:58	+ 4.30	44	+ 5:14	+ 4.30	55	+ 5:25	+ 4.30	61	+ 5:31	+ 4.30	39	+ 5:09	+ 4.30	33	+ 5:03
+ 4.45	17	+ 5:02	+ 4.45	44	+ 5:29	+ 4.45	28	+ 5:13	+ 4.45	43	+ 5:28	+ 4.45	55	+ 5:40	+ 4.45	61	+ 5:46	+ 4.45	39	+ 5:24	+ 4.45	33	+ 5:18
+ 5.00	**17**	**+ 5:17**	**+ 5.00**	**43**	**+ 5:43**	**+ 5.00**	**27**	**+ 5:27**	**+ 5.00**	**42**	**+ 5:42**	**+ 5.00**	**55**	**+ 5:55**	**+ 5.00**	**62**	**- 5:58**	**+ 5.00**	**40**	**+ 5:40**	**+ 5.00**	**33**	**+ 5:33**
+ 5.15	17	+ 5:32	+ 5.15	43	+ 5:58	+ 5.15	27	+ 5:42	+ 5.15	41	+ 5:56	+ 5.15	55	- 5:50	+ 5.15	63	- 5:42	+ 5.15	41	+ 5:56	+ 5.15	33	+ 5:48
+ 5.30	17	+ 5:47	+ 5.30	42	- 5:48	+ 5.30	26	+ 5:56	+ 5.30	40	- 5:50	+ 5.30	55	- 5:35	+ 5.30	64	- 5:26	+ 5.30	41	- 5:49	+ 5.30	33	- 5:57
+ 5.45	17	- 5:58	+ 5.45	41	- 5:34	+ 5.45	26	- 5:49	+ 5.45	39	- 5:36	+ 5.45	56	- 5:19	+ 5.45	65	- 5:10	+ 5.45	42	- 5:33	+ 5.45	33	- 5:42
+ 6.00	**17**	**- 5:43**	**+ 6.00**	**41**	**- 5:19**	**+ 6.00**	**25**	**- 5:35**	**+ 6.00**	**38**	**- 5:22**	**+ 6.00**	**56**	**- 5:04**	**+ 6.00**	**66**	**- 4:54**	**+ 6.00**	**42**	**- 5:18**	**+ 6.00**	**33**	**- 5:27**

Table C - Spitway to North Foreland via Princes Channel

Time to cover Sectors (in minutes) at 6.0 kts — All times relate to HW Sheerness — Springs

SOUTH BOUND

	C8 Spitway to Whitaker Spit			C7 Whitaker Spit to NE Maplin			C6 NE Maplin to Maplin Edge			C5 Maplin Edge to SW Barrow	
Time	Duration	Time at End of Sector	Time	Duration	Time at End of Sector	Time	Duration	Time at End of Sector	Time	Duration	Time at End of Sector
- 6.00	17	- 5:43	- 6.00	38	- 5:22	- 6.00	24	- 5:36	- 6.00	34	- 5:26
- 5.45	17	- 5:28	- 5.45	37	- 5:08	- 5.45	23	- 5:22	- 5.45	33	- 5:12
- 5.30	17	- 5:13	- 5.30	36	- 4:54	- 5.30	23	- 5:07	- 5.30	32	- 4:58
- 5.15	17	- 4:58	- 5.15	35	- 4:40	- 5.15	22	- 4:53	- 5.15	31	- 4:44
- 5.00	18	- 4:42	- 5.00	34	- 4:26	- 5.00	21	- 4:39	- 5.00	30	- 4:30
- 4.45	18	- 4:27	- 4.45	33	- 4:12	- 4.45	21	- 4:24	- 4.45	31	- 4:14
- 4.30	18	- 4:12	- 4.30	33	- 3:57	- 4.30	20	- 4:10	- 4.30	31	- 3:59
- 4.15	18	- 3:57	- 4.15	33	- 3:42	- 4.15	20	- 3:55	- 4.15	31	- 3:44
- 4.00	18	- 3:42	- 4.00	33	- 3:27	- 4.00	20	- 3:40	- 4.00	31	- 3:29
- 3.45	18	- 3:27	- 3.45	33	- 3:12	- 3.45	20	- 3:25	- 3.45	31	- 3:14
- 3.30	18	- 3:12	- 3.30	33	- 2:57	- 3.30	20	- 3:10	- 3.30	30	- 3:00
- 3.15	18	- 2:57	- 3.15	33	- 2:42	- 3.15	21	- 2:54	- 3.15	30	- 2:45
- 3.00	18	- 2:42	- 3.00	33	- 2:27	- 3.00	21	- 2:39	- 3.00	30	- 2:30
- 2.45	18	- 2:27	- 2.45	34	- 2:11	- 2.45	21	- 2:24	- 2.45	30	- 2:15
- 2.30	18	- 2:12	- 2.30	34	- 1:56	- 2.30	22	- 2:08	- 2.30	30	- 2:00
- 2.15	18	- 1:57	- 2.15	35	- 1:40	- 2.15	22	- 1:53	- 2.15	31	- 1:44
- 2.00	18	- 1:42	- 2.00	35	- 1:25	- 2.00	23	- 1:37	- 2.00	31	- 1:29
- 1.45	18	- 1:27	- 1.45	36	- 1:09	- 1.45	23	- 1:22	- 1.45	32	- 1:13
- 1.30	18	- 1:12	- 1.30	37	- 0:53	- 1.30	24	- 1:06	- 1.30	32	- 0:58
- 1.15	18	- 0:57	- 1.15	38	- 0:37	- 1.15	24	- 0:51	- 1.15	33	- 0:42
- 1.00	18	- 0:42	- 1.00	39	- 0:21	- 1.00	25	- 0:35	- 1.00	33	- 0:27
- 0.45	18	- 0:27	- 0.45	41	- 0:04	- 0.45	25	- 0:20	- 0.45	35	- 0:10
- 0.30	17	- 0:13	- 0.30	43	+ 0:13	- 0.30	26	- 0:04	- 0.30	36	+ 0:06
- 0.15	17	+ 0:02	- 0.15	45	+ 0:30	- 0.15	26	+ 0:11	- 0.15	38	+ 0:23
HW	17	+ 0:17	HW	47	+ 0:47	HW	26	+ 0:26	HW	39	+ 0:39
+ 0.15	17	+ 0:32	+ 0.15	48	+ 1:03	+ 0.15	27	+ 0:42	+ 0.15	42	+ 0:57
+ 0.30	18	+ 0:48	+ 0.30	50	+ 1:20	+ 0.30	28	+ 0:58	+ 0.30	45	+ 1:15
+ 0.45	18	+ 1:03	+ 0.45	52	+ 1:37	+ 0.45	29	+ 1:14	+ 0.45	48	+ 1:33
+ 1.00	18	+ 1:18	+ 1.00	54	+ 1:54	+ 1.00	31	+ 1:31	+ 1.00	50	+ 1:50
+ 1.15	18	+ 1:33	+ 1.15	54	+ 2:09	+ 1.15	31	+ 1:46	+ 1.15	53	+ 2:08
+ 1.30	19	+ 1:49	+ 1.30	55	+ 2:25	+ 1.30	31	+ 2:01	+ 1.30	56	+ 2:26
+ 1.45	19	+ 2:04	+ 1.45	55	+ 2:40	+ 1.45	31	+ 2:16	+ 1.45	59	+ 2:44
+ 2.00	19	+ 2:19	+ 2.00	56	+ 2:56	+ 2.00	32	+ 2:32	+ 2.00	62	+ 3:02
+ 2.15	19	+ 2:34	+ 2.15	55	+ 3:10	+ 2.15	32	+ 2:47	+ 2.15	60	+ 3:15
+ 2.30	19	+ 2:49	+ 2.30	54	+ 3:24	+ 2.30	32	+ 3:02	+ 2.30	59	+ 3:29
+ 2.45	19	+ 3:04	+ 2.45	54	+ 3:39	+ 2.45	32	+ 3:17	+ 2.45	58	+ 3:43
+ 3.00	19	+ 3:19	+ 3.00	53	+ 3:53	+ 3.00	32	+ 3:32	+ 3.00	57	+ 3:57
+ 3.15	18	+ 3:33	+ 3.15	52	+ 4:07	+ 3.15	32	+ 3:47	+ 3.15	56	+ 4:11
+ 3.30	18	+ 3:48	+ 3.30	51	+ 4:21	+ 3.30	32	+ 4:02	+ 3.30	54	+ 4:24
+ 3.45	18	+ 4:03	+ 3.45	50	+ 4:35	+ 3.45	31	+ 4:16	+ 3.45	52	+ 4:37
+ 4.00	18	+ 4:18	+ 4.00	49	+ 4:49	+ 4.00	31	+ 4:31	+ 4.00	50	+ 4:50
+ 4.15	17	+ 4:32	+ 4.15	48	+ 5:03	+ 4.15	30	+ 4:45	+ 4.15	49	+ 5:04
+ 4.30	17	+ 4:47	+ 4.30	47	+ 5:17	+ 4.30	29	+ 4:59	+ 4.30	47	+ 5:17
+ 4.45	17	+ 5:02	+ 4.45	46	+ 5:31	+ 4.45	29	+ 5:14	+ 4.45	46	+ 5:31
+ 5.00	17	+ 5:17	+ 5.00	45	+ 5:45	+ 5.00	28	+ 5:28	+ 5.00	44	+ 5:44
+ 5.15	17	+ 5:32	+ 5.15	44	+ 5:59	+ 5.15	27	+ 5:42	+ 5.15	42	+ 5:57
+ 5.30	17	+ 5:47	+ 5.30	43	- 5:47	+ 5.30	26	+ 5:56	+ 5.30	41	- 5:49
+ 5.45	17	- 5:58	+ 5.45	42	- 5:33	+ 5.45	25	- 5:50	+ 5.45	39	- 5:36
+ 6.00	17	- 5:43	+ 6.00	41	- 5:19	+ 6.00	25	- 5:35	+ 6.00	37	- 5:23

	C4 SW Barrow to Princes No 6			C3 Princes No 6 to Princes South			C2 Princes South to Margate Sand			C1 Margate Sand to North Foreland	
Time	Duration	Time at End of Sector	Time	Duration	Time at End of Sector	Time	Duration	Time at End of Sector	Time	Duration	Time at End of Sector
- 6.00	58	- 5:02	- 6.00	71	- 4:49	- 6.00	45	- 5:15	- 6.00	31	- 5:29
- 5.45	60	- 4:45	- 5.45	76	- 4:29	- 5.45	46	- 4:59	- 5.45	32	- 5:13
- 5.30	62	- 4:28	- 5.30	81	- 4:09	- 5.30	47	- 4:43	- 5.30	32	- 4:58
- 5.15	64	- 4:11	- 5.15	86	- 3:49	- 5.15	48	- 4:27	- 5.15	32	- 4:43
- 5.00	66	- 3:54	- 5.00	91	- 3:29	- 5.00	50	- 4:10	- 5.00	33	- 4:27
- 4.45	67	- 3:38	- 4.45	94	- 3:11	- 4.45	51	- 3:54	- 4.45	33	- 4:12
- 4.30	67	- 3:23	- 4.30	98	- 2:52	- 4.30	52	- 3:38	- 4.30	34	- 3:56
- 4.15	68	- 3:07	- 4.15	101	- 2:34	- 4.15	54	- 3:21	- 4.15	34	- 3:41
- 4.00	69	- 2:51	- 4.00	105	- 2:15	- 4.00	55	- 3:05	- 4.00	35	- 3:25
- 3.45	69	- 2:36	- 3.45	106	- 1:59	- 3.45	56	- 2:49	- 3.45	37	- 3:08
- 3.30	69	- 2:21	- 3.30	108	- 1:42	- 3.30	57	- 2:33	- 3.30	39	- 2:51
- 3.15	69	- 2:06	- 3.15	110	- 1:25	- 3.15	59	- 2:16	- 3.15	41	- 2:34
- 3.00	69	- 1:51	- 3.00	111	- 1:09	- 3.00	60	- 2:00	- 3.00	43	- 2:17
- 2.45	68	- 1:37	- 2.45	109	- 0:56	- 2.45	59	- 1:46	- 2.45	45	- 2:00
- 2.30	68	- 1:22	- 2.30	107	- 0:43	- 2.30	58	- 1:32	- 2.30	47	- 1:43
- 2.15	67	- 1:08	- 2.15	104	- 0:31	- 2.15	58	- 1:17	- 2.15	49	- 1:26
- 2.00	67	- 0:53	- 2.00	102	- 0:18	- 2.00	57	- 1:03	- 2.00	51	- 1:09
- 1.45	65	- 0:40	- 1.45	97	- 0:08	- 1.45	55	- 0:50	- 1.45	51	- 0:54
- 1.30	64	- 0:26	- 1.30	93	+ 0:03	- 1.30	53	- 0:37	- 1.30	51	- 0:39
- 1.15	63	- 0:12	- 1.15	88	+ 0:13	- 1.15	51	- 0:24	- 1.15	51	- 0:24
- 1.00	61	+ 0:01	- 1.00	84	+ 0:24	- 1.00	49	- 0:11	- 1.00	51	- 0:09
- 0.45	60	+ 0:15	- 0.45	79	+ 0:34	- 0.45	47	+ 0:02	- 0.45	50	+ 0:05
- 0.30	59	+ 0:29	- 0.30	74	+ 0:44	- 0.30	46	+ 0:16	- 0.30	48	+ 0:18
- 0.15	57	+ 0:42	- 0.15	69	+ 0:54	- 0.15	44	+ 0:29	- 0.15	47	+ 0:32
HW	56	+ 0:56	HW	64	+ 1:04	HW	42	+ 0:42	HW	46	+ 0:46
+ 0.15	55	+ 1:10	+ 0.15	61	+ 1:16	+ 0.15	41	+ 0:56	+ 0.15	44	+ 0:59
+ 0.30	54	+ 1:24	+ 0.30	58	+ 1:28	+ 0.30	40	+ 1:10	+ 0.30	42	+ 1:12
+ 0.45	54	+ 1:39	+ 0.45	55	+ 1:40	+ 0.45	39	+ 1:24	+ 0.45	41	+ 1:26
+ 1.00	53	+ 1:53	+ 1.00	52	+ 1:52	+ 1.00	37	+ 1:37	+ 1.00	39	+ 1:39
+ 1.15	53	+ 2:08	+ 1.15	52	+ 2:07	+ 1.15	37	+ 1:52	+ 1.15	38	+ 1:53
+ 1.30	52	+ 2:22	+ 1.30	51	+ 2:21	+ 1.30	36	+ 2:06	+ 1.30	37	+ 2:07
+ 1.45	52	+ 2:37	+ 1.45	50	+ 2:35	+ 1.45	35	+ 2:20	+ 1.45	36	+ 2:21
+ 2.00	52	+ 2:52	+ 2.00	49	+ 2:49	+ 2.00	35	+ 2:35	+ 2.00	35	+ 2:35
+ 2.15	52	+ 3:07	+ 2.15	49	+ 3:04	+ 2.15	34	+ 2:49	+ 2.15	34	+ 2:49
+ 2.30	52	+ 3:22	+ 2.30	50	+ 3:20	+ 2.30	34	+ 3:04	+ 2.30	33	+ 3:03
+ 2.45	52	+ 3:37	+ 2.45	50	+ 3:35	+ 2.45	34	+ 3:19	+ 2.45	32	+ 3:17
+ 3.00	52	+ 3:52	+ 3.00	50	+ 3:50	+ 3.00	34	+ 3:34	+ 3.00	31	+ 3:31
+ 3.15	53	+ 4:08	+ 3.15	51	+ 4:06	+ 3.15	34	+ 3:49	+ 3.15	31	+ 3:46
+ 3.30	53	+ 4:23	+ 3.30	51	+ 4:21	+ 3.30	35	+ 4:05	+ 3.30	31	+ 4:01
+ 3.45	53	+ 4:38	+ 3.45	52	+ 4:37	+ 3.45	35	+ 4:20	+ 3.45	31	+ 4:16
+ 4.00	53	+ 4:53	+ 4.00	52	+ 4:52	+ 4.00	36	+ 4:36	+ 4.00	31	+ 4:31
+ 4.15	54	+ 5:09	+ 4.15	54	+ 5:09	+ 4.15	37	+ 4:52	+ 4.15	31	+ 4:46
+ 4.30	54	+ 5:24	+ 4.30	55	+ 5:25	+ 4.30	37	+ 5:07	+ 4.30	31	+ 5:01
+ 4.45	54	+ 5:39	+ 4.45	56	+ 5:41	+ 4.45	38	+ 5:23	+ 4.45	31	+ 5:16
+ 5.00	54	+ 5:54	+ 5.00	57	+ 5:57	+ 5.00	39	+ 5:39	+ 5.00	31	+ 5:31
+ 5.15	54	- 5:51	+ 5.15	59	- 5:46	+ 5.15	40	+ 5:55	+ 5.15	31	+ 5:46
+ 5.30	55	- 5:35	+ 5.30	60	- 5:30	+ 5.30	41	- 5:49	+ 5.30	31	- 5:59
+ 5.45	55	- 5:20	+ 5.45	61	- 5:14	+ 5.45	41	- 5:34	+ 5.45	31	- 5:44
+ 6.00	55	- 5:05	+ 6.00	63	- 4:57	+ 6.00	42	- 5:18	+ 6.00	31	- 5:29

Table C - Spitway to North Foreland via Princes Channel

Neaps — All times relate to HW Sheerness — **Time to cover Sectors (in minutes) at 7.0 Kts**

SOUTH BOUND

	C8 Spitway to Whitaker Spit			C7 Whitaker Spit to NE Maplin			C6 NE Maplin to Maplin Edge			C5 Maplin Edge to SW Barrow			C4 SW Barrow to Princes No 6			C3 Princes No 6 to Princes South			C2 Princes South to Margate Sand			C1 Margate Sand to North Foreland	
Time	Duration	Time at End of Sector	Time	Duration	Time at End of Sector	Time	Duration	Time at End of Sector	Time	Duration	Time at End of Sector	Time	Duration	Time at End of Sector	Time	Duration	Time at End of Sector	Time	Duration	Time at End of Sector	Time	Duration	Time at End of Sector
- 6.00	14	- 5:46	- 6.00	34	- 5:26	- 6.00	21	- 5:39	- 6.00	31	- 5:29	- 6.00	49	- 5:11	- 6.00	59	- 5:01	- 6.00	37	- 5:23	- 6.00	29	- 5:31
- 5.45	14	- 5:31	- 5.45	33	- 5:12	- 5.45	21	- 5:24	- 5.45	30	- 5:15	- 5.45	50	- 4:55	- 5.45	61	- 4:44	- 5.45	38	- 5:07	- 5.45	29	- 5:16
- 5.30	14	- 5:16	- 5.30	33	- 4:57	- 5.30	20	- 5:10	- 5.30	30	- 5:00	- 5.30	51	- 4:39	- 5.30	62	- 4:28	- 5.30	38	- 4:52	- 5.30	29	- 5:01
- 5.15	14	- 5:01	- 5.15	32	- 4:43	- 5.15	20	- 4:55	- 5.15	29	- 4:46	- 5.15	51	- 4:24	- 5.15	63	- 4:12	- 5.15	39	- 4:36	- 5.15	29	- 4:46
- 5.00	14	- 4:46	- 5.00	32	- 4:28	- 5.00	19	- 4:41	- 5.00	29	- 4:31	- 5.00	52	- 4:08	- 5.00	65	- 3:55	- 5.00	39	- 4:21	- 5.00	29	- 4:31
- 4.45	14	- 4:31	- 4.45	31	- 4:14	- 4.45	19	- 4:26	- 4.45	28	- 4:17	- 4.45	53	- 3:52	- 4.45	67	- 3:38	- 4.45	40	- 4:05	- 4.45	29	- 4:16
- 4.30	14	- 4:16	- 4.30	31	- 3:59	- 4.30	19	- 4:11	- 4.30	28	- 4:02	- 4.30	53	- 3:37	- 4.30	68	- 3:22	- 4.30	40	- 3:50	- 4.30	30	- 4:00
- 4.15	14	- 4:01	- 4.15	31	- 3:44	- 4.15	19	- 3:56	- 4.15	27	- 3:48	- 4.15	53	- 3:22	- 4.15	70	- 3:05	- 4.15	41	- 3:34	- 4.15	30	- 3:45
- 4.00	14	- 3:46	- 4.00	31	- 3:29	- 4.00	19	- 3:41	- 4.00	27	- 3:33	- 4.00	54	- 3:06	- 4.00	72	- 2:48	- 4.00	41	- 3:19	- 4.00	30	- 3:30
- 3.45	14	- 3:31	- 3.45	31	- 3:14	- 3.45	19	- 3:26	- 3.45	27	- 3:18	- 3.45	54	- 2:51	- 3.45	73	- 2:32	- 3.45	42	- 3:03	- 3.45	31	- 3:14
- 3.30	15	- 3:15	- 3.30	31	- 2:59	- 3.30	19	- 3:11	- 3.30	27	- 3:03	- 3.30	54	- 2:36	- 3.30	74	- 2:16	- 3.30	42	- 2:48	- 3.30	32	- 2:58
- 3.15	15	- 3:00	- 3.15	31	- 2:44	- 3.15	19	- 2:56	- 3.15	28	- 2:47	- 3.15	54	- 2:21	- 3.15	75	- 2:00	- 3.15	43	- 2:32	- 3.15	32	- 2:43
- 3.00	15	- 2:45	- 3.00	31	- 2:29	- 3.00	19	- 2:41	- 3.00	28	- 2:32	- 3.00	54	- 2:06	- 3.00	76	- 1:44	- 3.00	43	- 2:17	- 3.00	33	- 2:27
- 2.45	15	- 2:30	- 2.45	32	- 2:13	- 2.45	19	- 2:26	- 2.45	28	- 2:17	- 2.45	54	- 1:51	- 2.45	76	- 1:29	- 2.45	43	- 2:02	- 2.45	34	- 2:11
- 2.30	15	- 2:15	- 2.30	32	- 1:58	- 2.30	20	- 2:10	- 2.30	28	- 2:02	- 2.30	53	- 1:37	- 2.30	75	- 1:15	- 2.30	43	- 1:47	- 2.30	35	- 1:55
- 2.15	15	- 2:00	- 2.15	32	- 1:43	- 2.15	20	- 1:55	- 2.15	29	- 1:46	- 2.15	53	- 1:22	- 2.15	75	- 1:00	- 2.15	43	- 1:32	- 2.15	35	- 1:40
- 2.00	15	- 1:45	- 2.00	32	- 1:28	- 2.00	20	- 1:40	- 2.00	29	- 1:31	- 2.00	53	- 1:07	- 2.00	75	- 0:45	- 2.00	43	- 1:17	- 2.00	36	- 1:24
- 1.45	15	- 1:30	- 1.45	33	- 1:12	- 1.45	20	- 1:25	- 1.45	29	- 1:16	- 1.45	53	- 0:52	- 1.45	73	- 0:32	- 1.45	42	- 1:03	- 1.45	36	- 1:09
- 1.30	15	- 1:15	- 1.30	33	- 0:57	- 1.30	21	- 1:09	- 1.30	30	- 1:00	- 1.30	52	- 0:38	- 1.30	71	- 0:19	- 1.30	41	- 0:49	- 1.30	36	- 0:54
- 1.15	15	- 1:00	- 1.15	34	- 0:41	- 1.15	21	- 0:54	- 1.15	30	- 0:45	- 1.15	52	- 0:23	- 1.15	69	- 0:06	- 1.15	40	- 0:35	- 1.15	36	- 0:39
- 1.00	15	- 0:45	- 1.00	34	- 0:26	- 1.00	21	- 0:39	- 1.00	30	- 0:30	- 1.00	51	- 0:09	- 1.00	67	+ 0:07	- 1.00	40	- 0:20	- 1.00	37	- 0:23
- 0.45	15	- 0:30	- 0.45	35	- 0:10	- 0.45	22	- 0:23	- 0.45	31	- 0:14	- 0.45	51	+ 0:06	- 0.45	65	+ 0:20	- 0.45	39	- 0:06	- 0.45	36	- 0:09
- 0.30	15	- 0:15	- 0.30	36	+ 0:06	- 0.30	22	- 0:08	- 0.30	31	+ 0:01	- 0.30	50	+ 0:20	- 0.30	62	+ 0:32	- 0.30	38	+ 0:08	- 0.30	36	+ 0:06
- 0.15	14	- 0:01	- 0.15	37	+ 0:22	- 0.15	22	+ 0:07	- 0.15	32	+ 0:17	- 0.15	49	+ 0:34	- 0.15	60	+ 0:45	- 0.15	37	+ 0:22	- 0.15	35	+ 0:20
HW	14	+ 0:14	HW	38	+ 0:38	HW	22	+ 0:22	HW	33	+ 0:33	HW	49	+ 0:49	HW	58	+ 0:58	HW	37	+ 0:37	HW	35	+ 0:35
+ 0.15	14	+ 0:29	+ 0.15	38	+ 0:53	+ 0.15	23	+ 0:38	+ 0.15	34	+ 0:49	+ 0.15	48	+ 1:03	+ 0.15	56	+ 1:11	+ 0.15	36	+ 0:51	+ 0.15	34	+ 0:49
+ 0.30	15	+ 0:45	+ 0.30	39	+ 1:09	+ 0.30	23	+ 0:53	+ 0.30	35	+ 1:05	+ 0.30	48	+ 1:18	+ 0.30	55	+ 1:25	+ 0.30	35	+ 1:05	+ 0.30	34	+ 1:04
+ 0.45	15	+ 1:00	+ 0.45	40	+ 1:25	+ 0.45	24	+ 1:09	+ 0.45	37	+ 1:22	+ 0.45	47	+ 1:32	+ 0.45	53	+ 1:38	+ 0.45	35	+ 1:20	+ 0.45	33	+ 1:18
+ 1.00	15	+ 1:15	+ 1.00	41	+ 1:41	+ 1.00	25	+ 1:25	+ 1.00	38	+ 1:38	+ 1.00	47	+ 1:47	+ 1.00	52	+ 1:52	+ 1.00	34	+ 1:34	+ 1.00	33	+ 1:33
+ 1.15	15	+ 1:30	+ 1.15	41	+ 1:56	+ 1.15	25	+ 1:40	+ 1.15	39	+ 1:54	+ 1.15	46	+ 2:01	+ 1.15	51	+ 2:06	+ 1.15	34	+ 1:49	+ 1.15	32	+ 1:47
+ 1.30	15	+ 1:45	+ 1.30	41	+ 2:11	+ 1.30	25	+ 1:55	+ 1.30	41	+ 2:11	+ 1.30	46	+ 2:16	+ 1.30	50	+ 2:20	+ 1.30	33	+ 2:03	+ 1.30	31	+ 2:01
+ 1.45	15	+ 2:00	+ 1.45	41	+ 2:26	+ 1.45	25	+ 2:10	+ 1.45	42	+ 2:27	+ 1.45	46	+ 2:31	+ 1.45	50	+ 2:35	+ 1.45	33	+ 2:18	+ 1.45	31	+ 2:16
+ 2.00	15	+ 2:15	+ 2.00	42	+ 2:42	+ 2.00	25	+ 2:25	+ 2.00	44	+ 2:44	+ 2.00	46	+ 2:46	+ 2.00	49	+ 2:49	+ 2.00	32	+ 2:32	+ 2.00	30	+ 2:30
+ 2.15	15	+ 2:30	+ 2.15	41	+ 2:56	+ 2.15	25	+ 2:40	+ 2.15	43	+ 2:58	+ 2.15	46	+ 3:01	+ 2.15	49	+ 3:04	+ 2.15	32	+ 2:47	+ 2.15	30	+ 2:45
+ 2.30	15	+ 2:45	+ 2.30	41	+ 3:11	+ 2.30	25	+ 2:55	+ 2.30	43	+ 3:13	+ 2.30	46	+ 3:16	+ 2.30	49	+ 3:19	+ 2.30	32	+ 3:02	+ 2.30	29	+ 2:59
+ 2.45	15	+ 3:00	+ 2.45	41	+ 3:26	+ 2.45	25	+ 3:10	+ 2.45	42	+ 3:27	+ 2.45	46	+ 3:31	+ 2.45	49	+ 3:34	+ 2.45	32	+ 3:17	+ 2.45	29	+ 3:14
+ 3.00	15	+ 3:15	+ 3.00	41	+ 3:41	+ 3.00	26	+ 3:26	+ 3.00	42	+ 3:42	+ 3.00	46	+ 3:46	+ 3.00	50	+ 3:50	+ 3.00	31	+ 3:31	+ 3.00	29	+ 3:29
+ 3.15	15	+ 3:30	+ 3.15	40	+ 3:55	+ 3.15	25	+ 3:40	+ 3.15	41	+ 3:56	+ 3.15	46	+ 4:01	+ 3.15	50	+ 4:05	+ 3.15	32	+ 3:47	+ 3.15	29	+ 3:44
+ 3.30	15	+ 3:45	+ 3.30	40	+ 4:10	+ 3.30	25	+ 3:55	+ 3.30	40	+ 4:10	+ 3.30	46	+ 4:16	+ 3.30	51	+ 4:21	+ 3.30	32	+ 4:02	+ 3.30	29	+ 3:59
+ 3.45	15	+ 4:00	+ 3.45	40	+ 4:25	+ 3.45	25	+ 4:10	+ 3.45	39	+ 4:24	+ 3.45	47	+ 4:32	+ 3.45	51	+ 4:36	+ 3.45	32	+ 4:17	+ 3.45	28	+ 4:13
+ 4.00	14	+ 4:14	+ 4.00	39	+ 4:39	+ 4.00	25	+ 4:25	+ 4.00	39	+ 4:39	+ 4.00	47	+ 4:47	+ 4.00	51	+ 4:51	+ 4.00	33	+ 4:33	+ 4.00	28	+ 4:28
+ 4.15	14	+ 4:29	+ 4.15	39	+ 4:54	+ 4.15	24	+ 4:39	+ 4.15	38	+ 4:53	+ 4.15	47	+ 5:02	+ 4.15	52	+ 5:07	+ 4.15	33	+ 4:48	+ 4.15	28	+ 4:43
+ 4.30	14	+ 4:44	+ 4.30	38	+ 5:08	+ 4.30	24	+ 4:54	+ 4.30	37	+ 5:07	+ 4.30	47	+ 5:17	+ 4.30	53	+ 5:23	+ 4.30	33	+ 5:03	+ 4.30	28	+ 4:58
+ 4.45	14	+ 4:59	+ 4.45	38	+ 5:23	+ 4.45	24	+ 5:09	+ 4.45	37	+ 5:22	+ 4.45	47	+ 5:32	+ 4.45	53	+ 5:38	+ 4.45	34	+ 5:19	+ 4.45	28	+ 5:13
+ 5.00	14	+ 5:14	+ 5.00	37	+ 5:37	+ 5.00	23	+ 5:23	+ 5.00	36	+ 5:36	+ 5.00	47	+ 5:47	+ 5.00	54	+ 5:54	+ 5.00	34	+ 5:34	+ 5.00	28	+ 5:28
+ 5.15	14	+ 5:29	+ 5.15	37	+ 5:52	+ 5.15	23	+ 5:38	+ 5.15	35	+ 5:50	+ 5.15	47	- 5:58	+ 5.15	55	- 5:50	+ 5.15	35	+ 5:50	+ 5.15	28	+ 5:43
+ 5.30	14	+ 5:44	+ 5.30	36	- 5:54	+ 5.30	22	+ 5:52	+ 5.30	34	- 5:56	+ 5.30	48	- 5:42	+ 5.30	55	- 5:35	+ 5.30	35	- 5:55	+ 5.30	28	+ 5:58
+ 5.45	14	+ 5:59	+ 5.45	36	- 5:39	+ 5.45	22	- 5:53	+ 5.45	33	- 5:42	+ 5.45	48	- 5:27	+ 5.45	56	- 5:19	+ 5.45	36	- 5:39	+ 5.45	28	- 5:47
+ 6.00	14	- 5:46	+ 6.00	35	- 5:25	+ 6.00	22	- 5:38	+ 6.00	32	- 5:28	+ 6.00	48	- 5:12	+ 6.00	57	- 5:03	+ 6.00	36	- 5:24	+ 6.00	28	- 5:32

C - 7 Kts — Table C - Spitway to North Foreland via Princes Channel — 7 Kts - C

Time to cover Sectors (in minutes) at 7.0 kts — All times relate to HW Sheerness — **Springs**

Time	C8 Spitway to Whitaker Spit Duration	C8 Time at End of Sector	Time	C7 Whitaker Spit to NE Maplin Duration	C7 Time at End of Sector	Time	C6 NE Maplin to Maplin Edge Duration	C6 Time at End of Sector	Time	C5 Maplin Edge to SW Barrow Duration	C5 Time at End of Sector	Time	C4 SW Barrow to Princes No 6 Duration	C4 Time at End of Sector	Time	C3 Princes No 6 to Princes South Duration	C3 Time at End of Sector	Time	C2 Princes South to Margate Sand Duration	C2 Time at End of Sector	Time	C1 Margate Sand to North Foreland Duration	C1 Time at End of Sector
- 6.00	14	- 5:46	- 6.00	33	- 5:27	- 6.00	21	- 5:39	- 6.00	30	- 5:30	- 6.00	49	- 5:11	- 6.00	60	- 5:00	- 6.00	38	- 5:22	- 6.00	27	- 5:33
- 5.45	14	- 5:31	- 5.45	33	- 5:12	- 5.45	20	- 5:25	- 5.45	29	- 5:16	- 5.45	50	- 4:55	- 5.45	63	- 4:42	- 5.45	38	- 5:07	- 5.45	27	- 5:18
- 5.30	15	- 5:15	- 5.30	32	- 4:58	- 5.30	19	- 5:11	- 5.30	28	- 5:02	- 5.30	52	- 4:38	- 5.30	67	- 4:23	- 5.30	39	- 4:51	- 5.30	27	- 5:03
- 5.15	15	- 5:00	- 5.15	31	- 4:44	- 5.15	18	- 4:57	- 5.15	27	- 4:48	- 5.15	53	- 4:22	- 5.15	70	- 4:05	- 5.15	40	- 4:35	- 5.15	28	- 4:47
- 5.00	15	- 4:45	- 5.00	30	- 4:30	- 5.00	18	- 4:42	- 5.00	26	- 4:34	- 5.00	54	- 4:06	- 5.00	73	- 3:47	- 5.00	41	- 4:19	- 5.00	28	- 4:32
- 4.45	15	- 4:30	- 4.45	30	- 4:15	- 4.45	18	- 4:27	- 4.45	26	- 4:19	- 4.45	55	- 3:50	- 4.45	75	- 3:30	- 4.45	42	- 4:03	- 4.45	28	- 4:17
- 4.30	15	- 4:15	- 4.30	29	- 4:01	- 4.30	17	- 4:13	- 4.30	25	- 4:05	- 4.30	56	- 3:34	- 4.30	78	- 3:12	- 4.30	43	- 3:47	- 4.30	29	- 4:01
- 4.15	15	- 4:00	- 4.15	29	- 3:46	- 4.15	17	- 3:58	- 4.15	24	- 3:51	- 4.15	57	- 3:18	- 4.15	80	- 2:55	- 4.15	44	- 3:31	- 4.15	29	- 3:46
- 4.00	15	- 3:45	- 4.00	29	- 3:31	- 4.00	17	- 3:43	- 4.00	23	- 3:37	- 4.00	57	- 3:03	- 4.00	82	- 2:38	- 4.00	45	- 3:15	- 4.00	30	- 3:30
- 3.45	15	- 3:30	- 3.45	29	- 3:16	- 3.45	17	- 3:28	- 3.45	24	- 3:21	- 3.45	57	- 2:48	- 3.45	84	- 2:21	- 3.45	46	- 2:59	- 3.45	31	- 3:14
- 3.30	15	- 3:15	- 3.30	29	- 3:01	- 3.30	17	- 3:13	- 3.30	24	- 3:06	- 3.30	57	- 2:33	- 3.30	86	- 2:04	- 3.30	46	- 2:44	- 3.30	32	- 2:58
- 3.15	15	- 3:00	- 3.15	29	- 2:46	- 3.15	18	- 2:57	- 3.15	25	- 2:50	- 3.15	57	- 2:18	- 3.15	88	- 1:47	- 3.15	47	- 2:28	- 3.15	33	- 2:42
- 3.00	16	- 2:44	- 3.00	29	- 2:31	- 3.00	18	- 2:42	- 3.00	25	- 2:35	- 3.00	57	- 2:03	- 3.00	89	- 1:31	- 3.00	48	- 2:12	- 3.00	35	- 2:25
- 2.45	15	- 2:30	- 2.45	30	- 2:15	- 2.45	18	- 2:27	- 2.45	26	- 2:19	- 2.45	57	- 1:48	- 2.45	88	- 1:17	- 2.45	48	- 1:57	- 2.45	36	- 2:09
- 2.30	15	- 2:15	- 2.30	30	- 2:00	- 2.30	19	- 2:11	- 2.30	26	- 2:04	- 2.30	56	- 1:34	- 2.30	87	- 1:03	- 2.30	48	- 1:42	- 2.30	38	- 1:52
- 2.15	15	- 2:00	- 2.15	30	- 1:45	- 2.15	19	- 1:56	- 2.15	26	- 1:49	- 2.15	56	- 1:19	- 2.15	86	- 0:49	- 2.15	47	- 1:28	- 2.15	40	- 1:35
- 2.00	15	- 1:45	- 2.00	31	- 1:29	- 2.00	20	- 1:40	- 2.00	27	- 1:33	- 2.00	56	- 1:04	- 2.00	85	- 0:35	- 2.00	47	- 1:13	- 2.00	41	- 1:19
- 1.45	15	- 1:30	- 1.45	31	- 1:14	- 1.45	20	- 1:25	- 1.45	27	- 1:18	- 1.45	55	- 0:50	- 1.45	82	- 0:23	- 1.45	46	- 0:59	- 1.45	41	- 1:04
- 1.30	15	- 1:15	- 1.30	32	- 0:58	- 1.30	20	- 1:10	- 1.30	28	- 1:02	- 1.30	54	- 0:36	- 1.30	78	- 0:12	- 1.30	44	- 0:46	- 1.30	42	- 0:48
- 1.15	15	- 1:00	- 1.15	32	- 0:43	- 1.15	21	- 0:54	- 1.15	28	- 0:47	- 1.15	53	- 0:22	- 1.15	74	- 0:01	- 1.15	43	- 0:32	- 1.15	42	- 0:33
- 1.00	15	- 0:45	- 1.00	33	- 0:27	- 1.00	21	- 0:39	- 1.00	29	- 0:31	- 1.00	52	- 0:08	- 1.00	71	+ 0:11	- 1.00	42	- 0:18	- 1.00	42	- 0:18
- 0.45	15	- 0:30	- 0.45	34	- 0:11	- 0.45	22	- 0:23	- 0.45	30	- 0:15	- 0.45	51	+ 0:06	- 0.45	67	+ 0:22	- 0.45	40	- 0:05	- 0.45	41	- 0:04
- 0.30	15	- 0:15	- 0.30	36	+ 0:06	- 0.30	22	- 0:08	- 0.30	31	+ 0:01	- 0.30	50	+ 0:20	- 0.30	63	+ 0:33	- 0.30	39	+ 0:09	- 0.30	40	+ 0:10
- 0.15	15	HW	- 0.15	37	+ 0:22	- 0.15	22	+ 0:07	- 0.15	32	+ 0:17	- 0.15	49	+ 0:34	- 0.15	60	+ 0:45	- 0.15	38	+ 0:23	- 0.15	39	+ 0:24
HW	15	+ 0:15	HW	39	+ 0:39	HW	22	+ 0:22	HW	33	+ 0:33	HW	48	+ 0:48	HW	56	+ 0:56	HW	37	+ 0:37	HW	38	+ 0:38
+ 0.15	15	+ 0:30	+ 0.15	40	+ 0:55	+ 0.15	23	+ 0:38	+ 0.15	35	+ 0:50	+ 0.15	48	+ 1:03	+ 0.15	54	+ 1:09	+ 0.15	36	+ 0:51	+ 0.15	37	+ 0:52
+ 0.30	15	+ 0:45	+ 0.30	41	+ 1:11	+ 0.30	24	+ 0:54	+ 0.30	37	+ 1:07	+ 0.30	47	+ 1:17	+ 0.30	51	+ 1:21	+ 0.30	35	+ 1:05	+ 0.30	36	+ 1:06
+ 0.45	15	+ 1:00	+ 0.45	43	+ 1:28	+ 0.45	25	+ 1:10	+ 0.45	39	+ 1:24	+ 0.45	46	+ 1:31	+ 0.45	49	+ 1:34	+ 0.45	34	+ 1:19	+ 0.45	35	+ 1:20
+ 1.00	15	+ 1:15	+ 1.00	44	+ 1:44	+ 1.00	26	+ 1:26	+ 1.00	41	+ 1:41	+ 1.00	46	+ 1:46	+ 1.00	47	+ 1:47	+ 1.00	33	+ 1:33	+ 1.00	34	+ 1:34
+ 1.15	16	+ 1:31	+ 1.15	45	+ 2:00	+ 1.15	26	+ 1:41	+ 1.15	44	+ 1:59	+ 1.15	45	+ 2:00	+ 1.15	46	+ 2:01	+ 1.15	32	+ 1:47	+ 1.15	33	+ 1:48
+ 1.30	16	+ 1:46	+ 1.30	45	+ 2:15	+ 1.30	26	+ 1:56	+ 1.30	46	+ 2:16	+ 1.30	45	+ 2:15	+ 1.30	45	+ 2:15	+ 1.30	32	+ 2:02	+ 1.30	32	+ 2:02
+ 1.45	16	+ 2:01	+ 1.45	45	+ 2:30	+ 1.45	26	+ 2:11	+ 1.45	48	+ 2:33	+ 1.45	45	+ 2:30	+ 1.45	45	+ 2:30	+ 1.45	31	+ 2:16	+ 1.45	31	+ 2:16
+ 2.00	16	+ 2:16	+ 2.00	46	+ 2:46	+ 2.00	27	+ 2:27	+ 2.00	51	+ 2:51	+ 2.00	45	+ 2:45	+ 2.00	44	+ 2:44	+ 2.00	30	+ 2:30	+ 2.00	30	+ 2:30
+ 2.15	16	+ 2:31	+ 2.15	45	+ 3:00	+ 2.15	27	+ 2:42	+ 2.15	50	+ 3:05	+ 2.15	45	+ 3:00	+ 2.15	44	+ 2:59	+ 2.15	30	+ 2:45	+ 2.15	29	+ 2:44
+ 2.30	16	+ 2:46	+ 2.30	45	+ 3:15	+ 2.30	27	+ 2:57	+ 2.30	49	+ 3:19	+ 2.30	45	+ 3:15	+ 2.30	44	+ 3:14	+ 2.30	30	+ 3:00	+ 2.30	28	+ 2:58
+ 2.45	16	+ 3:01	+ 2.45	45	+ 3:30	+ 2.45	27	+ 3:12	+ 2.45	49	+ 3:34	+ 2.45	45	+ 3:30	+ 2.45	44	+ 3:29	+ 2.45	30	+ 3:15	+ 2.45	28	+ 3:13
+ 3.00	16	+ 3:16	+ 3.00	44	+ 3:44	+ 3.00	27	+ 3:27	+ 3.00	48	+ 3:48	+ 3.00	45	+ 3:45	+ 3.00	45	+ 3:45	+ 3.00	29	+ 3:29	+ 3.00	27	+ 3:27
+ 3.15	16	+ 3:31	+ 3.15	44	+ 3:59	+ 3.15	27	+ 3:42	+ 3.15	46	+ 4:01	+ 3.15	45	+ 4:00	+ 3.15	45	+ 4:00	+ 3.15	30	+ 3:45	+ 3.15	27	+ 3:42
+ 3.30	15	+ 3:45	+ 3.30	43	+ 4:13	+ 3.30	27	+ 3:57	+ 3.30	45	+ 4:15	+ 3.30	45	+ 4:15	+ 3.30	45	+ 4:15	+ 3.30	30	+ 4:00	+ 3.30	26	+ 3:56
+ 3.45	15	+ 4:00	+ 3.45	42	+ 4:27	+ 3.45	27	+ 4:12	+ 3.45	43	+ 4:28	+ 3.45	46	+ 4:31	+ 3.45	46	+ 4:31	+ 3.45	31	+ 4:16	+ 3.45	26	+ 4:11
+ 4.00	15	+ 4:15	+ 4.00	42	+ 4:42	+ 4.00	26	+ 4:26	+ 4.00	42	+ 4:42	+ 4.00	46	+ 4:46	+ 4.00	46	+ 4:46	+ 4.00	31	+ 4:31	+ 4.00	26	+ 4:26
+ 4.15	15	+ 4:30	+ 4.15	41	+ 4:56	+ 4.15	26	+ 4:41	+ 4.15	41	+ 4:56	+ 4.15	46	+ 5:01	+ 4.15	47	+ 5:02	+ 4.15	32	+ 4:47	+ 4.15	26	+ 4:41
+ 4.30	15	+ 4:45	+ 4.30	40	+ 5:10	+ 4.30	25	+ 4:55	+ 4.30	40	+ 5:10	+ 4.30	46	+ 5:16	+ 4.30	48	+ 5:18	+ 4.30	32	+ 5:02	+ 4.30	26	+ 4:56
+ 4.45	15	+ 5:00	+ 4.45	39	+ 5:24	+ 4.45	24	+ 5:09	+ 4.45	39	+ 5:24	+ 4.45	46	+ 5:31	+ 4.45	49	+ 5:34	+ 4.45	33	+ 5:18	+ 4.45	26	+ 5:11
+ 5.00	15	+ 5:15	+ 5.00	38	+ 5:38	+ 5.00	24	+ 5:24	+ 5.00	38	+ 5:38	+ 5.00	47	+ 5:47	+ 5.00	50	+ 5:50	+ 5.00	33	+ 5:33	+ 5.00	26	+ 5:26
+ 5.15	15	+ 5:30	+ 5.15	37	+ 5:52	+ 5.15	23	+ 5:38	+ 5.15	37	+ 5:52	+ 5.15	47	- 5:58	+ 5.15	51	- 5:54	+ 5.15	34	+ 5:49	+ 5.15	26	+ 5:41
+ 5.30	15	+ 5:45	+ 5.30	37	- 5:53	+ 5.30	22	+ 5:52	+ 5.30	35	- 5:55	+ 5.30	47	- 5:43	+ 5.30	52	- 5:38	+ 5.30	35	- 5:55	+ 5.30	26	+ 5:56
+ 5.45	14	+ 5:59	+ 5.45	36	- 5:39	+ 5.45	22	- 5:53	+ 5.45	34	- 5:41	+ 5.45	47	- 5:28	+ 5.45	53	- 5:22	+ 5.45	35	- 5:40	+ 5.45	26	- 5:49
+ 6.00	14	- 5:46	+ 6.00	35	- 5:25	+ 6.00	21	- 5:39	+ 6.00	32	- 5:28	+ 6.00	47	- 5:13	+ 6.00	54	- 5:06	+ 6.00	36	- 5:24	+ 6.00	26	- 5:34

SOUTH BOUND

Table D - North Edinburgh, Crouch and Colne

Neaps

All times relate to HW Sheerness

Time to cover Sectors (in minutes) at 4.0 Kts

SOUTH BOUND

D8 — Colne Landfall to Spitway

Time	Duration	Time at End of Sector
- 6.00	71	- 4:49
- 5.45	72	- 4:33
- 5.30	74	- 4:16
- 5.15	75	- 4:00
- 5.00	76	- 3:44
- 4.45	77	- 3:28
- 4.30	77	- 3:13
- 4.15	78	- 2:57
- 4.00	78	- 2:42
- 3.45	78	- 2:27
- 3.30	79	- 2:11
- 3.15	79	- 1:56
- 3.00	79	- 1:41
- 2.45	78	- 1:27
- 2.30	77	- 1:13
- 2.15	76	- 0:59
- 2.00	76	- 0:44
- 1.45	73	- 0:32
- 1.30	70	- 0:20
- 1.15	67	- 0:08
- 1.00	64	+ 0:04
- 0.45	62	+ 0:17
- 0.30	59	+ 0:29
- 0.15	57	+ 0:42
HW	54	+ 0:54
+ 0.15	53	+ 1:08
+ 0.30	52	+ 1:22
+ 0.45	51	+ 1:36
+ 1.00	50	+ 1:50
+ 1.15	51	+ 2:06
+ 1.30	51	+ 2:21
+ 1.45	51	+ 2:36
+ 2.00	51	+ 2:51
+ 2.15	52	+ 3:07
+ 2.30	53	+ 3:23
+ 2.45	54	+ 3:39
+ 3.00	54	+ 3:54
+ 3.15	55	+ 4:10
+ 3.30	56	+ 4:26
+ 3.45	57	+ 4:42
+ 4.00	58	+ 4:58
+ 4.15	59	+ 5:14
+ 4.30	60	+ 5:30
+ 4.45	61	+ 5:46
+ 5.00	62	- 5:58
+ 5.15	64	- 5:41
+ 5.30	65	- 5:25
+ 5.45	66	- 5:09
+ 6.00	67	- 4:53

River Colne

D7 — Crouch Landfall to Whitaker Spit

Time	Duration	Time at End of Sector
- 6.00	74	- 4:46
- 5.45	79	- 4:26
- 5.30	84	- 4:06
- 5.15	89	- 3:46
- 5.00	94	- 3:26
- 4.45	94	- 3:11
- 4.30	95	- 2:55
- 4.15	95	- 2:40
- 4.00	95	- 2:25
- 3.45	94	- 2:11
- 3.30	93	- 1:57
- 3.15	92	- 1:43
- 3.00	90	- 1:30
- 2.45	87	- 1:18
- 2.30	83	- 1:07
- 2.15	79	- 0:56
- 2.00	75	- 0:45
- 1.45	73	- 0:32
- 1.30	70	- 0:20
- 1.15	68	- 0:07
- 1.00	65	+ 0:05
- 0.45	62	+ 0:17
- 0.30	59	+ 0:29
- 0.15	57	+ 0:42
HW	54	+ 0:54
+ 0.15	52	+ 1:07
+ 0.30	51	+ 1:21
+ 0.45	49	+ 1:34
+ 1.00	47	+ 1:47
+ 1.15	47	+ 2:02
+ 1.30	47	+ 2:17
+ 1.45	47	+ 2:32
+ 2.00	47	+ 2:47
+ 2.15	48	+ 3:03
+ 2.30	48	+ 3:18
+ 2.45	49	+ 3:34
+ 3.00	49	+ 3:49
+ 3.15	50	+ 4:05
+ 3.30	51	+ 4:21
+ 3.45	52	+ 4:37
+ 4.00	53	+ 4:53
+ 4.15	55	+ 5:10
+ 4.30	56	+ 5:26
+ 4.45	58	+ 5:43
+ 5.00	60	- 6:00
+ 5.15	61	- 5:44
+ 5.30	62	- 5:28
+ 5.45	63	- 5:12
+ 6.00	65	- 4:55

D6 — Whitaker Spit to Black Deep

Time	Duration	Time at End of Sector
- 6.00	189	- 2:51
- 5.45	190	- 2:35
- 5.30	191	- 2:19
- 5.15	192	- 2:03
- 5.00	194	- 1:46
- 4.45	192	- 1:33
- 4.30	190	- 1:20
- 4.15	188	- 1:07
- 4.00	186	- 0:54
- 3.45	181	- 0:44
- 3.30	177	- 0:33
- 3.15	173	- 0:22
- 3.00	169	- 0:11
- 2.45	165	HW
- 2.30	161	+ 0:11
- 2.15	157	+ 0:22
- 2.00	152	+ 0:32
- 1.45	148	+ 0:43
- 1.30	143	+ 0:53
- 1.15	139	+ 1:04
- 1.00	134	+ 1:14
- 0.45	131	+ 1:26
- 0.30	128	+ 1:38
- 0.15	125	+ 1:50
HW	122	+ 2:02
+ 0.15	121	+ 2:16
+ 0.30	119	+ 2:29
+ 0.45	118	+ 2:43
+ 1.00	117	+ 2:57
+ 1.15	117	+ 3:12
+ 1.30	117	+ 3:27
+ 1.45	117	+ 3:42
+ 2.00	117	+ 3:57
+ 2.15	119	+ 4:14
+ 2.30	121	+ 4:31
+ 2.45	123	+ 4:48
+ 3.00	125	+ 5:05
+ 3.15	128	+ 5:23
+ 3.30	131	+ 5:41
+ 3.45	134	+ 5:59
+ 4.00	137	- 5:43
+ 4.15	141	- 5:24
+ 4.30	144	- 5:06
+ 4.45	148	- 4:47
+ 5.00	152	- 4:28
+ 5.15	157	- 4:08
+ 5.30	162	- 3:48
+ 5.45	167	- 3:28
+ 6.00	172	- 3:08

D5 — Whitaker Spit to Barrow Deep

Time	Duration	Time at End of Sector
- 6.00	128	- 3:52
- 5.45	130	- 3:35
- 5.30	133	- 3:17
- 5.15	135	- 3:00
- 5.00	137	- 2:43
- 4.45	137	- 2:28
- 4.30	136	- 2:14
- 4.15	135	- 2:00
- 4.00	135	- 1:45
- 3.45	132	- 1:33
- 3.30	130	- 1:20
- 3.15	127	- 1:08
- 3.00	125	- 0:55
- 2.45	122	- 0:43
- 2.30	119	- 0:31
- 2.15	116	- 0:19
- 2.00	113	- 0:07
- 1.45	109	+ 0:04
- 1.30	106	+ 0:16
- 1.15	102	+ 0:27
- 1.00	99	+ 0:39
- 0.45	97	+ 0:52
- 0.30	94	+ 1:04
- 0.15	92	+ 1:17
HW	90	+ 1:30
+ 0.15	88	+ 1:43
+ 0.30	87	+ 1:57
+ 0.45	85	+ 2:10
+ 1.00	84	+ 2:24
+ 1.15	84	+ 2:39
+ 1.30	83	+ 2:53
+ 1.45	83	+ 3:08
+ 2.00	83	+ 3:23
+ 2.15	84	+ 3:39
+ 2.30	85	+ 3:55
+ 2.45	86	+ 4:11
+ 3.00	87	+ 4:27
+ 3.15	88	+ 4:43
+ 3.30	90	+ 5:00
+ 3.45	91	+ 5:16
+ 4.00	93	+ 5:33
+ 4.15	95	+ 5:50
+ 4.30	98	- 5:52
+ 4.45	100	- 5:35
+ 5.00	103	- 5:17
+ 5.15	106	- 4:59
+ 5.30	109	- 4:41
+ 5.45	111	- 4:24
+ 6.00	114	- 4:06

D4 — Whitaker Spit to East Barrow

Time	Duration	Time at End of Sector
- 6.00	57	- 5:03
- 5.45	59	- 4:46
- 5.30	60	- 4:30
- 5.15	62	- 4:13
- 5.00	64	- 3:56
- 4.45	64	- 3:41
- 4.30	64	- 3:26
- 4.15	65	- 3:10
- 4.00	65	- 2:55
- 3.45	65	- 2:40
- 3.30	64	- 2:26
- 3.15	64	- 2:11
- 3.00	63	- 1:57
- 2.45	62	- 1:43
- 2.30	61	- 1:29
- 2.15	59	- 1:16
- 2.00	58	- 1:02
- 1.45	56	- 0:49
- 1.30	55	- 0:35
- 1.15	53	- 0:22
- 1.00	51	- 0:09
- 0.45	50	+ 0:05
- 0.30	48	+ 0:18
- 0.15	47	+ 0:32
HW	45	+ 0:45
+ 0.15	44	+ 0:59
+ 0.30	43	+ 1:13
+ 0.45	42	+ 1:27
+ 1.00	41	+ 1:41
+ 1.15	41	+ 1:56
+ 1.30	41	+ 2:11
+ 1.45	41	+ 2:26
+ 2.00	41	+ 2:41
+ 2.15	41	+ 2:56
+ 2.30	41	+ 3:11
+ 2.45	42	+ 3:27
+ 3.00	42	+ 3:42
+ 3.15	43	+ 3:58
+ 3.30	44	+ 4:14
+ 3.45	44	+ 4:29
+ 4.00	45	+ 4:45
+ 4.15	46	+ 5:01
+ 4.30	47	+ 5:17
+ 4.45	48	+ 5:33
+ 5.00	49	+ 5:49
+ 5.15	50	- 5:55
+ 5.30	50	- 5:40
+ 5.45	51	- 5:24
+ 6.00	52	- 5:08

D3 — SW Sunk to NW Long Sand

Time	Duration	Time at End of Sector
- 6.00	50	- 5:10
- 5.45	49	- 4:56
- 5.30	47	- 4:43
- 5.15	46	- 4:29
- 5.00	45	- 4:15
- 4.45	45	- 4:00
- 4.30	45	- 3:45
- 4.15	45	- 3:30
- 4.00	45	- 3:15
- 3.45	45	- 3:00
- 3.30	46	- 2:44
- 3.15	46	- 2:29
- 3.00	47	- 2:13
- 2.45	49	- 1:56
- 2.30	50	- 1:40
- 2.15	52	- 1:23
- 2.00	54	- 1:06
- 1.45	56	- 0:49
- 1.30	59	- 0:31
- 1.15	61	- 0:14
- 1.00	64	+ 0:04
- 0.45	66	+ 0:21
- 0.30	68	+ 0:38
- 0.15	70	+ 0:55
HW	72	+ 1:12
+ 0.15	76	+ 1:31
+ 0.30	81	+ 1:51
+ 0.45	85	+ 2:10
+ 1.00	90	+ 2:30
+ 1.15	91	+ 2:46
+ 1.30	93	+ 3:03
+ 1.45	94	+ 3:19
+ 2.00	96	+ 3:36
+ 2.15	94	+ 3:49
+ 2.30	93	+ 4:03
+ 2.45	91	+ 4:16
+ 3.00	90	+ 4:30
+ 3.15	85	+ 4:40
+ 3.30	81	+ 4:51
+ 3.45	76	+ 5:01
+ 4.00	71	+ 5:11
+ 4.15	69	+ 5:24
+ 4.30	67	+ 5:37
+ 4.45	65	+ 5:50
+ 5.00	63	- 5:57
+ 5.15	61	- 5:44
+ 5.30	60	- 5:30
+ 5.45	58	- 5:17
+ 6.00	57	- 5:03

D2 — Long Sand to North Edinburgh

Time	Duration	Time at End of Sector
- 6.00	49	- 5:11
- 5.45	51	- 4:54
- 5.30	53	- 4:37
- 5.15	55	- 4:20
- 5.00	57	- 4:03
- 4.45	58	- 3:47
- 4.30	59	- 3:31
- 4.15	60	- 3:15
- 4.00	62	- 2:58
- 3.45	62	- 2:43
- 3.30	63	- 2:27
- 3.15	63	- 2:12
- 3.00	63	- 1:57
- 2.45	64	- 1:41
- 2.30	64	- 1:26
- 2.15	64	- 1:11
- 2.00	64	- 0:56
- 1.45	63	- 0:42
- 1.30	62	- 0:28
- 1.15	62	- 0:13
- 1.00	61	+ 0:01
- 0.45	59	+ 0:14
- 0.30	57	+ 0:27
- 0.15	55	+ 0:40
HW	53	+ 0:53
+ 0.15	51	+ 1:06
+ 0.30	49	+ 1:19
+ 0.45	46	+ 1:31
+ 1.00	44	+ 1:44
+ 1.15	42	+ 1:57
+ 1.30	40	+ 2:10
+ 1.45	38	+ 2:23
+ 2.00	37	+ 2:37
+ 2.15	36	+ 2:51
+ 2.30	35	+ 3:05
+ 2.45	34	+ 3:19
+ 3.00	33	+ 3:33
+ 3.15	33	+ 3:48
+ 3.30	33	+ 4:03
+ 3.45	33	+ 4:18
+ 4.00	33	+ 4:33
+ 4.15	34	+ 4:49
+ 4.30	35	+ 5:05
+ 4.45	36	+ 5:21
+ 5.00	37	+ 5:37
+ 5.15	39	+ 5:54
+ 5.30	40	- 5:50
+ 5.45	42	- 5:33
+ 6.00	43	- 5:17

D1 — North Edinburgh to East Margate

Time	Duration	Time at End of Sector
- 6.00	112	- 4:08
- 5.45	114	- 3:51
- 5.30	116	- 3:34
- 5.15	119	- 3:16
- 5.00	121	- 2:59
- 4.45	123	- 2:42
- 4.30	126	- 2:24
- 4.15	129	- 2:06
- 4.00	131	- 1:49
- 3.45	132	- 1:33
- 3.30	133	- 1:17
- 3.15	133	- 1:02
- 3.00	134	- 0:46
- 2.45	132	- 0:33
- 2.30	131	- 0:19
- 2.15	129	- 0:06
- 2.00	127	+ 0:07
- 1.45	124	+ 0:19
- 1.30	121	+ 0:31
- 1.15	118	+ 0:43
- 1.00	115	+ 0:55
- 0.45	112	+ 1:07
- 0.30	109	+ 1:19
- 0.15	106	+ 1:31
HW	103	+ 1:43
+ 0.15	102	+ 1:57
+ 0.30	100	+ 2:10
+ 0.45	98	+ 2:23
+ 1.00	96	+ 2:36
+ 1.15	95	+ 2:50
+ 1.30	94	+ 3:04
+ 1.45	93	+ 3:18
+ 2.00	92	+ 3:32
+ 2.15	92	+ 3:47
+ 2.30	92	+ 4:02
+ 2.45	92	+ 4:17
+ 3.00	92	+ 4:32
+ 3.15	93	+ 4:48
+ 3.30	93	+ 5:03
+ 3.45	94	+ 5:19
+ 4.00	94	+ 5:34
+ 4.15	96	+ 5:51
+ 4.30	98	- 5:52
+ 4.45	100	- 5:35
+ 5.00	102	- 5:18
+ 5.15	103	- 5:02
+ 5.30	104	- 4:46
+ 5.45	104	- 4:31
+ 6.00	105	- 4:15

Table D - North Edinburgh, Crouch and Colne

Time to cover Sectors (in minutes) at 4.0 kts — All times relate to HW Sheerness — Springs

SOUTH BOUND

D8 — Colne Landfall to Spitway

Time	Duration	Time at End of Sector
- 6.00	75	- 4:45
- 5.45	77	- 4:28
- 5.30	79	- 4:11
- 5.15	81	- 3:54
- 5.00	82	- 3:38
- 4.45	85	- 3:20
- 4.30	88	- 3:02
- 4.15	91	- 2:44
- 4.00	93	- 2:27
- 3.45	94	- 2:11
- 3.30	94	- 1:56
- 3.15	95	- 1:40
- 3.00	95	- 1:25
- 2.45	92	- 1:13
- 2.30	89	- 1:01
- 2.15	85	- 0:50
- 2.00	82	- 0:38
- 1.45	77	- 0:28
- 1.30	73	- 0:17
- 1.15	68	- 0:07
- 1.00	63	+ 0:03
- 0.45	60	+ 0:15
- 0.30	57	+ 0:27
- 0.15	53	+ 0:38
HW	50	+ 0:50
+ 0.15	48	+ 1:03
+ 0.30	47	+ 1:17
+ 0.45	46	+ 1:31
+ 1.00	45	+ 1:45
+ 1.15	45	+ 2:00
+ 1.30	45	+ 2:15
+ 1.45	46	+ 2:31
+ 2.00	46	+ 2:46
+ 2.15	47	+ 3:02
+ 2.30	48	+ 3:18
+ 2.45	49	+ 3:34
+ 3.00	50	+ 3:50
+ 3.15	52	+ 4:07
+ 3.30	53	+ 4:23
+ 3.45	54	+ 4:39
+ 4.00	55	+ 4:55
+ 4.15	57	+ 5:12
+ 4.30	58	+ 5:28
+ 4.45	60	+ 5:45
+ 5.00	62	- 5:58
+ 5.15	63	- 5:42
+ 5.30	65	- 5:25
+ 5.45	67	- 5:08
+ 6.00	68	- 4:52

River Colne

D7 — Crouch Landfall to Whitaker Spit

Time	Duration	Time at End of Sector
- 6.00	80	- 4:40
- 5.45	87	- 4:18
- 5.30	95	- 3:55
- 5.15	102	- 3:33
- 5.00	110	- 3:10
- 4.45	110	- 2:55
- 4.30	110	- 2:40
- 4.15	110	- 2:25
- 4.00	110	- 2:10
- 3.45	107	- 1:58
- 3.30	105	- 1:45
- 3.15	102	- 1:33
- 3.00	99	- 1:21
- 2.45	95	- 1:10
- 2.30	91	- 0:59
- 2.15	87	- 0:48
- 2.00	83	- 0:37
- 1.45	79	- 0:26
- 1.30	75	- 0:15
- 1.15	70	- 0:05
- 1.00	66	+ 0:06
- 0.45	62	+ 0:17
- 0.30	58	+ 0:28
- 0.15	54	+ 0:39
HW	49	+ 0:49
+ 0.15	47	+ 1:02
+ 0.30	45	+ 1:15
+ 0.45	43	+ 1:28
+ 1.00	41	+ 1:41
+ 1.15	41	+ 1:56
+ 1.30	40	+ 2:10
+ 1.45	40	+ 2:25
+ 2.00	40	+ 2:40
+ 2.15	41	+ 2:56
+ 2.30	41	+ 3:11
+ 2.45	42	+ 3:27
+ 3.00	43	+ 3:43
+ 3.15	44	+ 3:59
+ 3.30	46	+ 4:16
+ 3.45	47	+ 4:32
+ 4.00	48	+ 4:48
+ 4.15	50	+ 5:05
+ 4.30	53	+ 5:23
+ 4.45	55	+ 5:40
+ 5.00	57	+ 5:57
+ 5.15	59	- 5:46
+ 5.30	61	- 5:29
+ 5.45	63	- 5:12
+ 6.00	66	- 4:54

D6 — Whitaker Spit to Black Deep

Time	Duration	Time at End of Sector
- 6.00	220	- 2:20
- 5.45	220	- 2:05
- 5.30	220	- 1:50
- 5.15	219	- 1:36
- 5.00	219	- 1:21
- 4.45	214	- 1:11
- 4.30	210	- 1:00
- 4.15	205	- 0:50
- 4.00	200	- 0:40
- 3.45	194	- 0:31
- 3.30	188	- 0:22
- 3.15	181	- 0:14
- 3.00	175	- 0:05
- 2.45	169	+ 0:04
- 2.30	163	+ 0:13
- 2.15	157	+ 0:22
- 2.00	152	+ 0:32
- 1.45	146	+ 0:41
- 1.30	140	+ 0:50
- 1.15	134	+ 0:59
- 1.00	128	+ 1:08
- 0.45	125	+ 1:20
- 0.30	122	+ 1:32
- 0.15	118	+ 1:43
HW	115	+ 1:55
+ 0.15	114	+ 2:09
+ 0.30	113	+ 2:23
+ 0.45	111	+ 2:36
+ 1.00	110	+ 2:50
+ 1.15	110	+ 3:05
+ 1.30	110	+ 3:20
+ 1.45	111	+ 3:36
+ 2.00	111	+ 3:51
+ 2.15	113	+ 4:08
+ 2.30	115	+ 4:25
+ 2.45	117	+ 4:42
+ 3.00	119	+ 4:59
+ 3.15	123	+ 5:18
+ 3.30	127	+ 5:37
+ 3.45	131	+ 5:56
+ 4.00	135	- 5:45
+ 4.15	141	- 5:24
+ 4.30	146	- 5:04
+ 4.45	152	- 4:43
+ 5.00	158	- 4:22
+ 5.15	166	- 3:59
+ 5.30	174	- 3:36
+ 5.45	181	- 3:14
+ 6.00	189	- 2:51

D5 — Whitaker Spit to Barrow Deep

Time	Duration	Time at End of Sector
- 6.00	151	- 3:29
- 5.45	153	- 3:12
- 5.30	155	- 2:55
- 5.15	157	- 2:38
- 5.00	159	- 2:21
- 4.45	157	- 2:08
- 4.30	155	- 1:55
- 4.15	153	- 1:42
- 4.00	150	- 1:30
- 3.45	146	- 1:19
- 3.30	141	- 1:09
- 3.15	137	- 0:58
- 3.00	132	- 0:48
- 2.45	127	- 0:38
- 2.30	123	- 0:27
- 2.15	118	- 0:17
- 2.00	113	- 0:07
- 1.45	109	+ 0:04
- 1.30	105	+ 0:15
- 1.15	101	+ 0:26
- 1.00	97	+ 0:37
- 0.45	94	+ 0:49
- 0.30	90	+ 1:00
- 0.15	87	+ 1:12
HW	83	+ 1:23
+ 0.15	82	+ 1:37
+ 0.30	81	+ 1:51
+ 0.45	79	+ 2:04
+ 1.00	78	+ 2:18
+ 1.15	78	+ 2:33
+ 1.30	77	+ 2:47
+ 1.45	77	+ 3:02
+ 2.00	77	+ 3:17
+ 2.15	78	+ 3:33
+ 2.30	79	+ 3:49
+ 2.45	79	+ 4:04
+ 3.00	80	+ 4:20
+ 3.15	83	+ 4:38
+ 3.30	85	+ 4:55
+ 3.45	88	+ 5:13
+ 4.00	90	+ 5:30
+ 4.15	94	+ 5:49
+ 4.30	97	- 5:53
+ 4.45	101	- 5:34
+ 5.00	105	- 5:15
+ 5.15	109	- 4:56
+ 5.30	113	- 4:37
+ 5.45	117	- 4:18
+ 6.00	121	- 3:59

D4 — Whitaker Spit to East Barrow

Time	Duration	Time at End of Sector
- 6.00	61	- 4:59
- 5.45	64	- 4:41
- 5.30	67	- 4:23
- 5.15	70	- 4:05
- 5.00	73	- 3:47
- 4.45	73	- 3:32
- 4.30	74	- 3:16
- 4.15	75	- 3:00
- 4.00	76	- 2:44
- 3.45	75	- 2:30
- 3.30	74	- 2:16
- 3.15	73	- 2:02
- 3.00	72	- 1:48
- 2.45	70	- 1:35
- 2.30	67	- 1:23
- 2.15	65	- 1:10
- 2.00	63	- 0:57
- 1.45	60	- 0:45
- 1.30	58	- 0:32
- 1.15	55	- 0:20
- 1.00	52	- 0:08
- 0.45	50	+ 0:05
- 0.30	47	+ 0:17
- 0.15	45	+ 0:30
HW	43	+ 0:43
+ 0.15	42	+ 0:57
+ 0.30	40	+ 1:10
+ 0.45	39	+ 1:24
+ 1.00	38	+ 1:38
+ 1.15	38	+ 1:53
+ 1.30	37	+ 2:07
+ 1.45	37	+ 2:22
+ 2.00	37	+ 2:37
+ 2.15	37	+ 2:52
+ 2.30	38	+ 3:08
+ 2.45	38	+ 3:23
+ 3.00	39	+ 3:39
+ 3.15	40	+ 3:55
+ 3.30	41	+ 4:11
+ 3.45	42	+ 4:27
+ 4.00	43	+ 4:43
+ 4.15	44	+ 4:59
+ 4.30	45	+ 5:15
+ 4.45	46	+ 5:31
+ 5.00	48	+ 5:48
+ 5.15	48	- 5:57
+ 5.30	48	- 5:42
+ 5.45	48	- 5:27
+ 6.00	48	- 5:12

D3 — SW Sunk to NW Long Sand

Time	Duration	Time at End of Sector
- 6.00	45	- 5:15
- 5.45	43	- 5:02
- 5.30	42	- 4:48
- 5.15	40	- 4:35
- 5.00	39	- 4:21
- 4.45	39	- 4:06
- 4.30	39	- 3:51
- 4.15	39	- 3:36
- 4.00	39	- 3:21
- 3.45	39	- 3:06
- 3.30	40	- 2:50
- 3.15	41	- 2:34
- 3.00	41	- 2:19
- 2.45	44	- 2:01
- 2.30	46	- 1:44
- 2.15	48	- 1:27
- 2.00	51	- 1:09
- 1.45	55	- 0:50
- 1.30	59	- 0:31
- 1.15	63	- 0:12
- 1.00	67	+ 0:07
- 0.45	70	+ 0:25
- 0.30	73	+ 0:43
- 0.15	76	+ 1:01
HW	80	+ 1:20
+ 0.15	87	+ 1:42
+ 0.30	93	+ 2:03
+ 0.45	100	+ 2:25
+ 1.00	107	+ 2:47
+ 1.15	109	+ 3:04
+ 1.30	110	+ 3:20
+ 1.45	112	+ 3:37
+ 2.00	113	+ 3:53
+ 2.15	110	+ 4:05
+ 2.30	107	+ 4:17
+ 2.45	104	+ 4:29
+ 3.00	101	+ 4:41
+ 3.15	96	+ 4:51
+ 3.30	90	+ 5:00
+ 3.45	85	+ 5:10
+ 4.00	79	+ 5:19
+ 4.15	75	+ 5:30
+ 4.30	72	+ 5:42
+ 4.45	68	+ 5:53
+ 5.00	64	- 5:56
+ 5.15	61	- 5:44
+ 5.30	59	- 5:31
+ 5.45	57	- 5:18
+ 6.00	55	- 5:05

D2 — Long Sand to North Edinburgh

Time	Duration	Time at End of Sector
- 6.00	49	- 5:11
- 5.45	52	- 4:53
- 5.30	56	- 4:34
- 5.15	59	- 4:16
- 5.00	63	- 3:57
- 4.45	65	- 3:40
- 4.30	67	- 3:23
- 4.15	69	- 3:06
- 4.00	71	- 2:49
- 3.45	76	- 2:29
- 3.30	81	- 2:09
- 3.15	86	- 1:49
- 3.00	91	- 1:29
- 2.45	87	- 1:18
- 2.30	84	- 1:06
- 2.15	81	- 0:54
- 2.00	77	- 0:43
- 1.45	76	- 0:29
- 1.30	74	- 0:16
- 1.15	72	- 0:03
- 1.00	70	+ 0:10
- 0.45	66	+ 0:21
- 0.30	63	+ 0:33
- 0.15	60	+ 0:45
HW	56	+ 0:56
+ 0.15	53	+ 1:08
+ 0.30	49	+ 1:19
+ 0.45	45	+ 1:30
+ 1.00	42	+ 1:42
+ 1.15	39	+ 1:54
+ 1.30	37	+ 2:07
+ 1.45	35	+ 2:20
+ 2.00	33	+ 2:33
+ 2.15	32	+ 2:47
+ 2.30	31	+ 3:01
+ 2.45	30	+ 3:15
+ 3.00	29	+ 3:29
+ 3.15	29	+ 3:44
+ 3.30	29	+ 3:59
+ 3.45	29	+ 4:14
+ 4.00	29	+ 4:29
+ 4.15	30	+ 4:45
+ 4.30	31	+ 5:01
+ 4.45	32	+ 5:17
+ 5.00	33	+ 5:33
+ 5.15	35	+ 5:50
+ 5.30	37	- 5:53
+ 5.45	39	- 5:36
+ 6.00	41	- 5:19

D1 — North Edinburgh to East Margate

Time	Duration	Time at End of Sector
- 6.00	116	- 4:04
- 5.45	120	- 3:45
- 5.30	124	- 3:26
- 5.15	128	- 3:07
- 5.00	132	- 2:48
- 4.45	137	- 2:28
- 4.30	142	- 2:08
- 4.15	146	- 1:49
- 4.00	151	- 1:29
- 3.45	150	- 1:15
- 3.30	148	- 1:02
- 3.15	147	- 0:48
- 3.00	145	- 0:35
- 2.45	142	- 0:23
- 2.30	139	- 0:11
- 2.15	136	+ 0:01
- 2.00	132	+ 0:12
- 1.45	128	+ 0:23
- 1.30	124	+ 0:34
- 1.15	120	+ 0:45
- 1.00	116	+ 0:56
- 0.45	112	+ 1:07
- 0.30	109	+ 1:19
- 0.15	105	+ 1:30
HW	102	+ 1:42
+ 0.15	100	+ 1:55
+ 0.30	98	+ 2:08
+ 0.45	95	+ 2:20
+ 1.00	93	+ 2:33
+ 1.15	92	+ 2:47
+ 1.30	90	+ 3:00
+ 1.45	89	+ 3:14
+ 2.00	87	+ 3:27
+ 2.15	88	+ 3:43
+ 2.30	88	+ 3:58
+ 2.45	88	+ 4:13
+ 3.00	88	+ 4:28
+ 3.15	89	+ 4:44
+ 3.30	91	+ 5:01
+ 3.45	93	+ 5:18
+ 4.00	94	+ 5:34
+ 4.15	96	+ 5:51
+ 4.30	97	- 5:53
+ 4.45	99	- 5:36
+ 5.00	100	- 5:20
+ 5.15	102	- 5:03
+ 5.30	103	- 4:47
+ 5.45	104	- 4:31
+ 6.00	106	- 4:14

Table D - North Edinburgh, Crouch and Colne

Neaps — All times relate to HW Sheerness — **Time to cover Sectors (in minutes) at 5.0 Kts**

SOUTHBOUND

Time	D8 Colne Landfall to Spitway: Duration	D8: Time at End of Sector	Time	D7 Crouch Landfall to Whitaker Spit: Duration	D7: Time at End of Sector
-6.00	55	-5:05	-6.00	56	-5:04
-5.45	56	-4:49	-5.45	58	-4:47
-5.30	57	-4:33	-5.30	60	-4:30
-5.15	58	-4:17	-5.15	61	-4:14
-5.00	58	-4:02	-5.00	63	-3:57
-4.45	59	-3:46	-4.45	63	-3:42
-4.30	59	-3:31	-4.30	63	-3:27
-4.15	60	-3:15	-4.15	64	-3:11
-4.00	60	-3:00	-4.00	64	-2:56
-3.45	60	-2:45	-3.45	63	-2:42
-3.30	60	-2:30	-3.30	63	-2:27
-3.15	60	-2:15	-3.15	63	-2:12
-3.00	61	-1:59	-3.00	62	-1:58
-2.45	60	-1:45	-2.45	61	-1:44
-2.30	60	-1:30	-2.30	60	-1:30
-2.15	59	-1:16	-2.15	60	-1:15
-2.00	59	-1:01	-2.00	59	-1:01
-1.45	57	-0:48	-1.45	57	-0:48
-1.30	56	-0:34	-1.30	56	-0:34
-1.15	54	-0:21	-1.15	54	-0:21
-1.00	52	-0:08	-1.00	53	-0:07
-0.45	50	+0:05	-0.45	51	+0:06
-0.30	49	+0:19	-0.30	49	+0:19
-0.15	47	+0:32	-0.15	47	+0:32
HW	45	+0:45	HW	45	+0:45
+0.15	45	+1:00	+0.15	44	+0:59
+0.30	44	+1:14	+0.30	43	+1:13
+0.45	43	+1:28	+0.45	42	+1:27
+1.00	42	+1:42	+1.00	41	+1:41
+1.15	42	+1:57	+1.15	41	+1:56
+1.30	42	+2:12	+1.30	40	+2:10
+1.45	42	+2:27	+1.45	40	+2:25
+2.00	43	+2:43	+2.00	40	+2:40
+2.15	43	+2:58	+2.15	40	+2:55
+2.30	44	+3:14	+2.30	41	+3:11
+2.45	44	+3:29	+2.45	41	+3:26
+3.00	45	+3:45	+3.00	41	+3:41
+3.15	45	+4:00	+3.15	42	+3:57
+3.30	46	+4:16	+3.30	43	+4:13
+3.45	47	+4:32	+3.45	43	+4:28
+4.00	47	+4:47	+4.00	44	+4:44
+4.15	48	+5:03	+4.15	45	+5:00
+4.30	48	+5:18	+4.30	46	+5:16
+4.45	49	+5:34	+4.45	47	+5:32
+5.00	50	+5:50	+5.00	48	+5:48
+5.15	50	-5:55	+5.15	48	-5:57
+5.30	51	-5:39	+5.30	49	-5:41
+5.45	52	-5:23	+5.45	50	-5:25
+6.00	53	-5:07	+6.00	51	-5:09

River Colne

Time	D6 Whitaker Spit to Black Deep: Duration	D6: Time at End of Sector	Time	D5 Whitaker Spit to Barrow Deep: Duration	D5: Time at End of Sector
-6.00	141	-3:39	-6.00	97	-4:23
-5.45	142	-3:23	-5.45	99	-4:06
-5.30	144	-3:06	-5.30	101	-3:49
-5.15	146	-2:49	-5.15	103	-3:32
-5.00	147	-2:33	-5.00	104	-3:16
-4.45	147	-2:18	-4.45	104	-3:01
-4.30	146	-2:04	-4.30	104	-2:46
-4.15	145	-1:50	-4.15	104	-2:31
-4.00	145	-1:35	-4.00	104	-2:16
-3.45	142	-1:23	-3.45	103	-2:02
-3.30	140	-1:10	-3.30	101	-1:49
-3.15	138	-0:57	-3.15	100	-1:35
-3.00	136	-0:44	-3.00	98	-1:22
-2.45	133	-0:32	-2.45	97	-1:08
-2.30	130	-0:20	-2.30	95	-0:55
-2.15	127	-0:08	-2.15	93	-0:42
-2.00	124	+0:04	-2.00	92	-0:28
-1.45	121	+0:16	-1.45	89	-0:16
-1.30	118	+0:28	-1.30	86	-0:04
-1.15	114	+0:39	-1.15	83	+0:08
-1.00	111	+0:51	-1.00	80	+0:20
-0.45	109	+1:04	-0.45	79	+0:34
-0.30	107	+1:17	-0.30	77	+0:47
-0.15	104	+1:29	-0.15	75	+1:00
HW	102	+1:42	HW	73	+1:13
+0.15	101	+1:56	+0.15	73	+1:28
+0.30	100	+2:10	+0.30	72	+1:42
+0.45	99	+2:24	+0.45	71	+1:56
+1.00	97	+2:37	+1.00	70	+2:10
+1.15	97	+2:52	+1.15	70	+2:25
+1.30	97	+3:07	+1.30	70	+2:40
+1.45	97	+3:22	+1.45	69	+2:54
+2.00	97	+3:37	+2.00	69	+3:09
+2.15	98	+3:53	+2.15	70	+3:25
+2.30	99	+4:09	+2.30	70	+3:40
+2.45	100	+4:25	+2.45	71	+3:56
+3.00	101	+4:41	+3.00	71	+4:11
+3.15	103	+4:58	+3.15	73	+4:28
+3.30	105	+5:15	+3.30	74	+4:44
+3.45	107	+5:32	+3.45	75	+5:00
+4.00	109	+5:49	+4.00	76	+5:16
+4.15	111	-5:54	+4.15	78	+5:33
+4.30	113	-5:37	+4.30	79	+5:49
+4.45	116	-5:19	+4.45	81	-5:54
+5.00	118	-5:02	+5.00	82	-5:38
+5.15	121	-4:44	+5.15	83	-5:22
+5.30	124	-4:26	+5.30	85	-5:05
+5.45	126	-4:09	+5.45	86	-4:49
+6.00	129	-3:51	+6.00	87	-4:33

Time	D4 Whitaker Spit to East Barrow: Duration	D4: Time at End of Sector	Time	D3 SW Sunk to NW Long Sand: Duration	D3: Time at End of Sector
-6.00	44	-5:16	-6.00	42	-5:18
-5.45	45	-5:00	-5.45	41	-5:04
-5.30	46	-4:44	-5.30	40	-4:50
-5.15	47	-4:28	-5.15	39	-4:36
-5.00	49	-4:11	-5.00	38	-4:22
-4.45	49	-3:56	-4.45	38	-4:07
-4.30	49	-3:41	-4.30	38	-3:52
-4.15	49	-3:26	-4.15	38	-3:37
-4.00	49	-3:11	-4.00	38	-3:22
-3.45	49	-2:56	-3.45	38	-3:07
-3.30	49	-2:41	-3.30	38	-2:52
-3.15	49	-2:26	-3.15	39	-2:36
-3.00	48	-2:12	-3.00	39	-2:21
-2.45	48	-1:57	-2.45	40	-2:05
-2.30	47	-1:43	-2.30	41	-1:49
-2.15	46	-1:29	-2.15	42	-1:33
-2.00	46	-1:14	-2.00	43	-1:17
-1.45	45	-1:00	-1.45	44	-1:01
-1.30	43	-0:47	-1.30	46	-0:44
-1.15	42	-0:33	-1.15	48	-0:27
-1.00	41	-0:19	-1.00	50	-0:10
-0.45	40	-0:05	-0.45	51	+0:06
-0.30	39	+0:09	-0.30	52	+0:22
-0.15	38	+0:23	-0.15	53	+0:38
HW	37	+0:37	HW	55	+0:55
+0.15	37	+0:52	+0.15	56	+1:11
+0.30	36	+1:06	+0.30	57	+1:27
+0.45	35	+1:20	+0.45	58	+1:43
+1.00	34	+1:34	+1.00	59	+1:59
+1.15	34	+1:49	+1.15	60	+2:15
+1.30	34	+2:04	+1.30	60	+2:30
+1.45	34	+2:19	+1.45	61	+2:46
+2.00	34	+2:34	+2.00	61	+3:01
+2.15	34	+2:49	+2.15	61	+3:16
+2.30	34	+3:04	+2.30	61	+3:31
+2.45	34	+3:19	+2.45	61	+3:46
+3.00	34	+3:34	+3.00	60	+4:00
+3.15	35	+3:50	+3.15	59	+4:14
+3.30	35	+4:05	+3.30	58	+4:28
+3.45	36	+4:21	+3.45	57	+4:42
+4.00	36	+4:36	+4.00	56	+4:56
+4.15	37	+4:52	+4.15	54	+5:09
+4.30	38	+5:08	+4.30	53	+5:23
+4.45	38	+5:23	+4.45	52	+5:37
+5.00	39	+5:39	+5.00	50	+5:50
+5.15	39	+5:54	+5.15	49	-5:56
+5.30	40	-5:50	+5.30	48	-5:42
+5.45	41	-5:34	+5.45	47	-5:28
+6.00	41	-5:19	+6.00	46	-5:14

Time	D2 Long Sand to North Edinburgh: Duration	D2: Time at End of Sector	Time	D1 North Edinburgh to East Margate: Duration	D1: Time at End of Sector
-6.00	38	-5:22	-6.00	87	-4:33
-5.45	39	-5:06	-5.45	89	-4:16
-5.30	41	-4:49	-5.30	90	-4:00
-5.15	42	-4:33	-5.15	91	-3:44
-5.00	43	-4:17	-5.00	93	-3:27
-4.45	44	-4:01	-4.45	95	-3:10
-4.30	45	-3:45	-4.30	96	-2:54
-4.15	46	-3:29	-4.15	98	-2:37
-4.00	47	-3:13	-4.00	100	-2:20
-3.45	47	-2:58	-3.45	101	-2:04
-3.30	47	-2:43	-3.30	102	-1:48
-3.15	48	-2:27	-3.15	103	-1:32
-3.00	48	-2:12	-3.00	104	-1:16
-2.45	48	-1:57	-2.45	103	-1:02
-2.30	48	-1:42	-2.30	102	-0:48
-2.15	49	-1:26	-2.15	101	-0:34
-2.00	49	-1:11	-2.00	100	-0:20
-1.45	48	-0:57	-1.45	98	-0:07
-1.30	48	-0:42	-1.30	97	+0:07
-1.15	47	-0:28	-1.15	95	+0:20
-1.00	47	-0:13	-1.00	93	+0:33
-0.45	46	+0:01	-0.45	90	+0:45
-0.30	45	+0:15	-0.30	88	+0:58
-0.15	44	+0:29	-0.15	86	+1:11
HW	43	+0:43	HW	83	+1:23
+0.15	41	+0:56	+0.15	82	+1:37
+0.30	40	+1:10	+0.30	81	+1:51
+0.45	38	+1:23	+0.45	80	+2:05
+1.00	37	+1:37	+1.00	78	+2:18
+1.15	35	+1:50	+1.15	78	+2:33
+1.30	34	+2:04	+1.30	77	+2:47
+1.45	33	+2:18	+1.45	76	+3:01
+2.00	32	+2:32	+2.00	76	+3:16
+2.15	31	+2:46	+2.15	76	+3:31
+2.30	30	+3:00	+2.30	76	+3:46
+2.45	29	+3:14	+2.45	76	+4:01
+3.00	28	+3:28	+3.00	76	+4:16
+3.15	28	+3:43	+3.15	76	+4:31
+3.30	28	+3:58	+3.30	77	+4:47
+3.45	28	+4:13	+3.45	77	+5:02
+4.00	28	+4:28	+4.00	77	+5:17
+4.15	29	+4:44	+4.15	78	+5:33
+4.30	29	+4:59	+4.30	79	+5:49
+4.45	30	+5:15	+4.45	80	-5:55
+5.00	31	+5:31	+5.00	81	-5:39
+5.15	32	+5:47	+5.15	82	-5:23
+5.30	33	-5:57	+5.30	83	-5:07
+5.45	34	-5:41	+5.45	83	-4:52
+6.00	35	-5:25	+6.00	84	-4:36

D - 5 Kts

Table D - North Edinburgh, Crouch and Colne

5 Kts - D

Time to cover Sectors (in minutes) at 5.0 kts — All times relate to HW Sheerness — **Springs**

	D8			D7			D6			D5			D4			D3			D2			D1	
	Colne Landfall to Spitway			Crouch Landfall to Whitaker Spit			Whitaker Spit to Black Deep			Whitaker Spit to Barrow Deep			Whitaker Spit to East Barrow			SW Sunk to NW Long Sand			Long Sand to North Edinburgh			North Edinburgh to East Margate	
Time	*Duration*	*Time at End of Sector*	*Time*	*Duration*	*Time at End of Sector*	*Time*	*Duration*	*Time at End of Sector*	*Time*	*Duration*	*Time at End of Sector*	*Time*	*Duration*	*Time at End of Sector*	*Time*	*Duration*	*Time at End of Sector*	*Time*	*Duration*	*Time at End of Sector*	*Time*	*Duration*	*Time at End of Sector*
- 6.00	57	- 5:03	- 6.00	59	- 5:01	- 6.00	158	- 3:22	- 6.00	104	- 4:16	- 6.00	46	- 5:14	- 6.00	39	- 5:21	- 6.00	37	- 5:23	- 6.00	88	- 4:32
- 5.45	59	- 4:46	- 5.45	63	- 4:42	- 5.45	160	- 3:05	- 5.45	107	- 3:58	- 5.45	48	- 4:57	- 5.45	38	- 5:07	- 5.45	40	- 5:05	- 5.45	91	- 4:14
- 5.30	60	- 4:30	- 5.30	66	- 4:24	- 5.30	161	- 2:49	- 5.30	109	- 3:41	- 5.30	50	- 4:40	- 5.30	37	- 4:53	- 5.30	42	- 4:48	- 5.30	93	- 3:57
- 5.15	61	- 4:14	- 5.15	69	- 4:06	- 5.15	162	- 2:33	- 5.15	111	- 3:24	- 5.15	52	- 4:23	- 5.15	36	- 4:39	- 5.15	44	- 4:31	- 5.15	96	- 3:39
- 5.00	62	- 3:58	- 5.00	72	- 3:48	- 5.00	164	- 2:16	- 5.00	113	- 3:07	- 5.00	54	- 4:06	- 5.00	34	- 4:26	- 5.00	47	- 4:13	- 5.00	99	- 3:21
- 4.45	63	- 3:42	- 4.45	72	- 3:33	- 4.45	162	- 2:03	- 4.45	113	- 2:52	- 4.45	54	- 3:51	- 4.45	34	- 4:11	- 4.45	48	- 3:57	- 4.45	101	- 3:04
- 4.30	64	- 3:26	- 4.30	73	- 3:17	- 4.30	160	- 1:50	- 4.30	112	- 2:38	- 4.30	55	- 3:35	- 4.30	34	- 3:56	- 4.30	50	- 3:40	- 4.30	103	- 2:47
- 4.15	65	- 3:10	- 4.15	73	- 3:02	- 4.15	158	- 1:37	- 4.15	112	- 2:23	- 4.15	55	- 3:20	- 4.15	34	- 3:41	- 4.15	51	- 3:24	- 4.15	106	- 2:29
- 4.00	65	- 2:55	- 4.00	74	- 2:46	- 4.00	156	- 1:24	- 4.00	111	- 2:09	- 4.00	56	- 3:04	- 4.00	34	- 3:26	- 4.00	53	- 3:07	- 4.00	108	- 2:12
- 3.45	66	- 2:39	- 3.45	73	- 2:32	- 3.45	153	- 1:12	- 3.45	109	- 1:56	- 3.45	56	- 2:49	- 3.45	34	- 3:11	- 3.45	53	- 2:52	- 3.45	109	- 1:56
- 3.30	66	- 2:24	- 3.30	72	- 2:18	- 3.30	149	- 1:01	- 3.30	107	- 1:43	- 3.30	55	- 2:35	- 3.30	34	- 2:56	- 3.30	54	- 2:36	- 3.30	109	- 1:41
- 3.15	66	- 2:09	- 3.15	71	- 2:04	- 3.15	145	- 0:50	- 3.15	105	- 1:30	- 3.15	54	- 2:21	- 3.15	35	- 2:40	- 3.15	54	- 2:21	- 3.15	110	- 1:25
- 3.00	67	- 1:53	- 3.00	70	- 1:50	- 3.00	142	- 0:38	- 3.00	103	- 1:17	- 3.00	54	- 2:06	- 3.00	35	- 2:25	- 3.00	55	- 2:05	- 3.00	111	- 1:09
- 2.45	66	- 1:39	- 2.45	69	- 1:36	- 2.45	137	- 0:28	- 2.45	100	- 1:05	- 2.45	53	- 1:52	- 2.45	36	- 2:09	- 2.45	56	- 1:49	- 2.45	109	- 0:56
- 2.30	65	- 1:25	- 2.30	67	- 1:23	- 2.30	133	- 0:17	- 2.30	98	- 0:52	- 2.30	52	- 1:38	- 2.30	38	- 1:52	- 2.30	56	- 1:34	- 2.30	107	- 0:43
- 2.15	64	- 1:11	- 2.15	65	- 1:10	- 2.15	128	- 0:07	- 2.15	95	- 0:40	- 2.15	50	- 1:25	- 2.15	39	- 1:36	- 2.15	57	- 1:18	- 2.15	106	- 0:29
- 2.00	63	- 0:57	- 2.00	64	- 0:56	- 2.00	124	+ 0:04	- 2.00	93	- 0:27	- 2.00	49	- 1:11	- 2.00	40	- 1:20	- 2.00	57	- 1:03	- 2.00	104	- 0:16
- 1.45	61	- 0:44	- 1.45	61	- 0:44	- 1.45	120	+ 0:15	- 1.45	89	- 0:16	- 1.45	47	- 0:58	- 1.45	43	- 1:02	- 1.45	56	- 0:49	- 1.45	101	- 0:04
- 1.30	58	- 0:32	- 1.30	59	- 0:31	- 1.30	116	+ 0:26	- 1.30	86	- 0:04	- 1.30	46	- 0:44	- 1.30	46	- 0:44	- 1.30	55	- 0:35	- 1.30	99	+ 0:09
- 1.15	55	- 0:20	- 1.15	56	- 0:19	- 1.15	112	+ 0:37	- 1.15	83	+ 0:08	- 1.15	44	- 0:31	- 1.15	48	- 0:27	- 1.15	54	- 0:21	- 1.15	96	+ 0:21
- 1.00	52	- 0:08	- 1.00	54	- 0:06	- 1.00	108	+ 0:48	- 1.00	80	+ 0:20	- 1.00	42	- 0:18	- 1.00	51	- 0:09	- 1.00	53	- 0:07	- 1.00	94	+ 0:34
- 0.45	50	+ 0:05	- 0.45	51	+ 0:06	- 0.45	106	+ 1:01	- 0.45	77	+ 0:32	- 0.45	41	- 0:04	- 0.45	53	+ 0:08	- 0.45	51	+ 0:06	- 0.45	91	+ 0:46
- 0.30	47	+ 0:17	- 0.30	48	+ 0:18	- 0.30	103	+ 1:13	- 0.30	75	+ 0:45	- 0.30	39	+ 0:09	- 0.30	55	+ 0:25	- 0.30	49	+ 0:19	- 0.30	88	+ 0:58
- 0.15	45	+ 0:30	- 0.15	46	+ 0:31	- 0.15	101	+ 1:26	- 0.15	72	+ 0:57	- 0.15	38	+ 0:23	- 0.15	57	+ 0:42	- 0.15	47	+ 0:32	- 0.15	86	+ 1:11
HW	43	+ 0:43	HW	43	+ 0:43	HW	98	+ 1:38	HW	70	+ 1:10	HW	36	+ 0:36	HW	60	+ 1:00	HW	45	+ 0:45	HW	83	+ 1:23
+ 0.15	42	+ 0:57	+ 0.15	42	+ 0:57	+ 0.15	97	+ 1:52	+ 0.15	69	+ 1:24	+ 0.15	35	+ 0:50	+ 0.15	61	+ 1:16	+ 0.15	43	+ 0:58	+ 0.15	81	+ 1:36
+ 0.30	41	+ 1:11	+ 0.30	40	+ 1:10	+ 0.30	96	+ 2:06	+ 0.30	68	+ 1:38	+ 0.30	34	+ 1:04	+ 0.30	63	+ 1:33	+ 0.30	40	+ 1:10	+ 0.30	79	+ 1:49
+ 0.45	40	+ 1:25	+ 0.45	38	+ 1:23	+ 0.45	94	+ 2:19	+ 0.45	67	+ 1:52	+ 0.45	33	+ 1:18	+ 0.45	65	+ 1:50	+ 0.45	38	+ 1:23	+ 0.45	78	+ 2:03
+ 1.00	39	+ 1:39	+ 1.00	37	+ 1:37	+ 1.00	93	+ 2:33	+ 1.00	66	+ 2:06	+ 1.00	32	+ 1:32	+ 1.00	67	+ 2:07	+ 1.00	36	+ 1:36	+ 1.00	76	+ 2:16
+ 1.15	39	+ 1:54	+ 1.15	36	+ 1:51	+ 1.15	93	+ 2:48	+ 1.15	65	+ 2:20	+ 1.15	32	+ 1:47	+ 1.15	68	+ 2:23	+ 1.15	34	+ 1:49	+ 1.15	75	+ 2:30
+ 1.30	39	+ 2:09	+ 1.30	36	+ 2:06	+ 1.30	93	+ 3:03	+ 1.30	65	+ 2:35	+ 1.30	32	+ 2:02	+ 1.30	69	+ 2:39	+ 1.30	33	+ 2:03	+ 1.30	74	+ 2:44
+ 1.45	39	+ 2:24	+ 1.45	36	+ 2:21	+ 1.45	93	+ 3:18	+ 1.45	65	+ 2:50	+ 1.45	31	+ 2:16	+ 1.45	70	+ 2:55	+ 1.45	31	+ 2:16	+ 1.45	73	+ 2:58
+ 2.00	39	+ 2:39	+ 2.00	35	+ 2:35	+ 2.00	93	+ 3:33	+ 2.00	65	+ 3:05	+ 2.00	31	+ 2:31	+ 2.00	71	+ 3:11	+ 2.00	30	+ 2:30	+ 2.00	72	+ 3:12
+ 2.15	40	+ 2:55	+ 2.15	36	+ 2:51	+ 2.15	94	+ 3:49	+ 2.15	65	+ 3:20	+ 2.15	31	+ 2:46	+ 2.15	71	+ 3:26	+ 2.15	28	+ 2:43	+ 2.15	72	+ 3:27
+ 2.30	40	+ 3:10	+ 2.30	36	+ 3:06	+ 2.30	95	+ 4:05	+ 2.30	66	+ 3:36	+ 2.30	32	+ 3:02	+ 2.30	70	+ 3:40	+ 2.30	26	+ 2:56	+ 2.30	72	+ 3:42
+ 2.45	41	+ 3:26	+ 2.45	37	+ 3:22	+ 2.45	96	+ 4:21	+ 2.45	67	+ 3:52	+ 2.45	32	+ 3:17	+ 2.45	70	+ 3:55	+ 2.45	25	+ 3:10	+ 2.45	72	+ 3:57
+ 3.00	42	+ 3:42	+ 3.00	37	+ 3:37	+ 3.00	97	+ 4:37	+ 3.00	67	+ 4:07	+ 3.00	32	+ 3:32	+ 3.00	69	+ 4:09	+ 3.00	23	+ 3:23	+ 3.00	72	+ 4:12
+ 3.15	43	+ 3:58	+ 3.15	38	+ 3:53	+ 3.15	99	+ 4:54	+ 3.15	69	+ 4:24	+ 3.15	33	+ 3:48	+ 3.15	67	+ 4:22	+ 3.15	23	+ 3:38	+ 3.15	73	+ 4:28
+ 3.30	43	+ 4:13	+ 3.30	39	+ 4:09	+ 3.30	102	+ 5:12	+ 3.30	70	+ 4:40	+ 3.30	33	+ 4:03	+ 3.30	65	+ 4:35	+ 3.30	23	+ 3:53	+ 3.30	74	+ 4:44
+ 3.45	44	+ 4:29	+ 3.45	39	+ 4:24	+ 3.45	104	+ 5:29	+ 3.45	71	+ 4:56	+ 3.45	34	+ 4:19	+ 3.45	63	+ 4:48	+ 3.45	23	+ 4:08	+ 3.45	75	+ 5:00
+ 4.00	45	+ 4:45	+ 4.00	40	+ 4:40	+ 4.00	107	+ 5:47	+ 4.00	73	+ 5:13	+ 4.00	35	+ 4:35	+ 4.00	61	+ 5:01	+ 4.00	23	+ 4:23	+ 4.00	76	+ 5:16
+ 4.15	46	+ 5:01	+ 4.15	42	+ 4:57	+ 4.15	110	- 5:55	+ 4.15	75	+ 5:30	+ 4.15	35	+ 4:50	+ 4.15	59	+ 5:14	+ 4.15	24	+ 4:39	+ 4.15	77	+ 5:32
+ 4.30	47	+ 5:17	+ 4.30	43	+ 5:13	+ 4.30	114	- 5:36	+ 4.30	77	+ 5:47	+ 4.30	36	+ 5:06	+ 4.30	56	+ 5:26	+ 4.30	25	+ 4:55	+ 4.30	78	+ 5:48
+ 4.45	48	+ 5:33	+ 4.45	44	+ 5:29	+ 4.45	117	- 5:18	+ 4.45	80	- 5:55	+ 4.45	37	+ 5:22	+ 4.45	54	+ 5:39	+ 4.45	26	+ 5:11	+ 4.45	79	- 5:56
+ 5.00	49	+ 5:49	+ 5.00	46	+ 5:46	+ 5.00	120	- 5:00	+ 5.00	82	- 5:38	+ 5.00	38	+ 5:38	+ 5.00	51	+ 5:51	+ 5.00	27	+ 5:27	+ 5.00	80	- 5:40
+ 5.15	50	- 5:55	+ 5.15	47	- 5:58	+ 5.15	124	- 4:41	+ 5.15	84	- 5:21	+ 5.15	39	+ 5:54	+ 5.15	50	- 5:55	+ 5.15	28	+ 5:43	+ 5.15	81	- 5:24
+ 5.30	51	- 5:39	+ 5.30	49	- 5:41	+ 5.30	128	- 4:22	+ 5.30	86	- 5:04	+ 5.30	40	- 5:50	+ 5.30	48	- 5:42	+ 5.30	30	- 6:00	+ 5.30	82	- 5:08
+ 5.45	52	- 5:23	+ 5.45	50	- 5:25	+ 5.45	132	- 4:03	+ 5.45	89	- 4:46	+ 5.45	41	- 5:34	+ 5.45	46	- 5:29	+ 5.45	31	- 5:44	+ 5.45	83	- 4:52
+ 6.00	53	- 5:07	+ 6.00	52	- 5:08	+ 6.00	135	- 3:45	+ 6.00	91	- 4:29	+ 6.00	42	- 5:18	+ 6.00	45	- 5:15	+ 6.00	33	- 5:27	+ 6.00	83	- 4:37

River Colne

SOUTH BOUND

Table D - North Edinburgh, Crouch and Colne

Neaps

All times relate to HW Sheerness

Time to cover Sectors (in minutes) at 6.0 Kts

SOUTH BOUND

D8 – Colne Landfall to Spitway

Time	Duration	Time at End of Sector
- 6.00	45	- 5:15
- 5.45	46	- 4:59
- 5.30	46	- 4:44
- 5.15	47	- 4:28
- 5.00	47	- 4:13
- 4.45	48	- 3:57
- 4.30	48	- 3:42
- 4.15	48	- 3:27
- 4.00	49	- 3:11
- 3.45	49	- 2:56
- 3.30	49	- 2:41
- 3.15	49	- 2:26
- 3.00	49	- 2:11
- 2.45	49	- 1:56
- 2.30	49	- 1:41
- 2.15	48	- 1:27
- 2.00	48	- 1:12
- 1.45	47	- 0:58
- 1.30	46	- 0:44
- 1.15	45	- 0:30
- 1.00	44	- 0:16
- 0.45	43	- 0:02
- 0.30	41	+ 0:11
- 0.15	40	+ 0:25
HW	39	+ 0:39
+ 0.15	38	+ 0:53
+ 0.30	38	+ 1:08
+ 0.45	37	+ 1:22
+ 1.00	36	+ 1:36
+ 1.15	36	+ 1:51
+ 1.30	36	+ 2:06
+ 1.45	36	+ 2:21
+ 2.00	36	+ 2:36
+ 2.15	37	+ 2:52
+ 2.30	37	+ 3:07
+ 2.45	37	+ 3:22
+ 3.00	38	+ 3:38
+ 3.15	38	+ 3:53
+ 3.30	39	+ 4:09
+ 3.45	39	+ 4:24
+ 4.00	40	+ 4:40
+ 4.15	40	+ 4:55
+ 4.30	40	+ 5:10
+ 4.45	41	+ 5:26
+ 5.00	41	+ 5:41
+ 5.15	42	+ 5:57
+ 5.30	42	- 5:48
+ 5.45	43	- 5:32
+ 6.00	43	- 5:17

River Colne

D7 – Crouch Landfall to Whitaker Spit

Time	Duration	Time at End of Sector
- 6.00	45	- 5:15
- 5.45	47	- 4:58
- 5.30	48	- 4:42
- 5.15	49	- 4:26
- 5.00	51	- 4:09
- 4.45	51	- 3:54
- 4.30	51	- 3:39
- 4.15	51	- 3:24
- 4.00	51	- 3:09
- 3.45	51	- 2:54
- 3.30	51	- 2:39
- 3.15	51	- 2:24
- 3.00	50	- 2:10
- 2.45	50	- 1:55
- 2.30	49	- 1:41
- 2.15	49	- 1:26
- 2.00	48	- 1:12
- 1.45	47	- 0:58
- 1.30	46	- 0:44
- 1.15	45	- 0:30
- 1.00	44	- 0:16
- 0.45	43	- 0:02
- 0.30	42	+ 0:12
- 0.15	40	+ 0:25
HW	39	+ 0:39
+ 0.15	38	+ 0:53
+ 0.30	37	+ 1:07
+ 0.45	36	+ 1:21
+ 1.00	36	+ 1:36
+ 1.15	35	+ 1:50
+ 1.30	35	+ 2:05
+ 1.45	35	+ 2:20
+ 2.00	35	+ 2:35
+ 2.15	35	+ 2:50
+ 2.30	35	+ 3:05
+ 2.45	35	+ 3:20
+ 3.00	36	+ 3:36
+ 3.15	36	+ 3:51
+ 3.30	36	+ 4:06
+ 3.45	37	+ 4:22
+ 4.00	37	+ 4:37
+ 4.15	38	+ 4:53
+ 4.30	38	+ 5:08
+ 4.45	39	+ 5:24
+ 5.00	40	+ 5:40
+ 5.15	40	+ 5:55
+ 5.30	41	- 5:49
+ 5.45	42	- 5:33
+ 6.00	42	- 5:18

D6 – Whitaker Spit to Black Deep

Time	Duration	Time at End of Sector
- 6.00	113	- 4:07
- 5.45	114	- 3:51
- 5.30	116	- 3:34
- 5.15	117	- 3:18
- 5.00	119	- 3:01
- 4.45	118	- 2:47
- 4.30	118	- 2:32
- 4.15	118	- 2:17
- 4.00	118	- 2:02
- 3.45	116	- 1:49
- 3.30	115	- 1:35
- 3.15	113	- 1:22
- 3.00	112	- 1:08
- 2.45	110	- 0:55
- 2.30	108	- 0:42
- 2.15	106	- 0:29
- 2.00	105	- 0:15
- 1.45	102	- 0:03
- 1.30	100	+ 0:10
- 1.15	97	+ 0:22
- 1.00	95	+ 0:35
- 0.45	93	+ 0:48
- 0.30	91	+ 1:01
- 0.15	89	+ 1:14
HW	87	+ 1:27
+ 0.15	86	+ 1:41
+ 0.30	85	+ 1:55
+ 0.45	84	+ 2:09
+ 1.00	84	+ 2:24
+ 1.15	83	+ 2:38
+ 1.30	83	+ 2:53
+ 1.45	83	+ 3:08
+ 2.00	83	+ 3:23
+ 2.15	84	+ 3:39
+ 2.30	84	+ 3:54
+ 2.45	85	+ 4:10
+ 3.00	86	+ 4:26
+ 3.15	87	+ 4:42
+ 3.30	88	+ 4:58
+ 3.45	89	+ 5:14
+ 4.00	90	+ 5:30
+ 4.15	92	+ 5:47
+ 4.30	94	- 5:56
+ 4.45	95	- 5:40
+ 5.00	97	- 5:23
+ 5.15	99	- 5:06
+ 5.30	101	- 4:49
+ 5.45	103	- 4:32
+ 6.00	104	- 4:16

D5 – Whitaker Spit to Barrow Deep

Time	Duration	Time at End of Sector
- 6.00	76	- 4:44
- 5.45	77	- 4:28
- 5.30	78	- 4:12
- 5.15	79	- 3:56
- 5.00	80	- 3:40
- 4.45	80	- 3:25
- 4.30	80	- 3:10
- 4.15	80	- 2:55
- 4.00	80	- 2:40
- 3.45	79	- 2:26
- 3.30	79	- 2:11
- 3.15	78	- 1:57
- 3.00	78	- 1:42
- 2.45	77	- 1:28
- 2.30	76	- 1:14
- 2.15	75	- 1:00
- 2.00	74	- 0:46
- 1.45	72	- 0:33
- 1.30	71	- 0:19
- 1.15	69	- 0:06
- 1.00	68	+ 0:08
- 0.45	66	+ 0:21
- 0.30	65	+ 0:35
- 0.15	64	+ 0:49
HW	63	+ 1:03
+ 0.15	62	+ 1:17
+ 0.30	61	+ 1:31
+ 0.45	61	+ 1:46
+ 1.00	60	+ 2:00
+ 1.15	60	+ 2:15
+ 1.30	60	+ 2:30
+ 1.45	59	+ 2:44
+ 2.00	59	+ 2:59
+ 2.15	60	+ 3:15
+ 2.30	60	+ 3:30
+ 2.45	60	+ 3:45
+ 3.00	61	+ 4:01
+ 3.15	61	+ 4:16
+ 3.30	62	+ 4:32
+ 3.45	63	+ 4:48
+ 4.00	64	+ 5:04
+ 4.15	65	+ 5:20
+ 4.30	66	+ 5:36
+ 4.45	67	+ 5:52
+ 5.00	68	- 5:52
+ 5.15	69	- 5:36
+ 5.30	70	- 5:20
+ 5.45	71	- 5:04
+ 6.00	72	- 4:48

D4 – Whitaker Spit to East Barrow

Time	Duration	Time at End of Sector
- 6.00	35	- 5:25
- 5.45	36	- 5:09
- 5.30	37	- 4:53
- 5.15	38	- 4:37
- 5.00	39	- 4:21
- 4.45	39	- 4:06
- 4.30	39	- 3:51
- 4.15	40	- 3:35
- 4.00	40	- 3:20
- 3.45	40	- 3:05
- 3.30	40	- 2:50
- 3.15	39	- 2:36
- 3.00	39	- 2:21
- 2.45	39	- 2:06
- 2.30	38	- 1:52
- 2.15	38	- 1:37
- 2.00	38	- 1:22
- 1.45	37	- 1:08
- 1.30	36	- 0:54
- 1.15	35	- 0:40
- 1.00	35	- 0:25
- 0.45	34	- 0:11
- 0.30	33	+ 0:03
- 0.15	33	+ 0:18
HW	32	+ 0:32
+ 0.15	31	+ 0:46
+ 0.30	31	+ 1:01
+ 0.45	30	+ 1:15
+ 1.00	29	+ 1:29
+ 1.15	29	+ 1:44
+ 1.30	29	+ 1:59
+ 1.45	29	+ 2:14
+ 2.00	29	+ 2:29
+ 2.15	29	+ 2:44
+ 2.30	29	+ 2:59
+ 2.45	29	+ 3:14
+ 3.00	29	+ 3:29
+ 3.15	29	+ 3:44
+ 3.30	30	+ 4:00
+ 3.45	30	+ 4:15
+ 4.00	31	+ 4:31
+ 4.15	31	+ 4:46
+ 4.30	31	+ 5:01
+ 4.45	32	+ 5:17
+ 5.00	32	+ 5:32
+ 5.15	32	+ 5:47
+ 5.30	33	- 5:57
+ 5.45	33	- 5:42
+ 6.00	34	- 5:26

D3 – SW Sunk to NW Long Sand

Time	Duration	Time at End of Sector
- 6.00	36	- 5:24
- 5.45	36	- 5:09
- 5.30	35	- 4:55
- 5.15	34	- 4:41
- 5.00	33	- 4:27
- 4.45	33	- 4:12
- 4.30	33	- 3:57
- 4.15	33	- 3:42
- 4.00	33	- 3:27
- 3.45	33	- 3:12
- 3.30	33	- 2:57
- 3.15	33	- 2:42
- 3.00	33	- 2:27
- 2.45	34	- 2:11
- 2.30	34	- 1:56
- 2.15	35	- 1:40
- 2.00	36	- 1:24
- 1.45	37	- 1:08
- 1.30	38	- 0:52
- 1.15	39	- 0:36
- 1.00	41	- 0:19
- 0.45	41	- 0:04
- 0.30	42	+ 0:12
- 0.15	43	+ 0:28
HW	44	+ 0:44
+ 0.15	45	+ 1:00
+ 0.30	46	+ 1:16
+ 0.45	46	+ 1:31
+ 1.00	47	+ 1:47
+ 1.15	48	+ 2:03
+ 1.30	48	+ 2:18
+ 1.45	48	+ 2:33
+ 2.00	49	+ 2:49
+ 2.15	49	+ 3:04
+ 2.30	49	+ 3:19
+ 2.45	49	+ 3:34
+ 3.00	49	+ 3:49
+ 3.15	48	+ 4:03
+ 3.30	47	+ 4:17
+ 3.45	46	+ 4:31
+ 4.00	45	+ 4:45
+ 4.15	44	+ 4:59
+ 4.30	44	+ 5:14
+ 4.45	43	+ 5:28
+ 5.00	42	+ 5:42
+ 5.15	41	+ 5:56
+ 5.30	40	- 5:50
+ 5.45	39	- 5:36
+ 6.00	39	- 5:21

D2 – Long Sand to North Edinburgh

Time	Duration	Time at End of Sector
- 6.00	31	- 5:29
- 5.45	32	- 5:13
- 5.30	33	- 4:57
- 5.15	34	- 4:41
- 5.00	35	- 4:25
- 4.45	36	- 4:09
- 4.30	36	- 3:54
- 4.15	37	- 3:38
- 4.00	38	- 3:22
- 3.45	38	- 3:07
- 3.30	38	- 2:52
- 3.15	38	- 2:37
- 3.00	38	- 2:22
- 2.45	38	- 2:07
- 2.30	39	- 1:51
- 2.15	39	- 1:36
- 2.00	39	- 1:21
- 1.45	39	- 1:06
- 1.30	39	- 0:51
- 1.15	38	- 0:37
- 1.00	38	- 0:22
- 0.45	37	- 0:08
- 0.30	37	+ 0:07
- 0.15	36	+ 0:21
HW	35	+ 0:35
+ 0.15	34	+ 0:49
+ 0.30	33	+ 1:03
+ 0.45	32	+ 1:17
+ 1.00	31	+ 1:31
+ 1.15	30	+ 1:45
+ 1.30	29	+ 1:59
+ 1.45	28	+ 2:13
+ 2.00	27	+ 2:27
+ 2.15	26	+ 2:41
+ 2.30	25	+ 2:55
+ 2.45	25	+ 3:10
+ 3.00	24	+ 3:24
+ 3.15	24	+ 3:39
+ 3.30	23	+ 3:53
+ 3.45	23	+ 4:08
+ 4.00	23	+ 4:23
+ 4.15	24	+ 4:39
+ 4.30	24	+ 4:54
+ 4.45	25	+ 5:10
+ 5.00	25	+ 5:25
+ 5.15	26	+ 5:41
+ 5.30	27	+ 5:57
+ 5.45	28	- 5:47
+ 6.00	29	- 5:31

D1 – North Edinburgh to East Margate

Time	Duration	Time at End of Sector
- 6.00	72	- 4:48
- 5.45	73	- 4:32
- 5.30	73	- 4:17
- 5.15	74	- 4:01
- 5.00	75	- 3:45
- 4.45	76	- 3:29
- 4.30	77	- 3:13
- 4.15	77	- 2:58
- 4.00	78	- 2:42
- 3.45	79	- 2:26
- 3.30	79	- 2:11
- 3.15	80	- 1:55
- 3.00	80	- 1:40
- 2.45	80	- 1:25
- 2.30	80	- 1:10
- 2.15	80	- 0:55
- 2.00	80	- 0:40
- 1.45	78	- 0:27
- 1.30	77	- 0:13
- 1.15	76	+ 0:01
- 1.00	75	+ 0:15
- 0.45	74	+ 0:29
- 0.30	73	+ 0:43
- 0.15	71	+ 0:56
HW	70	+ 1:10
+ 0.15	69	+ 1:24
+ 0.30	68	+ 1:38
+ 0.45	67	+ 1:52
+ 1.00	66	+ 2:06
+ 1.15	66	+ 2:21
+ 1.30	65	+ 2:35
+ 1.45	65	+ 2:50
+ 2.00	64	+ 3:04
+ 2.15	64	+ 3:19
+ 2.30	64	+ 3:34
+ 2.45	64	+ 3:49
+ 3.00	64	+ 4:04
+ 3.15	65	+ 4:20
+ 3.30	65	+ 4:35
+ 3.45	65	+ 4:50
+ 4.00	65	+ 5:05
+ 4.15	66	+ 5:21
+ 4.30	67	+ 5:37
+ 4.45	67	+ 5:52
+ 5.00	68	- 5:52
+ 5.15	69	- 5:36
+ 5.30	69	- 5:21
+ 5.45	70	- 5:05
+ 6.00	70	- 4:50

Table D - North Edinburgh, Crouch and Colne

Time to cover Sectors (in minutes) at 6.0 kts

All times relate to HW Sheerness

Springs

SOUTH BOUND

D8 – Colne Landfall to Spitway

Time	Duration	Time at End of Sector
- 6.00	46	- 5:14
- 5.45	47	- 4:58
- 5.30	48	- 4:42
- 5.15	49	- 4:26
- 5.00	50	- 4:10
- 4.45	51	- 3:54
- 4.30	51	- 3:39
- 4.15	52	- 3:23
- 4.00	52	- 3:08
- 3.45	53	- 2:52
- 3.30	53	- 2:37
- 3.15	53	- 2:22
- 3.00	53	- 2:07
- 2.45	53	- 1:52
- 2.30	52	- 1:38
- 2.15	52	- 1:23
- 2.00	52	- 1:08
- 1.45	50	- 0:55
- 1.30	48	- 0:42
- 1.15	46	- 0:29
- 1.00	44	- 0:16
- 0.45	43	- 0:02
- 0.30	41	+ 0:11
- 0.15	39	+ 0:24
HW	37	+ 0:37
+ 0.15	36	+ 0:51
+ 0.30	36	+ 1:06
+ 0.45	35	+ 1:20
+ 1.00	34	+ 1:34
+ 1.15	34	+ 1:49
+ 1.30	34	+ 2:04
+ 1.45	34	+ 2:19
+ 2.00	34	+ 2:34
+ 2.15	34	+ 2:49
+ 2.30	35	+ 3:05
+ 2.45	35	+ 3:20
+ 3.00	36	+ 3:36
+ 3.15	36	+ 3:51
+ 3.30	37	+ 4:07
+ 3.45	37	+ 4:22
+ 4.00	38	+ 4:38
+ 4.15	39	+ 4:54
+ 4.30	39	+ 5:09
+ 4.45	40	+ 5:25
+ 5.00	40	+ 5:40
+ 5.15	41	+ 5:56
+ 5.30	42	- 5:48
+ 5.45	43	- 5:32
+ 6.00	44	- 5:16

River Colne

D7 – Whitaker Spit to Crouch Landfall

Time	Duration	Time at End of Sector
- 6.00	47	- 5:13
- 5.45	49	- 4:56
- 5.30	52	- 4:38
- 5.15	54	- 4:21
- 5.00	57	- 4:03
- 4.45	57	- 3:48
- 4.30	57	- 3:33
- 4.15	58	- 3:17
- 4.00	58	- 3:02
- 3.45	58	- 2:47
- 3.30	57	- 2:33
- 3.15	57	- 2:18
- 3.00	56	- 2:04
- 2.45	55	- 1:50
- 2.30	54	- 1:36
- 2.15	53	- 1:22
- 2.00	52	- 1:08
- 1.45	50	- 0:55
- 1.30	48	- 0:42
- 1.15	47	- 0:28
- 1.00	45	- 0:15
- 0.45	43	- 0:02
- 0.30	42	+ 0:12
- 0.15	40	+ 0:25
HW	38	+ 0:38
+ 0.15	37	+ 0:52
+ 0.30	35	+ 1:05
+ 0.45	34	+ 1:19
+ 1.00	33	+ 1:33
+ 1.15	33	+ 1:48
+ 1.30	32	+ 2:02
+ 1.45	32	+ 2:17
+ 2.00	31	+ 2:31
+ 2.15	32	+ 2:47
+ 2.30	32	+ 3:02
+ 2.45	32	+ 3:17
+ 3.00	32	+ 3:32
+ 3.15	33	+ 3:48
+ 3.30	33	+ 4:03
+ 3.45	34	+ 4:19
+ 4.00	34	+ 4:34
+ 4.15	35	+ 4:50
+ 4.30	36	+ 5:06
+ 4.45	37	+ 5:22
+ 5.00	38	+ 5:38
+ 5.15	39	+ 5:54
+ 5.30	40	- 5:50
+ 5.45	41	- 5:34
+ 6.00	43	- 5:17

D6 – Whitaker Spit to Black Deep

Time	Duration	Time at End of Sector
- 6.00	120	- 4:00
- 5.45	122	- 3:43
- 5.30	124	- 3:26
- 5.15	125	- 3:10
- 5.00	127	- 2:53
- 4.45	126	- 2:39
- 4.30	126	- 2:24
- 4.15	125	- 2:10
- 4.00	125	- 1:55
- 3.45	122	- 1:43
- 3.30	120	- 1:30
- 3.15	118	- 1:17
- 3.00	116	- 1:04
- 2.45	113	- 0:52
- 2.30	111	- 0:39
- 2.15	108	- 0:27
- 2.00	105	- 0:15
- 1.45	102	- 0:03
- 1.30	99	+ 0:09
- 1.15	96	+ 0:21
- 1.00	93	+ 0:33
- 0.45	91	+ 0:46
- 0.30	88	+ 0:58
- 0.15	86	+ 1:11
HW	83	+ 1:23
+ 0.15	82	+ 1:37
+ 0.30	81	+ 1:51
+ 0.45	79	+ 2:04
+ 1.00	78	+ 2:18
+ 1.15	78	+ 2:33
+ 1.30	78	+ 2:48
+ 1.45	78	+ 3:03
+ 2.00	78	+ 3:18
+ 2.15	78	+ 3:33
+ 2.30	79	+ 3:49
+ 2.45	80	+ 4:05
+ 3.00	81	+ 4:21
+ 3.15	83	+ 4:38
+ 3.30	84	+ 4:54
+ 3.45	86	+ 5:11
+ 4.00	88	+ 5:28
+ 4.15	91	+ 5:46
+ 4.30	93	- 5:57
+ 4.45	96	- 5:39
+ 5.00	98	- 5:22
+ 5.15	101	- 5:04
+ 5.30	103	- 4:47
+ 5.45	106	- 4:29
+ 6.00	108	- 4:12

D5 – Whitaker Spit to Barrow Deep

Time	Duration	Time at End of Sector
- 6.00	80	- 4:40
- 5.45	82	- 4:23
- 5.30	85	- 4:05
- 5.15	87	- 3:48
- 5.00	90	- 3:30
- 4.45	90	- 3:15
- 4.30	90	- 3:00
- 4.15	90	- 2:45
- 4.00	90	- 2:30
- 3.45	88	- 2:17
- 3.30	86	- 2:04
- 3.15	84	- 1:51
- 3.00	83	- 1:37
- 2.45	81	- 1:24
- 2.30	79	- 1:11
- 2.15	78	- 0:57
- 2.00	76	- 0:44
- 1.45	74	- 0:31
- 1.30	72	- 0:18
- 1.15	70	- 0:05
- 1.00	67	+ 0:07
- 0.45	65	+ 0:20
- 0.30	64	+ 0:34
- 0.15	62	+ 0:47
HW	60	+ 1:00
+ 0.15	59	+ 1:14
+ 0.30	58	+ 1:28
+ 0.45	58	+ 1:43
+ 1.00	57	+ 1:57
+ 1.15	56	+ 2:11
+ 1.30	56	+ 2:26
+ 1.45	56	+ 2:41
+ 2.00	56	+ 2:56
+ 2.15	56	+ 3:11
+ 2.30	57	+ 3:27
+ 2.45	57	+ 3:42
+ 3.00	58	+ 3:58
+ 3.15	59	+ 4:14
+ 3.30	60	+ 4:30
+ 3.45	61	+ 4:46
+ 4.00	62	+ 5:02
+ 4.15	63	+ 5:18
+ 4.30	65	+ 5:35
+ 4.45	66	+ 5:51
+ 5.00	68	- 5:52
+ 5.15	69	- 5:36
+ 5.30	70	- 5:20
+ 5.45	72	- 5:03
+ 6.00	73	- 4:47

D4 – Whitaker Spit to East Barrow

Time	Duration	Time at End of Sector
- 6.00	37	- 5:23
- 5.45	38	- 5:07
- 5.30	40	- 4:50
- 5.15	41	- 4:34
- 5.00	42	- 4:18
- 4.45	43	- 4:02
- 4.30	43	- 3:47
- 4.15	44	- 3:31
- 4.00	44	- 3:16
- 3.45	44	- 3:01
- 3.30	44	- 2:46
- 3.15	43	- 2:32
- 3.00	43	- 2:17
- 2.45	42	- 2:03
- 2.30	42	- 1:48
- 2.15	41	- 1:34
- 2.00	40	- 1:20
- 1.45	39	- 1:06
- 1.30	38	- 0:52
- 1.15	37	- 0:38
- 1.00	35	- 0:25
- 0.45	34	- 0:11
- 0.30	33	+ 0:03
- 0.15	32	+ 0:17
HW	31	+ 0:31
+ 0.15	30	+ 0:45
+ 0.30	29	+ 0:59
+ 0.45	28	+ 1:13
+ 1.00	27	+ 1:27
+ 1.15	27	+ 1:42
+ 1.30	27	+ 1:57
+ 1.45	27	+ 2:12
+ 2.00	26	+ 2:26
+ 2.15	26	+ 2:41
+ 2.30	27	+ 2:57
+ 2.45	27	+ 3:12
+ 3.00	27	+ 3:27
+ 3.15	28	+ 3:43
+ 3.30	28	+ 3:58
+ 3.45	29	+ 4:14
+ 4.00	29	+ 4:29
+ 4.15	30	+ 4:45
+ 4.30	30	+ 5:00
+ 4.45	31	+ 5:16
+ 5.00	31	+ 5:31
+ 5.15	32	+ 5:47
+ 5.30	33	- 5:57
+ 5.45	33	- 5:42
+ 6.00	34	- 5:26

D3 – SW Sunk to NW Long Sand

Time	Duration	Time at End of Sector
- 6.00	35	- 5:25
- 5.45	34	- 5:11
- 5.30	33	- 4:57
- 5.15	32	- 4:43
- 5.00	30	- 4:30
- 4.45	30	- 4:15
- 4.30	30	- 4:00
- 4.15	30	- 3:45
- 4.00	30	- 3:30
- 3.45	30	- 3:15
- 3.30	30	- 3:00
- 3.15	30	- 2:45
- 3.00	30	- 2:30
- 2.45	31	- 2:14
- 2.30	32	- 1:58
- 2.15	33	- 1:42
- 2.00	34	- 1:26
- 1.45	35	- 1:10
- 1.30	37	- 0:53
- 1.15	39	- 0:36
- 1.00	41	- 0:19
- 0.45	43	- 0:02
- 0.30	44	+ 0:14
- 0.15	46	+ 0:31
HW	47	+ 0:47
+ 0.15	49	+ 1:04
+ 0.30	50	+ 1:20
+ 0.45	51	+ 1:36
+ 1.00	52	+ 1:52
+ 1.15	53	+ 2:08
+ 1.30	54	+ 2:24
+ 1.45	55	+ 2:40
+ 2.00	56	+ 2:56
+ 2.15	55	+ 3:10
+ 2.30	55	+ 3:25
+ 2.45	55	+ 3:40
+ 3.00	55	+ 3:55
+ 3.15	54	+ 4:09
+ 3.30	52	+ 4:22
+ 3.45	51	+ 4:36
+ 4.00	49	+ 4:49
+ 4.15	48	+ 5:03
+ 4.30	46	+ 5:16
+ 4.45	44	+ 5:29
+ 5.00	43	+ 5:43
+ 5.15	42	+ 5:57
+ 5.30	40	- 5:50
+ 5.45	39	- 5:36
+ 6.00	38	- 5:22

D2 – Long Sand to North Edinburgh

Time	Duration	Time at End of Sector
- 6.00	30	- 5:30
- 5.45	32	- 5:13
- 5.30	34	- 4:56
- 5.15	35	- 4:40
- 5.00	37	- 4:23
- 4.45	38	- 4:07
- 4.30	39	- 3:51
- 4.15	40	- 3:35
- 4.00	42	- 3:18
- 3.45	42	- 3:03
- 3.30	42	- 2:48
- 3.15	43	- 2:32
- 3.00	43	- 2:17
- 2.45	43	- 2:02
- 2.30	44	- 1:46
- 2.15	45	- 1:30
- 2.00	45	- 1:15
- 1.45	44	- 1:01
- 1.30	44	- 0:46
- 1.15	43	- 0:32
- 1.00	42	- 0:18
- 0.45	41	- 0:04
- 0.30	40	+ 0:10
- 0.15	39	+ 0:24
HW	37	+ 0:37
+ 0.15	36	+ 0:51
+ 0.30	34	+ 1:04
+ 0.45	33	+ 1:18
+ 1.00	31	+ 1:31
+ 1.15	30	+ 1:45
+ 1.30	28	+ 1:58
+ 1.45	26	+ 2:11
+ 2.00	25	+ 2:25
+ 2.15	23	+ 2:38
+ 2.30	22	+ 2:52
+ 2.45	21	+ 3:06
+ 3.00	19	+ 3:19
+ 3.15	19	+ 3:34
+ 3.30	19	+ 3:49
+ 3.45	19	+ 4:04
+ 4.00	19	+ 4:19
+ 4.15	20	+ 4:35
+ 4.30	21	+ 4:51
+ 4.45	21	+ 5:06
+ 5.00	22	+ 5:22
+ 5.15	24	+ 5:39
+ 5.30	25	+ 5:55
+ 5.45	26	- 5:49
+ 6.00	28	- 5:32

D1 – North Edinburgh to East Margate

Time	Duration	Time at End of Sector
- 6.00	73	- 4:47
- 5.45	74	- 4:31
- 5.30	75	- 4:15
- 5.15	77	- 3:58
- 5.00	78	- 3:42
- 4.45	79	- 3:26
- 4.30	81	- 3:09
- 4.15	82	- 2:53
- 4.00	84	- 2:36
- 3.45	84	- 2:21
- 3.30	85	- 2:05
- 3.15	86	- 1:49
- 3.00	86	- 1:34
- 2.45	86	- 1:19
- 2.30	85	- 1:05
- 2.15	85	- 0:50
- 2.00	84	- 0:36
- 1.45	82	- 0:23
- 1.30	81	- 0:09
- 1.15	79	+ 0:04
- 1.00	78	+ 0:18
- 0.45	76	+ 0:31
- 0.30	74	+ 0:44
- 0.15	72	+ 0:57
HW	70	+ 1:10
+ 0.15	69	+ 1:24
+ 0.30	67	+ 1:37
+ 0.45	66	+ 1:51
+ 1.00	64	+ 2:04
+ 1.15	64	+ 2:19
+ 1.30	63	+ 2:33
+ 1.45	62	+ 2:47
+ 2.00	62	+ 3:02
+ 2.15	62	+ 3:17
+ 2.30	62	+ 3:32
+ 2.45	62	+ 3:47
+ 3.00	62	+ 4:02
+ 3.15	62	+ 4:17
+ 3.30	63	+ 4:33
+ 3.45	64	+ 4:49
+ 4.00	64	+ 5:04
+ 4.15	65	+ 5:20
+ 4.30	66	+ 5:36
+ 4.45	67	+ 5:52
+ 5.00	67	- 5:53
+ 5.15	68	- 5:37
+ 5.30	68	- 5:22
+ 5.45	69	- 5:06
+ 6.00	70	- 4:50

Table D - North Edinburgh, Crouch and Colne

Neaps

All times relate to HW Sheerness

Time to cover Sectors (in minutes) at 7.0 Kts

SOUTH BOUND

D8 — Colne Landfall to Spitway

Time	Duration	Time at End of Sector
- 6.00	38	- 5:22
- 5.45	39	- 5:06
- 5.30	39	- 4:51
- 5.15	39	- 4:36
- 5.00	40	- 4:20
- 4.45	40	- 4:05
- 4.30	40	- 3:50
- 4.15	41	- 3:34
- 4.00	41	- 3:19
- 3.45	41	- 3:04
- 3.30	41	- 2:49
- 3.15	41	- 2:34
- 3.00	41	- 2:19
- 2.45	41	- 2:04
- 2.30	41	- 1:49
- 2.15	41	- 1:34
- 2.00	41	- 1:19
- 1.45	40	- 1:05
- 1.30	39	- 0:51
- 1.15	39	- 0:36
- 1.00	38	- 0:22
- 0.45	37	- 0:08
- 0.30	36	+ 1:06
- 0.15	35	+ 0:50
HW	34	+ 0:34
+ 0.15	33	+ 0:48
+ 0.30	33	+ 1:03
+ 0.45	32	+ 1:17
+ 1.00	32	+ 1:32
+ 1.15	32	+ 1:47
+ 1.30	32	+ 2:02
+ 1.45	32	+ 2:17
+ 2.00	32	+ 2:32
+ 2.15	32	+ 2:47
+ 2.30	32	+ 3:02
+ 2.45	32	+ 3:17
+ 3.00	33	+ 3:33
+ 3.15	33	+ 3:48
+ 3.30	33	+ 4:03
+ 3.45	34	+ 4:19
+ 4.00	34	+ 4:34
+ 4.15	34	+ 4:49
+ 4.30	35	+ 5:05
+ 4.45	35	+ 5:20
+ 5.00	35	+ 5:35
+ 5.15	36	+ 5:51
+ 5.30	36	- 4:54
+ 5.45	36	- 5:09
+ 6.00	37	- 5:23

River Colne

D7 — Crouch Landfall to Whitaker Spit

Time	Duration	Time at End of Sector
- 6.00	38	- 5:22
- 5.45	39	- 5:06
- 5.30	40	- 4:50
- 5.15	41	- 4:34
- 5.00	42	- 4:18
- 4.45	42	- 4:03
- 4.30	43	- 3:47
- 4.15	43	- 3:32
- 4.00	43	- 3:17
- 3.45	43	- 3:02
- 3.30	43	- 2:47
- 3.15	42	- 2:33
- 3.00	42	- 2:18
- 2.45	42	- 2:03
- 2.30	41	- 1:49
- 2.15	41	- 1:34
- 2.00	41	- 1:19
- 1.45	40	- 1:05
- 1.30	39	- 0:51
- 1.15	39	- 0:36
- 1.00	38	- 0:22
- 0.45	37	- 0:08
- 0.30	36	+ 0:06
- 0.15	35	+ 0:20
HW	34	+ 0:34
+ 0.15	34	+ 0:49
+ 0.30	33	+ 1:03
+ 0.45	32	+ 1:17
+ 1.00	31	+ 1:31
+ 1.15	31	+ 1:46
+ 1.30	31	+ 2:01
+ 1.45	31	+ 2:16
+ 2.00	30	+ 2:30
+ 2.15	31	+ 2:46
+ 2.30	31	+ 3:01
+ 2.45	31	+ 3:16
+ 3.00	31	+ 3:31
+ 3.15	31	+ 3:46
+ 3.30	32	+ 4:02
+ 3.45	32	+ 4:17
+ 4.00	32	+ 4:32
+ 4.15	32	+ 4:47
+ 4.30	33	+ 5:03
+ 4.45	33	+ 5:18
+ 5.00	34	+ 5:34
+ 5.15	34	+ 5:49
+ 5.30	35	- 5:55
+ 5.45	36	- 5:39
+ 6.00	36	- 5:24

D6 — Whitaker Spit to Black Deep

Time	Duration	Time at End of Sector
- 6.00	94	- 4:26
- 5.45	96	- 4:09
- 5.30	97	- 3:53
- 5.15	98	- 3:37
- 5.00	99	- 3:21
- 4.45	99	- 3:06
- 4.30	99	- 2:51
- 4.15	99	- 2:36
- 4.00	99	- 2:21
- 3.45	98	- 2:07
- 3.30	97	- 1:53
- 3.15	96	- 1:39
- 3.00	95	- 1:25
- 2.45	94	- 1:11
- 2.30	93	- 0:57
- 2.15	92	- 0:43
- 2.00	90	- 0:30
- 1.45	88	- 0:17
- 1.30	86	- 0:04
- 1.15	84	+ 0:09
- 1.00	82	+ 0:22
- 0.45	80	+ 0:35
- 0.30	79	+ 0:49
- 0.15	78	+ 1:03
HW	76	+ 1:16
+ 0.15	76	+ 1:31
+ 0.30	75	+ 1:45
+ 0.45	74	+ 1:59
+ 1.00	73	+ 2:13
+ 1.15	73	+ 2:28
+ 1.30	73	+ 2:43
+ 1.45	73	+ 2:58
+ 2.00	73	+ 3:13
+ 2.15	73	+ 3:28
+ 2.30	74	+ 3:44
+ 2.45	74	+ 3:59
+ 3.00	75	+ 4:15
+ 3.15	76	+ 4:31
+ 3.30	77	+ 4:47
+ 3.45	78	+ 5:03
+ 4.00	79	+ 5:19
+ 4.15	80	+ 5:35
+ 4.30	81	+ 5:51
+ 4.45	82	- 5:53
+ 5.00	83	- 5:37
+ 5.15	84	- 5:21
+ 5.30	85	- 5:05
+ 5.45	86	- 4:49
+ 6.00	87	- 4:33

D5 — Whitaker Spit to Barrow Deep

Time	Duration	Time at End of Sector
- 6.00	64	- 4:56
- 5.45	65	- 4:40
- 5.30	65	- 4:25
- 5.15	66	- 4:09
- 5.00	67	- 3:53
- 4.45	67	- 3:38
- 4.30	67	- 3:23
- 4.15	67	- 3:08
- 4.00	67	- 2:53
- 3.45	67	- 2:38
- 3.30	66	- 2:24
- 3.15	66	- 2:09
- 3.00	65	- 1:55
- 2.45	65	- 1:40
- 2.30	64	- 1:26
- 2.15	63	- 1:12
- 2.00	63	- 0:57
- 1.45	62	- 0:43
- 1.30	61	- 0:29
- 1.15	59	- 0:16
- 1.00	58	- 0:02
- 0.45	57	+ 0:12
- 0.30	56	+ 0:26
- 0.15	55	+ 0:40
HW	54	+ 0:54
+ 0.15	54	+ 1:09
+ 0.30	53	+ 1:23
+ 0.45	53	+ 1:38
+ 1.00	52	+ 1:52
+ 1.15	52	+ 2:07
+ 1.30	52	+ 2:22
+ 1.45	52	+ 2:37
+ 2.00	52	+ 2:52
+ 2.15	52	+ 3:07
+ 2.30	52	+ 3:22
+ 2.45	52	+ 3:37
+ 3.00	53	+ 3:53
+ 3.15	53	+ 4:08
+ 3.30	54	+ 4:24
+ 3.45	54	+ 4:39
+ 4.00	55	+ 4:55
+ 4.15	56	+ 5:11
+ 4.30	57	+ 5:27
+ 4.45	57	+ 5:42
+ 5.00	58	+ 5:58
+ 5.15	59	- 5:46
+ 5.30	59	- 5:31
+ 5.45	60	- 5:15
+ 6.00	61	- 4:59

D4 — Whitaker Spit to East Barrow

Time	Duration	Time at End of Sector
- 6.00	30	- 5:30
- 5.45	30	- 5:15
- 5.30	31	- 4:59
- 5.15	32	- 4:43
- 5.00	33	- 4:27
- 4.45	33	- 4:12
- 4.30	33	- 3:57
- 4.15	33	- 3:42
- 4.00	33	- 3:27
- 3.45	33	- 3:12
- 3.30	33	- 2:57
- 3.15	33	- 2:42
- 3.00	33	- 2:27
- 2.45	33	- 2:12
- 2.30	32	- 1:58
- 2.15	32	- 1:43
- 2.00	32	- 1:28
- 1.45	31	- 1:14
- 1.30	31	- 0:59
- 1.15	30	- 0:45
- 1.00	30	- 0:30
- 0.45	29	- 0:16
- 0.30	29	- 0:01
- 0.15	28	+ 0:13
HW	28	+ 0:28
+ 0.15	27	+ 0:42
+ 0.30	26	+ 0:56
+ 0.45	26	+ 1:11
+ 1.00	25	+ 1:25
+ 1.15	25	+ 1:40
+ 1.30	25	+ 1:55
+ 1.45	25	+ 2:10
+ 2.00	25	+ 2:25
+ 2.15	25	+ 2:40
+ 2.30	25	+ 2:55
+ 2.45	25	+ 3:10
+ 3.00	25	+ 3:25
+ 3.15	25	+ 3:40
+ 3.30	26	+ 3:56
+ 3.45	26	+ 4:11
+ 4.00	26	+ 4:26
+ 4.15	26	+ 4:41
+ 4.30	27	+ 4:57
+ 4.45	27	+ 5:12
+ 5.00	27	+ 5:27
+ 5.15	28	+ 5:43
+ 5.30	28	+ 5:58
+ 5.45	29	- 5:46
+ 6.00	29	- 5:31

D3 — SW Sunk to NW Long Sand

Time	Duration	Time at End of Sector
- 6.00	32	- 5:28
- 5.45	31	- 5:14
- 5.30	31	- 4:59
- 5.15	30	- 4:45
- 5.00	29	- 4:31
- 4.45	29	- 4:16
- 4.30	29	- 4:01
- 4.15	29	- 3:46
- 4.00	29	- 3:31
- 3.45	29	- 3:16
- 3.30	29	- 3:01
- 3.15	29	- 2:46
- 3.00	29	- 2:31
- 2.45	29	- 2:16
- 2.30	30	- 2:00
- 2.15	30	- 1:45
- 2.00	30	- 1:30
- 1.45	31	- 1:14
- 1.30	32	- 0:58
- 1.15	33	- 0:42
- 1.00	34	- 0:26
- 0.45	35	- 0:10
- 0.30	36	+ 0:06
- 0.15	36	+ 0:21
HW	37	+ 0:37
+ 0.15	37	+ 0:52
+ 0.30	38	+ 1:08
+ 0.45	39	+ 1:24
+ 1.00	39	+ 1:39
+ 1.15	40	+ 1:55
+ 1.30	40	+ 2:10
+ 1.45	40	+ 2:25
+ 2.00	41	+ 2:41
+ 2.15	41	+ 2:56
+ 2.30	41	+ 3:11
+ 2.45	41	+ 3:26
+ 3.00	41	+ 3:41
+ 3.15	40	+ 3:55
+ 3.30	39	+ 4:09
+ 3.45	39	+ 4:24
+ 4.00	38	+ 4:38
+ 4.15	38	+ 4:53
+ 4.30	37	+ 5:07
+ 4.45	36	+ 5:21
+ 5.00	36	+ 5:36
+ 5.15	35	+ 5:50
+ 5.30	35	- 5:55
+ 5.45	34	- 5:41
+ 6.00	33	- 5:27

D2 — Long Sand to North Edinburgh

Time	Duration	Time at End of Sector
- 6.00	26	- 5:34
- 5.45	27	- 5:18
- 5.30	28	- 5:02
- 5.15	28	- 4:47
- 5.00	29	- 4:31
- 4.45	30	- 4:15
- 4.30	30	- 4:00
- 4.15	31	- 3:44
- 4.00	32	- 3:28
- 3.45	32	- 3:13
- 3.30	32	- 2:58
- 3.15	32	- 2:43
- 3.00	32	- 2:28
- 2.45	32	- 2:13
- 2.30	32	- 1:58
- 2.15	33	- 1:42
- 2.00	33	- 1:27
- 1.45	33	- 1:12
- 1.30	32	- 0:58
- 1.15	32	- 0:43
- 1.00	32	- 0:28
- 0.45	31	- 0:14
- 0.30	31	+ 0:01
- 0.15	31	+ 0:16
HW	30	+ 0:30
+ 0.15	29	+ 0:44
+ 0.30	29	+ 0:59
+ 0.45	28	+ 1:13
+ 1.00	27	+ 1:27
+ 1.15	26	+ 1:41
+ 1.30	25	+ 1:55
+ 1.45	24	+ 2:09
+ 2.00	23	+ 2:23
+ 2.15	23	+ 2:38
+ 2.30	22	+ 2:52
+ 2.45	21	+ 3:06
+ 3.00	20	+ 3:20
+ 3.15	20	+ 3:35
+ 3.30	20	+ 3:50
+ 3.45	20	+ 4:05
+ 4.00	20	+ 4:20
+ 4.15	20	+ 4:35
+ 4.30	21	+ 4:51
+ 4.45	21	+ 5:06
+ 5.00	22	+ 5:22
+ 5.15	22	+ 5:37
+ 5.30	23	+ 5:53
+ 5.45	24	- 5:51
+ 6.00	25	- 5:35

D1 — North Edinburgh to East Margate

Time	Duration	Time at End of Sector
- 6.00	61	- 4:59
- 5.45	62	- 4:43
- 5.30	62	- 4:28
- 5.15	63	- 4:12
- 5.00	63	- 3:57
- 4.45	64	- 3:41
- 4.30	65	- 3:25
- 4.15	65	- 3:10
- 4.00	66	- 2:54
- 3.45	66	- 2:39
- 3.30	67	- 2:23
- 3.15	67	- 2:08
- 3.00	68	- 1:52
- 2.45	67	- 1:38
- 2.30	67	- 1:23
- 2.15	67	- 1:08
- 2.00	67	- 0:53
- 1.45	66	- 0:39
- 1.30	66	- 0:24
- 1.15	65	- 0:10
- 1.00	64	+ 0:04
- 0.45	63	+ 0:18
- 0.30	62	+ 0:32
- 0.15	61	+ 0:46
HW	60	+ 1:00
+ 0.15	60	+ 1:15
+ 0.30	59	+ 1:29
+ 0.45	58	+ 1:43
+ 1.00	57	+ 1:57
+ 1.15	57	+ 2:12
+ 1.30	57	+ 2:27
+ 1.45	56	+ 2:41
+ 2.00	56	+ 2:56
+ 2.15	56	+ 3:11
+ 2.30	56	+ 3:26
+ 2.45	56	+ 3:41
+ 3.00	56	+ 3:56
+ 3.15	56	+ 4:11
+ 3.30	56	+ 4:26
+ 3.45	56	+ 4:41
+ 4.00	57	+ 4:57
+ 4.15	57	+ 5:12
+ 4.30	57	+ 5:27
+ 4.45	58	+ 5:43
+ 5.00	58	+ 5:58
+ 5.15	59	- 5:46
+ 5.30	59	- 5:31
+ 5.45	60	- 5:15
+ 6.00	60	- 5:00

Table D - North Edinburgh, Crouch and Colne

Time to cover Sectors (in minutes) at 7.0 kts

All times relate to HW Sheerness

Springs

Time	D8 Colne Landfall to Spitway: Duration	D8: Time at End of Sector	Time	D7 Crouch Landfall to Whitaker Spit: Duration	D7: Time at End of Sector	Time	D6 Whitaker Spit to Black Deep: Duration	D6: Time at End of Sector	Time	D5 Whitaker Spit to Barrow Deep: Duration	D5: Time at End of Sector
- 6.00	39	- 5:21	- 6.00	39	- 5:21	- 6.00	99	- 4:21	- 6.00	67	- 4:53
- 5.45	40	- 5:05	- 5.45	41	- 5:04	- 5.45	101	- 4:04	- 5.45	68	- 4:37
- 5.30	40	- 4:50	- 5.30	43	- 4:47	- 5.30	102	- 3:48	- 5.30	69	- 4:21
- 5.15	41	- 4:34	- 5.15	45	- 4:30	- 5.15	104	- 3:31	- 5.15	70	- 4:05
- 5.00	42	- 4:18	- 5.00	46	- 4:14	- 5.00	105	- 3:15	- 5.00	71	- 3:49
- 4.45	42	- 4:03	- 4.45	47	- 3:58	- 4.45	105	- 3:00	- 4.45	71	- 3:34
- 4.30	43	- 3:47	- 4.30	47	- 3:43	- 4.30	105	- 2:45	- 4.30	71	- 3:19
- 4.15	43	- 3:32	- 4.15	47	- 3:28	- 4.15	104	- 2:31	- 4.15	72	- 3:03
- 4.00	43	- 3:17	- 4.00	48	- 3:12	- 4.00	104	- 2:16	- 4.00	72	- 2:48
- 3.45	44	- 3:01	- 3.45	47	- 2:58	- 3.45	103	- 2:02	- 3.45	71	- 2:34
- 3.30	44	- 2:46	- 3.30	47	- 2:43	- 3.30	101	- 1:49	- 3.30	70	- 2:20
- 3.15	44	- 2:31	- 3.15	47	- 2:28	- 3.15	100	- 1:35	- 3.15	70	- 2:05
- 3.00	44	- 2:16	- 3.00	46	- 2:14	- 3.00	99	- 1:21	- 3.00	69	- 1:51
- 2.45	44	- 2:01	- 2.45	46	- 1:59	- 2.45	97	- 1:08	- 2.45	68	- 1:37
- 2.30	44	- 1:46	- 2.30	45	- 1:45	- 2.30	95	- 0:55	- 2.30	67	- 1:23
- 2.15	44	- 1:31	- 2.15	44	- 1:31	- 2.15	93	- 0:42	- 2.15	66	- 1:09
- 2.00	43	- 1:17	- 2.00	43	- 1:17	- 2.00	91	- 0:29	- 2.00	65	- 0:55
- 1.45	42	- 1:03	- 1.45	42	- 1:03	- 1.45	89	- 0:16	- 1.45	63	- 0:42
- 1.30	41	- 0:49	- 1.30	41	- 0:49	- 1.30	86	- 0:04	- 1.30	61	- 0:29
- 1.15	40	- 0:35	- 1.15	40	- 0:35	- 1.15	84	+ 0:09	- 1.15	60	- 0:15
- 1.00	38	- 0:22	- 1.00	39	- 0:21	- 1.00	81	+ 0:21	- 1.00	58	- 0:02
- 0.45	37	- 0:08	- 0.45	38	- 0:07	- 0.45	79	+ 0:34	- 0.45	57	+ 0:12
- 0.30	36	+ 1:06	- 0.30	36	+ 0:06	- 0.30	77	+ 0:47	- 0.30	56	+ 0:26
- 0.15	34	+ 0:49	- 0.15	35	+ 0:20	- 0.15	75	+ 1:00	- 0.15	54	+ 0:39
HW	33	+ 0:33	HW	34	+ 0:34	HW	73	+ 1:13	HW	53	+ 0:53
+ 0.15	32	+ 0:47	+ 0.15	33	+ 0:48	+ 0.15	72	+ 1:27	+ 0.15	52	+ 1:07
+ 0.30	32	+ 1:02	+ 0.30	32	+ 1:02	+ 0.30	71	+ 1:41	+ 0.30	51	+ 1:21
+ 0.45	31	+ 1:16	+ 0.45	31	+ 1:16	+ 0.45	70	+ 1:55	+ 0.45	51	+ 1:36
+ 1.00	30	+ 1:30	+ 1.00	30	+ 1:30	+ 1.00	69	+ 2:09	+ 1.00	50	+ 1:50
+ 1.15	30	+ 1:45	+ 1.15	29	+ 1:44	+ 1.15	69	+ 2:24	+ 1.15	50	+ 2:05
+ 1.30	30	+ 2:00	+ 1.30	29	+ 1:59	+ 1.30	69	+ 2:39	+ 1.30	50	+ 2:20
+ 1.45	30	+ 2:15	+ 1.45	28	+ 2:13	+ 1.45	69	+ 2:54	+ 1.45	49	+ 2:34
+ 2.00	30	+ 2:30	+ 2.00	27	+ 2:27	+ 2.00	69	+ 3:09	+ 2.00	49	+ 2:49
+ 2.15	30	+ 2:45	+ 2.15	28	+ 2:43	+ 2.15	69	+ 3:24	+ 2.15	50	+ 3:05
+ 2.30	30	+ 3:00	+ 2.30	28	+ 2:58	+ 2.30	70	+ 3:40	+ 2.30	50	+ 3:20
+ 2.45	31	+ 3:16	+ 2.45	28	+ 3:13	+ 2.45	70	+ 3:55	+ 2.45	50	+ 3:35
+ 3.00	31	+ 3:31	+ 3.00	28	+ 3:28	+ 3.00	71	+ 4:11	+ 3.00	50	+ 3:50
+ 3.15	31	+ 3:46	+ 3.15	29	+ 3:44	+ 3.15	72	+ 4:27	+ 3.15	51	+ 4:06
+ 3.30	32	+ 4:02	+ 3.30	29	+ 3:59	+ 3.30	74	+ 4:44	+ 3.30	52	+ 4:22
+ 3.45	32	+ 4:17	+ 3.45	30	+ 4:15	+ 3.45	75	+ 5:00	+ 3.45	53	+ 4:38
+ 4.00	33	+ 4:33	+ 4.00	30	+ 4:30	+ 4.00	76	+ 5:16	+ 4.00	53	+ 4:53
+ 4.15	33	+ 4:48	+ 4.15	31	+ 4:46	+ 4.15	78	+ 5:33	+ 4.15	54	+ 5:09
+ 4.30	34	+ 5:04	+ 4.30	31	+ 5:01	+ 4.30	80	+ 5:50	+ 4.30	55	+ 5:25
+ 4.45	34	+ 5:19	+ 4.45	32	+ 5:17	+ 4.45	81	- 5:54	+ 4.45	57	+ 5:42
+ 5.00	34	+ 5:34	+ 5.00	33	+ 5:33	+ 5.00	83	- 5:37	+ 5.00	58	+ 5:58
+ 5.15	35	+ 5:50	+ 5.15	33	+ 5:48	+ 5.15	85	- 5:20	+ 5.15	59	- 5:46
+ 5.30	36	- 4:54	+ 5.30	34	- 5:56	+ 5.30	87	- 5:03	+ 5.30	60	- 5:30
+ 5.45	37	- 5:08	+ 5.45	35	- 5:40	+ 5.45	88	- 4:47	+ 5.45	61	- 5:14
+ 6.00	37	- 5:23	+ 6.00	36	- 5:24	+ 6.00	90	- 4:30	+ 6.00	62	- 4:58

River Colne

Time	D4 Whitaker Spit to East Barrow: Duration	D4: Time at End of Sector	Time	D3 SW Sunk to NW Long Sand: Duration	D3: Time at End of Sector	Time	D2 Long Sand to North Edinburgh: Duration	D2: Time at End of Sector	Time	D1 North Edinburgh to East Margate: Duration	D1: Time at End of Sector
- 6.00	30	- 5:30	- 6.00	31	- 5:29	- 6.00	26	- 5:34	- 6.00	62	- 4:58
- 5.45	32	- 5:13	- 5.45	30	- 5:15	- 5.45	27	- 5:18	- 5.45	63	- 4:42
- 5.30	33	- 4:57	- 5.30	29	- 5:01	- 5.30	28	- 5:02	- 5.30	64	- 4:26
- 5.15	34	- 4:41	- 5.15	28	- 4:47	- 5.15	29	- 4:46	- 5.15	64	- 4:11
- 5.00	35	- 4:25	- 5.00	26	- 4:34	- 5.00	31	- 4:29	- 5.00	65	- 3:55
- 4.45	35	- 4:10	- 4.45	26	- 4:19	- 4.45	32	- 4:13	- 4.45	66	- 3:39
- 4.30	36	- 3:54	- 4.30	26	- 4:04	- 4.30	32	- 3:58	- 4.30	67	- 3:23
- 4.15	36	- 3:39	- 4.15	26	- 3:49	- 4.15	33	- 3:42	- 4.15	69	- 3:06
- 4.00	37	- 3:23	- 4.00	26	- 3:34	- 4.00	34	- 3:26	- 4.00	70	- 2:50
- 3.45	36	- 3:09	- 3.45	26	- 3:19	- 3.45	35	- 3:10	- 3.45	70	- 2:35
- 3.30	36	- 2:54	- 3.30	26	- 3:04	- 3.30	35	- 2:55	- 3.30	71	- 2:19
- 3.15	36	- 2:39	- 3.15	26	- 2:49	- 3.15	35	- 2:40	- 3.15	71	- 2:04
- 3.00	36	- 2:24	- 3.00	26	- 2:34	- 3.00	35	- 2:25	- 3.00	72	- 1:48
- 2.45	35	- 2:10	- 2.45	27	- 2:18	- 2.45	36	- 2:09	- 2.45	72	- 1:33
- 2.30	35	- 1:55	- 2.30	27	- 2:03	- 2.30	36	- 1:54	- 2.30	71	- 1:19
- 2.15	34	- 1:41	- 2.15	28	- 1:47	- 2.15	37	- 1:38	- 2.15	71	- 1:04
- 2.00	34	- 1:26	- 2.00	29	- 1:31	- 2.00	37	- 1:23	- 2.00	70	- 0:50
- 1.45	33	- 1:12	- 1.45	30	- 1:15	- 1.45	37	- 1:08	- 1.45	69	- 0:36
- 1.30	32	- 0:58	- 1.30	32	- 0:58	- 1.30	36	- 0:54	- 1.30	68	- 0:22
- 1.15	31	- 0:44	- 1.15	33	- 0:42	- 1.15	36	- 0:39	- 1.15	67	- 0:08
- 1.00	31	- 0:29	- 1.00	34	- 0:26	- 1.00	35	- 0:25	- 1.00	66	+ 0:06
- 0.45	30	- 0:15	- 0.45	36	- 0:09	- 0.45	35	- 0:10	- 0.45	65	+ 0:20
- 0.30	29	- 0:01	- 0.30	37	+ 0:07	- 0.30	34	+ 0:04	- 0.30	63	+ 0:33
- 0.15	28	+ 0:13	- 0.15	38	+ 0:23	- 0.15	33	+ 0:18	- 0.15	62	+ 0:47
HW	27	+ 0:27	HW	39	+ 0:39	HW	32	+ 0:32	HW	60	+ 1:00
+ 0.15	26	+ 0:41	+ 0.15	40	+ 0:55	+ 0.15	31	+ 0:46	+ 0.15	59	+ 1:14
+ 0.30	25	+ 0:55	+ 0.30	41	+ 1:11	+ 0.30	29	+ 0:59	+ 0.30	58	+ 1:28
+ 0.45	24	+ 1:09	+ 0.45	42	+ 1:27	+ 0.45	28	+ 1:13	+ 0.45	57	+ 1:42
+ 1.00	23	+ 1:23	+ 1.00	43	+ 1:43	+ 1.00	27	+ 1:27	+ 1.00	56	+ 1:56
+ 1.15	23	+ 1:38	+ 1.15	43	+ 1:58	+ 1.15	26	+ 1:41	+ 1.15	55	+ 2:10
+ 1.30	23	+ 1:53	+ 1.30	44	+ 2:14	+ 1.30	24	+ 1:54	+ 1.30	55	+ 2:25
+ 1.45	23	+ 2:08	+ 1.45	45	+ 2:30	+ 1.45	23	+ 2:08	+ 1.45	54	+ 2:39
+ 2.00	22	+ 2:22	+ 2.00	45	+ 2:45	+ 2.00	21	+ 2:21	+ 2.00	54	+ 2:54
+ 2.15	23	+ 2:38	+ 2.15	45	+ 3:00	+ 2.15	20	+ 2:35	+ 2.15	54	+ 3:09
+ 2.30	23	+ 2:53	+ 2.30	45	+ 3:15	+ 2.30	19	+ 2:49	+ 2.30	54	+ 3:24
+ 2.45	23	+ 3:08	+ 2.45	45	+ 3:30	+ 2.45	18	+ 3:03	+ 2.45	54	+ 3:39
+ 3.00	23	+ 3:23	+ 3.00	45	+ 3:45	+ 3.00	16	+ 3:16	+ 3.00	54	+ 3:54
+ 3.15	24	+ 3:39	+ 3.15	44	+ 3:59	+ 3.15	16	+ 3:31	+ 3.15	54	+ 4:09
+ 3.30	24	+ 3:54	+ 3.30	43	+ 4:13	+ 3.30	16	+ 3:46	+ 3.30	55	+ 4:25
+ 3.45	24	+ 4:09	+ 3.45	42	+ 4:27	+ 3.45	16	+ 4:01	+ 3.45	55	+ 4:40
+ 4.00	25	+ 4:25	+ 4.00	42	+ 4:42	+ 4.00	16	+ 4:16	+ 4.00	55	+ 4:55
+ 4.15	25	+ 4:40	+ 4.15	40	+ 4:55	+ 4.15	17	+ 4:32	+ 4.15	56	+ 5:11
+ 4.30	26	+ 4:56	+ 4.30	39	+ 5:09	+ 4.30	18	+ 4:48	+ 4.30	57	+ 5:27
+ 4.45	26	+ 5:11	+ 4.45	38	+ 5:23	+ 4.45	18	+ 5:03	+ 4.45	57	+ 5:42
+ 5.00	27	+ 5:27	+ 5.00	37	+ 5:37	+ 5.00	19	+ 5:19	+ 5.00	58	+ 5:58
+ 5.15	27	+ 5:42	+ 5.15	36	+ 5:51	+ 5.15	20	+ 5:35	+ 5.15	58	- 5:47
+ 5.30	28	+ 5:58	+ 5.30	35	- 5:55	+ 5.30	21	+ 5:51	+ 5.30	59	- 5:31
+ 5.45	28	- 5:47	+ 5.45	34	- 5:41	+ 5.45	22	- 5:53	+ 5.45	59	- 5:16
+ 6.00	29	- 5:31	+ 6.00	33	- 5:27	+ 6.00	24	- 5:36	+ 6.00	60	- 5:00

SOUTH BOUND

Table E - Swale and Medway to Ramsgate via Copperas Channel

Neaps — All times relate to HW Sheerness — **Time to cover Sectors (in minutes) at 4.0 kts**

Medway: E7, E6, E5 | Ignore for Medway: E4, E3 | Medway: E3, E2, E1 | Swale: E4, E3, E2, E1

EASTBOUND

	E7			E6			E5			E4			E3			E2			E1	
	Medway Channel to Spile			Spile to Kentish Flats			Kentish Flats to Copperas			Swale Landfall to Copperas			Copperas to SE Margate			SE Margate to North Foreland			North Foreland to Ramsgate	
Time	Duration	Time at End of Sector	Time	Duration	Time at End of Sector	Time	Duration	Time at End of Sector	Time	Duration	Time at End of Sector	Time	Duration	Time at End of Sector	Time	Duration	Time at End of Sector	Time	Duration	Time at End of Sector
- 6.00	**82**	**- 4:38**	**- 6.00**	**74**	**- 4:46**	**- 6.00**	**87**	**- 4:33**	**- 6.00**	**97**	**- 4:23**	**- 6.00**	**100**	**- 4:20**	**- 6.00**	**80**	**- 4:40**	**- 6.00**	**56**	**- 5:04**
- 5.45	82	- 4:23	- 5.45	75	- 4:30	- 5.45	88	- 4:17	- 5.45	100	- 4:05	- 5.45	102	- 4:03	- 5.45	83	- 4:22	- 5.45	55	- 4:50
- 5.30	83	- 4:07	- 5.30	75	- 4:15	- 5.30	90	- 4:00	- 5.30	103	- 3:47	- 5.30	105	- 3:45	- 5.30	86	- 4:04	- 5.30	55	- 4:35
- 5.15	83	- 3:52	- 5.15	76	- 3:59	- 5.15	91	- 3:44	- 5.15	106	- 3:29	- 5.15	107	- 3:28	- 5.15	89	- 3:46	- 5.15	55	- 4:20
- 5.00	**84**	**- 3:36**	**- 5.00**	**77**	**- 3:43**	**- 5.00**	**93**	**- 3:27**	**- 5.00**	**109**	**- 3:11**	**- 5.00**	**110**	**- 3:10**	**- 5.00**	**91**	**- 3:29**	**- 5.00**	**56**	**- 4:04**
- 4.45	83	- 3:22	- 4.45	76	- 3:29	- 4.45	93	- 3:12	- 4.45	109	- 2:56	- 4.45	112	- 2:53	- 4.45	93	- 3:12	- 4.45	56	- 3:49
- 4.30	83	- 3:07	- 4.30	76	- 3:14	- 4.30	94	- 2:56	- 4.30	110	- 2:40	- 4.30	113	- 2:37	- 4.30	95	- 2:55	- 4.30	57	- 3:33
- 4.15	82	- 2:53	- 4.15	76	- 2:59	- 4.15	94	- 2:41	- 4.15	110	- 2:25	- 4.15	115	- 2:20	- 4.15	96	- 2:39	- 4.15	60	- 3:15
- 4.00	**82**	**- 2:38**	**- 4.00**	**75**	**- 2:45**	**- 4.00**	**95**	**- 2:25**	**- 4.00**	**111**	**- 2:09**	**- 4.00**	**117**	**- 2:03**	**- 4.00**	**98**	**- 2:22**	**- 4.00**	**63**	**- 2:57**
- 3.45	82	- 2:23	- 3.45	75	- 2:30	- 3.45	95	- 2:10	- 3.45	111	- 1:54	- 3.45	117	- 1:48	- 3.45	99	- 2:06	- 3.45	66	- 2:39
- 3.30	81	- 2:09	- 3.30	75	- 2:15	- 3.30	95	- 1:55	- 3.30	110	- 1:40	- 3.30	118	- 1:32	- 3.30	99	- 1:51	- 3.30	69	- 2:21
- 3.15	81	- 1:54	- 3.15	74	- 2:01	- 3.15	95	- 1:40	- 3.15	110	- 1:25	- 3.15	118	- 1:17	- 3.15	100	- 1:35	- 3.15	74	- 2:01
- 3.00	**81**	**- 1:39**	**- 3.00**	**74**	**- 1:46**	**- 3.00**	**95**	**- 1:25**	**- 3.00**	**110**	**- 1:10**	**- 3.00**	**118**	**- 1:02**	**- 3.00**	**101**	**- 1:19**	**- 3.00**	**80**	**- 1:40**
- 2.45	81	- 1:24	- 2.45	74	- 1:31	- 2.45	94	- 1:11	- 2.45	108	- 0:57	- 2.45	116	- 0:49	- 2.45	99	- 1:06	- 2.45	86	- 1:19
- 2.30	81	- 1:09	- 2.30	74	- 1:16	- 2.30	92	- 0:58	- 2.30	106	- 0:44	- 2.30	114	- 0:36	- 2.30	98	- 0:52	- 2.30	91	- 0:59
- 2.15	80	- 0:55	- 2.15	74	- 1:01	- 2.15	91	- 0:44	- 2.15	105	- 0:30	- 2.15	112	- 0:23	- 2.15	96	- 0:39	- 2.15	95	- 0:40
- 2.00	**80**	**- 0:40**	**- 2.00**	**73**	**- 0:47**	**- 2.00**	**90**	**- 0:30**	**- 2.00**	**103**	**- 0:17**	**- 2.00**	**109**	**- 0:11**	**- 2.00**	**95**	**- 0:25**	**- 2.00**	**98**	**- 0:22**
- 1.45	79	- 0:26	- 1.45	72	- 0:33	- 1.45	88	- 0:17	- 1.45	100	- 0:05	- 1.45	105	HW	- 1.45	90	- 0:15	- 1.45	102	- 0:03
- 1.30	77	- 0:13	- 1.30	71	- 0:19	- 1.30	86	- 0:04	- 1.30	97	+ 0:07	- 1.30	101	+ 0:11	- 1.30	86	- 0:04	- 1.30	105	+ 0:15
- 1.15	76	+ 0:01	- 1.15	70	- 0:05	- 1.15	83	+ 0:08	- 1.15	93	+ 0:18	- 1.15	97	+ 0:22	- 1.15	81	+ 0:06	- 1.15	105	+ 0:30
- 1.00	**75**	**+ 0:15**	**- 1.00**	**68**	**+ 0:08**	**- 1.00**	**81**	**+ 0:21**	**- 1.00**	**90**	**+ 0:30**	**- 1.00**	**93**	**+ 0:33**	**- 1.00**	**77**	**+ 0:17**	**- 1.00**	**104**	**+ 0:44**
- 0.45	72	+ 0:27	- 0.45	66	+ 0:21	- 0.45	79	+ 0:34	- 0.45	86	+ 0:41	- 0.45	88	+ 0:43	- 0.45	73	+ 0:28	- 0.45	104	+ 0:59
- 0.30	70	+ 0:40	- 0.30	64	+ 0:34	- 0.30	77	+ 0:47	- 0.30	81	+ 0:51	- 0.30	84	+ 0:54	- 0.30	70	+ 0:40	- 0.30	104	+ 1:14
- 0.15	68	+ 0:53	- 0.15	62	+ 0:47	- 0.15	75	+ 1:00	- 0.15	76	+ 1:01	- 0.15	79	+ 1:04	- 0.15	66	+ 0:51	- 0.15	101	+ 1:26
HW	**66**	**+ 1:06**	**HW**	**60**	**+ 1:00**	**HW**	**73**	**+ 1:13**	**HW**	**72**	**+ 1:12**	**HW**	**74**	**+ 1:14**	**HW**	**63**	**+ 1:03**	**HW**	**99**	**+ 1:39**
+ 0.15	65	+ 1:20	+ 0.15	59	+ 1:14	+ 0.15	71	+ 1:26	+ 0.15	70	+ 1:25	+ 0.15	72	+ 1:27	+ 0.15	61	+ 1:16	+ 0.15	96	+ 1:51
+ 0.30	64	+ 1:34	+ 0.30	58	+ 1:28	+ 0.30	70	+ 1:40	+ 0.30	68	+ 1:38	+ 0.30	70	+ 1:40	+ 0.30	59	+ 1:29	+ 0.30	94	+ 2:04
+ 0.45	63	+ 1:48	+ 0.45	57	+ 1:42	+ 0.45	69	+ 1:54	+ 0.45	67	+ 1:52	+ 0.45	68	+ 1:53	+ 0.45	58	+ 1:43	+ 0.45	90	+ 2:15
+ 1.00	**63**	**+ 2:03**	**+ 1.00**	**57**	**+ 1:57**	**+ 1.00**	**68**	**+ 2:08**	**+ 1.00**	**65**	**+ 2:05**	**+ 1.00**	**66**	**+ 2:06**	**+ 1.00**	**56**	**+ 1:56**	**+ 1.00**	**85**	**+ 2:25**
+ 1.15	63	+ 2:18	+ 1.15	57	+ 2:12	+ 1.15	68	+ 2:23	+ 1.15	65	+ 2:20	+ 1.15	67	+ 2:22	+ 1.15	56	+ 2:11	+ 1.15	81	+ 2:36
+ 1.30	64	+ 2:34	+ 1.30	58	+ 2:28	+ 1.30	68	+ 2:38	+ 1.30	65	+ 2:35	+ 1.30	67	+ 2:37	+ 1.30	56	+ 2:26	+ 1.30	77	+ 2:47
+ 1.45	65	+ 2:50	+ 1.45	58	+ 2:43	+ 1.45	69	+ 2:54	+ 1.45	65	+ 2:50	+ 1.45	67	+ 2:52	+ 1.45	56	+ 2:41	+ 1.45	74	+ 2:59
+ 2.00	**66**	**+ 3:06**	**+ 2.00**	**59**	**+ 2:59**	**+ 2.00**	**69**	**+ 3:09**	**+ 2.00**	**65**	**+ 3:05**	**+ 2.00**	**67**	**+ 3:07**	**+ 2.00**	**56**	**+ 2:56**	**+ 2.00**	**72**	**+ 3:12**
+ 2.15	67	+ 3:22	+ 2.15	60	+ 3:15	+ 2.15	70	+ 3:25	+ 2.15	66	+ 3:21	+ 2.15	68	+ 3:23	+ 2.15	57	+ 3:12	+ 2.15	70	+ 3:25
+ 2.30	68	+ 3:38	+ 2.30	62	+ 3:32	+ 2.30	71	+ 3:41	+ 2.30	67	+ 3:37	+ 2.30	70	+ 3:40	+ 2.30	58	+ 3:28	+ 2.30	68	+ 3:38
+ 2.45	70	+ 3:55	+ 2.45	63	+ 3:48	+ 2.45	71	+ 3:56	+ 2.45	68	+ 3:53	+ 2.45	71	+ 3:56	+ 2.45	59	+ 3:44	+ 2.45	67	+ 3:52
+ 3.00	**71**	**+ 4:11**	**+ 3.00**	**64**	**+ 4:04**	**+ 3.00**	**72**	**+ 4:12**	**+ 3.00**	**69**	**+ 4:09**	**+ 3.00**	**72**	**+ 4:12**	**+ 3.00**	**60**	**+ 4:00**	**+ 3.00**	**66**	**+ 4:06**
+ 3.15	73	+ 4:28	+ 3.15	65	+ 4:20	+ 3.15	73	+ 4:28	+ 3.15	70	+ 4:25	+ 3.15	73	+ 4:28	+ 3.15	61	+ 4:16	+ 3.15	64	+ 4:19
+ 3.30	74	+ 4:44	+ 3.30	67	+ 4:37	+ 3.30	74	+ 4:44	+ 3.30	72	+ 4:42	+ 3.30	74	+ 4:44	+ 3.30	61	+ 4:31	+ 3.30	63	+ 4:33
+ 3.45	75	+ 5:00	+ 3.45	68	+ 4:53	+ 3.45	75	+ 5:00	+ 3.45	73	+ 4:58	+ 3.45	75	+ 5:00	+ 3.45	62	+ 4:47	+ 3.45	62	+ 4:47
+ 4.00	**77**	**+ 5:17**	**+ 4.00**	**69**	**+ 5:09**	**+ 4.00**	**76**	**+ 5:16**	**+ 4.00**	**74**	**+ 5:14**	**+ 4.00**	**76**	**+ 5:16**	**+ 4.00**	**63**	**+ 5:03**	**+ 4.00**	**61**	**+ 5:01**
+ 4.15	77	+ 5:32	+ 4.15	70	+ 5:25	+ 4.15	77	+ 5:32	+ 4.15	76	+ 5:31	+ 4.15	78	+ 5:33	+ 4.15	64	+ 5:19	+ 4.15	61	+ 5:16
+ 4.30	78	+ 5:48	+ 4.30	70	+ 5:40	+ 4.30	78	+ 5:48	+ 4.30	78	+ 5:48	+ 4.30	79	+ 5:49	+ 4.30	66	+ 5:36	+ 4.30	60	+ 5:30
+ 4.45	78	- 5:57	+ 4.45	71	+ 5:56	+ 4.45	79	- 5:56	+ 4.45	80	- 5:55	+ 4.45	81	- 5:54	+ 4.45	67	+ 5:52	+ 4.45	60	+ 5:45
+ 5.00	**79**	**- 5:41**	**+ 5.00**	**72**	**- 5:48**	**+ 5.00**	**80**	**- 5:40**	**+ 5.00**	**82**	**- 5:38**	**+ 5.00**	**82**	**- 5:38**	**+ 5.00**	**68**	**- 5:52**	**+ 5.00**	**60**	**- 6:00**
+ 5.15	79	- 5:26	+ 5.15	72	- 5:33	+ 5.15	81	- 5:24	+ 5.15	83	- 5:22	+ 5.15	84	- 5:21	+ 5.15	69	- 5:36	+ 5.15	60	- 5:45
+ 5.30	79	- 5:11	+ 5.30	72	- 5:18	+ 5.30	81	- 5:09	+ 5.30	84	- 5:06	+ 5.30	85	- 5:05	+ 5.30	70	- 5:20	+ 5.30	59	- 5:31
+ 5.45	79	- 4:56	+ 5.45	72	- 5:03	+ 5.45	82	- 4:53	+ 5.45	86	- 4:49	+ 5.45	86	- 4:49	+ 5.45	71	- 5:04	+ 5.45	57	- 5:18
+ 6.00	**79**	**- 4:41**	**+ 6.00**	**72**	**- 4:48**	**+ 6.00**	**83**	**- 4:37**	**+ 6.00**	**87**	**- 4:33**	**+ 6.00**	**88**	**- 4:32**	**+ 6.00**	**72**	**- 4:48**	**+ 6.00**	**57**	**- 5:03**

Table E - Swale and Medway to Ramsgate via Copperas Channel

Time to cover Sectors (in minutes) at 4.0 kts — All times relate to HW Sheerness — **Springs**

Medway (E7–E5) · Ignore for Medway (E4) · Medway (E3–E1) · Swale (E4–E1)

Time	E7 Medway Channel to Spile Duration	E7 Time at End of Sector	Time	E6 Spile to Kentish Flats Duration	E6 Time at End of Sector	Time	E5 Kentish Flats to Copperas Duration	E5 Time at End of Sector
- 6.00	**85**	**- 4:35**	**- 6.00**	**78**	**- 4:42**	**- 6.00**	**91**	**- 4:29**
- 5.45	87	- 4:18	- 5.45	79	- 4:26	- 5.45	93	- 4:12
- 5.30	88	- 4:02	- 5.30	80	- 4:10	- 5.30	94	- 3:56
- 5.15	89	- 3:46	- 5.15	81	- 3:54	- 5.15	96	- 3:39
- 5.00	**90**	**- 3:30**	**- 5.00**	**82**	**- 3:38**	**- 5.00**	**98**	**- 3:22**
- 4.45	89	- 3:16	- 4.45	81	- 3:24	- 4.45	98	- 3:07
- 4.30	88	- 3:02	- 4.30	81	- 3:09	- 4.30	99	- 2:51
- 4.15	88	- 2:47	- 4.15	80	- 2:55	- 4.15	100	- 2:35
- 4.00	**87**	**- 2:33**	**- 4.00**	**80**	**- 2:40**	**- 4.00**	**100**	**- 2:20**
- 3.45	86	- 2:19	- 3.45	79	- 2:26	- 3.45	100	- 2:05
- 3.30	86	- 2:04	- 3.30	79	- 2:11	- 3.30	100	- 1:50
- 3.15	85	- 1:50	- 3.15	78	- 1:57	- 3.15	100	- 1:35
- 3.00	**85**	**- 1:35**	**- 3.00**	**78**	**- 1:42**	**- 3.00**	**100**	**- 1:20**
- 2.45	84	- 1:21	- 2.45	77	- 1:28	- 2.45	98	- 1:07
- 2.30	84	- 1:06	- 2.30	77	- 1:13	- 2.30	97	- 0:53
- 2.15	83	- 0:52	- 2.15	76	- 0:59	- 2.15	96	- 0:39
- 2.00	**82**	**- 0:38**	**- 2.00**	**76**	**- 0:44**	**- 2.00**	**94**	**- 0:26**
- 1.45	80	- 0:25	- 1.45	74	- 0:31	- 1.45	92	- 0:13
- 1.30	78	- 0:12	- 1.30	72	- 0:18	- 1.30	89	- 0:01
- 1.15	76	+ 0:01	- 1.15	70	- 0:05	- 1.15	86	+ 0:11
- 1.00	**74**	**+ 0:14**	**- 1.00**	**68**	**+ 0:08**	**- 1.00**	**83**	**+ 0:23**
- 0.45	71	+ 0:26	- 0.45	65	+ 0:20	- 0.45	80	+ 0:35
- 0.30	67	+ 0:37	- 0.30	61	+ 0:31	- 0.30	76	+ 0:46
- 0.15	64	+ 0:49	- 0.15	58	+ 0:43	- 0.15	73	+ 0:58
HW	**60**	**+ 1:00**	**HW**	**55**	**+ 0:55**	**HW**	**69**	**+ 1:09**
+ 0.15	59	+ 1:14	+ 0.15	54	+ 1:09	+ 0.15	68	+ 1:23
+ 0.30	59	+ 1:29	+ 0.30	53	+ 1:23	+ 0.30	66	+ 1:36
+ 0.45	58	+ 1:43	+ 0.45	52	+ 1:37	+ 0.45	64	+ 1:49
+ 1.00	**57**	**+ 1:57**	**+ 1.00**	**51**	**+ 1:51**	**+ 1.00**	**62**	**+ 2:02**
+ 1.15	58	+ 2:13	+ 1.15	52	+ 2:07	+ 1.15	63	+ 2:18
+ 1.30	59	+ 2:29	+ 1.30	53	+ 2:23	+ 1.30	63	+ 2:33
+ 1.45	60	+ 2:45	+ 1.45	54	+ 2:39	+ 1.45	63	+ 2:48
+ 2.00	**61**	**+ 3:01**	**+ 2.00**	**55**	**+ 2:55**	**+ 2.00**	**63**	**+ 3:03**
+ 2.15	63	+ 3:18	+ 2.15	56	+ 3:11	+ 2.15	64	+ 3:19
+ 2.30	65	+ 3:35	+ 2.30	58	+ 3:28	+ 2.30	65	+ 3:35
+ 2.45	67	+ 3:52	+ 2.45	60	+ 3:45	+ 2.45	66	+ 3:51
+ 3.00	**69**	**+ 4:09**	**+ 3.00**	**62**	**+ 4:02**	**+ 3.00**	**67**	**+ 4:07**
+ 3.15	71	+ 4:26	+ 3.15	64	+ 4:19	+ 3.15	69	+ 4:24
+ 3.30	73	+ 4:43	+ 3.30	66	+ 4:36	+ 3.30	70	+ 4:40
+ 3.45	75	+ 5:00	+ 3.45	68	+ 4:53	+ 3.45	71	+ 4:56
+ 4.00	**77**	**+ 5:17**	**+ 4.00**	**69**	**+ 5:09**	**+ 4.00**	**73**	**+ 5:13**
+ 4.15	78	+ 5:33	+ 4.15	70	+ 5:25	+ 4.15	74	+ 5:29
+ 4.30	79	+ 5:49	+ 4.30	71	+ 5:41	+ 4.30	76	+ 5:46
+ 4.45	80	- 5:55	+ 4.45	72	+ 5:57	+ 4.45	78	- 5:57
+ 5.00	**81**	**- 5:39**	**+ 5.00**	**73**	**- 5:47**	**+ 5.00**	**79**	**- 5:41**
+ 5.15	81	- 5:24	+ 5.15	73	- 5:32	+ 5.15	81	- 5:24
+ 5.30	81	- 5:09	+ 5.30	74	- 5:16	+ 5.30	82	- 5:08
+ 5.45	81	- 4:54	+ 5.45	74	- 5:01	+ 5.45	83	- 4:52
+ 6.00	**81**	**- 4:39**	**+ 6.00**	**74**	**- 4:46**	**+ 6.00**	**84**	**- 4:36**

Time	E4 Swale Landfall to Copperas Duration	E4 Time at End of Sector	Time	E3 Copperas to SE Margate Duration	E3 Time at End of Sector	Time	E2 SE Margate to North Foreland Duration	E2 Time at End of Sector	Time	E1 North Foreland to Ramsgate Duration	E1 Time at End of Sector
- 6.00	**108**	**- 4:12**	**- 6.00**	**106**	**- 4:14**	**- 6.00**	**83**	**- 4:37**	**- 6.00**	**47**	**- 5:13**
- 5.45	111	- 3:54	- 5.45	110	- 3:55	- 5.45	88	- 4:17	- 5.45	47	- 4:58
- 5.30	114	- 3:36	- 5.30	114	- 3:36	- 5.30	92	- 3:58	- 5.30	46	- 4:44
- 5.15	117	- 3:18	- 5.15	118	- 3:17	- 5.15	97	- 3:38	- 5.15	47	- 4:28
- 5.00	**120**	**- 3:00**	**- 5.00**	**122**	**- 2:58**	**- 5.00**	**102**	**- 3:18**	**- 5.00**	**47**	**- 4:13**
- 4.45	121	- 2:44	- 4.45	124	- 2:41	- 4.45	103	- 3:02	- 4.45	48	- 3:57
- 4.30	122	- 2:28	- 4.30	126	- 2:24	- 4.30	105	- 2:45	- 4.30	49	- 3:41
- 4.15	122	- 2:13	- 4.15	128	- 2:07	- 4.15	107	- 2:28	- 4.15	53	- 3:22
- 4.00	**123**	**- 1:57**	**- 4.00**	**130**	**- 1:50**	**- 4.00**	**109**	**- 2:11**	**- 4.00**	**57**	**- 3:03**
- 3.45	122	- 1:43	- 3.45	131	- 1:34	- 3.45	110	- 1:55	- 3.45	62	- 2:43
- 3.30	122	- 1:28	- 3.30	131	- 1:19	- 3.30	111	- 1:39	- 3.30	66	- 2:24
- 3.15	121	- 1:14	- 3.15	131	- 1:04	- 3.15	112	- 1:23	- 3.15	78	- 1:57
- 3.00	**121**	**- 0:59**	**- 3.00**	**132**	**- 0:48**	**- 3.00**	**113**	**- 1:07**	**- 3.00**	**90**	**- 1:30**
- 2.45	118	- 0:47	- 2.45	128	- 0:37	- 2.45	110	- 0:55	- 2.45	101	- 1:04
- 2.30	115	- 0:35	- 2.30	123	- 0:27	- 2.30	107	- 0:43	- 2.30	113	- 0:37
- 2.15	112	- 0:23	- 2.15	119	- 0:16	- 2.15	104	- 0:31	- 2.15	117	- 0:18
- 2.00	**108**	**- 0:12**	**- 2.00**	**115**	**- 0:05**	**- 2.00**	**100**	**- 0:20**	**- 2.00**	**121**	**+ 0:01**
- 1.45	104	- 0:01	- 1.45	109	+ 0:04	- 1.45	95	- 0:10	- 1.45	125	+ 0:20
- 1.30	99	+ 0:09	- 1.30	104	+ 0:14	- 1.30	90	HW	- 1.30	128	+ 0:38
- 1.15	94	+ 0:19	- 1.15	98	+ 0:23	- 1.15	85	+ 0:10	- 1.15	126	+ 0:51
- 1.00	**89**	**+ 0:29**	**- 1.00**	**93**	**+ 0:33**	**- 1.00**	**79**	**+ 0:19**	**- 1.00**	**124**	**+ 1:04**
- 0.45	84	+ 0:39	- 0.45	86	+ 0:41	- 0.45	74	+ 0:29	- 0.45	122	+ 1:17
- 0.30	78	+ 0:48	- 0.30	80	+ 0:50	- 0.30	69	+ 0:39	- 0.30	120	+ 1:30
- 0.15	72	+ 0:57	- 0.15	74	+ 0:59	- 0.15	63	+ 0:48	- 0.15	122	+ 1:47
HW	**66**	**+ 1:06**	**HW**	**68**	**+ 1:08**	**HW**	**58**	**+ 0:58**	**HW**	**111**	**+ 1:51**
+ 0.15	64	+ 1:19	+ 0.15	65	+ 1:20	+ 0.15	56	+ 1:11	+ 0.15	106	+ 2:01
+ 0.30	61	+ 1:31	+ 0.30	62	+ 1:32	+ 0.30	53	+ 1:23	+ 0.30	101	+ 2:11
+ 0.45	58	+ 1:43	+ 0.45	60	+ 1:45	+ 0.45	51	+ 1:36	+ 0.45	96	+ 2:21
+ 1.00	**56**	**+ 1:56**	**+ 1.00**	**57**	**+ 1:57**	**+ 1.00**	**49**	**+ 1:49**	**+ 1.00**	**91**	**+ 2:31**
+ 1.15	56	+ 2:11	+ 1.15	58	+ 2:13	+ 1.15	49	+ 2:04	+ 1.15	86	+ 2:41
+ 1.30	56	+ 2:26	+ 1.30	58	+ 2:28	+ 1.30	49	+ 2:19	+ 1.30	81	+ 2:51
+ 1.45	56	+ 2:41	+ 1.45	58	+ 2:43	+ 1.45	49	+ 2:34	+ 1.45	78	+ 3:03
+ 2.00	**57**	**+ 2:57**	**+ 2.00**	**58**	**+ 2:58**	**+ 2.00**	**49**	**+ 2:49**	**+ 2.00**	**74**	**+ 3:14**
+ 2.15	58	+ 3:13	+ 2.15	60	+ 3:15	+ 2.15	50	+ 3:05	+ 2.15	70	+ 3:25
+ 2.30	59	+ 3:29	+ 2.30	61	+ 3:31	+ 2.30	51	+ 3:21	+ 2.30	66	+ 3:36
+ 2.45	61	+ 3:46	+ 2.45	63	+ 3:48	+ 2.45	52	+ 3:37	+ 2.45	65	+ 3:50
+ 3.00	**62**	**+ 4:02**	**+ 3.00**	**64**	**+ 4:04**	**+ 3.00**	**53**	**+ 3:53**	**+ 3.00**	**63**	**+ 4:03**
+ 3.15	64	+ 4:19	+ 3.15	66	+ 4:21	+ 3.15	55	+ 4:10	+ 3.15	62	+ 4:17
+ 3.30	66	+ 4:36	+ 3.30	68	+ 4:38	+ 3.30	56	+ 4:26	+ 3.30	61	+ 4:31
+ 3.45	68	+ 4:53	+ 3.45	70	+ 4:55	+ 3.45	58	+ 4:43	+ 3.45	60	+ 4:45
+ 4.00	**69**	**+ 5:09**	**+ 4.00**	**72**	**+ 5:12**	**+ 4.00**	**59**	**+ 4:59**	**+ 4.00**	**58**	**+ 4:58**
+ 4.15	72	+ 5:27	+ 4.15	74	+ 5:29	+ 4.15	61	+ 5:16	+ 4.15	57	+ 5:12
+ 4.30	75	+ 5:45	+ 4.30	76	+ 5:46	+ 4.30	62	+ 5:32	+ 4.30	56	+ 5:26
+ 4.45	78	- 5:57	+ 4.45	78	- 5:57	+ 4.45	64	+ 5:49	+ 4.45	55	+ 5:40
+ 5.00	**80**	**- 5:40**	**+ 5.00**	**80**	**- 5:40**	**+ 5.00**	**66**	**- 5:54**	**+ 5.00**	**54**	**+ 5:54**
+ 5.15	82	- 5:23	+ 5.15	82	- 5:23	+ 5.15	67	- 5:38	+ 5.15	53	- 5:52
+ 5.30	84	- 5:06	+ 5.30	83	- 5:07	+ 5.30	69	- 5:21	+ 5.30	54	- 5:36
+ 5.45	86	- 4:49	+ 5.45	85	- 4:50	+ 5.45	70	- 5:05	+ 5.45	49	- 5:26
+ 6.00	**88**	**- 4:32**	**+ 6.00**	**87**	**- 4:33**	**+ 6.00**	**72**	**- 4:48**	**+ 6.00**	**48**	**- 5:12**

EAST BOUND

Table E - Swale and Medway to Ramsgate via Copperas Channel

Neaps — All times relate to HW Sheerness — **Time to cover Sectors (in minutes) at 5.0 kts**

EAST BOUND

	Medway								Ignore for Medway / Swale			Medway / Swale								
	E7			E6			E5			E4			E3			E2			E1	
	Medway Channel to Spile			Spile to Kentish Flats			Kentish Flats to Copperas			Swale Landfall to Copperas			Copperas to SE Margate			SE Margate to North Foreland			North Foreland to Ramsgate	
Time	Duration	Time at End of Sector	Time	Duration	Time at End of Sector	Time	Duration	Time at End of Sector	Time	Duration	Time at End of Sector	Time	Duration	Time at End of Sector	Time	Duration	Time at End of Sector	Time	Duration	Time at End of Sector
- 6.00	64	- 4:56	- 6.00	58	- 5:02	- 6.00	68	- 4:52	- 6.00	73	- 4:47	- 6.00	76	- 4:44	- 6.00	62	- 4:58	- 6.00	47	- 5:13
- 5.45	64	- 4:41	- 5.45	59	- 4:46	- 5.45	68	- 4:37	- 5.45	74	- 4:31	- 5.45	77	- 4:28	- 5.45	63	- 4:42	- 5.45	47	- 4:58
- 5.30	65	- 4:25	- 5.30	59	- 4:31	- 5.30	69	- 4:21	- 5.30	76	- 4:14	- 5.30	78	- 4:12	- 5.30	64	- 4:26	- 5.30	46	- 4:44
- 5.15	65	- 4:10	- 5.15	59	- 4:16	- 5.15	70	- 4:05	- 5.15	77	- 3:58	- 5.15	79	- 3:56	- 5.15	66	- 4:09	- 5.15	47	- 4:28
- 5.00	65	- 3:55	- 5.00	60	- 4:00	- 5.00	70	- 3:50	- 5.00	78	- 3:42	- 5.00	80	- 3:40	- 5.00	67	- 3:53	- 5.00	47	- 4:13
- 4.45	65	- 3:40	- 4.45	60	- 3:45	- 4.45	70	- 3:35	- 4.45	78	- 3:27	- 4.45	81	- 3:24	- 4.45	67	- 3:38	- 4.45	47	- 3:58
- 4.30	65	- 3:25	- 4.30	59	- 3:31	- 4.30	71	- 3:19	- 4.30	79	- 3:11	- 4.30	82	- 3:08	- 4.30	68	- 3:22	- 4.30	47	- 3:43
- 4.15	65	- 3:10	- 4.15	59	- 3:16	- 4.15	71	- 3:04	- 4.15	79	- 2:56	- 4.15	82	- 2:53	- 4.15	68	- 3:07	- 4.15	49	- 3:26
- 4.00	65	- 2:55	- 4.00	59	- 3:01	- 4.00	71	- 2:49	- 4.00	80	- 2:40	- 4.00	83	- 2:37	- 4.00	69	- 2:51	- 4.00	51	- 3:09
- 3.45	64	- 2:41	- 3.45	59	- 2:46	- 3.45	71	- 2:34	- 3.45	80	- 2:25	- 3.45	85	- 2:20	- 3.45	69	- 2:36	- 3.45	52	- 2:53
- 3.30	64	- 2:26	- 3.30	59	- 2:31	- 3.30	71	- 2:19	- 3.30	80	- 2:10	- 3.30	87	- 2:03	- 3.30	70	- 2:20	- 3.30	54	- 2:36
- 3.15	64	- 2:11	- 3.15	58	- 2:17	- 3.15	71	- 2:04	- 3.15	80	- 1:55	- 3.15	89	- 1:46	- 3.15	70	- 2:05	- 3.15	57	- 2:18
- 3.00	64	- 1:56	- 3.00	58	- 2:02	- 3.00	71	- 1:49	- 3.00	80	- 1:40	- 3.00	91	- 1:29	- 3.00	71	- 1:49	- 3.00	59	- 2:01
- 2.45	64	- 1:41	- 2.45	58	- 1:47	- 2.45	71	- 1:34	- 2.45	79	- 1:26	- 2.45	89	- 1:16	- 2.45	70	- 1:35	- 2.45	62	- 1:43
- 2.30	64	- 1:26	- 2.30	58	- 1:32	- 2.30	70	- 1:20	- 2.30	79	- 1:11	- 2.30	87	- 1:03	- 2.30	70	- 1:20	- 2.30	65	- 1:25
- 2.15	63	- 1:12	- 2.15	58	- 1:17	- 2.15	70	- 1:05	- 2.15	78	- 0:57	- 2.15	85	- 0:50	- 2.15	69	- 1:06	- 2.15	66	- 1:09
- 2.00	63	- 0:57	- 2.00	58	- 1:02	- 2.00	69	- 0:51	- 2.00	77	- 0:43	- 2.00	82	- 0:38	- 2.00	69	- 0:51	- 2.00	67	- 0:53
- 1.45	63	- 0:42	- 1.45	57	- 0:48	- 1.45	68	- 0:37	- 1.45	76	- 0:29	- 1.45	80	- 0:25	- 1.45	67	- 0:38	- 1.45	68	- 0:37
- 1.30	62	- 0:28	- 1.30	57	- 0:33	- 1.30	67	- 0:23	- 1.30	74	- 0:16	- 1.30	78	- 0:12	- 1.30	65	- 0:25	- 1.30	70	- 0:20
- 1.15	61	- 0:14	- 1.15	56	- 0:19	- 1.15	66	- 0:09	- 1.15	72	- 0:03	- 1.15	75	HW	- 1.15	63	- 0:12	- 1.15	70	- 0:05
- 1.00	60	HW	- 1.00	55	- 0:05	- 1.00	65	+ 0:05	- 1.00	70	+ 0:10	- 1.00	73	+ 0:13	- 1.00	61	+ 0:01	- 1.00	70	+ 0:10
- 0.45	59	+ 0:14	- 0.45	54	+ 0:09	- 0.45	64	+ 0:19	- 0.45	68	+ 0:23	- 0.45	70	+ 0:25	- 0.45	59	+ 0:14	- 0.45	70	+ 0:25
- 0.30	57	+ 0:27	- 0.30	52	+ 0:22	- 0.30	62	+ 0:32	- 0.30	65	+ 0:35	- 0.30	68	+ 0:38	- 0.30	57	+ 0:27	- 0.30	70	+ 0:40
- 0.15	56	+ 0:41	- 0.15	51	+ 0:36	- 0.15	61	+ 0:46	- 0.15	63	+ 0:48	- 0.15	65	+ 0:50	- 0.15	55	+ 0:40	- 0.15	69	+ 0:54
HW	55	+ 0:55	HW	50	+ 0:50	HW	60	+ 1:00	HW	60	+ 1:00	HW	62	+ 1:02	HW	53	+ 0:53	HW	68	+ 1:08
+ 0.15	54	+ 1:09	+ 0.15	49	+ 1:04	+ 0.15	59	+ 1:14	+ 0.15	59	+ 1:14	+ 0.15	61	+ 1:16	+ 0.15	51	+ 1:06	+ 0.15	68	+ 1:23
+ 0.30	53	+ 1:23	+ 0.30	48	+ 1:18	+ 0.30	58	+ 1:28	+ 0.30	58	+ 1:28	+ 0.30	59	+ 1:29	+ 0.30	50	+ 1:20	+ 0.30	67	+ 1:37
+ 0.45	53	+ 1:38	+ 0.45	48	+ 1:33	+ 0.45	57	+ 1:42	+ 0.45	56	+ 1:41	+ 0.45	58	+ 1:43	+ 0.45	49	+ 1:34	+ 0.45	65	+ 1:50
+ 1.00	52	+ 1:52	+ 1.00	47	+ 1:47	+ 1.00	56	+ 1:56	+ 1.00	55	+ 1:55	+ 1.00	57	+ 1:57	+ 1.00	47	+ 1:47	+ 1.00	64	+ 2:04
+ 1.15	52	+ 2:07	+ 1.15	47	+ 2:02	+ 1.15	56	+ 2:11	+ 1.15	55	+ 2:10	+ 1.15	57	+ 2:12	+ 1.15	47	+ 2:02	+ 1.15	62	+ 2:17
+ 1.30	53	+ 2:23	+ 1.30	48	+ 2:18	+ 1.30	56	+ 2:26	+ 1.30	55	+ 2:25	+ 1.30	57	+ 2:27	+ 1.30	47	+ 2:17	+ 1.30	61	+ 2:31
+ 1.45	53	+ 2:38	+ 1.45	48	+ 2:33	+ 1.45	57	+ 2:42	+ 1.45	55	+ 2:40	+ 1.45	57	+ 2:42	+ 1.45	47	+ 2:32	+ 1.45	59	+ 2:44
+ 2.00	54	+ 2:54	+ 2.00	48	+ 2:48	+ 2.00	57	+ 2:57	+ 2.00	55	+ 2:55	+ 2.00	57	+ 2:57	+ 2.00	47	+ 2:47	+ 2.00	58	+ 2:58
+ 2.15	54	+ 3:09	+ 2.15	49	+ 3:04	+ 2.15	57	+ 3:12	+ 2.15	55	+ 3:10	+ 2.15	57	+ 3:12	+ 2.15	48	+ 3:03	+ 2.15	57	+ 3:12
+ 2.30	55	+ 3:25	+ 2.30	50	+ 3:20	+ 2.30	58	+ 3:28	+ 2.30	56	+ 3:26	+ 2.30	58	+ 3:28	+ 2.30	48	+ 3:18	+ 2.30	55	+ 3:25
+ 2.45	56	+ 3:41	+ 2.45	51	+ 3:36	+ 2.45	58	+ 3:43	+ 2.45	57	+ 3:42	+ 2.45	59	+ 3:44	+ 2.45	49	+ 3:34	+ 2.45	55	+ 3:40
+ 3.00	57	+ 3:57	+ 3.00	51	+ 3:51	+ 3.00	59	+ 3:59	+ 3.00	57	+ 3:57	+ 3.00	60	+ 4:00	+ 3.00	49	+ 3:49	+ 3.00	54	+ 3:54
+ 3.15	58	+ 4:13	+ 3.15	52	+ 4:07	+ 3.15	59	+ 4:14	+ 3.15	58	+ 4:13	+ 3.15	60	+ 4:15	+ 3.15	50	+ 4:05	+ 3.15	53	+ 4:08
+ 3.30	59	+ 4:29	+ 3.30	53	+ 4:23	+ 3.30	60	+ 4:30	+ 3.30	59	+ 4:29	+ 3.30	61	+ 4:31	+ 3.30	50	+ 4:20	+ 3.30	52	+ 4:22
+ 3.45	60	+ 4:45	+ 3.45	54	+ 4:39	+ 3.45	60	+ 4:45	+ 3.45	60	+ 4:45	+ 3.45	62	+ 4:47	+ 3.45	51	+ 4:36	+ 3.45	51	+ 4:36
+ 4.00	61	+ 5:01	+ 4.00	55	+ 4:55	+ 4.00	61	+ 5:01	+ 4.00	60	+ 5:00	+ 4.00	62	+ 5:02	+ 4.00	52	+ 4:52	+ 4.00	51	+ 4:51
+ 4.15	61	+ 5:16	+ 4.15	55	+ 5:10	+ 4.15	62	+ 5:17	+ 4.15	62	+ 5:17	+ 4.15	63	+ 5:18	+ 4.15	52	+ 5:07	+ 4.15	50	+ 5:05
+ 4.30	61	+ 5:31	+ 4.30	56	+ 5:26	+ 4.30	62	+ 5:32	+ 4.30	63	+ 5:33	+ 4.30	64	+ 5:34	+ 4.30	53	+ 5:23	+ 4.30	50	+ 5:20
+ 4.45	62	+ 5:47	+ 4.45	56	+ 5:41	+ 4.45	63	+ 5:48	+ 4.45	64	+ 5:49	+ 4.45	65	+ 5:50	+ 4.45	54	+ 5:39	+ 4.45	50	+ 5:35
+ 5.00	62	- 5:58	+ 5.00	57	+ 5:57	+ 5.00	64	- 5:56	+ 5.00	65	- 5:55	+ 5.00	66	- 5:54	+ 5.00	55	+ 5:55	+ 5.00	50	+ 5:50
+ 5.15	62	- 5:43	+ 5.15	57	- 5:48	+ 5.15	64	- 5:41	+ 5.15	68	- 5:37	+ 5.15	67	- 5:38	+ 5.15	55	- 5:50	+ 5.15	49	- 5:56
+ 5.30	62	- 5:28	+ 5.30	57	- 5:33	+ 5.30	65	- 5:25	+ 5.30	71	- 5:19	+ 5.30	68	- 5:22	+ 5.30	56	- 5:34	+ 5.30	49	- 5:41
+ 5.45	62	- 5:13	+ 5.45	57	- 5:18	+ 5.45	65	- 5:10	+ 5.45	74	- 5:01	+ 5.45	69	- 5:06	+ 5.45	57	- 5:18	+ 5.45	48	- 5:27
+ 6.00	63	- 4:57	+ 6.00	57	- 5:03	+ 6.00	66	- 4:54	+ 6.00	76	- 4:44	+ 6.00	70	- 4:50	+ 6.00	58	- 5:02	+ 6.00	48	- 5:12

Table E - Swale and Medway to Ramsgate via Copperas Channel

Time to cover Sectors (in minutes) at 5.0 kts — All times relate to HW Sheerness — **Springs**

Medway (E7–E5) | Ignore for Medway (E4) | Medway (E3–E1) | Swale (E4–E1)

	E7			E6			E5			E4			E3			E2			E1	
	Medway Channel to Spile			Spile to Kentish Flats			Kentish Flats to Copperas			Swale Landfall to Copperas			Copperas to SE Margate			SE Margate to North Foreland			North Foreland to Ramsgate	
Time	*Duration*	*Time at End of Sector*	Time	*Duration*	*Time at End of Sector*	Time	*Duration*	*Time at End of Sector*	Time	*Duration*	*Time at End of Sector*	Time	*Duration*	*Time at End of Sector*	Time	*Duration*	*Time at End of Sector*	Time	*Duration*	*Time at End of Sector*
- 6.00	**66**	**- 4:54**	**- 6.00**	**60**	**- 5:00**	**- 6.00**	**70**	**- 4:50**	**- 6.00**	**78**	**- 4:42**	**- 6.00**	**78**	**- 4:42**	**- 6.00**	**64**	**- 4:56**	**- 6.00**	**42**	**- 5:18**
- 5.45	67	- 4:38	- 5.45	61	- 4:44	- 5.45	71	- 4:34	- 5.45	81	- 4:24	- 5.45	81	- 4:24	- 5.45	66	- 4:39	- 5.45	41	- 5:04
- 5.30	67	- 4:23	- 5.30	62	- 4:28	- 5.30	71	- 4:19	- 5.30	84	- 4:06	- 5.30	84	- 4:06	- 5.30	68	- 4:22	- 5.30	41	- 4:49
- 5.15	68	- 4:07	- 5.15	62	- 4:13	- 5.15	72	- 4:03	- 5.15	87	- 3:48	- 5.15	88	- 3:47	- 5.15	70	- 4:05	- 5.15	41	- 4:34
- 5.00	**69**	**- 3:51**	**- 5.00**	**63**	**- 3:57**	**- 5.00**	**73**	**- 3:47**	**- 5.00**	**90**	**- 3:30**	**- 5.00**	**91**	**- 3:29**	**- 5.00**	**72**	**- 3:48**	**- 5.00**	**41**	**- 4:19**
- 4.45	68	- 3:37	- 4.45	63	- 3:42	- 4.45	74	- 3:31	- 4.45	90	- 3:15	- 4.45	92	- 3:13	- 4.45	73	- 3:32	- 4.45	41	- 4:04
- 4.30	68	- 3:22	- 4.30	63	- 3:27	- 4.30	74	- 3:16	- 4.30	91	- 2:59	- 4.30	93	- 2:57	- 4.30	74	- 3:16	- 4.30	42	- 3:48
- 4.15	68	- 3:07	- 4.15	62	- 3:13	- 4.15	75	- 3:00	- 4.15	91	- 2:44	- 4.15	95	- 2:40	- 4.15	75	- 3:00	- 4.15	44	- 3:31
- 4.00	**67**	**- 2:53**	**- 4.00**	**62**	**- 2:58**	**- 4.00**	**75**	**- 2:45**	**- 4.00**	**92**	**- 2:28**	**- 4.00**	**96**	**- 2:24**	**- 4.00**	**76**	**- 2:44**	**- 4.00**	**46**	**- 3:14**
- 3.45	67	- 2:38	- 3.45	62	- 2:43	- 3.45	75	- 2:30	- 3.45	92	- 2:13	- 3.45	97	- 2:08	- 3.45	76	- 2:29	- 3.45	49	- 2:56
- 3.30	67	- 2:23	- 3.30	61	- 2:29	- 3.30	75	- 2:15	- 3.30	92	- 1:58	- 3.30	98	- 1:52	- 3.30	77	- 2:13	- 3.30	51	- 2:39
- 3.15	67	- 2:08	- 3.15	61	- 2:14	- 3.15	75	- 2:00	- 3.15	92	- 1:43	- 3.15	99	- 1:36	- 3.15	78	- 1:57	- 3.15	56	- 2:19
- 3.00	**66**	**- 1:54**	**- 3.00**	**61**	**- 1:59**	**- 3.00**	**75**	**- 1:45**	**- 3.00**	**92**	**- 1:28**	**- 3.00**	**100**	**- 1:20**	**- 3.00**	**79**	**- 1:41**	**- 3.00**	**62**	**- 1:58**
- 2.45	66	- 1:39	- 2.45	60	- 1:45	- 2.45	75	- 1:30	- 2.45	90	- 1:15	- 2.45	98	- 1:07	- 2.45	78	- 1:27	- 2.45	67	- 1:38
- 2.30	66	- 1:24	- 2.30	60	- 1:30	- 2.30	74	- 1:16	- 2.30	88	- 1:02	- 2.30	96	- 0:54	- 2.30	77	- 1:13	- 2.30	72	- 1:18
- 2.15	65	- 1:10	- 2.15	60	- 1:15	- 2.15	74	- 1:01	- 2.15	86	- 0:49	- 2.15	94	- 0:41	- 2.15	76	- 0:59	- 2.15	77	- 0:58
- 2.00	**65**	**- 0:55**	**- 2.00**	**59**	**- 1:01**	**- 2.00**	**73**	**- 0:47**	**- 2.00**	**84**	**- 0:36**	**- 2.00**	**92**	**- 0:28**	**- 2.00**	**76**	**- 0:44**	**- 2.00**	**82**	**- 0:38**
- 1.45	64	- 0:41	- 1.45	58	- 0:47	- 1.45	72	- 0:33	- 1.45	81	- 0:24	- 1.45	88	- 0:17	- 1.45	73	- 0:32	- 1.45	88	- 0:17
- 1.30	62	- 0:28	- 1.30	57	- 0:33	- 1.30	70	- 0:20	- 1.30	78	- 0:12	- 1.30	84	- 0:06	- 1.30	70	- 0:20	- 1.30	93	+ 0:03
- 1.15	61	- 0:14	- 1.15	56	- 0:19	- 1.15	68	- 0:07	- 1.15	75	HW	- 1.15	80	+ 0:05	- 1.15	67	- 0:08	- 1.15	92	+ 0:17
- 1.00	**60**	**HW**	**- 1.00**	**55**	**- 0:05**	**- 1.00**	**67**	**+ 0:07**	**- 1.00**	**72**	**+ 0:12**	**- 1.00**	**75**	**+ 0:15**	**- 1.00**	**64**	**+ 0:04**	**- 1.00**	**92**	**+ 0:32**
- 0.45	58	+ 0:13	- 0.45	53	+ 0:08	- 0.45	64	+ 0:19	- 0.45	68	+ 0:23	- 0.45	71	+ 0:26	- 0.45	60	+ 0:15	- 0.45	91	+ 0:46
- 0.30	56	+ 0:26	- 0.30	51	+ 0:21	- 0.30	62	+ 0:32	- 0.30	64	+ 0:34	- 0.30	67	+ 0:37	- 0.30	57	+ 0:27	- 0.30	90	+ 1:00
- 0.15	54	+ 0:39	- 0.15	49	+ 0:34	- 0.15	60	+ 0:45	- 0.15	61	+ 0:46	- 0.15	63	+ 0:48	- 0.15	53	+ 0:38	- 0.15	87	+ 1:12
HW	**52**	**+ 0:52**	**HW**	**47**	**+ 0:47**	**HW**	**58**	**+ 0:58**	**HW**	**57**	**+ 0:57**	**HW**	**59**	**+ 0:59**	**HW**	**50**	**+ 0:50**	**HW**	**83**	**+ 1:23**
+ 0.15	51	+ 1:06	+ 0.15	46	+ 1:01	+ 0.15	57	+ 1:12	+ 0.15	55	+ 1:10	+ 0.15	57	+ 1:12	+ 0.15	48	+ 1:03	+ 0.15	79	+ 1:34
+ 0.30	50	+ 1:20	+ 0.30	45	+ 1:15	+ 0.30	55	+ 1:25	+ 0.30	53	+ 1:23	+ 0.30	55	+ 1:25	+ 0.30	47	+ 1:17	+ 0.30	76	+ 1:46
+ 0.45	49	+ 1:34	+ 0.45	44	+ 1:29	+ 0.45	54	+ 1:39	+ 0.45	51	+ 1:36	+ 0.45	53	+ 1:38	+ 0.45	45	+ 1:30	+ 0.45	73	+ 1:58
+ 1.00	**48**	**+ 1:48**	**+ 1.00**	**43**	**+ 1:43**	**+ 1.00**	**53**	**+ 1:53**	**+ 1.00**	**49**	**+ 1:49**	**+ 1.00**	**51**	**+ 1:51**	**+ 1.00**	**43**	**+ 1:43**	**+ 1.00**	**70**	**+ 2:10**
+ 1.15	49	+ 2:04	+ 1.15	44	+ 1:59	+ 1.15	53	+ 2:08	+ 1.15	49	+ 2:04	+ 1.15	51	+ 2:06	+ 1.15	43	+ 1:58	+ 1.15	67	+ 2:22
+ 1.30	49	+ 2:19	+ 1.30	44	+ 2:14	+ 1.30	53	+ 2:23	+ 1.30	49	+ 2:19	+ 1.30	51	+ 2:21	+ 1.30	43	+ 2:13	+ 1.30	64	+ 2:34
+ 1.45	50	+ 2:35	+ 1.45	45	+ 2:30	+ 1.45	53	+ 2:38	+ 1.45	49	+ 2:34	+ 1.45	51	+ 2:36	+ 1.45	43	+ 2:28	+ 1.45	62	+ 2:47
+ 2.00	**51**	**+ 2:51**	**+ 2.00**	**45**	**+ 2:45**	**+ 2.00**	**53**	**+ 2:53**	**+ 2.00**	**49**	**+ 2:49**	**+ 2.00**	**51**	**+ 2:51**	**+ 2.00**	**42**	**+ 2:42**	**+ 2.00**	**59**	**+ 2:59**
+ 2.15	52	+ 3:07	+ 2.15	46	+ 3:01	+ 2.15	54	+ 3:09	+ 2.15	50	+ 3:05	+ 2.15	52	+ 3:07	+ 2.15	43	+ 2:58	+ 2.15	57	+ 3:12
+ 2.30	53	+ 3:23	+ 2.30	47	+ 3:17	+ 2.30	54	+ 3:24	+ 2.30	51	+ 3:21	+ 2.30	53	+ 3:23	+ 2.30	44	+ 3:14	+ 2.30	54	+ 3:24
+ 2.45	54	+ 3:39	+ 2.45	49	+ 3:34	+ 2.45	55	+ 3:40	+ 2.45	52	+ 3:37	+ 2.45	53	+ 3:38	+ 2.45	44	+ 3:29	+ 2.45	53	+ 3:38
+ 3.00	**56**	**+ 3:56**	**+ 3.00**	**50**	**+ 3:50**	**+ 3.00**	**55**	**+ 3:55**	**+ 3.00**	**53**	**+ 3:53**	**+ 3.00**	**54**	**+ 3:54**	**+ 3.00**	**45**	**+ 3:45**	**+ 3.00**	**52**	**+ 3:52**
+ 3.15	57	+ 4:12	+ 3.15	51	+ 4:06	+ 3.15	56	+ 4:11	+ 3.15	54	+ 4:09	+ 3.15	56	+ 4:11	+ 3.15	46	+ 4:01	+ 3.15	51	+ 4:06
+ 3.30	58	+ 4:28	+ 3.30	52	+ 4:22	+ 3.30	57	+ 4:27	+ 3.30	55	+ 4:25	+ 3.30	57	+ 4:27	+ 3.30	47	+ 4:17	+ 3.30	50	+ 4:20
+ 3.45	60	+ 4:45	+ 3.45	54	+ 4:39	+ 3.45	58	+ 4:43	+ 3.45	56	+ 4:41	+ 3.45	58	+ 4:43	+ 3.45	48	+ 4:33	+ 3.45	49	+ 4:34
+ 4.00	**61**	**+ 5:01**	**+ 4.00**	**55**	**+ 4:55**	**+ 4.00**	**59**	**+ 4:59**	**+ 4.00**	**57**	**+ 4:57**	**+ 4.00**	**59**	**+ 4:59**	**+ 4.00**	**49**	**+ 4:49**	**+ 4.00**	**49**	**+ 4:49**
+ 4.15	61	+ 5:16	+ 4.15	56	+ 5:11	+ 4.15	60	+ 5:15	+ 4.15	59	+ 5:14	+ 4.15	60	+ 5:15	+ 4.15	50	+ 5:05	+ 4.15	48	+ 5:03
+ 4.30	62	+ 5:32	+ 4.30	56	+ 5:26	+ 4.30	61	+ 5:31	+ 4.30	61	+ 5:31	+ 4.30	62	+ 5:32	+ 4.30	51	+ 5:21	+ 4.30	47	+ 5:17
+ 4.45	63	+ 5:48	+ 4.45	57	+ 5:42	+ 4.45	62	+ 5:47	+ 4.45	62	+ 5:47	+ 4.45	63	+ 5:48	+ 4.45	52	+ 5:37	+ 4.45	47	+ 5:32
+ 5.00	**63**	**- 5:57**	**+ 5.00**	**58**	**+ 5:58**	**+ 5.00**	**63**	**- 5:57**	**+ 5.00**	**64**	**- 5:56**	**+ 5.00**	**64**	**- 5:56**	**+ 5.00**	**53**	**+ 5:53**	**+ 5.00**	**46**	**+ 5:46**
+ 5.15	64	- 5:41	+ 5.15	58	- 5:47	+ 5.15	64	- 5:41	+ 5.15	67	- 5:38	+ 5.15	66	- 5:39	+ 5.15	54	- 5:51	+ 5.15	45	- 6:00
+ 5.30	64	- 5:26	+ 5.30	58	- 5:32	+ 5.30	65	- 5:25	+ 5.30	71	- 5:19	+ 5.30	67	- 5:23	+ 5.30	55	- 5:35	+ 5.30	44	- 5:46
+ 5.45	64	- 5:11	+ 5.45	58	- 5:17	+ 5.45	66	- 5:09	+ 5.45	74	- 5:01	+ 5.45	68	- 5:07	+ 5.45	56	- 5:19	+ 5.45	43	- 5:32
+ 6.00	**64**	**- 4:56**	**+ 6.00**	**58**	**- 5:02**	**+ 6.00**	**66**	**- 4:54**	**+ 6.00**	**77**	**- 4:43**	**+ 6.00**	**69**	**- 4:51**	**+ 6.00**	**57**	**- 5:03**	**+ 6.00**	**42**	**- 5:18**

EAST BOUND

Table E - Swale and Medway to Ramsgate via Copperas Channel

Neaps — All times relate to HW Sheerness — **Time to cover Sectors (in minutes) at 6.0 kts**

Medway (E7–E5) · Ignore for Medway (E4) · Medway / Swale (E3–E1)

EAST BOUND

	E7			E6			E5			E4			E3			E2			E1	
	Medway Channel to Spile			Spile to Kentish Flats			Kentish Flats to Copperas			Swale Landfall to Copperas			Copperas to SE Margate			SE Margate to North Foreland			North Foreland to Ramsgate	
Time	Duration	Time at End of Sector	Time	Duration	Time at End of Sector	Time	Duration	Time at End of Sector	Time	Duration	Time at End of Sector	Time	Duration	Time at End of Sector	Time	Duration	Time at End of Sector	Time	Duration	Time at End of Sector
- 6.00	**52**	**- 5:08**	**- 6.00**	**48**	**- 5:12**	**- 6.00**	**56**	**- 5:04**	**- 6.00**	**60**	**- 5:00**	**- 6.00**	**62**	**- 4:58**	**- 6.00**	**51**	**- 5:09**	**- 6.00**	**41**	**- 5:19**
- 5.45	53	- 4:52	- 5.45	48	- 4:57	- 5.45	56	- 4:49	- 5.45	61	- 4:44	- 5.45	63	- 4:42	- 5.45	51	- 4:54	- 5.45	40	- 5:05
- 5.30	53	- 4:37	- 5.30	48	- 4:42	- 5.30	57	- 4:33	- 5.30	61	- 4:29	- 5.30	64	- 4:26	- 5.30	52	- 4:38	- 5.30	40	- 4:50
- 5.15	53	- 4:22	- 5.15	49	- 4:26	- 5.15	57	- 4:18	- 5.15	62	- 4:13	- 5.15	64	- 4:11	- 5.15	53	- 4:22	- 5.15	40	- 4:35
- 5.00	**54**	**- 4:06**	**- 5.00**	**49**	**- 4:11**	**- 5.00**	**57**	**- 4:03**	**- 5.00**	**63**	**- 3:57**	**- 5.00**	**65**	**- 3:55**	**- 5.00**	**54**	**- 4:06**	**- 5.00**	**40**	**- 4:20**
- 4.45	54	- 3:51	- 4.45	49	- 3:56	- 4.45	58	- 3:47	- 4.45	64	- 3:41	- 4.45	66	- 3:39	- 4.45	55	- 3:50	- 4.45	40	- 4:05
- 4.30	53	- 3:37	- 4.30	49	- 3:41	- 4.30	58	- 3:32	- 4.30	64	- 3:26	- 4.30	66	- 3:24	- 4.30	55	- 3:35	- 4.30	40	- 3:50
- 4.15	53	- 3:22	- 4.15	49	- 3:26	- 4.15	58	- 3:17	- 4.15	64	- 3:11	- 4.15	67	- 3:08	- 4.15	55	- 3:20	- 4.15	41	- 3:34
- 4.00	**53**	**- 3:07**	**- 4.00**	**49**	**- 3:11**	**- 4.00**	**58**	**- 3:02**	**- 4.00**	**64**	**- 2:56**	**- 4.00**	**67**	**- 2:53**	**- 4.00**	**55**	**- 3:05**	**- 4.00**	**42**	**- 3:18**
- 3.45	53	- 2:52	- 3.45	49	- 2:56	- 3.45	58	- 2:47	- 3.45	64	- 2:41	- 3.45	67	- 2:38	- 3.45	56	- 2:49	- 3.45	43	- 3:02
- 3.30	53	- 2:37	- 3.30	48	- 2:42	- 3.30	58	- 2:32	- 3.30	65	- 2:25	- 3.30	68	- 2:22	- 3.30	56	- 2:34	- 3.30	44	- 2:46
- 3.15	53	- 2:22	- 3.15	48	- 2:27	- 3.15	58	- 2:17	- 3.15	65	- 2:10	- 3.15	68	- 2:07	- 3.15	57	- 2:18	- 3.15	46	- 2:29
- 3.00	**52**	**- 2:08**	**- 3.00**	**48**	**- 2:12**	**- 3.00**	**58**	**- 2:02**	**- 3.00**	**65**	**- 1:55**	**- 3.00**	**69**	**- 1:51**	**- 3.00**	**57**	**- 2:03**	**- 3.00**	**48**	**- 2:12**
- 2.45	52	- 1:53	- 2.45	48	- 1:57	- 2.45	58	- 1:47	- 2.45	64	- 1:41	- 2.45	68	- 1:37	- 2.45	57	- 1:48	- 2.45	50	- 1:55
- 2.30	52	- 1:38	- 2.30	48	- 1:42	- 2.30	58	- 1:32	- 2.30	64	- 1:26	- 2.30	68	- 1:22	- 2.30	57	- 1:33	- 2.30	52	- 1:38
- 2.15	52	- 1:23	- 2.15	48	- 1:27	- 2.15	57	- 1:18	- 2.15	64	- 1:11	- 2.15	67	- 1:08	- 2.15	56	- 1:19	- 2.15	53	- 1:22
- 2.00	**52**	**- 1:08**	**- 2.00**	**48**	**- 1:12**	**- 2.00**	**57**	**- 1:03**	**- 2.00**	**63**	**- 0:57**	**- 2.00**	**67**	**- 0:53**	**- 2.00**	**56**	**- 1:04**	**- 2.00**	**54**	**- 1:06**
- 1.45	52	- 0:53	- 1.45	47	- 0:58	- 1.45	56	- 0:49	- 1.45	62	- 0:43	- 1.45	66	- 0:39	- 1.45	55	- 0:50	- 1.45	55	- 0:50
- 1.30	51	- 0:39	- 1.30	47	- 0:43	- 1.30	56	- 0:34	- 1.30	61	- 0:29	- 1.30	64	- 0:26	- 1.30	54	- 0:36	- 1.30	56	- 0:34
- 1.15	51	- 0:24	- 1.15	47	- 0:28	- 1.15	55	- 0:20	- 1.15	60	- 0:15	- 1.15	63	- 0:12	- 1.15	52	- 0:23	- 1.15	56	- 0:19
- 1.00	**50**	**- 0:10**	**- 1.00**	**46**	**- 0:14**	**- 1.00**	**54**	**- 0:06**	**- 1.00**	**58**	**- 0:02**	**- 1.00**	**61**	**+ 0:01**	**- 1.00**	**51**	**- 0:09**	**- 1.00**	**56**	**- 0:04**
- 0.45	49	+ 0:04	- 0.45	45	HW	- 0.45	53	+ 0:08	- 0.45	57	+ 0:12	- 0.45	59	+ 0:14	- 0.45	50	+ 0:05	- 0.45	56	+ 0:11
- 0.30	49	+ 0:19	- 0.30	44	+ 0:14	- 0.30	52	+ 0:22	- 0.30	55	+ 0:25	- 0.30	57	+ 0:27	- 0.30	48	+ 0:18	- 0.30	56	+ 0:26
- 0.15	48	+ 0:33	- 0.15	43	+ 0:28	- 0.15	52	+ 0:37	- 0.15	53	+ 0:38	- 0.15	55	+ 0:40	- 0.15	47	+ 0:32	- 0.15	56	+ 0:41
HW	**47**	**+ 0:47**	**HW**	**43**	**+ 0:43**	**HW**	**51**	**+ 0:51**	**HW**	**52**	**+ 0:52**	**HW**	**54**	**+ 0:54**	**HW**	**45**	**+ 0:45**	**HW**	**55**	**+ 0:55**
+ 0.15	46	+ 1:01	+ 0.15	42	+ 0:57	+ 0.15	50	+ 1:05	+ 0.15	51	+ 1:06	+ 0.15	52	+ 1:07	+ 0.15	44	+ 0:59	+ 0.15	55	+ 1:10
+ 0.30	45	+ 1:15	+ 0.30	41	+ 1:11	+ 0.30	49	+ 1:19	+ 0.30	50	+ 1:20	+ 0.30	51	+ 1:21	+ 0.30	43	+ 1:13	+ 0.30	55	+ 1:25
+ 0.45	45	+ 1:30	+ 0.45	41	+ 1:26	+ 0.45	49	+ 1:34	+ 0.45	49	+ 1:34	+ 0.45	50	+ 1:35	+ 0.45	42	+ 1:27	+ 0.45	54	+ 1:39
+ 1.00	**44**	**+ 1:44**	**+ 1.00**	**40**	**+ 1:40**	**+ 1.00**	**48**	**+ 1:48**	**+ 1.00**	**48**	**+ 1:48**	**+ 1.00**	**49**	**+ 1:49**	**+ 1.00**	**41**	**+ 1:41**	**+ 1.00**	**52**	**+ 1:52**
+ 1.15	45	+ 2:00	+ 1.15	40	+ 1:55	+ 1.15	48	+ 2:03	+ 1.15	48	+ 2:03	+ 1.15	49	+ 2:04	+ 1.15	41	+ 1:56	+ 1.15	51	+ 2:06
+ 1.30	45	+ 2:15	+ 1.30	40	+ 2:10	+ 1.30	48	+ 2:18	+ 1.30	47	+ 2:17	+ 1.30	49	+ 2:19	+ 1.30	41	+ 2:11	+ 1.30	50	+ 2:20
+ 1.45	45	+ 2:30	+ 1.45	41	+ 2:26	+ 1.45	48	+ 2:33	+ 1.45	47	+ 2:32	+ 1.45	49	+ 2:34	+ 1.45	41	+ 2:26	+ 1.45	49	+ 2:34
+ 2.00	**45**	**+ 2:45**	**+ 2.00**	**41**	**+ 2:41**	**+ 2.00**	**48**	**+ 2:48**	**+ 2.00**	**47**	**+ 2:47**	**+ 2.00**	**49**	**+ 2:49**	**+ 2.00**	**40**	**+ 2:40**	**+ 2.00**	**48**	**+ 2:48**
+ 2.15	46	+ 3:01	+ 2.15	41	+ 2:56	+ 2.15	48	+ 3:03	+ 2.15	48	+ 3:03	+ 2.15	49	+ 3:04	+ 2.15	41	+ 2:56	+ 2.15	48	+ 3:03
+ 2.30	46	+ 3:16	+ 2.30	42	+ 3:12	+ 2.30	49	+ 3:19	+ 2.30	48	+ 3:18	+ 2.30	50	+ 3:20	+ 2.30	41	+ 3:11	+ 2.30	47	+ 3:17
+ 2.45	47	+ 3:32	+ 2.45	42	+ 3:27	+ 2.45	49	+ 3:34	+ 2.45	48	+ 3:33	+ 2.45	50	+ 3:35	+ 2.45	42	+ 3:27	+ 2.45	46	+ 3:31
+ 3.00	**48**	**+ 3:48**	**+ 3.00**	**43**	**+ 3:43**	**+ 3.00**	**49**	**+ 3:49**	**+ 3.00**	**49**	**+ 3:49**	**+ 3.00**	**51**	**+ 3:51**	**+ 3.00**	**42**	**+ 3:42**	**+ 3.00**	**45**	**+ 3:45**
+ 3.15	48	+ 4:03	+ 3.15	44	+ 3:59	+ 3.15	50	+ 4:05	+ 3.15	49	+ 4:04	+ 3.15	51	+ 4:06	+ 3.15	42	+ 3:57	+ 3.15	45	+ 4:00
+ 3.30	49	+ 4:19	+ 3.30	44	+ 4:14	+ 3.30	50	+ 4:20	+ 3.30	50	+ 4:20	+ 3.30	52	+ 4:22	+ 3.30	43	+ 4:13	+ 3.30	44	+ 4:14
+ 3.45	49	+ 4:34	+ 3.45	45	+ 4:30	+ 3.45	51	+ 4:36	+ 3.45	50	+ 4:35	+ 3.45	52	+ 4:37	+ 3.45	43	+ 4:28	+ 3.45	44	+ 4:29
+ 4.00	**50**	**+ 4:50**	**+ 4.00**	**45**	**+ 4:45**	**+ 4.00**	**51**	**+ 4:51**	**+ 4.00**	**51**	**+ 4:51**	**+ 4.00**	**53**	**+ 4:53**	**+ 4.00**	**44**	**+ 4:44**	**+ 4.00**	**43**	**+ 4:43**
+ 4.15	50	+ 5:05	+ 4.15	46	+ 5:01	+ 4.15	51	+ 5:06	+ 4.15	52	+ 5:07	+ 4.15	53	+ 5:08	+ 4.15	44	+ 4:59	+ 4.15	43	+ 4:58
+ 4.30	51	+ 5:21	+ 4.30	46	+ 5:16	+ 4.30	52	+ 5:22	+ 4.30	53	+ 5:23	+ 4.30	54	+ 5:24	+ 4.30	45	+ 5:15	+ 4.30	42	+ 5:12
+ 4.45	51	+ 5:36	+ 4.45	46	+ 5:31	+ 4.45	52	+ 5:37	+ 4.45	53	+ 5:38	+ 4.45	55	+ 5:40	+ 4.45	45	+ 5:30	+ 4.45	42	+ 5:27
+ 5.00	**52**	**+ 5:52**	**+ 5.00**	**47**	**+ 5:47**	**+ 5.00**	**53**	**+ 5:53**	**+ 5.00**	**54**	**+ 5:54**	**+ 5.00**	**55**	**+ 5:55**	**+ 5.00**	**46**	**+ 5:46**	**+ 5.00**	**42**	**+ 5:42**
+ 5.15	52	- 5:53	+ 5.15	47	- 5:58	+ 5.15	53	- 5:52	+ 5.15	55	- 5:50	+ 5.15	54	- 5:51	+ 5.15	46	- 5:59	+ 5.15	42	+ 5:57
+ 5.30	52	- 5:38	+ 5.30	47	- 5:43	+ 5.30	54	- 5:36	+ 5.30	55	- 5:35	+ 5.30	53	- 5:37	+ 5.30	47	- 5:43	+ 5.30	42	- 5:48
+ 5.45	52	- 5:23	+ 5.45	47	- 5:28	+ 5.45	54	- 5:21	+ 5.45	56	- 5:19	+ 5.45	52	- 5:23	+ 5.45	47	- 5:28	+ 5.45	41	- 5:34
+ 6.00	**52**	**- 5:08**	**+ 6.00**	**47**	**- 5:13**	**+ 6.00**	**54**	**- 5:06**	**+ 6.00**	**57**	**- 5:03**	**+ 6.00**	**51**	**- 5:09**	**+ 6.00**	**48**	**- 5:12**	**+ 6.00**	**41**	**- 5:19**

E - 6 Kts — Table E - Swale and Medway to Ramsgate via Copperas Channel — 6 Kts - E

Time to cover Sectors (in minutes) at 6.0 kts — All times relate to HW Sheerness — **Springs**

EAST BOUND

Medway (E7, E6, E5) · Ignore for Medway (E4) · Swale (E4, E3, E2, E1) · Medway (E2, E1)

E7 — Medway Channel to Spile

Time	Duration	Time at End of Sector
-6.00	54	-5:06
-5.45	54	-4:51
-5.30	55	-4:35
-5.15	55	-4:20
-5.00	56	-4:04
-4.45	56	-3:49
-4.30	56	-3:34
-4.15	55	-3:20
-4.00	55	-3:05
-3.45	55	-2:50
-3.30	55	-2:35
-3.15	54	-2:21
-3.00	54	-2:06
-2.45	54	-1:51
-2.30	54	-1:36
-2.15	54	-1:21
-2.00	53	-1:07
-1.45	53	-0:52
-1.30	52	-0:38
-1.15	51	-0:24
-1.00	50	-0:10
-0.45	49	+0:04
-0.30	48	+0:18
-0.15	46	+0:31
HW	45	+0:45
+0.15	44	+0:59
+0.30	43	+1:13
+0.45	42	+1:27
+1.00	41	+1:41
+1.15	42	+1:57
+1.30	42	+2:12
+1.45	43	+2:28
+2.00	43	+2:43
+2.15	44	+2:59
+2.30	45	+3:15
+2.45	46	+3:31
+3.00	46	+3:46
+3.15	47	+4:02
+3.30	48	+4:18
+3.45	49	+4:34
+4.00	50	+4:50
+4.15	51	+5:06
+4.30	51	+5:21
+4.45	52	+5:37
+5.00	52	+5:52
+5.15	52	-5:53
+5.30	52	-5:38
+5.45	52	-5:23
+6.00	53	-5:07

E6 — Spile to Kentish Flats

Time	Duration	Time at End of Sector
-6.00	49	-5:11
-5.45	50	-4:55
-5.30	50	-4:40
-5.15	51	-4:24
-5.00	51	-4:09
-4.45	51	-3:54
-4.30	51	-3:39
-4.15	51	-3:24
-4.00	51	-3:09
-3.45	50	-2:55
-3.30	50	-2:40
-3.15	50	-2:25
-3.00	50	-2:10
-2.45	50	-1:55
-2.30	49	-1:41
-2.15	49	-1:26
-2.00	49	-1:11
-1.45	48	-0:57
-1.30	48	-0:42
-1.15	47	-0:28
-1.00	46	-0:14
-0.45	45	HW
-0.30	44	+0:14
-0.15	42	+0:27
HW	41	+0:41
+0.15	40	+0:55
+0.30	39	+1:09
+0.45	38	+1:23
+1.00	37	+1:37
+1.15	38	+1:53
+1.30	38	+2:08
+1.45	38	+2:23
+2.00	38	+2:38
+2.15	39	+2:54
+2.30	40	+3:10
+2.45	41	+3:26
+3.00	42	+3:42
+3.15	43	+3:58
+3.30	43	+4:13
+3.45	44	+4:29
+4.00	45	+4:45
+4.15	46	+5:01
+4.30	46	+5:16
+4.45	47	+5:32
+5.00	48	+5:48
+5.15	48	-5:57
+5.30	48	-5:42
+5.45	48	-5:27
+6.00	48	-5:12

E5 — Kentish Flats to Copperas

Time	Duration	Time at End of Sector
-6.00	57	-5:03
-5.45	58	-4:47
-5.30	58	-4:32
-5.15	59	-4:16
-5.00	59	-4:01
-4.45	60	-3:45
-4.30	60	-3:30
-4.15	61	-3:14
-4.00	61	-2:59
-3.45	61	-2:44
-3.30	61	-2:29
-3.15	61	-2:14
-3.00	61	-1:59
-2.45	61	-1:44
-2.30	60	-1:30
-2.15	60	-1:15
-2.00	60	-1:00
-1.45	59	-0:46
-1.30	58	-0:32
-1.15	57	-0:18
-1.00	56	-0:04
-0.45	54	+0:09
-0.30	53	+0:23
-0.15	51	+0:36
HW	50	+0:50
+0.15	49	+1:04
+0.30	48	+1:18
+0.45	47	+1:32
+1.00	46	+1:46
+1.15	46	+2:01
+1.30	46	+2:16
+1.45	45	+2:30
+2.00	45	+2:45
+2.15	46	+3:01
+2.30	46	+3:16
+2.45	47	+3:32
+3.00	47	+3:47
+3.15	48	+4:03
+3.30	48	+4:18
+3.45	49	+4:34
+4.00	49	+4:49
+4.15	50	+5:05
+4.30	51	+5:21
+4.45	52	+5:37
+5.00	52	+5:52
+5.15	53	-5:52
+5.30	54	-5:36
+5.45	54	-5:21
+6.00	55	-5:05

E4 — Swale Landfall to Copperas

Time	Duration	Time at End of Sector
-6.00	62	-4:58
-5.45	64	-4:41
-5.30	65	-4:25
-5.15	67	-4:08
-5.00	69	-3:51
-4.45	69	-3:36
-4.30	69	-3:21
-4.15	70	-3:05
-4.00	70	-2:50
-3.45	70	-2:35
-3.30	70	-2:20
-3.15	70	-2:05
-3.00	70	-1:50
-2.45	70	-1:35
-2.30	69	-1:21
-2.15	69	-1:06
-2.00	68	-0:52
-1.45	66	-0:39
-1.30	64	-0:26
-1.15	62	-0:13
-1.00	60	HW
-0.45	58	+0:13
-0.30	55	+0:25
-0.15	52	+0:37
HW	50	+0:50
+0.15	48	+1:03
+0.30	47	+1:17
+0.45	45	+1:30
+1.00	44	+1:44
+1.15	44	+1:59
+1.30	43	+2:13
+1.45	43	+2:28
+2.00	43	+2:43
+2.15	44	+2:59
+2.30	44	+3:14
+2.45	45	+3:30
+3.00	45	+3:45
+3.15	46	+4:01
+3.30	47	+4:17
+3.45	48	+4:33
+4.00	49	+4:49
+4.15	50	+5:05
+4.30	51	+5:21
+4.45	52	+5:37
+5.00	53	+5:53
+5.15	54	-5:51
+5.30	55	-5:35
+5.45	56	-5:19
+6.00	57	-5:03

E3 — Copperas to SE Margate

Time	Duration	Time at End of Sector
-6.00	63	-4:57
-5.45	65	-4:40
-5.30	66	-4:24
-5.15	68	-4:07
-5.00	70	-3:50
-4.45	70	-3:35
-4.30	71	-3:19
-4.15	72	-3:03
-4.00	73	-2:47
-3.45	73	-2:32
-3.30	74	-2:16
-3.15	74	-2:01
-3.00	75	-1:45
-2.45	74	-1:31
-2.30	74	-1:16
-2.15	73	-1:02
-2.00	73	-0:47
-1.45	70	-0:35
-1.30	68	-0:22
-1.15	65	-0:10
-1.00	63	+0:03
-0.45	60	+0:15
-0.30	57	+0:27
-0.15	54	+0:39
HW	51	+0:51
+0.15	50	+1:05
+0.30	48	+1:18
+0.45	47	+1:32
+1.00	45	+1:45
+1.15	45	+2:00
+1.30	45	+2:15
+1.45	45	+2:30
+2.00	45	+2:45
+2.15	45	+3:00
+2.30	46	+3:16
+2.45	46	+3:31
+3.00	47	+3:47
+3.15	48	+4:03
+3.30	49	+4:19
+3.45	49	+4:34
+4.00	50	+4:50
+4.15	51	+5:06
+4.30	52	+5:22
+4.45	53	+5:38
+5.00	54	+5:54
+5.15	53	-5:52
+5.30	52	-5:38
+5.45	52	-5:23
+6.00	51	-5:09

E2 — SE Margate to North Foreland

Time	Duration	Time at End of Sector
-6.00	51	-5:09
-5.45	53	-4:52
-5.30	55	-4:35
-5.15	56	-4:19
-5.00	58	-4:02
-4.45	58	-3:47
-4.30	59	-3:31
-4.15	60	-3:15
-4.00	60	-3:00
-3.45	61	-2:44
-3.30	61	-2:29
-3.15	62	-2:13
-3.00	62	-1:58
-2.45	62	-1:43
-2.30	62	-1:28
-2.15	61	-1:14
-2.00	61	-0:59
-1.45	59	-0:46
-1.30	57	-0:33
-1.15	55	-0:20
-1.00	53	-0:07
-0.45	51	+0:06
-0.30	48	+0:18
-0.15	46	+0:31
HW	44	+0:44
+0.15	42	+0:57
+0.30	41	+1:11
+0.45	39	+1:24
+1.00	38	+1:38
+1.15	38	+1:53
+1.30	38	+2:08
+1.45	37	+2:22
+2.00	37	+2:37
+2.15	38	+2:53
+2.30	38	+3:08
+2.45	38	+3:23
+3.00	39	+3:39
+3.15	39	+3:54
+3.30	40	+4:10
+3.45	41	+4:26
+4.00	42	+4:42
+4.15	42	+4:57
+4.30	43	+5:13
+4.45	44	+5:29
+5.00	44	+5:44
+5.15	45	-6:00
+5.30	46	-5:44
+5.45	47	-5:28
+6.00	47	-5:13

E1 — North Foreland to Ramsgate

Time	Duration	Time at End of Sector
-6.00	37	-5:23
-5.45	37	-5:08
-5.30	36	-4:54
-5.15	36	-4:39
-5.00	36	-4:24
-4.45	36	-4:09
-4.30	36	-3:54
-4.15	38	-3:37
-4.00	39	-3:21
-3.45	40	-3:05
-3.30	42	-2:48
-3.15	45	-2:30
-3.00	49	-2:11
-2.45	53	-1:52
-2.30	56	-1:34
-2.15	59	-1:16
-2.00	61	-0:59
-1.45	63	-0:42
-1.30	65	-0:25
-1.15	65	-0:10
-1.00	65	+0:05
-0.45	65	+0:20
-0.30	65	+0:35
-0.15	64	+0:49
HW	63	+1:03
+0.15	62	+1:17
+0.30	61	+1:31
+0.45	59	+1:44
+1.00	57	+1:57
+1.15	55	+2:10
+1.30	53	+2:23
+1.45	51	+2:36
+2.00	50	+2:50
+2.15	48	+3:03
+2.30	46	+3:16
+2.45	45	+3:30
+3.00	44	+3:44
+3.15	43	+3:58
+3.30	43	+4:13
+3.45	42	+4:27
+4.00	42	+4:42
+4.15	42	+4:57
+4.30	41	+5:11
+4.45	41	+5:26
+5.00	40	+5:40
+5.15	39	+5:54
+5.30	39	-5:51
+5.45	38	-5:37
+6.00	37	-5:23

Table E - Swale and Medway to Ramsgate via Copperas Channel

Neaps — All times relate to HW Sheerness — **Time to cover Sectors (in minutes) at 7.0 kts**

Medway (E7–E5) | Ignore for Medway (E4) | Medway (E3–E1) | Swale (E4–E1)

EASTBOUND

Time	E7 Medway Channel to Spile: Duration	E7 Time at End of Sector	Time	E6 Spile to Kentish Flats: Duration	E6 Time at End of Sector	Time	E5 Kentish Flats to Copperas: Duration	E5 Time at End of Sector	Time	E4 Swale Landfall to Copperas: Duration	E4 Time at End of Sector	Time	E3 Copperas to SE Margate: Duration	E3 Time at End of Sector	Time	E2 SE Margate to North Foreland: Duration	E2 Time at End of Sector	Time	E1 North Foreland to Ramsgate: Duration	E1 Time at End of Sector
- 6.00	**44**	**- 5:16**	**- 6.00**	**40**	**- 5:20**	**- 6.00**	**47**	**- 5:13**	**- 6.00**	**50**	**- 5:10**	**- 6.00**	**52**	**- 5:08**	**- 6.00**	**43**	**- 5:17**	**- 6.00**	**36**	**- 5:24**
- 5.45	45	- 5:00	- 5.45	41	- 5:04	- 5.45	48	- 4:57	- 5.45	51	- 4:54	- 5.45	53	- 4:52	- 5.45	44	- 5:01	- 5.45	35	- 5:10
- 5.30	45	- 4:45	- 5.30	41	- 4:49	- 5.30	48	- 4:42	- 5.30	52	- 4:38	- 5.30	53	- 4:37	- 5.30	44	- 4:46	- 5.30	35	- 4:55
- 5.15	45	- 4:30	- 5.15	41	- 4:34	- 5.15	48	- 4:27	- 5.15	52	- 4:23	- 5.15	54	- 4:21	- 5.15	45	- 4:30	- 5.15	35	- 4:40
- 5.00	**45**	**- 4:15**	**- 5.00**	**42**	**- 4:18**	**- 5.00**	**49**	**- 4:11**	**- 5.00**	**53**	**- 4:07**	**- 5.00**	**55**	**- 4:05**	**- 5.00**	**46**	**- 4:14**	**- 5.00**	**35**	**- 4:25**
- 4.45	45	- 4:00	- 4.45	41	- 4:04	- 4.45	49	- 3:56	- 4.45	53	- 3:52	- 4.45	55	- 3:50	- 4.45	46	- 3:59	- 4.45	35	- 4:10
- 4.30	45	- 3:45	- 4.30	41	- 3:49	- 4.30	49	- 3:41	- 4.30	54	- 3:36	- 4.30	56	- 3:34	- 4.30	46	- 3:44	- 4.30	35	- 3:55
- 4.15	45	- 3:30	- 4.15	41	- 3:34	- 4.15	49	- 3:26	- 4.15	54	- 3:21	- 4.15	56	- 3:19	- 4.15	47	- 3:28	- 4.15	36	- 3:39
- 4.00	**45**	**- 3:15**	**- 4.00**	**41**	**- 3:19**	**- 4.00**	**49**	**- 3:11**	**- 4.00**	**55**	**- 3:05**	**- 4.00**	**56**	**- 3:04**	**- 4.00**	**47**	**- 3:13**	**- 4.00**	**36**	**- 3:24**
- 3.45	45	- 3:00	- 3.45	41	- 3:04	- 3.45	49	- 2:56	- 3.45	55	- 2:50	- 3.45	56	- 2:49	- 3.45	47	- 2:58	- 3.45	37	- 3:08
- 3.30	45	- 2:45	- 3.30	41	- 2:49	- 3.30	49	- 2:41	- 3.30	55	- 2:35	- 3.30	57	- 2:33	- 3.30	47	- 2:43	- 3.30	38	- 2:52
- 3.15	45	- 2:30	- 3.15	41	- 2:34	- 3.15	49	- 2:26	- 3.15	55	- 2:20	- 3.15	57	- 2:18	- 3.15	48	- 2:27	- 3.15	39	- 2:36
- 3.00	**45**	**- 2:15**	**- 3.00**	**41**	**- 2:19**	**- 3.00**	**49**	**- 2:11**	**- 3.00**	**55**	**- 2:05**	**- 3.00**	**57**	**- 2:03**	**- 3.00**	**48**	**- 2:12**	**- 3.00**	**41**	**- 2:19**
- 2.45	45	- 2:00	- 2.45	41	- 2:04	- 2.45	49	- 1:56	- 2.45	54	- 1:51	- 2.45	57	- 1:48	- 2.45	48	- 1:57	- 2.45	42	- 2:03
- 2.30	45	- 1:45	- 2.30	41	- 1:49	- 2.30	49	- 1:41	- 2.30	54	- 1:36	- 2.30	57	- 1:33	- 2.30	48	- 1:42	- 2.30	44	- 1:46
- 2.15	45	- 1:30	- 2.15	41	- 1:34	- 2.15	49	- 1:26	- 2.15	54	- 1:21	- 2.15	57	- 1:18	- 2.15	48	- 1:27	- 2.15	44	- 1:31
- 2.00	**45**	**- 1:15**	**- 2.00**	**41**	**- 1:19**	**- 2.00**	**49**	**- 1:11**	**- 2.00**	**54**	**- 1:06**	**- 2.00**	**57**	**- 1:03**	**- 2.00**	**47**	**- 1:13**	**- 2.00**	**45**	**- 1:15**
- 1.45	44	- 1:01	- 1.45	40	- 1:05	- 1.45	48	- 0:57	- 1.45	53	- 0:52	- 1.45	55	- 0:50	- 1.45	47	- 0:58	- 1.45	46	- 0:59
- 1.30	44	- 0:46	- 1.30	40	- 0:50	- 1.30	48	- 0:42	- 1.30	52	- 0:38	- 1.30	54	- 0:36	- 1.30	46	- 0:44	- 1.30	47	- 0:43
- 1.15	44	- 0:31	- 1.15	40	- 0:35	- 1.15	47	- 0:28	- 1.15	51	- 0:24	- 1.15	53	- 0:22	- 1.15	45	- 0:30	- 1.15	47	- 0:28
- 1.00	**43**	**- 0:17**	**- 1.00**	**40**	**- 0:20**	**- 1.00**	**46**	**- 0:14**	**- 1.00**	**50**	**- 0:10**	**- 1.00**	**52**	**- 0:08**	**- 1.00**	**44**	**- 0:16**	**- 1.00**	**47**	**- 0:13**
- 0.45	43	- 0:02	- 0.45	39	- 0:06	- 0.45	46	+ 0:01	- 0.45	49	+ 0:04	- 0.45	51	+ 0:06	- 0.45	43	- 0:02	- 0.45	47	+ 0:02
- 0.30	42	+ 0:12	- 0.30	38	+ 0:08	- 0.30	45	+ 0:15	- 0.30	47	+ 0:17	- 0.30	50	+ 0:20	- 0.30	42	+ 0:12	- 0.30	47	+ 0:17
- 0.15	41	+ 0:26	- 0.15	38	+ 0:23	- 0.15	45	+ 0:30	- 0.15	46	+ 0:31	- 0.15	48	+ 0:33	- 0.15	40	+ 0:25	- 0.15	47	+ 0:32
HW	**41**	**+ 0:41**	**HW**	**37**	**+ 0:37**	**HW**	**44**	**+ 0:44**	**HW**	**45**	**+ 0:45**	**HW**	**47**	**+ 0:47**	**HW**	**39**	**+ 0:39**	**HW**	**46**	**+ 0:46**
+ 0.15	40	+ 0:55	+ 0.15	37	+ 0:52	+ 0.15	43	+ 0:58	+ 0.15	44	+ 0:59	+ 0.15	46	+ 1:01	+ 0.15	38	+ 0:53	+ 0.15	46	+ 1:01
+ 0.30	40	+ 1:10	+ 0.30	36	+ 1:06	+ 0.30	43	+ 1:13	+ 0.30	43	+ 1:13	+ 0.30	45	+ 1:15	+ 0.30	38	+ 1:08	+ 0.30	46	+ 1:16
+ 0.45	39	+ 1:24	+ 0.45	36	+ 1:21	+ 0.45	42	+ 1:27	+ 0.45	43	+ 1:28	+ 0.45	44	+ 1:29	+ 0.45	37	+ 1:22	+ 0.45	45	+ 1:30
+ 1.00	**39**	**+ 1:39**	**+ 1.00**	**35**	**+ 1:35**	**+ 1.00**	**42**	**+ 1:42**	**+ 1.00**	**42**	**+ 1:42**	**+ 1.00**	**43**	**+ 1:43**	**+ 1.00**	**36**	**+ 1:36**	**+ 1.00**	**45**	**+ 1:45**
+ 1.15	39	+ 1:54	+ 1.15	35	+ 1:50	+ 1.15	42	+ 1:57	+ 1.15	42	+ 1:57	+ 1.15	43	+ 1:58	+ 1.15	36	+ 1:51	+ 1.15	44	+ 1:59
+ 1.30	39	+ 2:09	+ 1.30	35	+ 2:05	+ 1.30	42	+ 2:12	+ 1.30	42	+ 2:12	+ 1.30	43	+ 2:13	+ 1.30	36	+ 2:06	+ 1.30	43	+ 2:13
+ 1.45	39	+ 2:24	+ 1.45	35	+ 2:20	+ 1.45	42	+ 2:27	+ 1.45	42	+ 2:27	+ 1.45	43	+ 2:28	+ 1.45	35	+ 2:20	+ 1.45	42	+ 2:27
+ 2.00	**39**	**+ 2:39**	**+ 2.00**	**35**	**+ 2:35**	**+ 2.00**	**42**	**+ 2:42**	**+ 2.00**	**41**	**+ 2:41**	**+ 2.00**	**43**	**+ 2:43**	**+ 2.00**	**35**	**+ 2:35**	**+ 2.00**	**42**	**+ 2:42**
+ 2.15	39	+ 2:54	+ 2.15	36	+ 2:51	+ 2.15	42	+ 2:57	+ 2.15	42	+ 2:57	+ 2.15	43	+ 2:58	+ 2.15	36	+ 2:51	+ 2.15	41	+ 2:56
+ 2.30	40	+ 3:10	+ 2.30	36	+ 3:06	+ 2.30	42	+ 3:12	+ 2.30	42	+ 3:12	+ 2.30	43	+ 3:13	+ 2.30	36	+ 3:06	+ 2.30	40	+ 3:10
+ 2.45	40	+ 3:25	+ 2.45	36	+ 3:21	+ 2.45	42	+ 3:27	+ 2.45	42	+ 3:27	+ 2.45	44	+ 3:29	+ 2.45	36	+ 3:21	+ 2.45	40	+ 3:25
+ 3.00	**41**	**+ 3:41**	**+ 3.00**	**37**	**+ 3:37**	**+ 3.00**	**43**	**+ 3:43**	**+ 3.00**	**42**	**+ 3:42**	**+ 3.00**	**44**	**+ 3:44**	**+ 3.00**	**36**	**+ 3:36**	**+ 3.00**	**39**	**+ 3:39**
+ 3.15	41	+ 3:56	+ 3.15	37	+ 3:52	+ 3.15	43	+ 3:58	+ 3.15	43	+ 3:58	+ 3.15	44	+ 3:59	+ 3.15	37	+ 3:52	+ 3.15	39	+ 3:54
+ 3.30	42	+ 4:12	+ 3.30	38	+ 4:08	+ 3.30	43	+ 4:13	+ 3.30	43	+ 4:13	+ 3.30	45	+ 4:15	+ 3.30	37	+ 4:07	+ 3.30	38	+ 4:08
+ 3.45	42	+ 4:27	+ 3.45	38	+ 4:23	+ 3.45	43	+ 4:28	+ 3.45	44	+ 4:29	+ 3.45	45	+ 4:30	+ 3.45	37	+ 4:22	+ 3.45	38	+ 4:23
+ 4.00	**43**	**+ 4:43**	**+ 4.00**	**39**	**+ 4:39**	**+ 4.00**	**44**	**+ 4:44**	**+ 4.00**	**44**	**+ 4:44**	**+ 4.00**	**46**	**+ 4:46**	**+ 4.00**	**38**	**+ 4:38**	**+ 4.00**	**38**	**+ 4:38**
+ 4.15	43	+ 4:58	+ 4.15	39	+ 4:54	+ 4.15	44	+ 4:59	+ 4.15	45	+ 5:00	+ 4.15	46	+ 5:01	+ 4.15	38	+ 4:53	+ 4.15	37	+ 4:52
+ 4.30	43	+ 5:13	+ 4.30	39	+ 5:09	+ 4.30	44	+ 5:14	+ 4.30	45	+ 5:15	+ 4.30	47	+ 5:17	+ 4.30	38	+ 5:08	+ 4.30	37	+ 5:07
+ 4.45	44	+ 5:29	+ 4.45	40	+ 5:25	+ 4.45	45	+ 5:30	+ 4.45	46	+ 5:31	+ 4.45	47	+ 5:32	+ 4.45	39	+ 5:24	+ 4.45	37	+ 5:22
+ 5.00	**44**	**+ 5:44**	**+ 5.00**	**40**	**+ 5:40**	**+ 5.00**	**45**	**+ 5:45**	**+ 5.00**	**46**	**+ 5:46**	**+ 5.00**	**47**	**+ 5:47**	**+ 5.00**	**39**	**+ 5:39**	**+ 5.00**	**37**	**+ 5:37**
+ 5.15	44	+ 5:59	+ 5.15	40	+ 5:55	+ 5.15	45	- 6:00	+ 5.15	47	- 5:58	+ 5.15	48	- 5:57	+ 5.15	39	+ 5:54	+ 5.15	37	+ 5:52
+ 5.30	44	- 5:46	+ 5.30	40	- 5:50	+ 5.30	46	- 5:44	+ 5.30	47	- 5:43	+ 5.30	48	- 5:42	+ 5.30	40	- 5:50	+ 5.30	37	- 5:53
+ 5.45	44	- 5:31	+ 5.45	40	- 5:35	+ 5.45	46	- 5:29	+ 5.45	48	- 5:27	+ 5.45	49	- 5:26	+ 5.45	40	- 5:35	+ 5.45	36	- 5:39
+ 6.00	**44**	**- 5:16**	**+ 6.00**	**40**	**- 5:20**	**+ 6.00**	**46**	**- 5:14**	**+ 6.00**	**48**	**- 5:12**	**+ 6.00**	**49**	**- 5:11**	**+ 6.00**	**41**	**- 5:19**	**+ 6.00**	**36**	**- 5:24**

E - 7 Kts   Table E - Swale and Medway to Ramsgate via Copperas Channel   7 Kts - E

Time to cover Sectors (in minutes) at 7.0 kts — All times relate to HW Sheerness — **Springs**

Medway (E7–E5) · Ignore for Medway (E4) · Medway (E3–E1) · Swale (E4–E1)

Time	E7 Medway Channel to Spile: Duration	E7: Time at End of Sector	Time	E6 Spile to Kentish Flats: Duration	E6: Time at End of Sector	Time	E5 Kentish Flats to Copperas: Duration	E5: Time at End of Sector
- 6.00	45	- 5:15	- 6.00	41	- 5:19	- 6.00	48	- 5:12
- 5.45	46	- 4:59	- 5.45	42	- 5:03	- 5.45	49	- 4:56
- 5.30	46	- 4:44	- 5.30	42	- 4:48	- 5.30	49	- 4:41
- 5.15	47	- 4:28	- 5.15	43	- 4:32	- 5.15	49	- 4:26
- 5.00	47	- 4:13	- 5.00	43	- 4:17	- 5.00	50	- 4:10
- 4.45	47	- 3:58	- 4.45	43	- 4:02	- 4.45	50	- 3:55
- 4.30	47	- 3:43	- 4.30	43	- 3:47	- 4.30	51	- 3:39
- 4.15	47	- 3:28	- 4.15	43	- 3:32	- 4.15	51	- 3:24
- 4.00	47	- 3:13	- 4.00	43	- 3:17	- 4.00	51	- 3:09
- 3.45	46	- 2:59	- 3.45	43	- 3:02	- 3.45	51	- 2:54
- 3.30	46	- 2:44	- 3.30	42	- 2:48	- 3.30	51	- 2:39
- 3.15	46	- 2:29	- 3.15	42	- 2:33	- 3.15	51	- 2:24
- 3.00	46	- 2:14	- 3.00	42	- 2:18	- 3.00	51	- 2:09
- 2.45	46	- 1:59	- 2.45	42	- 2:03	- 2.45	51	- 1:54
- 2.30	46	- 1:44	- 2.30	42	- 1:48	- 2.30	51	- 1:39
- 2.15	45	- 1:30	- 2.15	42	- 1:33	- 2.15	51	- 1:24
- 2.00	45	- 1:15	- 2.00	42	- 1:18	- 2.00	51	- 1:09
- 1.45	45	- 1:00	- 1.45	41	- 1:04	- 1.45	50	- 0:55
- 1.30	44	- 0:46	- 1.30	41	- 0:49	- 1.30	49	- 0:41
- 1.15	44	- 0:31	- 1.15	40	- 0:35	- 1.15	48	- 0:27
- 1.00	43	- 0:17	- 1.00	40	- 0:20	- 1.00	48	- 0:12
- 0.45	42	- 0:03	- 0.45	39	- 0:06	- 0.45	47	+ 0:02
- 0.30	41	+ 0:11	- 0.30	38	+ 0:08	- 0.30	45	+ 0:15
- 0.15	40	+ 0:25	- 0.15	37	+ 0:22	- 0.15	44	+ 0:29
HW	39	+ 0:39	HW	36	+ 0:36	HW	43	+ 0:43
+ 0.15	39	+ 0:54	+ 0.15	35	+ 0:50	+ 0.15	42	+ 0:57
+ 0.30	38	+ 1:08	+ 0.30	35	+ 1:05	+ 0.30	42	+ 1:12
+ 0.45	37	+ 1:22	+ 0.45	34	+ 1:19	+ 0.45	41	+ 1:26
+ 1.00	36	+ 1:36	+ 1.00	33	+ 1:33	+ 1.00	40	+ 1:40
+ 1.15	37	+ 1:52	+ 1.15	33	+ 1:48	+ 1.15	40	+ 1:55
+ 1.30	37	+ 2:07	+ 1.30	33	+ 2:03	+ 1.30	40	+ 2:10
+ 1.45	37	+ 2:22	+ 1.45	33	+ 2:18	+ 1.45	40	+ 2:25
+ 2.00	37	+ 2:37	+ 2.00	33	+ 2:33	+ 2.00	40	+ 2:40
+ 2.15	38	+ 2:53	+ 2.15	34	+ 2:49	+ 2.15	40	+ 2:55
+ 2.30	39	+ 3:09	+ 2.30	35	+ 3:05	+ 2.30	40	+ 3:10
+ 2.45	39	+ 3:24	+ 2.45	35	+ 3:20	+ 2.45	41	+ 3:26
+ 3.00	40	+ 3:40	+ 3.00	36	+ 3:36	+ 3.00	41	+ 3:41
+ 3.15	41	+ 3:56	+ 3.15	36	+ 3:51	+ 3.15	41	+ 3:56
+ 3.30	41	+ 4:11	+ 3.30	37	+ 4:07	+ 3.30	42	+ 4:12
+ 3.45	42	+ 4:27	+ 3.45	38	+ 4:23	+ 3.45	42	+ 4:27
+ 4.00	43	+ 4:43	+ 4.00	38	+ 4:38	+ 4.00	43	+ 4:43
+ 4.15	43	+ 4:58	+ 4.15	39	+ 4:54	+ 4.15	43	+ 4:58
+ 4.30	44	+ 5:14	+ 4.30	39	+ 5:09	+ 4.30	44	+ 5:14
+ 4.45	44	+ 5:29	+ 4.45	40	+ 5:25	+ 4.45	44	+ 5:29
+ 5.00	44	+ 5:44	+ 5.00	40	+ 5:40	+ 5.00	45	+ 5:45
+ 5.15	45	- 6:00	+ 5.15	40	+ 5:55	+ 5.15	45	- 6:00
+ 5.30	45	- 5:45	+ 5.30	41	- 5:49	+ 5.30	46	- 5:44
+ 5.45	45	- 5:30	+ 5.45	41	- 5:34	+ 5.45	46	- 5:29
+ 6.00	45	- 5:15	+ 6.00	41	- 5:19	+ 6.00	47	- 5:13

Time	E4 Swale Landfall to Copperas: Duration	E4: Time at End of Sector	Time	E3 Copperas to SE Margate: Duration	E3: Time at End of Sector	Time	E2 SE Margate to North Foreland: Duration	E2: Time at End of Sector	Time	E1 North Foreland to Ramsgate: Duration	E1: Time at End of Sector
- 6.00	52	- 5:08	- 6.00	53	- 5:07	- 6.00	43	- 5:17	- 6.00	33	- 5:27
- 5.45	53	- 4:52	- 5.45	54	- 4:51	- 5.45	44	- 5:01	- 5.45	33	- 5:12
- 5.30	54	- 4:36	- 5.30	55	- 4:35	- 5.30	46	- 4:44	- 5.30	32	- 4:58
- 5.15	56	- 4:19	- 5.15	57	- 4:18	- 5.15	47	- 4:28	- 5.15	32	- 4:43
- 5.00	57	- 4:03	- 5.00	58	- 4:02	- 5.00	48	- 4:12	- 5.00	32	- 4:28
- 4.45	57	- 3:48	- 4.45	59	- 3:46	- 4.45	49	- 3:56	- 4.45	32	- 4:13
- 4.30	58	- 3:32	- 4.30	59	- 3:31	- 4.30	49	- 3:41	- 4.30	32	- 3:58
- 4.15	58	- 3:17	- 4.15	60	- 3:15	- 4.15	49	- 3:26	- 4.15	33	- 3:42
- 4.00	59	- 3:01	- 4.00	60	- 3:00	- 4.00	50	- 3:10	- 4.00	34	- 3:26
- 3.45	59	- 2:46	- 3.45	61	- 2:44	- 3.45	50	- 2:55	- 3.45	34	- 3:11
- 3.30	59	- 2:31	- 3.30	61	- 2:29	- 3.30	51	- 2:39	- 3.30	35	- 2:55
- 3.15	59	- 2:16	- 3.15	62	- 2:13	- 3.15	52	- 2:23	- 3.15	38	- 2:37
- 3.00	59	- 2:01	- 3.00	62	- 1:58	- 3.00	52	- 2:08	- 3.00	41	- 2:19
- 2.45	59	- 1:46	- 2.45	62	- 1:43	- 2.45	52	- 1:53	- 2.45	44	- 2:01
- 2.30	58	- 1:32	- 2.30	61	- 1:29	- 2.30	52	- 1:38	- 2.30	46	- 1:44
- 2.15	58	- 1:17	- 2.15	61	- 1:14	- 2.15	52	- 1:23	- 2.15	48	- 1:27
- 2.00	58	- 1:02	- 2.00	61	- 0:59	- 2.00	51	- 1:09	- 2.00	50	- 1:10
- 1.45	56	- 0:49	- 1.45	59	- 0:46	- 1.45	50	- 0:55	- 1.45	52	- 0:53
- 1.30	55	- 0:35	- 1.30	57	- 0:33	- 1.30	48	- 0:42	- 1.30	54	- 0:36
- 1.15	53	- 0:22	- 1.15	56	- 0:19	- 1.15	47	- 0:28	- 1.15	53	- 0:22
- 1.00	52	- 0:08	- 1.00	54	- 0:06	- 1.00	45	- 0:15	- 1.00	53	- 0:07
- 0.45	50	+ 0:05	- 0.45	52	+ 0:07	- 0.45	44	- 0:01	- 0.45	53	+ 0:08
- 0.30	48	+ 0:18	- 0.30	50	+ 0:20	- 0.30	42	+ 0:12	- 0.30	53	+ 0:23
- 0.15	46	+ 0:31	- 0.15	48	+ 0:33	- 0.15	40	+ 0:25	- 0.15	53	+ 0:38
HW	44	+ 0:44	HW	46	+ 0:46	HW	38	+ 0:38	HW	52	+ 0:52
+ 0.15	42	+ 0:57	+ 0.15	44	+ 0:59	+ 0.15	37	+ 0:52	+ 0.15	51	+ 1:06
+ 0.30	41	+ 1:11	+ 0.30	43	+ 1:13	+ 0.30	36	+ 1:06	+ 0.30	51	+ 1:21
+ 0.45	40	+ 1:25	+ 0.45	42	+ 1:27	+ 0.45	35	+ 1:20	+ 0.45	49	+ 1:34
+ 1.00	39	+ 1:39	+ 1.00	40	+ 1:40	+ 1.00	34	+ 1:34	+ 1.00	48	+ 1:48
+ 1.15	39	+ 1:54	+ 1.15	40	+ 1:55	+ 1.15	34	+ 1:49	+ 1.15	47	+ 2:02
+ 1.30	39	+ 2:09	+ 1.30	40	+ 2:10	+ 1.30	33	+ 2:03	+ 1.30	45	+ 2:15
+ 1.45	38	+ 2:23	+ 1.45	40	+ 2:25	+ 1.45	33	+ 2:18	+ 1.45	44	+ 2:29
+ 2.00	38	+ 2:38	+ 2.00	40	+ 2:40	+ 2.00	33	+ 2:33	+ 2.00	43	+ 2:43
+ 2.15	39	+ 2:54	+ 2.15	40	+ 2:55	+ 2.15	33	+ 2:48	+ 2.15	41	+ 2:56
+ 2.30	39	+ 3:09	+ 2.30	40	+ 3:10	+ 2.30	33	+ 3:03	+ 2.30	40	+ 3:10
+ 2.45	39	+ 3:24	+ 2.45	41	+ 3:26	+ 2.45	34	+ 3:19	+ 2.45	39	+ 3:24
+ 3.00	40	+ 3:40	+ 3.00	41	+ 3:41	+ 3.00	34	+ 3:34	+ 3.00	39	+ 3:39
+ 3.15	40	+ 3:55	+ 3.15	42	+ 3:57	+ 3.15	34	+ 3:49	+ 3.15	38	+ 3:53
+ 3.30	41	+ 4:11	+ 3.30	42	+ 4:12	+ 3.30	35	+ 4:05	+ 3.30	37	+ 4:07
+ 3.45	42	+ 4:27	+ 3.45	43	+ 4:28	+ 3.45	36	+ 4:21	+ 3.45	37	+ 4:22
+ 4.00	42	+ 4:42	+ 4.00	44	+ 4:44	+ 4.00	36	+ 4:36	+ 4.00	37	+ 4:37
+ 4.15	43	+ 4:58	+ 4.15	44	+ 4:59	+ 4.15	37	+ 4:52	+ 4.15	36	+ 4:51
+ 4.30	44	+ 5:14	+ 4.30	45	+ 5:15	+ 4.30	37	+ 5:07	+ 4.30	36	+ 5:06
+ 4.45	45	+ 5:30	+ 4.45	46	+ 5:31	+ 4.45	38	+ 5:23	+ 4.45	36	+ 5:21
+ 5.00	45	+ 5:45	+ 5.00	46	+ 5:46	+ 5.00	38	+ 5:38	+ 5.00	35	+ 5:35
+ 5.15	46	- 5:59	+ 5.15	47	- 5:58	+ 5.15	39	+ 5:54	+ 5.15	35	+ 5:50
+ 5.30	47	- 5:43	+ 5.30	48	- 5:42	+ 5.30	39	- 5:51	+ 5.30	34	- 5:56
+ 5.45	48	- 5:27	+ 5.45	48	- 5:27	+ 5.45	40	- 5:35	+ 5.45	34	- 5:41
+ 6.00	49	- 5:11	+ 6.00	49	- 5:11	+ 6.00	40	- 5:20	+ 6.00	33	- 5:27

EAST BOUND

Table F - Queens Channel and Southwards to the Swale

Neaps — All times relate to HW Sheerness — Time to cover Sectors (in minutes) at 4.0 Kts

SOUTH & EAST

	F8			F7			F6			F5			F4			F3			F2			F1	
	SW Barrow to Red Sand			Red Sand to Spaniard			Spaniard to Swale Landfall			Spile to Spaniard			Spaniard to Wedge			Swale Landfall to Woolpack			Woolpack to Wedge			Wedge to Margate Sands	
Time	Duration	Time at End of Sector	Time	Duration	Time at End of Sector	Time	Duration	Time at End of Sector	Time	Duration	Time at End of Sector	Time	Duration	Time at End of Sector	Time	Duration	Time at End of Sector	Time	Duration	Time at End of Sector	Time	Duration	Time at End of Sector
- 6.00	69	- 4:51	- 6.00	34	- 5:26	- 6.00	32	- 5:28	- 6.00	93	- 4:27	- 6.00	153	- 3:27	- 6.00	93	- 4:27	- 6.00	82	- 4:38	- 6.00	65	- 4:55
- 5.45	69	- 4:36	- 5.45	34	- 5:11	- 5.45	32	- 5:13	- 5.45	94	- 4:11	- 5.45	158	- 3:07	- 5.45	94	- 4:11	- 5.45	85	- 4:20	- 5.45	67	- 4:38
- 5.30	70	- 4:20	- 5.30	34	- 4:56	- 5.30	31	- 4:59	- 5.30	96	- 3:54	- 5.30	162	- 2:48	- 5.30	95	- 3:55	- 5.30	88	- 4:02	- 5.30	68	- 4:22
- 5.15	70	- 4:05	- 5.15	34	- 4:41	- 5.15	31	- 4:44	- 5.15	97	- 3:38	- 5.15	167	- 2:28	- 5.15	97	- 3:38	- 5.15	92	- 3:43	- 5.15	70	- 4:05
- 5.00	71	- 3:49	- 5.00	34	- 4:26	- 5.00	30	- 4:30	- 5.00	98	- 3:22	- 5.00	172	- 2:08	- 5.00	98	- 3:22	- 5.00	95	- 3:25	- 5.00	71	- 3:49
- 4.45	71	- 3:34	- 4.45	34	- 4:11	- 4.45	30	- 4:15	- 4.45	97	- 3:08	- 4.45	175	- 1:50	- 4.45	98	- 3:07	- 4.45	98	- 3:07	- 4.45	73	- 3:32
- 4.30	72	- 3:18	- 4.30	35	- 3:55	- 4.30	30	- 4:00	- 4.30	97	- 2:53	- 4.30	177	- 1:33	- 4.30	99	- 2:51	- 4.30	101	- 2:49	- 4.30	74	- 3:16
- 4.15	72	- 3:03	- 4.15	35	- 3:40	- 4.15	30	- 3:45	- 4.15	96	- 2:39	- 4.15	180	- 1:15	- 4.15	99	- 2:36	- 4.15	103	- 2:32	- 4.15	76	- 2:59
- 4.00	72	- 2:48	- 4.00	35	- 3:25	- 4.00	30	- 3:30	- 4.00	95	- 2:25	- 4.00	182	- 0:58	- 4.00	100	- 2:20	- 4.00	106	- 2:14	- 4.00	77	- 2:43
- 3.45	72	- 2:33	- 3.45	35	- 3:10	- 3.45	30	- 3:15	- 3.45	95	- 2:10	- 3.45	180	- 0:45	- 3.45	100	- 2:05	- 3.45	107	- 1:58	- 3.45	81	- 2:24
- 3.30	72	- 2:18	- 3.30	35	- 2:55	- 3.30	30	- 3:00	- 3.30	95	- 1:55	- 3.30	179	- 0:31	- 3.30	99	- 1:51	- 3.30	108	- 1:42	- 3.30	85	- 2:05
- 3.15	73	- 2:02	- 3.15	35	- 2:40	- 3.15	30	- 2:45	- 3.15	94	- 1:41	- 3.15	177	- 0:18	- 3.15	99	- 1:36	- 3.15	109	- 1:26	- 3.15	89	- 1:46
- 3.00	73	- 1:47	- 3.00	35	- 2:25	- 3.00	30	- 2:30	- 3.00	94	- 1:26	- 3.00	175	- 0:05	- 3.00	99	- 1:21	- 3.00	110	- 1:10	- 3.00	93	- 1:27
- 2.45	72	- 1:33	- 2.45	35	- 2:10	- 2.45	30	- 2:15	- 2.45	93	- 1:12	- 2.45	171	+ 0:06	- 2.45	98	- 1:07	- 2.45	107	- 0:58	- 2.45	89	- 1:16
- 2.30	72	- 1:18	- 2.30	35	- 1:55	- 2.30	30	- 2:00	- 2.30	93	- 0:57	- 2.30	166	+ 0:16	- 2.30	97	- 0:53	- 2.30	105	- 0:45	- 2.30	85	- 1:05
- 2.15	72	- 1:03	- 2.15	35	- 1:40	- 2.15	30	- 1:45	- 2.15	92	- 0:43	- 2.15	162	+ 0:27	- 2.15	95	- 0:40	- 2.15	103	- 0:32	- 2.15	81	- 0:54
- 2.00	72	- 0:48	- 2.00	35	- 1:25	- 2.00	30	- 1:30	- 2.00	92	- 0:28	- 2.00	157	+ 0:37	- 2.00	94	- 0:26	- 2.00	101	- 0:19	- 2.00	78	- 0:42
- 1.45	71	- 0:34	- 1.45	35	- 1:10	- 1.45	31	- 1:14	- 1.45	89	- 0:16	- 1.45	152	+ 0:47	- 1.45	91	- 0:14	- 1.45	96	- 0:09	- 1.45	75	- 0:30
- 1.30	71	- 0:19	- 1.30	35	- 0:55	- 1.30	31	- 0:59	- 1.30	87	- 0:03	- 1.30	146	+ 0:56	- 1.30	89	- 0:01	- 1.30	91	+ 0:01	- 1.30	73	- 0:17
- 1.15	71	- 0:04	- 1.15	35	- 0:40	- 1.15	32	- 0:43	- 1.15	85	+ 0:10	- 1.15	140	+ 1:05	- 1.15	86	+ 0:11	- 1.15	87	+ 0:12	- 1.15	70	- 0:05
- 1.00	70	+ 0:10	- 1.00	34	- 0:26	- 1.00	32	- 0:28	- 1.00	83	+ 0:23	- 1.00	134	+ 1:14	- 1.00	84	+ 0:24	- 1.00	82	+ 0:22	- 1.00	68	+ 0:08
- 0.45	70	+ 0:25	- 0.45	34	- 0:11	- 0.45	33	- 0:12	- 0.45	80	+ 0:35	- 0.45	129	+ 1:24	- 0.45	81	+ 0:36	- 0.45	79	+ 0:34	- 0.45	65	+ 0:20
- 0.30	69	+ 0:39	- 0.30	34	+ 0:04	- 0.30	33	+ 0:03	- 0.30	77	+ 0:47	- 0.30	123	+ 1:33	- 0.30	79	+ 0:49	- 0.30	75	+ 0:45	- 0.30	62	+ 0:32
- 0.15	69	+ 0:54	- 0.15	33	+ 0:18	- 0.15	34	+ 0:19	- 0.15	74	+ 0:59	- 0.15	118	+ 1:43	- 0.15	77	+ 1:02	- 0.15	72	+ 0:57	- 0.15	60	+ 0:45
HW	68	+ 1:08	HW	33	+ 0:33	HW	35	+ 0:35	HW	72	+ 1:12	HW	113	+ 1:53	HW	74	+ 1:14	HW	68	+ 1:08	HW	57	+ 0:57
+ 0.15	68	+ 1:23	+ 0.15	33	+ 0:48	+ 0.15	36	+ 0:51	+ 0.15	70	+ 1:25	+ 0.15	109	+ 2:04	+ 0.15	73	+ 1:28	+ 0.15	66	+ 1:21	+ 0.15	55	+ 1:10
+ 0.30	67	+ 1:37	+ 0.30	32	+ 1:02	+ 0.30	37	+ 1:07	+ 0.30	69	+ 1:39	+ 0.30	106	+ 2:16	+ 0.30	71	+ 1:41	+ 0.30	63	+ 1:33	+ 0.30	53	+ 1:23
+ 0.45	67	+ 1:52	+ 0.45	32	+ 1:17	+ 0.45	38	+ 1:23	+ 0.45	68	+ 1:53	+ 0.45	102	+ 2:27	+ 0.45	70	+ 1:55	+ 0.45	60	+ 1:45	+ 0.45	51	+ 1:36
+ 1.00	67	+ 2:07	+ 1.00	32	+ 1:32	+ 1.00	39	+ 1:39	+ 1.00	67	+ 2:07	+ 1.00	99	+ 2:39	+ 1.00	69	+ 2:09	+ 1.00	57	+ 1:57	+ 1.00	48	+ 1:48
+ 1.15	66	+ 2:21	+ 1.15	32	+ 1:47	+ 1.15	39	+ 1:54	+ 1.15	68	+ 2:23	+ 1.15	98	+ 2:53	+ 1.15	69	+ 2:24	+ 1.15	56	+ 2:11	+ 1.15	47	+ 2:02
+ 1.30	66	+ 2:36	+ 1.30	32	+ 2:02	+ 1.30	39	+ 2:09	+ 1.30	69	+ 2:39	+ 1.30	96	+ 3:06	+ 1.30	69	+ 2:39	+ 1.30	55	+ 2:25	+ 1.30	46	+ 2:16
+ 1.45	66	+ 2:51	+ 1.45	32	+ 2:17	+ 1.45	40	+ 2:25	+ 1.45	70	+ 2:55	+ 1.45	95	+ 3:20	+ 1.45	69	+ 2:54	+ 1.45	54	+ 2:39	+ 1.45	45	+ 2:30
+ 2.00	66	+ 3:06	+ 2.00	32	+ 2:32	+ 2.00	40	+ 2:40	+ 2.00	70	+ 3:10	+ 2.00	93	+ 3:33	+ 2.00	70	+ 3:10	+ 2.00	52	+ 2:52	+ 2.00	44	+ 2:44
+ 2.15	66	+ 3:21	+ 2.15	32	+ 2:47	+ 2.15	39	+ 2:54	+ 2.15	72	+ 3:27	+ 2.15	94	+ 3:49	+ 2.15	71	+ 3:26	+ 2.15	53	+ 3:08	+ 2.15	44	+ 2:59
+ 2.30	66	+ 3:36	+ 2.30	32	+ 3:02	+ 2.30	39	+ 3:09	+ 2.30	74	+ 3:44	+ 2.30	95	+ 4:05	+ 2.30	72	+ 3:42	+ 2.30	53	+ 3:23	+ 2.30	44	+ 3:14
+ 2.45	66	+ 3:51	+ 2.45	32	+ 3:17	+ 2.45	39	+ 3:24	+ 2.45	75	+ 4:00	+ 2.45	95	+ 4:20	+ 2.45	72	+ 3:57	+ 2.45	54	+ 3:39	+ 2.45	44	+ 3:29
+ 3.00	66	+ 4:06	+ 3.00	32	+ 3:32	+ 3.00	38	+ 3:38	+ 3.00	77	+ 4:17	+ 3.00	96	+ 4:36	+ 3.00	73	+ 4:13	+ 3.00	54	+ 3:54	+ 3.00	45	+ 3:45
+ 3.15	66	+ 4:21	+ 3.15	33	+ 3:48	+ 3.15	38	+ 3:53	+ 3.15	79	+ 4:34	+ 3.15	99	+ 4:54	+ 3.15	74	+ 4:29	+ 3.15	55	+ 4:10	+ 3.15	46	+ 4:01
+ 3.30	66	+ 4:36	+ 3.30	33	+ 4:03	+ 3.30	37	+ 4:07	+ 3.30	80	+ 4:50	+ 3.30	102	+ 5:12	+ 3.30	75	+ 4:45	+ 3.30	57	+ 4:27	+ 3.30	47	+ 4:17
+ 3.45	66	+ 4:51	+ 3.45	33	+ 4:18	+ 3.45	37	+ 4:22	+ 3.45	82	+ 5:07	+ 3.45	105	+ 5:30	+ 3.45	76	+ 5:01	+ 3.45	58	+ 4:43	+ 3.45	48	+ 4:33
+ 4.00	66	+ 5:06	+ 4.00	33	+ 4:33	+ 4.00	37	+ 4:37	+ 4.00	84	+ 5:24	+ 4.00	108	+ 5:48	+ 4.00	77	+ 5:17	+ 4.00	60	+ 5:00	+ 4.00	49	+ 4:49
+ 4.15	66	+ 5:21	+ 4.15	33	+ 4:48	+ 4.15	36	+ 4:51	+ 4.15	84	+ 5:39	+ 4.15	112	- 5:53	+ 4.15	78	+ 5:33	+ 4.15	62	+ 5:17	+ 4.15	50	+ 5:05
+ 4.30	67	+ 5:37	+ 4.30	33	+ 5:03	+ 4.30	36	+ 5:06	+ 4.30	85	+ 5:55	+ 4.30	115	- 5:35	+ 4.30	80	+ 5:50	+ 4.30	64	+ 5:34	+ 4.30	52	+ 5:22
+ 4.45	67	+ 5:52	+ 4.45	33	+ 5:18	+ 4.45	35	+ 5:20	+ 4.45	86	- 5:49	+ 4.45	119	- 5:16	+ 4.45	81	- 5:54	+ 4.45	67	+ 5:52	+ 4.45	54	+ 5:39
+ 5.00	67	- 5:53	+ 5.00	33	+ 5:33	+ 5.00	35	+ 5:35	+ 5.00	87	- 5:33	+ 5.00	123	- 4:57	+ 5.00	82	- 5:38	+ 5.00	69	- 5:51	+ 5.00	55	+ 5:55
+ 5.15	67	- 5:38	+ 5.15	34	+ 5:49	+ 5.15	35	+ 5:50	+ 5.15	87	- 5:18	+ 5.15	126	- 4:39	+ 5.15	83	- 5:22	+ 5.15	70	- 5:35	+ 5.15	56	- 5:49
+ 5.30	67	- 5:23	+ 5.30	34	- 5:56	+ 5.30	34	- 5:56	+ 5.30	87	- 5:03	+ 5.30	129	- 4:21	+ 5.30	84	- 5:06	+ 5.30	72	- 5:18	+ 5.30	58	- 5:32
+ 5.45	67	- 5:08	+ 5.45	34	- 5:41	+ 5.45	34	- 5:41	+ 5.45	87	- 4:48	+ 5.45	133	- 4:02	+ 5.45	85	- 4:50	+ 5.45	74	- 5:01	+ 5.45	59	- 5:16
+ 6.00	68	- 4:52	+ 6.00	34	- 5:26	+ 6.00	34	- 5:26	+ 6.00	88	- 4:32	+ 6.00	136	- 3:44	+ 6.00	86	- 4:34	+ 6.00	75	- 4:45	+ 6.00	60	- 5:00

Southwards to Swale — The Queens Channel

Table F - Queens Channel and Southwards to the Swale

Time to cover Sectors (in minutes) at 4.0 kts — All times relate to HW Sheerness — **Springs**

	F8			F7			F6			F5	
	SW Barrow to Red Sand			Red Sand to Spaniard			Spaniard to Swale Landfall			Spile to Spaniard	
Time	*Duration*	*Time at End of Sector*	*Time*	*Duration*	*Time at End of Sector*	*Time*	*Duration*	*Time at End of Sector*	*Time*	*Duration*	*Time at End of Sector*
- 6.00	**70**	**- 4:50**	**- 6.00**	**35**	**- 5:25**	**- 6.00**	**32**	**- 5:28**	**- 6.00**	**99**	**- 4:21**
- 5.45	71	- 4:34	- 5.45	35	- 5:10	- 5.45	31	- 5:14	- 5.45	100	- 4:05
- 5.30	71	- 4:19	- 5.30	35	- 4:55	- 5.30	30	- 5:00	- 5.30	101	- 3:49
- 5.15	72	- 4:03	- 5.15	35	- 4:40	- 5.15	30	- 4:45	- 5.15	102	- 3:33
- 5.00	**73**	**- 3:47**	**- 5.00**	**35**	**- 4:25**	**- 5.00**	**29**	**- 4:31**	**- 5.00**	**103**	**- 3:17**
- 4.45	74	- 3:31	- 4.45	35	- 4:10	- 4.45	29	- 4:16	- 4.45	102	- 3:03
- 4.30	75	- 3:15	- 4.30	36	- 3:54	- 4.30	29	- 4:01	- 4.30	102	- 2:48
- 4.15	75	- 3:00	- 4.15	36	- 3:39	- 4.15	28	- 3:47	- 4.15	101	- 2:34
- 4.00	**76**	**- 2:44**	**- 4.00**	**36**	**- 3:24**	**- 4.00**	**28**	**- 3:32**	**- 4.00**	**100**	**- 2:20**
- 3.45	76	- 2:29	- 3.45	36	- 3:09	- 3.45	28	- 3:17	- 3.45	99	- 2:06
- 3.30	76	- 2:14	- 3.30	37	- 2:53	- 3.30	28	- 3:02	- 3.30	99	- 1:51
- 3.15	77	- 1:58	- 3.15	37	- 2:38	- 3.15	28	- 2:47	- 3.15	98	- 1:37
- 3.00	**77**	**- 1:43**	**- 3.00**	**37**	**- 2:23**	**- 3.00**	**29**	**- 2:31**	**- 3.00**	**97**	**- 1:23**
- 2.45	76	- 1:29	- 2.45	37	- 2:08	- 2.45	29	- 2:16	- 2.45	96	- 1:09
- 2.30	76	- 1:14	- 2.30	37	- 1:53	- 2.30	28	- 2:02	- 2.30	95	- 0:55
- 2.15	76	- 0:59	- 2.15	37	- 1:38	- 2.15	28	- 1:47	- 2.15	94	- 0:41
- 2.00	**75**	**- 0:45**	**- 2.00**	**36**	**- 1:24**	**- 2.00**	**28**	**- 1:32**	**- 2.00**	**93**	**- 0:27**
- 1.45	74	- 0:31	- 1.45	36	- 1:09	- 1.45	29	- 1:16	- 1.45	90	- 0:15
- 1.30	73	- 0:17	- 1.30	36	- 0:54	- 1.30	29	- 1:01	- 1.30	88	- 0:02
- 1.15	73	- 0:02	- 1.15	36	- 0:39	- 1.15	30	- 0:45	- 1.15	85	+ 0:10
- 1.00	**72**	**+ 0:12**	**- 1.00**	**35**	**- 0:25**	**- 1.00**	**31**	**- 0:29**	**- 1.00**	**82**	**+ 0:22**
- 0.45	71	+ 0:26	- 0.45	35	- 0:10	- 0.45	32	- 0:13	- 0.45	78	+ 0:33
- 0.30	70	+ 0:40	- 0.30	34	+ 0:04	- 0.30	33	+ 0:03	- 0.30	73	+ 0:43
- 0.15	69	+ 0:54	- 0.15	33	+ 0:18	- 0.15	34	+ 0:19	- 0.15	69	+ 0:54
HW	**68**	**+ 1:08**	**HW**	**33**	**+ 0:33**	**HW**	**35**	**+ 0:35**	**HW**	**65**	**+ 1:05**
+ 0.15	68	+ 1:23	+ 0.15	32	+ 0:47	+ 0.15	37	+ 0:52	+ 0.15	63	+ 1:18
+ 0.30	68	+ 1:38	+ 0.30	32	+ 1:02	+ 0.30	38	+ 1:08	+ 0.30	62	+ 1:32
+ 0.45	67	+ 1:52	+ 0.45	32	+ 1:17	+ 0.45	40	+ 1:25	+ 0.45	60	+ 1:45
+ 1.00	**67**	**+ 2:07**	**+ 1.00**	**31**	**+ 1:31**	**+ 1.00**	**42**	**+ 1:42**	**+ 1.00**	**59**	**+ 1:59**
+ 1.15	67	+ 2:22	+ 1.15	31	+ 1:46	+ 1.15	42	+ 1:57	+ 1.15	60	+ 2:15
+ 1.30	67	+ 2:37	+ 1.30	32	+ 2:02	+ 1.30	43	+ 2:13	+ 1.30	62	+ 2:32
+ 1.45	67	+ 2:52	+ 1.45	32	+ 2:17	+ 1.45	43	+ 2:28	+ 1.45	63	+ 2:48
+ 2.00	**67**	**+ 3:07**	**+ 2.00**	**32**	**+ 2:32**	**+ 2.00**	**44**	**+ 2:44**	**+ 2.00**	**64**	**+ 3:04**
+ 2.15	67	+ 3:22	+ 2.15	32	+ 2:47	+ 2.15	43	+ 2:58	+ 2.15	67	+ 3:22
+ 2.30	67	+ 3:37	+ 2.30	32	+ 3:02	+ 2.30	43	+ 3:13	+ 2.30	69	+ 3:39
+ 2.45	67	+ 3:52	+ 2.45	32	+ 3:17	+ 2.45	42	+ 3:27	+ 2.45	72	+ 3:57
+ 3.00	**67**	**+ 4:07**	**+ 3.00**	**32**	**+ 3:32**	**+ 3.00**	**42**	**+ 3:42**	**+ 3.00**	**74**	**+ 4:14**
+ 3.15	67	+ 4:22	+ 3.15	32	+ 3:47	+ 3.15	41	+ 3:56	+ 3.15	76	+ 4:31
+ 3.30	67	+ 4:37	+ 3.30	32	+ 4:02	+ 3.30	40	+ 4:10	+ 3.30	79	+ 4:49
+ 3.45	67	+ 4:52	+ 3.45	32	+ 4:17	+ 3.45	40	+ 4:25	+ 3.45	81	+ 5:06
+ 4.00	**66**	**+ 5:06**	**+ 4.00**	**33**	**+ 4:33**	**+ 4.00**	**39**	**+ 4:39**	**+ 4.00**	**84**	**+ 5:24**
+ 4.15	66	+ 5:21	+ 4.15	33	+ 4:48	+ 4.15	38	+ 4:53	+ 4.15	85	+ 5:40
+ 4.30	66	+ 5:36	+ 4.30	33	+ 5:03	+ 4.30	37	+ 5:07	+ 4.30	86	+ 5:56
+ 4.45	66	+ 5:51	+ 4.45	33	+ 5:18	+ 4.45	37	+ 5:22	+ 4.45	87	- 5:48
+ 5.00	**67**	**- 5:53**	**+ 5.00**	**33**	**+ 5:33**	**+ 5.00**	**36**	**+ 5:36**	**+ 5.00**	**89**	**- 5:31**
+ 5.15	67	- 5:38	+ 5.15	33	+ 5:48	+ 5.15	35	+ 5:50	+ 5.15	89	- 5:16
+ 5.30	67	- 5:23	+ 5.30	34	- 5:56	+ 5.30	35	- 5:55	+ 5.30	89	- 5:01
+ 5.45	67	- 5:08	+ 5.45	34	- 5:41	+ 5.45	34	- 5:41	+ 5.45	90	- 4:45
+ 6.00	**67**	**- 4:53**	**+ 6.00**	**34**	**- 5:26**	**+ 6.00**	**34**	**- 5:26**	**+ 6.00**	**90**	**- 4:30**

	F4			F3			F2			F1	
	Spaniard to Wedge			Swale Landfall to Woolpack			Woolpack to Wedge			Wedge to Margate Sands	
Time	*Duration*	*Time at End of Sector*	*Time*	*Duration*	*Time at End of Sector*	*Time*	*Duration*	*Time at End of Sector*	*Time*	*Duration*	*Time at End of Sector*
- 6.00	**170**	**- 3:10**	**- 6.00**	**96**	**- 4:24**	**- 6.00**	**86**	**- 4:34**	**- 6.00**	**68**	**- 4:52**
- 5.45	181	- 2:44	- 5.45	98	- 4:07	- 5.45	91	- 4:14	- 5.45	70	- 4:35
- 5.30	192	- 2:18	- 5.30	100	- 3:50	- 5.30	96	- 3:54	- 5.30	73	- 4:17
- 5.15	203	- 1:52	- 5.15	102	- 3:33	- 5.15	101	- 3:34	- 5.15	76	- 3:59
- 5.00	**214**	**- 1:26**	**- 5.00**	**104**	**- 3:16**	**- 5.00**	**107**	**- 3:13**	**- 5.00**	**78**	**- 3:42**
- 4.45	214	- 1:11	- 4.45	104	- 3:01	- 4.45	110	- 2:55	- 4.45	84	- 3:21
- 4.30	215	- 0:55	- 4.30	105	- 2:45	- 4.30	114	- 2:36	- 4.30	89	- 3:01
- 4.15	216	- 0:39	- 4.15	105	- 2:30	- 4.15	118	- 2:17	- 4.15	95	- 2:40
- 4.00	**216**	**- 0:24**	**- 4.00**	**106**	**- 2:14**	**- 4.00**	**122**	**- 1:58**	**- 4.00**	**100**	**- 2:20**
- 3.45	211	- 0:14	- 3.45	106	- 1:59	- 3.45	123	- 1:42	- 3.45	102	- 2:03
- 3.30	205	- 0:05	- 3.30	105	- 1:45	- 3.30	124	- 1:26	- 3.30	104	- 1:46
- 3.15	200	+ 0:05	- 3.15	105	- 1:30	- 3.15	125	- 1:10	- 3.15	106	- 1:29
- 3.00	**195**	**+ 0:15**	**- 3.00**	**105**	**- 1:15**	**- 3.00**	**126**	**- 0:54**	**- 3.00**	**107**	**- 1:13**
- 2.45	187	+ 0:22	- 2.45	103	- 1:02	- 2.45	121	- 0:44	- 2.45	104	- 1:01
- 2.30	179	+ 0:29	- 2.30	102	- 0:48	- 2.30	117	- 0:33	- 2.30	101	- 0:49
- 2.15	171	+ 0:36	- 2.15	100	- 0:35	- 2.15	113	- 0:22	- 2.15	98	- 0:37
- 2.00	**163**	**+ 0:43**	**- 2.00**	**98**	**- 0:22**	**- 2.00**	**109**	**- 0:11**	**- 2.00**	**94**	**- 0:26**
- 1.45	155	+ 0:50	- 1.45	95	- 0:10	- 1.45	104	- 0:01	- 1.45	89	- 0:16
- 1.30	147	+ 0:57	- 1.30	92	+ 0:02	- 1.30	98	+ 0:08	- 1.30	83	- 0:07
- 1.15	138	+ 1:03	- 1.15	89	+ 0:14	- 1.15	93	+ 0:18	- 1.15	78	+ 0:03
- 1.00	**130**	**+ 1:10**	**- 1.00**	**86**	**+ 0:26**	**- 1.00**	**87**	**+ 0:27**	**- 1.00**	**72**	**+ 0:12**
- 0.45	124	+ 1:19	- 0.45	82	+ 0:37	- 0.45	82	+ 0:37	- 0.45	68	+ 0:23
- 0.30	117	+ 1:27	- 0.30	78	+ 0:48	- 0.30	76	+ 0:46	- 0.30	63	+ 0:33
- 0.15	111	+ 1:36	- 0.15	74	+ 0:59	- 0.15	70	+ 0:55	- 0.15	59	+ 0:44
HW	**105**	**+ 1:45**	**HW**	**70**	**+ 1:10**	**HW**	**64**	**+ 1:04**	**HW**	**55**	**+ 0:55**
+ 0.15	102	+ 1:57	+ 0.15	68	+ 1:23	+ 0.15	61	+ 1:16	+ 0.15	52	+ 1:07
+ 0.30	99	+ 2:09	+ 0.30	66	+ 1:36	+ 0.30	57	+ 1:27	+ 0.30	49	+ 1:19
+ 0.45	95	+ 2:20	+ 0.45	64	+ 1:49	+ 0.45	53	+ 1:38	+ 0.45	46	+ 1:31
+ 1.00	**92**	**+ 2:32**	**+ 1.00**	**62**	**+ 2:02**	**+ 1.00**	**50**	**+ 1:50**	**+ 1.00**	**43**	**+ 1:43**
+ 1.15	87	+ 2:42	+ 1.15	62	+ 2:17	+ 1.15	48	+ 2:03	+ 1.15	42	+ 1:57
+ 1.30	82	+ 2:52	+ 1.30	62	+ 2:32	+ 1.30	47	+ 2:17	+ 1.30	41	+ 2:11
+ 1.45	76	+ 3:01	+ 1.45	63	+ 2:48	+ 1.45	46	+ 2:31	+ 1.45	40	+ 2:25
+ 2.00	**71**	**+ 3:11**	**+ 2.00**	**63**	**+ 3:03**	**+ 2.00**	**44**	**+ 2:44**	**+ 2.00**	**39**	**+ 2:39**
+ 2.15	76	+ 3:31	+ 2.15	64	+ 3:19	+ 2.15	45	+ 3:00	+ 2.15	39	+ 2:54
+ 2.30	80	+ 3:50	+ 2.30	65	+ 3:35	+ 2.30	45	+ 3:15	+ 2.30	39	+ 3:09
+ 2.45	85	+ 4:10	+ 2.45	66	+ 3:51	+ 2.45	46	+ 3:31	+ 2.45	39	+ 3:24
+ 3.00	**90**	**+ 4:30**	**+ 3.00**	**67**	**+ 4:07**	**+ 3.00**	**47**	**+ 3:47**	**+ 3.00**	**39**	**+ 3:39**
+ 3.15	93	+ 4:48	+ 3.15	69	+ 4:24	+ 3.15	49	+ 4:04	+ 3.15	41	+ 3:56
+ 3.30	97	+ 5:07	+ 3.30	71	+ 4:41	+ 3.30	51	+ 4:21	+ 3.30	42	+ 4:12
+ 3.45	100	+ 5:25	+ 3.45	72	+ 4:57	+ 3.45	52	+ 4:37	+ 3.45	43	+ 4:28
+ 4.00	**104**	**+ 5:44**	**+ 4.00**	**74**	**+ 5:14**	**+ 4.00**	**54**	**+ 4:54**	**+ 4.00**	**45**	**+ 4:45**
+ 4.15	109	- 5:56	+ 4.15	76	+ 5:31	+ 4.15	57	+ 5:12	+ 4.15	47	+ 5:02
+ 4.30	113	- 5:37	+ 4.30	78	+ 5:48	+ 4.30	60	+ 5:30	+ 4.30	49	+ 5:19
+ 4.45	118	- 5:17	+ 4.45	79	- 5:56	+ 4.45	63	+ 5:48	+ 4.45	51	+ 5:36
+ 5.00	**123**	**- 4:57**	**+ 5.00**	**81**	**- 5:39**	**+ 5.00**	**66**	**- 5:54**	**+ 5.00**	**53**	**+ 5:53**
+ 5.15	127	- 4:38	+ 5.15	83	- 5:22	+ 5.15	69	- 5:36	+ 5.15	55	- 5:50
+ 5.30	132	- 4:18	+ 5.30	84	- 5:06	+ 5.30	71	- 5:19	+ 5.30	57	- 5:33
+ 5.45	136	- 3:59	+ 5.45	86	- 4:49	+ 5.45	74	- 5:01	+ 5.45	59	- 5:16
+ 6.00	**141**	**- 3:39**	**+ 6.00**	**87**	**- 4:33**	**+ 6.00**	**76**	**- 4:44**	**+ 6.00**	**61**	**- 4:59**

Southwards to Swale — The Queens Channel

SOUTH & EAST

Table F - Queens Channel and Southwards to the Swale

Neaps — All times relate to HW Sheerness — **Time to cover Sectors (in minutes) at 5.0 Kts**

SOUTH & EAST

Time	F8 SW Barrow to Red Sand: Duration	F8: Time at End of Sector	Time	F7 Red Sand to Spaniard: Duration	F7: Time at End of Sector	Time	F6 Spaniard to Swale Landfall: Duration	F6: Time at End of Sector	Time	F5 Spile to Spaniard: Duration	F5: Time at End of Sector
- 6.00	55	- 5:05	- 6.00	27	- 5:33	- 6.00	26	- 5:34	- 6.00	71	- 4:49
- 5.45	55	- 4:50	- 5.45	27	- 5:18	- 5.45	26	- 5:19	- 5.45	72	- 4:33
- 5.30	55	- 4:35	- 5.30	27	- 5:03	- 5.30	25	- 5:05	- 5.30	73	- 4:17
- 5.15	56	- 4:19	- 5.15	27	- 4:48	- 5.15	25	- 4:50	- 5.15	73	- 4:02
- 5.00	56	- 4:04	- 5.00	27	- 4:33	- 5.00	24	- 4:36	- 5.00	74	- 3:46
- 4.45	56	- 3:49	- 4.45	27	- 4:18	- 4.45	24	- 4:21	- 4.45	73	- 3:32
- 4.30	56	- 3:34	- 4.30	27	- 4:03	- 4.30	24	- 4:06	- 4.30	73	- 3:17
- 4.15	57	- 3:18	- 4.15	28	- 3:47	- 4.15	24	- 3:51	- 4.15	73	- 3:02
- 4.00	57	- 3:03	- 4.00	28	- 3:32	- 4.00	24	- 3:36	- 4.00	73	- 2:47
- 3.45	57	- 2:48	- 3.45	28	- 3:17	- 3.45	24	- 3:21	- 3.45	72	- 2:33
- 3.30	57	- 2:33	- 3.30	28	- 3:02	- 3.30	24	- 3:06	- 3.30	72	- 2:18
- 3.15	57	- 2:18	- 3.15	28	- 2:47	- 3.15	24	- 2:51	- 3.15	72	- 2:03
- 3.00	57	- 2:03	- 3.00	28	- 2:32	- 3.00	24	- 2:36	- 3.00	72	- 1:48
- 2.45	57	- 1:48	- 2.45	28	- 2:17	- 2.45	24	- 2:21	- 2.45	71	- 1:34
- 2.30	57	- 1:33	- 2.30	28	- 2:02	- 2.30	24	- 2:06	- 2.30	71	- 1:19
- 2.15	57	- 1:18	- 2.15	28	- 1:47	- 2.15	24	- 1:51	- 2.15	71	- 1:04
- 2.00	57	- 1:03	- 2.00	28	- 1:32	- 2.00	24	- 1:36	- 2.00	71	- 0:49
- 1.45	56	- 0:49	- 1.45	28	- 1:17	- 1.45	24	- 1:21	- 1.45	70	- 0:35
- 1.30	56	- 0:34	- 1.30	28	- 1:02	- 1.30	25	- 1:05	- 1.30	69	- 0:21
- 1.15	56	- 0:19	- 1.15	28	- 0:47	- 1.15	25	- 0:50	- 1.15	68	- 0:07
- 1.00	56	- 0:04	- 1.00	27	- 0:33	- 1.00	26	- 0:34	- 1.00	67	+ 0:07
- 0.45	55	+ 0:10	- 0.45	27	- 0:18	- 0.45	26	- 0:19	- 0.45	65	+ 0:20
- 0.30	55	+ 0:25	- 0.30	27	- 0:03	- 0.30	26	- 0:04	- 0.30	63	+ 0:33
- 0.15	55	+ 0:40	- 0.15	27	+ 0:12	- 0.15	27	+ 0:12	- 0.15	62	+ 0:47
HW	55	+ 0:55	HW	26	+ 0:26	HW	27	+ 0:27	HW	60	+ 1:00
+ 0.15	54	+ 1:09	+ 0.15	26	+ 0:41	+ 0.15	28	+ 0:43	+ 0.15	59	+ 1:14
+ 0.30	54	+ 1:24	+ 0.30	26	+ 0:56	+ 0.30	28	+ 0:58	+ 0.30	58	+ 1:28
+ 0.45	54	+ 1:39	+ 0.45	26	+ 1:11	+ 0.45	29	+ 1:14	+ 0.45	57	+ 1:42
+ 1.00	53	+ 1:53	+ 1.00	25	+ 1:25	+ 1.00	30	+ 1:30	+ 1.00	56	+ 1:56
+ 1.15	53	+ 2:08	+ 1.15	25	+ 1:40	+ 1.15	30	+ 1:45	+ 1.15	57	+ 2:12
+ 1.30	53	+ 2:23	+ 1.30	25	+ 1:55	+ 1.30	30	+ 2:00	+ 1.30	57	+ 2:27
+ 1.45	53	+ 2:38	+ 1.45	25	+ 2:10	+ 1.45	31	+ 2:16	+ 1.45	57	+ 2:42
+ 2.00	53	+ 2:53	+ 2.00	25	+ 2:25	+ 2.00	31	+ 2:31	+ 2.00	58	+ 2:58
+ 2.15	53	+ 3:08	+ 2.15	26	+ 2:41	+ 2.15	31	+ 2:46	+ 2.15	59	+ 3:14
+ 2.30	53	+ 3:23	+ 2.30	26	+ 2:56	+ 2.30	30	+ 3:00	+ 2.30	60	+ 3:30
+ 2.45	53	+ 3:38	+ 2.45	26	+ 3:11	+ 2.45	30	+ 3:15	+ 2.45	61	+ 3:46
+ 3.00	53	+ 3:53	+ 3.00	26	+ 3:26	+ 3.00	30	+ 3:30	+ 3.00	62	+ 4:02
+ 3.15	53	+ 4:08	+ 3.15	26	+ 3:41	+ 3.15	30	+ 3:45	+ 3.15	63	+ 4:18
+ 3.30	53	+ 4:23	+ 3.30	26	+ 3:56	+ 3.30	29	+ 3:59	+ 3.30	64	+ 4:34
+ 3.45	53	+ 4:38	+ 3.45	26	+ 4:11	+ 3.45	29	+ 4:14	+ 3.45	65	+ 4:50
+ 4.00	53	+ 4:53	+ 4.00	26	+ 4:26	+ 4.00	29	+ 4:29	+ 4.00	66	+ 5:06
+ 4.15	53	+ 5:08	+ 4.15	26	+ 4:41	+ 4.15	29	+ 4:44	+ 4.15	67	+ 5:22
+ 4.30	53	+ 5:23	+ 4.30	26	+ 4:56	+ 4.30	28	+ 4:58	+ 4.30	68	+ 5:38
+ 4.45	53	+ 5:38	+ 4.45	26	+ 5:11	+ 4.45	28	+ 5:13	+ 4.45	68	+ 5:53
+ 5.00	53	+ 5:53	+ 5.00	26	+ 5:26	+ 5.00	28	+ 5:28	+ 5.00	69	- 5:51
+ 5.15	54	- 5:51	+ 5.15	27	+ 5:42	+ 5.15	28	+ 5:43	+ 5.15	69	- 5:36
+ 5.30	54	- 5:36	+ 5.30	27	+ 5:57	+ 5.30	27	+ 5:57	+ 5.30	69	- 5:21
+ 5.45	54	- 5:21	+ 5.45	27	- 5:48	+ 5.45	27	- 5:48	+ 5.45	69	- 5:06
+ 6.00	54	- 5:06	+ 6.00	27	- 5:33	+ 6.00	27	- 5:33	+ 6.00	69	- 4:51

Southwards to Swale

Time	F4 Spaniard to Wedge: Duration	F4: Time at End of Sector	Time	F3 Swale Landfall to Woolpack: Duration	F3: Time at End of Sector	Time	F2 Woolpack to Wedge: Duration	F2: Time at End of Sector	Time	F1 Wedge to Margate Sands: Duration	F1: Time at End of Sector
- 6.00	115	- 4:05	- 6.00	71	- 4:49	- 6.00	63	- 4:57	- 6.00	51	- 5:09
- 5.45	118	- 3:47	- 5.45	72	- 4:33	- 5.45	65	- 4:40	- 5.45	52	- 4:53
- 5.30	120	- 3:30	- 5.30	72	- 4:18	- 5.30	66	- 4:24	- 5.30	53	- 4:37
- 5.15	123	- 3:12	- 5.15	73	- 4:02	- 5.15	67	- 4:08	- 5.15	54	- 4:21
- 5.00	126	- 2:54	- 5.00	74	- 3:46	- 5.00	68	- 3:52	- 5.00	55	- 4:05
- 4.45	128	- 2:37	- 4.45	74	- 3:31	- 4.45	69	- 3:36	- 4.45	56	- 3:49
- 4.30	130	- 2:20	- 4.30	74	- 3:16	- 4.30	70	- 3:20	- 4.30	57	- 3:33
- 4.15	133	- 2:02	- 4.15	74	- 3:01	- 4.15	71	- 3:04	- 4.15	58	- 3:17
- 4.00	135	- 1:45	- 4.00	75	- 2:45	- 4.00	72	- 2:48	- 4.00	59	- 3:01
- 3.45	135	- 1:30	- 3.45	75	- 2:30	- 3.45	73	- 2:32	- 3.45	59	- 2:46
- 3.30	135	- 1:15	- 3.30	75	- 2:15	- 3.30	74	- 2:16	- 3.30	60	- 2:30
- 3.15	136	- 0:59	- 3.15	75	- 2:00	- 3.15	75	- 2:00	- 3.15	61	- 2:14
- 3.00	136	- 0:44	- 3.00	75	- 1:45	- 3.00	75	- 1:45	- 3.00	61	- 1:59
- 2.45	133	- 0:32	- 2.45	74	- 1:31	- 2.45	75	- 1:30	- 2.45	61	- 1:44
- 2.30	131	- 0:19	- 2.30	73	- 1:17	- 2.30	74	- 1:16	- 2.30	61	- 1:29
- 2.15	128	- 0:07	- 2.15	73	- 1:02	- 2.15	73	- 1:02	- 2.15	60	- 1:15
- 2.00	126	+ 0:06	- 2.00	72	- 0:48	- 2.00	72	- 0:48	- 2.00	60	- 1:00
- 1.45	122	+ 0:17	- 1.45	71	- 0:34	- 1.45	70	- 0:35	- 1.45	58	- 0:47
- 1.30	118	+ 0:28	- 1.30	70	- 0:20	- 1.30	69	- 0:21	- 1.30	57	- 0:33
- 1.15	114	+ 0:39	- 1.15	68	- 0:07	- 1.15	67	- 0:08	- 1.15	55	- 0:20
- 1.00	110	+ 0:50	- 1.00	67	+ 0:07	- 1.00	65	+ 0:05	- 1.00	53	- 0:07
- 0.45	107	+ 1:02	- 0.45	66	+ 0:21	- 0.45	63	+ 0:18	- 0.45	52	+ 0:07
- 0.30	103	+ 1:13	- 0.30	64	+ 0:34	- 0.30	61	+ 0:31	- 0.30	50	+ 0:20
- 0.15	100	+ 1:25	- 0.15	63	+ 0:48	- 0.15	58	+ 0:43	- 0.15	48	+ 0:33
HW	96	+ 1:36	HW	61	+ 1:01	HW	56	+ 0:56	HW	47	+ 0:47
+ 0.15	93	+ 1:48	+ 0.15	60	+ 1:15	+ 0.15	54	+ 1:09	+ 0.15	45	+ 1:00
+ 0.30	89	+ 1:59	+ 0.30	59	+ 1:29	+ 0.30	53	+ 1:23	+ 0.30	44	+ 1:14
+ 0.45	86	+ 2:11	+ 0.45	58	+ 1:43	+ 0.45	51	+ 1:36	+ 0.45	43	+ 1:28
+ 1.00	83	+ 2:23	+ 1.00	57	+ 1:57	+ 1.00	49	+ 1:49	+ 1.00	41	+ 1:41
+ 1.15	82	+ 2:37	+ 1.15	57	+ 2:12	+ 1.15	48	+ 2:03	+ 1.15	40	+ 1:55
+ 1.30	80	+ 2:50	+ 1.30	57	+ 2:27	+ 1.30	47	+ 2:17	+ 1.30	40	+ 2:10
+ 1.45	79	+ 3:04	+ 1.45	57	+ 2:42	+ 1.45	46	+ 2:31	+ 1.45	39	+ 2:24
+ 2.00	78	+ 3:18	+ 2.00	58	+ 2:58	+ 2.00	45	+ 2:45	+ 2.00	38	+ 2:38
+ 2.15	78	+ 3:33	+ 2.15	58	+ 3:13	+ 2.15	46	+ 3:01	+ 2.15	38	+ 2:53
+ 2.30	79	+ 3:49	+ 2.30	59	+ 3:29	+ 2.30	46	+ 3:16	+ 2.30	38	+ 3:08
+ 2.45	80	+ 4:05	+ 2.45	59	+ 3:44	+ 2.45	46	+ 3:31	+ 2.45	38	+ 3:23
+ 3.00	81	+ 4:21	+ 3.00	60	+ 4:00	+ 3.00	46	+ 3:46	+ 3.00	38	+ 3:38
+ 3.15	83	+ 4:38	+ 3.15	61	+ 4:16	+ 3.15	47	+ 4:02	+ 3.15	38	+ 3:53
+ 3.30	85	+ 4:55	+ 3.30	61	+ 4:31	+ 3.30	48	+ 4:18	+ 3.30	39	+ 4:09
+ 3.45	87	+ 5:12	+ 3.45	62	+ 4:47	+ 3.45	49	+ 4:34	+ 3.45	40	+ 4:25
+ 4.00	89	+ 5:29	+ 4.00	62	+ 5:02	+ 4.00	49	+ 4:49	+ 4.00	40	+ 4:40
+ 4.15	91	+ 5:46	+ 4.15	63	+ 5:18	+ 4.15	51	+ 5:06	+ 4.15	41	+ 4:56
+ 4.30	93	- 5:57	+ 4.30	64	+ 5:34	+ 4.30	52	+ 5:22	+ 4.30	42	+ 5:12
+ 4.45	95	- 5:40	+ 4.45	65	+ 5:50	+ 4.45	54	+ 5:39	+ 4.45	43	+ 5:28
+ 5.00	97	- 5:23	+ 5.00	65	- 5:55	+ 5.00	55	+ 5:55	+ 5.00	44	+ 5:44
+ 5.15	99	- 5:06	+ 5.15	66	- 5:39	+ 5.15	56	- 5:49	+ 5.15	45	- 6:00
+ 5.30	102	- 4:48	+ 5.30	67	- 5:23	+ 5.30	57	- 5:33	+ 5.30	46	- 5:44
+ 5.45	104	- 4:31	+ 5.45	67	- 5:08	+ 5.45	58	- 5:17	+ 5.45	47	- 5:28
+ 6.00	106	- 4:14	+ 6.00	68	- 4:52	+ 6.00	60	- 5:00	+ 6.00	48	- 5:12

The Queens Channel

F - 5 Kts

Table F - Queens Channel and Southwards to the Swale

5 Kts - F

Time to cover Sectors (in minutes) at 5.0 kts — All times relate to HW Sheerness — Springs

Time	F8 SW Barrow to Red Sand Duration	F8 Time at End of Sector	Time	F7 Red Sand to Spaniard Duration	F7 Time at End of Sector	Time	F6 Spaniard to Swale Landfall Duration	F6 Time at End of Sector	Time	F5 Spile to Spaniard Duration	F5 Time at End of Sector	Time	F4 Spaniard to Wedge Duration	F4 Time at End of Sector	Time	F3 Swale Landfall to Woolpack Duration	F3 Time at End of Sector	Time	F2 Woolpack to Wedge Duration	F2 Time at End of Sector	Time	F1 Wedge to Margate Sands Duration	F1 Time at End of Sector
- 6.00	55	- 5:05	- 6.00	28	- 5:32	- 6.00	26	- 5:34	- 6.00	74	- 4:46	- 6.00	121	- 3:59	- 6.00	73	- 4:47	- 6.00	66	- 4:54	- 6.00	52	- 5:08
- 5.45	55	- 4:50	- 5.45	27	- 5:18	- 5.45	25	- 5:20	- 5.45	75	- 4:30	- 5.45	125	- 3:40	- 5.45	74	- 4:31	- 5.45	68	- 4:37	- 5.45	54	- 4:51
- 5.30	56	- 4:34	- 5.30	27	- 5:03	- 5.30	24	- 5:06	- 5.30	76	- 4:14	- 5.30	129	- 3:21	- 5.30	75	- 4:15	- 5.30	70	- 4:20	- 5.30	55	- 4:35
- 5.15	57	- 4:18	- 5.15	27	- 4:48	- 5.15	24	- 4:51	- 5.15	77	- 3:58	- 5.15	133	- 3:02	- 5.15	76	- 3:59	- 5.15	72	- 4:03	- 5.15	57	- 4:18
- 5.00	57	- 4:03	- 5.00	27	- 4:33	- 5.00	23	- 4:37	- 5.00	78	- 3:42	- 5.00	137	- 2:43	- 5.00	77	- 3:43	- 5.00	74	- 3:46	- 5.00	59	- 4:01
- 4.45	58	- 3:47	- 4.45	28	- 4:17	- 4.45	23	- 4:22	- 4.45	78	- 3:27	- 4.45	143	- 2:22	- 4.45	78	- 3:27	- 4.45	76	- 3:29	- 4.45	60	- 3:45
- 4.30	58	- 3:32	- 4.30	28	- 4:02	- 4.30	23	- 4:07	- 4.30	77	- 3:13	- 4.30	148	- 2:02	- 4.30	78	- 3:12	- 4.30	77	- 3:13	- 4.30	62	- 3:28
- 4.15	58	- 3:17	- 4.15	28	- 3:47	- 4.15	23	- 3:52	- 4.15	77	- 2:58	- 4.15	153	- 1:42	- 4.15	79	- 2:56	- 4.15	79	- 2:56	- 4.15	64	- 3:11
- 4.00	59	- 3:01	- 4.00	28	- 3:32	- 4.00	22	- 3:38	- 4.00	77	- 2:43	- 4.00	159	- 1:21	- 4.00	79	- 2:41	- 4.00	81	- 2:39	- 4.00	65	- 2:55
- 3.45	59	- 2:46	- 3.45	29	- 3:16	- 3.45	23	- 3:22	- 3.45	76	- 2:29	- 3.45	157	- 1:08	- 3.45	79	- 2:26	- 3.45	84	- 2:21	- 3.45	66	- 2:39
- 3.30	59	- 2:31	- 3.30	29	- 3:01	- 3.30	23	- 3:07	- 3.30	76	- 2:14	- 3.30	156	- 0:54	- 3.30	79	- 2:11	- 3.30	87	- 2:03	- 3.30	68	- 2:22
- 3.15	59	- 2:16	- 3.15	29	- 2:46	- 3.15	23	- 2:52	- 3.15	75	- 2:00	- 3.15	155	- 0:40	- 3.15	79	- 1:56	- 3.15	91	- 1:44	- 3.15	69	- 2:06
- 3.00	59	- 2:01	- 3.00	29	- 2:31	- 3.00	23	- 2:37	- 3.00	75	- 1:45	- 3.00	154	- 0:26	- 3.00	79	- 1:41	- 3.00	94	- 1:26	- 3.00	70	- 1:50
- 2.45	59	- 1:46	- 2.45	29	- 2:16	- 2.45	23	- 2:22	- 2.45	74	- 1:31	- 2.45	148	- 0:17	- 2.45	78	- 1:27	- 2.45	91	- 1:14	- 2.45	69	- 1:36
- 2.30	59	- 1:31	- 2.30	29	- 2:01	- 2.30	23	- 2:07	- 2.30	74	- 1:16	- 2.30	143	- 0:07	- 2.30	78	- 1:12	- 2.30	88	- 1:02	- 2.30	69	- 1:21
- 2.15	59	- 1:16	- 2.15	29	- 1:46	- 2.15	23	- 1:52	- 2.15	73	- 1:02	- 2.15	138	+ 0:03	- 2.15	77	- 0:58	- 2.15	85	- 0:50	- 2.15	68	- 1:07
- 2.00	59	- 1:01	- 2.00	29	- 1:31	- 2.00	23	- 1:37	- 2.00	73	- 0:47	- 2.00	133	+ 0:13	- 2.00	77	- 0:43	- 2.00	81	- 0:39	- 2.00	68	- 0:52
- 1.45	58	- 0:47	- 1.45	28	- 1:17	- 1.45	23	- 1:22	- 1.45	71	- 0:34	- 1.45	127	+ 0:22	- 1.45	75	- 0:30	- 1.45	78	- 0:27	- 1.45	65	- 0:40
- 1.30	58	- 0:32	- 1.30	28	- 1:02	- 1.30	23	- 1:07	- 1.30	70	- 0:20	- 1.30	121	+ 0:31	- 1.30	73	- 0:17	- 1.30	75	- 0:15	- 1.30	62	- 0:28
- 1.15	57	- 0:18	- 1.15	28	- 0:47	- 1.15	24	- 0:51	- 1.15	68	- 0:07	- 1.15	115	+ 0:40	- 1.15	71	- 0:04	- 1.15	72	- 0:03	- 1.15	60	- 0:15
- 1.00	57	- 0:03	- 1.00	28	- 0:32	- 1.00	24	- 0:36	- 1.00	67	+ 0:07	- 1.00	110	+ 0:50	- 1.00	69	+ 0:09	- 1.00	69	+ 0:09	- 1.00	57	- 0:03
- 0.45	56	+ 0:11	- 0.45	28	- 0:17	- 0.45	25	- 0:20	- 0.45	64	+ 0:19	- 0.45	105	+ 1:00	- 0.45	66	+ 0:21	- 0.45	65	+ 0:20	- 0.45	54	+ 0:09
- 0.30	56	+ 0:26	- 0.30	27	- 0:03	- 0.30	26	- 0:04	- 0.30	61	+ 0:31	- 0.30	101	+ 1:11	- 0.30	64	+ 0:34	- 0.30	62	+ 0:32	- 0.30	51	+ 0:21
- 0.15	55	+ 0:40	- 0.15	27	+ 0:12	- 0.15	27	+ 0:12	- 0.15	58	+ 0:43	- 0.15	96	+ 1:21	- 0.15	61	+ 0:46	- 0.15	58	+ 0:43	- 0.15	49	+ 0:34
HW	55	+ 0:55	HW	26	+ 0:26	HW	27	+ 0:27	HW	56	+ 0:56	HW	92	+ 1:32	HW	59	+ 0:59	HW	54	+ 0:54	HW	46	+ 0:46
+ 0.15	54	+ 1:09	+ 0.15	26	+ 0:41	+ 0.15	28	+ 0:43	+ 0.15	55	+ 1:10	+ 0.15	87	+ 1:42	+ 0.15	58	+ 1:13	+ 0.15	52	+ 1:07	+ 0.15	44	+ 0:59
+ 0.30	54	+ 1:24	+ 0.30	26	+ 0:56	+ 0.30	29	+ 0:59	+ 0.30	53	+ 1:23	+ 0.30	83	+ 1:53	+ 0.30	56	+ 1:26	+ 0.30	49	+ 1:19	+ 0.30	42	+ 1:12
+ 0.45	54	+ 1:39	+ 0.45	25	+ 1:10	+ 0.45	30	+ 1:15	+ 0.45	52	+ 1:37	+ 0.45	78	+ 2:03	+ 0.45	55	+ 1:40	+ 0.45	47	+ 1:32	+ 0.45	40	+ 1:25
+ 1.00	53	+ 1:53	+ 1.00	25	+ 1:25	+ 1.00	32	+ 1:32	+ 1.00	51	+ 1:51	+ 1.00	73	+ 2:13	+ 1.00	53	+ 1:53	+ 1.00	44	+ 1:44	+ 1.00	38	+ 1:38
+ 1.15	53	+ 2:08	+ 1.15	25	+ 1:40	+ 1.15	32	+ 1:47	+ 1.15	52	+ 2:07	+ 1.15	72	+ 2:27	+ 1.15	53	+ 2:08	+ 1.15	43	+ 1:58	+ 1.15	37	+ 1:52
+ 1.30	53	+ 2:23	+ 1.30	25	+ 1:55	+ 1.30	33	+ 2:03	+ 1.30	52	+ 2:22	+ 1.30	70	+ 2:40	+ 1.30	53	+ 2:23	+ 1.30	42	+ 2:12	+ 1.30	36	+ 2:06
+ 1.45	53	+ 2:38	+ 1.45	25	+ 2:10	+ 1.45	33	+ 2:18	+ 1.45	53	+ 2:38	+ 1.45	68	+ 2:53	+ 1.45	53	+ 2:38	+ 1.45	41	+ 2:26	+ 1.45	35	+ 2:20
+ 2.00	53	+ 2:53	+ 2.00	25	+ 2:25	+ 2.00	34	+ 2:34	+ 2.00	54	+ 2:54	+ 2.00	66	+ 3:06	+ 2.00	53	+ 2:53	+ 2.00	40	+ 2:40	+ 2.00	34	+ 2:34
+ 2.15	53	+ 3:08	+ 2.15	25	+ 2:40	+ 2.15	33	+ 2:48	+ 2.15	55	+ 3:10	+ 2.15	68	+ 3:23	+ 2.15	54	+ 3:09	+ 2.15	40	+ 2:55	+ 2.15	34	+ 2:49
+ 2.30	53	+ 3:23	+ 2.30	25	+ 2:55	+ 2.30	33	+ 3:03	+ 2.30	57	+ 3:27	+ 2.30	69	+ 3:39	+ 2.30	54	+ 3:24	+ 2.30	41	+ 3:11	+ 2.30	34	+ 3:04
+ 2.45	53	+ 3:38	+ 2.45	26	+ 3:11	+ 2.45	33	+ 3:18	+ 2.45	58	+ 3:43	+ 2.45	70	+ 3:55	+ 2.45	55	+ 3:40	+ 2.45	41	+ 3:26	+ 2.45	34	+ 3:19
+ 3.00	53	+ 3:53	+ 3.00	26	+ 3:26	+ 3.00	32	+ 3:32	+ 3.00	60	+ 4:00	+ 3.00	71	+ 4:11	+ 3.00	56	+ 3:56	+ 3.00	41	+ 3:41	+ 3.00	34	+ 3:34
+ 3.15	53	+ 4:08	+ 3.15	26	+ 3:41	+ 3.15	32	+ 3:47	+ 3.15	61	+ 4:16	+ 3.15	74	+ 4:29	+ 3.15	57	+ 4:12	+ 3.15	42	+ 3:57	+ 3.15	35	+ 3:50
+ 3.30	53	+ 4:23	+ 3.30	26	+ 3:56	+ 3.30	31	+ 4:01	+ 3.30	63	+ 4:33	+ 3.30	77	+ 4:47	+ 3.30	58	+ 4:28	+ 3.30	43	+ 4:13	+ 3.30	36	+ 4:06
+ 3.45	53	+ 4:38	+ 3.45	26	+ 4:11	+ 3.45	31	+ 4:16	+ 3.45	65	+ 4:50	+ 3.45	80	+ 5:05	+ 3.45	59	+ 4:44	+ 3.45	44	+ 4:29	+ 3.45	36	+ 4:21
+ 4.00	53	+ 4:53	+ 4.00	26	+ 4:26	+ 4.00	31	+ 4:31	+ 4.00	66	+ 5:06	+ 4.00	82	+ 5:22	+ 4.00	60	+ 5:00	+ 4.00	46	+ 4:46	+ 4.00	37	+ 4:37
+ 4.15	53	+ 5:08	+ 4.15	26	+ 4:41	+ 4.15	30	+ 4:45	+ 4.15	67	+ 5:22	+ 4.15	86	+ 5:41	+ 4.15	61	+ 5:16	+ 4.15	48	+ 5:03	+ 4.15	39	+ 4:54
+ 4.30	53	+ 5:23	+ 4.30	26	+ 4:56	+ 4.30	30	+ 5:00	+ 4.30	68	+ 5:38	+ 4.30	90	- 6:00	+ 4.30	62	+ 5:32	+ 4.30	49	+ 5:19	+ 4.30	40	+ 5:10
+ 4.45	53	+ 5:38	+ 4.45	26	+ 5:11	+ 4.45	29	+ 5:14	+ 4.45	69	+ 5:54	+ 4.45	94	- 5:41	+ 4.45	64	+ 5:49	+ 4.45	51	+ 5:36	+ 4.45	41	+ 5:26
+ 5.00	53	+ 5:53	+ 5.00	26	+ 5:26	+ 5.00	28	+ 5:28	+ 5.00	70	- 5:50	+ 5.00	97	- 5:23	+ 5.00	65	- 5:55	+ 5.00	53	+ 5:53	+ 5.00	43	+ 5:43
+ 5.15	53	- 5:52	+ 5.15	27	+ 5:42	+ 5.15	28	+ 5:43	+ 5.15	70	- 5:35	+ 5.15	100	- 5:05	+ 5.15	66	- 5:39	+ 5.15	55	- 5:50	+ 5.15	44	+ 5:59
+ 5.30	53	- 5:37	+ 5.30	27	+ 5:57	+ 5.30	28	+ 5:58	+ 5.30	70	- 5:20	+ 5.30	103	- 4:47	+ 5.30	67	- 5:23	+ 5.30	57	- 5:33	+ 5.30	45	- 5:45
+ 5.45	54	- 5:21	+ 5.45	27	- 5:48	+ 5.45	27	- 5:48	+ 5.45	70	- 5:05	+ 5.45	105	- 4:30	+ 5.45	68	- 5:07	+ 5.45	58	- 5:17	+ 5.45	47	- 5:28
+ 6.00	54	- 5:06	+ 6.00	27	- 5:33	+ 6.00	27	- 5:33	+ 6.00	71	- 4:49	+ 6.00	108	- 4:12	+ 6.00	69	- 4:51	+ 6.00	60	- 5:00	+ 6.00	48	- 5:12

Southwards to Swale (F8–F6) — The Queens Channel (F5–F1)

SOUTH & EAST

F - 6 Kts — Table F - Queens Channel and Southwards to the Swale — 6 Kts - F

Neaps — All times relate to HW Sheerness — **Time to cover Sectors (in minutes) at 6.0 Kts**

SOUTH & EAST

	F8			F7			F6			F5			F4			F3			F2			F1	
	SW Barrow to Red Sand			Red Sand to Spaniard			Spaniard to Swale Landfall			Spile to Spaniard			Spaniard to Wedge			Swale Landfall to Woolpack			Woolpack to Wedge			Wedge to Margate Sands	
Time	Duration	Time at End of Sector	Time	Duration	Time at End of Sector	Time	Duration	Time at End of Sector	Time	Duration	Time at End of Sector	Time	Duration	Time at End of Sector	Time	Duration	Time at End of Sector	Time	Duration	Time at End of Sector	Time	Duration	Time at End of Sector
- 6.00	45	- 5:15	- 6.00	23	- 5:37	- 6.00	22	- 5:38	- 6.00	59	- 5:01	- 6.00	93	- 4:27	- 6.00	58	- 5:02	- 6.00	52	- 5:08	- 6.00	41	- 5:19
- 5.45	46	- 4:59	- 5.45	23	- 5:22	- 5.45	21	- 5:24	- 5.45	59	- 4:46	- 5.45	95	- 4:10	- 5.45	59	- 4:46	- 5.45	53	- 4:52	- 5.45	42	- 5:03
- 5.30	46	- 4:44	- 5.30	23	- 5:07	- 5.30	21	- 5:09	- 5.30	59	- 4:31	- 5.30	97	- 3:53	- 5.30	59	- 4:31	- 5.30	53	- 4:37	- 5.30	43	- 4:47
- 5.15	46	- 4:29	- 5.15	22	- 4:53	- 5.15	20	- 4:55	- 5.15	60	- 4:15	- 5.15	99	- 3:36	- 5.15	60	- 4:15	- 5.15	54	- 4:21	- 5.15	44	- 4:31
- 5.00	46	- 4:14	- 5.00	22	- 4:38	- 5.00	20	- 4:40	- 5.00	60	- 4:00	- 5.00	101	- 3:19	- 5.00	60	- 4:00	- 5.00	55	- 4:05	- 5.00	44	- 4:16
- 4.45	46	- 3:59	- 4.45	23	- 4:22	- 4.45	20	- 4:25	- 4.45	60	- 3:45	- 4.45	102	- 3:03	- 4.45	60	- 3:45	- 4.45	56	- 3:49	- 4.45	45	- 4:00
- 4.30	46	- 3:44	- 4.30	23	- 4:07	- 4.30	20	- 4:10	- 4.30	60	- 3:30	- 4.30	104	- 2:46	- 4.30	61	- 3:29	- 4.30	57	- 3:33	- 4.30	46	- 3:44
- 4.15	47	- 3:28	- 4.15	23	- 3:52	- 4.15	20	- 3:55	- 4.15	60	- 3:15	- 4.15	106	- 2:29	- 4.15	61	- 3:14	- 4.15	57	- 3:18	- 4.15	46	- 3:29
- 4.00	47	- 3:13	- 4.00	23	- 3:37	- 4.00	20	- 3:40	- 4.00	60	- 3:00	- 4.00	108	- 2:12	- 4.00	61	- 2:59	- 4.00	58	- 3:02	- 4.00	47	- 3:13
- 3.45	47	- 2:58	- 3.45	23	- 3:22	- 3.45	20	- 3:25	- 3.45	60	- 2:45	- 3.45	108	- 1:57	- 3.45	61	- 2:44	- 3.45	59	- 2:46	- 3.45	47	- 2:58
- 3.30	47	- 2:43	- 3.30	23	- 3:07	- 3.30	20	- 3:10	- 3.30	59	- 2:31	- 3.30	109	- 1:41	- 3.30	61	- 2:29	- 3.30	59	- 2:31	- 3.30	48	- 2:42
- 3.15	47	- 2:28	- 3.15	23	- 2:52	- 3.15	20	- 2:55	- 3.15	59	- 2:16	- 3.15	110	- 1:25	- 3.15	61	- 2:14	- 3.15	60	- 2:15	- 3.15	49	- 2:26
- 3.00	47	- 2:13	- 3.00	23	- 2:37	- 3.00	20	- 2:40	- 3.00	59	- 2:01	- 3.00	110	- 1:10	- 3.00	61	- 1:59	- 3.00	60	- 2:00	- 3.00	49	- 2:11
- 2.45	47	- 1:58	- 2.45	23	- 2:22	- 2.45	20	- 2:25	- 2.45	59	- 1:46	- 2.45	109	- 0:56	- 2.45	60	- 1:45	- 2.45	60	- 1:45	- 2.45	49	- 1:56
- 2.30	47	- 1:43	- 2.30	23	- 2:07	- 2.30	20	- 2:10	- 2.30	59	- 1:31	- 2.30	107	- 0:43	- 2.30	60	- 1:30	- 2.30	60	- 1:30	- 2.30	49	- 1:41
- 2.15	47	- 1:28	- 2.15	23	- 1:52	- 2.15	20	- 1:55	- 2.15	59	- 1:16	- 2.15	106	- 0:29	- 2.15	60	- 1:15	- 2.15	59	- 1:16	- 2.15	49	- 1:26
- 2.00	47	- 1:13	- 2.00	23	- 1:37	- 2.00	20	- 1:40	- 2.00	59	- 1:01	- 2.00	104	- 0:16	- 2.00	59	- 1:01	- 2.00	59	- 1:01	- 2.00	48	- 1:12
- 1.45	47	- 0:58	- 1.45	23	- 1:22	- 1.45	20	- 1:25	- 1.45	58	- 0:47	- 1.45	102	- 0:03	- 1.45	59	- 0:46	- 1.45	57	- 0:48	- 1.45	47	- 0:58
- 1.30	47	- 0:43	- 1.30	23	- 1:07	- 1.30	21	- 1:09	- 1.30	57	- 0:33	- 1.30	99	+ 0:09	- 1.30	58	- 0:32	- 1.30	56	- 0:34	- 1.30	46	- 0:44
- 1.15	46	- 0:29	- 1.15	23	- 0:52	- 1.15	21	- 0:54	- 1.15	57	- 0:18	- 1.15	96	+ 0:21	- 1.15	57	- 0:18	- 1.15	55	- 0:20	- 1.15	45	- 0:30
- 1.00	46	- 0:14	- 1.00	23	- 0:37	- 1.00	21	- 0:39	- 1.00	56	- 0:04	- 1.00	94	+ 0:34	- 1.00	56	- 0:04	- 1.00	54	- 0:06	- 1.00	44	- 0:16
- 0.45	46	+ 0:01	- 0.45	23	- 0:22	- 0.45	22	- 0:23	- 0.45	55	+ 0:10	- 0.45	91	+ 0:46	- 0.45	55	+ 0:10	- 0.45	52	+ 0:07	- 0.45	43	- 0:02
- 0.30	46	+ 0:16	- 0.30	22	- 0:08	- 0.30	22	- 0:08	- 0.30	54	+ 0:24	- 0.30	87	+ 0:57	- 0.30	54	+ 0:24	- 0.30	51	+ 0:21	- 0.30	42	+ 0:12
- 0.15	46	+ 0:31	- 0.15	22	+ 0:07	- 0.15	22	+ 0:07	- 0.15	52	+ 0:37	- 0.15	84	+ 1:09	- 0.15	53	+ 0:38	- 0.15	49	+ 0:34	- 0.15	41	+ 0:26
HW	45	+ 0:45	HW	22	+ 0:22	HW	23	+ 0:23	HW	51	+ 0:51	HW	81	+ 1:21	HW	52	+ 0:52	HW	48	+ 0:48	HW	40	+ 0:40
+ 0.15	45	+ 1:00	+ 0.15	22	+ 0:37	+ 0.15	23	+ 0:38	+ 0.15	50	+ 1:05	+ 0.15	79	+ 1:34	+ 0.15	51	+ 1:06	+ 0.15	47	+ 1:02	+ 0.15	39	+ 0:54
+ 0.30	45	+ 1:15	+ 0.30	22	+ 0:52	+ 0.30	24	+ 0:54	+ 0.30	50	+ 1:20	+ 0.30	77	+ 1:47	+ 0.30	51	+ 1:21	+ 0.30	45	+ 1:15	+ 0.30	38	+ 1:08
+ 0.45	45	+ 1:30	+ 0.45	21	+ 1:06	+ 0.45	24	+ 1:09	+ 0.45	49	+ 1:34	+ 0.45	75	+ 2:00	+ 0.45	50	+ 1:35	+ 0.45	44	+ 1:29	+ 0.45	37	+ 1:22
+ 1.00	45	+ 1:45	+ 1.00	21	+ 1:21	+ 1.00	25	+ 1:25	+ 1.00	48	+ 1:48	+ 1.00	72	+ 2:12	+ 1.00	49	+ 1:49	+ 1.00	43	+ 1:43	+ 1.00	36	+ 1:36
+ 1.15	44	+ 1:59	+ 1.15	21	+ 1:36	+ 1.15	25	+ 1:40	+ 1.15	48	+ 2:03	+ 1.15	71	+ 2:26	+ 1.15	49	+ 2:04	+ 1.15	42	+ 1:57	+ 1.15	35	+ 1:50
+ 1.30	44	+ 2:14	+ 1.30	21	+ 1:51	+ 1.30	25	+ 1:55	+ 1.30	49	+ 2:19	+ 1.30	70	+ 2:40	+ 1.30	49	+ 2:19	+ 1.30	41	+ 2:11	+ 1.30	34	+ 2:04
+ 1.45	44	+ 2:29	+ 1.45	21	+ 2:06	+ 1.45	25	+ 2:10	+ 1.45	49	+ 2:34	+ 1.45	69	+ 2:54	+ 1.45	49	+ 2:34	+ 1.45	41	+ 2:26	+ 1.45	34	+ 2:19
+ 2.00	44	+ 2:44	+ 2.00	21	+ 2:21	+ 2.00	26	+ 2:26	+ 2.00	49	+ 2:49	+ 2.00	68	+ 3:08	+ 2.00	49	+ 2:49	+ 2.00	40	+ 2:40	+ 2.00	33	+ 2:33
+ 2.15	44	+ 2:59	+ 2.15	21	+ 2:36	+ 2.15	25	+ 2:40	+ 2.15	50	+ 3:05	+ 2.15	69	+ 3:24	+ 2.15	49	+ 3:04	+ 2.15	40	+ 2:55	+ 2.15	33	+ 2:48
+ 2.30	44	+ 3:14	+ 2.30	21	+ 2:51	+ 2.30	25	+ 2:55	+ 2.30	51	+ 3:21	+ 2.30	69	+ 3:39	+ 2.30	50	+ 3:20	+ 2.30	40	+ 3:10	+ 2.30	33	+ 3:03
+ 2.45	44	+ 3:29	+ 2.45	21	+ 3:06	+ 2.45	25	+ 3:10	+ 2.45	51	+ 3:36	+ 2.45	70	+ 3:55	+ 2.45	50	+ 3:35	+ 2.45	40	+ 3:25	+ 2.45	33	+ 3:18
+ 3.00	44	+ 3:44	+ 3.00	22	+ 3:22	+ 3.00	25	+ 3:25	+ 3.00	52	+ 3:52	+ 3.00	70	+ 4:10	+ 3.00	51	+ 3:51	+ 3.00	40	+ 3:40	+ 3.00	32	+ 3:32
+ 3.15	44	+ 3:59	+ 3.15	22	+ 3:37	+ 3.15	25	+ 3:40	+ 3.15	53	+ 4:08	+ 3.15	71	+ 4:26	+ 3.15	51	+ 4:06	+ 3.15	40	+ 3:55	+ 3.15	33	+ 3:48
+ 3.30	44	+ 4:14	+ 3.30	22	+ 3:52	+ 3.30	24	+ 3:54	+ 3.30	54	+ 4:24	+ 3.30	73	+ 4:43	+ 3.30	51	+ 4:21	+ 3.30	41	+ 4:11	+ 3.30	33	+ 4:03
+ 3.45	44	+ 4:29	+ 3.45	22	+ 4:07	+ 3.45	24	+ 4:09	+ 3.45	54	+ 4:39	+ 3.45	74	+ 4:59	+ 3.45	52	+ 4:37	+ 3.45	41	+ 4:26	+ 3.45	34	+ 4:19
+ 4.00	44	+ 4:44	+ 4.00	22	+ 4:22	+ 4.00	24	+ 4:24	+ 4.00	55	+ 4:55	+ 4.00	75	+ 5:15	+ 4.00	52	+ 4:52	+ 4.00	42	+ 4:42	+ 4.00	34	+ 4:34
+ 4.15	44	+ 4:59	+ 4.15	22	+ 4:37	+ 4.15	24	+ 4:39	+ 4.15	55	+ 5:10	+ 4.15	77	+ 5:32	+ 4.15	53	+ 5:08	+ 4.15	43	+ 4:58	+ 4.15	35	+ 4:50
+ 4.30	44	+ 5:14	+ 4.30	22	+ 4:52	+ 4.30	24	+ 4:54	+ 4.30	56	+ 5:26	+ 4.30	79	+ 5:49	+ 4.30	53	+ 5:23	+ 4.30	44	+ 5:14	+ 4.30	35	+ 5:05
+ 4.45	44	+ 5:29	+ 4.45	22	+ 5:07	+ 4.45	23	+ 5:08	+ 4.45	56	+ 5:41	+ 4.45	81	- 5:54	+ 4.45	54	+ 5:39	+ 4.45	45	+ 5:30	+ 4.45	36	+ 5:21
+ 5.00	44	+ 5:44	+ 5.00	22	+ 5:22	+ 5.00	23	+ 5:23	+ 5.00	57	+ 5:57	+ 5.00	82	- 5:38	+ 5.00	54	+ 5:54	+ 5.00	46	+ 5:46	+ 5.00	37	+ 5:37
+ 5.15	45	- 6:00	+ 5.15	22	+ 5:37	+ 5.15	23	+ 5:38	+ 5.15	57	- 5:48	+ 5.15	83	- 5:22	+ 5.15	55	- 5:50	+ 5.15	47	- 5:58	+ 5.15	38	+ 5:53
+ 5.30	45	- 5:45	+ 5.30	22	+ 5:52	+ 5.30	23	+ 5:53	+ 5.30	57	- 5:33	+ 5.30	85	- 5:05	+ 5.30	55	- 5:35	+ 5.30	48	- 5:42	+ 5.30	38	- 5:52
+ 5.45	45	- 5:30	+ 5.45	22	- 5:53	+ 5.45	23	- 5:52	+ 5.45	57	- 5:18	+ 5.45	86	- 4:49	+ 5.45	56	- 5:19	+ 5.45	48	- 5:27	+ 5.45	39	- 5:36
+ 6.00	45	- 5:15	+ 6.00	23	- 5:37	+ 6.00	22	- 5:38	+ 6.00	57	- 5:03	+ 6.00	87	- 4:33	+ 6.00	56	- 5:04	+ 6.00	49	- 5:11	+ 6.00	40	- 5:20

Southwards to Swale (F8–F6) — The Queens Channel (F5–F1)

Table F - Queens Channel and Southwards to the Swale

Time to cover Sectors (in minutes) at 6.0 kts — All times relate to HW Sheerness — **Springs**

	F8		F7		F6		F5		F4		F3		F2		F1	
	SW Barrow to Red Sand		Red Sand to Spaniard		Spaniard to Swale Landfall		Spile to Spaniard		Spaniard to Wedge		Swale Landfall to Woolpack		Woolpack to Wedge		Wedge to Margate Sands	
Time	Duration	Time at End of Sector	Duration	Time at End of Sector	Duration	Time at End of Sector	Duration	Time at End of Sector	Duration	Time at End of Sector	Duration	Time at End of Sector	Duration	Time at End of Sector	Duration	Time at End of Sector
- 6.00	45	- 5:15	23	- 5:37	21	- 5:39	60	- 5:00	97	- 4:23	60	- 5:00	53	- 5:07	42	- 5:18
- 5.45	46	- 4:59	23	- 5:22	21	- 5:24	61	- 4:44	99	- 4:06	60	- 4:45	55	- 4:50	43	- 5:02
- 5.30	46	- 4:44	23	- 5:07	20	- 5:10	62	- 4:28	102	- 3:48	61	- 4:29	56	- 4:34	45	- 4:45
- 5.15	47	- 4:28	23	- 4:52	20	- 4:55	63	- 4:12	105	- 3:30	62	- 4:13	57	- 4:18	46	- 4:29
- 5.00	47	- 4:13	23	- 4:37	19	- 4:41	63	- 3:57	108	- 3:12	63	- 3:57	59	- 4:01	47	- 4:13
- 4.45	47	- 3:58	23	- 4:22	19	- 4:26	63	- 3:42	110	- 2:55	63	- 3:42	60	- 3:45	48	- 3:57
- 4.30	47	- 3:43	23	- 4:07	19	- 4:11	63	- 3:27	113	- 2:37	63	- 3:27	61	- 3:29	49	- 3:41
- 4.15	48	- 3:27	23	- 3:52	19	- 3:56	63	- 3:12	115	- 2:20	64	- 3:11	63	- 3:12	50	- 3:25
- 4.00	48	- 3:12	24	- 3:36	19	- 3:41	63	- 2:57	118	- 2:02	64	- 2:56	64	- 2:56	51	- 3:09
- 3.45	48	- 2:57	24	- 3:21	19	- 3:26	62	- 2:43	118	- 1:47	64	- 2:41	65	- 2:40	52	- 2:53
- 3.30	48	- 2:42	24	- 3:06	19	- 3:11	62	- 2:28	119	- 1:31	64	- 2:26	65	- 2:25	53	- 2:37
- 3.15	48	- 2:27	24	- 2:51	19	- 2:56	62	- 2:13	120	- 1:15	64	- 2:11	66	- 2:09	54	- 2:21
- 3.00	48	- 2:12	24	- 2:36	19	- 2:41	61	- 1:59	120	- 1:00	64	- 1:56	67	- 1:53	55	- 2:05
- 2.45	48	- 1:57	24	- 2:21	19	- 2:26	61	- 1:44	118	- 0:47	64	- 1:41	67	- 1:38	55	- 1:50
- 2.30	48	- 1:42	24	- 2:06	19	- 2:11	61	- 1:29	115	- 0:35	63	- 1:27	66	- 1:24	54	- 1:36
- 2.15	48	- 1:27	24	- 1:51	19	- 1:56	60	- 1:15	112	- 0:23	63	- 1:12	66	- 1:09	54	- 1:21
- 2.00	48	- 1:12	24	- 1:36	19	- 1:41	60	- 1:00	110	- 0:10	62	- 0:58	65	- 0:55	54	- 1:06
- 1.45	48	- 0:57	24	- 1:21	19	- 1:26	59	- 0:46	106	+ 0:01	61	- 0:44	63	- 0:42	52	- 0:53
- 1.30	48	- 0:42	24	- 1:06	19	- 1:11	58	- 0:32	102	+ 0:12	60	- 0:30	61	- 0:29	50	- 0:40
- 1.15	47	- 0:28	24	- 0:51	20	- 0:55	57	- 0:18	98	+ 0:23	59	- 0:16	59	- 0:16	49	- 0:26
- 1.00	47	- 0:13	23	- 0:37	20	- 0:40	56	- 0:04	94	+ 0:34	58	- 0:02	57	- 0:03	47	- 0:13
- 0.45	47	+ 0:02	23	- 0:22	21	- 0:24	54	+ 0:09	90	+ 0:45	56	+ 0:11	54	+ 0:09	45	HW
- 0.30	46	+ 0:16	23	- 0:07	21	- 0:09	52	+ 0:22	86	+ 0:56	54	+ 0:24	52	+ 0:22	43	+ 0:13
- 0.15	46	+ 0:31	22	+ 0:07	22	+ 0:07	51	+ 0:36	82	+ 1:07	52	+ 0:37	49	+ 0:34	41	+ 0:26
HW	46	+ 0:46	22	+ 0:22	23	+ 0:23	49	+ 0:49	78	+ 1:18	51	+ 0:51	47	+ 0:47	39	+ 0:39
+ 0.15	45	+ 1:00	22	+ 0:37	23	+ 0:38	48	+ 1:03	75	+ 1:30	50	+ 1:05	45	+ 1:00	38	+ 0:53
+ 0.30	45	+ 1:15	21	+ 0:51	24	+ 0:54	47	+ 1:17	72	+ 1:42	49	+ 1:19	43	+ 1:13	36	+ 1:06
+ 0.45	45	+ 1:30	21	+ 1:06	25	+ 1:10	46	+ 1:31	69	+ 1:54	47	+ 1:32	41	+ 1:26	35	+ 1:20
+ 1.00	44	+ 1:44	21	+ 1:21	26	+ 1:26	45	+ 1:45	66	+ 2:06	46	+ 1:46	40	+ 1:40	34	+ 1:34
+ 1.15	44	+ 1:59	21	+ 1:36	26	+ 1:41	45	+ 2:00	65	+ 2:20	46	+ 2:01	39	+ 1:54	33	+ 1:48
+ 1.30	44	+ 2:14	21	+ 1:51	27	+ 1:57	45	+ 2:15	63	+ 2:33	46	+ 2:16	38	+ 2:08	32	+ 2:02
+ 1.45	44	+ 2:29	21	+ 2:06	27	+ 2:12	46	+ 2:31	62	+ 2:47	46	+ 2:31	37	+ 2:22	31	+ 2:16
+ 2.00	44	+ 2:44	21	+ 2:21	27	+ 2:27	46	+ 2:46	61	+ 3:01	46	+ 2:46	36	+ 2:36	31	+ 2:31
+ 2.15	44	+ 2:59	21	+ 2:36	27	+ 2:42	47	+ 3:02	61	+ 3:16	46	+ 3:01	36	+ 2:51	30	+ 2:45
+ 2.30	44	+ 3:14	21	+ 2:51	27	+ 2:57	48	+ 3:18	62	+ 3:32	47	+ 3:17	36	+ 3:06	30	+ 3:00
+ 2.45	44	+ 3:29	21	+ 3:06	27	+ 3:12	49	+ 3:34	63	+ 3:48	47	+ 3:32	36	+ 3:21	30	+ 3:15
+ 3.00	44	+ 3:44	21	+ 3:21	27	+ 3:27	50	+ 3:50	63	+ 4:03	48	+ 3:48	36	+ 3:36	30	+ 3:30
+ 3.15	44	+ 3:59	21	+ 3:36	26	+ 3:41	51	+ 4:06	65	+ 4:20	48	+ 4:03	37	+ 3:52	30	+ 3:45
+ 3.30	44	+ 4:14	21	+ 3:51	26	+ 3:56	52	+ 4:22	67	+ 4:37	49	+ 4:19	38	+ 4:08	31	+ 4:01
+ 3.45	44	+ 4:29	21	+ 4:06	26	+ 4:11	54	+ 4:39	69	+ 4:54	50	+ 4:35	38	+ 4:23	31	+ 4:16
+ 4.00	44	+ 4:44	22	+ 4:22	25	+ 4:25	55	+ 4:55	71	+ 5:11	50	+ 4:50	39	+ 4:39	32	+ 4:32
+ 4.15	44	+ 4:59	22	+ 4:37	25	+ 4:40	55	+ 5:10	73	+ 5:28	51	+ 5:06	40	+ 4:55	33	+ 4:48
+ 4.30	44	+ 5:14	22	+ 4:52	24	+ 4:54	56	+ 5:26	76	+ 5:46	52	+ 5:22	42	+ 5:12	34	+ 5:04
+ 4.45	44	+ 5:29	22	+ 5:07	24	+ 5:09	57	+ 5:42	78	- 5:57	53	+ 5:38	43	+ 5:28	35	+ 5:20
+ 5.00	44	+ 5:44	22	+ 5:22	24	+ 5:24	58	+ 5:58	81	- 5:39	54	+ 5:54	44	+ 5:44	35	+ 5:35
+ 5.15	44	+ 5:59	22	+ 5:37	23	+ 5:38	58	- 5:47	82	- 5:23	54	- 5:51	46	- 5:59	37	+ 5:52
+ 5.30	44	- 5:46	22	+ 5:52	23	+ 5:53	58	- 5:32	84	- 5:06	55	- 5:35	47	- 5:43	38	- 5:52
+ 5.45	45	- 5:30	22	- 5:53	23	- 5:52	58	- 5:17	86	- 4:49	56	- 5:19	48	- 5:27	39	- 5:36
+ 6.00	45	- 5:15	23	- 5:37	22	- 5:38	58	- 5:02	87	- 4:33	57	- 5:03	50	- 5:10	40	- 5:20

Southwards to Swale (F8–F6) — The Queens Channel (F5–F1)

SOUTH & EAST

Table F - Queens Channel and Southwards to the Swale

Neaps — All times relate to HW Sheerness — Time to cover Sectors (in minutes) at 7.0 Kts

SOUTH & EAST

	F8			F7			F6			F5			F4			F3			F2			F1	
	SW Barrow to Red Sand			Red Sand to Spaniard			Spaniard to Swale Landfall			Spile to Spaniard			Spaniard to Wedge			Swale Landfall to Woolpack			Woolpack to Wedge			Wedge to Margate Sands	
Time	Duration	Time at End of Sector	Time	Duration	Time at End of Sector	Time	Duration	Time at End of Sector	Time	Duration	Time at End of Sector	Time	Duration	Time at End of Sector	Time	Duration	Time at End of Sector	Time	Duration	Time at End of Sector	Time	Duration	Time at End of Sector
-6.00	39	-5:21	-6.00	19	-5:41	-6.00	18	-5:42	-6.00	50	-5:10	-6.00	78	-4:42	-6.00	49	-5:11	-6.00	44	-5:16	-6.00	35	-5:25
-5.45	39	-5:06	-5.45	19	-5:26	-5.45	18	-5:27	-5.45	50	-4:55	-5.45	79	-4:26	-5.45	50	-4:55	-5.45	44	-5:01	-5.45	35	-5:10
-5.30	39	-4:51	-5.30	19	-5:11	-5.30	18	-5:12	-5.30	50	-4:40	-5.30	80	-4:10	-5.30	50	-4:40	-5.30	45	-4:45	-5.30	36	-4:54
-5.15	39	-4:36	-5.15	19	-4:56	-5.15	17	-4:58	-5.15	51	-4:24	-5.15	81	-3:54	-5.15	50	-4:25	-5.15	46	-4:29	-5.15	37	-4:38
-5.00	39	-4:21	-5.00	19	-4:41	-5.00	17	-4:43	-5.00	51	-4:09	-5.00	82	-3:38	-5.00	51	-4:09	-5.00	46	-4:14	-5.00	37	-4:23
-4.45	39	-4:06	-4.45	19	-4:26	-4.45	17	-4:28	-4.45	51	-3:54	-4.45	84	-3:21	-4.45	51	-3:54	-4.45	47	-3:58	-4.45	38	-4:07
-4.30	39	-3:51	-4.30	19	-4:11	-4.30	17	-4:13	-4.30	51	-3:39	-4.30	86	-3:04	-4.30	51	-3:39	-4.30	47	-3:43	-4.30	38	-3:52
-4.15	40	-3:35	-4.15	20	-3:55	-4.15	17	-3:58	-4.15	51	-3:24	-4.15	88	-2:47	-4.15	51	-3:24	-4.15	48	-3:27	-4.15	39	-3:36
-4.00	40	-3:20	-4.00	20	-3:40	-4.00	17	-3:43	-4.00	51	-3:09	-4.00	90	-2:30	-4.00	51	-3:09	-4.00	48	-3:12	-4.00	39	-3:21
-3.45	40	-3:05	-3.45	20	-3:25	-3.45	17	-3:28	-3.45	51	-2:54	-3.45	90	-2:15	-3.45	51	-2:54	-3.45	49	-2:56	-3.45	40	-3:05
-3.30	40	-2:50	-3.30	20	-3:10	-3.30	17	-3:13	-3.30	50	-2:40	-3.30	91	-1:59	-3.30	51	-2:39	-3.30	49	-2:41	-3.30	40	-2:50
-3.15	40	-2:35	-3.15	20	-2:55	-3.15	17	-2:58	-3.15	50	-2:25	-3.15	92	-1:43	-3.15	51	-2:24	-3.15	50	-2:25	-3.15	40	-2:35
-3.00	40	-2:20	-3.00	20	-2:40	-3.00	17	-2:43	-3.00	50	-2:10	-3.00	93	-1:27	-3.00	51	-2:09	-3.00	50	-2:10	-3.00	41	-2:19
-2.45	40	-2:05	-2.45	20	-2:25	-2.45	17	-2:28	-2.45	50	-1:55	-2.45	91	-1:14	-2.45	51	-1:54	-2.45	50	-1:55	-2.45	41	-2:04
-2.30	40	-1:50	-2.30	20	-2:10	-2.30	17	-2:13	-2.30	50	-1:40	-2.30	89	-1:01	-2.30	51	-1:39	-2.30	50	-1:40	-2.30	41	-1:49
-2.15	40	-1:35	-2.15	20	-1:55	-2.15	17	-1:58	-2.15	50	-1:25	-2.15	87	-0:48	-2.15	51	-1:24	-2.15	50	-1:25	-2.15	41	-1:34
-2.00	40	-1:20	-2.00	20	-1:40	-2.00	17	-1:43	-2.00	50	-1:10	-2.00	85	-0:35	-2.00	50	-1:10	-2.00	49	-1:11	-2.00	41	-1:19
-1.45	40	-1:05	-1.45	20	-1:25	-1.45	17	-1:28	-1.45	49	-0:56	-1.45	83	-0:22	-1.45	50	-0:55	-1.45	48	-0:57	-1.45	40	-1:05
-1.30	40	-0:50	-1.30	20	-1:10	-1.30	18	-1:12	-1.30	49	-0:41	-1.30	81	-0:09	-1.30	49	-0:41	-1.30	48	-0:42	-1.30	39	-0:51
-1.15	40	-0:35	-1.15	20	-0:55	-1.15	18	-0:57	-1.15	49	-0:26	-1.15	80	+0:05	-1.15	49	-0:26	-1.15	47	-0:28	-1.15	38	-0:37
-1.00	39	-0:21	-1.00	19	-0:41	-1.00	18	-0:42	-1.00	48	-0:12	-1.00	78	+0:18	-1.00	48	-0:12	-1.00	46	-0:14	-1.00	38	-0:22
-0.45	39	-0:06	-0.45	19	-0:26	-0.45	18	-0:27	-0.45	47	+0:02	-0.45	76	+0:31	-0.45	47	+0:02	-0.45	45	HW	-0.45	37	-0:08
-0.30	39	+0:09	-0.30	19	-0:11	-0.30	19	-0:11	-0.30	46	+0:16	-0.30	74	+0:44	-0.30	47	+0:17	-0.30	44	+0:14	-0.30	36	+0:06
-0.15	39	+0:24	-0.15	19	+0:04	-0.15	19	+0:04	-0.15	46	+0:31	-0.15	72	+0:57	-0.15	46	+0:31	-0.15	43	+0:28	-0.15	35	+0:20
HW	39	+0:39	HW	19	+0:19	HW	19	+0:19	HW	45	+0:45	HW	71	+1:11	HW	45	+0:45	HW	42	+0:42	HW	34	+0:34
+0.15	39	+0:54	+0.15	19	+0:34	+0.15	20	+0:35	+0.15	44	+0:59	+0.15	69	+1:24	+0.15	45	+1:00	+0.15	41	+0:56	+0.15	34	+0:49
+0.30	39	+1:09	+0.30	18	+0:48	+0.30	20	+0:50	+0.30	43	+1:13	+0.30	67	+1:37	+0.30	44	+1:14	+0.30	40	+1:10	+0.30	33	+1:03
+0.45	38	+1:23	+0.45	18	+1:03	+0.45	21	+1:06	+0.45	43	+1:28	+0.45	66	+1:51	+0.45	43	+1:28	+0.45	39	+1:24	+0.45	32	+1:17
+1.00	38	+1:38	+1.00	18	+1:18	+1.00	21	+1:21	+1.00	42	+1:42	+1.00	64	+2:04	+1.00	43	+1:43	+1.00	38	+1:38	+1.00	31	+1:31
+1.15	38	+1:53	+1.15	18	+1:33	+1.15	21	+1:36	+1.15	42	+1:57	+1.15	63	+2:18	+1.15	43	+1:58	+1.15	37	+1:52	+1.15	31	+1:46
+1.30	38	+2:08	+1.30	18	+1:48	+1.30	21	+1:51	+1.30	42	+2:12	+1.30	62	+2:32	+1.30	43	+2:13	+1.30	36	+2:06	+1.30	30	+2:00
+1.45	38	+2:23	+1.45	18	+2:03	+1.45	22	+2:07	+1.45	43	+2:28	+1.45	62	+2:47	+1.45	43	+2:28	+1.45	36	+2:21	+1.45	30	+2:15
+2.00	38	+2:38	+2.00	18	+2:18	+2.00	22	+2:22	+2.00	43	+2:43	+2.00	61	+3:01	+2.00	42	+2:42	+2.00	35	+2:35	+2.00	29	+2:29
+2.15	38	+2:53	+2.15	18	+2:33	+2.15	22	+2:37	+2.15	43	+2:58	+2.15	61	+3:16	+2.15	43	+2:58	+2.15	35	+2:50	+2.15	29	+2:44
+2.30	38	+3:08	+2.30	18	+2:48	+2.30	22	+2:52	+2.30	44	+3:14	+2.30	61	+3:31	+2.30	43	+3:13	+2.30	35	+3:05	+2.30	29	+2:59
+2.45	38	+3:23	+2.45	18	+3:03	+2.45	21	+3:06	+2.45	44	+3:29	+2.45	61	+3:46	+2.45	43	+3:28	+2.45	35	+3:20	+2.45	28	+3:13
+3.00	38	+3:38	+3.00	18	+3:18	+3.00	21	+3:21	+3.00	45	+3:45	+3.00	62	+4:02	+3.00	44	+3:44	+3.00	35	+3:35	+3.00	28	+3:28
+3.15	38	+3:53	+3.15	18	+3:33	+3.15	21	+3:36	+3.15	45	+4:00	+3.15	63	+4:18	+3.15	44	+3:59	+3.15	35	+3:50	+3.15	29	+3:44
+3.30	38	+4:08	+3.30	18	+3:48	+3.30	21	+3:51	+3.30	46	+4:16	+3.30	64	+4:34	+3.30	44	+4:14	+3.30	36	+4:06	+3.30	29	+3:59
+3.45	38	+4:23	+3.45	18	+4:03	+3.45	21	+4:06	+3.45	46	+4:31	+3.45	65	+4:50	+3.45	45	+4:30	+3.45	36	+4:21	+3.45	29	+4:14
+4.00	38	+4:38	+4.00	19	+4:19	+4.00	21	+4:21	+4.00	47	+4:47	+4.00	66	+5:06	+4.00	45	+4:45	+4.00	36	+4:36	+4.00	30	+4:30
+4.15	38	+4:53	+4.15	19	+4:34	+4.15	20	+4:35	+4.15	47	+5:02	+4.15	67	+5:22	+4.15	45	+5:00	+4.15	37	+4:52	+4.15	30	+4:45
+4.30	38	+5:08	+4.30	19	+4:49	+4.30	20	+4:50	+4.30	48	+5:18	+4.30	68	+5:38	+4.30	46	+5:16	+4.30	38	+5:08	+4.30	31	+5:01
+4.45	38	+5:23	+4.45	19	+5:04	+4.45	20	+5:05	+4.45	48	+5:33	+4.45	69	+5:54	+4.45	46	+5:31	+4.45	39	+5:24	+4.45	31	+5:16
+5.00	38	+5:38	+5.00	19	+5:19	+5.00	20	+5:20	+5.00	48	+5:48	+5.00	71	-5:49	+5.00	46	+5:46	+5.00	39	+5:39	+5.00	32	+5:32
+5.15	38	+5:53	+5.15	19	+5:34	+5.15	20	+5:35	+5.15	49	-5:56	+5.15	71	-5:34	+5.15	47	-5:58	+5.15	40	+5:55	+5.15	32	+5:47
+5.30	38	-5:52	+5.30	19	+5:49	+5.30	19	+5:49	+5.30	49	-5:41	+5.30	72	-5:18	+5.30	47	-5:43	+5.30	41	-5:49	+5.30	33	-5:57
+5.45	38	-5:37	+5.45	19	-5:56	+5.45	19	-5:56	+5.45	49	-5:26	+5.45	73	-5:02	+5.45	47	-5:28	+5.45	41	-5:34	+5.45	33	-5:42
+6.00	38	-5:22	+6.00	19	-5:41	+6.00	19	-5:41	+6.00	49	-5:11	+6.00	74	-4:46	+6.00	48	-5:12	+6.00	42	-5:18	+6.00	34	-5:26

Southwards to Swale — The Queens Channel

Table F - Queens Channel and Southwards to the Swale

Time to cover Sectors (in minutes) at 7.0 kts

All times relate to HW Sheerness

Springs

	F8			F7			F6			F5			F4			F3			F2			F1	
	SW Barrow to Red Sand			Red Sand to Spaniard			Spaniard to Swale Landfall			Spile to Spaniard			Spaniard to Wedge			Swale Landfall to Woolpack			Woolpack to Wedge			Wedge to Margate Sands	
Time	Duration	Time at End of Sector	Time	Duration	Time at End of Sector	Time	Duration	Time at End of Sector	Time	Duration	Time at End of Sector	Time	Duration	Time at End of Sector	Time	Duration	Time at End of Sector	Time	Duration	Time at End of Sector	Time	Duration	Time at End of Sector
- 6.00	**39**	**- 5:21**	**- 6.00**	**20**	**- 5:40**	**- 6.00**	**18**	**- 5:42**	**- 6.00**	**51**	**- 5:09**	**- 6.00**	**80**	**- 4:40**	**- 6.00**	**50**	**- 5:10**	**- 6.00**	**45**	**- 5:15**	**- 6.00**	**35**	**- 5:25**
- 5.45	39	- 5:06	- 5.45	19	- 5:26	- 5.45	18	- 5:27	- 5.45	51	- 4:54	- 5.45	81	- 4:24	- 5.45	51	- 4:54	- 5.45	46	- 4:59	- 5.45	36	- 5:09
- 5.30	39	- 4:51	- 5.30	19	- 5:11	- 5.30	17	- 5:13	- 5.30	52	- 4:38	- 5.30	83	- 4:07	- 5.30	51	- 4:39	- 5.30	47	- 4:43	- 5.30	37	- 4:53
- 5.15	39	- 4:36	- 5.15	19	- 4:56	- 5.15	17	- 4:58	- 5.15	53	- 4:22	- 5.15	85	- 3:50	- 5.15	52	- 4:23	- 5.15	48	- 4:27	- 5.15	38	- 4:37
- 5.00	**40**	**- 4:20**	**- 5.00**	**19**	**- 4:41**	**- 5.00**	**16**	**- 4:44**	**- 5.00**	**53**	**- 4:07**	**- 5.00**	**86**	**- 3:34**	**- 5.00**	**53**	**- 4:07**	**- 5.00**	**49**	**- 4:11**	**- 5.00**	**39**	**- 4:21**
- 4.45	40	- 4:05	- 4.45	20	- 4:25	- 4.45	16	- 4:29	- 4.45	53	- 3:52	- 4.45	89	- 3:16	- 4.45	53	- 3:52	- 4.45	50	- 3:55	- 4.45	40	- 4:05
- 4.30	40	- 3:50	- 4.30	20	- 4:10	- 4.30	16	- 4:14	- 4.30	53	- 3:37	- 4.30	91	- 2:59	- 4.30	53	- 3:37	- 4.30	51	- 3:39	- 4.30	41	- 3:49
- 4.15	40	- 3:35	- 4.15	20	- 3:55	- 4.15	16	- 3:59	- 4.15	53	- 3:22	- 4.15	94	- 2:41	- 4.15	53	- 3:22	- 4.15	52	- 3:23	- 4.15	41	- 3:34
- 4.00	**40**	**- 3:20**	**- 4.00**	**20**	**- 3:40**	**- 4.00**	**16**	**- 3:44**	**- 4.00**	**53**	**- 3:07**	**- 4.00**	**96**	**- 2:24**	**- 4.00**	**54**	**- 3:06**	**- 4.00**	**53**	**- 3:07**	**- 4.00**	**42**	**- 3:18**
- 3.45	41	- 3:04	- 3.45	20	- 3:25	- 3.45	16	- 3:29	- 3.45	53	- 2:52	- 3.45	97	- 2:08	- 3.45	54	- 2:51	- 3.45	53	- 2:52	- 3.45	43	- 3:02
- 3.30	41	- 2:49	- 3.30	20	- 3:10	- 3.30	16	- 3:14	- 3.30	52	- 2:38	- 3.30	98	- 1:52	- 3.30	54	- 2:36	- 3.30	54	- 2:36	- 3.30	44	- 2:46
- 3.15	41	- 2:34	- 3.15	20	- 2:55	- 3.15	16	- 2:59	- 3.15	52	- 2:23	- 3.15	99	- 1:36	- 3.15	54	- 2:21	- 3.15	55	- 2:20	- 3.15	44	- 2:31
- 3.00	**41**	**- 2:19**	**- 3.00**	**20**	**- 2:40**	**- 3.00**	**16**	**- 2:44**	**- 3.00**	**52**	**- 2:08**	**- 3.00**	**100**	**- 1:20**	**- 3.00**	**54**	**- 2:06**	**- 3.00**	**55**	**- 2:05**	**- 3.00**	**45**	**- 2:15**
- 2.45	41	- 2:04	- 2.45	20	- 2:25	- 2.45	16	- 2:29	- 2.45	52	- 1:53	- 2.45	99	- 1:06	- 2.45	53	- 1:52	- 2.45	55	- 1:50	- 2.45	45	- 2:00
- 2.30	41	- 1:49	- 2.30	20	- 2:10	- 2.30	16	- 2:14	- 2.30	51	- 1:39	- 2.30	98	- 0:52	- 2.30	53	- 1:37	- 2.30	55	- 1:35	- 2.30	45	- 1:45
- 2.15	41	- 1:34	- 2.15	20	- 1:55	- 2.15	16	- 1:59	- 2.15	51	- 1:24	- 2.15	96	- 0:39	- 2.15	53	- 1:22	- 2.15	54	- 1:21	- 2.15	45	- 1:30
- 2.00	**41**	**- 1:19**	**- 2.00**	**20**	**- 1:40**	**- 2.00**	**16**	**- 1:44**	**- 2.00**	**51**	**- 1:09**	**- 2.00**	**95**	**- 0:25**	**- 2.00**	**53**	**- 1:07**	**- 2.00**	**54**	**- 1:06**	**- 2.00**	**45**	**- 1:15**
- 1.45	41	- 1:04	- 1.45	20	- 1:25	- 1.45	16	- 1:29	- 1.45	50	- 0:55	- 1.45	92	- 0:13	- 1.45	52	- 0:53	- 1.45	53	- 0:52	- 1.45	44	- 1:01
- 1.30	40	- 0:50	- 1.30	20	- 1:10	- 1.30	17	- 1:13	- 1.30	50	- 0:40	- 1.30	88	- 0:02	- 1.30	51	- 0:39	- 1.30	51	- 0:39	- 1.30	42	- 0:48
- 1.15	40	- 0:35	- 1.15	20	- 0:55	- 1.15	17	- 0:58	- 1.15	49	- 0:26	- 1.15	85	+ 0:10	- 1.15	50	- 0:25	- 1.15	50	- 0:25	- 1.15	41	- 0:34
- 1.00	**40**	**- 0:20**	**- 1.00**	**20**	**- 0:40**	**- 1.00**	**17**	**- 0:43**	**- 1.00**	**48**	**- 0:12**	**- 1.00**	**81**	**+ 0:21**	**- 1.00**	**49**	**- 0:11**	**- 1.00**	**48**	**- 0:12**	**- 1.00**	**40**	**- 0:20**
- 0.45	40	- 0:05	- 0.45	20	- 0:25	- 0.45	18	- 0:27	- 0.45	47	+ 0:02	- 0.45	78	+ 0:33	- 0.45	48	+ 0:03	- 0.45	46	+ 0:01	- 0.45	39	- 0:06
- 0.30	40	+ 0:10	- 0.30	19	- 0:11	- 0.30	18	- 0:12	- 0.30	46	+ 0:16	- 0.30	75	+ 0:45	- 0.30	47	+ 0:17	- 0.30	45	+ 0:15	- 0.30	37	+ 0:07
- 0.15	39	+ 0:24	- 0.15	19	+ 0:04	- 0.15	19	+ 0:04	- 0.15	44	+ 0:29	- 0.15	72	+ 0:57	- 0.15	46	+ 0:31	- 0.15	43	+ 0:28	- 0.15	36	+ 0:21
HW	**39**	**+ 0:39**	**HW**	**19**	**+ 0:19**	**HW**	**19**	**+ 0:19**	**HW**	**43**	**+ 0:43**	**HW**	**68**	**+ 1:08**	**HW**	**44**	**+ 0:44**	**HW**	**41**	**+ 0:41**	**HW**	**34**	**+ 0:34**
+ 0.15	39	+ 0:54	+ 0.15	18	+ 0:33	+ 0.15	20	+ 0:35	+ 0.15	42	+ 0:57	+ 0.15	66	+ 1:21	+ 0.15	44	+ 0:59	+ 0.15	40	+ 0:55	+ 0.15	33	+ 0:48
+ 0.30	39	+ 1:09	+ 0.30	18	+ 0:48	+ 0.30	21	+ 0:51	+ 0.30	41	+ 1:11	+ 0.30	64	+ 1:34	+ 0.30	43	+ 1:13	+ 0.30	38	+ 1:08	+ 0.30	32	+ 1:02
+ 0.45	38	+ 1:23	+ 0.45	18	+ 1:03	+ 0.45	21	+ 1:06	+ 0.45	40	+ 1:25	+ 0.45	62	+ 1:47	+ 0.45	42	+ 1:27	+ 0.45	37	+ 1:22	+ 0.45	31	+ 1:16
+ 1.00	**38**	**+ 1:38**	**+ 1.00**	**18**	**+ 1:18**	**+ 1.00**	**22**	**+ 1:22**	**+ 1.00**	**40**	**+ 1:40**	**+ 1.00**	**59**	**+ 1:59**	**+ 1.00**	**41**	**+ 1:41**	**+ 1.00**	**35**	**+ 1:35**	**+ 1.00**	**30**	**+ 1:30**
+ 1.15	38	+ 1:53	+ 1.15	18	+ 1:33	+ 1.15	22	+ 1:37	+ 1.15	40	+ 1:55	+ 1.15	58	+ 2:13	+ 1.15	41	+ 1:56	+ 1.15	35	+ 1:50	+ 1.15	29	+ 1:44
+ 1.30	38	+ 2:08	+ 1.30	18	+ 1:48	+ 1.30	23	+ 1:53	+ 1.30	40	+ 2:10	+ 1.30	57	+ 2:27	+ 1.30	41	+ 2:11	+ 1.30	34	+ 2:04	+ 1.30	28	+ 1:58
+ 1.45	38	+ 2:23	+ 1.45	18	+ 2:03	+ 1.45	23	+ 2:08	+ 1.45	40	+ 2:25	+ 1.45	56	+ 2:41	+ 1.45	40	+ 2:25	+ 1.45	33	+ 2:18	+ 1.45	28	+ 2:13
+ 2.00	**37**	**+ 2:37**	**+ 2.00**	**18**	**+ 2:18**	**+ 2.00**	**23**	**+ 2:23**	**+ 2.00**	**40**	**+ 2:40**	**+ 2.00**	**55**	**+ 2:55**	**+ 2.00**	**40**	**+ 2:40**	**+ 2.00**	**33**	**+ 2:33**	**+ 2.00**	**27**	**+ 2:27**
+ 2.15	38	+ 2:53	+ 2.15	18	+ 2:33	+ 2.15	23	+ 2:38	+ 2.15	41	+ 2:56	+ 2.15	55	+ 3:10	+ 2.15	40	+ 2:55	+ 2.15	33	+ 2:48	+ 2.15	26	+ 2:41
+ 2.30	38	+ 3:08	+ 2.30	18	+ 2:48	+ 2.30	23	+ 2:53	+ 2.30	42	+ 3:12	+ 2.30	56	+ 3:26	+ 2.30	41	+ 3:11	+ 2.30	32	+ 3:02	+ 2.30	26	+ 2:56
+ 2.45	38	+ 3:23	+ 2.45	18	+ 3:03	+ 2.45	23	+ 3:08	+ 2.45	43	+ 3:28	+ 2.45	56	+ 3:41	+ 2.45	41	+ 3:26	+ 2.45	32	+ 3:17	+ 2.45	26	+ 3:11
+ 3.00	**38**	**+ 3:38**	**+ 3.00**	**18**	**+ 3:18**	**+ 3.00**	**23**	**+ 3:23**	**+ 3.00**	**43**	**+ 3:43**	**+ 3.00**	**57**	**+ 3:57**	**+ 3.00**	**41**	**+ 3:41**	**+ 3.00**	**32**	**+ 3:32**	**+ 3.00**	**25**	**+ 3:25**
+ 3.15	38	+ 3:53	+ 3.15	18	+ 3:33	+ 3.15	22	+ 3:37	+ 3.15	44	+ 3:59	+ 3.15	58	+ 4:13	+ 3.15	42	+ 3:57	+ 3.15	33	+ 3:48	+ 3.15	26	+ 3:41
+ 3.30	38	+ 4:08	+ 3.30	18	+ 3:48	+ 3.30	22	+ 3:52	+ 3.30	45	+ 4:15	+ 3.30	59	+ 4:29	+ 3.30	42	+ 4:12	+ 3.30	33	+ 4:03	+ 3.30	26	+ 3:56
+ 3.45	38	+ 4:23	+ 3.45	18	+ 4:03	+ 3.45	22	+ 4:07	+ 3.45	46	+ 4:31	+ 3.45	61	+ 4:46	+ 3.45	43	+ 4:28	+ 3.45	34	+ 4:19	+ 3.45	27	+ 4:12
+ 4.00	**38**	**+ 4:38**	**+ 4.00**	**18**	**+ 4:18**	**+ 4.00**	**22**	**+ 4:22**	**+ 4.00**	**47**	**+ 4:47**	**+ 4.00**	**62**	**+ 5:02**	**+ 4.00**	**43**	**+ 4:43**	**+ 4.00**	**34**	**+ 4:34**	**+ 4.00**	**28**	**+ 4:28**
+ 4.15	38	+ 4:53	+ 4.15	18	+ 4:33	+ 4.15	21	+ 4:36	+ 4.15	47	+ 5:02	+ 4.15	64	+ 5:19	+ 4.15	44	+ 4:59	+ 4.15	35	+ 4:50	+ 4.15	28	+ 4:43
+ 4.30	38	+ 5:08	+ 4.30	19	+ 4:49	+ 4.30	21	+ 4:51	+ 4.30	48	+ 5:18	+ 4.30	66	+ 5:36	+ 4.30	45	+ 5:15	+ 4.30	36	+ 5:06	+ 4.30	29	+ 4:59
+ 4.45	38	+ 5:23	+ 4.45	19	+ 5:04	+ 4.45	21	+ 5:06	+ 4.45	48	+ 5:33	+ 4.45	67	+ 5:52	+ 4.45	45	+ 5:30	+ 4.45	37	+ 5:22	+ 4.45	30	+ 5:15
+ 5.00	**38**	**+ 5:38**	**+ 5.00**	**19**	**+ 5:19**	**+ 5.00**	**20**	**+ 5:20**	**+ 5.00**	**49**	**+ 5:49**	**+ 5.00**	**69**	**- 5:51**	**+ 5.00**	**46**	**+ 5:46**	**+ 5.00**	**38**	**+ 5:38**	**+ 5.00**	**30**	**+ 5:30**
+ 5.15	38	+ 5:53	+ 5.15	19	+ 5:34	+ 5.15	20	+ 5:35	+ 5.15	49	- 5:56	+ 5.15	71	- 5:34	+ 5.15	46	- 5:59	+ 5.15	39	+ 5:54	+ 5.15	31	+ 5:46
+ 5.30	38	- 5:52	+ 5.30	19	+ 5:49	+ 5.30	20	+ 5:50	+ 5.30	49	- 5:41	+ 5.30	72	- 5:18	+ 5.30	47	- 5:43	+ 5.30	40	- 5:50	+ 5.30	32	- 5:58
+ 5.45	38	- 5:37	+ 5.45	19	- 5:56	+ 5.45	19	- 5:56	+ 5.45	49	- 5:26	+ 5.45	73	- 5:02	+ 5.45	48	- 5:27	+ 5.45	41	- 5:34	+ 5.45	33	- 5:42
+ 6.00	**38**	**- 5:22**	**+ 6.00**	**19**	**- 5:41**	**+ 6.00**	**19**	**- 5:41**	**+ 6.00**	**49**	**- 5:11**	**+ 6.00**	**75**	**- 4:45**	**+ 6.00**	**48**	**- 5:12**	**+ 6.00**	**42**	**- 5:18**	**+ 6.00**	**34**	**- 5:26**

Southwards to Swale

The Queens Channel

Table G - Medway, Sea Reach and Black Deep Connections

Neaps — All times relate to HW Sheerness — **Time to cover Sectors (in minutes) at 4.0 Kts**

SOUTH BOUND

	G8			G7	
	Long Sand Inner to Blk Deep No 8			Black Deep to Blk Deep No 8	
Time	Duration	Time at End of Sector	Time	Duration	Time at End of Sector
- 6.00	46	- 5:14	- 6.00	56	- 5:04
- 5.45	45	- 5:00	- 5.45	55	- 4:50
- 5.30	44	- 4:46	- 5.30	55	- 4:35
- 5.15	43	- 4:32	- 5.15	54	- 4:21
- 5.00	41	- 4:19	- 5.00	53	- 4:07
- 4.45	41	- 4:04	- 4.45	53	- 3:52
- 4.30	41	- 3:49	- 4.30	54	- 3:36
- 4.15	40	- 3:35	- 4.15	54	- 3:21
- 4.00	40	- 3:20	- 4.00	54	- 3:06
- 3.45	40	- 3:05	- 3.45	57	- 2:48
- 3.30	41	- 2:49	- 3.30	59	- 2:31
- 3.15	41	- 2:34	- 3.15	62	- 2:13
- 3.00	41	- 2:19	- 3.00	65	- 1:55
- 2.45	43	- 2:02	- 2.45	69	- 1:36
- 2.30	44	- 1:46	- 2.30	73	- 1:17
- 2.15	45	- 1:30	- 2.15	77	- 0:58
- 2.00	46	- 1:14	- 2.00	81	- 0:39
- 1.45	49	- 0:56	- 1.45	85	- 0:20
- 1.30	51	- 0:39	- 1.30	89	- 0:01
- 1.15	53	- 0:22	- 1.15	93	+ 0:18
- 1.00	56	- 0:04	- 1.00	98	+ 0:38
- 0.45	59	+ 0:14	- 0.45	101	+ 0:56
- 0.30	62	+ 0:32	- 0.30	105	+ 1:15
- 0.15	65	+ 0:50	- 0.15	109	+ 1:34
HW	68	+ 1:08	HW	112	+ 1:52
+ 0.15	70	+ 1:25	+ 0.15	114	+ 2:09
+ 0.30	72	+ 1:42	+ 0.30	117	+ 2:27
+ 0.45	74	+ 1:59	+ 0.45	119	+ 2:44
+ 1.00	75	+ 2:15	+ 1.00	121	+ 3:01
+ 1.15	75	+ 2:30	+ 1.15	119	+ 3:14
+ 1.30	75	+ 2:45	+ 1.30	118	+ 3:28
+ 1.45	75	+ 3:00	+ 1.45	116	+ 3:41
+ 2.00	75	+ 3:15	+ 2.00	114	+ 3:54
+ 2.15	74	+ 3:29	+ 2.15	112	+ 4:07
+ 2.30	72	+ 3:42	+ 2.30	109	+ 4:19
+ 2.45	71	+ 3:56	+ 2.45	107	+ 4:32
+ 3.00	70	+ 4:10	+ 3.00	104	+ 4:44
+ 3.15	69	+ 4:24	+ 3.15	102	+ 4:57
+ 3.30	67	+ 4:37	+ 3.30	99	+ 5:09
+ 3.45	65	+ 4:50	+ 3.45	96	+ 5:21
+ 4.00	63	+ 5:03	+ 4.00	93	+ 5:33
+ 4.15	61	+ 5:16	+ 4.15	88	+ 5:43
+ 4.30	60	+ 5:30	+ 4.30	83	+ 5:53
+ 4.45	58	+ 5:43	+ 4.45	78	- 5:57
+ 5.00	56	+ 5:56	+ 5.00	73	- 5:47
+ 5.15	54	- 5:51	+ 5.15	70	- 5:35
+ 5.30	53	- 5:37	+ 5.30	68	- 5:22
+ 5.45	52	- 5:23	+ 5.45	65	- 5:10
+ 6.00	51	- 5:09	+ 6.00	63	- 4:57

	G6			G5	
	SW Barrow to Sea Reach			SW Barrow to Medway	
Time	Duration	Time at End of Sector	Time	Duration	Time at End of Sector
- 6.00	68	- 4:52	- 6.00	110	- 4:10
- 5.45	66	- 4:39	- 5.45	107	- 3:58
- 5.30	65	- 4:25	- 5.30	105	- 3:45
- 5.15	63	- 4:12	- 5.15	102	- 3:33
- 5.00	61	- 3:59	- 5.00	100	- 3:20
- 4.45	60	- 3:45	- 4.45	99	- 3:06
- 4.30	59	- 3:31	- 4.30	98	- 2:52
- 4.15	59	- 3:16	- 4.15	97	- 2:38
- 4.00	58	- 3:02	- 4.00	96	- 2:24
- 3.45	58	- 2:47	- 3.45	96	- 2:09
- 3.30	58	- 2:32	- 3.30	97	- 1:53
- 3.15	58	- 2:17	- 3.15	97	- 1:38
- 3.00	58	- 2:02	- 3.00	97	- 1:23
- 2.45	59	- 1:46	- 2.45	99	- 1:06
- 2.30	60	- 1:30	- 2.30	100	- 0:50
- 2.15	61	- 1:14	- 2.15	102	- 0:33
- 2.00	62	- 0:58	- 2.00	103	- 0:17
- 1.45	63	- 0:42	- 1.45	106	+ 0:01
- 1.30	65	- 0:25	- 1.30	109	+ 0:19
- 1.15	66	- 0:09	- 1.15	112	+ 0:37
- 1.00	68	+ 0:08	- 1.00	115	+ 0:55
- 0.45	70	+ 0:25	- 0.45	119	+ 1:14
- 0.30	72	+ 0:42	- 0.30	124	+ 1:34
- 0.15	74	+ 0:59	- 0.15	128	+ 1:53
HW	76	+ 1:16	HW	132	+ 2:12
+ 0.15	79	+ 1:34	+ 0.15	138	+ 2:33
+ 0.30	83	+ 1:53	+ 0.30	144	+ 2:54
+ 0.45	87	+ 2:12	+ 0.45	150	+ 3:15
+ 1.00	91	+ 2:31	+ 1.00	156	+ 3:36
+ 1.15	94	+ 2:49	+ 1.15	158	+ 3:53
+ 1.30	97	+ 3:07	+ 1.30	160	+ 4:10
+ 1.45	100	+ 3:25	+ 1.45	162	+ 4:27
+ 2.00	103	+ 3:43	+ 2.00	163	+ 4:43
+ 2.15	102	+ 3:57	+ 2.15	162	+ 4:57
+ 2.30	102	+ 4:12	+ 2.30	160	+ 5:10
+ 2.45	101	+ 4:26	+ 2.45	158	+ 5:23
+ 3.00	101	+ 4:41	+ 3.00	157	+ 5:37
+ 3.15	99	+ 4:54	+ 3.15	154	+ 5:49
+ 3.30	97	+ 5:07	+ 3.30	150	- 6:00
+ 3.45	95	+ 5:20	+ 3.45	147	- 5:48
+ 4.00	93	+ 5:33	+ 4.00	144	- 5:36
+ 4.15	90	+ 5:45	+ 4.15	141	- 5:24
+ 4.30	87	- 6:03	+ 4.30	138	- 5:12
+ 4.45	84	- 5:51	+ 4.45	135	- 5:00
+ 5.00	81	- 5:39	+ 5.00	133	- 4:47
+ 5.15	79	- 5:26	+ 5.15	130	- 4:35
+ 5.30	78	- 5:12	+ 5.30	127	- 4:23
+ 5.45	77	- 4:58	+ 5.45	124	- 4:11
+ 6.00	75	- 4:45	+ 6.00	121	- 3:59

	G4			G3	
	Sea Reach to Medway			Sea Reach to Red Sand Tower	
Time	Duration	Time at End of Sector	Time	Duration	Time at End of Sector
- 6.00	47	- 5:13	- 6.00	70	- 4:50
- 5.45	46	- 4:59	- 5.45	73	- 4:32
- 5.30	45	- 4:45	- 5.30	75	- 4:15
- 5.15	44	- 4:31	- 5.15	78	- 3:57
- 5.00	43	- 4:17	- 5.00	81	- 3:39
- 4.45	43	- 4:02	- 4.45	84	- 3:21
- 4.30	42	- 3:48	- 4.30	88	- 3:02
- 4.15	41	- 3:34	- 4.15	91	- 2:44
- 4.00	40	- 3:20	- 4.00	95	- 2:25
- 3.45	40	- 3:05	- 3.45	95	- 2:10
- 3.30	40	- 2:50	- 3.30	95	- 1:55
- 3.15	40	- 2:35	- 3.15	95	- 1:40
- 3.00	40	- 2:20	- 3.00	95	- 1:25
- 2.45	41	- 2:04	- 2.45	93	- 1:12
- 2.30	41	- 1:49	- 2.30	92	- 0:58
- 2.15	41	- 1:34	- 2.15	91	- 0:44
- 2.00	42	- 1:18	- 2.00	90	- 0:30
- 1.45	43	- 1:02	- 1.45	86	- 0:19
- 1.30	43	- 0:47	- 1.30	82	- 0:08
- 1.15	44	- 0:31	- 1.15	79	+ 0:04
- 1.00	45	- 0:15	- 1.00	75	+ 0:15
- 0.45	46	+ 0:01	- 0.45	72	+ 0:27
- 0.30	47	+ 0:17	- 0.30	70	+ 0:40
- 0.15	48	+ 0:33	- 0.15	67	+ 0:52
HW	49	+ 0:49	HW	64	+ 1:04
+ 0.15	50	+ 1:05	+ 0.15	61	+ 1:16
+ 0.30	51	+ 1:21	+ 0.30	58	+ 1:28
+ 0.45	53	+ 1:38	+ 0.45	55	+ 1:40
+ 1.00	54	+ 1:54	+ 1.00	53	+ 1:53
+ 1.15	55	+ 2:10	+ 1.15	51	+ 2:06
+ 1.30	57	+ 2:27	+ 1.30	50	+ 2:20
+ 1.45	58	+ 2:43	+ 1.45	48	+ 2:33
+ 2.00	59	+ 2:59	+ 2.00	47	+ 2:47
+ 2.15	59	+ 3:14	+ 2.15	47	+ 3:02
+ 2.30	59	+ 3:29	+ 2.30	47	+ 3:17
+ 2.45	59	+ 3:44	+ 2.45	48	+ 3:33
+ 3.00	59	+ 3:59	+ 3.00	48	+ 3:48
+ 3.15	58	+ 4:13	+ 3.15	49	+ 4:04
+ 3.30	57	+ 4:27	+ 3.30	50	+ 4:20
+ 3.45	57	+ 4:42	+ 3.45	51	+ 4:36
+ 4.00	56	+ 4:56	+ 4.00	53	+ 4:53
+ 4.15	55	+ 5:10	+ 4.15	54	+ 5:09
+ 4.30	54	+ 5:24	+ 4.30	56	+ 5:26
+ 4.45	53	+ 5:38	+ 4.45	58	+ 5:43
+ 5.00	52	+ 5:52	+ 5.00	59	+ 5:59
+ 5.15	51	- 5:54	+ 5.15	60	- 5:45
+ 5.30	50	- 5:40	+ 5.30	61	- 5:29
+ 5.45	50	- 5:25	+ 5.45	62	- 5:13
+ 6.00	49	- 5:11	+ 6.00	63	- 4:57

	G2			G1	
	Medway to Red Sand Towers			Red Sand Tower to Princes No 6	
Time	Duration	Time at End of Sector	Time	Duration	Time at End of Sector
- 6.00	122	- 3:58	- 6.00	77	- 4:43
- 5.45	127	- 3:38	- 5.45	81	- 4:24
- 5.30	132	- 3:18	- 5.30	86	- 4:04
- 5.15	136	- 2:59	- 5.15	90	- 3:45
- 5.00	141	- 2:39	- 5.00	95	- 3:25
- 4.45	144	- 2:21	- 4.45	96	- 3:09
- 4.30	147	- 2:03	- 4.30	97	- 2:53
- 4.15	149	- 1:46	- 4.15	98	- 2:37
- 4.00	152	- 1:28	- 4.00	99	- 2:21
- 3.45	151	- 1:14	- 3.45	99	- 2:06
- 3.30	149	- 1:01	- 3.30	99	- 1:51
- 3.15	147	- 0:48	- 3.15	99	- 1:36
- 3.00	146	- 0:34	- 3.00	100	- 1:20
- 2.45	143	- 0:22	- 2.45	98	- 1:07
- 2.30	140	- 0:10	- 2.30	96	- 0:54
- 2.15	137	+ 0:02	- 2.15	95	- 0:40
- 2.00	135	+ 0:15	- 2.00	93	- 0:27
- 1.45	130	+ 0:25	- 1.45	88	- 0:17
- 1.30	126	+ 0:36	- 1.30	84	- 0:06
- 1.15	122	+ 0:47	- 1.15	79	+ 0:04
- 1.00	117	+ 0:57	- 1.00	75	+ 0:15
- 0.45	113	+ 1:08	- 0.45	72	+ 0:27
- 0.30	108	+ 1:18	- 0.30	68	+ 0:38
- 0.15	103	+ 1:28	- 0.15	65	+ 0:50
HW	99	+ 1:39	HW	61	+ 1:01
+ 0.15	93	+ 1:48	+ 0.15	59	+ 1:14
+ 0.30	88	+ 1:58	+ 0.30	57	+ 1:27
+ 0.45	83	+ 2:08	+ 0.45	55	+ 1:40
+ 1.00	77	+ 2:17	+ 1.00	53	+ 1:53
+ 1.15	75	+ 2:30	+ 1.15	53	+ 2:08
+ 1.30	73	+ 2:43	+ 1.30	53	+ 2:23
+ 1.45	71	+ 2:56	+ 1.45	53	+ 2:38
+ 2.00	69	+ 3:09	+ 2.00	53	+ 2:53
+ 2.15	71	+ 3:26	+ 2.15	53	+ 3:08
+ 2.30	72	+ 3:42	+ 2.30	54	+ 3:24
+ 2.45	73	+ 3:58	+ 2.45	55	+ 3:40
+ 3.00	75	+ 4:15	+ 3.00	55	+ 3:55
+ 3.15	77	+ 4:32	+ 3.15	56	+ 4:11
+ 3.30	80	+ 4:50	+ 3.30	57	+ 4:27
+ 3.45	83	+ 5:08	+ 3.45	59	+ 4:44
+ 4.00	85	+ 5:25	+ 4.00	60	+ 5:00
+ 4.15	88	+ 5:43	+ 4.15	61	+ 5:16
+ 4.30	90	- 6:00	+ 4.30	62	+ 5:32
+ 4.45	93	- 5:42	+ 4.45	63	+ 5:48
+ 5.00	95	- 5:25	+ 5.00	64	- 5:56
+ 5.15	98	- 5:07	+ 5.15	65	- 5:40
+ 5.30	101	- 4:49	+ 5.30	67	- 5:23
+ 5.45	103	- 4:32	+ 5.45	68	- 5:07
+ 6.00	106	- 4:14	+ 6.00	69	- 4:51

Table G - Medway, Sea Reach and Black Deep Connections

Time to cover Sectors (in minutes) at 4.0 kts — All times relate to HW Sheerness — **Springs**

SOUTH BOUND

G8 — Long Sand Inner to Blk Deep No 8

Time	Duration	Time at End of Sector
- 6.00	42	- 5:18
- 5.45	41	- 5:04
- 5.30	39	- 4:51
- 5.15	38	- 4:37
- 5.00	37	- 4:23
- 4.45	36	- 4:09
- 4.30	36	- 3:54
- 4.15	35	- 3:40
- 4.00	35	- 3:25
- 3.45	35	- 3:10
- 3.30	36	- 2:54
- 3.15	36	- 2:39
- 3.00	36	- 2:24
- 2.45	38	- 2:07
- 2.30	40	- 1:50
- 2.15	41	- 1:34
- 2.00	43	- 1:17
- 1.45	46	- 0:59
- 1.30	49	- 0:41
- 1.15	53	- 0:22
- 1.00	56	- 0:04
- 0.45	61	+ 0:16
- 0.30	66	+ 0:36
- 0.15	71	+ 0:56
HW	76	+ 1:16
+ 0.15	82	+ 1:37
+ 0.30	89	+ 1:59
+ 0.45	96	+ 2:21
+ 1.00	103	+ 2:43
+ 1.15	102	+ 2:57
+ 1.30	101	+ 3:11
+ 1.45	99	+ 3:24
+ 2.00	98	+ 3:38
+ 2.15	94	+ 3:49
+ 2.30	89	+ 3:59
+ 2.45	85	+ 4:10
+ 3.00	80	+ 4:20
+ 3.15	78	+ 4:33
+ 3.30	75	+ 4:45
+ 3.45	72	+ 4:57
+ 4.00	70	+ 5:10
+ 4.15	66	+ 5:21
+ 4.30	63	+ 5:33
+ 4.45	60	+ 5:45
+ 5.00	57	+ 5:57
+ 5.15	55	- 5:50
+ 5.30	53	- 5:37
+ 5.45	51	- 5:24
+ 6.00	49	- 5:11

G7 — Black Deep to Blk Deep No 8

Time	Duration	Time at End of Sector
- 6.00	45	- 5:15
- 5.45	44	- 5:01
- 5.30	43	- 4:47
- 5.15	42	- 4:33
- 5.00	41	- 4:19
- 4.45	42	- 4:03
- 4.30	42	- 3:48
- 4.15	43	- 3:32
- 4.00	43	- 3:17
- 3.45	47	- 2:58
- 3.30	50	- 2:40
- 3.15	54	- 2:21
- 3.00	57	- 2:03
- 2.45	63	- 1:42
- 2.30	69	- 1:21
- 2.15	75	- 1:00
- 2.00	81	- 0:39
- 1.45	87	- 0:18
- 1.30	94	+ 0:04
- 1.15	101	+ 0:26
- 1.00	107	+ 0:47
- 0.45	113	+ 1:08
- 0.30	119	+ 1:29
- 0.15	125	+ 1:50
HW	131	+ 2:11
+ 0.15	133	+ 2:28
+ 0.30	135	+ 2:45
+ 0.45	137	+ 3:02
+ 1.00	139	+ 3:19
+ 1.15	137	+ 3:32
+ 1.30	134	+ 3:44
+ 1.45	131	+ 3:56
+ 2.00	129	+ 4:09
+ 2.15	125	+ 4:20
+ 2.30	121	+ 4:31
+ 2.45	117	+ 4:42
+ 3.00	114	+ 4:54
+ 3.15	109	+ 5:04
+ 3.30	104	+ 5:14
+ 3.45	99	+ 5:24
+ 4.00	95	+ 5:35
+ 4.15	88	+ 5:43
+ 4.30	82	+ 5:52
+ 4.45	75	- 6:00
+ 5.00	68	- 5:52
+ 5.15	65	- 5:40
+ 5.30	61	- 5:29
+ 5.45	58	- 5:17
+ 6.00	55	- 5:05

G6 — SW Barrow to Sea Reach

Time	Duration	Time at End of Sector
- 6.00	66	- 4:54
- 5.45	63	- 4:42
- 5.30	61	- 4:29
- 5.15	58	- 4:17
- 5.00	56	- 4:04
- 4.45	55	- 3:50
- 4.30	53	- 3:37
- 4.15	52	- 3:23
- 4.00	51	- 3:09
- 3.45	51	- 2:54
- 3.30	51	- 2:39
- 3.15	51	- 2:24
- 3.00	51	- 2:09
- 2.45	53	- 1:52
- 2.30	54	- 1:36
- 2.15	55	- 1:20
- 2.00	56	- 1:04
- 1.45	58	- 0:47
- 1.30	60	- 0:30
- 1.15	63	- 0:12
- 1.00	65	+ 0:05
- 0.45	68	+ 0:23
- 0.30	71	+ 0:41
- 0.15	74	+ 0:59
HW	77	+ 1:17
+ 0.15	83	+ 1:38
+ 0.30	89	+ 1:59
+ 0.45	95	+ 2:20
+ 1.00	102	+ 2:42
+ 1.15	105	+ 3:00
+ 1.30	109	+ 3:19
+ 1.45	112	+ 3:37
+ 2.00	116	+ 3:56
+ 2.15	115	+ 4:10
+ 2.30	113	+ 4:23
+ 2.45	112	+ 4:37
+ 3.00	111	+ 4:51
+ 3.15	108	+ 5:03
+ 3.30	104	+ 5:14
+ 3.45	101	+ 5:26
+ 4.00	98	+ 5:38
+ 4.15	94	+ 5:49
+ 4.30	91	- 5:59
+ 4.45	88	- 5:47
+ 5.00	84	- 5:36
+ 5.15	82	- 5:23
+ 5.30	81	- 5:09
+ 5.45	79	- 4:56
+ 6.00	77	- 4:43

G5 — SW Barrow to Medway

Time	Duration	Time at End of Sector
- 6.00	104	- 4:16
- 5.45	102	- 4:03
- 5.30	99	- 3:51
- 5.15	97	- 3:38
- 5.00	95	- 3:25
- 4.45	93	- 3:12
- 4.30	92	- 2:58
- 4.15	91	- 2:44
- 4.00	90	- 2:30
- 3.45	91	- 2:14
- 3.30	91	- 1:59
- 3.15	91	- 1:44
- 3.00	91	- 1:29
- 2.45	93	- 1:12
- 2.30	95	- 0:55
- 2.15	97	- 0:38
- 2.00	99	- 0:21
- 1.45	103	- 0:02
- 1.30	107	+ 0:17
- 1.15	111	+ 0:36
- 1.00	115	+ 0:55
- 0.45	121	+ 1:16
- 0.30	128	+ 1:38
- 0.15	134	+ 1:59
HW	140	+ 2:20
+ 0.15	150	+ 2:45
+ 0.30	160	+ 3:10
+ 0.45	169	+ 3:34
+ 1.00	179	+ 3:59
+ 1.15	180	+ 4:15
+ 1.30	181	+ 4:31
+ 1.45	183	+ 4:48
+ 2.00	184	+ 5:04
+ 2.15	180	+ 5:15
+ 2.30	177	+ 5:27
+ 2.45	173	+ 5:38
+ 3.00	170	+ 5:50
+ 3.15	165	- 6:00
+ 3.30	160	- 5:50
+ 3.45	155	- 5:40
+ 4.00	150	- 5:30
+ 4.15	146	- 5:19
+ 4.30	142	- 5:08
+ 4.45	138	- 4:57
+ 5.00	134	- 4:46
+ 5.15	130	- 4:35
+ 5.30	126	- 4:24
+ 5.45	123	- 4:12
+ 6.00	119	- 4:01

G4 — Sea Reach to Medway

Time	Duration	Time at End of Sector
- 6.00	47	- 5:13
- 5.45	45	- 5:00
- 5.30	44	- 4:46
- 5.15	43	- 4:32
- 5.00	41	- 4:19
- 4.45	40	- 4:05
- 4.30	39	- 3:51
- 4.15	38	- 3:37
- 4.00	37	- 3:23
- 3.45	37	- 3:08
- 3.30	37	- 2:53
- 3.15	37	- 2:38
- 3.00	37	- 2:23
- 2.45	38	- 2:07
- 2.30	38	- 1:52
- 2.15	39	- 1:36
- 2.00	39	- 1:21
- 1.45	40	- 1:05
- 1.30	41	- 0:49
- 1.15	42	- 0:33
- 1.00	43	- 0:17
- 0.45	45	HW
- 0.30	46	+ 0:16
- 0.15	47	+ 0:32
HW	49	+ 0:49
+ 0.15	51	+ 1:06
+ 0.30	53	+ 1:23
+ 0.45	55	+ 1:40
+ 1.00	57	+ 1:57
+ 1.15	60	+ 2:15
+ 1.30	62	+ 2:32
+ 1.45	65	+ 2:50
+ 2.00	68	+ 3:08
+ 2.15	67	+ 3:22
+ 2.30	67	+ 3:37
+ 2.45	67	+ 3:52
+ 3.00	67	+ 4:07
+ 3.15	65	+ 4:20
+ 3.30	63	+ 4:33
+ 3.45	62	+ 4:47
+ 4.00	60	+ 5:00
+ 4.15	59	+ 5:14
+ 4.30	57	+ 5:27
+ 4.45	55	+ 5:40
+ 5.00	54	+ 5:54
+ 5.15	53	- 5:52
+ 5.30	52	- 5:38
+ 5.45	51	- 5:24
+ 6.00	50	- 5:10

G3 — Sea Reach to Red Sand Tower

Time	Duration	Time at End of Sector
- 6.00	72	- 4:48
- 5.45	79	- 4:26
- 5.30	86	- 4:04
- 5.15	92	- 3:43
- 5.00	99	- 3:21
- 4.45	101	- 3:04
- 4.30	103	- 2:47
- 4.15	106	- 2:29
- 4.00	108	- 2:12
- 3.45	107	- 1:58
- 3.30	106	- 1:44
- 3.15	105	- 1:30
- 3.00	105	- 1:15
- 2.45	103	- 1:02
- 2.30	101	- 0:49
- 2.15	99	- 0:36
- 2.00	96	- 0:24
- 1.45	92	- 0:13
- 1.30	88	- 0:02
- 1.15	84	+ 0:09
- 1.00	80	+ 0:20
- 0.45	76	+ 0:31
- 0.30	72	+ 0:42
- 0.15	68	+ 0:53
HW	64	+ 1:04
+ 0.15	60	+ 1:15
+ 0.30	56	+ 1:26
+ 0.45	51	+ 1:36
+ 1.00	47	+ 1:47
+ 1.15	46	+ 2:01
+ 1.30	44	+ 2:14
+ 1.45	42	+ 2:27
+ 2.00	41	+ 2:41
+ 2.15	41	+ 2:56
+ 2.30	41	+ 3:11
+ 2.45	41	+ 3:26
+ 3.00	41	+ 3:41
+ 3.15	43	+ 3:58
+ 3.30	44	+ 4:14
+ 3.45	46	+ 4:31
+ 4.00	47	+ 4:47
+ 4.15	50	+ 5:05
+ 4.30	52	+ 5:22
+ 4.45	55	+ 5:40
+ 5.00	57	+ 5:57
+ 5.15	59	- 5:46
+ 5.30	60	- 5:30
+ 5.45	61	- 5:14
+ 6.00	63	- 4:57

G2 — Medway to Red Sand Towers

Time	Duration	Time at End of Sector
- 6.00	132	- 3:48
- 5.45	142	- 3:23
- 5.30	151	- 2:59
- 5.15	161	- 2:34
- 5.00	170	- 2:10
- 4.45	171	- 1:54
- 4.30	172	- 1:38
- 4.15	173	- 1:22
- 4.00	174	- 1:06
- 3.45	172	- 0:53
- 3.30	169	- 0:41
- 3.15	166	- 0:29
- 3.00	164	- 0:16
- 2.45	159	- 0:06
- 2.30	154	+ 0:04
- 2.15	149	+ 0:14
- 2.00	143	+ 0:23
- 1.45	137	+ 0:32
- 1.30	131	+ 0:41
- 1.15	125	+ 0:50
- 1.00	118	+ 0:58
- 0.45	112	+ 1:07
- 0.30	107	+ 1:17
- 0.15	101	+ 1:26
HW	95	+ 1:35
+ 0.15	87	+ 1:42
+ 0.30	79	+ 1:49
+ 0.45	72	+ 1:57
+ 1.00	64	+ 2:04
+ 1.15	61	+ 2:16
+ 1.30	59	+ 2:29
+ 1.45	56	+ 2:41
+ 2.00	54	+ 2:54
+ 2.15	56	+ 3:11
+ 2.30	57	+ 3:27
+ 2.45	59	+ 3:44
+ 3.00	60	+ 4:00
+ 3.15	64	+ 4:19
+ 3.30	68	+ 4:38
+ 3.45	72	+ 4:57
+ 4.00	76	+ 5:16
+ 4.15	81	+ 5:36
+ 4.30	86	+ 5:56
+ 4.45	91	- 5:44
+ 5.00	95	- 5:25
+ 5.15	98	- 5:07
+ 5.30	100	- 4:50
+ 5.45	103	- 4:32
+ 6.00	106	- 4:14

G1 — Red Sand Tower to Princes No 6

Time	Duration	Time at End of Sector
- 6.00	84	- 4:36
- 5.45	90	- 4:15
- 5.30	96	- 3:54
- 5.15	102	- 3:33
- 5.00	108	- 3:12
- 4.45	109	- 2:56
- 4.30	110	- 2:40
- 4.15	111	- 2:24
- 4.00	112	- 2:08
- 3.45	112	- 1:53
- 3.30	112	- 1:38
- 3.15	112	- 1:23
- 3.00	111	- 1:09
- 2.45	108	- 0:57
- 2.30	104	- 0:46
- 2.15	100	- 0:35
- 2.00	97	- 0:23
- 1.45	92	- 0:13
- 1.30	86	- 0:04
- 1.15	81	+ 0:06
- 1.00	76	+ 0:16
- 0.45	71	+ 0:26
- 0.30	65	+ 0:35
- 0.15	60	+ 0:45
HW	55	+ 0:55
+ 0.15	52	+ 1:07
+ 0.30	49	+ 1:19
+ 0.45	47	+ 1:32
+ 1.00	44	+ 1:44
+ 1.15	44	+ 1:59
+ 1.30	44	+ 2:14
+ 1.45	44	+ 2:29
+ 2.00	43	+ 2:43
+ 2.15	45	+ 3:00
+ 2.30	46	+ 3:16
+ 2.45	47	+ 3:32
+ 3.00	49	+ 3:49
+ 3.15	51	+ 4:06
+ 3.30	52	+ 4:22
+ 3.45	54	+ 4:39
+ 4.00	56	+ 4:56
+ 4.15	58	+ 5:13
+ 4.30	59	+ 5:29
+ 4.45	61	+ 5:46
+ 5.00	63	- 5:57
+ 5.15	64	- 5:41
+ 5.30	66	- 5:24
+ 5.45	67	- 5:08
+ 6.00	69	- 4:51

Table G - Medway, Sea Reach and Black Deep Connections

Neaps | All times relate to HW Sheerness | **Time to cover Sectors (in minutes) at 5.0 Kts**

SOUTH BOUND

	G8			G7			G6			G5	
	Long Sand Inner to Blk Deep No 8			Black Deep to Blk Deep No 8			SW Barrow to Sea Reach			SW Barrow to Medway	
Time	Duration	Time at End of Sector	Time	Duration	Time at End of Sector	Time	Duration	Time at End of Sector	Time	Duration	Time at End of Sector
- 6.00	39	- 5:21	- 6.00	49	- 5:11	- 6.00	56	- 5:04	- 6.00	92	- 4:28
- 5.45	38	- 5:07	- 5.45	49	- 4:56	- 5.45	55	- 4:50	- 5.45	90	- 4:15
- 5.30	37	- 4:53	- 5.30	48	- 4:42	- 5.30	54	- 4:36	- 5.30	88	- 4:02
- 5.15	36	- 4:39	- 5.15	47	- 4:28	- 5.15	52	- 4:23	- 5.15	85	- 3:50
- 5.00	35	- 4:25	- 5.00	47	- 4:13	- 5.00	51	- 4:09	- 5.00	83	- 3:37
- 4.45	35	- 4:10	- 4.45	47	- 3:58	- 4.45	51	- 3:54	- 4.45	82	- 3:23
- 4.30	35	- 3:55	- 4.30	47	- 3:43	- 4.30	50	- 3:40	- 4.30	82	- 3:08
- 4.15	35	- 3:40	- 4.15	47	- 3:28	- 4.15	49	- 3:26	- 4.15	81	- 2:54
- 4.00	34	- 3:26	- 4.00	47	- 3:13	- 4.00	49	- 3:11	- 4.00	80	- 2:40
- 3.45	34	- 3:11	- 3.45	49	- 2:56	- 3.45	49	- 2:56	- 3.45	80	- 2:25
- 3.30	34	- 2:56	- 3.30	50	- 2:40	- 3.30	49	- 2:41	- 3.30	81	- 2:09
- 3.15	35	- 2:40	- 3.15	51	- 2:24	- 3.15	49	- 2:26	- 3.15	81	- 1:54
- 3.00	35	- 2:25	- 3.00	53	- 2:07	- 3.00	49	- 2:11	- 3.00	81	- 1:39
- 2.45	35	- 2:10	- 2.45	55	- 1:50	- 2.45	49	- 1:56	- 2.45	82	- 1:23
- 2.30	36	- 1:54	- 2.30	58	- 1:32	- 2.30	50	- 1:40	- 2.30	83	- 1:07
- 2.15	37	- 1:38	- 2.15	61	- 1:14	- 2.15	50	- 1:25	- 2.15	84	- 0:51
- 2.00	38	- 1:22	- 2.00	63	- 0:57	- 2.00	51	- 1:09	- 2.00	85	- 0:35
- 1.45	39	- 1:06	- 1.45	65	- 0:40	- 1.45	52	- 0:53	- 1.45	87	- 0:18
- 1.30	40	- 0:50	- 1.30	67	- 0:23	- 1.30	53	- 0:37	- 1.30	88	- 0:02
- 1.15	42	- 0:33	- 1.15	70	- 0:05	- 1.15	54	- 0:21	- 1.15	89	+ 0:14
- 1.00	43	- 0:17	- 1.00	72	+ 0:12	- 1.00	54	- 0:06	- 1.00	90	+ 0:30
- 0.45	45	HW	- 0.45	73	+ 0:28	- 0.45	56	+ 0:11	- 0.45	93	+ 0:48
- 0.30	47	+ 0:17	- 0.30	75	+ 0:45	- 0.30	57	+ 0:27	- 0.30	96	+ 1:06
- 0.15	49	+ 0:34	- 0.15	76	+ 1:01	- 0.15	58	+ 0:43	- 0.15	99	+ 1:24
HW	51	+ 0:51	HW	77	+ 1:17	HW	59	+ 0:59	HW	101	+ 1:41
+ 0.15	53	+ 1:08	+ 0.15	81	+ 1:36	+ 0.15	61	+ 1:16	+ 0.15	105	+ 2:00
+ 0.30	54	+ 1:24	+ 0.30	85	+ 1:55	+ 0.30	63	+ 1:33	+ 0.30	108	+ 2:18
+ 0.45	55	+ 1:40	+ 0.45	88	+ 2:13	+ 0.45	64	+ 1:49	+ 0.45	112	+ 2:37
+ 1.00	57	+ 1:57	+ 1.00	92	+ 2:32	+ 1.00	66	+ 2:06	+ 1.00	116	+ 2:56
+ 1.15	57	+ 2:12	+ 1.15	89	+ 2:44	+ 1.15	68	+ 2:23	+ 1.15	118	+ 3:13
+ 1.30	57	+ 2:27	+ 1.30	86	+ 2:56	+ 1.30	69	+ 2:39	+ 1.30	120	+ 3:30
+ 1.45	57	+ 2:42	+ 1.45	83	+ 3:08	+ 1.45	70	+ 2:55	+ 1.45	122	+ 3:47
+ 2.00	56	+ 2:56	+ 2.00	80	+ 3:20	+ 2.00	72	+ 3:12	+ 2.00	124	+ 4:04
+ 2.15	56	+ 3:11	+ 2.15	79	+ 3:34	+ 2.15	72	+ 3:27	+ 2.15	123	+ 4:18
+ 2.30	55	+ 3:25	+ 2.30	78	+ 3:48	+ 2.30	72	+ 3:42	+ 2.30	123	+ 4:33
+ 2.45	55	+ 3:40	+ 2.45	77	+ 4:02	+ 2.45	72	+ 3:57	+ 2.45	122	+ 4:47
+ 3.00	54	+ 3:54	+ 3.00	76	+ 4:16	+ 3.00	72	+ 4:12	+ 3.00	121	+ 5:01
+ 3.15	53	+ 4:08	+ 3.15	75	+ 4:30	+ 3.15	71	+ 4:26	+ 3.15	119	+ 5:14
+ 3.30	52	+ 4:22	+ 3.30	73	+ 4:43	+ 3.30	70	+ 4:40	+ 3.30	118	+ 5:28
+ 3.45	51	+ 4:36	+ 3.45	72	+ 4:57	+ 3.45	69	+ 4:54	+ 3.45	116	+ 5:41
+ 4.00	50	+ 4:50	+ 4.00	71	+ 5:11	+ 4.00	68	+ 5:08	+ 4.00	114	+ 5:54
+ 4.15	49	+ 5:04	+ 4.15	68	+ 5:23	+ 4.15	67	+ 5:22	+ 4.15	112	- 5:53
+ 4.30	47	+ 5:17	+ 4.30	65	+ 5:35	+ 4.30	66	+ 5:36	+ 4.30	110	- 5:40
+ 4.45	46	+ 5:31	+ 4.45	63	+ 5:48	+ 4.45	65	+ 5:50	+ 4.45	108	- 5:27
+ 5.00	45	+ 5:45	+ 5.00	60	- 6:00	+ 5.00	64	- 5:56	+ 5.00	105	- 5:15
+ 5.15	44	+ 5:59	+ 5.15	59	- 5:46	+ 5.15	63	- 5:42	+ 5.15	104	- 5:01
+ 5.30	43	- 5:47	+ 5.30	57	- 5:33	+ 5.30	62	- 5:28	+ 5.30	102	- 4:48
+ 5.45	42	- 5:33	+ 5.45	55	- 5:20	+ 5.45	61	- 5:14	+ 5.45	101	- 4:34
+ 6.00	41	- 5:19	+ 6.00	53	- 5:07	+ 6.00	60	- 5:00	+ 6.00	99	- 4:21

	G4			G3			G2			G1	
	Sea Reach to Medway			Sea Reach to Red Sand Tower			Medway to Red Sand Towers			Red Sand Tower to Princes No 6	
Time	Duration	Time at End of Sector	Time	Duration	Time at End of Sector	Time	Duration	Time at End of Sector	Time	Duration	Time at End of Sector
- 6.00	38	- 5:22	- 6.00	54	- 5:06	- 6.00	93	- 4:27	- 6.00	60	- 5:00
- 5.45	38	- 5:07	- 5.45	56	- 4:49	- 5.45	96	- 4:09	- 5.45	62	- 4:43
- 5.30	37	- 4:53	- 5.30	58	- 4:32	- 5.30	100	- 3:50	- 5.30	63	- 4:27
- 5.15	36	- 4:39	- 5.15	60	- 4:15	- 5.15	103	- 3:32	- 5.15	64	- 4:11
- 5.00	36	- 4:24	- 5.00	61	- 3:59	- 5.00	107	- 3:13	- 5.00	66	- 3:54
- 4.45	35	- 4:10	- 4.45	62	- 3:43	- 4.45	108	- 2:57	- 4.45	67	- 3:38
- 4.30	35	- 3:55	- 4.30	63	- 3:27	- 4.30	110	- 2:40	- 4.30	67	- 3:23
- 4.15	34	- 3:41	- 4.15	64	- 3:11	- 4.15	111	- 2:24	- 4.15	68	- 3:07
- 4.00	34	- 3:26	- 4.00	65	- 2:55	- 4.00	112	- 2:08	- 4.00	69	- 2:51
- 3.45	33	- 3:12	- 3.45	65	- 2:40	- 3.45	112	- 1:53	- 3.45	69	- 2:36
- 3.30	33	- 2:57	- 3.30	65	- 2:25	- 3.30	112	- 1:38	- 3.30	69	- 2:21
- 3.15	33	- 2:42	- 3.15	65	- 2:10	- 3.15	112	- 1:23	- 3.15	70	- 2:05
- 3.00	33	- 2:27	- 3.00	65	- 1:55	- 3.00	111	- 1:09	- 3.00	70	- 1:50
- 2.45	33	- 2:12	- 2.45	64	- 1:41	- 2.45	110	- 0:55	- 2.45	69	- 1:36
- 2.30	34	- 1:56	- 2.30	64	- 1:26	- 2.30	109	- 0:41	- 2.30	69	- 1:21
- 2.15	34	- 1:41	- 2.15	64	- 1:11	- 2.15	107	- 0:28	- 2.15	68	- 1:07
- 2.00	34	- 1:26	- 2.00	64	- 0:56	- 2.00	106	- 0:14	- 2.00	68	- 0:52
- 1.45	34	- 1:11	- 1.45	62	- 0:43	- 1.45	103	- 0:02	- 1.45	66	- 0:39
- 1.30	35	- 0:55	- 1.30	61	- 0:29	- 1.30	101	+ 0:11	- 1.30	64	- 0:26
- 1.15	35	- 0:40	- 1.15	60	- 0:15	- 1.15	98	+ 0:23	- 1.15	62	- 0:13
- 1.00	36	- 0:24	- 1.00	59	- 0:01	- 1.00	96	+ 0:36	- 1.00	60	HW
- 0.45	36	- 0:09	- 0.45	57	+ 0:12	- 0.45	92	+ 0:47	- 0.45	58	+ 0:13
- 0.30	37	+ 0:07	- 0.30	56	+ 0:26	- 0.30	89	+ 0:59	- 0.30	56	+ 0:26
- 0.15	38	+ 0:23	- 0.15	54	+ 0:39	- 0.15	85	+ 1:10	- 0.15	54	+ 0:39
HW	38	+ 0:38	HW	52	+ 0:52	HW	82	+ 1:22	HW	52	+ 0:52
+ 0.15	39	+ 0:54	+ 0.15	50	+ 1:05	+ 0.15	78	+ 1:33	+ 0.15	50	+ 1:05
+ 0.30	40	+ 1:10	+ 0.30	49	+ 1:19	+ 0.30	75	+ 1:45	+ 0.30	49	+ 1:19
+ 0.45	41	+ 1:26	+ 0.45	47	+ 1:32	+ 0.45	71	+ 1:56	+ 0.45	47	+ 1:32
+ 1.00	42	+ 1:42	+ 1.00	45	+ 1:45	+ 1.00	68	+ 2:08	+ 1.00	46	+ 1:46
+ 1.15	42	+ 1:57	+ 1.15	44	+ 1:59	+ 1.15	66	+ 2:21	+ 1.15	46	+ 2:01
+ 1.30	43	+ 2:13	+ 1.30	43	+ 2:13	+ 1.30	64	+ 2:34	+ 1.30	45	+ 2:15
+ 1.45	44	+ 2:29	+ 1.45	42	+ 2:27	+ 1.45	63	+ 2:48	+ 1.45	45	+ 2:30
+ 2.00	45	+ 2:45	+ 2.00	40	+ 2:40	+ 2.00	61	+ 3:01	+ 2.00	45	+ 2:45
+ 2.15	45	+ 3:00	+ 2.15	40	+ 2:55	+ 2.15	62	+ 3:17	+ 2.15	45	+ 3:00
+ 2.30	45	+ 3:15	+ 2.30	40	+ 3:10	+ 2.30	63	+ 3:33	+ 2.30	46	+ 3:16
+ 2.45	45	+ 3:30	+ 2.45	40	+ 3:25	+ 2.45	63	+ 3:48	+ 2.45	46	+ 3:31
+ 3.00	46	+ 3:46	+ 3.00	41	+ 3:41	+ 3.00	64	+ 4:04	+ 3.00	47	+ 3:47
+ 3.15	45	+ 4:00	+ 3.15	41	+ 3:56	+ 3.15	66	+ 4:21	+ 3.15	47	+ 4:02
+ 3.30	44	+ 4:14	+ 3.30	42	+ 4:12	+ 3.30	67	+ 4:37	+ 3.30	48	+ 4:18
+ 3.45	44	+ 4:29	+ 3.45	43	+ 4:28	+ 3.45	69	+ 4:54	+ 3.45	49	+ 4:34
+ 4.00	43	+ 4:43	+ 4.00	44	+ 4:44	+ 4.00	71	+ 5:11	+ 4.00	49	+ 4:49
+ 4.15	43	+ 4:58	+ 4.15	45	+ 5:00	+ 4.15	73	+ 5:28	+ 4.15	50	+ 5:05
+ 4.30	42	+ 5:12	+ 4.30	46	+ 5:16	+ 4.30	75	+ 5:45	+ 4.30	51	+ 5:21
+ 4.45	42	+ 5:27	+ 4.45	47	+ 5:32	+ 4.45	77	- 5:58	+ 4.45	51	+ 5:36
+ 5.00	41	+ 5:41	+ 5.00	48	+ 5:48	+ 5.00	78	- 5:42	+ 5.00	52	+ 5:52
+ 5.15	41	+ 5:56	+ 5.15	48	- 5:57	+ 5.15	80	- 5:25	+ 5.15	53	- 5:52
+ 5.30	40	- 5:50	+ 5.30	49	- 5:41	+ 5.30	81	- 5:09	+ 5.30	54	- 5:36
+ 5.45	40	- 5:35	+ 5.45	50	- 5:25	+ 5.45	82	- 4:53	+ 5.45	55	- 5:20
+ 6.00	39	- 5:21	+ 6.00	51	- 5:09	+ 6.00	83	- 4:37	+ 6.00	55	- 5:05

Table G - Medway, Sea Reach and Black Deep Connections

Time to cover Sectors (in minutes) at 5.0 kts — All times relate to HW Sheerness — Springs

	G8 Long Sand Inner to Blk Deep No 8			G7 Black Deep to Blk Deep No 8			G6 SW Barrow to Sea Reach			G5 SW Barrow to Medway			G4 Sea Reach to Medway			G3 Sea Reach to Red Sand Tower			G2 Medway to Red Sand Towers			G1 Red Sand Tower to Princes No 6	
Time	Duration	Time at End of Sector	Time	Duration	Time at End of Sector	Time	Duration	Time at End of Sector	Time	Duration	Time at End of Sector	Time	Duration	Time at End of Sector	Time	Duration	Time at End of Sector	Time	Duration	Time at End of Sector	Time	Duration	Time at End of Sector
- 6.00	37	- 5:23	- 6.00	42	- 5:18	- 6.00	55	- 5:05	- 6.00	88	- 4:32	- 6.00	38	- 5:22	- 6.00	55	- 5:05	- 6.00	98	- 4:22	- 6.00	64	- 4:56
- 5.45	36	- 5:09	- 5.45	42	- 5:03	- 5.45	53	- 4:52	- 5.45	85	- 4:20	- 5.45	37	- 5:08	- 5.45	58	- 4:47	- 5.45	103	- 4:02	- 5.45	66	- 4:39
- 5.30	35	- 4:55	- 5.30	41	- 4:49	- 5.30	51	- 4:39	- 5.30	82	- 4:08	- 5.30	36	- 4:54	- 5.30	61	- 4:29	- 5.30	108	- 3:42	- 5.30	69	- 4:21
- 5.15	34	- 4:41	- 5.15	40	- 4:35	- 5.15	50	- 4:25	- 5.15	80	- 3:55	- 5.15	35	- 4:40	- 5.15	64	- 4:11	- 5.15	113	- 3:22	- 5.15	72	- 4:03
- 5.00	33	- 4:27	- 5.00	39	- 4:21	- 5.00	48	- 4:12	- 5.00	77	- 3:43	- 5.00	35	- 4:25	- 5.00	67	- 3:53	- 5.00	118	- 3:02	- 5.00	74	- 3:46
- 4.45	32	- 4:13	- 4.45	39	- 4:06	- 4.45	47	- 3:58	- 4.45	76	- 3:29	- 4.45	34	- 4:11	- 4.45	68	- 3:37	- 4.45	120	- 2:45	- 4.45	75	- 3:30
- 4.30	32	- 3:58	- 4.30	39	- 3:51	- 4.30	46	- 3:44	- 4.30	75	- 3:15	- 4.30	33	- 3:57	- 4.30	70	- 3:20	- 4.30	121	- 2:29	- 4.30	76	- 3:14
- 4.15	31	- 3:44	- 4.15	40	- 3:35	- 4.15	46	- 3:29	- 4.15	74	- 3:01	- 4.15	32	- 3:43	- 4.15	71	- 3:04	- 4.15	122	- 2:13	- 4.15	77	- 2:58
- 4.00	31	- 3:29	- 4.00	40	- 3:20	- 4.00	45	- 3:15	- 4.00	72	- 2:48	- 4.00	32	- 3:28	- 4.00	73	- 2:47	- 4.00	124	- 1:56	- 4.00	78	- 2:42
- 3.45	31	- 3:14	- 3.45	42	- 3:03	- 3.45	45	- 3:00	- 3.45	73	- 2:32	- 3.45	31	- 3:14	- 3.45	73	- 2:32	- 3.45	123	- 1:42	- 3.45	78	- 2:27
- 3.30	31	- 2:59	- 3.30	44	- 2:46	- 3.30	45	- 2:45	- 3.30	73	- 2:17	- 3.30	31	- 2:59	- 3.30	72	- 2:18	- 3.30	122	- 1:28	- 3.30	78	- 2:12
- 3.15	31	- 2:44	- 3.15	45	- 2:30	- 3.15	45	- 2:30	- 3.15	73	- 2:02	- 3.15	31	- 2:44	- 3.15	72	- 2:03	- 3.15	121	- 1:14	- 3.15	78	- 1:57
- 3.00	31	- 2:29	- 3.00	47	- 2:13	- 3.00	44	- 2:16	- 3.00	73	- 1:47	- 3.00	31	- 2:29	- 3.00	72	- 1:48	- 3.00	120	- 1:00	- 3.00	79	- 1:41
- 2.45	32	- 2:13	- 2.45	51	- 1:54	- 2.45	45	- 2:00	- 2.45	75	- 1:30	- 2.45	31	- 2:14	- 2.45	72	- 1:33	- 2.45	118	- 0:47	- 2.45	77	- 1:28
- 2.30	33	- 1:57	- 2.30	55	- 1:35	- 2.30	46	- 1:44	- 2.30	76	- 1:14	- 2.30	31	- 1:59	- 2.30	71	- 1:19	- 2.30	116	- 0:34	- 2.30	76	- 1:14
- 2.15	34	- 1:41	- 2.15	59	- 1:16	- 2.15	46	- 1:29	- 2.15	78	- 0:57	- 2.15	32	- 1:43	- 2.15	70	- 1:05	- 2.15	114	- 0:21	- 2.15	75	- 1:00
- 2.00	35	- 1:25	- 2.00	63	- 0:57	- 2.00	47	- 1:13	- 2.00	79	- 0:41	- 2.00	32	- 1:28	- 2.00	69	- 0:51	- 2.00	112	- 0:08	- 2.00	74	- 0:46
- 1.45	37	- 1:08	- 1.45	66	- 0:39	- 1.45	48	- 0:57	- 1.45	82	- 0:23	- 1.45	33	- 1:12	- 1.45	68	- 0:37	- 1.45	108	+ 0:03	- 1.45	71	- 0:34
- 1.30	39	- 0:51	- 1.30	69	- 0:21	- 1.30	50	- 0:40	- 1.30	84	- 0:06	- 1.30	33	- 0:57	- 1.30	66	- 0:24	- 1.30	105	+ 0:15	- 1.30	68	- 0:22
- 1.15	41	- 0:34	- 1.15	73	- 0:02	- 1.15	51	- 0:24	- 1.15	87	+ 0:12	- 1.15	34	- 0:41	- 1.15	64	- 0:11	- 1.15	101	+ 0:26	- 1.15	64	- 0:11
- 1.00	43	- 0:17	- 1.00	76	+ 0:16	- 1.00	52	- 0:08	- 1.00	89	+ 0:29	- 1.00	35	- 0:25	- 1.00	63	+ 0:03	- 1.00	97	+ 0:37	- 1.00	61	+ 0:01
- 0.45	46	+ 0:01	- 0.45	81	+ 0:36	- 0.45	54	+ 0:09	- 0.45	93	+ 0:48	- 0.45	36	- 0:09	- 0.45	60	+ 0:15	- 0.45	93	+ 0:48	- 0.45	58	+ 0:13
- 0.30	49	+ 0:19	- 0.30	85	+ 0:55	- 0.30	56	+ 0:26	- 0.30	97	+ 1:07	- 0.30	36	+ 0:06	- 0.30	58	+ 0:28	- 0.30	89	+ 0:59	- 0.30	55	+ 0:25
- 0.15	53	+ 0:38	- 0.15	90	+ 1:15	- 0.15	58	+ 0:43	- 0.15	101	+ 1:26	- 0.15	37	+ 0:22	- 0.15	55	+ 0:40	- 0.15	85	+ 1:10	- 0.15	51	+ 0:36
HW	56	+ 0:56	HW	95	+ 1:35	HW	60	+ 1:00	HW	105	+ 1:45	HW	38	+ 0:38	HW	53	+ 0:53	HW	81	+ 1:21	HW	48	+ 0:48
+ 0.15	58	+ 1:13	+ 0.15	97	+ 1:52	+ 0.15	63	+ 1:18	+ 0.15	110	+ 2:05	+ 0.15	39	+ 0:54	+ 0.15	50	+ 1:05	+ 0.15	76	+ 1:31	+ 0.15	46	+ 1:01
+ 0.30	60	+ 1:30	+ 0.30	99	+ 2:09	+ 0.30	65	+ 1:35	+ 0.30	116	+ 2:26	+ 0.30	41	+ 1:11	+ 0.30	47	+ 1:17	+ 0.30	70	+ 1:40	+ 0.30	44	+ 1:14
+ 0.45	62	+ 1:47	+ 0.45	101	+ 2:26	+ 0.45	68	+ 1:53	+ 0.45	121	+ 2:46	+ 0.45	42	+ 1:27	+ 0.45	45	+ 1:30	+ 0.45	65	+ 1:50	+ 0.45	42	+ 1:27
+ 1.00	65	+ 2:05	+ 1.00	103	+ 2:43	+ 1.00	71	+ 2:11	+ 1.00	126	+ 3:06	+ 1.00	43	+ 1:43	+ 1.00	42	+ 1:42	+ 1.00	60	+ 2:00	+ 1.00	40	+ 1:40
+ 1.15	65	+ 2:20	+ 1.15	102	+ 2:57	+ 1.15	73	+ 2:28	+ 1.15	128	+ 3:23	+ 1.15	45	+ 2:00	+ 1.15	41	+ 1:56	+ 1.15	58	+ 2:13	+ 1.15	40	+ 1:55
+ 1.30	65	+ 2:35	+ 1.30	100	+ 3:10	+ 1.30	75	+ 2:45	+ 1.30	131	+ 3:41	+ 1.30	47	+ 2:17	+ 1.30	39	+ 2:09	+ 1.30	56	+ 2:26	+ 1.30	40	+ 2:10
+ 1.45	65	+ 2:50	+ 1.45	98	+ 3:23	+ 1.45	77	+ 3:02	+ 1.45	133	+ 3:58	+ 1.45	49	+ 2:34	+ 1.45	38	+ 2:23	+ 1.45	54	+ 2:39	+ 1.45	39	+ 2:24
+ 2.00	65	+ 3:05	+ 2.00	97	+ 3:37	+ 2.00	80	+ 3:20	+ 2.00	136	+ 4:16	+ 2.00	50	+ 2:50	+ 2.00	36	+ 2:36	+ 2.00	52	+ 2:52	+ 2.00	39	+ 2:39
+ 2.15	64	+ 3:19	+ 2.15	94	+ 3:49	+ 2.15	80	+ 3:35	+ 2.15	134	+ 4:29	+ 2.15	50	+ 3:05	+ 2.15	36	+ 2:51	+ 2.15	53	+ 3:08	+ 2.15	40	+ 2:55
+ 2.30	63	+ 3:33	+ 2.30	91	+ 4:01	+ 2.30	80	+ 3:50	+ 2.30	133	+ 4:43	+ 2.30	50	+ 3:20	+ 2.30	36	+ 3:06	+ 2.30	53	+ 3:23	+ 2.30	40	+ 3:10
+ 2.45	61	+ 3:46	+ 2.45	87	+ 4:12	+ 2.45	80	+ 4:05	+ 2.45	131	+ 4:56	+ 2.45	50	+ 3:35	+ 2.45	36	+ 3:21	+ 2.45	54	+ 3:39	+ 2.45	41	+ 3:26
+ 3.00	60	+ 4:00	+ 3.00	84	+ 4:24	+ 3.00	80	+ 4:20	+ 3.00	130	+ 5:10	+ 3.00	50	+ 3:50	+ 3.00	36	+ 3:36	+ 3.00	55	+ 3:55	+ 3.00	42	+ 3:42
+ 3.15	59	+ 4:14	+ 3.15	82	+ 4:37	+ 3.15	78	+ 4:33	+ 3.15	127	+ 5:22	+ 3.15	49	+ 4:04	+ 3.15	37	+ 3:52	+ 3.15	57	+ 4:12	+ 3.15	43	+ 3:58
+ 3.30	57	+ 4:27	+ 3.30	80	+ 4:50	+ 3.30	77	+ 4:47	+ 3.30	124	+ 5:34	+ 3.30	48	+ 4:18	+ 3.30	38	+ 4:08	+ 3.30	60	+ 4:30	+ 3.30	44	+ 4:14
+ 3.45	56	+ 4:41	+ 3.45	78	+ 5:03	+ 3.45	75	+ 5:00	+ 3.45	121	+ 5:46	+ 3.45	47	+ 4:32	+ 3.45	39	+ 4:24	+ 3.45	62	+ 4:47	+ 3.45	46	+ 4:31
+ 4.00	54	+ 4:54	+ 4.00	75	+ 5:15	+ 4.00	74	+ 5:14	+ 4.00	118	+ 5:58	+ 4.00	47	+ 4:47	+ 4.00	40	+ 4:40	+ 4.00	65	+ 5:05	+ 4.00	47	+ 4:47
+ 4.15	52	+ 5:07	+ 4.15	71	+ 5:26	+ 4.15	72	+ 5:27	+ 4.15	115	- 5:50	+ 4.15	45	+ 5:00	+ 4.15	41	+ 4:56	+ 4.15	68	+ 5:23	+ 4.15	48	+ 5:03
+ 4.30	50	+ 5:20	+ 4.30	67	+ 5:37	+ 4.30	70	+ 5:40	+ 4.30	112	- 5:38	+ 4.30	44	+ 5:14	+ 4.30	43	+ 5:13	+ 4.30	71	+ 5:41	+ 4.30	49	+ 5:19
+ 4.45	48	+ 5:33	+ 4.45	63	+ 5:48	+ 4.45	68	+ 5:53	+ 4.45	109	- 5:26	+ 4.45	43	+ 5:28	+ 4.45	44	+ 5:29	+ 4.45	74	+ 5:59	+ 4.45	50	+ 5:35
+ 5.00	46	+ 5:46	+ 5.00	58	+ 5:58	+ 5.00	66	- 5:54	+ 5.00	107	- 5:13	+ 5.00	42	+ 5:42	+ 5.00	46	+ 5:46	+ 5.00	77	- 5:43	+ 5.00	51	+ 5:51
+ 5.15	45	- 6:00	+ 5.15	56	- 5:49	+ 5.15	65	- 5:40	+ 5.15	105	- 5:00	+ 5.15	42	+ 5:57	+ 5.15	47	- 5:58	+ 5.15	78	- 5:27	+ 5.15	52	- 5:53
+ 5.30	43	- 5:47	+ 5.30	53	- 5:37	+ 5.30	64	- 5:26	+ 5.30	103	- 4:47	+ 5.30	41	- 5:49	+ 5.30	48	- 5:42	+ 5.30	79	- 5:11	+ 5.30	53	- 5:37
+ 5.45	42	- 5:33	+ 5.45	51	- 5:24	+ 5.45	62	- 5:13	+ 5.45	101	- 4:34	+ 5.45	40	- 5:35	+ 5.45	49	- 5:26	+ 5.45	81	- 4:54	+ 5.45	54	- 5:21
+ 6.00	40	- 5:20	+ 6.00	48	- 5:12	+ 6.00	61	- 4:59	+ 6.00	99	- 4:21	+ 6.00	40	- 5:20	+ 6.00	50	- 5:10	+ 6.00	82	- 4:38	+ 6.00	55	- 5:05

SOUTH BOUND

Table G - Medway, Sea Reach and Black Deep Connections

Neaps — All times relate to HW Sheerness — **Time to cover Sectors (in minutes) at 6.0 Kts**

SOUTH BOUND

	G8			G7			G6			G5	
	Long Sand Inner to Blk Deep No 8			Black Deep to Blk Deep No 8			SW Barrow to Sea Reach			SW Barrow to Medway	
Time	Duration	Time at End of Sector	Time	Duration	Time at End of Sector	Time	Duration	Time at End of Sector	Time	Duration	Time at End of Sector
-6.00	**33**	**-5:27**	**-6.00**	**43**	**-5:17**	**-6.00**	**47**	**-5:13**	**-6.00**	**77**	**-4:43**
-5.45	33	-5:12	-5.45	43	-5:02	-5.45	47	-4:58	-5.45	76	-4:29
-5.30	32	-4:58	-5.30	42	-4:48	-5.30	46	-4:44	-5.30	75	-4:15
-5.15	31	-4:44	-5.15	42	-4:33	-5.15	45	-4:30	-5.15	73	-4:02
-5.00	**31**	**-4:29**	**-5.00**	**41**	**-4:19**	**-5.00**	**44**	**-4:16**	**-5.00**	**72**	**-3:48**
-4.45	31	-4:14	-4.45	41	-4:04	-4.45	44	-4:01	-4.45	71	-3:34
-4.30	30	-4:00	-4.30	41	-3:49	-4.30	43	-3:47	-4.30	70	-3:20
-4.15	30	-3:45	-4.15	41	-3:34	-4.15	43	-3:32	-4.15	70	-3:05
-4.00	**30**	**-3:30**	**-4.00**	**41**	**-3:19**	**-4.00**	**42**	**-3:18**	**-4.00**	**69**	**-2:51**
-3.45	30	-3:15	-3.45	42	-3:03	-3.45	42	-3:03	-3.45	69	-2:36
-3.30	30	-3:00	-3.30	43	-2:47	-3.30	42	-2:48	-3.30	69	-2:21
-3.15	30	-2:45	-3.15	44	-2:31	-3.15	42	-2:33	-3.15	70	-2:05
-3.00	**30**	**-2:30**	**-3.00**	**45**	**-2:15**	**-3.00**	**42**	**-2:18**	**-3.00**	**70**	**-1:50**
-2.45	30	-2:15	-2.45	46	-1:59	-2.45	42	-2:03	-2.45	70	-1:35
-2.30	31	-1:59	-2.30	48	-1:42	-2.30	43	-1:47	-2.30	71	-1:19
-2.15	31	-1:44	-2.15	50	-1:25	-2.15	43	-1:32	-2.15	72	-1:03
-2.00	**31**	**-1:29**	**-2.00**	**52**	**-1:08**	**-2.00**	**43**	**-1:17**	**-2.00**	**72**	**-0:48**
-1.45	32	-1:13	-1.45	54	-0:51	-1.45	44	-1:01	-1.45	74	-0:31
-1.30	33	-0:57	-1.30	55	-0:35	-1.30	44	-0:46	-1.30	75	-0:15
-1.15	34	-0:41	-1.15	57	-0:18	-1.15	45	-0:30	-1.15	76	+0:01
-1.00	**35**	**-0:25**	**-1.00**	**58**	**-0:02**	**-1.00**	**46**	**-0:14**	**-1.00**	**77**	**+0:17**
-0.45	37	-0:08	-0.45	59	+0:14	-0.45	46	+0:01	-0.45	78	+0:33
-0.30	38	+0:08	-0.30	60	+0:30	-0.30	47	+0:17	-0.30	80	+0:50
-0.15	40	+0:25	-0.15	61	+0:46	-0.15	48	+0:33	-0.15	81	+1:06
HW	**41**	**+0:41**	**HW**	**62**	**+1:02**	**HW**	**49**	**+0:49**	**HW**	**83**	**+1:23**
+0.15	42	+0:57	+0.15	63	+1:18	+0.15	50	+1:05	+0.15	85	+1:40
+0.30	43	+1:13	+0.30	64	+1:34	+0.30	51	+1:21	+0.30	88	+1:58
+0.45	44	+1:29	+0.45	65	+1:50	+0.45	52	+1:37	+0.45	90	+2:15
+1.00	**45**	**+1:45**	**+1.00**	**66**	**+2:06**	**+1.00**	**54**	**+1:54**	**+1.00**	**93**	**+2:33**
+1.15	45	+2:00	+1.15	65	+2:20	+1.15	55	+2:10	+1.15	95	+2:50
+1.30	45	+2:15	+1.30	65	+2:35	+1.30	56	+2:26	+1.30	96	+3:06
+1.45	45	+2:30	+1.45	65	+2:50	+1.45	57	+2:42	+1.45	98	+3:23
+2.00	**45**	**+2:45**	**+2.00**	**65**	**+3:05**	**+2.00**	**58**	**+2:58**	**+2.00**	**100**	**+3:40**
+2.15	45	+3:00	+2.15	64	+3:19	+2.15	58	+3:13	+2.15	100	+3:55
+2.30	44	+3:14	+2.30	63	+3:33	+2.30	58	+3:28	+2.30	100	+4:10
+2.45	44	+3:29	+2.45	62	+3:47	+2.45	58	+3:43	+2.45	99	+4:24
+3.00	**44**	**+3:44**	**+3.00**	**62**	**+4:02**	**+3.00**	**58**	**+3:58**	**+3.00**	**99**	**+4:39**
+3.15	43	+3:58	+3.15	61	+4:16	+3.15	57	+4:12	+3.15	98	+4:53
+3.30	42	+4:12	+3.30	60	+4:30	+3.30	57	+4:27	+3.30	97	+5:07
+3.45	42	+4:27	+3.45	59	+4:44	+3.45	56	+4:41	+3.45	95	+5:20
+4.00	**41**	**+4:41**	**+4.00**	**58**	**+4:58**	**+4.00**	**56**	**+4:56**	**+4.00**	**94**	**+5:34**
+4.15	40	+4:55	+4.15	56	+5:11	+4.15	55	+5:10	+4.15	92	+5:47
+4.30	39	+5:09	+4.30	55	+5:25	+4.30	54	+5:24	+4.30	90	-6:00
+4.45	38	+5:23	+4.45	53	+5:38	+4.45	53	+5:38	+4.45	88	-5:47
+5.00	**38**	**+5:38**	**+5.00**	**51**	**+5:51**	**+5.00**	**53**	**+5:53**	**+5.00**	**86**	**-5:34**
+5.15	37	+5:52	+5.15	50	-5:55	+5.15	52	-5:53	+5.15	85	-5:20
+5.30	36	-5:54	+5.30	49	-5:41	+5.30	51	-5:39	+5.30	84	-5:06
+5.45	35	-5:40	+5.45	47	-5:28	+5.45	51	-5:24	+5.45	84	-4:51
+6.00	**35**	**-5:25**	**+6.00**	**46**	**-5:14**	**+6.00**	**50**	**-5:10**	**+6.00**	**83**	**-4:37**

	G4			G3			G2			G1	
	Sea Reach to Medway			Sea Reach to Red Sand Tower			Medway to Red Sand Towers			Red Sand Tower to Princes No 6	
Time	Duration	Time at End of Sector	Time	Duration	Time at End of Sector	Time	Duration	Time at End of Sector	Time	Duration	Time at End of Sector
-6.00	**32**	**-5:28**	**-6.00**	**44**	**-5:16**	**-6.00**	**75**	**-4:45**	**-6.00**	**49**	**-5:11**
-5.45	32	-5:13	-5.45	46	-4:59	-5.45	77	-4:28	-5.45	50	-4:55
-5.30	31	-4:59	-5.30	47	-4:43	-5.30	78	-4:12	-5.30	51	-4:39
-5.15	31	-4:44	-5.15	48	-4:27	-5.15	80	-3:55	-5.15	52	-4:23
-5.00	**30**	**-4:30**	**-5.00**	**49**	**-4:11**	**-5.00**	**82**	**-3:38**	**-5.00**	**53**	**-4:07**
-4.45	30	-4:15	-4.45	50	-3:55	-4.45	84	-3:21	-4.45	54	-3:51
-4.30	29	-4:01	-4.30	51	-3:39	-4.30	86	-3:04	-4.30	55	-3:35
-4.15	29	-3:46	-4.15	51	-3:24	-4.15	88	-2:47	-4.15	55	-3:20
-4.00	**28**	**-3:32**	**-4.00**	**52**	**-3:08**	**-4.00**	**90**	**-2:30**	**-4.00**	**56**	**-3:04**
-3.45	28	-3:17	-3.45	52	-2:53	-3.45	90	-2:15	-3.45	56	-2:49
-3.30	28	-3:02	-3.30	52	-2:38	-3.30	90	-2:00	-3.30	56	-2:34
-3.15	28	-2:47	-3.15	52	-2:23	-3.15	90	-1:45	-3.15	56	-2:19
-3.00	**28**	**-2:32**	**-3.00**	**52**	**-2:08**	**-3.00**	**90**	**-1:30**	**-3.00**	**56**	**-2:04**
-2.45	28	-2:17	-2.45	52	-1:53	-2.45	88	-1:17	-2.45	56	-1:49
-2.30	28	-2:02	-2.30	52	-1:38	-2.30	87	-1:03	-2.30	56	-1:34
-2.15	28	-1:47	-2.15	52	-1:23	-2.15	85	-0:50	-2.15	56	-1:19
-2.00	**29**	**-1:31**	**-2.00**	**51**	**-1:09**	**-2.00**	**83**	**-0:37**	**-2.00**	**55**	**-1:05**
-1.45	29	-1:16	-1.45	51	-0:54	-1.45	82	-0:23	-1.45	54	-0:51
-1.30	29	-1:01	-1.30	50	-0:40	-1.30	80	-0:10	-1.30	53	-0:37
-1.15	29	-0:46	-1.15	49	-0:26	-1.15	79	+0:04	-1.15	52	-0:23
-1.00	**30**	**-0:30**	**-1.00**	**49**	**-0:11**	**-1.00**	**77**	**+0:17**	**-1.00**	**51**	**-0:09**
-0.45	30	-0:15	-0.45	47	+0:02	-0.45	75	+0:30	-0.45	50	+0:05
-0.30	31	+0:01	-0.30	46	+0:16	-0.30	73	+0:43	-0.30	49	+0:19
-0.15	31	+0:16	-0.15	45	+0:30	-0.15	71	+0:56	-0.15	47	+0:32
HW	**32**	**+0:32**	**HW**	**44**	**+0:44**	**HW**	**69**	**+1:09**	**HW**	**46**	**+0:46**
+0.15	32	+0:47	+0.15	43	+0:58	+0.15	67	+1:22	+0.15	44	+0:59
+0.30	33	+1:03	+0.30	42	+1:12	+0.30	64	+1:34	+0.30	43	+1:13
+0.45	33	+1:18	+0.45	40	+1:25	+0.45	62	+1:47	+0.45	42	+1:27
+1.00	**34**	**+1:34**	**+1.00**	**39**	**+1:39**	**+1.00**	**59**	**+1:59**	**+1.00**	**40**	**+1:40**
+1.15	34	+1:49	+1.15	38	+1:53	+1.15	58	+2:13	+1.15	40	+1:55
+1.30	35	+2:05	+1.30	37	+2:07	+1.30	57	+2:27	+1.30	40	+2:10
+1.45	36	+2:21	+1.45	36	+2:21	+1.45	56	+2:41	+1.45	39	+2:24
+2.00	**37**	**+2:37**	**+2.00**	**35**	**+2:35**	**+2.00**	**54**	**+2:54**	**+2.00**	**39**	**+2:39**
+2.15	37	+2:52	+2.15	35	+2:50	+2.15	55	+3:10	+2.15	39	+2:54
+2.30	37	+3:07	+2.30	35	+3:05	+2.30	55	+3:25	+2.30	40	+3:10
+2.45	37	+3:22	+2.45	35	+3:20	+2.45	56	+3:41	+2.45	40	+3:25
+3.00	**37**	**+3:37**	**+3.00**	**35**	**+3:35**	**+3.00**	**56**	**+3:56**	**+3.00**	**40**	**+3:40**
+3.15	37	+3:52	+3.15	36	+3:51	+3.15	57	+4:12	+3.15	40	+3:55
+3.30	36	+4:06	+3.30	36	+4:06	+3.30	58	+4:28	+3.30	41	+4:11
+3.45	36	+4:21	+3.45	36	+4:21	+3.45	59	+4:44	+3.45	41	+4:26
+4.00	**36**	**+4:36**	**+4.00**	**37**	**+4:37**	**+4.00**	**60**	**+5:00**	**+4.00**	**42**	**+4:42**
+4.15	35	+4:50	+4.15	38	+4:53	+4.15	62	+5:17	+4.15	42	+4:57
+4.30	35	+5:05	+4.30	38	+5:08	+4.30	63	+5:33	+4.30	43	+5:13
+4.45	34	+5:19	+4.45	39	+5:24	+4.45	64	+5:49	+4.45	43	+5:28
+5.00	**34**	**+5:34**	**+5.00**	**40**	**+5:40**	**+5.00**	**66**	**-5:54**	**+5.00**	**44**	**+5:44**
+5.15	34	+5:49	+5.15	41	+5:56	+5.15	67	-5:38	+5.15	45	-6:00
+5.30	33	-5:57	+5.30	41	-5:49	+5.30	67	-5:23	+5.30	45	-5:45
+5.45	33	-5:42	+5.45	42	-5:33	+5.45	68	-5:07	+5.45	46	-5:29
+6.00	**32**	**-5:28**	**+6.00**	**42**	**-5:18**	**+6.00**	**69**	**-4:51**	**+6.00**	**46**	**-5:14**

Table G - Medway, Sea Reach and Black Deep Connections

Time to cover Sectors (in minutes) at 6.0 kts — All times relate to HW Sheerness — **Springs**

Time	G8 Long Sand Inner to Blk Deep No 8 Duration	G8 Time at End of Sector	G7 Black Deep to Blk Deep No 8 Duration	G7 Time at End of Sector	G6 SW Barrow to Sea Reach Duration	G6 Time at End of Sector	G5 SW Barrow to Medway Duration	G5 Time at End of Sector
- 6.00	32	- 5:28	39	- 5:21	47	- 5:13	75	- 4:45
- 5.45	31	- 5:14	38	- 5:07	46	- 4:59	73	- 4:32
- 5.30	30	- 5:00	37	- 4:53	44	- 4:46	71	- 4:19
- 5.15	30	- 4:45	37	- 4:38	43	- 4:32	69	- 4:06
- 5.00	29	- 4:31	36	- 4:24	42	- 4:18	67	- 3:53
- 4.45	28	- 4:17	36	- 4:09	41	- 4:04	66	- 3:39
- 4.30	27	- 4:03	36	- 3:54	41	- 3:49	66	- 3:24
- 4.15	27	- 3:48	36	- 3:39	40	- 3:35	65	- 3:10
- 4.00	26	- 3:34	36	- 3:24	39	- 3:21	64	- 2:56
- 3.45	26	- 3:19	37	- 3:08	39	- 3:06	64	- 2:41
- 3.30	26	- 3:04	38	- 2:52	39	- 2:51	64	- 2:26
- 3.15	26	- 2:49	39	- 2:36	39	- 2:36	64	- 2:11
- 3.00	26	- 2:34	40	- 2:20	39	- 2:21	64	- 1:56
- 2.45	27	- 2:18	43	- 2:02	39	- 2:06	65	- 1:40
- 2.30	28	- 2:02	46	- 1:44	40	- 1:50	66	- 1:24
- 2.15	29	- 1:46	48	- 1:27	40	- 1:35	67	- 1:08
- 2.00	30	- 1:30	51	- 1:09	40	- 1:20	68	- 0:52
- 1.45	31	- 1:14	54	- 0:51	41	- 1:04	70	- 0:35
- 1.30	32	- 0:58	56	- 0:34	42	- 0:48	72	- 0:18
- 1.15	33	- 0:42	58	- 0:17	43	- 0:32	73	- 0:02
- 1.00	34	- 0:26	61	+ 0:01	44	- 0:16	75	+ 0:15
- 0.45	37	- 0:08	63	+ 0:18	45	HW	77	+ 0:32
- 0.30	39	+ 0:09	64	+ 0:34	47	+ 0:17	80	+ 0:50
- 0.15	42	+ 0:27	66	+ 0:51	48	+ 0:33	82	+ 1:07
HW	44	+ 0:44	68	+ 1:08	49	+ 0:49	84	+ 1:24
+ 0.15	46	+ 1:01	69	+ 1:24	51	+ 1:06	88	+ 1:43
+ 0.30	47	+ 1:17	71	+ 1:41	53	+ 1:23	92	+ 2:02
+ 0.45	49	+ 1:34	72	+ 1:57	55	+ 1:40	96	+ 2:21
+ 1.00	51	+ 1:51	74	+ 2:14	56	+ 1:56	99	+ 2:39
+ 1.15	51	+ 2:06	73	+ 2:28	58	+ 2:13	102	+ 2:57
+ 1.30	51	+ 2:21	73	+ 2:43	60	+ 2:30	104	+ 3:14
+ 1.45	51	+ 2:36	73	+ 2:58	61	+ 2:46	106	+ 3:31
+ 2.00	51	+ 2:51	72	+ 3:12	63	+ 3:03	108	+ 3:48
+ 2.15	50	+ 3:05	71	+ 3:26	63	+ 3:18	107	+ 4:02
+ 2.30	50	+ 3:20	70	+ 3:40	63	+ 3:33	107	+ 4:17
+ 2.45	49	+ 3:34	69	+ 3:54	64	+ 3:49	106	+ 4:31
+ 3.00	48	+ 3:48	68	+ 4:08	64	+ 4:04	105	+ 4:45
+ 3.15	47	+ 4:02	66	+ 4:21	63	+ 4:18	103	+ 4:58
+ 3.30	46	+ 4:16	65	+ 4:35	62	+ 4:32	101	+ 5:11
+ 3.45	45	+ 4:30	63	+ 4:48	61	+ 4:46	99	+ 5:24
+ 4.00	44	+ 4:44	62	+ 5:02	60	+ 5:00	97	+ 5:37
+ 4.15	43	+ 4:58	59	+ 5:14	58	+ 5:13	95	+ 5:50
+ 4.30	41	+ 5:11	56	+ 5:26	57	+ 5:27	93	- 5:57
+ 4.45	40	+ 5:25	53	+ 5:38	56	+ 5:41	91	- 5:44
+ 5.00	39	+ 5:39	51	+ 5:51	55	+ 5:55	88	- 5:32
+ 5.15	37	+ 5:52	49	- 5:56	54	- 5:51	87	- 5:18
+ 5.30	36	- 5:54	47	- 5:43	53	- 5:37	86	- 5:04
+ 5.45	35	- 5:40	45	- 5:30	52	- 5:23	85	- 4:50
+ 6.00	34	- 5:26	43	- 5:17	51	- 5:09	84	- 4:36

Time	G4 Sea Reach to Medway Duration	G4 Time at End of Sector	G3 Sea Reach to Red Sand Tower Duration	G3 Time at End of Sector	G2 Medway to Red Sand Towers Duration	G2 Time at End of Sector	G1 Red Sand Tower to Princes No 6 Duration	G1 Time at End of Sector
- 6.00	32	- 5:28	44	- 5:16	76	- 4:44	51	- 5:09
- 5.45	31	- 5:14	47	- 4:58	81	- 4:24	53	- 4:52
- 5.30	31	- 4:59	49	- 4:41	85	- 4:05	55	- 4:35
- 5.15	30	- 4:45	51	- 4:24	89	- 3:46	57	- 4:18
- 5.00	30	- 4:30	53	- 4:07	93	- 3:27	59	- 4:01
- 4.45	29	- 4:16	54	- 3:51	94	- 3:11	60	- 3:45
- 4.30	28	- 4:02	55	- 3:35	95	- 2:55	61	- 3:29
- 4.15	27	- 3:48	56	- 3:19	97	- 2:38	61	- 3:14
- 4.00	27	- 3:33	58	- 3:02	98	- 2:22	62	- 2:58
- 3.45	26	- 3:19	58	- 2:47	97	- 2:08	62	- 2:43
- 3.30	26	- 3:04	57	- 2:33	97	- 1:53	62	- 2:28
- 3.15	26	- 2:49	57	- 2:18	97	- 1:38	62	- 2:13
- 3.00	26	- 2:34	57	- 2:03	96	- 1:24	62	- 1:58
- 2.45	26	- 2:19	57	- 1:48	95	- 1:10	62	- 1:43
- 2.30	26	- 2:04	57	- 1:33	94	- 0:56	61	- 1:29
- 2.15	27	- 1:48	56	- 1:19	93	- 0:42	60	- 1:15
- 2.00	27	- 1:33	56	- 1:04	92	- 0:28	60	- 1:00
- 1.45	27	- 1:18	55	- 0:50	89	- 0:16	58	- 0:47
- 1.30	28	- 1:02	53	- 0:37	86	- 0:04	57	- 0:33
- 1.15	28	- 0:47	52	- 0:23	84	+ 0:09	55	- 0:20
- 1.00	29	- 0:31	51	- 0:09	81	+ 0:21	53	- 0:07
- 0.45	29	- 0:16	50	+ 0:05	78	+ 0:33	51	+ 0:06
- 0.30	30	HW	48	+ 0:18	75	+ 0:45	49	+ 0:19
- 0.15	31	+ 0:16	46	+ 0:31	72	+ 0:57	46	+ 0:31
HW	31	+ 0:31	44	+ 0:44	69	+ 1:09	44	+ 0:44
+ 0.15	32	+ 0:47	43	+ 0:58	65	+ 1:20	42	+ 0:57
+ 0.30	33	+ 1:03	41	+ 1:11	62	+ 1:32	40	+ 1:10
+ 0.45	34	+ 1:19	39	+ 1:24	58	+ 1:43	38	+ 1:23
+ 1.00	35	+ 1:35	37	+ 1:37	54	+ 1:54	36	+ 1:36
+ 1.15	36	+ 1:51	36	+ 1:51	53	+ 2:08	36	+ 1:51
+ 1.30	37	+ 2:07	35	+ 2:05	51	+ 2:21	36	+ 2:06
+ 1.45	39	+ 2:24	34	+ 2:19	49	+ 2:34	35	+ 2:20
+ 2.00	40	+ 2:40	32	+ 2:32	48	+ 2:48	35	+ 2:35
+ 2.15	40	+ 2:55	32	+ 2:47	48	+ 3:03	35	+ 2:50
+ 2.30	40	+ 3:10	32	+ 3:02	49	+ 3:19	36	+ 3:06
+ 2.45	40	+ 3:25	32	+ 3:17	49	+ 3:34	36	+ 3:21
+ 3.00	40	+ 3:40	32	+ 3:32	49	+ 3:49	36	+ 3:36
+ 3.15	40	+ 3:55	32	+ 3:47	51	+ 4:06	37	+ 3:52
+ 3.30	39	+ 4:09	33	+ 4:03	53	+ 4:23	38	+ 4:08
+ 3.45	38	+ 4:23	33	+ 4:18	54	+ 4:39	39	+ 4:24
+ 4.00	38	+ 4:38	34	+ 4:34	56	+ 4:56	40	+ 4:40
+ 4.15	37	+ 4:52	35	+ 4:50	58	+ 5:13	41	+ 4:56
+ 4.30	36	+ 5:06	36	+ 5:06	60	+ 5:30	42	+ 5:12
+ 4.45	36	+ 5:21	37	+ 5:22	62	+ 5:47	42	+ 5:27
+ 5.00	35	+ 5:35	39	+ 5:39	64	- 5:56	43	+ 5:43
+ 5.15	34	+ 5:49	39	+ 5:54	65	- 5:40	44	+ 5:59
+ 5.30	34	- 5:56	40	- 5:50	66	- 5:24	45	- 5:45
+ 5.45	33	- 5:42	41	- 5:34	68	- 5:07	45	- 5:30
+ 6.00	33	- 5:27	42	- 5:18	69	- 4:51	46	- 5:14

SOUTH BOUND

Table G - Medway, Sea Reach and Black Deep Connections

Neaps

All times relate to HW Sheerness

Time to cover Sectors (in minutes) at 7.0 Kts

SOUTH BOUND

Time	G8 Long Sand Inner to Blk Deep No 8 Duration	G8 Time at End of Sector	Time	G7 Black Deep to Blk Deep No 8 Duration	G7 Time at End of Sector	Time	G6 SW Barrow to Sea Reach Duration	G6 Time at End of Sector	Time	G5 SW Barrow to Medway Duration	G5 Time at End of Sector
- 6.00	29	- 5:31	- 6.00	39	- 5:21	- 6.00	41	- 5:19	- 6.00	67	- 4:53
- 5.45	29	- 5:16	- 5.45	39	- 5:06	- 5.45	40	- 5:05	- 5.45	66	- 4:39
- 5.30	28	- 5:02	- 5.30	38	- 4:52	- 5.30	40	- 4:50	- 5.30	65	- 4:25
- 5.15	27	- 4:48	- 5.15	38	- 4:37	- 5.15	39	- 4:36	- 5.15	64	- 4:11
- 5.00	27	- 4:33	- 5.00	37	- 4:23	- 5.00	39	- 4:21	- 5.00	63	- 3:57
- 4.45	26	- 4:19	- 4.45	37	- 4:08	- 4.45	38	- 4:07	- 4.45	62	- 3:43
- 4.30	26	- 4:04	- 4.30	37	- 3:53	- 4.30	38	- 3:52	- 4.30	62	- 3:28
- 4.15	26	- 3:49	- 4.15	37	- 3:38	- 4.15	37	- 3:38	- 4.15	61	- 3:14
- 4.00	25	- 3:35	- 4.00	37	- 3:23	- 4.00	37	- 3:23	- 4.00	61	- 2:59
- 3.45	25	- 3:20	- 3.45	38	- 3:07	- 3.45	37	- 3:08	- 3.45	61	- 2:44
- 3.30	25	- 3:05	- 3.30	38	- 2:52	- 3.30	37	- 2:53	- 3.30	61	- 2:29
- 3.15	25	- 2:50	- 3.15	39	- 2:36	- 3.15	37	- 2:38	- 3.15	61	- 2:14
- 3.00	25	- 2:35	- 3.00	40	- 2:20	- 3.00	37	- 2:23	- 3.00	61	- 1:59
- 2.45	26	- 2:19	- 2.45	41	- 2:04	- 2.45	37	- 2:08	- 2.45	61	- 1:44
- 2.30	26	- 2:04	- 2.30	42	- 1:48	- 2.30	37	- 1:53	- 2.30	62	- 1:28
- 2.15	27	- 1:48	- 2.15	43	- 1:32	- 2.15	37	- 1:38	- 2.15	62	- 1:13
- 2.00	27	- 1:33	- 2.00	45	- 1:15	- 2.00	37	- 1:23	- 2.00	63	- 0:57
- 1.45	28	- 1:17	- 1.45	46	- 0:59	- 1.45	38	- 1:07	- 1.45	64	- 0:41
- 1.30	28	- 1:02	- 1.30	47	- 0:43	- 1.30	38	- 0:52	- 1.30	65	- 0:25
- 1.15	29	- 0:46	- 1.15	48	- 0:27	- 1.15	39	- 0:36	- 1.15	65	- 0:10
- 1.00	30	- 0:30	- 1.00	49	- 0:11	- 1.00	39	- 0:21	- 1.00	66	+ 0:06
- 0.45	31	- 0:14	- 0.45	49	+ 0:04	- 0.45	40	- 0:05	- 0.45	67	+ 0:22
- 0.30	32	+ 0:02	- 0.30	50	+ 0:20	- 0.30	40	+ 0:10	- 0.30	68	+ 0:38
- 0.15	33	+ 0:18	- 0.15	50	+ 0:35	- 0.15	41	+ 0:26	- 0.15	69	+ 0:54
HW	34	+ 0:34	HW	50	+ 0:50	HW	42	+ 0:42	HW	71	+ 1:11
+ 0.15	35	+ 0:50	+ 0.15	51	+ 1:06	+ 0.15	42	+ 0:57	+ 0.15	72	+ 1:27
+ 0.30	36	+ 1:06	+ 0.30	51	+ 1:21	+ 0.30	43	+ 1:13	+ 0.30	73	+ 1:43
+ 0.45	37	+ 1:22	+ 0.45	52	+ 1:37	+ 0.45	44	+ 1:29	+ 0.45	75	+ 2:00
+ 1.00	38	+ 1:38	+ 1.00	52	+ 1:52	+ 1.00	45	+ 1:45	+ 1.00	76	+ 2:16
+ 1.15	38	+ 1:53	+ 1.15	52	+ 2:07	+ 1.15	46	+ 2:01	+ 1.15	77	+ 2:32
+ 1.30	38	+ 2:08	+ 1.30	52	+ 2:22	+ 1.30	47	+ 2:17	+ 1.30	78	+ 2:48
+ 1.45	38	+ 2:23	+ 1.45	52	+ 2:37	+ 1.45	47	+ 2:32	+ 1.45	79	+ 3:04
+ 2.00	38	+ 2:38	+ 2.00	52	+ 2:52	+ 2.00	48	+ 2:48	+ 2.00	80	+ 3:20
+ 2.15	37	+ 2:52	+ 2.15	52	+ 3:07	+ 2.15	48	+ 3:03	+ 2.15	80	+ 3:35
+ 2.30	37	+ 3:07	+ 2.30	51	+ 3:21	+ 2.30	48	+ 3:18	+ 2.30	80	+ 3:50
+ 2.45	37	+ 3:22	+ 2.45	51	+ 3:36	+ 2.45	49	+ 3:34	+ 2.45	80	+ 4:05
+ 3.00	37	+ 3:37	+ 3.00	50	+ 3:50	+ 3.00	49	+ 3:49	+ 3.00	80	+ 4:20
+ 3.15	36	+ 3:51	+ 3.15	50	+ 4:05	+ 3.15	48	+ 4:03	+ 3.15	79	+ 4:34
+ 3.30	36	+ 4:06	+ 3.30	49	+ 4:19	+ 3.30	48	+ 4:18	+ 3.30	78	+ 4:48
+ 3.45	35	+ 4:20	+ 3.45	49	+ 4:34	+ 3.45	47	+ 4:32	+ 3.45	78	+ 5:03
+ 4.00	35	+ 4:35	+ 4.00	48	+ 4:48	+ 4.00	47	+ 4:47	+ 4.00	77	+ 5:17
+ 4.15	34	+ 4:49	+ 4.15	47	+ 5:02	+ 4.15	47	+ 5:02	+ 4.15	76	+ 5:31
+ 4.30	33	+ 5:03	+ 4.30	46	+ 5:16	+ 4.30	46	+ 5:16	+ 4.30	75	+ 5:45
+ 4.45	33	+ 5:18	+ 4.45	45	+ 5:30	+ 4.45	45	+ 5:30	+ 4.45	74	+ 5:59
+ 5.00	32	+ 5:32	+ 5.00	45	+ 5:45	+ 5.00	45	+ 5:45	+ 5.00	73	- 5:47
+ 5.15	32	+ 5:47	+ 5.15	44	+ 5:59	+ 5.15	44	+ 5:59	+ 5.15	73	- 5:32
+ 5.30	31	- 5:59	+ 5.30	43	- 5:47	+ 5.30	44	- 5:46	+ 5.30	72	- 5:18
+ 5.45	31	- 5:44	+ 5.45	42	- 5:33	+ 5.45	43	- 5:32	+ 5.45	72	- 5:03
+ 6.00	30	- 5:30	+ 6.00	41	- 5:19	+ 6.00	43	- 5:17	+ 6.00	71	- 4:49

Time	G4 Sea Reach to Medway Duration	G4 Time at End of Sector	Time	G3 Sea Reach to Red Sand Tower Duration	G3 Time at End of Sector	Time	G2 Medway to Red Sand Towers Duration	G2 Time at End of Sector	Time	G1 Red Sand Tower to Princes No 6 Duration	G1 Time at End of Sector
- 6.00	27	- 5:33	- 6.00	37	- 5:23	- 6.00	63	- 4:57	- 6.00	42	- 5:18
- 5.45	27	- 5:18	- 5.45	38	- 5:07	- 5.45	64	- 4:41	- 5.45	42	- 5:03
- 5.30	27	- 5:03	- 5.30	39	- 4:51	- 5.30	66	- 4:24	- 5.30	43	- 4:47
- 5.15	26	- 4:49	- 5.15	40	- 4:35	- 5.15	67	- 4:08	- 5.15	44	- 4:31
- 5.00	26	- 4:34	- 5.00	41	- 4:19	- 5.00	69	- 3:51	- 5.00	45	- 4:15
- 4.45	26	- 4:19	- 4.45	42	- 4:03	- 4.45	69	- 3:36	- 4.45	45	- 4:00
- 4.30	25	- 4:05	- 4.30	42	- 3:48	- 4.30	70	- 3:20	- 4.30	46	- 3:44
- 4.15	25	- 3:50	- 4.15	43	- 3:32	- 4.15	70	- 3:05	- 4.15	46	- 3:29
- 4.00	24	- 3:36	- 4.00	43	- 3:17	- 4.00	71	- 2:49	- 4.00	47	- 3:13
- 3.45	24	- 3:21	- 3.45	44	- 3:01	- 3.45	71	- 2:34	- 3.45	47	- 2:58
- 3.30	24	- 3:06	- 3.30	44	- 2:46	- 3.30	71	- 2:19	- 3.30	47	- 2:43
- 3.15	24	- 2:51	- 3.15	44	- 2:31	- 3.15	71	- 2:04	- 3.15	47	- 2:28
- 3.00	24	- 2:36	- 3.00	44	- 2:16	- 3.00	71	- 1:49	- 3.00	47	- 2:13
- 2.45	24	- 2:21	- 2.45	43	- 2:02	- 2.45	70	- 1:35	- 2.45	47	- 1:58
- 2.30	24	- 2:06	- 2.30	43	- 1:47	- 2.30	70	- 1:20	- 2.30	47	- 1:43
- 2.15	24	- 1:51	- 2.15	43	- 1:32	- 2.15	70	- 1:05	- 2.15	47	- 1:28
- 2.00	24	- 1:36	- 2.00	43	- 1:17	- 2.00	70	- 0:50	- 2.00	47	- 1:13
- 1.45	25	- 1:20	- 1.45	43	- 1:02	- 1.45	69	- 0:36	- 1.45	46	- 0:59
- 1.30	25	- 1:05	- 1.30	42	- 0:48	- 1.30	68	- 0:22	- 1.30	45	- 0:45
- 1.15	25	- 0:50	- 1.15	42	- 0:33	- 1.15	67	- 0:08	- 1.15	44	- 0:31
- 1.00	25	- 0:35	- 1.00	41	- 0:19	- 1.00	66	+ 0:06	- 1.00	43	- 0:17
- 0.45	26	- 0:19	- 0.45	40	- 0:05	- 0.45	64	+ 0:19	- 0.45	42	- 0:03
- 0.30	26	- 0:04	- 0.30	40	+ 0:10	- 0.30	63	+ 0:33	- 0.30	41	+ 0:11
- 0.15	27	+ 0:12	- 0.15	39	+ 0:24	- 0.15	61	+ 0:46	- 0.15	40	+ 0:25
HW	27	+ 0:27	HW	38	+ 0:38	HW	60	+ 1:00	HW	39	+ 0:39
+ 0.15	27	+ 0:42	+ 0.15	37	+ 0:52	+ 0.15	58	+ 1:13	+ 0.15	38	+ 0:53
+ 0.30	28	+ 0:58	+ 0.30	36	+ 1:06	+ 0.30	56	+ 1:26	+ 0.30	37	+ 1:07
+ 0.45	28	+ 1:13	+ 0.45	35	+ 1:20	+ 0.45	55	+ 1:40	+ 0.45	36	+ 1:21
+ 1.00	28	+ 1:28	+ 1.00	35	+ 1:35	+ 1.00	53	+ 1:53	+ 1.00	36	+ 1:36
+ 1.15	29	+ 1:44	+ 1.15	34	+ 1:49	+ 1.15	52	+ 2:07	+ 1.15	35	+ 1:50
+ 1.30	29	+ 1:59	+ 1.30	33	+ 2:03	+ 1.30	51	+ 2:21	+ 1.30	35	+ 2:05
+ 1.45	30	+ 2:15	+ 1.45	32	+ 2:17	+ 1.45	50	+ 2:35	+ 1.45	35	+ 2:20
+ 2.00	31	+ 2:31	+ 2.00	31	+ 2:31	+ 2.00	49	+ 2:49	+ 2.00	34	+ 2:34
+ 2.15	31	+ 2:46	+ 2.15	31	+ 2:46	+ 2.15	49	+ 3:04	+ 2.15	34	+ 2:49
+ 2.30	31	+ 3:01	+ 2.30	31	+ 3:01	+ 2.30	49	+ 3:19	+ 2.30	35	+ 3:05
+ 2.45	31	+ 3:16	+ 2.45	31	+ 3:16	+ 2.45	49	+ 3:34	+ 2.45	35	+ 3:20
+ 3.00	31	+ 3:31	+ 3.00	31	+ 3:31	+ 3.00	49	+ 3:49	+ 3.00	35	+ 3:35
+ 3.15	31	+ 3:46	+ 3.15	31	+ 3:46	+ 3.15	50	+ 4:05	+ 3.15	35	+ 3:50
+ 3.30	31	+ 4:01	+ 3.30	31	+ 4:01	+ 3.30	51	+ 4:21	+ 3.30	36	+ 4:06
+ 3.45	30	+ 4:15	+ 3.45	32	+ 4:17	+ 3.45	52	+ 4:37	+ 3.45	36	+ 4:21
+ 4.00	30	+ 4:30	+ 4.00	32	+ 4:32	+ 4.00	53	+ 4:53	+ 4.00	36	+ 4:36
+ 4.15	30	+ 4:45	+ 4.15	33	+ 4:48	+ 4.15	54	+ 5:09	+ 4.15	37	+ 4:52
+ 4.30	30	+ 5:00	+ 4.30	33	+ 5:03	+ 4.30	55	+ 5:25	+ 4.30	37	+ 5:07
+ 4.45	29	+ 5:14	+ 4.45	34	+ 5:19	+ 4.45	56	+ 5:41	+ 4.45	38	+ 5:23
+ 5.00	29	+ 5:29	+ 5.00	34	+ 5:34	+ 5.00	57	+ 5:57	+ 5.00	38	+ 5:38
+ 5.15	29	+ 5:44	+ 5.15	35	+ 5:50	+ 5.15	57	- 5:48	+ 5.15	38	+ 5:53
+ 5.30	28	+ 5:58	+ 5.30	35	- 5:55	+ 5.30	58	- 5:32	+ 5.30	39	- 5:51
+ 5.45	28	- 5:47	+ 5.45	36	- 5:39	+ 5.45	59	- 5:16	+ 5.45	39	- 5:36
+ 6.00	28	- 5:32	+ 6.00	36	- 5:24	+ 6.00	59	- 5:01	+ 6.00	39	- 5:21

Table G - Medway, Sea Reach and Black Deep Connections

Time to cover Sectors (in minutes) at 7.0 kts — All times relate to HW Sheerness — **Springs**

SOUTH BOUND

G8 – Long Sand Inner to Blk Deep No 8

Time	Duration	Time at End of Sector
- 6.00	28	- 5:32
- 5.45	27	- 5:18
- 5.30	26	- 5:04
- 5.15	25	- 4:50
- 5.00	24	- 4:36
- 4.45	24	- 4:21
- 4.30	23	- 4:07
- 4.15	23	- 3:52
- 4.00	23	- 3:37
- 3.45	22	- 3:23
- 3.30	22	- 3:08
- 3.15	22	- 2:53
- 3.00	22	- 2:38
- 2.45	23	- 2:22
- 2.30	24	- 2:06
- 2.15	25	- 1:50
- 2.00	25	- 1:35
- 1.45	26	- 1:19
- 1.30	27	- 1:03
- 1.15	28	- 0:47
- 1.00	29	- 0:31
- 0.45	31	- 0:14
- 0.30	32	+ 0:02
- 0.15	34	+ 0:19
HW	36	+ 0:36
+ 0.15	37	+ 0:52
+ 0.30	39	+ 1:09
+ 0.45	40	+ 1:25
+ 1.00	41	+ 1:41
+ 1.15	42	+ 1:57
+ 1.30	42	+ 2:12
+ 1.45	42	+ 2:27
+ 2.00	42	+ 2:42
+ 2.15	42	+ 2:57
+ 2.30	41	+ 3:11
+ 2.45	40	+ 3:25
+ 3.00	40	+ 3:40
+ 3.15	39	+ 3:54
+ 3.30	39	+ 4:09
+ 3.45	38	+ 4:23
+ 4.00	37	+ 4:37
+ 4.15	36	+ 4:51
+ 4.30	35	+ 5:05
+ 4.45	34	+ 5:19
+ 5.00	33	+ 5:33
+ 5.15	32	+ 5:47
+ 5.30	31	- 5:59
+ 5.45	31	- 5:44
+ 6.00	30	- 5:30

G7 – Black Deep to Blk Deep No 8

Time	Duration	Time at End of Sector
- 6.00	36	- 5:24
- 5.45	36	- 5:09
- 5.30	35	- 4:55
- 5.15	35	- 4:40
- 5.00	34	- 4:26
- 4.45	34	- 4:11
- 4.30	34	- 3:56
- 4.15	34	- 3:41
- 4.00	34	- 3:26
- 3.45	35	- 3:10
- 3.30	35	- 2:55
- 3.15	36	- 2:39
- 3.00	37	- 2:23
- 2.45	39	- 2:06
- 2.30	41	- 1:49
- 2.15	43	- 1:32
- 2.00	44	- 1:16
- 1.45	46	- 0:59
- 1.30	48	- 0:42
- 1.15	49	- 0:26
- 1.00	51	- 0:09
- 0.45	51	+ 0:06
- 0.30	52	+ 0:22
- 0.15	53	+ 0:38
HW	54	+ 0:54
+ 0.15	55	+ 1:10
+ 0.30	55	+ 1:25
+ 0.45	56	+ 1:41
+ 1.00	57	+ 1:57
+ 1.15	57	+ 2:12
+ 1.30	57	+ 2:27
+ 1.45	57	+ 2:42
+ 2.00	57	+ 2:57
+ 2.15	56	+ 3:11
+ 2.30	55	+ 3:25
+ 2.45	55	+ 3:40
+ 3.00	54	+ 3:54
+ 3.15	53	+ 4:08
+ 3.30	52	+ 4:22
+ 3.45	52	+ 4:37
+ 4.00	51	+ 4:51
+ 4.15	49	+ 5:04
+ 4.30	48	+ 5:18
+ 4.45	46	+ 5:31
+ 5.00	44	+ 5:44
+ 5.15	43	+ 5:58
+ 5.30	42	- 5:48
+ 5.45	40	- 5:35
+ 6.00	39	- 5:21

G6 – SW Barrow to Sea Reach

Time	Duration	Time at End of Sector
- 6.00	41	- 5:19
- 5.45	40	- 5:05
- 5.30	39	- 4:51
- 5.15	38	- 4:37
- 5.00	37	- 4:23
- 4.45	36	- 4:09
- 4.30	36	- 3:54
- 4.15	35	- 3:40
- 4.00	35	- 3:25
- 3.45	35	- 3:10
- 3.30	35	- 2:55
- 3.15	35	- 2:40
- 3.00	34	- 2:26
- 2.45	35	- 2:10
- 2.30	35	- 1:55
- 2.15	35	- 1:40
- 2.00	35	- 1:25
- 1.45	36	- 1:09
- 1.30	37	- 0:53
- 1.15	37	- 0:38
- 1.00	38	- 0:22
- 0.45	39	- 0:06
- 0.30	40	+ 0:10
- 0.15	41	+ 0:26
HW	42	+ 0:42
+ 0.15	43	+ 0:58
+ 0.30	44	+ 1:14
+ 0.45	46	+ 1:31
+ 1.00	47	+ 1:47
+ 1.15	48	+ 2:03
+ 1.30	50	+ 2:20
+ 1.45	51	+ 2:36
+ 2.00	52	+ 2:52
+ 2.15	52	+ 3:07
+ 2.30	53	+ 3:23
+ 2.45	53	+ 3:38
+ 3.00	53	+ 3:53
+ 3.15	52	+ 4:07
+ 3.30	52	+ 4:22
+ 3.45	51	+ 4:36
+ 4.00	50	+ 4:50
+ 4.15	49	+ 5:04
+ 4.30	48	+ 5:18
+ 4.45	47	+ 5:32
+ 5.00	46	+ 5:46
+ 5.15	46	- 5:59
+ 5.30	45	- 5:45
+ 5.45	44	- 5:31
+ 6.00	43	- 5:17

G5 – SW Barrow to Medway

Time	Duration	Time at End of Sector
- 6.00	65	- 4:55
- 5.45	64	- 4:41
- 5.30	63	- 4:27
- 5.15	61	- 4:14
- 5.00	60	- 4:00
- 4.45	59	- 3:46
- 4.30	58	- 3:32
- 4.15	58	- 3:17
- 4.00	57	- 3:03
- 3.45	57	- 2:48
- 3.30	57	- 2:33
- 3.15	57	- 2:18
- 3.00	57	- 2:03
- 2.45	58	- 1:47
- 2.30	58	- 1:32
- 2.15	59	- 1:16
- 2.00	60	- 1:00
- 1.45	61	- 0:44
- 1.30	62	- 0:28
- 1.15	63	- 0:12
- 1.00	65	+ 0:05
- 0.45	66	+ 0:21
- 0.30	68	+ 0:38
- 0.15	70	+ 0:55
HW	71	+ 1:11
+ 0.15	73	+ 1:28
+ 0.30	76	+ 1:46
+ 0.45	78	+ 2:03
+ 1.00	80	+ 2:20
+ 1.15	81	+ 2:36
+ 1.30	83	+ 2:53
+ 1.45	85	+ 3:10
+ 2.00	86	+ 3:26
+ 2.15	86	+ 3:41
+ 2.30	86	+ 3:56
+ 2.45	86	+ 4:11
+ 3.00	86	+ 4:26
+ 3.15	85	+ 4:40
+ 3.30	83	+ 4:53
+ 3.45	82	+ 5:07
+ 4.00	81	+ 5:21
+ 4.15	80	+ 5:35
+ 4.30	78	+ 5:48
+ 4.45	77	- 5:58
+ 5.00	75	- 5:45
+ 5.15	74	- 5:31
+ 5.30	73	- 5:17
+ 5.45	72	- 5:03
+ 6.00	71	- 4:49

G4 – Sea Reach to Medway

Time	Duration	Time at End of Sector
- 6.00	27	- 5:33
- 5.45	27	- 5:18
- 5.30	26	- 5:04
- 5.15	26	- 4:49
- 5.00	26	- 4:34
- 4.45	25	- 4:20
- 4.30	24	- 4:06
- 4.15	23	- 3:52
- 4.00	23	- 3:37
- 3.45	23	- 3:22
- 3.30	22	- 3:08
- 3.15	22	- 2:53
- 3.00	22	- 2:38
- 2.45	22	- 2:23
- 2.30	23	- 2:07
- 2.15	23	- 1:52
- 2.00	23	- 1:37
- 1.45	23	- 1:22
- 1.30	24	- 1:06
- 1.15	24	- 0:51
- 1.00	25	- 0:35
- 0.45	25	- 0:20
- 0.30	26	- 0:04
- 0.15	26	+ 0:11
HW	27	+ 0:27
+ 0.15	27	+ 0:42
+ 0.30	28	+ 0:58
+ 0.45	28	+ 1:13
+ 1.00	29	+ 1:29
+ 1.15	30	+ 1:45
+ 1.30	31	+ 2:01
+ 1.45	32	+ 2:17
+ 2.00	33	+ 2:33
+ 2.15	33	+ 2:48
+ 2.30	33	+ 3:03
+ 2.45	33	+ 3:18
+ 3.00	33	+ 3:33
+ 3.15	33	+ 3:48
+ 3.30	33	+ 4:03
+ 3.45	32	+ 4:17
+ 4.00	32	+ 4:32
+ 4.15	31	+ 4:46
+ 4.30	31	+ 5:01
+ 4.45	30	+ 5:15
+ 5.00	30	+ 5:30
+ 5.15	29	+ 5:44
+ 5.30	29	+ 5:59
+ 5.45	28	- 5:47
+ 6.00	28	- 5:32

G3 – Sea Reach to Red Sand Tower

Time	Duration	Time at End of Sector
- 6.00	37	- 5:23
- 5.45	39	- 5:06
- 5.30	40	- 4:50
- 5.15	42	- 4:33
- 5.00	44	- 4:16
- 4.45	45	- 4:00
- 4.30	46	- 3:44
- 4.15	47	- 3:28
- 4.00	48	- 3:12
- 3.45	48	- 2:57
- 3.30	47	- 2:43
- 3.15	47	- 2:28
- 3.00	47	- 2:13
- 2.45	47	- 1:58
- 2.30	47	- 1:43
- 2.15	47	- 1:28
- 2.00	46	- 1:14
- 1.45	46	- 0:59
- 1.30	45	- 0:45
- 1.15	44	- 0:31
- 1.00	43	- 0:17
- 0.45	42	- 0:03
- 0.30	41	+ 0:11
- 0.15	40	+ 0:25
HW	39	+ 0:39
+ 0.15	37	+ 0:52
+ 0.30	36	+ 1:06
+ 0.45	35	+ 1:20
+ 1.00	34	+ 1:34
+ 1.15	32	+ 1:47
+ 1.30	31	+ 2:01
+ 1.45	30	+ 2:15
+ 2.00	29	+ 2:29
+ 2.15	29	+ 2:44
+ 2.30	29	+ 2:59
+ 2.45	28	+ 3:13
+ 3.00	28	+ 3:28
+ 3.15	28	+ 3:43
+ 3.30	29	+ 3:59
+ 3.45	29	+ 4:14
+ 4.00	30	+ 4:30
+ 4.15	30	+ 4:45
+ 4.30	31	+ 5:01
+ 4.45	32	+ 5:17
+ 5.00	33	+ 5:33
+ 5.15	34	+ 5:49
+ 5.30	35	- 5:55
+ 5.45	35	- 5:40
+ 6.00	36	- 5:24

G2 – Medway to Red Sand Towers

Time	Duration	Time at End of Sector
- 6.00	64	- 4:56
- 5.45	66	- 4:39
- 5.30	68	- 4:22
- 5.15	71	- 4:04
- 5.00	73	- 3:47
- 4.45	74	- 3:31
- 4.30	75	- 3:15
- 4.15	76	- 2:59
- 4.00	77	- 2:43
- 3.45	77	- 2:28
- 3.30	77	- 2:13
- 3.15	76	- 1:59
- 3.00	76	- 1:44
- 2.45	76	- 1:29
- 2.30	75	- 1:15
- 2.15	75	- 1:00
- 2.00	74	- 0:46
- 1.45	73	- 0:32
- 1.30	71	- 0:19
- 1.15	70	- 0:05
- 1.00	69	+ 0:09
- 0.45	66	+ 0:21
- 0.30	64	+ 0:34
- 0.15	62	+ 0:47
HW	60	+ 1:00
+ 0.15	57	+ 1:12
+ 0.30	55	+ 1:25
+ 0.45	52	+ 1:37
+ 1.00	49	+ 1:49
+ 1.15	48	+ 2:03
+ 1.30	47	+ 2:17
+ 1.45	45	+ 2:30
+ 2.00	44	+ 2:44
+ 2.15	44	+ 2:59
+ 2.30	44	+ 3:14
+ 2.45	44	+ 3:29
+ 3.00	45	+ 3:45
+ 3.15	46	+ 4:01
+ 3.30	47	+ 4:17
+ 3.45	48	+ 4:33
+ 4.00	49	+ 4:49
+ 4.15	51	+ 5:06
+ 4.30	52	+ 5:22
+ 4.45	54	+ 5:39
+ 5.00	55	+ 5:55
+ 5.15	56	- 5:49
+ 5.30	57	- 5:33
+ 5.45	58	- 5:17
+ 6.00	59	- 5:01

G1 – Red Sand Tower to Princes No 6

Time	Duration	Time at End of Sector
- 6.00	43	- 5:17
- 5.45	44	- 5:01
- 5.30	46	- 4:44
- 5.15	48	- 4:27
- 5.00	49	- 4:11
- 4.45	50	- 3:55
- 4.30	50	- 3:40
- 4.15	51	- 3:24
- 4.00	51	- 3:09
- 3.45	51	- 2:54
- 3.30	51	- 2:39
- 3.15	51	- 2:24
- 3.00	52	- 2:08
- 2.45	51	- 1:54
- 2.30	51	- 1:39
- 2.15	51	- 1:24
- 2.00	50	- 1:10
- 1.45	49	- 0:56
- 1.30	47	- 0:43
- 1.15	46	- 0:29
- 1.00	44	- 0:16
- 0.45	43	- 0:02
- 0.30	41	+ 0:11
- 0.15	39	+ 0:24
HW	38	+ 0:38
+ 0.15	36	+ 0:51
+ 0.30	35	+ 1:05
+ 0.45	34	+ 1:19
+ 1.00	33	+ 1:33
+ 1.15	32	+ 1:47
+ 1.30	32	+ 2:02
+ 1.45	32	+ 2:17
+ 2.00	31	+ 2:31
+ 2.15	31	+ 2:46
+ 2.30	32	+ 3:02
+ 2.45	32	+ 3:17
+ 3.00	32	+ 3:32
+ 3.15	33	+ 3:48
+ 3.30	34	+ 4:04
+ 3.45	34	+ 4:19
+ 4.00	35	+ 4:35
+ 4.15	35	+ 4:50
+ 4.30	36	+ 5:06
+ 4.45	37	+ 5:22
+ 5.00	37	+ 5:37
+ 5.15	38	+ 5:53
+ 5.30	38	- 5:52
+ 5.45	39	- 5:36
+ 6.00	39	- 5:21

Table H - Harwich to Foulger's Gat and Sunk Head Connections

Neaps — All times relate to HW Sheerness — **Time to cover Sectors (in minutes) at 4.0 Kts**

SOUTH BOUND

	H8			H7			H6			H5			H4			H3			H2			H1	
	NE Gunfleet to Sunk Head			Goldmer Gat to Sunk Head			Sunk Head to Long Sand Inner			Harwich to The Naze			The Naze to Goldmer Gat			Goldmer Gat to Barrow No 2			Barrow No 2 to Black Deep			Long Sand Inner to Outer	
Time	Duration	Time at End of Sector	Time	Duration	Time at End of Sector	Time	Duration	Time at End of Sector	Time	Duration	Time at End of Sector	Time	Duration	Time at End of Sector	Time	Duration	Time at End of Sector	Time	Duration	Time at End of Sector	Time	Duration	Time at End of Sector
- 6.00	58	- 5:02	- 6.00	62	- 4:58	- 6.00	70	- 4:50	- 6.00	42	- 5:18	- 6.00	84	- 4:36	- 6.00	80	- 4:40	- 6.00	18	- 5:42	- 6.00	67	- 4:53
- 5.45	58	- 4:47	- 5.45	63	- 4:42	- 5.45	69	- 4:36	- 5.45	41	- 5:04	- 5.45	87	- 4:18	- 5.45	78	- 4:27	- 5.45	17	- 5:28	- 5.45	68	- 4:37
- 5.30	57	- 4:33	- 5.30	63	- 4:27	- 5.30	68	- 4:22	- 5.30	41	- 4:49	- 5.30	90	- 4:00	- 5.30	77	- 4:13	- 5.30	17	- 5:13	- 5.30	70	- 4:20
- 5.15	57	- 4:18	- 5.15	64	- 4:11	- 5.15	67	- 4:08	- 5.15	41	- 4:34	- 5.15	92	- 3:43	- 5.15	75	- 4:00	- 5.15	17	- 4:58	- 5.15	71	- 4:04
- 5.00	56	- 4:04	- 5.00	64	- 3:56	- 5.00	66	- 3:54	- 5.00	41	- 4:19	- 5.00	95	- 3:25	- 5.00	74	- 3:46	- 5.00	17	- 4:43	- 5.00	73	- 3:47
- 4.45	57	- 3:48	- 4.45	65	- 3:40	- 4.45	67	- 3:38	- 4.45	41	- 4:04	- 4.45	96	- 3:09	- 4.45	75	- 3:30	- 4.45	17	- 4:28	- 4.45	73	- 3:32
- 4.30	57	- 3:33	- 4.30	66	- 3:24	- 4.30	68	- 3:22	- 4.30	42	- 3:48	- 4.30	96	- 2:54	- 4.30	75	- 3:15	- 4.30	17	- 4:13	- 4.30	74	- 3:16
- 4.15	57	- 3:18	- 4.15	67	- 3:08	- 4.15	68	- 3:07	- 4.15	42	- 3:33	- 4.15	96	- 2:39	- 4.15	76	- 2:59	- 4.15	17	- 3:58	- 4.15	75	- 3:00
- 4.00	58	- 3:02	- 4.00	67	- 2:53	- 4.00	69	- 2:51	- 4.00	42	- 3:18	- 4.00	97	- 2:23	- 4.00	77	- 2:43	- 4.00	17	- 3:43	- 4.00	75	- 2:45
- 3.45	59	- 2:46	- 3.45	68	- 2:37	- 3.45	73	- 2:32	- 3.45	43	- 3:02	- 3.45	96	- 2:09	- 3.45	79	- 2:26	- 3.45	17	- 3:28	- 3.45	77	- 2:28
- 3.30	60	- 2:30	- 3.30	69	- 2:21	- 3.30	77	- 2:13	- 3.30	44	- 2:46	- 3.30	95	- 1:55	- 3.30	81	- 2:09	- 3.30	17	- 3:13	- 3.30	78	- 2:12
- 3.15	61	- 2:14	- 3.15	70	- 2:05	- 3.15	81	- 1:54	- 3.15	45	- 2:30	- 3.15	94	- 1:41	- 3.15	83	- 1:52	- 3.15	18	- 2:57	- 3.15	79	- 1:56
- 3.00	62	- 1:58	- 3.00	70	- 1:50	- 3.00	85	- 1:35	- 3.00	46	- 2:14	- 3.00	93	- 1:27	- 3.00	85	- 1:35	- 3.00	18	- 2:42	- 3.00	81	- 1:39
- 2.45	63	- 1:42	- 2.45	71	- 1:34	- 2.45	91	- 1:14	- 2.45	48	- 1:57	- 2.45	91	- 1:14	- 2.45	87	- 1:18	- 2.45	18	- 2:27	- 2.45	82	- 1:23
- 2.30	65	- 1:25	- 2.30	71	- 1:19	- 2.30	96	- 0:54	- 2.30	49	- 1:41	- 2.30	88	- 1:02	- 2.30	90	- 1:00	- 2.30	19	- 2:11	- 2.30	84	- 1:06
- 2.15	66	- 1:09	- 2.15	71	- 1:04	- 2.15	101	- 0:34	- 2.15	51	- 1:24	- 2.15	86	- 0:49	- 2.15	93	- 0:42	- 2.15	19	- 1:56	- 2.15	85	- 0:50
- 2.00	67	- 0:53	- 2.00	71	- 0:49	- 2.00	107	- 0:13	- 2.00	53	- 1:07	- 2.00	83	- 0:37	- 2.00	95	- 0:25	- 2.00	20	- 1:40	- 2.00	87	- 0:33
- 1.45	69	- 0:36	- 1.45	71	- 0:34	- 1.45	112	+ 0:07	- 1.45	54	- 0:51	- 1.45	82	- 0:23	- 1.45	100	- 0:05	- 1.45	20	- 1:25	- 1.45	86	- 0:19
- 1.30	71	- 0:19	- 1.30	71	- 0:19	- 1.30	117	+ 0:27	- 1.30	56	- 0:34	- 1.30	80	- 0:10	- 1.30	105	+ 0:15	- 1.30	21	- 1:09	- 1.30	85	- 0:05
- 1.15	73	- 0:02	- 1.15	71	- 0:04	- 1.15	122	+ 0:47	- 1.15	57	- 0:18	- 1.15	79	+ 0:04	- 1.15	110	+ 0:35	- 1.15	22	- 0:53	- 1.15	85	+ 0:10
- 1.00	75	+ 0:15	- 1.00	71	+ 0:11	- 1.00	127	+ 1:07	- 1.00	59	- 0:01	- 1.00	77	+ 0:17	- 1.00	115	+ 0:55	- 1.00	23	- 0:37	- 1.00	84	+ 0:24
- 0.45	78	+ 0:33	- 0.45	71	+ 0:26	- 0.45	133	+ 1:28	- 0.45	60	+ 0:15	- 0.45	76	+ 0:31	- 0.45	120	+ 1:15	- 0.45	23	- 0:22	- 0.45	82	+ 0:37
- 0.30	82	+ 0:52	- 0.30	72	+ 0:42	- 0.30	139	+ 1:49	- 0.30	61	+ 0:31	- 0.30	75	+ 0:45	- 0.30	125	+ 1:35	- 0.30	23	- 0:07	- 0.30	80	+ 0:50
- 0.15	86	+ 1:11	- 0.15	72	+ 0:57	- 0.15	144	+ 2:09	- 0.15	61	+ 0:46	- 0.15	74	+ 0:59	- 0.15	131	+ 1:56	- 0.15	23	+ 0:08	- 0.15	78	+ 1:03
HW	90	+ 1:30	HW	72	+ 1:12	HW	150	+ 2:30	HW	62	+ 1:02	HW	73	+ 1:13	HW	136	+ 2:16	HW	23	+ 0:23	HW	77	+ 1:17
+ 0.15	92	+ 1:47	+ 0.15	72	+ 1:27	+ 0.15	150	+ 2:45	+ 0.15	63	+ 1:18	+ 0.15	72	+ 1:27	+ 0.15	142	+ 2:37	+ 0.15	23	+ 0:38	+ 0.15	75	+ 1:30
+ 0.30	94	+ 2:04	+ 0.30	72	+ 1:42	+ 0.30	151	+ 3:01	+ 0.30	63	+ 1:33	+ 0.30	72	+ 1:42	+ 0.30	147	+ 2:57	+ 0.30	23	+ 0:53	+ 0.30	74	+ 1:44
+ 0.45	96	+ 2:21	+ 0.45	73	+ 1:58	+ 0.45	152	+ 3:17	+ 0.45	63	+ 1:48	+ 0.45	71	+ 1:56	+ 0.45	153	+ 3:18	+ 0.45	23	+ 1:08	+ 0.45	72	+ 1:57
+ 1.00	98	+ 2:38	+ 1.00	73	+ 2:13	+ 1.00	153	+ 3:33	+ 1.00	64	+ 2:04	+ 1.00	71	+ 2:11	+ 1.00	158	+ 3:38	+ 1.00	24	+ 1:24	+ 1.00	71	+ 2:11
+ 1.15	98	+ 2:53	+ 1.15	73	+ 2:28	+ 1.15	150	+ 3:45	+ 1.15	63	+ 2:18	+ 1.15	70	+ 2:25	+ 1.15	157	+ 3:52	+ 1.15	24	+ 1:39	+ 1.15	70	+ 2:25
+ 1.30	97	+ 3:07	+ 1.30	72	+ 2:42	+ 1.30	147	+ 3:57	+ 1.30	63	+ 2:33	+ 1.30	70	+ 2:40	+ 1.30	155	+ 4:05	+ 1.30	24	+ 1:54	+ 1.30	68	+ 2:38
+ 1.45	96	+ 3:21	+ 1.45	72	+ 2:57	+ 1.45	144	+ 4:09	+ 1.45	63	+ 2:48	+ 1.45	70	+ 2:55	+ 1.45	154	+ 4:19	+ 1.45	24	+ 2:09	+ 1.45	67	+ 2:52
+ 2.00	96	+ 3:36	+ 2.00	72	+ 3:12	+ 2.00	141	+ 4:21	+ 2.00	63	+ 3:03	+ 2.00	70	+ 3:10	+ 2.00	152	+ 4:32	+ 2.00	24	+ 2:24	+ 2.00	66	+ 3:06
+ 2.15	92	+ 3:47	+ 2.15	71	+ 3:26	+ 2.15	138	+ 4:33	+ 2.15	61	+ 3:16	+ 2.15	70	+ 3:25	+ 2.15	147	+ 4:42	+ 2.15	24	+ 2:39	+ 2.15	65	+ 3:20
+ 2.30	88	+ 3:58	+ 2.30	69	+ 3:39	+ 2.30	135	+ 4:45	+ 2.30	59	+ 3:29	+ 2.30	70	+ 3:40	+ 2.30	143	+ 4:53	+ 2.30	24	+ 2:54	+ 2.30	65	+ 3:35
+ 2.45	85	+ 4:10	+ 2.45	68	+ 3:53	+ 2.45	132	+ 4:57	+ 2.45	57	+ 3:42	+ 2.45	70	+ 3:55	+ 2.45	138	+ 5:03	+ 2.45	24	+ 3:09	+ 2.45	64	+ 3:49
+ 3.00	81	+ 4:21	+ 3.00	67	+ 4:07	+ 3.00	129	+ 5:09	+ 3.00	54	+ 3:54	+ 3.00	70	+ 4:10	+ 3.00	133	+ 5:13	+ 3.00	23	+ 3:23	+ 3.00	63	+ 4:03
+ 3.15	80	+ 4:35	+ 3.15	66	+ 4:21	+ 3.15	125	+ 5:20	+ 3.15	53	+ 4:08	+ 3.15	71	+ 4:26	+ 3.15	129	+ 5:24	+ 3.15	23	+ 3:38	+ 3.15	64	+ 4:19
+ 3.30	78	+ 4:48	+ 3.30	65	+ 4:35	+ 3.30	120	+ 5:30	+ 3.30	52	+ 4:22	+ 3.30	71	+ 4:41	+ 3.30	124	+ 5:34	+ 3.30	23	+ 3:53	+ 3.30	65	+ 4:35
+ 3.45	77	+ 5:02	+ 3.45	64	+ 4:49	+ 3.45	116	+ 5:41	+ 3.45	50	+ 4:35	+ 3.45	71	+ 4:56	+ 3.45	120	+ 5:45	+ 3.45	23	+ 4:08	+ 3.45	67	+ 4:52
+ 4.00	75	+ 5:15	+ 4.00	63	+ 5:03	+ 4.00	112	+ 5:52	+ 4.00	49	+ 4:49	+ 4.00	72	+ 5:12	+ 4.00	115	+ 5:55	+ 4.00	22	+ 4:22	+ 4.00	68	+ 5:08
+ 4.15	73	+ 5:28	+ 4.15	62	+ 5:17	+ 4.15	107	- 5:58	+ 4.15	49	+ 5:04	+ 4.15	73	+ 5:28	+ 4.15	112	- 5:53	+ 4.15	22	+ 4:37	+ 4.15	71	+ 5:26
+ 4.30	71	+ 5:41	+ 4.30	62	+ 5:32	+ 4.30	103	- 5:47	+ 4.30	49	+ 5:19	+ 4.30	74	+ 5:44	+ 4.30	108	- 5:42	+ 4.30	21	+ 4:51	+ 4.30	74	+ 5:44
+ 4.45	69	+ 5:54	+ 4.45	62	+ 5:47	+ 4.45	98	- 5:37	+ 4.45	49	+ 5:34	+ 4.45	75	- 6:00	+ 4.45	105	- 5:30	+ 4.45	21	+ 5:06	+ 4.45	78	- 5:57
+ 5.00	67	- 5:53	+ 5.00	61	- 5:59	+ 5.00	94	- 5:26	+ 5.00	49	+ 5:49	+ 5.00	76	- 5:44	+ 5.00	101	- 5:19	+ 5.00	20	+ 5:20	+ 5.00	81	- 5:39
+ 5.15	65	- 5:40	+ 5.15	61	- 5:44	+ 5.15	91	- 5:14	+ 5.15	48	- 5:57	+ 5.15	77	- 5:28	+ 5.15	98	- 5:07	+ 5.15	20	+ 5:35	+ 5.15	78	- 5:27
+ 5.30	64	- 5:26	+ 5.30	61	- 5:29	+ 5.30	87	- 5:03	+ 5.30	47	- 5:43	+ 5.30	78	- 5:12	+ 5.30	96	- 4:54	+ 5.30	19	+ 5:49	+ 5.30	76	- 5:14
+ 5.45	63	- 5:12	+ 5.45	61	- 5:14	+ 5.45	84	- 4:51	+ 5.45	46	- 5:29	+ 5.45	78	- 4:57	+ 5.45	93	- 4:42	+ 5.45	19	- 5:56	+ 5.45	74	- 5:01
+ 6.00	61	- 4:59	+ 6.00	61	- 4:59	+ 6.00	80	- 4:40	+ 6.00	45	- 5:15	+ 6.00	79	- 4:41	+ 6.00	91	- 4:29	+ 6.00	18	- 5:42	+ 6.00	71	- 4:49

Table H - Harwich to Foulger's Gat and Sunk Head Connections

Time to cover Sectors (in minutes) at 4.0 kts — All times relate to HW Sheerness — **Springs**

	H8			H7			H6			H5			H4			H3			H2			H1	
	NE Gunfleet to Sunk Head			Goldmer Gat to Sunk Head			Sunk Head to Long Sand Inner			Harwich to The Naze			The Naze to Goldmer Gat			Goldmer Gat to Barrow No 2			Barrow No 2 to Black Deep			Long Sand Inner to Outer	
Time	Duration	Time at End of Sector	Time	Duration	Time at End of Sector	Time	Duration	Time at End of Sector	Time	Duration	Time at End of Sector	Time	Duration	Time at End of Sector	Time	Duration	Time at End of Sector	Time	Duration	Time at End of Sector	Time	Duration	Time at End of Sector
- 6.00	55	- 5:05	- 6.00	64	- 4:56	- 6.00	54	- 5:06	- 6.00	38	- 5:22	- 6.00	95	- 4:25	- 6.00	71	- 4:49	- 6.00	18	- 5:42	- 6.00	66	- 4:54
- 5.45	54	- 4:51	- 5.45	65	- 4:40	- 5.45	53	- 4:52	- 5.45	38	- 5:07	- 5.45	98	- 4:07	- 5.45	70	- 4:35	- 5.45	18	- 5:27	- 5.45	69	- 4:36
- 5.30	54	- 4:36	- 5.30	66	- 4:24	- 5.30	51	- 4:39	- 5.30	38	- 4:52	- 5.30	101	- 3:49	- 5.30	68	- 4:22	- 5.30	18	- 5:12	- 5.30	71	- 4:19
- 5.15	54	- 4:21	- 5.15	68	- 4:07	- 5.15	50	- 4:25	- 5.15	37	- 4:38	- 5.15	104	- 3:31	- 5.15	66	- 4:09	- 5.15	18	- 4:57	- 5.15	74	- 4:01
- 5.00	53	- 4:07	- 5.00	69	- 3:51	- 5.00	49	- 4:11	- 5.00	37	- 4:23	- 5.00	107	- 3:13	- 5.00	64	- 3:56	- 5.00	18	- 4:42	- 5.00	76	- 3:44
- 4.45	53	- 3:52	- 4.45	70	- 3:35	- 4.45	50	- 3:55	- 4.45	38	- 4:07	- 4.45	107	- 2:58	- 4.45	65	- 3:40	- 4.45	19	- 4:26	- 4.45	77	- 3:28
- 4.30	54	- 3:36	- 4.30	71	- 3:19	- 4.30	51	- 3:39	- 4.30	38	- 3:52	- 4.30	108	- 2:42	- 4.30	66	- 3:24	- 4.30	19	- 4:11	- 4.30	79	- 3:11
- 4.15	54	- 3:21	- 4.15	72	- 3:03	- 4.15	52	- 3:23	- 4.15	38	- 3:37	- 4.15	108	- 2:27	- 4.15	67	- 3:08	- 4.15	19	- 3:56	- 4.15	80	- 2:55
- 4.00	54	- 3:06	- 4.00	73	- 2:47	- 4.00	54	- 3:06	- 4.00	39	- 3:21	- 4.00	108	- 2:12	- 4.00	67	- 2:53	- 4.00	19	- 3:41	- 4.00	81	- 2:39
- 3.45	56	- 2:49	- 3.45	74	- 2:31	- 3.45	59	- 2:46	- 3.45	40	- 3:05	- 3.45	106	- 1:59	- 3.45	70	- 2:35	- 3.45	19	- 3:26	- 3.45	83	- 2:22
- 3.30	57	- 2:33	- 3.30	74	- 2:16	- 3.30	65	- 2:25	- 3.30	41	- 2:49	- 3.30	104	- 1:46	- 3.30	72	- 2:18	- 3.30	19	- 3:11	- 3.30	85	- 2:05
- 3.15	58	- 2:17	- 3.15	75	- 2:00	- 3.15	71	- 2:04	- 3.15	42	- 2:33	- 3.15	102	- 1:33	- 3.15	75	- 2:00	- 3.15	19	- 2:56	- 3.15	88	- 1:47
- 3.00	59	- 2:01	- 3.00	76	- 1:44	- 3.00	76	- 1:44	- 3.00	44	- 2:16	- 3.00	99	- 1:21	- 3.00	78	- 1:42	- 3.00	19	- 2:41	- 3.00	90	- 1:30
- 2.45	61	- 1:44	- 2.45	76	- 1:29	- 2.45	85	- 1:20	- 2.45	46	- 1:59	- 2.45	97	- 1:08	- 2.45	82	- 1:23	- 2.45	20	- 2:25	- 2.45	92	- 1:13
- 2.30	63	- 1:27	- 2.30	76	- 1:14	- 2.30	94	- 0:56	- 2.30	48	- 1:42	- 2.30	94	- 0:56	- 2.30	86	- 1:04	- 2.30	20	- 2:10	- 2.30	94	- 0:56
- 2.15	65	- 1:10	- 2.15	76	- 0:59	- 2.15	103	- 0:32	- 2.15	50	- 1:25	- 2.15	91	- 0:44	- 2.15	91	- 0:44	- 2.15	20	- 1:55	- 2.15	97	- 0:38
- 2.00	67	- 0:53	- 2.00	76	- 0:44	- 2.00	111	- 0:09	- 2.00	53	- 1:07	- 2.00	89	- 0:31	- 2.00	95	- 0:25	- 2.00	20	- 1:40	- 2.00	99	- 0:21
- 1.45	69	- 0:36	- 1.45	76	- 0:29	- 1.45	122	+ 0:17	- 1.45	56	- 0:49	- 1.45	86	- 0:19	- 1.45	102	- 0:03	- 1.45	21	- 1:24	- 1.45	97	- 0:08
- 1.30	72	- 0:18	- 1.30	76	- 0:14	- 1.30	133	+ 0:43	- 1.30	58	- 0:32	- 1.30	84	- 0:06	- 1.30	108	+ 0:18	- 1.30	22	- 1:08	- 1.30	96	+ 0:06
- 1.15	74	- 0:01	- 1.15	76	+ 0:01	- 1.15	144	+ 1:09	- 1.15	61	- 0:14	- 1.15	81	+ 0:06	- 1.15	115	+ 0:40	- 1.15	23	- 0:52	- 1.15	94	+ 0:19
- 1.00	77	+ 0:17	- 1.00	76	+ 0:16	- 1.00	155	+ 1:35	- 1.00	64	+ 0:04	- 1.00	79	+ 0:19	- 1.00	121	+ 1:01	- 1.00	24	- 0:36	- 1.00	93	+ 0:33
- 0.45	83	+ 0:38	- 0.45	76	+ 0:31	- 0.45	161	+ 1:56	- 0.45	66	+ 0:21	- 0.45	78	+ 0:33	- 0.45	135	+ 1:30	- 0.45	24	- 0:21	- 0.45	90	+ 0:45
- 0.30	89	+ 0:59	- 0.30	77	+ 0:47	- 0.30	167	+ 2:17	- 0.30	67	+ 0:37	- 0.30	77	+ 0:47	- 0.30	148	+ 1:58	- 0.30	25	- 0:05	- 0.30	87	+ 0:57
- 0.15	95	+ 1:20	- 0.15	78	+ 1:03	- 0.15	173	+ 2:38	- 0.15	69	+ 0:54	- 0.15	76	+ 1:01	- 0.15	161	+ 2:26	- 0.15	25	+ 0:10	- 0.15	84	+ 1:09
HW	101	+ 1:41	HW	79	+ 1:19	HW	179	+ 2:59	HW	70	+ 1:10	HW	75	+ 1:15	HW	175	+ 2:55	HW	25	+ 0:25	HW	81	+ 1:21
+ 0.15	104	+ 1:59	+ 0.15	83	+ 1:38	+ 0.15	179	+ 3:14	+ 0.15	71	+ 1:26	+ 0.15	75	+ 1:30	+ 0.15	178	+ 3:13	+ 0.15	26	+ 0:41	+ 0.15	79	+ 1:34
+ 0.30	107	+ 2:17	+ 0.30	87	+ 1:57	+ 0.30	179	+ 3:29	+ 0.30	71	+ 1:41	+ 0.30	74	+ 1:44	+ 0.30	181	+ 3:31	+ 0.30	26	+ 0:56	+ 0.30	77	+ 1:47
+ 0.45	110	+ 2:35	+ 0.45	90	+ 2:15	+ 0.45	179	+ 3:44	+ 0.45	72	+ 1:57	+ 0.45	74	+ 1:59	+ 0.45	185	+ 3:50	+ 0.45	27	+ 1:12	+ 0.45	75	+ 2:00
+ 1.00	114	+ 2:54	+ 1.00	94	+ 2:34	+ 1.00	179	+ 3:59	+ 1.00	72	+ 2:12	+ 1.00	73	+ 2:13	+ 1.00	188	+ 4:08	+ 1.00	27	+ 1:27	+ 1.00	73	+ 2:13
+ 1.15	112	+ 3:07	+ 1.15	91	+ 2:46	+ 1.15	175	+ 4:10	+ 1.15	71	+ 2:26	+ 1.15	72	+ 2:27	+ 1.15	184	+ 4:19	+ 1.15	27	+ 1:42	+ 1.15	71	+ 2:26
+ 1.30	110	+ 3:20	+ 1.30	88	+ 2:58	+ 1.30	171	+ 4:21	+ 1.30	71	+ 2:41	+ 1.30	72	+ 2:42	+ 1.30	180	+ 4:30	+ 1.30	28	+ 1:58	+ 1.30	69	+ 2:39
+ 1.45	107	+ 3:32	+ 1.45	85	+ 3:10	+ 1.45	167	+ 4:32	+ 1.45	70	+ 2:55	+ 1.45	71	+ 2:56	+ 1.45	176	+ 4:41	+ 1.45	28	+ 2:13	+ 1.45	68	+ 2:53
+ 2.00	105	+ 3:45	+ 2.00	82	+ 3:22	+ 2.00	163	+ 4:43	+ 2.00	69	+ 3:09	+ 2.00	70	+ 3:10	+ 2.00	172	+ 4:52	+ 2.00	28	+ 2:28	+ 2.00	66	+ 3:06
+ 2.15	102	+ 3:57	+ 2.15	79	+ 3:34	+ 2.15	157	+ 4:52	+ 2.15	66	+ 3:21	+ 2.15	70	+ 3:25	+ 2.15	165	+ 5:00	+ 2.15	28	+ 2:43	+ 2.15	64	+ 3:19
+ 2.30	98	+ 4:08	+ 2.30	76	+ 3:46	+ 2.30	151	+ 5:01	+ 2.30	63	+ 3:33	+ 2.30	70	+ 3:40	+ 2.30	158	+ 5:08	+ 2.30	27	+ 2:57	+ 2.30	63	+ 3:33
+ 2.45	95	+ 4:20	+ 2.45	74	+ 3:59	+ 2.45	145	+ 5:10	+ 2.45	59	+ 3:44	+ 2.45	70	+ 3:55	+ 2.45	151	+ 5:16	+ 2.45	27	+ 3:12	+ 2.45	62	+ 3:47
+ 3.00	91	+ 4:31	+ 3.00	71	+ 4:11	+ 3.00	139	+ 5:19	+ 3.00	56	+ 3:56	+ 3.00	69	+ 4:09	+ 3.00	144	+ 5:24	+ 3.00	26	+ 3:26	+ 3.00	60	+ 4:00
+ 3.15	88	+ 4:43	+ 3.15	69	+ 4:24	+ 3.15	132	+ 5:27	+ 3.15	54	+ 4:09	+ 3.15	70	+ 4:25	+ 3.15	137	+ 5:32	+ 3.15	26	+ 3:41	+ 3.15	62	+ 4:17
+ 3.30	84	+ 4:54	+ 3.30	67	+ 4:37	+ 3.30	125	+ 5:35	+ 3.30	52	+ 4:22	+ 3.30	70	+ 4:40	+ 3.30	130	+ 5:40	+ 3.30	26	+ 3:56	+ 3.30	63	+ 4:33
+ 3.45	81	+ 5:06	+ 3.45	65	+ 4:50	+ 3.45	118	+ 5:43	+ 3.45	50	+ 4:35	+ 3.45	70	+ 4:55	+ 3.45	124	+ 5:49	+ 3.45	25	+ 4:10	+ 3.45	65	+ 4:50
+ 4.00	78	+ 5:18	+ 4.00	63	+ 5:03	+ 4.00	111	+ 5:51	+ 4.00	48	+ 4:48	+ 4.00	71	+ 5:11	+ 4.00	117	+ 5:57	+ 4.00	25	+ 4:25	+ 4.00	66	+ 5:06
+ 4.15	75	+ 5:30	+ 4.15	62	+ 5:17	+ 4.15	106	- 5:59	+ 4.15	48	+ 5:03	+ 4.15	72	+ 5:27	+ 4.15	112	- 5:53	+ 4.15	24	+ 4:39	+ 4.15	72	+ 5:27
+ 4.30	71	+ 5:41	+ 4.30	62	+ 5:32	+ 4.30	100	- 5:50	+ 4.30	47	+ 5:17	+ 4.30	73	+ 5:43	+ 4.30	108	- 5:42	+ 4.30	23	+ 4:53	+ 4.30	77	+ 5:47
+ 4.45	68	+ 5:53	+ 4.45	61	+ 5:46	+ 4.45	95	- 5:40	+ 4.45	47	+ 5:32	+ 4.45	74	+ 5:59	+ 4.45	103	- 5:32	+ 4.45	22	+ 5:07	+ 4.45	83	- 5:52
+ 5.00	65	- 5:55	+ 5.00	60	- 6:00	+ 5.00	90	- 5:30	+ 5.00	47	+ 5:47	+ 5.00	76	- 5:44	+ 5.00	98	- 5:22	+ 5.00	21	+ 5:21	+ 5.00	88	- 5:32
+ 5.15	63	- 5:42	+ 5.15	60	- 5:45	+ 5.15	84	- 5:21	+ 5.15	46	- 5:59	+ 5.15	77	- 5:28	+ 5.15	95	- 5:10	+ 5.15	20	+ 5:35	+ 5.15	84	- 5:21
+ 5.30	61	- 5:29	+ 5.30	60	- 5:30	+ 5.30	79	- 5:11	+ 5.30	45	- 5:45	+ 5.30	79	- 5:11	+ 5.30	92	- 4:58	+ 5.30	19	+ 5:49	+ 5.30	80	- 5:10
+ 5.45	60	- 5:15	+ 5.45	60	- 5:15	+ 5.45	74	- 5:01	+ 5.45	43	- 5:32	+ 5.45	80	- 4:55	+ 5.45	88	- 4:47	+ 5.45	19	- 5:56	+ 5.45	76	- 4:59
+ 6.00	58	- 5:02	+ 6.00	60	- 5:00	+ 6.00	68	- 4:52	+ 6.00	42	- 5:18	+ 6.00	81	- 4:39	+ 6.00	85	- 4:35	+ 6.00	18	- 5:42	+ 6.00	72	- 4:48

SOUTH BOUND

Table H - Harwich to Foulger's Gat and Sunk Head Connections

Neaps — All times relate to HW Sheerness — **Time to cover Sectors (in minutes) at 5.0 Kts**

SOUTH BOUND

Time	H8 NE Gunfleet to Sunk Head		H7 Goldmer Gat to Sunk Head		H6 Sunk Head to Long Sand Inner		H5 Harwich to The Naze	
	Duration	Time at End of Sector	Duration	Time at End of Sector	Duration	Time at End of Sector	Duration	Time at End of Sector
- 6.00	48	- 5:12	49	- 5:11	62	- 4:58	35	- 5:25
- 5.45	48	- 4:57	50	- 4:55	61	- 4:44	35	- 5:10
- 5.30	48	- 4:42	50	- 4:40	60	- 4:30	34	- 4:56
- 5.15	47	- 4:28	50	- 4:25	60	- 4:15	34	- 4:41
- 5.00	47	- 4:13	50	- 4:10	59	- 4:01	34	- 4:26
- 4.45	47	- 3:58	51	- 3:54	59	- 3:46	34	- 4:11
- 4.30	47	- 3:43	51	- 3:39	60	- 3:30	34	- 3:56
- 4.15	47	- 3:28	52	- 3:23	60	- 3:15	34	- 3:41
- 4.00	47	- 3:13	52	- 3:08	60	- 3:00	35	- 3:25
- 3.45	48	- 2:57	53	- 2:52	63	- 2:42	35	- 3:10
- 3.30	49	- 2:41	53	- 2:37	65	- 2:25	36	- 2:54
- 3.15	49	- 2:26	54	- 2:21	67	- 2:08	36	- 2:39
- 3.00	50	- 2:10	55	- 2:05	70	- 1:50	37	- 2:23
- 2.45	51	- 1:54	55	- 1:50	73	- 1:32	38	- 2:07
- 2.30	52	- 1:38	55	- 1:35	77	- 1:13	39	- 1:51
- 2.15	53	- 1:22	55	- 1:20	80	- 0:55	40	- 1:35
- 2.00	54	- 1:06	56	- 1:04	83	- 0:37	41	- 1:19
- 1.45	55	- 0:50	56	- 0:49	87	- 0:18	42	- 1:03
- 1.30	56	- 0:34	56	- 0:34	90	HW	43	- 0:47
- 1.15	57	- 0:18	56	- 0:19	93	+ 0:18	44	- 0:31
- 1.00	58	- 0:02	56	- 0:04	96	+ 0:36	46	- 0:14
- 0.45	60	+ 0:15	56	+ 0:11	99	+ 0:54	46	+ 0:01
- 0.30	61	+ 0:31	56	+ 0:26	102	+ 1:12	47	+ 0:17
- 0.15	62	+ 0:47	56	+ 0:41	104	+ 1:29	47	+ 0:32
HW	64	+ 1:04	56	+ 0:56	107	+ 1:47	48	+ 0:48
+ 0.15	65	+ 1:20	56	+ 1:11	109	+ 2:04	48	+ 1:03
+ 0.30	66	+ 1:36	56	+ 1:26	110	+ 2:20	48	+ 1:18
+ 0.45	67	+ 1:52	56	+ 1:41	112	+ 2:37	48	+ 1:33
+ 1.00	68	+ 2:08	56	+ 1:56	114	+ 2:54	49	+ 1:49
+ 1.15	67	+ 2:22	56	+ 2:11	112	+ 3:07	49	+ 2:04
+ 1.30	67	+ 2:37	56	+ 2:26	111	+ 3:21	49	+ 2:19
+ 1.45	67	+ 2:52	56	+ 2:41	110	+ 3:35	48	+ 2:33
+ 2.00	67	+ 3:07	55	+ 2:55	109	+ 3:49	48	+ 2:48
+ 2.15	66	+ 3:21	55	+ 3:10	107	+ 4:02	47	+ 3:02
+ 2.30	65	+ 3:35	54	+ 3:24	105	+ 4:15	46	+ 3:16
+ 2.45	64	+ 3:49	54	+ 3:39	103	+ 4:28	45	+ 3:30
+ 3.00	63	+ 4:03	53	+ 3:53	102	+ 4:42	44	+ 3:44
+ 3.15	62	+ 4:17	52	+ 4:07	99	+ 4:54	43	+ 3:58
+ 3.30	61	+ 4:31	52	+ 4:22	97	+ 5:07	42	+ 4:12
+ 3.45	60	+ 4:45	51	+ 4:36	95	+ 5:20	40	+ 4:25
+ 4.00	59	+ 4:59	51	+ 4:51	93	+ 5:33	39	+ 4:39
+ 4.15	58	+ 5:13	50	+ 5:05	88	+ 5:43	39	+ 4:54
+ 4.30	57	+ 5:27	50	+ 5:20	84	+ 5:54	39	+ 5:09
+ 4.45	56	+ 5:41	50	+ 5:35	80	- 5:55	39	+ 5:24
+ 5.00	54	+ 5:54	49	+ 5:49	76	- 5:44	39	+ 5:39
+ 5.15	53	- 5:52	49	- 5:56	74	- 5:31	39	+ 5:54
+ 5.30	52	- 5:38	49	- 5:41	72	- 5:18	38	- 5:52
+ 5.45	51	- 5:24	49	- 5:26	70	- 5:05	38	- 5:37
+ 6.00	50	- 5:10	49	- 5:11	68	- 4:52	37	- 5:23

Time	H4 The Naze to Goldmer Gat		H3 Goldmer Gat to Barrow No 2		H2 Barrow No 2 to Black Deep		H1 Long Sand Inner to Outer	
	Duration	Time at End of Sector	Duration	Time at End of Sector	Duration	Time at End of Sector	Duration	Time at End of Sector
- 6.00	65	- 4:55	68	- 4:52	14	- 5:46	54	- 5:06
- 5.45	66	- 4:39	67	- 4:38	14	- 5:31	55	- 4:50
- 5.30	66	- 4:24	66	- 4:24	14	- 5:16	56	- 4:34
- 5.15	67	- 4:08	65	- 4:10	13	- 5:02	57	- 4:18
- 5.00	68	- 3:52	63	- 3:57	13	- 4:47	58	- 4:02
- 4.45	68	- 3:37	64	- 3:41	13	- 4:32	58	- 3:47
- 4.30	68	- 3:22	64	- 3:26	13	- 4:17	58	- 3:32
- 4.15	69	- 3:06	64	- 3:11	13	- 4:02	59	- 3:16
- 4.00	69	- 2:51	65	- 2:55	13	- 3:47	59	- 3:01
- 3.45	69	- 2:36	66	- 2:39	14	- 3:31	60	- 2:45
- 3.30	68	- 2:22	67	- 2:23	14	- 3:16	61	- 2:29
- 3.15	68	- 2:07	68	- 2:07	14	- 3:01	61	- 2:14
- 3.00	68	- 1:52	70	- 1:50	14	- 2:46	62	- 1:58
- 2.45	67	- 1:38	72	- 1:33	15	- 2:30	63	- 1:42
- 2.30	66	- 1:24	74	- 1:16	15	- 2:15	65	- 1:25
- 2.15	66	- 1:09	75	- 1:00	15	- 2:00	66	- 1:09
- 2.00	65	- 0:55	77	- 0:43	16	- 1:44	67	- 0:53
- 1.45	64	- 0:41	80	- 0:25	16	- 1:29	67	- 0:38
- 1.30	64	- 0:26	82	- 0:08	17	- 1:13	66	- 0:24
- 1.15	63	- 0:12	84	+ 0:09	17	- 0:58	66	- 0:09
- 1.00	62	+ 0:02	87	+ 0:27	18	- 0:42	66	+ 0:06
- 0.45	61	+ 0:16	90	+ 0:45	18	- 0:27	65	+ 0:20
- 0.30	60	+ 0:30	94	+ 1:04	18	- 0:12	63	+ 0:33
- 0.15	59	+ 0:44	98	+ 1:23	18	+ 0:03	62	+ 0:47
HW	58	+ 0:58	101	+ 1:41	18	+ 0:18	61	+ 1:01
+ 0.15	58	+ 1:13	105	+ 2:00	18	+ 0:33	60	+ 1:15
+ 0.30	57	+ 1:27	108	+ 2:18	19	+ 0:49	59	+ 1:29
+ 0.45	57	+ 1:42	111	+ 2:36	19	+ 1:04	58	+ 1:43
+ 1.00	57	+ 1:57	114	+ 2:54	19	+ 1:19	57	+ 1:57
+ 1.15	56	+ 2:11	114	+ 3:09	19	+ 1:34	56	+ 2:11
+ 1.30	56	+ 2:26	114	+ 3:24	19	+ 1:49	55	+ 2:25
+ 1.45	56	+ 2:41	114	+ 3:39	19	+ 2:04	55	+ 2:40
+ 2.00	56	+ 2:56	114	+ 3:54	19	+ 2:19	54	+ 2:54
+ 2.15	56	+ 3:11	112	+ 4:07	19	+ 2:34	53	+ 3:08
+ 2.30	56	+ 3:26	109	+ 4:19	19	+ 2:49	53	+ 3:23
+ 2.45	56	+ 3:41	107	+ 4:32	19	+ 3:04	52	+ 3:37
+ 3.00	56	+ 3:56	105	+ 4:45	19	+ 3:19	51	+ 3:51
+ 3.15	57	+ 4:12	102	+ 4:57	18	+ 3:33	52	+ 4:07
+ 3.30	57	+ 4:27	99	+ 5:09	18	+ 3:48	52	+ 4:22
+ 3.45	57	+ 4:42	96	+ 5:21	18	+ 4:03	52	+ 4:37
+ 4.00	58	+ 4:58	93	+ 5:33	18	+ 4:18	52	+ 4:52
+ 4.15	58	+ 5:13	90	+ 5:45	17	+ 4:32	55	+ 5:10
+ 4.30	59	+ 5:29	87	+ 5:57	17	+ 4:47	58	+ 5:28
+ 4.45	59	+ 5:44	84	- 5:51	17	+ 5:02	60	+ 5:45
+ 5.00	60	- 6:00	81	- 5:39	16	+ 5:16	63	- 5:57
+ 5.15	61	- 5:44	79	- 5:26	16	+ 5:31	62	- 5:43
+ 5.30	61	- 5:29	78	- 5:12	15	+ 5:45	61	- 5:29
+ 5.45	62	- 5:13	76	- 4:59	15	- 6:00	59	- 5:16
+ 6.00	63	- 4:57	75	- 4:45	14	- 5:46	58	- 5:02

Table H - Harwich to Foulger's Gat and Sunk Head Connections

Time to cover Sectors (in minutes) at 5.0 kts | All times relate to HW Sheerness | **Springs**

	H8			H7			H6			H5			H4			H3			H2			H1	
	NE Gunfleet to Sunk Head			Goldmer Gat to Sunk Head			Sunk Head to Long Sand Inner			Harwich to The Naze			The Naze to Goldmer Gat			Goldmer Gat to Barrow No 2			Barrow No 2 to Black Deep			Long Sand Inner to Outer	
Time	Duration	Time at End of Sector	Time	Duration	Time at End of Sector	Time	Duration	Time at End of Sector	Time	Duration	Time at End of Sector	Time	Duration	Time at End of Sector	Time	Duration	Time at End of Sector	Time	Duration	Time at End of Sector	Time	Duration	Time at End of Sector
- 6.00	**46**	**- 5:14**	**- 6.00**	**50**	**- 5:10**	**- 6.00**	**52**	**- 5:08**	**- 6.00**	**32**	**- 5:28**	**- 6.00**	**68**	**- 4:52**	**- 6.00**	**62**	**- 4:58**	**- 6.00**	**14**	**- 5:46**	**- 6.00**	**53**	**- 5:07**
- 5.45	45	- 5:00	- 5.45	50	- 4:55	- 5.45	51	- 4:54	- 5.45	32	- 5:13	- 5.45	70	- 4:35	- 5.45	61	- 4:44	- 5.45	14	- 5:31	- 5.45	55	- 4:50
- 5.30	45	- 4:45	- 5.30	51	- 4:39	- 5.30	50	- 4:40	- 5.30	32	- 4:58	- 5.30	71	- 4:19	- 5.30	59	- 4:31	- 5.30	14	- 5:16	- 5.30	57	- 4:33
- 5.15	45	- 4:30	- 5.15	52	- 4:23	- 5.15	49	- 4:26	- 5.15	32	- 4:43	- 5.15	72	- 4:03	- 5.15	58	- 4:17	- 5.15	15	- 5:00	- 5.15	58	- 4:17
- 5.00	**44**	**- 4:16**	**- 5.00**	**52**	**- 4:08**	**- 5.00**	**48**	**- 4:12**	**- 5.00**	**32**	**- 4:28**	**- 5.00**	**73**	**- 3:47**	**- 5.00**	**57**	**- 4:03**	**- 5.00**	**15**	**- 4:45**	**- 5.00**	**60**	**- 4:00**
- 4.45	44	- 4:01	- 4.45	53	- 3:52	- 4.45	48	- 3:57	- 4.45	32	- 4:13	- 4.45	74	- 3:31	- 4.45	57	- 3:48	- 4.45	15	- 4:30	- 4.45	61	- 3:44
- 4.30	45	- 3:45	- 4.30	53	- 3:37	- 4.30	49	- 3:41	- 4.30	32	- 3:58	- 4.30	75	- 3:15	- 4.30	57	- 3:33	- 4.30	15	- 4:15	- 4.30	61	- 3:29
- 4.15	45	- 3:30	- 4.15	54	- 3:21	- 4.15	49	- 3:26	- 4.15	32	- 3:43	- 4.15	75	- 3:00	- 4.15	58	- 3:17	- 4.15	15	- 4:00	- 4.15	62	- 3:13
- 4.00	**45**	**- 3:15**	**- 4.00**	**55**	**- 3:05**	**- 4.00**	**50**	**- 3:10**	**- 4.00**	**32**	**- 3:28**	**- 4.00**	**76**	**- 2:44**	**- 4.00**	**58**	**- 3:02**	**- 4.00**	**15**	**- 3:45**	**- 4.00**	**63**	**- 2:57**
- 3.45	46	- 2:59	- 3.45	55	- 2:50	- 3.45	53	- 2:52	- 3.45	33	- 3:12	- 3.45	75	- 2:30	- 3.45	60	- 2:45	- 3.45	15	- 3:30	- 3.45	64	- 2:41
- 3.30	46	- 2:44	- 3.30	56	- 2:34	- 3.30	57	- 2:33	- 3.30	34	- 2:56	- 3.30	75	- 2:15	- 3.30	61	- 2:29	- 3.30	15	- 3:15	- 3.30	65	- 2:25
- 3.15	47	- 2:28	- 3.15	57	- 2:18	- 3.15	60	- 2:15	- 3.15	34	- 2:41	- 3.15	74	- 2:01	- 3.15	63	- 2:12	- 3.15	15	- 3:00	- 3.15	67	- 2:08
- 3.00	**48**	**- 2:12**	**- 3.00**	**58**	**- 2:02**	**- 3.00**	**63**	**- 1:57**	**- 3.00**	**35**	**- 2:25**	**- 3.00**	**74**	**- 1:46**	**- 3.00**	**65**	**- 1:55**	**- 3.00**	**15**	**- 2:45**	**- 3.00**	**68**	**- 1:52**
- 2.45	49	- 1:56	- 2.45	58	- 1:47	- 2.45	68	- 1:37	- 2.45	36	- 2:09	- 2.45	72	- 1:33	- 2.45	67	- 1:38	- 2.45	16	- 2:29	- 2.45	70	- 1:35
- 2.30	50	- 1:40	- 2.30	58	- 1:32	- 2.30	73	- 1:17	- 2.30	38	- 1:52	- 2.30	71	- 1:19	- 2.30	70	- 1:20	- 2.30	16	- 2:14	- 2.30	71	- 1:19
- 2.15	52	- 1:23	- 2.15	58	- 1:17	- 2.15	78	- 0:57	- 2.15	39	- 1:36	- 2.15	70	- 1:05	- 2.15	73	- 1:02	- 2.15	16	- 1:59	- 2.15	73	- 1:02
- 2.00	**53**	**- 1:07**	**- 2.00**	**58**	**- 1:02**	**- 2.00**	**83**	**- 0:37**	**- 2.00**	**41**	**- 1:19**	**- 2.00**	**69**	**- 0:51**	**- 2.00**	**75**	**- 0:45**	**- 2.00**	**16**	**- 1:44**	**- 2.00**	**75**	**- 0:45**
- 1.45	55	- 0:50	- 1.45	58	- 0:47	- 1.45	88	- 0:17	- 1.45	43	- 1:02	- 1.45	67	- 0:38	- 1.45	79	- 0:26	- 1.45	17	- 1:28	- 1.45	74	- 0:31
- 1.30	56	- 0:34	- 1.30	58	- 0:32	- 1.30	94	+ 0:04	- 1.30	45	- 0:45	- 1.30	66	- 0:24	- 1.30	83	- 0:07	- 1.30	18	- 1:12	- 1.30	73	- 0:17
- 1.15	58	- 0:17	- 1.15	58	- 0:17	- 1.15	99	+ 0:24	- 1.15	46	- 0:29	- 1.15	64	- 0:11	- 1.15	86	+ 0:11	- 1.15	18	- 0:57	- 1.15	73	- 0:02
- 1.00	**59**	**- 0:01**	**- 1.00**	**58**	**- 0:02**	**- 1.00**	**104**	**+ 0:44**	**- 1.00**	**48**	**- 0:12**	**- 1.00**	**63**	**+ 0:03**	**- 1.00**	**90**	**+ 0:30**	**- 1.00**	**19**	**- 0:41**	**- 1.00**	**72**	**+ 0:12**
- 0.45	61	+ 0:16	- 0.45	59	+ 0:14	- 0.45	108	+ 1:03	- 0.45	49	+ 0:04	- 0.45	62	+ 0:17	- 0.45	95	+ 0:50	- 0.45	19	- 0:26	- 0.45	70	+ 0:25
- 0.30	64	+ 0:34	- 0.30	59	+ 0:29	- 0.30	112	+ 1:22	- 0.30	51	+ 0:21	- 0.30	61	+ 0:31	- 0.30	101	+ 1:11	- 0.30	20	- 0:10	- 0.30	68	+ 0:38
- 0.15	66	+ 0:51	- 0.15	59	+ 0:44	- 0.15	116	+ 1:41	- 0.15	52	+ 0:37	- 0.15	60	+ 0:45	- 0.15	107	+ 1:32	- 0.15	20	+ 0:05	- 0.15	66	+ 0:51
HW	**68**	**+ 1:08**	**HW**	**60**	**+ 1:00**	**HW**	**121**	**+ 2:01**	**HW**	**53**	**+ 0:53**	**HW**	**59**	**+ 0:59**	**HW**	**112**	**+ 1:52**	**HW**	**20**	**+ 0:20**	**HW**	**64**	**+ 1:04**
+ 0.15	70	+ 1:25	+ 0.15	60	+ 1:15	+ 0.15	122	+ 2:17	+ 0.15	53	+ 1:08	+ 0.15	58	+ 1:13	+ 0.15	116	+ 2:11	+ 0.15	20	+ 0:35	+ 0.15	63	+ 1:18
+ 0.30	72	+ 1:42	+ 0.30	61	+ 1:31	+ 0.30	124	+ 2:34	+ 0.30	53	+ 1:23	+ 0.30	58	+ 1:28	+ 0.30	121	+ 2:31	+ 0.30	21	+ 0:51	+ 0.30	62	+ 1:32
+ 0.45	74	+ 1:59	+ 0.45	61	+ 1:46	+ 0.45	125	+ 2:50	+ 0.45	54	+ 1:39	+ 0.45	57	+ 1:42	+ 0.45	125	+ 2:50	+ 0.45	21	+ 1:06	+ 0.45	60	+ 1:45
+ 1.00	**76**	**+ 2:16**	**+ 1.00**	**62**	**+ 2:02**	**+ 1.00**	**127**	**+ 3:07**	**+ 1.00**	**54**	**+ 1:54**	**+ 1.00**	**57**	**+ 1:57**	**+ 1.00**	**129**	**+ 3:09**	**+ 1.00**	**22**	**+ 1:22**	**+ 1.00**	**59**	**+ 1:59**
+ 1.15	75	+ 2:30	+ 1.15	61	+ 2:16	+ 1.15	125	+ 3:20	+ 1.15	54	+ 2:09	+ 1.15	57	+ 2:12	+ 1.15	128	+ 3:23	+ 1.15	22	+ 1:37	+ 1.15	58	+ 2:13
+ 1.30	75	+ 2:45	+ 1.30	61	+ 2:31	+ 1.30	123	+ 3:33	+ 1.30	53	+ 2:23	+ 1.30	56	+ 2:26	+ 1.30	128	+ 3:38	+ 1.30	22	+ 1:52	+ 1.30	57	+ 2:27
+ 1.45	75	+ 3:00	+ 1.45	61	+ 2:46	+ 1.45	121	+ 3:46	+ 1.45	53	+ 2:38	+ 1.45	56	+ 2:41	+ 1.45	127	+ 3:52	+ 1.45	22	+ 2:07	+ 1.45	55	+ 2:40
+ 2.00	**75**	**+ 3:15**	**+ 2.00**	**61**	**+ 3:01**	**+ 2.00**	**119**	**+ 3:59**	**+ 2.00**	**53**	**+ 2:53**	**+ 2.00**	**56**	**+ 2:56**	**+ 2.00**	**126**	**+ 4:06**	**+ 2.00**	**22**	**+ 2:22**	**+ 2.00**	**54**	**+ 2:54**
+ 2.15	73	+ 3:28	+ 2.15	59	+ 3:14	+ 2.15	117	+ 4:12	+ 2.15	51	+ 3:06	+ 2.15	56	+ 3:11	+ 2.15	122	+ 4:17	+ 2.15	22	+ 2:37	+ 2.15	53	+ 3:08
+ 2.30	71	+ 3:41	+ 2.30	58	+ 3:28	+ 2.30	114	+ 4:24	+ 2.30	49	+ 3:19	+ 2.30	56	+ 3:26	+ 2.30	119	+ 4:29	+ 2.30	22	+ 2:52	+ 2.30	52	+ 3:22
+ 2.45	70	+ 3:55	+ 2.45	57	+ 3:42	+ 2.45	111	+ 4:36	+ 2.45	47	+ 3:32	+ 2.45	56	+ 3:41	+ 2.45	115	+ 4:40	+ 2.45	21	+ 3:06	+ 2.45	51	+ 3:36
+ 3.00	**68**	**+ 4:08**	**+ 3.00**	**55**	**+ 3:55**	**+ 3.00**	**109**	**+ 4:49**	**+ 3.00**	**45**	**+ 3:45**	**+ 3.00**	**56**	**+ 3:56**	**+ 3.00**	**111**	**+ 4:51**	**+ 3.00**	**21**	**+ 3:21**	**+ 3.00**	**50**	**+ 3:50**
+ 3.15	66	+ 4:21	+ 3.15	54	+ 4:09	+ 3.15	105	+ 5:00	+ 3.15	44	+ 3:59	+ 3.15	56	+ 4:11	+ 3.15	107	+ 5:02	+ 3.15	21	+ 3:36	+ 3.15	50	+ 4:05
+ 3.30	65	+ 4:35	+ 3.30	53	+ 4:23	+ 3.30	101	+ 5:11	+ 3.30	42	+ 4:12	+ 3.30	56	+ 4:26	+ 3.30	103	+ 5:13	+ 3.30	20	+ 3:50	+ 3.30	50	+ 4:20
+ 3.45	63	+ 4:48	+ 3.45	52	+ 4:37	+ 3.45	98	+ 5:23	+ 3.45	40	+ 4:25	+ 3.45	56	+ 4:41	+ 3.45	100	+ 5:25	+ 3.45	20	+ 4:05	+ 3.45	50	+ 4:35
+ 4.00	**61**	**+ 5:01**	**+ 4.00**	**51**	**+ 4:51**	**+ 4.00**	**94**	**+ 5:34**	**+ 4.00**	**38**	**+ 4:38**	**+ 4.00**	**57**	**+ 4:57**	**+ 4.00**	**96**	**+ 5:36**	**+ 4.00**	**20**	**+ 4:20**	**+ 4.00**	**50**	**+ 4:50**
+ 4.15	59	+ 5:14	+ 4.15	50	+ 5:05	+ 4.15	89	+ 5:44	+ 4.15	38	+ 4:53	+ 4.15	58	+ 5:13	+ 4.15	92	+ 5:47	+ 4.15	19	+ 4:34	+ 4.15	55	+ 5:10
+ 4.30	57	+ 5:27	+ 4.30	50	+ 5:20	+ 4.30	83	+ 5:53	+ 4.30	38	+ 5:08	+ 4.30	58	+ 5:28	+ 4.30	88	+ 5:58	+ 4.30	18	+ 4:48	+ 4.30	59	+ 5:29
+ 4.45	55	+ 5:40	+ 4.45	49	+ 5:34	+ 4.45	78	- 5:57	+ 4.45	38	+ 5:23	+ 4.45	59	+ 5:44	+ 4.45	84	- 5:51	+ 4.45	18	+ 5:03	+ 4.45	64	+ 5:49
+ 5.00	**53**	**+ 5:53**	**+ 5.00**	**49**	**+ 5:49**	**+ 5.00**	**73**	**- 5:47**	**+ 5.00**	**38**	**+ 5:38**	**+ 5.00**	**60**	**- 6:00**	**+ 5.00**	**80**	**- 5:40**	**+ 5.00**	**17**	**+ 5:17**	**+ 5.00**	**68**	**- 5:52**
+ 5.15	52	- 5:53	+ 5.15	49	- 5:56	+ 5.15	70	- 5:35	+ 5.15	38	+ 5:53	+ 5.15	61	- 5:44	+ 5.15	78	- 5:27	+ 5.15	16	+ 5:31	+ 5.15	66	- 5:39
+ 5.30	51	- 5:39	+ 5.30	48	- 5:42	+ 5.30	67	- 5:23	+ 5.30	37	- 5:53	+ 5.30	62	- 5:28	+ 5.30	76	- 5:14	+ 5.30	15	+ 5:45	+ 5.30	64	- 5:26
+ 5.45	49	- 5:26	+ 5.45	48	- 5:27	+ 5.45	64	- 5:11	+ 5.45	36	- 5:39	+ 5.45	63	- 5:12	+ 5.45	73	- 5:02	+ 5.45	15	- 6:00	+ 5.45	62	- 5:13
+ 6.00	**48**	**- 5:12**	**+ 6.00**	**48**	**- 5:12**	**+ 6.00**	**61**	**- 4:59**	**+ 6.00**	**36**	**- 5:24**	**+ 6.00**	**64**	**- 4:56**	**+ 6.00**	**71**	**- 4:49**	**+ 6.00**	**14**	**- 5:46**	**+ 6.00**	**59**	**- 5:01**

SOUTH BOUND

Table H - Harwich to Foulger's Gat and Sunk Head Connections

Neaps

All times relate to HW Sheerness

Time to cover Sectors (in minutes) at 6.0 Kts

SOUTH BOUND

	H8			H7			H6			H5			H4			H3			H2			H1	
	NE Gunfleet to Sunk Head			Goldmer Gat to Sunk Head			Sunk Head to Long Sand Inner			Harwich to The Naze			The Naze to Goldmer Gat			Goldmer Gat to Barrow No 2			Barrow No 2 to Black Deep			Long Sand Inner to Outer	
Time	Duration	Time at End of Sector	Time	Duration	Time at End of Sector	Time	Duration	Time at End of Sector	Time	Duration	Time at End of Sector	Time	Duration	Time at End of Sector	Time	Duration	Time at End of Sector	Time	Duration	Time at End of Sector	Time	Duration	Time at End of Sector
- 6.00	**41**	**- 5:19**	**- 6.00**	**41**	**- 5:19**	**- 6.00**	**55**	**- 5:05**	**- 6.00**	**30**	**- 5:30**	**- 6.00**	**53**	**- 5:07**	**- 6.00**	**59**	**- 5:01**	**- 6.00**	**12**	**- 5:48**	**- 6.00**	**45**	**- 5:15**
- 5.45	41	- 5:04	- 5.45	41	- 5:04	- 5.45	54	- 4:51	- 5.45	30	- 5:15	- 5.45	54	- 4:51	- 5.45	58	- 4:47	- 5.45	11	- 5:34	- 5.45	45	- 5:00
- 5.30	41	- 4:49	- 5.30	41	- 4:49	- 5.30	53	- 4:37	- 5.30	29	- 5:01	- 5.30	54	- 4:36	- 5.30	57	- 4:33	- 5.30	11	- 5:19	- 5.30	46	- 4:44
- 5.15	40	- 4:35	- 5.15	42	- 4:33	- 5.15	53	- 4:22	- 5.15	29	- 4:46	- 5.15	54	- 4:21	- 5.15	56	- 4:19	- 5.15	11	- 5:04	- 5.15	47	- 4:28
- 5.00	**40**	**- 4:20**	**- 5.00**	**42**	**- 4:18**	**- 5.00**	**52**	**- 4:08**	**- 5.00**	**29**	**- 4:31**	**- 5.00**	**55**	**- 4:05**	**- 5.00**	**55**	**- 4:05**	**- 5.00**	**11**	**- 4:49**	**- 5.00**	**48**	**- 4:12**
- 4.45	40	- 4:05	- 4.45	42	- 4:03	- 4.45	52	- 3:53	- 4.45	29	- 4:16	- 4.45	55	- 3:50	- 4.45	56	- 3:49	- 4.45	11	- 4:34	- 4.45	48	- 3:57
- 4.30	40	- 3:50	- 4.30	42	- 3:48	- 4.30	53	- 3:37	- 4.30	29	- 4:01	- 4.30	55	- 3:35	- 4.30	56	- 3:34	- 4.30	11	- 4:19	- 4.30	48	- 3:42
- 4.15	40	- 3:35	- 4.15	43	- 3:32	- 4.15	53	- 3:22	- 4.15	29	- 3:46	- 4.15	56	- 3:19	- 4.15	56	- 3:19	- 4.15	11	- 4:04	- 4.15	48	- 3:27
- 4.00	**40**	**- 3:20**	**- 4.00**	**43**	**- 3:17**	**- 4.00**	**53**	**- 3:07**	**- 4.00**	**29**	**- 3:31**	**- 4.00**	**56**	**- 3:04**	**- 4.00**	**56**	**- 3:04**	**- 4.00**	**11**	**- 3:49**	**- 4.00**	**49**	**- 3:11**
- 3.45	41	- 3:04	- 3.45	43	- 3:02	- 3.45	54	- 2:51	- 3.45	30	- 3:15	- 3.45	56	- 2:49	- 3.45	57	- 2:48	- 3.45	11	- 3:34	- 3.45	49	- 2:56
- 3.30	41	- 2:49	- 3.30	44	- 2:46	- 3.30	56	- 2:34	- 3.30	30	- 3:00	- 3.30	56	- 2:34	- 3.30	58	- 2:32	- 3.30	11	- 3:19	- 3.30	50	- 2:40
- 3.15	41	- 2:34	- 3.15	44	- 2:31	- 3.15	57	- 2:18	- 3.15	30	- 2:45	- 3.15	55	- 2:20	- 3.15	58	- 2:17	- 3.15	12	- 3:03	- 3.15	50	- 2:25
- 3.00	**42**	**- 2:18**	**- 3.00**	**45**	**- 2:15**	**- 3.00**	**59**	**- 2:01**	**- 3.00**	**31**	**- 2:29**	**- 3.00**	**55**	**- 2:05**	**- 3.00**	**59**	**- 2:01**	**- 3.00**	**12**	**- 2:48**	**- 3.00**	**51**	**- 2:09**
- 2.45	42	- 2:03	- 2.45	45	- 2:00	- 2.45	61	- 1:44	- 2.45	31	- 2:14	- 2.45	55	- 1:50	- 2.45	61	- 1:44	- 2.45	12	- 2:33	- 2.45	52	- 1:53
- 2.30	43	- 1:47	- 2.30	45	- 1:45	- 2.30	64	- 1:26	- 2.30	32	- 1:58	- 2.30	54	- 1:36	- 2.30	62	- 1:28	- 2.30	12	- 2:18	- 2.30	52	- 1:38
- 2.15	44	- 1:31	- 2.15	45	- 1:30	- 2.15	66	- 1:09	- 2.15	33	- 1:42	- 2.15	54	- 1:21	- 2.15	63	- 1:12	- 2.15	13	- 2:02	- 2.15	53	- 1:22
- 2.00	**44**	**- 1:16**	**- 2.00**	**46**	**- 1:14**	**- 2.00**	**68**	**- 0:52**	**- 2.00**	**33**	**- 1:27**	**- 2.00**	**54**	**- 1:06**	**- 2.00**	**65**	**- 0:55**	**- 2.00**	**13**	**- 1:47**	**- 2.00**	**54**	**- 1:06**
- 1.45	45	- 1:00	- 1.45	46	- 0:59	- 1.45	70	- 0:35	- 1.45	34	- 1:11	- 1.45	53	- 0:52	- 1.45	66	- 0:39	- 1.45	13	- 1:32	- 1.45	54	- 0:51
- 1.30	46	- 0:44	- 1.30	46	- 0:44	- 1.30	72	- 0:18	- 1.30	35	- 0:55	- 1.30	53	- 0:37	- 1.30	68	- 0:22	- 1.30	14	- 1:16	- 1.30	54	- 0:36
- 1.15	47	- 0:28	- 1.15	46	- 0:29	- 1.15	74	- 0:01	- 1.15	36	- 0:39	- 1.15	52	- 0:23	- 1.15	69	- 0:06	- 1.15	14	- 1:01	- 1.15	54	- 0:21
- 1.00	**48**	**- 0:12**	**- 1.00**	**46**	**- 0:14**	**- 1.00**	**76**	**+ 0:16**	**- 1.00**	**37**	**- 0:23**	**- 1.00**	**51**	**- 0:09**	**- 1.00**	**71**	**+ 0:11**	**- 1.00**	**15**	**- 0:45**	**- 1.00**	**54**	**- 0:06**
- 0.45	49	+ 0:04	- 0.45	46	+ 0:01	- 0.45	77	+ 0:32	- 0.45	37	- 0:08	- 0.45	51	+ 0:06	- 0.45	73	+ 0:28	- 0.45	15	- 0:30	- 0.45	53	+ 0:08
- 0.30	50	+ 0:20	- 0.30	46	+ 0:16	- 0.30	78	+ 0:48	- 0.30	38	+ 0:08	- 0.30	50	+ 0:20	- 0.30	74	+ 0:44	- 0.30	15	- 0:15	- 0.30	52	+ 0:22
- 0.15	51	+ 0:36	- 0.15	46	+ 0:31	- 0.15	79	+ 1:04	- 0.15	38	+ 0:23	- 0.15	49	+ 0:34	- 0.15	76	+ 1:01	- 0.15	15	HW	- 0.15	52	+ 0:37
HW	**52**	**+ 0:52**	**HW**	**46**	**+ 0:46**	**HW**	**80**	**+ 1:20**	**HW**	**39**	**+ 0:39**	**HW**	**49**	**+ 0:49**	**HW**	**78**	**+ 1:18**	**HW**	**15**	**+ 0:15**	**HW**	**51**	**+ 0:51**
+ 0.15	52	+ 1:07	+ 0.15	46	+ 1:01	+ 0.15	83	+ 1:38	+ 0.15	39	+ 0:54	+ 0.15	48	+ 1:03	+ 0.15	81	+ 1:36	+ 0.15	15	+ 0:30	+ 0.15	50	+ 1:05
+ 0.30	53	+ 1:23	+ 0.30	46	+ 1:16	+ 0.30	86	+ 1:56	+ 0.30	39	+ 1:09	+ 0.30	48	+ 1:18	+ 0.30	84	+ 1:54	+ 0.30	15	+ 0:45	+ 0.30	49	+ 1:19
+ 0.45	54	+ 1:39	+ 0.45	46	+ 1:31	+ 0.45	89	+ 2:14	+ 0.45	39	+ 1:24	+ 0.45	48	+ 1:33	+ 0.45	88	+ 2:13	+ 0.45	15	+ 1:00	+ 0.45	49	+ 1:34
+ 1.00	**54**	**+ 1:54**	**+ 1.00**	**46**	**+ 1:46**	**+ 1.00**	**91**	**+ 2:31**	**+ 1.00**	**39**	**+ 1:39**	**+ 1.00**	**47**	**+ 1:47**	**+ 1.00**	**91**	**+ 2:31**	**+ 1.00**	**16**	**+ 1:16**	**+ 1.00**	**48**	**+ 1:48**
+ 1.15	54	+ 2:09	+ 1.15	46	+ 2:01	+ 1.15	89	+ 2:44	+ 1.15	39	+ 1:54	+ 1.15	47	+ 2:02	+ 1.15	91	+ 2:46	+ 1.15	16	+ 1:31	+ 1.15	47	+ 2:02
+ 1.30	54	+ 2:24	+ 1.30	45	+ 2:15	+ 1.30	87	+ 2:57	+ 1.30	39	+ 2:09	+ 1.30	47	+ 2:17	+ 1.30	91	+ 3:01	+ 1.30	16	+ 1:46	+ 1.30	47	+ 2:17
+ 1.45	54	+ 2:39	+ 1.45	45	+ 2:30	+ 1.45	85	+ 3:10	+ 1.45	39	+ 2:24	+ 1.45	47	+ 2:32	+ 1.45	92	+ 3:17	+ 1.45	16	+ 2:01	+ 1.45	46	+ 2:31
+ 2.00	**54**	**+ 2:54**	**+ 2.00**	**45**	**+ 2:45**	**+ 2.00**	**82**	**+ 3:22**	**+ 2.00**	**39**	**+ 2:39**	**+ 2.00**	**47**	**+ 2:47**	**+ 2.00**	**92**	**+ 3:32**	**+ 2.00**	**16**	**+ 2:16**	**+ 2.00**	**45**	**+ 2:45**
+ 2.15	53	+ 3:08	+ 2.15	45	+ 3:00	+ 2.15	82	+ 3:37	+ 2.15	39	+ 2:54	+ 2.15	47	+ 3:02	+ 2.15	89	+ 3:44	+ 2.15	16	+ 2:31	+ 2.15	45	+ 3:00
+ 2.30	53	+ 3:23	+ 2.30	45	+ 3:15	+ 2.30	81	+ 3:51	+ 2.30	38	+ 3:08	+ 2.30	47	+ 3:17	+ 2.30	86	+ 3:56	+ 2.30	16	+ 2:46	+ 2.30	45	+ 3:15
+ 2.45	52	+ 3:37	+ 2.45	44	+ 3:29	+ 2.45	80	+ 4:05	+ 2.45	37	+ 3:22	+ 2.45	47	+ 3:32	+ 2.45	84	+ 4:09	+ 2.45	16	+ 3:01	+ 2.45	44	+ 3:29
+ 3.00	**52**	**+ 3:52**	**+ 3.00**	**44**	**+ 3:44**	**+ 3.00**	**79**	**+ 4:19**	**+ 3.00**	**37**	**+ 3:37**	**+ 3.00**	**47**	**+ 3:47**	**+ 3.00**	**81**	**+ 4:21**	**+ 3.00**	**15**	**+ 3:15**	**+ 3.00**	**44**	**+ 3:44**
+ 3.15	51	+ 4:06	+ 3.15	44	+ 3:59	+ 3.15	78	+ 4:33	+ 3.15	36	+ 3:51	+ 3.15	47	+ 4:02	+ 3.15	79	+ 4:34	+ 3.15	15	+ 3:30	+ 3.15	43	+ 3:58
+ 3.30	50	+ 4:20	+ 3.30	43	+ 4:13	+ 3.30	76	+ 4:46	+ 3.30	35	+ 4:05	+ 3.30	48	+ 4:18	+ 3.30	78	+ 4:48	+ 3.30	15	+ 3:45	+ 3.30	43	+ 4:13
+ 3.45	50	+ 4:35	+ 3.45	43	+ 4:28	+ 3.45	75	+ 5:00	+ 3.45	34	+ 4:19	+ 3.45	48	+ 4:33	+ 3.45	76	+ 5:01	+ 3.45	15	+ 4:00	+ 3.45	43	+ 4:28
+ 4.00	**49**	**+ 4:49**	**+ 4.00**	**42**	**+ 4:42**	**+ 4.00**	**74**	**+ 5:14**	**+ 4.00**	**33**	**+ 4:33**	**+ 4.00**	**48**	**+ 4:48**	**+ 4.00**	**75**	**+ 5:15**	**+ 4.00**	**15**	**+ 4:15**	**+ 4.00**	**43**	**+ 4:43**
+ 4.15	48	+ 5:03	+ 4.15	42	+ 4:57	+ 4.15	72	+ 5:27	+ 4.15	33	+ 4:48	+ 4.15	49	+ 5:04	+ 4.15	73	+ 5:28	+ 4.15	14	+ 4:29	+ 4.15	45	+ 5:00
+ 4.30	47	+ 5:17	+ 4.30	42	+ 5:12	+ 4.30	69	+ 5:39	+ 4.30	33	+ 5:03	+ 4.30	49	+ 5:19	+ 4.30	71	+ 5:41	+ 4.30	14	+ 4:44	+ 4.30	47	+ 5:17
+ 4.45	47	+ 5:32	+ 4.45	42	+ 5:27	+ 4.45	67	+ 5:52	+ 4.45	33	+ 5:18	+ 4.45	49	+ 5:34	+ 4.45	70	+ 5:55	+ 4.45	14	+ 4:59	+ 4.45	49	+ 5:34
+ 5.00	**46**	**+ 5:46**	**+ 5.00**	**41**	**+ 5:41**	**+ 5.00**	**65**	**- 5:55**	**+ 5.00**	**33**	**+ 5:33**	**+ 5.00**	**50**	**+ 5:50**	**+ 5.00**	**68**	**- 5:52**	**+ 5.00**	**13**	**+ 5:13**	**+ 5.00**	**52**	**+ 5:52**
+ 5.15	45	- 6:00	+ 5.15	41	+ 5:56	+ 5.15	63	- 5:42	+ 5.15	33	+ 5:48	+ 5.15	50	- 5:55	+ 5.15	67	- 5:38	+ 5.15	13	+ 5:28	+ 5.15	51	- 5:54
+ 5.30	44	- 5:46	+ 5.30	41	- 5:49	+ 5.30	62	- 5:28	+ 5.30	32	- 5:58	+ 5.30	51	- 5:39	+ 5.30	66	- 5:24	+ 5.30	13	+ 5:43	+ 5.30	50	- 5:40
+ 5.45	43	- 5:32	+ 5.45	41	- 5:34	+ 5.45	60	- 5:15	+ 5.45	32	- 5:43	+ 5.45	51	- 5:24	+ 5.45	65	- 5:10	+ 5.45	12	+ 5:57	+ 5.45	50	- 5:25
+ 6.00	**43**	**- 5:17**	**+ 6.00**	**41**	**- 5:19**	**+ 6.00**	**59**	**- 5:01**	**+ 6.00**	**32**	**- 5:28**	**+ 6.00**	**52**	**- 5:08**	**+ 6.00**	**64**	**- 4:56**	**+ 6.00**	**12**	**- 5:48**	**+ 6.00**	**49**	**- 5:11**

Table H - Harwich to Foulger's Gat and Sunk Head Connections

Time to cover Sectors (in minutes) at 6.0 kts

All times relate to HW Sheerness

Springs

H8 — NE Gunfleet to Sunk Head

Time	Duration	Time at End of Sector
- 6.00	40	- 5:20
- 5.45	39	- 5:06
- 5.30	39	- 4:51
- 5.15	38	- 4:37
- 5.00	38	- 4:22
- 4.45	38	- 4:07
- 4.30	38	- 3:52
- 4.15	38	- 3:37
- 4.00	38	- 3:22
- 3.45	39	- 3:06
- 3.30	39	- 2:51
- 3.15	40	- 2:35
- 3.00	40	- 2:20
- 2.45	41	- 2:04
- 2.30	42	- 1:48
- 2.15	43	- 1:32
- 2.00	44	- 1:16
- 1.45	45	- 1:00
- 1.30	46	- 0:44
- 1.15	47	- 0:28
- 1.00	48	- 0:12
- 0.45	50	+ 0:05
- 0.30	51	+ 0:21
- 0.15	53	+ 0:38
HW	54	+ 0:54
+ 0.15	56	+ 1:11
+ 0.30	57	+ 1:27
+ 0.45	58	+ 1:43
+ 1.00	60	+ 2:00
+ 1.15	60	+ 2:15
+ 1.30	60	+ 2:30
+ 1.45	59	+ 2:44
+ 2.00	59	+ 2:59
+ 2.15	58	+ 3:13
+ 2.30	57	+ 3:27
+ 2.45	56	+ 3:41
+ 3.00	55	+ 3:55
+ 3.15	54	+ 4:09
+ 3.30	53	+ 4:23
+ 3.45	52	+ 4:37
+ 4.00	50	+ 4:50
+ 4.15	49	+ 5:04
+ 4.30	48	+ 5:18
+ 4.45	47	+ 5:32
+ 5.00	45	+ 5:45
+ 5.15	44	+ 5:59
+ 5.30	43	- 5:47
+ 5.45	42	- 5:33
+ 6.00	41	- 5:19

H7 — Goldmer Gat to Sunk Head

Time	Duration	Time at End of Sector
- 6.00	41	- 5:19
- 5.45	41	- 5:04
- 5.30	42	- 4:48
- 5.15	42	- 4:33
- 5.00	42	- 4:18
- 4.45	43	- 4:02
- 4.30	43	- 3:47
- 4.15	44	- 3:31
- 4.00	44	- 3:16
- 3.45	45	- 3:00
- 3.30	45	- 2:45
- 3.15	46	- 2:29
- 3.00	47	- 2:13
- 2.45	47	- 1:58
- 2.30	47	- 1:43
- 2.15	47	- 1:28
- 2.00	48	- 1:12
- 1.45	48	- 0:57
- 1.30	48	- 0:42
- 1.15	48	- 0:27
- 1.00	48	- 0:12
- 0.45	48	+ 0:03
- 0.30	48	+ 0:18
- 0.15	48	+ 0:33
HW	48	+ 0:48
+ 0.15	48	+ 1:03
+ 0.30	48	+ 1:18
+ 0.45	49	+ 1:34
+ 1.00	49	+ 1:49
+ 1.15	49	+ 2:04
+ 1.30	49	+ 2:19
+ 1.45	49	+ 2:34
+ 2.00	48	+ 2:48
+ 2.15	48	+ 3:03
+ 2.30	47	+ 3:17
+ 2.45	46	+ 3:31
+ 3.00	45	+ 3:45
+ 3.15	45	+ 4:00
+ 3.30	44	+ 4:14
+ 3.45	43	+ 4:28
+ 4.00	42	+ 4:42
+ 4.15	42	+ 4:57
+ 4.30	42	+ 5:12
+ 4.45	41	+ 5:26
+ 5.00	41	+ 5:41
+ 5.15	41	+ 5:56
+ 5.30	41	- 5:49
+ 5.45	41	- 5:34
+ 6.00	40	- 5:20

H6 — Sunk Head to Long Sand Inner

Time	Duration	Time at End of Sector
- 6.00	48	- 5:12
- 5.45	47	- 4:58
- 5.30	46	- 4:44
- 5.15	45	- 4:30
- 5.00	45	- 4:15
- 4.45	45	- 4:00
- 4.30	45	- 3:45
- 4.15	45	- 3:30
- 4.00	46	- 3:14
- 3.45	48	- 2:57
- 3.30	50	- 2:40
- 3.15	52	- 2:23
- 3.00	54	- 2:06
- 2.45	57	- 1:48
- 2.30	61	- 1:29
- 2.15	65	- 1:10
- 2.00	68	- 0:52
- 1.45	71	- 0:34
- 1.30	74	- 0:16
- 1.15	77	+ 0:02
- 1.00	79	+ 0:19
- 0.45	83	+ 0:38
- 0.30	87	+ 0:57
- 0.15	90	+ 1:15
HW	94	+ 1:34
+ 0.15	96	+ 1:51
+ 0.30	97	+ 2:07
+ 0.45	99	+ 2:24
+ 1.00	100	+ 2:40
+ 1.15	99	+ 2:54
+ 1.30	98	+ 3:08
+ 1.45	97	+ 3:22
+ 2.00	95	+ 3:35
+ 2.15	93	+ 3:48
+ 2.30	91	+ 4:01
+ 2.45	88	+ 4:13
+ 3.00	86	+ 4:26
+ 3.15	84	+ 4:39
+ 3.30	82	+ 4:52
+ 3.45	80	+ 5:05
+ 4.00	78	+ 5:18
+ 4.15	74	+ 5:29
+ 4.30	71	+ 5:41
+ 4.45	67	+ 5:52
+ 5.00	63	- 5:57
+ 5.15	61	- 5:44
+ 5.30	58	- 5:32
+ 5.45	56	- 5:19
+ 6.00	54	- 5:06

H5 — Harwich to The Naze

Time	Duration	Time at End of Sector
- 6.00	28	- 5:32
- 5.45	28	- 5:17
- 5.30	27	- 5:03
- 5.15	27	- 4:48
- 5.00	27	- 4:33
- 4.45	27	- 4:18
- 4.30	27	- 4:03
- 4.15	27	- 3:48
- 4.00	27	- 3:33
- 3.45	28	- 3:17
- 3.30	28	- 3:02
- 3.15	29	- 2:46
- 3.00	29	- 2:31
- 2.45	30	- 2:15
- 2.30	31	- 1:59
- 2.15	32	- 1:43
- 2.00	33	- 1:27
- 1.45	34	- 1:11
- 1.30	36	- 0:54
- 1.15	37	- 0:38
- 1.00	39	- 0:21
- 0.45	40	- 0:05
- 0.30	40	+ 0:10
- 0.15	41	+ 0:26
HW	42	+ 0:42
+ 0.15	42	+ 0:57
+ 0.30	42	+ 1:12
+ 0.45	43	+ 1:28
+ 1.00	43	+ 1:43
+ 1.15	43	+ 1:58
+ 1.30	43	+ 2:13
+ 1.45	43	+ 2:28
+ 2.00	43	+ 2:43
+ 2.15	42	+ 2:57
+ 2.30	40	+ 3:10
+ 2.45	39	+ 3:24
+ 3.00	38	+ 3:38
+ 3.15	37	+ 3:52
+ 3.30	35	+ 4:05
+ 3.45	34	+ 4:19
+ 4.00	32	+ 4:32
+ 4.15	32	+ 4:47
+ 4.30	32	+ 5:02
+ 4.45	32	+ 5:17
+ 5.00	33	+ 5:33
+ 5.15	32	+ 5:47
+ 5.30	32	- 5:58
+ 5.45	31	- 5:44
+ 6.00	31	- 5:29

H4 — The Naze to Goldmer Gat

Time	Duration	Time at End of Sector
- 6.00	55	- 5:05
- 5.45	56	- 4:49
- 5.30	57	- 4:33
- 5.15	58	- 4:17
- 5.00	58	- 4:02
- 4.45	59	- 3:46
- 4.30	59	- 3:31
- 4.15	60	- 3:15
- 4.00	60	- 3:00
- 3.45	60	- 2:45
- 3.30	60	- 2:30
- 3.15	59	- 2:16
- 3.00	59	- 2:01
- 2.45	58	- 1:47
- 2.30	58	- 1:32
- 2.15	57	- 1:18
- 2.00	56	- 1:04
- 1.45	55	- 0:50
- 1.30	54	- 0:36
- 1.15	53	- 0:22
- 1.00	52	- 0:08
- 0.45	52	+ 0:07
- 0.30	51	+ 0:21
- 0.15	50	+ 0:35
HW	49	+ 0:49
+ 0.15	48	+ 1:03
+ 0.30	48	+ 1:18
+ 0.45	48	+ 1:33
+ 1.00	47	+ 1:47
+ 1.15	47	+ 2:02
+ 1.30	47	+ 2:17
+ 1.45	47	+ 2:32
+ 2.00	46	+ 2:46
+ 2.15	46	+ 3:01
+ 2.30	46	+ 3:16
+ 2.45	46	+ 3:31
+ 3.00	46	+ 3:46
+ 3.15	47	+ 4:02
+ 3.30	47	+ 4:17
+ 3.45	47	+ 4:32
+ 4.00	47	+ 4:47
+ 4.15	48	+ 5:03
+ 4.30	48	+ 5:18
+ 4.45	49	+ 5:34
+ 5.00	50	+ 5:50
+ 5.15	50	- 5:55
+ 5.30	51	- 5:39
+ 5.45	52	- 5:23
+ 6.00	52	- 5:08

H3 — Goldmer Gat to Barrow No 2

Time	Duration	Time at End of Sector
- 6.00	55	- 5:05
- 5.45	54	- 4:51
- 5.30	53	- 4:37
- 5.15	52	- 4:23
- 5.00	51	- 4:09
- 4.45	51	- 3:54
- 4.30	51	- 3:39
- 4.15	51	- 3:24
- 4.00	51	- 3:09
- 3.45	52	- 2:53
- 3.30	53	- 2:37
- 3.15	54	- 2:21
- 3.00	55	- 2:05
- 2.45	57	- 1:48
- 2.30	59	- 1:31
- 2.15	61	- 1:14
- 2.00	63	- 0:57
- 1.45	65	- 0:40
- 1.30	67	- 0:23
- 1.15	70	- 0:05
- 1.00	72	+ 0:12
- 0.45	75	+ 0:30
- 0.30	77	+ 0:47
- 0.15	80	+ 1:05
HW	83	+ 1:23
+ 0.15	87	+ 1:42
+ 0.30	92	+ 2:02
+ 0.45	96	+ 2:21
+ 1.00	101	+ 2:41
+ 1.15	100	+ 2:55
+ 1.30	100	+ 3:10
+ 1.45	100	+ 3:25
+ 2.00	100	+ 3:40
+ 2.15	98	+ 3:53
+ 2.30	95	+ 4:05
+ 2.45	93	+ 4:18
+ 3.00	91	+ 4:31
+ 3.15	88	+ 4:43
+ 3.30	85	+ 4:55
+ 3.45	82	+ 5:07
+ 4.00	79	+ 5:19
+ 4.15	76	+ 5:31
+ 4.30	73	+ 5:43
+ 4.45	71	+ 5:56
+ 5.00	68	- 5:52
+ 5.15	66	- 5:39
+ 5.30	64	- 5:26
+ 5.45	63	- 5:12
+ 6.00	61	- 4:59

H2 — Barrow No 2 to Black Deep

Time	Duration	Time at End of Sector
- 6.00	12	- 5:48
- 5.45	12	- 5:33
- 5.30	12	- 5:18
- 5.15	12	- 5:03
- 5.00	12	- 4:48
- 4.45	12	- 4:33
- 4.30	12	- 4:18
- 4.15	13	- 4:02
- 4.00	13	- 3:47
- 3.45	13	- 3:32
- 3.30	13	- 3:17
- 3.15	13	- 3:02
- 3.00	13	- 2:47
- 2.45	13	- 2:32
- 2.30	13	- 2:17
- 2.15	13	- 2:02
- 2.00	13	- 1:47
- 1.45	14	- 1:31
- 1.30	15	- 1:15
- 1.15	15	- 1:00
- 1.00	16	- 0:44
- 0.45	16	- 0:29
- 0.30	16	- 0:14
- 0.15	16	+ 0:01
HW	17	+ 0:17
+ 0.15	17	+ 0:32
+ 0.30	17	+ 0:47
+ 0.45	18	+ 1:03
+ 1.00	18	+ 1:18
+ 1.15	18	+ 1:33
+ 1.30	18	+ 1:48
+ 1.45	18	+ 2:03
+ 2.00	18	+ 2:18
+ 2.15	18	+ 2:33
+ 2.30	18	+ 2:48
+ 2.45	18	+ 3:03
+ 3.00	17	+ 3:17
+ 3.15	17	+ 3:32
+ 3.30	17	+ 3:47
+ 3.45	17	+ 4:02
+ 4.00	16	+ 4:16
+ 4.15	16	+ 4:31
+ 4.30	15	+ 4:45
+ 4.45	15	+ 5:00
+ 5.00	14	+ 5:14
+ 5.15	13	+ 5:28
+ 5.30	13	+ 5:43
+ 5.45	12	+ 5:57
+ 6.00	12	- 5:48

H1 — Long Sand Inner to Outer

Time	Duration	Time at End of Sector
- 6.00	44	- 5:16
- 5.45	46	- 4:59
- 5.30	47	- 4:43
- 5.15	48	- 4:27
- 5.00	50	- 4:10
- 4.45	50	- 3:55
- 4.30	50	- 3:40
- 4.15	51	- 3:24
- 4.00	51	- 3:09
- 3.45	52	- 2:53
- 3.30	53	- 2:37
- 3.15	54	- 2:21
- 3.00	55	- 2:05
- 2.45	56	- 1:49
- 2.30	57	- 1:33
- 2.15	58	- 1:17
- 2.00	60	- 1:00
- 1.45	59	- 0:46
- 1.30	59	- 0:31
- 1.15	59	- 0:16
- 1.00	59	- 0:01
- 0.45	57	+ 0:12
- 0.30	56	+ 0:26
- 0.15	55	+ 0:40
HW	54	+ 0:54
+ 0.15	53	+ 1:08
+ 0.30	52	+ 1:22
+ 0.45	51	+ 1:36
+ 1.00	50	+ 1:50
+ 1.15	49	+ 2:04
+ 1.30	48	+ 2:18
+ 1.45	47	+ 2:32
+ 2.00	46	+ 2:46
+ 2.15	45	+ 3:00
+ 2.30	44	+ 3:14
+ 2.45	43	+ 3:28
+ 3.00	43	+ 3:43
+ 3.15	42	+ 3:57
+ 3.30	42	+ 4:12
+ 3.45	41	+ 4:26
+ 4.00	41	+ 4:41
+ 4.15	44	+ 4:59
+ 4.30	48	+ 5:18
+ 4.45	52	+ 5:37
+ 5.00	56	+ 5:56
+ 5.15	54	- 5:51
+ 5.30	53	- 5:37
+ 5.45	52	- 5:23
+ 6.00	50	- 5:10

SOUTH BOUND

Table H - Harwich to Foulger's Gat and Sunk Head Connections

Neaps — All times relate to HW Sheerness — Time to cover Sectors (in minutes) at 7.0 Kts

SOUTH BOUND

Time	H8 NE Gunfleet to Sunk Head Duration	H8 Time at End of Sector	Time	H7 Goldmer Gat to Sunk Head Duration	H7 Time at End of Sector	Time	H6 Sunk Head to Long Sand Inner Duration	H6 Time at End of Sector	Time	H5 Harwich to The Naze Duration	H5 Time at End of Sector	Time	H4 The Naze to Goldmer Gat Duration	H4 Time at End of Sector	Time	H3 Goldmer Gat to Barrow No 2 Duration	H3 Time at End of Sector	Time	H2 Barrow No 2 to Black Deep Duration	H2 Time at End of Sector	Time	H1 Long Sand Inner to Outer Duration	H1 Time at End of Sector
- 6.00	36	- 5:24	- 6.00	35	- 5:25	- 6.00	48	- 5:12	- 6.00	25	- 5:35	- 6.00	45	- 5:15	- 6.00	52	- 5:08	- 6.00	10	- 5:50	- 6.00	38	- 5:22
- 5.45	36	- 5:09	- 5.45	35	- 5:10	- 5.45	47	- 4:58	- 5.45	25	- 5:20	- 5.45	45	- 5:00	- 5.45	51	- 4:54	- 5.45	10	- 5:35	- 5.45	39	- 5:06
- 5.30	35	- 4:55	- 5.30	35	- 4:55	- 5.30	47	- 4:43	- 5.30	25	- 5:05	- 5.30	46	- 4:44	- 5.30	50	- 4:40	- 5.30	10	- 5:20	- 5.30	40	- 4:50
- 5.15	35	- 4:40	- 5.15	35	- 4:40	- 5.15	46	- 4:29	- 5.15	25	- 4:50	- 5.15	46	- 4:29	- 5.15	50	- 4:25	- 5.15	9	- 5:06	- 5.15	40	- 4:35
- 5.00	35	- 4:25	- 5.00	36	- 4:24	- 5.00	46	- 4:14	- 5.00	25	- 4:35	- 5.00	46	- 4:14	- 5.00	49	- 4:11	- 5.00	9	- 4:51	- 5.00	41	- 4:19
- 4.45	35	- 4:10	- 4.45	36	- 4:09	- 4.45	46	- 3:59	- 4.45	25	- 4:20	- 4.45	46	- 3:59	- 4.45	49	- 3:56	- 4.45	9	- 4:36	- 4.45	41	- 4:04
- 4.30	35	- 3:55	- 4.30	36	- 3:54	- 4.30	46	- 3:44	- 4.30	25	- 4:05	- 4.30	47	- 3:43	- 4.30	49	- 3:41	- 4.30	9	- 4:21	- 4.30	41	- 3:49
- 4.15	35	- 3:40	- 4.15	36	- 3:39	- 4.15	46	- 3:29	- 4.15	25	- 3:50	- 4.15	47	- 3:28	- 4.15	49	- 3:26	- 4.15	9	- 4:06	- 4.15	41	- 3:34
- 4.00	35	- 3:25	- 4.00	36	- 3:24	- 4.00	46	- 3:14	- 4.00	25	- 3:35	- 4.00	47	- 3:13	- 4.00	49	- 3:11	- 4.00	9	- 3:51	- 4.00	41	- 3:19
- 3.45	35	- 3:10	- 3.45	37	- 3:08	- 3.45	47	- 2:58	- 3.45	25	- 3:20	- 3.45	47	- 2:58	- 3.45	50	- 2:55	- 3.45	10	- 3:35	- 3.45	42	- 3:03
- 3.30	35	- 2:55	- 3.30	37	- 2:53	- 3.30	48	- 2:42	- 3.30	26	- 3:04	- 3.30	47	- 2:43	- 3.30	50	- 2:40	- 3.30	10	- 3:20	- 3.30	42	- 2:48
- 3.15	36	- 2:39	- 3.15	37	- 2:38	- 3.15	50	- 2:25	- 3.15	26	- 2:49	- 3.15	47	- 2:28	- 3.15	51	- 2:24	- 3.15	10	- 3:05	- 3.15	42	- 2:33
- 3.00	36	- 2:24	- 3.00	38	- 2:22	- 3.00	51	- 2:09	- 3.00	26	- 2:34	- 3.00	47	- 2:13	- 3.00	52	- 2:08	- 3.00	10	- 2:50	- 3.00	43	- 2:17
- 2.45	36	- 2:09	- 2.45	38	- 2:07	- 2.45	53	- 1:52	- 2.45	27	- 2:18	- 2.45	46	- 1:59	- 2.45	52	- 1:53	- 2.45	10	- 2:35	- 2.45	43	- 2:02
- 2.30	37	- 1:53	- 2.30	38	- 1:52	- 2.30	54	- 1:36	- 2.30	27	- 2:03	- 2.30	46	- 1:44	- 2.30	53	- 1:37	- 2.30	11	- 2:19	- 2.30	44	- 1:46
- 2.15	37	- 1:38	- 2.15	38	- 1:37	- 2.15	56	- 1:19	- 2.15	28	- 1:47	- 2.15	46	- 1:29	- 2.15	54	- 1:21	- 2.15	11	- 2:04	- 2.15	45	- 1:30
- 2.00	38	- 1:22	- 2.00	39	- 1:21	- 2.00	58	- 1:02	- 2.00	28	- 1:32	- 2.00	46	- 1:14	- 2.00	55	- 1:05	- 2.00	11	- 1:49	- 2.00	46	- 1:14
- 1.45	39	- 1:06	- 1.45	39	- 1:06	- 1.45	60	- 0:45	- 1.45	29	- 1:16	- 1.45	45	- 1:00	- 1.45	57	- 0:48	- 1.45	11	- 1:34	- 1.45	46	- 0:59
- 1.30	39	- 0:51	- 1.30	39	- 0:51	- 1.30	61	- 0:29	- 1.30	30	- 1:00	- 1.30	45	- 0:45	- 1.30	58	- 0:32	- 1.30	12	- 1:18	- 1.30	46	- 0:44
- 1.15	40	- 0:35	- 1.15	39	- 0:36	- 1.15	63	- 0:12	- 1.15	30	- 0:45	- 1.15	44	- 0:31	- 1.15	59	- 0:16	- 1.15	12	- 1:03	- 1.15	46	- 0:29
- 1.00	40	- 0:20	- 1.00	39	- 0:21	- 1.00	64	+ 0:04	- 1.00	31	- 0:29	- 1.00	44	- 0:16	- 1.00	60	HW	- 1.00	13	- 0:47	- 1.00	46	- 0:14
- 0.45	41	- 0:04	- 0.45	39	- 0:06	- 0.45	65	+ 0:20	- 0.45	31	- 0:14	- 0.45	44	- 0:01	- 0.45	61	+ 0:16	- 0.45	13	- 0:32	- 0.45	45	HW
- 0.30	42	+ 0:12	- 0.30	39	+ 0:09	- 0.30	66	+ 0:36	- 0.30	32	+ 0:02	- 0.30	43	+ 0:13	- 0.30	63	+ 0:33	- 0.30	13	- 0:17	- 0.30	45	+ 0:15
- 0.15	42	+ 0:27	- 0.15	39	+ 0:24	- 0.15	67	+ 0:52	- 0.15	32	+ 0:17	- 0.15	42	+ 0:27	- 0.15	64	+ 0:49	- 0.15	13	- 0:02	- 0.15	44	+ 0:29
HW	43	+ 0:43	HW	39	+ 0:39	HW	68	+ 1:08	HW	32	+ 0:32	HW	42	+ 0:42	HW	65	+ 1:05	HW	13	+ 0:13	HW	43	+ 0:43
+ 0.15	44	+ 0:59	+ 0.15	39	+ 0:54	+ 0.15	69	+ 1:24	+ 0.15	32	+ 0:47	+ 0.15	42	+ 0:57	+ 0.15	66	+ 1:21	+ 0.15	13	+ 0:28	+ 0.15	43	+ 0:58
+ 0.30	44	+ 1:14	+ 0.30	39	+ 1:09	+ 0.30	70	+ 1:40	+ 0.30	33	+ 1:03	+ 0.30	41	+ 1:11	+ 0.30	67	+ 1:37	+ 0.30	13	+ 0:43	+ 0.30	42	+ 1:12
+ 0.45	45	+ 1:30	+ 0.45	39	+ 1:24	+ 0.45	70	+ 1:55	+ 0.45	33	+ 1:18	+ 0.45	41	+ 1:26	+ 0.45	69	+ 1:54	+ 0.45	13	+ 0:58	+ 0.45	42	+ 1:27
+ 1.00	45	+ 1:45	+ 1.00	38	+ 1:38	+ 1.00	71	+ 2:11	+ 1.00	33	+ 1:33	+ 1.00	41	+ 1:41	+ 1.00	70	+ 2:10	+ 1.00	13	+ 1:13	+ 1.00	41	+ 1:41
+ 1.15	45	+ 2:00	+ 1.15	38	+ 1:53	+ 1.15	71	+ 2:26	+ 1.15	33	+ 1:48	+ 1.15	41	+ 1:56	+ 1.15	70	+ 2:25	+ 1.15	13	+ 1:28	+ 1.15	41	+ 1:56
+ 1.30	45	+ 2:15	+ 1.30	38	+ 2:08	+ 1.30	70	+ 2:40	+ 1.30	33	+ 2:03	+ 1.30	41	+ 2:11	+ 1.30	70	+ 2:40	+ 1.30	13	+ 1:43	+ 1.30	40	+ 2:10
+ 1.45	45	+ 2:30	+ 1.45	38	+ 2:23	+ 1.45	70	+ 2:55	+ 1.45	33	+ 2:18	+ 1.45	40	+ 2:25	+ 1.45	71	+ 2:56	+ 1.45	14	+ 1:59	+ 1.45	40	+ 2:25
+ 2.00	45	+ 2:45	+ 2.00	38	+ 2:38	+ 2.00	70	+ 3:10	+ 2.00	33	+ 2:33	+ 2.00	40	+ 2:40	+ 2.00	71	+ 3:11	+ 2.00	14	+ 2:14	+ 2.00	39	+ 2:39
+ 2.15	45	+ 3:00	+ 2.15	38	+ 2:53	+ 2.15	69	+ 3:24	+ 2.15	33	+ 2:48	+ 2.15	40	+ 2:55	+ 2.15	70	+ 3:25	+ 2.15	14	+ 2:29	+ 2.15	39	+ 2:54
+ 2.30	44	+ 3:14	+ 2.30	38	+ 3:08	+ 2.30	68	+ 3:38	+ 2.30	32	+ 3:02	+ 2.30	41	+ 3:11	+ 2.30	69	+ 3:39	+ 2.30	13	+ 2:43	+ 2.30	38	+ 3:08
+ 2.45	44	+ 3:29	+ 2.45	38	+ 3:23	+ 2.45	68	+ 3:53	+ 2.45	32	+ 3:17	+ 2.45	41	+ 3:26	+ 2.45	69	+ 3:54	+ 2.45	13	+ 2:58	+ 2.45	38	+ 3:23
+ 3.00	44	+ 3:44	+ 3.00	37	+ 3:37	+ 3.00	67	+ 4:07	+ 3.00	32	+ 3:32	+ 3.00	41	+ 3:41	+ 3.00	68	+ 4:08	+ 3.00	13	+ 3:13	+ 3.00	37	+ 3:37
+ 3.15	43	+ 3:58	+ 3.15	37	+ 3:52	+ 3.15	66	+ 4:21	+ 3.15	31	+ 3:46	+ 3.15	41	+ 3:56	+ 3.15	67	+ 4:22	+ 3.15	13	+ 3:28	+ 3.15	37	+ 3:52
+ 3.30	43	+ 4:13	+ 3.30	37	+ 4:07	+ 3.30	65	+ 4:35	+ 3.30	30	+ 4:00	+ 3.30	41	+ 4:11	+ 3.30	66	+ 4:36	+ 3.30	13	+ 3:43	+ 3.30	37	+ 4:07
+ 3.45	42	+ 4:27	+ 3.45	37	+ 4:22	+ 3.45	64	+ 4:49	+ 3.45	29	+ 4:14	+ 3.45	41	+ 4:26	+ 3.45	65	+ 4:50	+ 3.45	13	+ 3:58	+ 3.45	37	+ 4:22
+ 4.00	42	+ 4:42	+ 4.00	36	+ 4:36	+ 4.00	63	+ 5:03	+ 4.00	28	+ 4:28	+ 4.00	41	+ 4:41	+ 4.00	63	+ 5:03	+ 4.00	13	+ 4:13	+ 4.00	36	+ 4:36
+ 4.15	41	+ 4:56	+ 4.15	36	+ 4:51	+ 4.15	61	+ 5:16	+ 4.15	28	+ 4:43	+ 4.15	42	+ 4:57	+ 4.15	62	+ 5:17	+ 4.15	12	+ 4:27	+ 4.15	38	+ 4:53
+ 4.30	41	+ 5:11	+ 4.30	36	+ 5:06	+ 4.30	60	+ 5:30	+ 4.30	28	+ 4:58	+ 4.30	42	+ 5:12	+ 4.30	61	+ 5:31	+ 4.30	12	+ 4:42	+ 4.30	40	+ 5:10
+ 4.45	40	+ 5:25	+ 4.45	36	+ 5:21	+ 4.45	58	+ 5:43	+ 4.45	28	+ 5:13	+ 4.45	42	+ 5:27	+ 4.45	60	+ 5:45	+ 4.45	12	+ 4:57	+ 4.45	42	+ 5:27
+ 5.00	40	+ 5:40	+ 5.00	36	+ 5:36	+ 5.00	56	+ 5:56	+ 5.00	28	+ 5:28	+ 5.00	42	+ 5:42	+ 5.00	59	+ 5:59	+ 5.00	11	+ 5:11	+ 5.00	44	+ 5:44
+ 5.15	39	+ 5:54	+ 5.15	36	+ 5:51	+ 5.15	55	- 5:50	+ 5.15	28	+ 5:43	+ 5.15	43	+ 5:58	+ 5.15	58	- 5:47	+ 5.15	11	+ 5:26	+ 5.15	43	+ 5:58
+ 5.30	38	- 5:52	+ 5.30	35	- 5:55	+ 5.30	53	- 5:37	+ 5.30	28	+ 5:58	+ 5.30	43	- 5:47	+ 5.30	57	- 5:33	+ 5.30	11	+ 5:41	+ 5.30	43	- 5:47
+ 5.45	38	- 5:37	+ 5.45	35	- 5:40	+ 5.45	52	- 5:23	+ 5.45	28	- 5:47	+ 5.45	44	- 5:31	+ 5.45	56	- 5:19	+ 5.45	10	+ 5:55	+ 5.45	43	- 5:32
+ 6.00	37	- 5:23	+ 6.00	35	- 5:25	+ 6.00	51	- 5:09	+ 6.00	28	- 5:32	+ 6.00	44	- 5:16	+ 6.00	55	- 5:05	+ 6.00	10	- 5:50	+ 6.00	42	- 5:18

H - 7 Kts

Table H - Harwich to Foulger's Gat and Sunk Head Connections

7 Kts - H

Time to cover Sectors (in minutes) at 7.0 kts — All times relate to HW Sheerness — Springs

	H8			H7			H6			H5	
	NE Gunfleet to Sunk Head			Goldmer Gat to Sunk Head			Sunk Head to Long Sand Inner			Harwich to The Naze	
Time	Duration	Time at End of Sector	Time	Duration	Time at End of Sector	Time	Duration	Time at End of Sector	Time	Duration	Time at End of Sector
- 6.00	35	- 5:25	- 6.00	35	- 5:25	- 6.00	43	- 5:17	- 6.00	24	- 5:36
- 5.45	34	- 5:11	- 5.45	35	- 5:10	- 5.45	42	- 5:03	- 5.45	24	- 5:21
- 5.30	34	- 4:56	- 5.30	35	- 4:55	- 5.30	41	- 4:49	- 5.30	23	- 5:07
- 5.15	34	- 4:41	- 5.15	36	- 4:39	- 5.15	41	- 4:34	- 5.15	23	- 4:52
- 5.00	33	- 4:27	- 5.00	36	- 4:24	- 5.00	40	- 4:20	- 5.00	23	- 4:37
- 4.45	33	- 4:12	- 4.45	36	- 4:09	- 4.45	40	- 4:05	- 4.45	23	- 4:22
- 4.30	33	- 3:57	- 4.30	36	- 3:54	- 4.30	40	- 3:50	- 4.30	23	- 4:07
- 4.15	33	- 3:42	- 4.15	37	- 3:38	- 4.15	40	- 3:35	- 4.15	23	- 3:52
- 4.00	34	- 3:26	- 4.00	37	- 3:23	- 4.00	41	- 3:19	- 4.00	23	- 3:37
- 3.45	34	- 3:11	- 3.45	37	- 3:08	- 3.45	42	- 3:03	- 3.45	24	- 3:21
- 3.30	34	- 2:56	- 3.30	38	- 2:52	- 3.30	44	- 2:46	- 3.30	24	- 3:06
- 3.15	34	- 2:41	- 3.15	38	- 2:37	- 3.15	45	- 2:30	- 3.15	25	- 2:50
- 3.00	35	- 2:25	- 3.00	39	- 2:21	- 3.00	47	- 2:13	- 3.00	25	- 2:35
- 2.45	35	- 2:10	- 2.45	39	- 2:06	- 2.45	49	- 1:56	- 2.45	26	- 2:19
- 2.30	36	- 1:54	- 2.30	39	- 1:51	- 2.30	52	- 1:38	- 2.30	27	- 2:03
- 2.15	37	- 1:38	- 2.15	40	- 1:35	- 2.15	55	- 1:20	- 2.15	27	- 1:48
- 2.00	37	- 1:23	- 2.00	40	- 1:20	- 2.00	58	- 1:02	- 2.00	28	- 1:32
- 1.45	38	- 1:07	- 1.45	40	- 1:05	- 1.45	60	- 0:45	- 1.45	29	- 1:16
- 1.30	39	- 0:51	- 1.30	40	- 0:50	- 1.30	62	- 0:28	- 1.30	30	- 1:00
- 1.15	40	- 0:35	- 1.15	40	- 0:35	- 1.15	65	- 0:10	- 1.15	31	- 0:44
- 1.00	41	- 0:19	- 1.00	40	- 0:20	- 1.00	67	+ 0:07	- 1.00	32	- 0:28
- 0.45	42	- 0:03	- 0.45	40	- 0:05	- 0.45	69	+ 0:24	- 0.45	33	- 0:12
- 0.30	43	+ 0:13	- 0.30	40	+ 0:10	- 0.30	70	+ 0:40	- 0.30	34	+ 0:04
- 0.15	44	+ 0:29	- 0.15	40	+ 0:25	- 0.15	72	+ 0:57	- 0.15	34	+ 0:19
HW	45	+ 0:45	HW	40	+ 0:40	HW	74	+ 1:14	HW	35	+ 0:35
+ 0.15	46	+ 1:01	+ 0.15	40	+ 0:55	+ 0.15	75	+ 1:30	+ 0.15	35	+ 0:50
+ 0.30	47	+ 1:17	+ 0.30	40	+ 1:10	+ 0.30	76	+ 1:46	+ 0.30	35	+ 1:05
+ 0.45	48	+ 1:33	+ 0.45	40	+ 1:25	+ 0.45	78	+ 2:03	+ 0.45	35	+ 1:20
+ 1.00	49	+ 1:49	+ 1.00	41	+ 1:41	+ 1.00	79	+ 2:19	+ 1.00	35	+ 1:35
+ 1.15	49	+ 2:04	+ 1.15	41	+ 1:56	+ 1.15	78	+ 2:33	+ 1.15	35	+ 1:50
+ 1.30	49	+ 2:19	+ 1.30	40	+ 2:10	+ 1.30	78	+ 2:48	+ 1.30	36	+ 2:06
+ 1.45	49	+ 2:34	+ 1.45	40	+ 2:25	+ 1.45	78	+ 3:03	+ 1.45	36	+ 2:21
+ 2.00	49	+ 2:49	+ 2.00	40	+ 2:40	+ 2.00	77	+ 3:17	+ 2.00	36	+ 2:36
+ 2.15	48	+ 3:03	+ 2.15	40	+ 2:55	+ 2.15	76	+ 3:31	+ 2.15	35	+ 2:50
+ 2.30	48	+ 3:18	+ 2.30	39	+ 3:09	+ 2.30	75	+ 3:45	+ 2.30	34	+ 3:04
+ 2.45	47	+ 3:32	+ 2.45	39	+ 3:24	+ 2.45	74	+ 3:59	+ 2.45	33	+ 3:18
+ 3.00	46	+ 3:46	+ 3.00	38	+ 3:38	+ 3.00	73	+ 4:13	+ 3.00	33	+ 3:33
+ 3.15	45	+ 4:00	+ 3.15	38	+ 3:53	+ 3.15	71	+ 4:26	+ 3.15	31	+ 3:46
+ 3.30	45	+ 4:15	+ 3.30	37	+ 4:07	+ 3.30	69	+ 4:39	+ 3.30	30	+ 4:00
+ 3.45	44	+ 4:29	+ 3.45	37	+ 4:22	+ 3.45	68	+ 4:53	+ 3.45	29	+ 4:14
+ 4.00	43	+ 4:43	+ 4.00	36	+ 4:36	+ 4.00	66	+ 5:06	+ 4.00	27	+ 4:27
+ 4.15	42	+ 4:57	+ 4.15	36	+ 4:51	+ 4.15	64	+ 5:19	+ 4.15	28	+ 4:43
+ 4.30	41	+ 5:11	+ 4.30	36	+ 5:06	+ 4.30	61	+ 5:31	+ 4.30	28	+ 4:58
+ 4.45	40	+ 5:25	+ 4.45	36	+ 5:21	+ 4.45	58	+ 5:43	+ 4.45	28	+ 5:13
+ 5.00	39	+ 5:39	+ 5.00	35	+ 5:35	+ 5.00	56	+ 5:56	+ 5.00	28	+ 5:28
+ 5.15	39	+ 5:54	+ 5.15	35	+ 5:50	+ 5.15	54	- 5:51	+ 5.15	28	+ 5:43
+ 5.30	38	- 5:52	+ 5.30	35	- 5:55	+ 5.30	52	- 5:38	+ 5.30	27	+ 5:57
+ 5.45	37	- 5:38	+ 5.45	35	- 5:40	+ 5.45	50	- 5:25	+ 5.45	27	- 5:48
+ 6.00	36	- 5:24	+ 6.00	35	- 5:25	+ 6.00	48	- 5:12	+ 6.00	27	- 5:33

	H4			H3			H2			H1	
	The Naze to Goldmer Gat			Goldmer Gat to Barrow No 2			Barrow No 2 to Black Deep			Long Sand Inner to Outer	
Time	Duration	Time at End of Sector	Time	Duration	Time at End of Sector	Time	Duration	Time at End of Sector	Time	Duration	Time at End of Sector
- 6.00	46	- 5:14	- 6.00	49	- 5:11	- 6.00	10	- 5:50	- 6.00	38	- 5:22
- 5.45	47	- 4:58	- 5.45	48	- 4:57	- 5.45	10	- 5:35	- 5.45	39	- 5:06
- 5.30	47	- 4:43	- 5.30	47	- 4:43	- 5.30	10	- 5:20	- 5.30	40	- 4:50
- 5.15	48	- 4:27	- 5.15	46	- 4:29	- 5.15	10	- 5:05	- 5.15	41	- 4:34
- 5.00	49	- 4:11	- 5.00	45	- 4:15	- 5.00	10	- 4:50	- 5.00	42	- 4:18
- 4.45	49	- 3:56	- 4.45	45	- 4:00	- 4.45	10	- 4:35	- 4.45	43	- 4:02
- 4.30	49	- 3:41	- 4.30	45	- 3:45	- 4.30	11	- 4:19	- 4.30	43	- 3:47
- 4.15	49	- 3:26	- 4.15	45	- 3:30	- 4.15	11	- 4:04	- 4.15	43	- 3:32
- 4.00	50	- 3:10	- 4.00	45	- 3:15	- 4.00	11	- 3:49	- 4.00	43	- 3:17
- 3.45	50	- 2:55	- 3.45	46	- 2:59	- 3.45	11	- 3:34	- 3.45	44	- 3:01
- 3.30	50	- 2:40	- 3.30	47	- 2:43	- 3.30	11	- 3:19	- 3.30	44	- 2:46
- 3.15	50	- 2:25	- 3.15	48	- 2:27	- 3.15	11	- 3:04	- 3.15	45	- 2:30
- 3.00	49	- 2:11	- 3.00	48	- 2:12	- 3.00	11	- 2:49	- 3.00	45	- 2:15
- 2.45	49	- 1:56	- 2.45	50	- 1:55	- 2.45	11	- 2:34	- 2.45	46	- 1:59
- 2.30	48	- 1:42	- 2.30	51	- 1:39	- 2.30	11	- 2:19	- 2.30	48	- 1:42
- 2.15	48	- 1:27	- 2.15	52	- 1:23	- 2.15	11	- 2:04	- 2.15	49	- 1:26
- 2.00	47	- 1:13	- 2.00	54	- 1:06	- 2.00	11	- 1:49	- 2.00	50	- 1:10
- 1.45	47	- 0:58	- 1.45	56	- 0:49	- 1.45	12	- 1:33	- 1.45	50	- 0:55
- 1.30	46	- 0:44	- 1.30	57	- 0:33	- 1.30	12	- 1:18	- 1.30	49	- 0:41
- 1.15	46	- 0:29	- 1.15	59	- 0:16	- 1.15	13	- 1:02	- 1.15	49	- 0:26
- 1.00	45	- 0:15	- 1.00	61	+ 0:01	- 1.00	13	- 0:47	- 1.00	49	- 0:11
- 0.45	44	- 0:01	- 0.45	63	+ 0:18	- 0.45	14	- 0:31	- 0.45	48	+ 0:03
- 0.30	43	+ 0:13	- 0.30	65	+ 0:35	- 0.30	14	- 0:16	- 0.30	48	+ 0:18
- 0.15	43	+ 0:28	- 0.15	67	+ 0:52	- 0.15	14	- 0:01	- 0.15	47	+ 0:32
HW	42	+ 0:42	HW	69	+ 1:09	HW	14	+ 0:14	HW	46	+ 0:46
+ 0.15	42	+ 0:57	+ 0.15	70	+ 1:25	+ 0.15	14	+ 0:29	+ 0.15	45	+ 1:00
+ 0.30	41	+ 1:11	+ 0.30	72	+ 1:42	+ 0.30	15	+ 0:45	+ 0.30	44	+ 1:14
+ 0.45	41	+ 1:26	+ 0.45	74	+ 1:59	+ 0.45	15	+ 1:00	+ 0.45	43	+ 1:28
+ 1.00	40	+ 1:40	+ 1.00	76	+ 2:16	+ 1.00	15	+ 1:15	+ 1.00	43	+ 1:43
+ 1.15	40	+ 1:55	+ 1.15	76	+ 2:31	+ 1.15	15	+ 1:30	+ 1.15	42	+ 1:57
+ 1.30	40	+ 2:10	+ 1.30	77	+ 2:47	+ 1.30	16	+ 1:46	+ 1.30	41	+ 2:11
+ 1.45	40	+ 2:25	+ 1.45	77	+ 3:02	+ 1.45	16	+ 2:01	+ 1.45	40	+ 2:25
+ 2.00	40	+ 2:40	+ 2.00	78	+ 3:18	+ 2.00	16	+ 2:16	+ 2.00	40	+ 2:40
+ 2.15	40	+ 2:55	+ 2.15	77	+ 3:32	+ 2.15	16	+ 2:31	+ 2.15	39	+ 2:54
+ 2.30	40	+ 3:10	+ 2.30	75	+ 3:45	+ 2.30	15	+ 2:45	+ 2.30	38	+ 3:08
+ 2.45	40	+ 3:25	+ 2.45	74	+ 3:59	+ 2.45	15	+ 3:00	+ 2.45	37	+ 3:22
+ 3.00	40	+ 3:40	+ 3.00	73	+ 4:13	+ 3.00	15	+ 3:15	+ 3.00	36	+ 3:36
+ 3.15	40	+ 3:55	+ 3.15	71	+ 4:26	+ 3.15	15	+ 3:30	+ 3.15	36	+ 3:51
+ 3.30	40	+ 4:10	+ 3.30	70	+ 4:40	+ 3.30	14	+ 3:44	+ 3.30	36	+ 4:06
+ 3.45	41	+ 4:26	+ 3.45	68	+ 4:53	+ 3.45	14	+ 3:59	+ 3.45	35	+ 4:20
+ 4.00	41	+ 4:41	+ 4.00	67	+ 5:07	+ 4.00	14	+ 4:14	+ 4.00	35	+ 4:35
+ 4.15	41	+ 4:56	+ 4.15	65	+ 5:20	+ 4.15	13	+ 4:28	+ 4.15	38	+ 4:53
+ 4.30	41	+ 5:11	+ 4.30	63	+ 5:33	+ 4.30	13	+ 4:43	+ 4.30	41	+ 5:11
+ 4.45	42	+ 5:27	+ 4.45	61	+ 5:46	+ 4.45	12	+ 4:57	+ 4.45	44	+ 5:29
+ 5.00	42	+ 5:42	+ 5.00	59	+ 5:59	+ 5.00	12	+ 5:12	+ 5.00	47	+ 5:47
+ 5.15	43	+ 5:58	+ 5.15	57	- 5:48	+ 5.15	11	+ 5:26	+ 5.15	46	- 5:59
+ 5.30	43	- 5:47	+ 5.30	56	- 5:34	+ 5.30	11	+ 5:41	+ 5.30	45	- 5:45
+ 5.45	44	- 5:31	+ 5.45	55	- 5:20	+ 5.45	10	+ 5:55	+ 5.45	45	- 5:30
+ 6.00	44	- 5:16	+ 6.00	53	- 5:07	+ 6.00	10	- 5:50	+ 6.00	44	- 5:16

SOUTH BOUND

Table I - Deben and Barrow Deep

Neaps — All times relate to HW Sheerness — **Time to cover Sectors (in minutes) at 4.0 Kts**

SOUTH BOUND

Time	I8 Deben Landfall to Cork Sand		Time	I7 Cork Sand to Goldmer Gat		Time	I6 Goldmer Gat to Gunfleet Spit		Time	I5 Gunfleet Spit to Barrow No 4	
	Duration	Time at End of Sector		Duration	Time at End of Sector		Duration	Time at End of Sector		Duration	Time at End of Sector
- 6.00	40	- 5:20	- 6.00	74	- 4:46	- 6.00	49	- 5:11	- 6.00	75	- 4:45
- 5.45	40	- 5:05	- 5.45	73	- 4:32	- 5.45	48	- 4:57	- 5.45	73	- 4:32
- 5.30	40	- 4:50	- 5.30	73	- 4:17	- 5.30	47	- 4:43	- 5.30	72	- 4:18
- 5.15	40	- 4:35	- 5.15	73	- 4:02	- 5.15	46	- 4:29	- 5.15	70	- 4:05
- 5.00	40	- 4:20	- 5.00	72	- 3:48	- 5.00	44	- 4:16	- 5.00	69	- 3:51
- 4.45	40	- 4:05	- 4.45	73	- 3:32	- 4.45	44	- 4:01	- 4.45	70	- 3:35
- 4.30	40	- 3:50	- 4.30	73	- 3:17	- 4.30	44	- 3:46	- 4.30	70	- 3:20
- 4.15	41	- 3:34	- 4.15	74	- 3:01	- 4.15	44	- 3:31	- 4.15	71	- 3:04
- 4.00	41	- 3:19	- 4.00	74	- 2:46	- 4.00	44	- 3:16	- 4.00	71	- 2:49
- 3.45	41	- 3:04	- 3.45	77	- 2:28	- 3.45	45	- 3:00	- 3.45	73	- 2:32
- 3.30	41	- 2:49	- 3.30	79	- 2:11	- 3.30	46	- 2:44	- 3.30	75	- 2:15
- 3.15	42	- 2:33	- 3.15	82	- 1:53	- 3.15	47	- 2:28	- 3.15	76	- 1:59
- 3.00	42	- 2:18	- 3.00	84	- 1:36	- 3.00	48	- 2:12	- 3.00	78	- 1:42
- 2.45	42	- 2:03	- 2.45	88	- 1:17	- 2.45	50	- 1:55	- 2.45	80	- 1:25
- 2.30	43	- 1:47	- 2.30	92	- 0:58	- 2.30	52	- 1:38	- 2.30	82	- 1:08
- 2.15	43	- 1:32	- 2.15	95	- 0:40	- 2.15	54	- 1:21	- 2.15	84	- 0:51
- 2.00	44	- 1:16	- 2.00	99	- 0:21	- 2.00	55	- 1:05	- 2.00	86	- 0:34
- 1.45	44	- 1:01	- 1.45	104	- 0:01	- 1.45	58	- 0:47	- 1.45	90	- 0:15
- 1.30	44	- 0:46	- 1.30	109	+ 0:19	- 1.30	60	- 0:30	- 1.30	94	+ 0:04
- 1.15	45	- 0:30	- 1.15	115	+ 0:40	- 1.15	63	- 0:12	- 1.15	98	+ 0:23
- 1.00	45	- 0:15	- 1.00	120	+ 1:00	- 1.00	66	+ 0:06	- 1.00	102	+ 0:42
- 0.45	46	+ 0:01	- 0.45	124	+ 1:19	- 0.45	68	+ 0:23	- 0.45	106	+ 1:01
- 0.30	46	+ 0:16	- 0.30	128	+ 1:38	- 0.30	71	+ 0:41	- 0.30	111	+ 1:21
- 0.15	46	+ 0:31	- 0.15	132	+ 1:57	- 0.15	74	+ 0:59	- 0.15	116	+ 1:41
HW	47	+ 0:47	HW	135	+ 2:15	HW	77	+ 1:17	HW	121	+ 2:01
+ 0.15	47	+ 1:02	+ 0.15	135	+ 2:30	+ 0.15	84	+ 1:39	+ 0.15	124	+ 2:19
+ 0.30	47	+ 1:17	+ 0.30	135	+ 2:45	+ 0.30	91	+ 2:01	+ 0.30	127	+ 2:37
+ 0.45	47	+ 1:32	+ 0.45	135	+ 3:00	+ 0.45	97	+ 2:22	+ 0.45	131	+ 2:56
+ 1.00	47	+ 1:47	+ 1.00	134	+ 3:14	+ 1.00	104	+ 2:44	+ 1.00	134	+ 3:14
+ 1.15	47	+ 2:02	+ 1.15	131	+ 3:26	+ 1.15	104	+ 2:59	+ 1.15	133	+ 3:28
+ 1.30	47	+ 2:17	+ 1.30	129	+ 3:39	+ 1.30	105	+ 3:15	+ 1.30	133	+ 3:43
+ 1.45	46	+ 2:31	+ 1.45	126	+ 3:51	+ 1.45	105	+ 3:30	+ 1.45	132	+ 3:57
+ 2.00	46	+ 2:46	+ 2.00	123	+ 4:03	+ 2.00	105	+ 3:45	+ 2.00	132	+ 4:12
+ 2.15	46	+ 3:01	+ 2.15	120	+ 4:15	+ 2.15	102	+ 3:57	+ 2.15	129	+ 4:24
+ 2.30	45	+ 3:15	+ 2.30	117	+ 4:27	+ 2.30	99	+ 4:09	+ 2.30	126	+ 4:36
+ 2.45	45	+ 3:30	+ 2.45	113	+ 4:38	+ 2.45	96	+ 4:21	+ 2.45	122	+ 4:47
+ 3.00	45	+ 3:45	+ 3.00	110	+ 4:50	+ 3.00	93	+ 4:33	+ 3.00	119	+ 4:59
+ 3.15	45	+ 4:00	+ 3.15	107	+ 5:02	+ 3.15	88	+ 4:43	+ 3.15	116	+ 5:11
+ 3.30	44	+ 4:14	+ 3.30	105	+ 5:15	+ 3.30	83	+ 4:53	+ 3.30	113	+ 5:23
+ 3.45	44	+ 4:29	+ 3.45	102	+ 5:27	+ 3.45	78	+ 5:03	+ 3.45	109	+ 5:34
+ 4.00	44	+ 4:44	+ 4.00	99	+ 5:39	+ 4.00	74	+ 5:14	+ 4.00	106	+ 5:46
+ 4.15	43	+ 4:58	+ 4.15	97	+ 5:52	+ 4.15	71	+ 5:26	+ 4.15	103	+ 5:58
+ 4.30	43	+ 5:13	+ 4.30	95	- 5:55	+ 4.30	68	+ 5:38	+ 4.30	100	- 5:50
+ 4.45	43	+ 5:28	+ 4.45	93	- 5:42	+ 4.45	66	+ 5:51	+ 4.45	97	- 5:38
+ 5.00	43	+ 5:43	+ 5.00	91	- 5:29	+ 5.00	63	- 5:57	+ 5.00	94	- 5:26
+ 5.15	42	+ 5:57	+ 5.15	88	- 5:17	+ 5.15	61	- 5:44	+ 5.15	92	- 5:13
+ 5.30	42	- 5:48	+ 5.30	85	- 5:05	+ 5.30	59	- 5:31	+ 5.30	89	- 5:01
+ 5.45	42	- 5:33	+ 5.45	83	- 4:52	+ 5.45	58	- 5:17	+ 5.45	87	- 4:48
+ 6.00	41	- 5:19	+ 6.00	80	- 4:40	+ 6.00	56	- 5:04	+ 6.00	85	- 4:35

Time	I4 Barrow No 4 to Barrow No 10		Time	I3 Barrow No 10 to North Oaze PHM		Time	I2 North Oaze PHM to Medway		Time	I1 Barrow No 10 to Red Sand	
	Duration	Time at End of Sector		Duration	Time at End of Sector		Duration	Time at End of Sector		Duration	Time at End of Sector
- 6.00	102	- 4:18	- 6.00	92	- 4:28	- 6.00	87	- 4:33	- 6.00	84	- 4:36
- 5.45	100	- 4:05	- 5.45	88	- 4:17	- 5.45	84	- 4:21	- 5.45	82	- 4:23
- 5.30	98	- 3:52	- 5.30	83	- 4:07	- 5.30	82	- 4:08	- 5.30	79	- 4:11
- 5.15	96	- 3:39	- 5.15	79	- 3:56	- 5.15	79	- 3:56	- 5.15	77	- 3:58
- 5.00	94	- 3:26	- 5.00	75	- 3:45	- 5.00	77	- 3:43	- 5.00	75	- 3:45
- 4.45	94	- 3:11	- 4.45	74	- 3:31	- 4.45	76	- 3:29	- 4.45	75	- 3:30
- 4.30	94	- 2:56	- 4.30	73	- 3:17	- 4.30	75	- 3:15	- 4.30	75	- 3:15
- 4.15	94	- 2:41	- 4.15	73	- 3:02	- 4.15	74	- 3:01	- 4.15	75	- 3:00
- 4.00	94	- 2:26	- 4.00	72	- 2:48	- 4.00	73	- 2:47	- 4.00	74	- 2:46
- 3.45	95	- 2:10	- 3.45	73	- 2:32	- 3.45	73	- 2:32	- 3.45	76	- 2:29
- 3.30	96	- 1:54	- 3.30	74	- 2:16	- 3.30	73	- 2:17	- 3.30	77	- 2:13
- 3.15	97	- 1:38	- 3.15	74	- 2:01	- 3.15	73	- 2:02	- 3.15	79	- 1:56
- 3.00	98	- 1:22	- 3.00	75	- 1:45	- 3.00	74	- 1:46	- 3.00	80	- 1:40
- 2.45	101	- 1:04	- 2.45	78	- 1:27	- 2.45	75	- 1:30	- 2.45	82	- 1:23
- 2.30	104	- 0:46	- 2.30	80	- 1:10	- 2.30	76	- 1:14	- 2.30	83	- 1:07
- 2.15	107	- 0:28	- 2.15	83	- 0:52	- 2.15	77	- 0:58	- 2.15	84	- 0:51
- 2.00	110	- 0:10	- 2.00	86	- 0:34	- 2.00	79	- 0:41	- 2.00	85	- 0:35
- 1.45	115	+ 0:10	- 1.45	90	- 0:15	- 1.45	81	- 0:24	- 1.45	87	- 0:18
- 1.30	120	+ 0:30	- 1.30	94	+ 0:04	- 1.30	83	- 0:07	- 1.30	88	- 0:02
- 1.15	125	+ 0:50	- 1.15	98	+ 0:23	- 1.15	85	+ 0:10	- 1.15	90	+ 0:15
- 1.00	129	+ 1:09	- 1.00	102	+ 0:42	- 1.00	87	+ 0:27	- 1.00	91	+ 0:31
- 0.45	138	+ 1:33	- 0.45	110	+ 1:05	- 0.45	89	+ 0:44	- 0.45	96	+ 0:51
- 0.30	146	+ 1:56	- 0.30	118	+ 1:28	- 0.30	92	+ 1:02	- 0.30	100	+ 1:10
- 0.15	154	+ 2:19	- 0.15	126	+ 1:51	- 0.15	95	+ 1:20	- 0.15	105	+ 1:30
HW	162	+ 2:42	HW	134	+ 2:14	HW	98	+ 1:38	HW	109	+ 1:49
+ 0.15	167	+ 3:02	+ 0.15	143	+ 2:38	+ 0.15	103	+ 1:58	+ 0.15	114	+ 2:09
+ 0.30	171	+ 3:21	+ 0.30	152	+ 3:02	+ 0.30	108	+ 2:18	+ 0.30	119	+ 2:29
+ 0.45	175	+ 3:40	+ 0.45	160	+ 3:25	+ 0.45	112	+ 2:37	+ 0.45	124	+ 2:49
+ 1.00	180	+ 4:00	+ 1.00	169	+ 3:49	+ 1.00	117	+ 2:57	+ 1.00	129	+ 3:09
+ 1.15	179	+ 4:14	+ 1.15	170	+ 4:05	+ 1.15	120	+ 3:15	+ 1.15	130	+ 3:25
+ 1.30	179	+ 4:29	+ 1.30	171	+ 4:21	+ 1.30	123	+ 3:33	+ 1.30	131	+ 3:41
+ 1.45	178	+ 4:43	+ 1.45	172	+ 4:37	+ 1.45	125	+ 3:50	+ 1.45	132	+ 3:57
+ 2.00	178	+ 4:58	+ 2.00	174	+ 4:54	+ 2.00	128	+ 4:08	+ 2.00	133	+ 4:13
+ 2.15	174	+ 5:09	+ 2.15	170	+ 5:05	+ 2.15	127	+ 4:22	+ 2.15	131	+ 4:26
+ 2.30	171	+ 5:21	+ 2.30	167	+ 5:17	+ 2.30	126	+ 4:36	+ 2.30	129	+ 4:39
+ 2.45	168	+ 5:33	+ 2.45	163	+ 5:28	+ 2.45	126	+ 4:51	+ 2.45	127	+ 4:52
+ 3.00	164	+ 5:44	+ 3.00	160	+ 5:40	+ 3.00	125	+ 5:05	+ 3.00	125	+ 5:05
+ 3.15	160	+ 5:55	+ 3.15	155	+ 5:50	+ 3.15	122	+ 5:17	+ 3.15	122	+ 5:17
+ 3.30	155	- 5:55	+ 3.30	150	+ 6:00	+ 3.30	120	+ 5:30	+ 3.30	119	+ 5:29
+ 3.45	151	- 5:44	+ 3.45	145	- 5:50	+ 3.45	117	+ 5:42	+ 3.45	116	+ 5:41
+ 4.00	146	- 5:34	+ 4.00	139	- 5:41	+ 4.00	115	+ 5:55	+ 4.00	114	+ 5:54
+ 4.15	142	- 5:23	+ 4.15	135	- 5:30	+ 4.15	112	- 5:53	+ 4.15	111	- 5:54
+ 4.30	139	- 5:11	+ 4.30	131	- 5:19	+ 4.30	109	- 5:41	+ 4.30	108	- 5:42
+ 4.45	135	- 5:00	+ 4.45	126	- 5:09	+ 4.45	107	- 5:28	+ 4.45	105	- 5:30
+ 5.00	131	- 4:49	+ 5.00	122	- 4:58	+ 5.00	104	- 5:16	+ 5.00	103	- 5:17
+ 5.15	127	- 4:38	+ 5.15	118	- 4:47	+ 5.15	102	- 5:03	+ 5.15	100	- 5:05
+ 5.30	123	- 4:27	+ 5.30	114	- 4:36	+ 5.30	100	- 4:50	+ 5.30	98	- 4:52
+ 5.45	119	- 4:16	+ 5.45	110	- 4:25	+ 5.45	98	- 4:37	+ 5.45	96	- 4:39
+ 6.00	114	- 4:06	+ 6.00	106	- 4:14	+ 6.00	97	- 4:23	+ 6.00	94	- 4:26

Table I - Deben and Barrow Deep

Time to cover Sectors (in minutes) at 4.0 kts — All times relate to HW Sheerness — **Springs**

	I8 Deben Landfall to Cork Sand			I7 Cork Sand to Goldmer Gat			I6 Goldmer Gat to Gunfleet Spit			I5 Gunfleet Spit to Barrow No 4			I4 Barrow No 4 to Barrow No 10			I3 Barrow No 10 to North Oaze PHM			I2 North Oaze PHM to Medway			I1 Barrow No 10 to Red Sand	
Time	Duration	Time at End of Sector	Time	Duration	Time at End of Sector	Time	Duration	Time at End of Sector	Time	Duration	Time at End of Sector	Time	Duration	Time at End of Sector	Time	Duration	Time at End of Sector	Time	Duration	Time at End of Sector	Time	Duration	Time at End of Sector
- 6.00	**39**	**- 5:21**	**- 6.00**	**63**	**- 4:57**	**- 6.00**	**44**	**- 5:16**	**- 6.00**	**66**	**- 4:54**	**- 6.00**	**95**	**- 4:25**	**- 6.00**	**77**	**- 4:43**	**- 6.00**	**82**	**- 4:38**	**- 6.00**	**78**	**- 4:42**
- 5.45	39	- 5:06	- 5.45	63	- 4:42	- 5.45	43	- 5:02	- 5.45	64	- 4:41	- 5.45	90	- 4:15	- 5.45	72	- 4:33	- 5.45	79	- 4:26	- 5.45	75	- 4:30
- 5.30	39	- 4:51	- 5.30	62	- 4:28	- 5.30	41	- 4:49	- 5.30	63	- 4:27	- 5.30	85	- 4:05	- 5.30	68	- 4:22	- 5.30	75	- 4:15	- 5.30	72	- 4:18
- 5.15	39	- 4:36	- 5.15	62	- 4:13	- 5.15	40	- 4:35	- 5.15	61	- 4:14	- 5.15	80	- 3:55	- 5.15	63	- 4:12	- 5.15	72	- 4:03	- 5.15	70	- 4:05
- 5.00	**39**	**- 4:21**	**- 5.00**	**61**	**- 3:59**	**- 5.00**	**38**	**- 4:22**	**- 5.00**	**59**	**- 4:01**	**- 5.00**	**74**	**- 3:46**	**- 5.00**	**58**	**- 4:02**	**- 5.00**	**69**	**- 3:51**	**- 5.00**	**67**	**- 3:53**
- 4.45	40	- 4:05	- 4.45	62	- 3:43	- 4.45	38	- 4:07	- 4.45	60	- 3:45	- 4.45	75	- 3:30	- 4.45	58	- 3:47	- 4.45	68	- 3:37	- 4.45	67	- 3:38
- 4.30	40	- 3:50	- 4.30	63	- 3:27	- 4.30	38	- 3:52	- 4.30	61	- 3:29	- 4.30	75	- 3:15	- 4.30	58	- 3:32	- 4.30	66	- 3:24	- 4.30	67	- 3:23
- 4.15	40	- 3:35	- 4.15	64	- 3:11	- 4.15	38	- 3:37	- 4.15	62	- 3:13	- 4.15	75	- 3:00	- 4.15	57	- 3:18	- 4.15	65	- 3:10	- 4.15	67	- 3:08
- 4.00	**40**	**- 3:20**	**- 4.00**	**65**	**- 2:55**	**- 4.00**	**38**	**- 3:22**	**- 4.00**	**63**	**- 2:57**	**- 4.00**	**75**	**- 2:45**	**- 4.00**	**57**	**- 3:03**	**- 4.00**	**64**	**- 2:56**	**- 4.00**	**66**	**- 2:54**
- 3.45	41	- 3:04	- 3.45	69	- 2:36	- 3.45	39	- 3:06	- 3.45	65	- 2:40	- 3.45	79	- 2:26	- 3.45	57	- 2:48	- 3.45	64	- 2:41	- 3.45	68	- 2:37
- 3.30	41	- 2:49	- 3.30	72	- 2:18	- 3.30	40	- 2:50	- 3.30	67	- 2:23	- 3.30	84	- 2:06	- 3.30	58	- 2:32	- 3.30	64	- 2:26	- 3.30	70	- 2:20
- 3.15	41	- 2:34	- 3.15	76	- 1:59	- 3.15	41	- 2:34	- 3.15	69	- 2:06	- 3.15	88	- 1:47	- 3.15	59	- 2:16	- 3.15	64	- 2:11	- 3.15	72	- 2:03
- 3.00	**42**	**- 2:18**	**- 3.00**	**79**	**- 1:41**	**- 3.00**	**42**	**- 2:18**	**- 3.00**	**71**	**- 1:49**	**- 3.00**	**92**	**- 1:28**	**- 3.00**	**60**	**- 2:00**	**- 3.00**	**64**	**- 1:56**	**- 3.00**	**74**	**- 1:46**
- 2.45	43	- 2:02	- 2.45	85	- 1:20	- 2.45	45	- 2:00	- 2.45	74	- 1:31	- 2.45	96	- 1:09	- 2.45	63	- 1:42	- 2.45	66	- 1:39	- 2.45	76	- 1:29
- 2.30	43	- 1:47	- 2.30	91	- 0:59	- 2.30	47	- 1:43	- 2.30	77	- 1:13	- 2.30	99	- 0:51	- 2.30	67	- 1:23	- 2.30	68	- 1:22	- 2.30	77	- 1:13
- 2.15	44	- 1:31	- 2.15	96	- 0:39	- 2.15	50	- 1:25	- 2.15	80	- 0:55	- 2.15	103	- 0:32	- 2.15	71	- 1:04	- 2.15	70	- 1:05	- 2.15	79	- 0:56
- 2.00	**44**	**- 1:16**	**- 2.00**	**102**	**- 0:18**	**- 2.00**	**52**	**- 1:08**	**- 2.00**	**83**	**- 0:37**	**- 2.00**	**107**	**- 0:13**	**- 2.00**	**74**	**- 0:46**	**- 2.00**	**71**	**- 0:49**	**- 2.00**	**81**	**- 0:39**
- 1.45	45	- 1:00	- 1.45	110	+ 0:05	- 1.45	56	- 0:49	- 1.45	89	- 0:16	- 1.45	114	+ 0:09	- 1.45	82	- 0:23	- 1.45	74	- 0:31	- 1.45	83	- 0:22
- 1.30	46	- 0:44	- 1.30	118	+ 0:28	- 1.30	59	- 0:31	- 1.30	95	+ 0:05	- 1.30	121	+ 0:31	- 1.30	89	- 0:01	- 1.30	77	- 0:13	- 1.30	86	- 0:04
- 1.15	46	- 0:29	- 1.15	126	+ 0:51	- 1.15	63	- 0:12	- 1.15	101	+ 0:26	- 1.15	128	+ 0:53	- 1.15	96	+ 0:21	- 1.15	80	+ 0:05	- 1.15	89	+ 0:14
- 1.00	**47**	**- 0:13**	**- 1.00**	**134**	**+ 1:14**	**- 1.00**	**66**	**+ 0:06**	**- 1.00**	**107**	**+ 0:47**	**- 1.00**	**135**	**+ 1:15**	**- 1.00**	**104**	**+ 0:44**	**- 1.00**	**83**	**+ 0:23**	**- 1.00**	**91**	**+ 0:31**
- 0.45	47	+ 0:02	- 0.45	141	+ 1:36	- 0.45	74	+ 0:29	- 0.45	114	+ 1:09	- 0.45	147	+ 1:42	- 0.45	121	+ 1:16	- 0.45	88	+ 0:43	- 0.45	98	+ 0:53
- 0.30	48	+ 0:18	- 0.30	149	+ 1:59	- 0.30	82	+ 0:52	- 0.30	121	+ 1:31	- 0.30	160	+ 2:10	- 0.30	139	+ 1:49	- 0.30	93	+ 1:03	- 0.30	105	+ 1:15
- 0.15	49	+ 0:34	- 0.15	156	+ 2:21	- 0.15	89	+ 1:14	- 0.15	128	+ 1:53	- 0.15	173	+ 2:38	- 0.15	157	+ 2:22	- 0.15	98	+ 1:23	- 0.15	113	+ 1:38
HW	**50**	**+ 0:50**	**HW**	**163**	**+ 2:43**	**HW**	**97**	**+ 1:37**	**HW**	**136**	**+ 2:16**	**HW**	**186**	**+ 3:06**	**HW**	**175**	**+ 2:55**	**HW**	**103**	**+ 1:43**	**HW**	**120**	**+ 2:00**
+ 0.15	50	+ 1:05	+ 0.15	161	+ 2:56	+ 0.15	104	+ 1:59	+ 0.15	142	+ 2:37	+ 0.15	193	+ 3:28	+ 0.15	188	+ 3:23	+ 0.15	110	+ 2:05	+ 0.15	129	+ 2:24
+ 0.30	50	+ 1:20	+ 0.30	158	+ 3:08	+ 0.30	111	+ 2:21	+ 0.30	148	+ 2:58	+ 0.30	200	+ 3:50	+ 0.30	200	+ 3:50	+ 0.30	117	+ 2:27	+ 0.30	139	+ 2:49
+ 0.45	50	+ 1:35	+ 0.45	156	+ 3:21	+ 0.45	117	+ 2:42	+ 0.45	154	+ 3:19	+ 0.45	207	+ 4:12	+ 0.45	213	+ 4:18	+ 0.45	124	+ 2:49	+ 0.45	149	+ 3:14
+ 1.00	**50**	**+ 1:50**	**+ 1.00**	**154**	**+ 3:34**	**+ 1.00**	**124**	**+ 3:04**	**+ 1.00**	**159**	**+ 3:39**	**+ 1.00**	**215**	**+ 4:35**	**+ 1.00**	**226**	**+ 4:46**	**+ 1.00**	**131**	**+ 3:11**	**+ 1.00**	**159**	**+ 3:39**
+ 1.15	50	+ 2:05	+ 1.15	148	+ 3:43	+ 1.15	123	+ 3:18	+ 1.15	156	+ 3:51	+ 1.15	211	+ 4:46	+ 1.15	222	+ 4:57	+ 1.15	136	+ 3:31	+ 1.15	158	+ 3:53
+ 1.30	49	+ 2:19	+ 1.30	142	+ 3:52	+ 1.30	123	+ 3:33	+ 1.30	152	+ 4:02	+ 1.30	207	+ 4:57	+ 1.30	219	+ 5:09	+ 1.30	141	+ 3:51	+ 1.30	157	+ 4:07
+ 1.45	49	+ 2:34	+ 1.45	137	+ 4:02	+ 1.45	122	+ 3:47	+ 1.45	148	+ 4:13	+ 1.45	203	+ 5:08	+ 1.45	215	+ 5:20	+ 1.45	146	+ 4:11	+ 1.45	157	+ 4:22
+ 2.00	**48**	**+ 2:48**	**+ 2.00**	**131**	**+ 4:11**	**+ 2.00**	**121**	**+ 4:01**	**+ 2.00**	**145**	**+ 4:25**	**+ 2.00**	**200**	**+ 5:20**	**+ 2.00**	**212**	**+ 5:32**	**+ 2.00**	**151**	**+ 4:31**	**+ 2.00**	**156**	**+ 4:36**
+ 2.15	48	+ 3:03	+ 2.15	127	+ 4:22	+ 2.15	116	+ 4:11	+ 2.15	140	+ 4:35	+ 2.15	194	+ 5:29	+ 2.15	203	+ 5:38	+ 2.15	147	+ 4:42	+ 2.15	151	+ 4:46
+ 2.30	47	+ 3:17	+ 2.30	122	+ 4:32	+ 2.30	112	+ 4:22	+ 2.30	136	+ 4:46	+ 2.30	188	+ 5:38	+ 2.30	195	+ 5:45	+ 2.30	144	+ 4:54	+ 2.30	145	+ 4:55
+ 2.45	47	+ 3:32	+ 2.45	117	+ 4:42	+ 2.45	107	+ 4:32	+ 2.45	131	+ 4:56	+ 2.45	182	+ 5:47	+ 2.45	187	+ 5:52	+ 2.45	140	+ 5:05	+ 2.45	140	+ 5:05
+ 3.00	**46**	**+ 3:46**	**+ 3.00**	**113**	**+ 4:53**	**+ 3.00**	**102**	**+ 4:42**	**+ 3.00**	**127**	**+ 5:07**	**+ 3.00**	**176**	**+ 5:56**	**+ 3.00**	**179**	**+ 5:59**	**+ 3.00**	**136**	**+ 5:16**	**+ 3.00**	**135**	**+ 5:15**
+ 3.15	46	+ 4:01	+ 3.15	109	+ 5:04	+ 3.15	97	+ 4:52	+ 3.15	122	+ 5:17	+ 3.15	170	- 5:55	+ 3.15	171	- 5:54	+ 3.15	132	+ 5:27	+ 3.15	131	+ 5:26
+ 3.30	45	+ 4:15	+ 3.30	106	+ 5:16	+ 3.30	91	+ 5:01	+ 3.30	117	+ 5:27	+ 3.30	164	- 5:46	+ 3.30	164	- 5:46	+ 3.30	128	+ 5:38	+ 3.30	127	+ 5:37
+ 3.45	45	+ 4:30	+ 3.45	103	+ 5:28	+ 3.45	86	+ 5:11	+ 3.45	113	+ 5:38	+ 3.45	158	- 5:37	+ 3.45	156	- 5:39	+ 3.45	124	+ 5:49	+ 3.45	122	+ 5:47
+ 4.00	**44**	**+ 4:44**	**+ 4.00**	**99**	**+ 5:39**	**+ 4.00**	**81**	**+ 5:21**	**+ 4.00**	**108**	**+ 5:48**	**+ 4.00**	**152**	**- 5:28**	**+ 4.00**	**148**	**- 5:32**	**+ 4.00**	**120**	**- 6:00**	**+ 4.00**	**118**	**+ 5:58**
+ 4.15	44	+ 4:59	+ 4.15	97	+ 5:52	+ 4.15	76	+ 5:31	+ 4.15	104	+ 5:59	+ 4.15	146	- 5:19	+ 4.15	142	- 5:23	+ 4.15	116	- 5:49	+ 4.15	114	- 5:51
+ 4.30	43	+ 5:13	+ 4.30	94	- 5:56	+ 4.30	72	+ 5:42	+ 4.30	100	- 5:50	+ 4.30	140	- 5:10	+ 4.30	136	- 5:14	+ 4.30	113	- 5:37	+ 4.30	110	- 5:40
+ 4.45	43	+ 5:28	+ 4.45	92	- 5:43	+ 4.45	67	+ 5:52	+ 4.45	96	- 5:39	+ 4.45	135	- 5:00	+ 4.45	131	- 5:04	+ 4.45	109	- 5:26	+ 4.45	107	- 5:28
+ 5.00	**42**	**+ 5:42**	**+ 5.00**	**90**	**- 5:30**	**+ 5.00**	**63**	**- 5:57**	**+ 5.00**	**92**	**- 5:28**	**+ 5.00**	**129**	**- 4:51**	**+ 5.00**	**125**	**- 4:55**	**+ 5.00**	**106**	**- 5:14**	**+ 5.00**	**103**	**- 5:17**
+ 5.15	42	+ 5:57	+ 5.15	85	- 5:20	+ 5.15	60	- 5:45	+ 5.15	89	- 5:16	+ 5.15	124	- 4:41	+ 5.15	119	- 4:46	+ 5.15	103	- 5:02	+ 5.15	100	- 5:05
+ 5.30	42	- 5:48	+ 5.30	81	- 5:09	+ 5.30	58	- 5:32	+ 5.30	86	- 5:04	+ 5.30	119	- 4:31	+ 5.30	114	- 4:36	+ 5.30	101	- 4:49	+ 5.30	98	- 4:52
+ 5.45	41	- 5:34	+ 5.45	76	- 4:59	+ 5.45	55	- 5:20	+ 5.45	83	- 4:52	+ 5.45	114	- 4:21	+ 5.45	108	- 4:27	+ 5.45	98	- 4:37	+ 5.45	95	- 4:40
+ 6.00	**41**	**- 5:19**	**+ 6.00**	**72**	**- 4:48**	**+ 6.00**	**53**	**- 5:07**	**+ 6.00**	**80**	**- 4:40**	**+ 6.00**	**109**	**- 4:11**	**+ 6.00**	**103**	**- 4:17**	**+ 6.00**	**96**	**- 4:24**	**+ 6.00**	**93**	**- 4:27**

SOUTH BOUND

Table I - Deben and Barrow Deep

Neaps — All times relate to HW Sheerness — **Time to cover Sectors (in minutes) at 5.0 Kts**

SOUTH BOUND

	I8 Deben Landfall to Cork Sand			I7 Cork Sand to Goldmer Gat			I6 Goldmer Gat to Gunfleet Spit			I5 Gunfleet Spit to Barrow No 4			I4 Barrow No 4 to Barrow No 10			I3 Barrow No 10 to North Oaze PHM			I2 North Oaze PHM to Medway			I1 Barrow No 10 to Red Sand	
Time	Duration	Time at End of Sector	Time	Duration	Time at End of Sector	Time	Duration	Time at End of Sector	Time	Duration	Time at End of Sector	Time	Duration	Time at End of Sector	Time	Duration	Time at End of Sector	Time	Duration	Time at End of Sector	Time	Duration	Time at End of Sector
- 6.00	32	- 5:28	- 6.00	63	- 4:57	- 6.00	42	- 5:18	- 6.00	63	- 4:57	- 6.00	85	- 4:35	- 6.00	75	- 4:45	- 6.00	71	- 4:49	- 6.00	70	- 4:50
- 5.45	32	- 5:13	- 5.45	62	- 4:43	- 5.45	41	- 5:04	- 5.45	62	- 4:43	- 5.45	84	- 4:21	- 5.45	73	- 4:32	- 5.45	69	- 4:36	- 5.45	68	- 4:37
- 5.30	32	- 4:58	- 5.30	62	- 4:28	- 5.30	40	- 4:50	- 5.30	61	- 4:29	- 5.30	82	- 4:08	- 5.30	70	- 4:20	- 5.30	68	- 4:22	- 5.30	67	- 4:23
- 5.15	32	- 4:43	- 5.15	62	- 4:13	- 5.15	40	- 4:35	- 5.15	60	- 4:15	- 5.15	80	- 3:55	- 5.15	68	- 4:07	- 5.15	66	- 4:09	- 5.15	65	- 4:10
- 5.00	32	- 4:28	- 5.00	62	- 3:58	- 5.00	39	- 4:21	- 5.00	59	- 4:01	- 5.00	79	- 3:41	- 5.00	66	- 3:54	- 5.00	64	- 3:56	- 5.00	63	- 3:57
- 4.45	32	- 4:13	- 4.45	62	- 3:43	- 4.45	38	- 4:07	- 4.45	59	- 3:46	- 4.45	79	- 3:26	- 4.45	65	- 3:40	- 4.45	64	- 3:41	- 4.45	63	- 3:42
- 4.30	32	- 3:58	- 4.30	62	- 3:28	- 4.30	38	- 3:52	- 4.30	60	- 3:30	- 4.30	79	- 3:11	- 4.30	65	- 3:25	- 4.30	63	- 3:27	- 4.30	63	- 3:27
- 4.15	33	- 3:42	- 4.15	62	- 3:13	- 4.15	38	- 3:37	- 4.15	60	- 3:15	- 4.15	79	- 2:56	- 4.15	64	- 3:11	- 4.15	62	- 3:13	- 4.15	63	- 3:12
- 4.00	33	- 3:27	- 4.00	63	- 2:57	- 4.00	38	- 3:22	- 4.00	60	- 3:00	- 4.00	79	- 2:41	- 4.00	64	- 2:56	- 4.00	62	- 2:58	- 4.00	63	- 2:57
- 3.45	33	- 3:12	- 3.45	64	- 2:41	- 3.45	39	- 3:06	- 3.45	61	- 2:44	- 3.45	80	- 2:25	- 3.45	64	- 2:41	- 3.45	62	- 2:43	- 3.45	63	- 2:42
- 3.30	33	- 2:57	- 3.30	65	- 2:25	- 3.30	39	- 2:51	- 3.30	62	- 2:28	- 3.30	81	- 2:09	- 3.30	64	- 2:26	- 3.30	62	- 2:28	- 3.30	64	- 2:26
- 3.15	33	- 2:42	- 3.15	67	- 2:08	- 3.15	40	- 2:35	- 3.15	63	- 2:12	- 3.15	81	- 1:54	- 3.15	65	- 2:10	- 3.15	62	- 2:13	- 3.15	65	- 2:10
- 3.00	33	- 2:27	- 3.00	68	- 1:52	- 3.00	40	- 2:20	- 3.00	64	- 1:56	- 3.00	82	- 1:38	- 3.00	65	- 1:55	- 3.00	62	- 1:58	- 3.00	66	- 1:54
- 2.45	34	- 2:11	- 2.45	71	- 1:34	- 2.45	41	- 2:04	- 2.45	66	- 1:39	- 2.45	84	- 1:21	- 2.45	67	- 1:38	- 2.45	63	- 1:42	- 2.45	67	- 1:38
- 2.30	34	- 1:56	- 2.30	73	- 1:17	- 2.30	42	- 1:48	- 2.30	67	- 1:23	- 2.30	86	- 1:04	- 2.30	68	- 1:22	- 2.30	63	- 1:27	- 2.30	68	- 1:22
- 2.15	34	- 1:41	- 2.15	75	- 1:00	- 2.15	43	- 1:32	- 2.15	68	- 1:07	- 2.15	88	- 0:47	- 2.15	70	- 1:05	- 2.15	64	- 1:11	- 2.15	69	- 1:06
- 2.00	35	- 1:25	- 2.00	78	- 0:42	- 2.00	45	- 1:15	- 2.00	70	- 0:50	- 2.00	90	- 0:30	- 2.00	72	- 0:48	- 2.00	65	- 0:55	- 2.00	69	- 0:51
- 1.45	35	- 1:10	- 1.45	81	- 0:24	- 1.45	46	- 0:59	- 1.45	72	- 0:33	- 1.45	92	- 0:13	- 1.45	74	- 0:31	- 1.45	66	- 0:39	- 1.45	70	- 0:35
- 1.30	35	- 0:55	- 1.30	84	- 0:06	- 1.30	48	- 0:42	- 1.30	74	- 0:16	- 1.30	95	+ 0:05	- 1.30	77	- 0:13	- 1.30	67	- 0:23	- 1.30	72	- 0:18
- 1.15	35	- 0:40	- 1.15	87	+ 0:12	- 1.15	49	- 0:26	- 1.15	76	+ 0:01	- 1.15	97	+ 0:22	- 1.15	80	+ 0:05	- 1.15	69	- 0:06	- 1.15	73	- 0:02
- 1.00	35	- 0:25	- 1.00	90	+ 0:30	- 1.00	51	- 0:09	- 1.00	78	+ 0:18	- 1.00	100	+ 0:40	- 1.00	83	+ 0:23	- 1.00	70	+ 0:10	- 1.00	74	+ 0:14
- 0.45	36	- 0:09	- 0.45	93	+ 0:48	- 0.45	53	+ 0:08	- 0.45	81	+ 0:36	- 0.45	104	+ 0:59	- 0.45	87	+ 0:42	- 0.45	72	+ 0:27	- 0.45	76	+ 0:31
- 0.30	36	+ 0:06	- 0.30	96	+ 1:06	- 0.30	55	+ 0:25	- 0.30	85	+ 0:55	- 0.30	109	+ 1:19	- 0.30	91	+ 1:01	- 0.30	73	+ 0:43	- 0.30	78	+ 0:48
- 0.15	36	+ 0:21	- 0.15	99	+ 1:24	- 0.15	57	+ 0:42	- 0.15	88	+ 1:13	- 0.15	113	+ 1:38	- 0.15	96	+ 1:21	- 0.15	75	+ 1:00	- 0.15	80	+ 1:05
HW	36	+ 0:36	HW	102	+ 1:42	HW	59	+ 0:59	HW	91	+ 1:31	HW	118	+ 1:58	HW	100	+ 1:40	HW	77	+ 1:17	HW	82	+ 1:22
+ 0.15	37	+ 0:52	+ 0.15	103	+ 1:58	+ 0.15	60	+ 1:15	+ 0.15	94	+ 1:49	+ 0.15	121	+ 2:16	+ 0.15	105	+ 2:00	+ 0.15	79	+ 1:34	+ 0.15	86	+ 1:41
+ 0.30	37	+ 1:07	+ 0.30	103	+ 2:13	+ 0.30	62	+ 1:32	+ 0.30	96	+ 2:06	+ 0.30	125	+ 2:35	+ 0.30	110	+ 2:20	+ 0.30	81	+ 1:51	+ 0.30	90	+ 2:00
+ 0.45	37	+ 1:22	+ 0.45	103	+ 2:28	+ 0.45	64	+ 1:49	+ 0.45	99	+ 2:24	+ 0.45	129	+ 2:54	+ 0.45	115	+ 2:40	+ 0.45	83	+ 2:08	+ 0.45	94	+ 2:19
+ 1.00	37	+ 1:37	+ 1.00	103	+ 2:43	+ 1.00	66	+ 2:06	+ 1.00	101	+ 2:41	+ 1.00	132	+ 3:12	+ 1.00	120	+ 3:00	+ 1.00	85	+ 2:25	+ 1.00	98	+ 2:38
+ 1.15	37	+ 1:52	+ 1.15	102	+ 2:57	+ 1.15	67	+ 2:22	+ 1.15	101	+ 2:56	+ 1.15	133	+ 3:28	+ 1.15	122	+ 3:17	+ 1.15	89	+ 2:44	+ 1.15	99	+ 2:54
+ 1.30	37	+ 2:07	+ 1.30	100	+ 3:10	+ 1.30	67	+ 2:37	+ 1.30	101	+ 3:11	+ 1.30	134	+ 3:44	+ 1.30	124	+ 3:34	+ 1.30	92	+ 3:02	+ 1.30	100	+ 3:10
+ 1.45	36	+ 2:21	+ 1.45	98	+ 3:23	+ 1.45	68	+ 2:53	+ 1.45	101	+ 3:26	+ 1.45	134	+ 3:59	+ 1.45	125	+ 3:50	+ 1.45	95	+ 3:20	+ 1.45	101	+ 3:26
+ 2.00	36	+ 2:36	+ 2.00	97	+ 3:37	+ 2.00	68	+ 3:08	+ 2.00	101	+ 3:41	+ 2.00	135	+ 4:15	+ 2.00	127	+ 4:07	+ 2.00	98	+ 3:38	+ 2.00	102	+ 3:42
+ 2.15	36	+ 2:51	+ 2.15	94	+ 3:49	+ 2.15	67	+ 3:22	+ 2.15	100	+ 3:55	+ 2.15	133	+ 4:28	+ 2.15	126	+ 4:21	+ 2.15	98	+ 3:53	+ 2.15	101	+ 3:56
+ 2.30	36	+ 3:06	+ 2.30	91	+ 4:01	+ 2.30	66	+ 3:36	+ 2.30	98	+ 4:08	+ 2.30	131	+ 4:41	+ 2.30	125	+ 4:35	+ 2.30	97	+ 4:07	+ 2.30	100	+ 4:10
+ 2.45	36	+ 3:21	+ 2.45	88	+ 4:13	+ 2.45	65	+ 3:50	+ 2.45	96	+ 4:21	+ 2.45	130	+ 4:55	+ 2.45	124	+ 4:49	+ 2.45	97	+ 4:22	+ 2.45	98	+ 4:23
+ 3.00	36	+ 3:36	+ 3.00	85	+ 4:25	+ 3.00	64	+ 4:04	+ 3.00	94	+ 4:34	+ 3.00	128	+ 5:08	+ 3.00	122	+ 5:02	+ 3.00	97	+ 4:37	+ 3.00	97	+ 4:37
+ 3.15	35	+ 3:50	+ 3.15	83	+ 4:38	+ 3.15	63	+ 4:18	+ 3.15	91	+ 4:46	+ 3.15	125	+ 5:20	+ 3.15	119	+ 5:14	+ 3.15	95	+ 4:50	+ 3.15	95	+ 4:50
+ 3.30	35	+ 4:05	+ 3.30	82	+ 4:52	+ 3.30	61	+ 4:31	+ 3.30	88	+ 4:58	+ 3.30	123	+ 5:33	+ 3.30	116	+ 5:26	+ 3.30	94	+ 5:04	+ 3.30	94	+ 5:04
+ 3.45	35	+ 4:20	+ 3.45	80	+ 5:05	+ 3.45	59	+ 4:44	+ 3.45	85	+ 5:10	+ 3.45	120	+ 5:45	+ 3.45	113	+ 5:38	+ 3.45	92	+ 5:17	+ 3.45	92	+ 5:17
+ 4.00	35	+ 4:35	+ 4.00	79	+ 5:19	+ 4.00	58	+ 4:58	+ 4.00	82	+ 5:22	+ 4.00	117	+ 5:57	+ 4.00	110	+ 5:50	+ 4.00	91	+ 5:31	+ 4.00	90	+ 5:30
+ 4.15	35	+ 4:50	+ 4.15	78	+ 5:33	+ 4.15	56	+ 5:11	+ 4.15	80	+ 5:35	+ 4.15	115	- 5:50	+ 4.15	107	- 5:58	+ 4.15	88	+ 5:43	+ 4.15	88	+ 5:43
+ 4.30	34	+ 5:04	+ 4.30	76	+ 5:46	+ 4.30	54	+ 5:24	+ 4.30	79	+ 5:49	+ 4.30	112	- 5:38	+ 4.30	104	- 5:46	+ 4.30	86	+ 5:56	+ 4.30	85	+ 5:55
+ 4.45	34	+ 5:19	+ 4.45	75	- 6:00	+ 4.45	53	+ 5:38	+ 4.45	77	- 5:58	+ 4.45	109	- 5:26	+ 4.45	101	- 5:34	+ 4.45	83	- 5:52	+ 4.45	83	- 5:52
+ 5.00	34	+ 5:34	+ 5.00	74	- 5:46	+ 5.00	51	+ 5:51	+ 5.00	75	- 5:45	+ 5.00	106	- 5:14	+ 5.00	97	- 5:23	+ 5.00	81	- 5:39	+ 5.00	81	- 5:39
+ 5.15	34	+ 5:49	+ 5.15	72	- 5:33	+ 5.15	50	- 5:55	+ 5.15	74	- 5:31	+ 5.15	104	- 5:01	+ 5.15	95	- 5:10	+ 5.15	80	- 5:25	+ 5.15	79	- 5:26
+ 5.30	34	- 5:56	+ 5.30	70	- 5:20	+ 5.30	49	- 5:41	+ 5.30	72	- 5:18	+ 5.30	101	- 4:49	+ 5.30	93	- 4:57	+ 5.30	79	- 5:11	+ 5.30	78	- 5:12
+ 5.45	34	- 5:41	+ 5.45	69	- 5:06	+ 5.45	47	- 5:28	+ 5.45	71	- 5:04	+ 5.45	99	- 4:36	+ 5.45	91	- 4:44	+ 5.45	78	- 4:57	+ 5.45	77	- 4:58
+ 6.00	33	- 5:27	+ 6.00	67	- 4:53	+ 6.00	46	- 5:14	+ 6.00	70	- 4:50	+ 6.00	96	- 4:24	+ 6.00	88	- 4:32	+ 6.00	77	- 4:43	+ 6.00	76	- 4:44

Table I - Deben and Barrow Deep

Time to cover Sectors (in minutes) at 5.0 kts — All times relate to HW Sheerness — Springs

SOUTH BOUND

Time	I8 Deben Landfall to Cork Sand: Duration	I8: Time at End of Sector	Time	I7 Cork Sand to Goldmer Gat: Duration	I7: Time at End of Sector	Time	I6 Goldmer Gat to Gunfleet Spit: Duration	I6: Time at End of Sector	Time	I5 Gunfleet Spit to Barrow No 4: Duration	I5: Time at End of Sector	Time	I4 Barrow No 4 to Barrow No 10: Duration	I4: Time at End of Sector	Time	I3 Barrow No 10 to North Oaze PHM: Duration	I3: Time at End of Sector	Time	I2 North Oaze PHM to Medway: Duration	I2: Time at End of Sector	Time	I1 Barrow No 10 to Red Sand: Duration	I1: Time at End of Sector
- 6.00	32	- 5:28	- 6.00	56	- 5:04	- 6.00	39	- 5:21	- 6.00	58	- 5:02	- 6.00	78	- 4:42	- 6.00	69	- 4:51	- 6.00	68	- 4:52	- 6.00	66	- 4:54
- 5.45	32	- 5:13	- 5.45	55	- 4:50	- 5.45	38	- 5:07	- 5.45	57	- 4:48	- 5.45	75	- 4:30	- 5.45	65	- 4:40	- 5.45	66	- 4:39	- 5.45	64	- 4:41
- 5.30	32	- 4:58	- 5.30	55	- 4:35	- 5.30	37	- 4:53	- 5.30	56	- 4:34	- 5.30	73	- 4:17	- 5.30	62	- 4:28	- 5.30	64	- 4:26	- 5.30	62	- 4:28
- 5.15	32	- 4:43	- 5.15	55	- 4:20	- 5.15	36	- 4:39	- 5.15	54	- 4:21	- 5.15	70	- 4:05	- 5.15	59	- 4:16	- 5.15	62	- 4:13	- 5.15	60	- 4:15
- 5.00	32	- 4:28	- 5.00	54	- 4:06	- 5.00	35	- 4:25	- 5.00	53	- 4:07	- 5.00	68	- 3:52	- 5.00	56	- 4:04	- 5.00	60	- 4:00	- 5.00	58	- 4:02
- 4.45	32	- 4:13	- 4.45	55	- 3:50	- 4.45	35	- 4:10	- 4.45	53	- 3:52	- 4.45	68	- 3:37	- 4.45	55	- 3:50	- 4.45	59	- 3:46	- 4.45	58	- 3:47
- 4.30	32	- 3:58	- 4.30	55	- 3:35	- 4.30	34	- 3:56	- 4.30	54	- 3:36	- 4.30	68	- 3:22	- 4.30	54	- 3:36	- 4.30	58	- 3:32	- 4.30	58	- 3:32
- 4.15	32	- 3:43	- 4.15	56	- 3:19	- 4.15	34	- 3:41	- 4.15	54	- 3:21	- 4.15	68	- 3:07	- 4.15	54	- 3:21	- 4.15	57	- 3:18	- 4.15	57	- 3:18
- 4.00	32	- 3:28	- 4.00	56	- 3:04	- 4.00	34	- 3:26	- 4.00	54	- 3:06	- 4.00	68	- 2:52	- 4.00	53	- 3:07	- 4.00	56	- 3:04	- 4.00	57	- 3:03
- 3.45	32	- 3:13	- 3.45	58	- 2:47	- 3.45	34	- 3:11	- 3.45	56	- 2:49	- 3.45	69	- 2:36	- 3.45	54	- 2:51	- 3.45	56	- 2:49	- 3.45	58	- 2:47
- 3.30	33	- 2:57	- 3.30	60	- 2:30	- 3.30	35	- 2:55	- 3.30	57	- 2:33	- 3.30	71	- 2:19	- 3.30	54	- 2:36	- 3.30	56	- 2:34	- 3.30	59	- 2:31
- 3.15	33	- 2:42	- 3.15	63	- 2:12	- 3.15	35	- 2:40	- 3.15	58	- 2:17	- 3.15	72	- 2:03	- 3.15	55	- 2:20	- 3.15	56	- 2:19	- 3.15	60	- 2:15
- 3.00	33	- 2:27	- 3.00	65	- 1:55	- 3.00	36	- 2:24	- 3.00	60	- 2:00	- 3.00	74	- 1:46	- 3.00	55	- 2:05	- 3.00	56	- 2:04	- 3.00	62	- 1:58
- 2.45	34	- 2:11	- 2.45	68	- 1:37	- 2.45	38	- 2:07	- 2.45	62	- 1:43	- 2.45	76	- 1:29	- 2.45	57	- 1:48	- 2.45	57	- 1:48	- 2.45	63	- 1:42
- 2.30	34	- 1:56	- 2.30	71	- 1:19	- 2.30	39	- 1:51	- 2.30	64	- 1:26	- 2.30	79	- 1:11	- 2.30	59	- 1:31	- 2.30	58	- 1:32	- 2.30	64	- 1:26
- 2.15	35	- 1:40	- 2.15	74	- 1:01	- 2.15	41	- 1:34	- 2.15	65	- 1:10	- 2.15	81	- 0:54	- 2.15	62	- 1:13	- 2.15	59	- 1:16	- 2.15	65	- 1:10
- 2.00	35	- 1:25	- 2.00	78	- 0:42	- 2.00	42	- 1:18	- 2.00	67	- 0:53	- 2.00	84	- 0:36	- 2.00	64	- 0:56	- 2.00	60	- 1:00	- 2.00	66	- 0:54
- 1.45	35	- 1:10	- 1.45	83	- 0:22	- 1.45	44	- 1:01	- 1.45	70	- 0:35	- 1.45	88	- 0:17	- 1.45	68	- 0:37	- 1.45	62	- 0:43	- 1.45	68	- 0:37
- 1.30	36	- 0:54	- 1.30	88	- 0:02	- 1.30	47	- 0:43	- 1.30	73	- 0:17	- 1.30	93	+ 0:03	- 1.30	72	- 0:18	- 1.30	64	- 0:26	- 1.30	70	- 0:20
- 1.15	36	- 0:39	- 1.15	93	+ 0:18	- 1.15	49	- 0:26	- 1.15	76	+ 0:01	- 1.15	97	+ 0:22	- 1.15	76	+ 0:01	- 1.15	66	- 0:09	- 1.15	71	- 0:04
- 1.00	36	- 0:24	- 1.00	98	+ 0:38	- 1.00	51	- 0:09	- 1.00	79	+ 0:19	- 1.00	102	+ 0:42	- 1.00	80	+ 0:20	- 1.00	67	+ 0:07	- 1.00	73	+ 0:13
- 0.45	37	- 0:08	- 0.45	102	+ 0:57	- 0.45	54	+ 0:09	- 0.45	84	+ 0:39	- 0.45	108	+ 1:03	- 0.45	87	+ 0:42	- 0.45	70	+ 0:25	- 0.45	76	+ 0:31
- 0.30	37	+ 0:07	- 0.30	106	+ 1:16	- 0.30	57	+ 0:27	- 0.30	89	+ 0:59	- 0.30	114	+ 1:24	- 0.30	95	+ 1:05	- 0.30	73	+ 0:43	- 0.30	79	+ 0:49
- 0.15	38	+ 0:23	- 0.15	109	+ 1:34	- 0.15	60	+ 0:45	- 0.15	94	+ 1:19	- 0.15	120	+ 1:45	- 0.15	103	+ 1:28	- 0.15	75	+ 1:00	- 0.15	82	+ 1:07
HW	38	+ 0:38	HW	113	+ 1:53	HW	63	+ 1:03	HW	99	+ 1:39	HW	127	+ 2:07	HW	110	+ 1:50	HW	78	+ 1:18	HW	85	+ 1:25
+ 0.15	38	+ 0:53	+ 0.15	113	+ 2:08	+ 0.15	66	+ 1:21	+ 0.15	102	+ 1:57	+ 0.15	134	+ 2:29	+ 0.15	121	+ 2:16	+ 0.15	82	+ 1:37	+ 0.15	91	+ 1:46
+ 0.30	38	+ 1:08	+ 0.30	113	+ 2:23	+ 0.30	69	+ 1:39	+ 0.30	105	+ 2:15	+ 0.30	140	+ 2:50	+ 0.30	132	+ 2:42	+ 0.30	87	+ 1:57	+ 0.30	97	+ 2:07
+ 0.45	38	+ 1:23	+ 0.45	113	+ 2:38	+ 0.45	72	+ 1:57	+ 0.45	108	+ 2:33	+ 0.45	147	+ 3:12	+ 0.45	143	+ 3:08	+ 0.45	92	+ 2:17	+ 0.45	103	+ 2:28
+ 1.00	39	+ 1:39	+ 1.00	113	+ 2:53	+ 1.00	75	+ 2:15	+ 1.00	111	+ 2:51	+ 1.00	154	+ 3:34	+ 1.00	154	+ 3:34	+ 1.00	97	+ 2:37	+ 1.00	109	+ 2:49
+ 1.15	38	+ 1:53	+ 1.15	110	+ 3:05	+ 1.15	79	+ 2:34	+ 1.15	111	+ 3:06	+ 1.15	154	+ 3:49	+ 1.15	154	+ 3:49	+ 1.15	99	+ 2:54	+ 1.15	110	+ 3:05
+ 1.30	38	+ 2:08	+ 1.30	107	+ 3:17	+ 1.30	83	+ 2:53	+ 1.30	110	+ 3:20	+ 1.30	153	+ 4:03	+ 1.30	155	+ 4:05	+ 1.30	102	+ 3:12	+ 1.30	111	+ 3:21
+ 1.45	38	+ 2:23	+ 1.45	105	+ 3:30	+ 1.45	86	+ 3:11	+ 1.45	110	+ 3:35	+ 1.45	153	+ 4:18	+ 1.45	155	+ 4:20	+ 1.45	105	+ 3:30	+ 1.45	112	+ 3:37
+ 2.00	37	+ 2:37	+ 2.00	102	+ 3:42	+ 2.00	90	+ 3:30	+ 2.00	109	+ 3:49	+ 2.00	153	+ 4:33	+ 2.00	156	+ 4:36	+ 2.00	108	+ 3:48	+ 2.00	113	+ 3:53
+ 2.15	37	+ 2:52	+ 2.15	99	+ 3:54	+ 2.15	85	+ 3:40	+ 2.15	107	+ 4:02	+ 2.15	149	+ 4:44	+ 2.15	151	+ 4:46	+ 2.15	107	+ 4:02	+ 2.15	110	+ 4:05
+ 2.30	37	+ 3:07	+ 2.30	96	+ 4:06	+ 2.30	81	+ 3:51	+ 2.30	104	+ 4:14	+ 2.30	145	+ 4:55	+ 2.30	145	+ 4:55	+ 2.30	106	+ 4:16	+ 2.30	108	+ 4:18
+ 2.45	37	+ 3:22	+ 2.45	93	+ 4:18	+ 2.45	77	+ 4:02	+ 2.45	102	+ 4:27	+ 2.45	141	+ 5:06	+ 2.45	140	+ 5:05	+ 2.45	105	+ 4:30	+ 2.45	106	+ 4:31
+ 3.00	36	+ 3:36	+ 3.00	90	+ 4:30	+ 3.00	72	+ 4:12	+ 3.00	99	+ 4:39	+ 3.00	137	+ 5:17	+ 3.00	135	+ 5:15	+ 3.00	104	+ 4:44	+ 3.00	104	+ 4:44
+ 3.15	36	+ 3:51	+ 3.15	88	+ 4:43	+ 3.15	70	+ 4:25	+ 3.15	96	+ 4:51	+ 3.15	133	+ 5:28	+ 3.15	130	+ 5:25	+ 3.15	102	+ 4:57	+ 3.15	101	+ 4:56
+ 3.30	36	+ 4:06	+ 3.30	85	+ 4:55	+ 3.30	67	+ 4:37	+ 3.30	93	+ 5:03	+ 3.30	129	+ 5:39	+ 3.30	125	+ 5:35	+ 3.30	99	+ 5:09	+ 3.30	99	+ 5:09
+ 3.45	36	+ 4:21	+ 3.45	83	+ 5:08	+ 3.45	65	+ 4:50	+ 3.45	90	+ 5:15	+ 3.45	125	+ 5:50	+ 3.45	121	+ 5:46	+ 3.45	97	+ 5:22	+ 3.45	96	+ 5:21
+ 4.00	35	+ 4:35	+ 4.00	80	+ 5:20	+ 4.00	62	+ 5:02	+ 4.00	86	+ 5:26	+ 4.00	121	- 5:59	+ 4.00	116	+ 5:56	+ 4.00	95	+ 5:35	+ 4.00	93	+ 5:33
+ 4.15	35	+ 4:50	+ 4.15	78	+ 5:33	+ 4.15	60	+ 5:15	+ 4.15	84	+ 5:39	+ 4.15	117	- 5:48	+ 4.15	112	- 5:53	+ 4.15	92	+ 5:47	+ 4.15	91	+ 5:46
+ 4.30	35	+ 5:05	+ 4.30	76	+ 5:46	+ 4.30	57	+ 5:27	+ 4.30	81	+ 5:51	+ 4.30	113	- 5:37	+ 4.30	108	- 5:42	+ 4.30	89	+ 5:59	+ 4.30	88	+ 5:58
+ 4.45	34	+ 5:19	+ 4.45	75	- 6:00	+ 4.45	54	+ 5:39	+ 4.45	78	- 5:57	+ 4.45	109	- 5:26	+ 4.45	104	- 5:31	+ 4.45	86	- 5:49	+ 4.45	85	- 5:50
+ 5.00	34	+ 5:34	+ 5.00	73	- 5:47	+ 5.00	52	+ 5:52	+ 5.00	75	- 5:45	+ 5.00	106	- 5:14	+ 5.00	100	- 5:20	+ 5.00	84	- 5:36	+ 5.00	83	- 5:37
+ 5.15	34	+ 5:49	+ 5.15	70	- 5:35	+ 5.15	50	- 5:55	+ 5.15	73	- 5:32	+ 5.15	103	- 5:02	+ 5.15	97	- 5:08	+ 5.15	82	- 5:23	+ 5.15	81	- 5:24
+ 5.30	34	- 5:56	+ 5.30	68	- 5:22	+ 5.30	48	- 5:42	+ 5.30	71	- 5:19	+ 5.30	100	- 4:50	+ 5.30	95	- 4:55	+ 5.30	81	- 5:09	+ 5.30	79	- 5:11
+ 5.45	33	- 5:42	+ 5.45	65	- 5:10	+ 5.45	46	- 5:29	+ 5.45	69	- 5:06	+ 5.45	97	- 4:38	+ 5.45	92	- 4:43	+ 5.45	79	- 4:56	+ 5.45	77	- 4:58
+ 6.00	33	- 5:27	+ 6.00	62	- 4:58	+ 6.00	44	- 5:16	+ 6.00	67	- 4:53	+ 6.00	94	- 4:26	+ 6.00	89	- 4:31	+ 6.00	78	- 4:42	+ 6.00	75	- 4:45

Table I - Deben and Barrow Deep

Neaps — All times relate to HW Sheerness — Time to cover Sectors (in minutes) at 6.0 Kts

SOUTH BOUND

Time	I8 Deben Landfall to Cork Sand: Duration	I8: Time at End of Sector	Time	I7 Cork Sand to Goldmer Gat: Duration	I7: Time at End of Sector	Time	I6 Goldmer Gat to Gunfleet Spit: Duration	I6: Time at End of Sector	Time	I5 Gunfleet Spit to Barrow No 4: Duration	I5: Time at End of Sector
- 6.00	27	- 5:33	- 6.00	54	- 5:06	- 6.00	37	- 5:23	- 6.00	55	- 5:05
- 5.45	27	- 5:18	- 5.45	54	- 4:51	- 5.45	36	- 5:09	- 5.45	54	- 4:51
- 5.30	27	- 5:03	- 5.30	54	- 4:36	- 5.30	35	- 4:55	- 5.30	53	- 4:37
- 5.15	27	- 4:48	- 5.15	53	- 4:22	- 5.15	35	- 4:40	- 5.15	52	- 4:23
- 5.00	27	- 4:33	- 5.00	53	- 4:07	- 5.00	34	- 4:26	- 5.00	52	- 4:08
- 4.45	27	- 4:18	- 4.45	53	- 3:52	- 4.45	34	- 4:11	- 4.45	52	- 3:53
- 4.30	27	- 4:03	- 4.30	54	- 3:36	- 4.30	33	- 3:57	- 4.30	52	- 3:38
- 4.15	27	- 3:48	- 4.15	54	- 3:21	- 4.15	33	- 3:42	- 4.15	52	- 3:23
- 4.00	27	- 3:33	- 4.00	54	- 3:06	- 4.00	33	- 3:27	- 4.00	52	- 3:08
- 3.45	27	- 3:18	- 3.45	55	- 2:50	- 3.45	33	- 3:12	- 3.45	53	- 2:52
- 3.30	27	- 3:03	- 3.30	56	- 2:34	- 3.30	34	- 2:56	- 3.30	53	- 2:37
- 3.15	28	- 2:47	- 3.15	57	- 2:18	- 3.15	34	- 2:41	- 3.15	54	- 2:21
- 3.00	28	- 2:32	- 3.00	58	- 2:02	- 3.00	34	- 2:26	- 3.00	55	- 2:05
- 2.45	28	- 2:17	- 2.45	59	- 1:46	- 2.45	35	- 2:10	- 2.45	56	- 1:49
- 2.30	28	- 2:02	- 2.30	61	- 1:29	- 2.30	36	- 1:54	- 2.30	57	- 1:33
- 2.15	28	- 1:47	- 2.15	62	- 1:13	- 2.15	37	- 1:38	- 2.15	58	- 1:17
- 2.00	29	- 1:31	- 2.00	64	- 0:56	- 2.00	37	- 1:23	- 2.00	59	- 1:01
- 1.45	29	- 1:16	- 1.45	66	- 0:39	- 1.45	38	- 1:07	- 1.45	60	- 0:45
- 1.30	29	- 1:01	- 1.30	67	- 0:23	- 1.30	39	- 0:51	- 1.30	61	- 0:29
- 1.15	29	- 0:46	- 1.15	69	- 0:06	- 1.15	41	- 0:34	- 1.15	63	- 0:12
- 1.00	29	- 0:31	- 1.00	71	+ 0:11	- 1.00	42	- 0:18	- 1.00	64	+ 0:04
- 0.45	29	- 0:16	- 0.45	72	+ 0:27	- 0.45	43	- 0:02	- 0.45	66	+ 0:21
- 0.30	30	- 0:00	- 0.30	74	+ 0:44	- 0.30	44	+ 0:14	- 0.30	67	+ 0:37
- 0.15	30	+ 0:15	- 0.15	75	+ 1:00	- 0.15	46	+ 0:31	- 0.15	69	+ 0:54
HW	30	+ 0:30	HW	76	+ 1:16	HW	47	+ 0:47	HW	71	+ 1:11
+ 0.15	30	+ 0:45	+ 0.15	77	+ 1:32	+ 0.15	48	+ 1:03	+ 0.15	72	+ 1:27
+ 0.30	30	+ 1:00	+ 0.30	77	+ 1:47	+ 0.30	50	+ 1:20	+ 0.30	73	+ 1:43
+ 0.45	30	+ 1:15	+ 0.45	77	+ 2:02	+ 0.45	51	+ 1:36	+ 0.45	74	+ 1:59
+ 1.00	30	+ 1:30	+ 1.00	78	+ 2:18	+ 1.00	52	+ 1:52	+ 1.00	75	+ 2:15
+ 1.15	30	+ 1:45	+ 1.15	77	+ 2:32	+ 1.15	53	+ 2:08	+ 1.15	76	+ 2:31
+ 1.30	30	+ 2:00	+ 1.30	76	+ 2:46	+ 1.30	53	+ 2:23	+ 1.30	76	+ 2:46
+ 1.45	30	+ 2:15	+ 1.45	75	+ 3:00	+ 1.45	54	+ 2:39	+ 1.45	76	+ 3:01
+ 2.00	30	+ 2:30	+ 2.00	75	+ 3:15	+ 2.00	54	+ 2:54	+ 2.00	76	+ 3:16
+ 2.15	30	+ 2:45	+ 2.15	73	+ 3:28	+ 2.15	54	+ 3:09	+ 2.15	75	+ 3:30
+ 2.30	30	+ 3:00	+ 2.30	72	+ 3:42	+ 2.30	53	+ 3:23	+ 2.30	75	+ 3:45
+ 2.45	30	+ 3:15	+ 2.45	71	+ 3:56	+ 2.45	52	+ 3:37	+ 2.45	74	+ 3:59
+ 3.00	29	+ 3:29	+ 3.00	70	+ 4:10	+ 3.00	52	+ 3:52	+ 3.00	73	+ 4:13
+ 3.15	29	+ 3:44	+ 3.15	69	+ 4:24	+ 3.15	51	+ 4:06	+ 3.15	72	+ 4:27
+ 3.30	29	+ 3:59	+ 3.30	68	+ 4:38	+ 3.30	50	+ 4:20	+ 3.30	70	+ 4:40
+ 3.45	29	+ 4:14	+ 3.45	67	+ 4:52	+ 3.45	49	+ 4:34	+ 3.45	69	+ 4:54
+ 4.00	29	+ 4:29	+ 4.00	66	+ 5:06	+ 4.00	47	+ 4:47	+ 4.00	68	+ 5:08
+ 4.15	29	+ 4:44	+ 4.15	65	+ 5:20	+ 4.15	46	+ 5:01	+ 4.15	67	+ 5:22
+ 4.30	29	+ 4:59	+ 4.30	64	+ 5:34	+ 4.30	45	+ 5:15	+ 4.30	65	+ 5:35
+ 4.45	29	+ 5:14	+ 4.45	63	+ 5:48	+ 4.45	44	+ 5:29	+ 4.45	64	+ 5:49
+ 5.00	28	+ 5:28	+ 5.00	62	- 5:58	+ 5.00	43	+ 5:43	+ 5.00	63	- 5:57
+ 5.15	28	+ 5:43	+ 5.15	61	- 5:44	+ 5.15	42	+ 5:57	+ 5.15	62	- 5:43
+ 5.30	28	+ 5:58	+ 5.30	60	- 5:30	+ 5.30	41	- 5:49	+ 5.30	61	- 5:29
+ 5.45	28	- 5:47	+ 5.45	59	- 5:16	+ 5.45	40	- 5:35	+ 5.45	60	- 5:15
+ 6.00	28	- 5:32	+ 6.00	58	- 5:02	+ 6.00	39	- 5:21	+ 6.00	59	- 5:01

Time	I4 Barrow No 4 to Barrow No 10: Duration	I4: Time at End of Sector	Time	I3 Barrow No 10 to North Oaze PHM: Duration	I3: Time at End of Sector	Time	I2 North Oaze PHM to Medway: Duration	I2: Time at End of Sector	Time	I1 Barrow No 10 to Red Sand: Duration	I1: Time at End of Sector
- 6.00	74	- 4:46	- 6.00	65	- 4:55	- 6.00	60	- 5:00	- 6.00	60	- 5:00
- 5.45	73	- 4:32	- 5.45	63	- 4:42	- 5.45	59	- 4:46	- 5.45	58	- 4:47
- 5.30	71	- 4:19	- 5.30	62	- 4:28	- 5.30	58	- 4:32	- 5.30	57	- 4:33
- 5.15	70	- 4:05	- 5.15	60	- 4:15	- 5.15	57	- 4:18	- 5.15	56	- 4:19
- 5.00	69	- 3:51	- 5.00	58	- 4:02	- 5.00	55	- 4:05	- 5.00	55	- 4:05
- 4.45	69	- 3:36	- 4.45	58	- 3:47	- 4.45	55	- 3:50	- 4.45	54	- 3:51
- 4.30	69	- 3:21	- 4.30	57	- 3:33	- 4.30	54	- 3:36	- 4.30	54	- 3:36
- 4.15	69	- 3:06	- 4.15	57	- 3:18	- 4.15	54	- 3:21	- 4.15	54	- 3:21
- 4.00	69	- 2:51	- 4.00	56	- 3:04	- 4.00	53	- 3:07	- 4.00	54	- 3:06
- 3.45	69	- 2:36	- 3.45	56	- 2:49	- 3.45	53	- 2:52	- 3.45	54	- 2:51
- 3.30	70	- 2:20	- 3.30	57	- 2:33	- 3.30	53	- 2:37	- 3.30	55	- 2:35
- 3.15	70	- 2:05	- 3.15	57	- 2:18	- 3.15	53	- 2:22	- 3.15	56	- 2:19
- 3.00	71	- 1:49	- 3.00	57	- 2:03	- 3.00	53	- 2:07	- 3.00	56	- 2:04
- 2.45	72	- 1:33	- 2.45	58	- 1:47	- 2.45	54	- 1:51	- 2.45	57	- 1:48
- 2.30	73	- 1:17	- 2.30	59	- 1:31	- 2.30	54	- 1:36	- 2.30	57	- 1:33
- 2.15	75	- 1:00	- 2.15	60	- 1:15	- 2.15	55	- 1:20	- 2.15	58	- 1:17
- 2.00	76	- 0:44	- 2.00	61	- 0:59	- 2.00	55	- 1:05	- 2.00	59	- 1:01
- 1.45	78	- 0:27	- 1.45	63	- 0:42	- 1.45	56	- 0:49	- 1.45	59	- 0:46
- 1.30	79	- 0:11	- 1.30	65	- 0:25	- 1.30	57	- 0:33	- 1.30	60	- 0:30
- 1.15	81	+ 0:06	- 1.15	67	- 0:08	- 1.15	58	- 0:17	- 1.15	61	- 0:14
- 1.00	83	+ 0:23	- 1.00	69	+ 0:09	- 1.00	59	- 0:01	- 1.00	61	+ 0:01
- 0.45	86	+ 0:41	- 0.45	71	+ 0:26	- 0.45	60	+ 0:15	- 0.45	63	+ 0:18
- 0.30	88	+ 0:58	- 0.30	74	+ 0:44	- 0.30	61	+ 0:31	- 0.30	64	+ 0:34
- 0.15	91	+ 1:16	- 0.15	76	+ 1:01	- 0.15	62	+ 0:47	- 0.15	66	+ 0:51
HW	94	+ 1:34	HW	79	+ 1:19	HW	63	+ 1:03	HW	67	+ 1:07
+ 0.15	97	+ 1:52	+ 0.15	83	+ 1:38	+ 0.15	65	+ 1:20	+ 0.15	69	+ 1:24
+ 0.30	100	+ 2:10	+ 0.30	87	+ 1:57	+ 0.30	66	+ 1:36	+ 0.30	71	+ 1:41
+ 0.45	103	+ 2:28	+ 0.45	91	+ 2:16	+ 0.45	68	+ 1:53	+ 0.45	72	+ 1:57
+ 1.00	106	+ 2:46	+ 1.00	95	+ 2:35	+ 1.00	69	+ 2:09	+ 1.00	74	+ 2:14
+ 1.15	107	+ 3:02	+ 1.15	97	+ 2:52	+ 1.15	70	+ 2:25	+ 1.15	75	+ 2:30
+ 1.30	107	+ 3:17	+ 1.30	98	+ 3:08	+ 1.30	71	+ 2:41	+ 1.30	75	+ 2:45
+ 1.45	108	+ 3:33	+ 1.45	100	+ 3:25	+ 1.45	73	+ 2:58	+ 1.45	76	+ 3:01
+ 2.00	109	+ 3:49	+ 2.00	101	+ 3:41	+ 2.00	74	+ 3:14	+ 2.00	77	+ 3:17
+ 2.15	108	+ 4:03	+ 2.15	101	+ 3:56	+ 2.15	74	+ 3:29	+ 2.15	76	+ 3:31
+ 2.30	107	+ 4:17	+ 2.30	100	+ 4:10	+ 2.30	74	+ 3:44	+ 2.30	75	+ 3:45
+ 2.45	106	+ 4:31	+ 2.45	100	+ 4:25	+ 2.45	74	+ 3:59	+ 2.45	75	+ 4:00
+ 3.00	104	+ 4:44	+ 3.00	99	+ 4:39	+ 3.00	74	+ 4:14	+ 3.00	74	+ 4:14
+ 3.15	103	+ 4:58	+ 3.15	97	+ 4:52	+ 3.15	73	+ 4:28	+ 3.15	73	+ 4:28
+ 3.30	101	+ 5:11	+ 3.30	95	+ 5:05	+ 3.30	72	+ 4:42	+ 3.30	73	+ 4:43
+ 3.45	99	+ 5:24	+ 3.45	93	+ 5:18	+ 3.45	71	+ 4:56	+ 3.45	72	+ 4:57
+ 4.00	97	+ 5:37	+ 4.00	91	+ 5:31	+ 4.00	71	+ 5:11	+ 4.00	71	+ 5:11
+ 4.15	95	+ 5:50	+ 4.15	88	+ 5:43	+ 4.15	70	+ 5:25	+ 4.15	70	+ 5:25
+ 4.30	93	- 5:57	+ 4.30	85	+ 5:55	+ 4.30	69	+ 5:39	+ 4.30	69	+ 5:39
+ 4.45	90	- 5:45	+ 4.45	82	- 5:53	+ 4.45	68	+ 5:53	+ 4.45	68	+ 5:53
+ 5.00	88	- 5:32	+ 5.00	79	- 5:41	+ 5.00	67	- 5:53	+ 5.00	67	- 5:53
+ 5.15	86	- 5:19	+ 5.15	77	- 5:28	+ 5.15	66	- 5:39	+ 5.15	66	- 5:39
+ 5.30	85	- 5:05	+ 5.30	76	- 5:14	+ 5.30	65	- 5:25	+ 5.30	65	- 5:25
+ 5.45	83	- 4:52	+ 5.45	75	- 5:00	+ 5.45	65	- 5:10	+ 5.45	64	- 5:11
+ 6.00	82	- 4:38	+ 6.00	74	- 4:46	+ 6.00	64	- 4:56	+ 6.00	63	- 4:57

Table I - Deben and Barrow Deep

Time to cover Sectors (in minutes) at 6.0 kts | All times relate to HW Sheerness | **Springs**

	I8			I7			I6			I5			I4			I3			I2			I1	
	Deben Landfall to Cork Sand			Cork Sand to Goldmer Gat			Goldmer Gat to Gunfleet Spit			Gunfleet Spit to Barrow No 4			Barrow No 4 to Barrow No 10			Barrow No 10 to North Oaze PHM			North Oaze PHM to Medway			Barrow No 10 to Red Sand	
Time	Duration	Time at End of Sector	Time	Duration	Time at End of Sector	Time	Duration	Time at End of Sector	Time	Duration	Time at End of Sector	Time	Duration	Time at End of Sector	Time	Duration	Time at End of Sector	Time	Duration	Time at End of Sector	Time	Duration	Time at End of Sector
- 6.00	**27**	**- 5:33**	**- 6.00**	**50**	**- 5:10**	**- 6.00**	**35**	**- 5:25**	**- 6.00**	**51**	**- 5:09**	**- 6.00**	**69**	**- 4:51**	**- 6.00**	**61**	**- 4:59**	**- 6.00**	**59**	**- 5:01**	**- 6.00**	**58**	**- 5:02**
- 5.45	27	- 5:18	- 5.45	49	- 4:56	- 5.45	34	- 5:11	- 5.45	50	- 4:55	- 5.45	67	- 4:38	- 5.45	58	- 4:47	- 5.45	57	- 4:48	- 5.45	56	- 4:49
- 5.30	26	- 5:04	- 5.30	49	- 4:41	- 5.30	33	- 4:57	- 5.30	49	- 4:41	- 5.30	65	- 4:25	- 5.30	56	- 4:34	- 5.30	55	- 4:35	- 5.30	54	- 4:36
- 5.15	26	- 4:49	- 5.15	49	- 4:26	- 5.15	32	- 4:43	- 5.15	48	- 4:27	- 5.15	63	- 4:12	- 5.15	54	- 4:21	- 5.15	54	- 4:21	- 5.15	53	- 4:22
- 5.00	**26**	**- 4:34**	**- 5.00**	**48**	**- 4:12**	**- 5.00**	**31**	**- 4:29**	**- 5.00**	**47**	**- 4:13**	**- 5.00**	**62**	**- 3:58**	**- 5.00**	**51**	**- 4:09**	**- 5.00**	**52**	**- 4:08**	**- 5.00**	**51**	**- 4:09**
- 4.45	26	- 4:19	- 4.45	49	- 3:56	- 4.45	31	- 4:14	- 4.45	48	- 3:57	- 4.45	61	- 3:44	- 4.45	51	- 3:54	- 4.45	52	- 3:53	- 4.45	51	- 3:54
- 4.30	27	- 4:03	- 4.30	49	- 3:41	- 4.30	31	- 3:59	- 4.30	48	- 3:42	- 4.30	61	- 3:29	- 4.30	50	- 3:40	- 4.30	51	- 3:39	- 4.30	50	- 3:40
- 4.15	27	- 3:48	- 4.15	49	- 3:26	- 4.15	30	- 3:45	- 4.15	48	- 3:27	- 4.15	61	- 3:14	- 4.15	50	- 3:25	- 4.15	50	- 3:25	- 4.15	50	- 3:25
- 4.00	**27**	**- 3:33**	**- 4.00**	**49**	**- 3:11**	**- 4.00**	**30**	**- 3:30**	**- 4.00**	**48**	**- 3:12**	**- 4.00**	**61**	**- 2:59**	**- 4.00**	**49**	**- 3:11**	**- 4.00**	**49**	**- 3:11**	**- 4.00**	**50**	**- 3:10**
- 3.45	27	- 3:18	- 3.45	51	- 2:54	- 3.45	30	- 3:15	- 3.45	49	- 2:56	- 3.45	62	- 2:43	- 3.45	49	- 2:56	- 3.45	49	- 2:56	- 3.45	51	- 2:54
- 3.30	27	- 3:03	- 3.30	52	- 2:38	- 3.30	31	- 2:59	- 3.30	50	- 2:40	- 3.30	63	- 2:27	- 3.30	50	- 2:40	- 3.30	49	- 2:41	- 3.30	51	- 2:39
- 3.15	27	- 2:48	- 3.15	53	- 2:22	- 3.15	31	- 2:44	- 3.15	50	- 2:25	- 3.15	64	- 2:11	- 3.15	50	- 2:25	- 3.15	49	- 2:26	- 3.15	52	- 2:23
- 3.00	**27**	**- 2:33**	**- 3.00**	**55**	**- 2:05**	**- 3.00**	**31**	**- 2:29**	**- 3.00**	**51**	**- 2:09**	**- 3.00**	**65**	**- 1:55**	**- 3.00**	**50**	**- 2:10**	**- 3.00**	**49**	**- 2:11**	**- 3.00**	**53**	**- 2:07**
- 2.45	28	- 2:17	- 2.45	57	- 1:48	- 2.45	32	- 2:13	- 2.45	53	- 1:52	- 2.45	66	- 1:39	- 2.45	51	- 1:54	- 2.45	50	- 1:55	- 2.45	54	- 1:51
- 2.30	28	- 2:02	- 2.30	59	- 1:31	- 2.30	33	- 1:57	- 2.30	54	- 1:36	- 2.30	68	- 1:22	- 2.30	53	- 1:37	- 2.30	50	- 1:40	- 2.30	54	- 1:36
- 2.15	29	- 1:46	- 2.15	61	- 1:14	- 2.15	34	- 1:41	- 2.15	55	- 1:20	- 2.15	70	- 1:05	- 2.15	54	- 1:21	- 2.15	51	- 1:24	- 2.15	55	- 1:20
- 2.00	**29**	**- 1:31**	**- 2.00**	**64**	**- 0:56**	**- 2.00**	**35**	**- 1:25**	**- 2.00**	**57**	**- 1:03**	**- 2.00**	**72**	**- 0:48**	**- 2.00**	**55**	**- 1:05**	**- 2.00**	**52**	**- 1:08**	**- 2.00**	**56**	**- 1:04**
- 1.45	29	- 1:16	- 1.45	66	- 0:39	- 1.45	37	- 1:08	- 1.45	59	- 0:46	- 1.45	74	- 0:31	- 1.45	58	- 0:47	- 1.45	53	- 0:52	- 1.45	57	- 0:48
- 1.30	29	- 1:01	- 1.30	69	- 0:21	- 1.30	38	- 0:52	- 1.30	61	- 0:29	- 1.30	77	- 0:13	- 1.30	61	- 0:29	- 1.30	54	- 0:36	- 1.30	58	- 0:32
- 1.15	29	- 0:46	- 1.15	72	- 0:03	- 1.15	40	- 0:35	- 1.15	63	- 0:12	- 1.15	80	+ 0:05	- 1.15	64	- 0:11	- 1.15	55	- 0:20	- 1.15	59	- 0:16
- 1.00	**30**	**- 0:30**	**- 1.00**	**74**	**+ 0:14**	**- 1.00**	**42**	**- 0:18**	**- 1.00**	**65**	**+ 0:05**	**- 1.00**	**82**	**+ 0:22**	**- 1.00**	**66**	**+ 0:06**	**- 1.00**	**57**	**- 0:03**	**- 1.00**	**61**	**+ 0:01**
- 0.45	30	- 0:15	- 0.45	76	+ 0:31	- 0.45	44	- 0:01	- 0.45	67	+ 0:22	- 0.45	87	+ 0:42	- 0.45	70	+ 0:25	- 0.45	58	+ 0:13	- 0.45	63	+ 0:18
- 0.30	30	HW	- 0.30	79	+ 0:49	- 0.30	46	+ 0:16	- 0.30	70	+ 0:40	- 0.30	91	+ 1:01	- 0.30	74	+ 0:44	- 0.30	60	+ 0:30	- 0.30	65	+ 0:35
- 0.15	31	+ 0:16	- 0.15	81	+ 1:06	- 0.15	48	+ 0:33	- 0.15	72	+ 0:57	- 0.15	95	+ 1:20	- 0.15	78	+ 1:03	- 0.15	62	+ 0:47	- 0.15	67	+ 0:52
HW	**31**	**+ 0:31**	**HW**	**83**	**+ 1:23**	**HW**	**50**	**+ 0:50**	**HW**	**75**	**+ 1:15**	**HW**	**99**	**+ 1:39**	**HW**	**82**	**+ 1:22**	**HW**	**64**	**+ 1:04**	**HW**	**69**	**+ 1:09**
+ 0.15	31	+ 0:46	+ 0.15	85	+ 1:40	+ 0.15	52	+ 1:07	+ 0.15	77	+ 1:32	+ 0.15	103	+ 1:58	+ 0.15	89	+ 1:44	+ 0.15	66	+ 1:21	+ 0.15	72	+ 1:27
+ 0.30	31	+ 1:01	+ 0.30	87	+ 1:57	+ 0.30	54	+ 1:24	+ 0.30	78	+ 1:48	+ 0.30	107	+ 2:17	+ 0.30	95	+ 2:05	+ 0.30	68	+ 1:38	+ 0.30	75	+ 1:45
+ 0.45	31	+ 1:16	+ 0.45	89	+ 2:14	+ 0.45	56	+ 1:41	+ 0.45	80	+ 2:05	+ 0.45	111	+ 2:36	+ 0.45	102	+ 2:27	+ 0.45	71	+ 1:56	+ 0.45	77	+ 2:02
+ 1.00	**31**	**+ 1:31**	**+ 1.00**	**90**	**+ 2:30**	**+ 1.00**	**59**	**+ 1:59**	**+ 1.00**	**82**	**+ 2:22**	**+ 1.00**	**115**	**+ 2:55**	**+ 1.00**	**108**	**+ 2:48**	**+ 1.00**	**73**	**+ 2:13**	**+ 1.00**	**80**	**+ 2:20**
+ 1.15	31	+ 1:46	+ 1.15	88	+ 2:43	+ 1.15	59	+ 2:14	+ 1.15	82	+ 2:37	+ 1.15	116	+ 3:11	+ 1.15	110	+ 3:05	+ 1.15	75	+ 2:30	+ 1.15	81	+ 2:36
+ 1.30	31	+ 2:01	+ 1.30	85	+ 2:55	+ 1.30	60	+ 2:30	+ 1.30	83	+ 2:53	+ 1.30	116	+ 3:26	+ 1.30	112	+ 3:22	+ 1.30	77	+ 2:47	+ 1.30	83	+ 2:53
+ 1.45	31	+ 2:16	+ 1.45	83	+ 3:08	+ 1.45	61	+ 2:46	+ 1.45	83	+ 3:08	+ 1.45	117	+ 3:42	+ 1.45	113	+ 3:38	+ 1.45	79	+ 3:04	+ 1.45	84	+ 3:09
+ 2.00	**31**	**+ 2:31**	**+ 2.00**	**81**	**+ 3:21**	**+ 2.00**	**62**	**+ 3:02**	**+ 2.00**	**83**	**+ 3:23**	**+ 2.00**	**118**	**+ 3:58**	**+ 2.00**	**115**	**+ 3:55**	**+ 2.00**	**81**	**+ 3:21**	**+ 2.00**	**85**	**+ 3:25**
+ 2.15	31	+ 2:46	+ 2.15	79	+ 3:34	+ 2.15	61	+ 3:16	+ 2.15	82	+ 3:37	+ 2.15	116	+ 4:11	+ 2.15	113	+ 4:08	+ 2.15	81	+ 3:36	+ 2.15	84	+ 3:39
+ 2.30	30	+ 3:00	+ 2.30	77	+ 3:47	+ 2.30	60	+ 3:30	+ 2.30	81	+ 3:51	+ 2.30	114	+ 4:24	+ 2.30	111	+ 4:21	+ 2.30	81	+ 3:51	+ 2.30	83	+ 3:53
+ 2.45	30	+ 3:15	+ 2.45	75	+ 4:00	+ 2.45	59	+ 3:44	+ 2.45	80	+ 4:05	+ 2.45	112	+ 4:37	+ 2.45	110	+ 4:35	+ 2.45	81	+ 4:06	+ 2.45	82	+ 4:07
+ 3.00	**30**	**+ 3:30**	**+ 3.00**	**73**	**+ 4:13**	**+ 3.00**	**58**	**+ 3:58**	**+ 3.00**	**78**	**+ 4:18**	**+ 3.00**	**111**	**+ 4:51**	**+ 3.00**	**108**	**+ 4:48**	**+ 3.00**	**81**	**+ 4:21**	**+ 3.00**	**81**	**+ 4:21**
+ 3.15	30	+ 3:45	+ 3.15	71	+ 4:26	+ 3.15	56	+ 4:11	+ 3.15	76	+ 4:31	+ 3.15	108	+ 5:03	+ 3.15	105	+ 5:00	+ 3.15	79	+ 4:34	+ 3.15	80	+ 4:35
+ 3.30	30	+ 4:00	+ 3.30	70	+ 4:40	+ 3.30	54	+ 4:24	+ 3.30	75	+ 4:45	+ 3.30	106	+ 5:16	+ 3.30	101	+ 5:11	+ 3.30	78	+ 4:48	+ 3.30	78	+ 4:48
+ 3.45	29	+ 4:14	+ 3.45	68	+ 4:53	+ 3.45	53	+ 4:38	+ 3.45	73	+ 4:58	+ 3.45	103	+ 5:28	+ 3.45	98	+ 5:23	+ 3.45	77	+ 5:02	+ 3.45	77	+ 5:02
+ 4.00	**29**	**+ 4:29**	**+ 4.00**	**67**	**+ 5:07**	**+ 4.00**	**51**	**+ 4:51**	**+ 4.00**	**71**	**+ 5:11**	**+ 4.00**	**100**	**+ 5:40**	**+ 4.00**	**95**	**+ 5:35**	**+ 4.00**	**75**	**+ 5:15**	**+ 4.00**	**75**	**+ 5:15**
+ 4.15	29	+ 4:44	+ 4.15	65	+ 5:20	+ 4.15	49	+ 5:04	+ 4.15	69	+ 5:24	+ 4.15	98	+ 5:53	+ 4.15	92	+ 5:47	+ 4.15	74	+ 5:29	+ 4.15	74	+ 5:29
+ 4.30	29	+ 4:59	+ 4.30	64	+ 5:34	+ 4.30	47	+ 5:17	+ 4.30	67	+ 5:37	+ 4.30	95	- 5:55	+ 4.30	89	+ 5:59	+ 4.30	72	+ 5:42	+ 4.30	72	+ 5:42
+ 4.45	29	+ 5:14	+ 4.45	63	+ 5:48	+ 4.45	45	+ 5:30	+ 4.45	65	+ 5:50	+ 4.45	92	- 5:43	+ 4.45	85	- 5:50	+ 4.45	71	+ 5:56	+ 4.45	70	+ 5:55
+ 5.00	**28**	**+ 5:28**	**+ 5.00**	**62**	**- 5:58**	**+ 5.00**	**44**	**+ 5:44**	**+ 5.00**	**63**	**- 5:57**	**+ 5.00**	**89**	**- 5:31**	**+ 5.00**	**82**	**- 5:38**	**+ 5.00**	**69**	**- 5:51**	**+ 5.00**	**68**	**- 5:52**
+ 5.15	28	+ 5:43	+ 5.15	60	- 5:45	+ 5.15	42	+ 5:57	+ 5.15	62	- 5:43	+ 5.15	87	- 5:18	+ 5.15	80	- 5:25	+ 5.15	68	- 5:37	+ 5.15	67	- 5:38
+ 5.30	28	+ 5:58	+ 5.30	58	- 5:32	+ 5.30	41	- 5:49	+ 5.30	60	- 5:30	+ 5.30	85	- 5:05	+ 5.30	78	- 5:12	+ 5.30	67	- 5:23	+ 5.30	66	- 5:24
+ 5.45	28	- 5:47	+ 5.45	56	- 5:19	+ 5.45	39	- 5:36	+ 5.45	59	- 5:16	+ 5.45	82	- 4:53	+ 5.45	76	- 4:59	+ 5.45	66	- 5:09	+ 5.45	65	- 5:10
+ 6.00	**28**	**- 5:32**	**+ 6.00**	**55**	**- 5:05**	**+ 6.00**	**38**	**- 5:22**	**+ 6.00**	**57**	**- 5:03**	**+ 6.00**	**80**	**- 4:40**	**+ 6.00**	**75**	**- 4:45**	**+ 6.00**	**65**	**- 4:55**	**+ 6.00**	**63**	**- 4:57**

SOUTH BOUND

Table I - Deben and Barrow Deep

Neaps — All times relate to HW Sheerness — **Time to cover Sectors (in minutes) at 7.0 Kts**

SOUTHBOUND

	I8			I7			I6			I5	
	Deben Landfall to Cork Sand			Cork Sand to Goldmer Gat			Goldmer Gat to Gunfleet Spit			Gunfleet Spit to Barrow No 4	
Time	Duration	Time at End of Sector	Time	Duration	Time at End of Sector	Time	Duration	Time at End of Sector	Time	Duration	Time at End of Sector
- 6.00	23	- 5:37	- 6.00	48	- 5:12	- 6.00	32	- 5:28	- 6.00	48	- 5:12
- 5.45	23	- 5:22	- 5.45	47	- 4:58	- 5.45	32	- 5:13	- 5.45	48	- 4:57
- 5.30	23	- 5:07	- 5.30	47	- 4:43	- 5.30	31	- 4:59	- 5.30	47	- 4:43
- 5.15	23	- 4:52	- 5.15	47	- 4:28	- 5.15	31	- 4:44	- 5.15	46	- 4:29
- 5.00	23	- 4:37	- 5.00	47	- 4:13	- 5.00	30	- 4:30	- 5.00	46	- 4:14
- 4.45	23	- 4:22	- 4.45	47	- 3:58	- 4.45	30	- 4:15	- 4.45	46	- 3:59
- 4.30	23	- 4:07	- 4.30	47	- 3:43	- 4.30	30	- 4:00	- 4.30	46	- 3:44
- 4.15	23	- 3:52	- 4.15	47	- 3:28	- 4.15	29	- 3:46	- 4.15	46	- 3:29
- 4.00	23	- 3:37	- 4.00	47	- 3:13	- 4.00	29	- 3:31	- 4.00	46	- 3:14
- 3.45	23	- 3:22	- 3.45	48	- 2:57	- 3.45	29	- 3:16	- 3.45	46	- 2:59
- 3.30	23	- 3:07	- 3.30	48	- 2:42	- 3.30	30	- 3:00	- 3.30	47	- 2:43
- 3.15	24	- 2:51	- 3.15	49	- 2:26	- 3.15	30	- 2:45	- 3.15	47	- 2:28
- 3.00	24	- 2:36	- 3.00	50	- 2:10	- 3.00	30	- 2:30	- 3.00	48	- 2:12
- 2.45	24	- 2:21	- 2.45	51	- 1:54	- 2.45	31	- 2:14	- 2.45	48	- 1:57
- 2.30	24	- 2:06	- 2.30	52	- 1:38	- 2.30	31	- 1:59	- 2.30	49	- 1:41
- 2.15	24	- 1:51	- 2.15	53	- 1:22	- 2.15	31	- 1:44	- 2.15	50	- 1:25
- 2.00	25	- 1:35	- 2.00	54	- 1:06	- 2.00	32	- 1:28	- 2.00	50	- 1:10
- 1.45	25	- 1:20	- 1.45	56	- 0:49	- 1.45	33	- 1:12	- 1.45	51	- 0:54
- 1.30	25	- 1:05	- 1.30	57	- 0:33	- 1.30	34	- 0:56	- 1.30	52	- 0:38
- 1.15	25	- 0:50	- 1.15	58	- 0:17	- 1.15	34	- 0:41	- 1.15	53	- 0:22
- 1.00	25	- 0:35	- 1.00	59	- 0:01	- 1.00	35	- 0:25	- 1.00	54	- 0:06
- 0.45	25	- 0:20	- 0.45	60	+ 0:15	- 0.45	36	- 0:09	- 0.45	55	+ 0:10
- 0.30	25	- 0:05	- 0.30	61	+ 0:31	- 0.30	37	+ 0:07	- 0.30	57	+ 0:27
- 0.15	25	+ 0:10	- 0.15	63	+ 0:48	- 0.15	38	+ 0:23	- 0.15	58	+ 0:43
HW	25	+ 0:25	HW	64	+ 1:04	HW	39	+ 0:39	HW	59	+ 0:59
+ 0.15	26	+ 0:41	+ 0.15	64	+ 1:19	+ 0.15	40	+ 0:55	+ 0.15	60	+ 1:15
+ 0.30	26	+ 0:56	+ 0.30	64	+ 1:34	+ 0.30	41	+ 1:11	+ 0.30	61	+ 1:31
+ 0.45	26	+ 1:11	+ 0.45	65	+ 1:50	+ 0.45	42	+ 1:27	+ 0.45	62	+ 1:47
+ 1.00	26	+ 1:26	+ 1.00	65	+ 2:05	+ 1.00	43	+ 1:43	+ 1.00	63	+ 2:03
+ 1.15	26	+ 1:41	+ 1.15	64	+ 2:19	+ 1.15	44	+ 1:59	+ 1.15	63	+ 2:18
+ 1.30	26	+ 1:56	+ 1.30	64	+ 2:34	+ 1.30	44	+ 2:14	+ 1.30	63	+ 2:33
+ 1.45	26	+ 2:11	+ 1.45	63	+ 2:48	+ 1.45	45	+ 2:30	+ 1.45	63	+ 2:48
+ 2.00	25	+ 2:25	+ 2.00	63	+ 3:03	+ 2.00	45	+ 2:45	+ 2.00	64	+ 3:04
+ 2.15	25	+ 2:40	+ 2.15	62	+ 3:17	+ 2.15	45	+ 3:00	+ 2.15	63	+ 3:18
+ 2.30	25	+ 2:55	+ 2.30	61	+ 3:31	+ 2.30	44	+ 3:14	+ 2.30	63	+ 3:33
+ 2.45	25	+ 3:10	+ 2.45	60	+ 3:45	+ 2.45	44	+ 3:29	+ 2.45	62	+ 3:47
+ 3.00	25	+ 3:25	+ 3.00	59	+ 3:59	+ 3.00	43	+ 3:43	+ 3.00	61	+ 4:01
+ 3.15	25	+ 3:40	+ 3.15	59	+ 4:14	+ 3.15	43	+ 3:58	+ 3.15	61	+ 4:16
+ 3.30	25	+ 3:55	+ 3.30	58	+ 4:28	+ 3.30	42	+ 4:12	+ 3.30	60	+ 4:30
+ 3.45	25	+ 4:10	+ 3.45	57	+ 4:42	+ 3.45	41	+ 4:26	+ 3.45	59	+ 4:44
+ 4.00	25	+ 4:25	+ 4.00	56	+ 4:56	+ 4.00	40	+ 4:40	+ 4.00	58	+ 4:58
+ 4.15	25	+ 4:40	+ 4.15	56	+ 5:11	+ 4.15	39	+ 4:54	+ 4.15	57	+ 5:12
+ 4.30	24	+ 4:54	+ 4.30	55	+ 5:25	+ 4.30	39	+ 5:09	+ 4.30	56	+ 5:26
+ 4.45	24	+ 5:09	+ 4.45	54	+ 5:39	+ 4.45	38	+ 5:23	+ 4.45	55	+ 5:40
+ 5.00	24	+ 5:24	+ 5.00	54	+ 5:54	+ 5.00	37	+ 5:37	+ 5.00	54	+ 5:54
+ 5.15	24	+ 5:39	+ 5.15	53	- 5:52	+ 5.15	36	+ 5:51	+ 5.15	53	- 5:52
+ 5.30	24	+ 5:54	+ 5.30	52	- 5:38	+ 5.30	35	- 5:55	+ 5.30	53	- 5:37
+ 5.45	24	- 5:51	+ 5.45	51	- 5:24	+ 5.45	35	- 5:40	+ 5.45	52	- 5:23
+ 6.00	24	- 5:36	+ 6.00	50	- 5:10	+ 6.00	34	- 5:26	+ 6.00	51	- 5:09

	I4			I3			I2			I1	
	Barrow No 4 to Barrow No 10			Barrow No 10 to North Oaze PHM			North Oaze PHM to Medway			Barrow No 10 to Red Sand	
Time	Duration	Time at End of Sector	Time	Duration	Time at End of Sector	Time	Duration	Time at End of Sector	Time	Duration	Time at End of Sector
- 6.00	64	- 4:56	- 6.00	56	- 5:04	- 6.00	52	- 5:08	- 6.00	52	- 5:08
- 5.45	63	- 4:42	- 5.45	55	- 4:50	- 5.45	51	- 4:54	- 5.45	51	- 4:54
- 5.30	62	- 4:28	- 5.30	54	- 4:36	- 5.30	50	- 4:40	- 5.30	50	- 4:40
- 5.15	61	- 4:14	- 5.15	52	- 4:23	- 5.15	49	- 4:26	- 5.15	49	- 4:26
- 5.00	60	- 4:00	- 5.00	51	- 4:09	- 5.00	49	- 4:11	- 5.00	48	- 4:12
- 4.45	60	- 3:45	- 4.45	50	- 3:55	- 4.45	48	- 3:57	- 4.45	48	- 3:57
- 4.30	60	- 3:30	- 4.30	50	- 3:40	- 4.30	48	- 3:42	- 4.30	48	- 3:42
- 4.15	60	- 3:15	- 4.15	50	- 3:25	- 4.15	47	- 3:28	- 4.15	47	- 3:28
- 4.00	60	- 3:00	- 4.00	49	- 3:11	- 4.00	47	- 3:13	- 4.00	47	- 3:13
- 3.45	60	- 2:45	- 3.45	49	- 2:56	- 3.45	47	- 2:58	- 3.45	48	- 2:57
- 3.30	60	- 2:30	- 3.30	49	- 2:41	- 3.30	47	- 2:43	- 3.30	48	- 2:42
- 3.15	61	- 2:14	- 3.15	50	- 2:25	- 3.15	47	- 2:28	- 3.15	48	- 2:27
- 3.00	61	- 1:59	- 3.00	50	- 2:10	- 3.00	47	- 2:13	- 3.00	49	- 2:11
- 2.45	62	- 1:43	- 2.45	51	- 1:54	- 2.45	47	- 1:58	- 2.45	49	- 1:56
- 2.30	63	- 1:27	- 2.30	51	- 1:39	- 2.30	47	- 1:43	- 2.30	50	- 1:40
- 2.15	64	- 1:11	- 2.15	52	- 1:23	- 2.15	48	- 1:27	- 2.15	50	- 1:25
- 2.00	65	- 0:55	- 2.00	53	- 1:07	- 2.00	48	- 1:12	- 2.00	51	- 1:09
- 1.45	67	- 0:38	- 1.45	54	- 0:51	- 1.45	49	- 0:56	- 1.45	51	- 0:54
- 1.30	68	- 0:22	- 1.30	56	- 0:34	- 1.30	49	- 0:41	- 1.30	52	- 0:38
- 1.15	69	- 0:06	- 1.15	57	- 0:18	- 1.15	50	- 0:25	- 1.15	52	- 0:23
- 1.00	71	+ 0:11	- 1.00	59	- 0:01	- 1.00	50	- 0:10	- 1.00	53	- 0:07
- 0.45	73	+ 0:28	- 0.45	61	+ 0:16	- 0.45	51	+ 0:06	- 0.45	54	+ 0:09
- 0.30	75	+ 0:45	- 0.30	63	+ 0:33	- 0.30	52	+ 0:22	- 0.30	55	+ 0:25
- 0.15	76	+ 1:01	- 0.15	65	+ 0:50	- 0.15	53	+ 0:38	- 0.15	56	+ 0:41
HW	78	+ 1:18	HW	67	+ 1:07	HW	54	+ 0:54	HW	57	+ 0:57
+ 0.15	80	+ 1:35	+ 0.15	69	+ 1:24	+ 0.15	55	+ 1:10	+ 0.15	58	+ 1:13
+ 0.30	82	+ 1:52	+ 0.30	71	+ 1:41	+ 0.30	56	+ 1:26	+ 0.30	59	+ 1:29
+ 0.45	84	+ 2:09	+ 0.45	73	+ 1:58	+ 0.45	57	+ 1:42	+ 0.45	60	+ 1:45
+ 1.00	85	+ 2:25	+ 1.00	75	+ 2:15	+ 1.00	58	+ 1:58	+ 1.00	62	+ 2:02
+ 1.15	87	+ 2:42	+ 1.15	76	+ 2:31	+ 1.15	59	+ 2:14	+ 1.15	62	+ 2:17
+ 1.30	88	+ 2:58	+ 1.30	76	+ 2:46	+ 1.30	60	+ 2:30	+ 1.30	63	+ 2:33
+ 1.45	90	+ 3:15	+ 1.45	77	+ 3:02	+ 1.45	61	+ 2:46	+ 1.45	63	+ 2:48
+ 2.00	91	+ 3:31	+ 2.00	78	+ 3:18	+ 2.00	62	+ 3:02	+ 2.00	64	+ 3:04
+ 2.15	90	+ 3:45	+ 2.15	78	+ 3:33	+ 2.15	62	+ 3:17	+ 2.15	64	+ 3:19
+ 2.30	88	+ 3:58	+ 2.30	78	+ 3:48	+ 2.30	62	+ 3:32	+ 2.30	63	+ 3:33
+ 2.45	87	+ 4:12	+ 2.45	77	+ 4:02	+ 2.45	62	+ 3:47	+ 2.45	63	+ 3:48
+ 3.00	85	+ 4:25	+ 3.00	77	+ 4:17	+ 3.00	62	+ 4:02	+ 3.00	62	+ 4:02
+ 3.15	84	+ 4:39	+ 3.15	76	+ 4:31	+ 3.15	61	+ 4:16	+ 3.15	62	+ 4:17
+ 3.30	83	+ 4:53	+ 3.30	75	+ 4:45	+ 3.30	61	+ 4:31	+ 3.30	61	+ 4:31
+ 3.45	82	+ 5:07	+ 3.45	74	+ 4:59	+ 3.45	60	+ 4:45	+ 3.45	61	+ 4:46
+ 4.00	81	+ 5:21	+ 4.00	73	+ 5:13	+ 4.00	60	+ 5:00	+ 4.00	60	+ 5:00
+ 4.15	79	+ 5:34	+ 4.15	71	+ 5:26	+ 4.15	59	+ 5:14	+ 4.15	59	+ 5:14
+ 4.30	78	+ 5:48	+ 4.30	70	+ 5:40	+ 4.30	58	+ 5:28	+ 4.30	59	+ 5:29
+ 4.45	77	- 5:58	+ 4.45	68	+ 5:53	+ 4.45	58	+ 5:43	+ 4.45	58	+ 5:43
+ 5.00	75	- 5:45	+ 5.00	67	- 5:53	+ 5.00	57	+ 5:57	+ 5.00	57	+ 5:57
+ 5.15	74	- 5:31	+ 5.15	66	- 5:39	+ 5.15	56	- 5:49	+ 5.15	56	- 5:49
+ 5.30	73	- 5:17	+ 5.30	65	- 5:25	+ 5.30	56	- 5:34	+ 5.30	56	- 5:34
+ 5.45	72	- 5:03	+ 5.45	64	- 5:11	+ 5.45	55	- 5:20	+ 5.45	55	- 5:20
+ 6.00	70	- 4:50	+ 6.00	63	- 4:57	+ 6.00	55	- 5:05	+ 6.00	54	- 5:06

Table I - Deben and Barrow Deep

Time to cover Sectors (in minutes) at 7.0 kts — All times relate to HW Sheerness — **Springs**

	I8 Deben Landfall to Cork Sand			I7 Cork Sand to Goldmer Gat			I6 Goldmer Gat to Gunfleet Spit			I5 Gunfleet Spit to Barrow No 4			I4 Barrow No 4 to Barrow No 10			I3 Barrow No 10 to North Oaze PHM			I2 North Oaze PHM to Medway			I1 Barrow No 10 to Red Sand	
Time	Duration	Time at End of Sector	Time	Duration	Time at End of Sector	Time	Duration	Time at End of Sector	Time	Duration	Time at End of Sector	Time	Duration	Time at End of Sector	Time	Duration	Time at End of Sector	Time	Duration	Time at End of Sector	Time	Duration	Time at End of Sector
- 6.00	**23**	**- 5:37**	**- 6.00**	**44**	**- 5:16**	**- 6.00**	**31**	**- 5:29**	**- 6.00**	**46**	**- 5:14**	**- 6.00**	**61**	**- 4:59**	**- 6.00**	**54**	**- 5:06**	**- 6.00**	**51**	**- 5:09**	**- 6.00**	**51**	**- 5:09**
- 5.45	23	- 5:22	- 5.45	44	- 5:01	- 5.45	30	- 5:15	- 5.45	45	- 5:00	- 5.45	60	- 4:45	- 5.45	53	- 4:52	- 5.45	50	- 4:55	- 5.45	49	- 4:56
- 5.30	23	- 5:07	- 5.30	44	- 4:46	- 5.30	30	- 5:00	- 5.30	44	- 4:46	- 5.30	59	- 4:31	- 5.30	51	- 4:39	- 5.30	49	- 4:41	- 5.30	48	- 4:42
- 5.15	23	- 4:52	- 5.15	44	- 4:31	- 5.15	29	- 4:46	- 5.15	43	- 4:32	- 5.15	57	- 4:18	- 5.15	49	- 4:26	- 5.15	47	- 4:28	- 5.15	47	- 4:28
- 5.00	**23**	**- 4:37**	**- 5.00**	**43**	**- 4:17**	**- 5.00**	**28**	**- 4:32**	**- 5.00**	**43**	**- 4:17**	**- 5.00**	**56**	**- 4:04**	**- 5.00**	**47**	**- 4:13**	**- 5.00**	**46**	**- 4:14**	**- 5.00**	**45**	**- 4:15**
- 4.45	23	- 4:22	- 4.45	43	- 4:02	- 4.45	27	- 4:18	- 4.45	43	- 4:02	- 4.45	55	- 3:50	- 4.45	46	- 3:59	- 4.45	46	- 3:59	- 4.45	45	- 4:00
- 4.30	23	- 4:07	- 4.30	44	- 3:46	- 4.30	27	- 4:03	- 4.30	43	- 3:47	- 4.30	55	- 3:35	- 4.30	46	- 3:44	- 4.30	45	- 3:45	- 4.30	45	- 3:45
- 4.15	23	- 3:52	- 4.15	44	- 3:31	- 4.15	26	- 3:49	- 4.15	43	- 3:32	- 4.15	55	- 3:20	- 4.15	45	- 3:30	- 4.15	45	- 3:30	- 4.15	45	- 3:30
- 4.00	**23**	**- 3:37**	**- 4.00**	**44**	**- 3:16**	**- 4.00**	**26**	**- 3:34**	**- 4.00**	**42**	**- 3:18**	**- 4.00**	**55**	**- 3:05**	**- 4.00**	**45**	**- 3:15**	**- 4.00**	**44**	**- 3:16**	**- 4.00**	**44**	**- 3:16**
- 3.45	23	- 3:22	- 3.45	45	- 3:00	- 3.45	26	- 3:19	- 3.45	43	- 3:02	- 3.45	56	- 2:49	- 3.45	45	- 3:00	- 3.45	44	- 3:01	- 3.45	45	- 3:00
- 3.30	23	- 3:07	- 3.30	45	- 2:45	- 3.30	26	- 3:04	- 3.30	44	- 2:46	- 3.30	56	- 2:34	- 3.30	45	- 2:45	- 3.30	44	- 2:46	- 3.30	45	- 2:45
- 3.15	23	- 2:52	- 3.15	46	- 2:29	- 3.15	27	- 2:48	- 3.15	44	- 2:31	- 3.15	57	- 2:18	- 3.15	44	- 2:31	- 3.15	44	- 2:31	- 3.15	46	- 2:29
- 3.00	**23**	**- 2:37**	**- 3.00**	**47**	**- 2:13**	**- 3.00**	**27**	**- 2:33**	**- 3.00**	**45**	**- 2:15**	**- 3.00**	**57**	**- 2:03**	**- 3.00**	**44**	**- 2:16**	**- 3.00**	**44**	**- 2:16**	**- 3.00**	**46**	**- 2:14**
- 2.45	24	- 2:21	- 2.45	49	- 1:56	- 2.45	28	- 2:17	- 2.45	46	- 1:59	- 2.45	59	- 1:46	- 2.45	45	- 2:00	- 2.45	44	- 2:01	- 2.45	47	- 1:58
- 2.30	24	- 2:06	- 2.30	51	- 1:39	- 2.30	29	- 2:01	- 2.30	47	- 1:43	- 2.30	60	- 1:30	- 2.30	46	- 1:44	- 2.30	44	- 1:46	- 2.30	47	- 1:43
- 2.15	24	- 1:51	- 2.15	52	- 1:23	- 2.15	29	- 1:46	- 2.15	48	- 1:27	- 2.15	61	- 1:14	- 2.15	47	- 1:28	- 2.15	45	- 1:30	- 2.15	48	- 1:27
- 2.00	**25**	**- 1:35**	**- 2.00**	**54**	**- 1:06**	**- 2.00**	**30**	**- 1:30**	**- 2.00**	**49**	**- 1:11**	**- 2.00**	**62**	**- 0:58**	**- 2.00**	**48**	**- 1:12**	**- 2.00**	**45**	**- 1:15**	**- 2.00**	**49**	**- 1:11**
- 1.45	25	- 1:20	- 1.45	56	- 0:49	- 1.45	31	- 1:14	- 1.45	50	- 0:55	- 1.45	64	- 0:41	- 1.45	50	- 0:55	- 1.45	46	- 0:59	- 1.45	50	- 0:55
- 1.30	25	- 1:05	- 1.30	58	- 0:32	- 1.30	33	- 0:57	- 1.30	52	- 0:38	- 1.30	66	- 0:24	- 1.30	53	- 0:37	- 1.30	47	- 0:43	- 1.30	50	- 0:40
- 1.15	25	- 0:50	- 1.15	60	- 0:15	- 1.15	34	- 0:41	- 1.15	53	- 0:22	- 1.15	68	- 0:07	- 1.15	55	- 0:20	- 1.15	48	- 0:27	- 1.15	51	- 0:24
- 1.00	**25**	**- 0:35**	**- 1.00**	**62**	**+ 0:02**	**- 1.00**	**35**	**- 0:25**	**- 1.00**	**55**	**- 0:05**	**- 1.00**	**70**	**+ 0:10**	**- 1.00**	**57**	**- 0:03**	**- 1.00**	**49**	**- 0:11**	**- 1.00**	**52**	**- 0:08**
- 0.45	26	- 0:19	- 0.45	63	+ 0:18	- 0.45	37	- 0:08	- 0.45	56	+ 0:11	- 0.45	73	+ 0:28	- 0.45	60	+ 0:15	- 0.45	50	+ 0:05	- 0.45	53	+ 0:08
- 0.30	26	- 0:04	- 0.30	65	+ 0:35	- 0.30	38	+ 0:08	- 0.30	58	+ 0:28	- 0.30	76	+ 0:46	- 0.30	63	+ 0:33	- 0.30	51	+ 0:21	- 0.30	55	+ 0:25
- 0.15	26	+ 0:11	- 0.15	67	+ 0:52	- 0.15	39	+ 0:24	- 0.15	60	+ 0:45	- 0.15	79	+ 1:04	- 0.15	66	+ 0:51	- 0.15	53	+ 0:38	- 0.15	56	+ 0:41
HW	**26**	**+ 0:26**	**HW**	**69**	**+ 1:09**	**HW**	**41**	**+ 0:41**	**HW**	**62**	**+ 1:02**	**HW**	**82**	**+ 1:22**	**HW**	**69**	**+ 1:09**	**HW**	**54**	**+ 0:54**	**HW**	**58**	**+ 0:58**
+ 0.15	26	+ 0:41	+ 0.15	69	+ 1:24	+ 0.15	43	+ 0:58	+ 0.15	63	+ 1:18	+ 0.15	85	+ 1:40	+ 0.15	73	+ 1:28	+ 0.15	56	+ 1:11	+ 0.15	60	+ 1:15
+ 0.30	27	+ 0:57	+ 0.30	70	+ 1:40	+ 0.30	44	+ 1:14	+ 0.30	65	+ 1:35	+ 0.30	88	+ 1:58	+ 0.30	76	+ 1:46	+ 0.30	57	+ 1:27	+ 0.30	62	+ 1:32
+ 0.45	27	+ 1:12	+ 0.45	70	+ 1:55	+ 0.45	46	+ 1:31	+ 0.45	66	+ 1:51	+ 0.45	91	+ 2:16	+ 0.45	80	+ 2:05	+ 0.45	59	+ 1:44	+ 0.45	64	+ 1:49
+ 1.00	**27**	**+ 1:27**	**+ 1.00**	**71**	**+ 2:11**	**+ 1.00**	**48**	**+ 1:48**	**+ 1.00**	**68**	**+ 2:08**	**+ 1.00**	**94**	**+ 2:34**	**+ 1.00**	**83**	**+ 2:23**	**+ 1.00**	**61**	**+ 2:01**	**+ 1.00**	**66**	**+ 2:06**
+ 1.15	27	+ 1:42	+ 1.15	70	+ 2:25	+ 1.15	48	+ 2:03	+ 1.15	68	+ 2:23	+ 1.15	95	+ 2:50	+ 1.15	86	+ 2:41	+ 1.15	62	+ 2:17	+ 1.15	67	+ 2:22
+ 1.30	26	+ 1:56	+ 1.30	69	+ 2:39	+ 1.30	49	+ 2:19	+ 1.30	68	+ 2:38	+ 1.30	96	+ 3:06	+ 1.30	88	+ 2:58	+ 1.30	64	+ 2:34	+ 1.30	68	+ 2:38
+ 1.45	26	+ 2:11	+ 1.45	68	+ 2:53	+ 1.45	50	+ 2:35	+ 1.45	68	+ 2:53	+ 1.45	97	+ 3:22	+ 1.45	91	+ 3:16	+ 1.45	65	+ 2:50	+ 1.45	69	+ 2:54
+ 2.00	**26**	**+ 2:26**	**+ 2.00**	**67**	**+ 3:07**	**+ 2.00**	**51**	**+ 2:51**	**+ 2.00**	**69**	**+ 3:09**	**+ 2.00**	**97**	**+ 3:37**	**+ 2.00**	**94**	**+ 3:34**	**+ 2.00**	**67**	**+ 3:07**	**+ 2.00**	**70**	**+ 3:10**
+ 2.15	26	+ 2:41	+ 2.15	66	+ 3:21	+ 2.15	50	+ 3:05	+ 2.15	68	+ 3:23	+ 2.15	96	+ 3:51	+ 2.15	93	+ 3:48	+ 2.15	67	+ 3:22	+ 2.15	69	+ 3:24
+ 2.30	26	+ 2:56	+ 2.30	65	+ 3:35	+ 2.30	49	+ 3:19	+ 2.30	67	+ 3:37	+ 2.30	95	+ 4:05	+ 2.30	92	+ 4:02	+ 2.30	67	+ 3:37	+ 2.30	69	+ 3:39
+ 2.45	26	+ 3:11	+ 2.45	63	+ 3:48	+ 2.45	48	+ 3:33	+ 2.45	66	+ 3:51	+ 2.45	94	+ 4:19	+ 2.45	91	+ 4:16	+ 2.45	67	+ 3:52	+ 2.45	68	+ 3:53
+ 3.00	**26**	**+ 3:26**	**+ 3.00**	**62**	**+ 4:02**	**+ 3.00**	**48**	**+ 3:48**	**+ 3.00**	**65**	**+ 4:05**	**+ 3.00**	**93**	**+ 4:33**	**+ 3.00**	**90**	**+ 4:30**	**+ 3.00**	**67**	**+ 4:07**	**+ 3.00**	**68**	**+ 4:08**
+ 3.15	25	+ 3:40	+ 3.15	61	+ 4:16	+ 3.15	46	+ 4:01	+ 3.15	64	+ 4:19	+ 3.15	91	+ 4:46	+ 3.15	87	+ 4:42	+ 3.15	66	+ 4:21	+ 3.15	66	+ 4:21
+ 3.30	25	+ 3:55	+ 3.30	59	+ 4:29	+ 3.30	45	+ 4:15	+ 3.30	63	+ 4:33	+ 3.30	89	+ 4:59	+ 3.30	84	+ 4:54	+ 3.30	65	+ 4:35	+ 3.30	65	+ 4:35
+ 3.45	25	+ 4:10	+ 3.45	58	+ 4:43	+ 3.45	44	+ 4:29	+ 3.45	61	+ 4:46	+ 3.45	87	+ 5:12	+ 3.45	81	+ 5:06	+ 3.45	64	+ 4:49	+ 3.45	64	+ 4:49
+ 4.00	**25**	**+ 4:25**	**+ 4.00**	**57**	**+ 4:57**	**+ 4.00**	**43**	**+ 4:43**	**+ 4.00**	**60**	**+ 5:00**	**+ 4.00**	**84**	**+ 5:24**	**+ 4.00**	**78**	**+ 5:18**	**+ 4.00**	**63**	**+ 5:03**	**+ 4.00**	**63**	**+ 5:03**
+ 4.15	25	+ 4:40	+ 4.15	56	+ 5:11	+ 4.15	42	+ 4:57	+ 4.15	59	+ 5:14	+ 4.15	82	+ 5:37	+ 4.15	76	+ 5:31	+ 4.15	62	+ 5:17	+ 4.15	62	+ 5:17
+ 4.30	25	+ 4:55	+ 4.30	55	+ 5:25	+ 4.30	40	+ 5:10	+ 4.30	57	+ 5:27	+ 4.30	80	+ 5:50	+ 4.30	74	+ 5:44	+ 4.30	61	+ 5:31	+ 4.30	61	+ 5:31
+ 4.45	24	+ 5:09	+ 4.45	54	+ 5:39	+ 4.45	39	+ 5:24	+ 4.45	56	+ 5:41	+ 4.45	78	- 5:57	+ 4.45	72	+ 5:57	+ 4.45	60	+ 5:45	+ 4.45	60	+ 5:45
+ 5.00	**24**	**+ 5:24**	**+ 5.00**	**53**	**+ 5:53**	**+ 5.00**	**38**	**+ 5:38**	**+ 5.00**	**54**	**+ 5:54**	**+ 5.00**	**76**	**- 5:44**	**+ 5.00**	**70**	**- 5:50**	**+ 5.00**	**59**	**+ 5:59**	**+ 5.00**	**58**	**+ 5:58**
+ 5.15	24	+ 5:39	+ 5.15	52	- 5:53	+ 5.15	37	+ 5:52	+ 5.15	53	- 5:52	+ 5.15	75	- 5:30	+ 5.15	68	- 5:37	+ 5.15	58	- 5:47	+ 5.15	57	- 5:48
+ 5.30	24	+ 5:54	+ 5.30	51	- 5:39	+ 5.30	35	- 5:55	+ 5.30	52	- 5:38	+ 5.30	73	- 5:17	+ 5.30	67	- 5:23	+ 5.30	57	- 5:33	+ 5.30	56	- 5:34
+ 5.45	24	- 5:51	+ 5.45	50	- 5:25	+ 5.45	34	- 5:41	+ 5.45	51	- 5:24	+ 5.45	71	- 5:04	+ 5.45	65	- 5:10	+ 5.45	56	- 5:19	+ 5.45	55	- 5:20
+ 6.00	**24**	**- 5:36**	**+ 6.00**	**48**	**- 5:12**	**+ 6.00**	**33**	**- 5:27**	**+ 6.00**	**50**	**- 5:10**	**+ 6.00**	**69**	**- 4:51**	**+ 6.00**	**64**	**- 4:56**	**+ 6.00**	**55**	**- 5:05**	**+ 6.00**	**54**	**- 5:06**

SOUTH BOUND

Table J - Suffolk to Essex Rivers, Sea Reach to North Oaze

Neaps | All times relate to HW Sheerness | **Time to cover Sectors (in minutes) at 4.0 Kts**

SOUTH BOUND

	J8			J7			J6			J5			J4			J3			J2			J1	
	Spitway to Crouch			North Oaze to Sea Reach No 1			Cork Sand Bcn to NE Gunfleet			Deben Landfall to The Naze			The Naze to Holland-on-sea			Holland-on-sea to Colne			Colne to Blackwater			The Naze to the Spitway	
Time	Duration	Time at End of Sector	Time	Duration	Time at End of Sector	Time	Duration	Time at End of Sector	Time	Duration	Time at End of Sector	Time	Duration	Time at End of Sector	Time	Duration	Time at End of Sector	Time	Duration	Time at End of Sector	Time	Duration	Time at End of Sector
- 6.00	56	- 5:04	- 6.00	47	- 5:13	- 6.00	67	- 4:53	- 6.00	81	- 4:39	- 6.00	64	- 4:56	- 6.00	100	- 4:20	- 6.00	57	- 5:03	- 6.00	143	- 3:37
- 5.45	54	- 4:51	- 5.45	45	- 5:00	- 5.45	67	- 4:38	- 5.45	80	- 4:25	- 5.45	63	- 4:42	- 5.45	98	- 4:07	- 5.45	56	- 4:49	- 5.45	142	- 3:23
- 5.30	53	- 4:37	- 5.30	44	- 4:46	- 5.30	67	- 4:23	- 5.30	80	- 4:10	- 5.30	62	- 4:28	- 5.30	96	- 3:54	- 5.30	55	- 4:35	- 5.30	141	- 3:09
- 5.15	51	- 4:24	- 5.15	43	- 4:32	- 5.15	66	- 4:09	- 5.15	80	- 3:55	- 5.15	61	- 4:14	- 5.15	94	- 3:41	- 5.15	54	- 4:21	- 5.15	140	- 2:55
- 5.00	50	- 4:10	- 5.00	41	- 4:19	- 5.00	66	- 3:54	- 5.00	80	- 3:40	- 5.00	60	- 4:00	- 5.00	93	- 3:27	- 5.00	53	- 4:07	- 5.00	139	- 2:41
- 4.45	50	- 3:55	- 4.45	41	- 4:04	- 4.45	67	- 3:38	- 4.45	81	- 3:24	- 4.45	60	- 3:45	- 4.45	92	- 3:13	- 4.45	52	- 3:53	- 4.45	140	- 2:25
- 4.30	50	- 3:40	- 4.30	40	- 3:50	- 4.30	67	- 3:23	- 4.30	82	- 3:08	- 4.30	60	- 3:30	- 4.30	92	- 2:58	- 4.30	52	- 3:38	- 4.30	141	- 2:09
- 4.15	49	- 3:26	- 4.15	40	- 3:35	- 4.15	68	- 3:07	- 4.15	83	- 2:52	- 4.15	60	- 3:15	- 4.15	92	- 2:43	- 4.15	51	- 3:24	- 4.15	142	- 1:53
- 4.00	49	- 3:11	- 4.00	39	- 3:21	- 4.00	69	- 2:51	- 4.00	83	- 2:37	- 4.00	60	- 3:00	- 4.00	91	- 2:29	- 4.00	51	- 3:09	- 4.00	143	- 1:37
- 3.45	50	- 2:55	- 3.45	39	- 3:06	- 3.45	71	- 2:34	- 3.45	85	- 2:20	- 3.45	61	- 2:44	- 3.45	92	- 2:13	- 3.45	51	- 2:54	- 3.45	146	- 1:19
- 3.30	50	- 2:40	- 3.30	39	- 2:51	- 3.30	73	- 2:17	- 3.30	86	- 2:04	- 3.30	62	- 2:28	- 3.30	92	- 1:58	- 3.30	51	- 2:39	- 3.30	150	- 1:00
- 3.15	51	- 2:24	- 3.15	39	- 2:36	- 3.15	75	- 2:00	- 3.15	88	- 1:47	- 3.15	63	- 2:12	- 3.15	93	- 1:42	- 3.15	51	- 2:24	- 3.15	153	- 0:42
- 3.00	51	- 2:09	- 3.00	39	- 2:21	- 3.00	77	- 1:43	- 3.00	89	- 1:31	- 3.00	63	- 1:57	- 3.00	94	- 1:26	- 3.00	51	- 2:09	- 3.00	156	- 0:24
- 2.45	52	- 1:53	- 2.45	39	- 2:06	- 2.45	79	- 1:26	- 2.45	92	- 1:13	- 2.45	65	- 1:40	- 2.45	96	- 1:09	- 2.45	52	- 1:53	- 2.45	162	- 0:03
- 2.30	53	- 1:37	- 2.30	39	- 1:51	- 2.30	82	- 1:08	- 2.30	94	- 0:56	- 2.30	66	- 1:24	- 2.30	99	- 0:51	- 2.30	52	- 1:38	- 2.30	169	+ 0:19
- 2.15	54	- 1:21	- 2.15	40	- 1:35	- 2.15	85	- 0:50	- 2.15	96	- 0:39	- 2.15	68	- 1:07	- 2.15	102	- 0:33	- 2.15	53	- 1:22	- 2.15	175	+ 0:40
- 2.00	55	- 1:05	- 2.00	40	- 1:20	- 2.00	87	- 0:33	- 2.00	99	- 0:21	- 2.00	69	- 0:51	- 2.00	105	- 0:15	- 2.00	54	- 1:06	- 2.00	181	+ 1:01
- 1.45	57	- 0:48	- 1.45	41	- 1:04	- 1.45	91	- 0:14	- 1.45	102	- 0:03	- 1.45	72	- 0:33	- 1.45	112	+ 0:07	- 1.45	56	- 0:49	- 1.45	191	+ 1:26
- 1.30	60	- 0:30	- 1.30	42	- 0:48	- 1.30	95	+ 0:05	- 1.30	106	+ 0:16	- 1.30	75	- 0:15	- 1.30	118	+ 0:28	- 1.30	59	- 0:31	- 1.30	202	+ 1:52
- 1.15	62	- 0:13	- 1.15	42	- 0:33	- 1.15	99	+ 0:24	- 1.15	110	+ 0:35	- 1.15	77	+ 0:02	- 1.15	125	+ 0:50	- 1.15	61	- 0:14	- 1.15	212	+ 2:17
- 1.00	64	+ 0:04	- 1.00	43	- 0:17	- 1.00	103	+ 0:43	- 1.00	114	+ 0:54	- 1.00	80	+ 0:20	- 1.00	132	+ 1:12	- 1.00	64	+ 0:04	- 1.00	222	+ 2:42
- 0.45	67	+ 0:22	- 0.45	44	- 0:01	- 0.45	106	+ 1:01	- 0.45	116	+ 1:11	- 0.45	86	+ 0:41	- 0.45	141	+ 1:36	- 0.45	67	+ 0:22	- 0.45	227	+ 3:02
- 0.30	70	+ 0:40	- 0.30	46	+ 0:16	- 0.30	110	+ 1:20	- 0.30	119	+ 1:29	- 0.30	91	+ 1:01	- 0.30	150	+ 2:00	- 0.30	70	+ 0:40	- 0.30	232	+ 3:22
- 0.15	73	+ 0:58	- 0.15	47	+ 0:32	- 0.15	113	+ 1:38	- 0.15	122	+ 1:47	- 0.15	97	+ 1:22	- 0.15	160	+ 2:25	- 0.15	74	+ 0:59	- 0.15	236	+ 3:41
HW	76	+ 1:16	HW	48	+ 0:48	HW	117	+ 1:57	HW	124	+ 2:04	HW	103	+ 1:43	HW	169	+ 2:49	HW	77	+ 1:17	HW	241	+ 4:01
+ 0.15	81	+ 1:36	+ 0.15	50	+ 1:05	+ 0.15	117	+ 2:12	+ 0.15	124	+ 2:19	+ 0.15	106	+ 2:01	+ 0.15	171	+ 3:06	+ 0.15	78	+ 1:33	+ 0.15	241	+ 4:16
+ 0.30	86	+ 1:56	+ 0.30	52	+ 1:22	+ 0.30	117	+ 2:27	+ 0.30	123	+ 2:33	+ 0.30	109	+ 2:19	+ 0.30	173	+ 3:23	+ 0.30	80	+ 1:50	+ 0.30	240	+ 4:30
+ 0.45	91	+ 2:16	+ 0.45	54	+ 1:39	+ 0.45	117	+ 2:42	+ 0.45	122	+ 2:47	+ 0.45	112	+ 2:37	+ 0.45	175	+ 3:40	+ 0.45	81	+ 2:06	+ 0.45	240	+ 4:45
+ 1.00	96	+ 2:36	+ 1.00	55	+ 1:55	+ 1.00	117	+ 2:57	+ 1.00	122	+ 3:02	+ 1.00	115	+ 2:55	+ 1.00	177	+ 3:57	+ 1.00	83	+ 2:23	+ 1.00	240	+ 5:00
+ 1.15	96	+ 2:51	+ 1.15	57	+ 2:12	+ 1.15	115	+ 3:10	+ 1.15	120	+ 3:15	+ 1.15	114	+ 3:09	+ 1.15	175	+ 4:10	+ 1.15	83	+ 2:38	+ 1.15	236	+ 5:11
+ 1.30	96	+ 3:06	+ 1.30	59	+ 2:29	+ 1.30	113	+ 3:23	+ 1.30	119	+ 3:29	+ 1.30	112	+ 3:22	+ 1.30	172	+ 4:22	+ 1.30	82	+ 2:52	+ 1.30	232	+ 5:22
+ 1.45	97	+ 3:22	+ 1.45	60	+ 2:45	+ 1.45	111	+ 3:36	+ 1.45	117	+ 3:42	+ 1.45	111	+ 3:36	+ 1.45	170	+ 4:35	+ 1.45	82	+ 3:07	+ 1.45	229	+ 5:34
+ 2.00	97	+ 3:37	+ 2.00	62	+ 3:02	+ 2.00	108	+ 3:48	+ 2.00	115	+ 3:55	+ 2.00	110	+ 3:50	+ 2.00	167	+ 4:47	+ 2.00	82	+ 3:22	+ 2.00	225	+ 5:45
+ 2.15	95	+ 3:50	+ 2.15	62	+ 3:17	+ 2.15	106	+ 4:01	+ 2.15	113	+ 4:08	+ 2.15	107	+ 4:02	+ 2.15	163	+ 4:58	+ 2.15	80	+ 3:35	+ 2.15	220	+ 5:55
+ 2.30	94	+ 4:04	+ 2.30	62	+ 3:32	+ 2.30	103	+ 4:13	+ 2.30	111	+ 4:21	+ 2.30	104	+ 4:14	+ 2.30	160	+ 5:10	+ 2.30	79	+ 3:49	+ 2.30	216	- 5:54
+ 2.45	93	+ 4:18	+ 2.45	62	+ 3:47	+ 2.45	100	+ 4:25	+ 2.45	109	+ 4:34	+ 2.45	102	+ 4:27	+ 2.45	156	+ 5:21	+ 2.45	77	+ 4:02	+ 2.45	211	- 5:44
+ 3.00	91	+ 4:31	+ 3.00	63	+ 4:03	+ 3.00	97	+ 4:37	+ 3.00	107	+ 4:47	+ 3.00	99	+ 4:39	+ 3.00	153	+ 5:33	+ 3.00	76	+ 4:16	+ 3.00	207	- 5:33
+ 3.15	87	+ 4:42	+ 3.15	62	+ 4:17	+ 3.15	95	+ 4:50	+ 3.15	105	+ 5:00	+ 3.15	97	+ 4:52	+ 3.15	149	+ 5:44	+ 3.15	74	+ 4:29	+ 3.15	202	- 5:23
+ 3.30	84	+ 4:54	+ 3.30	61	+ 4:31	+ 3.30	92	+ 5:02	+ 3.30	103	+ 5:13	+ 3.30	95	+ 5:05	+ 3.30	146	+ 5:56	+ 3.30	73	+ 4:43	+ 3.30	198	- 5:12
+ 3.45	80	+ 5:05	+ 3.45	60	+ 4:45	+ 3.45	90	+ 5:15	+ 3.45	101	+ 5:26	+ 3.45	93	+ 5:18	+ 3.45	142	- 5:53	+ 3.45	72	+ 4:57	+ 3.45	194	- 5:01
+ 4.00	76	+ 5:16	+ 4.00	59	+ 4:59	+ 4.00	87	+ 5:27	+ 4.00	99	+ 5:39	+ 4.00	91	+ 5:31	+ 4.00	138	- 5:42	+ 4.00	70	+ 5:10	+ 4.00	190	- 4:50
+ 4.15	74	+ 5:29	+ 4.15	58	+ 5:13	+ 4.15	85	+ 5:40	+ 4.15	97	+ 5:52	+ 4.15	89	+ 5:44	+ 4.15	135	- 5:30	+ 4.15	69	+ 5:24	+ 4.15	185	- 4:40
+ 4.30	72	+ 5:42	+ 4.30	56	+ 5:26	+ 4.30	84	+ 5:54	+ 4.30	96	- 5:54	+ 4.30	86	+ 5:56	+ 4.30	131	- 5:19	+ 4.30	68	+ 5:38	+ 4.30	181	- 4:29
+ 4.45	70	+ 5:55	+ 4.45	55	+ 5:40	+ 4.45	82	- 5:53	+ 4.45	94	- 5:41	+ 4.45	83	- 5:52	+ 4.45	128	- 5:07	+ 4.45	67	+ 5:52	+ 4.45	176	- 4:19
+ 5.00	68	- 5:52	+ 5.00	54	+ 5:54	+ 5.00	81	- 5:39	+ 5.00	92	- 5:28	+ 5.00	81	- 5:39	+ 5.00	125	- 4:55	+ 5.00	65	- 5:55	+ 5.00	172	- 4:08
+ 5.15	66	- 5:39	+ 5.15	53	- 5:52	+ 5.15	79	- 5:26	+ 5.15	90	- 5:15	+ 5.15	79	- 5:26	+ 5.15	136	- 4:29	+ 5.15	64	- 5:41	+ 5.15	168	- 3:57
+ 5.30	65	- 5:25	+ 5.30	52	- 5:38	+ 5.30	77	- 5:13	+ 5.30	88	- 5:02	+ 5.30	77	- 5:13	+ 5.30	147	- 4:03	+ 5.30	63	- 5:27	+ 5.30	164	- 3:46
+ 5.45	64	- 5:11	+ 5.45	51	- 5:24	+ 5.45	74	- 5:01	+ 5.45	86	- 4:49	+ 5.45	75	- 5:00	+ 5.45	159	- 3:36	+ 5.45	62	- 5:13	+ 5.45	161	- 3:34
+ 6.00	63	- 4:57	+ 6.00	50	- 5:10	+ 6.00	72	- 4:48	+ 6.00	84	- 4:36	+ 6.00	73	- 4:47	+ 6.00	170	- 3:10	+ 6.00	61	- 4:59	+ 6.00	157	- 3:23

Table J - Suffolk to Essex Rivers, Sea Reach to North Oaze

Time to cover Sectors (in minutes) at 4.0 kts — All times relate to HW Sheerness — **Springs**

SOUTH BOUND

Time	J8 Spitway to Crouch Duration	J8 Time at End of Sector	J7 North Oaze to Sea Reach No 1 Duration	J7 Time at End of Sector	J6 Cork Sand Bcn to NE Gunfleet Duration	J6 Time at End of Sector	J5 Deben Landfall to The Naze Duration	J5 Time at End of Sector	J4 The Naze to Holland-on-sea Duration	J4 Time at End of Sector	J3 Holland-on-sea to Colne Duration	J3 Time at End of Sector	J2 Colne to Blackwater Duration	J2 Time at End of Sector	J1 The Naze to the Spitway Duration	J1 Time at End of Sector
- 6.00	50	- 5:10	45	- 5:15	59	- 5:01	71	- 4:49	57	- 5:03	94	- 4:26	54	- 5:06	130	- 3:50
- 5.45	49	- 4:56	44	- 5:01	59	- 4:46	72	- 4:33	56	- 4:49	89	- 4:16	52	- 4:53	129	- 3:36
- 5.30	47	- 4:43	42	- 4:48	59	- 4:31	72	- 4:18	55	- 4:35	85	- 4:05	51	- 4:39	129	- 3:21
- 5.15	45	- 4:30	40	- 4:35	58	- 4:17	72	- 4:03	54	- 4:21	80	- 3:55	50	- 4:25	128	- 3:07
- 5.00	43	- 4:17	38	- 4:22	58	- 4:02	72	- 3:48	53	- 4:07	76	- 3:44	48	- 4:12	128	- 2:52
- 4.45	43	- 4:02	38	- 4:07	59	- 3:46	73	- 3:32	53	- 3:52	76	- 3:29	48	- 3:57	129	- 2:36
- 4.30	43	- 3:47	37	- 3:53	60	- 3:30	75	- 3:15	53	- 3:37	76	- 3:14	47	- 3:43	131	- 2:19
- 4.15	42	- 3:33	36	- 3:39	61	- 3:14	76	- 2:59	54	- 3:21	76	- 2:59	46	- 3:29	133	- 2:02
- 4.00	42	- 3:18	36	- 3:24	62	- 2:58	77	- 2:43	54	- 3:06	76	- 2:44	46	- 3:14	134	- 1:46
- 3.45	43	- 3:02	35	- 3:10	65	- 2:40	79	- 2:26	55	- 2:50	77	- 2:28	46	- 2:59	138	- 1:27
- 3.30	44	- 2:46	35	- 2:55	68	- 2:22	81	- 2:09	56	- 2:34	77	- 2:13	45	- 2:45	141	- 1:09
- 3.15	44	- 2:31	35	- 2:40	71	- 2:04	83	- 1:52	57	- 2:18	78	- 1:57	45	- 2:30	145	- 0:50
- 3.00	45	- 2:15	35	- 2:25	74	- 1:46	86	- 1:34	58	- 2:02	79	- 1:41	45	- 2:15	148	- 0:32
- 2.45	46	- 1:59	35	- 2:10	77	- 1:28	90	- 1:15	60	- 1:45	85	- 1:20	46	- 1:59	171	+ 0:06
- 2.30	48	- 1:42	36	- 1:54	81	- 1:09	93	- 0:57	62	- 1:28	91	- 0:59	47	- 1:43	193	+ 0:43
- 2.15	49	- 1:26	36	- 1:39	85	- 0:50	97	- 0:38	64	- 1:11	97	- 0:38	48	- 1:27	216	+ 1:21
- 2.00	50	- 1:10	36	- 1:24	88	- 0:32	101	- 0:19	66	- 0:54	102	- 0:18	49	- 1:11	238	+ 1:58
- 1.45	53	- 0:52	37	- 1:08	94	- 0:11	107	+ 0:02	70	- 0:35	114	+ 0:09	53	- 0:52	241	+ 2:16
- 1.30	56	- 0:34	39	- 0:51	101	+ 0:11	112	+ 0:22	74	- 0:16	126	+ 0:36	57	- 0:33	244	+ 2:34
- 1.15	59	- 0:16	40	- 0:35	107	+ 0:32	118	+ 0:43	77	+ 0:02	138	+ 1:03	61	- 0:14	246	+ 2:51
- 1.00	62	+ 0:02	41	- 0:19	114	+ 0:54	123	+ 1:03	81	+ 0:21	150	+ 1:30	64	+ 0:04	249	+ 3:09
- 0.45	69	+ 0:24	43	- 0:02	118	+ 1:13	126	+ 1:21	90	+ 0:45	161	+ 1:56	69	+ 0:24	256	+ 3:31
- 0.30	76	+ 0:46	44	+ 0:14	123	+ 1:33	129	+ 1:39	98	+ 1:08	172	+ 2:22	74	+ 0:44	262	+ 3:52
- 0.15	83	+ 1:08	46	+ 0:31	127	+ 1:52	132	+ 1:57	106	+ 1:31	183	+ 2:48	79	+ 1:04	268	+ 4:13
HW	90	+ 1:30	48	+ 0:48	132	+ 2:12	134	+ 2:14	115	+ 1:55	194	+ 3:14	85	+ 1:25	275	+ 4:35
+ 0.15	96	+ 1:51	51	+ 1:06	132	+ 2:27	133	+ 2:28	118	+ 2:13	196	+ 3:31	87	+ 1:42	272	+ 4:47
+ 0.30	101	+ 2:11	54	+ 1:24	131	+ 2:41	132	+ 2:42	122	+ 2:32	198	+ 3:48	90	+ 2:00	270	+ 5:00
+ 0.45	107	+ 2:32	57	+ 1:42	131	+ 2:56	132	+ 2:57	126	+ 2:51	199	+ 4:04	92	+ 2:17	267	+ 5:12
+ 1.00	112	+ 2:52	60	+ 2:00	130	+ 3:10	131	+ 3:11	129	+ 3:09	201	+ 4:21	94	+ 2:34	265	+ 5:25
+ 1.15	112	+ 3:07	63	+ 2:18	127	+ 3:22	128	+ 3:23	127	+ 3:22	196	+ 4:31	94	+ 2:49	258	+ 5:33
+ 1.30	112	+ 3:22	66	+ 2:36	123	+ 3:33	126	+ 3:36	124	+ 3:34	192	+ 4:42	93	+ 3:03	252	+ 5:42
+ 1.45	111	+ 3:36	68	+ 2:53	119	+ 3:44	124	+ 3:49	122	+ 3:47	188	+ 4:53	93	+ 3:18	245	+ 5:50
+ 2.00	111	+ 3:51	71	+ 3:11	115	+ 3:55	121	+ 4:01	120	+ 4:00	184	+ 5:04	92	+ 3:32	239	+ 5:59
+ 2.15	108	+ 4:03	71	+ 3:26	111	+ 4:06	118	+ 4:13	116	+ 4:11	178	+ 5:13	90	+ 3:45	232	- 5:53
+ 2.30	106	+ 4:16	72	+ 3:42	107	+ 4:17	116	+ 4:26	113	+ 4:23	173	+ 5:23	87	+ 3:57	226	- 5:44
+ 2.45	103	+ 4:28	72	+ 3:57	104	+ 4:29	113	+ 4:38	109	+ 4:34	167	+ 5:32	85	+ 4:10	219	- 5:36
+ 3.00	100	+ 4:40	72	+ 4:12	100	+ 4:40	110	+ 4:50	105	+ 4:45	162	+ 5:42	82	+ 4:22	212	- 5:28
+ 3.15	96	+ 4:51	70	+ 4:25	97	+ 4:52	107	+ 5:02	102	+ 4:57	156	+ 5:51	81	+ 4:36	206	- 5:19
+ 3.30	92	+ 5:02	69	+ 4:39	94	+ 5:04	104	+ 5:14	100	+ 5:10	151	- 5:59	79	+ 4:49	200	- 5:10
+ 3.45	88	+ 5:13	67	+ 4:52	91	+ 5:16	101	+ 5:26	97	+ 5:22	146	- 5:49	77	+ 5:02	194	- 5:01
+ 4.00	84	+ 5:24	65	+ 5:05	88	+ 5:28	99	+ 5:39	94	+ 5:34	141	- 5:39	75	+ 5:15	188	- 4:52
+ 4.15	80	+ 5:35	63	+ 5:18	86	+ 5:41	97	+ 5:52	90	+ 5:45	136	- 5:29	73	+ 5:28	183	- 4:42
+ 4.30	76	+ 5:46	61	+ 5:31	84	+ 5:54	95	- 5:55	87	+ 5:57	132	- 5:18	70	+ 5:40	177	- 4:33
+ 4.45	72	+ 5:57	59	+ 5:44	82	- 5:53	93	- 5:42	84	- 5:51	127	- 5:08	68	+ 5:53	171	- 4:24
+ 5.00	69	- 5:51	57	+ 5:57	80	- 5:40	91	- 5:29	81	- 5:39	123	- 4:57	66	- 5:54	166	- 4:14
+ 5.15	67	- 5:38	56	- 5:49	76	- 5:29	88	- 5:17	78	- 5:27	118	- 4:47	64	- 5:41	162	- 4:03
+ 5.30	65	- 5:25	54	- 5:36	73	- 5:17	84	- 5:06	75	- 5:15	114	- 4:36	63	- 5:27	158	- 3:52
+ 5.45	63	- 5:12	53	- 5:22	70	- 5:05	81	- 4:54	73	- 5:02	110	- 4:25	61	- 5:14	154	- 3:41
+ 6.00	61	- 4:59	51	- 5:09	66	- 4:54	78	- 4:42	70	- 4:50	106	- 4:14	59	- 5:01	150	- 3:30

Table J - Suffolk to Essex Rivers, Sea Reach to North Oaze

Neaps

All times relate to HW Sheerness

Time to cover Sectors (in minutes) at 5.0 Kts

SOUTH BOUND

	J8			J7			J6			J5			J4			J3			J2			J1	
	Spitway to Crouch			North Oaze to Sea Reach No 1			Cork Sand Bcn to NE Gunfleet			Deben Landfall to The Naze			The Naze to Holland-on-sea			Holland-on-sea to Colne			Colne to Blackwater			The Naze to the Spitway	
Time	Duration	Time at End of Sector	Time	Duration	Time at End of Sector	Time	Duration	Time at End of Sector	Time	Duration	Time at End of Sector	Time	Duration	Time at End of Sector	Time	Duration	Time at End of Sector	Time	Duration	Time at End of Sector	Time	Duration	Time at End of Sector
- 6.00	**47**	**- 5:13**	**- 6.00**	**38**	**- 5:22**	**- 6.00**	**57**	**- 5:03**	**- 6.00**	**67**	**- 4:53**	**- 6.00**	**54**	**- 5:06**	**- 6.00**	**82**	**- 4:38**	**- 6.00**	**47**	**- 5:13**	**- 6.00**	**121**	**- 3:59**
- 5.45	46	- 4:59	- 5.45	37	- 5:08	- 5.45	56	- 4:49	- 5.45	67	- 4:38	- 5.45	53	- 4:52	- 5.45	81	- 4:24	- 5.45	46	- 4:59	- 5.45	120	- 3:45
- 5.30	45	- 4:45	- 5.30	36	- 4:54	- 5.30	56	- 4:34	- 5.30	67	- 4:23	- 5.30	52	- 4:38	- 5.30	80	- 4:10	- 5.30	46	- 4:44	- 5.30	119	- 3:31
- 5.15	43	- 4:32	- 5.15	36	- 4:39	- 5.15	56	- 4:19	- 5.15	67	- 4:08	- 5.15	52	- 4:23	- 5.15	79	- 3:56	- 5.15	45	- 4:30	- 5.15	118	- 3:17
- 5.00	**42**	**- 4:18**	**- 5.00**	**35**	**- 4:25**	**- 5.00**	**56**	**- 4:04**	**- 5.00**	**67**	**- 3:53**	**- 5.00**	**51**	**- 4:09**	**- 5.00**	**77**	**- 3:43**	**- 5.00**	**44**	**- 4:16**	**- 5.00**	**117**	**- 3:03**
- 4.45	42	- 4:03	- 4.45	34	- 4:11	- 4.45	56	- 3:49	- 4.45	67	- 3:38	- 4.45	51	- 3:54	- 4.45	77	- 3:28	- 4.45	44	- 4:01	- 4.45	117	- 2:48
- 4.30	42	- 3:48	- 4.30	34	- 3:56	- 4.30	56	- 3:34	- 4.30	68	- 3:22	- 4.30	51	- 3:39	- 4.30	77	- 3:13	- 4.30	43	- 3:47	- 4.30	118	- 2:32
- 4.15	42	- 3:33	- 4.15	33	- 3:42	- 4.15	57	- 3:18	- 4.15	68	- 3:07	- 4.15	51	- 3:24	- 4.15	77	- 2:58	- 4.15	43	- 3:32	- 4.15	118	- 2:17
- 4.00	**42**	**- 3:18**	**- 4.00**	**33**	**- 3:27**	**- 4.00**	**57**	**- 3:03**	**- 4.00**	**69**	**- 2:51**	**- 4.00**	**51**	**- 3:09**	**- 4.00**	**76**	**- 2:44**	**- 4.00**	**43**	**- 3:17**	**- 4.00**	**119**	**- 2:01**
- 3.45	42	- 3:03	- 3.45	33	- 3:12	- 3.45	58	- 2:47	- 3.45	69	- 2:36	- 3.45	51	- 2:54	- 3.45	77	- 2:28	- 3.45	43	- 3:02	- 3.45	120	- 1:45
- 3.30	42	- 2:48	- 3.30	32	- 2:58	- 3.30	59	- 2:31	- 3.30	70	- 2:20	- 3.30	52	- 2:38	- 3.30	77	- 2:13	- 3.30	43	- 2:47	- 3.30	122	- 1:28
- 3.15	43	- 2:32	- 3.15	32	- 2:43	- 3.15	61	- 2:14	- 3.15	71	- 2:04	- 3.15	52	- 2:23	- 3.15	77	- 1:58	- 3.15	43	- 2:32	- 3.15	124	- 1:11
- 3.00	**43**	**- 2:17**	**- 3.00**	**32**	**- 2:28**	**- 3.00**	**62**	**- 1:58**	**- 3.00**	**72**	**- 1:48**	**- 3.00**	**53**	**- 2:07**	**- 3.00**	**78**	**- 1:42**	**- 3.00**	**43**	**- 2:17**	**- 3.00**	**125**	**- 0:55**
- 2.45	43	- 2:02	- 2.45	32	- 2:13	- 2.45	64	- 1:41	- 2.45	74	- 1:31	- 2.45	54	- 1:51	- 2.45	80	- 1:25	- 2.45	43	- 2:02	- 2.45	129	- 0:36
- 2.30	44	- 1:46	- 2.30	33	- 1:57	- 2.30	65	- 1:25	- 2.30	75	- 1:15	- 2.30	54	- 1:36	- 2.30	82	- 1:08	- 2.30	43	- 1:47	- 2.30	132	- 0:18
- 2.15	45	- 1:30	- 2.15	33	- 1:42	- 2.15	67	- 1:08	- 2.15	77	- 0:58	- 2.15	55	- 1:20	- 2.15	84	- 0:51	- 2.15	44	- 1:31	- 2.15	135	HW
- 2.00	**45**	**- 1:15**	**- 2.00**	**33**	**- 1:27**	**- 2.00**	**69**	**- 0:51**	**- 2.00**	**78**	**- 0:42**	**- 2.00**	**56**	**- 1:04**	**- 2.00**	**86**	**- 0:34**	**- 2.00**	**44**	**- 1:16**	**- 2.00**	**138**	**+ 0:18**
- 1.45	46	- 0:59	- 1.45	33	- 1:12	- 1.45	70	- 0:35	- 1.45	80	- 0:25	- 1.45	58	- 0:47	- 1.45	89	- 0:16	- 1.45	45	- 1:00	- 1.45	144	+ 0:39
- 1.30	48	- 0:42	- 1.30	34	- 0:56	- 1.30	72	- 0:18	- 1.30	82	- 0:08	- 1.30	60	- 0:30	- 1.30	93	+ 0:03	- 1.30	47	- 0:43	- 1.30	151	+ 1:01
- 1.15	49	- 0:26	- 1.15	34	- 0:41	- 1.15	74	- 0:01	- 1.15	83	+ 0:08	- 1.15	61	- 0:14	- 1.15	96	+ 0:21	- 1.15	48	- 0:27	- 1.15	157	+ 1:22
- 1.00	**50**	**- 0:10**	**- 1.00**	**35**	**- 0:25**	**- 1.00**	**76**	**+ 0:16**	**- 1.00**	**85**	**+ 0:25**	**- 1.00**	**63**	**+ 0:03**	**- 1.00**	**99**	**+ 0:39**	**- 1.00**	**50**	**- 0:10**	**- 1.00**	**163**	**+ 1:43**
- 0.45	52	+ 0:07	- 0.45	36	- 0:09	- 0.45	77	+ 0:32	- 0.45	88	+ 0:43	- 0.45	65	+ 0:20	- 0.45	105	+ 1:00	- 0.45	52	+ 0:07	- 0.45	168	+ 2:03
- 0.30	54	+ 0:24	- 0.30	36	+ 0:06	- 0.30	79	+ 0:49	- 0.30	90	+ 1:00	- 0.30	68	+ 0:38	- 0.30	111	+ 1:21	- 0.30	54	+ 0:24	- 0.30	173	+ 2:23
- 0.15	56	+ 0:41	- 0.15	37	+ 0:22	- 0.15	80	+ 1:05	- 0.15	93	+ 1:18	- 0.15	70	+ 0:55	- 0.15	117	+ 1:42	- 0.15	56	+ 0:41	- 0.15	178	+ 2:43
HW	**58**	**+ 0:58**	**HW**	**38**	**+ 0:38**	**HW**	**82**	**+ 1:22**	**HW**	**96**	**+ 1:36**	**HW**	**73**	**+ 1:13**	**HW**	**122**	**+ 2:02**	**HW**	**59**	**+ 0:59**	**HW**	**183**	**+ 3:03**
+ 0.15	60	+ 1:15	+ 0.15	39	+ 0:54	+ 0.15	84	+ 1:39	+ 0.15	95	+ 1:50	+ 0.15	74	+ 1:29	+ 0.15	125	+ 2:20	+ 0.15	60	+ 1:15	+ 0.15	184	+ 3:19
+ 0.30	62	+ 1:32	+ 0.30	40	+ 1:10	+ 0.30	86	+ 1:56	+ 0.30	95	+ 2:05	+ 0.30	76	+ 1:46	+ 0.30	128	+ 2:38	+ 0.30	61	+ 1:31	+ 0.30	184	+ 3:34
+ 0.45	63	+ 1:48	+ 0.45	41	+ 1:26	+ 0.45	88	+ 2:13	+ 0.45	95	+ 2:20	+ 0.45	78	+ 2:03	+ 0.45	130	+ 2:55	+ 0.45	62	+ 1:47	+ 0.45	185	+ 3:50
+ 1.00	**65**	**+ 2:05**	**+ 1.00**	**42**	**+ 1:42**	**+ 1.00**	**90**	**+ 2:30**	**+ 1.00**	**95**	**+ 2:35**	**+ 1.00**	**80**	**+ 2:20**	**+ 1.00**	**133**	**+ 3:13**	**+ 1.00**	**63**	**+ 2:03**	**+ 1.00**	**186**	**+ 4:06**
+ 1.15	65	+ 2:20	+ 1.15	44	+ 1:59	+ 1.15	88	+ 2:43	+ 1.15	94	+ 2:49	+ 1.15	79	+ 2:34	+ 1.15	132	+ 3:27	+ 1.15	63	+ 2:18	+ 1.15	184	+ 4:19
+ 1.30	65	+ 2:35	+ 1.30	45	+ 2:15	+ 1.30	85	+ 2:55	+ 1.30	93	+ 3:03	+ 1.30	79	+ 2:49	+ 1.30	131	+ 3:41	+ 1.30	63	+ 2:33	+ 1.30	182	+ 4:32
+ 1.45	65	+ 2:50	+ 1.45	46	+ 2:31	+ 1.45	82	+ 3:07	+ 1.45	92	+ 3:17	+ 1.45	79	+ 3:04	+ 1.45	130	+ 3:55	+ 1.45	63	+ 2:48	+ 1.45	179	+ 4:44
+ 2.00	**66**	**+ 3:06**	**+ 2.00**	**47**	**+ 2:47**	**+ 2.00**	**80**	**+ 3:20**	**+ 2.00**	**91**	**+ 3:31**	**+ 2.00**	**78**	**+ 3:18**	**+ 2.00**	**128**	**+ 4:08**	**+ 2.00**	**63**	**+ 3:03**	**+ 2.00**	**177**	**+ 4:57**
+ 2.15	65	+ 3:20	+ 2.15	47	+ 3:02	+ 2.15	78	+ 3:33	+ 2.15	89	+ 3:44	+ 2.15	77	+ 3:32	+ 2.15	126	+ 4:21	+ 2.15	62	+ 3:17	+ 2.15	174	+ 5:09
+ 2.30	64	+ 3:34	+ 2.30	48	+ 3:18	+ 2.30	77	+ 3:47	+ 2.30	87	+ 3:57	+ 2.30	76	+ 3:46	+ 2.30	124	+ 4:34	+ 2.30	61	+ 3:31	+ 2.30	171	+ 5:21
+ 2.45	64	+ 3:49	+ 2.45	48	+ 3:33	+ 2.45	76	+ 4:01	+ 2.45	85	+ 4:10	+ 2.45	74	+ 3:59	+ 2.45	121	+ 4:46	+ 2.45	60	+ 3:45	+ 2.45	169	+ 5:34
+ 3.00	**63**	**+ 4:03**	**+ 3.00**	**48**	**+ 3:48**	**+ 3.00**	**74**	**+ 4:14**	**+ 3.00**	**84**	**+ 4:24**	**+ 3.00**	**73**	**+ 4:13**	**+ 3.00**	**119**	**+ 4:59**	**+ 3.00**	**59**	**+ 3:59**	**+ 3.00**	**166**	**+ 5:46**
+ 3.15	62	+ 4:17	+ 3.15	47	+ 4:02	+ 3.15	73	+ 4:28	+ 3.15	82	+ 4:37	+ 3.15	72	+ 4:27	+ 3.15	117	+ 5:12	+ 3.15	58	+ 4:13	+ 3.15	163	+ 5:58
+ 3.30	61	+ 4:31	+ 3.30	47	+ 4:17	+ 3.30	72	+ 4:42	+ 3.30	81	+ 4:51	+ 3.30	71	+ 4:41	+ 3.30	115	+ 5:25	+ 3.30	57	+ 4:27	+ 3.30	160	- 5:50
+ 3.45	61	+ 4:46	+ 3.45	46	+ 4:31	+ 3.45	71	+ 4:56	+ 3.45	80	+ 5:05	+ 3.45	70	+ 4:55	+ 3.45	113	+ 5:38	+ 3.45	56	+ 4:41	+ 3.45	157	- 5:38
+ 4.00	**60**	**+ 5:00**	**+ 4.00**	**46**	**+ 4:46**	**+ 4.00**	**69**	**+ 5:09**	**+ 4.00**	**79**	**+ 5:19**	**+ 4.00**	**69**	**+ 5:09**	**+ 4.00**	**111**	**+ 5:51**	**+ 4.00**	**55**	**+ 4:55**	**+ 4.00**	**155**	**- 5:25**
+ 4.15	58	+ 5:13	+ 4.15	45	+ 5:00	+ 4.15	68	+ 5:23	+ 4.15	78	+ 5:33	+ 4.15	68	+ 5:23	+ 4.15	108	- 5:57	+ 4.15	55	+ 5:10	+ 4.15	152	- 5:13
+ 4.30	57	+ 5:27	+ 4.30	44	+ 5:14	+ 4.30	67	+ 5:37	+ 4.30	77	+ 5:47	+ 4.30	67	+ 5:37	+ 4.30	106	- 5:44	+ 4.30	54	+ 5:24	+ 4.30	149	- 5:01
+ 4.45	56	+ 5:41	+ 4.45	43	+ 5:28	+ 4.45	66	+ 5:51	+ 4.45	76	- 5:59	+ 4.45	66	+ 5:51	+ 4.45	104	- 5:31	+ 4.45	53	+ 5:38	+ 4.45	146	- 4:49
+ 5.00	**54**	**+ 5:54**	**+ 5.00**	**43**	**+ 5:43**	**+ 5.00**	**66**	**- 5:54**	**+ 5.00**	**75**	**- 5:45**	**+ 5.00**	**65**	**- 5:55**	**+ 5.00**	**101**	**- 5:19**	**+ 5.00**	**52**	**+ 5:52**	**+ 5.00**	**144**	**- 4:36**
+ 5.15	53	- 5:52	+ 5.15	42	+ 5:57	+ 5.15	64	- 5:41	+ 5.15	73	- 5:32	+ 5.15	63	- 5:42	+ 5.15	99	- 5:06	+ 5.15	52	- 5:53	+ 5.15	140	- 4:25
+ 5.30	52	- 5:38	+ 5.30	41	- 5:49	+ 5.30	63	- 5:27	+ 5.30	72	- 5:18	+ 5.30	62	- 5:28	+ 5.30	97	- 4:53	+ 5.30	51	- 5:39	+ 5.30	137	- 4:13
+ 5.45	51	- 5:24	+ 5.45	41	- 5:34	+ 5.45	62	- 5:13	+ 5.45	71	- 5:04	+ 5.45	61	- 5:14	+ 5.45	95	- 4:40	+ 5.45	50	- 5:25	+ 5.45	133	- 4:02
+ 6.00	**51**	**- 5:09**	**+ 6.00**	**40**	**- 5:20**	**+ 6.00**	**60**	**- 5:00**	**+ 6.00**	**70**	**- 4:50**	**+ 6.00**	**60**	**- 5:00**	**+ 6.00**	**93**	**- 4:27**	**+ 6.00**	**49**	**- 5:11**	**+ 6.00**	**130**	**- 3:50**

Table J - Suffolk to Essex Rivers, Sea Reach to North Oaze

Time to cover Sectors (in minutes) at 5.0 kts | All times relate to HW Sheerness | **Springs**

	J8			J7			J6			J5			J4			J3			J2			J1	
	Spitway to Crouch			North Oaze to Sea Reach No 1			Cork Sand Bcn to NE Gunfleet			Deben Landfall to The Naze			The Naze to Holland-on-sea			Holland-on-sea to Colne			Colne to Blackwater			The Naze to the Spitway	
Time	Duration	Time at End of Sector	Time	Duration	Time at End of Sector	Time	Duration	Time at End of Sector	Time	Duration	Time at End of Sector	Time	Duration	Time at End of Sector	Time	Duration	Time at End of Sector	Time	Duration	Time at End of Sector	Time	Duration	Time at End of Sector
- 6.00	44	- 5:16	- 6.00	38	- 5:22	- 6.00	51	- 5:09	- 6.00	61	- 4:59	- 6.00	50	- 5:10	- 6.00	76	- 4:44	- 6.00	45	- 5:15	- 6.00	113	- 4:07
- 5.45	42	- 5:03	- 5.45	36	- 5:09	- 5.45	51	- 4:54	- 5.45	61	- 4:44	- 5.45	49	- 4:56	- 5.45	74	- 4:31	- 5.45	44	- 5:01	- 5.45	112	- 3:53
- 5.30	41	- 4:49	- 5.30	35	- 4:55	- 5.30	51	- 4:39	- 5.30	61	- 4:29	- 5.30	48	- 4:42	- 5.30	72	- 4:18	- 5.30	43	- 4:47	- 5.30	111	- 3:39
- 5.15	40	- 4:35	- 5.15	34	- 4:41	- 5.15	51	- 4:24	- 5.15	61	- 4:14	- 5.15	47	- 4:28	- 5.15	70	- 4:05	- 5.15	42	- 4:33	- 5.15	111	- 3:24
- 5.00	38	- 4:22	- 5.00	33	- 4:27	- 5.00	50	- 4:10	- 5.00	61	- 3:59	- 5.00	46	- 4:14	- 5.00	68	- 3:52	- 5.00	41	- 4:19	- 5.00	110	- 3:10
- 4.45	38	- 4:07	- 4.45	32	- 4:13	- 4.45	51	- 3:54	- 4.45	62	- 3:43	- 4.45	46	- 3:59	- 4.45	68	- 3:37	- 4.45	41	- 4:04	- 4.45	111	- 2:54
- 4.30	38	- 3:52	- 4.30	32	- 3:58	- 4.30	51	- 3:39	- 4.30	63	- 3:27	- 4.30	46	- 3:44	- 4.30	68	- 3:22	- 4.30	40	- 3:50	- 4.30	111	- 2:39
- 4.15	37	- 3:38	- 4.15	31	- 3:44	- 4.15	52	- 3:23	- 4.15	64	- 3:11	- 4.15	46	- 3:29	- 4.15	68	- 3:07	- 4.15	40	- 3:35	- 4.15	112	- 2:23
- 4.00	37	- 3:23	- 4.00	31	- 3:29	- 4.00	52	- 3:08	- 4.00	64	- 2:56	- 4.00	47	- 3:13	- 4.00	68	- 2:52	- 4.00	39	- 3:21	- 4.00	113	- 2:07
- 3.45	37	- 3:08	- 3.45	30	- 3:15	- 3.45	54	- 2:51	- 3.45	66	- 2:39	- 3.45	47	- 2:58	- 3.45	68	- 2:37	- 3.45	39	- 3:06	- 3.45	115	- 1:50
- 3.30	38	- 2:52	- 3.30	30	- 3:00	- 3.30	56	- 2:34	- 3.30	67	- 2:23	- 3.30	48	- 2:42	- 3.30	69	- 2:21	- 3.30	39	- 2:51	- 3.30	117	- 1:33
- 3.15	38	- 2:37	- 3.15	30	- 2:45	- 3.15	58	- 2:17	- 3.15	68	- 2:07	- 3.15	48	- 2:27	- 3.15	69	- 2:06	- 3.15	39	- 2:36	- 3.15	119	- 1:16
- 3.00	38	- 2:22	- 3.00	30	- 2:30	- 3.00	59	- 2:01	- 3.00	70	- 1:50	- 3.00	49	- 2:11	- 3.00	70	- 1:50	- 3.00	39	- 2:21	- 3.00	121	- 0:59
- 2.45	39	- 2:06	- 2.45	30	- 2:15	- 2.45	62	- 1:43	- 2.45	72	- 1:33	- 2.45	50	- 1:55	- 2.45	73	- 1:32	- 2.45	39	- 2:06	- 2.45	125	- 0:40
- 2.30	40	- 1:50	- 2.30	30	- 2:00	- 2.30	64	- 1:26	- 2.30	74	- 1:16	- 2.30	51	- 1:39	- 2.30	75	- 1:15	- 2.30	40	- 1:50	- 2.30	130	- 0:20
- 2.15	41	- 1:34	- 2.15	30	- 1:45	- 2.15	67	- 1:08	- 2.15	76	- 0:59	- 2.15	53	- 1:22	- 2.15	78	- 0:57	- 2.15	40	- 1:35	- 2.15	134	- 0:01
- 2.00	42	- 1:18	- 2.00	30	- 1:30	- 2.00	69	- 0:51	- 2.00	78	- 0:42	- 2.00	54	- 1:06	- 2.00	81	- 0:39	- 2.00	41	- 1:19	- 2.00	138	+ 0:18
- 1.45	44	- 1:01	- 1.45	31	- 1:14	- 1.45	72	- 0:33	- 1.45	82	- 0:23	- 1.45	56	- 0:49	- 1.45	86	- 0:19	- 1.45	43	- 1:02	- 1.45	148	+ 0:43
- 1.30	45	- 0:45	- 1.30	32	- 0:58	- 1.30	74	- 0:16	- 1.30	85	- 0:05	- 1.30	58	- 0:32	- 1.30	92	+ 0:02	- 1.30	45	- 0:45	- 1.30	157	+ 1:07
- 1.15	47	- 0:28	- 1.15	32	- 0:43	- 1.15	77	+ 0:02	- 1.15	89	+ 0:14	- 1.15	61	- 0:14	- 1.15	97	+ 0:22	- 1.15	47	- 0:28	- 1.15	166	+ 1:31
- 1.00	49	- 0:11	- 1.00	33	- 0:27	- 1.00	80	+ 0:20	- 1.00	92	+ 0:32	- 1.00	63	+ 0:03	- 1.00	103	+ 0:43	- 1.00	49	- 0:11	- 1.00	176	+ 1:56
- 0.45	52	+ 0:07	- 0.45	34	- 0:11	- 0.45	84	+ 0:39	- 0.45	95	+ 0:50	- 0.45	67	+ 0:22	- 0.45	111	+ 1:06	- 0.45	53	+ 0:08	- 0.45	182	+ 2:17
- 0.30	55	+ 0:25	- 0.30	35	+ 0:05	- 0.30	88	+ 0:58	- 0.30	97	+ 1:07	- 0.30	70	+ 0:40	- 0.30	118	+ 1:28	- 0.30	56	+ 0:26	- 0.30	189	+ 2:39
- 0.15	58	+ 0:43	- 0.15	36	+ 0:21	- 0.15	93	+ 1:18	- 0.15	99	+ 1:24	- 0.15	74	+ 0:59	- 0.15	126	+ 1:51	- 0.15	60	+ 0:45	- 0.15	195	+ 3:00
HW	61	+ 1:01	HW	38	+ 0:38	HW	97	+ 1:37	HW	102	+ 1:42	HW	78	+ 1:18	HW	134	+ 2:14	HW	63	+ 1:03	HW	202	+ 3:22
+ 0.15	64	+ 1:19	+ 0.15	39	+ 0:54	+ 0.15	97	+ 1:52	+ 0.15	101	+ 1:56	+ 0.15	82	+ 1:37	+ 0.15	138	+ 2:33	+ 0.15	65	+ 1:20	+ 0.15	202	+ 3:37
+ 0.30	67	+ 1:37	+ 0.30	41	+ 1:11	+ 0.30	98	+ 2:08	+ 0.30	101	+ 2:11	+ 0.30	87	+ 1:57	+ 0.30	143	+ 2:53	+ 0.30	67	+ 1:37	+ 0.30	202	+ 3:52
+ 0.45	70	+ 1:55	+ 0.45	43	+ 1:28	+ 0.45	98	+ 2:23	+ 0.45	101	+ 2:26	+ 0.45	91	+ 2:16	+ 0.45	148	+ 3:13	+ 0.45	69	+ 1:54	+ 0.45	202	+ 4:07
+ 1.00	73	+ 2:13	+ 1.00	45	+ 1:45	+ 1.00	99	+ 2:39	+ 1.00	100	+ 2:40	+ 1.00	96	+ 2:36	+ 1.00	152	+ 3:32	+ 1.00	70	+ 2:10	+ 1.00	203	+ 4:23
+ 1.15	73	+ 2:28	+ 1.15	47	+ 2:02	+ 1.15	96	+ 2:51	+ 1.15	99	+ 2:54	+ 1.15	95	+ 2:50	+ 1.15	149	+ 3:44	+ 1.15	70	+ 2:25	+ 1.15	199	+ 4:34
+ 1.30	74	+ 2:44	+ 1.30	49	+ 2:19	+ 1.30	93	+ 3:03	+ 1.30	97	+ 3:07	+ 1.30	93	+ 3:03	+ 1.30	145	+ 3:55	+ 1.30	70	+ 2:40	+ 1.30	196	+ 4:46
+ 1.45	75	+ 3:00	+ 1.45	51	+ 2:36	+ 1.45	90	+ 3:15	+ 1.45	96	+ 3:21	+ 1.45	92	+ 3:17	+ 1.45	142	+ 4:07	+ 1.45	70	+ 2:55	+ 1.45	192	+ 4:57
+ 2.00	75	+ 3:15	+ 2.00	53	+ 2:53	+ 2.00	87	+ 3:27	+ 2.00	95	+ 3:35	+ 2.00	91	+ 3:31	+ 2.00	138	+ 4:18	+ 2.00	69	+ 3:09	+ 2.00	189	+ 5:09
+ 2.15	74	+ 3:29	+ 2.15	53	+ 3:08	+ 2.15	85	+ 3:40	+ 2.15	93	+ 3:48	+ 2.15	88	+ 3:43	+ 2.15	135	+ 4:30	+ 2.15	68	+ 3:23	+ 2.15	184	+ 5:19
+ 2.30	73	+ 3:43	+ 2.30	53	+ 3:23	+ 2.30	82	+ 3:52	+ 2.30	91	+ 4:01	+ 2.30	85	+ 3:55	+ 2.30	132	+ 4:42	+ 2.30	66	+ 3:36	+ 2.30	180	+ 5:30
+ 2.45	72	+ 3:57	+ 2.45	54	+ 3:39	+ 2.45	80	+ 4:05	+ 2.45	89	+ 4:14	+ 2.45	82	+ 4:07	+ 2.45	129	+ 4:54	+ 2.45	65	+ 3:50	+ 2.45	176	+ 5:41
+ 3.00	71	+ 4:11	+ 3.00	54	+ 3:54	+ 3.00	78	+ 4:18	+ 3.00	87	+ 4:27	+ 3.00	79	+ 4:19	+ 3.00	126	+ 5:06	+ 3.00	63	+ 4:03	+ 3.00	171	+ 5:51
+ 3.15	69	+ 4:24	+ 3.15	53	+ 4:08	+ 3.15	76	+ 4:31	+ 3.15	85	+ 4:40	+ 3.15	77	+ 4:32	+ 3.15	122	+ 5:17	+ 3.15	62	+ 4:17	+ 3.15	167	- 5:58
+ 3.30	68	+ 4:38	+ 3.30	52	+ 4:22	+ 3.30	74	+ 4:44	+ 3.30	84	+ 4:54	+ 3.30	76	+ 4:46	+ 3.30	119	+ 5:29	+ 3.30	61	+ 4:31	+ 3.30	163	- 5:47
+ 3.45	66	+ 4:51	+ 3.45	51	+ 4:36	+ 3.45	72	+ 4:57	+ 3.45	82	+ 5:07	+ 3.45	74	+ 4:59	+ 3.45	116	+ 5:41	+ 3.45	60	+ 4:45	+ 3.45	159	- 5:36
+ 4.00	64	+ 5:04	+ 4.00	50	+ 4:50	+ 4.00	70	+ 5:10	+ 4.00	80	+ 5:20	+ 4.00	73	+ 5:13	+ 4.00	113	+ 5:53	+ 4.00	58	+ 4:58	+ 4.00	155	- 5:25
+ 4.15	62	+ 5:17	+ 4.15	49	+ 5:04	+ 4.15	69	+ 5:24	+ 4.15	78	+ 5:33	+ 4.15	71	+ 5:26	+ 4.15	110	- 5:55	+ 4.15	57	+ 5:12	+ 4.15	151	- 5:14
+ 4.30	60	+ 5:30	+ 4.30	47	+ 5:17	+ 4.30	68	+ 5:38	+ 4.30	77	+ 5:47	+ 4.30	69	+ 5:39	+ 4.30	107	- 5:43	+ 4.30	56	+ 5:26	+ 4.30	148	- 5:02
+ 4.45	58	+ 5:43	+ 4.45	46	+ 5:31	+ 4.45	66	+ 5:51	+ 4.45	75	- 6:00	+ 4.45	67	+ 5:52	+ 4.45	104	- 5:31	+ 4.45	54	+ 5:39	+ 4.45	144	- 4:51
+ 5.00	55	+ 5:55	+ 5.00	45	+ 5:45	+ 5.00	65	- 5:55	+ 5.00	74	- 5:46	+ 5.00	65	- 5:55	+ 5.00	100	- 5:20	+ 5.00	53	+ 5:53	+ 5.00	140	- 4:40
+ 5.15	54	- 5:51	+ 5.15	44	+ 5:59	+ 5.15	63	- 5:42	+ 5.15	72	- 5:33	+ 5.15	63	- 5:42	+ 5.15	98	- 5:07	+ 5.15	52	- 5:53	+ 5.15	136	- 4:29
+ 5.30	52	- 5:38	+ 5.30	43	- 5:47	+ 5.30	61	- 5:29	+ 5.30	70	- 5:20	+ 5.30	61	- 5:29	+ 5.30	96	- 4:54	+ 5.30	51	- 5:39	+ 5.30	132	- 4:18
+ 5.45	51	- 5:24	+ 5.45	42	- 5:33	+ 5.45	59	- 5:16	+ 5.45	68	- 5:07	+ 5.45	60	- 5:15	+ 5.45	94	- 4:41	+ 5.45	49	- 5:26	+ 5.45	127	- 4:08
+ 6.00	50	- 5:10	+ 6.00	41	- 5:19	+ 6.00	57	- 5:03	+ 6.00	66	- 4:54	+ 6.00	58	- 5:02	+ 6.00	91	- 4:29	+ 6.00	48	- 5:12	+ 6.00	123	- 3:57

SOUTH BOUND

Table J - Suffolk to Essex Rivers, Sea Reach to North Oaze

Neaps — All times relate to HW Sheerness — Time to cover Sectors (in minutes) at 6.0 Kts

SOUTH BOUND

	J8			J7			J6			J5	
	Spitway to Crouch			North Oaze to Sea Reach No 1			Cork Sand Bcn to NE Gunfleet			Deben Landfall to The Naze	
Time	Duration	Time at End of Sector	Time	Duration	Time at End of Sector	Time	Duration	Time at End of Sector	Time	Duration	Time at End of Sector
- 6.00	40	- 5:20	- 6.00	32	- 5:28	- 6.00	49	- 5:11	- 6.00	57	- 5:03
- 5.45	39	- 5:06	- 5.45	32	- 5:13	- 5.45	48	- 4:57	- 5.45	57	- 4:48
- 5.30	38	- 4:52	- 5.30	31	- 4:59	- 5.30	48	- 4:42	- 5.30	57	- 4:33
- 5.15	38	- 4:37	- 5.15	30	- 4:45	- 5.15	48	- 4:27	- 5.15	57	- 4:18
- 5.00	37	- 4:23	- 5.00	30	- 4:30	- 5.00	48	- 4:12	- 5.00	57	- 4:03
- 4.45	37	- 4:08	- 4.45	29	- 4:16	- 4.45	48	- 3:57	- 4.45	57	- 3:48
- 4.30	36	- 3:54	- 4.30	29	- 4:01	- 4.30	48	- 3:42	- 4.30	58	- 3:32
- 4.15	36	- 3:39	- 4.15	28	- 3:47	- 4.15	48	- 3:27	- 4.15	58	- 3:17
- 4.00	36	- 3:24	- 4.00	28	- 3:32	- 4.00	49	- 3:11	- 4.00	58	- 3:02
- 3.45	36	- 3:09	- 3.45	28	- 3:17	- 3.45	49	- 2:56	- 3.45	59	- 2:46
- 3.30	36	- 2:54	- 3.30	28	- 3:02	- 3.30	50	- 2:40	- 3.30	59	- 2:31
- 3.15	37	- 2:38	- 3.15	27	- 2:48	- 3.15	51	- 2:24	- 3.15	60	- 2:15
- 3.00	37	- 2:23	- 3.00	27	- 2:33	- 3.00	52	- 2:08	- 3.00	61	- 1:59
- 2.45	37	- 2:08	- 2.45	27	- 2:18	- 2.45	53	- 1:52	- 2.45	62	- 1:43
- 2.30	37	- 1:53	- 2.30	27	- 2:03	- 2.30	54	- 1:36	- 2.30	63	- 1:27
- 2.15	38	- 1:37	- 2.15	28	- 1:47	- 2.15	55	- 1:20	- 2.15	63	- 1:12
- 2.00	38	- 1:22	- 2.00	28	- 1:32	- 2.00	57	- 1:03	- 2.00	64	- 0:56
- 1.45	39	- 1:06	- 1.45	28	- 1:17	- 1.45	58	- 0:47	- 1.45	66	- 0:39
- 1.30	40	- 0:50	- 1.30	28	- 1:02	- 1.30	59	- 0:31	- 1.30	67	- 0:23
- 1.15	41	- 0:34	- 1.15	29	- 0:46	- 1.15	60	- 0:15	- 1.15	68	- 0:07
- 1.00	41	- 0:19	- 1.00	29	- 0:31	- 1.00	61	+ 0:01	- 1.00	70	+ 0:10
- 0.45	43	- 0:02	- 0.45	30	- 0:15	- 0.45	63	+ 0:18	- 0.45	71	+ 0:26
- 0.30	44	+ 0:14	- 0.30	30	HW	- 0.30	64	+ 0:34	- 0.30	72	+ 0:42
- 0.15	46	+ 0:31	- 0.15	31	+ 0:16	- 0.15	65	+ 0:50	- 0.15	73	+ 0:58
HW	47	+ 0:47	HW	31	+ 0:31	HW	66	+ 1:06	HW	74	+ 1:14
+ 0.15	48	+ 1:03	+ 0.15	32	+ 0:47	+ 0.15	66	+ 1:21	+ 0.15	74	+ 1:29
+ 0.30	49	+ 1:19	+ 0.30	33	+ 1:03	+ 0.30	67	+ 1:37	+ 0.30	74	+ 1:44
+ 0.45	51	+ 1:36	+ 0.45	33	+ 1:18	+ 0.45	67	+ 1:52	+ 0.45	74	+ 1:59
+ 1.00	52	+ 1:52	+ 1.00	34	+ 1:34	+ 1.00	67	+ 2:07	+ 1.00	74	+ 2:14
+ 1.15	52	+ 2:07	+ 1.15	35	+ 1:50	+ 1.15	67	+ 2:22	+ 1.15	73	+ 2:28
+ 1.30	52	+ 2:22	+ 1.30	36	+ 2:06	+ 1.30	66	+ 2:36	+ 1.30	73	+ 2:43
+ 1.45	53	+ 2:38	+ 1.45	37	+ 2:22	+ 1.45	66	+ 2:51	+ 1.45	72	+ 2:57
+ 2.00	53	+ 2:53	+ 2.00	38	+ 2:38	+ 2.00	65	+ 3:05	+ 2.00	72	+ 3:12
+ 2.15	52	+ 3:07	+ 2.15	38	+ 2:53	+ 2.15	64	+ 3:19	+ 2.15	71	+ 3:26
+ 2.30	52	+ 3:22	+ 2.30	38	+ 3:08	+ 2.30	63	+ 3:33	+ 2.30	70	+ 3:40
+ 2.45	52	+ 3:37	+ 2.45	39	+ 3:24	+ 2.45	62	+ 3:47	+ 2.45	70	+ 3:55
+ 3.00	51	+ 3:51	+ 3.00	39	+ 3:39	+ 3.00	61	+ 4:01	+ 3.00	69	+ 4:09
+ 3.15	51	+ 4:06	+ 3.15	38	+ 3:53	+ 3.15	60	+ 4:15	+ 3.15	68	+ 4:23
+ 3.30	50	+ 4:20	+ 3.30	38	+ 4:08	+ 3.30	59	+ 4:29	+ 3.30	67	+ 4:37
+ 3.45	49	+ 4:34	+ 3.45	38	+ 4:23	+ 3.45	59	+ 4:44	+ 3.45	66	+ 4:51
+ 4.00	49	+ 4:49	+ 4.00	37	+ 4:37	+ 4.00	58	+ 4:58	+ 4.00	66	+ 5:06
+ 4.15	48	+ 5:03	+ 4.15	37	+ 4:52	+ 4.15	57	+ 5:12	+ 4.15	65	+ 5:20
+ 4.30	47	+ 5:17	+ 4.30	36	+ 5:06	+ 4.30	56	+ 5:26	+ 4.30	64	+ 5:34
+ 4.45	46	+ 5:31	+ 4.45	36	+ 5:21	+ 4.45	56	+ 5:41	+ 4.45	63	+ 5:48
+ 5.00	45	+ 5:45	+ 5.00	35	+ 5:35	+ 5.00	55	+ 5:55	+ 5.00	63	- 5:57
+ 5.15	45	- 6:00	+ 5.15	35	+ 5:50	+ 5.15	54	- 5:51	+ 5.15	62	- 5:43
+ 5.30	44	- 5:46	+ 5.30	34	- 5:56	+ 5.30	53	- 5:37	+ 5.30	61	- 5:29
+ 5.45	43	- 5:32	+ 5.45	34	- 5:41	+ 5.45	52	- 5:23	+ 5.45	60	- 5:15
+ 6.00	42	- 5:18	+ 6.00	33	- 5:27	+ 6.00	52	- 5:08	+ 6.00	59	- 5:01

	J4			J3			J2			J1	
	The Naze to Holland-on-sea			Holland-on-sea to Colne			Colne to Blackwater			The Naze to the Spitway	
Time	Duration	Time at End of Sector	Time	Duration	Time at End of Sector	Time	Duration	Time at End of Sector	Time	Duration	Time at End of Sector
- 6.00	47	- 5:13	- 6.00	71	- 4:49	- 6.00	40	- 5:20	- 6.00	105	- 4:15
- 5.45	46	- 4:59	- 5.45	70	- 4:35	- 5.45	39	- 5:06	- 5.45	104	- 4:01
- 5.30	45	- 4:45	- 5.30	69	- 4:21	- 5.30	39	- 4:51	- 5.30	103	- 3:47
- 5.15	45	- 4:30	- 5.15	68	- 4:07	- 5.15	38	- 4:37	- 5.15	102	- 3:33
- 5.00	44	- 4:16	- 5.00	67	- 3:53	- 5.00	38	- 4:22	- 5.00	101	- 3:19
- 4.45	44	- 4:01	- 4.45	67	- 3:38	- 4.45	38	- 4:07	- 4.45	101	- 3:04
- 4.30	44	- 3:46	- 4.30	67	- 3:23	- 4.30	37	- 3:53	- 4.30	101	- 2:49
- 4.15	44	- 3:31	- 4.15	67	- 3:08	- 4.15	37	- 3:38	- 4.15	101	- 2:34
- 4.00	44	- 3:16	- 4.00	67	- 2:53	- 4.00	37	- 3:23	- 4.00	101	- 2:19
- 3.45	44	- 3:01	- 3.45	67	- 2:38	- 3.45	37	- 3:08	- 3.45	102	- 2:03
- 3.30	44	- 2:46	- 3.30	67	- 2:23	- 3.30	37	- 2:53	- 3.30	103	- 1:47
- 3.15	45	- 2:30	- 3.15	67	- 2:08	- 3.15	37	- 2:38	- 3.15	105	- 1:30
- 3.00	45	- 2:15	- 3.00	68	- 1:52	- 3.00	37	- 2:23	- 3.00	106	- 1:14
- 2.45	45	- 2:00	- 2.45	69	- 1:36	- 2.45	37	- 2:08	- 2.45	108	- 0:57
- 2.30	46	- 1:44	- 2.30	70	- 1:20	- 2.30	37	- 1:53	- 2.30	110	- 0:40
- 2.15	47	- 1:28	- 2.15	71	- 1:04	- 2.15	37	- 1:38	- 2.15	112	- 0:23
- 2.00	47	- 1:13	- 2.00	73	- 0:47	- 2.00	37	- 1:23	- 2.00	114	- 0:06
- 1.45	48	- 0:57	- 1.45	75	- 0:30	- 1.45	38	- 1:07	- 1.45	117	+ 0:12
- 1.30	49	- 0:41	- 1.30	77	- 0:13	- 1.30	39	- 0:51	- 1.30	121	+ 0:31
- 1.15	51	- 0:24	- 1.15	79	+ 0:04	- 1.15	40	- 0:35	- 1.15	125	+ 0:50
- 1.00	52	- 0:08	- 1.00	82	+ 0:22	- 1.00	41	- 0:19	- 1.00	128	+ 1:08
- 0.45	53	+ 0:08	- 0.45	86	+ 0:41	- 0.45	42	- 0:03	- 0.45	133	+ 1:28
- 0.30	55	+ 0:25	- 0.30	90	+ 1:00	- 0.30	44	+ 0:14	- 0.30	137	+ 1:47
- 0.15	57	+ 0:42	- 0.15	93	+ 1:18	- 0.15	46	+ 0:31	- 0.15	141	+ 2:06
HW	58	+ 0:58	HW	97	+ 1:37	HW	47	+ 0:47	HW	145	+ 2:25
+ 0.15	60	+ 1:15	+ 0.15	100	+ 1:55	+ 0.15	48	+ 1:03	+ 0.15	147	+ 2:42
+ 0.30	61	+ 1:31	+ 0.30	102	+ 2:12	+ 0.30	49	+ 1:19	+ 0.30	148	+ 2:58
+ 0.45	63	+ 1:48	+ 0.45	105	+ 2:30	+ 0.45	50	+ 1:35	+ 0.45	150	+ 3:15
+ 1.00	64	+ 2:04	+ 1.00	107	+ 2:47	+ 1.00	51	+ 1:51	+ 1.00	152	+ 3:32
+ 1.15	64	+ 2:19	+ 1.15	106	+ 3:01	+ 1.15	51	+ 2:06	+ 1.15	150	+ 3:45
+ 1.30	63	+ 2:33	+ 1.30	106	+ 3:16	+ 1.30	51	+ 2:21	+ 1.30	148	+ 3:58
+ 1.45	63	+ 2:48	+ 1.45	105	+ 3:30	+ 1.45	51	+ 2:36	+ 1.45	147	+ 4:12
+ 2.00	63	+ 3:03	+ 2.00	104	+ 3:44	+ 2.00	51	+ 2:51	+ 2.00	145	+ 4:25
+ 2.15	62	+ 3:17	+ 2.15	103	+ 3:58	+ 2.15	50	+ 3:05	+ 2.15	143	+ 4:38
+ 2.30	61	+ 3:31	+ 2.30	101	+ 4:11	+ 2.30	49	+ 3:19	+ 2.30	141	+ 4:51
+ 2.45	61	+ 3:46	+ 2.45	99	+ 4:24	+ 2.45	49	+ 3:34	+ 2.45	139	+ 5:04
+ 3.00	60	+ 4:00	+ 3.00	97	+ 4:37	+ 3.00	48	+ 3:48	+ 3.00	137	+ 5:17
+ 3.15	59	+ 4:14	+ 3.15	96	+ 4:51	+ 3.15	48	+ 4:03	+ 3.15	135	+ 5:30
+ 3.30	58	+ 4:28	+ 3.30	95	+ 5:05	+ 3.30	47	+ 4:17	+ 3.30	133	+ 5:43
+ 3.45	58	+ 4:43	+ 3.45	94	+ 5:19	+ 3.45	46	+ 4:31	+ 3.45	131	+ 5:56
+ 4.00	57	+ 4:57	+ 4.00	92	+ 5:32	+ 4.00	46	+ 4:46	+ 4.00	129	- 5:51
+ 4.15	56	+ 5:11	+ 4.15	90	+ 5:45	+ 4.15	45	+ 5:00	+ 4.15	127	- 5:38
+ 4.30	55	+ 5:25	+ 4.30	88	+ 5:58	+ 4.30	45	+ 5:15	+ 4.30	125	- 5:25
+ 4.45	55	+ 5:40	+ 4.45	86	- 5:49	+ 4.45	44	+ 5:29	+ 4.45	123	- 5:12
+ 5.00	54	+ 5:54	+ 5.00	84	- 5:36	+ 5.00	44	+ 5:44	+ 5.00	121	- 4:59
+ 5.15	53	- 5:52	+ 5.15	83	- 5:22	+ 5.15	43	+ 5:58	+ 5.15	119	- 4:46
+ 5.30	52	- 5:38	+ 5.30	81	- 5:09	+ 5.30	43	- 5:47	+ 5.30	117	- 4:33
+ 5.45	51	- 5:24	+ 5.45	80	- 4:55	+ 5.45	42	- 5:33	+ 5.45	114	- 4:21
+ 6.00	50	- 5:10	+ 6.00	79	- 4:41	+ 6.00	41	- 5:19	+ 6.00	112	- 4:08

Table J - Suffolk to Essex Rivers, Sea Reach to North Oaze

Time to cover Sectors (in minutes) at 6.0 kts — All times relate to HW Sheerness — **Springs**

SOUTH BOUND

J8 — Spitway to Crouch

Time	Duration	Time at End of Sector
- 6.00	39	- 5:21
- 5.45	37	- 5:08
- 5.30	36	- 4:54
- 5.15	35	- 4:40
- 5.00	34	- 4:26
- 4.45	34	- 4:11
- 4.30	33	- 3:57
- 4.15	33	- 3:42
- 4.00	33	- 3:27
- 3.45	33	- 3:12
- 3.30	33	- 2:57
- 3.15	33	- 2:42
- 3.00	33	- 2:27
- 2.45	34	- 2:11
- 2.30	35	- 1:55
- 2.15	35	- 1:40
- 2.00	36	- 1:24
- 1.45	37	- 1:08
- 1.30	38	- 0:52
- 1.15	39	- 0:36
- 1.00	40	- 0:20
- 0.45	42	- 0:03
- 0.30	45	+ 0:15
- 0.15	47	+ 0:32
HW	49	+ 0:49
+ 0.15	51	+ 1:06
+ 0.30	53	+ 1:23
+ 0.45	55	+ 1:40
+ 1.00	57	+ 1:57
+ 1.15	58	+ 2:13
+ 1.30	58	+ 2:28
+ 1.45	59	+ 2:44
+ 2.00	60	+ 3:00
+ 2.15	59	+ 3:14
+ 2.30	58	+ 3:28
+ 2.45	57	+ 3:42
+ 3.00	57	+ 3:57
+ 3.15	56	+ 4:11
+ 3.30	55	+ 4:25
+ 3.45	53	+ 4:38
+ 4.00	52	+ 4:52
+ 4.15	51	+ 5:06
+ 4.30	49	+ 5:19
+ 4.45	48	+ 5:33
+ 5.00	46	+ 5:46
+ 5.15	45	- 6:00
+ 5.30	44	- 5:46
+ 5.45	43	- 5:32
+ 6.00	42	- 5:18

J7 — North Oaze to Sea Reach No 1

Time	Duration	Time at End of Sector
- 6.00	32	- 5:28
- 5.45	31	- 5:14
- 5.30	30	- 5:00
- 5.15	29	- 4:46
- 5.00	28	- 4:32
- 4.45	28	- 4:17
- 4.30	27	- 4:03
- 4.15	26	- 3:49
- 4.00	26	- 3:34
- 3.45	26	- 3:19
- 3.30	25	- 3:05
- 3.15	25	- 2:50
- 3.00	25	- 2:35
- 2.45	25	- 2:20
- 2.30	25	- 2:05
- 2.15	25	- 1:50
- 2.00	25	- 1:35
- 1.45	26	- 1:19
- 1.30	26	- 1:04
- 1.15	27	- 0:48
- 1.00	28	- 0:32
- 0.45	28	- 0:17
- 0.30	29	- 0:01
- 0.15	30	+ 0:15
HW	31	+ 0:31
+ 0.15	32	+ 0:47
+ 0.30	33	+ 1:03
+ 0.45	34	+ 1:19
+ 1.00	36	+ 1:36
+ 1.15	37	+ 1:52
+ 1.30	39	+ 2:09
+ 1.45	40	+ 2:25
+ 2.00	42	+ 2:42
+ 2.15	42	+ 2:57
+ 2.30	42	+ 3:12
+ 2.45	43	+ 3:28
+ 3.00	43	+ 3:43
+ 3.15	42	+ 3:57
+ 3.30	42	+ 4:12
+ 3.45	41	+ 4:26
+ 4.00	40	+ 4:40
+ 4.15	40	+ 4:55
+ 4.30	39	+ 5:09
+ 4.45	38	+ 5:23
+ 5.00	37	+ 5:37
+ 5.15	36	+ 5:51
+ 5.30	35	- 5:55
+ 5.45	34	- 5:41
+ 6.00	34	- 5:26

J6 — Cork Sand Bcn to NE Gunfleet

Time	Duration	Time at End of Sector
- 6.00	45	- 5:15
- 5.45	45	- 5:00
- 5.30	45	- 4:45
- 5.15	44	- 4:31
- 5.00	44	- 4:16
- 4.45	44	- 4:01
- 4.30	45	- 3:45
- 4.15	45	- 3:30
- 4.00	45	- 3:15
- 3.45	46	- 2:59
- 3.30	47	- 2:43
- 3.15	48	- 2:27
- 3.00	50	- 2:10
- 2.45	51	- 1:54
- 2.30	53	- 1:37
- 2.15	55	- 1:20
- 2.00	57	- 1:03
- 1.45	58	- 0:47
- 1.30	60	- 0:30
- 1.15	62	- 0:13
- 1.00	64	+ 0:04
- 0.45	66	+ 0:21
- 0.30	68	+ 0:38
- 0.15	70	+ 0:55
HW	71	+ 1:11
+ 0.15	72	+ 1:27
+ 0.30	73	+ 1:43
+ 0.45	73	+ 1:58
+ 1.00	74	+ 2:14
+ 1.15	73	+ 2:28
+ 1.30	72	+ 2:42
+ 1.45	71	+ 2:56
+ 2.00	70	+ 3:10
+ 2.15	68	+ 3:23
+ 2.30	67	+ 3:37
+ 2.45	65	+ 3:50
+ 3.00	64	+ 4:04
+ 3.15	63	+ 4:18
+ 3.30	61	+ 4:31
+ 3.45	60	+ 4:45
+ 4.00	59	+ 4:59
+ 4.15	58	+ 5:13
+ 4.30	57	+ 5:27
+ 4.45	56	+ 5:41
+ 5.00	55	+ 5:55
+ 5.15	53	- 5:52
+ 5.30	52	- 5:38
+ 5.45	51	- 5:24
+ 6.00	49	- 5:11

J5 — Deben Landfall to The Naze

Time	Duration	Time at End of Sector
- 6.00	53	- 5:07
- 5.45	53	- 4:52
- 5.30	53	- 4:37
- 5.15	53	- 4:22
- 5.00	53	- 4:07
- 4.45	54	- 3:51
- 4.30	54	- 3:36
- 4.15	55	- 3:20
- 4.00	55	- 3:05
- 3.45	56	- 2:49
- 3.30	57	- 2:33
- 3.15	58	- 2:17
- 3.00	59	- 2:01
- 2.45	60	- 1:45
- 2.30	62	- 1:28
- 2.15	63	- 1:12
- 2.00	64	- 0:56
- 1.45	66	- 0:39
- 1.30	68	- 0:22
- 1.15	70	- 0:05
- 1.00	72	+ 0:12
- 0.45	74	+ 0:29
- 0.30	75	+ 0:45
- 0.15	77	+ 1:02
HW	78	+ 1:18
+ 0.15	78	+ 1:33
+ 0.30	79	+ 1:49
+ 0.45	79	+ 2:04
+ 1.00	79	+ 2:19
+ 1.15	78	+ 2:33
+ 1.30	77	+ 2:47
+ 1.45	76	+ 3:01
+ 2.00	76	+ 3:16
+ 2.15	75	+ 3:30
+ 2.30	74	+ 3:44
+ 2.45	73	+ 3:58
+ 3.00	72	+ 4:12
+ 3.15	70	+ 4:25
+ 3.30	69	+ 4:39
+ 3.45	68	+ 4:53
+ 4.00	66	+ 5:06
+ 4.15	65	+ 5:20
+ 4.30	64	+ 5:34
+ 4.45	63	+ 5:48
+ 5.00	62	- 5:58
+ 5.15	61	- 5:44
+ 5.30	60	- 5:30
+ 5.45	58	- 5:17
+ 6.00	57	- 5:03

J4 — The Naze to Holland-on-sea

Time	Duration	Time at End of Sector
- 6.00	44	- 5:16
- 5.45	43	- 5:02
- 5.30	42	- 4:48
- 5.15	42	- 4:33
- 5.00	41	- 4:19
- 4.45	41	- 4:04
- 4.30	41	- 3:49
- 4.15	41	- 3:34
- 4.00	41	- 3:19
- 3.45	41	- 3:04
- 3.30	42	- 2:48
- 3.15	42	- 2:33
- 3.00	42	- 2:18
- 2.45	43	- 2:02
- 2.30	44	- 1:46
- 2.15	45	- 1:30
- 2.00	45	- 1:15
- 1.45	47	- 0:58
- 1.30	49	- 0:41
- 1.15	50	- 0:25
- 1.00	52	- 0:08
- 0.45	54	+ 0:09
- 0.30	57	+ 0:27
- 0.15	59	+ 0:44
HW	62	+ 1:02
+ 0.15	64	+ 1:19
+ 0.30	66	+ 1:36
+ 0.45	68	+ 1:53
+ 1.00	70	+ 2:10
+ 1.15	69	+ 2:24
+ 1.30	69	+ 2:39
+ 1.45	69	+ 2:54
+ 2.00	69	+ 3:09
+ 2.15	67	+ 3:22
+ 2.30	66	+ 3:36
+ 2.45	65	+ 3:50
+ 3.00	64	+ 4:04
+ 3.15	63	+ 4:18
+ 3.30	62	+ 4:32
+ 3.45	60	+ 4:45
+ 4.00	59	+ 4:59
+ 4.15	58	+ 5:13
+ 4.30	57	+ 5:27
+ 4.45	56	+ 5:41
+ 5.00	54	+ 5:54
+ 5.15	53	- 5:52
+ 5.30	52	- 5:38
+ 5.45	51	- 5:24
+ 6.00	49	- 5:11

J3 — Holland-on-sea to Colne

Time	Duration	Time at End of Sector
- 6.00	67	- 4:53
- 5.45	65	- 4:40
- 5.30	64	- 4:26
- 5.15	63	- 4:12
- 5.00	61	- 3:59
- 4.45	61	- 3:44
- 4.30	61	- 3:29
- 4.15	61	- 3:14
- 4.00	61	- 2:59
- 3.45	61	- 2:44
- 3.30	61	- 2:29
- 3.15	62	- 2:13
- 3.00	62	- 1:58
- 2.45	64	- 1:41
- 2.30	65	- 1:25
- 2.15	67	- 1:08
- 2.00	69	- 0:51
- 1.45	72	- 0:33
- 1.30	76	- 0:14
- 1.15	79	+ 0:04
- 1.00	82	+ 0:22
- 0.45	88	+ 0:43
- 0.30	93	+ 1:03
- 0.15	99	+ 1:24
HW	105	+ 1:45
+ 0.15	107	+ 2:02
+ 0.30	110	+ 2:20
+ 0.45	113	+ 2:38
+ 1.00	116	+ 2:56
+ 1.15	115	+ 3:10
+ 1.30	114	+ 3:24
+ 1.45	112	+ 3:37
+ 2.00	111	+ 3:51
+ 2.15	109	+ 4:04
+ 2.30	107	+ 4:17
+ 2.45	104	+ 4:29
+ 3.00	102	+ 4:42
+ 3.15	100	+ 4:55
+ 3.30	98	+ 5:08
+ 3.45	96	+ 5:21
+ 4.00	94	+ 5:34
+ 4.15	92	+ 5:47
+ 4.30	89	+ 5:59
+ 4.45	87	- 5:48
+ 5.00	85	- 5:35
+ 5.15	83	- 5:22
+ 5.30	81	- 5:09
+ 5.45	79	- 4:56
+ 6.00	77	- 4:43

J2 — Colne to Blackwater

Time	Duration	Time at End of Sector
- 6.00	39	- 5:21
- 5.45	38	- 5:07
- 5.30	37	- 4:53
- 5.15	37	- 4:38
- 5.00	36	- 4:24
- 4.45	36	- 4:09
- 4.30	35	- 3:55
- 4.15	35	- 3:40
- 4.00	34	- 3:26
- 3.45	34	- 3:11
- 3.30	34	- 2:56
- 3.15	34	- 2:41
- 3.00	34	- 2:26
- 2.45	34	- 2:11
- 2.30	34	- 1:56
- 2.15	35	- 1:40
- 2.00	35	- 1:25
- 1.45	36	- 1:09
- 1.30	37	- 0:53
- 1.15	39	- 0:36
- 1.00	40	- 0:20
- 0.45	43	- 0:02
- 0.30	45	+ 0:15
- 0.15	48	+ 0:33
HW	50	+ 0:50
+ 0.15	52	+ 1:07
+ 0.30	53	+ 1:23
+ 0.45	54	+ 1:39
+ 1.00	56	+ 1:56
+ 1.15	56	+ 2:11
+ 1.30	56	+ 2:26
+ 1.45	56	+ 2:41
+ 2.00	56	+ 2:56
+ 2.15	55	+ 3:10
+ 2.30	54	+ 3:24
+ 2.45	52	+ 3:37
+ 3.00	51	+ 3:51
+ 3.15	51	+ 4:06
+ 3.30	50	+ 4:20
+ 3.45	49	+ 4:34
+ 4.00	48	+ 4:48
+ 4.15	47	+ 5:02
+ 4.30	46	+ 5:16
+ 4.45	45	+ 5:30
+ 5.00	44	+ 5:44
+ 5.15	43	+ 5:58
+ 5.30	43	- 5:47
+ 5.45	42	- 5:33
+ 6.00	41	- 5:19

J1 — The Naze to the Spitway

Time	Duration	Time at End of Sector
- 6.00	100	- 4:20
- 5.45	99	- 4:06
- 5.30	98	- 3:52
- 5.15	97	- 3:38
- 5.00	96	- 3:24
- 4.45	96	- 3:09
- 4.30	97	- 2:53
- 4.15	97	- 2:38
- 4.00	97	- 2:23
- 3.45	99	- 2:06
- 3.30	100	- 1:50
- 3.15	101	- 1:34
- 3.00	102	- 1:18
- 2.45	105	- 1:00
- 2.30	108	- 0:42
- 2.15	110	- 0:25
- 2.00	113	- 0:07
- 1.45	118	+ 0:13
- 1.30	123	+ 0:33
- 1.15	128	+ 0:53
- 1.00	134	+ 1:14
- 0.45	140	+ 1:35
- 0.30	147	+ 1:57
- 0.15	154	+ 2:19
HW	160	+ 2:40
+ 0.15	161	+ 2:56
+ 0.30	162	+ 3:12
+ 0.45	163	+ 3:28
+ 1.00	164	+ 3:44
+ 1.15	161	+ 3:56
+ 1.30	159	+ 4:09
+ 1.45	156	+ 4:21
+ 2.00	154	+ 4:34
+ 2.15	151	+ 4:46
+ 2.30	148	+ 4:58
+ 2.45	145	+ 5:10
+ 3.00	142	+ 5:22
+ 3.15	139	+ 5:34
+ 3.30	136	+ 5:46
+ 3.45	133	+ 5:58
+ 4.00	130	- 5:50
+ 4.15	128	- 5:37
+ 4.30	125	- 5:25
+ 4.45	122	- 5:13
+ 5.00	119	- 5:01
+ 5.15	117	- 4:48
+ 5.30	114	- 4:36
+ 5.45	111	- 4:24
+ 6.00	108	- 4:12

Table J - Suffolk to Essex Rivers, Sea Reach to North Oaze

Neaps — All times relate to HW Sheerness — **Time to cover Sectors (in minutes) at 7.0 Kts**

SOUTH BOUND

	J8			J7			J6			J5			J4			J3			J2			J1	
	Spitway to Crouch			North Oaze to Sea Reach No 1			Cork Sand Bcn to NE Gunfleet			Deben Landfall to The Naze			The Naze to Holland-on-sea			Holland-on-sea to Colne			Colne to Blackwater			The Naze to the Spitway	
Time	Duration	Time at End of Sector	Time	Duration	Time at End of Sector	Time	Duration	Time at End of Sector	Time	Duration	Time at End of Sector	Time	Duration	Time at End of Sector	Time	Duration	Time at End of Sector	Time	Duration	Time at End of Sector	Time	Duration	Time at End of Sector
- 6.00	**35**	**- 5:25**	**- 6.00**	**28**	**- 5:32**	**- 6.00**	**42**	**- 5:18**	**- 6.00**	**50**	**- 5:10**	**- 6.00**	**41**	**- 5:19**	**- 6.00**	**63**	**- 4:57**	**- 6.00**	**35**	**- 5:25**	**- 6.00**	**92**	**- 4:28**
- 5.45	34	- 5:11	- 5.45	27	- 5:18	- 5.45	42	- 5:03	- 5.45	50	- 4:55	- 5.45	40	- 5:05	- 5.45	62	- 4:43	- 5.45	34	- 5:11	- 5.45	91	- 4:14
- 5.30	34	- 4:56	- 5.30	27	- 5:03	- 5.30	42	- 4:48	- 5.30	50	- 4:40	- 5.30	40	- 4:50	- 5.30	61	- 4:29	- 5.30	34	- 4:56	- 5.30	90	- 4:00
- 5.15	33	- 4:42	- 5.15	26	- 4:49	- 5.15	42	- 4:33	- 5.15	50	- 4:25	- 5.15	39	- 4:36	- 5.15	60	- 4:15	- 5.15	34	- 4:41	- 5.15	90	- 3:45
- 5.00	**32**	**- 4:28**	**- 5.00**	**25**	**- 4:35**	**- 5.00**	**42**	**- 4:18**	**- 5.00**	**50**	**- 4:10**	**- 5.00**	**39**	**- 4:21**	**- 5.00**	**60**	**- 4:00**	**- 5.00**	**33**	**- 4:27**	**- 5.00**	**89**	**- 3:31**
- 4.45	32	- 4:13	- 4.45	25	- 4:20	- 4.45	42	- 4:03	- 4.45	50	- 3:55	- 4.45	39	- 4:06	- 4.45	59	- 3:46	- 4.45	33	- 4:12	- 4.45	89	- 3:16
- 4.30	32	- 3:58	- 4.30	25	- 4:05	- 4.30	42	- 3:48	- 4.30	50	- 3:40	- 4.30	39	- 3:51	- 4.30	59	- 3:31	- 4.30	33	- 3:57	- 4.30	89	- 3:01
- 4.15	32	- 3:43	- 4.15	24	- 3:51	- 4.15	42	- 3:33	- 4.15	50	- 3:25	- 4.15	39	- 3:36	- 4.15	59	- 3:16	- 4.15	32	- 3:43	- 4.15	89	- 2:46
- 4.00	**32**	**- 3:28**	**- 4.00**	**24**	**- 3:36**	**- 4.00**	**42**	**- 3:18**	**- 4.00**	**50**	**- 3:10**	**- 4.00**	**39**	**- 3:21**	**- 4.00**	**59**	**- 3:01**	**- 4.00**	**32**	**- 3:28**	**- 4.00**	**89**	**- 2:31**
- 3.45	32	- 3:13	- 3.45	24	- 3:21	- 3.45	43	- 3:02	- 3.45	51	- 2:54	- 3.45	39	- 3:06	- 3.45	59	- 2:46	- 3.45	32	- 3:13	- 3.45	90	- 2:15
- 3.30	32	- 2:58	- 3.30	24	- 3:06	- 3.30	43	- 2:47	- 3.30	51	- 2:39	- 3.30	39	- 2:51	- 3.30	59	- 2:31	- 3.30	32	- 2:58	- 3.30	90	- 2:00
- 3.15	32	- 2:43	- 3.15	23	- 2:52	- 3.15	44	- 2:31	- 3.15	52	- 2:23	- 3.15	39	- 2:36	- 3.15	59	- 2:16	- 3.15	32	- 2:43	- 3.15	91	- 1:44
- 3.00	**32**	**- 2:28**	**- 3.00**	**23**	**- 2:37**	**- 3.00**	**44**	**- 2:16**	**- 3.00**	**52**	**- 2:08**	**- 3.00**	**39**	**- 2:21**	**- 3.00**	**59**	**- 2:01**	**- 3.00**	**32**	**- 2:28**	**- 3.00**	**91**	**- 1:29**
- 2.45	32	- 2:13	- 2.45	23	- 2:22	- 2.45	45	- 2:00	- 2.45	53	- 1:52	- 2.45	40	- 2:05	- 2.45	60	- 1:45	- 2.45	32	- 2:13	- 2.45	92	- 1:13
- 2.30	33	- 1:57	- 2.30	23	- 2:07	- 2.30	46	- 1:44	- 2.30	54	- 1:36	- 2.30	40	- 1:50	- 2.30	61	- 1:29	- 2.30	32	- 1:58	- 2.30	94	- 0:56
- 2.15	33	- 1:42	- 2.15	24	- 1:51	- 2.15	47	- 1:28	- 2.15	54	- 1:21	- 2.15	40	- 1:35	- 2.15	62	- 1:13	- 2.15	32	- 1:43	- 2.15	95	- 0:40
- 2.00	**33**	**- 1:27**	**- 2.00**	**24**	**- 1:36**	**- 2.00**	**48**	**- 1:12**	**- 2.00**	**55**	**- 1:05**	**- 2.00**	**41**	**- 1:19**	**- 2.00**	**63**	**- 0:57**	**- 2.00**	**32**	**- 1:28**	**- 2.00**	**97**	**- 0:23**
- 1.45	34	- 1:11	- 1.45	24	- 1:21	- 1.45	49	- 0:56	- 1.45	56	- 0:49	- 1.45	42	- 1:03	- 1.45	65	- 0:40	- 1.45	33	- 1:12	- 1.45	99	- 0:06
- 1.30	34	- 0:56	- 1.30	24	- 1:06	- 1.30	50	- 0:40	- 1.30	57	- 0:33	- 1.30	42	- 0:48	- 1.30	66	- 0:24	- 1.30	33	- 0:57	- 1.30	102	+ 0:12
- 1.15	35	- 0:40	- 1.15	25	- 0:50	- 1.15	51	- 0:24	- 1.15	58	- 0:17	- 1.15	43	- 0:32	- 1.15	68	- 0:07	- 1.15	34	- 0:41	- 1.15	104	+ 0:29
- 1.00	**35**	**- 0:25**	**- 1.00**	**25**	**- 0:35**	**- 1.00**	**52**	**- 0:08**	**- 1.00**	**59**	**- 0:01**	**- 1.00**	**44**	**- 0:16**	**- 1.00**	**69**	**+ 0:09**	**- 1.00**	**34**	**- 0:26**	**- 1.00**	**107**	**+ 0:47**
- 0.45	36	- 0:09	- 0.45	25	- 0:20	- 0.45	53	+ 0:08	- 0.45	59	+ 0:14	- 0.45	45	HW	- 0.45	72	+ 0:27	- 0.45	36	- 0:09	- 0.45	110	+ 1:05
- 0.30	37	+ 0:07	- 0.30	26	- 0:04	- 0.30	54	+ 0:24	- 0.30	60	+ 0:30	- 0.30	46	+ 0:16	- 0.30	74	+ 0:44	- 0.30	37	+ 0:07	- 0.30	114	+ 1:24
- 0.15	38	+ 0:23	- 0.15	26	+ 0:11	- 0.15	55	+ 0:40	- 0.15	61	+ 0:46	- 0.15	48	+ 0:33	- 0.15	76	+ 1:01	- 0.15	38	+ 0:23	- 0.15	117	+ 1:42
HW	**39**	**+ 0:39**	**HW**	**27**	**+ 0:27**	**HW**	**56**	**+ 0:56**	**HW**	**62**	**+ 1:02**	**HW**	**49**	**+ 0:49**	**HW**	**78**	**+ 1:18**	**HW**	**40**	**+ 0:40**	**HW**	**121**	**+ 2:01**
+ 0.15	40	+ 0:55	+ 0.15	27	+ 0:42	+ 0.15	56	+ 1:11	+ 0.15	62	+ 1:17	+ 0.15	50	+ 1:05	+ 0.15	80	+ 1:35	+ 0.15	40	+ 0:55	+ 0.15	122	+ 2:17
+ 0.30	41	+ 1:11	+ 0.30	28	+ 0:58	+ 0.30	56	+ 1:26	+ 0.30	62	+ 1:32	+ 0.30	51	+ 1:21	+ 0.30	81	+ 1:51	+ 0.30	41	+ 1:11	+ 0.30	123	+ 2:33
+ 0.45	42	+ 1:27	+ 0.45	28	+ 1:13	+ 0.45	57	+ 1:42	+ 0.45	62	+ 1:47	+ 0.45	52	+ 1:37	+ 0.45	83	+ 2:08	+ 0.45	42	+ 1:27	+ 0.45	125	+ 2:50
+ 1.00	**43**	**+ 1:43**	**+ 1.00**	**29**	**+ 1:29**	**+ 1.00**	**57**	**+ 1:57**	**+ 1.00**	**62**	**+ 2:02**	**+ 1.00**	**53**	**+ 1:53**	**+ 1.00**	**84**	**+ 2:24**	**+ 1.00**	**42**	**+ 1:42**	**+ 1.00**	**126**	**+ 3:06**
+ 1.15	43	+ 1:58	+ 1.15	29	+ 1:44	+ 1.15	57	+ 2:12	+ 1.15	62	+ 2:17	+ 1.15	53	+ 2:08	+ 1.15	84	+ 2:39	+ 1.15	42	+ 1:57	+ 1.15	125	+ 3:20
+ 1.30	44	+ 2:14	+ 1.30	30	+ 2:00	+ 1.30	56	+ 2:26	+ 1.30	61	+ 2:31	+ 1.30	53	+ 2:23	+ 1.30	84	+ 2:54	+ 1.30	42	+ 2:12	+ 1.30	124	+ 3:34
+ 1.45	44	+ 2:29	+ 1.45	31	+ 2:16	+ 1.45	56	+ 2:41	+ 1.45	61	+ 2:46	+ 1.45	53	+ 2:38	+ 1.45	84	+ 3:09	+ 1.45	42	+ 2:27	+ 1.45	123	+ 3:48
+ 2.00	**44**	**+ 2:44**	**+ 2.00**	**32**	**+ 2:32**	**+ 2.00**	**55**	**+ 2:55**	**+ 2.00**	**61**	**+ 3:01**	**+ 2.00**	**53**	**+ 2:53**	**+ 2.00**	**83**	**+ 3:23**	**+ 2.00**	**42**	**+ 2:42**	**+ 2.00**	**122**	**+ 4:02**
+ 2.15	44	+ 2:59	+ 2.15	32	+ 2:47	+ 2.15	54	+ 3:09	+ 2.15	60	+ 3:15	+ 2.15	52	+ 3:07	+ 2.15	82	+ 3:37	+ 2.15	42	+ 2:57	+ 2.15	121	+ 4:16
+ 2.30	44	+ 3:14	+ 2.30	32	+ 3:02	+ 2.30	54	+ 3:24	+ 2.30	60	+ 3:30	+ 2.30	52	+ 3:22	+ 2.30	81	+ 3:51	+ 2.30	42	+ 3:12	+ 2.30	119	+ 4:29
+ 2.45	43	+ 3:28	+ 2.45	32	+ 3:17	+ 2.45	53	+ 3:38	+ 2.45	59	+ 3:44	+ 2.45	51	+ 3:36	+ 2.45	80	+ 4:05	+ 2.45	41	+ 3:26	+ 2.45	118	+ 4:43
+ 3.00	**43**	**+ 3:43**	**+ 3.00**	**32**	**+ 3:32**	**+ 3.00**	**52**	**+ 3:52**	**+ 3.00**	**59**	**+ 3:59**	**+ 3.00**	**50**	**+ 3:50**	**+ 3.00**	**79**	**+ 4:19**	**+ 3.00**	**41**	**+ 3:41**	**+ 3.00**	**116**	**+ 4:56**
+ 3.15	43	+ 3:58	+ 3.15	32	+ 3:47	+ 3.15	51	+ 4:06	+ 3.15	58	+ 4:13	+ 3.15	50	+ 4:05	+ 3.15	79	+ 4:34	+ 3.15	40	+ 3:55	+ 3.15	115	+ 5:10
+ 3.30	42	+ 4:12	+ 3.30	32	+ 4:02	+ 3.30	51	+ 4:21	+ 3.30	57	+ 4:27	+ 3.30	49	+ 4:19	+ 3.30	78	+ 4:48	+ 3.30	40	+ 4:10	+ 3.30	114	+ 5:24
+ 3.45	42	+ 4:27	+ 3.45	32	+ 4:17	+ 3.45	50	+ 4:35	+ 3.45	57	+ 4:42	+ 3.45	49	+ 4:34	+ 3.45	77	+ 5:02	+ 3.45	39	+ 4:24	+ 3.45	112	+ 5:37
+ 4.00	**41**	**+ 4:41**	**+ 4.00**	**31**	**+ 4:31**	**+ 4.00**	**49**	**+ 4:49**	**+ 4.00**	**56**	**+ 4:56**	**+ 4.00**	**48**	**+ 4:48**	**+ 4.00**	**76**	**+ 5:16**	**+ 4.00**	**39**	**+ 4:39**	**+ 4.00**	**111**	**+ 5:51**
+ 4.15	41	+ 4:56	+ 4.15	31	+ 4:46	+ 4.15	49	+ 5:04	+ 4.15	56	+ 5:11	+ 4.15	48	+ 5:03	+ 4.15	75	+ 5:30	+ 4.15	38	+ 4:53	+ 4.15	109	- 5:56
+ 4.30	40	+ 5:10	+ 4.30	31	+ 5:01	+ 4.30	48	+ 5:18	+ 4.30	55	+ 5:25	+ 4.30	47	+ 5:17	+ 4.30	74	+ 5:44	+ 4.30	38	+ 5:08	+ 4.30	108	- 5:42
+ 4.45	39	+ 5:24	+ 4.45	30	+ 5:15	+ 4.45	48	+ 5:33	+ 4.45	55	+ 5:40	+ 4.45	47	+ 5:32	+ 4.45	73	+ 5:58	+ 4.45	38	+ 5:23	+ 4.45	106	- 5:29
+ 5.00	**39**	**+ 5:39**	**+ 5.00**	**30**	**+ 5:30**	**+ 5.00**	**47**	**+ 5:47**	**+ 5.00**	**54**	**+ 5:54**	**+ 5.00**	**46**	**+ 5:46**	**+ 5.00**	**72**	**- 5:48**	**+ 5.00**	**37**	**+ 5:37**	**+ 5.00**	**105**	**- 5:15**
+ 5.15	38	+ 5:53	+ 5.15	30	+ 5:45	+ 5.15	47	- 5:58	+ 5.15	53	- 5:52	+ 5.15	46	- 5:59	+ 5.15	71	- 5:34	+ 5.15	37	+ 5:52	+ 5.15	103	- 5:02
+ 5.30	38	- 5:52	+ 5.30	29	+ 5:59	+ 5.30	46	- 5:44	+ 5.30	53	- 5:37	+ 5.30	45	- 5:45	+ 5.30	70	- 5:20	+ 5.30	37	- 5:53	+ 5.30	102	- 4:48
+ 5.45	37	- 5:38	+ 5.45	29	- 5:46	+ 5.45	45	- 5:30	+ 5.45	52	- 5:23	+ 5.45	44	- 5:31	+ 5.45	69	- 5:06	+ 5.45	36	- 5:39	+ 5.45	100	- 4:35
+ 6.00	**36**	**- 5:24**	**+ 6.00**	**28**	**- 5:32**	**+ 6.00**	**45**	**- 5:15**	**+ 6.00**	**52**	**- 5:08**	**+ 6.00**	**44**	**- 5:16**	**+ 6.00**	**68**	**- 4:52**	**+ 6.00**	**36**	**- 5:24**	**+ 6.00**	**98**	**- 4:22**

Table J - Suffolk to Essex Rivers, Sea Reach to North Oaze

Time to cover Sectors (in minutes) at 7.0 kts — All times relate to HW Sheerness — Springs

	J8 Spitway to Crouch			J7 North Oaze to Sea Reach No 1			J6 Cork Sand Bcn to NE Gunfleet			J5 Deben Landfall to The Naze	
Time	Duration	Time at End of Sector	Time	Duration	Time at End of Sector	Time	Duration	Time at End of Sector	Time	Duration	Time at End of Sector
- 6.00	34	- 5:26	- 6.00	28	- 5:32	- 6.00	40	- 5:20	- 6.00	47	- 5:13
- 5.45	33	- 5:12	- 5.45	27	- 5:18	- 5.45	40	- 5:05	- 5.45	47	- 4:58
- 5.30	32	- 4:58	- 5.30	26	- 5:04	- 5.30	40	- 4:50	- 5.30	47	- 4:43
- 5.15	31	- 4:44	- 5.15	25	- 4:50	- 5.15	39	- 4:36	- 5.15	47	- 4:28
- 5.00	30	- 4:30	- 5.00	24	- 4:36	- 5.00	39	- 4:21	- 5.00	47	- 4:13
- 4.45	30	- 4:15	- 4.45	24	- 4:21	- 4.45	39	- 4:06	- 4.45	47	- 3:58
- 4.30	30	- 4:00	- 4.30	23	- 4:07	- 4.30	39	- 3:51	- 4.30	47	- 3:43
- 4.15	29	- 3:46	- 4.15	23	- 3:52	- 4.15	40	- 3:35	- 4.15	48	- 3:27
- 4.00	29	- 3:31	- 4.00	22	- 3:38	- 4.00	40	- 3:20	- 4.00	48	- 3:12
- 3.45	29	- 3:16	- 3.45	22	- 3:23	- 3.45	40	- 3:05	- 3.45	49	- 2:56
- 3.30	29	- 3:01	- 3.30	22	- 3:08	- 3.30	41	- 2:49	- 3.30	49	- 2:41
- 3.15	29	- 2:46	- 3.15	21	- 2:54	- 3.15	42	- 2:33	- 3.15	50	- 2:25
- 3.00	30	- 2:30	- 3.00	21	- 2:39	- 3.00	43	- 2:17	- 3.00	51	- 2:09
- 2.45	30	- 2:15	- 2.45	21	- 2:24	- 2.45	44	- 2:01	- 2.45	52	- 1:53
- 2.30	30	- 2:00	- 2.30	21	- 2:09	- 2.30	45	- 1:45	- 2.30	53	- 1:37
- 2.15	31	- 1:44	- 2.15	21	- 1:54	- 2.15	47	- 1:28	- 2.15	54	- 1:21
- 2.00	31	- 1:29	- 2.00	22	- 1:38	- 2.00	48	- 1:12	- 2.00	55	- 1:05
- 1.45	32	- 1:13	- 1.45	22	- 1:23	- 1.45	50	- 0:55	- 1.45	56	- 0:49
- 1.30	33	- 0:57	- 1.30	23	- 1:07	- 1.30	51	- 0:39	- 1.30	58	- 0:32
- 1.15	33	- 0:42	- 1.15	23	- 0:52	- 1.15	52	- 0:23	- 1.15	59	- 0:16
- 1.00	34	- 0:26	- 1.00	24	- 0:36	- 1.00	54	- 0:06	- 1.00	61	+ 0:01
- 0.45	36	- 0:09	- 0.45	24	- 0:21	- 0.45	55	+ 0:10	- 0.45	62	+ 0:17
- 0.30	37	+ 0:07	- 0.30	25	- 0:05	- 0.30	57	+ 0:27	- 0.30	63	+ 0:33
- 0.15	39	+ 0:24	- 0.15	26	+ 0:11	- 0.15	58	+ 0:43	- 0.15	64	+ 0:49
HW	41	+ 0:41	HW	26	+ 0:26	HW	60	+ 1:00	HW	65	+ 1:05
+ 0.15	42	+ 0:57	+ 0.15	27	+ 0:42	+ 0.15	60	+ 1:15	+ 0.15	65	+ 1:20
+ 0.30	44	+ 1:14	+ 0.30	28	+ 0:58	+ 0.30	61	+ 1:31	+ 0.30	66	+ 1:36
+ 0.45	45	+ 1:30	+ 0.45	29	+ 1:14	+ 0.45	61	+ 1:46	+ 0.45	66	+ 1:51
+ 1.00	47	+ 1:47	+ 1.00	30	+ 1:30	+ 1.00	62	+ 2:02	+ 1.00	66	+ 2:06
+ 1.15	47	+ 2:02	+ 1.15	31	+ 1:46	+ 1.15	61	+ 2:16	+ 1.15	65	+ 2:20
+ 1.30	48	+ 2:18	+ 1.30	32	+ 2:02	+ 1.30	61	+ 2:31	+ 1.30	65	+ 2:35
+ 1.45	49	+ 2:34	+ 1.45	33	+ 2:18	+ 1.45	60	+ 2:45	+ 1.45	64	+ 2:49
+ 2.00	49	+ 2:49	+ 2.00	34	+ 2:34	+ 2.00	59	+ 2:59	+ 2.00	64	+ 3:04
+ 2.15	49	+ 3:04	+ 2.15	35	+ 2:50	+ 2.15	58	+ 3:13	+ 2.15	63	+ 3:18
+ 2.30	48	+ 3:18	+ 2.30	35	+ 3:05	+ 2.30	57	+ 3:27	+ 2.30	62	+ 3:32
+ 2.45	48	+ 3:33	+ 2.45	35	+ 3:20	+ 2.45	55	+ 3:40	+ 2.45	61	+ 3:46
+ 3.00	47	+ 3:47	+ 3.00	36	+ 3:36	+ 3.00	54	+ 3:54	+ 3.00	61	+ 4:01
+ 3.15	46	+ 4:01	+ 3.15	35	+ 3:50	+ 3.15	53	+ 4:08	+ 3.15	60	+ 4:15
+ 3.30	46	+ 4:16	+ 3.30	35	+ 4:05	+ 3.30	52	+ 4:22	+ 3.30	59	+ 4:29
+ 3.45	45	+ 4:30	+ 3.45	34	+ 4:19	+ 3.45	51	+ 4:36	+ 3.45	58	+ 4:43
+ 4.00	44	+ 4:44	+ 4.00	34	+ 4:34	+ 4.00	50	+ 4:50	+ 4.00	57	+ 4:57
+ 4.15	43	+ 4:58	+ 4.15	33	+ 4:48	+ 4.15	49	+ 5:04	+ 4.15	56	+ 5:11
+ 4.30	42	+ 5:12	+ 4.30	33	+ 5:03	+ 4.30	49	+ 5:19	+ 4.30	55	+ 5:25
+ 4.45	41	+ 5:26	+ 4.45	32	+ 5:17	+ 4.45	48	+ 5:33	+ 4.45	54	+ 5:39
+ 5.00	40	+ 5:40	+ 5.00	31	+ 5:31	+ 5.00	47	+ 5:47	+ 5.00	54	+ 5:54
+ 5.15	39	+ 5:54	+ 5.15	31	+ 5:46	+ 5.15	46	- 5:59	+ 5.15	53	- 5:52
+ 5.30	38	- 5:52	+ 5.30	30	- 6:00	+ 5.30	45	- 5:45	+ 5.30	52	- 5:38
+ 5.45	37	- 5:38	+ 5.45	29	- 5:46	+ 5.45	44	- 5:31	+ 5.45	51	- 5:24
+ 6.00	36	- 5:24	+ 6.00	29	- 5:31	+ 6.00	44	- 5:16	+ 6.00	50	- 5:10

	J4 The Naze to Holland-on-sea			J3 Holland-on-sea to Colne			J2 Colne to Blackwater			J1 The Naze to the Spitway	
Time	Duration	Time at End of Sector	Time	Duration	Time at End of Sector	Time	Duration	Time at End of Sector	Time	Duration	Time at End of Sector
- 6.00	39	- 5:21	- 6.00	60	- 5:00	- 6.00	34	- 5:26	- 6.00	86	- 4:34
- 5.45	39	- 5:06	- 5.45	58	- 4:47	- 5.45	33	- 5:12	- 5.45	85	- 4:20
- 5.30	38	- 4:52	- 5.30	57	- 4:33	- 5.30	33	- 4:57	- 5.30	84	- 4:06
- 5.15	37	- 4:38	- 5.15	56	- 4:19	- 5.15	32	- 4:43	- 5.15	83	- 3:52
- 5.00	36	- 4:24	- 5.00	55	- 4:05	- 5.00	32	- 4:28	- 5.00	82	- 3:38
- 4.45	36	- 4:09	- 4.45	55	- 3:50	- 4.45	32	- 4:13	- 4.45	82	- 3:23
- 4.30	36	- 3:54	- 4.30	55	- 3:35	- 4.30	31	- 3:59	- 4.30	83	- 3:07
- 4.15	36	- 3:39	- 4.15	55	- 3:20	- 4.15	31	- 3:44	- 4.15	83	- 2:52
- 4.00	36	- 3:24	- 4.00	55	- 3:05	- 4.00	30	- 3:30	- 4.00	83	- 2:37
- 3.45	36	- 3:09	- 3.45	55	- 2:50	- 3.45	30	- 3:15	- 3.45	84	- 2:21
- 3.30	37	- 2:53	- 3.30	55	- 2:35	- 3.30	30	- 3:00	- 3.30	85	- 2:05
- 3.15	37	- 2:38	- 3.15	55	- 2:20	- 3.15	30	- 2:45	- 3.15	86	- 1:49
- 3.00	37	- 2:23	- 3.00	55	- 2:05	- 3.00	30	- 2:30	- 3.00	87	- 1:33
- 2.45	38	- 2:07	- 2.45	57	- 1:48	- 2.45	30	- 2:15	- 2.45	89	- 1:16
- 2.30	38	- 1:52	- 2.30	58	- 1:32	- 2.30	30	- 2:00	- 2.30	91	- 0:59
- 2.15	39	- 1:36	- 2.15	59	- 1:16	- 2.15	30	- 1:45	- 2.15	93	- 0:42
- 2.00	39	- 1:21	- 2.00	60	- 1:00	- 2.00	30	- 1:30	- 2.00	96	- 0:24
- 1.45	40	- 1:05	- 1.45	62	- 0:43	- 1.45	31	- 1:14	- 1.45	99	- 0:06
- 1.30	41	- 0:49	- 1.30	65	- 0:25	- 1.30	32	- 0:58	- 1.30	103	+ 0:13
- 1.15	43	- 0:32	- 1.15	67	- 0:08	- 1.15	33	- 0:42	- 1.15	107	+ 0:32
- 1.00	44	- 0:16	- 1.00	70	+ 0:10	- 1.00	34	- 0:26	- 1.00	110	+ 0:50
- 0.45	46	+ 0:01	- 0.45	73	+ 0:28	- 0.45	36	- 0:09	- 0.45	115	+ 1:10
- 0.30	47	+ 0:17	- 0.30	76	+ 0:46	- 0.30	38	+ 0:08	- 0.30	119	+ 1:29
- 0.15	49	+ 0:34	- 0.15	79	+ 1:04	- 0.15	40	+ 0:25	- 0.15	123	+ 1:48
HW	51	+ 0:51	HW	82	+ 1:22	HW	42	+ 0:42	HW	128	+ 2:08
+ 0.15	53	+ 1:08	+ 0.15	85	+ 1:40	+ 0.15	43	+ 0:58	+ 0.15	129	+ 2:24
+ 0.30	54	+ 1:24	+ 0.30	89	+ 1:59	+ 0.30	44	+ 1:14	+ 0.30	131	+ 2:41
+ 0.45	56	+ 1:41	+ 0.45	92	+ 2:17	+ 0.45	45	+ 1:30	+ 0.45	132	+ 2:57
+ 1.00	57	+ 1:57	+ 1.00	96	+ 2:36	+ 1.00	46	+ 1:46	+ 1.00	134	+ 3:14
+ 1.15	57	+ 2:12	+ 1.15	95	+ 2:50	+ 1.15	46	+ 2:01	+ 1.15	132	+ 3:27
+ 1.30	57	+ 2:27	+ 1.30	94	+ 3:04	+ 1.30	46	+ 2:16	+ 1.30	131	+ 3:41
+ 1.45	57	+ 2:42	+ 1.45	94	+ 3:19	+ 1.45	46	+ 2:31	+ 1.45	129	+ 3:54
+ 2.00	57	+ 2:57	+ 2.00	93	+ 3:33	+ 2.00	46	+ 2:46	+ 2.00	128	+ 4:08
+ 2.15	56	+ 3:11	+ 2.15	91	+ 3:46	+ 2.15	45	+ 3:00	+ 2.15	126	+ 4:21
+ 2.30	55	+ 3:25	+ 2.30	89	+ 3:59	+ 2.30	45	+ 3:15	+ 2.30	124	+ 4:34
+ 2.45	54	+ 3:39	+ 2.45	87	+ 4:12	+ 2.45	44	+ 3:29	+ 2.45	122	+ 4:47
+ 3.00	53	+ 3:53	+ 3.00	84	+ 4:24	+ 3.00	43	+ 3:43	+ 3.00	120	+ 5:00
+ 3.15	53	+ 4:08	+ 3.15	83	+ 4:38	+ 3.15	43	+ 3:58	+ 3.15	118	+ 5:13
+ 3.30	52	+ 4:22	+ 3.30	82	+ 4:52	+ 3.30	42	+ 4:12	+ 3.30	116	+ 5:26
+ 3.45	51	+ 4:36	+ 3.45	81	+ 5:06	+ 3.45	41	+ 4:26	+ 3.45	114	+ 5:39
+ 4.00	50	+ 4:50	+ 4.00	79	+ 5:19	+ 4.00	40	+ 4:40	+ 4.00	112	+ 5:52
+ 4.15	49	+ 5:04	+ 4.15	78	+ 5:33	+ 4.15	40	+ 4:55	+ 4.15	110	- 5:55
+ 4.30	48	+ 5:18	+ 4.30	76	+ 5:46	+ 4.30	39	+ 5:09	+ 4.30	108	- 5:42
+ 4.45	48	+ 5:33	+ 4.45	74	+ 5:59	+ 4.45	39	+ 5:24	+ 4.45	106	- 5:29
+ 5.00	47	+ 5:47	+ 5.00	73	- 5:47	+ 5.00	38	+ 5:38	+ 5.00	104	- 5:16
+ 5.15	46	- 5:59	+ 5.15	71	- 5:34	+ 5.15	37	+ 5:52	+ 5.15	102	- 5:03
+ 5.30	45	- 5:45	+ 5.30	70	- 5:20	+ 5.30	37	- 5:53	+ 5.30	100	- 4:50
+ 5.45	44	- 5:31	+ 5.45	68	- 5:07	+ 5.45	36	- 5:39	+ 5.45	98	- 4:37
+ 6.00	43	- 5:17	+ 6.00	67	- 4:53	+ 6.00	35	- 5:25	+ 6.00	96	- 4:24

SOUTH BOUND

Table K - Harwich to Ramsgate - Outside Route

Neaps

All times relate to HW Sheerness

Time to cover Sectors (in minutes) at 4.0 Kts

SOUTH BOUND

	K8			K7			K6			K5			K4			K3			K2			K1	
	Harwich to Cork Sand B'cn			Cork Sand B'cn to S Threshold			S Threshold to Long Sand Hd			Long S'nd Hd to Kentish Knock			Kentish Knock to South Knock			South Knock to Thanet			Thanet to North Foreland			North Foreland to Ramsgate	
Time	*Duration*	*Time at End of Sector*	*Time*	*Duration*	*Time at End of Sector*	*Time*	*Duration*	*Time at End of Sector*	*Time*	*Duration*	*Time at End of Sector*	*Time*	*Duration*	*Time at End of Sector*	*Time*	*Duration*	*Time at End of Sector*	*Time*	*Duration*	*Time at End of Sector*	*Time*	*Duration*	*Time at End of Sector*
- 6.00	**86**	**- 4:34**	**- 6.00**	**77**	**- 4:43**	**- 6.00**	**88**	**- 4:32**	**- 6.00**	**72**	**- 4:48**	**- 6.00**	**63**	**- 4:57**	**- 6.00**	**79**	**- 4:41**	**- 6.00**	**83**	**- 4:37**	**- 6.00**	**56**	**- 5:04**
- 5.45	86	- 4:19	- 5.45	77	- 4:28	- 5.45	89	- 4:16	- 5.45	72	- 4:33	- 5.45	63	- 4:42	- 5.45	77	- 4:28	- 5.45	81	- 4:24	- 5.45	55	- 4:50
- 5.30	86	- 4:04	- 5.30	77	- 4:13	- 5.30	89	- 4:01	- 5.30	72	- 4:18	- 5.30	62	- 4:28	- 5.30	74	- 4:16	- 5.30	79	- 4:11	- 5.30	55	- 4:35
- 5.15	86	- 3:49	- 5.15	77	- 3:58	- 5.15	90	- 3:45	- 5.15	72	- 4:03	- 5.15	61	- 4:14	- 5.15	75	- 4:00	- 5.15	79	- 3:56	- 5.15	55	- 4:20
- 5.00	**87**	**- 3:33**	**- 5.00**	**76**	**- 3:44**	**- 5.00**	**91**	**- 3:29**	**- 5.00**	**72**	**- 3:48**	**- 5.00**	**61**	**- 3:59**	**- 5.00**	**75**	**- 3:45**	**- 5.00**	**80**	**- 3:40**	**- 5.00**	**56**	**- 4:04**
- 4.45	86	- 3:19	- 4.45	77	- 3:28	- 4.45	91	- 3:14	- 4.45	74	- 3:31	- 4.45	62	- 3:43	- 4.45	76	- 3:29	- 4.45	80	- 3:25	- 4.45	56	- 3:49
- 4.30	86	- 3:04	- 4.30	78	- 3:12	- 4.30	92	- 2:58	- 4.30	75	- 3:15	- 4.30	62	- 3:28	- 4.30	76	- 3:14	- 4.30	81	- 3:09	- 4.30	57	- 3:33
- 4.15	86	- 2:49	- 4.15	79	- 2:56	- 4.15	92	- 2:43	- 4.15	77	- 2:58	- 4.15	63	- 3:12	- 4.15	78	- 2:57	- 4.15	83	- 2:52	- 4.15	60	- 3:15
- 4.00	**85**	**- 2:35**	**- 4.00**	**80**	**- 2:40**	**- 4.00**	**93**	**- 2:27**	**- 4.00**	**78**	**- 2:42**	**- 4.00**	**64**	**- 2:56**	**- 4.00**	**80**	**- 2:40**	**- 4.00**	**85**	**- 2:35**	**- 4.00**	**63**	**- 2:57**
- 3.45	85	- 2:20	- 3.45	82	- 2:23	- 3.45	93	- 2:12	- 3.45	81	- 2:24	- 3.45	66	- 2:39	- 3.45	82	- 2:23	- 3.45	87	- 2:18	- 3.45	66	- 2:39
- 3.30	84	- 2:06	- 3.30	84	- 2:06	- 3.30	93	- 1:57	- 3.30	85	- 2:05	- 3.30	68	- 2:22	- 3.30	84	- 2:06	- 3.30	89	- 2:01	- 3.30	69	- 2:21
- 3.15	83	- 1:52	- 3.15	85	- 1:50	- 3.15	93	- 1:42	- 3.15	88	- 1:47	- 3.15	70	- 2:05	- 3.15	87	- 1:48	- 3.15	92	- 1:43	- 3.15	74	- 2:01
- 3.00	**83**	**- 1:37**	**- 3.00**	**87**	**- 1:33**	**- 3.00**	**93**	**- 1:27**	**- 3.00**	**91**	**- 1:29**	**- 3.00**	**72**	**- 1:48**	**- 3.00**	**89**	**- 1:31**	**- 3.00**	**96**	**- 1:24**	**- 3.00**	**80**	**- 1:40**
- 2.45	81	- 1:24	- 2.45	88	- 1:17	- 2.45	92	- 1:13	- 2.45	95	- 1:10	- 2.45	75	- 1:30	- 2.45	92	- 1:13	- 2.45	99	- 1:06	- 2.45	86	- 1:19
- 2.30	79	- 1:11	- 2.30	88	- 1:02	- 2.30	92	- 0:58	- 2.30	100	- 0:50	- 2.30	78	- 1:12	- 2.30	94	- 0:56	- 2.30	102	- 0:48	- 2.30	91	- 0:59
- 2.15	77	- 0:58	- 2.15	89	- 0:46	- 2.15	92	- 0:43	- 2.15	104	- 0:31	- 2.15	81	- 0:54	- 2.15	99	- 0:36	- 2.15	106	- 0:29	- 2.15	95	- 0:40
- 2.00	**76**	**- 0:44**	**- 2.00**	**90**	**- 0:30**	**- 2.00**	**91**	**- 0:29**	**- 2.00**	**109**	**- 0:11**	**- 2.00**	**84**	**- 0:36**	**- 2.00**	**103**	**- 0:17**	**- 2.00**	**111**	**- 0:09**	**- 2.00**	**98**	**- 0:22**
- 1.45	75	- 0:30	- 1.45	91	- 0:14	- 1.45	91	- 0:14	- 1.45	114	+ 0:09	- 1.45	89	- 0:16	- 1.45	107	+ 0:02	- 1.45	115	+ 0:10	- 1.45	102	- 0:03
- 1.30	74	- 0:16	- 1.30	91	+ 0:01	- 1.30	92	+ 0:02	- 1.30	120	+ 0:30	- 1.30	93	+ 0:03	- 1.30	112	+ 0:22	- 1.30	120	+ 0:30	- 1.30	105	+ 0:15
- 1.15	74	- 0:01	- 1.15	92	+ 0:17	- 1.15	92	+ 0:17	- 1.15	126	+ 0:51	- 1.15	98	+ 0:23	- 1.15	116	+ 0:41	- 1.15	122	+ 0:47	- 1.15	105	+ 0:30
- 1.00	**73**	**+ 0:13**	**- 1.00**	**92**	**+ 0:32**	**- 1.00**	**92**	**+ 0:32**	**- 1.00**	**131**	+ 1:11	**- 1.00**	**102**	**+ 0:42**	**- 1.00**	**119**	**+ 0:59**	**- 1.00**	**123**	+ 1:03	**- 1.00**	**104**	**+ 0:44**
- 0.45	71	+ 0:26	- 0.45	94	+ 0:49	- 0.45	93	+ 0:48	- 0.45	134	+ 1:29	- 0.45	106	+ 1:01	- 0.45	123	+ 1:18	- 0.45	125	+ 1:20	- 0.45	104	+ 0:59
- 0.30	69	+ 0:39	- 0.30	96	+ 1:06	- 0.30	93	+ 1:03	- 0.30	136	+ 1:46	- 0.30	109	+ 1:19	- 0.30	127	+ 1:37	- 0.30	126	+ 1:36	- 0.30	104	+ 1:14
- 0.15	66	+ 0:51	- 0.15	98	+ 1:23	- 0.15	94	+ 1:19	- 0.15	139	+ 2:04	- 0.15	**113**	+ 1:38	- 0.15	128	+ 1:53	- 0.15	126	+ 1:51	- 0.15	101	+ 1:26
HW	**64**	**+ 1:04**	**HW**	**100**	**+ 1:40**	**HW**	**95**	**+ 1:35**	**HW**	**141**	**+ 2:21**	**HW**	**116**	**+ 1:56**	**HW**	**127**	**+ 2:07**	**HW**	**125**	**+ 2:05**	**HW**	**99**	**+ 1:39**
+ 0.15	63	+ 1:18	+ 0.15	101	+ 1:56	+ 0.15	96	+ 1:51	+ 0.15	140	+ 2:35	+ 0.15	117	+ 2:12	+ 0.15	128	+ 2:23	+ 0.15	124	+ 2:19	+ 0.15	96	+ 1:51
+ 0.30	63	+ 1:33	+ 0.30	101	+ 2:11	+ 0.30	97	+ 2:07	+ 0.30	138	+ 2:48	+ 0.30	117	+ 2:27	+ 0.30	130	+ 2:40	+ 0.30	123	+ 2:33	+ 0.30	94	+ 2:04
+ 0.45	63	+ 1:48	+ 0.45	102	+ 2:27	+ 0.45	98	+ 2:23	+ 0.45	136	+ 3:01	+ 0.45	118	+ 2:43	+ 0.45	131	+ 2:56	+ 0.45	122	+ 2:47	+ 0.45	90	+ 2:15
+ 1.00	**62**	**+ 2:02**	**+ 1.00**	**103**	**+ 2:43**	**+ 1.00**	**99**	**+ 2:39**	**+ 1.00**	**134**	**+ 3:14**	**+ 1.00**	**119**	**+ 2:59**	**+ 1.00**	**132**	**+ 3:12**	**+ 1.00**	**120**	**+ 3:00**	**+ 1.00**	**85**	**+ 2:25**
+ 1.15	63	+ 2:18	+ 1.15	101	+ 2:56	+ 1.15	98	+ 2:53	+ 1.15	131	+ 3:26	+ 1.15	118	+ 3:13	+ 1.15	131	+ 3:26	+ 1.15	119	+ 3:14	+ 1.15	81	+ 2:36
+ 1.30	63	+ 2:33	+ 1.30	100	+ 3:10	+ 1.30	98	+ 3:08	+ 1.30	127	+ 3:37	+ 1.30	117	+ 3:27	+ 1.30	129	+ 3:39	+ 1.30	118	+ 3:28	+ 1.30	77	+ 2:47
+ 1.45	63	+ 2:48	+ 1.45	99	+ 3:24	+ 1.45	98	+ 3:23	+ 1.45	123	+ 3:48	+ 1.45	116	+ 3:41	+ 1.45	127	+ 3:52	+ 1.45	117	+ 3:42	+ 1.45	74	+ 2:59
+ 2.00	**64**	**+ 3:04**	**+ 2.00**	**97**	**+ 3:37**	**+ 2.00**	**97**	**+ 3:37**	**+ 2.00**	**120**	**+ 4:00**	**+ 2.00**	**115**	**+ 3:55**	**+ 2.00**	**125**	**+ 4:05**	**+ 2.00**	**115**	**+ 3:55**	**+ 2.00**	**72**	**+ 3:12**
+ 2.15	64	+ 3:19	+ 2.15	96	+ 3:51	+ 2.15	96	+ 3:51	+ 2.15	117	+ 4:12	+ 2.15	112	+ 4:07	+ 2.15	123	+ 4:18	+ 2.15	114	+ 4:09	+ 2.15	70	+ 3:25
+ 2.30	65	+ 3:35	+ 2.30	94	+ 4:04	+ 2.30	95	+ 4:05	+ 2.30	113	+ 4:23	+ 2.30	109	+ 4:19	+ 2.30	121	+ 4:31	+ 2.30	113	+ 4:23	+ 2.30	68	+ 3:38
+ 2.45	65	+ 3:50	+ 2.45	92	+ 4:17	+ 2.45	94	+ 4:19	+ 2.45	110	+ 4:35	+ 2.45	106	+ 4:31	+ 2.45	118	+ 4:43	+ 2.45	111	+ 4:36	+ 2.45	67	+ 3:52
+ 3.00	**66**	**+ 4:06**	**+ 3.00**	**91**	**+ 4:31**	**+ 3.00**	**93**	**+ 4:33**	**+ 3.00**	**107**	**+ 4:47**	**+ 3.00**	**103**	**+ 4:43**	**+ 3.00**	**116**	**+ 4:56**	**+ 3.00**	**109**	**+ 4:49**	**+ 3.00**	**66**	**+ 4:06**
+ 3.15	67	+ 4:22	+ 3.15	89	+ 4:44	+ 3.15	92	+ 4:47	+ 3.15	104	+ 4:59	+ 3.15	100	+ 4:55	+ 3.15	114	+ 5:09	+ 3.15	107	+ 5:02	+ 3.15	64	+ 4:19
+ 3.30	68	+ 4:38	+ 3.30	88	+ 4:58	+ 3.30	92	+ 5:02	+ 3.30	102	+ 5:12	+ 3.30	97	+ 5:07	+ 3.30	111	+ 5:21	+ 3.30	106	+ 5:16	+ 3.30	63	+ 4:33
+ 3.45	70	+ 4:55	+ 3.45	87	+ 5:12	+ 3.45	91	+ 5:16	+ 3.45	99	+ 5:24	+ 3.45	94	+ 5:19	+ 3.45	109	+ 5:34	+ 3.45	104	+ 5:29	+ 3.45	62	+ 4:47
+ 4.00	**71**	**+ 5:11**	**+ 4.00**	**86**	**+ 5:26**	**+ 4.00**	**90**	**+ 5:30**	**+ 4.00**	**96**	**+ 5:36**	**+ 4.00**	**90**	**+ 5:30**	**+ 4.00**	**106**	**+ 5:46**	**+ 4.00**	**102**	**+ 5:42**	**+ 4.00**	**61**	**+ 5:01**
+ 4.15	72	+ 5:27	+ 4.15	85	+ 5:40	+ 4.15	90	+ 5:45	+ 4.15	94	+ 5:49	+ 4.15	87	+ 5:42	+ 4.15	105	- 6:00	+ 4.15	101	+ 5:56	+ 4.15	61	+ 5:16
+ 4.30	72	+ 5:42	+ 4.30	84	+ 5:54	+ 4.30	89	+ 5:59	+ 4.30	91	- 5:59	+ 4.30	83	+ 5:53	+ 4.30	103	- 5:47	+ 4.30	99	- 5:51	+ 4.30	60	+ 5:30
+ 4.45	73	+ 5:58	+ 4.45	83	- 5:52	+ 4.45	88	- 5:47	+ 4.45	88	- 5:47	+ 4.45	80	- 5:55	+ 4.45	101	- 5:34	+ 4.45	98	- 5:37	+ 4.45	60	+ 5:45
+ 5.00	**74**	**- 5:46**	**+ 5.00**	**83**	**- 5:37**	**+ 5.00**	**88**	**- 5:32**	**+ 5.00**	**85**	**- 5:35**	**+ 5.00**	**76**	**- 5:44**	**+ 5.00**	**99**	**- 5:21**	**+ 5.00**	**96**	**- 5:24**	**+ 5.00**	**60**	**- 6:00**
+ 5.15	75	- 5:30	+ 5.15	80	- 5:25	+ 5.15	85	- 5:20	+ 5.15	84	- 5:21	+ 5.15	75	- 5:30	+ 5.15	98	- 5:07	+ 5.15	95	- 5:10	+ 5.15	60	- 5:45
+ 5.30	76	- 5:14	+ 5.30	77	- 5:13	+ 5.30	83	- 5:07	+ 5.30	82	- 5:08	+ 5.30	73	- 5:17	+ 5.30	96	- 4:54	+ 5.30	93	- 4:57	+ 5.30	59	- 5:31
+ 5.45	77	- 4:58	+ 5.45	74	- 5:01	+ 5.45	80	- 4:55	+ 5.45	81	- 4:54	+ 5.45	72	- 5:03	+ 5.45	94	- 4:41	+ 5.45	86	- 4:49	+ 5.45	57	- 5:18
+ 6.00	**77**	**- 4:43**	**+ 6.00**	**71**	**- 4:49**	**+ 6.00**	**78**	**- 4:42**	**+ 6.00**	**79**	**- 4:41**	**+ 6.00**	**70**	**- 4:50**	**+ 6.00**	**92**	**- 4:28**	**+ 6.00**	**84**	**- 4:36**	**+ 6.00**	**57**	**- 5:03**

Table K - Harwich to Ramsgate - Outside Route

Time to cover Sectors (in minutes) at 4.0 kts

All times relate to HW Sheerness

Springs

	K8			K7			K6			K5	
	Harwich to Cork Sand B'cn			Cork Sand B'cn to S Threshold			S Threshold to Long Sand Hd			Long S'nd Hd to Kentish Knock	
Time	Duration	Time at End of Sector	Time	Duration	Time at End of Sector	Time	Duration	Time at End of Sector	Time	Duration	Time at End of Sector
- 6.00	96	- 4:24	- 6.00	76	- 4:44	- 6.00	90	- 4:30	- 6.00	62	- 4:58
- 5.45	96	- 4:09	- 5.45	75	- 4:30	- 5.45	92	- 4:13	- 5.45	62	- 4:43
- 5.30	96	- 3:54	- 5.30	75	- 4:15	- 5.30	93	- 3:57	- 5.30	62	- 4:28
- 5.15	97	- 3:38	- 5.15	75	- 4:00	- 5.15	94	- 3:41	- 5.15	62	- 4:13
- 5.00	97	- 3:23	- 5.00	75	- 3:45	- 5.00	95	- 3:25	- 5.00	62	- 3:58
- 4.45	96	- 3:09	- 4.45	76	- 3:29	- 4.45	95	- 3:10	- 4.45	64	- 3:41
- 4.30	95	- 2:55	- 4.30	78	- 3:12	- 4.30	95	- 2:55	- 4.30	66	- 3:24
- 4.15	94	- 2:41	- 4.15	79	- 2:56	- 4.15	96	- 2:39	- 4.15	69	- 3:06
- 4.00	93	- 2:27	- 4.00	81	- 2:39	- 4.00	96	- 2:24	- 4.00	71	- 2:49
- 3.45	92	- 2:13	- 3.45	83	- 2:22	- 3.45	95	- 2:10	- 3.45	75	- 2:30
- 3.30	91	- 1:59	- 3.30	85	- 2:05	- 3.30	95	- 1:55	- 3.30	80	- 2:10
- 3.15	90	- 1:45	- 3.15	87	- 1:48	- 3.15	95	- 1:40	- 3.15	84	- 1:51
- 3.00	89	- 1:31	- 3.00	90	- 1:30	- 3.00	94	- 1:26	- 3.00	89	- 1:31
- 2.45	86	- 1:19	- 2.45	90	- 1:15	- 2.45	94	- 1:11	- 2.45	95	- 1:10
- 2.30	83	- 1:07	- 2.30	91	- 0:59	- 2.30	93	- 0:57	- 2.30	102	- 0:48
- 2.15	80	- 0:55	- 2.15	91	- 0:44	- 2.15	93	- 0:42	- 2.15	108	- 0:27
- 2.00	77	- 0:43	- 2.00	91	- 0:29	- 2.00	93	- 0:27	- 2.00	115	- 0:05
- 1.45	77	- 0:28	- 1.45	93	- 0:12	- 1.45	93	- 0:12	- 1.45	134	+ 0:29
- 1.30	76	- 0:14	- 1.30	95	+ 0:05	- 1.30	93	+ 0:03	- 1.30	153	+ 1:03
- 1.15	75	- HW	- 1.15	96	+ 0:21	- 1.15	94	+ 0:19	- 1.15	172	+ 1:37
- 1.00	74	+ 0:14	- 1.00	98	+ 0:38	- 1.00	94	+ 0:34	- 1.00	192	+ 2:12
- 0.45	71	+ 0:26	- 0.45	101	+ 0:56	- 0.45	96	+ 0:51	- 0.45	195	+ 2:30
- 0.30	69	+ 0:39	- 0.30	103	+ 1:13	- 0.30	98	+ 1:08	- 0.30	199	+ 2:49
- 0.15	66	+ 0:51	- 0.15	106	+ 1:31	- 0.15	100	+ 1:25	- 0.15	202	+ 3:07
HW	63	+ 1:03	HW	109	+ 1:49	HW	102	+ 1:42	HW	206	+ 3:26
+ 0.15	63	+ 1:18	+ 0.15	110	+ 2:05	+ 0.15	103	+ 1:58	+ 0.15	203	+ 3:38
+ 0.30	62	+ 1:32	+ 0.30	110	+ 2:20	+ 0.30	104	+ 2:14	+ 0.30	201	+ 3:51
+ 0.45	61	+ 1:46	+ 0.45	110	+ 2:35	+ 0.45	105	+ 2:30	+ 0.45	199	+ 4:04
+ 1.00	60	+ 2:00	+ 1.00	111	+ 2:51	+ 1.00	106	+ 2:46	+ 1.00	197	+ 4:17
+ 1.15	61	+ 2:16	+ 1.15	108	+ 3:03	+ 1.15	105	+ 3:00	+ 1.15	179	+ 4:14
+ 1.30	61	+ 2:31	+ 1.30	106	+ 3:16	+ 1.30	104	+ 3:14	+ 1.30	161	+ 4:11
+ 1.45	61	+ 2:46	+ 1.45	103	+ 3:28	+ 1.45	103	+ 3:28	+ 1.45	144	+ 4:09
+ 2.00	62	+ 3:02	+ 2.00	101	+ 3:41	+ 2.00	101	+ 3:41	+ 2.00	126	+ 4:06
+ 2.15	62	+ 3:17	+ 2.15	99	+ 3:54	+ 2.15	100	+ 3:55	+ 2.15	121	+ 4:16
+ 2.30	62	+ 3:32	+ 2.30	96	+ 4:06	+ 2.30	98	+ 4:08	+ 2.30	117	+ 4:27
+ 2.45	63	+ 3:48	+ 2.45	94	+ 4:19	+ 2.45	96	+ 4:21	+ 2.45	113	+ 4:38
+ 3.00	63	+ 4:03	+ 3.00	92	+ 4:32	+ 3.00	95	+ 4:35	+ 3.00	108	+ 4:48
+ 3.15	65	+ 4:20	+ 3.15	90	+ 4:45	+ 3.15	94	+ 4:49	+ 3.15	105	+ 5:00
+ 3.30	66	+ 4:36	+ 3.30	89	+ 4:59	+ 3.30	93	+ 5:03	+ 3.30	101	+ 5:11
+ 3.45	68	+ 4:53	+ 3.45	87	+ 5:12	+ 3.45	92	+ 5:17	+ 3.45	98	+ 5:23
+ 4.00	69	+ 5:09	+ 4.00	86	+ 5:26	+ 4.00	91	+ 5:31	+ 4.00	94	+ 5:34
+ 4.15	70	+ 5:25	+ 4.15	85	+ 5:40	+ 4.15	86	+ 5:41	+ 4.15	91	+ 5:46
+ 4.30	71	+ 5:41	+ 4.30	84	+ 5:54	+ 4.30	82	+ 5:52	+ 4.30	87	- 6:03
+ 4.45	72	+ 5:57	+ 4.45	83	- 5:52	+ 4.45	77	- 5:58	+ 4.45	83	- 5:52
+ 5.00	73	- 5:47	+ 5.00	82	- 5:38	+ 5.00	72	- 5:48	+ 5.00	79	- 5:41
+ 5.15	75	- 5:30	+ 5.15	78	- 5:27	+ 5.15	76	- 5:29	+ 5.15	77	- 5:28
+ 5.30	77	- 5:13	+ 5.30	73	- 5:17	+ 5.30	80	- 5:10	+ 5.30	75	- 5:15
+ 5.45	78	- 4:57	+ 5.45	69	- 5:06	+ 5.45	83	- 4:52	+ 5.45	72	- 5:03
+ 6.00	80	- 4:40	+ 6.00	64	- 4:56	+ 6.00	87	- 4:33	+ 6.00	70	- 4:50

	K4			K3			K2			K1	
	Kentish Knock to South Knock			South Knock to Thanet			Thanet to North Foreland			North Foreland to Ramsgate	
Time	Duration	Time at End of Sector	Time	Duration	Time at End of Sector	Time	Duration	Time at End of Sector	Time	Duration	Time at End of Sector
- 6.00	56	- 5:04	- 6.00	64	- 4:56	- 6.00	72	- 4:48	- 6.00	47	- 5:13
- 5.45	55	- 4:50	- 5.45	60	- 4:45	- 5.45	69	- 4:36	- 5.45	47	- 4:58
- 5.30	55	- 4:35	- 5.30	56	- 4:34	- 5.30	66	- 4:24	- 5.30	46	- 4:44
- 5.15	54	- 4:21	- 5.15	57	- 4:18	- 5.15	66	- 4:09	- 5.15	47	- 4:28
- 5.00	53	- 4:07	- 5.00	57	- 4:03	- 5.00	66	- 3:54	- 5.00	47	- 4:13
- 4.45	54	- 3:51	- 4.45	58	- 3:47	- 4.45	66	- 3:39	- 4.45	48	- 3:57
- 4.30	55	- 3:35	- 4.30	59	- 3:31	- 4.30	66	- 3:24	- 4.30	49	- 3:41
- 4.15	56	- 3:19	- 4.15	62	- 3:13	- 4.15	70	- 3:05	- 4.15	53	- 3:22
- 4.00	57	- 3:03	- 4.00	66	- 2:54	- 4.00	74	- 2:46	- 4.00	57	- 3:03
- 3.45	59	- 2:46	- 3.45	69	- 2:36	- 3.45	77	- 2:28	- 3.45	62	- 2:43
- 3.30	62	- 2:28	- 3.30	73	- 2:17	- 3.30	81	- 2:09	- 3.30	66	- 2:24
- 3.15	64	- 2:11	- 3.15	79	- 1:56	- 3.15	88	- 1:47	- 3.15	78	- 1:57
- 3.00	67	- 1:53	- 3.00	85	- 1:35	- 3.00	95	- 1:25	- 3.00	90	- 1:30
- 2.45	72	- 1:33	- 2.45	90	- 1:15	- 2.45	103	- 1:02	- 2.45	101	- 1:04
- 2.30	76	- 1:14	- 2.30	96	- 0:54	- 2.30	110	- 0:40	- 2.30	113	- 0:37
- 2.15	81	- 0:54	- 2.15	104	- 0:31	- 2.15	116	- 0:19	- 2.15	117	- 0:18
- 2.00	85	- 0:35	- 2.00	112	- 0:08	- 2.00	123	+ 0:03	- 2.00	121	+ 0:01
- 1.45	92	- 0:13	- 1.45	119	+ 0:14	- 1.45	130	+ 0:25	- 1.45	125	+ 0:20
- 1.30	100	+ 0:10	- 1.30	127	+ 0:37	- 1.30	137	+ 0:47	- 1.30	128	+ 0:38
- 1.15	107	+ 0:32	- 1.15	136	+ 1:01	- 1.15	138	+ 1:03	- 1.15	126	+ 0:51
- 1.00	114	+ 0:54	- 1.00	145	+ 1:25	- 1.00	140	+ 1:20	- 1.00	124	+ 1:04
- 0.45	118	+ 1:13	- 0.45	153	+ 1:48	- 0.45	141	+ 1:36	- 0.45	122	+ 1:17
- 0.30	123	+ 1:33	- 0.30	162	+ 2:12	- 0.30	142	+ 1:52	- 0.30	120	+ 1:30
- 0.15	127	+ 1:52	- 0.15	162	+ 2:27	- 0.15	141	+ 2:06	- 0.15	115	+ 1:40
HW	132	+ 2:12	HW	161	+ 2:41	HW	139	+ 2:19	HW	111	+ 1:51
+ 0.15	133	+ 2:28	+ 0.15	161	+ 2:56	+ 0.15	138	+ 2:33	+ 0.15	106	+ 2:01
+ 0.30	133	+ 2:43	+ 0.30	161	+ 3:11	+ 0.30	136	+ 2:46	+ 0.30	101	+ 2:11
+ 0.45	134	+ 2:59	+ 0.45	156	+ 3:21	+ 0.45	134	+ 2:59	+ 0.45	96	+ 2:21
+ 1.00	135	+ 3:15	+ 1.00	151	+ 3:31	+ 1.00	132	+ 3:12	+ 1.00	91	+ 2:31
+ 1.15	133	+ 3:28	+ 1.15	146	+ 3:41	+ 1.15	130	+ 3:25	+ 1.15	86	+ 2:41
+ 1.30	130	+ 3:40	+ 1.30	141	+ 3:51	+ 1.30	128	+ 3:38	+ 1.30	81	+ 2:51
+ 1.45	128	+ 3:53	+ 1.45	137	+ 4:02	+ 1.45	126	+ 3:51	+ 1.45	78	+ 3:03
+ 2.00	125	+ 4:05	+ 2.00	132	+ 4:12	+ 2.00	123	+ 4:03	+ 2.00	74	+ 3:14
+ 2.15	121	+ 4:16	+ 2.15	128	+ 4:23	+ 2.15	120	+ 4:15	+ 2.15	70	+ 3:25
+ 2.30	116	+ 4:26	+ 2.30	123	+ 4:33	+ 2.30	118	+ 4:28	+ 2.30	66	+ 3:36
+ 2.45	112	+ 4:37	+ 2.45	119	+ 4:44	+ 2.45	115	+ 4:40	+ 2.45	65	+ 3:50
+ 3.00	108	+ 4:48	+ 3.00	115	+ 4:55	+ 3.00	112	+ 4:52	+ 3.00	63	+ 4:03
+ 3.15	103	+ 4:58	+ 3.15	112	+ 5:07	+ 3.15	109	+ 5:04	+ 3.15	62	+ 4:17
+ 3.30	99	+ 5:09	+ 3.30	108	+ 5:18	+ 3.30	106	+ 5:16	+ 3.30	61	+ 4:31
+ 3.45	95	+ 5:20	+ 3.45	106	+ 5:31	+ 3.45	104	+ 5:29	+ 3.45	60	+ 4:45
+ 4.00	90	+ 5:30	+ 4.00	103	+ 5:43	+ 4.00	102	+ 5:42	+ 4.00	58	+ 4:58
+ 4.15	86	+ 5:41	+ 4.15	101	+ 5:56	+ 4.15	100	+ 5:55	+ 4.15	57	+ 5:12
+ 4.30	82	+ 5:52	+ 4.30	99	- 5:51	+ 4.30	98	- 5:52	+ 4.30	56	+ 5:26
+ 4.45	77	- 5:58	+ 4.45	96	- 5:39	+ 4.45	96	- 5:39	+ 4.45	55	+ 5:40
+ 5.00	73	- 5:47	+ 5.00	93	- 5:27	+ 5.00	94	- 5:26	+ 5.00	54	+ 5:54
+ 5.15	71	- 5:34	+ 5.15	90	- 5:15	+ 5.15	92	- 5:13	+ 5.15	53	- 5:52
+ 5.30	69	- 5:21	+ 5.30	87	- 5:03	+ 5.30	90	- 5:00	+ 5.30	52	- 5:38
+ 5.45	66	- 5:09	+ 5.45	71	- 5:04	+ 5.45	77	- 4:58	+ 5.45	49	- 5:26
+ 6.00	64	- 4:56	+ 6.00	64	- 4:56	+ 6.00	74	- 4:46	+ 6.00	48	- 5:12

SOUTH BOUND

Table K - Harwich to Ramsgate - Outside Route

Neaps | All times relate to HW Sheerness | Time to cover Sectors (in minutes) at 5.0 Kts

SOUTH BOUND

	K8			K7			K6			K5			K4			K3			K2			K1	
	Harwich to Cork Sand B'cn			Cork Sand B'cn to S Threshold			S Threshold to Long Sand Hd			Long S'nd Hd to Kentish Knock			Kentish Knock to South Knock			South Knock to Thanet			Thanet to North Foreland			North Foreland to Ramsgate	
Time	Duration	Time at End of Sector	Time	Duration	Time at End of Sector	Time	Duration	Time at End of Sector	Time	Duration	Time at End of Sector	Time	Duration	Time at End of Sector	Time	Duration	Time at End of Sector	Time	Duration	Time at End of Sector	Time	Duration	Time at End of Sector
- 6.00	67	- 4:53	- 6.00	63	- 4:57	- 6.00	70	- 4:50	- 6.00	62	- 4:58	- 6.00	54	- 5:06	- 6.00	67	- 4:53	- 6.00	69	- 4:51	- 6.00	47	- 5:13
- 5.45	67	- 4:38	- 5.45	62	- 4:43	- 5.45	70	- 4:35	- 5.45	62	- 4:43	- 5.45	54	- 4:51	- 5.45	66	- 4:39	- 5.45	68	- 4:37	- 5.45	47	- 4:58
- 5.30	67	- 4:23	- 5.30	62	- 4:28	- 5.30	70	- 4:20	- 5.30	62	- 4:28	- 5.30	53	- 4:37	- 5.30	64	- 4:26	- 5.30	67	- 4:23	- 5.30	46	- 4:44
- 5.15	67	- 4:08	- 5.15	62	- 4:13	- 5.15	70	- 4:05	- 5.15	62	- 4:13	- 5.15	53	- 4:22	- 5.15	64	- 4:11	- 5.15	67	- 4:08	- 5.15	47	- 4:28
- 5.00	67	- 3:53	- 5.00	62	- 3:58	- 5.00	70	- 3:50	- 5.00	61	- 3:59	- 5.00	52	- 4:08	- 5.00	64	- 3:56	- 5.00	67	- 3:53	- 5.00	47	- 4:13
- 4.45	67	- 3:38	- 4.45	63	- 3:42	- 4.45	71	- 3:34	- 4.45	62	- 3:43	- 4.45	53	- 3:52	- 4.45	64	- 3:41	- 4.45	67	- 3:38	- 4.45	47	- 3:58
- 4.30	67	- 3:23	- 4.30	63	- 3:27	- 4.30	71	- 3:19	- 4.30	63	- 3:27	- 4.30	53	- 3:37	- 4.30	64	- 3:26	- 4.30	67	- 3:23	- 4.30	47	- 3:43
- 4.15	67	- 3:08	- 4.15	64	- 3:11	- 4.15	71	- 3:04	- 4.15	64	- 3:11	- 4.15	53	- 3:22	- 4.15	65	- 3:10	- 4.15	69	- 3:06	- 4.15	49	- 3:26
- 4.00	67	- 2:53	- 4.00	64	- 2:56	- 4.00	71	- 2:49	- 4.00	65	- 2:55	- 4.00	54	- 3:06	- 4.00	67	- 2:53	- 4.00	70	- 2:50	- 4.00	51	- 3:09
- 3.45	66	- 2:39	- 3.45	65	- 2:40	- 3.45	71	- 2:34	- 3.45	67	- 2:38	- 3.45	55	- 2:50	- 3.45	68	- 2:37	- 3.45	71	- 2:34	- 3.45	52	- 2:53
- 3.30	66	- 2:24	- 3.30	66	- 2:24	- 3.30	72	- 2:18	- 3.30	69	- 2:21	- 3.30	56	- 2:34	- 3.30	69	- 2:21	- 3.30	73	- 2:17	- 3.30	54	- 2:36
- 3.15	65	- 2:10	- 3.15	67	- 2:08	- 3.15	72	- 2:03	- 3.15	71	- 2:04	- 3.15	57	- 2:18	- 3.15	71	- 2:04	- 3.15	75	- 2:00	- 3.15	57	- 2:18
- 3.00	65	- 1:55	- 3.00	68	- 1:52	- 3.00	72	- 1:48	- 3.00	73	- 1:47	- 3.00	59	- 2:01	- 3.00	73	- 1:47	- 3.00	77	- 1:43	- 3.00	59	- 2:01
- 2.45	64	- 1:41	- 2.45	69	- 1:36	- 2.45	72	- 1:33	- 2.45	75	- 1:30	- 2.45	60	- 1:45	- 2.45	75	- 1:30	- 2.45	79	- 1:26	- 2.45	62	- 1:43
- 2.30	63	- 1:27	- 2.30	69	- 1:21	- 2.30	72	- 1:18	- 2.30	78	- 1:12	- 2.30	62	- 1:28	- 2.30	77	- 1:13	- 2.30	81	- 1:09	- 2.30	65	- 1:25
- 2.15	62	- 1:13	- 2.15	70	- 1:05	- 2.15	72	- 1:03	- 2.15	80	- 0:55	- 2.15	64	- 1:11	- 2.15	79	- 0:56	- 2.15	84	- 0:51	- 2.15	66	- 1:09
- 2.00	60	- 1:00	- 2.00	70	- 0:50	- 2.00	72	- 0:48	- 2.00	82	- 0:38	- 2.00	66	- 0:54	- 2.00	81	- 0:39	- 2.00	87	- 0:33	- 2.00	67	- 0:53
- 1.45	60	- 0:45	- 1.45	71	- 0:34	- 1.45	72	- 0:33	- 1.45	86	- 0:19	- 1.45	69	- 0:36	- 1.45	83	- 0:22	- 1.45	89	- 0:16	- 1.45	68	- 0:37
- 1.30	60	- 0:30	- 1.30	71	- 0:19	- 1.30	72	- 0:18	- 1.30	90	- 0:00	- 1.30	71	- 0:19	- 1.30	85	- 0:05	- 1.30	92	+ 0:02	- 1.30	70	- 0:20
- 1.15	60	- 0:15	- 1.15	71	- 0:04	- 1.15	72	- 0:03	- 1.15	94	+ 0:19	- 1.15	73	- 0:02	- 1.15	88	+ 0:13	- 1.15	94	+ 0:19	- 1.15	70	- 0:05
- 1.00	60	HW	- 1.00	71	+ 0:11	- 1.00	72	+ 0:12	- 1.00	98	+ 0:38	- 1.00	75	+ 0:15	- 1.00	91	+ 0:31	- 1.00	95	+ 0:35	- 1.00	70	+ 0:10
- 0.45	58	+ 0:13	- 0.45	72	+ 0:27	- 0.45	72	+ 0:27	- 0.45	100	+ 0:55	- 0.45	77	+ 0:32	- 0.45	94	+ 0:49	- 0.45	97	+ 0:52	- 0.45	70	+ 0:25
- 0.30	56	+ 0:26	- 0.30	73	+ 0:43	- 0.30	73	+ 0:43	- 0.30	103	+ 1:13	- 0.30	78	+ 0:48	- 0.30	97	+ 1:07	- 0.30	98	+ 1:08	- 0.30	70	+ 0:40
- 0.15	54	+ 0:39	- 0.15	73	+ 0:58	- 0.15	73	+ 0:58	- 0.15	105	+ 1:30	- 0.15	80	+ 1:05	- 0.15	98	+ 1:23	- 0.15	98	+ 1:23	- 0.15	69	+ 0:54
HW	52	+ 0:52	HW	74	+ 1:14	HW	73	+ 1:13	HW	108	+ 1:48	HW	81	+ 1:21	HW	100	+ 1:40	HW	97	+ 1:37	HW	68	+ 1:08
+ 0.15	52	+ 1:07	+ 0.15	75	+ 1:30	+ 0.15	74	+ 1:29	+ 0.15	107	+ 2:02	+ 0.15	83	+ 1:38	+ 0.15	101	+ 1:56	+ 0.15	96	+ 1:51	+ 0.15	68	+ 1:23
+ 0.30	52	+ 1:22	+ 0.30	75	+ 1:45	+ 0.30	74	+ 1:44	+ 0.30	106	+ 2:16	+ 0.30	86	+ 1:56	+ 0.30	102	+ 2:12	+ 0.30	96	+ 2:06	+ 0.30	67	+ 1:37
+ 0.45	51	+ 1:36	+ 0.45	75	+ 2:00	+ 0.45	74	+ 1:59	+ 0.45	105	+ 2:30	+ 0.45	88	+ 2:13	+ 0.45	101	+ 2:26	+ 0.45	95	+ 2:20	+ 0.45	65	+ 1:50
+ 1.00	51	+ 1:51	+ 1.00	76	+ 2:16	+ 1.00	74	+ 2:14	+ 1.00	104	+ 2:44	+ 1.00	90	+ 2:30	+ 1.00	100	+ 2:40	+ 1.00	94	+ 2:34	+ 1.00	64	+ 2:04
+ 1.15	51	+ 2:06	+ 1.15	75	+ 2:30	+ 1.15	74	+ 2:29	+ 1.15	101	+ 2:56	+ 1.15	88	+ 2:43	+ 1.15	99	+ 2:54	+ 1.15	93	+ 2:48	+ 1.15	62	+ 2:17
+ 1.30	51	+ 2:21	+ 1.30	75	+ 2:45	+ 1.30	74	+ 2:44	+ 1.30	99	+ 3:09	+ 1.30	86	+ 2:56	+ 1.30	98	+ 3:08	+ 1.30	93	+ 3:03	+ 1.30	61	+ 2:31
+ 1.45	52	+ 2:37	+ 1.45	74	+ 2:59	+ 1.45	74	+ 2:59	+ 1.45	97	+ 3:22	+ 1.45	84	+ 3:09	+ 1.45	97	+ 3:22	+ 1.45	92	+ 3:17	+ 1.45	59	+ 2:44
+ 2.00	52	+ 2:52	+ 2.00	73	+ 3:13	+ 2.00	73	+ 3:13	+ 2.00	94	+ 3:34	+ 2.00	82	+ 3:22	+ 2.00	95	+ 3:35	+ 2.00	91	+ 3:31	+ 2.00	58	+ 2:58
+ 2.15	52	+ 3:07	+ 2.15	73	+ 3:28	+ 2.15	73	+ 3:28	+ 2.15	92	+ 3:47	+ 2.15	81	+ 3:36	+ 2.15	94	+ 3:49	+ 2.15	91	+ 3:46	+ 2.15	57	+ 3:12
+ 2.30	52	+ 3:22	+ 2.30	72	+ 3:42	+ 2.30	73	+ 3:43	+ 2.30	89	+ 3:59	+ 2.30	80	+ 3:50	+ 2.30	92	+ 4:02	+ 2.30	90	+ 4:00	+ 2.30	55	+ 3:25
+ 2.45	53	+ 3:38	+ 2.45	71	+ 3:56	+ 2.45	72	+ 3:57	+ 2.45	86	+ 4:11	+ 2.45	79	+ 4:04	+ 2.45	90	+ 4:15	+ 2.45	88	+ 4:13	+ 2.45	55	+ 3:40
+ 3.00	53	+ 3:53	+ 3.00	70	+ 4:10	+ 3.00	72	+ 4:12	+ 3.00	84	+ 4:24	+ 3.00	78	+ 4:18	+ 3.00	87	+ 4:27	+ 3.00	86	+ 4:26	+ 3.00	54	+ 3:54
+ 3.15	54	+ 4:09	+ 3.15	70	+ 4:25	+ 3.15	72	+ 4:27	+ 3.15	82	+ 4:37	+ 3.15	76	+ 4:31	+ 3.15	85	+ 4:40	+ 3.15	85	+ 4:40	+ 3.15	53	+ 4:08
+ 3.30	55	+ 4:25	+ 3.30	69	+ 4:39	+ 3.30	72	+ 4:42	+ 3.30	81	+ 4:51	+ 3.30	74	+ 4:44	+ 3.30	82	+ 4:52	+ 3.30	83	+ 4:53	+ 3.30	52	+ 4:22
+ 3.45	56	+ 4:41	+ 3.45	69	+ 4:54	+ 3.45	71	+ 4:56	+ 3.45	79	+ 5:04	+ 3.45	72	+ 4:57	+ 3.45	82	+ 5:07	+ 3.45	82	+ 5:07	+ 3.45	51	+ 4:36
+ 4.00	56	+ 4:56	+ 4.00	68	+ 5:08	+ 4.00	71	+ 5:11	+ 4.00	78	+ 5:18	+ 4.00	71	+ 5:11	+ 4.00	81	+ 5:21	+ 4.00	81	+ 5:21	+ 4.00	51	+ 4:51
+ 4.15	57	+ 5:12	+ 4.15	68	+ 5:23	+ 4.15	71	+ 5:26	+ 4.15	76	+ 5:31	+ 4.15	69	+ 5:24	+ 4.15	80	+ 5:35	+ 4.15	81	+ 5:36	+ 4.15	50	+ 5:05
+ 4.30	57	+ 5:27	+ 4.30	67	+ 5:37	+ 4.30	71	+ 5:41	+ 4.30	74	+ 5:44	+ 4.30	67	+ 5:37	+ 4.30	80	+ 5:50	+ 4.30	80	+ 5:50	+ 4.30	50	+ 5:20
+ 4.45	58	+ 5:43	+ 4.45	67	+ 5:52	+ 4.45	70	+ 5:55	+ 4.45	72	+ 5:57	+ 4.45	65	+ 5:50	+ 4.45	79	- 5:56	+ 4.45	79	- 5:56	+ 4.45	50	+ 5:35
+ 5.00	58	+ 5:58	+ 5.00	67	- 5:53	+ 5.00	70	- 5:50	+ 5.00	71	- 5:49	+ 5.00	63	- 5:57	+ 5.00	77	- 5:43	+ 5.00	78	- 5:42	+ 5.00	50	+ 5:50
+ 5.15	59	- 5:46	+ 5.15	66	- 5:39	+ 5.15	70	- 5:35	+ 5.15	70	- 5:35	+ 5.15	62	- 5:43	+ 5.15	76	- 5:29	+ 5.15	77	- 5:28	+ 5.15	49	- 5:56
+ 5.30	59	- 5:31	+ 5.30	65	- 5:25	+ 5.30	70	- 5:20	+ 5.30	69	- 5:21	+ 5.30	61	- 5:29	+ 5.30	75	- 5:15	+ 5.30	78	- 5:12	+ 5.30	49	- 5:41
+ 5.45	60	- 5:15	+ 5.45	65	- 5:10	+ 5.45	70	- 5:05	+ 5.45	67	- 5:08	+ 5.45	59	- 5:16	+ 5.45	70	- 5:05	+ 5.45	71	- 5:04	+ 5.45	48	- 5:27
+ 6.00	61	- 4:59	+ 6.00	64	- 4:56	+ 6.00	70	- 4:50	+ 6.00	66	- 4:54	+ 6.00	58	- 5:02	+ 6.00	69	- 4:51	+ 6.00	70	- 4:50	+ 6.00	48	- 5:12

Table K - Harwich to Ramsgate - Outside Route

Time to cover Sectors (in minutes) at 5.0 kts — All times relate to HW Sheerness — **Springs**

Time	K8 Harwich to Cork Sand B'cn		Time	K7 Cork Sand B'cn to S Threshold		Time	K6 S Threshold to Long Sand Hd		Time	K5 Long S'nd Hd to Kentish Knock		Time	K4 Kentish Knock to South Knock		Time	K3 South Knock to Thanet		Time	K2 Thanet to North Foreland		Time	K1 North Foreland to Ramsgate	
	Duration	Time at End of Sector		Duration	Time at End of Sector		Duration	Time at End of Sector		Duration	Time at End of Sector		Duration	Time at End of Sector		Duration	Time at End of Sector		Duration	Time at End of Sector		Duration	Time at End of Sector
- 6.00	74	- 4:46	- 6.00	61	- 4:59	- 6.00	70	- 4:50	- 6.00	55	- 5:05	- 6.00	49	- 5:11	- 6.00	57	- 5:03	- 6.00	62	- 4:58	- 6.00	42	- 5:18
- 5.45	74	- 4:31	- 5.45	61	- 4:44	- 5.45	71	- 4:34	- 5.45	55	- 4:50	- 5.45	49	- 4:56	- 5.45	55	- 4:50	- 5.45	60	- 4:45	- 5.45	41	- 5:04
- 5.30	74	- 4:16	- 5.30	61	- 4:29	- 5.30	71	- 4:19	- 5.30	55	- 4:35	- 5.30	48	- 4:42	- 5.30	53	- 4:37	- 5.30	58	- 4:32	- 5.30	41	- 4:49
- 5.15	74	- 4:01	- 5.15	61	- 4:14	- 5.15	72	- 4:03	- 5.15	54	- 4:21	- 5.15	48	- 4:27	- 5.15	53	- 4:22	- 5.15	58	- 4:17	- 5.15	41	- 4:34
- 5.00	74	- 3:46	- 5.00	60	- 4:00	- 5.00	72	- 3:48	- 5.00	54	- 4:06	- 5.00	47	- 4:13	- 5.00	53	- 4:07	- 5.00	58	- 4:02	- 5.00	41	- 4:19
- 4.45	74	- 3:31	- 4.45	61	- 3:44	- 4.45	73	- 3:32	- 4.45	56	- 3:49	- 4.45	48	- 3:57	- 4.45	53	- 3:52	- 4.45	58	- 3:47	- 4.45	41	- 4:04
- 4.30	73	- 3:17	- 4.30	62	- 3:28	- 4.30	73	- 3:17	- 4.30	57	- 3:33	- 4.30	48	- 3:42	- 4.30	53	- 3:37	- 4.30	58	- 3:32	- 4.30	42	- 3:48
- 4.15	73	- 3:02	- 4.15	63	- 3:12	- 4.15	73	- 3:02	- 4.15	58	- 3:17	- 4.15	49	- 3:26	- 4.15	55	- 3:20	- 4.15	60	- 3:15	- 4.15	44	- 3:31
- 4.00	72	- 2:48	- 4.00	64	- 2:56	- 4.00	74	- 2:46	- 4.00	60	- 3:00	- 4.00	49	- 3:11	- 4.00	57	- 3:03	- 4.00	62	- 2:58	- 4.00	46	- 3:14
- 3.45	72	- 2:33	- 3.45	65	- 2:40	- 3.45	73	- 2:32	- 3.45	62	- 2:43	- 3.45	51	- 2:54	- 3.45	59	- 2:46	- 3.45	65	- 2:40	- 3.45	49	- 2:56
- 3.30	71	- 2:19	- 3.30	67	- 2:23	- 3.30	73	- 2:17	- 3.30	65	- 2:25	- 3.30	52	- 2:38	- 3.30	61	- 2:29	- 3.30	67	- 2:23	- 3.30	51	- 2:39
- 3.15	70	- 2:05	- 3.15	68	- 2:07	- 3.15	73	- 2:02	- 3.15	68	- 2:07	- 3.15	54	- 2:21	- 3.15	65	- 2:10	- 3.15	71	- 2:04	- 3.15	56	- 2:19
- 3.00	69	- 1:51	- 3.00	70	- 1:50	- 3.00	73	- 1:47	- 3.00	71	- 1:49	- 3.00	55	- 2:05	- 3.00	68	- 1:52	- 3.00	74	- 1:46	- 3.00	62	- 1:58
- 2.45	67	- 1:38	- 2.45	70	- 1:35	- 2.45	73	- 1:32	- 2.45	74	- 1:31	- 2.45	58	- 1:47	- 2.45	72	- 1:33	- 2.45	78	- 1:27	- 2.45	67	- 1:38
- 2.30	66	- 1:24	- 2.30	71	- 1:19	- 2.30	73	- 1:17	- 2.30	77	- 1:13	- 2.30	61	- 1:29	- 2.30	75	- 1:15	- 2.30	82	- 1:08	- 2.30	72	- 1:18
- 2.15	64	- 1:11	- 2.15	71	- 1:04	- 2.15	73	- 1:02	- 2.15	81	- 0:54	- 2.15	64	- 1:11	- 2.15	80	- 0:55	- 2.15	87	- 0:48	- 2.15	77	- 0:58
- 2.00	62	- 0:58	- 2.00	72	- 0:48	- 2.00	73	- 0:47	- 2.00	84	- 0:36	- 2.00	67	- 0:53	- 2.00	84	- 0:36	- 2.00	92	- 0:28	- 2.00	82	- 0:38
- 1.45	62	- 0:43	- 1.45	72	- 0:33	- 1.45	73	- 0:32	- 1.45	90	- 0:15	- 1.45	70	- 0:35	- 1.45	89	- 0:16	- 1.45	97	- 0:08	- 1.45	88	- 0:17
- 1.30	61	- 0:29	- 1.30	73	- 0:17	- 1.30	73	- 0:17	- 1.30	96	+ 0:06	- 1.30	73	- 0:17	- 1.30	93	+ 0:03	- 1.30	102	+ 0:12	- 1.30	93	+ 0:03
- 1.15	61	- 0:14	- 1.15	73	- 0:02	- 1.15	73	- 0:02	- 1.15	101	+ 0:26	- 1.15	77	+ 0:02	- 1.15	98	+ 0:23	- 1.15	103	+ 0:28	- 1.15	92	+ 0:17
- 1.00	60	HW	- 1.00	74	+ 0:14	- 1.00	73	+ 0:13	- 1.00	107	+ 0:47	- 1.00	80	+ 0:20	- 1.00	103	+ 0:43	- 1.00	105	+ 0:45	- 1.00	92	+ 0:32
- 0.45	58	+ 0:13	- 0.45	75	+ 0:30	- 0.45	74	+ 0:29	- 0.45	110	+ 1:05	- 0.45	84	+ 0:39	- 0.45	108	+ 1:03	- 0.45	107	+ 1:02	- 0.45	91	+ 0:46
- 0.30	56	+ 0:26	- 0.30	76	+ 0:46	- 0.30	75	+ 0:45	- 0.30	113	+ 1:23	- 0.30	88	+ 0:58	- 0.30	112	+ 1:22	- 0.30	108	+ 1:18	- 0.30	90	+ 1:00
- 0.15	54	+ 0:39	- 0.15	77	+ 1:02	- 0.15	76	+ 1:01	- 0.15	117	+ 1:42	- 0.15	92	+ 1:17	- 0.15	113	+ 1:38	- 0.15	107	+ 1:32	- 0.15	87	+ 1:12
HW	52	+ 0:52	HW	79	+ 1:19	HW	76	+ 1:16	HW	120	+ 2:00	HW	97	+ 1:37	HW	114	+ 1:54	HW	108	+ 1:48	HW	83	+ 1:23
+ 0.15	52	+ 1:07	+ 0.15	79	+ 1:34	+ 0.15	77	+ 1:32	+ 0.15	118	+ 2:13	+ 0.15	98	+ 1:53	+ 0.15	115	+ 2:10	+ 0.15	107	+ 2:02	+ 0.15	79	+ 1:34
+ 0.30	51	+ 1:21	+ 0.30	80	+ 1:50	+ 0.30	78	+ 1:48	+ 0.30	116	+ 2:26	+ 0.30	99	+ 2:09	+ 0.30	116	+ 2:26	+ 0.30	106	+ 2:16	+ 0.30	76	+ 1:46
+ 0.45	50	+ 1:35	+ 0.45	81	+ 2:06	+ 0.45	78	+ 2:03	+ 0.45	114	+ 2:39	+ 0.45	100	+ 2:25	+ 0.45	114	+ 2:39	+ 0.45	104	+ 2:29	+ 0.45	73	+ 1:58
+ 1.00	50	+ 1:50	+ 1.00	81	+ 2:21	+ 1.00	79	+ 2:19	+ 1.00	112	+ 2:52	+ 1.00	101	+ 2:41	+ 1.00	112	+ 2:52	+ 1.00	103	+ 2:43	+ 1.00	70	+ 2:10
+ 1.15	50	+ 2:05	+ 1.15	80	+ 2:35	+ 1.15	78	+ 2:33	+ 1.15	109	+ 3:04	+ 1.15	99	+ 2:54	+ 1.15	110	+ 3:05	+ 1.15	102	+ 2:57	+ 1.15	67	+ 2:22
+ 1.30	50	+ 2:20	+ 1.30	80	+ 2:50	+ 1.30	78	+ 2:48	+ 1.30	105	+ 3:15	+ 1.30	98	+ 3:08	+ 1.30	109	+ 3:19	+ 1.30	101	+ 3:11	+ 1.30	64	+ 2:34
+ 1.45	50	+ 2:35	+ 1.45	79	+ 3:04	+ 1.45	78	+ 3:03	+ 1.45	102	+ 3:27	+ 1.45	97	+ 3:22	+ 1.45	106	+ 3:31	+ 1.45	100	+ 3:25	+ 1.45	62	+ 2:47
+ 2.00	51	+ 2:51	+ 2.00	78	+ 3:18	+ 2.00	77	+ 3:17	+ 2.00	98	+ 3:38	+ 2.00	96	+ 3:36	+ 2.00	103	+ 3:43	+ 2.00	99	+ 3:39	+ 2.00	59	+ 2:59
+ 2.15	51	+ 3:06	+ 2.15	76	+ 3:31	+ 2.15	76	+ 3:31	+ 2.15	95	+ 3:50	+ 2.15	93	+ 3:48	+ 2.15	100	+ 3:55	+ 2.15	98	+ 3:53	+ 2.15	57	+ 3:12
+ 2.30	51	+ 3:21	+ 2.30	75	+ 3:45	+ 2.30	76	+ 3:46	+ 2.30	93	+ 4:03	+ 2.30	90	+ 4:00	+ 2.30	97	+ 4:07	+ 2.30	97	+ 4:07	+ 2.30	54	+ 3:24
+ 2.45	51	+ 3:36	+ 2.45	74	+ 3:59	+ 2.45	75	+ 4:00	+ 2.45	90	+ 4:15	+ 2.45	87	+ 4:12	+ 2.45	94	+ 4:19	+ 2.45	95	+ 4:20	+ 2.45	53	+ 3:38
+ 3.00	51	+ 3:51	+ 3.00	72	+ 4:12	+ 3.00	74	+ 4:14	+ 3.00	87	+ 4:27	+ 3.00	84	+ 4:24	+ 3.00	92	+ 4:32	+ 3.00	94	+ 4:34	+ 3.00	52	+ 3:52
+ 3.15	52	+ 4:07	+ 3.15	71	+ 4:26	+ 3.15	73	+ 4:28	+ 3.15	84	+ 4:39	+ 3.15	81	+ 4:36	+ 3.15	89	+ 4:44	+ 3.15	91	+ 4:46	+ 3.15	51	+ 4:06
+ 3.30	53	+ 4:23	+ 3.30	70	+ 4:40	+ 3.30	73	+ 4:43	+ 3.30	82	+ 4:52	+ 3.30	78	+ 4:48	+ 3.30	86	+ 4:56	+ 3.30	89	+ 4:59	+ 3.30	50	+ 4:20
+ 3.45	54	+ 4:39	+ 3.45	70	+ 4:55	+ 3.45	72	+ 4:57	+ 3.45	80	+ 5:05	+ 3.45	75	+ 5:00	+ 3.45	85	+ 5:10	+ 3.45	87	+ 5:12	+ 3.45	49	+ 4:34
+ 4.00	55	+ 4:55	+ 4.00	69	+ 5:09	+ 4.00	72	+ 5:12	+ 4.00	77	+ 5:17	+ 4.00	72	+ 5:12	+ 4.00	83	+ 5:23	+ 4.00	85	+ 5:25	+ 4.00	49	+ 4:49
+ 4.15	56	+ 5:11	+ 4.15	68	+ 5:23	+ 4.15	72	+ 5:27	+ 4.15	75	+ 5:30	+ 4.15	69	+ 5:24	+ 4.15	82	+ 5:37	+ 4.15	84	+ 5:39	+ 4.15	48	+ 5:03
+ 4.30	56	+ 5:26	+ 4.30	67	+ 5:37	+ 4.30	71	+ 5:41	+ 4.30	72	+ 5:42	+ 4.30	67	+ 5:37	+ 4.30	80	+ 5:50	+ 4.30	82	+ 5:52	+ 4.30	47	+ 5:17
+ 4.45	57	+ 5:42	+ 4.45	67	+ 5:52	+ 4.45	71	+ 5:56	+ 4.45	70	+ 5:55	+ 4.45	64	+ 5:49	+ 4.45	78	- 5:57	+ 4.45	81	- 5:54	+ 4.45	47	+ 5:32
+ 5.00	57	+ 5:57	+ 5.00	66	- 5:54	+ 5.00	70	- 5:50	+ 5.00	67	- 5:53	+ 5.00	61	- 5:59	+ 5.00	76	- 5:44	+ 5.00	80	- 5:40	+ 5.00	46	+ 5:46
+ 5.15	59	- 5:46	+ 5.15	65	- 5:40	+ 5.15	70	- 5:35	+ 5.15	66	- 5:39	+ 5.15	59	- 5:46	+ 5.15	74	- 5:31	+ 5.15	78	- 5:27	+ 5.15	45	- 6:00
+ 5.30	60	- 5:30	+ 5.30	65	- 5:25	+ 5.30	70	- 5:20	+ 5.30	64	- 5:26	+ 5.30	58	- 5:32	+ 5.30	72	- 5:18	+ 5.30	76	- 5:14	+ 5.30	44	- 5:46
+ 5.45	61	- 5:14	+ 5.45	64	- 5:11	+ 5.45	70	- 5:05	+ 5.45	62	- 5:13	+ 5.45	56	- 5:19	+ 5.45	62	- 5:13	+ 5.45	65	- 5:10	+ 5.45	43	- 5:32
+ 6.00	62	- 4:58	+ 6.00	63	- 4:57	+ 6.00	69	- 4:51	+ 6.00	61	- 4:59	+ 6.00	54	- 5:06	+ 6.00	60	- 5:00	+ 6.00	64	- 4:56	+ 6.00	42	- 5:18

SOUTH BOUND

Table K - Harwich to Ramsgate - Outside Route

Neaps — All times relate to HW Sheerness — **Time to cover Sectors (in minutes) at 6.0 Kts**

SOUTH BOUND

	K8 Harwich to Cork Sand B'cn			K7 Cork Sand B'cn to S Threshold			K6 S Threshold to Long Sand Hd			K5 Long S'nd Hd to Kentish Knock			K4 Kentish Knock to South Knock			K3 South Knock to Thanet			K2 Thanet to North Foreland			K1 North Foreland to Ramsgate	
Time	Duration	Time at End of Sector	Time	Duration	Time at End of Sector	Time	Duration	Time at End of Sector	Time	Duration	Time at End of Sector	Time	Duration	Time at End of Sector	Time	Duration	Time at End of Sector	Time	Duration	Time at End of Sector	Time	Duration	Time at End of Sector
- 6.00	55	- 5:05	- 6.00	53	- 5:07	- 6.00	58	- 5:02	- 6.00	54	- 5:06	- 6.00	47	- 5:13	- 6.00	58	- 5:02	- 6.00	59	- 5:01	- 6.00	41	- 5:19
- 5.45	55	- 4:50	- 5.45	53	- 4:52	- 5.45	58	- 4:47	- 5.45	54	- 4:51	- 5.45	47	- 4:58	- 5.45	57	- 4:48	- 5.45	59	- 4:46	- 5.45	40	- 5:05
- 5.30	55	- 4:35	- 5.30	52	- 4:38	- 5.30	58	- 4:32	- 5.30	54	- 4:36	- 5.30	46	- 4:44	- 5.30	56	- 4:34	- 5.30	58	- 4:32	- 5.30	40	- 4:50
- 5.15	55	- 4:20	- 5.15	52	- 4:23	- 5.15	58	- 4:17	- 5.15	53	- 4:22	- 5.15	46	- 4:29	- 5.15	56	- 4:19	- 5.15	58	- 4:17	- 5.15	40	- 4:35
- 5.00	55	- 4:05	- 5.00	52	- 4:08	- 5.00	58	- 4:02	- 5.00	53	- 4:07	- 5.00	45	- 4:15	- 5.00	56	- 4:04	- 5.00	58	- 4:02	- 5.00	40	- 4:20
- 4.45	55	- 3:50	- 4.45	53	- 3:52	- 4.45	58	- 3:47	- 4.45	54	- 3:51	- 4.45	46	- 3:59	- 4.45	55	- 3:50	- 4.45	58	- 3:47	- 4.45	40	- 4:05
- 4.30	55	- 3:35	- 4.30	53	- 3:37	- 4.30	59	- 3:31	- 4.30	54	- 3:36	- 4.30	46	- 3:44	- 4.30	55	- 3:35	- 4.30	58	- 3:32	- 4.30	40	- 3:50
- 4.15	55	- 3:20	- 4.15	53	- 3:22	- 4.15	59	- 3:16	- 4.15	55	- 3:20	- 4.15	46	- 3:29	- 4.15	56	- 3:19	- 4.15	59	- 3:16	- 4.15	41	- 3:34
- 4.00	55	- 3:05	- 4.00	53	- 3:07	- 4.00	59	- 3:01	- 4.00	56	- 3:04	- 4.00	46	- 3:14	- 4.00	57	- 3:03	- 4.00	59	- 3:01	- 4.00	42	- 3:18
- 3.45	55	- 2:50	- 3.45	54	- 2:51	- 3.45	59	- 2:46	- 3.45	57	- 2:48	- 3.45	47	- 2:58	- 3.45	58	- 2:47	- 3.45	60	- 2:45	- 3.45	43	- 3:02
- 3.30	54	- 2:36	- 3.30	55	- 2:35	- 3.30	59	- 2:31	- 3.30	58	- 2:32	- 3.30	48	- 2:42	- 3.30	59	- 2:31	- 3.30	61	- 2:29	- 3.30	44	- 2:46
- 3.15	54	- 2:21	- 3.15	56	- 2:19	- 3.15	59	- 2:16	- 3.15	59	- 2:16	- 3.15	49	- 2:26	- 3.15	60	- 2:15	- 3.15	63	- 2:12	- 3.15	46	- 2:29
- 3.00	53	- 2:07	- 3.00	56	- 2:04	- 3.00	59	- 2:01	- 3.00	61	- 1:59	- 3.00	49	- 2:11	- 3.00	61	- 1:59	- 3.00	64	- 1:56	- 3.00	48	- 2:12
- 2.45	53	- 1:52	- 2.45	57	- 1:48	- 2.45	59	- 1:46	- 2.45	62	- 1:43	- 2.45	51	- 1:54	- 2.45	63	- 1:42	- 2.45	65	- 1:40	- 2.45	50	- 1:55
- 2.30	52	- 1:38	- 2.30	57	- 1:33	- 2.30	59	- 1:31	- 2.30	64	- 1:26	- 2.30	52	- 1:38	- 2.30	64	- 1:26	- 2.30	67	- 1:23	- 2.30	52	- 1:38
- 2.15	51	- 1:24	- 2.15	58	- 1:17	- 2.15	60	- 1:15	- 2.15	66	- 1:09	- 2.15	53	- 1:22	- 2.15	65	- 1:10	- 2.15	68	- 1:07	- 2.15	53	- 1:22
- 2.00	50	- 1:10	- 2.00	58	- 1:02	- 2.00	60	- 1:00	- 2.00	68	- 0:52	- 2.00	55	- 1:05	- 2.00	67	- 0:53	- 2.00	70	- 0:50	- 2.00	54	- 1:06
- 1.45	50	- 0:55	- 1.45	58	- 0:47	- 1.45	60	- 0:45	- 1.45	69	- 0:36	- 1.45	56	- 0:49	- 1.45	68	- 0:37	- 1.45	71	- 0:34	- 1.45	55	- 0:50
- 1.30	50	- 0:40	- 1.30	58	- 0:32	- 1.30	60	- 0:30	- 1.30	71	- 0:19	- 1.30	58	- 0:32	- 1.30	69	- 0:21	- 1.30	72	- 0:18	- 1.30	56	- 0:34
- 1.15	50	- 0:25	- 1.15	59	- 0:16	- 1.15	60	- 0:15	- 1.15	73	- 0:02	- 1.15	59	- 0:16	- 1.15	71	- 0:04	- 1.15	73	- 0:02	- 1.15	56	- 0:19
- 1.00	50	- 0:10	- 1.00	59	- 0:01	- 1.00	60	HW	- 1.00	75	+ 0:15	- 1.00	61	+ 0:01	- 1.00	72	+ 0:12	- 1.00	74	+ 0:14	- 1.00	56	- 0:04
- 0.45	49	+ 0:04	- 0.45	59	+ 0:14	- 0.45	60	+ 0:15	- 0.45	76	+ 0:31	- 0.45	62	+ 0:17	- 0.45	73	+ 0:28	- 0.45	75	+ 0:30	- 0.45	56	+ 0:11
- 0.30	47	+ 0:17	- 0.30	60	+ 0:30	- 0.30	60	+ 0:30	- 0.30	78	+ 0:48	- 0.30	63	+ 0:33	- 0.30	74	+ 0:44	- 0.30	75	+ 0:45	- 0.30	56	+ 0:26
- 0.15	46	+ 0:31	- 0.15	60	+ 0:45	- 0.15	60	+ 0:45	- 0.15	79	+ 1:04	- 0.15	64	+ 0:49	- 0.15	73	+ 0:58	- 0.15	75	+ 1:00	- 0.15	56	+ 0:41
HW	44	+ 0:44	HW	60	+ 1:00	HW	60	+ 1:00	HW	80	+ 1:20	HW	65	+ 1:05	HW	75	+ 1:15	HW	75	+ 1:15	HW	55	+ 0:55
+ 0.15	44	+ 0:59	+ 0.15	61	+ 1:16	+ 0.15	61	+ 1:16	+ 0.15	80	+ 1:35	+ 0.15	66	+ 1:21	+ 0.15	76	+ 1:31	+ 0.15	75	+ 1:30	+ 0.15	55	+ 1:10
+ 0.30	44	+ 1:14	+ 0.30	61	+ 1:31	+ 0.30	61	+ 1:31	+ 0.30	80	+ 1:50	+ 0.30	66	+ 1:36	+ 0.30	76	+ 1:46	+ 0.30	74	+ 1:44	+ 0.30	55	+ 1:25
+ 0.45	43	+ 1:28	+ 0.45	61	+ 1:46	+ 0.45	61	+ 1:46	+ 0.45	79	+ 2:04	+ 0.45	67	+ 1:52	+ 0.45	76	+ 2:01	+ 0.45	74	+ 1:59	+ 0.45	54	+ 1:39
+ 1.00	43	+ 1:43	+ 1.00	62	+ 2:02	+ 1.00	61	+ 2:01	+ 1.00	79	+ 2:19	+ 1.00	67	+ 2:07	+ 1.00	76	+ 2:16	+ 1.00	74	+ 2:14	+ 1.00	52	+ 1:52
+ 1.15	43	+ 1:58	+ 1.15	61	+ 2:16	+ 1.15	61	+ 2:16	+ 1.15	78	+ 2:33	+ 1.15	67	+ 2:22	+ 1.15	75	+ 2:30	+ 1.15	73	+ 2:28	+ 1.15	51	+ 2:06
+ 1.30	43	+ 2:13	+ 1.30	61	+ 2:31	+ 1.30	61	+ 2:31	+ 1.30	76	+ 2:46	+ 1.30	67	+ 2:37	+ 1.30	75	+ 2:45	+ 1.30	73	+ 2:43	+ 1.30	50	+ 2:20
+ 1.45	43	+ 2:28	+ 1.45	61	+ 2:46	+ 1.45	61	+ 2:46	+ 1.45	75	+ 3:00	+ 1.45	66	+ 2:51	+ 1.45	74	+ 2:59	+ 1.45	73	+ 2:58	+ 1.45	49	+ 2:34
+ 2.00	44	+ 2:44	+ 2.00	60	+ 3:00	+ 2.00	60	+ 3:00	+ 2.00	74	+ 3:14	+ 2.00	66	+ 3:06	+ 2.00	73	+ 3:13	+ 2.00	72	+ 3:12	+ 2.00	48	+ 2:48
+ 2.15	44	+ 2:59	+ 2.15	60	+ 3:15	+ 2.15	60	+ 3:15	+ 2.15	73	+ 3:28	+ 2.15	66	+ 3:21	+ 2.15	73	+ 3:28	+ 2.15	72	+ 3:27	+ 2.15	48	+ 3:03
+ 2.30	44	+ 3:14	+ 2.30	59	+ 3:29	+ 2.30	60	+ 3:30	+ 2.30	72	+ 3:42	+ 2.30	65	+ 3:35	+ 2.30	72	+ 3:42	+ 2.30	71	+ 3:41	+ 2.30	47	+ 3:17
+ 2.45	44	+ 3:29	+ 2.45	59	+ 3:44	+ 2.45	60	+ 3:45	+ 2.45	70	+ 3:55	+ 2.45	64	+ 3:49	+ 2.45	71	+ 3:56	+ 2.45	71	+ 3:56	+ 2.45	46	+ 3:31
+ 3.00	44	+ 3:44	+ 3.00	58	+ 3:58	+ 3.00	60	+ 4:00	+ 3.00	69	+ 4:09	+ 3.00	63	+ 4:03	+ 3.00	70	+ 4:10	+ 3.00	70	+ 4:10	+ 3.00	45	+ 3:45
+ 3.15	45	+ 4:00	+ 3.15	58	+ 4:13	+ 3.15	60	+ 4:15	+ 3.15	68	+ 4:23	+ 3.15	62	+ 4:17	+ 3.15	69	+ 4:24	+ 3.15	69	+ 4:24	+ 3.15	45	+ 4:00
+ 3.30	46	+ 4:16	+ 3.30	58	+ 4:28	+ 3.30	59	+ 4:29	+ 3.30	67	+ 4:37	+ 3.30	61	+ 4:31	+ 3.30	68	+ 4:38	+ 3.30	69	+ 4:39	+ 3.30	44	+ 4:14
+ 3.45	46	+ 4:31	+ 3.45	57	+ 4:42	+ 3.45	59	+ 4:44	+ 3.45	66	+ 4:51	+ 3.45	60	+ 4:45	+ 3.45	68	+ 4:53	+ 3.45	68	+ 4:53	+ 3.45	44	+ 4:29
+ 4.00	47	+ 4:47	+ 4.00	57	+ 4:57	+ 4.00	59	+ 4:59	+ 4.00	65	+ 5:05	+ 4.00	59	+ 4:59	+ 4.00	67	+ 5:07	+ 4.00	68	+ 5:08	+ 4.00	43	+ 4:43
+ 4.15	47	+ 5:02	+ 4.15	57	+ 5:12	+ 4.15	59	+ 5:14	+ 4.15	64	+ 5:19	+ 4.15	57	+ 5:12	+ 4.15	67	+ 5:22	+ 4.15	67	+ 5:22	+ 4.15	43	+ 4:58
+ 4.30	47	+ 5:17	+ 4.30	56	+ 5:26	+ 4.30	59	+ 5:29	+ 4.30	63	+ 5:33	+ 4.30	56	+ 5:26	+ 4.30	66	+ 5:36	+ 4.30	67	+ 5:37	+ 4.30	42	+ 5:12
+ 4.45	48	+ 5:33	+ 4.45	56	+ 5:41	+ 4.45	59	+ 5:44	+ 4.45	61	+ 5:46	+ 4.45	55	+ 5:40	+ 4.45	66	+ 5:51	+ 4.45	66	+ 5:51	+ 4.45	42	+ 5:27
+ 5.00	48	+ 5:48	+ 5.00	56	+ 5:56	+ 5.00	59	+ 5:59	+ 5.00	60	- 6:00	+ 5.00	53	+ 5:53	+ 5.00	65	- 5:55	+ 5.00	65	- 5:55	+ 5.00	42	+ 5:42
+ 5.15	49	- 5:56	+ 5.15	55	- 5:50	+ 5.15	58	- 5:47	+ 5.15	59	- 5:46	+ 5.15	52	- 5:53	+ 5.15	64	- 5:41	+ 5.15	65	- 5:40	+ 5.15	42	+ 5:57
+ 5.30	49	- 5:41	+ 5.30	55	- 5:35	+ 5.30	58	- 5:32	+ 5.30	59	- 5:31	+ 5.30	52	- 5:38	+ 5.30	63	- 5:27	+ 5.30	64	- 5:26	+ 5.30	42	- 5:48
+ 5.45	49	- 5:26	+ 5.45	54	- 5:21	+ 5.45	58	- 5:17	+ 5.45	58	- 5:17	+ 5.45	51	- 5:24	+ 5.45	60	- 5:15	+ 5.45	61	- 5:14	+ 5.45	41	- 5:34
+ 6.00	50	- 5:10	+ 6.00	54	- 5:06	+ 6.00	58	- 5:02	+ 6.00	57	- 5:03	+ 6.00	50	- 5:10	+ 6.00	59	- 5:01	+ 6.00	60	- 5:00	+ 6.00	41	- 5:19

Table K - Harwich to Ramsgate - Outside Route

Time to cover Sectors (in minutes) at 6.0 kts — All times relate to HW Sheerness — Springs

	K8			K7			K6			K5			K4			K3			K2			K1	
	Harwich to Cork Sand B'cn			Cork Sand B'cn to S Threshold			S Threshold to Long Sand Hd			Long S'nd Hd to Kentish Knock			Kentish Knock to South Knock			South Knock to Thanet			Thanet to North Foreland			North Foreland to Ramsgate	
Time	*Duration*	*Time at End of Sector*	*Time*	*Duration*	*Time at End of Sector*	*Time*	*Duration*	*Time at End of Sector*	*Time*	*Duration*	*Time at End of Sector*	*Time*	*Duration*	*Time at End of Sector*	*Time*	*Duration*	*Time at End of Sector*	*Time*	*Duration*	*Time at End of Sector*	*Time*	*Duration*	*Time at End of Sector*
- 6.00	60	- 5:00	- 6.00	51	- 5:09	- 6.00	58	- 5:02	- 6.00	49	- 5:11	- 6.00	44	- 5:16	- 6.00	51	- 5:09	- 6.00	54	- 5:06	- 6.00	37	- 5:23
- 5.45	60	- 4:45	- 5.45	51	- 4:54	- 5.45	58	- 4:47	- 5.45	49	- 4:56	- 5.45	43	- 5:02	- 5.45	50	- 4:55	- 5.45	53	- 4:52	- 5.45	37	- 5:08
- 5.30	60	- 4:30	- 5.30	51	- 4:39	- 5.30	59	- 4:31	- 5.30	49	- 4:41	- 5.30	43	- 4:47	- 5.30	48	- 4:42	- 5.30	52	- 4:38	- 5.30	36	- 4:54
- 5.15	60	- 4:15	- 5.15	51	- 4:24	- 5.15	59	- 4:16	- 5.15	48	- 4:27	- 5.15	42	- 4:33	- 5.15	48	- 4:27	- 5.15	52	- 4:23	- 5.15	36	- 4:39
- 5.00	60	- 4:00	- 5.00	51	- 4:09	- 5.00	59	- 4:01	- 5.00	48	- 4:12	- 5.00	42	- 4:18	- 5.00	48	- 4:12	- 5.00	52	- 4:08	- 5.00	36	- 4:24
- 4.45	60	- 3:45	- 4.45	51	- 3:54	- 4.45	59	- 3:46	- 4.45	49	- 3:56	- 4.45	42	- 4:03	- 4.45	47	- 3:58	- 4.45	51	- 3:54	- 4.45	36	- 4:09
- 4.30	60	- 3:30	- 4.30	52	- 3:38	- 4.30	60	- 3:30	- 4.30	50	- 3:40	- 4.30	42	- 3:48	- 4.30	47	- 3:43	- 4.30	51	- 3:39	- 4.30	36	- 3:54
- 4.15	59	- 3:16	- 4.15	52	- 3:23	- 4.15	60	- 3:15	- 4.15	51	- 3:24	- 4.15	43	- 3:32	- 4.15	49	- 3:26	- 4.15	53	- 3:22	- 4.15	38	- 3:37
- 4.00	59	- 3:01	- 4.00	53	- 3:07	- 4.00	60	- 3:00	- 4.00	51	- 3:09	- 4.00	43	- 3:17	- 4.00	50	- 3:10	- 4.00	54	- 3:06	- 4.00	39	- 3:21
- 3.45	58	- 2:47	- 3.45	54	- 2:51	- 3.45	60	- 2:45	- 3.45	53	- 2:52	- 3.45	44	- 3:01	- 3.45	51	- 2:54	- 3.45	55	- 2:50	- 3.45	40	- 3:05
- 3.30	58	- 2:32	- 3.30	55	- 2:35	- 3.30	60	- 2:30	- 3.30	55	- 2:35	- 3.30	45	- 2:45	- 3.30	53	- 2:37	- 3.30	57	- 2:33	- 3.30	42	- 2:48
- 3.15	57	- 2:18	- 3.15	56	- 2:19	- 3.15	60	- 2:15	- 3.15	57	- 2:18	- 3.15	46	- 2:29	- 3.15	55	- 2:20	- 3.15	59	- 2:16	- 3.15	45	- 2:30
- 3.00	57	- 2:03	- 3.00	57	- 2:03	- 3.00	60	- 2:00	- 3.00	59	- 2:01	- 3.00	47	- 2:13	- 3.00	58	- 2:02	- 3.00	62	- 1:58	- 3.00	49	- 2:11
- 2.45	55	- 1:50	- 2.45	57	- 1:48	- 2.45	60	- 1:45	- 2.45	61	- 1:44	- 2.45	49	- 1:56	- 2.45	60	- 1:45	- 2.45	64	- 1:41	- 2.45	53	- 1:52
- 2.30	54	- 1:36	- 2.30	58	- 1:32	- 2.30	60	- 1:30	- 2.30	64	- 1:26	- 2.30	51	- 1:39	- 2.30	62	- 1:28	- 2.30	67	- 1:23	- 2.30	56	- 1:34
- 2.15	53	- 1:22	- 2.15	58	- 1:17	- 2.15	60	- 1:15	- 2.15	66	- 1:09	- 2.15	53	- 1:22	- 2.15	65	- 1:10	- 2.15	70	- 1:05	- 2.15	59	- 1:16
- 2.00	52	- 1:08	- 2.00	59	- 1:01	- 2.00	60	- 1:00	- 2.00	68	- 0:52	- 2.00	55	- 1:05	- 2.00	68	- 0:52	- 2.00	73	- 0:47	- 2.00	61	- 0:59
- 1.45	52	- 0:53	- 1.45	59	- 0:46	- 1.45	60	- 0:45	- 1.45	71	- 0:34	- 1.45	57	- 0:48	- 1.45	70	- 0:35	- 1.45	75	- 0:30	- 1.45	63	- 0:42
- 1.30	51	- 0:39	- 1.30	59	- 0:31	- 1.30	60	- 0:30	- 1.30	74	- 0:16	- 1.30	59	- 0:31	- 1.30	73	- 0:17	- 1.30	78	- 0:12	- 1.30	65	- 0:25
- 1.15	51	- 0:24	- 1.15	60	- 0:15	- 1.15	61	- 0:14	- 1.15	77	+ 0:02	- 1.15	62	- 0:13	- 1.15	75	HW	- 1.15	79	+ 0:04	- 1.15	65	- 0:10
- 1.00	51	- 0:09	- 1.00	60	HW	- 1.00	61	+ 0:01	- 1.00	79	+ 0:19	- 1.00	64	+ 0:04	- 1.00	78	+ 0:18	- 1.00	81	+ 0:21	- 1.00	65	+ 0:05
- 0.45	50	+ 0:05	- 0.45	61	+ 0:16	- 0.45	61	+ 0:16	- 0.45	83	+ 0:38	- 0.45	66	+ 0:21	- 0.45	81	+ 0:36	- 0.45	82	+ 0:37	- 0.45	65	+ 0:20
- 0.30	48	+ 0:18	- 0.30	62	+ 0:32	- 0.30	61	+ 0:31	- 0.30	87	+ 0:57	- 0.30	68	+ 0:38	- 0.30	83	+ 0:53	- 0.30	83	+ 0:53	- 0.30	65	+ 0:35
- 0.15	46	+ 0:31	- 0.15	62	+ 0:47	- 0.15	62	+ 0:47	- 0.15	91	+ 1:16	- 0.15	69	+ 0:54	- 0.15	85	+ 1:10	- 0.15	83	+ 1:08	- 0.15	64	+ 0:49
HW	45	+ 0:45	HW	63	+ 1:03	HW	62	+ 1:02	HW	95	+ 1:35	HW	71	+ 1:11	HW	88	+ 1:28	HW	82	+ 1:22	HW	63	+ 1:03
+ 0.15	44	+ 0:59	+ 0.15	64	+ 1:19	+ 0.15	63	+ 1:18	+ 0.15	94	+ 1:49	+ 0.15	72	+ 1:27	+ 0.15	90	+ 1:45	+ 0.15	82	+ 1:37	+ 0.15	62	+ 1:17
+ 0.30	43	+ 1:13	+ 0.30	64	+ 1:34	+ 0.30	63	+ 1:33	+ 0.30	93	+ 2:03	+ 0.30	73	+ 1:43	+ 0.30	92	+ 2:02	+ 0.30	81	+ 1:51	+ 0.30	61	+ 1:31
+ 0.45	43	+ 1:28	+ 0.45	65	+ 1:50	+ 0.45	63	+ 1:48	+ 0.45	91	+ 2:16	+ 0.45	73	+ 1:58	+ 0.45	90	+ 2:15	+ 0.45	81	+ 2:06	+ 0.45	59	+ 1:44
+ 1.00	42	+ 1:42	+ 1.00	65	+ 2:05	+ 1.00	64	+ 2:04	+ 1.00	90	+ 2:30	+ 1.00	74	+ 2:14	+ 1.00	89	+ 2:29	+ 1.00	80	+ 2:20	+ 1.00	57	+ 1:57
+ 1.15	42	+ 1:57	+ 1.15	65	+ 2:20	+ 1.15	64	+ 2:19	+ 1.15	87	+ 2:42	+ 1.15	74	+ 2:29	+ 1.15	87	+ 2:42	+ 1.15	79	+ 2:34	+ 1.15	55	+ 2:10
+ 1.30	43	+ 2:13	+ 1.30	64	+ 2:34	+ 1.30	63	+ 2:33	+ 1.30	84	+ 2:54	+ 1.30	73	+ 2:43	+ 1.30	85	+ 2:55	+ 1.30	79	+ 2:49	+ 1.30	53	+ 2:23
+ 1.45	43	+ 2:28	+ 1.45	64	+ 2:49	+ 1.45	63	+ 2:48	+ 1.45	82	+ 3:07	+ 1.45	73	+ 2:58	+ 1.45	83	+ 3:08	+ 1.45	78	+ 3:03	+ 1.45	51	+ 2:36
+ 2.00	43	+ 2:43	+ 2.00	63	+ 3:03	+ 2.00	63	+ 3:03	+ 2.00	79	+ 3:19	+ 2.00	73	+ 3:13	+ 2.00	82	+ 3:22	+ 2.00	78	+ 3:18	+ 2.00	50	+ 2:50
+ 2.15	43	+ 2:58	+ 2.15	62	+ 3:17	+ 2.15	62	+ 3:17	+ 2.15	77	+ 3:32	+ 2.15	71	+ 3:26	+ 2.15	80	+ 3:35	+ 2.15	77	+ 3:32	+ 2.15	48	+ 3:03
+ 2.30	43	+ 3:13	+ 2.30	61	+ 3:31	+ 2.30	62	+ 3:32	+ 2.30	75	+ 3:45	+ 2.30	70	+ 3:40	+ 2.30	79	+ 3:49	+ 2.30	76	+ 3:46	+ 2.30	46	+ 3:16
+ 2.45	43	+ 3:28	+ 2.45	60	+ 3:45	+ 2.45	61	+ 3:46	+ 2.45	73	+ 3:58	+ 2.45	69	+ 3:54	+ 2.45	77	+ 4:02	+ 2.45	75	+ 4:00	+ 2.45	45	+ 3:30
+ 3.00	43	+ 3:43	+ 3.00	60	+ 4:00	+ 3.00	61	+ 4:01	+ 3.00	71	+ 4:11	+ 3.00	68	+ 4:08	+ 3.00	75	+ 4:15	+ 3.00	73	+ 4:13	+ 3.00	44	+ 3:44
+ 3.15	44	+ 3:59	+ 3.15	59	+ 4:14	+ 3.15	61	+ 4:16	+ 3.15	70	+ 4:25	+ 3.15	66	+ 4:21	+ 3.15	73	+ 4:28	+ 3.15	72	+ 4:27	+ 3.15	43	+ 3:58
+ 3.30	44	+ 4:14	+ 3.30	58	+ 4:28	+ 3.30	60	+ 4:30	+ 3.30	68	+ 4:38	+ 3.30	64	+ 4:34	+ 3.30	71	+ 4:41	+ 3.30	70	+ 4:40	+ 3.30	43	+ 4:13
+ 3.45	45	+ 4:30	+ 3.45	58	+ 4:43	+ 3.45	60	+ 4:45	+ 3.45	67	+ 4:52	+ 3.45	62	+ 4:47	+ 3.45	70	+ 4:55	+ 3.45	69	+ 4:54	+ 3.45	42	+ 4:27
+ 4.00	46	+ 4:46	+ 4.00	57	+ 4:57	+ 4.00	60	+ 5:00	+ 4.00	65	+ 5:05	+ 4.00	60	+ 5:00	+ 4.00	69	+ 5:09	+ 4.00	68	+ 5:08	+ 4.00	42	+ 4:42
+ 4.15	46	+ 5:01	+ 4.15	57	+ 5:12	+ 4.15	59	+ 5:14	+ 4.15	63	+ 5:18	+ 4.15	58	+ 5:13	+ 4.15	68	+ 5:23	+ 4.15	68	+ 5:23	+ 4.15	42	+ 4:57
+ 4.30	46	+ 5:16	+ 4.30	56	+ 5:26	+ 4.30	59	+ 5:29	+ 4.30	61	+ 5:31	+ 4.30	56	+ 5:26	+ 4.30	67	+ 5:37	+ 4.30	67	+ 5:37	+ 4.30	41	+ 5:11
+ 4.45	47	+ 5:32	+ 4.45	56	+ 5:41	+ 4.45	59	+ 5:44	+ 4.45	60	+ 5:45	+ 4.45	54	+ 5:39	+ 4.45	66	+ 5:51	+ 4.45	65	+ 5:50	+ 4.45	41	+ 5:26
+ 5.00	47	+ 5:47	+ 5.00	55	+ 5:55	+ 5.00	59	+ 5:59	+ 5.00	58	+ 5:58	+ 5.00	52	+ 5:52	+ 5.00	64	- 5:56	+ 5.00	64	- 5:56	+ 5.00	40	+ 5:40
+ 5.15	48	- 5:57	+ 5.15	55	- 5:50	+ 5.15	58	- 5:47	+ 5.15	57	- 5:48	+ 5.15	51	- 5:54	+ 5.15	63	- 5:42	+ 5.15	63	- 5:42	+ 5.15	39	+ 5:54
+ 5.30	49	- 5:41	+ 5.30	54	- 5:36	+ 5.30	58	- 5:32	+ 5.30	56	- 5:34	+ 5.30	50	- 5:40	+ 5.30	62	- 5:28	+ 5.30	62	- 5:28	+ 5.30	39	- 5:51
+ 5.45	50	- 5:25	+ 5.45	54	- 5:21	+ 5.45	58	- 5:17	+ 5.45	54	- 5:21	+ 5.45	49	- 5:26	+ 5.45	55	- 5:20	+ 5.45	57	- 5:18	+ 5.45	38	- 5:37
+ 6.00	50	- 5:10	+ 6.00	53	- 5:07	+ 6.00	58	- 5:02	+ 6.00	53	- 5:07	+ 6.00	47	- 5:13	+ 6.00	53	- 5:07	+ 6.00	57	- 5:03	+ 6.00	37	- 5:23

SOUTH BOUND

Table K - Harwich to Ramsgate - Outside Route

Neaps — All times relate to HW Sheerness — Time to cover Sectors (in minutes) at 7.0 Kts

SOUTHBOUND

	K8 Harwich to Cork Sand B'cn			K7 Cork Sand B'cn to S Threshold			K6 S Threshold to Long Sand Hd			K5 Long S'nd Hd to Kentish Knock	
Time	Duration	Time at End of Sector	Time	Duration	Time at End of Sector	Time	Duration	Time at End of Sector	Time	Duration	Time at End of Sector
- 6.00	47	- 5:13	- 6.00	46	- 5:14	- 6.00	50	- 5:10	- 6.00	48	- 5:12
- 5.45	47	- 4:58	- 5.45	45	- 5:00	- 5.45	50	- 4:55	- 5.45	48	- 4:57
- 5.30	47	- 4:43	- 5.30	45	- 4:45	- 5.30	50	- 4:40	- 5.30	47	- 4:43
- 5.15	47	- 4:28	- 5.15	45	- 4:30	- 5.15	50	- 4:25	- 5.15	47	- 4:28
- 5.00	47	- 4:13	- 5.00	45	- 4:15	- 5.00	50	- 4:10	- 5.00	47	- 4:13
- 4.45	47	- 3:58	- 4.45	45	- 4:00	- 4.45	50	- 3:55	- 4.45	47	- 3:58
- 4.30	47	- 3:43	- 4.30	45	- 3:45	- 4.30	50	- 3:40	- 4.30	48	- 3:42
- 4.15	47	- 3:28	- 4.15	46	- 3:29	- 4.15	50	- 3:25	- 4.15	48	- 3:27
- 4.00	47	- 3:13	- 4.00	46	- 3:14	- 4.00	50	- 3:10	- 4.00	48	- 3:12
- 3.45	46	- 2:59	- 3.45	46	- 2:59	- 3.45	50	- 2:55	- 3.45	49	- 2:56
- 3.30	46	- 2:44	- 3.30	47	- 2:43	- 3.30	50	- 2:40	- 3.30	50	- 2:40
- 3.15	46	- 2:29	- 3.15	47	- 2:28	- 3.15	51	- 2:24	- 3.15	51	- 2:24
- 3.00	45	- 2:15	- 3.00	48	- 2:12	- 3.00	51	- 2:09	- 3.00	52	- 2:08
- 2.45	45	- 2:00	- 2.45	48	- 1:57	- 2.45	51	- 1:54	- 2.45	53	- 1:52
- 2.30	44	- 1:46	- 2.30	49	- 1:41	- 2.30	51	- 1:39	- 2.30	55	- 1:35
- 2.15	44	- 1:31	- 2.15	49	- 1:26	- 2.15	51	- 1:24	- 2.15	56	- 1:19
- 2.00	43	- 1:17	- 2.00	49	- 1:11	- 2.00	51	- 1:09	- 2.00	57	- 1:03
- 1.45	43	- 1:02	- 1.45	50	- 0:55	- 1.45	51	- 0:54	- 1.45	59	- 0:46
- 1.30	43	- 0:47	- 1.30	50	- 0:40	- 1.30	51	- 0:39	- 1.30	60	- 0:30
- 1.15	43	- 0:32	- 1.15	50	- 0:25	- 1.15	51	- 0:24	- 1.15	61	- 0:14
- 1.00	43	- 0:17	- 1.00	50	- 0:10	- 1.00	51	- 0:09	- 1.00	63	+ 0:03
- 0.45	42	- 0:03	- 0.45	50	+ 0:05	- 0.45	51	+ 0:06	- 0.45	64	+ 0:19
- 0.30	41	+ 0:11	- 0.30	50	+ 0:20	- 0.30	51	+ 0:21	- 0.30	65	+ 0:35
- 0.15	40	+ 0:25	- 0.15	51	+ 0:36	- 0.15	51	+ 0:36	- 0.15	66	+ 0:51
HW	38	+ 0:38	HW	51	+ 0:51	HW	52	+ 0:52	HW	67	+ 1:07
+ 0.15	38	+ 0:53	+ 0.15	51	+ 1:06	+ 0.15	52	+ 1:07	+ 0.15	67	+ 1:22
+ 0.30	38	+ 1:08	+ 0.30	52	+ 1:22	+ 0.30	52	+ 1:22	+ 0.30	66	+ 1:36
+ 0.45	38	+ 1:23	+ 0.45	52	+ 1:37	+ 0.45	52	+ 1:37	+ 0.45	66	+ 1:51
+ 1.00	37	+ 1:37	+ 1.00	52	+ 1:52	+ 1.00	52	+ 1:52	+ 1.00	66	+ 2:06
+ 1.15	37	+ 1:52	+ 1.15	52	+ 2:07	+ 1.15	52	+ 2:07	+ 1.15	65	+ 2:20
+ 1.30	37	+ 2:07	+ 1.30	52	+ 2:22	+ 1.30	52	+ 2:22	+ 1.30	64	+ 2:34
+ 1.45	38	+ 2:23	+ 1.45	51	+ 2:36	+ 1.45	52	+ 2:37	+ 1.45	63	+ 2:48
+ 2.00	38	+ 2:38	+ 2.00	51	+ 2:51	+ 2.00	52	+ 2:52	+ 2.00	62	+ 3:02
+ 2.15	38	+ 2:53	+ 2.15	51	+ 3:06	+ 2.15	51	+ 3:06	+ 2.15	62	+ 3:17
+ 2.30	38	+ 3:08	+ 2.30	50	+ 3:20	+ 2.30	51	+ 3:21	+ 2.30	61	+ 3:31
+ 2.45	38	+ 3:23	+ 2.45	50	+ 3:35	+ 2.45	51	+ 3:36	+ 2.45	60	+ 3:45
+ 3.00	38	+ 3:38	+ 3.00	50	+ 3:50	+ 3.00	51	+ 3:51	+ 3.00	59	+ 3:59
+ 3.15	39	+ 3:54	+ 3.15	49	+ 4:04	+ 3.15	51	+ 4:06	+ 3.15	58	+ 4:13
+ 3.30	39	+ 4:09	+ 3.30	49	+ 4:19	+ 3.30	51	+ 4:21	+ 3.30	57	+ 4:27
+ 3.45	39	+ 4:24	+ 3.45	49	+ 4:34	+ 3.45	51	+ 4:36	+ 3.45	57	+ 4:42
+ 4.00	40	+ 4:40	+ 4.00	49	+ 4:49	+ 4.00	51	+ 4:51	+ 4.00	56	+ 4:56
+ 4.15	40	+ 4:55	+ 4.15	48	+ 5:03	+ 4.15	50	+ 5:05	+ 4.15	55	+ 5:10
+ 4.30	40	+ 5:10	+ 4.30	48	+ 5:18	+ 4.30	50	+ 5:20	+ 4.30	54	+ 5:24
+ 4.45	41	+ 5:26	+ 4.45	48	+ 5:33	+ 4.45	50	+ 5:35	+ 4.45	53	+ 5:38
+ 5.00	41	+ 5:41	+ 5.00	48	+ 5:48	+ 5.00	50	+ 5:50	+ 5.00	53	+ 5:53
+ 5.15	41	+ 5:56	+ 5.15	47	- 5:58	+ 5.15	50	- 5:55	+ 5.15	52	- 5:53
+ 5.30	42	- 5:48	+ 5.30	47	- 5:43	+ 5.30	50	- 5:40	+ 5.30	51	- 5:39
+ 5.45	42	- 5:33	+ 5.45	47	- 5:28	+ 5.45	50	- 5:25	+ 5.45	51	- 5:24
+ 6.00	42	- 5:18	+ 6.00	47	- 5:13	+ 6.00	50	- 5:10	+ 6.00	50	- 5:10

	K4 Kentish Knock to South Knock			K3 South Knock to Thanet			K2 Thanet to North Foreland			K1 North Foreland to Ramsgate	
Time	Duration	Time at End of Sector	Time	Duration	Time at End of Sector	Time	Duration	Time at End of Sector	Time	Duration	Time at End of Sector
- 6.00	42	- 5:18	- 6.00	51	- 5:09	- 6.00	52	- 5:08	- 6.00	36	- 5:24
- 5.45	41	- 5:04	- 5.45	50	- 4:55	- 5.45	51	- 4:54	- 5.45	35	- 5:10
- 5.30	41	- 4:49	- 5.30	49	- 4:41	- 5.30	51	- 4:39	- 5.30	35	- 4:55
- 5.15	40	- 4:35	- 5.15	49	- 4:26	- 5.15	51	- 4:24	- 5.15	35	- 4:40
- 5.00	40	- 4:20	- 5.00	49	- 4:11	- 5.00	51	- 4:09	- 5.00	35	- 4:25
- 4.45	40	- 4:05	- 4.45	49	- 3:56	- 4.45	50	- 3:55	- 4.45	35	- 4:10
- 4.30	40	- 3:50	- 4.30	48	- 3:42	- 4.30	50	- 3:40	- 4.30	35	- 3:55
- 4.15	40	- 3:35	- 4.15	49	- 3:26	- 4.15	51	- 3:24	- 4.15	36	- 3:39
- 4.00	41	- 3:19	- 4.00	50	- 3:10	- 4.00	52	- 3:08	- 4.00	36	- 3:24
- 3.45	41	- 3:04	- 3.45	50	- 2:55	- 3.45	52	- 2:53	- 3.45	37	- 3:08
- 3.30	42	- 2:48	- 3.30	51	- 2:39	- 3.30	53	- 2:37	- 3.30	38	- 2:52
- 3.15	42	- 2:33	- 3.15	52	- 2:23	- 3.15	54	- 2:21	- 3.15	39	- 2:36
- 3.00	43	- 2:17	- 3.00	53	- 2:07	- 3.00	55	- 2:05	- 3.00	41	- 2:19
- 2.45	44	- 2:01	- 2.45	54	- 1:51	- 2.45	56	- 1:49	- 2.45	42	- 2:03
- 2.30	45	- 1:45	- 2.30	55	- 1:35	- 2.30	57	- 1:33	- 2.30	44	- 1:46
- 2.15	46	- 1:29	- 2.15	56	- 1:19	- 2.15	58	- 1:17	- 2.15	44	- 1:31
- 2.00	47	- 1:13	- 2.00	57	- 1:03	- 2.00	59	- 1:01	- 2.00	45	- 1:15
- 1.45	48	- 0:57	- 1.45	58	- 0:47	- 1.45	60	- 0:45	- 1.45	46	- 0:59
- 1.30	49	- 0:41	- 1.30	59	- 0:31	- 1.30	61	- 0:29	- 1.30	47	- 0:43
- 1.15	50	- 0:25	- 1.15	60	- 0:15	- 1.15	62	- 0:13	- 1.15	47	- 0:28
- 1.00	51	- 0:09	- 1.00	60	HW	- 1.00	62	+ 0:02	- 1.00	47	- 0:13
- 0.45	52	+ 0:07	- 0.45	61	+ 0:16	- 0.45	63	+ 0:18	- 0.45	47	+ 0:02
- 0.30	53	+ 0:23	- 0.30	62	+ 0:32	- 0.30	64	+ 0:34	- 0.30	47	+ 0:17
- 0.15	54	+ 0:39	- 0.15	63	+ 0:48	- 0.15	63	+ 0:48	- 0.15	47	+ 0:32
HW	55	+ 0:55	HW	63	+ 1:03	HW	63	+ 1:03	HW	46	+ 0:46
+ 0.15	55	+ 1:10	+ 0.15	64	+ 1:19	+ 0.15	63	+ 1:18	+ 0.15	46	+ 1:01
+ 0.30	55	+ 1:25	+ 0.30	64	+ 1:34	+ 0.30	63	+ 1:33	+ 0.30	46	+ 1:16
+ 0.45	56	+ 1:41	+ 0.45	64	+ 1:49	+ 0.45	63	+ 1:48	+ 0.45	45	+ 1:30
+ 1.00	56	+ 1:56	+ 1.00	64	+ 2:04	+ 1.00	62	+ 2:02	+ 1.00	45	+ 1:45
+ 1.15	56	+ 2:11	+ 1.15	63	+ 2:18	+ 1.15	62	+ 2:17	+ 1.15	44	+ 1:59
+ 1.30	56	+ 2:26	+ 1.30	63	+ 2:33	+ 1.30	62	+ 2:32	+ 1.30	43	+ 2:13
+ 1.45	56	+ 2:41	+ 1.45	63	+ 2:48	+ 1.45	61	+ 2:46	+ 1.45	42	+ 2:27
+ 2.00	55	+ 2:55	+ 2.00	62	+ 3:02	+ 2.00	61	+ 3:01	+ 2.00	42	+ 2:42
+ 2.15	55	+ 3:10	+ 2.15	62	+ 3:17	+ 2.15	61	+ 3:16	+ 2.15	41	+ 2:56
+ 2.30	55	+ 3:25	+ 2.30	61	+ 3:31	+ 2.30	61	+ 3:31	+ 2.30	40	+ 3:10
+ 2.45	54	+ 3:39	+ 2.45	60	+ 3:45	+ 2.45	60	+ 3:45	+ 2.45	40	+ 3:25
+ 3.00	54	+ 3:54	+ 3.00	60	+ 4:00	+ 3.00	60	+ 4:00	+ 3.00	39	+ 3:39
+ 3.15	53	+ 4:08	+ 3.15	59	+ 4:14	+ 3.15	59	+ 4:14	+ 3.15	39	+ 3:54
+ 3.30	52	+ 4:22	+ 3.30	58	+ 4:28	+ 3.30	59	+ 4:29	+ 3.30	38	+ 4:08
+ 3.45	51	+ 4:36	+ 3.45	58	+ 4:43	+ 3.45	58	+ 4:43	+ 3.45	38	+ 4:23
+ 4.00	50	+ 4:50	+ 4.00	58	+ 4:58	+ 4.00	58	+ 4:58	+ 4.00	38	+ 4:38
+ 4.15	49	+ 5:04	+ 4.15	57	+ 5:12	+ 4.15	58	+ 5:13	+ 4.15	37	+ 4:52
+ 4.30	48	+ 5:18	+ 4.30	57	+ 5:27	+ 4.30	57	+ 5:27	+ 4.30	37	+ 5:07
+ 4.45	47	+ 5:32	+ 4.45	56	+ 5:41	+ 4.45	57	+ 5:42	+ 4.45	37	+ 5:22
+ 5.00	46	+ 5:46	+ 5.00	56	+ 5:56	+ 5.00	56	+ 5:56	+ 5.00	37	+ 5:37
+ 5.15	46	- 5:59	+ 5.15	55	- 5:50	+ 5.15	56	- 5:49	+ 5.15	37	+ 5:52
+ 5.30	45	- 5:45	+ 5.30	55	- 5:35	+ 5.30	55	- 5:35	+ 5.30	37	- 5:53
+ 5.45	44	- 5:31	+ 5.45	52	- 5:23	+ 5.45	53	- 5:22	+ 5.45	36	- 5:39
+ 6.00	44	- 5:16	+ 6.00	51	- 5:09	+ 6.00	52	- 5:08	+ 6.00	36	- 5:24

K - 7 Kts

Table K - Harwich to Ramsgate - Outside Route

7 Kts - K

Time to cover Sectors (in minutes) at 7.0 kts

All times relate to HW Sheerness

Springs

Time	K8		Time	K7		Time	K6		Time	K5		Time	K4		Time	K3		Time	K2		Time	K1	
	Harwich to Cork Sand B'cn			Cork Sand B'cn to S Threshold			S Threshold to Long Sand Hd			Long S'nd Hd to Kentish Knock			Kentish Knock to South Knock			South Knock to Thanet			Thanet to North Foreland			North Foreland to Ramsgate	
Time	Duration	Time at End of Sector	Time	Duration	Time at End of Sector	Time	Duration	Time at End of Sector	Time	Duration	Time at End of Sector	Time	Duration	Time at End of Sector	Time	Duration	Time at End of Sector	Time	Duration	Time at End of Sector	Time	Duration	Time at End of Sector
- 6.00	50	- 5:10	- 6.00	44	- 5:16	- 6.00	50	- 5:10	- 6.00	44	- 5:16	- 6.00	39	- 5:21	- 6.00	46	- 5:14	- 6.00	48	- 5:12	- 6.00	33	- 5:27
- 5.45	51	- 4:54	- 5.45	44	- 5:01	- 5.45	50	- 4:55	- 5.45	44	- 5:01	- 5.45	39	- 5:06	- 5.45	45	- 5:00	- 5.45	47	- 4:58	- 5.45	33	- 5:12
- 5.30	51	- 4:39	- 5.30	44	- 4:46	- 5.30	50	- 4:40	- 5.30	44	- 4:46	- 5.30	38	- 4:52	- 5.30	44	- 4:46	- 5.30	47	- 4:43	- 5.30	32	- 4:58
- 5.15	51	- 4:24	- 5.15	44	- 4:31	- 5.15	50	- 4:25	- 5.15	43	- 4:32	- 5.15	38	- 4:37	- 5.15	43	- 4:32	- 5.15	46	- 4:29	- 5.15	32	- 4:43
- 5.00	51	- 4:09	- 5.00	44	- 4:16	- 5.00	50	- 4:10	- 5.00	43	- 4:17	- 5.00	37	- 4:23	- 5.00	43	- 4:17	- 5.00	46	- 4:14	- 5.00	32	- 4:28
- 4.45	51	- 3:54	- 4.45	44	- 4:01	- 4.45	51	- 3:54	- 4.45	44	- 4:01	- 4.45	38	- 4:07	- 4.45	43	- 4:02	- 4.45	46	- 3:59	- 4.45	32	- 4:13
- 4.30	50	- 3:40	- 4.30	44	- 3:46	- 4.30	51	- 3:39	- 4.30	44	- 3:46	- 4.30	38	- 3:52	- 4.30	42	- 3:48	- 4.30	46	- 3:44	- 4.30	32	- 3:58
- 4.15	50	- 3:25	- 4.15	45	- 3:30	- 4.15	51	- 3:24	- 4.15	45	- 3:30	- 4.15	38	- 3:37	- 4.15	43	- 3:32	- 4.15	46	- 3:29	- 4.15	33	- 3:42
- 4.00	50	- 3:10	- 4.00	45	- 3:15	- 4.00	51	- 3:09	- 4.00	45	- 3:15	- 4.00	38	- 3:22	- 4.00	44	- 3:16	- 4.00	47	- 3:13	- 4.00	34	- 3:26
- 3.45	49	- 2:56	- 3.45	46	- 2:59	- 3.45	51	- 2:54	- 3.45	47	- 2:58	- 3.45	39	- 3:06	- 3.45	45	- 3:00	- 3.45	48	- 2:57	- 3.45	34	- 3:11
- 3.30	49	- 2:41	- 3.30	47	- 2:43	- 3.30	51	- 2:39	- 3.30	48	- 2:42	- 3.30	39	- 2:51	- 3.30	46	- 2:44	- 3.30	49	- 2:41	- 3.30	35	- 2:55
- 3.15	48	- 2:27	- 3.15	47	- 2:28	- 3.15	51	- 2:24	- 3.15	49	- 2:26	- 3.15	40	- 2:35	- 3.15	48	- 2:27	- 3.15	51	- 2:24	- 3.15	38	- 2:37
- 3.00	48	- 2:12	- 3.00	48	- 2:12	- 3.00	51	- 2:09	- 3.00	51	- 2:09	- 3.00	41	- 2:19	- 3.00	50	- 2:10	- 3.00	53	- 2:07	- 3.00	41	- 2:19
- 2.45	47	- 1:58	- 2.45	49	- 1:56	- 2.45	51	- 1:54	- 2.45	52	- 1:53	- 2.45	42	- 2:03	- 2.45	51	- 1:54	- 2.45	55	- 1:50	- 2.45	44	- 2:01
- 2.30	46	- 1:44	- 2.30	49	- 1:41	- 2.30	51	- 1:39	- 2.30	54	- 1:36	- 2.30	43	- 1:47	- 2.30	53	- 1:37	- 2.30	57	- 1:33	- 2.30	46	- 1:44
- 2.15	45	- 1:30	- 2.15	50	- 1:25	- 2.15	51	- 1:24	- 2.15	56	- 1:19	- 2.15	45	- 1:30	- 2.15	55	- 1:20	- 2.15	59	- 1:16	- 2.15	48	- 1:27
- 2.00	44	- 1:16	- 2.00	50	- 1:10	- 2.00	51	- 1:09	- 2.00	58	- 1:02	- 2.00	46	- 1:14	- 2.00	57	- 1:03	- 2.00	61	- 0:59	- 2.00	50	- 1:10
- 1.45	44	- 1:01	- 1.45	50	- 0:55	- 1.45	52	- 0:53	- 1.45	60	- 0:45	- 1.45	48	- 0:57	- 1.45	59	- 0:46	- 1.45	63	- 0:42	- 1.45	52	- 0:53
- 1.30	44	- 0:46	- 1.30	50	- 0:40	- 1.30	52	- 0:38	- 1.30	62	- 0:28	- 1.30	50	- 0:40	- 1.30	61	- 0:29	- 1.30	65	- 0:25	- 1.30	54	- 0:36
- 1.15	44	- 0:31	- 1.15	51	- 0:24	- 1.15	52	- 0:23	- 1.15	64	- 0:11	- 1.15	52	- 0:23	- 1.15	63	- 0:12	- 1.15	66	- 0:09	- 1.15	53	- 0:22
- 1.00	44	- 0:16	- 1.00	51	- 0:09	- 1.00	52	- 0:08	- 1.00	66	+ 0:06	- 1.00	53	- 0:07	- 1.00	65	+ 0:05	- 1.00	67	+ 0:07	- 1.00	53	- 0:07
- 0.45	43	- 0:02	- 0.45	51	+ 0:06	- 0.45	52	+ 0:07	- 0.45	67	+ 0:22	- 0.45	55	+ 0:10	- 0.45	67	+ 0:22	- 0.45	68	+ 0:23	- 0.45	53	+ 0:08
- 0.30	42	+ 0:12	- 0.30	52	+ 0:22	- 0.30	52	+ 0:22	- 0.30	69	+ 0:39	- 0.30	56	+ 0:26	- 0.30	69	+ 0:39	- 0.30	69	+ 0:39	- 0.30	53	+ 0:23
- 0.15	40	+ 0:25	- 0.15	52	+ 0:37	- 0.15	53	+ 0:38	- 0.15	71	+ 0:56	- 0.15	57	+ 0:42	- 0.15	67	+ 0:52	- 0.15	68	+ 0:53	- 0.15	53	+ 0:38
HW	39	+ 0:39	HW	53	+ 0:53	HW	53	+ 0:53	HW	72	+ 1:12	HW	59	+ 0:59	HW	71	+ 1:11	HW	69	+ 1:09	HW	52	+ 0:52
+ 0.15	38	+ 0:53	+ 0.15	53	+ 1:08	+ 0.15	53	+ 1:08	+ 0.15	72	+ 1:27	+ 0.15	59	+ 1:14	+ 0.15	71	+ 1:26	+ 0.15	68	+ 1:23	+ 0.15	51	+ 1:06
+ 0.30	38	+ 1:08	+ 0.30	54	+ 1:24	+ 0.30	53	+ 1:23	+ 0.30	72	+ 1:42	+ 0.30	60	+ 1:30	+ 0.30	72	+ 1:42	+ 0.30	68	+ 1:38	+ 0.30	51	+ 1:21
+ 0.45	37	+ 1:22	+ 0.45	54	+ 1:39	+ 0.45	54	+ 1:39	+ 0.45	72	+ 1:57	+ 0.45	60	+ 1:45	+ 0.45	72	+ 1:57	+ 0.45	67	+ 1:52	+ 0.45	49	+ 1:34
+ 1.00	37	+ 1:37	+ 1.00	55	+ 1:55	+ 1.00	54	+ 1:54	+ 1.00	72	+ 2:12	+ 1.00	61	+ 2:01	+ 1.00	71	+ 2:11	+ 1.00	67	+ 2:07	+ 1.00	48	+ 1:48
+ 1.15	37	+ 1:52	+ 1.15	54	+ 2:09	+ 1.15	54	+ 2:09	+ 1.15	70	+ 2:25	+ 1.15	61	+ 2:16	+ 1.15	71	+ 2:26	+ 1.15	67	+ 2:22	+ 1.15	47	+ 2:02
+ 1.30	37	+ 2:07	+ 1.30	54	+ 2:24	+ 1.30	54	+ 2:24	+ 1.30	69	+ 2:39	+ 1.30	61	+ 2:31	+ 1.30	70	+ 2:40	+ 1.30	66	+ 2:36	+ 1.30	45	+ 2:15
+ 1.45	37	+ 2:22	+ 1.45	54	+ 2:39	+ 1.45	53	+ 2:38	+ 1.45	67	+ 2:52	+ 1.45	61	+ 2:46	+ 1.45	69	+ 2:54	+ 1.45	66	+ 2:51	+ 1.45	44	+ 2:29
+ 2.00	37	+ 2:37	+ 2.00	53	+ 2:53	+ 2.00	53	+ 2:53	+ 2.00	66	+ 3:06	+ 2.00	60	+ 3:00	+ 2.00	68	+ 3:08	+ 2.00	65	+ 3:05	+ 2.00	43	+ 2:43
+ 2.15	37	+ 2:52	+ 2.15	53	+ 3:08	+ 2.15	53	+ 3:08	+ 2.15	65	+ 3:20	+ 2.15	59	+ 3:14	+ 2.15	67	+ 3:22	+ 2.15	65	+ 3:20	+ 2.15	41	+ 2:56
+ 2.30	37	+ 3:07	+ 2.30	52	+ 3:22	+ 2.30	53	+ 3:23	+ 2.30	63	+ 3:33	+ 2.30	59	+ 3:29	+ 2.30	66	+ 3:36	+ 2.30	64	+ 3:34	+ 2.30	40	+ 3:10
+ 2.45	37	+ 3:22	+ 2.45	51	+ 3:36	+ 2.45	52	+ 3:37	+ 2.45	62	+ 3:47	+ 2.45	58	+ 3:43	+ 2.45	65	+ 3:50	+ 2.45	63	+ 3:48	+ 2.45	39	+ 3:24
+ 3.00	37	+ 3:37	+ 3.00	51	+ 3:51	+ 3.00	52	+ 3:52	+ 3.00	61	+ 4:01	+ 3.00	57	+ 3:57	+ 3.00	63	+ 4:03	+ 3.00	62	+ 4:02	+ 3.00	39	+ 3:39
+ 3.15	37	+ 3:52	+ 3.15	50	+ 4:05	+ 3.15	52	+ 4:07	+ 3.15	59	+ 4:14	+ 3.15	55	+ 4:10	+ 3.15	62	+ 4:17	+ 3.15	61	+ 4:16	+ 3.15	38	+ 3:53
+ 3.30	38	+ 4:08	+ 3.30	50	+ 4:20	+ 3.30	51	+ 4:21	+ 3.30	58	+ 4:28	+ 3.30	54	+ 4:24	+ 3.30	61	+ 4:31	+ 3.30	60	+ 4:30	+ 3.30	37	+ 4:07
+ 3.45	38	+ 4:23	+ 3.45	49	+ 4:34	+ 3.45	51	+ 4:36	+ 3.45	57	+ 4:42	+ 3.45	53	+ 4:38	+ 3.45	60	+ 4:45	+ 3.45	59	+ 4:44	+ 3.45	37	+ 4:22
+ 4.00	39	+ 4:39	+ 4.00	49	+ 4:49	+ 4.00	51	+ 4:51	+ 4.00	56	+ 4:56	+ 4.00	51	+ 4:51	+ 4.00	59	+ 4:59	+ 4.00	59	+ 4:59	+ 4.00	37	+ 4:37
+ 4.15	39	+ 4:54	+ 4.15	49	+ 5:04	+ 4.15	51	+ 5:06	+ 4.15	55	+ 5:10	+ 4.15	50	+ 5:05	+ 4.15	58	+ 5:13	+ 4.15	58	+ 5:13	+ 4.15	36	+ 4:51
+ 4.30	40	+ 5:10	+ 4.30	48	+ 5:18	+ 4.30	51	+ 5:21	+ 4.30	53	+ 5:23	+ 4.30	49	+ 5:19	+ 4.30	57	+ 5:27	+ 4.30	57	+ 5:27	+ 4.30	36	+ 5:06
+ 4.45	40	+ 5:25	+ 4.45	48	+ 5:33	+ 4.45	50	+ 5:35	+ 4.45	52	+ 5:37	+ 4.45	47	+ 5:32	+ 4.45	56	+ 5:41	+ 4.45	56	+ 5:41	+ 4.45	36	+ 5:21
+ 5.00	40	+ 5:40	+ 5.00	48	+ 5:48	+ 5.00	50	+ 5:50	+ 5.00	51	+ 5:51	+ 5.00	46	+ 5:46	+ 5.00	55	+ 5:55	+ 5.00	56	+ 5:56	+ 5.00	35	+ 5:35
+ 5.15	41	+ 5:56	+ 5.15	47	- 5:58	+ 5.15	50	- 5:55	+ 5.15	50	- 5:55	+ 5.15	45	- 6:00	+ 5.15	55	- 5:50	+ 5.15	55	- 5:50	+ 5.15	35	+ 5:50
+ 5.30	41	- 5:49	+ 5.30	47	- 5:43	+ 5.30	50	- 5:40	+ 5.30	49	- 5:41	+ 5.30	44	- 5:46	+ 5.30	54	- 5:36	+ 5.30	56	- 5:34	+ 5.30	34	- 5:56
+ 5.45	42	- 5:33	+ 5.45	46	- 5:29	+ 5.45	50	- 5:25	+ 5.45	48	- 5:27	+ 5.45	43	- 5:32	+ 5.45	49	- 5:26	+ 5.45	50	- 5:25	+ 5.45	34	- 5:41
+ 6.00	42	- 5:18	+ 6.00	46	- 5:14	+ 6.00	50	- 5:10	+ 6.00	47	- 5:13	+ 6.00	42	- 5:18	+ 6.00	47	- 5:13	+ 6.00	49	- 5:11	+ 6.00	33	- 5:27

SOUTH BOUND